D0915248

THE BUILDINGS OF SCOTLAND

EDITOR: COLIN MCWILLIAM
CONSULTANT EDITOR: JOHN NEWMAN

EDINBURGH

JOHN GIFFORD, COLIN MCWILLIAM AND DAVID WALKER

To Dad
XMAS 84
Ben + Senga

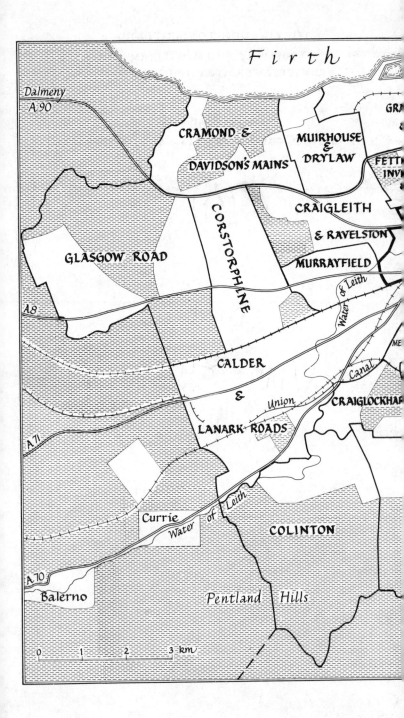

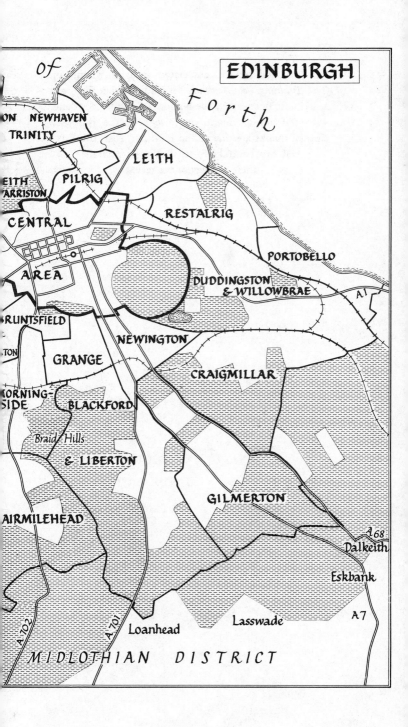

All work and services associated with the writing of *The Buildings of Scotland*, including historical research, are financed by the National Trust for Scotland with the aid of donations raised for the purpose. Special thanks are due to the Pilgrim Trust, the Russell Trust and the Scottish Arts Council for their support of the series.

Edinburgh

BY
JOHN GIFFORD,
COLIN McWILLIAM
AND
DAVID WALKER
MEDIEVAL BUILDINGS
BY CHRISTOPHER WILSON

THE BUILDINGS OF SCOTLAND

PENGUIN BOOKS

Penguin Books Ltd, Harmondsworth, Middlesex, England
Viking Penguin Inc., 40 West 23rd Street, New York, New York 10010, U.S.A.
Penguin Books Australia Ltd, Ringwood, Victoria, Australia
Penguin Books Canada Ltd, 2801 John Street, Markham, Ontario, Canada L3R 1B4
Penguin Books (N.Z.) Ltd, 182–190 Wairau Road, Auckland 10, New Zealand

First published 1984

ISBN 071.068 X
ISBN 0 14 0710.68 X

Copyright © John Gifford, Colin McWilliam and David Walker, 1984
All rights reserved

Made and printed in Great Britain by
Butler & Tanner Ltd, Frome and London

Set in Monophoto Plantin

Except in the United States of America,
this book is sold subject to the condition
that it shall not, by way of trade or otherwise,
be lent, re-sold, hired out, or otherwise circulated
without the publisher's prior consent in any form of
binding or cover other than that in which it is
published and without a similar condition
including this condition being imposed
on the subsequent purchaser

DEDICATED TO
NIKOLAUS PEVSNER
1902–83
EDITOR-IN-CHIEF OF
THE BUILDINGS OF SCOTLAND
DOCTOR OF LETTERS
OF
HERIOT-WATT UNIVERSITY, EDINBURGH

CONTENTS

For orientation see the maps on pp. 2–3 and 78–9
and the contents lists on pp. 77, 449, and 483

EDITOR'S FOREWORD

BY COLIN MCWILLIAM

The Edinburgh volume is a joint effort. The number and variety of buildings and the abundance of untapped research material made this inevitable if the job was to be done in a reasonable time. But who wrote what? Here I shall follow the example of Sir Nikolaus Pevsner in some volumes of The Buildings of England, *and explain what happened.*

Of all that has been written about Edinburgh, the nearest to a comprehensive roll-call of all interesting buildings, without restriction as to date or type, is the Secretary of State's Descriptive List of Buildings of Special Architectural or Historic Interest, *originally drawn up by the late Ian G. Lindsay (assisted by Alan Reiach), and later completely revised by Catherine Cruft and again by David Walker, who, as Principal Inspector of Historic Buildings in the Scottish Development Department, still has it under review. David Walker was thus the natural choice to write this volume, and had drafted a large part of the central area (including the New Town) before it became clear that he would not have time to finish. Dr Christopher Wilson became responsible for castles as well as churches of pre-1560 date. John Gifford wrote nearly all the Old Town and South Side, and the hitherto little-known territory of Leith. I wrote – or rewrote in updated and somewhat shorter form – almost all the rest of the central area. In the outer areas, I wrote all the church descriptions and most of the rest, but John Gifford was responsible for Corstorphine, Craigleith and Ravelston, Cramond and Davidson's Mains, Fairmilehead, and Glasgow Road, and also for a number of country houses. For special contributions I am grateful to Dr Graham Ritchie and Dr Gordon Maxwell of the Royal Commission on the Ancient and Historical Monuments of Scotland* (Prehistoric and Roman Edinburgh) and Professor Gordon Craig of the Department of Geological Science in the University of Edinburgh (Topography and Building Materials).*

Preparation began, as always, with a trawl through printed sources. Katherine Michaelson, who carried out much of the research for Sir Nikolaus Pevsner's original London *volumes, gave much help in the early stages. John Gifford checked the architectural journals from end to end for Scottish material, including Edinburgh entries, and dug carefully through a number of general periodicals, of which the* Edinburgh Evening Courant *proved most*

---

* Hereafter shortened to RCAHMS.

*valuable, providing much evidence to clothe the bare bones of 'ar-
chitect and date'. A difficulty arose with secondary printed sources.
Books about Edinburgh and its buildings are legion, but few of
them are based on research into primary material, virtually none
on the sort of wider research that discovers information in unexpected places. For us this work has been done very largely by John
Gifford, and I must also thank our research assistant Yvonne Hill-
yard for pursuing many further inquiries on buildings I came across
in outer Edinburgh, whose architects seemed to deserve rediscovery.
Between us we have found most of the answers.*

*The decision to dig deeper into the city's huge resources of pri-
mary material, and to look again at buildings in the light of what
we found, resulted in long delay and sorely tried the patience not
only of our publishers but of our sponsors and managers, the National Trust for Scotland. It was a Trust initiative, typical of an
organization which has done so much for the cause of preservation
in Scotland, which led to the beginning of* The Buildings of Scotland *series. The Trust wrote to Sir Nikolaus Pevsner, offering to
underwrite the series if he would organize the writing. The Trust
raises and administers the funds necessary for research, travelling,
and other expenses, without which the project could not proceed.
Without such backing this book would not have been written.*

*Next I must thank the owners and curators of books and docu-
ments we have used. It is impossible to name them all, or to put
them in order of precedence, but I must mention the staff of the
Scottish Record Office, the National Library of Scotland, the
Edinburgh Room and Art Library at the Central Public Library,
the City Archivist Dr Walter Makey, and Mr James Cruickshank
who pursued many dusty queries in the Dean of Guild records. We
owe much to the* RCAHMS, *including their Secretary John Dunbar,
and especially to Catherine Cruft, Ian Gow and Richard Emerson
(now Inspector of Historic Buildings, Scottish Development Department) of the National Monuments Record for Scotland, their
public archive. Iain McIvor and Dr Richard Fawcett of the Ancient Monuments Inspectorate have been constantly helpful. Joe
Rock made freely available the result of his researches into Edinburgh's late Georgian and early Victorian building history. Other
scholars who must also be thanked include the Rev. Ian Dunlop
with his wide knowledge of Edinburgh churches, Rhona Moodie
and Sax Shaw for information about stained glass, and David
Stewart and David Thomson for allowing us to quote freely from
their* Survey of Edinburgh Organs.

*In thanking the private and corporate owners who gave us access
to their property we must also acknowledge the help of those who
answered the typical question 'Do you know the name of the architect?' Many of them did, and many took a lot of trouble consulting their own records on this and other matters. Here I must
emphasize as firmly as ever that* the mention of a building in this
volume in no way implies any right of public access. *Some
owners, and particularly ministers and church officers, volunteered
that they would be glad to admit any interested person by advance
appointment.*

Another point, repeated in every foreword in the 'Buildings' series, is that we shall be grateful to any reader who is able to tell us of an error, or better still correct it. These books do not follow the normal scholarly practice of giving references to sources of information. Since this might double the size of a volume, it is done only in special cases, e.g. when other writers are directly quoted or have supplied a considerable body of facts from their own work still in preparation. However we, the authors, do take responsibility for what we write, and have tried to make it clear when there are problems of interpretation. We shall of course do our best to answer questions from those who want to follow up our necessarily brief description. A steady trickle of inquiries is already dealt with (including some on buildings not yet mentioned), and in the event of publication acknowledgement is made to the Buildings of Scotland Research Unit and/or the individual researcher with whom the inquirer is put in touch. The Unit is housed in the Edinburgh College of Art through the generosity of the Board of Governors and the Principal, Gavin Ross, who is a Buildings of Scotland enthusiast.

Last but not least, I must acknowledge the hard work of those who were involved in the preparation of the text and illustrations. The typing was done by Nancy Douglas, Vanessa Emerson, Anne Ferguson, Christine McWilliam, Margaret Morris, Rosalind Munro, Vera Steel and Louise Wheatley. Judy Nairn and Judith Wardman hacked resolutely through tropical forests of information, gave valuable advice and prepared the text for the printer. The maps were done with great patience and sympathy by Reg Piggott, and the line drawings by Richard Andrews and John Hutchinson.

In content the most obvious novelty is the inclusion of the names of a large number of builders and craftsmen. For reference, all these are lumped together with architects, painters and sculptors, stained-glass artists and others, in the Index of Artists. We have not automatically mentioned everyone whose name was attached to a building, but the earlier the date, the more names have been sought and included. We have certainly not mentioned every building for which we found a date and architect, but some examples of no great merit are included because they are typical, e.g. a small shopping centre in an inter-war housing development – and often the houses too; some of them are worthy of inclusion by any standard. Broadly, the length of an entry indicates our view of the importance of a building, though sometimes an entry is inflated by an unusually complex building history or kept slim by an unusually straightforward one. The subjective comments are our own, and I must stress that a lukewarm judgement should not be used in evidence against a building which may give great pleasure to its owners or be of great value in its context.

In the gazetteer the City of Edinburgh (within the boundary as it existed before 1975, and thus filling the gap left by the Lothian volume) is divided into central and outer areas and then subdivided into sections (see the maps at the beginning and the contents pages). The numbered sections of the central area (each with its own map) begin with the Old Town and then follow a fairly logical sequence

*of both time and place. Those in the outer area are arranged al-
phabetically. It is hard to draw exact boundaries in this way
because topography, historic ownership patterns, architectural
character and man-made severance lines, which all have to be taken
into account, are often contradictory. So the boundaries are a compromise in which convenience of visiting is a prime consideration.
The names have again been chosen for convenience; not every resident in any given section would necessarily agree with the title
that has been chosen for it.*

*Major buildings are given, as usual, at the start of each section,
with the Castle, St Giles, the Law Courts and Holyrood given
pride of place at the beginning of the Old Town. Churches are
given by their names at the time of writing, but if they have been
closed or secularized we have reverted to their original ones. Some
secularized churches are commonly known by their new names (e.g.
West Register House or Queen's Hall) and are included under
these names as public buildings, each with a cross reference from
the list of churches. In the last resort one can always refer to the
Index of Streets and Buildings; for this I must thank Judith
Wardman and John Gifford, and for the Index of Artists John
Gifford. After the major buildings, the others are described by the
traditional perambulations, by an alphabetical index of streets, or
by a general essay; the choice is dictated by the character of each
section.*

ACKNOWLEDGEMENTS FOR THE PLATES

We are grateful to the following for permission to reproduce
photographs:
Rowand Anderson Partnership: 47
City of Edinburgh District Council: 71
Country Life: 66, 67, 69
John Dewar: 3, 6, 57
Nicholas Groves-Raines: 131
A. L. Hunter: 28
Robert Hurd & Partners: 111
A. F. Kersting: 33, 36, 44, 45, 52, 65, 79, 81, 84, 86, 89, 92,
    97, 106, 108, 109, 117, 120, 122, 124
Michael Laird & Partners: 110
Colin McWilliam: 5, 31, 37, 62, 64, 73, 80, 94, 112, 118, 119,
    121, 128, 130
Robert Matthew, Johnson-Marshall & Partners: 102
Morris & Steedman: 132
National Monuments Record of Scotland: 13, 14, 15, 18, 58
Scott Robertson: 40
Joe Rock: 2, 7, 9, 10, 11, 16, 20, 21, 24, 25, 26, 27, 29, 30,
    32, 34, 35, 38, 39, 41, 43, 46, 48, 50, 51, 53, 54, 55, 56, 61,
    68, 70, 72, 75, 78, 82, 85, 88, 90, 91, 93, 95, 96, 98, 99,
    103, 104, 105, 107, 113, 114, 115, 116, 123, 125, 126, 127,
    129
Scotsman Publications: 1
Scottish Development Department, Crown Copyright: 12,
    59, 60
Sir Basil Spence, Glover & Ferguson: 101
Christopher Wilson: 4, 8, 17, 19, 22, 23, 42, 49, 74, 76, 77,
    83, 87, 100 and on p. 165

Pl. 63 is reproduced by Gracious Permission of Her Majesty
The Queen.

The plates are indexed in the indexes of artists and buildings
on pp. 689 ff., and references to them are given by numbers
in the margin of the text.

INTRODUCTION

THE CITY OF EDINBURGH

This introduction to the buildings of Edinburgh must begin
with a picture of the city as a whole, and some idea of what will
be found here. It is a city of just under half a million,* formerly
the seat of the Scottish parliament and still the centre of Scottish government, church and law. Public institutions and
professional services are the most visible part of its life-style.
Industry tends to be connected with these services (e.g. traditionally in printing, now in electronics). Business has a distinguished old face (the banks) and the usual anonymous new one.
Trade, which gave substance to the city and style to its own
port-town of Leith, is now less conspicuous.

Edinburgh's extraordinary site, and the hard sandstone which 1, 6
is its dominant building material, are explained in geological
terms in the next article. Site and buildings together produce
townscape – from the most predictable to the most improbable
and spectacular, and often both at once. Similarly the architecture, having established a reliable norm of type and style,
is apt to burst out into displays of genius and waywardness.
The Scottish system of land ownership, and how its discipline contributed to the character of Edinburgh, are explained
below.

As the name‡ implies, the original site was strategic. The
Castle rock is the most defensible (though second in height to
Arthur's Seat) of the group of distinctively shaped hills that
protrude from the coastal plain at its narrowest point, where
the Moorfoot–Pentland range comes closest to the Forth estuary. This was the natural strongpoint guarding the SE entry into
Scotland, though hardly the ideal starting-point for a town – let
alone a large city. The only adjacent site for development was
the long ridge descending vulnerably to the E. Down it, from
the Castle to Holyrood, runs the long street known from the 3

* This figure applies to the city as it was in 1975 and as described in this
volume. The present boundary of the City of Edinburgh District takes in South
Queensferry and Kirkliston, Ratho and Balerno, and these are described in the
Lothian volume.

‡ The first two syllables of 'Edinburgh' probably come from the Gaelic *Din
Eidyn* (Dunedin), both of whose parts have the meaning of a fort. There is a
doubtful connexion with the Northumbrian king Edwin, who ruled Lothian in
the early C7. *Burg* is a stronghold and thence a town.

c16 as the Royal Mile. The upper section consists of Castlehill and Lawnmarket and then High Street with the medieval burgh kirk of St Giles, the mercat cross, the c17 Parliament Hall and the seat of the Scottish justiciary. The lower bears the name of the old burgh of Canongate whose feudal superior was the Abbot of Holyrood, and still has its c16 tolbooth as well as its post-Reformation parish kirk. The Royal Mile has an exceptional wealth (by British standards) of c16–17 houses built for nobles who wanted to be near the court and, in the case of the royal (i.e. mercantile) burgh of Edinburgh, for merchants. Equally important from an early date, and often just as grand in their appointments, are the tenements fronting the main street or the wynds, or lining the rear courts. Many of them rise to an astonishing height from the lower slopes of the ridge.

This densely built-up spur of rock, with the Castle at its head and the palace at its foot, forms the historic image of the city as it was seen by c17 and early c18 engravers. Their vantagepoint was Blackford Hill, from which one can still see the same half-natural, half-man-made profile against the background of the Forth and the hills of Fife, but with the s suburbs in the foreground in place of the open country.

Major expansion did not take place till the mid c18 – piecemeal to the s but regular on the level ridge of the Town's land to the N, made accessible by draining and bridging the Nor' Loch. Across the Nor' Loch valley (now containing gardens and the railway) is the First New Town, starting with Princes Street – the principal route transfixing the city in a straight line from E to W, and a long promenade from which to view a great natural theatre of architecture, cut in two by the Grecian galleries of the Mound. In one part the Castle rock dominates; in the other the main parts are played by Georgian and Victorian buildings on the slopes of the Old Town – tenements of prosaic or quirky silhouette, Gothic towers and steeples, civic porticos, palaces of commerce.

Princes Street forms the s and Queen Street the N edge of the symmetrically planned First New Town, which was built up from E to W in the last quarter of the c18. Adam designed a great town-house in Queen Street, Chambers another in St Andrew Square, which is answered at the other end by Adam's almost perfectly surviving Charlotte Square. For the rest, there is an even balance between the original more or less distinguished Georgian houses and prestigious Victorian and Edwardian commercial redevelopment – all together producing a remarkable unity within the regular gridiron plan.

More new towns followed in the early c19, each distinct in itself but carefully joined to its neighbours. Today 'the New Town' is the collective name for all these developments, which together form an area of continuous Georgian layout and architecture stretching 1 km. to the N from Princes Street and some 3 km. from E to W (First New Town to Calton, Central Area Nos. 4–12 in the gazetteer). Henry-Russell Hitchcock calls it 'the most extensive example of a Romantic Classical city in the world'.* In some of the new towns the romance seems accidental – the picturesque result of imposing formal plans on uneven ground. In others (especially the Calton) it is deliberate, realizing the advantages of good sites, open outlook and tree-planting.

Not only in what is called the New Town but also on the city outskirts, and further afield along the main roads, almost all landowners eventually put up their ground for development – i.e. they offered building sites for sale, with a more or less exact description of what was to be built. So there is a close connexion between the pattern of suburban development and that of the large and small estates (some corporately held) that surrounded the city on all sides. Often the street names identify the former owner or his property, which may have been just a modest villa with a garden. Some properties (e.g. those in the South West area) were built up with urban terraces like the New Town, some were for villas, like the compact Blacket estate round Newington House, and some were for both, like Inverleith. The Georgian seaside resort of Portobello has a particularly engaging mixture. Many schemes were popular and thus quickly finished according to plan, but some went slowly and were subject to new fashions or lowered standards. Others achieved only a fragment of what was intended, and still others found no takers at all. It depended mainly on the landowner's success in predicting the demand and judging the best time to advertise.

Villa schemes allowed much flexibility of individual design, and the Georgian layout at Trinity continued to attract the best sort of villa over a very long period. The early Victorian scheme at Greenhill (Morningside) was followed by a continuous belt to the S of the city, ending with the charming part-Edwardian suburb of Colinton. These are all durable buildings, and the long-term demand was eventually satisfied; equivalent C20 excellence is very hard to find. Meantime from the 1880s came the massive invasion and infiltration of another type – the Victorian tenement, from the grandest in Marchmont, bay-windowed and turreted, to the most economical on the industrial E side, where the feeling of Victorian Edinburgh is still strong. Development was now much more than self-help for land-owners, or investment on the side; it was very big business indeed.

Thus apart from various old settlements engulfed by the growth of the city (the parish centres with their friendly mixture of buildings, their old graveyards and sometimes their original churches), Edinburgh outside the Old Town consists of a number of neighbourhoods, most of which have a distinct identity of building type, character and class. How was this local conformity produced and enforced? The most important factor has been the feudal Scottish system of land ownership, which lasted from the Middle Ages till quite recently. All land, in theory at least, belonged to the Crown, which granted 'feus' (estates or

---

* *Architecture, Nineteenth and Twentieth Centuries*, Pelican History of Art.

plots) in perpetuity to vassals-in-chief, in return for services
(feudal duties) specified in the charter. Conditions as to how the
land could be used might also be specified. Usually the vassal-
in-chief could in turn grant feus (strictly speaking, sub-feus),
again specifying services and conditions – and so on *ad infini-
tum*. By the C17 nearly all feu duties were changed into annual
money payments, and the feus were being sold. But this did not
make the possession of a feu into the equivalent of a freehold.
Anyone buying or inheriting a feu had to go on paying feu duty,
and was still bound by the attached conditions. From the late
C18 these conditions were often very detailed, requiring houses
or tenements to be built in conformity with elevations provided
by the feudal superior. Even for villas there were at least detailed guidelines. Different superiors varied in the strictness of
their control, both of the initial development and later alterations. In most cases the collection of duties has now been sold
as an investment, and it is possible for the feuar* to pay a lump
sum and cease payment. Some superiors, especially the old corporate ones, still exercise a degree of control over use and development, but their powers are subsidiary to those of the planning authority.

Another disciplinary influence has been the control of building standards and safety by the Dean of Guild. The exact function of the office varied from one Scottish burgh to another, as
also did the title, which means the head of the guild of merchants. In Edinburgh the earliest minutes of the Dean of Guild
Court go back to 1529 and are concerned with property rights.
In 1584 it was appointed to adjudicate between neighbouring
proprietors, and in 1674 it was empowered to grant or reject
petitions for new building or alteration, and to see that dangerous buildings were made safe. This has done much to ensure
substantial building and also to prevent flimsy additions such as
upper-floor bathrooms stuck on to the backs of Georgian terraces – though not, unfortunately, the ground-floor shops that
project from some of their fronts. In 1975 the office of Dean of
Guild ceased, and its main job was taken over (as elsewhere in
Scotland) by a director of building control. Its limited aesthetic
functions (e.g. the insistence on certain materials in certain
areas) had already passed to the planning authority, whose other
responsibilities include the protection of listed buildings and
the preservation and enhancement of character in conservation
areas. Much of what is described in this volume would be in
less good shape – or would not have survived at all – without
the planners' intervention.

---

* The feuar is the one who buys and then owns the feu, feuing it from the
superior. Confusingly, feuing is also the word applied to the function of the
superior – but not in this volume.

TOPOGRAPHY AND BUILDING MATERIALS

BY G. Y. CRAIG

Edinburgh has the most spectacular landscape of any in Britain. Just beyond its s boundary lies the great barrier of the Pentland Hills. Caerketton Hill (440 m.) looms over the little village of Swanston, and from here 10 km. to the N the coastal plain slopes down to the Firth of Forth and the harbours of Granton, Leith and Newhaven. Edinburgh, which has now absorbed these places, chose a much more difficult site – the middle hills of the group that stand up suddenly from the low ground of the plain. Like many towns, it occupies a strategic point on a traffic route. But the original strategy that led to its foundation was defensive – not to assist access but to block it.

All this eventful terrain rests on a complicated geological jigsaw of sediments, extinct volcanoes, lava flows and igneous intrusions, its pattern emphasized by the differential weathering of hard and soft rocks. The high ground consists of hard igneous rocks such as the old volcanic cores of Arthur's Seat and the Castle rock, the igneous intrusion such as Salisbury Crags and Corstorphine Hill, and the abundant lava flows which form most of the Pentlands and the Braids, Craiglockhart Hill, Calton Hill and the slopes of Arthur's Seat. The lower ground is mostly sandstones and mudstones, limestones and coals. During the Ice Age the topography was further modified by ice which moved from W to E, shaping the crag-and-tail structures of the Castle rock and Royal Mile (flanked by the low ground of Nor' Loch and Grassmarket), Blackford Hill and Lady Road, the Braid Hills and Liberton. In each case the crag is formed of solid rock and the tail is composed of glacial debris. Remnants of glacial lakes include what was the Nor' Loch below the Castle, the Meadows, and the lower part of Corstorphine.

The oldest rocks of the Devonian period, mostly lava flows, form much of the Pentland and Braid Hills and Blackford Hill. The younger Devonian rocks are water-laid reddish-brown sandstones and are clearly seen along the new Edinburgh by-pass near Redford Barracks. During early Carboniferous times the volcanoes of Arthur's Seat and the Castle rock were active; lava flows and ash falls covered Edinburgh and its neighbourhood. When the volcanic activity ceased, sands and organically rich muds were deposited in shallow lakes by rivers draining from the mountains. Limestones were formed in lagoons, and from time to time tropical coal forests grew over much of the area. The sands brought down by these rivers a little over three hundred million years ago are now beds of sandstone. Close inspection of almost any sandstone building will show traces of the origin of the stone (*see* Fig. 1); both ripple-marks and cross-bedding are visible on the W pier of the E entry to the City Chambers, on adjacent stones.

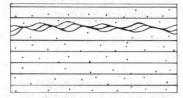 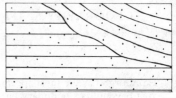

Fig. 1   Sandstone beds with ripple marks formed by a current of water moving from right to left.

Sandstone beds showing erosion by a later current of water which has deposited sand at an angle to the older bedding.

Edinburgh's sandstones provided the main source of building material till well into the C20. In its strict geological sense, sandstone is a term that defines the grain size of a sedimentary rock (2 mm. down to 0·062 mm.), not its mineral composition. The sandstones in the Edinburgh area are composed of grains of quartz, with subsidiary minerals such as mica and feldspar. In spite of obvious differences in colour and the ability to resist decay, most sandstones contain at least ninety per cent quartz.

The cement which binds the grains of quartz (sand) together is critical, both for ease of quarrying the stone and for its subsequent durability. Craigleith sandstone has a siliceous cement, and was hard to quarry and work but resistant to weathering (e.g. in Charlotte Square). Other sandstones are cemented by lime or by iron oxide. They were cheaper to buy and easier to dress, but have decayed more rapidly in Edinburgh's climate and atmosphere. Unintentionally spectacular examples of the weathering of many building stones used in Edinburgh (including those from further afield) can be seen in the sandstone piers erected in 1886 on each side of Melville Drive at the w entry to the Meadows. The name of the parent quarry was engraved on each stone, but some names have completely disappeared, despite renewal after threat of structural failure. These piers also show a variety of polished (perfectly smooth) and broached (horizontally tooled) finishes, but not the droving that characterizes a broached Georgian stone with a thin margin of toolmarks at right angles to the edge, or the rock-faced finishes of many Georgian basements and Victorian baronial tenements.

The geographical distribution of the main sandstone beds and quarries in or near Edinburgh is shown in Fig. 2. The main formations quarried for building are the Upper Old Red Sandstone (Devonian) at Craigmillar, whose stone was used for the original work at George Heriot's School, and in the Carboniferous system the Craigleith, Ravelston, Hailes, Dunnet and Binny sandstones. But names can be confusing. 'Craigleith' sandstone was quarried at Craigleith and also at Blackhall, Craigcrook, Granton and Barnton Park. 'Hailes' sandstone came from Hailes and Redhall. 'Binny', an important siliceous sandstone, was quarried in many places to the w of Edinburgh besides Binny itself, near Uphall in West Lothian. The name implies certain qualities, rather than the actual source; even in

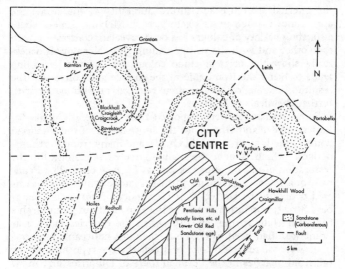

Fig. 2 Simplified geological map of the Edinburgh area
with the main sandstone beds and quarries.

one quarry the sandstone varies greatly in composition, colour
and performance. Apart from these famous names and types,
sandstones were quarried to a lesser extent from the rocks of
the limestone group in the Midlothian coalfield to the s of Edinburgh and from the coal measures in Midlothian and West
Lothian (e.g. Fauldhouse).

The predominantly grey colour of most Edinburgh sandstones is deceptive because the uniformly weathered outer layers
hide a surprising range of colours. Few of the sandstones in
their fresh state can be called grey. A rock colour chart shows
that they vary in colour from pinkish grey (some Craigleith)
through yellowish brown (Craigleith, Hailes, Craigmillar) and
greyish orange (Binny, Hailes and Ravelston) to dusky brown
(Ravelston). Less than one per cent of iron in the rock will
provide shades of yellow, brown, red, or even green, according
to the compounds formed. Carbon derived from plant material
provides the shades of grey, as in many examples of Hailes
sandstone which have closely spaced grey laminae of plant fragments separating the yellowish brown layers of sandstone. It
also contributes just as much as airborne soot to the darkening
of stone surfaces on finished buildings, because of deposits of
dead algae.

Uniformity of weathering brings a pleasing unity of appearance, silver-grey overall, to buildings (especially terraces) built
of different stones, and to the city as a whole. The process
known as cleaning usually involves not only the removal of
superficial dirt but the chemical bleaching or mechanical removal of the weathered surface layers. Whatever its effect on

the internal structure and future durability of the stone, the appearance is often unsatisfactory, as in Melville Street, where a startling variety of colours has been revealed, contrasting with each other and with the still prevailing grey. Nor does it necessarily show the original stone colour, for chemical cleaning tends to bring the iron oxide to the surface and conversely the resulting orange colour is often reduced or eliminated with further chemical applications.

Some sandstones were imported from Fife (e.g. Cullalo for Fettes College and Grange for the substructure of the Victorian dome at the University's Old Quad), and many from Northumberland, which is now the main source of sandstone for the restoration of old buildings as well as for new ones. The Prudham quarry, near Hexham, furnished stone which has weathered badly on the Heriot-Watt University's frontage in Chambers Street, but rather better at the University of Edinburgh's McEwan Hall. In the late C19, when the quarries in or near Edinburgh had been worked out, the most noticeable importations were of red sandstone of Locharbriggs type brought by rail from quarries in the Permian rocks of Dumfriesshire in SW Scotland. Formed under desert conditions, these stones are the remains of ancient, wind-blown sand dunes later cemented by iron oxide; they have very well rounded grains (without the flakes of mica that lie along the bedding plane in Edinburgh sandstone), and great sweeps of wind-blown cross-beds are visible on many of the cut faces. By the beginning of the C20 Edinburgh's townscape was studded with red buildings, nonconformist in colour if not in style, and the two rival railway companies were rushing up their giant hotels at opposite ends of Princes Street – the North British in yellow Northumberland stone, the Caledonian more conventional in design but eyecatching in its pink Dumfriesshire colour. But stone remained the rule. Even the Prudential Assurance company had to abandon its red-brick trademark in favour of Dumfriesshire stone on a speckly brown Peterhead granite base.

Limestones are extremely rare (e.g. the Portland stone of Commercial Union Insurance in George Street) and granite even more so (e.g. the Guardian Royal Exchange office). But polished granite for shopfronts became popular in the late C19 and the repertoire has subsequently increased with all manner of polished sheets of (mostly imported) rock such as blue syenite, green slate, marbles and diorite. They fulfil the role of geological wallpaper and no more need be said of them.

The first systematic paving of Edinburgh streets took place in the early C19, and the material used was dolerite (a very hard igneous rock otherwise known as basalt or whin), split into oblong setts. Whin chips appear on the footpath round Moray Place gardens (and small pins of the same material are used to stabilize the mortar joints in some of the houses on the W side of George Square). But the more usual footpath covering was with slabs of Edinburgh or Arbroath stone and later (when rail transport made it possible) dark grey slabs from Caithness. The railways also brought grey and orange granite setts from Aberdeenshire for the main carriageways, and large areas of setts, both granite and whin, survive. Footpaths, however, are largely resurfaced with concrete slabs; the recent paving of the Parliament Square with Caithness slabs is exceptional.

Scotland, and Edinburgh in particular, is famous for its slated roofs, the size and exposure of each course of slates diminishing towards the top. Slates are highly compacted muds, which break along a cleavage formed when the rocks were strongly folded, and the great majority of those in Edinburgh were imported by sea from the huge quarries of Easdale and Ballachulish. Welsh slate, sometimes purple, seems to have been introduced in late Georgian or early Victorian times. Later, along with the red stones of sw Scotland, came the pale green slates of Cumberland, but never in great quantities (e.g. at the Fire Station in Lauriston Place).

Brick is merely a postscript. Edinburgh and its surroundings have plenty of clay and the coal to burn it, but until the mid c19 brick never appears as a facing material, and then only in out-of-the-way locations (e.g. at Rosemount Buildings, Gardner's Crescent). However, it frequently crops up in useful minor applications such as the building or replacement of chimneys (for which it is better than stone in areas where formal appearance is not important) and for partition walls in Georgian houses and tenements as well as garden walls for villas and country houses. A special temporary brickwork was set up for the building of Colinton House in 1801. The exception to this secondary role for brick is, of course, Portobello, with its brickworks, tile-works and potteries. Portobello Tower, stuck with bits and pieces of old stone buildings like a red-brick scrapscreen, is a nice if rather lonely gesture against Edinburgh's conformity.

Sandstones used in Edinburgh

CRAIGMILLAR (Edinburgh)	George Heriot's School, original work
CRAIGLEITH (Edinburgh)	City Chambers, principal building
	University Old Quadrangle
	N side of Charlotte Square
	St Andrew's and St George's Church
	West Register House (St George's Church)
	Parliament Square and the Law Courts
	Leith Town Hall
HAILES (Edinburgh) Hailes Quarry	
	New College (Blue Hailes)
	Royal Infirmary (Pink Hailes)

Redhall Quarry	St John's Episcopal Church, original work
	St Paul's Episcopal Church, original work
	Lothian Road Church
BINNY (West Lothian)	
Binny Quarry	Scott monument
	Tolbooth Church
	Donaldson's School
	General Post Office, principal building
Hermand Quarry	Bank of Scotland, 103 George Street
Dalmeny Quarry	100 Princes Street
	Bank of Scotland, 66 George Street
	Palmerston Place, E side
Humbie Quarry	Royal Scottish Academy, newer work
	Steeple of Tron Church
RED SANDSTONE (Dumfriesshire)	
Locharbriggs Quarry	Caledonian Hotel
	Edinburgh College of Art
Corncockle Quarry	Milton House School
Corsehill Quarry	70 Princes Street
	Scottish National Portrait Gallery

PREHISTORIC AND ROMAN EDINBURGH*

BY GORDON S. MAXWELL AND J. N. GRAHAM RITCHIE

The boundary of a modern city is an artificial framework within which to examine the remains of man's ancient past, for it owes little to the geographical factors that determined the pattern of past human activity. The prehistory of Edinburgh mirrors that of Lothian generally; the same fundamental trends in social development, early technology and economic life can be discerned in the City's surviving monuments and finds as in those of the larger Region. It is difficult to imagine the topography of Edinburgh without buildings, the slopes of the Old and New Towns covered by forests of oak and deciduous trees, and the lochs and streams (now filled in or carefully piped) in marshy hollows between the ridges that still dominate the city; but such was the environment in early prehistory.

In the sixth and fifth millennia B.C. the earliest settlers wandered freely along the shores of the Forth in search of game or

---

* Some sites are within the Edinburgh District but outside the area covered by this volume; their former county location is given in brackets.

exploiting the beds of shellfish that formed one staple item of their diet, though there is scanty evidence of their passage – a few flints from their hunting implements. Similarly, our only indication of the presence of those communities that introduced stock-rearing and agriculture in the fourth millennium B.C. is provided by some of the stone axes with which they made clearings in the scrub and tree-cover for their small farms.

There are no settlement sites for the period immediately following c. 2000 B.C., and centres of population have to be guessed at by the distribution of burial cists and standing stones. Groups of cists or cremations in cinerary urns found on the banks of the Water of Leith, e.g. at Juniper Green, and on the Braid Hills and at Fairmilehead, are likely to indicate small and fairly permanent hamlets of farmers with some knowledge of bronze metallurgy. Such villages were almost certainly undefended and comprised no more than clusters of round timber houses and barns. Without the lasting traces of ramparts or stonework to betray their presence, settlements like these are discovered only by accident. Several cists were discovered in the middle of the last century during the building of Lennox Street and Oxford Terrace (Dean), and in 1823 two crouched inhumations were found in cists in front of St Mary's Church, Bellevue Crescent (Northern New Town). Several urns containing cremations were unearthed during the construction of the north pier of the Dean Bridge. Portable objects such as bronzes are less certain indications of areas of settlement, but it has been suggested that the axes of Late Bronze Age date that have been found along the lower reaches of the Water of Leith point to the existence of a port or a small trading station somewhere between Stockbridge and the Dean Village.

Within Edinburgh the most impressive monument of second-millennium date is the Caiystane (Fairmilehead), a rugged sandstone monolith decorated with a number of worn cup-marks; there are two smaller standing stones at Ravenswood Avenue and Kingsinch School (Gilmerton). The Buckstone (Fairmilehead) is traditionally associated with the Barony of Penicuik, but there is no evidence for the date of its erection. Only one prehistoric cairn still survives, that at Galachlaw (Fairmilehead), but several burial mounds were destroyed in the C18 and C19, including those on Figgate Muir (Leith) and at Fairmilehead. There are, however, several large cairns or barrows near Edinburgh, e.g. at Earl Cairnie in Dalmeny Park (formerly West Lothian) and Newbridge (formerly Midlothian). The site at Newbridge consists of a large earthen barrow surrounded by a series of standing stones, but these are not concentric and do not form a stone circle; an outlying stone a little distance to the east of the barrow may have been part of the same setting. The Catstane near Turnhouse (formerly West Lothian) bears an early Christian inscription but may be of Bronze Age date; it later formed the focus for a series of long-cist burials in the middle of the first millennium A.D. Apart from the rather uncertain examples of cup-marks on the Caiystane, there are several cup-marked rocks in the area, including those from the Braid Hills and Saughtonhall (Calder Road), now in the National Museum of Antiquities of Scotland (decorated cist slabs from Craigie Hill and Carlowrie (formerly West Lothian) have been lost); several expanses of cup-marked and cup-and-ring-marked rock may be seen on Tormain Hill (Ratho). Although such decorated stones are usually ascribed to the second millennium B.C., both earlier and later examples have been found.

In the later first millennium B.C. the importance of the area becomes apparent. Iron Age fortifications and settlements are still to be seen in Holyrood Park (Old Town), on Blackford Hill and on Wester Craiglockhart Hill (all in a poor state of preservation). The concentration of forts in Holyrood Park suggests that this was an area of particularly intensive occupation, incorporating at least four defended settlements of the Celtic tribe known to the Romans as the Votadini. Other extensive Iron Age fortifications exist on the summit of Craigie Hill (in Dalmeny Park, formerly West Lothian), a flat-topped ridge defended on one side by a series of walls and on the other by the natural crags. Although the walls are now denuded, their positions are clearly marked, as are several hut-circles in the interior.

Excavations at the now-destroyed fort on Kaimes Hill (near Dalmahoy, formerly Midlothian) revealed something of the complex structural history of such sites. Initially the hilltop was enclosed by a single stone-faced rampart which may have been built as early as the C6 B.C.; behind the stone facing the core was simply earth and rubble made more stable by a lacing of timber beams. When this rampart collapsed, the fort was provided with a new rubble wall, and may also have been strengthened by the addition of two outer ramparts built to enclose a larger area than that of the earlier fort. At this period too the fort was additionally protected by a series of pointed stones set upright in the ground outside the rampart to impede attacking cavalry. This type of defence, known as *chevaux de frise*, may be paralleled at Dreva and Cademuir Hill, SW of Peebles (Borders), and is a reminder of the aristocratic and warlike nature of Celtic society. The best preserved hut-circle on Kaimes Hill measured about 11·6 m. overall and consisted of the substantial stone footings for a timber and turf hut.

The finds from such settlement sites, comprising sherds of coarse pottery, iron knives, stone lamps and stone pounders, give little impression of the sophistication of Celtic art. There are, however, two superb examples of Celtic craftsmanship from Edinburgh, a bronze armlet from Wester Craiglockhart Hill and a sword scabbard from Mortonhall,* dating to the first two centuries A.D. The decoration of this fine scabbard, which is accentuated by the use of two different-coloured bronze alloys in its manufacture, demonstrates the remarkable skill of which

---

* Now in the National Museum of Antiquities in Edinburgh.

Celtic bronzesmiths were capable. Just how much may still be found was shown in 1969 when, on the southern slopes of Arthur's Seat above Samson's Ribs, the chance discovery of a Roman signet ring* with a sardonyx intaglio led to the identification of a hitherto unrecorded Iron Age fort.

Our knowledge of the advance of the ROMANS into southern Scotland, and the subsequent occupation, has been amplified by a number of significant discoveries since the writing in 1977 of the *Lothian* volume of *The Buildings of Scotland*. In particular the identification of a hitherto unknown fort at Elginhaugh (Midlothian), opposite the Roman temporary camp at Eskbank, has furnished important new evidence of the scheme of things in Edinburgh during the CI A.D.

One of the major results of the campaigns of Agricola in 77–83 was the establishment of Dere Street, the main arterial route from the Tyne to the Forth *via* Newstead and Lauderdale. Elginhaugh was the bridgehead fort which guarded its crossing of the North Esk, and the air photographs that revealed the existence of the fort also showed beyond doubt that the N continuation of Dere Street was indicated by the line of the A7. It would thus appear that for more than 6 km. the modern road has preserved the route of its ancient predecessor, still exhibiting the point-to-point alignment that was the hallmark of Roman military engineering. Basically the surviving road consists of two straight sections with a single major change of direction at the summit of Gilmerton Hill. When it 'disappears' at the Nether Liberton traffic lights it is on a heading which would have taken it along the S shore of the former Burgh Loch (now the Meadows) towards a crossing of the Water of Leith near the present Dean Village. The ultimate destination, at least in the second (Antonine) occupation of Scotland in A.D. 140–63, was the Roman fort of Cramond at the mouth of the river Almond. It is possible that in the CI the Romans did not avail themselves of Cramond's harbourage, preferring to drive on to the Forth–Clyde isthmus by a more inland route. In that case, the road may have changed its alignment on the high ground to the W of the Castle rock and proceeded W, perhaps for several miles, on a line approximately that of the present Edinburgh–Glasgow road. Some confirmation is provided by the Roman milestone discovered in the C17 near Newbridge‡ (formerly Midlothian) where the A8 crosses the river Almond, and two Roman marching-camps found in 1980 at Gogar Green (formerly Midlothian) just to the S of the modern road. Whatever the precise course of this W extension of Dere Street, there can be no doubt that it once traversed the heart of the present city. Indeed its proximity to Din Eidyn (the Castle rock) may have contributed to the use of the rock as a centre of Votadinian power in the post-Roman period.

* Now in the National Museum of Antiquities in Edinburgh.

‡ The milestone is now reckoned to have been found near its original position and not (as previously believed) to have been brought to Newbridge from Cramond.

The occupation of 140-63 saw the establishment of the Antonine Wall between Forth and Clyde - a frontier barrier of turf guarded by nineteen forts and intermediate 'milecastles'. Its flanks were protected by forts and fortlets (all apparently new foundations) along the s banks of both estuaries, those on the Forth being at Carriden and Inveresk (*see The Buildings of Scotland: Lothian*), with Cramond between. The Roman site at Cramond (the name means 'Fort on the Almond') comprised a stone-vaulted *castellum*, an extensive extramural settlement, and very probably a harbour, though no trace of it survives.

The existence of a Roman station at Cramond was long suspected because of the discovery over the years of Roman coins, pottery and inscriptions, but the exact site remained unknown until the excavations of 1954-66. The fort, measuring 165 m. by 140 m. (2·3 ha.) was found to have been occupied during three separate phases: twice in the Antonine period (140-63) and once at the beginning of the c3 Severan period. Throughout its life the fort was defended by a clay rampart 7 m. thick, revetted externally by a stone wall, with double ditches affording additional protection on the E and probably the S. Only the eastern part of the *praetentura* (the forward area of the fort) and the front of the range of principal buildings was uncovered during excavation, but sufficient evidence was obtained to show conclusively that in all three phases the *praetentura* had workshops (*fabricae*) but apparently no barracks, while the central range contained, in addition to the customary *principia* (headquarters building), *praetorium* (commandant's residence), and *horrea retentura* (granaries), a very robustly built magazine. As only limited areas of the *retentura* (the rear of the fort) have been examined, it is impossible to say how large a garrison was required to operate this works-depot and stores-base, but altars found here testify to the presence at some time of the thousand-strong *cohors I Tungrorum* and the five hundred-strong *cohors V Gallorum*. A bath-house was discovered outside the fort to the NW during excavations for a private house, and subsequent building works revealed that the extramural settlement, previously known to exist outside the E rampart of the fort, also extended some distance to the N and S. No structural traces of a C1 *castellum* have yet been found, and the context of early coins discovered in the neighbourhood of Cramond has yet to be defined; there is, however, definite evidence for an occupation of the fort and settlement, in a form not yet fully understood, at some time later than the Severan period.

In 1975-8 further excavations confirmed the complex nature of the surrounding settlement and located a second bath-house in a particularly fine state of preservation some 80 m. to the N of the fort. Additional evidence was thereby furnished of the extent of the brief c2 occupation (109-212) when Cramond and Carpow on the Tay were isolated outposts of the Roman province during and after the campaigns of the emperor Septimius Severus. Late in the c3 or probably early in the c4 Roman pottery was again being used - whether by native inhabitants or by a temporary military presence cannot yet be determined. Of the traditions alleging a Roman occupation of sites in the city centre (e.g. the Calton Hill and Nether Bow) little can be said save that they are still without archaeological foundation; the original provenance of the carving of triple mother goddesses found at Colinton is unknown.

There is no archaeological evidence for the important change in status that may be suspected in the middle of the first millennium A.D. when Din Eidyn (Edinburgh) became the capital of the British kingdom of the Gododdin (the earlier Votadini). This triumph was short-lived, as Din Eidyn fell to the Anglian invaders after a siege in 638. By the mid C7 the Forth had become the boundary between the Pictish kingdom to the north and the Angles to the south. The centre of power at this time is assumed to be the Castle rock, the natural citadel from which the warriors of Gododdin set forth to make an abortive attack on the Angles at Catraeth (usually identified as Catterick) and commemorated in a series of heroic elegies known as *Y Gododdin*. There are now no traces of the royal hall of Mynyddog, the British king whose seat Din Eidyn was, nor of the halls of the later Anglian chieftains. The symbol-stone found to the N of the Castle (if its original setting was hereabouts) may indicate the presence of some Christian Picts in the British kingdom of Gododdin about this time. Further afield are the fortifications on Dalmahoy Hill (formerly Midlothian) which may date from the middle of the first millennium A.D., and the secondary stone-walled fort overlying the N end of the earlier structure at Craigie Hill, Dalmeny, which has been compared to it. More evidence of the increasing strength of Christianity can be seen in a cemetery to one side of the Catstane, near Turnhouse (formerly Midlothian), with an inscription of the late C5 or early C6; and in long-cist cemeteries at Parkburn (Lasswade) and Gogarburn (Glasgow Road). These cemeteries, like the Bronze Age cist burials two millennia earlier, suggest settled communities living close by, but no trace of houses or villages has yet been discovered. All of them, like the continuing civil settlement at Cramond, now lie within the City of Edinburgh District.

MEDIEVAL CHURCHES

BY CHRISTOPHER WILSON

According to an anonymous monk of Durham writing in the early C12, the Northumbrian monastery of Lindisfarne had an outpost of some kind at Edinburgh in the mid C9. It has been suggested that St Cuthbert's church goes back to that time, although nothing so early has survived or been recorded there.

A church or chapel must have been among the royal buildings occupying the Castle rock in the later C11, but 'St Margaret's Chapel' was built at least twenty years after her death in 1093.
12 Its Anglo-Norman ROMANESQUE details include chevron of the kind apparently first used at Durham Cathedral c.1110-20. The plan is peculiar in that the apse of the chancel does not register externally. Parallels on this scale seem to be lacking, but squared apses were used in the choir aisles of quite a number of the greater Anglo-Norman churches, Durham included. Also unusual in so small a building is the use of stone vaulting over each compartment, a half-dome in the apse, a barrel-vault in the nave.

Before the Reformation St Giles was the only parish church in the royal burgh and its foundation no doubt coincided with that of the burgh itself around 1130. Today only one early/ mid-C12 capital survives, but until 1796 the nave was entered from the High Street through a large Romanesque portal carved by the same sculptors as Dalmeny church, Lothian. The chances are that this door was *in situ* and that the C12 St Giles was aisled and cruciform, like its late medieval successor and the later C12 St Nicholas, Aberdeen. Of Edinburgh's three known Romanesque churches, Holyrood is the only one to be documented: the foundation took place in 1128 and a charter of not later than 1136 includes a gift of timber for the buildings. All that remains above ground is the E processional door, typical of its date, with details not very different from those of the chancel arch of St Margaret's Chapel. The church itself, known only from excavations, had a flat E end, transepts each with a single rectangular chapel, and an aisleless nave – a plan best known from the primitive Cistercian churches at Waverley (1128) and Tintern (1131). In this case the source must be the church begun in 1125 at the Augustinian Merton Priory in Surrey, the 'mother house' of Holyrood in the sense that the first detachment of canons came from there. When Holyrood founded its own burgh (the Canongate) in 1140, the parishioners used the nave of the abbey church, as they did until 1688. Within the boundaries of modern Edinburgh, Duddingston has a good example of a C12 village church, much cut about by later work. The shortness of the nave and the closely spaced buttresses create boxy, upright proportions that cannot be matched in any other Norman parish church in Lothian. The original chancel arch and corbel tables remain, but the interesting s door has decayed very badly. Still recognizable is the group of small low-relief figures on the l. jamb shaft, a totally unarchitectural approach to sculpture paralleled in the small figures flanking the s door at Dalmeny.

The EARLY GOTHIC nave of Holyrood is Edinburgh's only building from that period, but it is a work of the highest value.
14 The w front, sadly mutilated as it is, can claim even international importance, for its central section had huge windows screened by open arcading on the same principle as the much later C13 w front of Strasbourg Cathedral. But the sources of

Strasbourg are French not English and the Holyrood screen-work was not taken up in England or Scotland. The source of the idea is probably the two-layer arcading in the aisles of St Hugh's Choir at Lincoln, a design which many early C13 architects were content to develop far more modestly. This extreme originality shows itself also in the basic shape of the W front. The N tower, like its demolished S counterpart, stands outside and in advance of the aisles so that only one corner is joined to the body of the church. There are no exact parallels, but the Romanesque W fronts at Lindisfarne (*c.* 1130) and Rochester (*c.* 1160) use relatively small turrets in much the same way. Lindisfarne may indeed have been in the Holyrood master's mind, for there too, in more modest form, is a double wall passage over the W door. The towers are covered with horizontal bands of blind arcading – a commonplace of C13 English W fronts. The spandrels, on the other hand, have the rare motif of heads in roundels, for which the best English parallels are probably the heads in quatrefoils on the tomb of Archbishop Hubert Walter of Canterbury †1205. The lintel of the portal has rows of roundels framing angels' busts, a charming design but vitiated by carving of wretched quality. A date of *c.* 1220 would suit all this. The oldest work at Holyrood is the N aisle wall, a sumptuously detailed Transitional design showing only the most cautious approach to the mature Early English style inaugurated at Lincoln in 1192. In the rest of the nave this toe-in-the-water attitude to E.E. was abandoned, and practically everything was taken direct from Lincoln. This applies both to major features like the triforium and to minor ones like the concave-sided vault shafts. The foliage carving too is the fully developed stiff-leaf popularized by Lincoln. It is nothing short of a disaster that the most distinctive feature of the design, the high vault, no longer exists. It was arranged in sexpartite compartments over every bay, as in both E and W transepts at Lincoln, and it must have created a strong rhythmic contrast with the wide arcades below. But in spite of so many detailed borrowings, the Holyrood nave is in spirit poles apart from Lincoln. It is an integrated and consistently executed design whereas Lincoln is experimental and varied: it has elegant, rather dry details and balanced proportions but none of the quirkinesses and crudities of Lincoln. This is a notable instance of contemporaries using the same formal language for entirely different ends.

From the FOURTEENTH CENTURY there is again just a single major monument, the rebuilding of St Giles. Unfortunately, the dating evidence leaves much to be desired. The nave must have been up by *c.* 1370, because a contract of 1387 exists for the building on of a new S aisle. A useful *terminus ante quem* for the transepts is provided by the addition of St John's Chapel to the N transept in or before 1395. The ample aisled choir may have been built in preparation for the Town Council's attempt in 1419 to have St Giles raised to collegiate rank. But notwithstanding variations in the date of its parts, St Giles was, by the

early C15, a stylistically homogeneous building on a regular
plan.* The choir was of four aisled bays, the nave of five, there
was a central tower, and, as at Glasgow Cathedral, the transepts
did not project beyond the aisles. The arcades were extremely
conservative with their chamfered arches, octagonal piers and
waterholding bases. The transepts and choir, if not the nave,
were covered by the pointed tunnel-vaults with surface ribs so
beloved of Scottish Late Gothic designers, though here the lateral cells were slightly domical as in the presbytery at Melrose
Abbey of 1385 etc. The central space of the choir had as yet no
clearstorey, only a vault like those in the aisles. The effect of
three broad parallel volumes vaulted at the same level must have
been extremely impressive and the nearest equivalent in Scotland to a German Late Gothic hall church. Among the earliest
of many piecemeal additions to this basic plan was the Chapel
of St John already mentioned. It has details more sophisticated
than the only other Perp work in the district, the windows at
Corstorphine in the s chapel of c. 1400 and the chancel of c. 1429
or c. 1444. These two examples hardly alter the general picture
of independence from England in the late Middle Ages.

The FIFTEENTH and EARLY SIXTEENTH CENTURIES were
the most productive for church building in Edinburgh. The
choir of St Giles was remodelled c. 1453 by rebuilding the two
E bays and adding a clearstorey with a fine tierceron vault. The
new piers have capitals and bases of a curious prismatic type
17 (already used in the Albany Aisle of c. 1401–10) which seems to
be peculiar to St Giles. They reappear in the Preston Aisle s of
the choir (begun 1455) and the later and very similar s aisles of
the nave.

18 Apart from additions to St Giles, the most important project
after the mid C15 was the choir of Trinity College Church
founded by James II's Queen, Mary of Gueldres. Work had
begun by 1460 and continued to the end of the century. The
transepts were built c. 1530 but the nave was never started. The
choir has three aisled bays plus a three-sided apse, the earliest
in Scotland after that at Crossraguel Priory (Ayrshire) of
c. 1440. The s aisle was entered through a porch of the shallow
type of Roslin Chapel and St Salvator's Chapel, St Andrews.
As rebuilt on a new site in 1872 the church has no aisles, porch
or transepts, yet it is still recognizable as the most accomplished
building of its date in Scotland. The two-storey elevation, the
graceful tierceron-vault and many of the mouldings are very
close to the contemporary parts of the choir of St Giles. Only
the piers are quite different: four shafts and four chamfered
pieces. Among the rarer features of Trinity College Church on
its old site were the flying buttresses. At Holyrood massive
flyers were added by Abbot Crawford (1460–83) when he replaced the original C13 vaults.

Easily the most original late C15 building in Edinburgh was
the double-decker chapel of hexagonal plan built c. 1477–87 for

* The impression of homogeneity might have been lessened had the tracery
survived.

James III on the S side of Restalrig Parish Church. Sadly, only 21 the lower storey survives. It is exactly like a chapter house, with a rib-vault branching from a central pier; indeed, the early C13 chapter house at Holyrood could have been the inspiration, though it was octagonal. The vault is in plan a six-pointed star divided into twelve equilateral triangles of the same size. From fragments it is known that the upper vault was of the same plan, but as there was no central column the effect would have been that of a German Late Gothic 'net-vault'. The hexagonal shape was used also for St Margaret's Well (originally at Restalrig, now at Holyrood Park), but the vault plan here is more conventional. After the completion of the hexagon chapel a start was made on adding a large aisled choir to the adjacent parish church, but it seems that the scheme died with James III. The existing church at Restalrig is a plain rectangular building probably of the early C15. More enjoyable is Corstorphine church 20 of c. 1400–30 with its curiously disjointed silhouette. The chancel and S chapel are single tunnel-vaulted compartments with heavy buttresses and the Perp tracery already mentioned. The fat W tower carries a suitably dumpy stone spire similar to the big stair-turret on the S transept at Melrose Abbey.

The one large-scale project initiated in the late C15 was St Mary, Leith, the parish church in all but name (and now in fact known as the South Leith Parish Church). Royal gifts were made specifically to the 'new church' in 1487 and 1503. Rivalry with Edinburgh is detectable in the choice of a cruciform plan with a central tower. The E parts were destroyed in 1560 and the aisled seven-bay nave heavily restored in 1847–8. The octagonal W crossing piers still exist and square-headed clearstorey windows are recorded, but the one aesthetically impressive survival, the six-light W window, is now at Loch Awe, Argyll. Its rather static grouping of mouchettes looks forward to loop tracery, the final development (some would say decadence) of Gothic window design. There are still cusps here, but the loop tracery of c. 1530 at Trinity College is typical in its lack of them. Chapels were still being added to St Giles at the beginning of the C16 (Chepman Aisle, St Anthony's Aisle, Holy Blood Aisle, all on the S side), but the outstanding achievement of the years 16 around 1500 was the crown spire added to the central tower. This is another of the few exceptions to the general insularity of Scottish architecture in this period, for the idea of a spire composed of flying buttresses carrying a pinnacle or lantern was first evolved in England. The lost example at St Mary-le-Bow in London is undated, but that at St Nicholas, Newcastle, probably belongs to the 1470s. Crown spires quickly became a Scottish speciality, but their chronology is hazy because precise dates are lacking for St Giles and its destroyed rivals at Haddington and Linlithgow. The crown at King's College, Aberdeen, finished by 1505, looks like a simplified copy of St Giles.

By way of mopping up, mention should be made of the very fragmentary St Anthony's Chapel in Holyrood Park. The date is presumably C15 but the exact function is a mystery. It was a vaulted room of three bays with an upper room over the W end, possibly for a priest. Collections of late medieval architectural fragments which deserve more attention than they can be given in *The Buildings of Scotland* are at Swanston Cottage (Fairmilehead), and the Astley Ainslie Hospital (Grange). Some at least may be from the many medieval religious foundations that have disappeared without trace. A full list of these is given in Cowan and Easson, *Medieval Religious Houses: Scotland* (London, 1976), but it is perhaps worth mentioning here that Edinburgh has lost three friaries (Dominican, Franciscan and Carmelite), a house of Dominican nuns (Sciennes), a collegiate church (St Mary in the Fields, the 'Kirk o' Field', on the site of the university) and no fewer than nine hospitals. The Hospital of St Mary Magdalen in the Cowgate survived the Reformation, but little more than the simple rectangular plan of its chapel goes back to the foundation of *c.* 1537.

Of medieval FURNISHINGS in Edinburgh churches hardly anything remains. Corstorphine church has a fine three-seater sedilia integral with the structure of the chancel. At Holyrood is a late C15 stone screen between the N nave aisle and the transept. The scraps of stained glass excavated from time to time at Holyrood are, with the exception of a C13 head, too fragmentary to be of aesthetic interest, but would no doubt repay study, if only to establish where Edinburgh's wealthiest religious foundation recruited glass painters in the C14. At this period the probable answer is England. An English sculptor is documented at Holyrood in 1372, when William Patrington (who had earlier worked on St Stephen's Chapel in Westminster Palace) had licence to come to Scotland to make the tomb of David II.

By the mid C15 Scottish patrons were turning to the Low Countries; the superb painted panels from a retable in Trinity College Church (now National Gallery), long attributed to *Hugo van der Goes* and his workshop, are the main surviving evidence for this reorientation. A fine panel from a late C15 stone retable, representing Extreme Unction and presumably one of a series of the Seven Sacraments, was found in 1859 in a close immediately N of St Giles (now National Museum of Antiquities). The Fetternear Banner (also Museum of Antiquities), thought to have been made for the Chapel of the Confraternity of the Holy Blood in St Giles, appears to date from the 1550s when (as the Dean of Guild accounts show) St Giles was being extensively refurbished. In the Magdalen Chapel is the only pre-Reformation stained glass in Scotland which survives in the building for which it was made. It is also very late, between 1542 and 1553. One roundel has a Renaissance arabesque frame. The brass eagle lectern, probably Flemish, given to Holyrood Abbey between 1524 and 1543 by Bishop Crichton of Dunkeld, was looted in 1544 by the English commander, Sir Richard Lee, who presented it to St Stephen's at St Albans, Hertfordshire, where it remains. A brass font from Holyrood, also removed by Lee, was at St Albans Abbey until the Civil War.

All the royal tombs at Holyrood have been destroyed, so for MONUMENTS Corstorphine must take first place. Of three wall-tombs to members of the Forrester family, the best, architecturally at least, is that to Sir John Forrester II †*c*. 1454. St Giles has several empty tomb recesses, the earliest in the Albany Aisle of *c*. 1401–10, the best and best preserved that from the Holy Blood Aisle of *c*. 1518. The brass to the Regent Moray in St Giles is a palimpsest with part of two figures of a late C15 couple wearing long gowns. The style and the quality make a Flemish origin likely. None of the few remaining grave slabs is outstanding in any way. Holyrood has the biggest collection, including one of *c*. 1300 with only the name in fine Lombardic letters. The foundress of the Magdalen Chapel died in 1533 but her tomb slab, unlike the stained glass she commissioned, shows no sign of Renaissance influence.

POST-REFORMATION CHURCHES

After the Scottish Reformation of 1560 existing parish churches continued in use, awkwardly adapted to new forms of worship. Preaching of the Word was now an integral if not the only part of every service. Village churches were rearranged, usually with the pulpit placed in the middle of one of the long walls of the unaisled nave; the chancel was abandoned or made over to a landowner for his family 'aisle'* in which he could set up his own gallery and/or burial vault. In larger churches, galleries could be erected in the nave aisles. Edinburgh's largest, St Giles, was divided among several congregations, each able to hear its own minister in his own pulpit.

No new church was built in Edinburgh until the EARLY SEVENTEENTH CENTURY. Greyfriars (1602–20) was decidedly 24 old-fashioned, with an aisled nave and W tower but without a chancel, a feature now redundant. There were no galleries, and the pulpit was placed against one pier of the S arcade. The lumpy Late Gothic style of the exterior was no more progressive. When the Tron Church was begun by *John Mylne Jun.* 23 sixteen years later, the design implications of the new form of worship had been assimilated. The plan was a T with the pulpit in the middle of the long wall of the cross-bar opposite the broad S aisle. Galleries enabled the congregation to be stacked in two tiers within range of the minister's voice. The style was rather Dutch (classical mixed with Gothic survival). The ogee-roofed belfry and spire of the tower over the entrance are very similar to those added to Holyrood Abbey in 1633 and St 22 Ninian, Leith, in 1675. Much less stylish than the Tron was

---

* The Scottish term for a wing or private part of a church, derived from the use of 'aisle' to describe a chantry chapel.

Cramond Parish Church, a village church rebuilt (except for its C15 W tower) as a broad box with two small transeptal aisles.

The LATE SEVENTEENTH CENTURY produced only one new
26-7 town church – Canongate (1688–91) – and this is a puzzle. *James Smith*'s design was imposed on the Town Council by Government order and its cruciform plan with a N (liturgical E) apse makes little sense in terms of the Protestant worship of the time. Perhaps conversion into a Roman Catholic church was envisaged. The shaped s gable was a common feature of the better class of country house, however, and the fat Tuscan columns of the nave are more Dutch than Roman, so the style gives little clue. Catholicism can hardly have been a factor in the design of Edinburgh's only EARLY EIGHTEENTH CENTURY church, New Greyfriars (1722), so its conservatism is striking: *Alexander McGill* simply restored the two fire-damaged W bays of the existing building and added a further two on the same nave-and-aisles plan and in the same Gothic survival style. In contrast, his vestry and porch are up-to-date Palladian.

Church building took off in the LATER EIGHTEENTH CENTURY. Chapels were built for overflow Church of Scotland congregations, for those who had left the Established Church after the Secession of 1733, and for other sects. Of these simple piend-roofed preaching-boxes the Friends' Meeting House, Pleasance (1791), is one of the few survivors. Even the large St Cuthbert's Parish Church (1744) was very plain till its steeple was added in 1789. Much more ambitious was *John Baxter Jun.*'s Cowgate Chapel, now St Patrick (R.C.), built in 1771–4 for a rich Episcopalian congregation.* Its plan was that of the large galleried preaching-box, with the addition of a small domed apse protruding from the middle of the long E wall. What was startling was its size, and the intended but never completed magnificence of its temple front and domed steeple. Another much smaller but identically planned Episcopalian chapel, St Peter, Roxburgh Place (1790–1), is startling for its lack of ostentation: occupying the two lower floors of a tenement, it is hardly noticeable as a church.

Centrally planned churches, logical developments of the preaching-box, form a recurrent theme of Scottish post-Reformation architecture. The first in Edinburgh was the octagonal Methodist Chapel, Low Calton (demolished), built in 1765. Then came Major *Andrew Frazer*'s oval St Andrew (now St
28 Andrew and St George) in George Street, 1785, for the Church of Scotland, and *James Adam*'s octagonal clearstoried St George, York Place, 1794 for the Episcopalians. The most sumptuous would have been *Robert Adam*'s temple-fronted and domed St George, Charlotte Square, the plan a Greek cross with a round central space under the dome and four ovals forming galleried aisles.

* This was an Anglican congregation in communion with the Church of England and also 'qualified', i.e. its priest had taken the oath of allegiance to George III. The non-juring Scottish bishops did not acknowledge the Hanoverian monarchy till 1792, after the death of Prince Charles Edward.

The New Town and suburban developments of the EARLY NINETEENTH CENTURY brought a corresponding demand for new churches. Except for the stolid Greek cross substituted by 29 *Robert Reid* for Adam's scheme at St George (1811) and *W.H. Playfair's* octagonal St Stephen (1828), the Presbyterians and other Protestant sects reverted to the galleried rectangle. But unadventurous planning did not mean dull exteriors. They fall into three main types. Pedimented temple-fronts (often with a classical steeple) are to be seen at North Leith (1816), Brough-ton Place (1820), Hope Park (1823, now Queen's Hall), St Mary 30 Bellevue (1824), St Thomas Junction Road (1825), and St Andrew Place (1827); villa-fronts at Nicolson Square Methodist Church (1815), St Mark's Episcopal in Portobello* (1824), and Lothian Road Church (1831); and neo-Gothic façades or more ambitious compositions at Liberton (1815), Nicolson Street 35 (1820), and Greenside (1838). Inside, architectural display is concentrated on the pulpit (e.g. that at St Mary Bellevue with 31 its domed sounding-board), which is sometimes raised to a terrific height; at North Leith the minister preached from gallery level.

The near-universal custom that a church must be designed primarily for preaching was broken by two Episcopalian churches, St John, Princes Street, and St George (now St Paul 32-3 and St George), York Place, both begun in 1816. Each had an aisled nave and a substantial one-bay chancel marked off by a chancel arch. These churches also herald the serious Gothic revival, for they are in a surprisingly scholarly Perp, *William Burn* at St John borrowing from Harrison's St Nicholas, Liverpool (1811), and Pinch's St Mary, Bathwick (1814), *Archibald Elliot* at St Paul from King's College Chapel, Cambridge, and Beverley Minster. Both churches had stained glass from their first years. Among later Gothic churches those of *John Henderson*, e.g. at Newhaven (1836) and Morningside 34 (1838), are less well informed but not without charm, and his Holy Trinity (Episcopal) (1837) is quite adequate for its important scenic role at the end of the Dean Bridge.

The MID NINETEENTH CENTURY was a great church-building period for Scotland. In the Disruption of 1843 a third of the ministers and as many laymen left the Established Church of Scotland to form the Free Church. Four years later the various Secession churches came together as the United Presbyterian Church. This ordering of Presbyterianism into three well-organized factions came at a time when Edinburgh was growing steadily, and within a few years doctrinal rivalry was matched by architectural rivalry, each denomination trying to build bigger and better churches than either of the others. Curiously at this time of theological ferment, there was no Presbyterian equivalent of the Anglican arguments about the appropriateness of architectural styles for churches. Greek was no longer ad-

* St Mark was even designed so that it could be converted into a villa.

missible,* but Gothic and Italian Renaissance styles were
adopted by congregations apparently oblivious of their connexion with the unreformed church of the Middle Ages or
37 the Counter-Reformation papacy. *David Bryce* gave St Mark's
Unitarian Church in Castle Terrace a surprisingly Mannerist
frontage in 1834. In the case of Free St George's he produced
a Gothic design for a site in Castle Terrace and an Italian
Baroque one for a site in Shandwick Place. The choice of
Shandwick Place gave the Free Church an unashamedly Italian
building. Less swaggering but just as Italianate is Palmerston
Place Church by *Peddie & Kinnear*, built for the United Presbyterians in 1873.

Gothic was the more popular style; its drawback was that it
was not easily adapted as a dress for the dominant preaching-
box plan. The simplest solution, especially easy when only the
gable showed to the street, was to follow the example of *Gillespie
Graham* in Nicolson Street and provide a firescreen front unrelated to what lay behind (e.g. at its crudest Lauriston Place
U.P. Church of 1859, the design seemingly taken from one of
A.W.N. Pugin's examples of what was to be avoided). A popular alternative was to bisect the broad gable of the preaching-
box with a tower apparently corresponding to the width of a
nave. This was used by *Gillespie Graham* (assisted by *Pugin*
36 himself, 1839–44) at the Tolbooth Church, which marks the
summit of the early Victorian Gothic revival in Edinburgh –
and equally of two of the city's finest vistas. A variant was to
expose the middle of the gable but with stair-towers each side
pretending that they are hiding aisles. Unusually honest was
Thomas Hamilton's New North Free Church (1846–8), where
no serious attempt was made to hide the breadth of the gable
or, for that matter, to design an authentically Gothic building.
Of later and more creative innovations the most exciting are
Peddie & Kinnear's fiercely detailed Pilrig-Dalmeny Church
40 (1861) and *F. T. Pilkington*'s powerful Barclay-Bruntsfield
(1862–4), its double-galleried ovoid plan disguised externally by
a massive N steeple and 'chancels' on each side.

The Episcopalians had no difficulty in combining plan and
style. They had accepted the Tractarian movement with enthusiasm, and adopted Catholic arrangement inside Gothic
structures as self-evidently desirable. In general their ideal was
the English rural parish church of the C13 or C14, perhaps most
43 fully expressed in *Slater & Carpenter*'s St Peter, Lutton Place
(1857). A specifically Scottish allusion (to the W front of Dunblane Cathedral) was made by *G. G. Scott* at St James, Leith
45 (1863), and his St Mary's Episcopal Cathedral (begun in 1874)
includes quotations from Dunblane, Holyrood, and the Border

---

* In Edinburgh the equation of Greek and pagan had been made in 1816 by
opponents of the scheme to build a reproduction of the Parthenon as the National
Monument of Scotland. *Archibald Elliot*'s Broughton Place Church (1820) has a
Doric temple-front, but no other church so explicitly Greek was to be built in the
city. In Glasgow, on the other hand, Greek churches were built till the end of the
C19.

abbeys. Externally more austere is St Michael and All Saints, 42
Brougham Street, by *Rowand Anderson* (1866–78), an Anglo-
Catholic mission church with adjoining clergy house, hall,
school and nunnery. Inside, ritualism was generally accepted
and FURNISHINGS lavish. Reredoses might be carved with the
Crucifixion (e.g. in St Mary's Cathedral) or the Annunciation
(e.g. *Burges*'s reredos in St Michael and All Saints), or painted
with the Madonna and Child (e.g. in Old St Paul). Lecterns,
pulpits and bench-pews followed Camdenian principles. By the
later C19 the reservation of the Sacrament was not uncommon,
though more often in a locked aumbry or sacrament house (after
Scottish medieval custom) than in a tabernacle on the altar.
Stained glass was commonplace. Services were musical and
organs a necessary accompaniment.* Only the Irvingites' Cath- 41
olic Apostolic Church by *Rowand Anderson* (1873) rivalled the
quality of Episcopalian fittings.

The Roman Catholics had few churches and no discernible
style other than a preference for large and cheap auditoria with
marble-clad sanctuaries, e.g. the huge Perp-fronted preaching-
box of St Mary's Cathedral by *Gillespie Graham* (1813), *Pugin
& Hansom*'s Gothic St Mary Star of the Sea, Leith (1853–4),
and Father *Richard Vaughan*'s Italianate Church of the Sacred
Heart (1860).

The richness of Episcopalian appointments may have embol-
dened Presbyterians to enliven the drab interiors that were a
background to their preaching, praying and still unaccompanied
singing. STAINED GLASS, banished from Presbyterian churches
since the Reformation, was reintroduced by the Church of Scotland at Glasgow Cathedral in 1854 and reached Edinburgh in
1857 when Old Greyfriars was restored. It then spread to the
Free and United Presbyterian Churches, where it soon developed from abstract or near-abstract designs to representations of Old and New Testament scenes and even of isolated
saints. More colour was introduced by stencilled WALL DECOR-
ATION, which survives only in a few Episcopal churches (e.g. St
James, Goldenacre) and fewer still Presbyterian (e.g. Barclay-
Bruntsfield). ORGANS, less obviously idolatrous than stained
glass, were more controversial. Again Old Greyfriars was the
pioneer; its introduction of an organ in 1865 was sanctioned by
the General Assembly of the Church of Scotland in the following year. Edinburgh's first U.P. organ came in 1874, its first
Free Church organ in 1889. Once admitted, the instrument was
often given pride of place behind a central pulpit (e.g. at
Barclay-Bruntsfield or Pilrig-Dalmeny). Organ, pulpit and
communion table were sometimes designed as a single formidable ensemble, particularly loathed by high-minded church re-
storers of the C20 (e.g. at Canongate, where this arrangement
was abolished in 1948). Of surviving examples the most awesome is at the now disused church of North Morningside.

---

* Episcopalians never doubted the propriety of organs. Old St Paul's Chapel
(demolished) had one as early as 1717, and an organ was provided for the Cowgate
Chapel from the start.

In the LATE NINETEENTH CENTURY Presbyterian church planning was brought into line with 'broad' Anglican practice by the restoration of St Giles (from 1870) as a single parish church and the would-be Westminster Abbey of Scotland. Gothic layout with aisles and chancel was now acceptable, e.g. at Mayfield (originally Free) Church of 1876 and Craigmillar Park of 1878, even though the arcaded aisles were mere passages for access and the chancel was used to house the organ. A fillip was given to Gothic planning by the foundation in 1886 of the Aberdeen (later Scottish) Ecclesiological Society, which advocated the placing of the communion table at a focal point (preferably a chancel), flanked by pulpit and font. Edinburgh's most lavish interpretation of this arrangement is in the classical church of St Cuthbert, Princes Street, by *Hippolyte Blanc*, 1892–5. In its large E apse (the word was often used as a Presbyterian synonym for chancel, irrespective of shape), oak choir-stalls frame the view of the marble communion table. The semicircular wall is lined with elders' stalls beneath an outsize high relief of Leonardo's Last Supper, the chancel arch flanked by a sumptuous marble pulpit on one side, an eagle lectern and a font (with a copy of Michelangelo's Bruges Madonna) on the other. Complaints were made about popishness,* but this arrangement (if not this richness) of furnishings was to become the norm. In many churches the need for a memorial after the First World War was to be the excuse for rearranging the 'sanctuary' along ecclesiological lines, or at least for installing an oak communion table with discreet Lorimerian carving,‡ in unhappy contrast with the stained pitch-pine of the Victorian pulpit and organ case.

Every new suburban congregation in late Victorian Edinburgh wanted a distinctive church, but few obtained a distinguished one. The E.E. St Michael, Slateford, by *John Honeyman* of Glasgow (1883) stands head and shoulders above the rest. *Rowand Anderson* set a standard of easy excellence at Braid Road Free Church (1890) and the Episcopal churches at Inverleith and Colinton. In 1886 *Washington Browne* gave the U.P. congregation at Braid an octagonal auditorium like a tastefully updated Italian baptistery – an unusual reversion from the nave-and-aisles theme to the central plan. Other churches speak with many tongues but without sustained inspiration or scholarship – early French at Bruntsfield Evangelical Church (originally U.P., 1882), later French in the Morningside and Mayfield Churches of *Hippolyte Blanc*, giant Lombardic at Priestfield (also U.P., 1877) in Newington. All make their bold contribution to the local townscape, many to the skyline.

In the TWENTIETH CENTURY ecclesiology was guided and eventually superseded by the idea of simplicity. The late Victorian enthusiasm for church history led to a rediscovery of Scots Late Gothic, e.g. in *George Henderson*'s crown-spired

---

* It was pointed out that even if a frieze of the Last Supper was not *prima facie* idolatrous, Leonardo da Vinci had been a Roman Catholic.

‡ Mostly by the firms of *Scott Morton & Co.*, *Nathaniel Grieve* and *Whytock & Reid*.

Craiglockhart Parish Church (1899), the Elder Memorial (United Free) Church by the prolific and inventive *Sydney Mitchell & Wilson* (1901), and Lady Glenorchy's Church by *MacGibbon & Ross* (1908). The quest for purity led back to the Romanesque, which had a special appeal for rationally minded churchgoers in the still expanding suburbs. St Anne, Corstorphine, by *MacGregor Chalmers* was the most ambitious (1912), *Ramsay R. Traquair*'s Christian Science Church at Inverleith the most sophisticated (1910), *J. M. Dick Peddie*'s little Episcopal church at Cramond the most basic (1912). At Church Hill (Morningside), by now a showground of church styles, *Lorimer* devised a hybrid Italian manner for St Peter (R.C.) in 1906. Its keynote was simplicity – charmingly picturesque outside, majestic inside. Nearby stands Morningside United (originally Congregational, 1927), a bland Early Christian version of the same theme by *James McLachlan*. But Gothic died hard, the revived Late Scots style becoming steadily more mannered in the years up to 1939. *J. T. Walford* at St John (R.C.), Portobello, in 1906, *Lorimer* at the Thistle Chapel of St Giles (1909) and *Leslie Grahame Thomson* at the Reid Memorial Church (1929) all cultivated the tall, blunt profile and the studied contrast between big, plain walls and patches of intricate carving. Natural materials were revered. Two fragments of suburban churches are worth seeing for their plainer, less affected approach: St Ninian (R.C.), Restalrig, of 1929 by *Giles G. Scott*, and St Salvador (Episcopal), Saughton, of 1939 by *Tarbolton & Ochterlony*, who also designed the Warriors' Chapel at Old St Paul (Episcopal) in 1924.

Most churches since the 1930s have been built in new housing areas under the Church of Scotland and other extension schemes. In the pre-war layout at Granton five churches were sited in a multi-denominational parade along Boswall Parkway, but after 1945 churches were built on more scattered sites and (as in the C19) it is hard to guess their allegiance from architectural style alone. The hopefulness of post-war Britain is best conveyed by *Basil Spence*'s St Andrew, Clermiston (1957). Three of the best are at Fairmilehead: Colinton Mains by *Ian Lindsay* (1954) in the tradition of the plain Georgian kirk, St John by *Alan Reiach* (1956) elegantly Scandinavian, and St Mark (R.C.) by *Peter Whiston* in the same year, a plain building but an unmistakably sacred one – the most elusive quality of all. Central planning is rare in Edinburgh's new churches (but see St David, Broomhouse Crescent), gratuitous expressionism almost non-existent. The prevalent harled brick is not only cheap but timeless, bridging the notorious gap between traditional and modern.

The sheer quantity of C19 and C20 STAINED GLASS helps to make up for its general lack of outstanding quality, and many a severe or downright dismal interior is brought to life by a set of richly coloured windows commemorating past members of the congregation with appropriate saints and biblical scenes. The stained-glass revival begins with the Episcopalians, in the sombre line-up of saints by *Eginton* (1816) at St John, Princes Street. *Clayton & Bell* provided more cheerful ones (1882), and did the original glass at St Peter, Lutton Place; they were joined at St Mary's Cathedral by *Burlison & Grylls*. *Wailes* was another Episcopalian standby, starting in 1849 with St Paul and St George, York Place. The Roman Catholics began gaily with St Margaret's Convent, Grange (1835), but for the most part they depended on *Hardman* and the Munich studios.

Ever reliable but never brilliant, the *Ballantines** were purveyors of any approved style to any denomination, the quality apparently varying according to price. Thus the early Victorian parish churches of Morningside and Newhaven were filled (from the 1850s) with darkly instructive bible stories, the Free churches of Salisbury (Grange) and Pilrig (in the 1860s) with non-idolatrous decoration, and the Episcopal church of St John, Princes Street, with a more elaborate and richly coloured version of the same type. Ballantines were responsible for a number of comprehensive schemes, e.g. at St Giles, at Christ Church (Episcopal), Morningside, and at St Cuthbert, Princes Street, where their perfectly competent windows are boring in the company of a David and Goliath by *Tiffany* of New York (*c.* 1900). Their swan-song was at the Reid Memorial Church (*c.* 1930), where they provided exactly the right watery tones for the tall E window. Another universal provider was *Kempe*; one of his best Edinburgh windows (1899) is at St Oswald in Merchiston, now used as a school hall.

The earlier C20, with the exceptions noted below, is a period of pale (sometimes white) glass, thin drawing and a pronounced lack of sentiment; doubtless there was an element of reaction, but few individual artists worked out a personal language to replace the Victorian conventions. *Margaret Chilton* and *Marjorie Kemp* had a large practice but their work seems deliberately dry. Craigmillar Park, Newington, has some of their more affectionate work (mainly of the 1930s). In the later C20 *William Wilson*'s name is practically everywhere. His monogram and lively lettering style are always attached to brilliantly coloured and rather crowded windows, of which those at St Luke, East Fettes Avenue (late 1950s), are among the last he designed himself; his later windows are by his assistants, including *John Blyth*, who is still working today.

Some lovely windows are worth seeking out. They tend to be grouped together, so this obviously personal selection is not in chronological sequence. Two masterpieces, for example, lighten the present murk of St Giles: the flame-and-blue palette and beautiful drawing of *Burne-Jones* in the N aisle (1888) and the brittle, dazzling vision of *Douglas Strachan* in the N transept (1922). Strachan's work under Lorimer's direction at the Scottish National War Memorial at the Castle (*c.* 1924) shows impressive restraint. *Nathaniel Bryson*'s pensive Annunciation (1880) at St Mary, Bellevue, is a revolutionary work for its date.

* This spelling is found in the Post Office directories. They usually signed their windows *Ballantyne*.

Of two windows by *Henry Holiday* (both 1899), that in Holy Trinity at the Dean Bridge is inaccessible, but the other at St Cuthbert (Episcopal), Colinton, is at eye-height and of more than enough quality to contain its deep sentiment.

Southward to Newington. The Glasgow artists *William Meikle* (1900), *Oscar Paterson* (1912) and *Guthrie & Wells* (1922) are all represented at Mayfield. The huge Lombardic Priestfield has a First World War memorial window by *Alexander Strachan* (Douglas's brother) and a charming set by *Mary Wood* and *Douglas Hamilton* (1921) illustrating the trees of the Bible. Further west at North Morningside (disused in 1984), a spectacular collection including *Chilton* and *Kemp* in Art Nouveau and primitive moods (1925–30), an awe-inspiring *John Duncan* war memorial (1935) and some excellent *William Wilson*. The very simple lights by *Gabriel Loire* (1970) in the nearby Archiepiscopal Chapel are the finest post-war glass in the city. Down to Greenbank, where *Alexander Strachan*'s Pilgrim's Progress (1934) is among the most convincing narrative work of its time. In the western suburbs St Anne, Corstorphine, owes its internal character to a scheme by the *Websters* of the *Stephen Adam Studio*, Glasgow (from 1917). For simple jollity one can end with *Sax Shaw*'s testimonial to a retired organist at Restalrig Parish Church (1979). There is little other evidence (except in the occasional modern pub window) that the art of stained glass is still alive in Edinburgh.

Declining and uniting congregations have produced an acute problem of REDUNDANCY in Scotland in general, but most of all in Edinburgh, half of whose churches are now little more than valuable artistic assets and townscape luxuries. Secularization has been particularly successful at the old Hope Park Chapel (now Queen's Hall) and at St George in Charlotte Square (now West Register House) despite the inevitable loss of a rather dull interior. At the Lothian Road Church and the Albany Street Chapel the shell has likewise been saved, but good interiors sacrificed. Gothic churches are harder to convert, both because of their architectural image and their internal design; few of them can admit a new floor as easily as the Free church which is now the Cluny Church Centre in Morningside.

GRAVEYARDS, CEMETERIES, MONUMENTS AND STATUES

In 1581 the reformed Church of Scotland forbade burial within churches. In country parishes the ban was often circumvented by lairds who took over the chancel or added 'aisles' for their gallery and burial vault. Although a burial took place in St Giles as late as 1765, and Holyrood Abbey (out of use as a church

after 1688) was an aristocratic resting place, the ban was
generally effective in town churches. CHURCH MONUMENTS of
the SIXTEENTH TO EIGHTEENTH CENTURIES are consequently few. Renaissance influence seems to have been strong
in the Moray monument in St Giles of 1569 (known only from
sketches). The monument to Jane Countess of Eglinton †1596
in Holyrood Abbey set the tone for the early C17 Greyfriars
Churchyard monuments. Its origin is the medieval tomb recess,
but without an effigy and with detail hopefully classical. With
John Schoerman's monument to Viscount Belhaven †1639 (also
at Holyrood) comes the next stage in the development of Scottish classicism. The tomb recess has become a flashy Corinthian
aedicule frame, unusual for a recumbent effigy. Much less grand
but equally accomplished is the Artisan Mannerist frame for the
inscription to Lady Yester †1647, now in Greyfriars Church.
From the C18 only the pedimented and richly decorated monument of 1703 to George, Earl of Sutherland, in Holyrood and
the vast stone inscription frame in South Leith Parish Church
made by *George Jameson* for James Jameson †1760 are memorable. Very little too from the EARLY NINETEENTH CENTURY:
only the carved panels by *John Flaxman* in St Cuthbert and St
John, Princes Street, are worth singling out. VICTORIAN busts
of ministers are plentiful. More interesting are the Gothic effigies of John Noble †1867 in St Mary Star of the Sea, Leith,
and Dean Montgomery †1900 by *Pittendrigh MacGillivray* in
St Mary's Episcopal Cathedral. Best of all are the Jacobean
Renaissance canopied effigies of Montrose (by *R. Rowand Anderson*, 1887-9) and Argyll (by *Sydney Mitchell & Wilson*,
1894-5) in St Giles, erected as part of the late C19 attempt to
make St Giles the Westminster Abbey of Scotland. That explains the church's vast array of wall monuments, *Augustus St
Gaudens*'s languid Robert Louis Stevenson of 1904 eclipsing all
the rest.

C16 Edinburgh had few GRAVEYARDS – St Giles (now covered by Parliament Square), Holyrood, Greyfriars (opened in
1562), St Cuthbert and South Leith, plus the rural churchyards
of Liberton, Restalrig, Duddingston, Colinton and Cramond.
To the number were added North Leith in 1664, Canongate in
1688, Old Calton in 1718, and New Calton and Newington Old
in 1820, as well as a few smaller burial grounds attached to
chapels. Stealing of bodies for use in the university's anatomy
classes had become enough of a scandal by the 1820s for
WATCHTOWERS (e.g. at St Cuthbert, New Calton, and Newington Old) to be built. Victorian ideas of propriety and property demanded that the middle classes should own their graves
in perpetuity: in the 1840s large, shrubberied CEMETERIES were
laid out on picturesque lines (Warriston, Dean, Dalry, Rosebank and Grange) followed in the 1880s by the Eastern and
Seafield Cemeteries and by Mount Vernon (R.C.) in 1913.
Then came CREMATORIA – Warriston (1928) and Seafield
(1938) both in subdued cinema style, and *Basil Spence*'s expressionist Mortonhall in 1964.

The connexion between a burial plot and monument, so obvious to the Victorians, was less clear in the C16 and C17. In 1603 the Town Council ordered the removal of unauthorized grave-slabs from Greyfriars Churchyard, but the first of a remarkable series of WALL MONUMENTS (not necessarily adjacent to their burial places) was allowed in 1606. This (to John Jackson) is Gothic survival, a tomb recess without an effigy. By 1610 the illiterate classicism of the Countess of Eglinton's monument in Holyrood had been superimposed upon the medieval form. By 1619 the masons seem to have established which way up consoles should be. With the monuments to Gilbert Primrose †1616 and Sir Robert Denniston of Mountjoy of 1626 the tomb recess changed into a classical reredos above an altar base. This became the standard pattern continuing well into the C18, often on a huge scale (e.g. the Bannatyne monument of 1635) and sometimes with emblematic figures (e.g. Religion and Justice on the Foulis of Ravelston monument of 1636). Grisly symbols of 49 mortality (Father Time, an hourglass, skulls, and well-fed cherubs lounging on heaps of bones) relieve the classicism. From the early C18 monuments stepped down from the walls to stand above the graves. The graveyards of rural parishes now within the City boundaries contain plenty of headstones and tablestones, often with naïf Baroque or Rococo carving. Spirited reminders of death and of the trade of the deceased (e.g. the farming scene on William Straiton's monument in Liberton Churchyard) add to the interest. Politer late C18 monuments take the form of pedestals, obelisks and urns. The Victorians extended the repertoire with truncated columns and runic crosses.

Walled ENCLOSURES for family burial plots were built from 1680, sometimes containing a free-standing monument. Of these the most ambitious is that of William Little (1680-3) in Greyfriars Churchyard; a canopy with figures at the corners covering a recumbent effigy. That of John Bayne (1684-5), also in Greyfriars, is similar but with a standing effigy. The first proper 51 MAUSOLEUM, again in Greyfriars, was built c. 1685-91 for Sir 50 George Mackenzie of Rosehaugh, a show-off piece of classicism by *James Smith*. The opportunity to display architectural skill on the small scale offered by a mausoleum was grasped characteristically by *John* and *Robert Adam*, whose mausoleum for their father (Greyfriars, 1753) combined filial piety with professional advertisement. *Robert Adam*'s David Hume Mausoleum 53 (Old Calton Burying Ground, 1777), a severe Roman drum, introduced a new vocabulary to Scottish architecture. The early C19 shift to Neo-Classical brutalism found uncompromising expression in the Dugald Stewart Mausoleum (Canongate) of 1828. The later C19 mausolea are less concerned to lead architectural fashion but they can be distinctly weird: none more so than the Robertson mortuary chapel (by *Henry S. Liefchild*, c. 1865) in Warriston Cemetery, a Gothic shrine for an effigy suffused in ruby light from the stained-glass roof.

Commemorative ARCHITECTURAL MONUMENTS were built

by public subscription and show shifts in public taste. In 1807
52 *Robert Burn* designed an inverted telescope for Calton Hill to
commemorate Nelson. In 1823 it was joined by the twelve columns (all that got built) of *C. R. Cockerell* and *W. H. Playfair*'s
National Monument, the 'Parthenon restored' intended as a
memorial to the dead of the Napoleonic Wars and an example
of correct architectural taste. The success of the Greek style was
54 confirmed by the monuments to Playfair, Burns and Dugald
Stewart which went up on Calton Hill in the next ten years.
But Neo-Classicism was not without its opponents. A vociferous minority had denounced the National Monument as pagan
and unScottish. Gothic was the style they wanted, and with the
Scott Monument of 1840 they triumphed: the style was specified in the competition which led to the adoption of *G. M.
Kemp*'s design for the huge shrine dominating Princes Street.
A Gothic shrine of a much starker nature was provided by
Robert S. Lorimer for the Scottish National War Memorial of
1924. Built on the summit of the Castle rock, its prickly Scottish
exterior conceals a beautifully cool setting for the monuments
to individual regiments. Architecturally it led nowhere.

Public monuments were meant to emphasize Edinburgh's status as a capital city. Just as effective for this are its STATUES.
The earliest (in Parliament Square) is of Charles II as a
mounted Caesar. Put up in 1685, it is the best work in lead of
its date in Britain. Almost as impressive and much more of a
portrait is *James Hill*'s bronze statue of George II (1755) at the
Royal Infirmary. The formal layout of the First New Town was
an invitation to erect statues along its central axis. In the early
c19 they duly came, beginning with *Forrest*'s Viscount Melville
(1822) skyed on a copy of Trajan's Column in St Andrew
Square. *Chantrey*'s swaggering George IV (1831) and aloof
William Pitt (1833) followed, and *John Steell*'s Thomas Chalmers took the last site in George Street in 1878. Two years
before, Steell's equestrian bronze of the Prince Consort had
been unveiled as the centrepiece of Charlotte Square. In the
late c19 and early c20 the open s side of Princes Street acquired
its parade of well-sited statues, among them the brooding Sir
James Simpson (by *William Brodie*, 1877) and the alert horse
56 and rider of *W. Birnie Rhind*'s Royal Scots Greys Monument
(1906). *John Rhind*'s William Chambers of 1891 gives Chambers
Street a Parisian panache. The centre of Coates Crescent is
admirably filled by *Pittendrigh MacGillivray*'s figure of W. E.
Gladstone (1916) surrounded by naked boys. The prestige of
important buildings was marked by a statue in front, e.g.
Thomas Campbell's figure of the Earl of Hopetoun with his horse
(1824) in the Royal Bank of Scotland forecourt in St Andrew
55 Square, *John Steell*'s mounted Duke of Wellington (1852) outside Register House, and his Alexander and Bucephalus (1832;
cast, 1883) in the City Chambers courtyard. Less a complement
to the architecture than an expression of the institution's ethos
is *Birnie Rhind*'s Fettes College War Memorial (1919), beautifully executed and horribly sentimental.

MEDIEVAL TOWER HOUSES,
CASTLES AND PALACES

BY CHRISTOPHER WILSON

Mainly because of the scorched earth policy pursued by the Scots in the Wars of Independence, the Lowlands can show extraordinarily few castles earlier than the late C14. Edinburgh Castle's only building that pre-dates the general dismantling carried out in 1313 is the little Romanesque chapel traditionally but wrongly regarded as the oratory used by St Margaret. Other buildings mentioned in C13 and C14 sources (hall, chambers, counting house etc.) stood near St Margaret's Chapel, at the summit of the Castle rock, but it is impossible to form an impression even of their general arrangement. The main chapel of the castle, St Mary's Church, stood where the Scottish National War Memorial stands now. A continuous circuit of stone walls existed certainly in the early C14 and probably as early as 1093, so Edinburgh Castle must be counted one of the earliest if not the earliest of Scotland's CASTLES OF ENCLOSURE. The N, S and W sides of the rock are so sheer that the defences on those sides must always have been comparatively simple, as they are still.

The great remodelling of the castle under David II and his immediate successors probably included an outer circuit of walls below the rock, but the main effort was concentrated on the defences towards the east, the easiest approach. David's Tower (1368–77) jutted forward from the eastern curtain to command both the city and the main entrance to the castle, but it also contained the private apartments of the king. If it were not part of a larger defensive scheme, one would unhesitatingly call David's Tower a tower house. Its L-plan and ground-floor entrance make it look like a tower house, and its combination of compact comfort and defensive strength made it function very much like one. But how should the resemblance be interpreted? Was this basically a tower house incorporated in a castle of enclosure or was it an original conception and hence the prototype Scottish tower house? Some of the pele towers of the English Border are earlier (e.g. Corbridge, Northumberland, c. 1300), so the building type was presumably known in Scotland around the same time. On the other hand, the earliest Scottish tower houses actually surviving date from the years following the start of David's Tower, which they resemble more than the squatly proportioned earlier English peles. David's Tower was of course ideally situated to be influential, for, until its destruction in the 1573 siege, it was the highest object in the Edinburgh skyline. Its ultimate ancestry is not at all obvious. Its blocky outline was reminiscent of Anglo-Norman keeps, but these are usually placed within a circuit of walls, not on the perimeter.

Exceptions are Richmond (*c.* 1146–71) and Helmsley (*c.* 1186–1227) in North Yorkshire, either of which could have been seen by David II. C13 cylindrical versions of the type are at Barnard Castle, Co. Durham (*c.* 1230–40), and Bothwell, Lanarkshire (last quarter of the C13). The other great tower on the town side of Edinburgh Castle, the Constable's Tower beside the main entrance (begun 1375), was also a cylinder, but then it was almost certainly a remodelling of an earlier round tower. Rectangularity was the rule in late medieval Scotland, and when built upon sheer rock, as here, the corners of rectangular towers were hardly vulnerable to mining, the threat which had encouraged the spread of round towers in the C13.

The influence of David's Tower is very palpable at Craigmillar, the finest of Edinburgh's TOWER HOUSES. The L-plan, the siting over a cliff and the carefully protected ground-floor entrance are all obvious borrowings. Two other important Edinburgh towers, Merchiston and Liberton, are also founded on rock, though their sites are less strong and, perhaps as a consequence, they have the common feature of first-floor entrances reached originally by easily dismountable wooden stairs. The internal arrangements of these three, and of the Bishop of Dunkeld's tower at Cramond, differ in detail but conform to the general pattern of vaulted and fireproof basement for storage (and even emergency shelter for livestock), hall on the first floor and private rooms above that. Craigmillar and Liberton have the extra security of vaulting immediately under the stone slab roof. Perhaps the most individual piece of internal planning is Craigmillar's turnpike stair which twice changes direction to confuse an attacker. At Liberton the progress of intruders entering through the basement would have been hampered by having to cross the hall to continue the ascent. The absence of machicolations from Craigmillar and Liberton suggests respectively early date and relatively low social standing. The machicolations and conical stair turret at Merchiston (before 1495) impart the more finished look which became general after 1500 and which in the early C17 was considered the hallmark of a gentleman's house.

The present dour aspect of Edinburgh's towers makes it difficult to see them for what they were, the luxurious suburban retreats of the city patriciate. Harling still adheres to Liberton as a reminder of lost external crispness, and at Craigmillar some shreds of medieval paint are all that survives to conjure up cheerful interiors long vanished. The most enduring internal decorations are chimney pieces and aumbries, and these often provide the best clues to dating when documentary evidence is lacking, as it usually is. The fireplace at Craigmillar is based, at several removes, on a late C14 French type used for example in the donjon at Vincennes (finished *c.* 1373), a relationship which effectively vetoes the date of *c.* 1374 often mooted. At Liberton, the depressed ogees of the aumbries recall the doors in the turrets of the Holyrood gatehouse built in 1502.

Improved comfort and privacy preoccupied patrons and

builders of late medieval secular architecture throughout Europe, although in Scotland the constraints imposed by defensive considerations were unusually severe. Within a castle of enclosure there was obviously more scope for improving amenities, and during the course of the C15 the major state and domestic apartments of Edinburgh Castle were re-sited round a spacious quadrangle formed to the s of the pre-existing St Mary's Church. This entailed raising a terrace on tiered cellarage – an adumbration of the spectacular under-buildings of C18 and C19 Edinburgh. The near-regularity of the courtyard (now called Crown Square) has no secular parallels, unless one invokes the much more well-like courtyard at Linlithgow Palace, Lothian, of 1423 etc. Crown Square's earliest surviving building is the Great Chamber of *c.* 1445, standing beside and communicating with David's Tower. The ample provision of fireplaces, the three oriels facing the town (cf. Linlithgow Palace N front) and a solitary ribbed ceiling are all that remains to indicate that this must have been the most opulently appointed secular building of its century in Edinburgh. The king's great chamber which gave this block its name was the apartment where the king dined in state, rather than in the great hall as in earlier centuries. The hall on the s side of Crown Square was probably built *c.* 1496–1511, and it is odd to find that it was originally entered broadside on rather than at the 'low' end by the kitchens – assuming that there were kitchens in the w range demolished in the 1573 siege.

The open timber roof of the Edinburgh Castle hall is now in a class of its own, though the hall at Stirling Castle had a roof almost identical, and Linlithgow's hall must have had one just as ambitious. There is no point of resemblance to the only other medieval great hall roof surviving in Scotland, at Darnaway Castle, Grampian. The Edinburgh roof, probably by *John Drummond*, is a complex and decidedly odd design, even allowing for its partial scrambling in the C19 restoration. The basic aim was clearly to emulate the greatest of all medieval timber roofs, the hammerbeam roof of Westminster Hall (1394–8), but instead of Westminster's massive arched principals, which impart rhythmic as well as structural cohesion, there are irregularly half-polygonal trusses formed from the same thin timbers as the common rafters. The stone corbels that carry the wall posts of the roof reveal influence from a very different quarter. All are leafy classical scrolls carved with a single Antique motif (e.g. urns, putti, busts), and one has James IV's monogram. So *prima facie* this is the earliest RENAISSANCE ARCHITECTURAL ORNAMENT in Britain, pre-dating by at least a decade Benedetto da Maiano's roundels of 1521 at Hampton Court, London, and even anticipating by a few years Torrigiano's tomb of Henry VII in Westminster Abbey (1512–18). The use of isolated Antique motifs is about as far as the French had moved towards classicism by the first decade of the C16, so if the Edinburgh great hall corbels really do belong to the years 1496–1511 they are of European significance. None of the histories of Scottish architecture mentions them, perhaps because there must remain a suspicion that they were made during the reign of James V, whose buildings use Renaissance motifs from 1538 onwards. No other building put up for James IV shows any sign of dissatisfaction with the Late Gothic; indeed *Walter Merlioun*'s Holyrood gatehouse of 1502 was indistinguishable from earlier monastic gateways, and its totally traditional rib vault sprang from elaborate bell capitals still essentially of C13 type.

The enlargement of the Palace within Edinburgh Castle is reflected on a more modest scale at Craigmillar, the seat of the rich merchant family of Preston. The prerequisite for expansion here was the rectangular curtain wall with the date 1508 over its vulnerably large entrance. Despite its big round angle turrets, generously provided with gunloops (some of them of the keyhole type used in the Holyrood gatehouse), the curtain can be regarded as an exceptionally imposing variant of the traditional barmkin. Not much remains of the first buildings erected against the curtain, but it is clear that from the start hugely expanded kitchen quarters opened off the screens end of the hall in the tower, and the private apartments were reached from the high table end. A second curtain probably added in response to the 1544 English invasion gives shelter to the (pre-existing?) chapel and no doubt to numerous timber outbuildings that have left no visible trace.

The disaster of Flodden in 1513 was followed by fifteen years during which royal patronage of PALACE BUILDING was virtually non-existent. In 1528 James V inaugurated his effective personal rule by building at Holyrood what was in essence a very grand tower house, ashlar-faced, freestanding and with a drawbridge on one long side. The intention may have been to impart a martial air to the rambling palace that had grown piecemeal from the abbey's w range during the preceding century. Such grandiose isolated towers were popular in the late Middle Ages, especially in England (e.g. Tattershall, Lincolnshire, begun 1435). The big round corner turrets with conical roofs look more French than English (cf. e.g. the donjon at Vincennes, finished *c.* 1373), but the immediate source for their detail was probably the Forework of *c.* 1500 at Stirling Castle. The only advanced thing about the Holyrood Tower is the astonishingly assertive way in which it elbows out the w front of the abbey church – a foretaste of an attitude soon to lead James V to divert ecclesiastical revenues into the palace-building programme which made him the greatest builder of all Scottish kings. The intimidating exterior of the tower concealed handsome state rooms from which two ceilings survive, although they may have been renewed after the 1544 sack. They are still Gothic in that they are ribbed, but their patterns (grids of rectangles and hexagons) can perhaps be seen as intimations of classical coffering.

The new works begun at Holyrood in 1535, three years after the completion of the tower, mark a complete about-turn, not only stylistically, but in the conception of what a royal residence should be. The tower became attached to the N end of a long symmetrical façade dominated by tall rectangular windows and with nothing more defensive about it than its crenellated parapet and its echo of gatehouse turrets in the paired semicircular bay-windows flanking the entrance. These bays and the polygonal ones further out show an awareness of Tudor palaces such as Richmond, London (1500-5), and Henry VIII's parts of Hampton Court (1531-6), and the overall symmetry could also be paralleled in England by this time, e.g. in the entrance fronts of Thornbury Castle, Gloucestershire, c. 1511-21, and Sutton Place, Surrey, c. 1536. Independence from England's still-Gothic architecture is apparent in the square heads to the windows and the individual lights. In this and their proportions, the Holyrood windows probably derive from the S elevation of the great hall at the Castle. In its single-minded exploitation of glazing and in its lack of ornament the Holyrood façade anticipated by forty years or so the over-glazed façades of English late C16 'prodigy houses' such as Wollaton (1580-8) or Hardwick (1590-7). If, as seems very likely, the tower of 1528-32 was to have been balanced by another at the S end – a project only realized in the 1670s – the general impression would have recalled French châteaux such as Bury (1511-24) or Chambord (begun 1519) where long, generously windowed façades are stretched out like flat screens between massive military-looking angle towers. The likeness may well be fortuitous, for the more surely identifiable sources are Scottish and English and none of the early views suggests Renaissance decoration comparable to what appeared at other royal houses in the wake of James's French visit of 1536-7. The contemporary courtyard at Holyrood was quieter in its elevations, with large angle turnpikes modelled on Linlithgow where rebuilding was in progress during the same years. If the Sienese humanist Aeneas Sylvius (later Pope Pius II) had visited Edinburgh in 1535 rather than 1435 he would not have written, even rhetorically, that Nuremberg's merchants were better housed than the king of Scotland.

Only the Crown could afford to make a clean break with the medieval concept of the defensible house – a process already under way in 1505 when James IV's English bride was received at a specially remodelled Holyrood Palace, rather than at what Bishop Douglas of Dunkeld called the 'windy and richt unpleasand castell and royk'. In 1540, when James V's Holyrood was completed, the demoting of the Castle to the status of a military installation went a step further with the conversion of St Mary's Church into a munitions store. The English invasion of 1544 prompted a lightning modernization of David II's defences designed to bring the castle into the artillery age. The 9-m.-thick artillery curtain stretching from the Constable's Tower to David's Tower and a second shorter curtain at a higher level were both replaced after the 1573 siege. All that remains visible of the 1544 work is a small part of the lower curtain: a single open-backed casemate and one of its two wide-mouthed loops.

MANSIONS

From the mid C16 the town of Edinburgh was ringed by country houses. Really these were villas – houses built on small estates, sometimes no bigger than large gardens, whose income was often insufficient to finance the maintenance, let alone the building cost, of the mansion house. For some, especially nobles and politicians whose main estates were at a distance from Edinburgh, these houses provided a convenient base close to the capital but giving greater privacy than could a house inside the town.* For others, such as lawyers and merchants, they were houses where children could be safely reared and where the owner could relax for a long weekend or commute into town. For both lawyers and merchants the associated land could provide both status and a safe if not very lucrative investment. Of much the same character as these rural villas were a few town houses blessed with extensive gardens. Their approach from the street, usually through a small courtyard, hardly differed from the approach through a courtyard of office-houses to almost any laird's house in the countryside.

These late C16–early C17 villas followed generally the type of the standard laird's house. They were mostly L-plan, with a first-floor hall and one or more chambers approached by a broad turnpike stair placed either in the jamb (e.g. Craigentinny House of c. 1600) or the re-entrant angle (e.g. Brunstane House or Caroline Park, both of c. 1585). Development of the L plan by the addition of a second jamb to form a sort of Z, common among Grampian tower houses, is represented in Edinburgh by the late C16 Bruntsfield House, whose jambs take the form of towers projecting from the NE and SW corners of the main block. Defence was not a serious consideration, the gun loops commanding entrance doors being symbols more of status than of military purpose. Gun loops abound at Liberton House (c. 1600) but its main rooms are on the ground floor, like those of Tweeddale House (c. 1576) in the middle of the Old Town.

These Edinburgh villas display none of that fantastic elaboration of turrets which marks the final development of the tower house elsewhere in Scotland. Solid comfort is the keynote, and elaboration is confined to Artisan Mannerist pedimented dormer-heads, or frames for armorial panels. Inside, late C16 tempera-painted beamed ceilings, decorated with flowers, animals and grotesque figures (e.g. the surviving beams at Caroline Park), gave way in the 1630s to modelled plasterwork, as at Moray House, whose compartmented ceilings are filled with

---

* This probably explains why the second and third Dukes of Argyll bought respectively Caroline Park and Brunstane although they also possessed a very large apartment in the Palace of Holyroodhouse. The same phenomenon of Scottish nobles owning large villas within easy commuting distance of the capital was also true of their houses near London in the C18, when Petersham became an enclave for Scottish potentates (see The Buildings of England: London 2: South).

individual emblems (figures, fruit, heraldic emblems and flowers), or at Brunstane, where stiff foliaged friezes survive.

Civil war in the 1640s, and the Cromwellian military government of the 1650s, when Scotland was ruled as an English
province, brought a virtual halt to the building of country
houses and villas near Edinburgh. Demand for new or enlarged
houses of this type resumed after 1660, when the restoration of
the monarchy restored also the Scottish Parliament and Privy
Council. By now the L-plan laird's house was old-fashioned,
not least because any house of pretension had expanded to include a state or show apartment (drawing room, bedchamber
and closet) approached by a scale-and-platt stair. *Sir William
Bruce*'s plan for Holyroodhouse with its two royal apartments
was a model for those wishing to impress fellow politicians,
lawyers or merchants. But although the principle of the Holyrood plan was accepted, its textbook classicism found no following. Instead, a Scottish predilection for emphasizing gables,
long established by the crowstep tradition, was given a new
vitality. Partly, this was a logical development of the L-plan
house. With the addition of a second, mirror-image L plan the
house became a U shape, whose open courtyard could be filled
with a grand entrance hall and staircase or, when the U was
very large (e.g. Caroline Park), closed as a quadrangle. The
entrance front of houses of this type presented twin gables grip-
ping a flat-roofed balustraded centre. This seems to have been
the form intended by Bruce in an unexecuted scheme for Brunstane House prepared in 1672, and had made its first appearance
in Edinburgh a few years earlier with Hillhousefield (now
demolished), whose shaped gables clasped a lower centrepiece.
The example of Hillhousefield was followed by Prestonfield 65
House in 1681 and Cammo House (demolished) in 1693. Much
gawkier is the 1685 N front of Caroline Park, but its S front, 64
remodelled in 1696 with boldly projecting ogee-roofed corner
towers and a pedimented first-floor doorpiece, introduces a tight
centre-and-ends treatment with something of a French note to
it.

Ogee-roofed pavilions (but of small projection) were provided
also by *James Smith* on the rear of Queensberry House (*c.* 1685),
an exceptionally grand town house whose restrained centre and
boldly projecting wings enclosing a forecourt are reminiscent of
Clarendon House in London. Queensberry House lost its internal finishings in 1808, but Caroline Park and Prestonfield House
both have heavily modelled plaster ceilings, coarse versions of
those at Holyrood. At Prestonfield the magnificent carved chimneypiece in the Tapestry Room and the stamped leather hang-
ings of the Leather Room contribute to the late C17 decorative
ideal of crowded richness.

The building of Craigiehall, designed by *Sir William Bruce*
c. 1695, marks the emergence of the rectangular piend-roofed
house type which was to dominate C18 Edinburgh country-
house and villa design. Craigiehall itself was a grand house with
a pedimented two-bay centrepiece and a lavish interior, but

scaled-down versions were to be built for the next hundred years. It is at first sight surprising that very few subsequent Edinburgh houses copied Craigiehall's expansion of this central corps-de-logis with flanking pavilions (though this was the basic C18 type a few miles further from the town centre; *see The Buildings of Scotland: Lothian*), but the villa character of the Edinburgh country houses meant that less service accommodation was required. One house which did have service pavilions was Morton House of 1702 or 1707, but they flank the gate-piers and are not linked by quadrants to the house itself. Drylaw House of 1718, which did without pavilions, is of the Craigiehall type at its simplest – two storeys and basement with six-bay fronts, but with no projection or pediment to mark the centre. Such reticence was abandoned by *William Adam*, whose front
66 for The Drum (1726) combines overall rustication with cornices, pediments and pilasters. The huge central Venetian window finally pushes the design across the border dividing exuberance from vulgarity. The indiscipline extends to *Samuel*
67 *Calderwood*'s entrance-hall stucco work but is brought under some control in the drawing room, where *Thomas Clayton* seems to have been the plasterer. Stucco work was also the glory of *William Adam*'s remodelling of Brunstane House in the 1740s but used less overpoweringly, even the huge armorial overmantel in the parlour seeming quite in company with the panelling and classical landscapes over the doors.

Overemphasis of the front elevation's centrepiece becomes enjoyably ludicrous at Murrayfield House (*c.* 1735), whose broken pediment is bracketed up above the eaves. A similar effect is given to the humbler Hermits and Termits (1734) by the central chimney gablet with its own set of skewputts. By 1758, when *James Robertson* designed Redhall, the central pediment had settled down to eaves level but was still emphasized by
68 large urns. So too was the pediment of Gayfield House (by *Charles* and *William Butter*, 1763), whose shaped gables give it an agreeably old-fashioned look. Sober respectability and bland good taste characterize the flat-fronted Mortonhall (1769), even the stuccoed cove of its top-floor library carefully restrained. Much plainer are Inverleith House (by *David Henderson*, 1774), whose central bay is filled with the flattened bow of the stair-tower, or Chapel House of *c.* 1750 and Beechwood of 1780, where the centre is marked only by the entrance door but the parapets carry a procession of urns.

The most sophisticated of small mid C18 villas were built for judges. The severe boxes with rusticated door and window surrounds designed by *William Adam* for Lord Minto *c.* 1738 and *John Adam* for Lord Milton in 1756 must have shocked by their plainness. Both have been demolished, as has John Adam's Hawkhill (1757) for the bachelor Lord Alemoor, its exterior very restrained with the pedimented centrepiece containing a Venetian door, but its main rooms decorated with wall paintings and enriched ceilings.

The grandest of all C18 Edinburgh villas is *William Cham-*

bers's Duddingston House of 1763. Its temple-fronted style was 69 revolutionary, with a giant Corinthian portico leading to a ground-floor *piano nobile* (the basement having been omitted), its centre filled by the huge stair-hall. The shallow relief of the plasterwork confirms the shift from Artisan Baroque to Neo-Classicism. Duddingston's classicism extends to the pedimented ranges and Doric colonnades of the set-back stable court, and further out to a Doric temple in the park.

In 1771 Chambers designed a villa for Sir Lawrence Dundas. Its site was in the middle of the E side of St Andrew Square. In front, where Craig's plan of the First New Town had shown a church, was a forecourt, the adjoining houses taking on the visual role of advanced pavilions. Behind was a large garden laid out as a park. The house itself is a beautifully detailed 116 version of the Palladian villa of Marble Hill type, showing how much more a major architect and very rich client could achieve than had been done with a design of the same derivation at Mortonhall two years before. By contrast, the exterior of *Robert Adam*'s townhouse for Baron Orde at No. 8 Queen Street is of an austerity which recalls Milton House, although the ceilings inside are far from plain. Both the Dundas and Orde town houses could have stood quite well in isolation had the planned New Town failed to be built. That is not true of the Charlotte Square houses but even their urban façades conceal plasterwork which could just as well have decorated a contemporary country house. Ceilings in Nos. 1 and 6 Charlotte Square are virtually identical with those added to Mortonhall in the 1790s.

Robert Adam's castellated town house for Adam Fergusson, also intended for Queen Street, was not built, nor was his castle-villa design for Sunnyside (now Kingston Grange) at Liberton. The Adam castellated style in Edinburgh is now best represented by the Hermitage of Braid (1785), a very plain little villa dressed up with a castellated parapet and diminutive pep-perpot turrets. The same style was used with greater efficiency but less charm for Craigroyston House, *c.* 1800. Nevertheless classicism retained its supremacy for the first years of the C19, Colinton House (by *Thomas Harrison*, 1801) and Comiston House (1815) both still using a Greek vocabulary with a refined Italian accent. Full-blooded Neo-Classical brutalism was per-haps too extreme an idiom for owners of small estates playing at being country gentlemen, although it made an occasional appearance in suburban streets. The only fully Italianate villa, and a most accomplished one, was Belmont by *W. H. Playfair*, 1828.

The early C19 revolution in country-house planning, which divided houses into areas for house-parties, family and servants, requested, if it did not demand, a more varied elevational treat-ment than was easily provided by a classical or even Italianate style. Picturesque Tudor was the garb for Muirhouse of 1832, 70 but *William Burn*'s Jacobean additions to Lauriston Castle 71 (1827), because they were designed to complement the old house, introduced Edinburgh to the virtues of Baronialism. The invitation was taken up in 1836 by *Playfair*, who designed a baronial house, all the more convincing because of its reliance on form rather than detail, at Bonaly for Lord Cockburn, a judge and would-be arbiter of Edinburgh taste. Romantic composition and an abundance of Scottish detail, combined with large bay-windows, characterize the next generation of the baronial movement, exemplified by two houses, Salisbury Green of 1860 and St Leonard's of 1869, both designed for members of the Nelson family by *John Lessels*. The baronial idiom did not extend inside, where Jacobean entrance halls give way to an eclecticism of style in which the French C18 just wins. Equally large but more routine is Southfield at Liberton, designed by *John Chesser* in 1875. Much more original is *F. T. Pilkington*'s Craigend (now Kingston Clinic), baronial in outline but French Gothic in detail.

The country-house villa close to Edinburgh was now out of fashion. Railways had made accessible more distant estates where lawyers and merchants could play at being lairds. It is the more surprising to find in 1905, at *William R. Reid*'s Easter Park, a return to the classiest type of late Georgian villa, faultlessly executed and quite devoid of feeling.

The full complement of ANCILLARY BUILDINGS was rarely provided for Edinburgh's country houses, and the spread of housing has removed much of what did exist. The heavily rusticated late C17 GATE-PIERS at Caroline Park have lost their scrolled finials. Slightly less heavy and topped with urns are the early C18 piers to Castle Gogar. Duddingston House wins again for sheer style, its late C18 park entrance (now damaged) presenting round-arched footgates linked by concave screen walls to the rosetted main piers. A curiosity is the stable block ('The Drummond Scrolls') of Redford House, built *c.* 1884 with scrolls and pilasters rescued from William Adam's Royal Infirmary.

At Duddingston the STABLES form part of the office court joined to the house. At Mortonhall, they are placed obliquely across a lawn from the house, the attenuated Doric columns of the pedimented entrance giving the courtyard front a nervous energy. At Cammo, still further from the house, they are more heavily classical, with an octagonal tower. Prestonfield House has a circular court by *James Gillespie Graham* (1816).

DOOCOTS housing pigeons to provide winter meat were an almost automatic appendage to a laird's house. Among the largest in Edinburgh is a C16 beehive doocot at Corstorphine. In the C17 and C18, the lectern or lean-to type was standard, but doocots were regarded also as decorative features, so the one at Edmonstone House was given a spire and the octagonal doocot at Redhall House (1756) incorporates a huge C16 armorial panel.

BELVEDERES were built as incidents in the landscape and also as buildings from which to admire the view. At Morton House the belvedere of *c.* 1700 is a plain rectangle but with drum towers on the front towards the mansion house. Much smarter was the circular Craigiehall Temple of 1759 with its outsize late C17 or early C18 porch as an entrance to the upstairs banqueting room. Here the owner and his friends could dine and look out over the parkland.

OLD TOWN TENEMENTS

The burgh of Edinburgh's constricted site meant that as its population increased the original burgess tofts or strips of land were subdivided. But there was a limit to the number of houses which could be built side by side, quite apart from the desirability of keeping some garden ground. The alternative, taken up in C16 Edinburgh, was to build houses on top of each other, i.e. to build tenements.*

The earliest surviving tenement in Edinburgh is John Knox 113 House, two houses, one above the other, with a ground-floor shop. The internal plan of each flat – a hall and chamber, supplemented by small rooms in the projecting wooden galleries and attic – was typical of any Edinburgh house of the period. Less typical is the beamed second-floor ceiling's lively tempera decoration, showing that this was a building of some pretension. Two early C17 tenements, Gladstone's Land and Moubray 111 House, show just as strongly that tenement life was for the prosperous, who, by living above the ground floor, could avoid the worst of the street noise and smell. Both have painted decoration on ceilings and walls, and Moubray House has also a modelled plaster first-floor ceiling. The sill-courses linking the windows of their stone fronts (replacements for wooden galleries) are characteristic of Edinburgh's early C17 tenements.

In the late C17 considerable rebuilding of houses took place, encouraged by the Town Council's grant in 1674 of a seventeen-year exemption from taxes on any new stone-fronted building which replaced a timber-fronted one. Thirty years earlier, the Council had acquired the power to compulsorily purchase derelict property, and this was now used to put together sizeable parcels of land for sale to developers. In comparison with their predecessors, the scale of these new developers' tenements, such as the demolished Robertson's Land (1674) and Milne's Square (1684) and the surviving Milne's Court (1690), was huge. The style showed a disciplined regularity which could be thought of as classical were it not for the eruption into a display of chimneys and gablets above the wall-head (e.g. the back of Milne's Court). Individual flats were often of five or six rooms and could have as many as twelve, finished with appropriate lavishness.

---

*The word tenement originally denoted a holding of land. In time it came to mean a flatted block (originally and confusingly called a 'land').

The pattern of tenement development set in the 1670s continued in the C18 with the creation of James Court (1723),
78 Chessels Court (*c.* 1748) and, grandest of all, Royal Exchange
Square (now the City Chambers) in 1753. Interior decoration
with classical paintings set in the panelling was of a standard at
least equal to what could be found in a small country house.
Sometimes, as in the demolished tenement at the head of Craig's
Close, it was very much grander. There, the rooms had expensively stuccoed overmantels above carved chimneypieces. An
evocative picture of luxury is given by the sale advertisement*
of 1763 for a four-bedroom flat in James Court which had 'two
genteel well finished public rooms, each above 18 feet long, with
handsome marble chimneys and hearths ... and one of the
rooms ornamented with a Chinese temple, Apollo and the
Muses, &c.'

TERRACES

Unified TERRACE DESIGN began with the tenements of St
James's Square (1773), just outside the First New Town proper,
and Merchant Street (1774) in the Old Town; the designer of
both was *James Craig*. Then came the shops and tenements
lining South Bridge (1786), symmetrically composed as palace
fronts with simply defined centrepieces and end pavilions. By
this time the First New Town was well under way. A standard
type of single house frontage had been adopted in it with three
bays, three storeys and basement. Here and there a single house
or larger unit was symmetrical, and giant pilasters and twin bow
windows were becoming fashionable as marks of status in
addition to rusticated ground floors and special doorpieces. But
Craig's monumental layout had not yet been matched by formal
grouping, except in the middle of the E side of St Andrew
Square and in the effective vernacular of the gables on the
corners of each of the cross-streets. Complete unity, with whole
blocks formally designed and formally related, eventually came
with *Robert Adam*'s design for the elevations of Charlotte
Square, commissioned by the City in 1791.
117   In Charlotte Square Adam used his sophisticated classical
vocabulary to combine the rows of houses into a civic composition whose climax is reached in the pedimented centrepieces
of the N and S sides. Never again was the hierarchy of different
parts so carefully expressed, monotony so scrupulously avoided.
The palace front remained the dominant type of terrace for
many years to come, though two innovations appeared from the
beginning of the C19: the introduction of attic storeys on top of
the centrepiece and end pavilions, which were usually built as

* In *Edinburgh Evening Courant*, 12 February 1763.

tenements; and the linking of pavilion frontages at street corners. The building up of all the sides of a block in a formal layout is much more frequent here than e.g. in Bath. The problems of detail that arose at the corner itself were most bluntly solved in the Moray Estate, where *Gillespie Graham*, seeking an effect of sustained magnificence, simply joined his giant pilasters 122 to form a corner pier, at whatever angle the layout demanded. The deliberate emphasis of a pavilion by means of a pyramidal roof is seen in Charlotte Square (though not quite as Adam intended) but not otherwise till much later – and most dramatically – in Gardner's Crescent. Quadrant (i.e. quarter-round) corners are common enough on simply detailed blocks but rare on grander ones, except in *Playfair*'s Calton scheme, and in *Robert Brown*'s splendid Haddington Place, further down Leith Walk. A bowed (half-round) corner was used at the acute angle of West Maitland Street and an octagonal pavilion at the corner of Lauriston Street.

The most persistently repeated motif of Charlotte Square was the projecting centrepiece with a subsidiary projecting bay on each side. *Reid* used it in the Northern New Town – without orders in Heriot Row, without a pediment in Great King Street, 119 and without either in London Street. *Robert Burn* used a stretched and simplified version in Forth Street, and dropped the projecting side bays in Picardy Place – an arrangement repeated without orders in Broughton Place. In Ann Street the dominant six-bay centrepiece is pedimented overall, with seven pilasters. Playfair moved right away from the theme of the dominant centrepiece, absorbing it into the regular rhythm of the façades of Royal Circus and Royal Terrace (though it is still 121, 124 marked by an attic storey), and omitting it altogether in Regent Terrace; the same was done in Rutland Square. Gardner's Crescent has no centrepiece, but the whole curved façade has the implication of a giant order. The less emphatic centrepieces on the E side of Charlotte Square (no projection in the middle) were splendidly echoed in the contemporary tenement of Gayfield Place, imitated in the W section of Heriot Row, and adapted for the pavilions of the Coates estate in the Western New Town.

A major break with Adam's basically Palladian theme occurred in St Bernard's Crescent, where the rusticated ground floor disappears and the giant Greek Doric order of the massive centrepiece comes down to pavement level, with a ground-floor Doric colonnade on each side. In the same year (1823) *Playfair* used a coupled ground-floor colonnade at Hillside Crescent in the Calton estate, and in 1825 it was repeated with Ionic columns in *Robert Brown*'s Hope estate. Doric-columned doorpieces were first used in *Thomas Brown*'s Royal Crescent, then in Playfair's Regent Terrace. Projecting porches were pioneered by *Burn* in his Henderson Row tenements, quickly followed by Playfair's Brunswick Street porches, which are also Ionic but of much ampler projection, their cornices linked by cantilevered balconies. All these late Georgian developments, compared with

Charlotte Square, illustrate the move from late C18 variety to early C19 Neo-Classical consistency.

The Victorian continuation of the Western New Town maintained its overall discipline and many of its established motifs (e.g. the pavilion design, and the three-bay balcony, translated from wrought into cast iron) but introduced a richer vocabulary of detail, e.g. in the segmental headed windows and bracketed cornices of Chester Street (1862–70) and the triple first-floor arcades of Rothesay Place (1872). Then came the bay-windows. The W side of Drumsheugh Gardens has rectangular bays with refined Neo-Classical detail, and Eglinton Crescent has canted bays telescoped out of the top of curved bows. Regular dormers were introduced as part of the design of Manor Place (later section, 1864). Only in the peripheral Magdala and Douglas Crescents do they join in the jolly free-for-all of the gingerbread terrace in less dignified quarters of the town.

HOUSE PLANNING in Edinburgh terraces is based on a type developed in the late C18 and used with occasional variations to the end of the C19. Its keynotes are the first-floor drawing room and the basement area. Earth excavated from the foundations was piled up in front to form an elevated street, and retained by vaulted cellars under the pavements. Earlier builders in the First New Town were not restricted as to width, and some of the plans are exceptional. The grandest is *Adam*'s No. 8 Queen Street for Baron Orde (1770), virtually a five-bay villa with a central staircase (plus a service stair) and rooms all round. The ground floor was called the parlour storey, the dining room being on one side of the front door, the study on the other, and the parlour itself to the rear. Overhead were the principal storey and bedchamber storey. The mansard-roofed attic is probably original, but nonetheless an afterthought. The subsequent act of 1785 laid down maximum roof pitches and ruled out dormer windows to the front, but dormers still grew and multiplied with picturesque effect throughout the First New Town. Often they take the form of bow-fronted, slate-hung boxes with conical roofs, giving full height and width to the attic room within.

The standard three-bay house is entered by a fanlit front door in the left- or right-hand bay, reached by a bridge over the area. The dining room is lit by windows in the other two bays, and the entrance hall (often the most showy feature of the house) goes past it into the top-lit stairwell, which has gracefully cantilevered stone flights, cast-iron balusters and a mahogany-veneered handrail. On the first floor the drawing room usually runs the whole width of the front, and to the rear each floor has one large room (parlour or main bedroom on either level), plus a small room to the back of the stairwell, which may continue upwards to a further (bedroom) storey before ending with a more or less ornamental skylight – often a dome with a conical glass roof sticking up in the central roof-valley. At the bottom, the stair goes less ceremoniously down to the servants' quarters in the basement, the kitchen usually being under the dining room. In most terraces the houses are paired, so that the flues are concentrated in alternate party walls.

Internal differences are mostly in detail, e.g. in the plan of the stairwell or the sideboard end of the dining room. Some drawing rooms have only two windows (conforming with the dining room underneath), but a more frequent variant is the full-width room with a backward jamb forming an L. Both arrangements caused problems by impinging on the middle space where the upper floors had water closets and (from early Victorian times) fixed baths. Common sewers were provided by the Town Council in the First New Town, but in later developments this job seems to have fallen to the builders; the results in the early years of the Northern New Town were particularly disastrous, the sewers under the streets having been laid piecemeal. Back gardens (used as drying greens and bounded by stone walls) were entered from basements or, where the terrace was built along a very steep slope, from sub-basements.

Houses and tenements jostled each other in the early days of the First New Town, but soon began to be formally combined (*see* the introduction to Queen Street). Main door and common stair tenements, i.e. houses with flats or more houses on top, were popular in better-class districts; they make up a large part of the N-S streets in the First and virtually all those in the Northern New Town. Where a block was built up on adjacent sides, the tenement, with its more flexible room layout, solved the problem of the corners where there was little or no wall space for windows at the rear. The FLATS, reached by the spartan common stair, have a fine and sometimes inconsequent spaciousness and a wonderful variety of outlook. Kitchen and W.C. are near the front door, the grandest rooms furthest away. The poorer streets had a higher proportion of flats, and their planning and outlook were less generous, some being placed back-to-back, with only one aspect.

SUBURBAN VILLAS AND TENEMENTS OF THE NINETEENTH AND TWENTIETH CENTURIES

In the early C19 many of the small estates ringing Edinburgh were laid out for building development. Tenements and terraced houses were favoured on land close to the town but did not find a market on more distant estates. On these, the detached or semi-detached villa in its own garden could offer a feeling of spaciousness and a hint of rural delight to offset the disadvantage of being some way from the town centre.

Unlike its prototype, the late c18 villa-mansion, the suburban
villa was part of a street, its view interrupted and often bounded
by garden walls and the houses opposite. The quality of the
neighbours and their houses was consequently important to the
intending villa-owner. To reassure purchasers and maintain the
value of unsold plots the developing landowner could and did
impose conditions on what was to be built. In a few cases, e.g.
Claremont Park, Leith (1827), elevations were provided. More
generally, the siting of the house on the plot was stipulated, as
was the minimum cost of building. Commercial use was usually
forbidden, together with most forms of livestock.

Until the 1840s it was easiest to find buyers for plots on or
near a carriage-road to the town centre. Newington (e.g. Minto
Street), parts of Grange, Bruntsfield, and Inverleith (e.g. Inverleith Row) were popular. So too were Leith Links, convenient for the town of Leith as well as Edinburgh, the seaside
resort of Portobello, and the lands of Trinity, with spectacular
views over the Forth. The standard design was the late-Georgian box, often dressed up with a rusticated ground floor or a
columned doorpiece, but some were more ambitious. Gothic
House, York Road (Granton, Newhaven and Trinity), is engag-
ingly lumpy Tudor-Gothick, whilst a group in Boswall Road
(Granton, Newhaven and Trinity) is uncompromisingly Greek.
Just as Greek and even more original is Arthur Lodge in Dalkeith Road (Newington).

Population growth led to steady expansion of the early villa
areas. By the 1860s speculative builders usually gave their plain
Georgian-survival boxes a bay-window projection, often two-
storeyed so as to serve both the ground-floor dining room and
the first-floor drawing room. The resulting asymmetry is disconcerting. The bay-window was much more happily incorporated in more expensive baronial villas, of which Avallon,
Clinton Road (Morningside), of c. 1862 is among the best.
Cottage-picturesque provided a pacific alternative although
128 *James Gowans*, e.g. at Lammerburn, Napier Road (Bruntsfield
and Merchiston), gave it a manic mathematical precision. Gowans worked on a carefully considered modular system. Just as
systematic in their expression of plan-forms are *F. T. Pilkington*'s rogue Ruskinian villas in Dick Place (Grange) of the 1860s.
In 1872 at Dean Park House, Queensferry Road (Dean), Pilkington turned to a confident Second Empire style, imitated
with less competence in a number of large houses by *Edward
Calvert* along Colinton Road.

Development of the railway system in the later c19 produced
new suburbs, sometimes, as at Corstorphine, Colinton, or Barnton, leapfrogging over open fields. Semi-rural seclusion comfortably close to urban convenience found architectural expression in Arts and Crafts or Edwardian free style. A Scottish
accent might be given by crowsteps or the emphasis of a stair-
tower (e.g. *R. S. Lorimer*'s Westfield, Pentland Avenue, Colinton, of 1897), but hard-edged baronial was relaxing into Jacobean Scots Renaissance (the Scottish Queen Anne), most suc-

cessfully perhaps in *John Kinross*'s houses at Oswald Road and
Mortonhall Road (Grange). English half-timbering and red tiles
abound in Barnton, whose inhabitants could go home from the
golf club and hardly notice the difference. Art Nouveau, perhaps too consciously advanced for Edinburgh, makes rare
appearances in Clermiston Road (Corstorphine) and Pentland 130
Terrace (Fairmilehead).

All except the most exclusive suburbs are invaded or hard-
pressed by tenements. In their plainest form, as working-class
housing, they are placed between or beside the railway tracks.
Although *Pilkington*'s West Fountainbridge block of 1864
shows what invention could do on a low budget, 'architecture'
was expensive and generally reserved for the middle classes.
Just like the Victorian villa, the Victorian tenement of pretension required a bay-window to make the most of available light
and give the main room a feeling of space quite disproportionate
to the extra floor area. Tall narrow blocks, their insistently repetitive bay-windows breaking into crowsteps, give Marchmont
(Bruntsfield and Merchiston) its air of oppressive solidity. In
Comely Bank Avenue (Dean) the uniform rhythm down a steep
slope is stomach-turning. The larger scale and relaxed confidence of *George Washington Browne*'s block in Bruntsfield Place
(Bruntsfield and Merchiston) of 1887, midway between the late
C19 Scottish tenement and the London mansion flats, make it
exceptional.

After the First World War a class division between villas for
the owner-occupiers and tenements for local-authority tenants
appeared. In general, the villas were mean and the tenements
plain – the first because they were speculative developments,
the second as if to show that every penny of ratepayers' money
had been accounted for. Not that the local-authority housing
was necessarily cheap, but the 1930s' *City Architect's Department*'s predilection for hungry-jointed rubble gave it a Puritan-
ical dourness. The Modern Movement was introduced by *Kininmonth & Spence* at 46a Dick Place (Grange) in 1933 and
Lismhor, Easter Belmont Road (Murrayfield), in 1935, but
neither has quite the moral commitment of the best contemporary work in England. Less stylish but more serious-minded
are *Neil & Hurd*'s flats of 1936 in Ravelston Garden (Craigleith
and Ravelston).

Since 1950 large local-authority housing developments have
been built both in the inner suburbs and on the edge of the
city. They are characterized by generous layout and acceptance
of the need for high-rise blocks. The architecture of the earlier
tall blocks, e.g. Maidencraig Court (Craigleith and Ravelston),
Gracemount (Blackford and Liberton) or Dumbiedykes (Old
Town), now looks spinsterish. By contrast, *Shaw-Stewart, Baikie & Perry*'s Leith Fort development has strength, but its bare
concrete is much too brutal. Houses of the post-Second World
War period have included few which are exciting – decent but
dull architect's designs picked up ten years later by the speculative builders. Buildings of excellence exist but have made a

merit of being invisible to the stroller along the street. *Morris & Steedman*'s Avisfield, Cramond Road North (Cramond), not only hides but encloses a courtyard for further privacy. Is such
132 self-effacement really necessary? The same firm's Nos. 65–67 Ravelston Dykes Road (Craigleith and Ravelston) gives the unexpected punchy accent which every good suburb should have.

PUBLIC AND COMMERCIAL BUILDINGS

This account is in mainly chronological order until about 1815. Later buildings are described according to type, including the commercial architecture that so often – especially in Victorian and Edwardian Edinburgh – aspired to public status.

The C15 mercat cross to the E of St Giles survives only as a fragment incorporated in a replica. The grim Old Tolbooth that half blocked the High Street to the NW (C14 with later additions) survives only in legend. Sir Walter Scott called it 'The Heart of Midlothian', and when it was pulled down in 1817* he took its doorway and keys away to Abbotsford. The next (James VI) generation of public buildings expressed civic strength in the Scottish baronial turrets and pointed roofs of the Canongate Tolbooth and the Netherbow Port (the city's E gate, remodelled in 1606 and demolished in 1764). Of the polyglot Renaissance style of Charles I's reign there was the façade of Parliament House to the SW of St Giles, and there still is the fantastic,
76-7 four-square prodigy of Heriot's School, whose building went on to the end of the C17 – the first of the 'pauper palaces' endowed in the wills of Edinburgh magnates. The grandest of the guild halls is that of the Tailors (1621); the Skinners in 1643 and the Candlemakers as late as 1722 were content with domestic-looking Scots vernacular. One of the first regular and symmetrical public buildings is *James Smith*'s Surgeons' Hall (1697). A former church, St Mary's Chapel off the High Street, used as the hall of the building trades, acquired a pedimented front in 1737 (demolished for South Bridge).

Edinburgh's C18 emergence as a modern capital began with an important pair of public buildings, *William Adam*'s Infirmary (1738, largely demolished in 1882) and then the new Ex-
78 change‡ (the City Chambers, 1753), both with open forecourts in the Dutch Palladian manner, and the former harking back to Wren, with a ponderous scrolled attic. The next step was *William Mylne*'s North Bridge giving access to the site of the

---

*Its successor was *Elliot*'s gaol (see Calton, Public Buildings, St Andrew's House).

‡A public building in its original conception but when first built largely a tenement block.

projected New Town (1763, later rebuilt). Its line was prolonged to the s of High Street by the multi-arched South Bridge
(1785), and near this are *Robert Mylne*'s St Cecilia's Hall (1761),
with an oval auditorium but only a modest façade (now altered)
to Niddry Street, and the old Royal High School (1777), whose
only pretension is its pedimented porch. But fronting the bridge
is *Robert Adam*'s monumental façade to the University of Edin- 80
burgh's Old Quad – his and the city's most magnificent work of
architecture (1789). His Register House (1774), closing the N 79
end of the North Bridge vista, is a design of less force but
greater suavity – and it is almost complete. The First New
Town's other c18 public building, *John Henderson*'s Assembly 81
Rooms in George Street (1782), was approved by a perceptive
committee but its original splendid austerity was unpopular.
The portico added by *Burn* belongs to the doldrum post-Adam
school of design, as does the unexciting classical screen which 85
Robert Reid began in 1803 to unroll round Parliament Square.
In Leith the story was different. The Assembly Rooms (1809)
are post-Adam Neo-Classical, and so is Trinity House (1816).
The revolution came with *Reid*'s Customs House (1810), mas- 83
sive and blockish with recessed giant Greek Doric columns. Its
sequel was disappointing, but fun – the Neo-Classical parody
of *R. & R. Dickson*'s town hall (1827).

The Nelson Monument (1807) is an oddity. After the victory 52
year of 1815, and further stimulated by George IV's visit in
1822, Edinburgh was seized by the enthusiasm to create great
architecture. The civic image was Grecian, starting with *Elliot*'s
bridge-borne vista of Waterloo Place and then adopting a proud 9
Neo-Classicism with no vestige of the city's long Palladian allegiance. Siting was all-important. The first two Greek Doric
temples were started in 1822, one on Calton Hill (*Playfair* and
Cockerell's National Monument, never finished) and the other 52
halfway along the open side of Princes Street (Playfair's Royal
Institution, now Royal Scottish Academy). 88

Then came the SCHOOLS. John Watson's by *William Burn* 86
(1825), for boarding and teaching the orphans of professional
people, is the ultimate refinement of his master Smirke's Greek
Doric manner. Burn's Edinburgh Academy (1823) owes its primitive simplicity to cost constraints, but its subtlety to his
understanding of that constant Neo-Classical problem – how to
reconcile a portico with a long façade. The decisive – if extravagant – solution was *Thomas Hamilton*'s at the Royal High 87
School (1825). The LEARNED SOCIETIES also found a Neo-
Classical image. *Playfair*'s observatory for the Astronomical
Society (1818) stands on the very summit of the Calton, with
four identical porticos forming a Greek cross at the cardinal
points of the observation dome. His Surgeons' Hall (1829, in 90
succession to Smith's) is an Ionic temple toeing the line of
Nicolson Street. By contrast, *Hamilton*'s Royal College of Phy- 89
sicians (1844) is a tall solid block continuous with the house
fronts of Queen Street, its public importance neatly symbolized
by a shrine-like two-storey porch.

Many Georgian BRIDGES in central Edinburgh help to solve the traffic problems of the hilly site, and provide a bonus in the form of multi-level townscape. North and South Bridges were followed by Regent Bridge to the E (1815). The 1827 Improvement Act fixed the line of the road up the Mound to High Street, where it went on as George IV Bridge, with the old West Bow realigned as a feeder (Victoria Street) from Grassmarket. In the same year the Western Approach scheme provided a road (Johnston Terrace) along the S face of the Castle rock, descending to the spectacular King's Bridge. Finally *Telford*'s Dean Bridge (1831) over the Water of Leith valley. Although most of the cost was borne by the landowner, who wanted to make his estate more accessible from the centre, it still serves a much larger purpose as the principal NW outlet from the city and further S. The wide-span North Bridge replacement (1894) breaks with the Georgian stone tradition but is complemented by Edwardian Baroque architecture at the Old Town end. Outside the centre the two finest bridges – the viaducts carrying the railway and the Union Canal – run parallel to each other at Slateford.

The origin of the late Georgian civic building was the temple; that of the Victorian house of business or ease (*negotium* or *otium*) was the palazzo. Edinburgh's distinguished CLUBS were in Princes Street and had distinguished buildings. *William Burn*'s New Club (1834, lengthened by *Bryce*) was designed after Barry's Travellers' and before his Reform Club in Pall Mall, London.* Except for the porch, it was even more severely astylar, the effect in no way diminished by bay-windows and crowning balustrade. The glass panes were large, the stonework detail hard and confident. Its successor on the same site (1966) shows some awareness of past dignity but is perched above shops. To the W two other palazzi survive as shells, both asymmetrical and bay-windowed – *Peddie & Kinnear*'s University Club (1866) Grecian in detail, *Rowand Anderson*'s Conservative Club (1882) fastidious early Renaissance.

BANKS took some time to find their palazzo image. Edinburgh's first purpose-built bank of any importance was the head office of the Bank of Scotland on the Mound, which originally (1801) looked like a country house stranded on a precipice. Others resembled villas, e.g. the bow-fronted Leith Bank in Bernard Street and the modest but solid Commercial Bank (1813) in New Assembly Close, High Street. In 1825 the Royal Bank of Scotland moved into the former Dundas mansion in St Andrew Square. By the time *Peddie* had added the telling hall to the rear (1857, in an enriched Soane manner, with star-pierced dome), the stampede of head offices into the First New Town was almost complete. *Rhind*'s Graeco-Roman temple for

---

Charles Barry was later consulted on the design of the adjacent building in Princes Street, Rhind's Life Association Assurance office (1855), which was the Edinburgh counterpart of Parnell & Smith's Army and Navy Club (1848). Both represented the full Venetian Baroque fruiting of the Victorian palazzo; both are destroyed.

the Commercial Bank in George Street (1846, now Royal Bank) 107
has a telling hall of Greek cross plan confidently adapted from
the model of Burn & Bryce's nearby music hall. In the same
year *Bryce* gave the British Linen Bank their Roman Baroque 108
head office in St Andrew Square (now Bank of Scotland), an
opulent development from his Edinburgh & Leith Bank (1841,
now Clydesdale) in George Street. It has a telling hall to match
its frontage, and a solemn, club-like staircase in between. The
Bank of Scotland's own head office remained on the Mound but
was transformed by Bryce (1864) to match its site. One of his
last works, the Edinburgh head office of the Glasgow-based
Union Bank (1874), recalls the austerity of the New Club. The
palazzo theme continues with *Peddie & Kinnear*'s Bank of Scot- 109
land New Town office in George Street (1883) and then well
into the C20,* the only innovation being a tendency to big
American-style entrances, e.g. at *Mewès & Davis*'s National
Bank in St Andrew Square (1936, now Royal Bank), until at
William Paterson's Trustee Savings Bank in Hanover Street
(1939) the whole building becomes one great portal and the
style reverts to Neo-Greek. After 1945 the only important bank
building is *Michael Laird*'s computer centre for the Royal Bank
in Dundas Street (1978). It is excellent in its context, though
structural-aesthetic purists object to its three-decker sandwich
alternately of stone and uninterrupted glass. More important
surely is the fact that a bank may put up a distinctive building,
but a distinctive style of bank architecture is a thing of the past.

INSURANCE OFFICES quickly adopted the palazzo idea, but
then increasingly felt obliged to move with the times, using
style as a medium of competition. In George Street *Bryce*'s
Edinburgh Life Assurance (1843), in the dignified New Club
manner, has survived as the Royal Society of Edinburgh. His
great symmetrical palazzo for the Western Bank in St Andrew
Square (1846) was taken over after the bank's failure by the
Scottish Widows Fund, who demolished it in 1960 and then
vacated its successor. Competition intensified towards the end
of the C19, and corner sites in the First New Town were in hot
demand. The Prudential came to Edinburgh with plans for a
red-brick Gothic office but were allowed only a pink stone one
(1892). Scottish Equitable replied across St Andrew Square
(1899) with pink Jacobean by *Peddie & Washington Browne*.
Standard Life used the same architects but had played safe
(1897), rationalizing their old buildings into a traditional palazzo, large but surprisingly pretty. Edinburgh Life built a new
George Street office on the Hanover Street corner (1908, now
Commercial Union), boisterous in Portland stone with a copper
dome. Pearl bought a truly C20 building which respected
George Street's conventions (1924); Caledonian (1938, now
Guardian) built one which defied them. *Michael Laird*'s exten-
sions of Standard Life (from 1964) explored the alternative 110

*Washington Browne's branch of the British Linen Bank in his François I
manner (1902, now Bank of Scotland), at the corner of George and Frederick
Streets, is an exceptional departure from the palazzo rule.

idioms of curtain wall and strong verticality. Otherwise mediocrity ruled; Scottish Provident's would-be modernity, which destroyed another palazzo and interrupted the building line of St Andrew Square (1961), can just be excused on grounds of enthusiasm. Perhaps shocked by the times, the Scottish Widows left their C20 palazzo (1962) and moved to the edge of town, into a large piece of brown glass sculpture (1972) – equally immaculate and aloof – by the same architects, *Basil Spence, Glover & Ferguson.*

Victorian GOVERNMENT ARCHITECTURE begins with *Play-fair*'s National Gallery (1848), austere Ionic to the R.S.A.'s rich Doric. The palazzo theme, in its High Victorian establishment version, then takes over with *Robert Matheson*'s New Register House (1858) and G.P.O. (1861). *Captain Fowke*'s opulent

96-7 screen to the big birdcage of the Royal Scottish Museum (also 1861) is arcaded Italian, with effective colour variation and a good deal of subtlety. The palm houses at the Royal Botanic Garden are largely Matheson's work (from 1856). His successors at the Office of Works, *Robertson* and then *Oldrieve*, were good caretakers and adapters (e.g. at the Law Courts and Register House) but less distinguished in new buildings. Robertson's Royal Observatory on Blackford Hill (1892) is purple-faced authoritarian, but at Portobello Post Office (1904) he broke out of official pomposity into quite pretty Jacobean. An important but lonely challenge had come earlier with *Rowand Anderson*'s Venetian-French Gothic National Portrait Gallery (1885). Paid for by the owner of *The Scotsman* with the encouragement of Lord Bute, this was a belated acknowledgement of the force of Ruskin's diatribe against the city's confirmed classicism (*Edinburgh Lectures*, 1856). The cardboard scenic-Gothic of Playfair's Free Church College on the Mound (1846, now New College) also excited Ruskin's rage. Whatever would he have said of the brute classicism of the United Free Church office (1909, now Church of Scotland) in George Street?

Government buildings of the C20 are dominated by the giant
100 presence of *Tait*'s St Andrew's House (1936), with which Edinburgh (in contrast to London) might claim to be part of the inter-war architectural community of Europe. But there is little else of distinction. The Sheriff Court and its equally dreary contemporary (1934), the National Library on the site of Bryce's old courthouse, are twin tombstones of Scottish architecture. *Stokes*'s telephone exchange in Rose Street (1901, but actually for a private company) is worth a look, and so is *Stewart Sim*'s in Fountainbridge (1949, but still in a pre-war manner). Such jobs are now given to private architects, without much raising the average standard; the Post Office Letter Sorting Office in Brunswick Road (1980) is little more than smart packaging, of a quality we should be able to take for granted. LOCAL AUTHORITY ARCHITECTURE comes mainly under other headings (sports, hospitals, schools, housing); but here must be mentioned the François I Central Library with which *Washington*
99 *Browne* did credit to a challenging site on George IV Bridge

(1887); and, simply because it was a rare adventure, the City Architect *Robert Morham*'s fire station in Lauriston Place (1897), whose hose-tower would never be mistaken (as are those of its successors) for the tower of a contemporary church.

HOTELS of modest size, adapted from existing houses, were the general rule till the later C19; No. 6 Charlotte Square was well known as Oman's Hotel. An exception was the Waterloo in Waterloo Place (1816), purpose-built with large public rooms as well as bedrooms. The Cockburn at the corner of Market Street (1865) was handier for the station, and when a new speculative block was finished in West Register Street just across Princes Street (1862), its accommodation and swanky French appearance made it ideal for the Café Royal Hotel and its associated restaurant. Princes Street itself, with the view and the railway, became a parade of hotels of ever increasing size; *David Bryce Jun.*'s Star (demolished) of 1861 was a giant version of the New Club over shops; the former Palace at Nos. 108–110 (1869), the first with a mansard roof, is modest in scale compared with e.g. the vast, splendiferous Old Waverley, which had lifts to its six floors (1883). One hotel specialist was *J. Macintyre Henry*, who designed the Royal British (1896). Another was *W. Hamilton Beattie*, with the former Clarendon at Nos. 104–106 (1875) and subsequently the colossal North British (1895). The Caledonian Station Hotel at the other end of Princes Street, by *Peddie & Washington Browne* for the rival railway company (1899), is just as big – and bright pink – but at least there is room for it on the ground. Beattie's Carlton at the far end of North Bridge (1898) makes good use of the site and partly retrieves his reputation. The absence of C19 hotels on the picturesque outskirts is surprising, suggesting that to the tourist Edinburgh was still mainly a transit point. The Craiglockhart Hydropathic Institution (1877), which looked and indeed was rather like a hospital, is now a college. Beattie's baronial Braid Hills Hotel (1886) has done better. Of C20 hotels, only the Post House at Corstorphine has any of the sense of occasion which is the essence of hotel architecture.

SHOPS – as opposed to markets – for everyday necessities are largely a C19 invention. The Luckenbooths – lock-up shops which lined the passage formed by a row of old houses to the N of St Giles – included a number of bookshops; all were demolished in 1817. Some early C19 Old Town shops have two-level frontages, with additional display windows on the first floor. In the First New Town ground-floor shops were already being inserted in houses by the end of the C18. An easy way was simply to add a doorpiece (preferably in the centre bay, as at No. 38 George Street) and enlarge the windows. New access had to be provided to the upper floors of houses if they were still to be lived in. In the 1820s pilastered shopfronts became very popular, e.g. in Rose and Thistle Streets, and were included in some terraces in the other new towns from the start, e.g. along most of William Street. In Stockbridge, Deanhaugh Street and St Stephen Street have shops on both basement and 104

ground-floor levels. A grander alternative to pilasters was a colonnade set slightly forward from the ground-floor windows, as
103 at No. 45 George Street, which was refronted for Blackwoods
in 1829. By that time the arcade was beginning to supersede the
pilastrade for new building. The arched shops of Elm Row have
all been changed, but many survive on the South Side and,
most notably, in Victoria Street.

The earliest conversions of ground floors into shops retained
the basement area (where it existed) and the bridge. The next
stage was to pave over the area, lowering the ground floor to the
same level and thus producing a very lofty shop with a columned or pilastered front (e.g. Blackwoods) or an early Victorian triple picture-frame of moulded stone (e.g. No. 139 Princes
Street). Sometimes the whole frontage was brought up to date
– upper storeys as well. Increasingly in the later C19 the introduction of wide-span girders enabled the shop to push right out
over the area, and the treatment of display windows bore less
and less relation to the architecture above. In the early C20 the
last stage was reached, and whole new buildings were allowed
to project to the old front area line. Inside, a feature of the
grander Edinburgh shops was the rear saloon, built over the old
back garden and lit by roof lights. The best of many survivors
is at No. 87 George Street (1835) by *David Bryce*. Behind John
Lessels's frontage at No. 110 Princes Street is perhaps the oldest
(1869) example of an even more spectacular type – the galleried
saloon.

First of the complete new mercantile buildings was *Beattie*'s
Venetian Gothic stationery warehouse in West Register Street
(1864), exceptional in type as well as style. Large redevelopments, when they came, were not for specialist but for depart-
106 ment stores, starting with Beattie's huge Jenners (1893), whose
complex Bodleian façade and multi-storey saloon astonished the
city. It was followed by *J.J. Burnet*'s two giants – the Professional & Civil Service at No. 80 George Street (1903) and
Forsyth's in Princes Street (1906, now Burtons). The only notable inter-war stores were Cleghorn's at the corner of George
and Castle Streets (1924, now the Pearl) and the curtain-walled
Co-op in Bread Street (1937) – an annexe to a fine palazzo store
which just pre-dates Jenners.

THEATRES are now few. Most famous was the Theatre Royal
in Shakespeare Square (1769–1860) on the site of the G.P.O.,
and the most regrettable casualty is *Matcham*'s Empire Palace
of Varieties in Nicolson Street (1891, now replaced) with its
movable roof. The much altered West End Theatre in Castle
Terrace (1875) was demolished to make way for an opera house
that never came. The shells of a dozen others are noted in the
gazetteer. The survivors are *Phipps*'s elegant Royal Lyceum
(1883, 1,200 seats) and *Swanston* and *Davidson*'s jolly King's
Theatre (1905, now 1,530 seats). *Fairweather*'s big Playhouse in
Leith Walk (1927, originally 3,048 seats) was designed as a
dual-purpose cinema-theatre and is now so used, after a prolonged closure. *Bowhill Gibson*'s former County Cinema in

tobello (1938) has unhappily lost most of its Art Deco finery. Of concert halls, the clever Beaux-Arts Usher Hall (1910) and the contemporary Freemasons' Hall command respect rather than admiration. Queen's Hall, converted from a Georgian church, has won both.

SPORTS BUILDINGS must include public baths of any sort, first those built for subscribers – e.g. the beautiful Seafield Baths (1810, long altered), the eccentric Warrender Baths (1886) and the Moorish Drumsheugh Baths (1882) – and then the city's baths, e.g. the indoor (1898) and apparently doomed outdoor baths (1934) at Portobello. The Royal Commonwealth 102 Pool was Edinburgh's real introduction to modern architecture, and the Meadowbank Sports Centre was its worthy contemporary (1968). In the suburbs it is worth seeking out such Edwardian golf clubhouses as have not yet been ruined by brewers' extensions, e.g. Kingsknowe (1909).

HOSPITALS are numerous. The name first belonged, of course, to private foundations for certain groups in need of charitable help, in George Heriot's tradition. Such originally was John Watson's (*see* Schools, above). Others were *Thomas Hamilton*'s mannered Baroque Dean Orphanage close by (1831), 91 and *Playfair*'s great Jacobean palace, Donaldson's School 92 (1841), both of which by today's ideas seem to offer more by way of commemoration than comfort. The discursive reader of this book will find no shortage of facilities aimed by Victorian benefactors at less fortunate citizens. More recently a popular cause has been the provision of day clubs for old people, e.g. in the converted C17 Dalry House and in Lamb's House, Leith, 112 and at the new Stockbridge House.

Edinburgh's early Georgian Royal Infirmary (*see* above) was supplemented by *Bryce*'s Surgical Hospital (1848, now in other use), but both were superseded by his new Royal Infirmary (1876). Its style is baronial, its plan in accordance with Florence Nightingale's reforms – parallel pavilions projecting from each side of a long corridor on three levels. Fronting the Meadows, it engulfed George Watson's Hospital and subsequently obliterated the Merchant Maiden Hospital; its own replacement has begun. The other large, purpose-built hospital is *Robert Morham*'s City Hospital to the S (1896); its factory-like blocks with huge ventilators are linked by covered ways. *Washington Browne*'s hospital for Sick Children (1892), across the Meadows from the Infirmary, is Jacobean and much more cheerful. Two Edinburgh hospitals began in a different role (both 1867); the baronial City Poor House is now Greenlea Old People's Home, and St Cuthbert's Parish Poor House became the Western General. The Northern General (1893) started as a Fever Hospital for Leith, with separate single-storey wards of red and yellow brick; the Royal Victoria Hospital (1894) was a consumptive hospital with an open layout of chalet-like wards, now nearly all replaced. Liberton has a typical example of the shallow V-plan cottage hospital (1906). Edinburgh's earliest surviving mental hospital is the massive Royal Edinburgh by *Burn*

(1839), like an illustration on one side of one of Pugin's *Contrasts*. What comes on the other side is not Gothic, however, but the polychrome François I of *Sydney Mitchell & Wilson*'s Craighouse (1896), its main block and subsidiary houses demonstrating the restorative effects of architecture and landscape. Moreover it is beautifully kept. The history of post-1945 hospital architecture is elsewhere marred by a policy that took the worst of both worlds, retaining old buildings but subjecting them to piecemeal extension with a defiance of their character that often seems deliberate. So to see the brave new world of hospital architecture one does not go where most money has been spent (e.g. the clutter of the Western General) but to smaller, outlying hospitals whose extension has been more sensibly planned. *John Holt*, the Hospital Board's own architect, made a successful addition at Liberton (1963). Decent buildings have been commissioned from private architects, e.g. *Alan Reiach* at the Royal Victoria (1966) and *Michael Laird* at the Astley Ainslie (children's block, 1963); but the most impressive single work is the lecture theatre and prosthetic department added to the Princess Margaret Rose Hospital by *Morris & Steedman* (1960).

SCHOOLS are Edinburgh's most characteristic public buildings as soon as one leaves the central area. The private sector has two great Victorian monuments – *Rhind*'s many-turreted Jacobethan Stewart's College (1848) and *Bryce*'s French-baronial Fettes College (1864), down the hill from it. But the combination of enforced economy with first the dead classicism of the C20, then with its other various trends, has produced indifferent results; the Merchant Company's George Watson's College (1930) and Mary Erskine School (1965) make the point. In the public sector the important date is that of the Scottish Education Act, 1872. Before it, the education of children was the job of parish schools in the country, burgh schools in towns; in Edinburgh there was also a particularly strong charitable element. Early Victorian schools include the ambitious neo-Gothic Dr Bell's School in Leith; George Heriot's School in Cowgate, which was one of the first and architecturally the best of many offshoots from the old foundation; and the little parish school by the church at Davidson's Mains; all were built *c.* 1840. Dr Guthrie's old Ragged School (1850) still stands in Ramsay Lane (*see* Old Town, Royal Mile, Castlehill).

The Edinburgh School Board set up when the 1872 Act superseded the burgh arrangements, took over a few of the existing buildings and built a great many more – all marked by their own carved stone roundel of Education with her pupils. Pioneer examples include *Rowand Anderson*'s superb Stockbridge School (1874) and *W. L. Moffat*'s Leith Walk School (1875), both Gothic. From the 1880s the Board had its own architect, *Robert Wilson*, and although he was a good hand at Gothic (e.g. Marchmont Road, 1882) and deferred to the Scots tradition in Canongate (Milton House School, 1886), he developed a school style known even then as Queen Anne – of

frequently amazing invention and grandeur, but cheerful and
beautifully detailed withal. *John A. Carfrae* assisted him in the
1890s and then succeeded him, producing the most remarkable
of this type, the Leith Academy Annexe in Albion Road (1903),
surely the sign of a policy that put some of the best architecture
in some of the least favoured places. Carfrae introduced a no
less inventive Board School Baroque style, e.g. at Boroughmuir 95
and Tollcross Schools, 1911. The typical Board School is symmetrical – girls on one side, boys on the other, and sometimes
an elevated central hall crowned with a ventilator – but many
are asymmetrically composed. Leith had its own Board with its
own architect, *James Simpson*, followed by *George Craig*, whose
Trinity Academy (1891) does not quite match performance with
ambition. Inter-war schools – generally arid places of symmetrical factory aspect by the City Architect *E. J. MacRae* – are
relieved by two important works of *Reid & Forbes*; the Neo-
Classical Royal High Primary (1931) and the more fashionably
contemporary Castlebrae High (1937).

Post-war schools have suffered from the politics of teaching
methods and of architectural style, but not from the transfer of
responsibility from City to Region in 1975. Firrhill High by
Robert Matthew, Johnson-Marshall (1957) typifies the brave new
school, its composition as good as its intentions and slightly
better than its construction, spoiled by poor maintenance and
piecemeal additions.* *William Kininmonth*'s James Gillespie's
High School (1964) is unusually well built and nicely related to
the old tower which is its centrepiece. The CLASP building
system, which could have brought organized maintenance and
a desirably uniform image to more schools, is best used at
Kingsinch by *Law & Dunbar-Nasmith* (1968). A number of
Special Schools under the new Regional regime (notably near
Redhall House, Craiglockhart) are modest and practical.

The UNIVERSITY OF EDINBURGH's largest Victorian development was *Rowand Anderson*'s Pisan collegiate Medical
School (following a competition of 1874) to the w of the Old
Quad and thus well related to the new Royal Infirmary site. In
1920 development began on a large open area to the s which is
now chockablock with sixty years of assorted science buildings,
shrubs and heaths keeping an uneasy peace between. As to the
post-war growth of the Arts faculties, a difficult decision had to
be made – development to the E of the Old Quad or to the w,
where the University's existing buildings included its obvious
centre, the McEwan Hall. It was decided to go w, and ambitious
plans were made in days when sound Georgian buildings were
less valued than they are now. In sum, George Square and
Buccleuch Place have been mocked but not all destroyed, and
the University has acquired a mixture of buildings including
one undoubtedly worthy one (*Basil Spence, Glover & Ferguson*'s
Library) and two very tall ones, plus an additional traffic-free 101
space.

*But the same firm's Dunfermline College of Physical Education near Cramond
(1964) has fared much better.

CENTRAL AREA

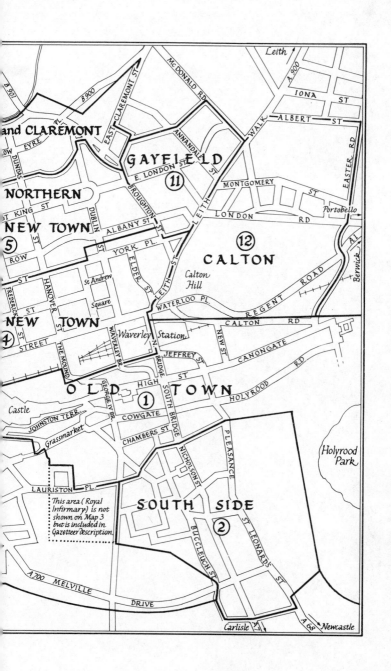

I. OLD TOWN

INTRODUCTION

David I founded the royal burgh of Edinburgh c. 1130, and gave leave to the canons of Holyrood to found their own burgh of Canongate in 1140.* These were new towns, designed to attract craftsmen and merchants. The ground each side of the old High Street was divided into 'tofts' in the form of strips running down the slopes of the ridge. Each was allotted to one burgess who had to build a house on it within a year and a day. Perhaps as early as the C14 some tofts were sub-divided, and by the end of the C15 most contained several 'lands' (buildings) – either 'forelands' fronting the street or 'backlands' reached by a passage or close at the side. Occasionally a foreland was built across two tofts, and the entrance to the backlands was by a 'pend' (a passage through the ground floor of a building).

By 1500 the High Street was continuously built up, the Canongate had buildings in each toft, and the suburbs of Grassmarket and Cowgate outside the town walls were in existence. The C16 saw a massive rebuilding, given special impetus after the Earl of Hertford's sack of Edinburgh in 1544. In this reconstruction the forelands (now generally tenement blocks) on the N side of the Royal Mile seem to have been allowed to encroach on the street by about 20 ft (6 m.), and further living space was gained by cantilevering wooden galleries out above the ground floor at front or back. Later in the century began the stone refronting of the galleries. Mansions were usually built towards the back of the tofts, away from the squalor of the main street.

The fear of fire brought increased Town Council control. After 1621 roofs on new properties had to be tiled or slated, and from 1674 new buildings facing the High Street had to be stone-fronted. In the same year regular fenestration and 'piazzas', i.e. ground-floor arcades, were recommended.

The major innovation of the C17 was the amalgamation of tofts and their redevelopment as courts surrounded by tenements, following an Act of 1644 which gave the Town Council power of compulsory purchase over derelict property. Parliament Close was rebuilt on these lines after 1675, and the climax was reached with Royal Exchange Square (*see* Public Buildings, City Chambers, below) in 1754-7.

From 1763, when the North Bridge was built across the North Loch, new roads were cut through the medieval pattern of tofts and closes. The South Bridge, with a unified scheme of

*The feudal superiority over Canongate passed to lay commendators of Holyrood after 1560. In 1636 it was bought by the burgh of Edinburgh although Canongate was not formally incorporated in the City until 1856.

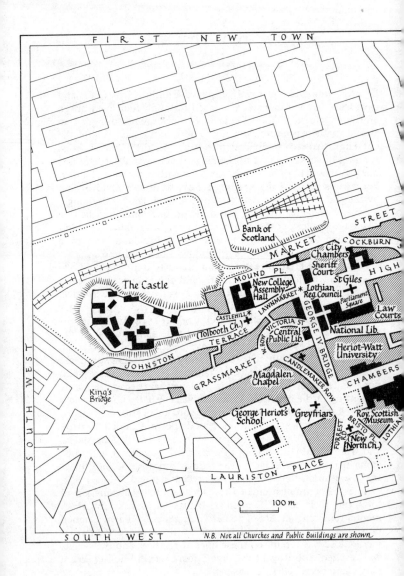

FIRST NEW TOWN

Bank of
Scotland

MARKET STREET

COCKBURN

City
Chambers

Sheriff
Court

MOUND PL.

New College
Assembly
Hall

HIGH

St Giles

Lothian
Reg. Council

The Castle

LAWNMARKET

GEORGE IV BRIDGE

Parliament
Square

Law
Courts

CASTLEHILL

(Tolbooth Ch.)

VICTORIA ST

Central
Public Lib.

National Lib.

TERRACE

W. BOW

Heriot-Watt
University

JOHNSTON

GRASSMARKET

Magdalen
Chapel

CANDLEMAKER ROW

CHAMBERS

King's
Bridge

George Heriot's
School

Greyfriars

Roy. Scottish
Museum

FORREST

BRISTO

New
(North Ch.)

LOTHIAN

SOUTH WEST

LAURISTON PLACE

0   100 m

SOUTH WEST   N.B. Not all Churches and Public Buildings are shown

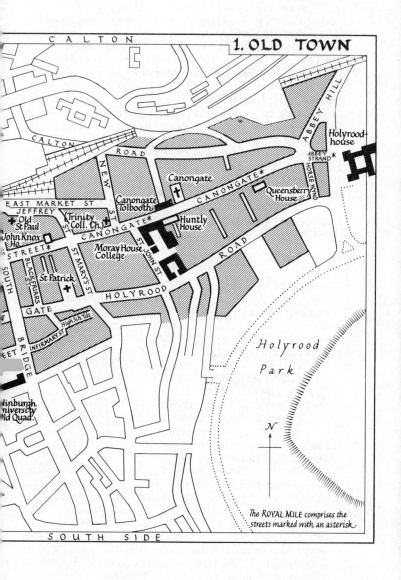

1. OLD TOWN

CALTON

CALTON ROAD

NEW ST

Canongate

CANONGATE*

Canongate Tolbooth

EAST MARKET ST

JEFFREY

Old St Paul*

John Knox Ho.

Trinity Coll. Ch.*

STREET*

CANONGATE*

ST MARY'S ST

ST JOHN ST

Moray House College

Huntly House

Queensberry House

ABBEY HILL

Holyrood house

ABBEY STRAND *

HORSE WYND

CANONGATE

ROAD

BLACKFRIARS

St Patrick

HOLYROOD

GATE

Infirmary St

High Sch. Yds

BRIDGE

Edinburgh University Old Quad.

Holyrood

Park

N

The ROYAL MILE comprises the streets marked with an asterisk

SOUTH SIDE

tenements, went up in 1785–8. After the 1827 Improvement Act better access was provided to the s by George IV Bridge and Victoria Street, and to the w by the King's Bridge and Johnston Terrace. Buildings along these streets were intended to be in the 'Old Flemish' style.

The 1827 Improvement Act's concern for the character of the Old Town was maintained in the 1867 Improvement Act, which provided for ten new streets to open up insanitary closes and replace the worst of the slums with model tenements in the Baronial style. Improvements in the 1890s again concentrated on clearance to give more light into closes, but Sir Patrick Geddes succeeded in reconstructing many of the better c16–18 buildings as university halls of residence.

In the 1930s extensive rebuilding of Canongate was begun by the Town Council. Hungry-pointed rubble and a few scrolled skewputts were thought sufficient gestures towards conservation. After 1950 further rebuilding of Canongate was carried out in a much more colourful style, some old fronts being retained, others rebuilt in replica though not necessarily on their old sites.

TOWN WALLS

The burgh of Edinburgh must have been enclosed soon after its foundation, if only to prevent smuggling. A West Gate is mentioned before 1180, a South Gate in 1214 and the Netherbow Port in 1369. The first wall, perhaps itself replacing a palisade, gave way to the slightly more extensive KING'S WALL c. 1450–75. In 1514, after the Battle of Flodden, James V ordered the walls to be strengthened. The Town took the opportunity to enclose the suburbs of Grassmarket and Cowgate with the FLODDEN WALL, more a defence against smugglers than against the English. Much of it was not really new – along St Mary's Street and Leith Wynd the houses were fortified; elsewhere, garden walls were incorporated. Bastions at the corners gave a martial flourish. In 1620 TELFER'S WALL (named after its mason *John Tailefer*) was built to enclose 10 acres bought by the Town in 1618. Military purpose appeared in 1650 when *John Mylne* and *John Scott* strengthened the walls with artillery emplacements. More gun-platforms were built under Colonel *Theodore Dury*'s direction in 1715. By the later c18 the walls were redundant. In 1762 leave was given to demolish the bastions of the Telfer Wall which obstructed the new road of Lauriston Place. In 1764 the Netherbow Port was pulled down to improve the traffic-flow of the Royal Mile, and from the 1770s the walls were gradually demolished.

Little survives. In Vennel, a crenellated sw bastion of the Flodden Wall, of purplish rubble from Bruntsfield Links. The pair of crosslet gunloops in the w face remain; and another in the fragmentary n face. In the s face only one crosslet, the other replaced by a door c. 1810 and then by a window in 1876. To the s a stretch of the rubble Telfer Wall. Much larger orangey stones. In Heriot Place an c18 gateway.

Scanty remains of the Flodden Wall in n walls of houses in Bristo Port. In Drummond Street a sizeable amount but with the top courses removed in 1772. Splayed corner to the Pleasance. There was a bastion here; the blocked arch was probably the c17 door to its lower part.

EDINBURGH CASTLE

In its time the Castle has had many functions – fortress, royal residence, ordnance factory, record office, repository for the regalia, barracks, prison and ancient monument. It has been quicker to accept new uses than to discard old, and for most of its recorded history it has housed disparate and sometimes incongruous activities. Even today it is a barracks as well as an ancient monument and not only a monument but also a tourist attraction.

Of the first fortification of the Castle rock nothing is known. The site is naturally defensive, the high w end of a long spur of basaltic rock. Its identification with the site of the c6 hall at Din Eidyn where feasted the warhost of King Mynyddog is probable enough. From other Dark Age sites can be conjectured a wall round the summit and an outer wall, certainly at the easier w and e approaches. After the death of St Margaret, Queen of Scotland, in 1093 the Castle appears as a rather colourless stage-set in the chronicles of her sanctity. From these we know that it was fortified, the main defence being to the e but with a wall at the w. There was a royal residence with an oratory and there was also a church (St Mary's), perhaps an Anglian foundation. The buildings seem to have been on the summit, at whose nw corner the chapel dedicated to St Margaret was built in the c12.

During the Wars of Independence Edinburgh Castle changed hands four times between 1296 and 1341. The defences were dismantled in 1313 but repaired in 1335, and were further strengthened with stone-throwing machines in 1342. The return of David II from English captivity in 1356 marks the beginning of a great building programme which was to stretch over nearly two hundred years. This was the golden age of the Castle as fortress and royal residence. In 1361 a new well was sunk to the n of the Castle rock and a tower (the Wellhouse Tower) built to defend it. A new gate-tower (the Constable's Tower) at the ne of the curtain was built in 1375–9. The royal residence was moved s of the summit to David's Tower, built in 1368–77. Following this the ground s of St Mary's Church, which had been reconstructed in 1366, was raised on a series of vaults and sub-vaults to make a flat court, now Crown Square. The King's Great Chamber built s of David's Tower in 1434–5 and rebuilt after the siege of 1445 may have formed the nucleus of the existing range of buildings on the e side of the court (the Palace). The Great Hall on the s side of the court existed by

1458, but the present building in that position was put up either
c. 1496–1511 or at about the same time as the Register House of
1540–2 which links it to the Palace. After James V's death in
1542 the Castle was abandoned as the royal residence at Edinburgh in favour of Holyrood; Queen Mary's confinement for
the birth of James VI in the Castle was quite exceptional. By
the end of the C15 the Castle had acquired a new function that
must have made it unattractive to reside in; it had become an
ordnance factory. This began in 1464 when James III improved
the access road for artillery and built a furnace. By 1498 there
was a House of Artillery, possibly on the w side of Crown
Square. The old Hall on the summit had become an arsenal by
1515, when a foundry was built against its n wall. In 1539–40
St Mary's Church was converted into a munitions store.

The Castle was not seriously threatened during the Earl of
Hertford's invasion in 1544, but later in the same year the E
defences were strengthened with a new rampart from David's
Tower to the Constable's Tower. Above this was built a second
battery stretching from St Mary's Church to St Margaret's
Chapel. Below these projected the Spur, a massive W-shaped
defence guarding the approach. In 1573 the Castle fell to the
English army sent to aid the anti-Marian forces. During the
siege the Spur and the whole of the E front between David's
Tower and the Constable's Tower were shot to pieces, the garrison surrendering after the collapse of the upper storeys of
David's Tower had blocked the Fore Well. Repairs were made
over the next fifteen years. The Spur and curtain wall were
rebuilt, a new gate-tower (the Portcullis Gate) replaced the
Constable's Tower, and a great new artillery defence (the Half
Moon Battery) was wrapped round the surviving lower portion
of David's Tower.

In 1617 the symbolic role of the Castle as a royal residence
was briefly re-established when James VI, during his return
visit to Scotland, held court in the Palace block, reconstructed
for the occasion. But it was only symbolic – the King slept at
Holyrood. The Castle continued to be a fortress – an immensely
strong one whose guns commanded not only the town to the E
but also the approaches to it from w, n and s. In 1640 it fell to
the Covenanting army after a three-month siege in which the
defences, particularly the Spur, were badly damaged. Repair
followed, but the Spur was demolished in 1648 as being too
expensive of manpower. After a second three-month siege in
1650, work continued on re-casting the lower defences to the E.
In 1662 the gun-embrasures of the Half Moon Battery were
strengthened. A scheme of 1675 by *John Slezer* for additional
fortification was partly carried out in 1677–80, when the ground
inside the w wall was graded and levelled and the re-casting of
the E defences continued. Repair followed yet another siege in
1689. The appearance of a French squadron in the Forth in
1708 led to further work directed by *Captain Theodore Dury*.
Five-gun emplacements (Butt's Battery and Dury's Battery)
were built at the w and s, and a vast hornwork ('*le grand secret*')

was begun to the E. Not much of the hornwork had been built when it was abandoned in 1710. In 1730-7 the whole of the perimeter wall to the W and S was rebuilt, and in 1742 the dry ditch across the E front was finally completed.

The maintenance of a standing army after the mid C17 gave the Castle a new function. From 1650 the Great Hall was used as a barracks, and in 1737 it was subdivided with intermediate floors. An officers' barracks was built in 1708 and houses for the governor, master gunner and storekeeper in 1742. After the completion of a new powder-magazine and ordnance store in 1754, the old St Mary's Church, long used as an ordnance store, was demolished and the North Barracks built on its site. The massive New Barracks were completed in 1799, when the Great Hall became a military hospital. The Castle's barrack function was further developed by the use of the vaults under Crown Square to house prisoners of war, a practice which began in 1757 and continued until 1814.

In 1753 had begun the creation of the Esplanade, a parade-ground in front of the Castle on the approach from the town. It was widened in 1816 and given decorative railings and walls. The Castle's function as a fortress was over. It remained a barracks throughout the C19 but was seen more and more as a monument. The Royal Engineers responsible for the buildings came to champion this idea of the Castle, and schemes for restoration of the old parts and baronialization of the newer are the theme of the century. In 1818 the Honours (regalia) of Scotland were rediscovered in the chest where they had lain since the Act of Union of 1707. They were placed on public view, a keeper was appointed to look after them and the maintenance of the Regalia Room transferred from the War Office to the Office of Works. In 1829 Mons Meg, the great cannon which had become a symbol for Scottish patriotism, was moved from the Tower of London to Edinburgh Castle. Then in 1845 the antiquarian Daniel Wilson identified a storehouse at the W end of the garrison chapel as St Margaret's Chapel. This was acclaimed as the very oratory in which St Margaret had worshipped. Prompted by the Society of Antiquaries of Scotland, the War Office demolished the garrison chapel and restored St Margaret's Chapel in 1851-2, its maintenance being taken over subsequently by the Office of Works. In 1853 *Colonel Richard Moody* replaced a Georgian guardhouse with one disguised as a bastion, and within two years *Robert Billings* had been commissioned to design a new chapel to replace the North Barracks on the site of St Mary's Church. Lord Panmure became Secretary for War in 1855 and immediately dismissed Billings, but this was the result of a dislike of Billings, not of the concept of the Castle as a monument, for which the restoration of the architectural primacy of the summit was of the greatest importance. Panmure championed a scheme by Colonel Moody for a new church on the North Barracks site and for an armoury in the form of a keep to the N of St Margaret's Chapel. The plans were approved by the Queen and Prince Consort, and the North

Barracks had been unroofed by 1858, when the Government fell
and the scheme was abandoned. Undeterred by this setback
Moody put forward a much more ambitious scheme in 1859.
The massive and uncompromisingly Georgian New Barracks
dominating the w view had been attacked for years as out of
keeping with the historic character of the Castle.* The 1859
report was accompanied by designs by *Francis T. Dollman* for
re-casting the New Barracks and the Munition House and Ordnance Stores in a style more French château than Scottish castle
but undeniably picturesque. None of this was executed. The
proposal for a keep on the summit was resurrected in 1864 with
David Bryce's scheme for a keep as a memorial to the Prince
Consort. Unfortunately the Queen wished Albert's monument
'to stand by itself unconnected with any other work', and the
presence of St Margaret's Chapel was sufficient to rule out the
Castle as a suitable site. In 1863 the North Barracks were reconstructed (for the same use), with Billings providing baronial
detail. Twenty years later private enterprise took the initiative.
Major James Gore Booth, R.E., showed Lord Napier and Ettrick the medieval roof of the subdivided Great Hall surviving
above the Georgian ceiling. Lord Napier wrote to *The Scotsman*
urging restoration of the Great Hall. By 1885 William Nelson
the publisher had promised to finance restoration of the Great
Hall and Portcullis Gate and a second restoration of St Margaret's Chapel, *Hippolyte Blanc* being employed as architect.
Blanc's unscholarly scheme for remodelling the Portcullis Gate
was greeted with enthusiasm by the War Office, Town Council
and Cockburn Association (Edinburgh's already vociferous
amenity society) and in silence by the Society for the Protection
of Ancient Buildings.‡ Work began in October 1886 and was
complete the next year. No objection was made to Blanc's
scheme for the Great Hall; only the problem of finding alternative hospital accommodation delayed the start of work until
February 1887. St Margaret's Chapel was the responsibility not
of the War Office but of the Office of Works. Predictably the
approval of a committee was required, and the committee would
approve only a much more limited scheme than Blanc had proposed. Work on the chapel had not begun at the time of Nelson's death in September 1887, but a codicil to his will bound
his executors to complete the restoration already begun, and
work on the Great Hall continued. It did not bind them to pay
for work which he had only intended to carry out, and since
they 'looked with disapproval at his expenditure on a subject
bringing in no return', the scheme for St Margaret's Chapel
was dropped. Meanwhile the War Office made its own contribution to the Castle by providing a new gatehouse and drawbridge. The intention had been to add to the picturesque
character of the Castle, but the design was so pared on grounds
of cost that it was not made public until after tenders had been
accepted. The w view of the Castle continued a subject for

* 'Look at the west side of the Castle and shudder', wrote Lord Cockburn.
‡ Blanc was the S.P.A.B.'s local correspondent.

improvement. Blanc provided sketch-designs for reconstruction of the New Barracks in 1887 and 1893. Finally in 1897 the War Office baronialized the Armoury as a hospital.

The development of the idea of the Castle as a monument reached its height at the end of the First World War. In October 1918 the Secretary for Scotland stated that after the war the Castle would no longer be needed to house any large body of troops, and appointed a committee 'to consider and report upon the utilisation of Edinburgh Castle for the purposes of a Scottish National War Memorial'. The committee recommended the building of a shrine on the summit and the conversion of existing buildings into regimental museums. The New Barracks could, it suggested, be turned into a new National Museum of Antiquities. The report of the committee's architectural adviser, *Robert Lorimer*, was prophetic in its approach to the Georgian buildings, proposing internal adaptation but respect for the exterior,* except for the New Barracks. But even here Lorimer proposed only the removal of chimneys and a vertical linking of windows. The shrine was built in 1924–7 as the Scottish National War Memorial. The conversion of barracks buildings into museums followed, and the Castle is now a museum, a monument and a shrine. But soldiers are still present, housed in the New Barracks, which remain as Georgian as ever.

FORTIFICATIONS

Of the medieval defences little is left. An irregularly curved bastion on the W of the Lang Stairs probably began as the gatehouse guarding the approach to the summit. Its C18 parapet encloses a cemetery for officers' dogs. S of the Great Hall is late C14 walling under a Georgian battlement. Below the Castle on the N is the WELLHOUSE TOWER built in 1362 as a combined defence for the well and gatehouse at the W entry to the outer ward. Its rubble walls, built into the sloping ground, stand to a height of two storeys on the N, E and S sides. Doors to both floors in the SE corner. Two deeply splayed windows with chamfered arrises on the S, looking into the passage between the tower and the rock. In the rock, the masonry surround for the gate-bolt. Seventy feet above this is the CRANE SEAT, a stone platform from which to drop missiles on attackers. Diagonally attached to the NE corner of the tower is a square jamb, probably containing the well itself. Stretching NE from here is a short length of the ward wall beginning with a semicircular bastion, perhaps a late medieval reconstruction to form a gun platform.

The E side of the Castle is dominated by the massive semicircle of the HALF MOON BATTERY built round the lower floors of David's Tower in 1573–88, its bulk relieved by

---

*Lorimer changed his mind in 1927 when the Office of Works architect prepared a scheme for the conversion of the interior of the old officers' barracks into a museum whilst keeping the front. Lorimer then put forward a counter-proposal for a new building designed by himself.

string-courses. In it, an early c16 gun loop N of David's Tower
has been reopened. Parapet with segment-headed gun embrasures rebuilt in 1689–95. To its N the contemporary FORE-
WALL BATTERY runs NW to the Portcullis Gate. In front, the
dry ditch begun in the 1630s, its masonwork finally completed
by *John Romer* a century later. c17 walling on the W of the
summit. Below the summit, DURY'S BATTERY on the N and
BUTT'S BATTERY on the S, built by *Theodore Dury* in 1708–
13. Of his ambitious hornwork, LE GRAND SECRET, just a
short stretch outside the N perimeter. The N and W PERIM-
ETER WALLS were rebuilt by *Romer* in 1730–7. Pepperpot
sentry-boxes corbelled out at the corners and martial-looking
garderobes add a touch of romance.

DESCRIPTION

The approach is across the ESPLANADE. The railings on the N
and the low wall punctuated by dummy turrets and sentry
boxes are of 1816. On the N side a row of MONUMENTS. 78th
Highlanders by *R. Rowand Anderson*, 1861. Celtic cross with
an elephant at the base. Stepped pedestal. – Earl Haig. Equestrian bronze on a rocky base, by *G. E. Wade*, 1922–3. – Colonel Kenneth Douglas Mackenzie. Richly carved Celtic cross
by *John Steell*, 1875. – Much more routine the Celtic cross to
the Scottish Horse by *Stewart McGlashan & Son*, 1905. –
Frederick, Duke of York. Bronze statue by *Thomas Campbell*,
1839. – Ensign Ewart, by *William H. Kininmonth*, 1938.
Block of grey Swedish granite. – Peterhead granite obelisk to
72nd Duke of Albany's Own Highlanders by *McDonald, Field
& Co.*, 1882–3.

From the Esplanade the Castle is entered across a DRAW-
BRIDGE and through a tepidly castellated GATEHOUSE. Both
are of 1887–8, by *R. Lawson Scott* of the *Royal Engineers
Department*, London. The canopied niches flanking the
entrance-arch are by *Robert S. Lorimer*, 1929. In them, STA-
TUES of Bruce (by *Thomas J. Clapperton*) and Wallace (by
Alexander Carrick). On the walls of the arch, c17 carved
reliefs of artillery. The road climbs round to the r. of the
summit. The first incident is the early c19 INNER BARRIER.
Only its broad gate-piers remain, the N one attached to the
rubble mass of the GUARDHOUSE built in 1853 by (Colonel)
Richard C. Moody, very defensive, with a massive gun loop.
Then the PORTCULLIS GATE, built to replace the Constable's
Tower destroyed in 1573. The lowest stage was completed by
December 1577, when *William McDowell*, Master of Work,
was paid for 'bigging of the inner yett' of Edinburgh Castle,
and it seems that no more than this stage was at first intended.
It forms a strong barrier across the road with two outer doors,
a portcullis and an inner door. Ashlar barrel-vault. The main
front uses classical motifs ignorantly, though with considerable conviction. Two tiers of spindly pilasters, tenuously

Tuscan, flank the roll-moulded segmental arch. The inner pilasters of the upper pairs branch out into two concentric hoodmoulds, and their capitals are extended inwards as rectangular labels. A string-course running the whole width of the gate divides all this from a vestigial pediment, with lions sitting on its ends and a relatively correct pedimented aedicule. The pilasters are Ionic, but the entablature has triglyphs alternating with hearts and mullets (armorial devices of the Regent Morton). The shield with the royal arms is a replacement of 1887. The original portcullis quickly rusted 'in default of ane hous', so in 1583 *Robert Drummond*, Master of Works, prepared estimates for adding two storeys to the gate in which to house both the portcullis and the Captain of the Castle. The work was executed in 1584 under the direction of *William Schaw*. The new upper storeys were plain under a crenellated parapet. Flat roof designed as a gun-emplacement. In the mid C18 the top floor was rebuilt with a pitched roof. It was rebuilt again in 1886-7 to *Hippolyte Blanc*'s design; he was trying to restore the Portcullis Gate 'as nearly as possible, in accordance with the appearance as built by David II', i.e. to give the C16 Portcullis Gate the top of the C14 Constable's Tower. Heavy corbelled parapet with angle rounds to the N, containing a stone-slabbed pitched roof. Inside, a plain tunnel-vaulted portcullis room. Set into the vault a toy portcullis – just a strip of iron with spikes, like the top of a railing inverted. On the second floor a tunnel-vault in soapy ashlar by Blanc. Here is stored a small collection of medieval ARCHITECTURAL FRAGMENTS, including pieces of tracery from St Mary's Church found when the Scottish National War Memorial was built.

Immediately beyond the Portcullis Gate a steep flight of steps, the LANG STAIRS, provides the principal access to the summit.* ST MARGARET'S CHAPEL occupies the highest part of the Castle rock. From at least the early C14 it was regarded as the chapel in which St Margaret († 1093) had worshipped. The architectural evidence rules out a date earlier than *c.* 1110. Externally it is an irregular rectangle approximately 10 × 5 m. Three windows in the s wall, none in the N and one each in the E and W. The heads are single pieces of stone. Only the E window and one on the s are unrestored. Much of the rock foundation has been cut away on the s, E and W sides, and these are now underpinned with masonry quite different from the squared ashlar of the original work. Later masonry also at the wall-heads. The C18 roof-shape, piended at the E, was retained by (Colonel) *George Phillpots* and *Maximilian Grant* in their restoration of 1851-2. The N door is of 1939 by *J. Wilson Paterson*, discreet and with no risk of being mistaken for original work. Contrary to what the exterior suggests, the chancel is apsidal within.

*Visitors are now (1984) directed to approach the summit through Foog's Gate to the w.

Apses squared to the outside quite often terminated the choir aisles of major Norman and Anglo-Norman churches (e.g. Durham Cathedral or St Etienne at Caen), but parallels on this scale are lacking. Off-centre E window, plain semi-dome vault. Chancel-arch of two orders, with chevron archivolts, chip-carved label and scallop capitals. The shafts are monoliths, replaced in 1851–2. The tunnel-vault of the nave is of the same date, but there was evidence for an earlier vault of the same type; the inward curve on the stones from which the window heads are made proves that there was originally a vault here. – STAINED GLASS. Single figures (William Wallace and SS. Andrew, Ninian, Columba and Margaret), by *Douglas Strachan*, 1922. The saints are icons of jewel-like intensity, Wallace a dramatic figure in fiery colours.

In the Forewall Battery to the SE of St Margaret's Chapel is the FORE WELL, the original well of the Castle. Its round parapet dates from 1913. The Half Moon Battery to the S encloses substantial remains of the two lower storeys of DAVID'S TOWER, the dominant feature of the castle until its destruction in 1573. As built in 1368–77 the tower was L-shaped, like so many late Scottish tower houses. The jamb projected from the W end of the S side, and the re-entrant angle originally sheltered a narrow barbican. The entrance is now at the NW corner, where there was a turnpike stair giving access to the upper storeys and also, no doubt, to the older Palace buildings between St Margaret's Chapel and St Mary's Church. From here a passage runs along the W side of the tower, its first exit being to the room that fills the ground floor except for the jamb, now subdivided by early C17 tunnel-vaulted water cisterns. Nearly all the N wall has been demolished. The passage continues down to the lobby in the jamb. In the W wall a deep recess with a pointed tunnel-vault on transverse ribs, possibly a porter's lodge. At first-floor level the lobby is tunnel-vaulted and from its W wall a C15 passage equipped with a privy leads through to the Palace block. In the S wall is a doorway with a pit in its floor to trap the unwary. It opened on to a bretasche and thence to the head of a curtain wall. This runs S for only a few metres before being interrupted by the Half Moon Battery. The rock face appears at the bottom of the cleft-like spaces between David's Tower and the Half Moon. At ground-floor level the E wall of the lobby is pierced by a narrow passage leading from the barbican, its entrance an almost triangular pointed arch formed of two stones. Of the late C14 barbican only footings remain. In its E side was a gate leading to a path down to the town. Later in the Middle Ages the barbican was demolished and the re-entrant angle filled in so as to make the tower rectangular. The first-floor-level barrel-vault is of this period. At the E end of the northernmost C17 water cistern is one of the casemates of the artillery curtain begun in 1544. The big ovoid gunport commanding the Old Town was blocked by the building of the Half Moon Battery in 1574 and reopened c. 1913. The segmental tunnel-vault over the casemate is probably of 1574.

sw of David's Tower is the block known as the PALACE. It formed the E side of Crown Square, all of whose buildings originally belonged to the late medieval palace. Like the ranges s and w of the square it rests on vaulted undercrofts whose purpose was to maximize the level area s of St Mary's Church. Whether the E, s and w ranges were all planned at once is not clear. The Palace occupies the site of the c15 Great Chamber. A Great Chamber presupposes a Great Hall, and in the 1430s this could still have been in David's Tower,* or it may have stood on the site of the present hall, s of Crown Square. The Palace is a double pile, rubble-built. The few medieval features remaining indicate a c15 date, perhaps later rather than earlier. Besides the Great Chamber it must have contained rooms for other members of the royal family. Originally the Palace ended well short of the s side of the Great Hall, and a straight joint marks it off from the L-shaped infilling of the angle between Palace and hall. The angle building may not be much later than the Palace, as it has a very similar corbelled-out parapet. The attic windows and battlements shown in c17 views were absorbed into a Georgian reroofing and raising of the wall-head. On the E front, the show front to the town, are the stumps of three c15 oriels, two corbelled out from the wall face, one on a polygonal stem rising from the rock. A similar group of oriels is on the N front of Linlithgow Palace. The N half of the Palace was remodelled in 1615–17 as a ceremonial royal lodging for James VI. *James Murray* was Master of Works and may well have made the design. A second storey was raised on the old walls and given great emphasis with a cannon-studded battlemented parapet. At the E corners are square turrets whose ogee-profiled lead roofs were reinstated in 1939. Only towards the N end was the old attic storey removed entirely – the new parts of the E front are ashlar-faced. Three wide bays, the thin pediments over the windows carved with swags and crowns by *William Wallace*. The openings were originally divided by a single mullion and transom. Segmental pediment to the central second-floor window. Flanking it are moulded frames, the l. one enclosing a relief of the Honours of Scotland, the r. one empty but until 1652 enclosing the royal arms. The rubble-built N front expresses a hierarchy of function. Its central stair-tower marks the boundary between royal apartments in the E division of the double pile and official accommodation in the w division. The upper floors of the royal lodging have large mullioned and transomed windows and pediments carved with royal emblems, whereas the official block is slightly lower and severely plain. One tall blocked medieval window survives. The stair-tower is octa-

---

* A 'lord's hall' and 'mid chamber' in the tower are mentioned in 1517, a 'cloisset' (i.e. an oratory) in 1488. Kitchens were being built nearby in 1382.

gonal in plan and ogee-roofed. The NW corner is linked to
the War Memorial by an arch placed high up, the purpose of
which is not obvious. On the W front to Crown Square a
central stair-tower is again the main accent. Originally ogee-
roofed, it was raised by two storeys of ashlar in toy fort style
c. 1820. It has at least the merit of diverting attention from
the discrepancy between the four official floors on the l. and
the three-storey royal lodging to the r. The stair leads to the
first-floor Regalia Room, apparently built at the outset as a
vaulted strongroom with its entrance guarded by a yett. The
Perp wooden panelling on walls and vault is of 1848. To the
s of the royal lodging the much-reconstructed medieval Palace
reappears. The entrance is a round arched door with rusticated quoins arranged radially at the head and a continuous
roll moulding (partly cut away). Above the door is a strapwork cartouche with the date of James VI's birth here, 1566,
and the monogram MAH (for Mary and Henry, Lord Darnley). The cartouche is awkwardly placed in a rectangular
frame which was previously filled with a panel dated 1633,
according to one of the extremely accurate survey drawings
made in 1754 for the Board of Ordnance. 1633 was the year
of Charles I's coronation at Holyrood and could well be the
date of the door. The original position of the 1566 datestone
is unknown. Inside, two stone fireplaces in the outer chamber.
Large and plain at the E wall, moulded with an aumbry above
at the s. The closet at the SE was the actual birthplace of
James VI, and in 1617 *John Anderson* was paid £100 Scots
for 'painting the rowme quhair his Majestie was borne'. Late
medieval wooden ceiling of four compartments with provision
for a central boss. Painted thistles at the corners of each compartment, and the initials MR and IR in alternate compartments. The boards covering the upper part of the walls are
painted with the date of James VI's birth and a large representation of the royal arms of Scotland above the inscription:

> Lord Jesu Chryst that Crounit was with Thornse
> Preserve the Birth quhais Badgie heir is borne.
> And send Hir Sonce Successione to Reigne still
> Lang in this Realme, if that it be Thy will
> Als Grant O lord quhat ever of Hir proseed
> Be to Thy Glorie Honer and Prais sobeid.

The panelling below is of c. 1700, imported in 1848. The NE
ground-floor rooms retain two C15 or early C16 fireplaces
with elided capitals and bases to the side shafts and flat hoods,
the latter suggesting a date c. 1500 rather than earlier. The
northernmost room on the E side connects with the first floor
of David's Tower. W of this room is the kitchen of 1615–17.
Two wide segmental fireplaces and a two-bay Georgian arcade across the middle of the room.

On the s side of Crown Square, next to the Palace, is the
REGISTER HOUSE built by *John Merlioun* in 1540–2. Its
stone slab roof was replaced in the late C18 by a slated garret,

but parts of the earlier wall-head survive on the s front. The rest of the s side of the square is occupied by the GREAT HALL, whose present state, as restored by *Hippolyte J. Blanc* in 1887-91, may be compared to the 1754 Board of Ordnance survey. Blanc's four windows on the N side follow the original arrangement in being placed high up and linked by a moulded sill-course. The original ones were only half as high, and their sill-course was in line with that of the Register House. Under the sill-course was a row of corbels that must have carried the roof of a wooden pentice along the whole s side of the square (cf. the former pentice on the courtyard front of the Great Hall at Stirling Castle). The structural and visual continuity between the Register House and the Great Hall suggests that both are James V's work, but the stylistic evidence does not allow one to decide between his reign and that of his father. The original parapet had the very long merlons used at Linlithgow church, Lothian, from the late C15 to the early 1530s, and the crowsteps on the end gables (most of the w one original) have copings of triangular section like those on James IV's Princes Tower at Stirling and James V's gatehouse of 1537-41 at Falkland Palace. The Falkland gateway also provides a parallel for the wide segmental door in the middle of the N wall, now built up. This seems to have been the original entrance, for there was no evidence of any opening in the traditional position at the lower end of the hall, where Blanc inserted a Late Gothic door. The s elevation is again mostly by Blanc, but old views and Blanc's pre-restoration drawings show that the evidence was clearer than on the N side. There are four big upright windows two lights wide and three high, like those shown in C17 views of James V's w front at Holyroodhouse, 1535-6. Gothic hankerings are entirely absent. As on the N side, Blanc gave the parapet closely spaced merlons.

The interior is Blanc's creation except for the hammerbeam 59 roof, and even this has been altered. In the late C18 the original hammerbeams were truncated and the members immediately above and below removed. The 1754 survey shows that the hammerbeams ended in carved beasts, had only single braces below and carried vertical struts rising to meet the kerb principals (the beams parallel with the lower parts of the rafters) at the points where Blanc added structurally redundant diagonal members. The struts now on the hammerbeams take the place of braces answering those between the lower collars and the kerb principals. Blanc's alterations have given the roof a very disjointed appearance. If, as seems likely, he did not know the 1754 survey, he would have had to base his reconstruction entirely on the peg holes and mortices left in the kerb principals after the removal of the original struts and braces. The longitudinal stability provided by the hammerbeams and their supports is reinforced by purlins under the upper collars and others over the lower collars and kerb principals. No assessment of the place of the roof in

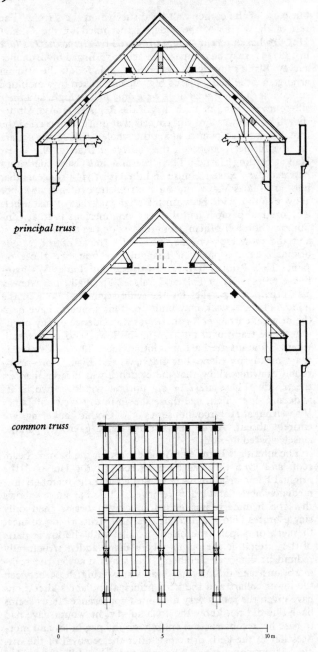

principal truss

common truss

partial longitudinal section

Edinburgh Castle,
roof of Great Hall, reconstruction of original state

the development of Scottish medieval carpentry can be attempted, because hardly any other medieval roofs have survived in Scotland. Nevertheless, it is clear that the intention was to create a version of the greater English hammerbeam roofs, in which a system of straight braces substitutes for the arched braces normally used over hammerbeams. Perhaps timbers of the massive size needed for arched braces were not available. There are many other departures from English practice, the most fundamental being the use of thin square-sectioned timbers for the main trusses as well as for the common rafters. This also gives the roof more than a passing resemblance to a matchstick model.

The date of the roof, as of the whole hall, is very hard to decide. A virtually identical roof once covered the Great Hall at Stirling, the walls of which are dated to James IV's reign on stylistic grounds. But there is no reason, so far as the present state of knowledge goes, why a roof built for James V should look much different from one made for his father. In fact the designer of the roof, whether it dates from the first or the fourth decade of the c16, was probably *John Drummond*, named king's principal carpenter in 1531 and active between 1507 and 1541 at most of the major royal residences, including the Castle. The main reason for crediting James IV with the Edinburgh roof is the presence of the monogram I R 4 on one of the corbels that carry the wall posts. There are no surviving documents which refer unambiguously to building or rebuilding the hall, but payments for timber in 1496, including four props for the hall, and a final payment for slating in 1511 have been interpreted as indications that the roof, if not the entire hall, had been renewed between these dates. The main obstacle to accepting a date in James IV's reign is the unequivocally Renaissance character of the scrolled roof corbels. It is usually stated that the earliest Renaissance architectural ornament in Scotland is that on the courtyard façades at Falkland Palace, but the possibility that the Edinburgh corbels are earlier by about thirty years cannot be ruled out. Classical motifs would probably have been known by c. 1500-10 in Scotland from such imports as French and Netherlandish tapestries and illuminated books, and the Pope's gift of a new State Sword in 1507 may not have been the only instance of direct contact with Italian Renaissance decorative art. A date c. 1496-1511 for the corbels would put Scotland momentarily abreast of France on the path to Renaissance architecture, although by 1511 French architects were applying the orders to whole elevations (e.g. Gaillon, 1508), something not attempted in Scotland before the Falkland courtyard. The absence of any other signs of Scottish interest in Renaissance motifs (other than Roman lettering) before the 1530s may argue against the early date; alternatively it could reflect the virtual drying up of royal patronage after 1513, the year of Flodden. The plainly mullioned and transomed s windows, reminiscent of English mid-c16 to early C17 work, are possible at the beginning of the C16 if the inspiration was coming from French secular architecture (e.g. the hall of the house of Jacques Cœur, Bourges, 1443–51). The main elevations of James IV's hall at Stirling are as matter-of-fact as the elevations of the Edinburgh hall, and nearly as devoid of Gothic feeling, but the ornamental accents remain purely Gothic. One way out of the dilemma is to suggest that James V modernized a hall built by James IV, setting up the I R 4 monogram to commemorate his father's contribution. The existence of two building phases is suggested by Blanc's report of a change in the masonry and by the still visible thinning of the walls at corbel level. It is even possible that the roof is James IV's, taken down and re-erected on raised walls.

The big hooded fireplace in the E wall was based by Blanc on an early C15 example at Borthwick, Lothian. On the hood are lumpy statues by *John Rhind*, an afterthought suggested by Lord Napier. They represent May, Flora, Aurora and Venus, in reference to Dunbar's *The Thistle and the Rose*,* written to celebrate the marriage of Margaret Tudor and James IV. By Blanc are the richly Late Gothic panelling and W screen, their details based closely on the choir stalls of King's College Chapel, Aberdeen. Carved window seats in the S embrasures and shutters to the lower divisions of the windows. Heraldic STAINED GLASS, 1887–91.

On the W side of Crown Square there would have been kitchens etc. serving the Great Hall. In this position is now the SCOTTISH UNITED SERVICES MUSEUM, built in 1708 by *Captain Theodore Dury* as officers' barracks. Parallel piend-roofed two-storey ranges with a slit of a courtyard between. Unaltered rear, skied on medieval vaults. Paired first-floor windows at the Crown Square front, but the ground-floor fenestration now muddled and the NE corner sliced off in 1924. Interior gutted to form the museum in 1928–30 by *J. Wilson Paterson*. The vaults and sub-vaults under the W range are entered from a corridor to the N. The nearest things to datable features are the wide segmental doors (cf. the N entrance of the Great Hall). The W room has been divided lengthwise and bread-ovens were installed in the E division. Only their pointed doors remain (cf. Craigmillar Castle). In the W division two pretty cast-iron grates with the arms of George III. From 1757 to 1814 the larger cellars were used as a gaol for prisoners of war; the large S window of the E cellar has bars of prodigious thickness. From 1650 they were barracks, and the remains of wooden galleries probably dating from then have been removed only very recently. The original use was no doubt as stores. The series of vaults further E is entered from the narrow terrace running

*Hail May, hail Flora, hail Aurora schene
  Hail Princess Nature, hail Venus Luvis Quene.

(The portrayal of Princess Nature was thought too difficult.)

under the s front. A solitary-confinement cell retains its Georgian fittings.

On the N side of Crown Square, the SCOTTISH NATIONAL WAR MEMORIAL, whose craggy Gothic aspect is due to *Robert S. Lorimer*, 1924–7. The biggest part is a U-shaped range built as the double-pile North Barracks in 1755, reusing the masonry of St Mary's Church. Unroofed in 1857, the barracks were reconstructed in 1863 by *Robert Billings* and *Captain Belfield*, the centre of the s half being demolished to form a U-shape with applied baronial detail.

In 1918 a committee was appointed by the Secretary for Scotland 'to consider and report upon the utilisation of Edinburgh Castle for the purposes of a Scottish National War Memorial'. The first recommendation of the committee's report in 1919 was the construction of 'a dedicated building or shrine erected on the apex of the Castle Rock, practically on the spot on which stood the ancient church built by King David I'. Lorimer had been appointed architect to the committee and his report was appended to theirs, together with his design, which contained the essential elements of his final scheme. The aim was three-fold: a national shrine, memorials to the different branches of the Scottish services, and some way of recording the individuals killed in the Great War.* For the regimental memorials Lorimer proposed a cloister on the site of the North Barracks. From this cloister a porch was to extend to the N leading to a tall octagonal shrine on the apex of the Castle rock, 'the centre round which Scottish history, in all its rugged and varied picturesqueness, has revolved'. Protests at the height of the proposed shrine and worries about cost led to much revision before approval was given in 1924. In the final scheme the regimental memorials were placed in a Hall of Honour (a conflation of the ideas of the cloister and Hall of Valour) formed by reconstructing the North Barracks. The shrine with its semi-octagonal apse was built to open directly from the N side of the Hall, the porch in line with it on the s side.

Outside, the rubble masonry of the barracks (now the Hall of Honour) survives. The detail is all Lorimer's. Parapet jumping up as a battlement at the corners and centre of each section. All openings contained in stilted segmental arches with heavy trefoil cusps, a detail borrowed from the Palace block at Stirling Castle. E-shaped s front to Crown Square. Broad canopied niches with small statues at the wings. In each link two windows below a smaller niche with a statue. At the centre a semicircular flight of steps to the tower, its front a vast arch in which is set the canopied porch beneath a colossal statue. Statues of a lion and unicorn flank the entrance. At the top, huge winged-lion gargoyles under

---

*This record was eventually provided by inscribing the names on Rolls of Honour placed in a casket in the shrine, but Lorimer's original recommendation (supported by the committee) was that it might be combined with the conversion of the officers' barracks on the w side of Crown Square into a Hall of Valour.

twisted-column pedestals surmounted by heraldic lions. Beneath them, the royal arms set in a depressed ogee arch. At
the E and W fronts a niche with a statue flanked by windows
under a single canopy, at the N a niche and statue on each
side of the projecting shrine. This is very vertical and very
strong. Battered ashlar buttresses rise from the rock. On
them, carved pairs of angels bearing shields. At the gable a
carved relief. From here the crowstepped S gable of the shrine
is seen to rise abruptly above the Hall. The scheme of,
SCULPTURE is expressive of this being *the* Scottish National
War Memorial. At the wings of the S front figures of Valour
and Justice by *Alexander Carrick*. At the links, Peace and
Mercy by *George Salvesen*. Above the porch, Survival of the
Spirit by *Percy Portsmouth*. The rather smooth lion and uni-
corn⋆ flanking the entrance, the gargoyles of the tower, the
heraldic lions above and the massive carved corbels (the lion
and eagle and the lion and the lamb) are by *Phyllis Bone*,‡ as
are all the carved corbels. The royal arms are by *C. d'O.
Pilkington Jackson*. – At the E and W flanks figures of Knowledge by *Alice Meredith Williams* and Freedom by *Percy
Portsmouth*. – Flanking the shrine, figures of Sacrifice by
Portsmouth and Truth by *Alice Meredith Williams*. – On the
shrine the heraldic angels and the relief of the Calling of St
Andrew all by *Alice Meredith Williams*. – Carved badges of
the Scottish regiments and corps by *Pilkington Jackson*.

INTERIOR. Low groin-vaulted porch. Roof bosses deeply
carved by *Pilkington Jackson*. Primary-coloured heraldic
STAINED GLASS by *Douglas Strachan*. Over the door to the
Hall of Honour, sculpture of the Pelican in Piety by *Morris
and Alice Meredith Williams*. Once through the porch the
architectural direction is hesitant. Ahead is the shrine, to E
and W the long transepts of the Hall of Valour, their panelled
concrete tunnel-vaults barely interrupted by the thin groin
vault of the crossing. The nine bays of the Hall are marked
by octagonal piers with capitals of ossified foliage (carved by
Thomas Beattie) set slightly in front of the walls. Frieze
carved with the names of Great War battlefields. In each bay
a round-arched architrave with a boldly projecting keyblock.
Along the N wall the architraves are frames for regimental
memorials above altars. In the two bays each side of the
crossing they frame stained-glass windows on the S. At the
end bays they are arches into S chapels, whose S walls repeat
the treatment of the N walls of the Hall. Stained glass at the
end walls of the Hall and chapels. The pale STAINED GLASS
is all by *Strachan*. Figurative roundels depicting aspects of
the war. – MONUMENTS. The Memorials to Scottish Regiments by *Pilkington Jackson*. – W chapel. Bronze reliefs to the
Women's Services (angels flanked by Charity and Sympathy)

⋆ '... They should look all right, hoary and venerable, in about 200 years', said
The Builder.

‡ Phyllis Bone and Alice Meredith Williams produced models for stone carving.
The carving itself is by *Donaldson & Burns*.

and Nursing Services (nurses with a stretcher party) by *Alice Meredith Williams*. – Mercantile Marine Memorial by *Pilkington Jackson*. Stone with a painted relief of ships. – Chaplains to the Forces. Bronze relief of a field-communion by *Hazel Kennedy*. – E chapel. Yeomanry Memorial. A large bronze trophy by *Pilkington Jackson*. – Bronze reliefs by *Alexander Carrick* for the Royal Artillery and Royal Engineers. – London, Liverpool and South African Scots Memorial. Bronze of a soldier by *Morris and Alice Meredith Williams*. – On the N walls of the chapels, roundels carved with animals which served in the war. – At the entrance to the E chapel, the Earl Haig Memorial, a bronze portrait bust by *Pilkington Jackson*, 1928.

Tall arch to the shrine, its broad moulded architrave carved with angels (by *Pilkington Jackson*). Inside, it is carved (also by Jackson) with trees bearing the arms of the Dominions. Wrought-iron GATES with thistle finials by *Thomas Hadden*. Elaborate groin vault springing from slender shafts. Central boss of the apse carved with trumpeting angels. From it hangs a painted wooden figure of St Michael modelled by *Alice Meredith Williams* and carved by *W. & A. Clow*. Beneath it bare rock thrusts through the floor of Ailsa Craig granite. On the rock a granite altar. At its corners kneeling bronze angels by *Alice Meredith Williams* pray round the steel CASKET which contains the Rolls of Honour. The casket is by *Thomas Hadden*, its bronze figures (SS. Margaret and Andrew with angels) by *Alice Meredith Williams*. Under the windows a bronze frieze of combatants of all ranks and branches of the forces by *Morris and Alice Meredith Williams*. Above the windows, low-relief panels of the planets designed by *Douglas Strachan* and carved by *George Salvesen*. – STAINED GLASS in deep cool colours by *Strachan*. A symbolic scheme representing the Birth of War at the W, the Overthrow of Tyranny at the E and Peace and Thanksgiving in the apse. On leaving the shrine is seen above the door to the porch a figure of Reveille by *Pilkington Jackson*, 1930. Bronze, partly overlaid with gold and silver. Coloured panel behind representing the elements.

At the W of the summit beside the round-arched C17 FOOG'S GATE a late C19 crowstepped FIRE STATION and two CISTERNS disguised as defences. One is a dumpy round tower by *H.M. Office of Works*, 1907, the other a squat Greek cross, c.1880. At the SE of the Lower Ward is the MILITARY PRISON, 1840–2. The heavy forestair at the S and the crowstep-gabled top floor were added, together with a rear wing, in 1880. But the severe block-pedimented door at the E opens into a gem of an early Victorian prison. Two tiers of cells with a central stair to the gallery. At the E wall a round-arched window at gallery level contained in a semi-elliptical over-arch.

At the SW of the Castle the NEW BARRACKS built in 1796. Ponderously classical three-storey and attic E front with a

pediment at the two-bay centre but lightened by guttae below
the mutuled cornice. Roman Doric columned porches at
centre and ends linked by balustrades in front of the area to
the l., and a bridge of round arches to the r. These are the
only indication that there are extra floors below the level of
the parade ground. From the w all is visible – an unadorned
five-storey and basement mass. The round arches of the
sub-structure were filled in and the verandah added at the
rear in 1893.

N of the New Barracks the GOVERNOR'S HOUSE by *Dugal
Campbell*, 1742. Two storeys and attic above a basement and
sub-basement; it was in fact three houses. The governor was
housed in the five-bay centre, the lower three-bay wings were
for the storekeeper and the master gunner. The wings are
decently utilitarian, but the centre block is dignified with
heavy rusticated pilaster-strips, massive crowsteps and a deep
parapet. Raised keyblocks at the windows. Pedimented porch
and dormers.

To the NE large mid-c18 rustic urns announce the road to
the HOSPITAL. Its genesis was a powder magazine designed
by *William Skinner* and built by *John Adam* in 1747-8. In
1753-4 were added N and S wings projecting E to form a
courtyard, its E side closed by a wall. Gateway flanked by
stone sentry-boxes linked by a cast-iron overthrow. Plans for
reconstruction of the complex as a military hospital were prepared by *E. Ingress Bell* in 1893 and executed with some
amendments by *T. Ivor-Moore* in 1897. The sentry-boxes
were reused but pushed off-axis to the l. by a bleak baronial
kitchen. The magazine was demolished. In its place a heavily
corbelled imperial stair to a terrace. The N and S ranges were
baronialized, the S range half-heartedly. Despite a corbelled
parapet and crowsteps, most of the arcaded ground floor and
first floor are recognizably Georgian. The N block was heightened and the new detail applied conscientiously. The result
is insipid.

On Mills Mount to the E the one-storey TEAROOM was
built as cart-sheds in 1746. *Dugal Campbell*'s design shows as
now a five-gabled front but with the gables pedimented and
with two cart-entrances in each. The front is now just dull.
Inside, the original cart-shed structure.

ST GILES CATHEDRAL (HIGH CHURCH)

16 St Giles has four personalities: the vast medieval Burgh Kirk,
the late Georgian Gothic casing of the exterior, the dour Victorian 'restoration' of the interior, and finally the character of
the reformed worship that was quite at home in the various
post-Reformation subdivisions but is still somewhat embarrassed by the complex and sullenly impressive spaces of a

pseudo-cathedral.* The late medieval tower and its crown spire, a rugged but graceful Old Town landmark, survives and triumphs over these vicissitudes.

Throughout the Middle Ages St Giles was the only parish church in the burgh of Edinburgh: hence its ample scale and its situation mid-way down the High Street. The first church on the site was probably begun soon after the founding of the burgh around 1130, and certainly well before the earliest documentary reference in 1178. Only a single scallop capital has survived from the C12, but until 1796 the N entrance to the nave was a large mid-C12 portal decorated with many of the same motifs as the door at Dalmeny (Lothian). Dalmeny dates from c.1140–66, a likely date for the original w parts of St Giles. Apart from this door, the church was entirely rebuilt during the two hundred years before the Reformation.

The earliest phases were the most productive and included four out of five bays of the choir, the crossing with the lower stage of the tower, the innermost bays of the transepts, and all five bays of the nave. Unfortunately, very little of this is firmly dated. According to Wyntoun and the *Scotichronicon*, St Giles was burned during the sack of Edinburgh by the English in 1385. But most of the fabric must have survived because in 1387 the Town Council contracted with three masons to add a row of chapels to the s of an existing nave. The contract mentions that the nave had then (as now) five bays and stood w of a central tower, so it had probably been built by c.1370 at the latest. The transepts can be dated before 1395, by which year a chapel had been added on the N. The choir was probably complete when in 1419 the Council applied to have St Giles made collegiate, claiming to have spent between 5,000 and 6,000 gold crowns on the fabric. The second (successful) application in 1467 followed a remodelling of the choir in which the two E bays were rebuilt more lavishly and a clearstorey was raised over the central vessel. Heraldic evidence gives a starting date of c.1453. Probably as a consequence of raising the choir, the central tower was heightened and given its crown spire shortly before 1500. In the meantime, the cruciform plan established c.1370–1420 was being extended piecemeal as chapels were added for private individuals and confraternities. Those with fairly firm dates are: St John's Aisle (N of N transept) in or before 1395; Albany Aisle between 1401 and 1410; Preston Aisle begun 1455; Chepman Aisle begun 1507, consecrated 1513; Holy Blood Aisle (s of outer s nave aisle) completed by 1518. Expansion to the N was limited by the High Street, but to the s space was available in the churchyard which extended as far as the Cowgate.

In 1560 the medieval screens and furnishings were destroyed and the three w bays taken over as an annexe to the

---

*The title 'cathedral' has only been strictly correct for the years 1633–8 and 1661–89. The present Church of Scotland minister (1984) is striving to reconcile the existing church and its use.

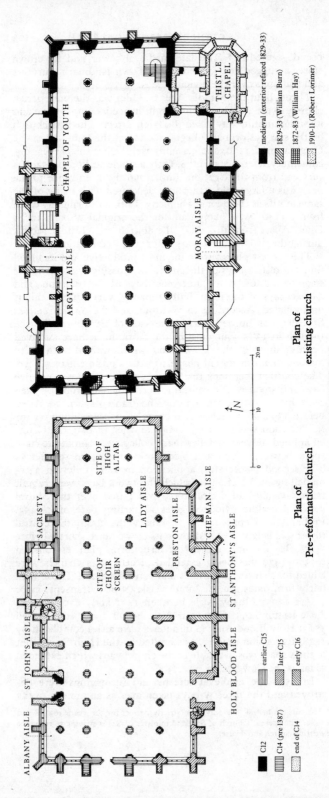

ST GILES CATHEDRAL

Plan of
existing church

Plan of
Pre-reformation church

CHAPEL OF YOUTH

ARGYLL AISLE

MORAY AISLE

THISTLE
CHAPEL

■ medieval (exterior refaced 1829-33)
▨ 1829-33 (William Burn)
▦ 1872-83 (William Hay)
▨ 1910-11 (Robert Lorimer)

ALBANY AISLE

ST JOHN'S AISLE

SACRISTY

SITE OF
CHOIR SCREEN

SITE OF HIGH ALTAR

LADY AISLE

PRESTON AISLE

CHEPMAN AISLE

ST ANTHONY'S AISLE

HOLY BLOOD AISLE

■ C12
▤ C14 (pre 1387)
▦ end of C14
▦ earlier C15
▨ later C15
▨ early C16

N

0   10   20m

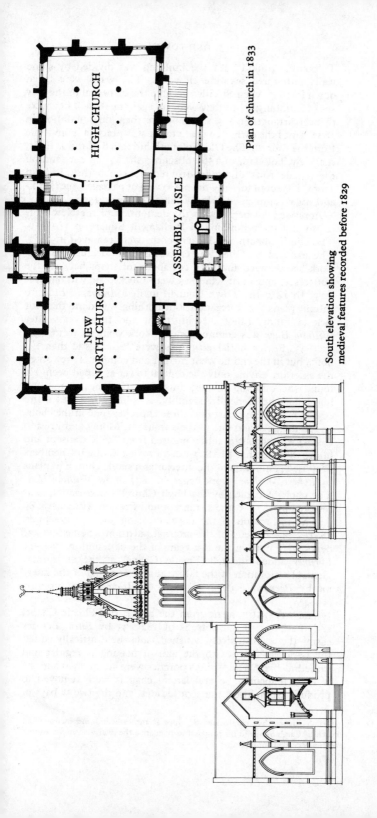

HIGH CHURCH

NEW NORTH CHURCH

ASSEMBLY AISLE

Plan of church in 1833

South elevation showing
medieval features recorded before 1829

Tolbooth. Around 1581 the building was divided by stone walls into three separate churches. The walls were taken down in 1633 when St Giles became the cathedral of the new see of Edinburgh, but they went up again in 1639. They were to be rearranged many times before their final abolition in 1882. Until the early C19 the exterior was practically invisible from the N or W. The Old Tolbooth hid much of the W front, the New Tolbooth of 1561 obscured the SW corner, and on the N side rows of timber-fronted 'luckenbooths' (lock-up shops) left room for only the narrowest of passages, the 'stink-and style' complained of by William Dunbar c. 1500.

Improvement began with the demolition of the New Tolbooth and the rebuilding of Parliament Square in 1807–10. The Old Tolbooth and luckenbooths were removed in 1817. The exposed St Giles was embarrassingly decrepit. Stonework had decayed and been cut about for shops between the buttresses, and most windows were blocked or without tracery. In 1817 the Town Council invited *Archibald Elliot* to submit plans for restoration, but nothing was done then for lack of funds. Elliot died in 1823, and three years later *William Burn* was commissioned. Work went on from 1829 to 1833. Burn's initial proposals were less drastic than Elliot's, but in the end he went further and completely reworked the exterior, leaving only the central tower as it had been. He found the building divided into four churches, a meeting house for the General Assembly, a police office and a fire engine house. He recast it as three churches (one in the choir, one in the nave and one in the S transept, Moray and Preston Aisles) with a central lobby entered from the N transept and filling the crossing. In 1867 Lord Provost William Chambers proposed restoration of the interior as a single church to plans by *Robert Morham*; work began in 1871 under *William Hay*. The choir, occupied by the High Church congregation, was restored in 1871–3, the S transept and Preston Aisle in 1878–9. The restoration of the nave, crossing and N transept in 1881–3 saw the end of the internal partitions. Some low annexes were built in the last years of the C19, and in 1909–11 *Lorimer* added the tall Thistle Chapel at the SE corner. General restoration of the fabric and re-ordering of the interior by *Bernard Feilden, Simpson & Brown*, is in progress (1984).

The EXTERIOR, apart from the tower, the Thistle Chapel and the late C19 outshots, is of 1829–33 by *Burn*. Besides casing the walls in steely polished ashlar he drastically edited the basic structure with the aim of making it regular and cathedral-like.* The N and S porches were suppressed and the W door reopened. Several lateral chapels were removed to produce symmetrical transept façades, and the two W bays of

---

* Elliot's report had emphasized St Giles as the cathedral and metropolitan church of Edinburgh, and his proposal to regularize the plan was similar to that eventually carried out by Burn.

the outer s nave aisle taken down to make a regular w front and more space in Parliament Square. The choir clearstorey was repeated at the nave and transepts, and all four were given cusped stone cresting copied from the original on the choir aisles. All windows except the central one in the E wall received rather thin flowing tracery, the patterns as much English Dec as Scottish Late Gothic, and buttresses became more uniform in size and placing. Differences between the several phases of building were thus smoothed out.

The tour starts at the w front, a symmetrical five-part composition completely disguising the asymmetrical disposition of the interior. The w window of what one reads as the outer N aisle (Albany Aisle) has been replaced with a pair of niches under blind tracery, a feature repeated on the other side to take up the difference in width between the s aisle and its new w window. The parapet hides the discrepancy of the roofs. The w doorway, replacing Burn's, is by *William Hay*, with sculpture by *John Rhind*, 1884. Trumeau and tympanum with a fine relief of St Giles, and flanking the arch small figures of personages from its history. Three gablets above, rather casually related to the rest of the design. The door itself is deeply recessed, richly carved and basically Dec in style. Burn's front to the curtailed outer s aisle has a door under an oriel with ogee lights and a shield-bearing angel corbel, replicas of those on the demolished s porch: he had at first intended to re-use the original stonework. Then on the s flank a low vestry by *Hay*, 1883, with a later ogee-headed door and window, very Lorimer-style. Burn balanced the Chepman Aisle E of the transept with a w chapel on the site of the E bay of the Holy Blood Aisle. s transept window crudely blocked,* and a Lorimerian organ chamber addition of the 1930s below, with a nicely carved panel of choirboys. To the E a low organ-chamber by *Hay*, 1883; cusped loop tracery and crocketed pinnacles.

Now the THISTLE CHAPEL by *Lorimer*, 1909–11, very tall and narrow, with three bays and a three-sided apse. This was Lorimer's first excursion into full-dress Gothic, and not surprisingly he turned for inspiration to the work of G. F. Bodley, his former master and the doyen of Late C19 English Goths. Particularly Bodleian are the Late Dec tracery, the sheer wall surfaces below the windows, and the deep, gabled buttresses that do not break the horizontal line of the parapet. The dense, blocky ornament, on the other hand, is typical of Lorimer. Most surprising is the heavy sloping plinth out of which the buttresses grow: something very similar can be seen at the E end of Chartres Cathedral, where it solves problems caused by the retention of an older substructure. Lorimer's adoption of this form for its own sake exemplifies his love of the massive and elemental. The roof-like aspect of the plinth is reinforced by small lucarnes that light (or at least

* Removal of the blocking is intended (1984).

ventilate) the basement. In the central bay of the apse a single
lancet and a canopied figure of St Andrew breaking into the
parapet. Heavy buttress at the sw corner carried up as an
octagonal spirelet, its top stage panelled with ogees. Over the
w door a panel of the pelican in her piety. Above, an oriel
with a heavily carved hoodmould. Crowstepped w gable. Between the e end of the chapel and the s choir aisle is the
ante-chapel, reached by a broad flight of steps and through a
round-arched c15 door which originally led from the s porch
into the nave.* Three orders of shafts, foliage capitals, elided
bases and abaci. Hoodmould with carved terminations, crockets and fleuron. More fleuron between the archivolts. The
jambs have been shortened by at least two courses. Above, a
rich heraldic frieze with sculpture by *Joseph Hayes*.

The e end of the CHOIR was already symmetrical and therefore acceptable to Burn, though he did add buttresses where
there had been none before. In the central window he copied
the existing tracery, which was probably a renewal of the
original c15 pattern:‡ five lights under a huge tear-drop shape
framing a mouchette, two circles and a larger circle divided
into three segments by almond shapes – an oddly undecided
design, neither Geometric nor Curvilinear. The half-way
transom and the ogee heads to the lights below it are Burn
innovations. On the n side of the choir a c17 armorial panel
of the Napiers of Merchiston, the inscription framed by
strapwork threaded through with fruit and beasts. Then a
ladies' vestry, quite low, by *MacGibbon & Ross*, 1891; on its
canted corner a niche with a much-crocketed canopy. The n
transept, like the s, appears as if flanked by arcaded aisle bays
rather than spatially separate compartments. The e aisle
(originally vestry) succeeds the much rebuilt mid-c16 sacristy. On the w the Argyll Aisle, extended n by Burn. The n
door has a broad segmental arch under a frieze of blank
shields. The subdivisions are by *Hay*, 1881–3. Also by Hay
the low Session House of 1883 to the w, with crocketed pinnacles and cusped loop tracery.

The CENTRAL TOWER with its late c15 spire is (after the
Castle) the best known object in the skyline of the Old Town.
In the lower stage of c. 1400 single Y-traceried openings with
deep, twice-chamfered splays. The upper stage and crown
spire were of one build, its date unfortunately unrecorded.§
In each face three closely spaced, obtusely pointed lancets
with cusped heads. The crown is in essence a big pinnacle
carried on eight flying buttresses springing from the corners
and the centres of the sides – an idea almost certainly derived
from the spire of St Nicholas, Newcastle (*c.* 1474), which may

---

* It had been re-used by Burn in a partition wall and was moved to the e front
of the Preston Aisle in 1883.

‡ The tracery, already in a dangerous state in 1555, was restored by *John Mylne
Jun.* about a century later.

§ A possible pointer is the re-imposition of fines applied to unspecified building
works at St Giles in 1486.

in turn have been modelled on the long-destroyed spire of the old St Mary-le-Bow, in London. The main differences at St Giles are the lack of big angle pinnacles, and the flyers springing from the sides as well as the corners. The destroyed crown at Linlithgow (also undated) may have marked a transitional stage, as it had only diagonal flyers and relatively small angle pinnacles.

Despite the English origin of the idea, its realization here has the ruggedness and compact outline characteristic of Scottish Late Gothic. Deep buttresses with many set-offs and stubby pinnacles start from corbels below the parapet and so exceed in width the tower itself. Parapet of pierced quatrefoils with a cresting of upturned half-quatrefoils. The flyers have similar cresting, and pinnacles half way up, except the central one on the E which carries steps connecting the cylindrical stair-turret to the topmost spire. The half-way pinnacles belong to the repairs which *John Mylne Jun.* carried out in 1648 at a cost of 2,700 merks. The meeting of the flyers is marked by a foliage boss and a circular rib above which Mylne's chunky Carolean Gothic takes over. An octagonal gangway, with a pierced parapet and eight pinnacles, surrounds the shank of the main pinnacle with its eight banded antae followed by eight shafts carrying the finial with its four cherubs' heads and the snub-beaked weathercock made by *Alexander Hunyman* in 1567. A festive note missing since *c.* 1800 is the series of metal vanes with gilded balls that capped the pinnacles. Gordon of Rothiemay's engraving of 1647 seems to show them, so perhaps they were an original feature.*

INTERIOR. The CHOIR is the finest piece of late medieval parish church architecture in Scotland. Although of two periods, it gives an appearance of consistency. The original choir of *c.* 1400 had four aisled bays, the S aisle (Lady Chapel) considerably wider than the N. Uniquely in Scotland, it was designed on the hall principle, i.e. with side aisles and centre aisle of equal height. Perhaps this scheme was used in preference to the usual basilica form because it needed only moderate height and left clear the original belfry openings in the crossing tower. This presupposes that the crossing is earlier than the choir, which cannot be proved. However a parallel may be drawn with the hall choirs of Bristol Cathedral and the Temple Church, London, both of which were limited in height by older work adjoining on the W.

Of this hall phase remain the three W bays of the arcades and of the N and S choir aisles. Simply chamfered arches carried on tall octagonal columns with plainly moulded capitals, the bases still of C13 'waterholding' type.‡ The aisle vaults are theoretically pointed tunnels with transverse and

* Spindles fitted in the 1980s restoration will allow these ornaments to be replaced in the future.

‡ These and most other bases in the building were greatly renewed by *Hay*. Fortunately he retained enough of the originals to authenticate their design.

diagonal ribs applied as surface decoration, but the courses of the infilling are laid so as to produce a slightly domical effect with the lateral cells billowing outwards. Originally the central vessel also had this kind of vault: parts of some of its springers remain below the later vault shafts. Above the E arch of the crossing, traces of the original vault and roof-line under a stepped string-course.

The second phase involved rebuilding the two E bays of the choir and raising a clearstorey over the main vessel. The shields on the new piers and responds provide a date *c.* 1453. Detail is consistently richer and more wholeheartedly Late Gothic than in the older parts. The arcade arches have hollows and rolls with fillet flanking a flat inner order. The piers are of a particularly elegant type that recurs several times at St Giles but seems to be unknown elsewhere* - eight filleted shafts separated by arrises. The S capitals have an octagonal main abacus and three-sided subsidiary abaci, with foliage between, which combine to form a second octagon with indentations at each angle. Under the lower abaci are little heads on the free-standing piers and fashionably dressed ladies at the E responds. The bases make the transition from subsidiary to main elements in much the same way as the capitals. At the base of the shafts a band of carved foliage. The two E bays of the aisles have proper lateral cells to their vaults, allowing taller windows than in the W bays. Near the E end of the N aisle a simple C15 tomb recess with an almost triangular depressed arch.‡ At the S aisle's E end, a stone staircase by *Bernard Feilden, Simpson & Brown*, 1981–2. The high vault of the central vessel springs from thin shafts on corbels set some distance above the piers. Longitudinal and lateral ridge-ribs and one pair of tiercerons to each cell. Big bosses at all intersections, some pierced for lamp chains.

The CHAPEL OF YOUTH at the W end of the N aisle was formed out of Burn's vestry as a memorial to William Chambers by *MacGibbon & Ross*, 1889–91. Theirs is the tall arch opening from the aisle and the vault with ridge-ribs. The large central boss is medieval and had been found lying outside the church. In the W wall the late C14 window of St John's Chapel, which formerly occupied the E two-thirds of the N part of the present transept (*see* below). Corbels carved with a lion's head and a rosette were found above this window in 1889–91 and reset on the responds of the arch from the choir aisle.

The PRESTON AISLE, S of the three W bays of the S choir aisle, was begun by the Town Council in 1455. A boss with the arms of Patrick Hepburn, Lord Hailes, Provost in 1487, indicates a slow rate of building despite the Council's undertaking to finish within seven years. Sir William Preston of Gourton had presented an arm-bone of St Giles to the church

* The nearest approximation is the chapter house at Glenluce Abbey, Dumfries and Galloway.
‡ When it was uncovered in 1871–3 traces of painted decoration were reported.

c. 1450, and his commemorative brass was also paid for by the Council. The aisle is separated from the choir by an arcade resembling that of the E choir bays, though simpler in detail. The tierceron-vault is also very like the high vault of the choir, so one may well be dealing with two works by the same designer. The vault shafts are stopped short by carved corbels. In the E wall a door to the Thistle Chapel (*see* below). On the l. a re-set medieval stone carved with an angel bearing the burgh arms.

Opening out of the W bay of the Preston Aisle is the CHEPMAN AISLE founded by Walter Chepman, the first Scottish printer. Permission to build was granted in 1507 and consecration took place in 1513. The entrance arch (as one can tell by the glazing-grooves) is a window of the Preston Aisle deprived of its tracery and extended downwards. Pointed tunnel-vault aligned N to S and decorated with surface ribs. On the boss Chepman's arms impaling those of his first wife. In the centre of the W wall a corbel carved with the eagle of St John to whom the chapel was dedicated.

The CROSSING may well be the one mentioned in a contract of 1387. Nevertheless the capitals, bases and arches of its stout octagonal piers are all much like those in the early C15 parts of the choir. Vault with two sets of ridge-ribs and a circular bell-hole. In the NORTH TRANSEPT a clearstorey and plaster tierceron-vault by *Burn*. As first built it was only one bay deep and so did not project beyond the aisles (cf. Glasgow Cathedral). Its tunnel-vault, of the same type as the first work in the choir, fitted directly over the crossing arch: the springing can be made out above the arch into the nave aisle, and a corbel with a piece of the NW diagonal rib remains *in situ* beneath a C19 corbelled-out spiral stair. The simply detailed arches into the choir and nave aisles are largely original. Beneath the gallery in the present N bay of the transept, a VESTIBULE separated from the church by a stone screen by *William Hay*, 1881–3, with an ogee-arched door and many crocketed pinnacles. Open screens and ceiling by *Esmé Gordon*, 1940. Originally the W third of the N transept bay was occupied by a spiral stair. The rest contained the two-bay St John's Chapel. To the l. of Hay's screen a fragment of rather Perp-looking wall arcade.

More definitely Perp are the remains of ST JOHN'S CHAPEL, founded by 1395. Best seen from the gallery, they consist of part of the E wall and its N window (now opening into the Chapel of Youth) and the central springer of the vault. The frame has typically Perp mouldings: rear-arch of ogee section separated from the mullions by a deep casement. Transom with miniature battlements on the E side. In 1889–91 *MacGibbon & Ross* most perversely inserted Curvilinear tracery based on a window in the S aisle of Dunkeld Cathedral. Flanking the window damaged image-niches. The remains of the vault indicate another variation on the theme of tunnel-vaults with applied ribs. The depressed pointed wall-rib finds its closest parallel in the prime example of Perp in Scotland, the presbytery of Melrose Abbey, Borders (rebuilt after 1385).

The SOUTH TRANSEPT, like the N transept, did not origin-ally project beyond the nave aisles. This first bay of c. 1400 still has its low tunnel-vault. Below the broad transverse arch and square foliage corbels by *Burn* are the medieval corbels, awkwardly reset when the arches into the Preston Aisle and outer nave aisle were widened. The first extension of the transept presumably followed completion of the first phase of the choir, whose aisles are much wider than were the C14 nave aisles. The building of the Preston Aisle and the S nave aisles must have necessitated further extension, the Lauder and Chepman Aisles yet another. One or more of these added bays was St Anthony's Aisle, whose vault was taken as a model for the choir of Midcalder Church, Lothian, in 1542. The present clearstorey and plaster vault over the whole of the transept are by *Burn*.

The NAVE is archaeologically the most complicated part of the church. Standing in the main vessel one sees an elevation superficially similar to the choir, with tall octagonal piers, a clearstorey and a tierceron-vault. But the clearstorey and plaster vault are *Burn*'s[*] and the arcades are *Hay*'s of 1881–3, incorporating some re-used medieval masonry in their arches. They replaced Burn's arcades (of the same height but with piers copied from the Albany Aisle), which in turn had succeeded C14 arcades with much lower octagonal piers. Remains of the original arcades *in situ* are confined to the W piers of the crossing: on the NW pier the moulded capital of the E respond which once continued round to the S face (rough tooling shows where it has been dressed off), and on the SW side of the SW crossing pier a short piece of arch, simply chamfered like the choir arcades. The two E arches of the S arcade are partly medieval work *in situ*, presumably survivors from an abortive scheme to make the nave arcades as high as those of the choir:‡ Hay's arcade conforms with them. Contemporary with the original arcades are the walls below Burn's clearstorey. Blocked medieval clearstorey win-dows remain on the S wall; the N was unlit (cf. the nave of Holy Rude, Stirling). The medieval high vault probably sur-vived until 1829: from the marks it has left one can see that it obscured the clearstorey. Presumably the nave was origin-ally timber-roofed.

The vault of the NORTH AISLE is structurally one with that of the ALBANY AISLE opening out of its two W bays. Simple quadripartite pattern, the rib profiles richer in the W bays and Albany Aisle. The pier of the Albany Aisle inspired those in the choir and Preston Aisle. On its capital are the arms of Robert Duke of Albany †1420 and Archibald fourth Earl of

---

[*] The vault shafts and corbels are by *Hay*.

‡ Burn's estimate for remodelling the arcades mentions eight piers but only eight arches.

Douglas †1424 which give the chapel its name and its date of between 1401 and 1410. One wonders whom the chapel was intended to commemorate: Albany was buried at Dunfermline and Douglas in Tours Cathedral. In the N wall a very heavily restored round-arched tomb recess. E of the Albany Aisle was the N porch, its upper floor reached by a small pointed door (now framing the Second Battalion Royal Scots Fusiliers Memorial). The bay E of this was a chapel (see the straight joint against the pier dividing it from the Argyll Aisle). The arch into the ARGYLL AISLE corresponds to the original height of the nave arcades, and its details show it to be not much later. Of the original vault only springers and a boss carved with a dragon remain. The present vault is part of *Hay*'s restoration of 1881-3. On the W wall a Norman scallop capital found in 1880. It belonged to a triple shaft and possibly comes from decorative wall arcading (cf. e.g. the chapter house at Wenlock Priory, Shropshire).

The inner and outer SOUTH NAVE AISLES were built together, probably soon after the Preston Aisle which they closely resemble in detail. They must have been recently completed in 1510 when an altar of All Saints, St Thomas and St Apollonia was being installed at the W end of the inner aisle, between the W door and an altar newly founded by Sir Alexander Lauder at the W end of the outer aisle.* Tall piers of Preston Aisle type. On the E respond a shield with a flaming heart. Original quadripartite vault in the inner aisle, plaster tierceron-vault by *Burn* in the outer. In the W wall of the inner aisle the line of the blocked medieval window is still visible: the window inserted by Burn to regularize his W front is off centre.

The MORAY CHAPEL opening out of the E bay of the outer aisle was formed by *Hay* out of a heating chamber by *Burn*. It occupies part of the site of the chapel completed by 1518 for the merchant confraternity of the Holy Blood: C18 views of the exterior show the two windows of the chapel with loop tracery typical of the early C16. In it, an elaborate Late Gothic tomb recess which stood at the centre of the S wall of the chapel. Low depressed pointed arch with rich cusping, flanking pinnacles and a heavy finial. Pre-1829 drawings show it enclosed in a stepped frame bounded by foliage carving. The shields on the label and finial bear the Arma Christi. Flanking the finial, nice reliefs of a lion and a dragon.‡

* The two S aisles have often been identified with the five chapels contracted for in 1387. Stylistically this is impossible, and in any case their details do not tally with those in the contract, which specifies that the masons *John Primrose, John of Scone*, and *John Skuyer* were to build five bays between the W wall of the nave and the SW pier of the crossing, the vaulting to be modelled on that of the N nave aisle at Holyrood. But the existing S aisles have had not five but ten bays of vaulting, all with ridge-ribs such as never existed at Holyrood. Moreover the contract makes no mention of the two W windows and the four piers. The Lauder Aisle is usually said to have stood W of the S porch, but early views and plans show that no chapel has ever occupied this position.

‡ The capital from the pier on the N side of the Lauder Aisle is now at Cathlaw House near Linlithgow (*see Buildings of Scotland: Lothian*). The foliage of the capital is of the same workmanship as the tomb recess.

FURNISHINGS. Before 1560 there were numerous subsidiary altars,* many placed against pillars and no doubt most
enclosed by wooden screens. Nothing of this remains. The
furnishings reflect post-1867 attempts to emulate a cathedral.
Until recently the effect was 'High Presbyterian' (i.e. Low
Anglican). Rearrangement began in 1982. Under the crossing,
octagonal PULPIT by *John Rhind* to *William Hay*'s design,
1883, of Caen stone elaborately and badly carved. - On the
N, canopied oak SCREEN and REREDOS (formerly in outer S
aisle of nave) by *Lorimer & Matthew*, 1927-32. - Above the
E crossing arch large painted ROYAL ARMS of George II dated
1736. - The Albany Aisle was refurnished by *Esmé Gordon* in
1951 as a War Memorial Chapel. Neo-Jacobean oak COM-
MUNION TABLE by *Whytock & Reid*. - Above it a cross with
stone panels of the Elements by *Elizabeth Dempster*. - LAMP
OF REMEMBRANCE by *Thomas Hadden*, a red glass bowl set
in a steel version of the St Giles crown spire. - The furnishings of the Chapel of Youth are by *Lorimer*, 1927-9. REREDOS
with a heavy frame enclosing a painted low relief of the Adoration of the Angels by *Alice and Morris Meredith Williams*.
- PENDANT LAMP with inset panels of stained glass by *Douglas Strachan*. - Wrought-iron FONT BRACKET. Open SCREEN
of oak. - The N aisle's E end has been separated off as a chapel
with a wrought-iron SCREEN (formerly in the outer S aisle of
the nave) by *F. A. Skidmore*, 1883. - The chapel's COMMU-
NION TABLE, which used to occupy the position of the high
altar, is by *Robert S. Lorimer*, 1910, lengthened in 1953. Front
with carved and painted panels set in arcading. - S choir aisle:
ROYAL PEW of oak originally by *William Hay*, 1885, recast
by *Esmé Gordon* in 1952-3. - S transept: ORGAN originally of
1883 by *Ingram & Co.*, much enlarged by them in 1890 and
rebuilt by *Henry Willis*, using the old pipes, in 1938-40. -
ORGAN CASE of 1938-40 by *Esmé Gordon*, executed by *Scott
Morton & Co.*, a tall stepped arrangement with carved figures
of Jubal and two angels by *Elizabeth Dempster*. - Wrought-
iron SCREEN to the outer S aisle of the nave; thistle finials and
a cross at the centre by *F. A. Skidmore*, 1883. - Outer S aisle:
oak PULPIT by *R. Rowand Anderson*, 1888, octagonal with
linenfold panelling and a tall steepled canopy. - FONT by
John Rhind, 1883, a kneeling angel holding out a large shell,
after Thorwaldsen's font at Copenhagen. - At the W end of
the nave the old ROYAL PEW of 1873 by *John Taylor & Son*
from *Hay*'s design, canopied, with cusped and finialled gablets. Central cross between crowned pinnacles, a lion and
unicorn sitting at the ends.

STATUE. John Knox, unappealing life-size bronze by *J.
Pittendrigh MacGillivray*, 1904-5.

MONUMENTS. The overwhelming majority are of the late
C19, reflecting Chambers's declared aim of creating a Scottish

---

* The exact number cannot be calculated as a large number of altars had several
dedications, only one of which appears in many references.

Westminster Abbey. Not all worth mention. NORTH AISLE, w wall. 3rd Battalion The Royal Scots South African War Memorial, *c.* 1905; mannered artisan Renaissance aedicule, an angel leaning over the top. – Royal Scots Greys Abu Klea Memorial, *c.* 1890; chunky Celtic cross with gilt bronze scrollwork. – Queen's Own Cameron Highlanders South African War Memorial by *W. S. Black*, 1905; an aedicule with axes for columns. – ALBANY AISLE, w wall. First World War Memorial, a bronze relief by *H. S. Gamley*, 1924; an angel crowns a naked soldier carrying a carefully placed flag. – N wall. 16th (S) Battalion The Royal Scots First World War Memorial, designed by *Lorimer* and carved by *Pilkington Jackson*; stone figure of St Michael. – NORTH AISLE, N wall. 72nd Duke of Albany's Own Highlanders, *c.* 1870; Commissioners' Perp Survival crowned with reversed trophies. – ARGYLL AISLE. Monument to Archibald Marquess of Argyll † 1661, by *Sydney Mitchell & Wilson*, 1894–5. Jacobean, of marble and alabaster carved by *Thomas Beveridge*. Recumbent effigy (by *Charles McBride*) on a sarcophagus. Canopy with Ionic columns, the pediment broken by Argyll arms. – NORTH PORCH, w wall. Rev. Robert Nisbet † 1874, designed by *John Chesser* and executed by *A. Wallace*; Gothic, of marble and alabaster with a relief portrait. – E wall. George Lorimer † 1865, by *David Bryce Jun.*, 1867; large and mannerist. – Aglionby Ross Carson † 1850, by *Peter Slater*, 1856, of marble; Literature mourning the loss of one of her disciples. – S wall. William Hay † 1888, bronze medallion portrait by *John Rhind*, 1890. – CHAPEL OF YOUTH. Sir William Smith † 1914, founder of the Boys' Brigade; bronze with a portrait in low relief. – NORTH CHOIR AISLE. Edward Maxwell Salvesen † 1915; bronze portrait bust by *H. S. Gamley*. – Royal Army Medical Corps First World War Memorial; bronze relief of a ministering angel. – Elsie Maud Inglis † 1917; of stone; prim angels standing on top of the inscribed tablet. – 94th (City of Edinburgh) H.A.A. Regiment Second World War Memorial, by *Basil Spence*.

SOUTH CHOIR AISLE, E wall. Church of Scotland Chaplains Second World War Memorial by *Henshaw*; bronze tablet with low relief of St Andrew. – S wall. John Inglis † 1891 by *R. Rowand Anderson*, 1892–3. Jacobean marble and alabaster Ionic aedicule with obelisk finials and coat of arms. – James Cameron Lees † 1913, bronze relief bust by *Pilkington Jackson*, 1931. – W of the N entrance to the Thistle Chapel, a monument (A. W. Williamson) to the same design by *Pilkington Jackson*, 1936. – PRESTON AISLE. Arthur Penrhyn Stanley † 1881; bronze portrait, a replica of the memorial by *Mary Grant* in St George's Chapel, Windsor. – R. S. Lorimer † 1929, by *Alexander N. Paterson*, 1932; stone tablet in a Lorimerian frame. – Below, fragments of medieval tombstones. – CHEPMAN AISLE, E wall. James Graham, Marquess of Montrose, † 1650, by *John* and *W. Birnie Rhind* from designs by *R. Rowand Anderson*, 1887–9. Richly polychrome

Jacobean in alabaster, marble and gilt bronze. A recumbent effigy on a sarcophagus under a round arch, its soffit panelled and studded with rosettes; crowning aedicule with putti. – s wall. William Hay of Delgaty † 1650, 1888, tablet in strapwork frame under large coat of arms. – w wall. Walter Chepman † 1523, by *F. A. Skidmore* to *Hay*'s design, 1879; bronze incised with portraits of Adam and Eve and a thistle and rose border. – MORAY CHAPEL. James Stewart Earl of Moray † 1569, by *David Cousin*, 1864, the design based on sketches of the original monument of 1569.* Mannered Renaissance aedicule, incorporating the brass plate of the original, the inscription by George Buchanan engraved by *James Gray*, goldsmith. The plate is a palimpsest re-using the middle of a late C15 brass.‡

SOUTH AISLE. Robert Fergusson, a bronze relief-portrait by *Pittendrigh MacGillivray*. – Margaret O. W. Oliphant † 1897; another relief by *MacGillivray* (1908) but gilt. – John Stuart Blackie † 1895; stone panel with a relief portrait. – Thomas Chambers † 1882; broken-pedimented tablet with a bronze portrait by *Pilkington Jackson*, 1923. – Also by *Pilkington Jackson*, 1923, the relief of John Brown † 1882. – OUTER SOUTH AISLE, w wall. Robert Louis Stevenson † 1894, by *Augustus St Gaudens*, 1904; life-size bronze relief of the writer sitting on a chaise-longue. – INNER SOUTH AISLE. Royal Scots Boer War Memorial by *W. Birnie Rhind*, 1903; bronze high relief of soldiers storming a kopje. Aedicular marble frame by *T. Duncan Rhind*, a figure of Glory in the pediment. – 5th Battalion The Royal Scots First World War Memorial by *Pilkington Jackson* and *Frank C. Mears*, c. 1920 with bronze figures. – SOUTH AISLE, w wall. 93rd Sutherland Highlanders Indian Mutiny Memorial by *William Brodie*, c. 1860; soldiers flanking a pylon. – 78th Highland Regiment, by *John Steell*, 1850; relief of a female mourning over a large urn decorated with a carved elephant. – Gen. Sir William Lockhart † 1900, high relief marble bust by *George Frampton*, 1903. – 92nd Gordon Highlanders, bronze tablet with Victory and a dead soldier, by *Frederic Shields*, 1885.

STAINED GLASS. A scheme for the CHOIR was suggested by J. Noel Paton and Robert Herdman, and executed in 1874–7 by *James Ballantine & Son* under *Herdman*'s supervision. Scenes from the life of Christ in the N aisle, the Crucifixion and Ascension in the great E window, the Resurrection in the E window of the S aisle and the Prodigal Son next to it. Brown is the dominant colour. – Much better is the other window in the s choir aisle (Scottish saints) by *Karl Parsons*, after 1913. – In the clearstorey, heraldic glass by *Ballantine*, 1877–92, except the E window on the N side by *David Small*, 1879; figures of saints by *Douglas Strachan*, 1932–5. – PRES-

---

* Destroyed at the end of the C18.

‡ On the back figures of civilians wearing long robes. They turn slightly towards each other – a late C15 to early C16 motif. Excellent workmanship, probably Flemish, but the inscription in Scots.

TON AISLE. E window (Pentecost) by *Ballantine & Gardiner*, 1895. – Memorial window to Lords High Commissioner (St Peter and St John before the High Priest above, the First Council of Jerusalem below) by *Ballantine & Gardiner*, 1895–1900. – Beside it, scenes from the life of St Paul, by *Ballantine & Son*, 1881. – CHEPMAN AISLE. Heraldic glass by *Ballantine & Son*, 1888. – CHAPEL OF YOUTH. Two windows (scenes from the life of John the Baptist, Solomon dedicating and Zerubbabel rebuilding the Temple) by *Ballantine & Gardiner*, 1892 and 1894. – NORTH TRANSEPT. Expressionist glass (Christ walking on the water) by *Strachan*, 1922. – Clearstorey window by *William Wilson*, 1954. – ARGYLL AISLE. Heraldic glass by the *Glass Stainers' Co.*, 1895. – MORAY CHAPEL. *Ballantine & Son* again, 1881 (assassination and funeral of the Regent Moray), the familiar brown colour all-pervasive. – OUTER SOUTH NAVE AISLE. Wauchope memorial window (David and Jonathan) by *Ballantine & Gardiner*, 1900–1. – More welcome the window (saints and Old Testament heroes) to J. R. Findlay † 1898, by *C. E. Kempe*. – In the oriel W window, heraldic glass by *Ballantine & Son*, 1883. – ALBANY AISLE. A folksy window designed by *Francis Spear* and painted by *Arthur Pearce*, 1957. – The other window (parables of the wise and foolish virgins and of the talents) by *Ballantine & Son*, 1876, and soberly brown. – NAVE. In the S aisle, scenes from the life of Joseph by *Ballantine & Gardiner*, 1898, and from the life of Moses by *Andrew Ballantine*, 1886. – The W window of the aisle (Old Testament figures) by *Burlison & Grylls* is much better. – In the N aisle, Christian Virtues by *Daniel Cottier*, 1890, and Scottish saints by *Oscar Paterson*, 1906. – W window (Israelites crossing the Jordan and Old Testament heroines) by *Edward Burne-Jones*, executed by *Morris & Co.*, 1886. By far the best in flaming reds and deep blue. – Great W window (Prophets) by *Cottier*, 1886.*

THISTLE CHAPEL. 1909–11. *Lorimer*'s interior is a stunningly rich ensemble to which stone carving, furnishings and glass contribute nearly as much as architecture. The project originated with a bequest by the eleventh Earl of Leven of £40,000 to be applied to the restoration of Holyrood Abbey as a chapel for the Order of the Thistle. This was not allowed, so a chapel was added to St Giles instead. It is the private chapel of a private order with no provision for spectators – an introverted celebration of the Order and only secondarily of God. The low two-bay antechapel has a very shallow vault springing from slim shafts. Between the ribs cusped panels and at every intersection large bosses (their foliage including thistles, roses and shamrocks) carved, like the rest of the stone sculpture, by *Joseph Hayes*. E and W doors with continuously moulded Tudor arches. The similar N and S arches have heav-

---

*A new window has been commissioned (1984) from *Leifur Breidfjord*. It will commemorate Robert Burns.

ily carved cusps; in the E bay they frame inscribed panels. Arch opening N into the S aisle of the choir filled with wrought iron by *Thomas Hadden*. In the arch opposite, a deeply cut relief of the Leven arms in an ogee frame and a much richer and deeper ogee through which one enters the main chapel.

The chapel is 13 m. high but only 11·5 m. long and 5·5 m. wide. Vault with steep branching tiercerons and a flattened crown overlaid with a dense mesh of liernes (cf. the Lady Chapel at Ely, St George's Chapel at Windsor Castle). The bosses are so large and so numerous that the liernes are nearly lost to sight. In the W bays of the N wall blind tracery encloses heraldic carving complementing the heraldic STAINED GLASS by *Louis Davis* to *Lorimer*'s designs. The E window (St Andrew) is by *Douglas Strachan*. But the dominant decoration is the WOODWORK by *Nathaniel Grieve & Co.*, carved by *W. & A. Clow*. At the E end, comparatively restrained linenfold panelling under a canopy of cusped ogees and a pierced cresting. Round the other three sides the KNIGHTS' STALLS, their gorgeous steepled canopies carried on slim twisted columns. Only the general arrangement follows English late medieval precedent. As on the stalls of the Garter Knights at Windsor, a sword hangs in front of each spire and a mantled and crested coronet is set on top. The SOVEREIGN'S STALL at the W end is larger. In its canopy figures of SS. Margaret, Columba and Kentigern; on the desk front the royal arms of Scotland. Rich carving is not confined to the canopies. Particularly enjoyable are the well-fed beasts on the arm-rests. At the back of each stall, enamelled armorial plates, the original ones by *Phoebe Traquair*. – COMMUNION TABLE (memorial to George V) by *John F. Matthew*, 1943. Originally only the Chair of Investiture stood here. – MEMORIAL to George VI by *Esmé Gordon*, 1962. Inscribed slab with the royal arms, set in the floor of Ailsa Craig and Iona marble. In the undercroft, STAINED GLASS (The Creation) by *Christian Shaw*, 1982.

THE LAW COURTS

Ponderous Adamesque wallpaper by *Robert Reid*, 1803–38, hems in the small civic space to the N of St Giles and disguises a very complex mass of building including the Parliament House, Court of Session, High Court of Justiciary, Advocates' Library, Signet Library and Library of Solicitors before the Supreme Court.

In 1532 James V reformed the Scottish judicial system by establishing the Court of Session as the supreme civil court with its judges (Lords of Session) organized as Senators of the College of Justice. Cases were decided by the whole court, although a single judge (the Lord Ordinary) sat alone for short periods to deal with minor aspects of a case. Except in times of plague the Court of Session was settled in Edinburgh, by then the usual meeting place of Parliament, which used the Court of Session's accommodation for its brief sittings.

Housing for the court was provided by the Town of Edinburgh, whose prosperity was much increased by the sizeable legal community and visiting litigants. The court sat in the Old Tolbooth until 1560 when the judges threatened to move to St Andrews unless they were given a better home. The Town Council then fitted up the w end of St Giles for them, but in 1632 Charles I ordered an end to this profanation. Frightened that 'the lack of convenient and fitt roumes within this burgh' might cause the court to leave Edinburgh, the Council built Parliament House in 1632-40 on the site of the manses of the ministers of St Giles. The King's Master of Works, *James Murray*, was paid 'for drawin of the modell', its external detail very similar to that of the Palace block at the Castle. The new building was L-shaped with a great hall (the Parliament or Outer House) where Parliament could meet and the Lord Ordinary sat. On the ground floor of the jamb of the L was a chamber (the Inner House) where the Court of Session sat. Above was the Court of Exchequer which after the Act of Union (1707) took over the Treasury Chambers built E of the jamb in 1680.

The great hall and chamber arrangement was already inconvenient by the end of the C17 when several Lords Ordinary were sitting simultaneously in the draughty Parliament House. A small concession to their comfort was the screening off of the N end as a lobby and Bailie (Town Council) Court in the early C18. There was also pressure for more accommodation. In 1662-89 most of the national records were moved into the Laigh Hall under Parliament House; their number increased with each lawsuit. There was also a demand for library space in or near the law courts. The Faculty of Advocates (barristers) began to form a library in 1682; in 1701 they were allowed to house it in the s end of the Laigh Hall. Libraries outside the building were begun by the two solicitors' Societies, the Writers to the Signet in 1722 and the Solicitors to the Supreme Court in 1784.

In 1789 storage space was gained when the official records were moved to the new Register House (*see* First New Town, Public Buildings); it was probably as a result of having persuaded the Government to spend money on Register House that the Barons of the Court of Exchequer commissioned *Robert Adam* to produce a scheme for reconstructing or rebuilding the E jamb of Parliament House and the adjacent Treasury Building. Adam's proposals of 1791 were thought 'more magnificent than was necessary'* but presaged later development. He suggested an addition to the w for a new Inner House and libraries for the Advocates and Writers, making the E wing the Bailie Court and Town Court offices and the Outer (Parliament) House the preserve of the Lords Ordinary. In 1798 the Bailie Court left for Royal Exchange Square and the partition in the Outer House was removed.

In 1803 the Treasury approved the replacement of the 1680

* They also failed to provide new accommodation for the Court of Exchequer.

Treasury Chambers with a new Exchequer Court, and the re-construction of the Inner House. *Robert Reid*'s scheme, carried out in 1804-6, also proposed the refronting of the E side and jamb of Parliament House and a new library block to the NW. Changes in the legal system in 1805-8 split the Court of Session into two Divisions, each with its own Outer House of Lords Ordinary and Inner House or court of appeal. As a result, a second Inner House court was added W of the Outer House. At the same time Parliament House was refaced and the library block begun. Its shell was completed in 1811, but in 1812 both Advocates and Writers decided that their library interiors should be designed by *William Stark*.* Two courtrooms for Lords Ordinary were added s of Parliament House by *Archibald Elliot* in 1818-20, and tenement property E of the Exchequer Court was bought for more accommodation and further expansion.

In 1824 fires destroyed all of Parliament Square‡ E of the Courts and damaged Reid's new Exchequer Court. Fear of more fires starting in new speculatively built tenements led the Treasury to buy all land to the s, E and w; Sir William Forbes & Co. sold their bank only on condition that the Treasury paid for a new one SE of Parliament Square. Expansion on the newly acquired land began in 1827. By 1830 the E range (Court of Exchequer) was complete, and by 1838 the s range was up, providing a Justiciary Court and replacing the C17 Inner House with two new Inner House courts.§ Meanwhile the Advocates sold their library to the Writers and built a new one W of Parliament House in 1829-33.

The sitting of Lords Ordinary in Parliament House ended in 1844 when *William Nixon* provided four new Outer House courtrooms to the s, on the site of Elliot's two courtrooms of 1818-20. Sir William Forbes's new bank of 1827-30 was con-verted into a Jury Court and offices in 1881-6. In 1888-92 a SW addition was built for the library of the Solicitors to the Supreme Court,‖ and in 1907-9 the Outer House courts were remodelled and extended. Extra courts were made from the Enrolling Room and the office of the Receiver of Crown Rents in 1952-4.

DESCRIPTION

The frontages to Parliament Square are all by *Reid*, quoting Adam's unexecuted designs for the University quadrangle (e.g. the quadrants) and Leith Street (e.g. the Ionic colon-nades over arcades). The SIGNET LIBRARY facing West Par-liament Square states the theme. Rusticated ground floor with deep over-arches. Centrepiece with attached Ionic columns between slightly advanced bays; pedimented first-floor win-

---

* Stark died in 1813.
‡ Then Parliament Close.
§ The Second Division Court of 1808-9, thus made redundant, became part of the Advocates' Library in 1840 and was rebuilt in 1856.
‖ Which had been in the Laigh Hall since 1846.

dows and panelled parapets interrupting the balustrade. Statues were meant to stand on the centrepiece. Round the corner in Parliament Square, Reid's refacing of PARLIAMENT HOUSE repeats the centrepiece with five bays instead of seven, and the over-arches become a loggia. Firm-bosomed sphinxes on the ends. Then the SW quadrant with more Ionic columns forming a loggia over which a large royal coat of arms was intended. Reid's 1803 scheme provided only a six-bay S range, with sphinxes on the ends, but in 1827–38 the E bay was swallowed up in a boldly projecting temple-front centrepiece (Ionic columns again), beyond which a mirror-image of the 1803 design was wrapped round the SE corner of the square. The force of the original conception is exhausted by this stretching and the centrepiece is too flabby to save it. Minor excitement in the loggia, which is punctuated by saucer domes in the projecting bays.

In Fishmarket Close to the E, Sir William Forbes & Co.'s Bank (now JURY COURT block) by *William Burn*, 1827–30. Tall and plain, of whinstone, with round-arched upper windows. The severe S elevation of Reid's work is set back from Cowgate. To its SW the red sandstone SOLICITORS' LIBRARY by *James B. Dunn*, 1888–92. Five unadorned storeys (flats over shops) crowned with a great hall in an early C16 manner. Huge oriel windows, gargoyles and clustered chimneys, and an octagonal turret at the corner. From George IV Bridge a glimpse of the rubble back of *James Murray*'s Parliament House of 1632–40. From it projects the ADVOCATES' LIBRARY begun by *W. H. Playfair* in 1829, the bay-windows added by *Robert Matheson* in 1856 looking N to the back of the Signet Library.

The central door to the LAW COURTS in Parliament Square is for judges. Anta-pilastered Judges' Entrance Hall.* To its S the Conference or Robing Room. Coffered ceiling with Greek key bands. Jacobean chimneypiece of *c.* 1885, probably by *William Adams*. Public entrance in the W quadrant. Two-storey Lobby reconstructed by *W. T. Oldrieve*, 1907, with a Neo-Classical compartmented ceiling. On the E the Crown Office Stair, top-lit from a pendentived dome; on the S the Main or Box Corridor, also reconstructed by *Oldrieve* and dead plain. At its end, a tall balconied archway to the South Stair (leading to the Laigh Hall and Solicitors' Library).

W of the Lobby is PARLIAMENT HOUSE of 1632–40. Great hammerbeam roof of Danish oak made in 1637–9 by *John* 75 *Scott*, Master Wright to the Town of Edinburgh. The roof itself is almost flat, the hammerbeams forming trusses with alternate broad and narrow intervals between. Stone corbels carved with vigorous portraits, castles (including Edinburgh Castle) and beasts, perhaps by *Alexander Mylne*. In the E wall two round-arched recesses flanking the Lobby door, the r. one made in 1752 for the statue of Duncan Forbes, the l. one

---

* One bay has been divided off.

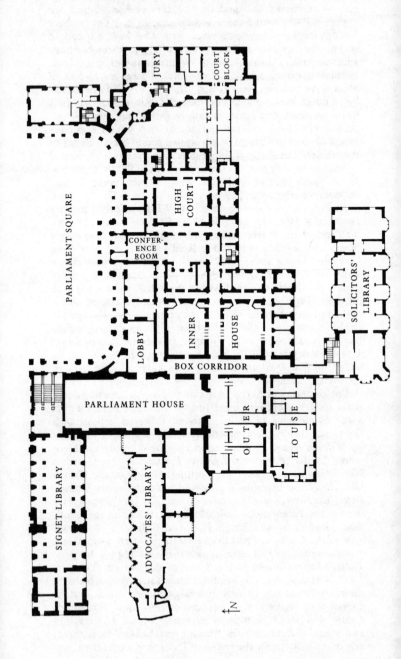

in 1819 for a Lord Ordinary's bench by *Archibald Elliot*, who added Gothick woodwork to the recesses* and door; their present severe appearance was probably part of *Robert Matheson*'s alterations of 1868-70. Of that date the late Gothic tracery in the windows.‡ Heraldic stained glass in the windows by *James Ballantine & Son*,§ 1870. Large s window, semi-elliptically arched, with glass designed by *Wilhelm von Kaulbach* and executed by *Maximilian Ainmiller* of Munich, 1866-8 – a colourful scene of James V founding the College of Justice. In the w wall, three heavily varnished chimney-pieces by *William Adams*, cabinetmaker and antique dealer. The one in the middle, made in 1880, incorporates c17 Italian woodwork; segmental-arched fireplace framed by Madonna and Child caryatids in front of Ionic pilasters. Deep entablature of Jacobean reliefs. Above, herms and caryatids framing two architectural panels, and in the centre panel a bas-relief of Christ giving the keys to St Peter. On top, a shaped broken pediment of Caroline type. The two smaller fireplaces are of 1884, the r. one with a bas-relief of scenes from 'The Merchant of Venice'.

STATUES. On the N wall, Viscount Melville (1818) and Robert Dundas (1824), both by *Chantrey*. – In the NE corner Lord Cockburn by *William Brodie*, 1863. – Along the E wall a dramatic Duncan Forbes about to give judgement, by *Roubiliac*, 1752; in the recesses Lord Jeffrey (1855) and Lord President Boyle (1860) both by *John Steell*; Lord President Blair by *Chantrey*, 1815. – On the w wall Sir Walter Scott, modelled in 1832 and carved in 1835 by *John Greenshields*. – Numerous BUSTS by *Brodie* and *Steell*; Henry Erskine (†1817) by *Turnerelli*. Outside the s door statues of Justice and Mercy by *Alexander Mylne*, 1637. Originally they stood over the main entrance.

Under Parliament House is the LAIGH HALL completed in 1634. Two aisles with a central arcade. Octagonal piers and simply chamfered round arches. Flat ceilings, the w one ribbed.

On the N is the SIGNET LIBRARY. The door from Parliament Square opens into a vestibule. On the r., the Lower (original Signet) Library by Stark, 1812-18. Nave-and-aisles arrangement, but each aisle-bay has its own saucer dome pushing up above the height of the nave ceiling. Corinthian-columned screen at the E dividing off a transverse 'sanctuary'. Until 1833 there was a wall on the l. of the vestibule and on its other side the Upper (original Advocates') Library entrance-cum-stair-hall. On both libraries coming into the possession of the Writers to the Signet, *William Burn* removed the wall and built a new imperial stair, opening on the first floor through a Corinthian-columned screen, by *W. H.*

* The r. recess now also housed a Lord Ordinary.
‡ The original tracery seems to have been of the Tron Church type (*see* below: Churches).
§ Design and execution superintended by *Sir George Harvey*, P.R.S.A.

83 *Playfair*, 1819–20, into the upper vestibule, whose coffered
dome is a prelude to the glory beyond. The Upper Library
extends the full length of the building, and Stark's mastery
is shown in his transformation of a potentially oppressive
tunnel into a marvellously light space. Again it is Corinthian
(the column capitals carved by *John Steell*), with nave and
aisles, but half way along transepts extend beyond the book-
shelves to N and S. Top-lit crossing marked by pilastered
piers. Screens into the transepts. The central saucer dome
was painted by *Thomas Stothard* in 1821 with Apollo and the
Muses, historians, philosophers and poets (ancient and modern). The longitudinal thrust of the design is maintained by
the line of anthemion-balustraded balconies running behind
the columns. The balcony crosses the E wall but was removed
from the W end in 1889 to make way for a STAINED GLASS
window by *James Ballantine & Son* commemorating Queen
Victoria's Diamond Jubilee.

On the S side of the Courts, *Dunn*'s SOLICITORS' LI-
BRARY of 1888–92. Nave and aisles again, but opulent rather
than enjoyable. Jacobean pilasters at the ends of the carrels.
Partly glazed elliptical ceiling. STAINED GLASS portraits of
lawyers by *Ballantine*.

S of Parliament House is the OUTER HOUSE. Of the four
Ordinary court-rooms provided by *William Nixon* in 1844 the
W pair (Nos. VII and VIII) are largely unaltered – simple
rectangles with the console-canopied benches in recesses
under a pilastrade of windows. Grained woodwork. In 1907–
9 *Oldrieve* threw the two E courts into one (No. VI), re-using
Nixon's furnishings, driving a corridor through their W end
to his new block to the S. In this is the panelled Oak Court
(No. IX), its bench in a coved recess under a segmental pediment. Coved ceiling of shallow compartments rising into a
glazed pendentive dome. Oak Library adjoining, also of 1907–
9; *Oldrieve*'s idiosyncratic Renaissance style, with a circular
roof-light.

E of Parliament House, the INNER HOUSE with nearly
identical First and Second Division Courts by *Reid*, 1838.
All-round galleries, carried on cast-iron piers at the deep end,
on consoles at the sides, and forming canopies over the bench.
Stone niches for stoves flank the judges' seats. Round-arched
clearstorey windows. Ribbed ceilings, with Jacobean pendants in the First Division Court, ventilation panels in the
Second Division. E of the central courtyard, the HIGH
COURT OF JUSTICIARY is of 1835, again by *Reid*. Very
similar to the other Inner House courts but used for criminal
cases, so there are no bookcases on the bench. Gallery fronts
with long Greek-key panels. Compartmented ceiling with
large bosses, lots of gilding and Greek-key ventilator panels.
Trapdoor from the dock to the cell-corridor built in 1836.

A bridge of 1885 links the court complex to Forbes' Bank,
originally entered only from the E quadrant of Parliament
Square. Of *Burn*'s work of 1827–30 the austere domed En-

trance Hall survives. Splendid iron doors. *W. W. Robertson* converted the Telling Room into Court No. IV in 1885. Coupled Corinthian columns framing the bench; pilasters opposite. Coved ceiling with pendants.

HOLYROOD ABBEY, PALACE OF HOLYROODHOUSE AND HOLYROOD PARK

INTRODUCTION

David I founded the abbey of Holyrood in 1128. Proximity to a major royal castle and royal burgh, coupled with the fact that the abbey was a royal foundation (perhaps with its guesthouse intended from the start to house the king), gave Holyrood prestige. In 1177 the papal legate Vivian held a council at the abbey, and twelve years later the nobles and prelates of Scotland met there to discuss raising a ransom for William the Lion. The early C12 church was rebuilt on a lavish scale *c.* 1195–1230. Robert I held a parliament here in 1326, and Exchequer grants for the provision of kitchen utensils and wine in 1329 suggest that by then Holyrood was used as a royal residence. The royal connexion was firmly established by 1370 when David II was buried in the choir – the first of a number of kings to be interred there.* In the C15 Holyrood was clearly a royal residence as well as an abbey. James II was born at Holyrood in 1426, crowned there in 1437, married there in 1449 and buried there in 1460. The guesthouse occupied by the King probably stood on the site of the present N range of the palace, immediately W of the abbey church and cloister. In 1449 the Exchequer Rolls record that building materials were brought to Holyrood 'ad fabricam regis'; presumably additions to the guesthouse. In 1501–5, in anticipation of his marriage to Margaret Tudor, James IV built virtually a new palace including a S tower, chapel, gallery, royal apartments and gatehouse. Already the shape of the present Holyroodhouse seems evident: a quadrangle W of the abbey cloister, with the chapel probably formed from part of the old guesthouse in the N range, the Queen's Apartment sited in the S range. S tower near the site of the present SW tower. Probably there was already a subsidiary court of officials' lodgings S of the main quadrangle and a kitchen court to the E behind the monastic refectory (by now the hall) on the S side of the abbey cloisters. The palace was completed with a lion house in 1512.

James IV's palace was followed by that of his son. Between 1528 and 1532 James V added to the N range of the palace the present NW tower containing sets of royal apartments for the king and queen, one above the other. In 1535–6 the W and S ranges of the quadrangle were reconstructed or rebuilt. A new chapel was made in the S range, the old chapel becoming the

* The last royal personage to be buried in the choir, in 1566, was Henry Lord Darnley, husband of Mary Queen of Scots.

Council Chamber. In the w range a ceremonial suite of outer chamber, mid chamber and wardrobe led to the king's private chamber and bedchamber in the tower. An outside stair in the sw corner of the courtyard served both ranges, acting as a hinge for the plan. A concern for architecture was evident: the w front had canted bay-windows at the ends and bowed windows at the centre, nearly symmetrical except for the lack of a sw tower to balance that at the nw.

During the Earl of Hertford's invasion of 1544 Holyrood was pillaged and burned. The abbey church was patched up, but in 1559 its altars were destroyed by the Reformers and thereafter the monastic buildings were left to decay. Only the nave of the church continued in use as the parish church of Canongate; the choir and transepts were demolished in 1570. A substantial amount of unspecified building work, perhaps including reconstruction of the n and e ranges of the quadrangle, was carried out between 1554 and 1566. In 1590 a 'new gallerie quarter' of officials' lodgings is mentioned. In preparation for James VI's visit to Scotland in 1617 the chapel in the s range was recast and redecorated, and in 1622-3 the Chancellor's Lodging in the court to the s was enlarged. Major repairs to the abbey church and palace were made before Charles I's coronation at Holyrood in 1633. In 1650, when Cromwellian troops were quartered in the palace, the building was badly damaged by a fire which started in the e range. As a result, most of the palace seems to have been abandoned except for the w range, which was reconstructed and heightened in 1658-9.

The Restoration of 1660 restored not just the monarchy but also Scotland's Parliament and Privy Council. Holyrood, a barracks during the Protectorate, became a palace again. In 1661 the Privy Council voted money to patch up the w range and nw tower for the use of the King's Commissioner to the Scottish Parliament. A full survey of the palace was made by *John Mylne Jun.* in 1663, and at last in 1670 the Privy Council voted £30,000 for the repair of Holyroodhouse and Stirling Castle. The next year plans for a virtual rebuild of the n, e and s sides of the main court of Holyrood were prepared by *William Bruce*, the King's Surveyor-General, in collaboration with the King's Master Mason, *Robert Mylne*. The existing quadrangular shape was accepted; it had to be, since the abbey church at the ne and the Chancellor's Court at the s were still in use, as were the w range and nw tower. A sw tower containing a chapel was to balance the nw tower, as had been proposed in Charles I's reign. The new ranges were to be carefully classical, with superimposed orders of pilasters. All this was much as carried out. Internally the plan was a muddle, perhaps the result of a hasty expansion of an earlier brief for rebuilding the e range to cover reconstruction of the whole palace. All the first floor would have been filled by three awkwardly planned sets of royal apartments (one each for the king and queen and the third presumably for the Duke of York).

After criticism from Charles II a second scheme was prepared, its planning admirably lucid. A state stair in the SW corner, inside the building (not outside as in James V's palace), was the hinge for the planning of the *piano nobile*. At the top of the stair were doors to the Council Chamber in the SW tower (Charles II having refused a chapel), to the Queen's Apartment running along the W range to end in the NW tower, and to the Great (King's) Apartment running along the inner side of the S range and the whole of the E range, overlooking a new privy garden on the site of the abbey cloister.* A privy gallery along the inner side of the N range linked the Great and Queen's Apartments. Both royal apartments were planned as a suite of rooms leading from a Guard Hall through a Presence Chamber, where was to stand a canopied chair of state, to a Privy Chamber, the decoration progressively increasing in richness the more 'private' the room (i.e. the more honoured the visitor who was admitted to it). The richness of the Privy Chamber was at least equalled by the last two rooms of the ceremonial sequence, the Antechamber and the Bedchamber. It is only with the Closet beyond the Bedchamber that a room which is private in the modern sense is reached, and here the decoration was for pleasure rather than an assertion of monarchical power. Important as they were, the royal apartments took up only part of the palace. The rest was designed to provide lodgings to be occupied normally by officers of state, in which the King's retinue could be billeted during a royal visit.

Work began in July 1671, and the NW tower and Lobby in the W range had been fitted out by 1672 when the Earl of Lauderdale took up residence at Holyrood as Commissioner to Parliament. By December 1674 the N range was virtually complete inside and out, the E range roofed and mostly floored (the plasterwork of its principal rooms in progress), the S range was being roofed, and most of the walling of the SW tower had been built. In 1675 Lord Hatton, Lord Treasurer Depute and Lauderdale's brother, was granted a lodging within the palace, soon followed by the Marquess of Atholl, Lord Privy Seal, and other officers. 1676 saw a major change in the scheme. The Earl of Kincardine, who had urged economy, was at last dismissed from the Privy Council and Lauderdale, the proponent of an extravagant display palace, was in effective control of Scottish affairs. It was now decided to rebuild the C16 W range between the two towers, to extend the new Queen's Apartment N of the NW tower with a new Bedchamber and Closet‡ above a Queen's Kitchen, and to build a new King's Kitchen block (balancing the abbey church and appropriately Gothic in style§) at the SE. In May 1678 Bruce's appointment as Surveyor-General was cancelled, 'now the said Building and reparations are (upon the matter) finished', and in October Hatton took on administrative

---

* The old privy garden had been N of the NW tower.

‡ An alternative interpretation of the purpose of these rooms is that they were the Queen's Wardrobe and Lady in Waiting's Room. In the C18 the putative Bedchamber was the Duchess of Hamilton's bedroom.

§ If William Adam's engraving in *Vitruvius Scoticus* is to be trusted.

oversight of the completion of the work. In 1678–9 the exterior, except for the King's Kitchen, was finished, and the last of the plasterwork and panelling in the Great Apartment completed. Royalty in the persons of James Duke of York and his duchess, Mary of Modena, came to Holyrood in 1679 to escape anti-Catholic agitation in England. The duke occupied the Great Apartment, the duchess the Queen's Apartment whose Guard Hall and Presence Chamber were still unfinished. The intended Queen's Presence Chamber was fitted up as a Roman Catholic chapel for Mary of Modena blocking the planned progression from the State Stair and muddying the clarity of Bruce's plan.

In 1686 James VII ordered conversion of the Council Chamber into a Roman Catholic chapel and in 1687 commandeered the abbey church as a chapel for the revived Order of the Thistle.* The Chancellor's Lodging in the court to the s was made over to the Jesuits, and the Chancellor was rehoused in the main quadrangle. In December 1688 the new fittings of the Chapel Royal and abbey church were destroyed by a Protestant mob, and the Jesuit college sacked.

After the Act of Union (1707) there was no Scottish Privy Council to occupy the Council Chamber, no Scottish Parliament and so no Commissioner to occupy the Great Apartment. Holyroodhouse became a tenement of exclusive flats for noblemen who had acquired grants of lodging there. For the Dukes of Hamilton and Argyll, Hereditary Keepers of the Palace and of the Household, these were by virtue of their office. For others like the Earls of Breadalbane lodgings in the palace were a mark of royal favour. All regarded them as virtually their private property. The Great Apartment was left empty and neglected‡ but the Queen's Apartment had been taken over by the Duke of Hamilton as early as *c.* 1682. The ground to the s and w of the palace was built over as lodgings for debtors (the 'Abbey Lairds') availing themselves of the right of sanctuary within the precincts of the abbey.§ Royalty came back to Holyrood in 1745 in the person of Prince Charles Edward (Bonnie Prince Charlie), but he occupied the Duke of Hamilton's apartment rather than the Great Apartment and used the Gallery in the N range rather than the rooms of state in the s range for his receptions. In 1796 the Great Apartment was again occupied by royalty, but this time by a debt-ridden foreign exile, the comte d'Artois (brother of Louis XVI), for whom Holyrood was a refuge from his creditors.

The rebirth of Holyrood as a palace came with George IV's visit to Scotland in 1822. The King actually slept at Dalkeith House‖ but held a levée, court and drawing room at Holyrood. The old Guard Hall of the Great Apartment was fitted out as a Presence Chamber, the throne being placed against the w

---

* *James Smith* was architect for the fitting out of this Thistle Chapel; *William Morgan* and *Grinling Gibbons* were responsible for the carving.
‡ '... dirty as stables' complained John Wesley in 1780.
§ The abbey precincts were taken as including Holyrood Park.
‖ But a bed was placed in the bedchamber of the Great Apartment at Holyrood.

wall, and the old Council Chamber was used as the King's Privy Chamber. The sequence of rooms now began with the Gallery and proceeded through the Great Apartment in reverse order to that intended by Bruce. Before he left, George IV ordered repair of the palace but, in accord with the romanticism of the time, stated that 'Queen Mary's apartments' (the C16 royal apartments in the NW tower) 'should be preserved sacred from every alteration'. Between 1824 and 1834 nearly £25,000 was spent on repairs under the direction of *Robert Reid*. The King's Kitchen at the SE had been long since removed, but the Chancellor's Court had been demolished only just before George IV's visit. Reid's scheme completed the clearance of buildings S of the Palace and removed from the NW tower the 1676–9 N addition, by then known as Lord Robert Stewart's House. The SE corner of the palace was rebuilt and the S front refaced with ashlar. W of the palace were built a new gaol and courthouse for the Bailie of Holyrood Abbey* and a new royal stables. The garden was extended round three sides of the palace. On completion of these repairs Holyrood regained something of the viceregal function it had lost in 1707. Since 1834 the Lord High Commissioner to the General Assembly of the Church of Scotland has used some of the Great Apartment during the sitting of the Assembly. In 1835 restoration of the roofless‡ abbey church as a hall for the General Assembly was proposed. *James Gillespie Graham*§ prepared plans but they were thought too expensive to execute.

On Queen Victoria's first visit to Holyrood in 1842 the 1822 back-to-front processional route through the Great Apartment was institutionalized and *William Nixon* made designs for an enriched ceiling for the old Guard Hall, now fixed as the Throne Room. A Jacobean ceiling by *Robert Matheson* was installed in 1855–6. The original function of the Royal Apartment was now lost and it became an inconvenient collection of drawing rooms with the Throne Room doubling as a dining room. During the Victorian period the Crown at last got possession of the lodgings of the officers of state except for the apartment of the Duke of Hamilton, and even he gave up the W range and the NW tower in 1852. In 1854 the 'Historical Apartments' in the tower were opened to the public on a regular basis. The change from a Restoration to a Victorian palace was completed in 1871 when a private suite for the Queen was formed in the second-floor rooms formerly occupied by the Duke of Argyll. The setting of the palace and abbey were also brought under royal control. The rights of the Earl of Haddington as Hereditary Keeper of Holyrood Park were bought out in 1843. St Anthony's Loch was formed and lodges built in 1855–7. The palace garden was further extended, and in 1860–2 the forecourt to the W of the palace tidied up, a new guardroom and stables replacing a brewery.

* The Bailie exercised legal control over the debtors within the Abbey precincts.
‡ The roof had collapsed in 1768.
§ Nominally; the drawings are actually by *A. W. N. Pugin*.

PALATIVM REGIVM EDINENSE,
quod & Cænobium S. Crucis.
The royal palace of holy rood-hous. by *J.G.*

Palace of Holyroodhouse
w front before the fire of 1650
(after Gordon of Rothiemay)

The proposal of 1906 to convert the abbey church into a
Thistle Chapel was rejected on the grounds that the new stonework required would destroy its value as a historical document. The forecourt was made bleaker and grander as a memorial to Edward VII in 1920-2. Since 1911, when the West
Drawing Room in the sw tower was panelled, Victorian
decoration has been replaced in a more subdued taste, respecting Holyroodhouse as a late C17 palace.

ABBEY CHURCH

The buildings begun when the abbey was founded in 1128 have
disappeared apart from one doorway and the excavated plan
of the church. For a royal foundation the design was surprisingly modest: an aisleless nave about 6 m. wide, short transepts, each with one rectangular chapel, and a short
straight-ended choir. There can be no doubt that the model
was the identically planned church begun in 1125 at Merton
Priory, Surrey, the home monastery of the first Augustinian
canons brought to Holyrood by David I. Shortly before 1200
work began on the cathedral-sized church whose nave alone
survives. There is unfortunately no documentation at all for
this building, but the evidence of style allows one to date the
earliest parts *c.* 1195 and the latest *c.* 1230. First came the N

nave wall, basically a Transitional design but with a few touches that show an awareness of St Hugh's Choir at Lincoln (begun 1192). The W front was built next, probably in the opening years of the C13. Its eccentrically placed towers and screened windows are unparalleled elsewhere in Britain, although extreme originality is a general characteristic of major early C13 façades in England. In the main body of the nave, the last part to be built, the debt to Lincoln is once more very clear, but the connexions are now mostly with the transepts that followed on from St Hugh's Choir. Comparisons with the church which is in many ways the masterpiece of the Early English style are not to Holyrood's disadvantage, for the C13 work here is of the highest order aesthetically – a fact not so widely known as it might be. The destroyed transepts and choir preceded the nave in the usual way, although the few remaining scraps are C14 to C15 reworking. Abbot Crawford (1460-83) was credited in the early C16 with rebuilding the church completely; though this is clearly untrue, he may have done much in the E parts. In the nave he replaced the C13 vaults and added flying buttresses. His successor Abbot Bellenden (1487-1503) covered the roof with lead.

The choir and transepts were demolished in 1570, but the nave was retained because it had always served as the parish church of the Canongate burgh. A major overhaul was carried

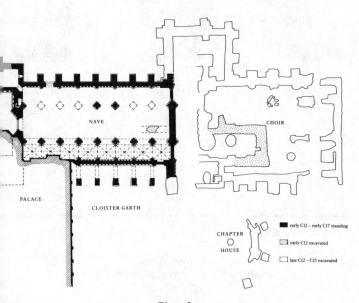

Plan of
Holyrood Abbey

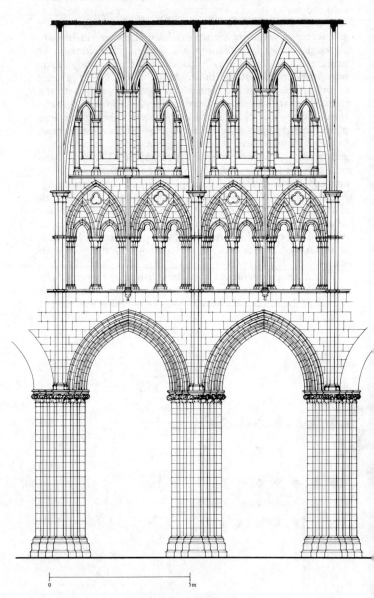

Holyrood Abbey,
reconstruction of internal elevation of nave

out in advance of Charles I's coronation in 1633, and many of the changes then made to the W and E fronts are still in evidence. The designs were probably drawn up by *James Murray* and *Anthony Alexander*, joint Masters of Works. After the removal of the Canongate parishioners in 1687 and the destruction of the Chapel Royal fittings in the following year, the building suffered a long period of neglect. In 1768 a stone slab roof laid over the high vault ten years earlier brought about the collapse of the vault, the clearstorey and most of the lower storeys on the N side. In 1906 and 1945 restoration schemes were rejected on the grounds that too much stonework would have to be added. Such timidity seems regrettable, since clear evidence was available for the appearance of the destroyed parts. Lack of authenticity in some of the fabric would have done little to harm a design that owes none of its authority to lively execution or charm of surface texture. No-one could say that the ruins are aesthetically satisfactory in their present state. They are too little varied in grouping to be picturesque yet fragmentary enough to detract from the monumentality of the palace.

INTERIOR. The normal procedure of describing exterior before interior is reversed here as visitors usually enter the church directly from the NE corner of the palace and then see only a small part of the exterior. The NORTH AISLE wall is the oldest part of the Gothic rebuilding. Windows are big single lancets with nook-shafts and wide, shallow splays. The wall arcade has the rather archaic motif of intersecting round arches (but cf. e.g. St Andrews Cathedral, *c.* 1160, and Jesus College Chapel, Cambridge, *c.* 1220). The arches have many shallow mouldings including keeled rolls. In the hollows tiny nailheads and above the springings curious discs where one would expect head stops. Identical discs appear on the late C12 intersecting wall arcade in the refectory at Saint-Wandrille in Normandy, a comparison which must imply that other examples have been lost. The vault has gone except for the wall ribs and the lowest parts of the springings, both of which must belong to Abbot Crawford's work. The vault shafts are triplets, the centre ones keeled, the others circular. They have fat shaft-rings and round abaci. Bases are not yet waterholding. The capitals include many permutations of waterleaf, crockets and rudimentary stiff-leaf. The sophisticated Lincoln types of stiff-leaf are absent. In fact there are only two motifs of Lincoln derivation: the systematic use of edge-bedded monoliths for wall arcades, nook-shafts and minor vault-shafts; and the bench-like plinth carried on round the vault-shafts exactly as in St Hugh's Choir at Lincoln. This description holds good as far as the NW bay, where the intersecting arcade ends abruptly with an ordinary pointed arch. There is no real break in the masonry, and it seems unlikely that any significant pause in building occurred here. Probably a new master mason with more advanced ideas had taken over. But if that were the case, his activities must have been confined to the W wall of the nave and the W front, because the rest of the nave is different again in style.*

The piers illustrate this second and more fundamental change. The W responds have square as well as round abaci, slightly waterholding bases, high plinths and detached shafts – that is, the forms are still basically those of the N aisle. The free-standing piers on the other hand are wholly E.E. They have pronouncedly waterholding bases, abaci are all round, there are no detached shafts, and in general the forms are less bulky. The section – a stepped core with four shafts in the main directions, eight slimmer ones between – stands outside the usual run of E.E. pier types, but something very similar is in the E transepts at Lincoln.‡

The arcades occupied exactly half the original height of the elevation, 30 feet out of 60. The main arches are sparingly moulded so that the orders remain distinct. The triforium is copied from the Lincoln transepts, although the main arches are much more acutely pointed. It has two double units per bay, alternately pointed and trefoiled sub-arches, spandrels with foiled shapes and shafting alternately circular and polygonal. The main vault-shafts are in threes and begin above the capitals of the piers, but there are also single shafts§ corbelled out over the apexes of the arcades whose function was to receive the intermediate ribs of sexpartite vaulting. This was not the classic French type of sexpartite vault, in which the alternation of the ribs combines with alternately strong and weak supports to form double bays. The intermediate ribs here were not reflected in the plan, so in terms of structural logic there was no justification for them. Of relatively few precedents for sexpartite vaults over single bays the most important on the Continent are Vézelay (choir) and Ávila, in Britain Lincoln (E and W transepts) and St Davids (nave). Unquestionably Lincoln was where the Holyrood mason saw them, for C18 drawings and fragments *in situ* show that he also reproduced a peculiar Lincoln form of clearstorey with four lancets per bay cut into pairs by intermediate ribs.‖ When the nave elevations were intact, with their upper parts marking double time to the arcades below, the affinity with the E parts of Lincoln would have been far more obvious than it is now. Not that the Holyrood designer was merely a talented plagiarist. Certainly his elevations have nothing of the robust inventiveness of Lincoln, but there are tall, elegant proportions and a fastidious clarity of articulation which few C13 buildings in England can match. The E.E. period, like

* The presence of earlier work at the W end of the nave suggests that the Romanesque nave was left standing while the new building went up around it; only after it had been demolished would the S aisle be built, and after that the central vessel.

‡ The surviving westernmost pier differs from the rest in having a core with chamfered rather than stepped projections between the shafts.

§ They have wide fluting, another specifically Lincoln trait.

‖ The very obtuse curvature of the intermediate ribs is paralleled in the aisle vaults of the W transepts at Lincoln.

any other, included artists who were primarily innovators as well as those whose achievement lay in consolidating and refining. The Holyrood master belongs to the second category, and his work is no less valuable for that.

The scheme of the SOUTH AISLE is basically as in the N aisle except for the plain pointed wall arcades. The capitals now have mature stiff-leaf of excellent quality. The vault is a late medieval rebuild – see the thin rib profiles, the small bosses and the omission of wall ribs. Part of the W processional door is visible in the third bay from the W. The easternmost bay is nearly filled by the royal vault and the Hamilton vault. Some of the capitals and window heads here have been crudely redone in the C15 or early C16. The central vessel now ends with the blocked W arch of the crossing. On either side, at clearstorey level, single C15 corbels remain from Abbot Crawford's replacement of the high vault. The big five-light window with ogee reticulated tracery was put in during the 1633 restoration and renewed in 1816. It is a remarkably convincing performance for the early C17, though no more so than the chapel windows at Heriot's Hospital. Of the same period, but less convincing, is the Y-tracery in the arch that formerly opened from the N aisle into the transept. Below it is a late C15 stone screen with the arms of Abbot Crawford. Straight-topped door between blind cusped arches, small roundels with blind tracery, a cornice with foliage trails and on top a pierced parapet with odd triangular-headed lights.

The W wall of the NAVE is filled by the off-centre rear arch of the W door (with the only dogtooth so far) and by two quite exceptionally large lancets. In front of them runs a wall-passage formerly with a trefoil-arched parapet. The vault is returned between the windows in a quasi-sexpartite way. The segmental heads of the lancets and the masonry above are of 1633. They cut across blocked wall-passages which could be made to connect with planks (see the slots in the window jambs). The lancets rose considerably higher than the openings framed by the W wall ribs of the vault (cf. the clearstorey of St Hugh's Choir).

The EXTERIOR is usually inaccessible apart from the WEST 14 FRONT. Unfortunately this has fared no better than the nave, and a considerable effort of the imagination is required to visualize its original state. The top storeys of the towers were taken off in the 1633 repairs, the S tower and part of the centre section of the front went to make way for the NE corner of Charles II's palace, and finally the whole upper half of the centre section was destroyed in the collapse of 1768. As first built, the front consisted of a tripartite centrepiece corresponding to the nave and aisles, with N and S towers treated more like outsize turrets than conventional towers in that they were unbuttressed and attached to the nave only by one corner. In the C13 this scheme was unique, but it had appeared at Lindisfarne Priory as long ago as c. 1140 and

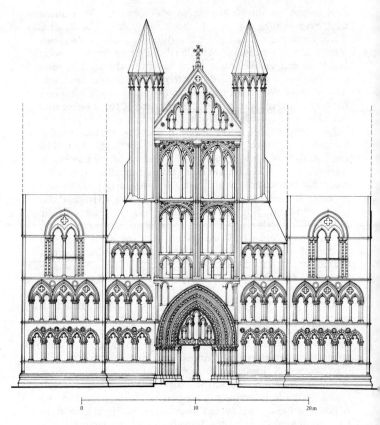

Holyrood Abbey,
reconstruction of west front in original state

then at Rochester Cathedral *c.* 1160. The difference in date
does not invalidate these connexions, especially as the two
outstanding E.E. w fronts, Wells and Peterborough, also hark
back to designs older by a century and more.

The surviving tower is lavishly decorated with blind arcading on its w and s faces. Detailing here and throughout the
w front is rather heavy, and in this respect closer to the N
aisle than to the rest of the nave. The lower tier has single

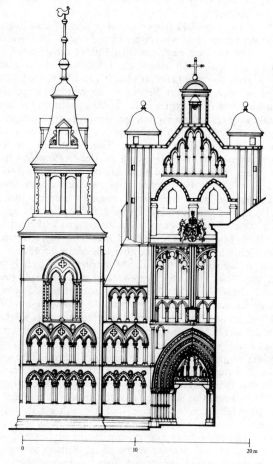

Holyrood Abbey,
reconstruction of west front after repairs of 1633

arches with foliage instead of mouldings, cusps decorated
with balls, and in the spandrels large heads not at all delicate
in their carving. The upper tier is plainer, with coupled
arches and quatrefoils under larger arches. Above this, on all
four sides, a large window of two lights plus a quatrefoil
under one arch, the jambs with grossly oversized ball decoration. According to a drawing of 1544, both towers had a
further storey crowned with short spires, probably of timber.

In the 1633 repairs the tower received a belfry which was widely copied later, e.g. at St Ninian's, Leith, and the original Tron steeple.

The remaining aisle front has three tiers of arcading, the two lower continuing the system of the tower. The heads on the bottom tier are replacements, but of what date? 1633 seems most likely, and indeed the youth with the ringlets is close in style to some heads at Heriot's and Winton, Lothian.

The w door is almost French in its cavernous recession, though all details are typically E.E. Many shafts on the jambs, capitals with beasts among foliage, voussoirs with deeply undercut stiff-leaf (some of it arranged in pyramid formations), dogtooth framing the tympanum. The tympanum itself has been shortened and is carried on a wooden beam with Charles I's cypher, which in turn rests on corbels with grotesque putti. Over this is the original lintel: two long stones covered by alternately large and small roundels framing busts of angels, their wings overlapping and filling the odd spaces. Their state of preservation is amazingly good, their quality execrable. There are five stepped niches in the tympanum, larger niches in the spandrels either side of the door.

The extraordinary size of the w windows has already been commented on, as has the presence of a wall-passage opening towards the interior. So it comes as a surprise to find a second passage outside the window.* This bold hollowing out of the wall was stressed by screening the windows with a kind of grille formed of tiers of open arcading – like E.E. clearstoreys turned inside out, with the difference that the divisions of the arcading are not repeated in the windows behind. The source of the idea may have been St Hugh's Choir, where the wall arcade has two layers of arcading set in a syncopated rhythm. However, it must be admitted that the visual effect is not very like the Lincoln arcade, or indeed any other C13 English design.

Although apparently not influential, the Holyrood front is interesting as the nearest approach in Britain to the free-standing screenwork developed from the end of the C13 on the w fronts at Strasbourg and Cologne. The first tier of the arcading has short triple shafts, and functions as a parapet. The second tier was much higher and originally fitted under large segmental arches – an unexpected form, but less of an obstruction to the windows behind than tall pointed arches would have been. The arches now enclose outsize C17 fleur-de-lys cusps (cf. James V's work at Stirling Castle) which cut across the shafts retained from the arcading. Originally, the arcades, with the windows and the inner and outer passages, rose to the base of the gable. The gable itself had stepped lancets and was flanked by tall turrets. The small part of the s turret remaining indicates a curious plan: a twenty-four-

---

* The w front at Lindisfarne is a precedent for the double wall-passage, as for the arrangement of the towers. The Lindisfarne passages, however, are not combined with large windows.

sided polygon with shafts in the centres of alternate sides. Between the windows a tablet in a strapwork frame records Charles I's restoration.

The N aisle windows have nook-shafts with capitals similar to those inside. The voussoirs have the ball motif. The tall buttresses, due to Abbot Crawford (1460–83), originally received flyers from the high vault. They have stumpy pinnacles, worn armorial panels and image niches with dainty canopies. The N door is a rather tired design of the same period: round arch with ogee hoodmould, flanking pinnacles, niches over. The aisle has been roofed with stone slabs.

Laid out on the grass are the foundations of the CHOIR. It was aisled for its whole length (six bays) and had a straight E end, i.e. the plan of Ripon, Whitby and many North of England churches of the late C12 and early C13. Fragments of late C12 keeled shafts re-used in the blocking of the W crossing arch probably come from the choir piers. A chapel added to the S aisle is still recognizable, as are the choir and transepts of the Romanesque church. Of the CROSSING the W responds of the N and S arches remain. Over the blocked W arch are slight traces of a vault. The drawing of 1544 shows no central tower.

The W walls of the TRANSEPTS are still partly readable. In the N transept the arch from the aisle and the lowest courses of the W walls belong, like the crossing, to the final phase of the nave and so are later than the adjacent N aisle wall. There is also a clear break between the external plinths of the nave and the N transept, and stretches of a plinth identical to the latter are still visible at several points among the foundations of the choir. These details indicate an extensive late medieval reworking of the E parts. The rest of the N transept is archaizing Late Gothic, probably late C14 or early C15. Thin vault-shafts followed by a length of trefoil-arched wall arcading with re-used C13 bases. Blank wall above this, then the jamb of a tall window with mouldings that give away the late date. Over the aisle arch part of a triple clearstorey unit. In the S transept the aisle arch is only partly C13, see the mouldings and the capitals with heads among bossy foliage. The arcading here is cinquefoiled, again with C13 bases. Finally, a window jamb with mouldings more obviously Late Gothic than that of the corresponding window in the N transept. Both transepts had three bays with E aisles.

S of the S transept was the CHAPTER HOUSE, a polygon with a central column (cf. Lincoln again). Its foundations are not exposed. The CLOISTER lay S of the nave. What was the back wall of the N walk has arcading grouped in fives under wide arches. The capitals are mostly by the same carvers as those of the wall arcade inside. Others are late medieval replacements. The E processional door, a survival from the first church, is a representative mid-C12 piece in two orders, the outer with scalloped capitals. Chevron on both arch orders, hoodmould with two rows of billet arranged chequerwise.

The surviving base is C13. Three bays of the S aisle wall are encroached on by the palace, three have their original windows, and two have crude late medieval windows formerly with Y-tracery. But the dominant accent in the S view is Abbot Crawford's buttressing. The flyers from the high vault have gone, but there are still tall pinnacled buttresses linked by flyers to another more massive set standing in the cloister garth. These are not preserved to their full height. They have the marks of lean-to roofs and their inner faces have blind arcading made to match the open arcades that stretched between them. The original aisle buttresses are of slight projection with a single set-off. The aisle roof is now much too low and exposes the wide relieving arches of the triforium.

MONUMENTS. Outside, at the N transept, a pedimented monument to Alexander Mylne †1643. Latin inscription with an English translation:

STAY PASSENGER, HERE FAMOUS MILNE DOTH REST.
WORTHY TO BE IN AEGYPT'S MARBLE DREST.
WHAT MYRON OR APELLES, COULD HAVE DONE
IN BRASSE OR PAINTRY HEE COULD THAT IN STONE.
BUT THRETTY YEARES HEE BLAMELESS LIVED; OLD AGE
HE DID BETRAY; AND IN'S PRIME LEFT THIS STAGE . . .

The monument was restored by *Robert Mylne* in 1776 and moved here in 1857. – Inside the W tower, Robert Douglas, Viscount Belhaven, †1639, by *John Schoerman*. Black and white marble Corinthian aedicule enclosing a recumbent statue.* Coat of arms in the pediment. – N aisle of nave. Medieval coffins and slabs. Among them, Sibilla de Stratun with fine Lombardic lettering of *c.* 1300 and Robert Ross †1409, incised with a chalice. Fragment from altar tomb of *c.* 1500. Ogee-arched panel flanked by crowned shields, one with the Arma Christi. It may come from one of the royal tombs in the choir. – Bishop George Wishart †1671. Large aedicule missing its columns, the segmental pediment broken by a coat of arms. Headless cherubs on the pediment. It looks the work of *Robert Mylne*. – George Earl of Sutherland by *James Smith*,‡ 1703. Aedicular with an open pediment. Low-relief thistles with coroneted family names at the columns. Crisply carved coat of arms. – Jane Countess of Eglinton †1596. Basket-arched recess between stumpy Composite pilasters on a tomb-chest (cf. similar tombs at Greyfriars). – At the E wall, Thomas Lowes †1812. The inscription begins by calling him

One instance among thousands.
Of the uncertainty of human life.
And the instability of earthly possessions
And enjoyments.

*Adam White points out that the effigy is remarkably similar to that of Sir Dudley Carleton, Viscount Dorchester, in Westminster Abbey, made in 1640 by Nicholas Stone, for whom Schoerman worked.
‡ Probably James Smith II (d. 1705).

– In the E bay of the S aisle the Royal Vault, now empty of
tombs. – Next to it the Roxburghe Aisle, an early C17 mausoleum with very flat pilasters and entablature. – At the pier in
front of this, an aedicule to Adam Bothwell †1593. Fluted
Doric pilasters and a segmental pediment carved with a coat
of arms. – To the W incised slabs. Among them, Margat
Bakster †1592, with a coat of arms, a hammer and a skull. –
Beside it a slab to John [   ] †1543 with a cross, compasses
and tools. – Memorial to Euphemia Stewart †1817 consoled
out from the wall and topped by a broad obelisk. Arms at the
apex, urn at the base.

PALACE

The grand approach – not from the Royal Mile but from Abbeyhill to the N – was made in 1856–7 when a carriage-drive
to Palace Yard was sliced across the C16 Privy Garden to the
NW. Left in unhappy isolation is a late C16 garden pavilion
known as QUEEN MARY'S BATH. Two storeys of rubble with
a rounded N corner, its upper floor corbelled out as a fat
turret. More corbelling-out of the upper floor at the S end of
the E side, but here with individual corbels, some of oak. The
effect is more weird than picturesque. PALACE YARD is enclosed at N and S by the SCOTTISH NATIONAL MEMORIAL
TO EDWARD VII by *George Washington Browne*,* 1920–2.
Huge wrought-iron screens and gates. Subsidiary gates at the
W entrance from Abbey Strand. The ironwork was made
under the direction of *J. Starkie Gardner*, a lavish version of
Tijou's work at Hampton Court. Gigantic piers with lion and
unicorn finials at the carriage-gates. Other piers near-copies
of late C17 ones at Caroline Park, but with their scrolled
spires supporting crowns. Bronze STATUE of Edward VII by
H. S. Gamley, tucked away in the NW corner. In the centre
of the forecourt, the octagonal FOUNTAIN is by *Robert
Matheson*, 1858–9, a variant of the 1628‡ Cross Well at Linlithgow. Lions' masks at the lowest stage. Above, a crown
spire with pinnacles and buttresses. The small statues of historical figures designed by *Charles Doyle* and carved by *John
Thomas* have all the charm and much of the appearance of
garden gnomes.§ On the W of Palace Yard immediately S of
Abbey Strand is the ABBEY COURTHOUSE, virtually rebuilt
in 1822–3 by *Robert Reid*; the blind arcading at its N wall
however survives from the Holyrood GATEHOUSE built by
Walter Merlioun in 1502 and demolished in 1753. It was a
two-storey building with a rib-vaulted pend, battlemented

* The memorial is a cheaper version of Browne's design of 1912 which would
have enclosed the N and S sides of the forecourt with semicircles of masonry and
iron. Grand approach from the N. At the S a sculpture of Edward VII receiving
a wreath and laurels from figures of Peace and Concord.
‡ This was replaced by a replica in 1807.
§ '... a confused and miserable mixture, ugly in outline and puerile in detail',
said *The Builder*.

rounds at three corners and a stair-tower at the SE. In the
arcading a re-set panel carved with the arms of James V,
probably the one which was in the W gable. The stair-tower
survives, its present appearance dating from *Robert Matheson*'s reconstruction of 1857 though the flattened ogee arch of
its door is genuine enough. S of the courthouse a re-used
Mannerist door, probably made for one of the royal visits of
1617 or 1633. Frieze with a thistle and rose at the ends of an
exuberant scroll. Pediment broken by the royal arms. STA-
BLES and GUARDROOM by *Matheson*, 1860–2. At their entrance, conical-roofed drum towers of Falkland type hark
back to James V's Holyrood.

62   The outside of the PALACE is substantially the creation of
Bruce and *Mylne* but with the untidy outbuildings to N and

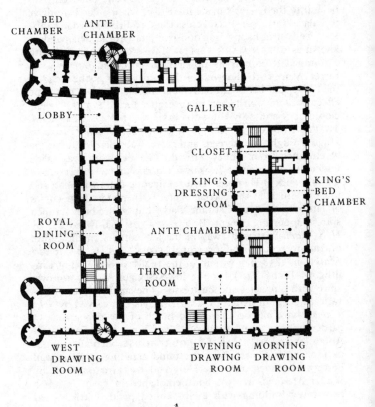

Palace of Holyroodhouse,
plan of first floor

s cleared away. What should have been a revelation of correct classicism contrasting with the surrounding huddle is now too obviously a careful copying from pattern books. Four ranges round a courtyard about 29 m. square. The w end of the abbey church muscles into the NE corner. Projecting towers at the NW and SW. The NW tower, not quite at right angles to the rest, built by *John Ayton*, Master Mason, for James V in 1528–32, is a massive tower house and still very defensive. Rectangular with chunky round towers at three corners. There used to be a corbelled-out turret at the join of the SE corner with the earlier N range. Gunloops at the ground floor, small horizontal windows at the third floor and a corbelled parapet with battlements. A drawbridge, probably on the S side, was the original entrance.

But the tower is also a palace and consciously architectural. String-courses mark the different floors and large windows light the King's and Queen's Apartments at first and second floors. The panels carved with the arms of James V and Mary of Guise are replacements of 1906, the arms of James V copied from the armorial panel now at the abbey gatehouse. The corner towers are topped by cap-houses with conical bell-cast roofs. The original finials carved with lions and miniature turrets, replaced with crowns by 1647,* were again replaced by ball-finials in 1676. The balancing SW tower by *Bruce*, 1671–6, repeats the C16 design even to the gunloops, but without the armorial panels and with a very peaceful round-arched door. The W range linking the towers is of only two storeys with a deep mutuled cornice and balustrade. Plain ashlar walling except at the centre. Here the entrance to the courtyard is set in an aedicule. Coupled Roman Doric columns, the pediment broken by an octagonal crowned cupola, its clock-face dated 1680. Dolphins support the sides of the pediment, ladies holding garlands recline upon it. At the frieze, metopes carved with the cypher of Charles II, crossed thistles, the Honours of Scotland‡ and crossed saltires. Above the corniced doorway a huge relief of the royal arms carved from a full-size drawing made by *Jacob de Witt* in 1677.

The N and s elevations to the garden are almost unadorned. The S front, originally of rubble, was refaced with ashlar, as part of *Robert Reid*'s reconstruction in 1824–6, the date of the superimposed orders of its three E bays. E elevation of seventeen bays with carefully detailed superimposed pilaster orders. It must have looked less flat when seen as a deeply recessed centre between the Gothic-revival kitchen and the abbey church.

Inside the quadrangle, superimposed orders of pilasters all round. Round-arched loggia with small consoled keyblocks. The three centre bays of the E front are slightly advanced§

* If Gordon of Rothiemay's elevation is to be trusted.
‡ i.e. the regalia of the Scottish Kings.
§ Bruce's first scheme of 1671 showed advanced centres at the N and S ranges also.

and pedimented. Tympanum carved with the monogram of Charles II and his coat of arms (again from a cartoon by *de Witt*). Metopes of the lowest frieze carved with the Honours of Scotland and crowned thistles. Pier at the NW corner inscribed

FVN BE RO MYLNE MM 1671

In the centre of the courtyard a stone LAMP STANDARD, a version of the 1633 sundial in the Palace Gardens (*see* below), by *W. T. Oldrieve*, 1908, the lamps based on C17 Scottish ones at Nuneham, Oxfordshire.

The door at the SW corner of the quadrangle opens directly into the STATE STAIRCASE, a square two-storey stair-hall with an easy well-stair round three sides. Dumpy stone balusters as if squashed by the weight of the handrail. Ceiling by *John Houlbert*, 1678–9. High-relief foliage at the frieze. Consoled mutule cornice. The flat of the ceiling is heavily enriched with circles of foliage. In the corners, well-clad angels blowing trumpets and holding crowns and swords. At the first floor, corniced doorcases with very tall and stiff acanthus-leaf friezes. In the SW tower is the WEST DRAWING ROOM (originally Council Chamber for the Privy Council of Scotland). Ceiling by *Houlbert* in partnership with *George Dunsterfield*, 1674. Large rectangular central compartment framed by heavily modelled borders. At the outer border arabesques and figures, among them cherubs playing with lions. Then oak leaves, then fat and droopy acanthus leaves. At the end compartments strawberry-leaf-bordered panels in the centres and foliage. Oak panelling designed by *W. T. Oldrieve* and made by *Scott Morton & Co.*, 1910–11, very C17, with bolection friezes and cornices at the doors. Festoons at the chimneypiece.

The first room in the S range is the THRONE ROOM (originally Guard Hall). Panelling and enriched ceiling by *J. Wilson Paterson*, 1927, a bloodless attempt to emulate late C17 work. The grey marble chimneypiece survives from *Robert Matheson*'s redecoration of 1856. Then the EVENING DRAWING ROOM (originally Presence Chamber). Oak panelling by *Wilson Paterson*, c. 1930, with modest architraves at the doors and festoons at the overmantel. Ceiling by *John Houlbert*, 1675–6. Roses in wreaths at the corners. Modestly moulded border enclosing a large plain centre.

The MORNING DRAWING ROOM (originally Privy Chamber) is much richer. Fluted Corinthian pilasters framing the fireplace. Overmantel with big festoons of foliage and a painting by *de Witt* set in a bay-leaved frame. Corniced doorcases with lugged architraves and acanthus-leaf friezes. All this woodwork is by *Alexander Eizat*, 1677, except the festoons carved by *Jan van Santvoort*. Ceiling by *Houlbert*, 1675–6. Arabesque frieze and bracketed cornice. On the flat, deeply moulded plasterwork with lavish foliage and cherubs holding the Honours of Scotland above CR monograms in wreaths. A door at the l. opens into the Antechamber. Ceiling by *Houlbert* and *Dunsterfield*, 1674-5. Central foliaged circle set in a bracketed octagon. More foliage at the border. Wreaths and cartouches in the corners. Panelling by *Eizat*, 1677. Pilastered chimneypiece with a painting by *de Witt* in the overmantel.

Then the KING'S BEDCHAMBER at the centre of the E range and the climax of the procession through the Great Apartment. Ceiling by *Houlbert* and *Dunsterfield*, entirely filled with heavily moulded foliaged decoration and emblems of kingship. In the central oval a painting by *de Witt*. Panelling by *Eizat*, 1677. Heavy chimneypiece with lion-headed caryatid jambs carved by *van Santvoort*, who also did the massive swagged drapery around the painting by *de Witt* in the overmantel. N of the bedchamber is a LOBBY off which opens to the W the STOOL ROOM, both with ceilings by *Houlbert*, 1678. Then the CLOSET. Very grand but much more relaxed. Coved ceiling by *Houlbert*, 1678. Shells at the corners of the cove. The royal arms and CR monogram set in drapery pulled back by cherubs in the centre of each side. On the flat a circle of oak-leaves at the centre and trophies in the corners. Panelling by *Eizat*, 1677, with carved work again by *van Santvoort*. Foliaged capitals at the pilasters of the chimneypiece. In the overmantel another painting by *de Witt* flanked by trophies. Behind these rooms in the E range are the PAGE OF OF THE BACKSTAIRS' ROOM, the KING'S DRESSING ROOM and WARDROBE. Panelling by *Wilson Paterson*, c. 1930. In the Dressing Room, ceiling with modestly foliaged enrichment by *Houlbert*, 1678. Displayed in the Wardrobe are fragments of MEDIEVAL STAINED GLASS found on top of the S aisle vault of the abbey church in 1909. Most of the recognizable pieces are early C14. The arrangement is by *Douglas Strachan*, 1914.

The whole of the inner side of the N range is filled with the GALLERY. It is something of a puzzle. In 1671 Charles II had ordered that 'a little gallerie for a passage be made betwixt his Majesties old appartement [in the NW tower] and his great new appartement to the East'. What was provided was not a passage but a gallery larger than the Privy Gallery which Bruce had first proposed, a suggestion which the King did 'much dislike'. The explanation for the size of the Gallery may be quite simply that this was the cheapest way to provide a direct link between the Great Apartment and the new Queen's Apartment to the W. The spine-wall of the N range is almost certainly the N wall of the C16 palace and probably of the medieval abbey guesthouse. Retention of this wall in the 1670s meant that it was impossible to provide both a 'little gallerie' and rooms on the inner side of the range unless either the gallery or the rooms were windowless. The gallery is panelled. Lugged architraves and bolection friezes at the corniced doorcases. Chimney surrounds with Doric friezes framed by giant Ionic pilasters. But otherwise the 'panelling' is only timber lining on which are planted picture-frames (by *James*

McFarland, 1684). In the frames, portraits of Scottish kings from Fergus (*fl. c.* 330 B.C.) to James VII, all by *de Witt*, who had been commissioned in 1684 'to make them like unto the Originalls which are to be given to him'. Surely the framed pictures must originally have been canted forward from the wall, but then why only lining and not panelling on the walls? The ceiling is by *George Hay*, 1968, using motifs from late C17 ceilings in the palace. N of the W bay of the Gallery, a scale-and-platt stair; wrought-iron balustrade of 1672 with crowned thistles and CR monograms.

At its W end the Gallery opens into the lobby, the King's Wardrobe in the C16, refitted by *Bruce* as the QUEEN'S PRIVY CHAMBER, with its W wall rebuilt after the new ceiling had been made. The ceiling of 1671–2 provided by *James Baine*, wright, is much more slackly detailed than the Houlbert and Dunsterfield work of a couple of years later. Bay-leaf frieze. On the flat, a foliaged circle with a star at the centre. Ovals with the CR monogram in the corners. Panelling with lugged architraves and bolection friezes at the doorcases. Fireplace framed in fluted Ionic pilasters. Adjoining, in the NW tower, is the C16 King's Outer Chamber, remodelled by *Bruce* as the QUEEN'S ANTECHAMBER, with its floor and ceiling raised about 0·6 m. Panelled, with Ionic pilasters at the fireplace. Ceiling provided by *Baine*, 1672. Foliaged centre oval and large wreaths in the middle of each side of the border. The floor and ceiling of the King's Inner Chamber were also raised in the 1671–2 remodelling for use as the QUEEN'S BEDCHAMBER. Superimposed pilasters flanking the fireplace. The basket-arched marble chimneypiece is the only survivor of William Adam's 1740 alteration of the tower for the Dukes of Hamilton. A very narrow turnpike stair* leads to the room above, a replacement for the straight C16 stair.

A broad C16 turnpike in the NE turret of the tower leads to MARY QUEEN OF SCOTS' OUTER CHAMBER. Fragment of tempera-painted frieze probably of 1617 by *Matthew Gooderick*.‡ Compartmented wooden ceiling probably of 1528–32 or perhaps of *c.* 1545. In the outer compartments foliaged roundels containing crowned IR and MR initials. In the centre compartments similar roundels, but with shields with the royal arms of James V, Mary Queen of Scots, and Henri II, and the arms of François II as Dauphin of France. On the centre intersection of the ribs the arms of Mary of Guise. The coats of arms must be of 1558–9§ but they are not *in situ* and seem to have been pressed into service in 1617 as part of a scheme for making the ceiling grander. At the E wall the reveal of a C16 window opened up in 1906. Doric pilastered chimneypiece of 1671–2; Dutch tiles in the fireplace. In MARY QUEEN OF SCOTS' INNER CHAMBER another wooden ceiling of the earlier C16, divided into compartments by spokes radiating

---

* This stair also served the demolished N extension of 1676–8.

‡ Gooderick was paid 'for painting his Majesteis chamberis at Hallirudhous'.

§ i.e. after Mary's marriage to the Dauphin and before his accession.

from a central boss. The initials MR and IR on the boss are again probably of 1617. Painted initials (CR and CP for Charles I and Charles Prince of Wales) and heraldic devices, presumably dating from Charles I's visit in 1633. Another deep tempera-painted frieze of the same character as in the Outer Chamber and again probably by *Gooderick*, 1617, in blacks and greys with the Honours of Scotland, arabesques and cornucopias between guilloche borders. Chimneypiece of 1671–2 with superimposed pilasters and a pedimented overmantel.

The splendid domestic rooms in the rest of the palace were the lodgings of the officers of state and lack (now at least) the logical progression through successive stages of display which marks the old royal apartments. A scattering of ceilings by *Houlbert* and *Dunsterfield* with the familiar foliaged enrichment. Only the ROYAL DINING ROOM in the W range, refitted by 1792 as the Duke of Hamilton's Music Room, introduces an unequivocal new note. Much sophistication but little excitement. Rosettes at the frieze. Ionic screen *in antis* at one end. Chimneypiece a pastiche of 1910, probably the date for the opening up of the dummy windows in its E wall.

The GARDENS reached their present size in 1857 with the incorporation of the site of St Ann's Yards (the old Chancellor's Court) on the S of the palace. Tall RAILINGS on the W side. WALLS on the N, S and E, the E wall disguised from the garden side by a sloping turfed rampart. N of the palace a SUNDIAL by *John Mylne Sen.*, 1633. Hexagonal base of three steps with panelled risers. Bulbous octagonal column with acanthus leaves at the base and a faceted polyhedron capital, its under surfaces carved with heraldry and other devices, the upper surfaces hollowed out as dials, their grotesque gnomons replacements by *W. T. Oldrieve*, 1908.

At the NW corner of the gardens is CROFT-AN-RIGH, an L-shaped mansion house, rubble-built, with angle-turrets at the SW corner of the main block and flanking the fat chimneystack of the gable of the SE jamb. The main block is early C17; the jamb could well be a rebuild of the late C17.★ At the first floor of the main block a moulded plaster ceiling of the earlier C17, compartmented into circles and squares containing lions, griffons, a half-naked man and other devices.‡

HOLYROOD PARK was extended to roughly its present boundaries in 1541–2. Picturesque LODGES by *Robert Matheson*, 1857. Near the St Leonards Lodge a FOUNTAIN by *Robert Morham*, 1886. Pink Peterhead granite; octagonal basin with a bulbous column decorated with bronze lions' masks (by *D. W. Stevenson*). The bronze unicorn finial is missing. SE of the palace and set into the slope beside Queen's Drive is ST MARGARET'S WELL, a late medieval conduit moved here from Restalrig in 1859. The concrete forecourt and green-painted

---

★ Gordon of Rothiemay's map of 1647 shows the house T-shaped, not L-shaped as now. Probably this was the house owned by William Graham, Earl of Airth, which was burnt, at least in part, *c.* 1680.

‡ The large room under the ceiling has been subdivided.

railings are unpromising, but inside is a small hexagonal room with a pretty rib-vault carried on a round column. The water escapes through a spout in the mouth of a grotesque mask (now mostly cement). The hexagonal plan recalls James III's chapel (St Triduana's Well) at Restalrig of c. 1477-87. E of this is ST ANTHONY'S CHAPEL, a shattered ruin perched on a crag above St Margaret's Loch. The purpose and date are not recorded. It was a late medieval vaulted room of three quadripartite bays springing from corbels. Lancets in the E bays, a door in the W. Over the W end was a room with one oblong window, reached by a stair W of the chapel proper; the stair, partly accommodated below a quadrant arch in the thickness of the N wall, was lit by small rectangular windows. To the SW of the chapel part of a wall containing a cupboard butts up against a large boulder.

ARCHAEOLOGY. The remains of four prehistoric forts in Holyrood Park suggest that the area was a major centre in the final centuries of the first millennium B.C. and early centuries A.D. The surviving walls are not always easy to trace. Arthur's Seat, Dunsapie, Salisbury Crags, the best-preserved of the four and defended by an extensive stone-faced rampart and Samson's Ribs. The most impressive of the groups of cultivation terraces in Holyrood Park are those on the E flank of Arthur's Seat, both above and below Queen's Drive; these terraced strips were formerly narrow ploughed fields and may be of Dark Age or medieval date. An irregular pile of stones beside the Duke's Walk, near the N entrance to the park, is close to the spot where Nicol Muschat of Boghall murdered his wife in 1720.

CHURCHES

AUGUSTINE BRISTO CONGREGATIONAL CHURCH, George IV Bridge. 1857-61 by *J., W. H. & J. M. Hay*. Best Liverpudlian free style, boldly mixing Romanesque, Renaissance and late Classical motifs. Gable front with the slightly projecting centre carried up as a solidly buttressed tower. In its base the round-arched main entrance (now a window), its V-tailed voussoirs alternately enriched with incised panels. Wooden tracery in the round-arched four-light window above. The tower ends in eight ball-finials. Frivolous pagoda spire of three diminishing octagonal stages; at the second, a boldly cantilevered balcony with ironwork balustrade. More ironwork at the pinnacles and nave. The flank, with pilaster strips and acroteria, plunges down into Merchant Street as a rock-faced basement.

Five-bay interior. Galleries on three sides, the space beneath them partitioned into offices. Composite hammerbeam and kingpost roof. The cast-iron columns set close to the walls are a structural afterthought (though inserted before completion), by *David Bryce*. – PULPIT. Broad rectangle with colonnettes. – ORGAN by *A.E. Ingram*, 1929. – In the N stair-hall a marble BUST of William Lindsay Alexander by *John Hutchison*, 1885.

CANONGATE CHURCH, Canongate. In 1687 James VII gave orders for the nave of Holyrood Abbey to be converted from the parish church of the burgh of Canongate into a chapel for the Order of the Thistle. The next year the Lords Commissioners of the Treasury asked *James Smith* for a design for a new church and ordered the Town Council to have it built under Smith's supervision. Paid for out of money mortified by Thomas Moodie in 1649 for erecting a church in the Grassmarket, it was opened in 1691. The plan – unique among C17 Scottish churches – is a Latin cross with an aisled three-bay nave, transepts, short chancel and apse. Aisles are not surprising: they had been built at Greyfriars earlier in the C17. Here they are of the same width as those of Holyrood Abbey and may have been planned for the re-erection of the congregation's dismantled galleries. But the chancel and transepts make no sense in the context of reformed worship.* These are not 'aisles' (i.e. wings) for lairds' or trades' lofts, nor is the chancel a communion aisle (i.e. one in which the communicants sat at long tables). Was this a deliberate attempt to build a church adaptable for Roman Catholic practice?

s front of ashlar, the curving skews of the aisles reaching 26 up to the shaped gable of the nave. Roman Doric portico flanked by doors with lugged architraves and pediments. At the gallery level two round-arched windows under a circular window. Lavishly carved royal arms of William III at the top. Between the windows, the arms of Thomas Moodie above an inscribed tablet flanked by cherubs' heads, a deeply cut swag of fruit below. Round-headed windows in the harled flanks. No clearstorey. In the piend-roofed transepts the windows repeat the arrangement of the gable. Two lights in the apse under a flattened dagger, all in a semi-elliptical arch. The vestries flanking the chancel were built on the site of demolished vestries as part of *Ian G. Lindsay*'s 1946–54 restoration. Inside, a vestibule under the s gallery with Roman Doric columned screens to E and W.

In the church itself, round-arched nave arcades on Roman 27 Doric columns halted by tall pilastered piers flanking the larger arches into the transepts. Lindsay's restoration removed E and W galleries, reopened the apse and lowered the s gallery. The nave ceiling, a segmental-arched vault of 1817, was hidden by acoustic tiles in 1961. – PULPIT. Made for the Territorial Free Church in 1847. Sounding-board by *Esmé Gordon*, 1961. – CLOCK, s gallery. 1817, the face flanked by lion and unicorn supporters. – ORGAN by *Norman & Beard*, 1910, moved here in 1960. – SCULPTURE. Christus Victor in the War Memorial Chapel and the Penitence of St Hubert of

---

* Although the Church of Scotland was episcopally governed in 1688 its worship was severely Protestant.

1962 in the E aisle, both by *Josephina de Vasconcellos*. – In the
W aisle, a bronze bust of Charles Warr †1969 by *Diona Murray*. – Mid-C17 BENEFACTION BOARD in the vestibule.

The CHURCHYARD was laid out in 1688. No shortage of
MONUMENTS. First those on the walls of the church. W transept: Alexander and John Runciman, erected by the Royal
Scottish Academy, 1866. Relief portrait busts by *William
Brodie*. – N end: a small broken-segmental-pedimented aedi-
cule. Monogrammed cartouche in the tympanum. Coat of
arms above. It looks *c.* 1700. One scroll flanking the pilasters
just visible in the harling. – E wall: Thomas Wilkie †1711.
Tablet supported by an angel-corbel, the pilasters of the
frame almost hidden by the drapery of another angel above.
On top an urn-finialled aedicule containing a book. –
Alexander Ramsay †1764. Tablet with a consoled pediment.
The inscription seems to have been recut.

W side of the churchyard. At the S corner Jardine and
Drummond Burial Ground. Stepped screen wall with tablets,
the earliest 1797. – Adam Smith †1790. Wall-monument, the
tablet set in a round-arched recess with fluted spandrels. Keyblock carved with a head. – Elegant early C19 urns on pedestals to James Spadin †1793, Bishop Keith †1756 and Janet
Cox †1821. – Robert Duncan †1758. Tall panelled pedestal
with cherub-heads at the corners of the entablature and a ball
finial. – Obelisk at James Aitken's lair. Dated 1766. – George
Chalmers †1836. Large obelisk with attenuated urn finial. –
In front of the pedimented entrance to an enclosure against
the W wall a table-stone on sturdy baluster legs to Mary
Irvine †1817. – Early C19 Roman Doric columns at the en-
trance to the Hamilton enclosure. – In front, headstone to
Robert Fergusson †1774, set up by Robert Burns in 1789.
Burns wrote the inscription:

> No sculptur'd Marble here nor pompous lay
> No storied Urn nor animated Bust
> This simple Stone directs Pale Scotia's way
> To pour her sorrows o'er her Poet's Dust

– Mid-C18 headstone to Agnes Mouat, wife of Robert Rutherford. Fluted pilasters and a swagged shaped top. Carvings
of a cherub's head, skull and hourglass. – Fat obelisk of 1801
for Sir Thomas Calder †1760. – In the W wall of the churchyard a realistic carving of skull and crossbones. – Wall-monument to Robert Boog †1766. Obelisk above a tablet framed
with a cutler's tools and skulls. – In front, segmental-pedimented headstone erected by the Society of Coachdrivers in
Canongate, 1765. In the tympanum a skull. Below the inscription, relief of a coach crossing a bridge. – In the churchyard wall a late-C17 segmental pediment broken by an hourglass. Skull and crossbones in the tympanum. – Burial
enclosure of James Blair †1790. Pilastered and pedimented
front with an urn at the apex of the pediment. – In front a
very large and very elegant urn on a pedestal. *c.* 1800.

To the N a lower part of the churchyard. At the E of the wall dividing it from the main body of the cemetery a pedimented gateway by *Alexander McGill*, 1722, to the burial ground of the earls of Marchmont. - On the S side of the wall a couple of pedimented surrounds to doors to lairs. Lugged architraves and bolection-moulded friezes; *c.* 1700. - Inside the S division of the churchyard, along the N and S walls, rows of small enclosures of 1828-41. - At the NW corner mausoleum of Dugald Stewart, 1828. Massive blocks of droved ashlar. Semi-elliptical-pedimented front. Entrance set in flat orderless pilasters with console-capitals and a slab-cornice. - In the centre of this division monument to soldiers who died at Edinburgh Castle, by *James Wright & Son*, 1880, a tall column of polished red granite with an elided capital topped by a cross. The style was described by *The Scotsman* as Byzantine. The inscription says:

DEATH CALLED THEM AWAY FROM THE MARTIAL RANKS
AND SAD WAS EACH COMRADE'S TREAD
AS THEY BORE THEM ALONG TO THE MARCH IN SAUL
MIDST CROWDS TO THEIR LONELY BED

BUT THEIR COUNTRY'S SONS WILL AROUND THIS STONE
OFT SPEAK OF THE DEEDS OF THE BRAVE
AND GRATEFULLY LOOK ON THE GRASSY SOD
THAT GROWS O'ER THE SOLDIERS' GRAVE

Immediately N of the church in the central division of the graveyard James Hunter †1801. Pedestal and urn. - To the NW of this, Private William Wilkins †1819 'in consequence of an injury of the Head, caused by the falling of his horse in a Charge at the conclusion of a review on the sands of Portobello'. - At the E wall of this division mausoleum of Sir William Fettes †1836. Heavily detailed Greek cross with a round-arched entrance in each arm. Groin-vault inside. - Immediately to the N, tablet to John Frederick Lampe †1751. Skull and crossbones at the bottom. Curvilinear top carved with cherubs holding a musical score. - Wall-monument at the burial place of John Douglas †1753. Consoled open pediment with a garlanded head in the tympanum. Among those commemorated is Janet Douglas †1786:

Beneath this Turff her Corps does ly
whoe's Virtues Grac'd humanity
And while on earth her Beauty shone
bewail'd by all now that She's gone

- Below the terrace, the Boylan monument, *c.* 1880. Very Gothic but not very good. Lucarned spire on a pedestal. Statue of St John at the NW.

E division of the churchyard. In the W wall, Hugh William Williams †1829 by *John Lessels*, *c.* 1860. Large aedicule with paired pilasters. Acroterion at the pediment. Inscription tablets of polished red granite, that to Williams with a bronze relief portrait by *John Steell*, 1863. - John Mitchell, dated

1792. Polished ashlar recess set in a rock-faced surround. –
s wall: Roman Doric aedicule to Benjamin Bell †1806, the
tablet set in a broadly keyblocked round arch with rosettes in
the spandrels. – E wall: Alexander McCrae †1796. Pointed-
arched recess in a large rock-faced slab of masonry. In the
recess a broad obelisk carved with a flattish tomb. – Small
tablet to Lord Craig †1813. Corbels with guttae. Fluted frieze
with rosettes. Urn on the top. – Clarinda. Bronze relief by
H. S. Gamley, 1909. – Then, three large pilastered aedicules
set side by side. The best is the monument built by James
Drybrough, 1794, very stark, with exaggerated entasis at the
pilasters and a block pediment. – More delicate is John Stobie
†1792. Masonry strips for pilasters, an incised band at the
frieze and acroteria at the ends of the pediment. – Alexander
Young †1842 is very conventional by comparison. – Heavy
classical aedicule to William Gibsone †1807, dated 1820. –
Adamesque classical monument to David Willison †1798.
Segmental-arched and keyblocked recess containing a tomb-
chest. Above the centre of the cornice a swagged panel and a
saucer dome. – N wall. Early C19 mausoleum with paired anta
pilasters at the corners and Empire garlands at the frieze.

Immediately sw of the church is the BURGH CROSS. The
octagonal shaft is probably C16; base, capital and cross head
of 1888.*

ELIM PENTECOSTAL CHURCH (originally Reformed Presbyterian), George IV Bridge. Precise Curvilinear Gothic by
Charles Leadbetter, 1859. Flat ashlar front with a crested gable
over the 'nave' window and the walling carried up as a small
pinnacled tower over the door at the l. The rear to Candlemaker Row is an acutely-pointed V. Inside, U-galleried auditorium. Foliaged corbels carry the ribs of the ceiling. –
PULPIT with a tent-shaped spire over the sounding-board.

GREYFRIARS CHURCH, Candlemaker Row. A long Gothic-sur-
vival box whose building history is all-important. In 1562
Queen Mary granted the garden of the Greyfriars monastery
to the Town as a cemetery to relieve the over-full churchyard
of St Giles. After the Reformation the parish of Edinburgh
was divided into four districts‡ and the building of a new
church to serve the sw district was proposed in 1595. In 1601
the Greyfriars cemetery was found 'maist meitt' as the site.
Building had begun by 1602, when *Clement Russell* was described as 'maister of wark to the Kirk begun in the buriell
plaice'. In the same year it was decided that the church should
be 120 ft by 60 ft (36 m. by 18 m.) and that 'the hewin wark of
the butrages and durris' of the convent at Sciennes should be
re-used. Work seems to have continued in 1603–4, with *Patrick Cochrane* as master of works, and then stopped. A move
towards resumption was made in 1611 when the Town Council 'appoynted, votet and condescendit that the kirk foundet

* The base is that provided for the Mercat Cross (*see* Public Buildings, below)
in 1866 and superseded in 1885.
‡ They became parishes in 1598.

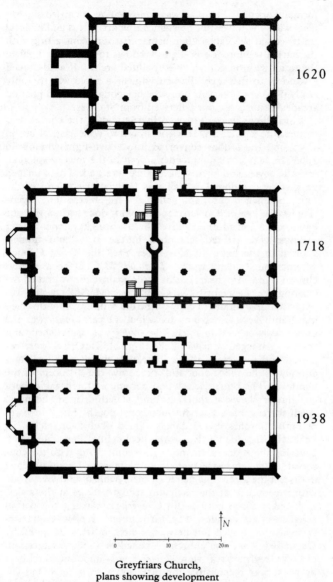

1620

1718

1938

↑N

0   10   20m

Greyfriars Church,
plans showing development

in the buriall yaird suld be bigget with pilleris', but it was
only in December 1612 that they approved the resolution of
the kirk session that 'the wark of bigging of the kirk in the
buriall yaird sall gang forward with all convenient expedi-
tioun' and appointed a treasurer for it. A date-stone of 1614
at the E gable suggests that considerable progress had been
made by then, but it was not until 1620 that Greyfriars was

formally opened. The plan was conservative, an aisled six-bay nave with a w tower but no chancel. Doors at N, S and E. Solid buttresses at the flanks, their ashlar masonry contrasting with the harled walling. Three-light windows to the S, two-light to the N, all with broadly-splayed pointed arches. Round-arched **24** E window to the nave. The curvilinear E gable was the only really progressive touch. Were the octagonal piers and pointed arcades inside consciously derived from St Giles?

Furnishings were destroyed in 1650 when the church was turned into a barracks. It was restored to ecclesiastical use in 1653, and the S door converted into a two-light window in 1696. In May 1718 gunpowder stored in the tower exploded, and the tower and two w bays were wrecked. The damaged bays were abandoned, a wall was built at the w end of the four undamaged ones, and galleries were erected to compensate for the loss of floor-space. The old N door was moved one bay to the E and adorned with a cherub-head keystone. Plaster ceilings were erected, coombed in the aisles and tunnel-vaulted in the nave. In November 1718 the Town Council commissioned plans from *Alexander McGill* for a second church (New Greyfriars) to be built against the w end of the existing one (henceforth Old Greyfriars). McGill's design was ready within a month (a copy of the old building on a reversed plan) and New Greyfriars, for which *Gilbert Smith* was the mason, was opened in 1721. The tower was demolished, and the two damaged w bays of the original Greyfriars were repaired and two more added, repeating those of the existing church, as did the N door and (probably) the Y-tracery of the windows. The buttressed w end became a Dutch gable, with curvilinear skews at the aisles and a pediment at the nave. Against the gable a low semi-octagonal porch. The buttresses of both churches received ball-topped obelisk-pinnacles. In 1722 *McGill* added a two-storey pedimented Palladian porch covering the N doors, its modernity contrasting with the conservatism of the rest. Channelled masonry and round-arched doors. At the same time he recast the E gable of Old Greyfriars with a pediment at the nave and straight skews at the aisles.

In 1845 a fire gutted Old Greyfriars, causing the partial collapse of its arcades. The furnishings of New Greyfriars were also destroyed but new ones were quickly designed by *David Bryce* and the church reopened in 1846. 'Restoration' of Old Greyfriars was slow. *James Smith*, appointed architect in 1845, was responsible for little more than removing the roof and demolishing the arcades. In 1856-7 *David Cousin* transformed the building into an aisleless box under a single-span roof of quite different outline from the original. The windows were filled with ashlar pierced by lancets.

The two congregations united in 1929 and a scheme of reconstruction by *Henry F. Kerr* followed from 1931 to 1938, the tercentenary of the signing of the National Covenant inside Greyfriars. The arcades of Old Greyfriars were rebuilt, its roof restored and its gable brought back to its 1722 appearance. The windows however were left alone. Inside, the galleries and dividing wall were removed and a timber ceiling was erected over the six bays of the original church. The plaster vaults of the two w bays were left, marked off by an arch as not really belonging to the church of the Covenant. Bryce's woodwork was re-used to form a w gallery.

FURNISHINGS. A High Presbyterian arrangement with communion tables standing like altars at the ends of nave and aisles. – Nave COMMUNION TABLE by *Herbert L. Honeyman*, 1912, recast by *George Hay* in 1951. – Behind it, PANELLING of 1912 by *Honeyman*. – Also of 1912 *Honeyman*'s large octagonal PULPIT, C17-style with a sounding-board. – FONT. Carved marble pedestal and fluted basin which do not seem to match, bought in Rome and said to date from the Apostolic age. – Nave LECTERN, 1893. Chunky wooden eagle. – Brass EAGLE LECTERN in the s aisle. – ORGAN by *D. & T. Hamilton*, 1866, moved here from Park Church, Glasgow, in 1889 and rebuilt by *Gray & Davison* in 1938. – STAINED GLASS. In the four E bays (Old Greyfriars) the first painted glass in an Edinburgh Presbyterian church since the Reformation, bright abstract designs with some figurative roundels, all by *Ballantine & Allan*, 1857, except for the even more garish Anderson Memorial Window in the N aisle by *Francis Barnett*. – Less strident the w window (Resurrection) by *A. Ballantine & Gardiner*, 1898, and the Gardiner Memorial Window (SS. Helen and Margaret of Scotland) by *Marjorie Kemp*, c. 1938. – MONUMENTS. By far the best is the mid-C17 tablet in the s aisle to Margaret Lady Yester †1647, moved here from Lady Yester's Church in 1938. Artisan Mannerist aedicule with emblems of mortality above, and below the inscription:

> IT'S NEIDLES TO ERECT A MARBLE TOMBE
> THE DAYLIE BREAD THAT FOR THE HUNGRY WOMBE
> AND BREAD OF LYF THY BOUNTIE HATH PROVYDED
> FOR HUNGRIE SOULES ALL TYMES TO BE DIVYDED
> WORLD LASTING MONIMENTIS SHALL REARE
> THAT SHAL ENDURE TIL CHRIST HIMSELFE APPEARE
> POS'D WAS THY LYF PREPAIR'D THY HAPPIE END
> NOTHING IN EITHER WAS WITHOUT COMMEND
> LET IT BE THE CAIR OF AL THAT LIVE THEREFTER
> TO LIVE & DIE LIKE MARGARET LADY YESTER
> WHO DIED · 15 · MARCH 1647 · HER AGE 75

– N aisle. Robert Lee †1868, a high relief of the angel of the Resurrection by *John Hutchison*, 1870. – William Robertson †1883, portrait bust by *John Hutchison*, 1883.

GREYFRIARS CHURCHYARD boasts the best collection of C17 monuments in Scotland. In 1562 Queen Mary granted the garden of the Greyfriars convent to the Town as a burial ground. In 1636 the churchyard was extended to the s beyond the present s wall to the line of the Telfer Wall along Lauriston Place. In 1703 a w strip of this (now known as the Covenanters' Prison) was divided off. w extension of 1798.

The Town Council tried to keep strict control over burials

and monuments. In 1591 it resolved that no one was to be
buried in Greyfriars yard 'without avyse of the Counsell', and
in 1603 'that na staynes aucht to be infixet or sett at ony
graiffes in the buriall yaird', ordering 'the baillies to caus
remove the samyn'. However in 1606 John Jackson was allowed to build a monument to his father 'provyding the sam
be maid alangs and upoun the wall of the said buriall'. This
established the pattern of development until the C18, with
wall-monuments along the boundary, the rest being kept for
grass and trees. Permission to erect memorials was condi-
tional on the payment of a substantial sum towards the support of the poor, and at least until the 1620s control over
design was given to the Dean of Guild.

At the E gable of the church, a realistically grisly memorial
to James Borthwick, Deacon of the Surgeons (†1676, having
acquired the plot in 1670). A St Andrew's cross formed by a
skeleton and a scythe. Surgical instruments in the border. –
At the W gable, James Penman †1773, a swagged marble
tablet under a cherub's head. Skull and crossbones at the
base. – Inscription to Daniel Wilkie †1838,

A BRIGHT EXAMPLE OF EVERY MINISTERIAL VIRTUE.
AND IN WHOM BOTH THE GRACES OF THE CHRISTIAN
AND THE ACCOMPLISHMENTS OF THE GENTLEMAN
WERE MOST ATTRACTIVELY BLENDED.

N wall of the church. Thomas Robertson †1686; leave to
set the monument up in the church was given in 1687 and it
was moved here in 1883. Angels flanking a Corinthianesque
aedicule, the concave pediment broken by a coat of arms.
Skulls on the pediment. Inscription tablet carved as drapery
held in a dragon's mouth. – John Carmichael †1785. Flat-
topped obelisk with concave sides and a relief portrait. On
the base a relief of Heriot's School. – Near the E end of this
wall C17 graveslabs from inside the church.

E wall of the churchyard, N of the main entrance. Mausoleum of John Law †1712 and his wife Isabella Cunningham
†1703 (the plot was granted to Law in that year). The inscription records the monument as built by his son and restored in
1803. Two-stage entrance with lugged architrave door under
a pedimented tablet. Flanking tablets with cherubs' heads and
carved bones. – Next, two of a series built in 1610–20, their
design apparently the responsibility of the Deans of Guild
(i.e. *Richard Doby*, 1610–12, and *David Aikinheid*, 1613–20):
essentially medieval (a basket-arched recess over a tomb-
chest) but with details culled from Serlio. James Harley
†1617, erected in 1619. Within the head of the arch a band of
Vitruvian scrollwork. Baluster columns at the base, arabesqued octagonal columns above, and upside-down consoles
supporting the entablature. Frieze with triglyphs and rosettes.
On top, an inscribed panel with symbols of death. – Beside it,
another early C17 tomb (with a later inscription to Elizabeth
48   Purves †1847) may belong to Alexander Miller †1616, de-

signed by *David Aikinheid* in the same year. Almost identical to the Harley monument. Scrolled pediment of *c.* 1801; the squat obelisks could be original. – In front of these, two free-standing classical monuments: Margaret Nasmyth †1811, a tall pedestal with an urn, 1820, and James Struthers †1807, a large urn carved with foliage. – Sir Robert Denniston of Mountjoy, dated 1626 and less Gothic in feeling than the earlier tombs. Corinthian columns with individual entablatures. Pedimented aedicule broken by a coat of arms above. Plenty of strapwork detail. – Partly buried beside this (and now bearing a tablet to Thomas Spens), Alexander Beatton †1672 by *Robert Mylne*, 1674–5. Corinthian aedicule, the pediment broken by a coat of arms; fragmentary figures sitting on top. Drapery inscription-tablet held in a lion's mouth. – John Nasmyth of Posso †1613. Licence to build was given in 1612 and it is dated 1614. Taller recess than usual, to accommodate a headless effigy of Nasmyth sitting up in his tomb. Flying angels on the wall behind. Rusticated and arabesqued pilasters, attenuated because of the height. – Epitaph to John Macfarlane set in the tomb of Richard Doby †1612. Licence was given in 1613, and Doby's epitaph is said to have been dated 1614. Pilasters as at Nasmyth's tomb, but shorter. Consoled frieze with rosettes and faceted blocks. Strapwork panel above. – John Laing, 1614. Same pilasters as for Doby and Nasmyth. Consoled frieze with triglyphs and faceted blocks. Two tiers of panels on top, the lower flanked by emblems of death. – George Hunter †1835, dated 1837. Free-standing and very mannered, Italian in outline and artisan in detail. High base bearing a tomb, the scroll-pedimented top broken by cartouches at front and back. – Wall-monument with inscription to Robert Kerr, built for John and Isaac Morrison and dated 1615. Fluted pilasters with squidgy acanthus-leaf capitals and Ionic volutes. Triglyphs and rosettes at the frieze, and a triple-obelisk finial. – Beside it, a very eroded tomb, also apparently of John Morrison, and of the general early C17 type. Semicircular pediment. – Ray's tomb (licence to build, 1610). Pilasters of the Morrison tomb type. Triglyphs and rosettes at the frieze. Early C19 blocking-course. – George Heriot †1610 (the year when the licence was granted), 'the forme and plaice thairof to be appoyntit' by *Richard Doby.* *John Simson* was the mason and *William Cokie* was paid for gilding. Vertical, diagonal and fishbone fluting at the pilasters. Triglyphs and faceted blocks at the frieze. On top, two-stage inscription-panel with segmental pediment. – The last of the early C17 series, now with a tablet to Adam Drummond, was probably built for William Mauld. Pilasters of the Morrison and Ray tomb type. Triglyphs at the frieze. – Near by, Lady Catherine Paulet †1740 by *James Stuart*, 1775–6. Elegant obelisk supporting an urn. – James Murray of Deuchar †1649, built in 1650. Large inscription tablet set in a frame. On top, an aedicule, its pediment broken by a coat of arms; piers carved with lions, their mouths stuffed with drapery. – To the

N an early C19 frame. Rosettes at the bottom corners and guttae at the centre of the entablature under an urn. – Some way to the N, Sir Hugh McCulloch of Pilton † 1688, set up by his nephew James McCulloch, following Sir Hugh's instruction of 1688 that it was to bear his arms with his name and that of his wife. Sir Hugh's further instruction that it was to be like the Catherine Tod or Young monuments (both at the W wall) was not followed very carefully. Torches flank the Corinthian aedicule. Above the scrolled pediment, coat of arms in a small aedicule. Cartouche for the inscription. – MARTYRS' MONUMENT. Built in 1706 to commemorate the Covenanters. The tall Ionic aedicule flanked by scrolls is of 1771. So is the inscription:

> Halt passenger, take heed what you do see,
> This tomb doth shew, for what some men did die.
> Here lies interr'd the dust of those who stood
> 'Gainst perjury, resisting unto blood,
> Adhering to the Covenants, and laws
> Establishing the same: which was the cause
> Their lives were sacrific'd unto the lust
> Of Prelatists abjur'd. Though here their dust
> Lies mixt with murderers, and other crew,
> Whom justice justly did to death pursue,
> But as for them, no cause was to be found
> Worthy of death, but only they were found,
> Constant and stedfast, zealous, witnessing,
> For the Prerogatives of CHRIST their KING.
> Which Truths were seal'd by famous Guthrie's head,
> And all along to Mr. Renwick's blood.
> They did endure the wrath of enemies,
> Reproaches, torments, deaths and injuries.
> But yet they're those who from such troubles came,
> And now triumph in glory with the LAMB

N wall. Bayne of Pitcarley enclosure, 1684–5, with a moulded door. Inside, a mausoleum. Shallow ogee dome with a swagged urn. Round-arched openings with very old-fashioned stumpy Corinthianesque pilasters. In an arched recess at the back, a statue of John Bayne † 1681. The effect decidedly spooky. – Mausoleum of the Trotters of Mortonhall, dated 1709, the year it was begun by *Robert Mylne*, to be finished after his death in 1710 by *William Mylne*. Ashlar gabled front with a moulded door.

W wall. A series of mid- and late-C17 wall-monuments, extravagant, tall aedicules, their inspiration more from architectural title-pages than from actual buildings. First Magdalen McMath † 1674. Pediment broken by coat of arms. Piers at the corners framing outrageously twisted columns. – Beside it, the very grand tomb built by Janet McMath in 1635 for her husband Thomas Bannatyne † 1635. Twisted columns again. Above the main aedicule was a smaller one (now on the ground) framing a pudgy cherub, his hands resting on an hourglass and a skull and with a view of Edinburgh behind him. Inscription:

IF THOU LIST THAT PASSEST BY
KNOW WHO IN THIS TOMBE DOTH LY
THOMAS BANNATYN ABROAD
AND AT HOME WHO SERVED GOD
THOUGH NO CHILDREN HE POSSEST
YET THE LORD WITH MEANES HIM BLIST
HE ON THEM DID WELL DISPOSE
LONG ERE DEATH HIS EYES DID CLOSE
FOR THE POORE HIS HELPING HAND
AND HIS FRIENDS HIS KYNDNES FAND
AND ON HIS DEARE BEDFELLOW
IENNET MAKMATH HE DID BESTOW
OUT OF HIS LOVELIE AFFECTION
A FIT AND GOODLIE PORTION
THANKFULL SHE HER SELF TO PROVE
FOR A SIGNE OF MUTUALL LOVE
DID NOR PAINES NOR CHARGES SPAIR
TO SET UP THIS FABRICK FAIR
AS ARTEMISE THAT NOBLE FRAME
TO HER DEAR MAUSOLUS NAME

– Very similar, the monument to George Foulis of Ravelston 49
†1633 by *William Ayton*, 1636. Headless figures of Religion
and Justice in shell-headed niches flank the Ionic aedicule
containing relief portraits of Foulis and his wife, their hands
clasped beneath a grinning skull. On top, a smaller aedicule
with caryatid columns and broken pediment, carved with a
cherub and hourglass. – Henryson monument, built for Sir 49
Thomas Henryson, 1636. Large Corinthian aedicule supported by corbels at the ends and an angel's wings at the
centre. Strapwork and drapery mixed in the frame of the
inscription. Coat of arms in the small aedicule above. – John
Byres of Coates †1629 by *William Wallace*. Broken-pedi- 49
mented Corinthian aedicule containing a keyblocked round-
arched recess, its tympanum carved with symbols of death
and resurrection. Strapwork at the base. – Gilbert Primrose
†1616. Paired baluster-columns. On the cornice, between
heraldic lions, a strapworked inscription panel under a coat
of arms. – At the W end of the terrace separating the upper
and lower burial-grounds, a tunnel-vaulted burial-chamber
of *c.* 1700. – In the retaining wall to the E, architectural fragments, among them a C15 capital from Trinity College
Church, with foliage and human heads, and the carved head
of a man from a C17 tomb. – Also against the retaining wall,
Henry Mackenzie †1831. Massive consoles and a block pediment but no entablature.

In the upper burial-ground, an obelisk to Charles Jackson
†1783, built in 1803, its front carved with an urn embraced
by a snake. – On the wall behind, John Jackson †1606 (the
year of the licence to build). Still Gothic, with a pointed arch
recess between pinnacled pilasters, their bases fluted. At the
base, round-headed arcading with heads in the panels. – Archibald Tod †1656, dated the same year. Emblems of death
at the sides. Open pediment with a coat of arms and ball-

finials. Worn inscription at the base:

> HEIR [WORTHY] PROVEST TOD DOTH LIE
> WHO DIED AND YET WHO DID NOT DIE
> HIS GOLDEN NAME IN FAMES FAIRE ROLE
> CL[AIMES THE] LIFE RENT TACK OF A SOUL . . .

– Two badly eroded early C17 square-arched tomb-recesses lead to the monument of James Chalmers †1675. It is of that date, and its similarities to the Beatton and Mylne monuments point to *Robert Mylne* as the architect. Tall Corinthian aedicule. Scrolls at the sides, carved with angels and emblems of death. Inscription recut in 1834. – Anne Scott. Early C19 tablet, badly weathered, in a round arch. Fluted imposts and sunburst tympanum. – Elizabeth Paton †1676, wife of John Cunningham of Enterkine. Licence to build, 1677. Vast aedicule flanked by figures of Adam and Eve wearing castles on their heads. Coupled Corinthian columns; pediment broken by a coat of arms. Urns at apex and sides. Inscription panel framed with mixed strapwork and drapery and set in a round-arched recess. In the tympanum, a jolly skeleton between Father Time and a cherub with a skull. – Catharine Tod †1679 (the year of the licence). Tripartite, with fluted Corinthian columns. In the centre an alert skeleton crowned by angels. Mourning figures at the sides; at the base a cherub reposing on a skull.

In the W extension of the churchyard, solidly prosperous monuments of the early to mid C19, mostly classical, eminently decent and not very interesting.

The W wall of the old churchyard continues with the monument to Alexander Gibson Wright †1793. Acanthus capital pilasters, and a coat of arms set in a concave pediment with vase finial. – Alexander Henderson †1646. Free-standing; a pier with a swagged urn. The inscriptions were recut *c.* 1690. Among them:

> Reader, bedew thine eyes,
> Not for the dust here lyes,
> It quicken shall again
> And ay in joy remain:
> But for thyself, the Church & states,
> Whose woes this dust prognosticates.

– Behind, William Carstaires †1727. The design was provided by *Joseph Cave*, engraver to the Scottish Mint, and executed under his direction by *Andrew Miller*. Restored by *John Hutchison*, 1876. Tall segmental-pedimented Corinthian aedicule. Outsize scrolls at the sides, badly weathered. At the base, a skeleton lying in the tomb. – Young monument. Licence granted to Thomas Kinkaid, husband of Mary Young, 1679. Caryatids support the entablature. Strapwork inscription panel with the resurrection of the body (or rather skeleton). – Mausoleum of William Robertson †1793. A domed square with Roman Doric pilasters at the corners. Round-

arched openings with fluted keyblocks and spandrels. Inside,
the pendentives spring from corbels with guttae. - Mausoleum of William Adam †1748 by *John Adam*, 1753. Round-
arched entrance at the E, thermal openings at N and S formed
by later infilling under the arches. Entablature with rams'
skulls and rosettes between the triglyphs. Dome inside, carried on a circular cornice. Large inscription panels, the principal one at the W with a portrait bust of William Adam and
a tomb-chest, its front carved with Hopetoun House with
ruined portico (*see The Buildings of Scotland: Lothian*).

Broken pedimented gateway into the COVENANTERS'
PRISON. Burial enclosures line its E and W walls. The W begins
with an inscription to John Learmonth (†1858) set in an early
C18 Corinthianesque aedicule with putti standing on scrolls
at the sides. - Warrender of Bruntsfield enclosure, dated 1710;
consoled open pediment over the door and heavy rusticated
quoins. - Broad pedimented monument to Robert Blair
(†1811) with coupled anta pilasters. - McAulay enclosure.
Permission to build it was given in 1738; on its W wall an
eroded tablet with a large egg-and-dart border and a Mylne-
type grotesque head at the bottom. - Joseph Black (†1799),
an urn-topped monument of 1805. Round-arched recess for
the inscription tablet (originally marble, replaced in sandstone, 1894). Serpents on the panelled piers, the keystone a
carved head, a fluted sunburst above the arch. - Late C18
Sceales enclosure; huge leafy scrolls beside the pedimented
round-arched entrance. - Whytt enclosure; Ionic pilasters and
a segmental pediment at the door, dated 1764. - Carnegy
enclosure; early C18, with ham-fisted Ionic pilasters at the
door. Coat of arms above cornice. - In the middle of the S
wall a large Corinthianesque aedicule to Hugh Cunningham
(†1710), the segmental pediment broken by a coat of arms. -
On the E wall, a vast monument by *William Jameson*, 1781,
commemorating John Dalrymple (†1779). Under the consoled open pediment, a high-relief draped urn flanked by
up-ended torches. - To its N an enclosure bought by James
Rutherford in 1825; the pedimented gable looks of that date.
- Pitcairn enclosure; Ionic doorpiece probably early C19 but
old-fashioned. - Innes enclosure; powerful early C19 Neo-
Classical with a Doric frieze and modillion cornice topped by
an urn. - Mausoleum of Adam Brown who acquired the plot
in 1711; artisan mannerist pilasters at the segmentally gabled
door, tunnel-vaulted interior. - Another large aedicule of C17
type forming the monument of Sir James McLurg (†1717),
its inscription a long list of his benefactions. Reclining cherubs on the sides of the pediment, and a pedimented coat of
arms overall. - To the N a plain enclosure with a pedimented
tablet to William Wardrop, dated 1726.

S wall of the old churchyard. Munro enclosure, dated 1819.
Entrance framed by very thin panelled pilasters with guttae
below square panelled capitals and a tall fluted frieze. - Dalzell enclosure. Channelled ashlar front with pediment. Inside,

wall-monument to Andrew Dalzell †1806. Tomb-chest under
an obelisk carved with an urn. – Enclosure of Patrick Millar
of Dalswinton. Pedimented entrance dated 1779. – Mausoleum of Sir George Mackenzie of Rosehaugh, the most advanced architectural work of its period in Scotland, completed
in time for his funeral in 1691. The mason and probably also
the designer was *James Smith*.* The inspiration is from Bra-
mante's Tempietto of S. Pietro in Montorio, illustrated in
Palladio's *Quattro Libri*. Corinthian-columned and ogee-
domed with an urn finial, it is really an octagon under the
circular cornice, but the tall shell-headed niches on each face
(except that of the entrance) distract the eye from its actual
form. Circular interior, lit by windows in the ribbed dome.
The inscription panel in the large recess on the s dates from
R. Rowand Anderson's restoration in 1892. – Enclosure of Sir
William Forbes. Pedimented entrance dated 1775, the year
Forbes acquired the land. Early C19 Gothic tomb recess in
the s wall. – Forrester enclosure, dated 1701. Coat of arms
over the entrance and flanking emblems of death. – More such
emblems on the w wall of the Lumsdaine of Innergelly enclosure. – Mausoleum of William Little of Liberton, 1680–3.
An oblong Corinthian peristyle with an ogee-domed roof and
draped urn, with figures of Justice, Mercy, Faith and Love at
the corners, covers a stiffly realistic recumbent effigy. Iron
railings at the N of the enclosure by *Thomas Sibbald*, 1770. –
Blind oculi flank the entrance to the Falconer of Phesdo enclosure, 1742. On its s wall, a tablet to Sir James Falconer
†1706 with a bracketed pediment. – Shed-like Ferguson of
Pitfour mausoleum, dated 1775. – Pediment over the entrance
to the Hunter Blair enclosure, 1787. – In the Mackenzie enclosure, monument to Colonel Alexander Mackenzie †1796.
Roman Doric pilasters at the ends; consoled segmental pediment over the centre. – At the E wall, immediately s of the
main entrance, John Mylne †1667; a tall Corinthian aedicule
by *Robert Mylne*, 1674. A mantelled coat of arms with cherub
supporters breaks the segmental pediment. Scrolls at the
sides. Inscription panel held in the mouth and paws of a lion.
Latin inscription and, below, one in English beginning

> Great artisan, grave Senator, JOHN MILNE
> Renown'd for learning, prudence, parts, and skill,
> Who in his life Vitruvius' art had shown,
> Adorning others' monuments: his own
> Can have no other beauty, than his name,
> His memory and everlasting fame.

Cartouche at the base inscribed:

> Reader, JOHN MILNE, who maketh the fourth John,
> And by descent, from father unto son,
> Sixth master mason to a royal race
> Of seven successive Kings, sleeps in this place.

* Smith's sketchbooks have been seen as a putative source for English Palladianism; *see* Howard Colvin, 'A Scottish Origin for English Palladianism?',
Architectural History, xvii (1974).

Inscriptions to members of the Mylne family are carved on the columns, with a curious effect. Semicircle of railings in front with spearhead and urn finials set up by *Robert Mylne*, 1779.

At the main entrance to the churchyard, obelisk-pinnacled GATEPIERS, probably *c.* 1840. LODGE of 1840 with a semi-octagonal end and lozenge-paned windows.

HOLYROOD FREE CHURCH, Horse Wynd. Secularized. By *John Henderson*, 1850. Simplest Gothic with a prominent bell-cote. Four-bay gableted flank.

LADY YESTER'S CHURCH, Infirmary Street. Secularized. By *William Sibbald*, 1803–5. Shaped gable front, a squatter version of Canongate Church (*see* above) but with pinnacles and window-tracery of 1640s' Gothic type, the main window copied from the W window of the previous Lady Yester's Church built in 1644–7.

MAGDALEN CHAPEL, Cowgate. A C16 almshouse chapel, later converted into the convening hall of the Incorporation of Hammermen. Michael MacQueen †1537 bequeathed £700 Scots towards the cost of building the chapel and providing accommodation for a chaplain and seven bedesmen 'who should continuallie pour forth prayers to Almighty God'. Further contributions did not materialize, so MacQueen's widow Janet Rynd had to put up another £2,000. Work was in progress by January 1541, and completed by 1544. The confirmation charter of 1547 provided for the patronage of the hospital (dedicated to St Mary Magdalene) to pass to the Incorporation of Hammermen (metalworkers) after Janet Rynd's death, which took place in 1553. The next year Isobel MacQueen made a further endowment of £50 Scots with which was built the 'croce-hous', a new lodging for the bedesmen. After the Reformation of 1560 the bedesmen continued to be housed and to pray (in a Protestant form), but the chapel seems to have suffered considerably and its furnishings to have been destroyed. It underwent major repairs in 1601 and again in 1613–17, the second phase including the building of a front wall to the Cowgate, with a grand columned entrance. In 1618 the Hammermen decided to rebuild a spirelet on the cross-house in a different position, but ordered the building committee 'to avys with ye Kingis master of work for bigging thairof on ye best and maist comedious fassonn'. What advice *James Murray* gave is not known, but in 1620 the Hammermen decided to build a steeple 'befoir ye greit doir of ye chappell'.

Of the outside of the chapel of 1541–4 only the rubble S wall and E gable are visible. In the S wall three windows, enlarged in 1625. In 1725 the W window (formerly above a door) was lowered to correspond (nearly) with the other two. High up at the W end an opening to a doocot between ceiling and roof, probably of 1625. The N front to Cowgate is dominated by the steeple built by *John Tailefer*, mason, and *Robert Wilson*, wright, in 1620–5. Ashlar tower of five stages

marked by string courses. Corbelled and battlemented parapet with two cannon-spouts at each face. Lead-covered spire
with ogee head; gilded globe and weathercock. At the w window below the belfry a sundial on the lintel. The round-
arched door and hoodmoulded window above are by *Richard
Crichton*, 1816–17 (the date of his two-storey Tudor
committee-room extension at the l.). Above the door a scrolly
pediment broken by a panel with the initials of Michael Mac-
Queen and Janet Rynd, their impaled arms divided by the
crowned hammer of the Hammermen, and the date 1553. On
the sides of the pediment, small figures of a bedesman and a
hammerman. The carving was done in 1615 (*John Sawer* was
paid for 'drawing of ye crown upone ye stane' and *Alexander
Wat* for masonwork) to form the top of the columned gateway
in the forewall. It was moved here in 1649 and a pediment
added to the armorial panel. To the r. of the steeple, the
Livingstone Memorial Medical Mission building by *Robert
Raeburn*, 1877–8, quotes from Crichton's 1816 addition.

Inside the tower the c16 entrance door to the chapel,
moulded with shields on the lintel. The chapel itself is a
broad single cell. Shallow c16 chancel-step between the E
part and the nave. Chancel filled with two semicircular tiers
of seats by *William Eizat*, wright, in 1725. The back of the
lower tier was painted by *Alexander Boswall* with the arms of
the trades which formed the Incorporation of Hammermen,
the shields linked by painted festoons of chains. In front of
this tier a wrought-iron RAILING incorporating the hammer
insignia, also 1725. Along the E wall and two-thirds of the N
wall, arcaded PANELLING. Round arches, all with lily and
whorl decoration in the spandrels, but the modelling and
pilasters of various types and probably dates: some at least
must be of before 1615 when *George Stewart* wrote the records of benefactions on 'ye tabillis about ye lang buird', but
most of the inscriptions have been rewritten over older ones,*
probably in 1813 when it was decided 'that the wooden work
should be painted'.‡ – High up on the w wall, plaster ROUN-
DEL with the Hammermen's insignia, probably 1813. – On
the w wall a PANEL painted with the City arms, perhaps the
work for which *Walter Melville*, 'herauld painter', was paid
in 1708–9. – Above it, a moulded stone PANEL dated 1624
and inscribed

> LORD   BLES
> THE   HAMMER
> MEN-PA   TRONS OF
> THIS HOSPITAL

---

* In general, by copying each old inscription on to the adjacent panel, whose
own original inscription had been covered with black paint.

‡ But *Alexander Boswall* was to 'varnish and refresh the painting of the Mortifications' in 1725.

The barrel-vaulted ceiling introduced in 1615 by *David Brown*, wright, seems to have covered only the E part of the chapel, since it was decided in 1725 to carry 'the arched roof above the place of meeting' to the w.* – STAINED GLASS. Four mid-C16 heraldic roundels in the central S window, virtually the only pre-Reformation glass in Scotland other than recent importations and excavated fragments. Royal Arms of Scotland and of Queen Mary of Guise above the arms of MacQueen and of MacQueen impaling Kerr. The wide range and brilliance of the colour are typical of early-to-mid-C16 glass outside Scotland. The bold design is supported by delicate drawing (e.g. the savages' heads in the MacQueen arms). Sophisticated technique, with pieces of one colour inserted into fields of another, the yellow staining of white glass exposed by abrading the ruby or blue flash, and very careful cutting, particularly in the Royal Arms. Several intrusions, e.g. the crescent moon and inky sky in the thistle border of the Royal Arms. The arabesque frame round the panel of MacQueen impaling Kerr is upside down, and the frame of the MacQueen panel has been replaced by plain glass, two pieces from a rectangular arabesque frame, and one fragment showing sickles lying on the ground (presumably from a lost narrative panel). – TOMBSTONE of Janet Rynd at the SE. Slab carved with her coat of arms and an inscribed border. The

Magdalen Chapel, stained glass,
the arms of Queen Mary of Guise

* The 1725 painting of the ceiling by *Alexander Boswall* 'with Skye colour with clouds and a sin gilded in the center' no longer survives.

edge of the slab is moulded so this may have been an altar-tomb.* – Brass CHANDELIER, early C18.

NEW NORTH FREE CHURCH, at the gusset of Bristo Place and Forrest Road. Disused. Thinly detailed early Dec rectangle by *Thomas Hamilton*, 1846–8. Wide N gable looking along George IV Bridge, with a porch whose open gablet is continued as blind tracery wrapped round the semi-octagonal stair-towers. U-plan gallery and single-span arch-braced roof. The congregation found it 'an ugly inconvenient church'.

OLD ST PAUL‡ (Episcopal), Jeffrey Street. A very distinctive church by *Hay & Henderson*, 1880–1905, on a narrow slope between Carrubbers Close and the even gloomier North Gray's Close. What it shows to the world is the high, buttressed gable of the N (liturgical E) end, including the chancel with three tall lancets above (the floor level indicated by an interlaced blind arcade), and the church hall on the level of Jeffrey Street below. A two-stage bellcote astride the roof is set back above the chancel arch, under the precipitous shadow of the Old Town.

The site is that of the wool store hurriedly occupied by the congregation after their expulsion from St Giles in 1689, but this became ruinous and in 1876 *R. Rowand Anderson* produced a scheme which probably influenced the final one. By 1880 enough money had been raised to start building, but now to a design by *William Hay* (another pupil of George Gilbert Scott) largely executed by his partner *George Henderson*. The chancel and N part of the nave were built by 1883, the S half in 1889–90, and the Seabury Chapel on the S side of the nave in 1904–5. Finally in 1924–6 *Matthew M. Ochterlony* designed the Warriors' Chapel in place of the W chancel aisle; the blunt gable of grey stone, squared and hammer-dressed, projects abruptly to one side of the original E.E. gable and contrasts with its yellower ashlar and steeper pitch.

In the stone-faced interior the relationship of spaces and levels is highly dramatic, as is the contrast between the sombre and sturdy architecture and its rich furnishings. Chancel small but lofty, with high-up N lancets. On its E a massive shaft of polished granite supports the two arches of the surviving aisle, occupied by the organ. The inner splay of the chancel arch is supported by smaller shafts on corbels. From it projects an iron ROOD SCREEN of delicate Art Nouveau fantasy; this and its polychrome marble base, along with the brown and white marble steps and floor of the chancel, were probably added in 1905. Following the Gerona arrangement, the width of the nave (12·2 m.) equals the combined width of the chancel and its aisles. Nave 27·5 m. long, divided into seven bays by wall shafts on very tall pedestals. From their capitals, intended to be foliated but never carved, spring

* As claimed by the RCAHMS. The alternative view is that it was raised when the platform in which it is set was built in 1725.
‡ The title distinguishes it from its namesake in York Place.

arched trusses with grotesque heads of beasts at two levels, those at the wall-head holding tie-rods in their mouths. The roof structure and plain timber lining are stained dark brown. E wall with an unbroken row of plain lancets. W wall partly altered, and not quite satisfactorily, for the SEABURY CHAPEL extension; this is like a low aisle, with truncated windows of Dec tracery forming a clearstorey overhead. The two S bays however are splendidly treated. From the long raised platform entered from Carrubbers Close there is a further ascent within the S wall, re-emerging on a balustered timber gallery across the arch which mirrors that of the chancel. This is the route to the vestry, necessitated by its unusual position on the much higher ground at the S (liturgical W) end. The vestry itself is now housed in the LAURIE MEMORIAL BUILDING by *Shaw-Stewart, Baikie & Perry*, 1960–2, well composed and detailed, with a timber Crucifixion on the harled wall overlooking a small garden. In the church itself the last major alteration, Ochterlony's work of 1924–6, done as a war memorial, begins with the entrance from Jeffrey Street. Then the CALVARY STAIR of three flights, beautifully contained within chisel-dressed walls under a segmental vault. The top landing opens into the nave. The WARRIORS' CHAPEL, alongside the chancel and screened from it by late Gothic tracery, is lined with very plain masonry on which the names are recorded in bronze Roman letters, with a continuous stone wall-bench below. Flags are hung under the compartmented oak wagon roof.

Henderson's furnishings are still *in situ*. – ALTAR. Rich neo-Norman, of wood. Over it the late Gothic pinnacles of the gilt TRIPTYCH rise 8 m. from the floor. Carved in oak to Henderson's design by *John Gibson*, who also did the angels holding scrolls, the triptych incorporates some forty figures by *Sebastian Zwink* of Oberammergau. *Doig & McKechnie* did the gilding. In the centre a copy of Benvenuto da Siena's enthroned Madonna and Child (National Gallery of Scotland). – CHOIR STALLS. Three canopied bays with ringed shafts on each side, poppyheads and griffons in front; all dark stained, as is the octagonal PULPIT. The congregation have chairs, not pews. – In the Seabury Chapel another gilded TRIPTYCH by *Henderson*. – SCULPTURE. In the middle of the E nave wall a Michelangelesque Madonna and Child in stone by *Louis R. Deuchars*. – At the head of the Calvary Stair, a Crucifixion by *Alfred Hardiman*, 1926. – ORGAN by *Henry Willis & Sons*, 1879, brought here from the Cathedral Song School in 1888; rebuilt by Willis in 1936, 1960 and 1969. – STAINED GLASS. Over the altar three lights (Crucifixion, St Paul and St Columba) and the vesica above by *Cox & Sons, Buckley & Co.*, 1895. – In the Seabury Chapel three lights (Bishop Seabury's vocation as priest and carpenter) by *Percy Bacon Bros.*, 1907, and three (Annunciation, Nativity, Presentation) by *Karl Parsons*, before 1945.

ST COLUMBA BY THE CASTLE (Episcopal), Johnston Terrace.

By *John Henderson*, 1846-7. A sturdy little village church. Buttressed nave of four bays with shafted and stepped triple lancets. No aisles. One-bay chancel with a trefoil-headed two-light window and diagonally set buttresses. The diminutive NW tower is a sham with no S wall; its W wall is an adjoining chimneyhead. In the tower a cusped door with a trefoil-headed window above, and a two-light 'belfry' opening. Battlemented parapet. The interior is even simpler. Triple arcade dividing the vestibule and organ gallery from the nave. Skimpily collar-braced roof. Chancel arch of a single large order. – Plain SEDILIA in the chancel. – SACRAMENT HOUSE. A cusp-arched aumbry given a bronze door *c.* 1914. – Stone ALTAR. – REREDOS of *c.* 1935, set in panelling of *c.* 1914. – The blocked E window has been filled with a MURAL (Christ enthroned) by *John Busby*, 1959. – In the other windows late-C19 PAINTED GLASS. – FONT. Stone bowl carved in rich relief. – ORGAN by *James Conacher & Sons*, 1880, rebuilt in 1965 by *N. P. Mander*.

ST COLUMBA'S FREE CHURCH (originally Free St John's), Johnston Terrace. Endearingly lumpy Gothic by *Thomas Hamilton*, 1845. Five-bay 'nave' with full-height three-bay 'aisles', all with double-pitched roofs. Pinnacles at the nave gable and the ends of the aisles. Two-storey ashlar flank to Johnston Terrace, with fat lancets lighting the galleries and round windows set in blind arcading below. The coursed rubble back to Victoria Terrace is similarly treated but has a basement (originally a school) in the fall of the ground. Steeply pointed hoodmoulds over the basement windows. Inside, open-spandrelled wooden arches on slim cast-iron piers. Late Tudor double-hammerbeam roof with pendant arches linking the purlins. Galleries with crested fronts in the 'aisles' and E bay. The W (Moderator's) gallery is of 1908, when *John Burnet & Son* altered the church to serve as the Free Church Assembly Hall. Arcaded front breaking into Hamilton's central pulpit with its flurry of Flemish pinnacles. – MONUMENT to Thomas Guthrie by *William Brodie*, 1873.

ST FRANCIS (R.C.), Lothian Street. Perp front of 1834 in the manner of *James Gillespie Graham*, the nave and aisles marked by pinnacled buttresses. Well-foliaged ogee hoodmould at the door. Three-light nave window above flanked by two-light windows for the aisles. The church behind was rebuilt as halls with a church above in 1937.

ST JOHN, Victoria Street. Secularized. By *George Smith*, 1838-40. Less like a church than three bays of a Jacobean country house. Strapwork scrolls link the outer bays to the taller advanced centre with its shaped gable, shallow rectangular oriel and round-arched door with crowned human-head labels. Interior floored over at gallery level.

ST PATRICK (R.C.), Cowgate. Built in 1772-4 as a 'qualified'* Episcopal chapel. *John Baxter Jun.* was the architect, *William*

---

* i.e. its clergy took the Oath of Allegiance to George III.

Wright the contractor. As first built, it was a large two-storey rectangle with a semi-octagonal apse at the E flank and a tower with a domed octagonal belfry (cf. St Andrew, Glasgow) astride the S gable for which a pedimented Roman Doric portico was planned but not built; nor was a small N portico. Simple detail with keyblocked windows, round-arched above, segment-headed below. The church was bought by the Roman Catholics in 1856. Pedimented W porch, with inappropriate foliaged capitals at the door, added in 1890, when the flanking ground-floor windows were deepened. In 1898 the interior was re-aligned and a new sanctuary built to the N, by *J. Graham Fairley* and externally self-effacing. Not so *Reginald Fairlie*'s S front of 1929, a triumphal arch built out to the line of the intended portico. Niches with statues of SS. Patrick and Bridget beside the entrance, fussy windows in the slab-ends, and a balustered parapet. The original gable (refaced) plays the part of a recessed pediment. Inside not much of the original plan survives. There was a gallery round three sides; the altar stood in the apse and the pulpit in front of the N gallery. The E and N foci still conflict. Segmental E apse-arch with giant fluted pilasters and extravagant triglyphs. Half-domed apse ceiling, later paint covering The Ascension by *Alexander Runciman*. His wall panels (the Prodigal Son, Christ and the Samaritan Woman, Moses and Elijah) survive. In the curved wall a Venetian window. Fairley's marble-panelled N sanctuary copies Baxter's pilasters on a larger scale, with an arch in Corinthian pilasters framing the crucifix in a pedimented aedicule. Flanking chapels of 1924–5, with Ionic pilasters and much marble. The Roman-Doric-columned S gallery has survived, panelled and boldly bracketed.

Mortuary chapel at the SE, clumsy Wrenaissance by *Alexander McWilliam*, 1921. – Large Baroque marble FONT. – STAINED GLASS. In St Patrick's Chapel, colourful abstract designs by *Francis Barnett*, 1856. – In the baptistery a late C19 Baptism of Christ. – ORGAN by *Muir, Wood & Co.*, 1819, rebuilt by *Small, Bruce & Co.* in 1835, and by *Frederick Holt* in 1867.

SEVENTH-DAY ADVENTIST CHURCH (originally Evangelical Union), Bristo Place. Two-storey hall-front in bright red sandstone by *Sydney Mitchell & Wilson*, 1900. C17 Scots Classical with a large shaped gable of Canongate Church type and Corinthian pilasters copied from the Tron Church. From the Tron also the tracery of the windows. Art Nouveau-ish green tiles on the stair-hall walls. The church is on the first floor. Compartmented segmental vault, N gallery with bracketed front; E gallery set behind a two-bay arcade, with its own segmental vaults at right angles to the main roof. – ORGAN by *Gray & Davison*, 1900.

TOLBOOTH CHURCH (VICTORIA HALL), Castlehill. Disused 36 (1984). Stunningly sited and beautifully detailed Gothic by *James Gillespie Graham* and *A. W. N. Pugin*, 1839–44, designed and built to serve both as a church for the Tolbooth congregation and as the meeting hall of the General Assembly of the Church of Scotland. The shape is still that of the aisleless Georgian box church with a tower stuck on to the E gable, but the scale is vast and the detail correctly Dec. Two storeys with the ground floor (filled with committee rooms) serving as a basement for the church-cum-hall above. Squat three-light windows on the ground floor, vast four-light windows for the church, all hoodmoulded and with the same quatrefoil tracery. Pierced parapet. At the buttressed flanks clustered pinnacles with huge octagonal pinnacles at the corner buttresses, richly crocketed. Discreet sw addition in the same style by *Hardy & Wight*, 1893. The steeple dominates, 74 m. high, its design closely related to Pugin's second scheme for St George, Southwark, and the ideal parish church of *The True Principles of Christian Architecture*. Richly crocketed gablet over the continuously moulded door. Then a huge six-light window at each face. Small, gableted clock-stage. Above, the two-stage belfry is carried up as very tall lucarnes for the spire, which is linked to the great pinnacled buttresses of the tower by flyers. Diapered bands at the upper stages of the spire.

In the vestibule a stone rib-vault. Inner vestibule with a diagonally-ribbed ceiling. Staircases off each side; in front, a corridor runs the length of the building. At its w end a stair-hall by *Hardy & Wight*, 1893. Imperial stair with bowed landing and cast-iron balustrades. Flat ribbed ceiling with a central lantern. The church takes up the whole of the first floor, a vast space roofed in a single span with a very flat-arched rib-vault of plaster. Four-centred arches spring from clustered piers to form a screen across the E bay. Here, the platform designed by *Gillespie Graham* and *Pugin* as the THRONE BENCH for the Lord High Commissioner to the General Assembly was converted by *Robert Matheson* in 1857–8 to serve also as a pulpit, the spired canopy brought forward as a sounding-board. Richly traceried E screen by *Gillespie Graham* and *Pugin*. – U-plan GALLERY by *Matheson*, 1858–9.* – ORGAN above the platform by *Hope-Jones & Co.*, 1902, with a thinly traceried case. – Mildly Art Nouveau ELECTROLIERS by *Charles Henshaw*, 1905. – In the upper hall (by *Hardy & Wight*, 1893) a straight-coved and elaborately ribbed ceiling.

18 TRINITY COLLEGE CHURCH, Chalmers Close. Mary of Gueldres, James II's queen, founded the college in 1460 or slightly earlier. The site was in the valley between the Old Town and the Calton Hill, on the w side of Leith Wynd. Work on the church began immediately and continued to the end of the century. Despite a renewed burst of activity in the early 1530s, the nave was never begun.‡ The choir and tran-

---

* Originally there was a gallery at the w end only.

‡ A papal indulgence of 1531 mentions the choir as complete, so it is likely that the transepts were in hand during the 1530s. Their loop tracery was appropriate for that date.

septs were a parish church from *c.* 1580 till 1848* when the North British Railway bought the site and the building was dismantled under the supervision of *David Bryce*; the stones, carefully numbered, were deposited on the Calton Hill. Rebuilding on the present site between the High Street and Jeffrey Street began only in 1872, by which time many stones had been pilfered: this was given as the reason for recreating no more than the main body of the choir without aisles or transepts. *John Lessels* used it as the cross bar of a T-plan church with the stalk on the N side (demolished in 1964).

Before it was taken down the choir was three bays long with an apse, aisles and a clearstorey with flying buttresses. On the N side was a two-storey sacristy, on the S a shallow vaulted porch squeezed in between buttresses (cf. e.g. Roslin Chapel, Lothian). The transepts were single compartments projecting slightly beyond the line of the aisles, and the crossing tower was low, with a saddleback roof aligned E to W. The traces of the nave on the W face of the transept showed that it was to be uniform with the choir.

The present external appearance is unimpressive apart from the apse, whose huge lancets and deep buttresses are seen to best advantage from Trunk's Close. The general arrangement and the plan – five sides of an octagon shallower than wide – follow the original design, but there have been several changes of detail; the most important are the lowering in pitch of the centre window head, the removal of evidence for tracery, and the addition to the buttresses of niches which belonged to the aisle buttresses. Reset over the windows are bits of capitals not used in 1872. On the SE face of the apse and the S side of the choir, gargoyles and two cornices of which parts must come from the aisles or transepts. In the S wall three clearstorey windows above three former aisle windows. The tracery is not original.‡ Many stones in the jambs and heads still have the key numbers painted on before the dismantling. In the W wall a large four-light window from one of the end walls of the transept, somewhat shortened and minus a transom. The simple loop tracery looks early C16, and this must be the date of two pieces of capitals set above the window. Both have shields with initials in Roman characters, IB on one, ID on the other (for John Brady, provost from 1502, and John Dingwall, provost 1525–32?). In the gable a cusped oculus from the W wall of one of the transepts. The N wall was rebuilt without windows on account of the new N wing, which projected where there is now harling. The outermost parts of the two E bays of the arcade protrude from the wall. Reset high up are two pieces of capital from the crossing piers and two pieces of niche canopies.

* The pre-1848 appearance of the church is preserved in a number of engravings and drawings, notably the plates in vol. II of Billings' *Baronial and Ecclesiastical Antiquities* (1847). The Edinburgh Room of the Edinburgh Central Public Library has a book of photographs showing the exterior immediately before demolition.

‡ Before 1849 the only old tracery in the choir was in the N clearstorey and the E window of the N aisle, all of two lights below a mouchette.

Even in its curtailed state, the interior is recognizably the
noblest of any Scottish collegiate church. It is a lofty space
about twice as high as broad, divided into three narrow bays
plus the apse. The arcades account for half the elevation. The
piers have, or had until they were walled up, four filleted
shafts in the cardinal directions with four chamfered pieces
between. Bell bases and crisp foliage capitals with shields and
grotesque masks. Arch mouldings virtually identical with
those of the contemporary E choir bays at St Giles. Clearstorey windows existed originally on the N side as well as on
the S. Tierceron vault with ridge ribs in both directions and
large, well carved bosses. The apse vault continues the system
of the straight bays, with two short extra ribs pushed in between the meeting of the apse ribs and the transverse rib of
the adjacent straight bay. The vault shafts rest on carved
corbels some way above the arcade capitals. Between the windows of the apse two image brackets. It seems to have escaped
mention in the literature that the elevation is very like that of
St Mary, Haddington: the only major difference is that the
proportions here are consistently taller. How then does one
define the relationship? It is tempting to regard the royal
church as the model and the less sophisticated Haddington as
the copy. Unfortunately the dates are inconclusive. Trinity
College was certainly in building by 1460, but at Haddington
we do not know for certain when work started, only that in
1462 the owners of the benefice promised an annual payment
to the fabric.

Reset at the W end of the N wall the former sacristy door
(minus a richly decorated hoodmould). – Framed by the door,
a large canopied PISCINA from the N wall of the sacristy, the
jambs with Perp capitals C19. – In the W wall a very fine C15
FIREPLACE from a house in Sandilands Close demolished
when the church was rebuilt. Jamb-shafts with fillet and
bands of foliage between. Knobbly foliage on the bases. On
each of the capitals two pairs of seated figures, male and
female – obviously domestic scenes but the subjects are not
clear. The only comparably sculpted fireplace is in the S range
at Linlithgow Palace. The hood is C19. – In the close S of the
church several CARVED STONES including two pieces of capitals, niche canopies and corbels either from niches or the
choir aisle vaults.* – The sole survivors of the original furnishings, the pair of PAINTED PANELS from an altarpiece
attributed to *Hugo van der Goes* (now in the National Gallery
of Scotland), are the most impressive evidence remaining for
the very extensive Scottish patronage of Flemish art in the
C15.

23 TRON CHURCH, High Street. Disused. A hybrid of the C17-
19 but a most superior one. It was built by *John Mylne Jun.*,
principal master-mason to the Crown and the Town, and

* Further collections of carved stones not re-used are at the Lady Stair's House
Museum (*see* Royal Mile, Lawnmarket) and at Craigcrook Castle (*see* Craigleith
and Ravelston: Mansion).

Tron Church, 1753
(after William Whitland)

John Scott, master wright, in 1636–47 to house a congregation ejected when St Giles became a cathedral. Not surprisingly it was up-to-date in style and plan. T-shaped, with a S aisle opposite the pulpit and a barely projecting tower over the door at the centre of the N front. Galleries at E and W and a 'small' S gallery. Stylistically, Gothic survival and classical elements mingled. Round-arched traceried windows with raised voussoirs supporting triangular pediments. Buttresses with obelisk pinnacles at the outer bays. Obelisk pinnacles again at the centre, this time carried on fluted Ionic pilasters with panelled lower parts, seemingly of direct Dutch derivation. Also Dutch is the treatment of the round-arched and corniced door in the centre under a cartouche inscribed

> ÆDEM HANC CHRISTO ET
> ECCLESIÆ SACRARUNT
> CIVES EDINBURGENSI
> ANNO MDCXLI

Above, a keyblocked round window under an open pediment, its tympanum carved by *Alexander Mylne* with the Town arms. A short spire* was added to the tower by *Thomas Sandilands* in 1671. Something of the sort was probably intended from the start. The plain doors flanking the centre were slapped in 1718.

In the major reconstruction of 1785–7 by *John Baxter Jun.* (part of the works to form South Bridge and Hunter Square) the S aisle was demolished, the buttresses removed, and the body of the church shortened from five to three bays. In fact only half of each of the end bays was lopped off, the half-bays being disguised with coupled pilasters copied from those at the centre. The gables were given a 'nave-and-aisles' treatment with obelisk finials on shallow pediments. Tracery of the most convincing mid-C17 sort in the windows. At the S the centre is very slightly advanced and pedimented. More C17-type tracery in its three-light window, which is blind below gallery level, the ashlar infilling formerly painted as lattice-glazing. In the fire of 1824 the steeple was burned and subsequently demolished to the level of the main entablature. In 1828 it was rebuilt to a new and considerably taller design by *R. & R. Dickson*, mixing mid-C17 classical and Gothic survival with Georgian classicism. Two tall stages. The lower is square with channelled pilasters and a mid-C17 traceried window at each face. Above the parapet, scrolled clock-faces and octagonal corner piers linked by round-arched flying buttresses to the tall octagonal upper stage. Then a smaller octagon with round openings and a stone spire of St Martin-in-the-Fields derivation. The steeple was largely refaced in *Andrew Renton*'s restoration of 1974–6.

The interior has been gutted. It had a gallery round three

---

* Of timber covered with lead and 'after the form of the [Holyrood] Abay Kirk steeple but 10 feet higher', in outline it was very similar to the spire surviving at Stirling Town House.

sides and the pulpit at the N. At the base of the tower the mid-C17 porch with a turnpike stair (the original access to the galleries) at the NW corner. Semicircular arches springing from giant Roman Doric columns open to E, W and S, the S arch twice the width of the others and moulded with an undulating curve. Similarly moulded arch to the S aisle, on Roman Doric half-columns, with on each side the remains of small round-arched windows. – The ROOF is fully the equal of that in Parliament Hall. Both are by *John Scott* and both of hammerbeam type, but here of sexfoil rather than cinquefoil profile and expressing the roof outside rather than trussing an almost flat roof. – STAINED GLASS. E and W windows (scenes from the Life of Christ) by *James Ballantine & Son*, 1870 and 1872. – S windows (David, Moses and Elijah) by *Ballantine & Gardiner*, c. 1900. – Window at the NW (Christ as the Sower and Good Shepherd) by *Ballantine & Gardiner*, c. 1890. – Excavation has revealed the remains of Marlin's Wynd, a close of the later C16.

PUBLIC BUILDINGS

CANONGATE TOLBOOTH, Canongate. The tower was built in 74 1591, the courtroom block to the E at the same time or soon after. This is Canongate's expression of burghal pride, so the tower above its vaulted pend to Tolbooth Wynd has conical-roofed bartizans at the front with quatrefoil gunloops, and a conical spire rising from flattened broaches. Splayed gunloops in the wall of the tower at the same level. Not very practical, but an impressive display. Panel above the pend arch inscribed with the date 1591, the Burgh motto PATRIAE ET POSTERIS and the initials SLB for Sir Lewis Bellenden, the lay successor of the Abbots of Holyrood and the superior of the Burgh. Burgh arms on the lintel of the window above. A large clock, dated 1884, sticks out over the street on scrolled wrought-iron brackets. Forestair and lean-to stair-turret in the angle of the courtroom block, which is quite domestic but has a rectangular oriel at the E end, partly balancing the tower. In the centre of the block, a large pedimented frame with upright thistles at the corners and a blowsy crowned thistle at the apex, the tympanum inscribed

I R 6   IUSTICIA ET PIETAS VALIDE SUNT PRINCIPIS ARCES

In this frame the Burgh arms. They are late C19, as is a good deal of the rest of the courthouse block, which acquired its appearance in *Robert Morham*'s restoration of 1875. He provided a new roof of steeper pitch, and a parapet, and replaced three piended dormers with four steeply pedimented ones (as shown in Gordon of Rothiemay's elevational map of 1647). The ground floor is very largely his, the rear almost entirely. Inside, the whole of the first and attic floors were thrown into one (now a museum).

CASTLEHILL RESERVOIR, Castlehill. Long low ashlar block by
  *Rendel & Beardmore,** 1849–50. Channelled base. Pedimented door to Castlehill. In the middle of the Ramsay Garden front, an Italianate tower on a blind basement. On the w
  wall an Art Nouveau DRINKING FOUNTAIN by *John Duncan*,
  1894, commemorating the execution of witches near this spot.
  Bronze relief of witches' heads entwined by a snake.
CASTLEHILL SCHOOL, Castlehill. By *Robert Wilson*, 1896.
  Lumpy baronial with red sandstone dressings. Built into the
  E wall on to Boswell's Court, an early C16 ogee-arched door
  from the Duchess of Gordon's House.
78 CITY CHAMBERS, High Street. The only C18 public building
  in the Royal Mile, large and decorous round a forecourt. In
  1753 an Act was passed 'for erecting several publick buildings
  in the City of Edinburgh', including a covered merchants'
  exchange.‡ In August of that year the Town Council adopted
  a scheme by *John Adam*, but appointed as contractors§ the
  'Gentlemen of Mary's Chappel', a consortium of tradesmen
  including the architect *John Fergus*. The agreement signed in
  June 1754 was accompanied by Fergus's elevation, a modification of Adam's scheme.
    Adam designed a three-sided courtyard open to High
  Street on the s; plain four-storey ranges with Gibbs surrounds at the first-floor and cornices at the second-floor windows, the only flourish a pediment with urns and sculptured
  tympanum in the middle. Arcaded ground floor to the court;
  and shops in the E and w ranges. The N arcade provided a
  loggia for the exchange. At the s ends of the E and w ranges,
  Venetian windows in round-headed over-arches. Fergus's
  amendments added punch. He emphasized the centrepiece
  with fluted Corinthian pilasters and reduced its third-floor
  windows to horizontal openings in the frieze.‖ The s side of
  the court was closed with a one-storey arcaded screen of
  shops, giving the air of a French *hôtel*. On the w side it proved
  impossible to buy the substantial tenement of Writers Court,
  which broke slightly forward from part of the building line.
  Fergus tried to disguise this by slightly advancing the four
  equivalent N bays of the E side, but his proposal for wooden
  pilasters on the front of Writers Court and stone pilasters on
  the answering part of the E side was dropped. At the back the
  ground falls abruptly and the building is an unadorned twelve
  storeys, the centre and the E end bay slightly advanced. No
  attempt here to camouflage the continuing presence of
  Writers Court at the w.

  * Playfair's pupil *James Leslie* was the engineer in charge.
  ‡ The proposals which led to the Act were much more ambitious, including
  provision of a meeting place for the Convention of Royal Burghs, a Council
  Chamber for the City, an official residence for the Lord Provost, an Advocates
  Library and a Register House, all in the same building.
  § The Adam design was commissioned in 1752. John and Robert Adam seem to
  have tendered unsuccessfully for the building contract.
  ‖ Fergus's contract elevation showed a shallower entablature above the windows,
  and unfluted pilasters.

When completed in 1761 the City Chambers housed only one public office: the upper floors of the N range were leased to the Government as a Customs House and the rest was used as shops, coffee-houses, printing-offices and flats. The Town Council got a toehold in the W block in 1762, took over the N range as City Chambers in 1811, and between 1849 and 1893 bought the entire building. In 1898-9 *Robert Morham* remodelled the Writers Court section, carefully matching its courtyard front with the N bays of the E range, but in a different stone. Less careful was his rebuilding of the S screen as a groin-vaulted open arcade in 1900-1: the depth was reduced to a uniform one bay, the bays next the ends advanced as carriage entrances, and a large sculptured coat of arms placed over the centre.* At the same time Morham refronted the S end of the W range (already altered) in a free interpretation of the C18 scheme, with a tripartite window under a fanlight. In 1901-4 he pushed out a NW extension, Edwardian Baroque with a columned aedicule at the centre top-floor window and sculpture above. Finally in 1930-4 *E.J. MacRae* extended the High Street front with wings to E and W, picking up motifs from the existing buildings. A segmental-pedimented doorpiece (by *John Lessels*, 1859) at the S end of the E range became the motif for the E wing.

INTERIOR. The main C18 feature was the entrance from the centre of the N range into the great staircase leading to the first-floor boardroom of the Customs House. The present character of vestibule and stair-hall is chiefly due to *MacRae*, who in 1936-8 panelled the walls and enlarged the windows, filling them with bright stained glass (SS. Giles, Cuthbert, Margaret and Malcolm Canmore) by *Margaret Chilton*. Above courtyard level the stair is of 1753-61, with turned balusters and moulded handrails; its continuation downwards was begun by *Morham* in 1875. The broken-pedimented doorpiece on the first floor is the entrance to an anteroom which served the two front rooms, but now opens E through a Corinthian-columned screen by *David Cousin*, 1859, into the Old Council Room, the C18 Customs House. Pine panelling with a modillion cornice and coved ceiling. Broken pediments with Rococo enriched friezes at the doors, and a scrolled overmantel. In one of the niches for sculpture in the E wall a C17 figure. The Dunedin Room to the W was made *c.* 1870 (from two earlier rooms) by *Cousin*, with a compartmented classical ceiling; wainscoting by *Scott Morton & Co.*, 1955. Imported into the Lord Provost's Room in 1936 (together with the Dutch tiles in the fireplace) a pine and gesso Leith chimneypiece of *c.* 1780, with slim columned shafts and a rose and thistle frieze. In Committee Room A in the E range, a coved ceiling and pompous plain wainscoting by *Morham*, 1889. In the S first-floor room of the W range a splendid C18 chimneypiece. Consoled fireplace surround and

* In 1980-1 the screen was extensively refaced, and the crowning urns renewed by *Dick Reid*.

scrolled overmantel painted with the City arms; pulvinated
frieze and broken pediment. At the N of the W range, rooms
of 1898-9. Wainscoting and a green marble chimneypiece in
the Councillors' Smoke Room. Armorial stained glass by
Margaret Chilton and *Marjorie Kemp*, 1932. The Dining
Room attempts splendour with pairs of fluted Ionic pilasters.
Wall paintings of historical scenes by *William Hole*, 1903-9.
The New Council Room of 1901-4 is the grandest of the
Morham interiors, rectangular, with the end bays divided off
by Ionic columns. Central square top-lit from a coffered
dome with rosettes at the lower tiers and stained glass above.
Ceiling above the public gallery with five shallow groin-
vaults. Armorial chimneypiece, mahogany wainscoting and an
armorial frieze in olive-green and gold. The Public Office on
the ground floor of the W range was built in 1898-9 as the
new Burgh Courtroom, neo-Baroque, with coupled pilasters
and oak wainscoting. Ionic columns at the N end, the site of
the bench. Baroque doorpiece in the W wall. The Adamesque
woodwork in the E wall looks later. Under the building substantial remains of the early C16 MARY KING'S CLOSE.

In the courtyard, STATUE of Alexander and Bucephalus by
John Steell, modelled in 1832 but not cast until 1883, and
moved here from St Andrew Square in 1916. Classical but
far from frigid.

DUCHESS OF GORDON'S SCHOOL, Horse Wynd. Jacobean of
1846. Converted into chauffeurs' quarters for Holyroodhouse,
c. 1920.

99 EDINBURGH CENTRAL PUBLIC LIBRARY, George IV Bridge.
By *G. Washington Browne*, 1887-90, realizing the picturesque
capabilities of the François I manner. Taller main block a
Greek cross on plan, the corner filled in with gabled jambs.
E front pilastered, arched and panelled like a simpler version
of François I's villa at Moret, and reached by its own bridge
from the street, since it actually stands in Cowgate four storeys below. Wrought-iron GATES by *Thomas Tait*. Steep pavilion roof with triple-pedimented dormers on four sides,
crowned with a two-stage octagonal lantern derived from the
Hôtel d'Écoville at Caen. To the r. a full-height jamb (its aedicular dormer from the same source) pushing forward to the
street, and in the angle a turret with dome and drum (Saint-
Germain-en-Laye). The S elevation to Cowgate is severe till
it reaches the higher level of George IV Bridge. Inside, the
landing hall lies straight across the vestibule, which has a
Doric screen at each end. The main staircase to the N is a
broad dog-leg with delicate half-balusters planted on square
posts. At the upper landing an aedicular recess with a bust of
Andrew Carnegie by *Charles McBride*, 1891. Corinthian arcades to W and E, and a compartmented ceiling with little
pendants. One of the doorways in the S wall is from the (E)
entry to Sir Thomas Hope's house in Cowgate, inscribed
TECUM HABITA 1616. The other opens into the reference
hall, of Greek cross plan with pilastered arcades across each

arm. Domed ceiling, with glazed coffers lit from the dormers above. At second basement level, a doorway from the w entry to Hope's house, inscribed AT HOSPES HUMO, leads to the Scottish Library, with its plain Ionic columns. The mezzanine, added in 1958, houses the Edinburgh Library.

EDINBURGH DENTAL HOSPITAL, Chambers Street. Tired Renaissance by *Begg & Lorne Campbell*, 1925-7, borrowing details (literally in the case of the l. pilaster) from the adjacent block. Recessed canted-bay attic windows hint at modernism. The original pedimented doorpiece was removed in 1952-4 as part of the alterations by *R. Rowand Anderson, Kininmonth & Paul*, whose rear extension has the same massing as *R. Rowand Anderson & Balfour Paul*'s unexecuted scheme of 1937.

FREE CHURCH COLLEGE AND H. M. COMMISSARY OFFICE, North Bank Street. Jacobean by *David Cousin*, 1858-63. Large five-storey and attic front divided into two unequal parts by a pavilion-roofed tower. Symmetrical E part with strapwork pediments and a conical-roofed centre turret at the head. Richer detail at the tower and W part, with tall strapworked aedicules at the second floor, segmental pediments at the third. Bartizan at the corner. The back half of the building is higher, with an elaborate turreted tower on the r. The rear to James Court is very plain, still Georgian except for a small and bleak E tower.

Inside, a vestibule with Artisan Mannerist Roman Doric pilasters and a stained-glass window by *James Ballantine*. The main room is the Presbytery Hall, with rectangular alcoves at each end. Panelling with coupled Corinthian pilasters, fluted and strapworked. Strapwork frieze. Artisan Mannerist chimneypiece. The woodwork by *J. R. Swann*, incorporating two mid-C18 over-door panels. Coved ceiling with strapwork and pendants. In the W window stained glass (Reforming Divines) by *Ballantine*, 1862. The Common Hall is also panelled. Ionic chimneypieces, festooned frieze and barrel-vaulted ceiling with gridiron ribs. It looks c. 1880.

GEORGE IV BRIDGE. By *Thomas Hamilton*, 1829-34, providing the s approach to the city under the 1827 Improvement Act. Built up on both sides as an elevated street, but with two open spans. Over Cowgate a round arch on oblong piers; groin-vault. Over Merchant Street a semi-elliptical vault under a ring-arch. Cast-iron railing with anthemion quatrefoils, replaced beside the National Library of Scotland (*see* below) with stone balusters as part of the library design.

GEORGE HERIOT'S SCHOOL (main entry now from Lauriston 76 Place). A prodigy of Scots Renaissance architecture on a platform site to the s of the Castle and the Old Town. It was started in 1628 by *William Wallace* (principal master mason to the crown from 1617) and finished c. 1700. The royal goldsmith and banker George Heriot † 1624 had left £23,625 sterling for the building of a hospital, i.e. a charity school, on a site at the foot of Gray's Close. One of the three 'overseers and supervisors' named in Heriot's will was his nephew Walter Balcanquall, subsequently Dean of Rochester. His was the choice of the plan, which is that of a palace in Serlio's seventh Book of Architecture, *c.* 1550.* As realized on the new site purchased from the Town, it is 49 m. square with large corner towers, and contains a 28 m. square courtyard with stair-turrets in the internal angles. The main differences from its model are that the arcaded ground-floor 'piazza' is omitted from the S (chapel) and W (refectory) sides, and the stair-turrets are quasi-octagonal; so are the additional central turrets on the E and W sides and the chapel bay on the S.

Work began in 1628 at the NW tower, and seems to have reached first-floor level by 1631 when Wallace died; his mason's mark, a saltire cross with a heart at the top right, is frequent on the pilastered N arcade of the courtyard. His former assistant *William Ayton* (with *John Watt*) went on till 1639 when the income from the bequest failed for a time. In 1642 (when Watt died) the spectacular but troublesome lead ogee roofs on the two N towers were dismantled and the attic between them built up, incorporating the existing dormers. In 1644 Ayton contracted to build the square belfry of the entrance tower and in 1648 *John Mylne Jun.*, master mason, and *John Scott*, master wright, suggested taking down the SW tower roof, but it was not till the end of the century that the two S towers were given flat roofs like those at the N. Cromwell requisitioned the building as a military hospital after the Battle of Dunbar (1650), but thirty boys in regulation sad-russet and black hats at last took up residence in 1659. The chapel was fitted out from that at the Leith Citadel in 1673, and in 1676 the top of the entrance tower was to be built to the drawing 'condescended upon be Sir William Bruce'. It may have been this design that *Robert Mylne* and *James Smith* agreed to build in 1684, but nothing happened until 1693, when *Robert Mylne* contracted to build the octagonal dome and lantern.

The elevations of Heriot's Hospital have large corner towers four storeys high and two bays wide. Otherwise they have nothing in common with the Serlio design (superimposed orders over a rusticated basement). Precedents for the detail and composition can be found in the corner-towered houses of Jacobean England such as Audley End (1603). The single-light aedicular windows‡ are characteristic of Wallace's earlier work at Edinburgh Castle and Linlithgow Palace, Lothian, but at Heriot's he disposed them with impressive authority, generally emphasizing the intermediate wall-space. The Laudian Gothic windows of the chapel may not be his design but are used in the same way, save for the central bay whose tall windows are higher than the wall itself, ending

---

* This was first noted by Sir John Summerson, *Architecture in Britain 1530–1830* (Pelican History of Art).

‡ Hippolyte Blanc (1906) compared their two hundred and nine pediments and strapwork heads, and found only two the same.

with a large ogee half-dome.* Far larger were the four ogee roofs (recalling Danish examples) which formerly crowned the profusion of lesser domes and turrets; without them the corner towers with their bartizans and gargoyles have an almost military baldness. Hybrid and incomplete as it is, this is a palace indeed, its jackdaw invention transcended by the four-square magnificence of the whole.

The best approach today is from the w gate of Greyfriars' Churchyard. An entry between walled parterres originally led to the entrance (N) front which is built entirely of Ravelston stone – not only the buckle quoins and other dressings but the ashlar wall between (the other outer walls, formerly harled, were faced with Craigleith stone by *Alexander Black* in 1833). In the entrance tower a two-stage centrepiece with paired Roman Doric columns on each side of the rusticated pend arch. In the frieze, reliefs of goldsmithing, Charity, and Heriot's boys. Above, obelisks and strapwork and a twisty-columned aedicule containing George Heriot's initials and heraldry, with the star and roses that are repeated all over the building. Massive timber doors, and a vaulted pend into the court. On the rear wall a life-size statue of Heriot by *Robert Mylne* in an aediculed niche, with the inscription CORPORIS HAEC, ANIMI EST HOC OPUS EFFIGIES (This statue represents my body, this work my soul). A sundial overhead, and royal portrait busts in cartouches above the second-floor windows, whose moulded base and entablature are continuous. More sundials on the central chimney gables of the E and W sides of the court, the chimneys throughout being of Wallace's type with concave octagonal shafts. On the W side the refectory doorway (rusticated Roman Doric with suppressed pilasters) from Vignola's Farnese villa at Caprarola.‡ On the S, opposite the courtyard entry, the pedimented Corinthian doorway of the chapel from Francini's Book of Architecture, 1631, at the base of an ogee-roofed oriel turret. On each side, as on the outer S front, a big œil-de-bœuf above a Gothic window.

The CHAPEL furnishings are now Puginian Gothic by *James Gillespie Graham*, 1837, with big arched trusses and a cusped ceiling. Patterned glazing in jewel colours. The former REFECTORY (west laigh hall) has a giant flat-arched Renaissance fireplace of stone at each end. Over a door a plain Grecian monument to James Denholm † 1822. Ceiling with bold square and cross compartments, possibly a restoration by *Playfair*. COUNCIL CHAMBER in the SW tower, furnished in 1690. Oak panelling, with Corinthian pilasters framing the moulded fireplace and overmantel, which has the Heriot arms in a carved leafy cartouche with swags. Tunnel-vaulted CHARTER ROOM adjacent. The other ground-floor rooms, and

* Gordon of Rothiemay's drawing (1647) anticipated a Gothic crown in this position.

‡ These sources were first noted by Alistair Rowan in *Country Life*, 6 March 1975.

those on the upper floors, were much altered by *John Anderson* in 1908 when the school was adapted for day pupils (total capacity now 1500).

GATEHOUSE on the S axis, in Lauriston Place, by *William H. Playfair*, 1829. A deep archway in full-dress Heriot's style with pepperpots and waterspouts and flanking lodges. Also by Playfair the balustrated terrace round the main building. The rest clockwise, starting at the SW corner of the large N playground. The HALL by *Donald A. Gow*, 1893, has plenty of Heriot's detail but its lanterned tower is a scaled-down parody of the original and a fussy entry to the 26 by 15 m. hammerbeamed hall itself. The CHEMISTRY BLOCK by *John Anderson*, 1911, is subtler; a big symmetrical front with a central oriel, its C17 quotations fewer and more telling. The single-storey PREPARATORY DEPARTMENT by *Reid & Forbes*, 1933, sticks to their own Art Deco classical style but its rubbly three-storey wing facing the Vennel has an effectively stepped parapet. The SCIENCE BLOCK by *John Chesser*, 1887, is an enlargement of *Alexander Black*'s Primary School (1838) with the entrance tower re-assembled at a higher level – an unpretentious miniature in the Heriot's style. SWIMMING POOL of 1856, the roof of its covered entry slanting downhill to the pool itself. WAR MEMORIAL to the E by *James B. Dunn*, 1922, a pelican-topped column on a balustraded platform.

HERIOT-WATT UNIVERSITY,* Chambers Street. A shambling public building begun by *David Rhind* for the Watt Institute in 1872. Originally five bays with standard Renaissance detail, a French-roofed entrance pavilion on the l., all following *David Cousin*'s elevation for the N side of Chambers Street. This elevation was disregarded by Cousin himself when he added the Phrenological Museum on the w. Just two bays, on the l. a canted bay-window with heads as keystones. The Institute took over the Museum in 1885. Alterations and extensions of 1886–8 by *John Chesser* were paid for by the George Heriot Trust; entrance pavilion rebuilt on a more opulent scale with columns at the rope-moulded door and first-floor bow window, a hammering cherub in the scrolly broken pediment and a wrought-iron crown on the French pavilion roof. Above the main door, BUSTS of George Heriot and Leonard Horner. To its r., bronze STATUE of James Watt by *Peter Slater*, 1854, copied from the seated figure by *Chantrey*. Chesser's E and W additions are in the Cousin manner. Rear wing by *Esmé Gordon*, 1952, linking to a bleak barracks fronting Cowgate (by *E. J. MacRae*, 1932–4).

INFIRMARY STREET BATHS, Infirmary Street. Rough Italianate, by *Robert Morham*, 1885–7.

KING'S BRIDGE, carrying Johnston Terrace (*see* Other Streets,

---

* Founded in 1821 as the School of Arts for the spare-time teaching of science relevant to the trades. In 1851 it became known as the Watt Institution and School of Art (after James Watt) and in 1855 as the Heriot-Watt College. It received its charter in 1966. The main campus is at Riccarton (*see The Buildings of Scotland: Lothian*).

below) over King's Stables Road. By *Thomas Hamilton*, 1829–32. A long, wide tunnel-vault of channelled masonry, the arches emerging obliquely from the grassy embankment and sweeping down to four pedestals with tall obelisks.

LOTHIAN REGION CHAMBERS, George IV Bridge and Parliament Square. Originally Midlothian County Council Buildings. Flabby Palladian by *J. Macintyre Henry*, 1900–5. Rusticated ground floor carrying pedimented temple fronts on the W and N, but it is the heavy windows which dominate. On the E, a giant order but no pediment. Instead, a deep frieze carved by *W. Birnie Rhind* with high reliefs of Agriculture, Mining and Fishing, a foretaste of Socialist Realism.

Holyrood revival is the dominant style inside. Marble pilastered entrance hall with a columned screen to the inner hall which opens on the l. into the stair-hall. Wrought iron balustrade with back-to-back winged ladies. Tall coved ceiling above a *putti*-rich frieze, more French Renaissance than Caroline. On the first floor, Ionic arcade dividing off a corridor to offices on the W and the courtroom in a lower S block. On the E is the Council Chamber. Elliptical tunnel vault with moulded plaster panels (like all the plasterwork, by *A. Hunter*). Fluted Corinthian pilasters along the walnut panelling and a pediment above the door.

LOTHIAN REGIONAL COUNCIL HEADQUARTERS, George IV Bridge. By *Robert Matthew, Johnson-Marshall & Partners*, 1968. Alternate horizontals of ashlar cladding and wood-framed windows disturbed off-centre by a recessed lift tower. No attempt to provide a stop at the Lawnmarket corner. Angular continuation of the curve of Victoria Terrace; the smooth line of Victoria Street below is inexplicably carried on in hammer-dressed stone.

MERCAT CROSS, High Street. By *Sydney Mitchell*, 1885, an octagonal shaft with a unicorn finial placed on top of an octagonal drum. But Mitchell did not begin from nothing. The capital is early C15, carved with dragons amid foliage. Both the capital and its shaft had been used in a rebuilding of the cross by *John Tailefer* and *John Mylne Sen.* in 1617, and were preserved (the shaft broken in pieces) after that cross was removed in 1756. In 1866 they were re-erected near the present site;* the unicorn (by *John Rhind* after a design by *James Drummond*) was added in 1869. The drum provided in 1885 was intended to be a near-replica of Tailefer and Mylne's drum of 1617 but Mitchell had only one late-C18 engraving to follow. It is smaller than its prototype – unavoidably, since the breaking of the 6m. shaft in 1756 had left usable fragments measuring only 4·25m.; Mitchell slimmed the shaft to preserve the proportions. The detailing of the drum looks rather too carefully Artisan Mannerist. Ionic columns at the corners and keyblocked round-headed

* On a simple stepped base, now supporting the Canongate Cross (*see* Canongate Parish Church, above).

arches at the faces. Above the door a Latin inscription composed by W. E. Gladstone who had paid for the work. Deep
parapet with corbelled angle-rounds. At the faces, heraldic
panels. The arms of Edinburgh were copied from a panel of
the 1617 cross but the other panels which had human heads
were not copied.* The present shaft is a replacement by the
City Architect's Department, 1970.

MILTON HOUSE SCHOOL, Canongate. By *Robert Wilson*,
1886. Red sandstone dressings and a crowstepped bellcote
gable. In the central stair-hall four large landscape panels by
William Delacour, 1758, survivors of *John Adam*'s Milton
House of 1755-8.

MORAY HOUSE COLLEGE OF EDUCATION, Holyrood Road.
A large building by *A. K. Robertson*, 1910-13. Unexciting
English Baroque front. In the courtyard, the main feature is
a Dutch Colonial gable between octagonal towers. To the E,
the pantiled C17 garden pavilion of Moray House (*see* Royal
Mile: Canongate, below). Round-arched openings with fan-
tailed voussoirs. Heraldic beasts used to sit on the ends. N of
the main quadrangle, a gateway with a strapwork pediment
of *c*. 1845. To the NE the Practice School, plainest Neo-Georgian by *Frank Wood*, 1932. Dalhousie Land, near the top of
St John's Street, is modern-traditional by *Gordon & Dey*,
1960-3. Charteris Land (1971) and St Mary's Land and
Chessel's Land (1980) by the same architects across the street
are more brutal but no better. Neo-Fascist gymnasium on the
s side of Holyrood Road, by *Gordon & Dey* again, 1968-70,
its huge flight of steps a test of fitness. Former Old Kirk on
the N side by *Anderson & Browne*, 1881-2: studied Scots style
with a canted bay between conical-roofed drum towers, badly
altered as part of the college.

NATIONAL LIBRARY OF SCOTLAND, George IV Bridge.
Timid classical modern by *Reginald Fairlie*,‡ designed in
1934-6, only the steel frame built by 1939, completed in
1950-5 by *A. R. Conlon*, who simplified some detail. Seven
storeys of book-stack below the bridge, to which there is a
long two-stage front with lower wings. Ground-floor windows high up above a rusticated base, then a very tall windowless upper stage with shallow pilasters framing flattish
sculpture. Tall figures by *Hew Lorimer*, the roundels above
by *Elizabeth Dempster*. Royal arms over the door by *Scott
Sutherland*. Figure panels on the wings by *James Barr*. Panels
on the N and S faces of the wings by *Maxwell Allan*. Interior
equally indeterminate in style. Huge engraved-glass stair window by *Helen Monro* to *Conlon*'s design. The reading room
was given a crudely modern gallery in 1973.

NEW COLLEGE AND ASSEMBLY HALL, Mound Place. By
William H. Playfair, 1845-50, built as a church (Free High
Church) and theological college for the Free Church.

* The arms and four other panels had been built into a wall at Abbotsford,
Borders, where they survive.
‡ Fairlie described it as 'frigid serenity'.

Cardboard-cutout Tudor front, the ecclesiastical towers of its gatehouse sited on the axis of Playfair's Royal Scottish Academy below and framing the spire of the Church of Scotland's Assembly Hall (*see* Tolbooth Church, above). The set-back lower tower at the l. hides the protruding gable of the church. Deliberately thin detail to emphasize the verticals of the design, thinnest of all at the pinnacled angle-buttresses whose polished ashlar contrasts with the stugged ashlar of the main walling. Groin-vaulted pend arch into the quadrangle. This is very collegiate, the church taking the traditional place of the chapel range, but with the Assembly Hall spire used as a focus for the s side. The inner front of the gatehouse forms a second gatehouse, the towers presented to the outside becoming boldly projecting octagonal towers of the Eton or St John's College (Cambridge) type. Opposite, a flight of steps flanked by tall ogee-roofed towers leads up towards the spire. (But the spire is not on the central axis of the quadrangle and the insistence on it as a focus is unsettling.) In the quadrangle, a bronze statue of John Knox by *John Hutchison*, 1895. In the N range was the Library, now Martin Hall. Flat ceiling with elaborate geometrical pattern of moulded ribs. War Memorial window by *Douglas Strachan*, 1922. In the old Free High Church, a Jacobean roof with pendants at the tie-beams, now painted in grey, blue, red and gold. Woodwork by *A. Lorne Campbell*, 1934-6, provided on the conversion into a library. Stained glass by *Douglas Strachan*, 1911-34.

The steps from the s of the quadrangle lead to the ASSEMBLY HALL, by *David Bryce*, 1858-9. To the quadrangle it shows only a pair of depressed-arch doors, an alteration by *Sydney Mitchell & Wilson*. The back facing Castlehill, extended E by *J. M. Dick Peddie* in 1885 and raised to two storeys (again by *Peddie*) in 1902-3, is now sub-Lorimer Gothic. The main entrance leads into the Assembly Hall corridor, originally open to the sky, later remodelled as a cloister with depressed arches. In it a low-relief bronze of John White by *P. Mortimer* and two C16 lintels from Sempill House. The hall consists of a very broad and low nave and aisles, covered by a giant brown-stained roof with barely any concession to elegance. Square timber columns with cantilever brackets carry trusses of huge span dividing the roof into four compartments. Boarding with pendants at the inner compartments, skylights at the outer. U-plan gallery round the Moderator's dais. The committee-room extension at the E was incorporated into the hall in 1902-3. Stained glass (David) by *Douglas Strachan*.

w of the Assembly Hall the RAINY HALL by *Sydney Mitchell & Wilson*, 1899-1900. Perp N front. Inside, walls panelled to a height of 3 m. with painted shields at the top of the panels. More shields at the corbels, from which springs the elaborate painted and gilded hammerbeam roof. All this is by *James Clark* to the architect's specification. At the E end a bronze low-relief of Robert Rainy by *David Wissaert*, 1915.

NORTH CANONGATE INFANT SCHOOL, New Street. Queen Anne style in red sandstone, by *Robert Wilson*, 1900-1. Two shaped gables and a cupola bellcote.

OLD HIGH SCHOOL, High School Yards. By *Alexander Laing*, 1777, a long two-storey piend-roofed block of droved ashlar. Pedimented Roman Doric portico in the centre. Advanced ends. At the back, the off-centre tower was heightened and given an ogee lead roof by *R. Rowand Anderson & Balfour Paul* in 1906-7.

OLD SURGEONS' HALL, Surgeons Square. By *James Smith*, 1697. Originally a two-storey and nine-bay piend-roofed block with semi-octagonal towers at the ends. An extra floor was added in the C19 and the first-floor windows enlarged. The door's lugged architrave is C17, its pediment a replacement.*

OLD SURGICAL HOSPITAL, Drummond Street. A long Renaissance block by *David Bryce*, 1848-53. Linked wall-head chimneys at the end pavilions. At the centrepiece, a scroll-sided pediment of della Porta inspiration; the pedimented dormers of the links are smaller versions of this. Groin-vaulted carriage-pend under the large rear wing by *Rowand Anderson & Balfour Paul*, 1906-7. At the NW a surviving if altered pavilion of *William Adam*'s Infirmary of 1738-48. Horizontal first-floor windows and rusticated quoins. Also from the Infirmary the fluted and heavily rusticated GATE-PIERS on the S axis. Wonderfully elaborate urns carved with grotesque heads and foliaged swags. They were moved here in 1906-7 when *Rowand Anderson & Balfour Paul* built the SCREEN WALL.

POLICE CHAMBERS, Parliament Square. By *William Nixon*, 1845-9. A sober stop to the Law Courts. Plain classical with a Doric porch. Round-headed attic windows give an Italianate hint.

REID SCHOOL OF MUSIC, Teviot Row. Unfussy Italianate by *David Cousin*, 1858. Concert Hall inside with a coffered semi-elliptical tunnel vault. – ORGAN by *Jorgen Ahrend*, 1978, its case by *Ian G. Lindsay & Partners*.

96 ROYAL SCOTTISH MUSEUM, Chambers Street. Big-scale Lombardic Renaissance by *Francis Fowke*, 1861, the centre and E part (with a bridge link to the university museum) built under *Robert Matheson* by 1865, the main block finished in 1871-5, the W wing (with a simplified flank) built under *W. W. Robertson* in 1885-9. Two-storey main block with balustrades and urns, advanced three-storey wings with deep cornices and red Roman-tiled roofs, all on a massive channelled base that deepens with the long slope of the street. Superimposed pilaster orders throughout, and pilastered ground-floor windows in the wings. All other windows arcaded, with red sandstone shafts, varied both in their grouping and their glazing. In the wings the arcades are directly

* The original pediment is now built into Surgeons' Hall (*see* South Side).

glazed; in the main block they stand free, the glass set back in a second rank of arches and revealing arched galleries within. In the centrepiece the glazing is still more deeply recessed. Main entrance reached by broad steps from the street. In the spandrels portrait busts of Victoria and Albert, Watt, Darwin, Michelangelo and Newton, on the parapet of Natural History, Science and Applied Art, all by *John Rhind*, 1859.

The GREAT HALL in the main block is a huge elegant bird- 97 cage of glass and iron, 82 m. by 21 m. high, with galleried aisles and a lofty nave spanned by stilted timber arches on slender iron columns. Iron balustrades of miniature stilted arches run round the galleries and up the staircases which are concentric with the apsidal ends. Between the façade and the great hall are spacious galleries or 'cloisters', on the ground floor with a long vista of transverse arches and the original pavement of tile and mosaic in good strong colours. Similar pavement in the great hall replaced by polished travertine as part of the new decorative scheme in 1971. More iron-framed halls to the s and in the wings, but less dramatic, and further halls and a staircase to the s, dry Neo-Classical by *W. T. Oldrieve*, 1910-14. Extension to the sw fronting Brighton Street by *H.M. Office of Works*, 1934-7. Lecture theatre by *Stewart Sim* in a fussy Festival-of-Britain style, 1958-61.

ST CECILIA'S HALL, Cowgate. Built for the Musical Society of Edinburgh in 1761-3 from *Robert Mylne*'s design under *George Paterson*'s supervision. The front is to Niddry Street, two storeys with a pedimented centre and console-corniced doorpiece. The asymmetrical harled bays each side were originally hidden by buildings forming a small court. The hall was bought by the Grand Lodge in 1809 and the plain two-storey block fronting Cowgate added in 1812. The resulting L-plan was filled out to a rectangle in 1966-8 by *Ian G. Lindsay & Partners* for the University of Edinburgh, with curtain-walling on a stone base. Inside, the ground floor of the original building forms three nearly equal compartments. The N two, opening into each other with semi-elliptical arches, form the Laigh Hall. To the s the foyer, with a Roman Doric columned screen and Imperial stair. Slim fluted balusters. On the first floor is the Concert Room, its oval shape restored in 1966-8, with a shallow oval dome.

ST PATRICK'S R.C. PRIMARY SCHOOL, Drummond Street. Symmetrical blocky Scots Renaissance with crowsteps and some mild Art Nouveau touches, by *John A. Carfrae*, 1905-6. Red sandstone with white stone dressings.

SALVATION ARMY HOSTEL (former Heriot's Trust school, Cowgate). In the C17 style of George Heriot's Hospital, by *Alexander Black*, 1840. Strapwork pediments over the first-floor windows of the main block; its arcaded ground floor was originally open as a covered playground. Taller projecting jamb at the SE with steep pediments over the second-floor windows and ogee-roofed bartizans.

SHERIFF COURTHOUSE, Lawnmarket. A large three-storey block on an island site by *A. J. Pitcher* and *J. Wilson Paterson* of *H.M. Office of Works*, 1934–7. Grim Neo-Georgian. Keyblocked openings in the rusticated ground floor, with a heavy bracketed cornice over the entrance. Shallower keyblocked windows above. Centrepiece with Roman Doric piers and a figure of Justice by *Alexander Carrick* in the pediment. The flanks are even less friendly. Antiseptic interior, the Roman Doric pilastered entrance hall lined with marble, Early Georgian style woodwork in the courts.

SOUTH BRIDGE. By *Robert Kay*,* 1785–8; *Alexander Laing* was the contractor. Nineteen arches but only the one across Cowgate is left open. On the E side of this arch, a mutuled cornice and railed parapet. It was widened to the W in 1929.

SOUTH BRIDGE PRIMARY SCHOOL, Infirmary Street. School Board Gothic by *Robert Wilson*, 1885. Tall and narrow with a bellcote at the centre gable. Extravagantly stilted arches at the first-floor windows.

80 UNIVERSITY OF EDINBURGH OLD QUAD, South Bridge and Chambers Street. The outside of the quadrangle is by *Robert Adam*, 1789, his greatest public work, the inside by *William H. Playfair*, 1819–27. There are overlaps between the two stages, but all the magnificent Greek Revival interiors are Playfair's. The dome is of 1879.

In 1785 it was agreed that the profits from feus along the proposed South Bridge should go to the building of a New College (i.e. University), for the Old College‡ was now decrepit. Adam's grandiose scheme for both bridge and college (1786) was not adopted, but he successfully sued the City for his fees and finally obtained the university job with a new and expanded brief. His final scheme had two courtyards, the first oblong (professors' residences), the second square (library, museum, graduation hall and teaching rooms), with a chapel between. Building began in 1789 with *John Paterson* in charge, but stopped in 1793 after the outbreak of the Napoleonic war and the death of Adam and of his cousin William Robertson, Principal of the University. A plan for economical completion submitted in 1810 by *Robert Reid* was dropped when government approval was at last obtained in 1815, but a competition was advertised on the lines he had suggested, 'leaving out the south front and the cross building which formed a small court in the original plan – regard always being had to the part already executed and to the preservation of the architecture of Mr Adam as far as practicable'.§ Playfair proposed that the dome should be built as Adam designed

---

* *Robert Adam* prepared a scheme in 1785 and Kay's design was modified in the light of Adam's comments in 1786.

‡ The University was founded by James VI in 1582. The name 'Old College' is now naturally, if confusingly, applied to the Adam-Playfair building.

§ The conditions were soon revised, and the omission of the s range and cross range was left to the discretion of competitors. *William Adam Jun.*, *William Burn*, *Richard Crichton*, *Archibald Elliot*, *Thomas Hamilton*, *James Milne* and *John Paterson* submitted designs, as well as Playfair.

it (a small-scale finial to the monumental E entrance); the large dome eventually built is however by *R. Rowand Anderson*, 1879, with a gilded figure of Youth bearing the torch of Learning by *John Hutchison*.

Nothing in Scotland is grander than Adam's ENTRANCE FRONT. 69 m. long, its massing enhanced by the upward slope of South Bridge from N to S, it has a major and two minor archways framed by Roman Doric columns and flanked by advanced distyle porticos of the same order, all giant monoliths of Craigleith stone. The entry is awe-inspiring. Plain domical vault in the centre, three groin-vaults on each side. Over the arches a great lunette,* and above the cornice a wide panel with inscription '... ARCHITECTO ROBERTO ADAM'. Three-bay links and pavilions, the windows set closer at the ends. By skilful juggling of the window-cornices and pediments, both first and second floors have the aspect of main storeys; the third floor is just a plain frieze with plain oblong windows punched in it. The N and S FRONTS (109 m. long) have end pavilions with Venetian over columned tripartite windows. The N side, originally facing the narrow lane of North College Street, follows Adam's design. At first only the E pavilion had its rusticated base and median guilloche frieze, but in 1888 *Anderson* suitably embellished the W and the pedimented intermediate pavilions as part of the architecture of Chambers Street. On the S side Playfair modified and subdued Adam's grand centrepiece and intermediate pavilions to suit his own larger library. On the W FRONT a more subtle change: the entablatures of the three Venetian windows in Adam's museum-block design are carried across their deeply arched centres, with a surprisingly Baroque result.

In the QUADRANGLE, Playfair repeated at the other three corners the Ionic-columned NW quadrant he inherited from Adam. His somewhat changed design for the W museum block (e.g. with doubled pilasters at the ends) is still an insufficient climax for his own splendid N and S elevations, their end-to-end Corinthian pilasters twice modulated into pedimented colonnades over the faculty entrances. The E side, an unhappy version of Adam's front with insufficient leg-room, is rendered still more inadequate by the ponderous dome overhead. There is no evidence of what Playfair intended for the courtyard. Peripheral balustraded terrace built before 1851 (possibly by *Thomas Brown*, as the City was still wholly responsible for the fabric) with far too many stairways. At the W end *Lorimer*'s worthy but boring War Memorial (1922) behind the central arch is an unsatisfactory focus. The stair was unsuitably modified c. 1960. The central area remains unpaved.

Of the INTERIORS, very few were completed by 1793.

---

* Kedleston is the obvious precursor of this arrangement, but Sir John Summerson has noted its connexion with a sketch design for a palace front drawn by Adam in 1758. Adam's 1786 scheme had a triumphal arch in the middle of the entrance screen.

Playfair's work is here described in chronological order.
Major changes since 1965 are by *Ian G. Lindsay & Partners*.
In the E RANGE Playfair made the unfinished professors'
houses to the N of the entrance into Society and teaching
rooms, and replanned most of the space to the S as a Senate
Hall, grand staircase, and Principal's house. The house at the
far S end was finished according to Adam and allotted to the
Librarian. In the so-called OLD SENATE ROOM on the ground
floor (mainly the work of *Robert Morham*, who converted the
houses for administrative use in 1883) the columnar screen
may have been moved from Playfair's Senate Hall, where
only the friezes and chimneypiece survive. Screens were also
removed from the former Theological Library over the entrance.

In the W (originally museum) RANGE Playfair's Lower
Museum, now the NEW SENATE ROOM, is a Greek Doric
temple inside out, recalling Soane at the Bank of England.
Seven bays by three, the columns engaged except for the two
at the N end which are a screen to an eighth bay with a
compartmented ceiling. At the ends, simple staircases to the
palatial ANTEROOM. Three groin-vaulted bays, lit by the
three Venetian windows of the W elevation and divided by
coupled pilasters with coffered arches. The centre bay opens
into the Upper Museum, which houses the permanent collections of the TALBOT RICE ARTS CENTRE. Again three bays
with coupled pilasters, the showcases (now plain alcoves) carried deftly behind them on two levels by means of a consoled
balcony. Top-lighting (more generous over the centre bay)
and a pair of Ionic columns forming a screen at each end. To
the S the former Chemistry Classroom, where only the ceiling
remained *in situ* before conversion to a gallery for temporary
exhibitions in 1974, with two new balconies.

In the N RANGE the octagonal classroom is the upper part
of *Adam*'s Anatomy Theatre, re-furnished by Playfair when
he raised the floor to form the Anatomy Museum (long vanished) underneath. Adam's NW staircase survives. Playfair's
Natural Philosophy Classroom, a square-domed cube, was
abolished as a fire hazard in 1975–6.

The S RANGE was built in 1826–7. On the ground floor
Playfair's Lower Library has been subdivided and the effect
of his austerely pilastered Graduation Hall, now the PUBLIC
OFFICE, is impaired by a recent mezzanine floor along the S
side. It is flanked by two halls, the W one (originally the
Students' Hall) impressive in scale but already altered before
the recent insertion of a balcony. The E hall leads to the
LIBRARY STAIR, plain cantilevered flights ascending to the
pilastered upper level, the landing carried by a wide arch with
octagonal coffers (cf. Chambers's Strand Staircase at Somerset House). Plain trabeated ceiling (the beams not corresponding with the antae) with a central light. Hence to the
UPPER LIBRARY. Eleven bays of broad pilasters carried outwards as two-storey book-stacks. A coffered vault from end

to end, and at each end two Ionic columns as a screen to a top-lit anteroom. In the sense that it is no longer used for its original purpose, or for any other except ceremonial, this great Neo-Classical room is now a monument, i.e. it has rightly been preserved. Some other rooms have been converted for modern use in an explicitly modern way.

WEST BOW WELL, West Bow. Built by *Robert Mylne* under the supervision of *Sir William Bruce*, 1674, a square ashlar box with a panelled concave pyramid roof and swagged urn finial. The cast-iron door in the W face is a replacement of 1861, when the other sides were dressed up with a basin and horse trough and carving by *John Rhind*.

THE ROYAL MILE

CASTLEHILL

N SIDE. At the top the ultra-picturesque and colourful RAMSAY GARDEN, designed as a Town-and-Gown hall of residence and block of flats for Professor Patrick Geddes, and faithful to his organic and improvisatory principles. From W to E, the first stage is by *S. Henbest Capper*, 1892, the second by *Sydney Mitchell*, 1893 (incorporating Ramsay Lodge, the eccentric self-designed house of the poet *Allan Ramsay*, c. 1740), and the third again by *Mitchell*, 1894 (incorporating a mid-C18 terrace), all in a mixture of harl and timber, grey slates, red tiles and red sandstone. Scots baronial and English cottage styles are combined to make the most of the steep and commanding site. Mixed sash and casement windows, with glazing of Georgian proportion. Capper's L-plan W range is the most Scottish: a cluster of gabled towers, the largest laden with a doubly jettied oriel and clasped by a battlemented stair-turret, the others linked by iron balconies at different levels. On the E (courtyard) side a dizzy round tower with a circular balcony and a conical roof, the windows vertically linked by heraldic panels. Beside it, a wall covered with 'pigeon-houses'. Then Mitchell takes over with a Scots gable corbelled out from different planes. At its base an intricate timber porch of Dietterlin type. Stair-tower with carved overdoors (cherubs as mason, farmer and blacksmith) giving access to iron balconies like welfare housing. Half-timbered gable overhead. On the N side the symmetry of the two remaining pilasters of the Ramsay Lodge centrepiece is respected. Action is then resumed in a stair-tower with spirally ascending windows. A projecting jamb helps to define the court; a bold splay (with affronted dragon corbels above) invites you into it. Nos. 1–3 Ramsay Garden are of 1768 with rubble masonry and architraved doors, but overlaid with red sandstone forestairs and fancy ironwork. In the middle of the

long N frontage overlooking Princes Street is the octagon of
RAMSAY LODGE, its massive stepped buttresses by *Robert
W. Billings*,* top floor and pyramidal roof by *Mitchell*. The
dominant W tower defers to it with a corner splay. More
substantial E tower of red sandstone with late Gothic enrichment over the windows. Inside, Common Room painted by
John Duncan, *c*. 1897, with scenes from Celtic and Scottish
history, in an appropriately Celtic Revival style. On the N of
Nos. 1–3 jettied attics added by Mitchell, the glazing carried
right into the apex of each gable. The old E gable he left
severely alone.

In MOUND PLACE, overlooking Princes Street to the E of
Ramsay Garden, the two plain late C18 tenements with late
C19 pedimented dormers were restored in 1977–9 by *Ian G.
Lindsay & Partners*. Broad chimney-gable at the wall-head of
No. 1. Artisan Mannerist pend arch of *c*. 1850 at PATRICK
GEDDES HALL; inside, well-finished flats with Corinthian
pilastered sideboard recesses. On the E side of RAMSAY
LANE the former TOLBOOTH PARISH SCHOOLS by *Patrick
Wilson*, dated 1837, with a very slightly projecting three-sto-
rey rectangular bay in a shaped and pinnacled gable. Then
the former DR GUTHRIE'S RAGGED SCHOOL, more force-
fully Jacobean, by *David Rhind*, 1850. Hoodmoulded windows in the shaped gable and an open bible over the door.

At Nos. 543–549 Castlehill the four harled lower floors of
the OUTLOOK TOWER‡ survive from a pair of three-bay tenements of the earlier C17. The windows of the r. building had
sill-courses jumping up as lintel-courses over the small stair
windows. Some of the first-floor lintel-course remains but the
second- and third-floor windows have been altered to line
through with those of the l. tenement. C17 moulded door at
the r. In the reconstruction of 1853 as Short's Observatory
(probably by *David Rhind*) the side and rear walls were rebuilt in stugged ashlar and the top floor replaced by two new
floors with a window canted across the SW angle Above, a
corbelled and battlemented parapet with rounds at the angles,
and within it an octagonal domed cap-house of wood which
still houses Geddes's camera obscura. W door, probably of
1686, brought here in 1955 from Woolmet House, Midlothian, demolished two years before. The arms of the Biggars of
Woolmet break through the pediment.

Behind the very plain early C19 tenement of Nos. 357–359
Castlehill a late C17 house, rubble-built, with a SE stair-tower
and a stout wall-head chimney to SEMPILL'S CLOSE on the
W. The late-C17 and early-C18 panelling inside did not sur-

---

*Billings altered Ramsay Lodge in 1856 for Lord Murray. The terrace and
lodge that he added to the NW fell into the valley, but his crazily heavy gate and
stairway still exist.

‡ The Outlook Tower is associated with the name of Patrick Geddes who
bought it in 1892. He fitted it up as 'the world's first sociological laboratory,
nucleus of the University of the Future for all neo-technic thinking and teaching
and for the future Encyclopaedia Civica'. None of this survives.

vive the reconstruction by *Ian G. Lindsay & Partners*, 1980. The short NW jamb ending with a semi-octagonal stair-tower is a fragment of a C17 mansion demolished *c.* 1965 for a kitchen extension to New College.* Stair-door lintel inscribed:

> PRAISED BE THE LORD, MY
> GOD, MY STRENGTH, & MY REDEEMER
> ANNO DOM 1638

On the lintel of the door next to it:

> SEDES MANET OPTIMA COELO. 1638

Beyond Sempill's Close the rear of New College (*see* above) continues the N side of Castlehill.

S SIDE. E of the Esplanade is CANNONBALL HOUSE.‡ Late C16 front block, the short crowstepped rear wing built for Alexander Mure, 1630, stepped down in the slope of the ground. On the W front a pedimented dormer-head with the date and initials of Mure and his wife. In the re-entrant angle of the L a low wing of the later C17 with a pend arch on moulded corbelling. In the mid C18 the original front block was extended to the E and remodelled with a roof of shallower pitch, both sides being given two pairs of wall-head gablets with lintel-courses over the attic windows suggesting pediments. Finally in 1913 the building was reconstructed by *John A. Carfrae* as an annexe to Castlehill School. He removed part of the C18 E addition, reducing the number of gablets to three on each side and supplying a new E gable with heavy Scots Renaissance detail and two very deep windows. The doorway was remodelled with a C17 lintel inscribed NOSCI TEIPSUM (from elsewhere in the building) to bring it into harmony with the serpentine parapets of the short forestair.

Beyond Castlehill School (*see* above) BOSWELL'S COURT (No. 352 Castlehill) built for Thomas Lowthian *c.* 1600, a large tenement with finialled dormer-heads rising from the wall, the r. three linked together and separated from the others by a later chimney (possibly C18). Moulded second- and third-floor string-courses. In 1895 the two lower floors were converted by *Hardy & Wight* into committee rooms for the General Assembly, with an architraved and corniced surround to the close entry and new windows to the ground floor which was covered with channelled stucco. In the rear court a double-gabled jamb, the E gable with a few crowsteps, the W with a complete set from 1895. In the stair-tower in the re-entrant angle a door lintel carved with a shield, a merchant's mark and the initials TL. On a panel to its l. the initials RM and RY and the motto O LORD (IN THE) IS A(L) MI

---

* Two lintels from the house have been re-used in the Assembly Hall corridor (*see* Public Buildings, New College and Assembly Hall).

‡ The name comes from the cannonball embedded in the W gable; how it came there is uncertain.

TRAIST. The yellow stucco applied in 1895 looks horribly bald. For the former Tolbooth Church *see* above.

LAWNMARKET

N SIDE. After the rear of New College comes MILNE'S COURT. In 1690 *Robert Mylne* demolished closes to form a courtyard bounded by existing structures on the E and W. On the N and S he built vast double piles (converted to university halls in a reconstruction by *Ian G. Lindsay & Partners*, 1966–70). The S tenement (PHILIP HENMAN HALL) presents a six-storey-and-attic ashlar front to Lawnmarket, the windows regular except for very narrow closet windows at the ends (their leaded lights over wooden shutters restored in 1966–70), the three chimneystacks along the roof-ridge also regular. The only enrichments are the scrolled skewputts and rusticated pend entry (encroached on by shopfronts) with triglyph frieze and broken pediment dated 1690. Five swept dormers, increased to a monotonous twelve in 1966–70. Timber lift-tower at the W gable 1966–70. To the court a rubble elevation with a touch of Scots Mannerism where the two middle bays shoot up into a tall crowstepped half-gable. Moulded door-piece belonging to *J. A. Williamson*'s partial reconstruction of 1914. The rooms inside were end-on to the frontage. Original scale-and-platt stair. The symmetry of Mylne's rubble-fronted N tenement (EDWARD SALVESEN HALL), five storeys with crowstep-gabled ends and architraved doorpiece, does not extend to the chimneys. The rear elevation, towering above the Library Hall of New College to look down on Princes Street, breaks into a Mannerist display of five wall-head gables, the end ones colossal chimneystacks pierced by windows. In the reconstruction of 1966–70 moulded chimneypieces (some with carved detail) were kept and much of the C17 panelling was re-used; in one room are fluted Corinthian pilasters and a rich cornice. The W side of the court (demolished in 1883) is now minimally enclosed by the harled flank of an extension to New College and a single-bay five-storey N block of 1966–70. On the E side the early C17 N block, with an octagonal stair-tower and crowstepped gable, was shortened by two bays in 1966–70 and a S block tactfully added.

E of Milne's Court the much larger JAMES COURT. In 1723–7 *James Brownhill* followed Mylne's precedent by removing closes to form a courtyard, building a massive double tenement on the N side. He kept the earlier buildings facing Lawnmarket but these were rebuilt (except for Gladstone's Land) with plain ashlar fronts in 1795. Their well-finished flats are approached from James Court by cramped turnpike stairs, and at No. 11 by a giddy geometrical stair built on a

very tight radius. The rear wing at Nos. 503–505 Lawnmarket
and No. 13 James Court, built for John Allan at the same
time as the front block, has tripartite windows at the gable.
The truncated harled wing at Nos. 493–495 Lawnmarket/3–
5 James Court, five storeys with a very irregular stair-turret
and outshot at the N end, looks C16 or C17. The timber-
framed upper floors at the NE corner and balconies on the E
flank belong to the remodelling for Patrick Geddes by *S.
Henbest Capper*, 1892.

The earliest part of GLADSTONE'S LAND (property of the
National Trust for Scotland) is the C16* rear wing in James
Court. Four storeys, basement and attic, with a stair-turret
under a lean-to roof at the E corner of the crowstepped N
gable. On the E flank a jettied and double-gabled outshot of
plastered timber and a SE jamb (rebuilt *c.* 1740, and reduced
by two storeys and covered with a flat roof in *Frank C.
Mears*'s restoration of 1934–6). This L-plan house, with balconies and oriels facing Lawnmarket, was bought in 1617 by
Thomas Gladstone who extended it to the S over the next few
years in at least two stages – the first (completed by 1620)
producing a new front block 5·6m. deep with a room on each
floor above a ground-floor shop, galleries to Lawnmarket and
a turnpike stair in the SW corner; the second an ashlar front,
probably on the line of the projecting galleries. Gladstone's
front is a dramatically tall slab, only 7m. across but of five III
storeys and attic in height. Three windows linked by sill-
courses, the r. two paired, with tiny additional windows for
the stair at the l. The fourth-floor windows rise into two
unequal gablets pierced by generous openings to the attic,
and all except the stair-bay is supported by a pair of round-
headed arches with a circular central pier, restored by *Mears*
in 1934–6. Curved forestair to the first-floor stair-door, the
wall immediately over it carried out to full width by steep
corbels following the line of the stair inside. Fixed leaded
windows in the original checks, with shutters beneath, were
restored in the first- and second-floor windows by *Robert
Hurd & Partners* in 1979–80; more conjectural was their design for the timber shopfront set back behind the arcade.

Inside Gladstone's Land a great deal survives. At the SE
corner of the C16 rear wing, a narrow vaulted ground-floor
room seems to have been a lobby to the main block from the
open ground floor of its original jamb. In the first-floor back
room an original chimneypiece with a re-used lintel. In the
C18 jamb a panelled room with a china cupboard and a
moulded stone chimneypiece. The front room is of outstanding interest. In its N wall (i.e. the front wall of the C16 house)
a segmental-arched recess, a pair of doors and a window,
relics of the orielled and balconied front. Above, a painted
C17 frieze of vases of flowers in an arcade with coupled pilasters. Painted arabesques on the window shutters and on the

---

* The RCAHMS found evidence of still earlier masonry at the original S gable.

beamed ceiling* along with fruit and flowers. A heavy transverse beam between ashlar pilasters (the E one fragmentary)
spans the full-width opening into the front extension – formerly a timber-fronted gallery. Similar beamed ceiling, and
gaily decorated timber lintels to the windows overlooking
Lawnmarket. The second-floor front room is almost an exact
repeat, its ceiling conveniently dated 1620. In the N wall of
the room above, a painted dado in the arched recess and a
painted architrave to the door beside it, the ceiling more
boldly patterned with animals and birds: among them, in the
front part, a gled (hawk) perched on a stone. Chimneypiece
dated 1620. On the fourth floor more traces of painted decoration.‡

On the N side of James Court stood the massive double
tenement built by *James Brownhill* in 1723–7, a double pile
of five storeys, attic, and basement to the court, and, taking
advantage of the fall of the ground, a full eight storeys and
attic to North Bank Street. A jamb at each end, narrower at
the E, returned to the S. After a fire in 1857 the W tenement
was rebuilt as the Free Church College (*see* Public Buildings,
above). The W half of the E tenement, badly damaged by the
fire, was reconstructed by *David Cousin* in 1858–65 as further
offices. The S front to James Court remained largely unaltered
so that the E tenement still reads as a whole, the windows
grouped three and three with a central crowstepped gablet; a
short splay softens the join with the jamb which has been
raised one storey in brick. Less unified front to North Bank
Street. To the W Cousin altered floor heights, corniced the
windows, and flanked the central gablet with tall angle-turrets, treating it as a link between the unabashed Victorian of
the new offices and the unaltered, starkly unadorned Georgian
to the E. Inside, two flats had§ early-C18 panelling and chimneypieces of William Adam type; only the marks of the
planted carved detail of the slightly grander upper flat remained.

To the E of James Court LADY STAIR'S CLOSE, its small
front block to Lawnmarket dull neo-C17 infill of the 1890s
when demolition left the close as little more than a hiccup
between James Court and Wardrop's Court. On its W side
LADY STAIR'S HOUSE, built for Sir Walter Gray of Pitten-
drum in 1622‖ and in 1893, at Patrick Geddes's instigation,
bought from the City by the fifth Earl of Rosebery, a descen-
dant of Gray. Restoration by *George S. Aitken*, an imaginative

---

* Part of the design is the same as that on a ceiling in the 'Palace' at Culross,
Fife. In both cases the original clear colours are distorted by the absorption of
wax applied with protective intent in the 1930s. The painted decoration was
extended in simplified form by *R. L. Snowden*, 1979–80.

‡ The remains of a painted ceiling, late C17 panelling and a bolection-moulded
fireplace were discovered in the third-floor N room (and removed) in 1934–6 when
the upper part of the rear wing was converted into flats.

§ The panelling was removed in 1979 with a view to restoration. It has not been
put back.

‖ It was bought by Elizabeth, Dowager Countess of Stair, in 1719.

reinterpretation of early c17 Scots architecture, completed in 1897. The City had made the demolition of the N and S wings of *c.* 1700 a condition of the sale; a W wing of *c.* 1725 was also demolished. Remains of Gray's house include the lower-two-thirds of the stair-tower with an excellent moulded door-piece (lintel dated 1622 and carved with the initials of Sir William Gray and Geida or Egidia Smith, his wife) and the half-pediment of a dormer-head abutting it at the SE; on the E flank another half-pediment of a dormer-head abutting the N chimney; most of the masonry but not the shape of the S chimney, and parts of the pedimented centre window. Gables completely rebuilt; the N one crowstepped with a turret at the E corner and balconies in a three-storey arched recess, the S one quieter, with a trefoil-pedimented oriel and an elaborately corbelled wrought-iron balcony. The corbelling at the SE splay was chamfered and given a balcony to support, and the stair-tower, which had been cut to the slope of the roof, was enthusiastically reconstructed with a round ogee roof and an extra storey. On the E front new ground-floor windows, on the N the first- and second-floor windows linked as tall tran-somed openings,* and the wall-head chimneystack covered with a pedimented grid of heraldry and dates. To the W a new canted link to the NE block of James Court. Elaborately Jacobean interior. In the E wall of the large galleried hall an original chimneypiece (the hood restored by Aitken) with moulded jambs and bell capitals. In another room a chimney-piece from Cannonball House (*see* Castlehill, S side, above). On the E side of the close only the late Georgian rear wing of Nos. 7–9 Bank Street remains. Its front block was remodelled and extended to the E by *John G. Adams*, 1895–6, in stodgy English Jacobean with a silly pepperpot turret.

E of Lady Stair's Close is WARDROP'S COURT, formed in the 1890s by removing closes between two tiny courts, War-drop's at the NW and Paterson's at the SE. Nos. 453–461 Lawnmarket, by *S. Henbest Capper* for Patrick Geddes, 1892, is a clever evocation of its timber-fronted predecessor: a near-symmetrical façade with a fireclay balustraded podium, two-storey oriels on corbels sculptured with emblems of the arts, sciences and crafts, and a triple-gabled oversailing top-hamper. The carved dragon brackets at the entry to the court are a happy afterthought. Next a plain late c18 tenement, followed by No. 435 Lawnmarket built for Andrew Paterson and John Henderson, wrights, in 1703. Central gablet and a jolly two-storey pub front of 1894 by *P. L. Henderson*, ar-caded to Lawnmarket and extending across the gable and part of the long rear wing in BANK STREET, the new thoroughfare cut through the closes in 1798. Here, Nos. 17–20 are plainest c17. Inside Wardrop's Court, *Capper*'s utilitarian rear ele-vation of Nos. 453–461 Lawnmarket with access balconies

---

* There had been quite a lot of brick infill, but it is doubtful whether this justified Aitken's treatment.

and a circular stair-tower. The fussy rubble stair replacing
the moulded doorpiece at the rear of No. 435 Lawnmarket
and the flat roof on the adjoining rear wing of Nos. 17–20
Bank Street belong to *Robert Hurd*'s restoration of 1950. On
the N side of the court BLACKIE HOUSE, a late-C17 tenement
of the Milne's Court type but shallower in plan, remodelled
in 1894 under the auspices of Geddes as a university hall in
memory of Professor J. S. Blackie, was sold in 1950 and
turned back into flats by *Robert Hurd*. Harled front to Wardrop's Court, divided in two by the off-centre stair-bays. One
of the original moulded stair-doors survives, and the keyblocked window above it is a memento of the first-floor entry
and forestair of 1894; box dormers of 1950. In the principal
rooms, panelling (some of 1950) and bolection-moulded
chimneypieces. The North Bank Street front was given the
Geddes picturesque treatment with asymmetrically disposed
two-storey oriels (the centre one with a terracotta portrait of
Blackie flanked by a thistle and harp), a gabled top-hamper
of plastered timber jettied out on a cavetto cornice, and
ground-floor shops with a balustraded parapet of Capper's
Lawnmarket type. To the E the corner of a plain tenement of
c. 1810 was turned into a bow with a four-storey oriel in a
late-C19 attempt to ease the flow of traffic into Bank Street.

S SIDE. Across the opening of Johnston Terrace the tenements
of the UPPER BOW: Nos. 5–8 by *Thomas Moncur*, 1882, set
back with a corbelled chimney; Nos. 1–4 Upper Bow and
Nos. 338–40 Lawnmarket by *J. Russell Walker*, 1884–6, with
shaped and crowstepped gablets and a three-storey oriel at
the canted corner. Much more lavish crowstep-gabled front
to No. 330 Lawnmarket by *Thomas P. Marwick*, 1883. Elaborate shopfront, third-floor chequered corbel-course with
cannon-spouts. Scrolled broken pediments over the door and
fourth-floor window and a diminutive broken pediment at the
apex of the gable. Five-storey-and-attic rubble-fronted tenement at Nos. 322–328 built for George Riddell, a wright, in
1726. Regular fenestration with small end windows and curvilinear wall-head gablets repeating those of Nos. 312–320 to
the E. Rusticated red sandstone surround of the pend arch to
RIDDLE'S CLOSE added by *S. Henbest Capper* in his reconstruction of Riddle's Close and Court in 1893 for Patrick
Geddes. Before 1893 the close was a narrow gorge; the demolition of the block on the E and of all but the octagonal
stair-tower of the rear wing of Nos. 322–328 Lawnmarket has
turned it into a bleak backland.

At the S end of the close RIDDLE'S COURT, built *c.* 1590*
by Bailie John McMorran, reputedly the richest merchant of
his time. He built two L-shaped three-storey blocks (each
containing a house) enclosing three sides of the tiny court,
and at the E end, running N along the close, a jamb demolished in 1893 of which the splayed entrance and the respond

---

* On the W side of the court is the date 1587, but McMorran was anxious to
rebuild 'ane auld ruinous hous' here in 1590.

of a door to its N survive. At the wall from which the jamb extended, a picturesque pentice stair by *Capper*. The short stretch of walling originally designed to be exposed to the close is adorned with string-courses, but its main feature is the round arch to the barrel-vaulted pend, with *Capper*'s inscription VIVENDO DISCIMUS in its unmoulded front. To the court the N block presents a polite appearance with regularly spaced second-floor windows, its moulded string-courses carried round the house occupying the W and S sides of the court, supposedly McMorran's own. The splay across the SW corner has a door, its moulded string-course of a cornice carried E over a pair of doors with stylized thistle finials at the end of the S range which here rises to a pedimented gable. Beneath it a string-course runs over to the splayed angle, steps up and stops. The E half, with projecting voussoirs forming a hood over the first-floor window, plus a cannon spout to the l., was only of two storeys and attic; it was raised to three storeys probably in the late C17. Perhaps late-C17 also is the small one-storey-and-attic building which fills the E side of the court, courteously picking up the first-floor string-course of the main block and stepping it over the tall ground-floor window. Exceptional interiors make this group one of the best surviving examples of mercantile high life from the C16 to the C18. In the first-floor W room of the N range the open-beam ceiling painted in tempera with a stencil pattern of cherubs' heads and double-headed eagles cannot be much after 1590. On the floor above, two rooms refitted in the mid and late C17. In the E room, some panelling and Ionic pilasters which look C17 framing an enriched early-C18 chimneypiece and overmantel. Square room to the W more complete, handsomely panelled, with a wide segmental-arched recess in the N wall and on the W an architraved overmantel above the shouldered chimneypiece. Moulded plaster ceiling dated 1648, consisting of a large circle surrounded by smaller circles and semicircles containing thistle, rose, lion and nimbus motifs.

The planning of the McMorran house on the S and W of Riddle's Court is unusual. Main block to the S, an uneven double pile with a narrow range in front and a broad one behind.* The door at the re-entrant angle leads not to the turnpike stair but to a passage running diagonally SW past the stair to give access to the kitchen in the W jamb and to what is now the Orwell Hall at the S.‡ The turnpike stair is reached through the door beside the splay (the door to its E gave access to cellarage below). In the principal rooms on the first floor, early C18 panelling and plain or bolection-moulded marble chimneypieces. Early or mid-C17 plaster ceiling in the SE room, its moulded ribs forming square, circle and

* The RCAHMS thought the S block a C17 addition. This would mean that the block fronting the court was very narrow.

‡ The S front, rebuilt when Victoria Street and Terrace went up, is described as part of Victoria Terrace (*see* below).

concave-sided diamond patterns with thistles, roses, berries and acorns. Compartmented and elaborately painted ceiling in the room to the w by *Thomas Bonnar*, 1898. The court was restored by *J. Wilson Paterson* in 1964.

Tenement block at Nos. 312–320 Lawnmarket, built by the merchant Thomas Fisher *c.* 1700. Its curvilinear gablets were the prototypes for those at Nos. 322–328. Ashlar-fronted and with windows grouped 1-3-3-1. *John Shearer*'s reconstruction of 1964 as the Carnegie Trust's Scottish Central Library banished shops from the ground floor, which was built up in ashlar and given a prissy broken pediment above the door. The interior was gutted. The broad rear wing with octagonal stair-tower was restored: this and the rear of Roman Eagle Hall with its semicircular stair-turret form FISHER'S CLOSE. Nos. 306–310 Lawnmarket, quite possibly late C16 in origin, have an early-C17 ashlar front 2 m. in front of the old building line, perhaps replacing a projecting timber front. Near-symmetrical, with a central stair rising to a steep crow-stepped gablet flanked by pairs of windows rising to single gablets: these stood up more emphatically before the wall-head was raised and the roof pitch altered in the late C19.

The broad pend into BRODIE'S CLOSE is narrowed by a former bakehouse on the w. Behind the block fronting Lawn-market, a low two-storey building on the E. On the w the old ROMAN EAGLE HALL, a substantial late-C16 three-storey mansion made T-shaped in the C17 when a lower three-storey wing was built across the close which runs under it through a broad segmental pend. The close thus forms two courts, the N no more than a light-well, the S now a large courtyard for the Lothian Regional Council Headquarters. Seen from the S it is the most atmospheric of Edinburgh's closes. At the N end of the mansion a gabled stair-tower, its moulded door cornice supporting a rounded turret which serves as a corbel for the jettied upper stages. The main front probably had first-floor timber galleries,* of which only putative traces remain. First-floor windows altered. In the pend under the E wing two doors breaking as lunettes into the vault give access to the ground-floor storage space. Elliptically arched vault with two of its three ribs surviving. On the first floor the ROMAN EAGLE HALL, made from three rooms. To the N a boarded ceiling of identical square compartments with applied cusp-tracery. A C16 date has been suggested,‡ but *c.* 1820–50 seems more likely. The moulded plaster ceilings of the middle and S sections, dated 1645 and 1646, are genuine enough. In the first, St John's crosses in Greek crosses surrounding a small central foliaged circle; in the second, petal shapes intricately arranged. At Nos. 300–302 Lawnmarket a C17 tenement. Two pairs of first-floor windows, three widely spaced ones on the second floor. Upper floors rebuilt in the late C19, jettied out

---

* There may also have been galleries at the rear of Nos. 306–310 Lawnmarket.
‡ By the RCAHMS.

under a tall gable with a bracketed jerkin head over the garret window. At the corner of George IV Bridge the Lothian Regional Council Headquarters (*see* Public Buildings, above).

HIGH STREET

Nos. 381–179, N SIDE. After the Sheriff Courthouse (*see* Public Buildings, above) and the corner of St Giles Street, the N side of High Street begins with Nos. 367–381, its late-C18 ashlar front a veneer applied to two tenements (the upper windows more closely set at the originally timber-fronted E tenement). Both of six storeys, all except the E bays of the three lower floors reconstructed *c.* 1800 as two tall floors. Ground-floor shopfronts and a first-floor pilastrade with rosettes on the capitals. In BYRES CLOSE behind, the W tenement is revealed as one wing of a very large H-shaped block of the C17. The N range, now roofless, with an arch across the close, was heightened and remodelled in the late C18. (Inside the court to the W of the cross-bar of the H, a built-up C17 dormer window with a merchant's mark in a panel, say the RCAHMS.) On the E side of the close a second rear wing which looks mainly C17. Running E from its N gable another tenement, again C17. Original window-openings on the two lower floors; bleak mid-C19 lintels on the first floor. It may have been the jamb of Adam Bothwell's House (*see* below) whose window-less flank continues the line of the close.

E of Byres Close the block at Nos. 351–363 High Street is the first of a pair of rubble-built double tenements of *c.* 1735, symmetrical, the windows grouped four and four each side of the arched entry to Advocates Close. Central gablet and flanking swept dormers removed in 1956. Restoration is proposed (1984). Inside, surprisingly complete interiors of the early C18. Basket-arched stone chimneypieces with key-blocked lintels and panelled jambs set flush with the fielded panelling, as is the curvilinear-arched chimneypiece on the second floor. In ADVOCATES CLOSE is the stair-tower to the W half of the front block (without its candlesnuffer roof), its N face corbelled out from just above the ground. Built for the C17 block running down the W side of the close (now demolished), it was adapted to serve also the C18 front block. A door in the tower was its original entrance. It shares a jamb with a door to the ground floor. Behind, at a higher level, another C17 door, presumably the original first-floor entrance reached by a forestair. High up in the exposed mutual gable with the front block, one massive corbel of an early-C17 fire-place. On the opposite side of the close the six-storey tenement incorporated into the front block was built for Clement Cor in 1590. On the moulded doorpieces to the ground-floor storage his initials and those of his wife Helen Bellenden. One lintel is inscribed BLISSIT·BE·GOD·OF·AL·HIS·GIFTIS, the other SPES·ALTERA·VITÆ·1590. A forestair led to the first-

floor door at the N end. Inside, a straight flight of steps
leading to the turnpike stair. To the N of Cor's tenement the
house built by Nicol Edgar, merchant burgess, c. 1615, three
storeys and attic, raised to four storeys in the C18. A monogrammed skewputt at the l. shows the original eaves-line.
Ground-floor chamfered doorpieces, all with crude new lintels. The main entrance was the moulded first-floor door,
originally with a forestair. Sill-courses linked the windows on
second-floor and attic level. To the N a large plain baronial
block of 1882, but its doorpiece has clustered shafts which
look genuine C15, probably jambs of a fireplace. Opposite and
set back, the four-storey ADAM BOTHWELL'S HOUSE built
for Sir William Dick of Braid c. 1630.* Canted three-sided N
gable with large windows at each face. Semicircular pediments to the top windows, inscribed with quotations from
Horace and Ovid. The bottoms of similar pediments survive
on the E flank, at whose S end a half-arch presumably marks
the position of the first-floor door reached by a forestair. Was
the adjoining block a jamb of Adam Bothwell's House?‡
Further down the close a crenellated and bartizaned block of
c. 1890. Nos. 343–349 High Street at the head of Roxburgh
Close (now closed) was the sister block to Nos. 351–363 but
reduced to three bays in 1930. At the l. a tall arched stair-
door with a round window above. Panelled rooms inside.

After the long stretch of the City Chambers (*see* Public
Buildings, above), ANCHOR CLOSE. On the E side two modest rubble-built C17 fronts, both originally four-storey, hide
brick buildings behind. Fronting High Street Nos. 221–241,
c. 1795, replaced tenements demolished as unsafe. The polished ashlar stonework reveals their common date, the asymmetry of design their differing origins.§ Each tenement has
the same number of floors as its predecessor. The block begins with a narrow three-bay pedimented frontage, originally
six-storey, the lower three floors reconstructed as late-C19
two-storey shops. Balustered aprons to the second-floor windows. Then an unadorned three-bay section, originally five
storeys and attic with a prominent dormer (lower floors again
reconstructed as two-storey shops), followed by a five-
storey-and-attic tenement, nine bays wide with an off-centre
stair-bay. Inside, a narrow geometrical half-turn stair above
the first floor. Rubble rear wing to NORTH FOULIS CLOSE,
perhaps C17. At Nos. 217–219 High Street another polished
ashlar front of c. 1800. Tripartite windows in the gable of its
rear wing suggest flats of some class. Then an early-C18 six-
storey-and-attic block (Nos. 213–215), rubble-built, with a
cavetto eaves-course and scrolled skewputts. The rear much
altered, with access-balconies added. Behind it, between

* Bishop Adam Bothwell died in 1593.

‡ No trace of an internal stair survives in the gutted interior of Adam Bothwell's
House, and without the jamb it was not a large house.

§ Under Scots law it is possible to own air-space. In cases such as this new
tenements reproduced the number of floors of their predecessors.

LYON'S CLOSE and JACKSON'S CLOSE, a rubble block made shapeless by demolition but with a chamfered opening of *c.* 1700. At Nos. 197-207 High Street a tall early-to-mid-C18 tenement, approximately symmetrical, with windows grouped each side of small closet openings and a broad chimney-gable in the middle. A chamfered opening with a blank panel above leads to FLESHMARKET CLOSE. Here the back wing has neatly disposed chamfered openings (some enlarged). A short second back wing fronts Cockburn Street. The whole block was restored by the *City Architect's Department* in 1978-81. Across Cockburn Street the ROYAL BANK OF SCOTLAND (No. 179 High Street), tough baronial by *John McLachlan*, 1892-3. Canted corner corbelled out above the third floor as a circular turret. Within the parapet rises a conical-roofed cap-house with segmental-pedimented windows. On the S and W fronts tall round-arched ground-floor windows, heavily bracketed balconies and off-centre oriels on the first floor, broad crowstepped gablets at the top (with a conical-roofed bartizan to Cockburn Street). Then the Scotsman building (*see* North Bridge, below) leads to the North Bridge corner.

Nos. 190-126, S SIDE. The S side begins with the public buildings of Parliament Square and then St Giles' Cathedral (for all these *see* above). At the NW corner of the square, a large pyramid-roofed WELL of 1835. In the square, STATUES. Fifth Duke of Buccleuch, an authoritative bronze by *J. Edgar Boehm*, 1887-8. The figure was too large for the pedestal designed by *Rowand Anderson*, so the top stage of cresting was left off. Cresting at the lower stages by *D. W.* and *W. G. Stevenson*; bronze panels of the history of the Scott family by *Clark Stanton*; panels of incidents in the Duke's life by *Stuart Burnett* and his virtues by *W. Birnie Rhind*. – In the middle of the square Charles II, a life-size equestrian lead statue of the King as a Caesar. It was supplied in 1685 by *James Smith*, Surveyor of the King's Works, but is an import, probably from Holland. Pedestal 1835, a near replica of the one designed and executed by *Robert Mylne*, incorporating the marble inscription tablet of 1685.* The statue itself was restored in 1824-35 and again by *H. S. Gamley*, 1922, and *E. R. Bevan*, 1951-2.

OLD FISHMARKET CLOSE runs S under the Police Chambers (*see* above). On its E side two late Georgian four-storey tenements. Facing High Street Nos. 188-190, designed as the Edinburgh Evening Courant offices by *George Smith*, 1845, in his best 1827 Improvement Act 'Flemish' (i.e. Jacobean) style, a narrow four-storey-and-attic front with strapwork first-floor pediments and second-floor cornices. At the top a neat corbelled gablet enclosing a hoodmoulded bipartite window. A pend arch leads to BORTHWICK'S CLOSE, which

---

* The pedestal design in Edinburgh Public Library seems to be by Mylne. The Latin inscription was composed by William Clerk, advocate.

begins as a slit only 1·7 m. wide between the back wings of High Street buildings. The narrow pend to the s allows a view of a shallow bow projecting from one of the Old Fish-market Close tenements.

E of Borthwick's Close High Street continues E to Hunter Square with tenements rebuilt soon after a fire of 1824. At Nos. 166–168 a first-floor pilastrade. To the l. an early Victorian shopfront with three arches on slender cast-iron columns. At the head of the close the CROSS WELL of 1785, with an awkwardly stepped top. Rear wing to OLD ASSEMBLY CLOSE with splayed corners and a semi-octagonal stair-tower. Down the close on the w side the old GEORGE HERIOT'S HOSPITAL SCHOOL by *Alexander Black*, 1839–40, thrifty Jacobean with details taken from its parent institution. Original main door in the flank of the rear wing, corniced with a strapwork head. Above, an inscription panel framed with more strapwork. At the foot of the close TRON SQUARE, really two squares, by the *City Engineer's Department*, 1899. Harled brickwork with pedimented dormer-heads as a gesture to architecture. Nos. 156–164 High Street were built in a single operation, but the inconsistent window-heights prove that separate tenements occupied the site before the 1824 fire. The ground and first floors of Nos. 160–164 achieve a smart unity of design with round-arched doors flanking a two-storey 'shopfront' with superimposed Roman Doric pilasters. Round-arched first-floor windows with intersecting-traceried astragals. Balustered aprons at the centre bays.* The cast-iron Gothick doorpiece (inscribed Mary's Chapel) at the entry to Burnet's Close was made by the *New Shotts Iron Co.* in 1814.

At Nos. 148–154 High Street (originally Clamshell Land) a pilastered and corniced door with a shell on the entablature. The tenement beyond is dominated by a pub with a François-I-style entrance of *c.* 1890, excellent except that it destroys the impact of the Ionic-columned and pedimented entrance to NEW ASSEMBLY CLOSE – really a court formed by the demolition of a rear wing of the N block. It is filled to the s by the EDINBURGH WAX MUSEUM, built in 1813–14 by *James Gillespie Graham* as the Commercial Bank, a heavily monumental two-storey-and-basement villa with railings at the area and an overthrow lampholder. Blind windows in the narrow slab ends. Coupled giant Roman Doric columns at the centre. Heavy parapet overall. Oddly, it is placed just off the axis of the close opening. Austerely detailed interior. To the r. of the spacious entrance hall a broad semi-elliptical consoled arch opens into the domed stair-hall. In the ground-floor front room at the E a marble chimneypiece with Roman Doric columns. At the rear a much reconstructed early C18 wing used as the Assembly Rooms from 1736 to

---

* The front is a replica of the pre-1824 front, or perhaps it was retained despite the fire.

1784. In STEVENLAWS CLOSE to the E a plain three-storey-
and-attic house with a wall-head gablet and random fenestration. Two tripartite windows suggest that it was reconstructed *c.* 1825. This part of High Street ends with
Nos. 126–140 of *c.* 1825–30, the original ashlar front now
harled but with a rubble-faced ground floor and wrought-iron
grilles in compensation. The corner block of Hunter Square
follows (*see* Other Streets, South Bridge, below).

Nos. 151–133, N SIDE. From under the E end of the corner block
with North Bridge (*see* Other Streets, below) runs CARRUB-
BERS CLOSE. On its E side the HOUSE OF BISHOP SPOT-
TISWOOD, a dreary model tenement of 1864 with a few baronial touches. Below it, Old St Paul's Episcopal Church (*see*
Churches, above). E of Carrubbers Close a small disaster area
with only the two lower floors of tenements surviving. At
Nos. 127–132 (originally by *Thomas Bonnar*, 1813) a two-
storey arcaded pub-front by *P. L. Henderson*, 1901. In
NORTH GRAY'S CLOSE the roofless and partly demolished
rear wing of No. 125 High Street with a pair of roll-moulded
doorways dated 1581. Then Nos. 109–119 High Street, a very
large tenement by *A. W. Macnaughtan*, 1902, sub-Geddes-
picturesque, incorporating a lintel of 1612 on the second floor
and a C17 armorial stone over the entrance to Bailie Fyfe's
Close. The scale drops again at Nos. 97–103 (by *Robert
Paterson*, 1862, largely refaced 1981), symmetrical with a
crowstepped chimney-gable. Under the central oriel a carved
portrait head by *John Rhind*. The inscription 'HEAVE AWA'
CHAPS, I'M NO DEAD YET' commemorates the rescue of a
boy buried in the collapse of the previous building on the
site, of which the six-storey rear wing to PAISLEY'S CLOSE
survives, rubble with chamfered openings. Half-columns at
the scale-and-platt stair. It must be of *c.* 1700. High Street is
almost halted by the vast CARRUBBERS CLOSE MISSION, by
John Armstrong, 1883, with giant Corinthian columns clumping across the front.* Long brick flank to CHALMERS
CLOSE. Inside, a bronze tablet to Sir Alexander Russell Simpson, by *H. S. Gamley*. Further down Chalmers Close is Trinity College Church (*see* Churches, above). In High Street a
parapeted building of *c.* 1840 with a second-floor sill-course
abuts Moubray House (Nos. 51–53). In front, the corniced
FOUNTAIN WELL of 1813, with guttae at the corners.

The front of MOUBRAY HOUSE is of *c.* 1630, a rubble-built
four-storey-and-attic variant of Gladstone's Land (*see* Lawnmarket, above) with a plain C19 shop on the ground floor and
an early C19 corniced doorpiece at the head of the forestair.
As at Gladstone's Land the sill-courses linking the three
closely spaced windows on the first and second floors jump
up to form moulded lintels at the small stair-windows on
the l. The arbitrarily placed third-floor window has been

* 'A miserable production, exhibiting in a feeble-forcible manner the most commonplace details of the style of Palladio,' said *The Builder*.

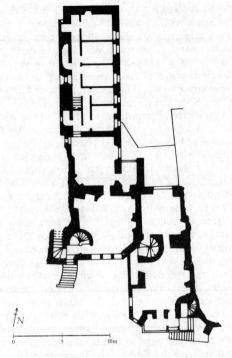

Moubray House and John Knox House,
plan of first floor

deepened. To its l. a gabled and jettied timber-fronted attic.★
The similarity between Moubray House and Gladstone's
Land is not confined to the fronts: their pear-shaped stairs
are the same, and their development probably followed a
similar course. In 1529 Andrew Moubray, a wright, is recorded as having built a 'new' tenement on the site – perhaps
the rubble-built three-storey-and-attic rear wing of the
present house, crowstep-gabled with massive corbelled projections for stairs on the flank to TRUNK's CLOSE. It must
have been extended s towards High Street in the later C16.
The line of the new frontage is marked by the moulded
door-jamb on the E side of Trunk's Close, set back from the
present front and aligned with the point from which that
front splays out from the mutual gable with John Knox
House to the E. The upper floors probably had timber-fronted
galleries jettied out perhaps to the present building-line; rebuilding of the front in stone then followed. In the first-floor
front room a mid-C17 plaster ceiling with moulded ribs and

★ Originally oak-boarded with scallop-edged bargeboards.

terms, cherubs' heads and floral motifs, and a heraldic device
of a cinquefoil flanked by a crescent and crown. Above the N
fireplace an inserted fragment of plasterwork dated 1630,
painted with a cartouche enclosing the arms of Pringle of
Galashiels. Replica fireplace in the E wall. Flanking late C17
pine pilasters brought from the room below. The wooden
barrel-vaulted attic ceiling was painted with architectural and
fruit designs similar to those at Gladstone's Land. Traces of
painted decoration survive on the walls. There is some evidence that the adjoining third-floor room originally rose
through two storeys with a timber barrel-vault.

Beyond Moubray House, JOHN KNOX HOUSE,* improb- 113
ably picturesque but largely genuine C16, projects S to stop
the view down High Street. It began as a medieval two-storey
house, probably with a projecting stair. This was heightened,
and a new front block built, probably when Christina Arres
conveyed the house to her son John in 1525, or perhaps after
the Earl of Hertford's sack of Edinburgh in 1544. It forms a
roughly rectangular three-storey building plus attic and garret. The core is of rubble. Jettied timber balconies on the
front block's W face seem to have existed from the start. The
timber galleries on the S may be later; the skewed ground
floor on this side, ashlar-faced and with three moulded windows, is clearly an encroachment on the street but must pre-
date the richly detailed, full-height ashlar façade that replaced
the timber galleries on the S half of the W front. The garlanded coat of arms flanked by the initials IM and MA (for
James Mosman and Mariota Arres) provides a fairly firm date
for this last part of the C16 work: between 1556 when Mariota
Arres inherited and 1573 when her husband James Mosman
was executed for treason. Splayed corner butt-jointed into the
ground floor of the S front. Shopfront of three close-spaced
windows and a door, all under an entablature inscribed
LYFE·GOD·ABUFE·AL·AND·YI·NYCHTBOUR·AS·YI·SELF.
Moulded windows above. The first-floor window of the W
front is a remarkable example of Scottish C16 classicism,
Doric-pilastered with small urn finials flanking a blind round
panel, and is flanked by tiny garlands. At the NW corner of
the splay, a sundial under a carved relief of Moses pointing
to the sun hidden in a cloud inscribed

ΘΕΟΣ

DEUS

GOD

The carving was restored by *A. Handyside Ritchie* in 1850.
Boxy gabled outshots, probably C17 additions, interrupt the
roof-line of the galleries. Main roof pantiled, 1981. Forestair
at the S of *c.* 1840 replacing and perhaps re-using the materials
of an earlier one which had also served a house to the E. C18

* The connexion with Knox is disputed but the legend ensured the preservation
of the house.

sash-windows were reproduced in *James Smith*'s restoration
of 1850, and again later. Originally there were leaded lights
with shutters beneath. Inside, two turnpike stairs, one in the
centre of the w wall serving the first and second floors, the
other rising from the first-floor entrance at the s to the attic.
Two main rooms on each floor. Roll-moulded chimneypieces
on the first floor. In the s fireplace Dutch tiles decorated with
large vases of flowers. Attached to one wall a late-C18 miniature pulpit formerly placed round the figure of Moses outside
so that it looked like a figure of Knox preaching. Open-beam
ceiling in the s room on the second floor with early-C17 tempera decoration. On the w wall a painting of Cain and Abel,
c. 1640, derived from a Cologne Bible of *c.* 1480 and said to
have formed part of a ceiling at the mansion of Dean. Arcaded
oak and pine panelling of three designs. The C16 panels, probably imported, some with Corinthianesque pilasters and a
marquetry frieze, others with superimposed Doric pilasters,
were 'perfected' by the carver *Walter Davidson* in *Thomas &
Peter Hamilton*'s restoration of 1853. Panels at the NE designed
by *Hippolyte Blanc* and made by *Whytock, Reid & Co.*, 1886:
fluted Doric pilasters with rosettes at the entablature. Roll-
moulded chimneypiece shortened, the moulding recut. In it
a mish-mash of Dutch and Flemish tiles. In the s gallery a
fireplace with more tiles depicting the Last Supper, and more
scraps of C16 panelling, some arcaded. Above the fireplace
three panels with a lion rampant and the date 31 OCTOBER AD
1561. In the back room more Flemish tiles (the Crucifixion
twice and the figure of a priest) in the fireplace. Stained glass,
including a portrait of John Knox, by *James Ballantine*, 1853.
Plain panelling by *Hippolyte Blanc*, 1886.

   To the E of John Knox House the NETHERBOW CENTRE
by *Harry Taylor*, 1971–2, a feeble quotation from the C16.
Then baronial tenements by *John Lessels*, *c.* 1870.

Nos. 122–2, S SIDE. After the Bank of Scotland (*see* Other
Streets, South Bridge, below) a yawning gap with no known
future.* At the E corner of Blackfriars Street, No. 60 High
Street and Nos. 1–3 Blackfriars Street by *Robert Morham*,
1873, adapting a design by *David Cousin* and *John Lessels*.
Five storeys and attic with a crowstepped gable and two-storey oriel to Blackfriars Street. Two-bay front to High Street,
with a gablet of the Gladstone's Land type at the l. Nos. 44–
48 High Street routine baronial by *Thomas P. Marwick*, 1887.
Then Nos. 36–42, the lower storeys of a pair of lopped C17
tenements. Inside No. 34, remains of a theatre of *c.* 1760.
Coved ceiling with enriched saucer cupolas. Proscenium arch
at the s end. Early C18 five-storey-and-attic rear wing
(MUSEUM OF CHILDHOOD) showing to SOUTH GRAY'S
CLOSE a six-bay front with the windows arranged 1–2–2–1

---

* A harled neo-vernacular design by *Covell Matthews & Partners* received planning permission in 1980 but was withdrawn in 1981. Housing for *Barratt* is
proposed (1984).

and a wall-head gablet, to HYNDFORD CLOSE a moulded door. Interior recast in 1956 by the *City Architect's Department*. Lopped Georgian at Nos. 26–32, narrow-fronted mid-C19 austerity at No. 24, and a large joyless cinema (by *Charles Mitchell*, 1927–9) at Nos. 18–20. A tall and narrow early C18 gableted front at Nos. 14–16.

A pend arch opens into TWEEDDALE COURT, initially bleak and unpromising. Iron balconies on the back of the High Street block which has lost its W rear wing. To the W the flank of the cinema, to the E the rear wing of Nos. 10–12 High Street (*see* below). Ahead a high wall with early C19 Gothick gates opening into the court beyond. Here is TWEEDDALE HOUSE, fascinating both for the complexity of its building and the eminence of its architects. The C16 main block to the S was built by Neil Laing, Keeper of the Signet. A W stair-tower seems to have projected into the Court, and probably a small yard on the S front was enclosed by a screen wall, i.e. the existing wall in which a moulded window survives to the l. of the present front door, its lintel inscribed NL and ED (for Neil Laing and his wife Elizabeth Danielstoune). John Laing inherited Tweeddale House in 1585, and by 1602 had added a 'dwelling hous' to the N, probably building on top of the screen wall to convert his father's house into a double pile. In 1664 the property was bought by *Sir William Bruce*, who recast it. In 1670 Bruce sold the buildings to the second Earl (later first Marquess) of Tweeddale who also bought the tenement immediately to the N which had been built for David Richardson *c.* 1600. *George Hooms*, mason, and *James Baine*, wright, made extensive repairs in 1671–4, probably rebuilding the timber and stud front wall of Richardson's tenement in stone. The main block was recast by *John Harrway*, mason, and *Alexander Hay*, wright, in 1687. In 1750 *John Adam* reported that the house was in an appalling state,* but his suggestion that it be demolished and a smaller one built was not accepted; it was reconstructed in 1752–3 by *John* and *Robert Adam*; *Charles Mack* was the mason and *Thomas Dunlop* the wright. The stair-tower was lowered to fit under the new bellcast roof, wall heights, windows and doors were altered and the court entrance shifted from the l. bay to its present central position with a new Gibbsian doorpiece. In 1782 the mason-architect *John Hay* rebuilt the N gable and E wall of the N wing in brick. At the same time the main block's interior was brought up to date with marble chimneypieces supplied by *John Adam*. In 1791 Tweeddale House became the head office of the British Linen Bank who probably added the porch and extended the s range to the W. The house then passed to Oliver & Boyd, printers

---

* 'There is not one single thing within the Doors of it that can be of use in the repairs, or can be allow'd to stand as they are. The rooff is so bad, that a new one must inevitably be put on next Spring, and the Floors, Ceilings, Doors, Sashes, Shutters, & every thing must be made new, so that nothing would be saved but the walls.'

and publishers, who altered the interior again and added large
workshops (now demolished) to the s.

The two-storey front to the court is plain but the l. part of
the first floor, rebuilt in 1752, is set at an uneasy angle to the
supporting C16 yard wall below in which is a door (made a
window in 1752) dated 1576. Roman Doric porch of c. 1800
sheltering the Gibbsian doorpiece of 1753. The front of the
three-storey N wing is of five regular bays with a Victorian
hoist to an enlarged first-floor window.

Inside, in the original N house wall, Neil Laing's entrance
door with his and his wife's initials, the date 1576, and the
words THE·FEIR·OF·THE·LORD·PRESERVITH·THE·LYFE. In
the room behind, presumably the Hall, arched buffet recesses.
In the chamber to the E, an aumbry painted with a guilloche
design. N windows set high up in the wall were blocked by
John Laing's addition: the tunnel-vault of the entrance hall
is presumably his, and so too the first-floor chimneypiece
above. Of the late C17 there is not much evidence except for
a few fireplaces and the moulded door into the N wing. In
what had been the High Dining Room on the first floor a
ceiling of 1782 by *James Nisbet*. Shallow Adamesque enrichment with a swagged cove and large central oval, diagonally
crossed by bow-tied cords. In the medallions at their ends,
figures of music and agriculture. The walls were lined in 1827
with chunky classical bookcases with pilasters and vertically
sliding glass doors. Set back from the bookcases are pilastered
doorpieces with (E) a block pediment and (N) a crenellated
parapet. In the room to the E more neo-classical detail of the
same date. Bookcase doors panelled with round arches and
Empire garlands. Classical frieze on the wall above. Brutal
marble chimneypiece. Otherwise two curiosities. In the attic
can be seen the bellcast roof of 1752–3 under the straight
pitched roof of c. 1800. In one of the two groin-vaulted
ground-floor rooms of the W extension, a serpentine flue and
parallel iron safety-rails (almost like a railway) set into the
stone-flagged door. Were these the 'holes' cut by *Lewis A.
Wallace* 'in the Pavement in Dampning Room for the reception of the timber Tubes from the Dampning tubs' for Oliver
& Boyd in 1838?

On the W side of Tweeddale Court a shed said to have been
a sedan-chair house.* On the E, a five-storey tenement, built
by *William Brodie*, wright, in 1783. Tracery of c. 1500 in the
fanlight over the door from World's End Close. In High
Street, a plain five-storey late-C18 tenement (Nos. 10–12)
followed at Nos. 2–8 by a large ashlar-fronted block of c. 1800
at the corner of St Mary's Street. Of its ground-floor shopfronts the panelled anta-pilasters on the W and the round-
arched openings on the E must be original. Consoled sills
above the first floor – unusual for the date.

*The story is persistent, but from what is known of Edinburgh sedan chairs it
is unlikely.

CANONGATE

Nos. 291–249, N SIDE. To the E of the crowstepped CANON-
GATE CHRISTIAN INSTITUTE (by *R. Paterson & Son*, 1877-
8) and the dour Gothic of the former CANONGATE U.P.
CHURCH of 1869, the MOROCCO LAND redevelopment by
Robert Hurd, 1956–7. It kicks off with MOROCCO LAND itself
at No. 267, the near-replica in rubble, with a centre gablet, of
an early C18 tenement which stood rather to the E of the
present site and was a storey higher. To it belonged the half-
length figure of a Moor on the l. of the front. The remainder
of the scheme is a determinedly gay attempt to express the
variety of Old Town life in an idiom both unmistakably modern and undeniably nostalgic – a busy amalgam of render,
rubble, timber and harl with jettying, arcading, balconies and
varied planes. Calmer back elevations, still with a variety of
materials, but the windows uniformly of the astragalled pivot
type.

Nos. 254–202, S SIDE. Except for the W building this is a redevelopment by *Robert Hurd & Partners*, 1958–66. The plain
rubble front of Nos. 250–254 (dated 1700) was kept, minus its
top storey and chimneys. The rendered mid-C18 front with a
centre gablet at Nos. 246–248 also lost a storey. The rebuilt
Nos. 242–244 maintain the full height of four tall storeys and
an attic, repeating the centre gablet and round-arched windows of the 1769 front, but in aggressively squared and
rock-faced rubble. Large basket-arched pend, an incongruously grand prelude to the utilitarian new stair. Behind,
the protruding rear wing became no more than a minimal
projection but with vases at the ends of its gable.

CHESSELS COURT is now reached through the arcades of
Nos. 234–240, rendered and pantiled but bravely dispensing
with astragals at the windows. A rear wing forms the E side of
the court. On the W side No. 4, earlier C18 with a centre
chimneyed gablet, and No. 8 with an octagonal stair-tower.
The court is dominated by CHESSELS BUILDINGS, put up
c. 1745 as mansion flats, a harled three-storey-and-basement
block. All the middle windows round-arched and rusticated
over a heavily rusticated door, the centre further stressed by
the chimneyed gable. Unequal wings of *c.* 1765 project at each
side, the E with a lugged architrave and cornice at the door,
the W with an octagonal stair-tower. Many original interiors
(notably on the ground and first floors), with panelling, pulvinated friezes on the chimneypieces, overmantels painted
with romantic scenes in the manner of *Norie*, and doorcases
with swags of fruit. Back in Canongate E of Chessels Court,
Nos. 206–208 are by *E. J. MacRae*, 1931, Nos. 202–204 by
Robert Hurd & Partners, 1965–7.

Nos. 231–169, N SIDE. At the corner of New Street the wing of
THE OLD SAILOR'S ARK by *Tarbolton & Ochterlony*, 1934-
6, preserves the street line but the main block, of crazy-paved
rubble with a broad pilastered doorpiece, is set back. Down

New Street the frontage is of red brick without frills.
Nos. 221–229 Canongate, of rubble with gablets and scrolled
skewputts to relieve the monotony, are by *E. J. MacRae*, 1930.
Nos. 171–197, the Tolbooth Area Redevelopment by *Robert
Hurd*, 1954–8, starts at No. 197 with SHOEMAKERS' LAND,
the rebuilt front of half the tenement reconstructed by the
Incorporation of Cordiners in 1725 (the other half went in
1882). The early-C19 parapet and cornice were kept in the
1954 rebuilding. Above the door at the E (originally centre) a
panel moved here in 1882, carved with the emblem of the
Cordiners and inscribed: 'Blessed is he that wisely doth the
poor man's case consider.' Rubble infill connects this to
Nos. 189–191, a rebuilt and rendered late-C17 front with a
massive central chimney, the windows paired on each side of
a moulded surround – a convenient frame for the plaque announcing a Saltire Society Housing Award in 1958.

At BIBLE LAND (Nos. 183–187) the almost entirely rebuilt
front of a double tenement put up by the Incorporation of
Cordiners in 1677. Five storeys with an ogee dome above the
central stair. On the E half the gablets are conjectural. On the
W a pair of large gablets, one with curved skews, both with
stumpy pinnacles. Above the door a pedimented cartouche
dated 1677 with the Cordiners' emblem of a crowned shoemaker's rounding-knife flanked by cherubs' heads. Below, an
open book inscribed:

> BEhold how good a thing it is
> and how becoming well
> Together such as brethren are
> in unity to dwell
> IT IS AN HONOUR FOR MEN TO CEASE FROM STRIFE

Nos. 171–181 are modern vernacular, a mixture of render, ashlar
and rubble. Central gablet. At the rear those buildings which
do not enjoy replica frontages have circular stair-towers of
C18 type. The low piend-roofed brick buildings of the late
C19 GLADSTONE'S COURT and the surviving ranges of the
old GASWORKS to its NW bring a straightforward honesty to
the backlands. The redevelopment comes to an end against a
small early C17 tenement with a projecting flat-fronted stair-
tower and crescent-and-thistle finials at the gablets. On its top
floor, a beamed ceiling painted with arabesques. It now forms
part of the Canongate Tolbooth (*see* Public Buildings, above).
Nos. 200–142, S SIDE. No. 200 is a replica of 1956–7 by *Gordon
& Dey* of a harled early C17 front, with gableted dormer-
heads on the second floor and a row of gabled dormers at the
attic. At the rear in Old Playhouse Close the cartouche on the
moulded door to the round stair-tower reads:

> AI   IEHOVA DEDIT   IS
> HOSPITIUM TERRIS, CÆLICA REGNA DABIT
> ANNO [   ]

Snecked rubble front to No. 190, with a broad gablet, probably C17, remodelled in the C18. After the harled block of

No. 188, Nos. 176–184 (originally 1755) are a heavy-handed reconstruction of 1955 by *Gordon & Dey*. First- and second-floor windows have been united with single architraves topped by scrolled pediments. Behind, in ST JOHN'S STREET, LODGE CANONGATE KILWINNING, incorporating a late C17 wing with a circular stair-tower at one end. Main block of 1736-7. *James Aitken* was the wright; *Joseph Enzer* the plasterer. Windowless lodge room. Recess in the s wall designed by *James Fergus*, 1757, as a setting for the ORGAN by *John Snetzler*, rebuilt by *Charles & Frederick Hamilton* in 1912. Female head in the broken pediment of the case. On the N and s walls painted life-size figures of Burns, Scott, Byron, and Shakespeare. Master's chair of before 1786, with an ogee-arched and pinnacled semi-octagonal Gothic canopy. In the refectory, shields with emblems of the trades at the ends of the beams imported from the Tolbooth in 1912. To the s a mid-C18 three-storey, four-bay house with a front garden.

Back in Canongate, MORAY HOUSE, built *c.* 1625 by 114 Mary, Dowager Countess of Home (the name came from her daughter Margaret, Countess of Moray, to whom it passed in 1643). The main w block with its tall gable and balcony on massive carved corbels was certainly built by Lady Home, whose arms are in one of the strapwork pediments above the upper windows. The s gable was originally almost a repeat, with rather more classical pediments; balcony long since gone. In the middle of the w front a stair-tower flanked by tall pairs of diagonally set chimneys. The E wing to the street had been built by 1647; three storeys, the ground-floor openings now built up and the upper windows linked by sill-courses. The extra windows and lowered first-floor windowsills date fom its conversion to a school in 1849. At the rear a plain C18 block. The close is entered through a pair of exaggeratedly tall obelisks set on massive piers of clustered shafts. To the w a crowstepped C19 gate-lodge. Inside, the original turnpike stair ends in a moulded balustrade on which a central column supports the saucer ceiling with moulded ribs and enrichments. In the Cromwell Room to the s, panelling with allegorical paintings (probably late C18) and an original plaster ceiling, domical, with ribs rising to a saucer at the top. Each of its four compartments is divided into a number of small panels with low reliefs of lions, griffons, sprays of flowers, figures and fleurs-de-lis. In the Balcony Room to the N a grander ceiling, domical again, the ribs meeting at a central pendant to which their progress has been punctuated half way up by further pendants. Compartments with heavier strapwork. In the panels many of the same motifs as in the Cromwell Room, but with cherubs and some more ambitiously grotesque figures such as a naked lady standing in a thicket.

Nondescript tenements of *c.* 1860 at Nos. 154-166 Canongate lead to HUNTLY HOUSE MUSEUM. The name is misleading – it was never a great town house and its connexion with the Gordons of Huntly is only that the Duchess of Gor-

don had a flat here in the mid C18. By 1517 there were three
small houses side by side. They were united in 1570 when the
E house was rebuilt above a vaulted pend and a new front
block built 3 m. closer to the street. Rubble ground floor,
corbelled-out ashlar first floor. The bases of the pedimented
dormer-heads of the first-floor windows survive, and at the
rear a tripartite window with low sidelights under the beginning of a pedimented gablet, squashed by the later top-hamper. Also of 1570 a single-storey-and-attic kitchen extension
to the S (the fireplace and associated salt-cellar survive inside).
In 1647 the house was bought by the Incorporation of Hammermen, who converted the attic above the new kitchen into
a convening house and then, in 1671, employed *Robert Mylne*
to consult with their masons and wrights about the enlargement of the front block, which was let as flats. The tenement
was then raised by two timber-framed and harled storeys with
three broad gables to the street, jettied out above the eaves-
line of the existing building. Minor alterations included a
scale-and-platt stair to the E at the foot of the turnpike that
begins from the first floor; a lugged and corniced entrance
from the rear; and another door of similar type (now a window) in the rear wing at Bakehouse Close, which was increased in height. To the S a pair of three-storey tenements of
1648, with timber-clad gabled projections to BAKEHOUSE
CLOSE, were incorporated with Huntly House in the restoration by *Frank C. Mears*, 1927–32, when the upper storeys of
1671 were replicated and the building converted to a museum.
A panel was placed at the front, inscribed: ANTIQUA TAMEN
T.B.W. 1932 [for Sir Thomas B. Whitson, Lord Provost]. This
matches the replicas of earlier panels inscribed:

> HODIE MIHI CRAS TIBI CUR IGITUR CURAS 1570
> UT TU LINGUÆ TUÆ SIC EGO MEAR[UM] AURIU[M]
> DOMINUS SUM
> CONSTANTI PECTORI RES MORTALIUM UMBRA
> SPES ALTERA VITÆ

Inside is a wealth of simply moulded stone fireplaces and
some panelled rooms, their woodwork partly already existing
in the house, and partly (in the S wing) early C18 from demolished Edinburgh houses. The best is an early-C18 panelled
room with lugged architraves and cornices at the doors. A
fragment of late-C16 fielded oak survives *in situ*. Also late-C16
are painted beams from Pinkie House, Musselburgh. The adjoining small C17 tenement, with its gable and balustraded
parapet, was restored in 1962–5 by *Ian G. Lindsay & Partners*
and incorporated into the museum.

Immediately E of Huntly House, set well back from the
street, is ACHESON HOUSE, a town house begun in 1633 by
Sir Archibald Acheson, Secretary of State, which later became a tenement. It was bought by the Marquess of Bute in
1935 and restored by *Neil & Hurd* in 1936–7. The present
main entrance from Canongate, with a crowstepped gable and

first-floor balcony reinstated in 1937, is really the side, originally hidden by buildings fronting the street. The real front is
to Bakehouse Close, set back behind a small forecourt of
which the kitchen wing forms the s side and the rectangular
stair-tower and entrance break forward at the N. Courtyard
entered through a moulded door dated 1679 from the demolished Elphinstone House. The pediment over the stair-tower
door, broken by the Acheson crest of a cock standing on a
trumpet, bears the date 1633 and a monogram of the initials
of Acheson and his wife Margaret Hamilton, their initials
appearing separately at the pedimented dormerheads with
rose and thistle finials. The crowstepped gable of the stair-
tower is of 1936–7, a conjectural completion of the original
architect's unexecuted design,* copied from the stair gable of
No. 142 Canongate. Above the entrance to the N courtyard,
through a door brought from Anchor Close, is the inscription
·O·LORD·IN·THE·IS·AL·MY·TRAIST·; and over the door from
the s courtyard to the house, also from Anchor Close,
·THE·LORD·IS·ONLY·MY·SUPORT. Spacious interior. Large
dining room on the ground floor. Drawing room above with
small rooms off to the N; to the s a kitchen wing with bedrooms above. Massive fireplaces, in the dining room with a
replica cornice of 1936–7. Of the same date the beamed ceiling, the beams mostly from the old roof. In the drawing room
another huge C17 fireplace, and shallow moulded plasterwork
of earlier-C17 type by *C. d'O. Pilkington Jackson*, executed by
Fisher, 1937. In the first-floor room above the kitchen a stone
chimneypiece, its lintel a replica except for the arabesque
frieze which is repeated in the decoration of the timber ceiling
by *Miles Johnston*, 1937. In the room above, the pine panelling and panelled timber ceiling with carvings of the regalia
of Scotland (to commemorate the Coronation of 1937) by *C.
d'O. Pilkington Jackson* are part of the restoration. The principal stair is a stone turnpike, an C18 replacement, its
wrought-iron balustrade by *Thomas Hadden*, 1936–7. Timber
stair from the first floor, the silhouette dumb-bell balusters
mostly copies from some of *c.* 1700 found embedded in a
lath-and-plaster partition.

Nos. 139–11, N SIDE. E of Canongate Church (*see* Churches,
above), non-architecture of the 1870s and 1920s leads to aggressive architecture of 1966 by *Basil Spence, Glover & Ferguson*, rubble, concrete and harl with concrete arcaded canopies at the front and clumsy concrete balconies at the back.
Earlier buildings imprisoned behind: in PANMURE CLOSE
the piend-roofed C18 CADELL HOUSE; in LITTLE LOCH-
END CLOSE the late C17 PANMURE HOUSE, L-plan with
crowstepped gables, once occupied by Adam Smith. Between
the two new blocks fronting Canongate is REID'S COURT.
The house filling its N side, restored by *Ian G. Lindsay &*

---

*Evidence was found during the restoration that a gable had been intended
although the tower was finished with a catslide roof. See Robert Hurd, *A History
of Acheson House*, 1952.

Partners in 1958–9 as the CANONGATE MANSE, is early-C18 of two storeys with scrolled skewputts. Piend-roofed wings were added in the later C18. Decent panelling inside. On the E side of Reid's Court a late-C18 house with a fluted frieze at the corniced doorpiece. To the E a low-pitch gable and Art Deco doorpiece stuck on to the recreation hall of Whitefoord House. Then a plain early C19 tenement and an early C18 four-storey house. In one of the first-floor rooms a dado and key-pattern frieze and a china cupboard with Rococo plaster-work in its spandrels and semi-dome.

The pair of plain ashlar gatepiers to GALLOWAY'S ENTRY belong to WHITEFOORD HOUSE, designed by *Robert Mylne* in 1769 and built for Sir John Whitefoord of Blairgunan and Ballochmyle, a simple harled rectangle of three storeys and basement with a pedimented Roman Doric porch to the r. and a cavetto eaves-cornice. The quoins are cement, ill-advised embellishments; even more unfortunate is the Neo-Georgian extension at the E gable. Inside, only the stair with its cast- and wrought-iron balusters survived the gutting of *c.* 1850 when it became a type-foundry. Sharing its W gable is the near-contemporary but slightly smaller CALLANDER HOUSE, built for Sir John Callander of Craigforth. Ground floor completely altered, but original quoins survive, largely hidden by an escape-stair clasping the W gable. To the rear in Calton Road the GATEWAY and LODGES (the W one enlarged), originally pyramid-roofed cubes linked by a screen-wall with a depressed arch and flanking doorways.

To the E, fronting Canongate, the new front to WHITE-HORSE CLOSE by *Frank Mears & Partners*, 1961–4, modern vernacular with an awkwardly detailed arcade on the ground floor. The close itself is much more enjoyable, so blatantly fake that it can be acquitted of any intention to deceive. A court built for Laurence Ord in the late C17, its buildings focused on the inn at the N end, was bought in 1889 by Dr Barbour and his sister, and reconstructed by *James Jerdan* as working-class housing, then even more extensively by *Frank Mears & Partners* in 1962. The W side is now a very plain row of harled two-storey houses, the E side very self-consciously picturesque, the N end a Hollywood dream of the C17. Even the datestone of 1623 joins in the fantasy; it used to read 1523 but was recut *c.* 1930 to give a more plausible date. The advantages of harling as a cover-up for modern brickwork are nowhere better displayed. Next, the dry-dashed backside of ROBERTSON'S COURT by *Frank Mears & Partners*, 1972, intrudes into the street, which ends with the three crowstepped gablets of Nos. 11–15, 1697, over-enthusiastically harled in the restoration of 1972–6 by *Robert Hurd & Partners*.

Nos. 126–2, S SIDE. In the front of No. 126, almost entirely rebuilt with a battlemented parapet, a pedimented panel dated 1685. Then plain later C19 baronial at Nos. 120–124, plain would-be gentility in the tall brewery entrance at No. 112 by

Blyth & Blyth, 1958–9, rubble and gablets at Nos. 100–110 by *E.J. MacRae*, 1930, and poorest Georgian survival of *c.* 1890 at Nos. 94–98. After Milton House School (*see* above) comes the 1953 replica of the 1624 front of NISBET OF DIR-LETON'S HOUSE (Nos. 82–84), with a broad crowstep gable at the l. and a crowstep-gabled stair-tower in the re-entrant angle. Above the door a re-used moulded lintel with the inscription:

1619 PAX·INTRANTIBUS
DZK SALUS·EXEUNTIBUS

O Lord I put my trust in thee, let nothing work me [har]m.

To its r. another re-used stone inscribed:

16 NISI 19   BLISSIT·BE·
DOMINS   GOD·IN·ALL·
FRUSTRA   HIS·GIFTIS

A harled block projecting over a rubble ground floor (by *Ian G. Lindsay & Partners*, 1962–4) is followed by QUEENS-BERRY HOUSE which, despite its justifiably barracks-like appearance, is of the greatest interest. Begun in 1681 by Charles Maitland, Lord Hatton, brother and heir to the Duke of Lauderdale, with *James Smith* as mason,* it was complete by 1686 when Maitland, by then Earl of Lauderdale, sold 'the great mansion' to the first Duke of Queensberry. Converted into flats in the C18, in 1803 it was sold to the Board of Ordnance for a barracks, and raised by a storey in 1808. In 1832 it became a People's Refuge and is now a hospital. What we know of its original appearance makes the absence of an elevation drawing the more tantalizing. Then as now it was of F-plan with full-height advanced wings enclosing the entry from the N, and lower, square pavilions at the angles of the S front. Daniel Wilson‡ wrote that before the alterations of 1808 the main block 'had a French roof, with storm windows in the style of the palace of Versailles'. So a mansard roof studded with wall-head dormers is indicated.§ Wilson made no mention of decorative treatment of the gables of the wings, and the presumption must be that they too were man-sarded, giving the house something of the look of Stoke Edith but not of any contemporary Scottish building. The rear pavilions had ogee roofs – replaced, apparently in the late C18, by piended roofs. Single-storey rusticated porch, with blind attic between the two wings, of *c.* 1700; presumably the round-arched rusticated doorways on the inner faces of the wings were the original means of access to the interior, whose reputedly sumptuous fittings (carving by *Alexander Eizat*) were sold to the Earl of Wemyss *c.* 1808. In front, a well dated 1817. Canongate ends with a whimper towards Holyrood. The office block at the corner of Horse Wynd, 1971,

* Information from Mr John Dunbar.
‡ Sir Daniel Wilson, *Memorials of Edinburgh*, 1848.
§ A Sandby drawing of 1799 shows a couple of shaped dormer-heads at the rear.

makes no terminal impact, for it is harled towards Canongate
but ashlar-fronted towards the Palace because a modicum of
formal dress is expected in face of royalty.

ABBEY STRAND

Two buildings only. The harled four-storey w one, restored by
Thomas Ross in 1916, began as a late C15 or early C16 tenement of three storeys and attic with two two-room dwellings
on each floor. The line of the crowstepped gable is still trace-
able at the w and a skewputt remains at the E. Each half had
its own forestair to the first floor (the E stair-door with
moulded jambs is still in position) and a corbelled-out stair-
turret to the floors above. After the sack of Edinburgh in 1544
the building was reconstructed and extended N by 3.3 m., the
turret stairs were removed, and a new stair-tower serving the
whole structure was put up at the back. Large contemporary
first-floor windows with moulded jambs checked for leaded
lights with shutters beneath. The second-floor windows seem
to be late C17. In Ross's restoration an additional storey and
attic of the early C19 were replaced by a lower storey, its
windows rising into gableted dormer-heads. Curiously, the
Georgian band-course was kept.

The two-storey building to the E began with a mid-C16 extension of the w tenement, maintaining the original building
line. Wrapped round the s and E of this small outshot an
early-C17 L-shaped two-storey addition with three unequal
crowstepped gables to the front. The present ground floor
with a large pend arch on the r., and the extension of the
simple C17 compartmented ceiling at the first floor, are due
to *H.M. Office of Works*, 1935. Pantiled rear wing with forestair.

OTHER STREETS

ABBEYHILL

Red sandstone former POLICE STATION by *Robert Morham*,
1896, one storey with corner towers and conical-roofed cap-
houses. Corbelled and battlemented parapet.

ABBEYHILL CRESCENT

Harled low-rise housing by *J. & F. Johnston & Partners*,
1967–8. Awkward use of different roof-pitches.

BANK STREET

On the w the backs and flanks of buildings fronting Lawnmarket, James Court (*see* Royal Mile, Lawnmarket, above) and

North Bank Street; on the E the flank of the Sheriff Court-house (*see* Public Buildings, above). At the N end, standing forward from the Old Town to lord it over the New, the Roman Baroque head office of the BANK OF SCOTLAND, sub-stantially by *David Bryce* from 1863. The site was bought in 1800. The original building, designed by *Robert Reid* and *Richard Crichton* in 1801 and built by *William Sibbald Jun.* in 1802-6, was not generally admired; particular fault was found with the N front, despite the screen wall intended to mask its excessive height. First *Thomas Hamilton* and then *Peddie & Kinnear* provided recasting schemes. Finally in 1863 *David Bryce* was appointed; his design was executed by *William Beattie & Son* in 1864-70 with sculpture by *John Rhind*. To the S facing Bank Street much of Reid and Crichton's front survives, of two storeys plus a blind third. Rusticated ground floor and pilastered first floor. The centrepiece, with middle bay set back behind columns *in antis* and balustrade inter-rupted by a carved coat of arms, is characteristic of Reid. The delicacy of the Corinthian order is not. This polite 'villa' was transformed by Bryce into a Baroque monument, with full-height wings on the S embracing a one-storey entrance range. The detail is far from polite. Ground-floor masonry chan-nelled with vermiculated bands. On the wings coupled Cor-inthian half-columns, the pediments broken by circular attic windows, scrolled and segmentally pedimented. Bryce re-placed Reid and Crichton's central dome with one derived from Pietro da Cortona, on a tall octagonal drum with lozenge-shaped windows and topped by a lantern (the scrolls at its base by *Kinnear & Peddie*, 1883) crowned with a statue of Fame. Bryce's wings extend halfway back across the flanks, where their ends are carried up as towers with open-arched top stages of clustered Corinthian columns. Segmental pedi-ments from which rise domes, fishscale-slated and crowned with statues. The N front was refaced, with vermiculated ma-sonry at the basement, bands of vermiculation at the ground floor, and a Corinthian order above. Reid and Crichton's centrepiece of a broad canted bay became a stepped three-bay composition with huge round-arched windows rising through two storeys, the centre bay framed by coupled Corinthian columns, the segmental pediment broken by coupled caryatids bearing a smaller broken pediment (an echo of Visconti's New Louvre). Parapet adorned with vigorous sculpture which with the dome forms a composition equally effective from any viewpoint. In 1878, after Bryce's death, the screen wall (for which he had designed domed terminal pavilions) was re-placed by *Peddie & Kinnear* with a pilastered retaining wall rising from a massive plinth of hammer-dressed masonry to a terrace with large open-arched pavilions. Inside the Bank, a simple vestibule leads to a flat-ceilinged two-storey stair-hall by Bryce, on the general plan of Reid and Crichton; three compartments with the stair at the E, its timber balustrade carried along the cantilevered N landing and picked up again on the w side where a first-floor corridor opens into the hall. Opposite the entrance, a Corinthian-pilastered doorpiece with a *sopraporte* clock opens into the telling room. Pedimented doorpiece of 1802–6 from the landing to a balcony. The telling room itself originally rose through two storeys to a (surviving*) coved ceiling, with lunettes, on huge Baroque consoles.

On the steep angle to the w of the Bank, the BLACK WATCH (SOUTH AFRICAN WAR) MEMORIAL by *W. Birnie Rhind*, 1908–10, a bronze soldier on a massive red granite plinth with Doric entablature.

BLACKFRIARS STREET

Formerly Blackfriars Wynd, widened to the E after the 1867 Improvement Act. On the w side at No. 8, REGENT MORTON'S HOUSE, four storeys of the early C16 raised by a floor in the C17. At the N end a stair-tower. Ogee-pedimented doorpiece; in the tympanum a crowned shield with unicorn supporters. Timber galleries projected from the Blackfriars Street front until 1860. Deeply splayed first-floor windows, apparently repositioned. Inside, a C16 chimneypiece, its columned jambs still Gothic in character. Beside it an ogee-headed niche with a crowned shield. At No. 50 a large four-storey-and-attic block by *Archibald Macpherson*, 1901–2, near-symmetrical, with baronial upperworks and a Renaissance door. Then a plain late C18 rubble-built tenement with a splayed corner to Cowgate.

On the E side Nos. 5–9 after the corner block to High Street is a four-storey-and-attic interpretation of Gladstone's Land,‡ 1873 by *Robert Morham* adapting a *Cousin* and *Lessels* design. Then Nos. 11–15 by *David Clunas*, again from a *Cousin* and *Lessels* design. Central wall-head chimney and gableted dormer-heads. The old BLACKFRIARS STREET U.P. CHURCH by *Robert Morham*,§ 1870–1, has a double-gabled front. Thin late Gothic tower squeezed in at the l. Then Nos. 23–29, a four-storey-and-attic tenement of 1870–1 by *Clunas* from a *Cousin* design. Baronial with gableted dormer-heads. Strongly corbelled rectangular oriel canted across the corner.

Set back from the street, CROSS HOUSE, built in 1643 as the Skinners' Hall. Originally approached from a close to the N it looks like a nobleman's town house. Three storeys and attic of rubble, T-plan, the stem running w towards Blackfriars Street and extended further w by a plain tenement of *c.* 1800. In the N re-entrant angle a large octagonal stair-tower. Architraved door with small corbelled lugs and cornice. Chamfered arrises at the windows. Plain ashlar pedimented dormers, one with a spherical finial. At the w corner of the N gable a small

---

*It is threatened with mutilation (1984).

‡ *See* Royal Mile, Lawnmarket, above.

§ The plans are signed 'for D. Cousin, Robert Morham jun.', but contemporary references and the style suggest that Morham was responsible.

splay, presumably a lookout into the close. The rear to South Gray's Close more altered: central wall-head chimney lopped, the sills of its flanking dormers lowered and extra windows slapped in the wall. From the crowstepped s gable extends a long and starkly utilitarian range built *c.* 1850 after the house's conversion into the United Industrial School. Inside, a couple of C17 stone fireplace surrounds on the first floor and a later-C18 wooden chimneypiece with urns and a central motif of flowers. Further conversion into housing by the *City Architect's Department*, 1981.

s of the entry to Cross House, Blackfriars Street continues with two blocks of 1870–1 (*Clunas* following a *Cousin* design). Central wall-head gables and a splayed corner to the N. Then an infill block by the *City Architect's Department*, 1979–81, and a drab tenement by *William Mackenzie*, 1873. At the s end the LODGE JOURNEYMEN MASONS by *Andrew Kerr*, 1870–1, idiosyncratic baronial with a shallow but energetically corbelled rectangular oriel.

BLAIR STREET *see* SOUTH BRIDGE

BRIGHTON STREET

A cul-de-sac closed by the diagonally set rear of the Royal Scottish Museum (*see* above). After the corner blocks of Lothian Street, five-storey tenements of *c.* 1820, droved ashlar with only a first-floor belt-course for relief. At the N end a fragment of wall and a half-pilaster, scanty remains of a chapel of 1827.

BRISTO PLACE AND BRISTO PORT

In BRISTO PORT a couple of early C19 three-storey warehouses incorporating some masonry of the Flodden Wall (*see* Town Walls, above). On the E side of BRISTO PLACE a droved ashlar early-C19 tenement followed by an equally plain late-C18 rendered block. Then the Seventh-Day Adventist Church (*see* above). At the SW corner baronial tenements of 1871–2, part of a scheme extending from Teviot Place and Forrest Road.

BROWNS PLACE *see* GRASSMARKET

CALTON ROAD

Later C19 pagoda-roofed kiln at No. 34, the old BALMORAL BREWERY.

CANDLEMAKER ROW

Named after the candlemakers who were forced to settle here,
out of the centre of the town, in 1654. The w side begins at
the main entrance to Greyfriars Churchyard with a two-
storey-and-attic building of c.1828, quite unassuming behind
its pilastered pub-front (by *Dunn & Findlay*, 1893). Then
CANDLEMAKERS' HALL by *James Watson*, 1722. Rubble.
Four storeys and three bays with a gabled stair-tower at the
l. Moulded doorpiece with an eroded armorial panel above,
the mantling of the arms still visible. In the old convening
room on the top floor, fielded pine panelling painted with
records of mortifications. Restored in 1929 by *E.J. MacRae*,
together with the adjoining Nos. 40–42, originally two C17
tenements (Henry's Land and Binny of Nisbet's Land) bought
by the Incorporation of Candlemakers in 1733–4. Soon after,
the two lower floors were reconstructed and two new upper
floors built, with a central stair-tower flanked by large wall-
head chimneys; the piend roof looks later. At No. 44 a front
of c.1900. Wide recessed canted bay-window on the first floor,
broad eaves and a long dormer. Next, a couple of tenements
of the earlier C18, restored by *MacRae* in 1930 and again by
Simpson & Brown in 1978–9. The second restoration faithfully respected the first, so the hungry-jointed rubble remains
as an architectural appeal for Oxfam. The ashlar gabled
dormer-heads cannot be original. At Nos. 50–54, broad wall-
head chimneys and windows grouped 1-3-1. Genteel neo-
Georgian shopfronts by *MacRae*. After plain mid-C19 Georgian survival (Nos. 56–62) the wall of Greyfriars Churchyard
takes over.

The E side of Candlemaker Row is mostly the backs of buildings
on George IV Bridge, but after the corner block with Merchant Street a five-storey-and-attic rubble tenement (Nos. 39–
43) of c.1765, symmetrical, with windows grouped 1-2-1, a
chimney-gablet and rusticated quoins. Narrow round-arched
central door. To its r. a diminutive door with Ionic columns,
acanthus leaves at their necks.

CANONGATE *see* ROYAL MILE

CASTLEHILL *see* ROYAL MILE

CHAMBERS STREET

A broad street driven through the sites of three C18 squares*
under the 1867 City Improvement Act and named after the
Lord Provost. In the centre, STATUE of William Chambers,
1888–91 by *John Rhind*.‡ On the base (designed by *Hippolyte*

* Adam Square at the NE, Argyle Square and Brown Square.
‡ Or nominally so. The panache suggests his son *W. Birnie Rhind*.

Blanc) low reliefs of Literature, Liberality and Perseverance. On the S side, Edinburgh University Old Quad and the Royal Scottish Museum (*see* Public Buildings, above). Elevations prepared for the whole N side by *David Cousin* in a Renaissance style, more French than Italian, were much modified in execution. At the corner of South Bridge a large block by *John Lessels* and *John Paterson*, 1873, now shorn of ornamental dormers. Next, modernistic Neo-Classical (ADAM HOUSE) by *William H. Kininmonth*, 1954-5, the name not a sick joke but commemorating Adam Square. Then three bays of unmodified *Cousin* elevation (executed by *Lessels*, 1885); punchy detail with a broken segmental pediment at the dormer-head to Chambers Street. Splayed corner and long flank to Guthrie Street.

Across Guthrie Street the UNIVERSITY STAFF CLUB by *Lessels*, 1875, has lost most of its sparse detail. CHAMBERS HOUSE (originally Normal School) is by *David Rhind*, 1878-9, with a massive console-pedimented door. Then the former TRON FREE CHURCH of 1876-7 by *R. Thornton Shiells* and typically Lombardic Romanesque except for the pavilion-roofed end bay which defers to Cousin's scheme. Beside it the mansarded MINTO HOUSE (No. 20) by *Peter L. Henderson*, built in 1878 as an extra-mural women's department of the University, follows Cousin's elevation. On the r. a French-roofed pavilion with a pedimented window and Corinthian-columned doorpiece. First-floor windows with cornices and balustered aprons. Then a narrow frontage by *Ian G. Lindsay & Partners*, 1971, coyly set back with alternating bands of glass and glass-reinforced plastic. Bold canopy over the entrance in case it gets missed. Beyond are Heriot-Watt University and Edinburgh Dental Hospital and School (*see* Public Buildings, above).

COCKBURN STREET

A serpentine curve formed in 1856 to provide a more direct access to Waverley Station from the S. About thirty blocks were built between 1859 and 1864 to the designs of *Peddie & Kinnear*. Their control gives Cockburn Street its cohesion but the individual buildings are resourcefully varied, including baronial of the David Bryce school for the main accents. Large angle towers guard the entrance from Waverley Bridge, the W one octagonal and gabled with a spired roof, the E one (which housed the entrance to the Cockburn Hotel) beginning round and then corbelled out to a rectangular cap-house. First-floor balcony to Market Street, convex-curved front to Cockburn Street with a restless profusion of detail stopped against a gable. In the gable a canted and extravagantly corbelled oriel, the corbels rising from the sculptured head and arms of a grinning magician.

Opposite at Nos. 18-20, circular angle-turrets corbelled out to the square, one with a pyramid roof, the other with a gable. Nos. 26–30 were built as offices for *The Scotsman* (with a boldly carved relief of its masthead), a storey higher than the prevailing three-storey-and-attic scale. Twin gables, the windows set in giant corbelled overarches. Across the road the ADELPHI HOTEL at Nos. 47–53, more elaborately detailed. At the corners semicircular turrets corbelled to the square, with fishscale-slated roofs. Round towers at Nos. 52 and 63, one corbelled to the square, the other conical-roofed, mark the interruption of Fleshmarket Close. Then on the E side the rear of *Dunn & Findlay*'s Scotsman building, 1899–1902 (*see also* North Bridge, below), continuing the style of the Royal Bank of Scotland to the s (*see* Royal Mile, High Street, above) so convincingly that the difference in date and architect is imperceptible.

COWGATE

Cowgate eases out of the SE corner of the Grassmarket. On the s side, at COWGATEHEAD, unexciting baronial tenements by *Edward Calvert*, 1871. On the N the larger but even less exciting GREYFRIARS HOTEL, 1930 by *E. J. MacRae* and typically rubbly. Next to this the former COWGATEHEAD FREE CHURCH, 1861, with a late Gothic octagonal tower. Opposite, the conical-roofed corner-turret is the best part of *Thomas P. Marwick*'s 1902–3 extension of the LIVINGSTONE INSTITUTE for the Edinburgh Medical Missionary Society. Beyond the Magdalen Chapel (*see* Churches, above), the vast backsides of buildings fronting George IV Bridge, and after the bridge itself (*see* Public Buildings, above) the backs of the buildings of Parliament Square and Chambers Street. On the r., set unpromisingly behind a car park, TAILORS' HALL, built in 1621 and raised to four storeys in 1757. It has been distinctly smart, with a stair-tower projecting at the NE corner and sill-courses linking the first- and second-floor windows. Of the first-floor hall, which had its own central entrance reached by a forestair, the ogee-headed moulded architrave of the door survives. Above the moulded door of the stair-tower which served the floors above, the date 1621 and an inscription

TO THE GLORIE · OF GOD · AND VERTEWIS · RENOWNE ·
THE CWMPANIE · OF · TAILZEOVRS WITHIN THIS · GOOD TOVNE
FOR MEITING · OF · THAIR · CRAFT · THIS · HAL · HES · ERECTED ·
IN TRVST · IN · GODS · GOODNES TO · BE · BLIST AND PROTECTED ·

The pedimented dormer-head of the tower, though embedded in C18 masonry, still adds a touch of ostentation. Fleurs-de-lis at the apex and base and scrolls at the sides. The tympanum is inscribed

GOD GIVE HIS BLISING
TO THE TAILZER CRAFT
IN THE GOOD TOVN OF
EDINBURGH

At the bottom of OLD FISHMARKET CLOSE the PEOPLE'S
PALACE by *Robert Wilson*, built in 1888 as the Edinburgh
Sabbath Free Breakfast Mission. Red sandstone front with
crowstepped gablets of different sizes and a pedimented
dormer-head. On the r. after College Wynd the WILKIE
HOUSE THEATRE, originally the Cowgate Free Church by
Patrick Wilson, 1859-60. Routine Dec, the gable front interrupted at the r. by a tower with a small broached spire. A
long mid-C19 warehouse with a round-arched ground-floor
arcade leads to South Bridge (q.v.). After the bridge, to the N
St Cecilia's Hall (*see* Public Buildings, above). To the S,
ROBERTSON'S CLOSE. On its W side a pair of rubble tenements, the N one early C18, four storeys with chamfered margins. Beside it an early-C17 three-storey house of seven bays
with an octagonal stair-tower at the centre and chamfered
windows. Gablets formerly flanked the tower. At the back, to
South Niddry Wynd, a crowstepped chimney-gablet. Restored by *Nicholas Groves-Raines*, 1981-2.

On the N side of Cowgate after Blackfriars Street, ST ANN'S
COMMUNITY CENTRE, its W extension of 1931 a feeble
paraphrase of the original school by *Robert Morham*, 1879-80,
two storeys with advanced gabled ends and a centre
chimney-gablet. Gothic detail. Beyond St Patrick's R.C.
Church (*see* above) the old GATEWAY to the stables of Tweeddale House, moved from a nearby site in 1977, a broad
round-headed carriage-arch flanked by foot-gates. The
present hungry pointing makes it hard to credit it as the work
of *William Adam*, 1736-7. Opposite, vast red sandstone tenements of *c.* 1890. Sparing Scots detail at the wall-head. At the
corner of the Pleasance the SALVATION ARMY HOSTEL (*see*
Public Buildings, above) by *Alexander Black*, 1840 (originally
a Heriot Foundation School).

DUMBIEDYKES

LOCHVIEW COURT and HOLYROOD COURT by the *City Architect*, 1959-64, are a pair of ten- and eleven-storey blocks,
very Festival of Britain and rather dated. To the S the DUM-
BIEDYKES CHILDREN'S CENTRE, mid-C18 with a bell-cast
platform roof. Two-storey, three-bay front with a tripartite
centre window above a tripartite door. To the W of Dumbiedykes a development of harled flats with pitched roofs by the
City Architect, 1964.

FORREST HILL AND FORREST ROAD *see* Addenda

GEORGE IV BRIDGE

From the junction with Lawnmarket at the N end the street
begins with public buildings: Lothian Regional Council

Headquarters on the w and their Chambers on the e, followed by the National Library of Scotland. For these and for the bridge itself *see* Public Buildings, above. On the w side No. 3 at the corner of Victoria Street is by *John Henderson*, 1836-7, in the 'old Flemish style' specified by the Edinburgh Improvements Act of 1827, i.e. with strapwork pediments above the first-floor windows and a pierced parapet with urns at the ends. Balconied doorpieces on the ground floor, the s one with a sculptured group (Caledonia with her children) by *A. Handyside Ritchie*, *c.*1840. After the Central Public Library (*see* above) a long block (Nos. 9-16) by *R. Thornton Shiells*, 1868, late classical of Glasgow character with pilastered shopfronts, heavily architraved upper windows linked by incised lines, and delicate neo-Greek cast-ironwork between the pedimented dormers. 'Old Flemish' reappears at the PROTESTANT INSTITUTE (Nos. 17-19) by *Patrick Wilson*, 1860, and with more refined detail at Nos. 21-25 of *c.*1845. The Elim Pentecostal Church (q.v.) is followed by astylar blocks by *Smith & Hardy*, the end one of *c.*1845, a wedge-shaped, bowed end over a single-storey wooden shop at the acute angle with Candlemaker Row. Here stands the GREYFRIARS BOBBY FOUNTAIN by *William Brodie* for Baroness Burdett-Coutts, 1872, a diminutive (life-size) bronze sculpture of the faithful terrier in the middle of a granite basin once filled with water, now with concrete. On the e side of the street Augustine Bristo Church (q.v.) is flanked with austere three-storey ashlar blocks by *Smith & Hardy*, Nos. 31-39 of *c.*1850, Nos. 46-55 of 1861, their moulded arrises a mere token of 'Old Flemish'. At the corner of Chambers Street the BANK OF SCOTLAND by *Lessels & Taylor*, 1906, agreeable mid-Victorian Renaissance with a quadrant corner under a Frenchy domical roof; only the smaller details hint at its real date.*

GRASSMARKET

A long rectangle, its e side formed by West Bow. At the e end in front of the public lavatories of *c.*1900 the COVENANTERS' MEMORIAL, a circular masonry table of 1937, the walls and railings of 1953-4 to designs by the *City Engineer*.

Nos. 1-13, w END. No. 1 of *c.*1875, at the corner of King's Stables Road, was made aggressively baronial with a three-storey corner turret by *J. W. Maclean*, 1898. Baronial detail applied to a symmetrical design with a central chimney-gablet at Nos. 3-7 of *c.*1880; above its Gothic-pilastered shopfront, panels with the arms of the Edinburgh and Glasgow Bank. The tenement at Nos. 9-13 is by *George Beattie & Son*, 1874, with large crowstepped gablets and a canted corner to West Port.

* It was doubtless designed in conformity with David Cousin's proposals for the site thirty years earlier.

Nos. 15-89, S SIDE. At the foot of the Vennel the bulk of the
Salvation Army Hostel in West Port overpowers Nos. 15-19,
a small block by *E.J. MacRae*, 1929. The design is derived
from its late-C18 predecessor but it is taller, the central windows do not line through, there is no chimney on the broad
central gablet and the rubble is hungrily pointed. It was said
by Robert Hurd in *The Architects' Journal* (2 April 1930) to
'combine the best features of the old elevation with direct
expression of the new planning'. The new planning won. On
the W side of the VENNEL behind is the old PORTSBURGH
CHURCH by *Archibald Scott*, 1828, a piend-roofed box with
an arcaded porch at the front and tall round-arched windows
at the rear. It is proposed (1984) to replace this with a brick-
faced building designed by *Matthew, Hamilton & Maclean*.
To the S a mid-C19 open-pedimented arch to Wemyss Terrace. Opposite, the three-sided court of BROWNS PLACE with
plain early-C19 tenements on the E, on the N an early-C19
house with fly-over stair across the basement and an anta-
pilastered doorpiece, and on the S the gable of George Heriot's
School preparatory department (*see* Public Buildings, above).
Back in the Grassmarket, Nos. 21-29 are by *George Fox*, 1859-
63, four storeys with a row of small gablets at the eaves.
Beyond, the MOUNTBATTEN BUILDING by *G.L. Walls &
Partners*, 1969, its crushing scale and cheerless aggregate panels hardly redeemed by the glass boxes protruding near each
end. It is a merciless bully to Nos. 37-41 by *David Cousin*,
1858, the small but richly detailed Jacobean front block of the
old Heriot Brewery, with an ogee-roofed turret at the r. and
a spired tower at the l. Strapwork pediments over the corniced
doors and rose and thistle finials at the centre dormer-heads.
The scale is kept by the dreary block to its E by *E.J. MacRae*,
1929. Across Heriot Bridge the scale rises again with UBERIOR
HOUSE by *Covell Matthews & Partners*, 1972. It tries to fit in
with the Old Town but its massive harled stair-towers are
merely oafish. Nos. 63-85 were built as tenements in 1875 to
John Lessels' design, a mixture of Georgian survival at the
lower floors and thin baronial at the top, with crowstepped
gablets and chimneys (now truncated) climbing up the wall-
face. *MacGibbon & Ross* carried out the central section, converted to a lodging house in 1889-90 by *James Jerdan*. His are
the doorpiece of early C17 type and brick stair-tower at the
rear. The old CASTLE BREWERY by *George Beattie & Son*,
1875 (turned into mining laboratories by *John Anderson*,
Superintendent of Works for George Heriot's Trust, in 1926),
is now part of Heriot-Watt University for whom the Pharmacology Building was designed by *G.L. Walls & Partners*,
1964. The S side of Grassmarket finishes with Nos. 87-89 by
David Sutherland & Sons, 1871, a small splay-fronted block
with crowstepped dormer-heads.
Nos. 2-98, N SIDE. Guarding the exit of King's Stables Road
the former ROBERTSON MEMORIAL CHURCH of 1884, spare
Gothic with a spired corner turret, by *Hardy & Wight*, who

also designed the associated baronial tenement at Nos. 6–8.
Nos. 10–14 by *J. A. McWilliam*, 1914, a tall three storeys with
corniced openings at the ground floor and scrolled centre
gablets. The BEEHIVE INN (by *John Paterson*, 1867–8)
follows, Georgian survival in shape but dressed up with
hammer-dressed snecked rubble and crowsteps. Then a dead
plain droved-ashlar tenement of *c*. 1800 makes a foil for the
late-C18 harled double tenement at Nos. 30–40. Central pend
arch, a broad chimney gablet crowning each half. Red sandstone intrudes at the late-C19 No. 42 with an agreeable
round-arched shopfront. The large gap E of Castle Wynd is
being filled (1984) with a busy post-modern tenement by *Calthrop & Mars* who won the Grassmarket Area Housing
Association's competition of 1980. The new block abuts the
austere four- and five-storey droved ashlar fronts of *c*. 1800 at
Nos. 60–68 (No. 60 with an elaborately bracketed late-C19
shopfront). Droved ashlar continues at the chimney-gableted
late C18 Nos. 70–72. Nos. 74–82, rebuilt in 1929–30 to designs
by *E. J. MacRae* (keeping the doorpiece dated 1634), were
two tenements, probably C17 in origin, the l. of two bays with
a prominent wall-head chimney, the r, with a crowstepped
gablet and stair-tower protruding at the r. MacRae unified
this pair with the use of hungrily-pointed rubble, moved the
stair-tower to the centre and widened it, and in compensation
narrowed both frontages (the l. one lost its chimney). The
result was acclaimed in the *The Architects' Journal* in 1930:
'The charming elevation ... is full of interest and is an improvement on the old one.' Late-C19 blocks with crowstepped
gablets, and an oriel at the GRASSMARKET MISSION HALL
(by *James Lessels*, 1890), lead to the corner of West Bow.

GREYFRIARS PLACE

Just two vernacular tenements conspicuously sited at the top of
Candlemaker Row. Nos. 1–3 faced with droved ashlar in the
mid C19. Nos. 4–6 *c*. 1790 with a rubble front; in the broad
chimney-gablet a Venetian window with a blind, keyblocked
centre.

HIGH STREET *see* ROYAL MILE

HOLYROOD ROAD

N SIDE. For Moray House College of Education *see* Public
Buildings, above. At the HOLYROOD BREWERY (No. 71) a
tall tower with a corbelled and battlemented parapet, dated
1872. On its l. another tower but very half-heartedly martial:
not surprising since it is of 1931, by *J. A. McWilliam*. On
the r. a broad crowstepped gable (flat detail, but 1936–7

was rather late for crowsteps) by *Charles E. Tweedie*.
QUEENSBERRY LODGE by *James W. Smith*, 1865, was erected
for the 'safe accommodation and reformation of females ad-
dicted to habits of drunkenness'. Crowstepped gables and a
restless second-floor string-course. The corbelled stair-turret
at the corner tower led to a flat roof 'for air and exercise
without leaving the house'. Crowstep-gabled LODGE to
Queensberry House by *C.S.S. Johnston*, 1881. Behind it a
severely plain early-C19 hospital block built when Queensberry House (*see* Royal Mile; Canongate, above) was a barracks. Then the 1903 offices of the ABBEY BREWERY (Nos.
107-109), asymmetrical Scots Renaissance. Tower to the l.,
crowstepped gable with a canted oriel to the r. The last building stripped neo-Georgian under a 'mansard' roof, by *Gordon
& Dey*, 1961.

s SIDE. Even less. The ashlar gatepiers of the GASWORKS of
1857 survive beside the PARK ALE STORES. Front block by
Blyth & Blyth, in two stages, 1946 and 1953. An attempt at
Modern Movement style, but in hammer-dressed masonry so
as not to frighten the dray-horses.

HUNTER SQUARE *see* SOUTH BRIDGE

INFIRMARY STREET

On the s side South Bridge School and Infirmary Street Baths
(*see* Public Buildings, above). On the N, after the corner block
with South Bridge, a plain early-C19 tenement. Then the
former Lady Yester's Church (*see* above), 1803-5 by *William
Sibbald*, who also designed its pavilions (built as shops), the
r. one now raised to two storeys. Round-arched keyblocked
openings. No. 13 by *Thomas Brown* was built as a Secession
chapel in 1822. Only one of each pair of anta-pilasters survives at the pedimented centre. Pilastered one-storey protu-
berance of *c.* 1900 across the front.

JEFFREY STREET

Plain tenements of 1888-92 with a routine baronial flourish at
the wall-head lead round from Canongate. A beefy baronial
villa by *James Lessels*, 1886,* at No. 39 is better. Broad crowstepped gable with a canted oriel at the r., nudged by an ample
conical-roofed turret. Then a large office development by
Michael Laird, 1963, a lumpy arrangement of concrete-aggre-
gate panels. A fag-end baronial tenement at Nos. 97-99 by
Hamilton Paterson, 1889, leads to Old St Paul's Church (*see*
above).

* Information from the Old Town Survey team.

JOHNSTON TERRACE

The main element of *Thomas Hamilton*'s Western Approach scheme of 1827. Starting at the E end, St Columba's Free Church (q.v.) on the S side is followed by the severe curved frontage of Nos. 1–13 by *Smith & Hardy*, 1862, later partly raised by a fourth floor. For St Columba's Episcopal Church, *see* Churches, above. Then Nos. 14–15 by *George Smith*, 1844–5, built as a school. Jacobean, two storeys and three bays to the front. Broad shaped gable at the centre with paired doorpieces under a single strapwork pediment. Oriel corbelled out at the top, and more strapwork at the flanking ground-floor windows. Two gables at the rear overlooking Grassmarket with asymmetrically placed chimneys. To the W a long free-standing block, now CASTLECLIFF WORKSHOPS, built as soldiers' married quarters in 1872–3. Its straightforward military architecture, quite plain except for the access balconies, was thought unworthy of the site and in 1874 *Robert Morham* added the Rhenish pavilions at the corners and centre and the crowstepped towers along the fronts. The N side of Johnston Terrace is dominated by the long flank of Tolbooth Church and the rear of Castlehill School (*see* Churches and Public Buildings, above). Gableted tenement (No. 16) at the corner of Castle Wynd North by *Smith & Hardy*, 1864, its stepped front up the Wynd complementing the rear wing of Cannonball House (*see* Royal Mile, Castlehill, above).

LOTHIAN STREET

Laid out *c.* 1800. Nos. 29–53 are droved ashlar tenements of that date. Round-arched ground-floor windows and doors. Belt-courses above.

MARKET STREET

At the E end the CITY ART CENTRE, designed as part of The Scotsman offices by *Dunn & Findlay*, 1899–1902. English Baroque. Six storeys and attic. Giant round-headed arches on octagonal piers uniting the ground and first floors, giant segmental-headed over-arches above. Dormers with alternately triangular and segmental pediments. Interior converted for exhibition purposes by the *City Architect's Department*, 1979. A stab at classicism was thought appropriate, so columns have been introduced. Near the W end a bleak baronial building by *John G. Adams*, 1897–9. One of its bartizans has escaped to sit on Nos. 15–17, a tenement of *c.* 1825, raised from three storeys to five *c.* 1865–70. Across Cockburn Street, Nos. 19–21 are by *Stewart Kaye*, 1928, incorporating a reconstructed block of 1871. Timid modernism diluted with a few dregs of Edwardian classicism.

MERCHANT STREET

A classy cul-de-sac which has come down in the world and had George IV Bridge built across it. Laid out in 1774 by *James Craig*, who also provided elevations. Probably by Craig is the splay-fronted N corner-block with Candlemaker Row, four storeys and attic, rubble with rusticated quoins. Gablets on both fronts, a round-arched window in the narrower gablet to Candlemaker Row, architraved and corniced doorpiece to Merchant Street. Then four-storey plus basement and attic tenements by *Robert Burn*, *c.*1810. Droved ashlar fronts. Heavy keyblocks and imposts at the pend-openings. Pilastered main doors, Roman Doric at Nos. 3 and 5, acanthus-leaf capitals and a fluted frieze at Nos. 9-10. Nos. 17-19 George IV Bridge have been built on top of No. 5.

MOUND PLACE *see* ROYAL MILE: CASTLEHILL

NEW STREET

The E side is the BUS GARAGE, 1927, red brick with no attempt at architecture.

NORTH BRIDGE

A redevelopment following the widening of the North Bridge itself in 1894-7 (*see* First New Town, Public Buildings). The competition was won by *J. N. Scott* and *J. A. Williamson* in 1896, but only the general outline of their scheme was followed. The E side begins at the High Street corner with the ROYAL BANK OF SCOTLAND by *Sydney Mitchell & Wilson*, 1898, its free Scots Renaissance setting the tone. To North Bridge a gable flanked by comfortable round towers, an aedicule at the chimney. Heavily machicolated parapet. Broad canted oriels set in two-storey round-arched recesses continue along the High Street front, where another motif appears: triangular-pedimented dormer-heads containing segmental pediments broken by pinnacles. After the corner North Bridge continues with a lower block by *Mitchell & Wilson*. At the centre a pedimented gable broken by a chimney. Recessed oriels and double-pedimented dormer-heads again. Then a long, near-symmetrical block by *W. Hamilton Beattie*,[*] 1898, using Mitchell & Wilson's motifs, but meanly, and omitting the machicolation altogether. Aediculed centre gable with scrolled sides, flanked by circular turrets. Turrets at the ends. The style continues at Beattie's CARLTON HOTEL overlooking the valley. On its N front a gable flanked by copper-domed towers. A lower block sneaks off to the SE.

---

[*] Nominally. Really by his partner, *A. R. Scott.*

The whole w side of North Bridge is filled with the SCOTSMAN
BUILDINGS by *Dunn & Findlay*, 1899–1902. English
Baroque of the Belcher type. At the corner of High Street, an
octagonal domed turret corbelled out above the first floor. To
High Street a narrow front with a three-storey canted oriel
and an aedicular pedimented gablet. The long North Bridge
façade is treated as five blocks. Giant overarches and a pedimented gablet at the first; stripped detail and a tall aedicular
gablet follow. At the broad centrepiece a pedimented gable
clasped by round turrets and rising to octagonal top stages,
copper-domed. Coat of arms in the tympanum. Below, canted
oriels set in three-storey overarches. Above the entrance to
the Arcade an allegorical figure by *W. Birnie Rhind* breaks
the segmental pediment. The ARCADE itself is V-shaped with
a leaded glass dome at the heel of the V. Mosaic ceilings at
the straight sections. The front to North Bridge continues
with bipartite windows. In the final section the offices of The
Scotsman, treated with due solemnity. Three tall round-
headed arches at the ground floor to North Bridge, their transoms carved with thistles and other foliage. The N front exploits its position – the Old Town overawing the New. Steep
gable between octagonal turrets, their stone domes topped
with Atlas figures. Tall segmental-pedimented aedicule at the
attic; in it, a figure of Peace by *Frederick E. E. Schenk*. Above,
figures of Mercury by *Joseph Hayes* flanking an obelisk. Giant
recessed Ionic order on the second and third floors. Blocked
aedicules on the second floor with figures of Night and Day
(by *Hayes* after Michelangelo) reclining on pediments. Vast
carving of the masthead of The Scotsman above the ground
floor. Low link to a boldly advanced pavilion at the r., with
copper-domed towers framing the N front. The building has
a further four floors below the level of North Bridge. From
the terrace across the N front Market Street is reached by a
Blois-type stair-tower with wrought-iron grilles in bold depressed arches. The Public Office of The Scotsman is
mahogany-panelled with a boldly bracketed gallery round all
four sides. Marble piers in the centre, and a compartmented
ceiling moulded in late C17 style.

ST GILES STREET

An L-shape. The E–W section was formed in 1802 as part of the
siteworks of the Bank of Scotland (*see* Bank Street, above).
The s leg was not punched through closes to join High Street
to the s until 1869. Its w side is the flank of the Sheriff Courthouse (*see* Public Buildings, above). The E side begins at the
High Street corner with Nos. 2–10 by *Thomas Gibson*, 1872.
Baronial with a spirelet at the corner, the two lower floors
unified as a two-tier shop with shouldered openings. Original
interior (once the Glasgow Herald office), with a panelled oak
ceiling and book presses. Nos. 12–18 by *David Bryce* for the

Edinburgh Courant, 1871–2, have his characteristic motif of twin centre gablets interlocking on a segmental-pedimented dormer-head. Tough Jacobean detail. Also by *Bryce* Nos. 20–24, built as the Daily Review offices in 1872–3, near-symmetrical, four storeys and attic, with twin gables flanking a pair of dormer-heads. First-floor pilastrade. To the N there are two storeys below the street, so this is a giant six storeys and attic rising to twin gables and pepperpot turrets.

ST MARY'S STREET

A creation of the 1867 Improvement Act, formed by widening St Mary Wynd in 1868–9. The W side begins with a late-C18 five-storey survivor of the Wynd at Nos. 3–11. Seven bays with windows grouped 3-1-3 and a chimney-gablet. Pub front to the r. by *R. Thornton Shiells & Thomson*, 1891. Segmental arches with twisted columns and sculptured spandrels. Carved heads of Bacchus on the frieze. Then squared-up baronial with red sandstone dressings at Nos. 13–17, by *J. B. Dunn*, 1889. Scots Renaissance dormer-heads at Nos. 19–25, by *T. P. Marwick*, 1889–90. The BEN LINE BUILDING stretches S to Cowgate, broken into four blocks by narrow recessed bays, the centre two set slightly back. Horizontal bands of glazing divided vertically by thin metal strips: straightforward enough except that some panes arbitrarily drop below the rest into the slate cladding. Hammer-dressed synthetic stone and a harled tower are unnecessary concessions to Old Town vernacular. By *Moira & Moira & Wann*, 1975–7.

E side all of 1869 by *David Cousin* and *John Lessels*, predictably baronial. It begins well at the Canongate corner with No. 2: five storeys with a canted corner corbelled out to a crowstepped gable with a two-storey oriel. The St Mary's Street front ends with a rectangular tower broached to an octagonal spirelet. Beyond, the scale drops to four storeys. Conical-roofed turret and trefoil-pedimented dormer at Nos. 6–8. A pair of strapwork-pedimented windows in the crowstepped gablet of Nos. 10–14 are followed by ST MARY'S HALL, a segmentally pedimented aedicule in its crowstepped gablet. Tall first floor with mullioned and transomed windows under a jerky hoodmould. Below Boyd's Entry the invention falters. Flat-fronted tenements with dormer-heads and crowstepped gablets. At the canted corner to Cowgate a flourish of pepperpot turrets.

SOUTH BRIDGE, HUNTER SQUARE AND BLAIR STREET

A development promoted by the Commissioners for the South Bridge from 1786. (For the bridge itself *see* Public Buildings, above.) Unified three-storey-and-attic frontages by *Robert*

Kay. HUNTER SQUARE was formed round the remodelled
Tron Church (q.v.), with South Bridge and Blair Street running into it from the s. The s block at Nos. 10–11 Hunter
Square is mostly intact. Giant Roman Doric pilasters, triglyph frieze, and an overall pediment with a thermal window.
On the ground floor a Victorian François I broken-pedimented door and chunky shopfront. On the w side Nos. 1–2
on the corner of High Street are pedimented to N and E.
Fluted frieze with rosettes and thermal windows in the pediments. Beside them Nos. 3–4 intrude into Kay's scheme,
designed and built in 1788–90 by *John Baxter Jun*. as the
Merchant Company Hall, with three large bays where Kay
had provided for seven. Fluted second-floor band-course,
studded with rosettes, threaded through giant fluted Roman
Doric pilasters. Round-arched first-floor windows set in
over-arches. Bracketed cornice and balustrade overall. Rusticated ground floor reconstructed in 1898 by *J. M. Dick Peddie* with artisan Ionic doorpieces. Inside, the hall was on the
first floor. Its enriched pine chimneypiece has been moved to
the ground floor. The block beyond (Nos. 7–8) acquired an
extra storey and chunky Italianate detail *c.* 1860.

The pediment of Nos. 1–7 BLAIR STREET answers that of the
High Street corner. Original round-arched ground-floor
openings. An early C19 fluted Doric doorpiece on the r. To
the s, Blair Street runs downhill to Cowgate. On the E side
the rubble backs (rather altered) of buildings fronting South
Bridge. Overall pediments with thermal windows in the end
blocks, the others with pedimented gablets. Plentiful Venetian windows. On the w side at Nos. 7–15 a superior ashlar-
fronted tenement with a pedimented gablet and round-arched
ground-floor openings. At Nos. 17–23 (with an added floor)
every other window is tripartite. A very plain block, reconstructed with a mansard, carries on towards Cowgate. A large
selection of enamelled advertisements on its front.

The E side of Hunter Square is formed by the buildings at the
beginning of SOUTH BRIDGE. At the corner of High Street
the copper-roofed BANK OF SCOTLAND by *W.J. Walker
Todd*, 1923, inter-war classical with a channelled ground
floor. Giant columns and a pediment to High Street, pilasters
to South Bridge. Along the rest of South Bridge, appalling
shopfronts. Above them some architecture. Nos. 4–6 were
refronted *c.* 1860 with shouldered arches and a bracketed
cornice. Next door at Nos. 7–9 a coarse bracketed cornice sits
on top of the original dentils. The pediment of Nos. 10–12
has been lost by the addition of another floor, with rusticated
quoins. Then a drab inter-war classical frame followed by a
plain original block dressed up with Victorian architraves.
The adjacent wall-head is raised on each side of a pedimented
gablet. Plain blocks lead to the gap overlooking Cowgate.
Here the tenements on each side were pedimented on both
main fronts and the lines of the Cowgate pediments survive
against the added top floors. The E side continues plain and

rather altered to Infirmary Street. Corner block originally
pedimented to W and S, but again the roof has been raised. A
recognizably original stretch next to Drummond Street, with
pedimented ends. The W side of South Bridge between Hunter Square and Cowgate has kept its pediments, but Nos.
100–106 have been recast in crudest Art Deco. [Inside however the old GOLDSMITHS HALL runs transversely across
the building. Compartmented shallow oval dome on pendentives. Screens of unfluted Ionic columns *in antis* at the ends.]
Beyond Cowgate a block unified with Chambers Street (*see*
above) and beyond Chambers Street Edinburgh University
Old Quad (*see* Public Buildings, above).

UPPER BOW *see* ROYAL MILE: LAWNMARKET

VENNEL *see* GRASSMARKET

VICTORIA STREET, VICTORIA TERRACE AND WEST BOW

Until the C19 West Bow was a precipitous Z-shaped street
leading from the Grassmarket to the Upper Bow at the foot
of Castlehill. The line of its final lunge up the hill to the N is
now marked by steps. Victoria Street and Victoria Terrace
are of 1829–34, part of *Thomas Hamilton*'s 1827 Improvement
Act scheme for new W and S approaches to the Old Town.
The lower part of West Bow was left, but Hamilton's new
street-line continues E (as Victoria Street) up to the new
George IV Bridge. On the N side of the new street a curving
terrace of shops, its flat roof a footpath from George IV
Bridge to Johnston Terrace and a base for Victoria Terrace
(the backs of the closes behind Lawnmarket).

VICTORIA TERRACE begins with the jagged profile of Lothian
Regional Council Headquarters (*see* Public Buildings, above).
Then BADEN POWELL HOUSE by *Paterson & Shiells*, built
as a Primitive Methodist Chapel in 1865. Italian Gothic gabled front with three tall windows and a cantilevered gablet
over the door. The spired belfry over the stair-bay at the r.
has been demolished. Nos. 5–6 are the rebuilt rear of Riddle's
Court (*see also* Royal Mile, Lawnmarket, above), thrifty
Jacobean with an arcaded ground floor and crowstepped
gablets, by *George Smith*, *c.* 1840. KIRK HOUSE E of Upper
Bow, again by *Paterson & Shiells*, 1865, was built as an
Original Secession chapel, carried over the footpath on a
round-arched arcade.* Italian Gothic with two tiers of
round-arched windows and crocketed gables. Then the backs
of St Columba's Free Church (*see* above) and of the buildings
fronting Johnston Terrace.

The N side of VICTORIA STREET, the plinth of the terrace, is

* This piazza was formerly repeated at the E end of the terrace.

one sweep of painted ashlar. Or was; the hammer-dressed base of Lothian Regional Council Headquarters is now an unhappy beginning. But after it, Hamilton's scheme (modified by *George Smith*) is intact. Uniform cornice-line but a steeply sloping site so that it is one-storey at the E end and three-storey at the W. Fat roll-moulded round-arched shop-windows at Nos. 8–20; mezzanines at the W end. Then, after the steps to Upper Bow, two storeys with narrower round-arched and keyblocked first-floor windows with early C17 detail. A full three storeys at Nos. 34–36, the windows of the upper floors set in giant arches repeating the detail of the preceding block. Simple architraves at Nos. 38–46.

Victoria Street is halted and joined to WEST BOW by one bay containing a stair (No. 87 West Bow) by *George Smith*, 1850, a most tactful solution of how to link old and new; ashlar-fronted to conform with the new, but crowstepped in sympathy with its other neighbour downhill. The four-storey-and-attic No. 89 West Bow is late C17. Windows grouped 2–1 and linked by sill-courses. Flight-hole for doves in the crowstepped centre gablet. Inside, late-C17 bolection-moulded wooden chimneypieces and plenty of panelling, mostly mid-C18 but some of the late C17 with lugged-architraved doorpieces. Ground-floor shopfront by *George Fox*, 1863. House and shop at Nos. 91–93 West Bow built by Thomas Crockett of Johnstounburn *c.* 1705. Five storeys; in the curvilinear gable two oval flight-holes for doves. Lintel and sill-courses combine with the raised stone margins of the windows to divide the four-bay front into panels of glass and rendering. The windows of the l. bay blocked up, probably in the mid C18. Early-C19 anta-pilastered door at the r. Inside, heavy plaster roundels enclosing truncated pendants at the ceilings of the stair. Moulded wooden balusters. Mid-C18 fielded panelling in all the front rooms, with panelled pilasters framing basket-arched stone chimneypieces. Round-arched and keyblocked china cupboard in a corner of a room on the first floor. Remains of simpler early C18 panelling in closets. Next Nos. 95–99, a harled tenement built by Janet McMath (widow of James Johnston, poultryman) in 1729, the date inscribed in the open pediment of the shop door. Five storeys, near-symmetrical, with windows grouped 1–3–1, but a pair of different-sized gablets, the r. one with a chimney, the l. with a C19 fleur-de-lis finial. The scale drops to three storeys and attic at Nos. 101–105. The base of its fleur-de-lis finial at the chunky crowstepped gablet is dated 1561; the C17 seems more likely. Paired windows and a forestair at the r. This side of West Bow ends with the five-storey-and-attic No. 107. Half a door lintel inscribed [BLESSED BE] GOD FOR AL HIS GIFTIS 1616 provides a credible date. Gable front to West Bow, originally with string-courses jumping up over the stair windows at the r. in the fashion of Gladstone's Land or Moubray House (*see* Royal Mile: Lawnmarket *and* High Street, above). The front to Grassmarket looks an early C18 reconstruction (regular fenestration and a gablet), but a stair-tower at the l. supports a C17 origin.

The s side of VICTORIA STREET begins with the convex-fronted INDIA BUILDINGS by *David Cousin*, 1864. Large and purposeful. The first bay a tall and narrow gable, its rich Scots Renaissance detail setting the tone for a grand five-bay section halted by a stark tower with bartizan and cap-house. The excitement over, strapwork pediments lead to a solid crowstepped gable with a two-storey oriel. Inside the main door, a long corridor-staircase leading through a series of arches to a domed and balconied rotunda. Except for the former St John's Church (*see* above), the street continues with very plain 1840s tenements (Nos. 5-7 by *David Bryce*) - only a suspicion of the 'Old Flemish' detail specified in the Improvement Act. Round the corner marking the approach to Grassmarket, the old WEST BOW takes over at Nos. 94-96, early C18, its central gablet with a flight-hole, the hungry jointing of its rubble front a witness of its restoration by *E. J. MacRae* in 1930. Harled frontage to Nos. 98-102 by *T. Waller Marwick*, 1964-8, meant to be a replica of the large late-C18 tenement which stood here. Its twin gablets were reproduced, but not their chimneys, or those of the gables. Chunky stair-tower at the back. By now Grassmarket has opened out to the w. Nos. 104-106 by *A. W. Macnaughtan*, 1879, tries hard to impress. Crowstepped gablet flanked by pedimented dormer-heads. Bold Jacobean detail, the upper windows set in giant over-arches. West Bow ends with a pair of tenements of the 1790s. Quoins at the corners and round-arched ground-floor openings. Centre gablet at Nos. 110-112. Behind, plain early C19 warehouses, now the TRAVERSE THEATRE.

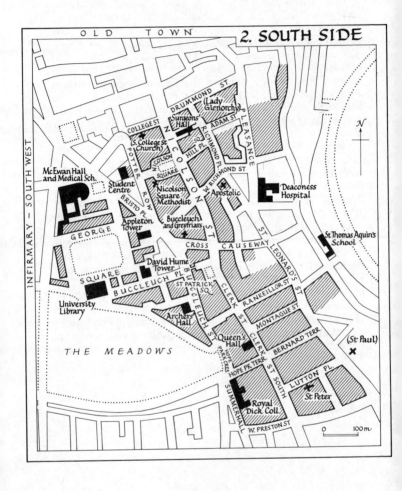

OLD TOWN

2. SOUTH SIDE

N

INFIRMARY – SOUTH WEST

DRUMMOND ST

(Lady Glenorchy)

COLLEGE ST

Surgeons' Hall

ADAM ST

RICHMOND PL.

HILL PL.

PLEASANCE

(S. College st Church)

POTTER ROW

NICOLSON SQUARE

NICOLSON ST

W. RICHMOND ST

McEwan Hall and Medical Sch.

Student Centre

Nicolson Square Methodist

Apostolic

Deaconess Hospital

BRISTO PL.

GEORGE

Appleton Tower

Buccleuch and Greyfriars

ST. LEONARD'S ST

St Thomas Aquin's School

CROSS CAUSEWAY

David Hume Tower

CLERK ST

SQUARE

BUCCLEUCH

ST. PATRICK SQ.

BUCCLEUCH ST

RANKEILLOR ST

University Library

Archers' Hall

MONTAGUE ST

BERNARD TERR.

THE MEADOWS

Queen's Hall

CLERK ST

HOPE PK. TERR.

HOPE PK CRES.

(St Paul)
×

LUTTON PL.

SUMMERHALL

Royal Dick Coll.

CLERK ST SOUTH

St Peter

W. PRESTON ST

0   100 m

The University and tenement area S of the Old Town. By the mid C18 there existed here a number of small estates, some with villas, and a straggle of tenements along Potterrow. After 1757, when Lady Nicolson offered building feus along the line of Nicolson Street, the estates began to be developed for tenements and, in George Square, terraced houses. A riding school designed by *Robert Adam* (since replaced by Surgeons' Hall) was built in 1764, Assembly Rooms in Buccleuch Place in 1783, and the South Bridge linking Nicolson Street to the Old and New Towns (*see* Old Town: Public Buildings) in 1788. For a time George Square was the most fashionable address in Edinburgh, but by 1800 the South Side had been eclipsed by the First New Town and its C19 development was respectable rather than smart, the workmanlike grid of streets giving little opportunity for calculated townscape effect and the fragmented ownership denying it any obvious centre.

Late C19 and early C20 decline was accompanied by some commercial rebuilding. Inter-war municipal housing, by *E. J. MacRae* and typically rubbly, took over a large chunk on the E. Most of the NW corner, including two-thirds of George Square, was flattened and partly rebuilt for the University of Edinburgh's post-war expansion. Conservation of the South Side is the present fashion, and has begun (1984) to cure the planning blight inflicted on the area E of Nicolson Street by the abortive scheme for a Bridges relief road.

CHURCHES

APOSTOLIC CHURCH, Davie Street. Built as an Original Secession chapel in 1813. Plain classic two-storey rectangle. Recessed entrance with a broad screen of Greek Doric columns *in antis*. Galleried interior reconstructed by *George Washington Browne*, 1886, with an enriched ceiling.★

BAPTIST CHAPEL, Pleasance. Disused. A piend-roofed rectangle of 1811 refronted and given Romanesque detail *c.* 1880, when it was owned by a United Presbyterian congregation.

BUCCLEUCH AND GREYFRIARS FREE CHURCH, West Cross-causeway. Vigorous Dec by *J., W. H. & J. M. Hay*, 1856-7. W front with a huge steeple. Massive diagonal buttresses and a very squat belfry at the tower; two tiers of lucarnes at the broached spire. The lower parts of the single-span roof mis-

---

★ This did not survive much-needed roof repairs, 1981.

leadingly suggest aisles. Inside, a braced collar roof of laminated timber. W gallery extended forward and the space beneath partitioned off in the reconstruction by *McLaren, Murdoch & Hamilton*, 1981.

BUCCLEUCH PARISH CHURCH, Chapel Street. Disused. Built as a chapel-of-ease in 1755–6; N aisle with a small ball finial added *c*. 1810. Reconstruction by *David MacGibbon*, 1866, provided an unappealing Gothic gable-front with a spired turret, and an apse at the S flank. – Some late C18 MONUMENTS in the graveyard.

CHURCH OF CHRIST (originally Church of Scotland), St Leonards. By *John Lessels*, 1880. Flat Scots Gothic front pretending that there is an aisled nave behind. Tower with a corbelled parapet and small spire on the l. of the gable; on its r. a parapet. Inside, a wagon roof with hammerbeam trusses. U-shaped gallery on cast-iron columns. – ORGAN by *Forster & Andrews*, 1880.

COLLEGE STREET UNITED PRESBYTERIAN, South College Street. Disused. Graeco-Italian by *Patrick Wilson*, 1856. Temple front centrepiece above shell-headed ground-floor windows. In the end bays, heavy bracketed balconies above massive round-arched doors.

FRIENDS' MEETING HOUSE, Pleasance. Disused. A piend-roofed box of 1791 built by *Alexander Paterson*, mason, and *Thomas Dott*, wright. Pedimented off-centre door. To the W a small graveyard opened in 1680. Late C18 pyramid-topped gatepiers.

HOPE PARK CONGREGATIONAL CHURCH, Hope Park Terrace. Disused. Lombardy Romanesque by *Sutherland & Walker*, 1875–6, with a small tower over the entrance. Horseshoe-galleried interior.

KIRK O'FIELD, Pleasance. Built as Charteris Memorial Church in 1910–12. Late Scots Gothic by *James B. Dunn*. NW tower, its red-tiled spire peeping up from the corbelled and battlemented parapet. Lorimerian vine enrichment on the vestibule ceiling. Wagon-roofed nave with W gallery. – MEMORIAL to A. H. Charteris † 1908. Bronze tablet with low relief bust by *P. M. C. Archibald*, cast by *Montacutelli Bros.*, Paris.

LADY GLENORCHY'S, Roxburgh Place. Disused. An ambitious scheme built in two stages. First, the buttressed halls at the N by *MacGibbon & Ross*, 1908–10. At one end the base of an intended steeple; at the other, the round-arched main entrance under an oriel, based on C15 work at St Giles'. The aisled church by *P. MacGregor Chalmers*, 1912–13, continues the late Scots Gothic idiom. Mouchette and Flamboyant traceried windows. Inside, stone arcades and a chancel.

NICOLSON SQUARE METHODIST CHURCH, Nicolson Square. A secular-looking church by *Thomas Brown*, 1815–16, set diagonally across the corner of the square behind a forecourt. Two-storey front based on Adam's design for the W block of the University. Rusticated ground floor. Set-back centre with an arcade and pilastered first floor under a balustrade. In the end bays, overarched Venetian windows. Inside, fluted cast-iron columns support the U-plan gallery, the small pilasters on its panelled front an embellishment by *Henry F. Kerr*, 1893. Ionic pilasters on the upper part of the walls. Inappropriate late Gothic oak PULPIT by *P. MacGregor Chalmers*, 1913, brought here from Lady Glenorchy's Church (*see* above) in 1974. – ORGAN by *Forster & Andrews*, 1864, rebuilt by *Ingram* in 1911, in a tripartite Corinthian aediculed case. – EPWORTH HALLS to the E by *Cousin, Ormiston & Taylor*, 1914–15; an unhappy intrusion.

NICOLSON STREET CHURCH, Nicolson Street. Disused. Large Perp firescreen front* by *James Gillespie Graham*, 1820. The body of the church bears no relation to the façade. Interior reconstructed by *J. R. McKay*, 1932.

ROXBURGH FREE CHURCH (now The King Khalid bin Abdul Aziz of Saudi Arabia Symposium Hall), Hill Square. Lumpy Gothic by *Thomas Hamilton*, 1846–7. Converted to a lecture hall by *James Parr & Partners*, 1982.

ST PAUL'S NEWINGTON, South Clerk Street. Originally Newington Free Church. Strong boxy late Scots Gothic front by *Henry & Maclennan*, 1907. The church behind, built to *David Cousin*'s design in 1843, was recast in 1847 when the E end was partitioned off as a school and the rest of the building heightened, with galleries in the aisles. Inside, pointed arcades on cast-iron columns. Depressed arch into the chancel, formed in 1907. – ORGAN by *C. & F. Hamilton*, 1902, rebuilt by *Ingram* in 1908. – STAINED GLASS. Three windows in the N aisle. One (War Memorial) by *James Ballantine II*, 1921; the others similar in style.

ST PETER (Episcopal), Lutton Place. A large and beautiful Geometric church by *William Slater* of *Slater & Carpenter*, 1857–65. Aisled nave, buttressed NE vestry, NW steeple, narthex and octagonal baptistery. The continuous roof of the nave and semi-octagonal chancel is broken only by a (truncated) flèche. The lean-to roofs of the buttressed aisles reach nearly to the nave eaves, so there is no clearstorey. Stark tower of two huge stages, the first with a statue of St Peter by *Dorothy M. McKay*, 1935, over the tall entrance arch, the second with lancet openings to the belfry which is reached by a stair-turret on the E face. Spire 56 m. high, diapered with bands of ornament and cinquefoils.

Prosperous Tractarian interior. A lofty porch in the tower, 43 then the flat-roofed narthex like a cloister opening W into the vaulted baptistery, E into the church. Broad five-bay nave arcade on polished Peterhead granite piers with minimally projecting stiff-leaf capitals. The aisles continue a further bay to flank the choir but have their own 'chancel arches'. In the E bay of the S aisle the organ chamber. Stencilled decoration

---

* Crocketed pinnacles removed during (but not by) the Scottish Civic Trust Conference, 1980.

of the braced collar-beam nave and aisle roofs by *G. H. Potts*;
the chancel roof was painted with sacred symbols on a blue
ground, the wall with panels of the Evangelists and the Agnus
Dei on a damask ground,* both by *George Dobie & Son*,
1890.

Expensive FURNISHINGS of 1865. Round Caen stone PUL-
PIT on marble shafts by *Poole*. – CHOIR STALLS carved by
Forsyth. – Elaborate scheme of encaustic TILES in the chancel
by *Minton & Co*. – STAINED GLASS. Chancel windows by
Clayton & Bell, 1865 in good strong colours. – In the E bay
of the N aisle the Duncan memorial window (The Servants of
the Lord) by *Isobel Goudie*, 1935. – The next two windows of
this aisle and the three E windows of the S aisle by *Clayton
& Bell c.* 1865–80. – More tasteful, but no better, the Bax-
endine memorial window (SS. George and Andrew), after
1918, and the Dawson and Robertson window (Post-Resur-
rection scenes), *c.* 1930. – In the baptistery, one light (Blessed
are the Pure in Heart) after 1898. – ORGAN by *Frederick Holt*,
1865; rebuilt by *Scovell* in 1913 and by *Rushworth & Dreaper*
in 1959–60.

PUBLIC BUILDINGS

ARCHERS' HALL, Buccleuch Street. Built in two stages, and it
shows. The r. half, by *Alexander Laing*, 1776–7, was a tall
piend-roofed block. In 1900 *A. F. Balfour Paul* blocked its
upper windows and extended it S in a different coloured stone.
Balfour Paul's new door under a heavy scroll-pedimented
armorial panel is an unsatisfactory balance for the first-floor
Venetian window of the addition. His off-centre cupola makes
matters worse. Expensive but bloodless early-C18-style interior.

DEACONESS HOSPITAL, Pleasance. By *Hardy & Wight*, in two
stages: red sandstone with the most perfunctory Gothic detail,
1894; equally dreary grey crowstepped extension, 1897. One
floor added to first block in reconstruction by *A. F. Balfour
Paul*, 1934.

GEORGE WATSON'S LADIES' COLLEGE (now UNIVERSITY
OF EDINBURGH PSYCHOLOGY DEPARTMENT), George
Square. A makeshift trying to impress: an L-shaped building
by *MacGibbon & Ross*, 1876, extended E by the same architects in 1890–3 to form a U, the original block recast in the
pedestrian French Renaissance style of the addition, and the
courtyard filled with a one-storey glass-roofed hall. Stone
screen-front more tensely French classical with pedimented
entrance. Admirably dull, had not the return wings to George
Square been one of four and one of three bays. The chance
to produce symmetry was missed by *Peter L. Henderson* in
his addition of 1902 – tired Renaissance pretending that it

---

* Now hidden by curtains (1984).

does not belong to its dowdy parent. In 1910–11 *George Washington Browne* tried to make something of the w wing, extending it from four to nine bays. Powerful centre with a Venetian window rising into the segmental pediment, its tympanum carved with the arms of the Merchant Company whose school this was.

HERIOT'S SCHOOL, Davie Street. By *John Chesser*, 1875. Plentiful detail of early C17 George Heriot's School type. Ogee-roofed rounds at the gabled centre. Extension at the r. of 1887, repeating the detail but muddying the design.

NEW COLLEGE MISSION, Pleasance. By *Henry F. Kerr*, 1891–3, and looking like two buildings. At the l. a tall narrow tenement, symmetrical, with three-storey gabled oriels. At the r. the broad gable of a hall with chapel above. Five-light window with Scots late Gothic tracery.

PLEASANCE TRUST, Pleasance. By *J. Inch Morrison*, 1925–38. Rubbly Scots C17 style with most roofs pantiled. Hall range on the N side of the courtyard with massive battered buttresses and large gableted dormer-heads with finials.

QUEEN'S HALL, South Clerk Street. Built by *Robert Brown*, 1823, as the Hope Park Chapel of Ease, a less extravagant version of Thomas Brown's contemporary St Mary, Bellevue Crescent (*see* Northern New Town). Two-storey pilastered and pedimented villa front with a domed three-stage steeple to show that it was a church. The round arches of the windows and doors are quoted with jarring effect in the new screen walls by *Robert Hurd & Partners*, 1978–9, part of the conversion to a concert hall. Inside, a round vestibule flanked by stair-halls. D-shaped auditorium, its gallery on cast-iron columns with acanthus-leaf capitals. Round-headed windows for the gallery, segment-headed below. Circles and foliaged roses on the ceiling. – In place of the pulpit a CHAMBER ORGAN (by *William Gray*, 1810, restored by *Christopher Dickens*, 1978–9) provides the focal point. – In the stair-halls, late C18 BOARDS painted with the Commandments, Lord's Prayer and Creed, brought here from Buccleuch Parish Church (*see* above) in 1950.

ROYAL (DICK) VETERINARY COLLEGE, Summerhall. Fag-end Wrenaissance by *David McArthy*, 1909–16, the front a dreary frame of columns and pediments. Inside, the pompous stair-hall is an epitome of bourgeois smugness, its Glasgow-style STAINED GLASS incorporating a medallion of William Dick, 1923. In the courtyard, a lumpy STATUE of Dick by *John Rhind*, 1883. Additions by *Alan Reiach, Eric Hall & Partners*, 1969–71. On the N an awkward ribbed tower. On the SE a glazed brick block forming a platform for a carved recumbent horse of *c.* 1835.*

ST LEONARD'S SCHOOL, Forbes Street. Disused. Plain; by *Robert Wilson*, 1879.

* This crowned the centre of the original Dick Veterinary College in Clyde Street.

St Thomas Aquins School, St Leonard's Lane. By *J. A. Carfrae*, 1913. Long, grand front with plentiful Scots Renaissance detail, overlooking Holyrood Park. Tower, more aggressive, at the s end.

90 Surgeons' Hall, Nicolson Street. A T-plan Ionic temple by *W. H. Playfair*, 1829-32. Across the front of the site, a channelled screen wall containing pedimented foot-gates with outsize scroll buttresses. At its ends, square piers with tripod incense-burners. In the middle the wall forms a base for the six fluted columns of the Hall's pedimented portico. Scrolly honeysuckle in the tympanum, honeysuckle and lotus frieze. Huge consoles support the entrance door pediment. The ends of the T are pedimented with giant attached piers, but do not stand out as they should from the central range whose first floor was thickened in *A. F. Balfour Paul*'s reconstruction of 1908-9, the additions carried on Doric columns. At the same time the Hall was joined by a bridge to Nos. 7-9 Hill Square at the SE and a door pediment dated 1697 from the Old Surgeons' Hall (*see* Old Town, Public Buildings) re-used in their W front. On the NE a detached classroom block of *c.* 1850 with a steep pediment.

Inside, a round two-storey coffer-domed vestibule. First-floor gallery on very flat consoles. Ahead, two rooms *en suite* made by Balfour Paul from the original Fellows' Hall. In the Reception Room, doorcases with shallow block pediments on huge consoles look like Playfair work re-used. The Librarians' Room ceiling has delicate leaf enrichment and a broad rectangular arch with heavy foliaged consoles for the broad bay pushed out in 1908-9. Then the Lister Room (originally Lecture Hall) with panelling of 1908-9 by *Scott Morton & Co.* The President's Room carries on its simple late C17 character. Flush-panelled Council Room by *Robert Hurd & Partners*, *c.* 1960. On the N, the East Reading Room made out of a waiting room, bedroom and kitchen. Four bays, three groin-vaulted and one with a barrel-vault. A corridor joins this to the octagonal NW stair-hall. On its half-landing, armorial stained glass of 1897. In the first-floor Fellows' Hall (originally West Museum), more Balfour Paul work with flat arches of the Librarians' Room type opening into his N and S extensions. In the middle he produced a coved ceiling with a glazed saucer-dome and leafy enrichment at the corners. In the Museum Playfair's austerity survives. Nave-and-aisle plan with pilastered piers; compartmented ceiling. Galleries in the aisles and across the ends. In the Hill Square extension, two museum rooms of 1908-9: one combines Playfairian piers and galleries with a Wrenaissance ceiling; the other, made by removing a floor, is disconcertingly slit-like.

University of Edinburgh George Square Redevelopment. A major expansion of the University's city-centre buildings. The overall layout by *Charles Holden*, 1947, was modified by *Basil Spence* in 1955 and by *Percy Johnson-Marshall* in 1962 and 1980. The whole of the s and most of the N and E sides of George Square have been rebuilt, the streets to NE obliterated, making way for new buildings. On the N side of the square, two blocks by *W. N. W. Ramsay.*[*] The PHARMACOLOGY DEPARTMENT of 1968, simultaneously stodgy and fussy. W of George Watson's Ladies College (*see* Public Buildings), the HUGH ROBSON BUILDING of 1978 repeats the formula but with the advantage of greater length. In the SE corner of the square, the UNIVERSITY LIBRARY by 101 *Basil Spence, Glover & Ferguson*, 1965–7. Mannered Modern Movement at its best. Rectangular tier of six shelves. Behind them, continuous glazing. Balcony fronts resting on exposed concrete 'beam ends', a conceit, since they form no part of the main structure. The balconies are not for recreation but to shield the students and books inside from the sun – not obviously necessary on the N side, but narrow functionalism must sometimes defer to style. Inside, cool two-storey entrance hall with louvred teak walls. Then a group at the SE corner of the square by *Robert Matthew, Johnson-Marshall & Partners.* GEORGE SQUARE THEATRE, 1967, is of only two storeys, the ground floor a stem for the massive overhanging lecture room above, its shape expressing the raked seating inside. Decent good manners are shown by the four-storey glass and ashlar horizontals of the ADAM FERGUSON and WILLIAM ROBERTSON BUILDINGS of 1964–7. Set back from the corner, the DAVID HUME TOWER of 1960–3, confidently detailed, fourteen storeys of dark grey slate and ashlar. Narrow S stair-tower with a fully glazed front to give a touch of excitement. Low NE lecture hall. In Crichton Street, the carefully detailed eleven-storey APPLETON TOWER by *Alan Reiach, Eric Hall & Partners*, 1963–6. Alternating horizontals of mosaic and glass gripped by a glazed stair-tower behind. To the N, STUDENT CENTRE of 1966–73 by *Morris & Steedman*. On the r. a boxy block raised on stilts, one jamb and the lintel of each of the upper-floor windows boldly canted. Ribbed concrete towers at the ends. Low block on the l., its soggy 'Plexiglass' dome a black contrast to the white concrete. Very effective in strong sunlight; lumpish in rain. On its S is to be built (1984) the DENTAL HOSPITAL, also by *Morris & Steedman*, in a friendly neo-Fascist style.

UNIVERSITY OF EDINBURGH MEDICAL SCHOOL AND McEWAN HALL, Teviot Place. A large Venetian Cinquecento complex designed by *R. Rowand Anderson* in 1874 and built in two stages, the Medical School in 1876–86, the McEwan Hall in 1888–97. Three-storey Medical School buildings round two courtyards. Red-tiled roofs. The front to Teviot Place is long and regular. Channelled ground floor; second-floor pilastrade. In the middle a pend arch under a balconied aedicule flanked by pedimented shell-headed niches. On top, a round-headed pediment derived from the

church of San Zaccaria. Tower at the W end; at the E the base
of an uncompleted San-Marco-type campanile. The W flank
much more relaxed, stepping confidently down Meadow
Walk as a succession of rectangles with one large bow. (S
extension by *W. N. W. Ramsay*, 1958–60.)

Inside the main courtyard, variety. The N range reproduces
the street front but without the six E bays, so the archway is
off-centre. On the W, a palazzo. A corbelled stair-turret
breaks the S range into two unequal parts. On the r., giant
over-arches; on the l., just two bays of beautifully decorated
bipartite windows. Door into a groin-vaulted hall. The E
range is again divided by a stair-tower hard against the pedimented porch of a severe palazzo-front. In the SE corner, a
pend to Park Place. Here symmetry returns. The two lower
floors of the seven centre bays are set back under a third floor
carried on round arches springing from huge consoles (cf. the
Palazzo Fava, Bologna). Aedicular monument to Archbishop
Tait designed by *Anderson* with a bronze bust by *Mario
Raggi*, 1885.

98   The D-plan McEwan Hall is a magnificent petrified blanc-
mange with a shallow ribbed dome and lantern. Niches meant
for statues in the straight buttresses. Blind second-floor arcading in red sandstone above a shallow-carved frieze. Semicircular pediment over the E door, its tympanum with a relief
of a degree-giving ceremony.

Inside, a groin-vaulted brick-faced corridor runs round the
curve of the D. At its SW end, a groin-vaulted vestibule into
a stair-hall. Slightly curving dog-leg stair under a moulded
saucer dome carried on corbelled vaulting. On the landing,
an arcade and more vaulting. All this decorated with heraldry.

The hall's plan was based on the 'form of the ancient Greek
theatre as best suited for an auditorium and one likely to
ensure good acoustic results' – a D with a shallow rectangular
apse in the straight side. Two tiers of balustraded galleries
behind giant arcades carrying the half-dome of the roof.
Opulent painted decoration by *William M. Palin*, 1892–7. On
the dome, figures of the Arts and Sciences. Over the proscenium arch to the apse, 'The Temple of Fame' with enthroned
goddesses of Science, Art and Literature. On the r. of the
arch is Minerva receiving the McEwan Hall; on the l. Fame
Crowning Success. On the splayed ingoes, figures of Perseverance, Intelligence, Imagination and Experience. Organ in
a Baroque case by *Robert Hope-Jones*, 1897, rebuilt by *Henry
Willis & Sons* in 1953.

The forecourt to the E is a formal paved layout by *Andrew
Mackie* of *Percy Johnson-Marshall & Associates*, 1980–2.
Planting contained in simulated stone walls, their coping
scooped up at every change in level. Stone-based Venetian
lantern contemporary with the hall.

UNIVERSITY OF EDINBURGH STUDENTS' UNION, Teviot
Place. By *Sydney Mitchell & Wilson*, 1887–8. Early C16 Scots
style with a crowstepped gable clasped by drum towers of the

Falkland or Holyrood type but with large windows. Large late Gothic traceried windows. By the same architects the w extension of 1902–5, still early C16 style but a great hall instead of a gatehouse. Slender corner turrets. In the gabled E bay a five-light second-floor window, semi-elliptically arched, with a balcony. The C16 character extends inside. Circular stair in the w tower leading to the Debating Hall. Shallow-pitched hammerbeam roof. In the w extension a galleried library. The room above has a tunnel-vault with bands of vine decoration.

MANSION

HERMITS AND TERMITS, St Leonards. A neat harled house built for William Clifton, Solicitor of Excise, in 1734. The front windows build up as a pyramid from the five-bay ground floor through the three-bay first floor to a chimney gablet. Scrolled skewputts. Inside, panelled entrance hall. Dining room on the r., panelled with pilasters framing the china cupboard. Geometric stair with turned mahogany balusters; large clamshell on the ceiling above. Another panelled room on the first floor.

PERAMBULATION

Starting at the N end of NICOLSON STREET, on the E side a trio of tenements of *c.* 1790, with open-pedimented chimney gablets, which form the w flank of a development on land offered to feuars by Dr Alexander Monro from 1788 and complete by *c.* 1800. The scheme was for tenements round three sides of a large stableyard, with coach-houses and stables on the fourth. To DRUMMOND STREET the austerity of droved ashlar is relieved by ground-floor over-arches at Nos. 12–21. *Robert Burn* was architect of one of these, and *Simon Fraser*, mason, built Nos. 16–19, including the arched pend to the stableyard. Nos. 3–5 ROXBURGH PLACE, by *James Playfair,** 1791–2, conform in overall height with the surrounding five-storey buildings, but have instead of the three lower storeys the two-storey frontage of the former St Peter's Episcopal Chapel, with overarched Venetian‡ windows above a rusticated ground floor. Inside, side galleries on Roman Doric columns. The flats above were not finished internally until *c.* 1805, probably also the date of the Tuscan-columned doorpiece to the common stair. To the s, the LISTER INSTITUTE by *Rowand Anderson, Kininmonth & Paul,* 1962, two blocks faced with aggregate panels and joined by a glazed link. On the E side No. 8 is by *Sydney Greenwood* (Chief

* Or, conceivably, by his brother John Playfair, the mathematician.
‡ All three are Venetian (1984), but the outer windows seem to have been originally tripartite under huge fanlights.

Architect, National Coal Board), 1967; the rest is occupied by Lady Glenorchy's Church (*see* Churches, above). After Roxburgh Place, Drummond Street continues with a development for which feus were sold by Francis Braidwood from *c.* 1800. Four-storey and basement tenements, their ground floors channelled except at Nos. 28-31. Round the corner in ROXBURGH STREET, the height drops by a floor. Here Nos. 1-7 on the E side show a modification of the scheme: two-storey-and-basement houses with a mutuled cornice and a couple of pilastered doorpieces. But the fragments of their neighbours show that the original scheme continued both in Roxburgh Street and in Drummond Street on whose N side is St Patrick's (R.C.) Primary School (*see* Public Buildings, above).

Back in Nicolson Street, the w side begins with a tall tenement of *c.* 1790. Then the old EMPIRE THEATRE by *William & T.R. Milburn*, 1927. Joyless Art Deco outside; inside, a huge space with a dome in the coffered ceiling, term columns at the boxes and an urn in a sunburst over the proscenium. Plate glass in a free Renaissance frame at Nos. 37-41 by *Peter L. Henderson*, 1899. Opposite is Surgeons' Hall (*see* Public Buildings, above). To the r. opens NICOLSON SQUARE, developed from 1765. Of that date are the tenements along the N side. Cherrycock-pointed squared rubble at Nos. 2 and 7-11; a boldly projecting cornice and balcony at Nos. 4-6. The NW corner jinks as if to form a street out of the square. Here, a classy tenement with a pilastered door to the common stair in the centre, and above it a round-arched window with astragals intersecting to form pointed panes. An open-pedimented gablet on each side. At the w end of the square, tenements of *c.* 1765 formed part of an H-shaped block which lost its crossbar when MARSHALL STREET was formed in 1877; the two surviving ranges were given Scots Renaissance jambs and crowsteps. Inside, a great deal of fielded panelling and chimneypieces with shouldered lintels. At the sw corner of the square the Methodist Church (*see* above). Nos. 33-34 at the corner with Nicolson Street gained a jolly half-timbered and gabled top-hamper with an angle-turret *c.* 1870. In the garden of the square, the BRASSFOUNDERS' COLUMN designed by *James Gowans* for the International Exhibition, 1886. The small statue of a brassfounder is by *John S. Rhind*.

In Nicolson Street late C18 tenements on the E side are halted by the red Corncockle sandstone of the ROYAL BANK by *Thomas P. Marwick*, 1902, François I, with an octagonal turret at the corner to Hill Place. HILL PLACE and HILL SQUARE were built on land offered to feuars by James Hill from 1808. At the w end of Hill Place were small tenements. Then a grander scheme of unified design at Hill Square. Into this gentility intrude a concrete corner of the Lister Institute and the old Roxburgh Free Church (*see* Churches, above). Nicolson Street continues across Hill Place with plain early C19 tenements abruptly followed by Nos. 52-58, a slab of green aggregate panels with thin ribs by *Mottram, Patrick, Whitehorn & Dalgleish*, 1963. Decent post-modern block by *Richard E. Moira & James Wann*, 1982, on the corner of WEST RICHMOND STREET where early C19 tenements on the S side lead to DAVIE STREET, with the Apostolic Church and Heriot's School (q.v.), and RICHMOND PLACE. Here, the red brick ROYAL BLIND ASYLUM workshops are by *Peddie & Washington Browne*, 1886–8. Off-centre crow-stepped gablet and colonnettes at the windows.

Tenements of *c.* 1770 on the W side of Nicolson Street turn the corner into WEST NICOLSON STREET with a Gibbsian door-piece at No. 1. No. 17 is grander, with a basket-arched pend and an open-pedimented gablet. Opposite are the remains of the SOUTHERN MARKETS of 1824, pilastered entrances with attached columns in a Georgian Norman style. To the S, Nicolson Street Church (*see* Churches, above).

The E side of Nicolson Street between West Richmond Street and East Crosscauseway, once an agreeable medley of the late C18 and early C19, was redeveloped in 1979–81. Some fronts were retained and others rebuilt, supposedly in replica. *Norman Gray* was the architect. In EAST CROSSCAUSEWAY at the corner with HOWDEN STREET, the Scots Renaissance FISHER'S BUILDINGS by *T.P. Marwick*, 1885–8. The SIMON SQUARE CENTRE to their N was built in 1887 as the office block of a foundry. Hammer-dressed masonry and crowstepped gablets.

After Crosscauseway, Nicolson Street becomes ST PATRICK STREET. The rubble tenements facing each other at its beginning were built by William Archibald, slater, *c.* 1780. Then, on the E side, a rough ashlar tenement leading to large rendered tenements with chimneyed gablets built by Archibald in partnership with James Aikman, mason, *c.* 1785, and a roofless building of the same date. These form the E side of ST PATRICK SQUARE. On its N side, only a polite neo-Georgian block of 1938 at the E corner. The S and W sides were begun *c.* 1800 to a unified scheme with rusticated ground floors, the unity disturbed by the taller and slightly projecting Nos. 35–39.

The line of Nicolson Street is continued S by CLERK STREET, built on Major John Hope's estate from *c.* 1810. Droved ashlar tenements, their front elevations by *Robert Brown*. The white-tiled ODEON CINEMA is an intruder, Garage Art Deco by *W. E. Trent*, 1930, but with a lavish 'Greek Theatre' interior lit by stars in the sky ceiling. Brown's scheme for the Hope Estate continues with RANKEILLOR STREET and MONTAGUE STREET, where building began in 1812. Of this date are the plain tenements with rusticated ground floor along the N sides of both streets and a short stretch of the S side of Rankeillor Street. In Rankeillor Street the unified design is broken by Nos. 12–14 of *c.* 1820, with lower tripartite ground-floor windows. Development resumed in the 1860s with bay-windowed tenements in Rankeillor Street.

The Queen's Hall (*see* Public Buildings, above) marks the beginning of SOUTH CLERK STREET, a development on Sir Robert Preston's estate from *c.* 1830. Georgian and Georgian survival mixed with 1871 bay-windows at Nos. 12–32. On the E side St Paul's Newington Church (*see* Churches, above). On the W, the old SOUTHERN LITERARY INSTITUTE (Nos. 34–42), Italianate bluster by *Robert Paterson*, 1871.* The Georgian survival of South Clerk Street is carried on at Nos. 1–19 LUTTON PLACE, 1852–9, with rusticated ground floors and anta-pilastered doorpieces. The rest of Lutton Place, except for St Peter (*see* Churches, above), is filled with a simpler scheme of tenements with channelled ground floors, 1863–71, extending S into Oxford Street. At the S end of South Clerk Street WEST PRESTON STREET moves off to the W. On its N side plain tenements, Nos. 2–18 by *Thomas Brown*, 1824, the rest completed in the same style in 1851, lead to SUMMERHALL PLACE, built in 1835, with a Roman Doric columned and pedimented door at No. 5. For the Royal Dick Veterinary College, *see* Public Buildings, above. To the N, the bay-windows of HOPE PARK TERRACE (1863) give way at HOPE PARK CRESCENT (*c.* 1860) to a scheme still of the Rankeillor Street Georgian type.

The E side of BUCCLEUCH STREET kicks off with a couple of tenements of *c.* 1780. A gablet at No. 130 with chimneystacks like ears and a gabled centre at the back; round-arched windows in the gablet of Nos. 118–124. Then dreary late Victorian tenements relieved by two buildings of *c.* 1770, No. 92 and the pantiled Nos. 76–78. BOROUGHLOCH LANE leads to the old BOROUGHLOCH BREWERY by *Lessels & Taylor*, 1897. Red sandstone with a few Baronial touches towards the Meadows. To its E NORTH MEADOW LANE runs past late Georgian stables to HOPE PARK SQUARE, where No. 6 of *c.* 1725 has a broad scrolled pediment and round-headed second-floor windows with hoodmoulds. Inside, a panelled room with pilasters framing the fireplace and a shell-headed china-cupboard. W of Hope Park Square, the old BUCCLEUCH PARISH SCHOOL by *George Smith*, 1839, Tudor, with an octagonal bellcote and strapwork pediments. Back in Buccleuch Street, the Archers' Hall (*see* above) on the l. On the r., contrasting tenements: Nos. 75–77 rubble, *c.* 1770, Nos. 53–57 stripped Scots Renaissance in red sandstone, *c.* 1890, No. 49 hungry-pointed rubble by *E. J. MacRae*, 1935. Opposite the entry to Buccleuch Place, Nos. 27–29 of *c.* 1770, with a Venetian window in the gablet.

BUCCLEUCH PLACE is the grandest street in the South Side, more than 18 m. broad. It was laid out by *James Brown* as a continuation of his George Square development (*see* below). Feus were sold from 1779. On the S side, main door and common stair tenement blocks of four storeys, basement and

---

* 'We have seldom seen a more weakly detailed and ill-proportioned elevation,' said *The Builder*.

attic. Droved ashlar, most with shallow-projecting rusticated quoins. Nos. 1-6 are by *James Brown, c.* 1790. Channelled ground floor except at the slightly recessed stair bays. Roman Doric columned doorpieces at Nos. 3 and 5 and, with an open pediment, at No. 6. Roman Doric pilastered doors in the outer bays of Nos. 7-13. In the centre, three anta-pilastered doors under a common cornice rising to form a pediment in the middle. This block was built in 1786-7 by *John Simpson* and *Alexander Deans,* wrights. Roman Doric pilasters at the entrances to the main door flats of Nos. 14-16, 1783. The rear wing of this block was occupied by the 'George's Square Assembly Rooms'* (later converted to housing). The very grand tenement of Nos. 17-19 was built by Jonathan Fulwood, *c.* 1780-90. Roman Doric columns at the main flat entrances. In the centre, pairs of Gothick-glazed Venetian windows. Columned doors sharing a cornice at Nos. 20-21. The N side of the street was never fully developed, for its w half was bounded by the garden walls of George Square houses. Then, tenements of *c.* 1820 at Nos. 30-35. No. 36 was not built until 1872-3. Canted corner to Buccleuch Street where it links up with a pair of *c.* 1775 tenements. Opposite, more late C18 tenements, Nos. 1-5 BUCCLEUCH STREET decidedly vernacular. At the corner of CHAPEL STREET and West Nicolson Street, a large front garden. Behind it is PEAR TREE HOUSE, built for William Reid, a merchant, *c.* 1747. Pedimented gablet and scrolled skewputts. In the rear extension a pompous late Victorian boardroom. To its N, Nos. 27-53 WEST NICOLSON STREET and 4-16 CHAPEL STREET were built *c.* 1820, with round-arched shop windows and doors. Beyond, in Chapel Street, tall late C18 round gatepiers with fluted necks and belted ball-finials‡ announce CHAPEL HOUSE, built by *Richard Frame,* mason, *c.* 1750. Urns and swagged tureens on its parapet. Interior gutted for conversion to a mosque by *Ian G. Lindsay & Partners,* 1982.

CRICHTON STREET leads w past the Appleton Tower to GEORGE SQUARE. The whole of the N and s sides and half the E side are now filled by C20 University buildings and the old George Watson's Ladies' College (for all these *see* Public Buildings, above), paying no attention to each other or to the Georgian survivors. Laid out in 1766 by *James Brown,* the square was the most ambitious scheme of unified architectural 115 character yet attempted in Edinburgh. Not that ambition went very far. Terraced houses on all four sides, each side divided into two blocks by a narrow lane which was central except at the N side; here a wider off-centre gap preserved the s view from Ross (or Bristo) House. Brown kept a certain control over height and design. *Michael Nasmyth* was the builder of at least some houses. The W side starts at its N end

---

* Here, according to Lord Cockburn (1779-1854), was 'in my youth the whole fashionable dancing, as indeed the fashionable everything'.

‡ One is missing.

with two-storey and basement houses at Nos. 16–22,* 1767–74. Cherrycock-pointed Craigmillar rubble. Then, No. 23A, 1779, a one-storey and-basement villa built across the centre lane. Three bays with round-headed over-arches, a Venetian window in the centre. s of this the houses have three storeys. Nos. 23–27 (1770–5) continue the cherrycock pointing and Craigmillar stone, but with Roman Doric and Ionic columned doorpieces and rusticated quoins. Droved ashlar at Nos. 28 and 29. Bolection frieze at the corniced doorpiece of No. 28, 1779. No. 29 of 1770 is more pretentious: round-arched door with an elaborate fanlight flanked by windows set in over-arches. The N half of the E side of the square was built in 1774–9. Only No. 60 is of Craigmillar rubble; the rest are of droved Craigleith ashlar, all of three storeys and basement, with Roman Doric and fluted Ionic columned doorpieces.

* No. 20 was raised to three storeys c. 1900.

3. SOUTH WEST

This area has no single historical identity. The earliest development was Portsburgh* (outside the city, to the w of Grassmarket), extending up West Port to the Main Point junction where
the old roads to Glasgow (now East Fountainbridge) and Linlithgow (now Bread Street) branched off to the w. All this became notoriously poor and squalid (the cattle market was on the
site now occupied by the Edinburgh College of Art), and was
later a stamping ground for Victorian housing reformers.

The patchwork of individual estates to the w and s of Portsburgh was developed from the late c18 onwards, starting with
Ponton Street and Semple Street which bear the names of their
sometime owners. Many had hopeful Georgian layouts, but
apart from the lonely masterpiece of Gardner's Crescent their
design was unexciting and only the sites fronting the main
thoroughfares were attractive to Georgian builders. The most
important estate was that of the Grindlays of Orchardfield
(extending as far s as the old Linlithgow Road) for which the
Merchant Company adopted *William Burn*'s layout in 1820.
Burn also provided the plan and some very similar elevations in
1822 for the estate of Major James Weir between the Linlithgow
and Glasgow roads, where feuing had begun in 1810. Both
schemes included rubble-fronted artisan tenements over shops.
In the next development to the s a similar row of tenements (in
Home Street) was the only executed part of the scheme prepared by *James Gillespie Graham* for James Home Rigg of
Downfield, Tarvit and Morton on part of the lands of Drumdryan House, and offered for feuing in 1810. Here the present
line of Brougham Street was fixed in 1857 and the rest laid out
ten years later, with Lonsdale Place fronting the meadows instead of the intended Morton Crescent. For the rest, the gaps
left by Georgian builders gave plenty of opportunities for Victorian enterprise to commission some of the most eccentric and
personal architecture to be seen in Edinburgh or anywhere else.
For convenience the South-West area includes the great Victorian complex of the Royal Infirmary, though as a teaching
hospital its links with the University of Edinburgh, and thus
with the South Side, are strong.

* From 1649 to 1856 Portsburgh was a separate but subservient barony extending right along the City's s boundary. The name survives in this part, which
should strictly be called West Portsburgh.

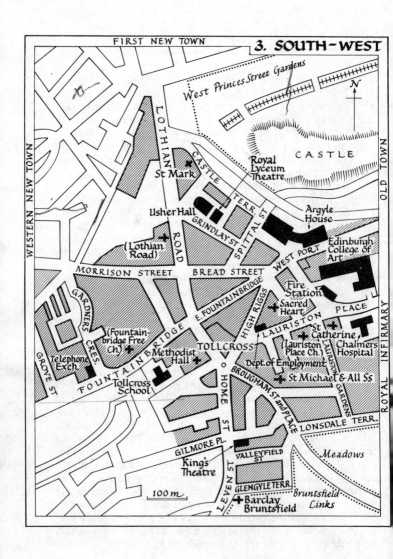

3. SOUTH-WEST

FIRST NEW TOWN

WESTERN NEW TOWN

West Princes Street Gardens

N

CASTLE

OLD TOWN

Royal Lyceum Theatre

St Mark

CASTLE TERR.

Usher Hall

SPITTAL ST.

Argyle House

(Lothian Road)

GRINDLAY ST

West Port

Edinburgh College of Art

LOTHIAN

ROAD

MORRISON STREET   BREAD STREET

Fire Station

Sacred Heart

HIGH RIGGS

LAURISTON   PLACE

E. FOUNTAINBRIDGE

St Catherine

GARDNERS CRES.

(Fountain-bridge Free Ch.)

FOUNTAINBRIDGE

Methodist Hall

TOLLCROSS

(Lauriston Place Ch.)

Chalmers Hospital

LAURISTON GARDENS

Telephone Exch.

Dept. of Employment

St Michael & All Ss

GROVE ST

Tollcross School

HOME ST

BROUGHAM ST and PLACE

LONSDALE TERR.

ROYAL INFIRMARY

GILMORE PL.

King's Theatre

VALLEYFIELD ST

Meadows

LEVEN ST

GLENGYLE TERR.

Bruntsfield Links

100 m

Barclay Bruntsfield

CHURCHES

BARCLAY-BRUNTSFIELD CHURCH (originally Free Church), 40
Barclay Place. Powerful Ruskinian Gothic by *Frederick T.
Pilkington*, 1862–4, the heavily corbelled and lucarned spire
rising to 76 m. to dominate the S view from Tollcross and the
city's whole SW skyline. Miss Barclay bequeathed the money
for its building. Exceptionally, the description must start inside. In the heart-shaped auditorium two tiers of galleries
with carved barley-sugar fronts follow the curve of the
broader N end. Massive square piers rise through them. The
sides of the heart are interrupted by columns with early
French capitals, the upper walls nipped in to make a trefoil
plan with chancel and flanking transepts. The two piers and
two columns carry the square roof. Intersecting trusses with
arch-braces, colonnette queen-posts and a mutual king-post
with a florid leafy pendant. Wooden rib-vaults over the transepts, radial rafters over the chancel. – Bow-fronted marble
PULPIT by *Pilkington*. – Above it the ORGAN by *R. Hope-
Jones*, 1896, rebuilt by *Lawton* in 1906 and by *Hilsdon* in
1969. Lacy Gothic organ case by *Sydney Mitchell*, who also
supervised the bright stencilled decoration of the roof by
James Clark. – Pilkington himself altered the seating in 1880.
Outside, the basic shape is just perceptible amid the corbelled angles, arches and stair-towers that fill every crevice in
the tight perimeter. Very complex roof system, rising from
bell-cast to steeply pyramidal and hooding every wall-head
save that of the big N gable with its rose window (cf. the N
transept at Lincoln) to light the upper gallery beneath a
cusped over-arch of red sandstone. Hammer-dressed masonry
with polychrome voussoirs. CARVING by *Pearce*, equally
effective whether strengthening the masonry's harsh impact
or refining it (e.g. in the delicate Venetian tracery or swept
corbels), but much of it unfortunately left in block. The
church has been vulnerable to the weather, losing all the iron
finials that originally resolved its craggy silhouette. More seriously, one of the slated lucarnes was blown down in 1969
and all four were replaced in grey fibreglass by *Stewart Tod*.
– HALLS attached to the E side, by *Sydney Mitchell & Wilson*,
1891; round-arched, with a round turret, high-spirited yet
relatively tame. The yellow sandstone has decayed.

FOUNTAINBRIDGE FREE CHURCH, Fountainbridge. Disused.
Lanceted Gothic by *Patrick Wilson* (the housing architect,
and designer of the adjacent Chalmers Buildings), opened in
1854. Workaday but well composed, with a gabled porch and
three-stage battlemented tower. Porch extension and hall to
the W by *Robert Raeburn*, 1887.

LAURISTON PLACE UNITED PRESBYTERIAN CHURCH, Lauriston Place. Disused. 1859, by *Archibald Scott*. A soot-
blackened E.E. gable with lancets and pyramid pinnacles.

LOTHIAN ROAD CHURCH (originally United Associate Synod
Church). Now Film House. Nominally by *William Burn* but

actually by his principal assistant *David Bryce*, 1830–1. A very secular and urban frontage of five bays with rusticated ground floor, the end bays framed by giant antae. The U-plan gallery and Tower-of-the-Winds columns supporting a segmental ceiling (*see* St Mark's, below) were removed in the conversion of 1978–81 by the *Waters Jamieson Partnership*.

METHODIST CENTRAL HALL, Earl Grey Street. 1899–1901 by *Dunn & Findlay* in a François I manner. Hall frontage with mullioned and transomed windows between Corinthian pilasters, gabled offices to the l. with a copper-clad corner dome, a band of Gothic enrichment running along the top of the ground-floor shops and proliferating over the corner entrance. Interior more impressive, with a curved and ribbed ceiling on arches rising from Ionic columns, the space under the gallery partitioned off by *Maclennan & Cunningham* in 1936. – Large ORGAN in a plain case at the E end by *H. S. Vincent*, 1904, rebuilt by *C. P. Scovell* in 1930, enlarged by *J. W. Walker* in 1958: further rebuilt in 1970 and enlarged in 1974 by *R. L. Smith*. – GLASS of Glasgow Art Nouveau type, mostly clear but with flashes of pale green, orange and purple.

SACRED HEART (R.C.), Lauriston Street. Designed as a temporary church (for later conversion to a hall) by *Richard Vaughan*, 1860, with a broad pedimented front. Inside, a large simple box lined with pilasters and top-lit by four domed lanterns. In 1884 *Archibald Macpherson* formed the apsidal chancel whose balustered screens remain, but in 1900 the two outer arches and the arcade round the apse were replaced with a weak Greek order. – Marble PULPIT, and perhaps the chapels flanking the apse, by *S. Henbest Capper*, 1895. – Large PAINTINGS of the Stations of the Cross by *Peter Rauth*, 1872–4, line the windowless walls and dominate the interior. – ORGAN by *C. P. Scovell* for Roseburn Free Church (*see* Western New Town), 1907, rebuilt here by *Rushworth & Dreaper* in 1963 and again in 1974. – HALL and priest's house to the SE by *Archibald Macpherson*, 1909.

ST CATHERINE'S CONVENT OF MERCY (R.C.), Lauriston Gardens. *David Cousin* designed the original convent, finished in 1860. Hammer-dressed masonry, the W entrance tower (now minus cresting) seen above the wall in Lauriston Gardens, the S front relieved by semi-dormers and a rigid ground-floor string-course jumping up at the canted staircase bay. Inside, a corridor with massive beams austerely profiled. N addition by *Archibald Macpherson*, 1887, a little more cheerful, with the same external masonry and a corridor with ribbed ceiling forming a three-sided indoor cloister with the old one. CHAPEL with shaped and pedimented W gable. The interior a long and impressive rectangle, with woodwork by *Whytock & Reid*. Arcaded stalls with continuous canopies against the N and S walls; refined C16-type carving and commemorative inlays. A recessed gallery to the S, a raked aisle to the N (now blocked) for schoolchildren. – Neo-Classical

REREDOS with Corinthian columns flanked by niches and pilasters. – ORGAN by *Bevington & Sons*, 1958.

ST MARK'S UNITARIAN CHURCH, Castle Terrace. 1834–5 by 37
David Bryce, who saw how Baroque composition and mannered detail could enliven a flat frontage on this conspicuous site. Against the channelled ground floor a broken-pedimented doorpiece, columns on pilasters. Above, the giant pilasters are doubled on each side of the wider central bay. In all three bays arched windows with florid pediments. Deep bracketed cornice and a mannered skyline with boldly profiled and inscribed centre panel. Galleried U-plan interior with twin stair-halls at the E (Castle Terrace) end; iron columns support the arched ceiling. Similar in fact to the destroyed Lothian Road Church interior, but with Mannerist touches in detail. – Of *Bryce*'s PULPIT only the octagonal sounding-board survives, with spires and finials. – ORGAN at the E end by *A. E. Ingram.*, 1911, in a late Stuart case.

ST MICHAEL AND ALL SAINTS (Episcopal, formerly All 42
Saints), Brougham Street. Originally a mission church of St John, Princes Street. Early Gothic, with lancets and plate tracery, by *R. Rowand Anderson*, 1866–78, well grouped on each side of the obtuse corner: to the E the aisled and transepted church with its long roof parallel to Panmure Place; to the W the three-storey parsonage (now in different use) with a Gothic top-floor balcony in its tall gable to Brougham Street. Between them a two-storey lean-to narthex whose corner turret is the pivot of the composition; a tower was originally intended here. Inside, the nave, with an arcaded W gallery, is separated from the splay-ended chancel by longer wall-shafts.* Dark red masonry with plastered (formerly patterned) walls. Nave arches of square section with French leaf-capitals on round piers, followed by the larger transept arches and then by two small arches with a central angel capital on each side of the chancel. Lanceted clearstorey and wagon roof overall. Lady Chapel with an apsidal E end (an addition of *c*. 1875), entered from the N transept by three low arches (the capitals left in block).

REREDOS at the high altar. Gothic, by *C. E. Kempe*, *c*. 1900, with tall spindly tracery framing pictures of saints and a central spire over a carved group of the Holy Family with shepherds.‡ – PULPIT. Hexagonal, of carved wood on a single baluster base. Mannered C17 Renaissance with figures of Hope, Justice etc. at the corners. Brought from St Michael, Hill Square (*see* Roxburgh Free Church, South Side, Churches), in 1965. – HIGH ALTAR. White marble, housing relics of St Francis de Sales and St Catherine of Siena. – ALTARPIECES. In the Lady Chapel (formerly at the high

---

* The original wrought-iron screen (removed *c*. 1965) did not detract from the continuity of nave and chancel but emphasized the dramatic sideways view into the N transept.

‡ The figures, imported from Oberammergau, are too large for the niche they occupy; perhaps it originally contained a Crucifixion.

altar) by *William Burges*, *c.* 1869. Large-scale, vigorous carving of the Annunciation, observed through thick foliage by
Moses and Gideon. - At the NW corner of the church another
(formerly at St Michael) by *Hamilton More-Nisbet*, *c.* 1910.
Red and gold, with scenes from the life of Our Lady in rib-
vaulted niches, and central Crucifixion. - STAINED GLASS.
In the chancel, three lights of deep blue and purple (the
Crucifixion moved from the centre to the S side, the flanking
angels still *in situ*), by *William Wailes*, *c.* 1870. In the transept
windows, sombre greenish panels (Nativity etc. to the N,
Crucifixion etc. to the S). - In the W bay of the N aisle two
lights (SS. Andrew and Margaret, St Mary) by *C. E. Kempe*,
after 1875. - At the W end of the S aisle, one light in similar
but less accomplished style (Christ and St Drostan), after
1876.

Former SCHOOL to the rear, fronting Glen Street. Also by
Anderson, and now (1984) being converted to flats.

PUBLIC BUILDINGS

ARGYLE HOUSE, West Port, Lady Lawson Street and Spittal
Street. A very large office building by *Michael Laird & Partners*, 1966-9, but not obtrusive or pompous. Tall slabs of
rough-faced units forming an L, the shorter limb set back
from Lady Lawson Street on a building line not subsequently
followed. Lower block with ashlar pylons facing Lady Lawson Street and Spittal Street, deferring to the view of the
castle. All the detail bluff but elegant, with neatly bevelled
sills and skyline.

CHALMERS* HOSPITAL, Lauriston Place. 1861 by *Peddie &
Kinnear*. Long wings flanking a tall centre block which has
slim spiral shafts carved into the corners of the polished ashlar. *The Builder* says that this finish was chosen for the building 'so as to secure it externally from any impurity which
might attach to it'.

DEPARTMENT OF EMPLOYMENT, 174 Lauriston Place. A labour exchange in the squared-up authoritarian classic style of
the *Office of Works* under *W. T. Oldrieve*, 1912-13. The stone
detail carved by *Joseph Hayes* is a labour of high quality if
not of love.

EDINBURGH COLLEGE OF ART, Lauriston Place. Beaux-Arts
Classical in red sandstone by *J. M. Dick Peddie*, 1906 (the E
wing 1910), like the École Militaire but without a formal space
in front (the Fire Station came first). Giant Roman Doric
order at the pedimented centrepiece, simpler pavilions, all
with deep French roofs of green-grey slate. Inside, a monumental staircase at the centre; to the E the galleried SCULP-
TURE COURT with arcade below, coupled Ionic columns
above. To the E the ARCHITECTURE BUILDING by *Ralph*

---

* Not Dr Thomas Chalmers the reforming churchman, but George Chalmers
the plumber who died in 1836 leaving money for the hospital.

Cowan, 1961, smooth grey slabs, the courtyard elevations altered and enlarged, but an impressive tower of studio glazing seen from West Port. To the SW (on Lauriston Place) the HUNTER BUILDING (Planning and Crafts), by *H. Anthony Wheeler*, 1972. Smooth red sandstone, boldly composed.

FIRE STATION, Lauriston Place. Elegant *fin-de-siècle* Renaissance in red sandstone, by the City Architect *Robert Morham*, 1897–1901. Ogee-domed corner tower, and a square hose-drying tower whose tapering head with blocked columns has unhappily been half-removed. Tenement shell for fire-practice by Morham's successor *J. A. Williamson*, 1913.

KING'S THEATRE, Leven Street. 1905–6 by *J. D. Swanston* of Kirkcaldy and *James Davidson* of Coatbridge, two minor architects with some experience of theatre design. A red sandstone front, rather Glaswegian, with a pedimented oriel between coupled Ionic columns. The main entrance has lost its canopy but kept its bevelled glass doors with bronze handles inlaid with enamel pictures. The general effect of the auditorium is much more confident, despite the uneven quality of the plasterwork. Scroll-pedimented proscenium. Three tiers of boxes on each side, in three bays divided by giant orders above term figures of Comedy and Tragedy. Sky-painted saucer-dome above. Of three concave-fronted galleries, without pillars, the topmost has been removed with some loss of character. Circulation and ancillary rooms formally planned and well detailed. Stained-glass door-panels in Glasgow style (from the studio of *Stephen Adam*?). Gilded figures on pediments in the upper foyer.

ROYAL INFIRMARY OF EDINBURGH, Lauriston Place. Scots Baronial by *David Bryce*. Begun in 1872 and finished by his nephew *John Bryce*, 1876–9, it succeeded *William Adam*'s Royal Infirmary (1738) and Bryce's own Surgical Hospital (1849–53).* The site was agreed in 1867. The building was compromised initially by the decision to retain the existing fabric of George Watson's Hospital (*see* below), later by all manner of additions and makeshift alterations. But Bryce's tough, bluff design still wins, its picturesque symmetry equally effective on the Lauriston Place elevation, with the turreted ends of four surgical pavilions and tall central entrance tower, and in the prospect of the medical pavilions across the Meadows. Florence Nightingale's principles of open layout were adopted and her detailed approval obtained. The rock-faced baronial style, disciplined by a narrow budget (£340,000 the final cost for 500 beds), suits it well. Paired turrets with lucarned roofs at the ends of the pavilions, crow-stepped chimney-gables on the flanks, spired ventilators

* The old Infirmary was off Infirmary Street. Bryce reported adversely to the managers on its structure in 1864. It was also too small, but its main functional defect, under-ventilation, was shared by Bryce's own Surgical Hospital (*see* Old Town, Public Buildings), and there was some pressure for the employment of an outside architect. After the demolition of the old Infirmary in 1884, its gatepiers were re-erected near the Old Surgical Hospital and its main architectural features re-used at Redford House (*see* Outer Area, Colinton, Mansions).

above (those to Lauriston Place have lost their spires). All very confident, with large shoulder-framed windows where functionally necessary. Stone piers separate the N side from Lauriston Place. Low Italianate LODGE by *John Lessels* in front of the central block, which has a symmetrically corbelled entrance tower and a 41 m. slated spire. Inscriptions over the door, copied in 1885 from those at the old Infirmary. Also from the old Infirmary, STATUE to the W of George II in Roman dress, by *James Hill*, 1755.

Behind this central range (but not quite parallel with it) the remnant of GEORGE WATSON'S HOSPITAL by *William Adam*, 1738–41. Nothing is left of its high French-roofed centre, but the bowed end of the W pavilion and the N elevation of the E pavilion (all of three storeys, with quoins and triple keyblocked windows) can still be seen, the rest obscured by the two parallel wings (portentously classical, with scrolled chimneystacks) added by *John Lessels* in 1857, and by later work. The CHAPEL is in a grand first-floor room in the W wing, with a compartmented ceiling and corner roundels of the Seasons painted by *Bonnar*.

The most obvious interference with Bryce's composition is at the NW corner, where the Pathology block was given an extra storey in the later C19. The principal C19 additions are otherwise easily recognizable as such, and are here given their original names. All are by the later Infirmary architects, *Sydney Mitchell & Wilson*. LAUNDRY to the W, 1896, following Bryce's style. Boiler-house CHIMNEY, 1895, 53 m. high, red brick with corbelled and pedimented octagon head, the stone dressings blackened by smoke. Entering at the W gate one sees the single-storey ISOLATION WARD (now the cafeteria), simple red brick, 1885. To the E of it the NURSES' HOME, 1890, a picturesque quadrangle on a small scale like a Flemish almshouse, red brick banded with stone. To the W a group of two large Flemish blocks with splayed and lanterned ends, the S one originally EAR, NOSE AND THROAT, the taller N one OPTICAL. Both 1900, both yellow sandstone. Further to the S the red sandstone DIAMOND JUBILEE PAVILION, 1897, adding a basically similar but more intricate elevation to the row of surgical pavilions seen from the Meadows. The Blaxter-faced block to the W, related to the general massing but little else, is the new SIMPSON MEMORIAL MATERNITY PAVILION* by the Infirmary's resident architect *Thomas W. Turnbull*, 1935 (*James Miller* of Glasgow consultant), steel-framed, the other elevations austerely faced with concrete blocks. FLORENCE NIGHTINGALE NURSES' HOME to the N of it (also by *Turnbull*, 1935, with more concrete slabs) occupies the site of *William Burn*'s Merchant Maiden Hospital, 1816, taken over by George Watson's after they sold their building to the Infirmary in 1871. The EYE PAVILION on the W side of Chalmers Street is an unhappily shoddy block by

---

* For the old building *see* below, Lauriston Place.

Alison & Hutchison, 1971; the REPRODUCTIVE BIOLOGY
BUILDING on the E side, crisp and elegant, is by *Robert Matthew, Johnson-Marshall & Partners*, 1977. Equally elegant,
with a lead-faced attic and beautifully modulated windows
from end to end, is their REDEVELOPMENT PHASE ONE, designed in 1965. A tall, shiny chimney of four connected steel
flues rises out of the central well. This building occupies the
site of a Georgian terrace, and subsequent phases are intended
(1984) to replace all the pre-1935 Infirmary buildings.

ROYAL LYCEUM THEATRE, Grindlay Street. By *C. J. Phipps*
for Howard & Wyndham, 1883. Channelled stucco front,
with a pedimented centrepiece whose Corinthian order is
wrapped round the corner to appear spasmodically in Cornwall Street. In the foyer, two carved wood monkeys dressed
as beggars. In the auditorium (originally designed to hold
1,950) three tiers of galleries, the lower two with running
classical relief, the lowest continued to form three boxes
marked with richer cast-iron columns. Consoled proscenium,
a painting of Apollo and the Muses by *Ballard* in the tympanum above. Circular ceiling, with radial Adamesque ornament. The theatre was lit by electricity from the start.

TELEPHONE EXCHANGE, Fountainbridge and Gardner's Crescent. Accomplished new architecture by *Stewart Sim* of the
Ministry of Works, 1949–52, in full command of the corner
site. A slab with vertically emphasized windows (for switch-
gear) linked by a glazed staircase to a bow-ended office block,
all stone clad, with good detail.

TOLLCROSS SCHOOL, West Tollcross. Typically imaginative
free-Renaissance by *John A. Carfrae*, 1911. Two-storeyed
T-plan, built of smooth and rock-faced masonry in two
colours. Symmetrical S front, divided into bays by banded
chimneystack pilasters, with lively variations in the window
arrangement on each side. In the centre a single-storey loggia
with blind arcade and pineapple finials. Tall piended roof,
the ventilator with a gay scroll-pedimented lantern.

USHER HALL, Lothian Road. A notable Beaux-Arts performance by *J. Stockdale Harrison** of Leicester, 1910–14, executed with the utmost suavity and precision in Darney stone.
Andrew Usher the brewer had given £100,000 for a concert
hall in 1896, and after much argument the site eventually
chosen was an awkward wedge at an oblique angle to Lothian
Road, where a suitably imposing frontage was required. Harrison's answer is a horseshoe-plan auditorium lined with access corridors. Five projecting wings (three entrances, two for
cloakrooms) are regularly disposed round the curve and tied
to the central mass by horizontal channelling; then a plain,
heavy attic, and finally a strongly modelled drum and
copper-green dome.

This arrangement allows the main entrance to be placed on

---

* Harrison won the open competition, but his drawings show elevations somewhat different from those executed, which owe something to *E. A. Rickards*'s
unsuccessful design.

the main axis of the building (its stature increased by the fall in the ground) while another entrance directly faces Lothian Road. Each entrance is flanked by pairs of Roman Doric columns attached to the channelled masonry, their entablature pushed up into a curve by a deeply rusticated archway in which the projecting canopy and other bronzework were made to Harrison's design by the *Bromsgrove Guild*. Set against the attic over the columns is sculpture by various hands. The city arms on the main entrance are by *W. Birnie Rhind*, the crouching Michelangelesque figures over the other two by *Crossland MacClure*, representing (l. to r.) the Music of the Woods and the Sea, Municipal Beneficence and the Soul of Music. *Hubert Paton* did the shallower relief lion-mask keystones of the arches – the only explicitly witty detail on the building. Lastly on the cloakroom wing along Grindlay Street, which looks like a compact miniature beside the lofty makeshift of the Lyceum Theatre, two more heroic figures: Musical Inspiration and Achievement, by *H. S. Gamley*.

Inside the building the access and foyer areas are spacious but friendly, almost domestic in scale, with Carolean plaster-work. Colourful materials are discreetly used, e.g. yellow Siena marble for the pilasters in the Crush Halls and the panelling of the staircase. In the Upper Crush Hall relief panels by *H. S. Gamley*, who also did the overdoor medallions of poets and composers in the pilastered corridors; portrait bust of Andrew Usher in the lower one. In these areas some survivors of the gilt light fittings made by *Singer & Sons* and *Charles Henshaw*. Large AUDITORIUM with room for 2,900, for all its gilding admirably simple, presided over by the giant Ionic order of the proscenium – very French-looking, fluted and elaborately reeded, with swagged capitals. Curving round over the stalls two cantilevered tiers of reinforced concrete designed by *F. A. MacDonald & Partners*. The roof structure is more obviously expressed in beamed compartments. Plaster centrepiece by *Thomas Beattie* framing, in place of the original glazed oculus, a perforated convex bowl for air-conditioning. Set back in the proscenium over raked seats the organ by *Norman & Beard*; case by *Adam Currie* with woodcarving by *John S. Gibson*; splendid festive centrepiece with trumpeting angels, but long diffuse wings, the end pilasters reeded with organ-pipes.

STREETS

BREAD STREET

The numbers start at the W end. On the N side, as far as No. 33, four-storey rubble tenements with arched doors and altered ground-floor shops, designed by *William Burn* for the Merchant Company's Grindlay Estate and finished by 1825. Beyond Spittal Street, Nos. 47–77, a long, crisply detailed

tenement by *T. P. Marwick*, 1907, with corbelled chimneys
and oriels. On the s side *Burn*'s grander design (on Major
Weir's estate) sweeps round from Lothian Road. The rest is
ST CUTHBERT'S CO-OPERATIVE ASSOCIATION: in the
middle Victorian, a strongly modelled palazzo by *John
McLachlan*, 1892, exactly repeated to the r. by *T. P. Marwick*
in 1898; to the E Edwardian in spirit (1914 in date), a preposterous, emaciated frontage with columns and a dome at
the acute angle, again by *Marwick*; to the w genuinely modern, a simple curtain wall by his son *T. Waller Marwick*,
1937, unhappily spoiled by the subsequent painting of the
back of the glass.

CASTLE TERRACE AND CAMBRIDGE STREET

CASTLE TERRACE is one-sided and serpentine, facing the Castle rock. No. 1, with giant *antae* on the front, was built (and
perhaps designed) by the architect *John Clark*, c. 1824, on St
Cuthbert's glebe. In 1825 *William Burn* produced a new
feuing-plan of this part of the Grindlay Estate, taking in the
glebe and allowing for the proposed new w approaches to the
Old Town, including Castle Terrace itself, whose roadway
was laid in 1831. Clearly the original intention* was to build
a quadrant frontage, then a straight range between pavilions.
Nos. 3 and 4 in the quadrant were built *c.* 1831, but in 1834
St Mark's Unitarian Church (q.v.) took the place intended
for the first pavilion. The straight range at Nos. 8-12 is by
David Bryce Jun. and the second pavilion (No. 13) by *John
Watherston*, both apparently to the original design. But in the
same year, 1859, the gap in the quadrant (Nos. 5-7) was filled
with two-storey houses whose lugged architraves imitate
those of the church. Finally the N side of CAMBRIDGE
STREET was started in 1863, with an attic storey added to the
original elevation.

After the vacant block (*see below*) the astonishing tenement designed by *James Gowans*, 1868, on his own very personal
principles, with a pair of stone-crowned towers as the main
centrepiece and a steep stone gable on the Spittal Street
corner. Battered basement, banded masonry, serried cross-
sections at every opening, a silhouette of hardly believable
picturesqueness – it would be mad if it were not so large, so
logical and so beautifully built. Gowans planned a similar
block between Cornwall Street and Cambridge Street, but in
1875 he changed his mind and built a theatre (the interior by
Pilkington & Bell) which later became the United Presbyterian Synod Hall and later still a cinema. Its façade, whose

---

* Who was the designer? *Hamilton* produced elevations (apparently for Castle
Terrace) in 1825, *Burn* in 1826. Burn was in charge of the Merchant Company's
feuing arrangements till *c.* 1845 when Hamilton succeeded him. This does not
confirm Burn's authorship of the original scheme, but it certainly looks like his
work.

gigantic arcade exploited its place in the distant view from
Princes Street, was flanked by two buildings of almost equal
scale, *Robert Wilson*'s School Board Office and *MacGibbon
& Ross*'s Parish Council office (both 1886). All three were
demolished in 1965-9 to make way for a new opera house
that was never built.*

EARL GREY STREET

Part of Major Weir's estate. Nothing is left of the original buildings here or in RIEGO STREET. On the W side Nos. 16-34,
a tall commercial-Classic block by *Hillier, Parker, May &
Rowden*, surveyors, 1934. At the Tollcross corner the Methodist Central Hall (*see* Churches, above).

FOUNTAINBRIDGE, PONTON STREET AND GROVE STREET

The first part is called EAST FOUNTAINBRIDGE. After Main
Point House (*see* West Port), Nos. 1-11 on the S side are a
survival of old Portsburgh, a much altered early C18 tenement
with wall-headed chimney-stalk. Then the swanky frontage
of the former Royal Circus Theatre by *George Gilroy*, 1886,
with an arcade breaking up into the pediment. The circular
auditorium and central stage are lost. On the N side, developed from 1822 by Major Weir, four-storey rubble tenements at Nos. 36-46 by *William Burn*, with smooth ground
floors and arched doorways. Nos. 20-34 similar, but overlaid
with the back windows of the Co-op (*see* Bread Street).
After Lothian Road the numbers continue along WEST FOUN-
TAINBRIDGE. Nos. 89-95 on the S side are the former EDIN-
BURGH INDUSTRIAL BRIGADE HOME by *Frank W.
Simon*, 1898, symmetrical, with mullioned windows and baronial
corner turrets. Its red brick rear wing was demolished in
1982. Next door the former CENTRAL MEAT MARKET by
W.H. Grey, 1890; common brick with Corncockle dressings
and white tile pilasters. On the N side of Fountainbridge
another former meat market at Nos. 56-58 by *Robert Morham*, 1884, a three-arched frontage with bulls' heads under
the pediment. Then CHALMERS BUILDINGS, a three-storey
range of artisan housing at right angles to the street by *Patrick
Wilson*, 1854, and his adjacent Fountainbridge Free Church
(*see* Churches, above). At No. 92 the offices of ST CUTH-
BERT'S WHOLESALE ASSOCIATION, turreted and dormered
baronial by *Hippolyte J. Blanc*, 1880. To the rear the polychrome brick bakery of *c.* 1880; also the massive dairy block

---

* *William H. Kininmonth*'s opera house design of 1965 was monumental Art
Deco, *Robert Matthew, Johnson-Marshall & Partners*' design of 1972 an elegant
pyramid. *Roland Wedgwood*'s hotel design was given outline approval in 1978 but
not built. 1984 has seen a revival of interest in the opera house project, with a
new design by *John Richards*.

running back to Morrison Street, 1922, and the commercial-Classic frontage of the funeral department in Semple Street, *c*. 1930, both by *T.P. Marwick & Son*. Opposite the Telephone Exchange (*see* Public Buildings, above) the TELECOM OFFICE of 1977, five lumpish storeys of yellow blockwork unrelated to the street or anything else. Numerous buildings on both sides for SCOTTISH & NEWCASTLE BREWERS, but not much architecture; the TARTAN CLUB by *Hugh Martin & Partners*, 1970, with smart pale grey aggregate panels, and in Gilmore Park the brewhouse and boiler house (with cylindrical concrete tank) of the NEW FOUNTAIN BREWERY by the company's architect *Charles Wakefield-Brand*, 1971.

Nos. 158–164 West Fountainbridge turn the corner into GROVE STREET with a three-storey hammer-dressed tenement by *Frederick T. Pilkington*, 1864. Arched shops, arched windows above, all with Ruskinian leafy capitals. On each elevation a broad chimney tapered up into the bell-cast roof. Frail dormers with twisty wooden baluster frames. Nos. 70–76 Grove Street, similar but less wild in composition, were built *c*. 1865 as a Working Men's Home. Nos. 48–68, four-storey tenements for the Fountainbridge Church (and other) Building Associations by *Paterson & Shiells*, 1863, are plain but quite sophisticated with shouldered windows at the third storey and corbelled eaves above the fourth. On the opposite (E) side the former West Fountainbridge Hall by *George Beattie & Son*, 1872, erected by the Barclay Church congregation; 'a heavy example of the chamfer and splay Gothic sort' (*The Builder*). At No. 97 the four-storey frontage of the former Martin's Bakery by *Alan Goodwin*, 1935, commercial-Classic with no frills. At the N end of the street a hopeful Georgian effort: two- and three-storey houses with basements and rusticated ground floors, all *c*. 1820, Nos. 19–25 on the E side, Nos. 2–18 turning the corner into Morrison Street.

GARDNER'S CRESCENT

A simple and subtle master-work by *R. & R. Dickson* for William Gardner, 1822. One unbroken arc of fifty-two bays. Segmental-topped ground-floor openings, giant orders stripped of all detail, third-floor attic above the cornice, the continuity emphasized by horizontal glazing. At the N end a square pyramid-roofed tower rising to a picturesque high point between the crescent and the asymmetrical pavilion whose turret turns the corner into Morrison Street.

Facing the crescent on a lower level, two mid-C19 artisan housing developments. First ROSEBANK COTTAGES by *Alexander McGregor* for James Gowans, 1853. Six blocks of 'flatted cottages' for 'the better class of mechanics' (*The Builder*); ground-floor flats entered on one side, upper-floor flats by outside stairs on the other. ROSEMOUNT BUILDINGS, 1859, is a three-storey quadrangle of red and yellow brick containing ninety-six flats. Fire-proof stair-towers at the corners. habilitation by *Roland Wedgwood Associates*, 1980, the herringbone metal balconies a puzzling new feature.

GLENGYLE TERRACE *see* VALLEYFIELD STREET

GLEN STREET *see* LAURISTON PLACE

GROVE STREET *see* FOUNTAINBRIDGE

HERIOT PLACE *see* LAURISTON PLACE

HOME STREET

On the E side a long row of four-storey artisan tenements, rubble-faced but Georgian in scale, built *c.* 1820 on J. Home Rigg's estate. On the W side two tall tenements next to Lochrin Place on the old Haig estate of Lochrin by *Dunn & Findlay* for James Anderson, 1897. Pyramidally roofed central tower, ogee-roofed corner bays.

KEIR STREET *see* LAURISTON PLACE

LADY LAWSON STREET *see* WEST PORT

LAURISTON PARK *see* LAURISTON PLACE

LAURISTON PLACE

An old road on the former S perimeter of the city. To the E the long institutional spread of the Royal Infirmary and Chalmers Hospital facing Heriot's School, the Edinburgh College of Art, and the swanky red Fire Station (*see* Public Buildings, above). To the W, compact C19 housing developments on the big gardens of vanished C18 villas. On the N side, W of Heriot's, a large four-storey Georgian block built piecemeal but with consistent detail (e.g. the rusticated ground floors) over the Keir Estate. Nos. 6–14, with a bowed corner to Heriot Place, were built for William Laurie by *John Ferrier*, *c.* 1814. Superimposed two-storey flats at Nos. 10–14. Nos. 16–36, erected in 1819 across the front garden of the Keirs' mid-C18 house demolished two years earlier, are slightly taller, with advanced centre and ends. Four houses at Nos. 38–44, part of a development by *Miller & Lorimer*, who also built Nos. 22–32, KEIR STREET, *c.* 1810, with a subtly spaced elevation, and the NW corner block at Nos. 14–20, 1821. In Nos. 2–10 (1832) some elaborate Grecian interiors, e.g. the ground-floor and basement flat at No. 6. The E elevation is formed by tenements at Nos. 2–14 Heriot Place. Spiral common stair at the NE corner. The entire block was repaired (removing the late-C19 projecting shops along Lauriston Place) and internally improved in 1977–81 by *T. M. Gray Associates* for the Lister Housing Co-operative.

Next on the N side LAURISTON HOUSE, a perfunctory concrete-slab office by *Rowand Anderson, Kininmonth & Paul*, 1960. In LAURISTON STREET the R.C. church of the Sacred Heart (*see* Churches, above), and GOLDBERGS store by *J. & F. Johnston & Partners*, 1960, its E and W proscenium fronts refaced with tiles in 1978. Nos. 40–46, a four-storey tenement with pilastered doorpieces, turn the corner into Nos. 106–110 Lauriston Place with an octagonal tower, arcaded on the ground floor. On the S side of Lauriston Place, LAURISTON GARDENS begins with St Catherine's Convent (on the site of Lauriston Lodge) and the former Lauriston U.P. Church (*see* Churches, above). The S part belongs to the Drumdryan Estate (*see* Valleyfield Street, below). No. 79 Lauriston Place, originally the Simpson Memorial Maternity Pavilion, now the SCHOOL OF RADIOLOGY, symmetrical lucarned Gothic with a central gablet and flèche, by *MacGibbon & Ross*, 1879, is on the site of the C18 villa of the Hogs of Newliston. On its grounds LAURISTON PARK and GLEN STREET were built up with 'respectable' (*The Builder*) but high-density tenements of plain design by *R. Thornton Shiells*, revised by *David MacGibbon*, 1869.

LAURISTON STREET *see* LAURISTON PLACE

LEVEN STREET

For the King's Theatre, *see* Public Buildings, above. The plain mid-Victorian tenement at Nos. 8–12 contains BENNET'S BAR by *George Lyle*, 1891, one of Edinburgh's best pub interiors, Jacobethan with the S wall's mirrors framed by tiled pictures (by *William B. Simpson & Sons* of London) and set in a round-arched arcade. Glasgow-type stained glass incorporating brewers' advertisements.

LEVEN TERRACE *see* VALLEYFIELD STREET

LOTHIAN ROAD

On the W side the long red sandstone façade of the CALEDON-IAN HOTEL* rivals the North British in size if not in ostentation. The three arches with coupled monolithic Corinthian columns, designed as a monumental entrance to the station in 1890–3 by *Kinnear & Peddie*, were incorporated in 1899–

---

* The Caledonian Railway terminus was laid out in 1847 by *William Tite*. His grand Italianate station was not built.

1903 by *J. M. Dick Peddie & G. Washington Browne* into their new V-plan hotel, which embraced the train-shed. Ground floor with more pairs of Corinthian columns and a grand procession of thermal mezzanine windows under a deep cornice, the tall roof dizzily gabled with two-storey François I dormers, the three intermediate storeys nondescript and unrelated. The station closed in 1965, and in 1970-1 the V of the hotel was made into an A with a workaday red-brick link. Typical Browne interior in a gentlemanly manner of *c*. 1700, the only big formal effect the imperial staircase (balustrade oddly replaced with cast bronze tree-trunks in an elaborate redecoration of 1958 by *Robert & Roger Nicholson*). The SHERATON HOTEL is by *Crerar & Partners*, 1982. Vestigially classical, with a lop-sided stone-faced E elevation and a forecourt, both studiously ignoring the axis of the Usher Hall. Then, Film House (the former Lothian Road Church, *see* Churches, above), which is linked by a Victorian tenement to *William Burn*'s plain corner-block at Nos. 112-116. Beyond Morrison Street the monster LOTHIAN HOUSE by *Stewart Kaye*, an expanded and degraded Art Deco version of Burnet & Tait's Kodak House in Kingsway, London. A stone relief of a barge commemorates the canal basin of Port Hopetoun.

The E side begins with the entries to St John's and St Cuthbert's churches (*see* First New Town: Churches). The cylindrical watch-tower belongs to St Cuthbert's churchyard. After the corner block of Castle Terrace (built on St Cuthbert's glebe) the CALEY CINEMA. Monumental entrance by *J. S. Richardson & J. R. McKay*, 1922-3; stained glass and mansard roof added in 1928 by *John McKissack* along with the sombre palazzo wing and ground-floor shops. Of the next three blocks, designed in 1848 (i.e. when *Thomas Hamilton* was acting for the Merchant Company on the Grindlay Estate), the four-storey one on the corner of Cornwall Street was not built till 1864. After the Usher Hall (*see* Public Buildings, above) Nos. 71-103 by *David MacGibbon* (Hamilton's successor), 1864, tactfully complete the plain palace-front started by *William Burn* with Nos. 105-123 (1820-5). Nos. 125-165 (originally Downie Place), by *Burn* working for Major Weir, are more elaborate; corniced windows in the middle of the centrepiece, and a quadrant opening into Bread Street.

MORRISON STREET

A diffident Georgian start with Nos. 10-32 on the N side, spoiled by the shopfronts. At No. 76 a rubbly block by the *City Architect's Department*, 1932, determined to set a virtuous example. On the S side Nos. 85-107, the four- and five-storey introduction to Gardner's Crescent (*see* above). Rehabilitation of the corner flats by *McLeod & Traub*, 1980.

At No. 174 another rubble tenement by the *City Architect*,
1939, and then a smug Georgian fragment at Nos. 176–180,
built in the mid C19 to *James Haldane*'s scheme (for the w
end of the street *see* Western New Town). On the s side the
totally unrelated office block of the AMALGAMATED UNION
OF ENGINEERING WORKERS in plum-coloured brick by
Marshall Morrison & Associates, 1973, and behind it the
equally irrelevant red brick of the St David's Terrace flats for
the Fountainbridge Housing Association by the *Building Design Consortium*, 1979.

PORTSBURGH SQUARE *see* WEST PORT

RIEGO STREET *see* EARL GREY STREET

SPITTAL STREET AND GRINDLAY STREET

Mostly dull four-storey tenements of the 1860s, but with some
relief. In SPITTAL STREET the sharply gabled flank of *James
Gowans*'s big block (*see* Castle Terrace, above). The Albert
Buildings Association contributed Nos. 1–7 in pure late Geor-
gian style, which they qualified only by paired windows at
ALBERT BUILDINGS (Nos. 12–20), 1860–3. The adjacent
CLAN ALPINE BUILDINGS, 1864, go over the edge into
Victorian detail. In GRINDLAY STREET a touch of class at
Nos. 20–42 by *C. G. H. Kinnear*, 1866, the block at Nos. 30–
42 with enriched tripartite windows. To the rear the former
Artillery Drill Hall, now the Heriot-Watt University Union.
Across the street the Royal Lyceum Theatre (*see* Public
Buildings, above).

VALLEYFIELD STREET, GLENGYLE TERRACE AND LEVEN
TERRACE

A scheme of 1815 for the Drumdryan Estate (the lands of Valleyfield and Leven Lodge, originally Drumdryan) came to
nothing, and this part of the property was developed in 1867–
70 by the builders *W. & D. McGregor* with four-storey tenements designed by *David MacGibbon* in the style of
Alexander 'Greek' Thomson. 'Flat, but unfortunately not un-
profitable' was *The Builder*'s comment. VALLEYFIELD
STREET has a flat string-course jumping up to link the first-
floor windows. GLENGYLE TERRACE, the most expensive
with its open s view, is a strong, nearly symmetrical composition, the main members clearly defined and delicately
chip-carved. Only the tall, pointed roofs on the corner of
LEVEN TERRACE are alien to the Thomson theme. Former
AGRICULTURAL HALL of 1868 in Valleyfield Street, with
arched and pedimented centre.

WEST PORT AND LADY LAWSON STREET

WEST PORT is a narrow chasm, eroded by planning-blight, curving up from the West Port proper (i.e. the city gate at the SW corner of the Grassmarket) to the once important junction of Main Point. On the N side is PORTSBURGH SQUARE, balconied housing of 1900 by the *City Engineer's Department*, with fancy red sandstone dormers and a pepper-pot at the SW corner, renovated by *T. M. Gray Associates* in 1978-80. Then a block by *Barratt*, 1984, with comically mis-applied baronial detail. The huge Argyle House (*see* Public Buildings, above) conforms with some difficulty to a wider road plan subsequently abandoned. Nos. 137-145, hammer-dressed tenements built in 1882 under the City Improvement Acts of 1866-7, have good baronial skylines and a fish-scale conical roof on the corner of LADY LAWSON STREET, where Nos. 6-30 (and Nos. 46-52 to the S, all part of the same scheme) are the only buildings of note.

The S side of WEST PORT begins at the bottom with the SALVATION ARMY WOMEN'S HOSTEL, dry Art Nouveau in red sandstone by *John Hamilton* of Glasgow, 1910. Its neighbour at Nos. 18-26 is by *John Robertson*, 1878. Then No. 28, a harled symmetrical tenement with C18 allusions designed in 1936 for the Edinburgh West Ark Housing Trust by the City Architect *E. J. MacRae*. The three plain gables with tall Gothic windows belong to the former WEST PORT FREE CHURCH, founded by Dr Chalmers himself in 1844. No. 50, stolid and crowstepped, was designed by *Robert Morham*, 1882, as a combined Police and Fire Station. Nos. 62-76 of 1887 are more cheerfully Scotch, with red sandstone dress-ings, by *David McArthy* for the Association for Improving the Dwellings of the Poor. No. 70 was the wash-house and factor's office. Over the main door a reinstated stone with the wreathed emblem of the Cordiners, inscribed

> Behold how Good a thing it is
> And how becoming well,
> Together such as brethren are
> In unity to dwell
> AD 1696

Across Lady Lawson Street WEST PORT HOUSE, a nine-storey townscape-stopper by *Stanley Poole Associates*, 1967. MAIN POINT HOUSE (No. 4 High Riggs) closes the vista unperturbed, with a delicately consoled bay-window and a modillion cornice. Built *c.* 1770, apparently with the present arrangement of house-over-shop, it acquired its pub-frontage in 1897 and the extra storey on the bay in 1906, both from *J. Macintyre Henry*. Upper floors subdivided *c.* 1906 and further divided in 1979-80 with the loss of much original detail.

4. FIRST NEW TOWN

For convenience, this section includes not only the rectangle of the First New Town proper, but to the s Princes Street Gardens, The Mound and Waverley Station; and to the NE the St James Centre and the whole of York Place.

The First New Town was begun in 1767, gradually built up from E to W, and finished (except for most of Charlotte Square) by the end of the C18. Both in its layout and its street names it celebrates the idea of the United Kingdom under George III. The gridiron plan, doubly symmetrical, has four great merits. First, it makes ideal use of the site, with its main axis (George Street) lying along the natural ridge. Second, it leaves open the spectacular views to the N and s, seen not only from Queen Street and Princes Street but also, architecturally framed, from George Street itself. Third, it offered from the start unequalled opportunities for architectural realization, whether by means of single buildings, axially sited monuments or formal compositions. Much of it has been redeveloped in the course of its change from a residential to a commercial quarter, but the original Georgian buildings still predominate over Victorian and C20 replacements, and all of them profit from the geometric discipline of Craig's plan. Finally, it is contained at its E and W ends; this, more than any other factor, has helped to preserve its identity through more than two centuries of change.

The initiative for this bold expansion came from Lord Provost Drummond, who from the start of his first term of office (1725) had set his heart on the draining of the Nor' Loch and the development of Bearford's Parks (bought by the Town in 1716). In 1752 *Proposals* were published embodying his ideas for the improvement and extension of the city. In 1753 they became an Act of Parliament. Five years later more land was acquired and in 1759 the drainage of the loch began, enabling the foundation stone of the North Bridge to be laid by Drummond in 1763. Further purchases over the next two years brought the greater part of the New Town site into the City's hands, and in March 1766, the year of Drummond's death, an advertisement was published for the submission of plans. Six were sent in, and on 2 August the Lord Provost and *John Adam* chose that of *James Craig*. The Extension of Royalty Act was passed in the following year and Craig's plan, redrawn after consultation with John Adam, Lord Kaimes and others, was formally adopted in July.

The revised plan involved canalizing the Nor' Loch as an ornamental water, with gardens to the N of it, and further to the N a long rectangular New Town on a gridiron plan. The out-

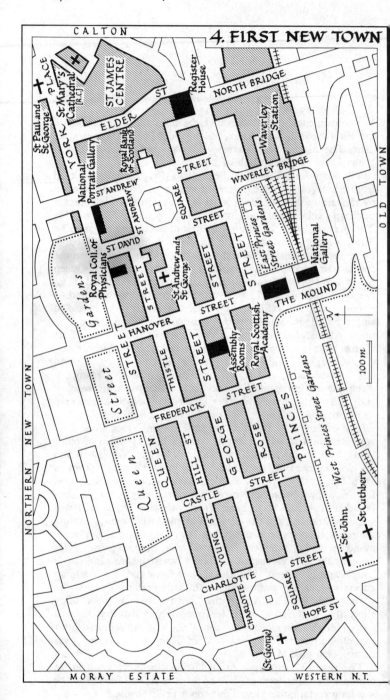

ermost streets, Princes Street on the s and Queen Street on the
n, were to be 80 ft (24 m.) wide and built up on one side only,
their houses enjoying the view. The central vista, George Street
on the crown of the ridge, was to be 100 ft (30 m.) wide, with St
Andrew Square at its e end and St George's (subsequently
Charlotte) Square at its w. Between the main e to w streets
there were to be humbler ones, Thistle and Rose, for a respectable middle class. Intersecting all of them were to be the n–s
streets, St David, St Andrew, Hanover, Frederick, Charlotte
and Hope (the first and last two not yet named), which like
Princes and Queen Streets, were to be 80 ft wide. These dimensions include the footpaths 10 ft (3 m.), but not the basement
areas whose width was fixed at 8 ft (2·4 m).

What were the sources of Craig's plan? Youngson* has suggested the French town of Richelieu with its two axial squares
(1633) as a possible prototype, and Bath as a precedent for
one-sided streets. Craig would certainly have known about
Inigo Jones's Covent Garden with its axially sited church
(1630), and must have read the paper written in 1728 by the
Earl of Mar (exiled for his part in the 1715 rising) which clearly
envisages an axial layout and open prospects to n and s. But he
also had the advice of *John Adam* who, with his father, had
planned Inveraray, Argyll, in 1747. Although Inveraray's narrow site precluded a gridiron and only needed one square, its
central street, axial square and back streets, and its single-sided
outer street (overlooking Loch Fyne), are all echoed in Craig's
layout.

CHURCHES

Charlotte Street Baptist Chapel, w end of Rose
Street. Tall and dryly Wrenish, by *J.A. Arnott & J. Inch
Morrison*, who won the competition of 1908 for the replacement of the Georgian building. A thousand-seat chapel and
two large halls.

St Andrew and St George (formerly St Andrew), George   28
Street. Designed by Major *Andrew Frazer‡* of the Royal Engineers, 1782–4. The 51 m. steeple, probably also designed by
Frazer, was built by *Alexander Stevens* in 1787.§ The site,
fixed in 1780 following the loss of the intended one in St
Andrew Square, was already developed along its n side when
the Town bought it back, and this shallow space suited the
oval (or strictly elliptical) plan of which this seems to be the
first important example in the U.K.; All Saints, Newcastle,
was not designed till 1786. To this simple droved masonry

* *The Making of Classical Edinburgh*, 1966.
‡ Frazer was appointed Scottish Engineer-in-Chief in 1779.
§ William Sibbald won a competition for its design in 1785 but the building
contract was not made for a further two years, and Mr Howard Colvin points out
that there is a portrait of Frazer holding an elevation of the church with the
steeple very much as built.

form is attached a tetrastyle Corinthian portico of smooth ashlar, raised on only a couple of steps so that the columns stand practically on the same level as the life of the street. Columns, mouldings and steps are of Craigleith, the ashlar of Redhall stone. The steeple stands well on the portico but is decidedly less original, the spire and splayed middle stage being obviously Gibbsian.

Inside, the oval plan is complemented by the ceiling (concentric ovals surrounded by husk garlands) and by the curving panelled gallery (with original pews) on Roman Ionic columns. The other pews are mainly late-c19. The PULPIT has undergone repeated changes since it was first put up in front of a screened-off session house and vestry (*John Young* built permanent accommodation at the back in 1788, since altered). Its present appearance (1984), without its Georgian sounding-board or staircase, is due to *Esmé Gordon*, who redecorated the church in 1953 and added the finicky plaster ornament to the ceiling of the vestibule. Here it is worth climbing the gallery stairs in order to see their upward continuation, clinging to the median walls on each side before they come together for a dizzy leap to the belfry. – COMMUNION TABLE. Late c18 in style if not in date, with consoled corners. – ORGAN to the S, over the gallery, by *Peter Conacher* of Huddersfield, 1881, rebuilt by *Rushworth & Dreaper*, 1967. – STAINED GLASS. To the N six windows (the Evangelists, David and Isaiah) by *Ballantine*, 1890, the colours distorted by amber plating. – To the S, one window (the Beatitudes) by *Alfred A. Webster*, 1913, and one (the Son of Man) by *Douglas Strachan*, 1934. – In 1976 *Robert Hurd & Partners* adapted the cellar for social use as the UNDERCROFT, and in 1979 they added the new stair leading to it from a glazed extension of the vestibule.

ST CUTHBERT'S PARISH CHURCH, entered from Lothian Road. A large mixed Renaissance church by *Hippolyte J. Blanc*, 1892–5, keeping the late-c18 steeple of its predecessor. The site, well below the level of Princes Street and picturesquely unrelated to any of the Georgian formalities to the N, is that of a still earlier building. The medieval St Cuthbert, first mentioned in 1127 (possibly a foundation of St Margaret), was the church of a large parish surrounding the old city. After the Reformation the long nave, with a staged tower in its S flank, became the 'Little Kirk', and the choir was submerged in a mass of additions of which one – the Nisbet of Dean vault of 1692 – survives on the N.

By 1772 the kirk was dangerous, and in 1773–5 (following a competition) the architect-builder *James Weir* of Tollcross built a preaching-box with two tiers of galleries reached by stairs in the pedimented W projection. In 1787–90 the ground to the N was drained for an extension of the burial ground, and in 1789–90 *Alexander Stevens* built the spire which he probably designed himself, Gibbsian with Adamish detail. By 1888 the church had become unsafe, and Blanc was appointed; he first proposed to recase it, but eventually a rebuild was decided upon, maintaining the general proportions but greatly increasing the size. The result, with a pair of Baroque W towers flanking the domed apse, is best seen from the lower level of Princes Street Gardens. This view succeeds by sheer swank; all the others show an uneasy compromise, for snecked stonework and C15–16 Renaissance detail do not suit the austere kirk style, and the great bulk and divergent roof pitch are at odds with the Georgian steeple.

The interior is better. A new entrance on the S side of Blanc's church leads into a vestibule extending right across the W end, with spacious gallery stairs ascending to a landing on whose W wall a screened wooden stair of confident Renaissance detail is cantilevered out, giving access to the tower. The body of the church is vast but plain, with a U-plan gallery, very deep at the W end, supported by Corinthian-esque columns. Compartmented ceiling. Two wide arches open into transepts, wider indeed than the apsed chancel in which most of the splendour is concentrated.

The FURNISHINGS are extraordinary. The mosaic floor and *Blanc*'s STALLS (scroll-topped for the choir and congregation, intricate Renaissance for the elders) were ready for the dedication in 1894. So was the white marble COMMUNION TABLE divided by Corinthian pilasters, in its three compartments a cross of green Aventurine marble with a golden crocodolyte centre and porphyry infill, flanked by panels of lapis lazuli and mother-of-pearl. Further items followed. – LECTERN. Bronze angel by *D.W. Stevenson*, 1895. – PULPIT. 1897–8 by *Blanc* again, on four red marble columns from S. Ambrogio in Verona, with verde antico panels, the front one bearing a relief of the Angel of the Gospel. – ORGAN, filling the N transept (and hiding its glass) as well as both arms of the chancel. 1899 by *R. Hope-Jones*, in rather feeble cases designed by *Blanc*, rebuilt by *Norman & Beard* in 1928 and by *J.W. Walker* in 1957. – In 1906–8 Blanc installed the alabaster WALL FRIEZE in the apse, a modified version of Leonardo's Last Supper in high relief by *Bridgeman* of Lichfield, curiously divided in three by the pilasters which were retained and clad in orangey-red Verona marble. – FONT devised by *Thomas Armstrong* (Keeper of Fine Art in the South Kensington Museum), 1907–8, a hexagonal bowl of one piece of polished white marble based on della Quercia's in Siena Cathedral, with a gilded bronze profile portrait by *MacGill*. Upon it (the bowl is actually a trough round the edge) a copy of Michelangelo's Bruges Madonna. – In 1928 *J. Inch Morrison* faced the chancel pilasters to match those of the apse.

MURALS. On the apse vault Christ in Glory by *Robert Hope*. – On the chancel vault the four evangelists by *Gerald E. Moira*. – On the spandrels of the chancel arch two angels with a Sanctus inscription by *John Duncan*, 1931. Each stage of this scheme is slightly more brash in style and rather less suited in colour to the exotic natural materials of the ensemble. The colours of *Duncan*'s huge painting on the w wall over the gallery (St Cuthbert on Lindisfarne Island) are relatively quiet. – STAINED GLASS. The Kirk Session in 1893 decided on 'a general and harmonious scheme of scriptural subjects applying to the whole church'. It mainly consists of large-scale figures in early Renaissance tabernacle frames, nearly all by the same firm, e.g. the E window on the N under the gallery (Ruth and Naomi) signed and dated '*A. Ballantyne & Gardiner* 1904', and the centre window above it (scenes from the life of Abraham) commemorating Alexander Ballantine himself, †1904. – To the l. the one notable exception, a window of bold composition and richly variegated colour (David and Goliath) by *Tiffany* of New York, after 1900. – Finally two lights (the Crucifixion and St Cuthbert) by *Douglas Strachan*, 1922, at the N and S ends of the WAR MEMORIAL CHAPEL by *P. MacGregor Chalmers*, 1921. The chapel walls are lined with exotic marbles, the apse with gold mosaic.

MONUMENTS. In the vestibule a vesica panel to the children of Francis Redfern (Christ blessing little children) by *John Flaxman*, 1802, and a Mannerist wall tablet of 1842 to John Napier of Merchiston, reproducing the title page of his book of logarithms. – On the stairs the aedicular monuments of Rocheid of Inverleith †1737 and Watson of Muirhouse †1774. – On the upper vestibule wall a good pair of wall sarcophagi on lion's feet, 1841, commemorating two ministers, William Paul and Sir Henry Moncrieff Wellwood, the latter at least by *Wallace & Whyte*. – To the l. of the chancel arch a portrait bust of the Rev. John Paul †1873 by *William Brodie*; to the r. the white marble Art Nouveau McLaren memorial by *George Frampton*, 1907, with a low-relief portrait. – On the N under the gallery a Renaissance tablet to Alexander Ballantine by *A. F. Balfour Paul*, 1907. – At the w end the 1939–45 WAR MEMORIAL, an early Renaissance screen by *Ian G. Lindsay*, 1950, harmonizing with Blanc's woodwork.

Large CHURCHYARD. HALLS by *Charles McArthy & Watson*, who won the competition of 1893; in a sort of rock-faced Queen Anne, replacing MacGibbon & Ross's buildings because of railway works. – WATCH HOUSE at the corner of Lothian Road dated 1827, circular, of two storeys with a crenellated top. – TOOL HOUSE, further along King's Stables Road, wedge-shaped, in even sadder condition. – MONUMENTS. Of some hundreds worthy of notice, the commonest are enclosures and back-to-back mural monuments in rows. – To the SW of the church a group of early-C18 enclosures. – To the W the three-bay pedimented monument with waffle rustication to John Grant of Kilgraston †1795, an example of late-C18 elegance. – Hamilton enclosures, early-C19 Greek Doric. – Enclosure of Neil MacVicar †1818, with square Thrasyllus order, probably by *William Burn*; similar wall-monument W of the church to George Winton, architect,

†1823. – Of Victorian work, the three-bay Gothic mausoleum of the Gordons of Cluny by *David Bryce*, carved by *P. B. Smith*, is near Lothian Road. – George Lorimer †1865. Baroque Ionic aedicule. – The best figure sculpture, commemorating the Rev. David Dickson in the blind arch at the base of the tower, is by *A. Handyside Ritchie*, 1844.

ST GEORGE (Episcopal), York Place. Now a warehouse. Originally castellated Gothic by *James Adam*, 1792–4, with battlemented and pepperpotted entrance tower and canted wings to match the octagonal clearstorey behind. Inside, eight slim clustered piers carrying the gallery, gaily crocketed ogee arches, and a plaster rib-vault with a classical roundel for a chandelier. It is virtually a copy of George Dance's St Bartholomew-the-Less (1789, replaced 1823) in London. In 1934 *John Jerdan* altered the front with two large display windows, leaving only the doorpiece with coupled octagonal columns and acanthus capitals, and floored the whole inside on the level of the gallery front. For some of the surviving furnishings *see* St Paul and St George, below.

ST GEORGE, Charlotte Square. *See* West Register House, Public Buildings, below.

ST JOHN (Episcopal), at the W end of Princes Street. Revived Perp by *William Burn*, and not only a good termination for the street but a remarkably convincing Gothic exercise for its date, 1815–18. The £18,000 cost was raised by Bishop Sandford from donations and an issue of shares. Undercroft projecting to the S as a terrace over a cloister arcade. The church is of eight clearstoried bays with buttresses and pinnacles. The end bays have elaborately corbelled niches instead of windows. W tower, originally with single belfry windows and an octagonal lantern (derived from Harrison's church at Liverpool) which blew down during construction. The double-windowed belfry improved the tower, and the only uncertainty of design is in the heavy pinnacles and the perfunctory moulding of the doorway at the base. In the E bay was the original chancel, with a wheel window glazed by *William Raphael Eginton*. A burial enclosure with canted E end extends another five bays.

In 1865 *G. Gilbert Scott* was called in to make changes in accordance with liturgical developments, but two years later only slight alterations were carried out by *Peddie & Kinnear*, including the removal of the galleries flanking the altar. In 1879–82 they extended the chancel within Burn's burial enclosure by one aisleless bay and a three-sided apse, sympathetic with the older work but much more refined. The large vestry hall to the SE by *J. M. Dick Peddie & Forbes Smith*, 1914–16, and the Morning Chapel between this and the chancel by *W. J. Walker Todd*, 1934–5, are manifestly later additions (e.g. with snecked masonry), but neither is conspicuously sited.

Burn's interior was a masterpiece in its time, and is still better now. Tall arcades with clustered shafts, each pier end-

32

ing with a leaning-out figure of the penitent Magdalen (an odd economy of specification) as a label-stop. Thin clear-storey wall-shafts run up into fan-vaults of the same diameter as the central pendant fans; these, like the ribbed aisle vaults, are of course of plaster. Peddie & Kinnear's chancel, with its slightly steeper stone arch, is more serious and more intricate in detail; the vault has an elaborate pattern of lierne ribs.

FURNISHINGS. Pews, pulpit and aisle panelling are all Neo-Perp by *Peddie & Kinnear*, 1867. In 1913 *J. M. Dick Peddie & Forbes Smith* removed the varnish, added the sounding-board over the pulpit and the tabernacle cover to the 1857 marble font, and set back the W gallery within the tower. Their handsome screen of East Anglian type was re-moved in 1974 but the rood still hangs above. They also refurnished the chancel, with canopied stalls and panelling inspired by King's College Chapel in Aberdeen, but the re-redos is by *Kinnear & Peddie*, 1889, a stone Gothic triptych carved by *James Kerr*, with tile pictures (Christ, St John and St Mary) by *W. B. Simpson & Sons* of London. *J. S. Gibson* was their woodcarver. – ORGAN to the N, 1901 by *Willis & Sons*, rebuilt by *Rushworth & Dreaper* in 1930 and modified by *R. C. Goldsmith* in 1974. – In the MORNING CHAPEL *Todd* designed the furnishings, including the low cambered roof of Scots oak, the wings of angels forming a heavily undercut pattern in the cornice; the carvers were *Scott Morton* and *Andrew Lunn*. Iron gates by *Ian G. Lindsay*. – MEMORIALS. In the aisles the disciplined series of mid-C19 marble wall-monuments, Gothic and neo-Tudor, many commemorating officers lost in the Crimean war, are perfectly suited to Burn's architecture. – S aisle, E end: Gothic wall-tabernacle to Mrs Mary Arbuthnot, with two mourning figures, by *John Flax-man*, 1822–3. – In the chancel *G. Gilbert Scott*'s memorial to Dean Ramsay, 1867, bronze, enamel and coloured stones, by *Skidmore*. – STAINED GLASS. In the chancel the main part of *Eginton*'s original E window (twelve saints, very hard in colour) was re-set in the new N and S windows in 1882. – E and SE apse windows by *Clayton & Bell*, 1882, NE window by *Heaton, Butler & Bayne*, 1886, all of three lights (scenes from the life of Christ). – In the nave mainly *Ballantine* work from the mid C19 onwards in brightly coloured 'mosaic' glass. – The lower parts of both the westernmost aisle windows, each of three lights, are by *James Ballantine II*, 1935. – DEAN RAMSAY MEMORIAL, outside the church, to the W. A cross of Shap granite, 7·3 m. high, by *R. Rowand Anderson*, 1878,* with Celtic bronze reliefs by *Skidmore*.

ST MARY'S CATHEDRAL (R.C.), at the S end of Broughton Street. The handsomely sited neo-Perp gable front is all that remains of the Catholic chapel (it became the cathedral in 1878) by *James Gillespie Graham*, 1813.‡ Facing E (liturgically

* In 1874 a statue by *John Steell* under a canopy by *Burges* had been proposed.
‡ The original interior lacked most of its intended ornament through want of funds, unlike that of Graham's contemporary R.C. chapel in Glasgow.

w), it has diagonal buttresses and pinnacles, and a parapet pierced over the nave, plain over the aisles. Door with dripstone heads carved by *Thomas Campbell*. Only the small extensions to N and S give any hint of the extraordinary interior, the nave spanning the whole width of Graham's original church, and the combined width of nave and aisles exceeding their length. The chancel and its aisles run into the nave, Gerona fashion. All this came after the fire that destroyed the S Cloister Chapel in 1891. In that year *John Biggar* designed the nave arcade, with paired clearstorey windows, cylindrical piers and moulded capitals. Biggar retained Graham's roofline but it was found oppressively low, so in 1932 *Reid & Forbes* raised the side walls as far as the E front would allow, and added an upper clearstorey of circular windows, giving Biggar's clearstorey the look of a sort of glazed triforium. The wide span was bridged with a sensational roof: giant crowned angels in polychrome painted wood (carved by *Scott Morton*) act as corbels, their wings stretched up into broad arches. They are highly stylized, a more substantial equivalent of the Art Deco cinema architecture of the time, as are the massive brackets for hanging lights in nave and chancel. Biggar had also designed a chancel (and two towers, never built), but it was *Buchanan & Bennett* who in 1895 made the triple opening in the W (liturgical E) wall of the nave and erected the three-bay chancel with quatrefoil piers and the aisleless semi-octagonal apse. Their low-pitch hammerbeam roof is less satisfactory.

FURNISHINGS. BALDACCHINO by *Reginald Fairlie*, 1928, gabled Gothic in polished stone, with marble pillars. – Central ALTAR by *R. Rowand Anderson*, 1876 (from the former Catholic Apostolic Church, *see* Gayfield, Bellevue Reformed Baptist Church). Grandly panelled with Derbyshire and Whitehaven alabaster. – Brass eagle LECTERN from the same source. – Stalls and THRONE adapted by *Buchanan & Bennett* from earlier work. – PULPIT by *Reid & Forbes*, not quite so showy as their other things. – PAINTING on the W nave wall (the Annunciation) by *Louis Beyart*, 1932. – STATIONS OF THE CROSS on the S aisle wall by *Mayer* of Munich. – LADY ALTAR at the end of the S aisle by *Robert S. Lorimer*, 1905, white marble with a white and gold reredos, the Madonna in a canopied niche. – ORGAN by *E. Lawton* of Aberdeen, 1932. – STAINED GLASS in the chancel clearstorey. Two windows of two lights each (the Crucifixion and the Annunciation) by *Hardman*; the rest from a Munich studio. In 1976–8 *T. Harley Haddow & Partners* removed Buchanan & Bennett's SE baptistery and the porch that covered Graham's doorway, both of 1895 and badly weathered. The new stone BAPTISTERY is starkly hexagonal, with a good modern interior of brick. A broad stone terrace, carried right across the site and stepping down to the street, makes an effectively simple base for the whole group.

To the W of the cathedral (and used as its halls from 1935

to 1978) is the massive piend-roofed block of the former St
James Place Relief Church, 1800, a stern seven-bay
front with three deep archways in the pedimented centrepiece. Round and square-arched openings alternate curiously
in its four storeys.

33 St Paul and St George (Episcopal, formerly St Paul), York
Place. Neo-Perp with corner turrets, by *Archibald Elliot*,
1816–18. The contractor was the Leith architect-builder
Thomas Beattie. The congregation moved here from the
Cowgate Chapel (*see* Old Town, St Patrick), subsequently
uniting with St George (*see* above). Originally of seven bays,
the E bay containing the sanctuary; the new sanctuary, and
additional aisleless bay, are by *Kinnear & Peddie*, 1891–2.
Elliot's church is remarkable, considering its date, for the
delicacy and scholarship of its detail both inside and out. The
regular bay design, well suited to its position at the end of
York Place, resembles that of a late medieval parish church
in England. Tall crenellated aisles (allowing for galleries) with
three-light windows, and a clearstorey with pierced crenellations, all buttressed and pinnacled. Lofty octagonal angle-
turrets derived from those at St Mary, Beverley, exactly reproduced (with some of the old stonework) at the new E end,
along with Elliot's five-light E window in between. Near the
W door (a scholarly design compared with that of St John,
Princes Street, *see* above) a delicate Gothic lamp-post of cast
iron by *Laidlaw* of Glasgow.

The interior is equally conscientious and effective. Four-
centred arches on tall clustered stone piers. Panelled canted
timber ceilings with pierced timber arches springing from
wall-shafts. In 1891–2 *Kinnear & Peddie* removed the aisle
galleries, making the church splendidly spacious, and changed
the old chancel into the choir, opening up the plaster rib-
vaulted SE porch. Theirs is presumably the very basic ORGAN
CASE in the equivalent N aisle bay, and certainly the tiled
floors throughout. Otherwise all the furnishings (except
where noted) are by *J. M. Dick Peddie & Forbes Smith*, 1911–
14, including the octagonal Perp PULPIT with sounding-
board, the ROOD SCREEN and CHOIR STALLS with canted
canopies, and in the sanctuary the traceried panelling, SEDI-
LIA, and carved wood REREDOS (Christ and little children,
with St Paul and St Cuthbert). – From old St George's are
the brass LECTERN and (at the W end) the BOX PEW of Sir
Walter Scott and the white marble FONT, hexagonal, with a
traceried base and a panelled basin with three reliefs of graceful late-C18 character (Christ being baptized, blessing little
children, and with the woman of Samaria). – ALTARPIECE
and other furnishings in the S aisle chapel by *Harold O. Tarbolton*, 1922, carved and gilded. – ORGAN by *Snetzler*, 1774,
moved from the Cowgate Chapel (*see* Old Town, St Patrick)
and rebuilt here by *J. Bruce* in 1818, rebuilt by *D. & T.
Hamilton* in 1870, rebuilt and further enlarged by *Harrison
& Harrison* in 1906.

STAINED GLASS. At the W end ten lights moved from the old E window (the evangelists and St Paul above, Melchizedek, Moses, SS. John the Baptist, Peter and Andrew below), by *Wailes*, 1849; hard browns and reds against vivid blues. – In the E sanctuary ten lights (Christ in glory, with scenes from his Birth to the Transfiguration) by *Heaton, Butler & Bayne*, 1891–2. – Also a number by *Ballantine & Gardiner*, all of six lights: N chancel window (Saints) 1898, s aisle third bay from W (the Light of the World) 1896, fifth bay (Acts of Mercy) after 1892, sixth bay (Gethsemane, and Magdalen at Christ's feet) 1894, and N side of W end (Blessed are they that do His Commandments) 1898. – MONUMENTS. In the s aisle Archibald Alison †1845, a marble relief of figures mourning at a tomb, by *John Steell*. – At the W end General Tytley †1880, marble tablet with medallion bust by *D. W. Stevenson*. – On the chancel N wall Bishop Terrot †1875, an ogee Gothic tabernacle by *David Bryce*.

SECOND CHURCH OF CHRIST SCIENTIST, Young Street. *See* Thistle Street.

PUBLIC BUILDINGS

ASSEMBLY ROOMS AND MUSIC HALL, George Street. The 81 pompous Roman Doric portico and arcaded base projecting into the street are appropriate for a public building and useful as a shelter, but they are not what *John Henderson* intended. Plans for assembly rooms in the New Town, to be built by subscription on a site given by the City, had been invited in December 1781. Although Henderson's design (even in its most economical form) was to cost £2,000 more than had been raised, Lord Moray's committee resolved in July 1782 to adopt it without alteration, and the building was opened in 1787. The outside effect can still be judged by subtracting the portico: square openings in a channelled base, corniced upper windows surmounted by blank recesses, all repeated through seven wide bays without variation or emphasis save for the doubling of the giant Roman Doric pilasters at the ends. It was a work of advanced continental Classicism stemming directly from Henderson's studies in Rome, far too severe for British taste. Robert Adam made ambitious plans for remodelling it, but these came to nothing. Even in 1811 it was described as 'heavy and inelegant',* and in 1817–18 the portico was put on by *William Burn*, who, with his partner *David Bryce*, was responsible for the Music Hall of 1843 behind. In 1865 some alterations were made by *Bryce* to plans made eight years before, and at the same time the ballroom apse was built out into the portico, further compromising Henderson's design. Finally, in 1906–7, *R. Rowand Anderson & A. F. Balfour Paul* bridged the side lanes with pend arches and filled up the site with long flanking rooms.

* Alexander Campbell, *Journey from Edinburgh through Parts of North Britain.*

There have been many changes inside, but the principal interiors remain. Low vestibule with depressed arches inserted by *John Bryce* in 1883, flanked at the far end by twin stair-halls; the iron balusters date from 1843, but the other finishings are relatively recent. Upstairs the SALOON, a domed square lined with Roman Doric columns, is presumably by *Henderson* with later titivations. The plan of the BALLROOM is also Henderson's (possibly altered by his father David in 1786–7), a magnificent apartment 28 by 13 m. along the front of the building and 12 m. high to the concave ceiling, which is like a diorama, with rounded ends. The three large plaster roses for the chandeliers were added by *John Baxter Jun.*, in 1796. So too were the fluted and filleted Corinthian pilasters. These were originally at absolutely regular intervals, but in 1865 the central ones were pushed out sideways to make room for the orchestra apse to the N and a shell-headed doorway to the S. *Anderson & Paul*'s side rooms are a mixture of late Caroline and William Adam (cf. the Library at Pollok House, Glasgow).

Burn & Bryce's MUSIC HALL to the S is an impressive affair, for whose design there was no precedent in Scotland in 1843; George Murray's City Hall in Glasgow (1840) was of standard rectangular shape with a U-plan gallery. Here the site was square, and Burn made the most of it with a Greek-cross plan; platform in the S arm, gallery in the N. Ancillary rooms were packed into the corners. Segmentally vaulted ceilings with Bryce's characteristic pattern of square and cross-shaped coffers. Shallow central dome on pendentives, with big coffers with rosettes. A huge gas sun-burner hanging in the middle.

FREEMASONS' HALL, George Street. 1910–12 (replacing the earlier hall by *David Bryce*), the most important work of *A. Hunter Crawford*, who was later to join the family baking firm as house-architect. Externally it is early-C18 revival with a giant order of channelled pilasters, the big central doorway surmounted by *H. S. Gamley*'s figure of St Andrew. *The Builder* said it lacked courage (a refreshing quality for that period?), but nothing could be more assured than the interior: vestibule with black marble columns, staircase with superimposed orders, and the hall itself like a five-bay temple with low aisles. The pendant wreath light fittings are original and all the woodwork is by *Scott Morton*, including the splendid case for the ORGAN by *Brindley & Foster*, 1913.

NATIONAL GALLERY, The Mound, to the S of what is now the Royal Scottish Academy and (because of the road line) not quite axial with it. Like the Academy, designed by *Playfair* for the Board of Manufactures, who in 1848 obtained an Act of Parliament for a Treasury grant of £30,000 to go with their own £20,000. The building had to accommodate the National Gallery in one half and the Academy in the other, a duality expressed in the double porticos to N and S and the central portico (of the higher, transverse block) on each flank, breaking forward from the blank pilastrade – all very austere and abstract with unfluted orders, though relieved (or compromised?) by the crowning balustrade. Cost was crucial, especially in view of the expensive foundation required, and the magnificent Doric scheme put up by the Academy's secretary *Thomas Hamilton* was thus impracticable. Playfair's own first design was very severe indeed; still Doric, with pilastrade flanks and end porticos only, i.e. too strictly Neo-Classical for the taste of the late 1840s. The composition of his executed Ionic design owes something to a scheme (with an arcade of shops) by *Archibald Elliot II*, possibly from a sketch by *Alexander Trotter* who put it forward in 1829.* Picturesque towers at the corners of the transverse central block were shown in Playfair's 1850 design but dropped in 1853; the building was finished in the following year.

Inside, there was originally an entrance hall at each end; the R.S.A. had the E range of galleries, the National Gallery the W, all octagonal except those at the N end which were also made into octagons in 1911-12 when *W. T. Oldrieve* completely refitted the building for the exclusive use of the National Gallery. Entrance hall with white marble antae, arched inner vestibule, oval staircase to the new upper galleries. Graceful columned screens along the central vista, and walnut doors and dadoes. In 1960 the *Department of the Environment* formed a second, though relatively clumsy and impoverished, arrangement of stair and galleries at the S end. For the further (downward) expansion of 1975-8 the Department wisely forsook the classical idiom, only to choose one that hovers expensively between the 1930s and 1950s; there is no attempt to emulate the well defined spaces upstairs. The new rooms, built out under the widened E terrace, are lit by windows carefully detailed to appear nothing more than a long horizontal slit.

NATIONAL PORTRAIT GALLERY, Queen Street. Orangey-red at the E end of Queen Street's weathered grey, this Venetian Gothic palace, designed by *R. Rowand Anderson* for the joint use of the Portrait Gallery and the National Museum of Antiquities, was built in 1885-90 for £50,000, a gift to the nation (i.e. to the Board of Manufactures) by J. R. Findlay, the owner of the *Scotsman* newspaper. Its architectural sources are mixed. The big centrepiece and blank upper wall (for top-lit galleries) recall the Doges' Palace, but the bay design (plain arches on the ground floor, paired windows above) is derived from Anderson's own published studies, e.g. of Figeac and Cordes, and the pierced parapet comes from his old master George Gilbert Scott. Most pervasive of all is the architectural taste of the third Marquess of Bute as shown in the new Mount Stuart (Isle of Bute) which Anderson had designed for him in 1880, including his liking for the red

---

* This in turn came from a scheme for a public building on the Mound made by Playfair himself in 1820.

sandstone of Dumfries-shire. Here this stone is equally effective, though spoiled by the decay and consequent loss of
much Gothic detail from the centre and ends of the building
where it is so tellingly concentrated.*

The copious SCULPTURE has fared better. At the head of
the arched and gabled centrepiece stands History over the
Scottish arms (the latter from a C14 manuscript), below them
Scotland between Industry and Religion, and under the windows three reliefs of Stone and Bronze Age craftsmen, the
Fine Arts and the Sciences. The whole ensemble is flanked
by pinnacled (and formerly crocketed) buttresses with more
figures in niches, all by *W. Birnie Rhind*, 1892-3, as is the
group in the central niche on the E end: Queen Mary between
Bishop Leslie and Maitland of Lethington. Other figures are
by *C. McBride, D. W. & W. Grant Stevenson, John Hutchison*
and *Pittendrigh MacGillivray*, most of them in the massive
octagonal turrets‡ that emphasize the corners. The rear (S)
elevation to the lane is plainer but no less considered. The
pointed cylindrical chimney is like those drawn by Anderson
at Figeac and Bayeux.

The grandeur of the interior is concentrated in the two-
storey central hall, where the red sandstone columns and
corner piers have gilded foliage capitals carved by chosen
students of the Edinburgh College of Art in 1897. Over the
arcade a frieze of celebrities from Scottish history, and set
back on the upper level a series of early historical scenes,
all by *William Hole*, 1887-1901. Sir James Caw§ gave them
qualified praise: 'a happy compromise between the rival
claims of decoration and representation and, if rather wanting
in terms of colour ... one of the most notable examples of
mural decoration ever accomplished in this country.' Decoratively they are indeed successful, best viewed from below,
their colours looming, like those of tapestries, above a well of
dark red brickwork. The ceiling survives to aid this Victorian
evocation of Scottish history, drab green between the timber
beams, the stars in their constellations picked out in gold.
The hall is flanked by twin stairways with vaulted top landings. The galleries are plain two-aisled halls, those on the
Antiquities (E) side less altered. The Library of the Society
of Antiquaries of Scotland remains intact on the second floor.
On that stair is a stained-glass window with medallion portraits of contemporary antiquaries (including Anderson, Bute
and Findlay) by *W. G. Boss* to *Anderson*'s design, 1895. Armorial windows in the hall by *Margaret Chilton* and *Marjorie
Kemp*, 1932.

NORTH BRIDGE. The present bridge, like the reconstruction
of Waverley Station (*see* below), was designed by *Cunningham, Blyth & Westland*, 1894-7. The original North

* Removal of the parapet and pinnacles, which had become unsafe (1980), is to
be followed by restoration.

‡ The original scheme had even larger circular towers at the ends.

§ *Scottish Painting, Past and Present*, 1908.

Bridge, giving access from the Old Town across the valley to the N, had been the first step in the making of the New Town. Its foundation stone was laid in 1763, but plans were not invited for another two years, and *William Mylne*'s three-arched stone bridge was not finished till 1772, after many mishaps. In 1873 the *Stevensons* widened it to 57 ft (17 m.), but this was hardly enough, and the expansion of the North British Railway was hampered by its piers; the new bridge was essential to the station rebuilding. 525 ft (160 m.) from end to end, it achieves an even gradient between High Street and Princes Street with three wide spans, each of six arched iron girders (made by *William Arrol & Co.*) on masonry piers. Detailing by *Robert Morham*, who gave the piers canted ends with festooned tops, and filled the spandrels with cast-iron arcading beneath a consoled and festooned entablature. On the E side of the parapet the MEMORIAL of the King's Own Scottish Borderers, four giant freestone figures by *Birnie Rhind*, 1906.

For buildings of North Bridge address, *see* Old Town, Other Streets.

NORTH BRITISH HOTEL. This huge structure (counted here as a public building) was part and parcel of the new North Bridge, for which the demolition of a pleasant range by *Richard Crichton* had been necessary, and the pride of the N.B. Railway. Quadrangular in plan, aggressive in bulk, C16 Franco-German in detail, it was designed by *W. Hamilton Beattie* in a competition of 1895 whose result is said to have been influenced by Charles Jenner, Beattie's client on the other side of Princes Street. *John J. Burnet* and *R. Rowand Anderson* (the architect of Glasgow's splendid Central Hotel for the Caledonian Railway) also took part, but Beattie had undeniably designed more hotels than any British architect then living. Completed in 1902, its bulbous 58-m. clock tower, probably Edinburgh's most familiar landmark after the Castle and the Scott Monument, never fails to shock because of its intrusion into a townscape which did not need a large new feature at all – even a better one than this. The crowded Princes Street front of which it forms the centrepiece is certainly the least good; the open W and S faces with their massively wrought skyline and extravagant bows and balconies are enjoyable. Inside, it is equally a mixture: the entrance hall passable Free Renaissance, the domed central saloon or Palm Court charmless Neo-Georgian, the large ground-floor rooms clumsy, with some excruciating detail. Like Beattie's building for Jenner, it is largely of fireproof construction, with floors by *Stuart's Granolithic*.

REGISTER HOUSE, E end of Princes Street. *Robert Adam*'s long 79 frontage with corner turrets stands austerely elegant at the entry from the Old Town to the New. Begun in 1774 (just before Somerset House in London), it was the first important government building in the U.K. since Kent's Horse Guards. A proper home for Scotland's public records had been proposed in 1722. Forty years later the English architect *Robert Baldwin* furnished a plan for a square one-storey building of fireproof construction with a central dome, but a site could not be agreed. In 1769 the City gave most of the necessary ground at the far end of the North Bridge, where the presence of a public building was likely to encourage development in the New Town. Adam, who was Architect of the King's Works with responsibility for Scotland, had been formally appointed the year before. By 1771 he had produced his plan for a domed rotunda within a quadrangle 200 by 155 ft (61 by 47 m.) overall, amplifying Baldwin's idea but owing much more to his own unexecuted scheme for Syon House. The foundation stone was laid on 27 June 1774. *John Adam* (resident in Edinburgh) was jointly responsible for supervision with his younger brother, *James Salisbury* was clerk of works, and the masons were *John Wilson* and *David Henderson*. The stone was to come from Craigleith and Hailes. The N part of the quadrangle was omitted meantime, but even so more money had to be voted by Parliament in 1778 to finish the carcase, which then stood empty for six years until a further grant was forthcoming for finishings and fittings. The clock and wind vane by *Vulliamy* of London were installed in the E and W turrets in 1790, and in the following year the interior of the dome was painted.

By the start of the Napoleonic war (1803) the completed section had cost £31,000, but by its end it was already inadequate. *Archibald Elliot* was consulted in 1816 and made plans, but nothing was done except some excavation of the s terrace for basement windows. The N part was carried out in 1822–34 by *Robert Reid*. The rest is a story of erosion – firstly of Adam's layout in front, with the object of widening the entry to Leith Street. In 1842 *Thomas Hamilton* as architect to the Paving Board made a plan for setting back the front area wall. Seven years later, after much argument, *David Bryce* did the work with the necessary minimum of change, but in 1890–1 *W. W. Robertson* had to push the wall back further and square off the staircase. The second sort of erosion occurred through the abrasive cleaning of the exterior stonework, with some inevitable loss of quality, in 1969.

The character of Register House is that of the dignified civil servant, fastidiously dressed. The basic formula is Palladian, a *piano nobile* over rusticated arches. The novelty is in the simplicity of its treatment, e.g. the expanse of plain wall between and above the upper windows, and the tall (but not giant) Corinthian columns of the centrepiece repeated at the ends. This cool authority is not Palladian but Neo-Classical in spirit, well attuned to the strong quadrangular form of the whole. The grace-notes that characterize Adam the decorator are few but telling, e.g. the fluted frieze with paterae that becomes a single panel over the central order, the chaste geometric turrets (miniatures of the main building), and the little roundel of the Royal Arms (originally of Liardet's cement) fixed in the pediment like a seal. All this must be imagined not as the elevated street façade that it is today, but as Adam saw it – the only one of his public buildings that he did in fact see virtually complete – standing back on a paved platform, the 'movement' of the original curved stair answering the curve of the dome.

Adam's interior was very simply finished except for the dome, and to this day most of the rooms have plain (fireproof) tunnel-vaults. Groin-vaulted entrance hall. *Reid* coffered the ceilings of the corridors, using rosettes over the passage to the rotunda; the gilded metal gates are his too. The ROTUNDA itself is a magnificent Roman space, 70 ft (21 m.) high from floor to oculus and 50 ft (15 m.) in diameter, its arcaded drum lined with the calf-bound folios of the Register of Sasines. The dome overhead gives a plain field to eight roundels and then decreases in scale but grows in intricacy towards the light. Designed in 1785 and executed by *Thomas Clayton Jun.*, the plasterwork underwent its latest redecoration (after considerable research) in 1973–4. Severely impressive E and W staircases, with screens of almost Vanbrughian arches below and tunnel-vaults overall; unfortunately both stairwells now house lifts. In the Lord Clerk Register's Room in the centre of the S front only an enriched frieze, a grey marble chimneypiece, and a statue of George III by *Anne Seymour Damer*, 1795.

Reid's interiors are much more elaborately finished than Adam's, and in their own way very good. The N STAIR is a double cantilever in a curved space, high and narrow, formed by gutting Adam's offices on the N side of the rotunda from top to bottom. The Historical Search Room (originally the Antiquarian Room) to which it leads has two storeys of bookcases and a balcony. Very rich neo-Greek ceiling like that of the staircase. Unhappily the mahogany furniture made for the building by *Trotter* has had to be replaced for utility's sake both in this room and in the rotunda.

The WELLINGTON STATUE in front of Register House is 55 by *John Steell*, 1848. The Duke sat for his bust and ordered two casts of it (for Apsley House and Eton). He also demonstrated his riding style; the heroic pose (supported on hind legs and tail) must have set unusual problems when the cast was made in 1852 and set up by *James Gowans* on the red Aberdeen granite pedestal designed by *David Bryce* as part of the 1849 alterations.

NEW REGISTER HOUSE, set back behind Adam's building and really in West Register Street, was designed by *Robert Matheson* in his most accomplished Italianate manner in 1858–63, for the registration of births, deaths and marriages which became compulsory in 1855. Internally it follows Adam's plan of rectangle and central dome, translated into a huge cast-iron bookstack and cantilevered galleries.

THE BACK DOME, connected by a basement passage to the back of Adam's building, is also by *Matheson*, 1869–71, and

its interior is based on the same structural scheme. THE SAS-
INE OFFICE at the NE corner of the group once formed
Nos. 27–31 St James's Square. Decent addition by the Office
of Works architect *W. T. Oldrieve* in 1902–4.

89 ROYAL COLLEGE OF PHYSICIANS, Nos. 9–10 Queen Street.
A Neo-Classical monument by *Thomas Hamilton*, 1844, taking the place of the single house acquired by the college in
the previous year for £2,750 after selling their old hall for
£30,000. Public status and changed fashion are deftly acknowledged without violence to the discipline of the street.
The front is basically simple and symmetrical: a wall in place
of area railings, with cast-iron lamps (by the *Shotts Foundry**)
bearing miniature gilded cocks and cut-glass bowls (by *Osler*
of Birmingham); a perfectly smooth façade set very slightly
forward from its neighbours, with two storeys in place of
their three, and an anthemion and palmette frieze at their
cornice level; a blind attic storey returned at the ends to give
a solid dimension to the whole; and finally a deep cornice set
with lion masks. On the front, a two-stage open Tower-of-
the-Winds structure supporting statues of Hippocrates and
Aesculapius, and between them a Corinthian aedicule bearing
a statue of Hygeia, all by *A. Handyside Ritchie*. Flanking
windows set in heavy architraves, with bracketed sills and
block cornices below, consoled cornices above.

The solemnity continues in a procession of internal spaces.
Square vestibule. Doors with engraved glass panels, flanked
by lamp-standards, lead into the inner hall with its Tower-
of-the-Winds columns and thence to the STAIR HALL, lit
from above by engraved Indian red glass (by *Chance Brothers*). The walls were originally marbled. Imperial stair, the
handrail supported by heavy gilt scrolls, ascending between
cylindrical pedestals to which putti and bronze urns were
added in 1854. At the landing before the stair divides, a massive doorpiece opens straight into the HALL, lined with Corinthian columns (gilt capitals on ochre-marbled shafts) and
originally five bays across and three deep. In 1865–6 *David
Bryce* increased the three bays to seven, thus bringing the
long axis in line with the approach. Hamilton's columns and
caryatid attic were repeated, and the original roundel portraits
of great physicians modelled by *Lazzaroni* in 1845 were supplemented by *George McCallum* and *Brucciani*. The plasterwork of the interlocking compartments of Bryce's ceiling was
modelled by *James Anderson*, the glass of the cove engraved
by *David Smith*. Bookcases by *Morrison & Co.* line the walls
of the aisles, which were originally marbled above.

To the SE (at the back of No. 8 Queen Street, acquired in
1864) the NEW LIBRARY, built to *Bryce*'s design in 1876–7
under the supervision of his nephew *John Bryce*. Segmental
ceiling (modelled by *James Annan*) with square coffers of
engraved glass. Stall-presses by *Whytock & Reid* projecting

---

* Dr Michael Rowe kindly supplied the names of artists and craftsmen.

beneath the balcony. In the N (formerly external) wall a carved stone roundel from the old Physicians' Hall. The other rooms in Hamilton's building are less grand, but the FRONT LIBRARY and PRESIDENT'S ROOM on the ground floor have bookcases by *Trotter*, of oak and walnut respectively. UPPER LIBRARY lined with discreet Renaissance woodwork by *J. Inch Morrison*. On the stair, the model for *James Craig*'s Physicians' Hall in George Street.

ROYAL SCOTTISH ACADEMY, The Mound. Greek Doric, by 88 *William H. Playfair*, 1822–6 and 1831–6, for the Board of Manufactures and Fisheries, accommodating the Royal Society, the Institution for the Encouragement of the Fine Arts and the Society of Antiquaries. The original building had octastyle porticos to N and S, the corner blocks defined by antae and containing steeply battered pedestals for sculptural groups (never supplied), nine columns along each side, and a perfectly plain parapet overall to hide the roof lights. This austere temple contained a series of galleries along the middle and two ranges of rooms, on two storeys, along each side. Built of Culallo and Craigleith stone, it cost £16,879. In 1831 Playfair was asked to enlarge it. He increased the length to sixteen columns and considerably enriched the whole design, enlarging the corner blocks with distyle porticos and sphinxes facing E and W, and adding wreaths to the triglyph frieze and tendrilly carving to the tympana of the main pediments. The N pediment, which he advanced by another rank of columns, was crowned in 1844 by the seated statue of Queen Victoria (her robes 'draped so as to give a general idea of Britannia') by *John Steell*. The final cost was of the order of £40,000.

The interior is not at all as Playfair designed it. In 1909–11 *W. T. Oldrieve* of the *Office of Works* adapted it for the Academy as part of an extensive re-organization which included the building of the new Edinburgh College of Art (*see* South West, Public Buildings) and the purchase of Nos. 22–24 George Street for the Royal Society, the Antiquaries having left for Queen Street in 1890 (*see* National Portrait Gallery, above). Oldrieve fitted in a new staircase and upper-level galleries in a simple Grecian style that accords well with Playfair's work (the coved concrete ceilings are by *L. G. Mouchel & Partners*) and rebuilt the NE corner, whose pile foundation had failed; *R. Rowand Anderson* had dealt with similar trouble at the NW corner in 1898.

WAVERLEY STATION. Although the earlier railway buildings have virtually disappeared, a brief history is necessary. There were originally three termini, operated by three companies. The North British and the Edinburgh & Glasgow railways, which lay end-to-end along the S side of Canal Street* (its line that of the present entrance ramp), were started in 1844

---

* The name is a survival of Craig's unexecuted project for a canal in the Nor' Loch valley.

as soon as Trinity College Church (*see* Old Town) and the objections of the Princes Street proprietors were out of the way. *William H. Playfair* designed the high retaining walls and the tunnel under The Mound, and may also have advised on the design of the original Waverley Bridge (a triple rock-faced arch) and the joint station which fronted it – a low, arcaded block straddling the lines. In its time this was one of the best groups of railway architecture in Britain. The engineer was *John Miller*, the architect probably *David Bell*. The third terminus, with a station to the N of Canal Street – that of the Edinburgh, Perth & Dundee Railway, opened in 1847 – was at right angles to the others, and its lines disappeared under Princes Street and the New Town to link with the Edinburgh, Leith & Newhaven terminus (opened in 1842) at Scotland Street.

In 1866 the North British, having absorbed the other two companies, held a competition to rationalize the layout. It was won by *Charles Jopp*, whose scheme was carried out by the company's engineer *James Bell* in 1868–74. He closed the Scotland Street tunnel, demolished most of the old station buildings, and substituted twelve lines of through track with three wide platforms, covering the whole area with transverse valley roofs, fully glazed. Most of them still exist, carried on lattice girders between slim iron columns cast by *Hannah, Donald & Wilson*. The opening of suburban links in 1884 and the Forth Bridge in 1892 necessitated further work. Beneath the wide span of the new North Bridge (*see* above) the engineers *Cunningham, Blyth & Westland* designed the large two-storey building, elaborately pilastered, that surrounds the BOOKING HALL. Here the panelled and domed ceiling with wrought-iron grilles has survived, but the central booking office of varnished timber was removed in a partial remodelling of 1970. In 1894–6 the same engineers constructed the present WAVERLEY BRIDGE with heavy plate girders on forty-two cast-iron columns; this second rebuilding incorporates the pierced iron parapets of the first, a lattice girder structure of 1870–3 by *James Bell*. They also built the present entry and exit ramps, with stocky Ionic balusters, and the arcaded PARCELS OFFICE between them. The surviving wings of the old station building were removed, but the salvaged front of one of them was used by *Robert Morham* for the N front of what is now (1984) the INFORMATION OFFICE on the corner of Waverley Bridge and Market Street.

The 1866 plan (*see* above) displaced the Vegetable Market which lay to the S of the railway lines in the shadow of the North Bridge. The replacement, designed by the City Superintendent of Works *Robert Morham*, was built in 1874–6 to the N of the new Waverley Station (partly over the site of the former Perth & Dundee Station), with a big U-plan hall whose central row of cast-iron columns supported a roof-garden on the level of Princes Street. Later called the Waverley Market, it became unsafe and was nearly all demolished in 1974. The site is now being developed (1984) with a shopping mall by *Building Design Partnership* on a scheme of triangular prisms, with triangular fins poking up through the street-level deck.

WEST REGISTER HOUSE (originally St George's Church), w 29 side of Charlotte Square. Not begun until 1811, *Robert Reid* adopting *Adam*'s 1791 scheme of portico, dome and flanking pavilions, but making it bolder in mass and simpler in detail – the latter no doubt in the cause of economy. His rash verbal estimate was £18,000, but even with further savings the cost had risen to £23,675 when the church was opened in 1814. 'It is certainly a pity that the Adam design was not used' said the *Scots Magazine*.

What were Reid's changes? For Adam's projecting portico (with pediment) he substituted a simple Ionic order *in antis*, altering the coupled columns to single ones by omitting the pedestals and enlarging the shafts; entablature and parapet are correspondingly deeper. From the pavilions he removed Adam's pilasters, and also the small domes on peristyle drums; in their place Reid's drawing shows two rather French-looking clock-stages supported by maidens and crowned with flam-beaux, but these were not carried out. Finally he re-designed the dome and also the drum, whose peristyle Adam had inter-rupted with four pedimented faces. Reid's version is simpler and loftier: a slim, Neo-Classical edition of the dome of St Paul's (though clad in green copper), complete with a *tem-pietto* lantern. All in all the result has a plain monumentality which is less kind to the scale of the flanking terraces in the square, but undoubtedly more effective in closing the vista of George Street as it now exists, with its larger buildings of the late C19 and early C20.

The rear elevation to Randolph Place is impressively sim-ple, with a Venetian window and lunette above, and shows that the interior was of Greek-cross plan. It had already been drastically altered before 1960, when severe structural defects, caused by the combined use of wood and stone underneath the dome, led to acquisition by the Crown. The present in-terior is by *R. Saddler* of the *Ministry of Public Building and Works*, who began the work of consolidation and adaptation in 1964. Document storage on five floors. Two-storey ENTRANCE, with an exhibition room below and a research room on the mezzanine above, all seen through three arched openings in which plate glass has taken the place of the huge panelled doors, and clearly announcing the C20 secularization of the building.

STREETS

CASTLE STREET

The feuing of sites began in 1792, and in the next couple of years the whole street was built up with high-class main door

tenements and a few houses. In the s section later shops have
done much damage, e.g. to the tenements at Nos. 9–13;
Nos. 15–19 now have only the remnants of Corinthian pilasters at the centre and ends. James Gillespie Graham had his
office in the main door flat at No. 15. On the w side Nos. 4–8
had an intricately detailed double-bow front till 1889, when
the N half was replaced with a showy and crowded Renaissance design by *Thomas Leadbetter* for the Scottish American
Mortgage Company. Good doorpiece at No. 10, with low-
relief heads over Corinthian pilasters; *Alexander Reid* and his
son *Robert Reid* lived here, and may have had something to
do with the building. On the first floor of No. 22 at the corner
of Rose Street a noteworthy ceiling with a centre fan, at No. 28
a single house development; both are rarities in the N–s streets
of the First New Town. Fewer added shopfronts in this
quarter of the street; at Nos. 26 and 32 two decent mid-c19
ones with canted ends.

The N section is a beautiful late-c18 ensemble, virtually unaltered except for the redevelopment at the SE (*see* No. 107
George Street) which spoiled the complete set of gabled
118   corner blocks. The six double-bow fronts (double main door
tenements as usual) are interesting both for their differences
in design and for their slight variations in siting; there seems
to have been doubt about whether the main wall or the fronts
of the bows should conform to the building line. The most
famous is that at Nos. 39–43, built in 1793 by *Robert Wright*
and *James McKain*, with a pedimented Corinthian centrepiece, slightly old-fashioned in detail, between the bows; Sir
Walter Scott lived at No. 39 from 1802 to 1826, but the first-
floor flat at No. 41 has the best rooms, including a drawing
room with Corinthian pilasters. The two fronts on each side
of Hill Street are plainer versions, the one to the s sadly
lumbered with a mansard. Then at Nos. 57–61 a superbly
decorated version, less ambitious than Nos. 39–43 but of far
greater refinement; widely spaced balusters under the first-
floor windows, a fluted frieze above, and triglyphs under the
eaves. The doorpiece has the same mannerism as No. 48 and
its successors in Queen Street: the elided entablature is set
back over the doorway. Both pairs of bow fronts on the other
(w) side are of the plainer type, but Nos. 42–46 give equal
status to all three doors, arched between four pilasters, and
the N half of Nos. 54–58 has kept a handsome set of cast-iron
balconies. The two houses in the NW quarter of the street (in
fact a double main door tenement numbered 48–52, with a
common stair in the s block serving the upper flats), were
built in 1792 for Thomas Cranstoun and Captain Brown by
John & James Williamson and *Andrew Crawford*. They are
almost twin fronts, with identical Roman Doric doorpieces
and architraved first-floor windows over balustrades (as at
Nos. 57–61); but not quite, for on the second floor the s windows are thinly pilastered, the N ones plain, with the slight
suggestion of an entablature, and three sets of tiny guttae over

each. Few shops, but discreet; the pub at No. 34a has a basement frontage with pilasters. The only commercial outbreak
is towards the NW corner, pleasant enough with its continuous
modillioned cornice, but with one shopfront nastily infilled.

CHARLOTTE SQUARE

Charlotte Square is the grand finale of the First New Town, the
last section to be built and the only one designed as a single
unified scheme. The architect was *Robert Adam*.

Craig's plan showed the square,* but an adjoining proprietor,
the Earl of Moray, owned a right of servitude over the NW
corner (the angled w end of Queen Street shows the old boundary line). In 1787 Robert Kay, the architect of the buildings
along South Bridge, was paid for a drawing for the square (presumably elevations), but the Moray servitude caused this
scheme to be dropped in favour of a circus or crescent.‡ By
March 1791 agreement with the Earl of Moray seemed to have
been reached§ and it was finally decided to have a square, but
to a new design. The Lord Provost requested of *Robert Adam*
elevations 'not much ornamented but with an elegant Simplicity
Such as the north Front of the College'. The original N elevation of the University Old Quad (*see* Old Town, Public Buildings) was at that time a simple affair indeed, facing onto a lane.
If not a joke, the brief was a warning to Adam not to repeat the
elaborate grandeur of his schemes for Leith Street and South
Bridge which had proved too expensive to build. Characteristically, Adam did not stick to the letter of his instructions, but
the design made in 1791 was sufficiently restrained to be feas-
ible, and the site was at the fashionable end of town. The feus
on the N side were offered for sale within days of Adam's death
in March 1792, and in May 1795 the premium of 10 guineas
offered to the first feuar to roof a house in the square was paid
to the builder *David Hay*. In 1796, feus on the E and S sides
were offered for sale, the w side following in 1803. A circular
garden in the middle was levelled in the same year and laid out
to a plan by *William Weir* in 1808. St George (*see* Public Buildings, West Register House, above), the w climax of the First
New Town, was begun (not to Adam's design) in 1811, and by
1820 the square was complete.

The GARDEN in the centre was enlarged as an octagon in 1873.
Railings of 1947, inappropriate despite their anthemions. AL-
BERT MEMORIAL in the middle,‖ 9·1 m. high, with a bronze
equestrian statue of the prince in field marshal's uniform by
John Steell, appointed after a competition in 1865 and

* But showed it as St George's Square. The name was changed in 1786 to avoid
confusion with George Square on the South Side.

‡ It was perhaps in connexion with this that the plasterer-architect *James Nisbet*
produced drawings.

§ But the formal agreement was not made until 1804; till then it was doubtful
if the NW corner could be built.

‖ The Charlotte Square site was an afterthought. Holyrood Park had been the
generally preferred site.

knighted at the unveiling in 1876. Peterhead granite base by *David Bryce* with corner groups of figures by *William Brodie* (the Nobility), *D. W. Stevenson* (Science and Learning), *Clark Stanton* (the Army and Navy), and *Stevenson** again (Labour). On the third stage bas-reliefs (including the opening of the Great Exhibition) by *Brodie* and *Ritchie*.

117 N SIDE (Nos. 1–11). A row of eleven houses composed as a 100 m. palace-front of uncommon finesse and grandeur in which movement is always complemented by stillness, repetition by variety, plainness by intricacy. Vertically, the stonework graduates from rock-faced basement to regular ground-floor rustication, then flat polished ashlar on the first and second floors. Horizontally this flat plane is dominant throughout the twenty-one bays, the rhythm maintained by not-quite-semicircular window heads through the ground floor of the pavilions and links. Pavilions slightly advanced, each with a doorway between overarched Venetian windows (Adam showed three windows), very broad pilasters above, and a crowning sphinx in front of the pyramidal roof. Centrepiece‡ with four pairs of attached columns (Adam's own version of Corinthian), the ground floor breaking forward beneath each outer pair to unite the inner pairs whose frieze of inverted garlands is interrupted by a plain panel at the very centre. Statues were meant to stand on the pediment. Only the centre bay of the ground floor is arched. At the first floor, single windows alternating with overarched tripartite windows like those of the pavilions; the sidelights of the outer two were built up in the C19.§ No drawings for the end elevations survive. The w one is plain, but the e has overarched first-floor windows linked with a fluted frieze, and on the chimney-head, flanked by balustrades, a serpentine fluted panel like a Roman sarcophagus; not very well related to the main front, but entirely in the spirit of late Adam. The execution at least was by *Alexander Stevens*, who built the whole e pavilion.

The interior of No. 1 is among the best in Edinburgh. *Stevens* designed Nos. 1 and 2 as two ingeniously interlocked houses (not the one very large house originally proposed for each pavilion), himself living at No. 1. Very small entrance hall leading straight into a rectangular stairwell, unusual both

* Following a sketch by *George McCallum*.

‡ A sketch in the Soane Museum illustrates the evolution of this seven-bay centrepiece which is quoted in many later palace-fronts in Edinburgh. It shows three broad bays (modelled on the w centrepiece of Portland Place, London, but refined in proportion) alternating with four narrow bays which have a distyle order and are crowned with sphinxes. In the final scheme of 1791 the sphinxes are omitted and the two distyle bays in the middle linked by a pediment in the manner of the Royal Society of Arts building at the Adelphi. In execution the centre bay was emphasized by enriching the tympanum over the first-floor tripartite window.

§ Numerous C19 alterations (e.g. lettering at No. 6, lowered sills and four large dormers) were rectified by the fourth Marquess of Bute, mainly in 1924–7 after he had acquired Nos. 5–8 (the first three now the property of the National Trust for Scotland).

for its lighting (from a window in each landing) and for its elegant wrought-iron balustrade of trelliswork panels supporting the sinuous handrail. Ceiling with a fan in concave husk garlands. Dining room on the l. with an arched sideboard recess between tall reeded shafts of segmental section. The room on the r. is entered through a Gothic-astragalled glass screen (the large opening was formed in 1957) made by *Whytock & Reid* in 1968 when *Robert Hurd & Partners* restored the house; its ceiling is the fashionable late C18 garlanded oval, with corn-ears shooting from the centre. In the first-floor drawing room above, a ceiling worthy of Adam (a simpler version existed at No. 31 Portland Place, London) with an eight-point star set in a circle. *James Henderson* seems to have been the plasterer. Here and elsewhere, ornamented pine chimneypieces of a slightly earlier date than the house, imported in 1968. At that date No. 1 was joined at all levels with No. 2, whose distinctive feature is a square stairwell overlooked by an open passage with a central column. The two first-floor front rooms were remodelled c. 1840 with heavy Greek detail.

No. 5 was put up by the architect-builders *Adam & Charles Russell* before 1796, and sold by them to John Grant of Rothiemurchus. It was probably quite plain until 1903, when it was bought by the fourth Marquess of Bute, for whom *A. F. Balfour Paul* replaced the woodwork of the front library and most of the stair with oak of late-Stuart/early-Georgian design and remodelled the two (communicating) first-floor drawing rooms in the Adam manner, albeit a little heavily. Front-drawing-room ceiling a copy of Adam's 1769 ceiling for Lady Bute's dressing room at Luton Hoo, its semi-realistic Edwardian colouring still complete. Back-drawing-room ceiling of similar type. Large marble chimneypieces of c. 1905, their roundels with carved cherubs probably by *Louis Deuchars*.

No. 6 was built by the shoemaker Orlando Hart by 1798. Sir John Sinclair, master mind of the *Statistical Account of Scotland*, became its third owner in 1806. T-plan entrance hall with a rosetted ceiling. At the far end a consoled white marble chimneypiece. It looks early C19. Dining room at the back with a complex circle-patterned ceiling. E of the main axis, and rather isolated, a spacious stairwell. The first-floor drawing room is one of the finest rooms of the brief post-Adam period in Edinburgh. Ceiling with long swagged oval and corner fans. White marble chimneypiece, a little small in scale but with a lovely reclining Galatea attended by dolphins on the centre panel.

No. 7 was built by *Edmund Butterworth* in 1796 and sold to John Lamont of Lamont. Originally (to judge by the unaltered rooms) quite plain inside, it is important today as THE GEORGIAN HOUSE, opened in 1975 by the National Trust for Scotland, the two main floors and basement decorated and furnished in simulation of their late-C18 state. Architectural

work (largely unseen) by *W. Schomberg Scott*; the rest by the
Trust's Curator *David Learmont*, with *R. L. Snowden* of the
DoE. as colour-consultant and *J. & T. Harvey* as decorators.
On the ground floor all the original cornices survive, with
rows of upright leaves. Restored stone-flagged floors in the
entrance hall and oblong stairwell; the separating screen may
not be original. The reeded black marble chimneypiece of the
dining room looks like an early replacement. In the room
behind (now the principal bedroom), a contemporary wood-
and-composition chimneypiece (rose and convolvulus frieze)
from Tarvit House, Fife. Stone stair lit by a swagged oval
skylight. The two first-floor rooms connect. Bracketed Victorian cornices replaced in 1975 with a husk frieze and a
cornice with a deep fascia less like 1796 than fifty years before
or after. Was this a deliberate change of policy? Drawing-
room chimneypiece moved here in 1975 from No. 5; white
marble with variegated Ionic columns of curious inverted entasis and a central roundel of cherubs. Presumably it is of
c. 1905. The one in the rear parlour is again from Tarvit, this
time with oval paterae. The kitchen at the back of the basement has been re-equipped with an open range and stone
sink. The stone-compartmented wine cellar is original.

The interior of No. 8 was embellished in a Dixhuitième
manner in 1897-8 when Dr T. R. Ronald had the rear bow
rebuilt as a canted bay. In the ground-floor rooms, geometrically patterned original ceilings. Thin reliefs of Louis-Seize
feeling have been added to the walls; figures at the front,
medallions and griffons at the back. On the ceiling of the
first-floor (rear) drawing room a rich Edwardian version of
the familiar oval motif. Figures with roundels on the walls.
Elaborate chimneypiece with oval overmantel. In No. 9 the
front ground-floor room has an oval-pattern ceiling with
figure reliefs.

W SIDE (Nos. 12-23). Adam's 1791 design for two identical
blocks each side of St George's church was largely carried
out after 1803, when the buyers of feus were allowed to have
taller windows than those shown by Adam – a privilege already given to the feuars of the S and E sides. Each block is
a short palace-front. The end pavilions are variants of those
on the N side with narrower pilasters (Ionic this time) and
rectangular ground-floor windows. Attached Ionic columns
on the five-bay centrepiece, its wide middle bay with a giant
first-floor tripartite window under a segmental fan of glass.
Below, a Roman Doric porch which should contain three
doors but only has two (the central dummy left out). Devia-
tions from the Adam design as regards doors and windows
are quite eclipsed by what has happened to the roof-line: the
pyramid roofs at the centre and ends are lost in a continuous
ridge which was broken by early C20 attics each side of the
church and by clumsy additions on Nos. 15-16. Interiors
mostly quite plain (e.g. *William Sibbald*'s own house at
No. 13). In No. 17 the front rooms have enriched ceilings, an

elongated octagon design on the ground floor, an oval above. The first-floor ceiling in No. 18 is of circled type. In No. 23 two ceilings with fans in the corners, probably of *c.* 1905 when the decorator *Charles W. Swanson* fitted up the house as his showrooms.

S SIDE (Nos. 24–32). A repeat of the N side with larger windows and no sphinxes on the end pavilions, but the tripartite windows in the centrepiece are intact. In the end elevations, concave shouldered chimney gables with thermal windows, a favourite detail of *Robert Reid*. Well finished but plain interiors.

E SIDE (Nos. 33–46). A lower-key version of the W side, designed without the central porches and tripartite windows but the centrepiece supposed to have an attic storey with a large lunette window;* the attic storey was omitted when *Robert Reid* redesigned the centrepieces in 1810. The N terrace is further upset by a porch added by *John Watherston & Sons* in 1902, the S by the mid-Victorian mansard of the Roxburgh Hotel. The two-bay No. 44 was designed by *Robert Reid* for himself, with an exceptional interior. Ground-floor front room, perhaps used for business, bowed on the window wall facing the square. In the dining room behind screens of Ionic columns *in antis* framing the sideboard recess and centre window. Coomb-shape ceiling with Greek-key border. Pendentive dome over the stair, whose top landing is answered by a balcony across the well.

ELDER STREET *see* YORK PLACE

FREDERICK STREET

The first feu was taken in 1786, and by 1792 the street had nearly filled up with main door tenements, mostly of plain droved ashlar but including two of the double-bowed kind. Almost all the original fronts survive over the shops, which came on the scene in the early C19 and have been replaced in most cases with later ones.

In the S section the workaday regularity of the E side is impressive, but the only notable shopfront is Dicksons the gunsmiths at No. 21, late C19 with excellent gilded lettering. On the W side some shops have run to two storeys, e.g. at Nos. 12–16 where the pilastered first-floor projection, decent in itself, has nearly swamped a double bow. The oddest alteration is at Nos. 30–32, which in 1900 grew upwards into an eccentric skyline with Lorimer-style dormers, and forwards into a spindly first-floor display case; it is either by *Victor D. Horsburgh* or *Francis W. Deas.*‡ In 1903 came the pleasant

---

* Adam's elevation shows the links without rusticated ground floors, but rustication had appeared on the prescribed elevation by 1807.

‡ Both these architects lived at the address given on the drawings, and both were closely connected with Robert Lorimer.

Edwardian Renaissance building at Nos. 5–7 by *Dunn & Findlay*, formerly the Queen's Club; twin oriel bays and a pedimented gable.

N of George Street on the E side a clear run of early C19 shops on ground-floor level. At Nos. 37–41 it is a simple matter of pilasters and an Ionic doorpiece applied to the existing openings. No. 47 is the same only plainer, and the glazing has been altered in both cases. But between them the shopfront at No. 45 is complete, a continuous Ionic colonnade of stone with classical iron cresting over the cornice, inserted in 1823 for William & Robert Hill (later Hill Thomsons). The upper W side has fared less well. After the corner building (*see* No. 74 George Street), VICTORIA CHAMBERS, another *Dunn & Findlay* job of 1903, this time with some female figures squeezed into the gables, and at the other end a pseudo-rubble corner block by *Covell Matthews & Partners*, 1966. The plain block between them at Nos. 44–48 still has one nice shopfront with slim cast-iron Corinthian columns. At the N end towards Queen Street the Georgian buildings are of superior class and relatively little spoiled. Nos. 51–55 include a single house (a rarity in these streets) which still has its rusticated ground floor. Likewise on the W side some ground floors have been left without shops, including that of the double-bow frontage at Nos. 58–62 which has no rustication.

GEORGE STREET, E TO W

7 NOS. 1–31 (N SIDE – St Andrew Square to Hanover Street). A good start with the STANDARD LIFE ASSURANCE building, restrained neo-Palladian by *J. M. Dick Peddie & G. Washington Browne*, built in three stages from 1897 to 1901 (1825 on the frieze is the date of the company's foundation) as the old buildings were demolished. This, plus the re-use of the large pediment from *David Bryce*'s 1839 building, explains its unusual proportions. The smallness of the Corinthian order supporting the pediment is camouflaged by a frieze of putti under the main cornice (Browne was a master of Renaissance detail), and the only real awkwardness is the absence of linking balustrades between the pedestals. The pediment SCULPTURE by *John Steell* represents the Wise and Foolish Virgins, it being supposed that the five wise ones would have insured themselves. The interior shows a new departure. A small public area, arched and pilastered with a variety of coloured marbles, is approached round a corner through a groin-vaulted vestibule; rich but informal, and suitable for the discussion of private matters, without trying to awe the client. The next building is Standard Life's Phase Three Extension by *Michael Laird & Partners*, 1975, based on the second-phase elevation in St Andrew Square but this time with a curiously sloping ground-floor window treatment and the facia enriched with SCULPTURE, a modern version of the

same theme of the Ten Virgins in a bronze relief by *Gerald Laing*. Part of the same phase was the complete internal re-building of No. 13, which is by *W. Hamilton Beattie* of *George Beattie & Sons*, designed for the Royal Insurance Company in 1898, Renaissance in style, but of far greater refinement than his North British Hotel, and a good end-piece for this interesting group. Tucked in behind it is Standard Life's 110 Phase One Extension, again by *Michael Laird & Partners*, 1964, a fastidiously detailed curtain wall whose one positive assertion is its colour, the dark green panels complementing the grey of the windows and the livelier grey of the stone buildings round about.

After St Andrew (*see* Churches, above), the GEORGE HOTEL, which grew Topsy-fashion from the three houses built on the site by *John Young* in the early 1780s. In 1840 *David Bryce* added a tetrastyle Corinthian portico to No. 19. In 1879 *MacGibbon & Ross* extended the same treatment over Nos. 15 and 17 for the Caledonian Insurance Company, in a remodelling that provided hotel accommodation on the upper floors. But they spoiled the effect with a weak Renaissance doorway and an absurdly fussy attic (an afterthought by their clients). In 1903 *R. H. Watherston* substituted rusticated arches for the ground-floor pilastrade. The whole building became the George Hotel in 1950. Inside, MacGibbon & Ross were responsible for the long vestibule with its coarse hybrid columns, but did much better in the dining room – originally the main business hall in the grand Edinburgh tradition. It is square, with composite columns and dome; four non-structural columns were removed in 1969. Extension E of the hotel to the rear by *Henry Wylie*, 1967, seven storeys high (ten less than the tower scheme of 1958 which was stopped by a Public Inquiry), with horizontal bands of pale stone cladding, alternating with the windows and their brown aluminium trim. Cleverly planned single-storey corridor link, with windows facing the street; altogether a decent standard for commercial architecture in the New Town.

The CLYDESDALE BANK at the Hanover Street corner, a prime example of *David Bryce*'s Graeco-Roman manner, was designed for the Edinburgh & Leith Bank, the first (S) half in 1841 as a private commission, the N half in 1847 when Bryce had become Burn's partner in charge of their Edinburgh office and the bank had become the Edinburgh & Glasgow. But it is a single composition, with a giant Corinthian order on the upper floors; pilasters all round, and pairs of columns set forward of them on the George Street side only (a Glasgow theme, cf. David Hamilton's theatre in Queen Street, now demolished). On the later part a shell-headed porch, an intimation of Bryce's later banks in Italian Renaissance style. The original front area has been lost along with Bryce's interior.

NOS. 2–26 (S SIDE – St Andrew Square to Hanover Street). First and very much foremost (though its address is in the square) is the GUARDIAN ROYAL EXCHANGE INSURANCE building by *L. Grahame Thomson* and *Frank J. Connell* for the Caledonian Insurance Company, 1938-40, faced with near-white granite over a black arcaded base, the set-back attic roof originally tiled. Big but gentle, with a touch of Scandinavian conviction in the Art Deco detail, e.g. the tall oriel over the corner splay, flanked by columns bearing bronze figures by the *Henshaws*. Beneath them the entrance, with the ground floor planned on its diagonal axis, a public area with reeded marble columns leading to the staircase with stained glass by *William Wilson*. On the first floor a fine boardroom with apsidal ends and more columns.

Nos. 4-6, by *Watson, Salmond & Gray*, 1962, have a sparse but stodgy classical front. At the LIFE ASSOCIATION OF SCOTLAND (successor to the old Princes Street office) *Mottram Patrick Whitehorn Dalgleish & Partners* in 1966 dispensed with classicism altogether and substituted a fussy and boxy system of articulation in grey marbles. Then the free-standing ROYAL BANK OF SCOTLAND with its huge portico, originally the head office of the Commercial Bank. It is by *David Rhind*, who was appointed architect in 1843. The building was opened in 1847. The site is that of *James Craig*'s Physicians' Hall (1775), which would have made a head office as grand as the Royal Bank's in St Andrew Square, but it was decided to build anew on the largest possible scale. Rhind's frontage is directly based on Playfair's original scheme for the Surgeons' Hall (*see* South Side, Public Buildings), but the portico is entered directly, not through the flanking gateways, and moreover the style is not Greek but the richest Graeco-Roman, with arched and keystoned upper windows and a Corinthian portico. Pedimental SCULPTURE modelled by *James Wyatt* of London and carved by *A. Handyside Ritchie*; a central figure of Caledonia, flanked by Prudence, Agriculture, Commerce, Enterprise, Mechanical Science and Learning, powerfully composed in high relief. The thickly wreathed cast-iron side gates are original, but not the lamp-standards or the flashy bronzework of the main door, or the plate glass in the front windows; Rhind's well proportioned glazing can still be seen on the sides of the building. Inside, the first big space is a top-lit square hall with superimposed Ionic columns – fluted above, smooth scagliola below. From its aisles twin staircases with gilded anthemion balusters ascend to the first-floor offices. Beyond is the magnificent telling hall, a Greek cross with arched ceilings and coffered central dome. This basic plan had already been used in Edinburgh, but Rhind greatly elaborated it with columned screens at the entry to each arm of the cross, a Fortuna Virilis frieze, rich anthemion decoration on the pendentives and an apsed end to the s arm. The columns were originally marbled wood, but in 1885 the Commercial Bank's new architect *Sydney Mitchell* re-faced them in Devonshire marble veined with grey and red, with black Belgian granite bases and bronze capitals. His

107

also are the marble mosaic floors, black, red and grey, with arabesques and the arms of the Bank.

No. 16 (the site feued by *James Craig* in 1779) consists of original houses altered in the early C19, with good Victorian shopfronts. No. 18, designed for Dowells the auctioneers in 1879 by *W. Hamilton Beattie*, is an elaborate but not exciting aggregation of superimposed pilaster orders and debased early Renaissance motifs which *The Builder* described as inspired 'from Heidelberg' and *The British Architect* as C16 French. The most interesting feature is the use of iron for window mullions and transoms. Behind this frontage the whole building was remodelled by *Robert Hurd & Partners* in 1978.

The ROYAL SOCIETY OF EDINBURGH at Nos. 22–24 occupies the building designed for the Edinburgh Life Assurance Company in 1843 by *William Burn & David Bryce* and adapted for the Society's use by *W. T. Oldrieve* in 1909. It has an Italian palace-front in the manner of Burn's New Club in Princes Street (now demolished), with the same sharp Grecian handling of Roman detail. In the old business hall (now the foyer) a screen of Roman Ionic columns. Otherwise the interior, which originally also housed the Edinburgh Subscription Library, is typical of Burn's austere classicism.*

The COMMERCIAL UNION INSURANCE building at the corner of Hanover Street, designed by *J. M. Dick Peddie* in 1908–9 for the Edinburgh Life Assurance Company in succession to their office next door, is large in scale in a restrained Edwardian Renaissance manner, with a giant unfluted Ionic order taking in the upper floors. On the circled corner a consoled drum and big copper dome surmounted by *Percy Portsmouth*'s bronze statue of Prudence. Portland stone was a curious choice, being George Street's first departure from Edinburgh sandstone except for T. Duncan Rhind's wild red frontage at No. 83. In the business hall Roman Doric columns of pavonazzo marble with entablatures elided. The stair, with the heavy balusters of the time, leads by a panelled corridor to a grand first-floor board room with a fine late C18 marble chimneypiece probably from the original house on this site, a neo-Adam ceiling, and wall panels of crimson Utrecht velvet from the company's old office next door.

GEORGE IV STATUE, at the George Street–Hanover Street intersection. Bronze, commemorating his visit to Edinburgh in 1822, by *Francis Chantrey*, 1831.

NOS. 33–69 (N SIDE - Hanover Street to Frederick Street). First a long run of original but altered and heightened houses, some of the alterations of great interest. Nos. 39–41 were reconstructed and refaced as a pair, with an extra storey, in 1830. No. 41 has a first-floor bay-window of 1875 by *John Lessels*, and in 1881 *Hippolyte J. Blanc* remodelled and extended the ground floor for William Johnstone & Co. in his rare Italian Renaissance manner (he had been in Robert

---

* Restored, with some alterations, by *Robert Hurd & Partners*, 1982–3.

Matheson's office); it has a richly coved saloon with Doric columns. Nos. 43–45 were similarly refaced and heightened by *Thomas Hamilton** for William Blackwood in 1829. The Ionic ground-floor colonnade of No. 45 was continued along the other house as well; the present Corinthian colonnade at No. 43 is by *A. W. Macnaughtan*, 1897. But No. 45 remained in use as Blackwood's office till 1972, the front shop lined with bookcases, then an Ionic screen leading to a further shelf-lined corridor and on to the square saloon with saucer-dome skylight and monumental chimneypiece. Its walls were red and the woodwork throughout was a venerable mahogany brown, but the decoration and much else was altered by *Covell Matthews Partnership* in 1974. No. 47 was raised and refaced in 1830–1, and in 1880 the ground floor was grandly extended by *John Bryce* for the jeweller James Crichton. A screen of Corinthian columns opens into a large rectangular saloon with a segmental ceiling coffered in the David Bryce manner. No. 49 has a heavy built-out front of two storeys, inter-war classic by *John Kinross & J. Inch Morrison*, 1921. The two lower floors of No. 51 were refaced with elegant Renaissance detail by *George Beattie & Sons* in 1877. Nos. 53–63 retain most of their original appearance, their plain ashlar marked off by rusticated strips at the party walls and common stairs. A good pair of plain Victorian shopfronts at Nos. 59a and 61, the latter containing an Ionic screen from the original late Georgian shop conversion.

No. 65 has a tall, narrow frontage of pink Dumfries-shire stone, late Gothic–early Renaissance, by *J. N. Scott & A. Lorne Campbell*, 1907–8. No. 67, a modest Italianate front of four storeys, beautifully proportioned, by *Peddie & Kinnear* for the Crown Insurance Company, 1867, has lost much of its detail, including the roof cresting. Finally the BANK OF SCOTLAND at No. 69, designed in 1905 by *G. Washington Browne* (*Dick Peddie & Washington Browne*) in his own authoritative François I manner for the British Linen Bank. Four storeys with mullioned and transomed windows curving into Frederick Street, articulated by panelled pilaster orders. Browne's telling room woodwork was entirely replaced in the internal reconstruction by *Henry Wylie & Partners*, 1964.

Nos. 30–68 (S SIDE – Hanover Street to Frederick Street). More original houses with stuck-on shops, the corner one as usual a block of flats but exceptional in having a chimney gable with two windows at the wallhead facing George Street. No. 38 has an elegant late Georgian shopfront without projection. Central door with Ionic columns reached by steps, as if it were still a house. No. 52 has a piend roof in deference to the Assembly Rooms (*see* Public Buildings, above) and so does No. 58, which also boasts a Georgian shopfront and a delicately moulded ceiling of late Adam type in the (subdivided) room overhead. The BANK OF SCOTLAND at Nos. 62–

---

* Information from Joe Rock.

66, designed by *David Bryce* in 1874 as the Edinburgh head office of the Glasgow-based Union Bank, was finished after his death in May 1876 by his nephew *John Bryce*. Long front with three Ionic porches, Corinthian first-floor aedicules, and a panelled and bracketed cornice. The High Renaissance austerity recalls Bryce's work of thirty years before. *William Beattie & Sons* were the contractors and the carver was *John Rhind*. In 1977 the bank's architect *Thomas Alexander* carefully restored and cleaned the front and modified the interior, the work of *John Bryce*, completed in 1878. In the public space four Peterhead granite Corinthian columns. The telling room is top-lit from the cove of the elaborate ceiling. Original floor tiles remain under the carpet, but the counter has been redesigned. No. 68, the SUN ALLIANCE ASSURANCE building by *T. Waller Marwick (T.P. Marwick & Sons)*, 1955, has two fashionably framed-up elevations meeting perfunctorily at the corner of Frederick Street with an ugly splay.

WILLIAM PITT STATUE, at the George Street–Frederick Street intersection. Bronze, by *Francis Chantrey*, 1833.

Nos. 71–105 (N SIDE – Frederick Street to Castle Street). The Edwardian Baroque fantasy at No. 71 is the former Gresham House by *T.P. Marwick*, 1908. Its corner splay grows into an octagonal tower with leaning-out term figures and a copper dome. Ground floor refaced. Nos. 73–75 is the latest and possibly the last redevelopment of a Georgian house in the street, by *George Walls & Partners*, 1974. Then a run of variously altered Georgian fronts, interrupted by the purposely outrageous projection of No. 83, the work of *Hamilton Paterson & Rhind*, 1901; a pity the wide red sandstone arch of its two-storey display window has been cut off at the knees with a long facia. At No. 87 is the most impressive and interesting of all George Street shop interiors, 1835 by *David Bryce* for the jewellers J. & G. Hunter Marshall, luxurious but modest in scale, with Corinthian columns punctuating its spaces and forming a screen at the end of the rear saloon. No. 89 has a tall and elaborate Renaissance front by *Cousin, Ormiston & Taylor*, a central arch rising into the gable. Then at last an unextended late-c18 house at No. 91 (the prosaic doorpiece is a recent replacement for the old tripartite one); good early Victorian railings and lamp-standard. No. 93 was reconstructed and refronted in 1833 by *Thomas Hamilton*.* In 1980–2 *Robert Hurd & Partners* restored the lower part of his design, removing *A.W. Macnaughtan*'s top-heavy portico of 1900 and reproducing the first-floor veranda with slim iron pillars. Of Hamilton's rooms, the chaste and splendid saloon at the rear has been demolished, the first-floor drawing room (ingeniously Grecian, with an earlier marble chimneypiece) restored. No. 95 was designed by *David Bryce* in 1840 as the Refuge Insurance building, the upper part and the balconied ground-floor projection united in one composition.

* Hamilton's work and the subsequent alterations were done for the grocer Andrew Melrose, who lived over his own shop.

The next three buildings should be seen together, for all
109   belong to the BANK OF SCOTLAND. In the middle the office
of 1883–5 by *J. M. Dick Peddie*, designed to assert the bank's
presence in the New Town; conservatively palatial in form,
beautifully refined in detail. As an afterthought the right-
hand bay, instead of a balancing porch, was given an arch like
the rest but with a tympanum delicately carved by *D. W.
Stevenson*. Telling room at the front, pure Neo-Classical, with
Corinthian columns and coffered ceiling, but again with some
graceful touches. In 1975 the bank commissioned *Robert
Hurd & Partners* not only to redecorate the interior but to
expand the office space with the help of the two adjacent
properties. The site of Nos. 97–99 was redeveloped with a
smooth-faced 'Georgian' house-front to balance the real one
at No. 105, though the latter's embellishments and shopfront
(now blocked up) of *c.* 1850 are rather inconsistently retained.* The ROYAL INSURANCE building at No. 107 on the
Castle Street corner is by *S. W. Edgar* of *Dick Peddie &
McKay*, 1969, distilled from the comments of various con-
sultative bodies. The loss of the original house in this context
was a disaster.

Nos. 74–102 (S SIDE – Frederick Street to Castle Street). An
original corner with a shiny new shop. Then No. 76, a complete Georgian house with a clumsy mansard and other later
trimmings; plain interior. The Edwardian giant at Nos. 78–80
was built in 1903–7 to the design of *John J. Burnet* for the
Professional & Civil Service Supply Association – a sort of
Harrods with club facilities. Granted its preposterous size,
this is a fine thing indeed: a lofty entrance formed as a recessed portico in a framing architrave, an upper giant order
(the sales floors) starting from the eaves height of the adjacent
houses, and finally its own eaves gallery with heroic caryatids
(the restaurant) between terminal domes. All this is Burnet's
distillation of Edwardian Baroque out of his own adventurous
Waterloo Chambers (1899) in Glasgow. About 1936 the Co-
op filled up the recessed proscenium entrance with bald Art
Deco granite, but in 1972 *Ian Burke Associates* restored it as
far as possible, with columns of slightly wobbly outline cased
in fibreglass. The interior, representing a high peak of Edwardian store planning, was totally removed in the conversion
to modern office use, but the rear elevation, an early modern
masterwork with its glass curtain walls between white glazed
brick pylons and its delivery bays on basement level, can still
be seen (though modified) in Rose Street Lane.

Now a row of late-C18 houses transformed in different
ways. The first two are now one, reconstructed in 1973 for
the NORTHERN LIGHTHOUSE BOARD by *Rowand Anderson,
Kininmonth & Paul*. At No. 82 the protruding shop was removed and the lower wall restored on its proper line, though

---

* There was also a real Georgian house at Nos. 97–99, concealed by *Kinnear
& Peddie*'s gabled Renaissance frontage of 1885.

without a front door, and at No. 84 the original precision of
the Ionic doorpiece was somewhat impaired by cleaning; over
it is a model lighthouse, lit up at night. The next house was
updated in 1832 with a shop below and saloon behind. No. 88
was remodelled in 1876 by *Peddie & Kinnear* with a spacious
shop interior, No. 90 in 1847 for the decorator D. R. Hay
with an elaborate undercut frieze and big urns on the parapet.
At No. 92 the shopfront and mullioned windows look as if
they had been put together from a building kit, a transformation in American stick-style by *MacGibbon & Ross* (the
upper part for use as their own office) in 1879; unfortunately
the pagoda-like bay-window lacks its original fancy ironwork
and the interior has been lost by fire. No. 94 has been completely rebuilt (for a change), as offices with a busy classical
front, by *Kinnear & Peddie*, 1882; the early-Georgian-revival
shop is of 1929. For the Freemasons' Hall *see* Public Buildings, above.

The PEARL ASSURANCE building at the end was Edinburgh's first gentle introduction to the modern movement.
The corner part, designed by *Alfred G. Lochhead* in 1924–5
for Cleghorn's store, recalls two of his masters: Burnet in its
vertical integration, Lorimer in the simplified scroll pediment
on the corner splay. *Basil Spence* (then of Rowand Anderson,
Paul & Partners) extended it in 1937–8 as planned, but added
the set-back attic with chamfered piers like Tait's at St Andrew's House. On the splay he substituted a window for the
intended coat of arms, and on the w elevation he unfortunately modified Lochhead's staircase bay; the junction with
the stonework of Frederick Street itself is regrettably careless.
Ground floor altered with coarse detailing in black and red
granite by *James Davidson & Son* of Coatbridge, 1956.

THOMAS CHALMERS STATUE, at the George Street–Castle
Street intersection. 1878 by *John Steell*, who had modelled a
bust for an unexecuted memorial in 1847. Bronze, on a red
granite plinth.

Nos. 109–141 (N SIDE – Castle Street to Charlotte Square).
Quite ordinary until No. 115, the only survivor of a trio built
c. 1790. Its fluted Corinthian pilasters and delicately swagged
frieze were formerly matched on No. 119, the house in the
middle having no pilasters. Projecting shop of 1883 removed
and ground floor approximately restored by *Covell Matthews
Partnership*, 1978–80. First-floor front drawing room retained, its elegant plasterwork clumsily reinstated.*

The CHURCH OF SCOTLAND office is one of the giants of
George Street, built in 1909–11 for the recently formed
United Free Church of Scotland, and the last work of *Sydney
Mitchell.*‡ Its novelty was not well received, and he retired
leaving *E. A. O. Auldjo Jamieson*, who probably had a large

* The plaster detail resembles that at Leuchie House, East Lothian, by *James
Nisbet. The Builder* (1883) attributed these houses to Robert Adam.

‡ It is very like Henry Hare's unsuccessful design for Colchester Town Hall,
illustrated in Alistair Service, *Edwardian Architecture*, 1977.

hand in the design, to carry on the practice with *J. A. Arnott*. Theirs is the E extension of 1932–3 (following the union of the United Free Church and the Church of Scotland in 1929), but the balancing extension to the W was not built even though No. 125 was bought for the purpose. All quite elegant in a ponderous Scandinavian way. Ground floor of granite, with triple arcades resting on Greek Doric columns of Paestum or Delos type, the doorway crowned with a double window and a great burning bush in bronze. Upper wall freestone, with two storeys of triple-arched windows punched into the channelled masonry under a Roman Doric eaves gallery. Metal-faced cornice and two ranks of metal-headed dormers in a large mansard. Interior very simple except for the solemn punctuation of corridors and staircase with black-shafted Roman Doric columns. Very plain CHAPEL by *Ian G. Lindsay*, 1953, the four windows filled with stained glass (the Evangelists) by *A. L. Russel*.

The tall classical frontage of No. 123, square and prosaic in detail, is of 1880 by *Peddie & Kinnear* for the Scottish Amicable and the Scottish American Investment Companies. Its neighbour No. 125 has the best intact Georgian house-front in the street, with the original fanlight in the arch of its pilastered doorpiece. In the entrance hall an Adamish ceiling and wall medallions with figures in relief. Additions at the back by *Robert Matheson* for the Board of Supervision, 1856, extended further by *George Morham* in 1898. Original houses of *c.* 1790 at Nos. 127–141, their ground floors later built out. In 1973–4 *Robert Hurd & Partners* restored Nos. 127–129 with one arched doorway in place of two triple doorpieces that had been there before. The same firm was responsible for the clever horizontal division of the richly coved mid-Victorian saloon at the back of No. 135 to form a tea room.

Nos. 104–138 (S SIDE – Castle Street to Charlotte Square). Still good things of the early 1790s, beginning with a main door tenement and a house, both complete except for the over-cleaning of the stonework. At Nos. 108–110 the doorpiece of the ground-floor and basement flat has pilasters of a kind of Corinthian, and lampholders and extinguishers in front. Fairly plain interior with good chimneypieces. No. 112, built in 1790 by *James Hill* and *Alexander Porteous*, has an architraved doorpiece with the original fanlight. Front hall and drawing room have Adamish ceilings and the dining room is panelled. CARRON HOUSE, Nos. 114–116, is by *Morris & Steedman*, 1963, the two upper storeys reinterpreting the Georgian balance of vertical and horizontal by means of upright fins overlaying the vertical cross bands – both of travertine marble. The next house has a built-out shop, and then comes the long frontage of Nos. 120–124, the former TONTINE BUILDING,* by *James Nisbet*, 1792. Still unfin-

---

* Tontine: a shared annuity, from which the survivors get more profit as the others die off.

ished at the Napoleonic War, it was cheaply fitted out as a cavalry barracks and then became a government office. The upper front survives with its centrepiece of Composite pilasters, but the arcaded ground floor has gone.* The frontage of Nos. 126–128 was taken down and rebuilt in 1973–5 as part of an office development by *R. Seifert*, adding a large mansard and an impossibly wide 'Georgian' doorway but not eliminating the ground-floor projection. Mannered ELECTRICITY BOARD office at No. 130 by *Gordon & Dey*, 1960, with sculptures of electrical subjects by *Tom Whalen*. The pedimented N and S corner blocks are part of Charlotte Square (*see* above).

HANOVER STREET

The first feu was taken in 1784, and after a slow start the street was finished by 1790, mostly with main door and common stair tenements in droved ashlar now much altered and even redeveloped for commercial use; the S end in particular is unworthy of the tremendous vista that it frames (*see* The Mound). Some buildings, e.g. a tenement on the E side built by *Robert Brown* before 1788, had shops from the start. On the E side Nos. 3–11, with some really old-fashioned classical detail (pulvinated frieze and triple keyblocks) on the first-floor windows. The only fault of the decent neo-Georgian front of Nos. 15–19, by *James McLachlan* for Crawfords the caterers, 1930, is its projection from the proper building line. Splendiferous corner block at Nos. 29–33 with a blocked De l'Orme-type order on the shopfronts, by *John Watherston & Sons*, 1881. Nos. 45–51 remodelled complete with shops in 1868 by *David Cousin*, using unexpectedly blockish detail with incised carving. On the W side of the street, two examples of the gentler and earlier type of conversion at Nos. 38 and 54; no building-out, so you can walk up into the ground-floor shop or down into the basement one. Otherwise the street is dominated by two bank buildings.

The first, the MERCHANTS' HALL and its twin to the S, designed for the City of Glasgow Bank by *David Bryce Jun.* (a nephew of his namesake) in 1865–6, had a symmetrical front with canted bay-windows attached to the advanced ends, richly but very fastidiously detailed, e.g. in the Corinthian pilastered angles of the bays and the deep foliage frieze running all round under the eaves. The jaded palate of *The Builder* found it, for some reason, 'stale and commonplace', and anyway only the N half was built at the time; it was finished in 1901 by *T. P. Marwick*, but with inferior stone. In 1959 *L. Grahame MacDougall* made the best of a bad job, restoring most of the S half and substituting a very plain doorway for the hopelessly decayed porch with coupled Cor-

* But the fronts of Nos. 118–124 are to be restored (1984) in a redevelopment which will retain the remarkable geometrical stair in No. 118.

inthian columns that was exactly the same as the older surviving one. In the N part the original telling room, now the
MERCHANTS' HALL, lit by a glass-coffered dome and formerly lined with coupled Corinthian columns now removed
on three sides; their position is indicated by putti in the attic
demonstrating the attributes of Trade, Industry and the Arts.
The good detail of the stair-hall and other rooms is at least
partly due to *MacGibbon & Ross*, who adapted the building
for the Merchants in 1879. Hall in the S part also designed
for banking use, with a glass dome and Corinthian screen,
but the detailing by *Marwick* relatively coarse.

The Edinburgh branch of the TRUSTEE SAVINGS BANK
further downhill is by *William Paterson* of *Oldrieve, Bell &
Paterson*, 1939. Monumental American Neo-Classical in the
McKim tradition, a tall cubic mass with giant recessed columns of a simplified Bassae order on the Hanover Street
elevation, but charming Italian Renaissance detail. Interior of
the same scale, cool and reserved.

The N section of Hanover Street begins on the E side with No.
71, a narrow palace-front built in one operation with the
extension of the Clydesdale Bank by *David Bryce*, 1847.
Pedimented porch, pulvinated laurel friezes on the upper
windows. Also shop with pilasters and Neo-Georgian glazing
inserted in the ground floor of Nos. 73–77. Then Nos. 79–89,
the oldest survivor of the First New Town double-bowed
type (there was an earlier one in Princes Street), described in
the *Edinburgh Evening Courant* sale notice of 14 May 1787 as
'lately built by *Mr John Young*, architect'. Five windows wide
between the bows; in the pedimented centre bay the common
stair door. Pairs of shopfronts, both good of their kind, chop
off the ground floor on each side. Nos. 101–107 were given a
handsome shop frontage of nine arches *c.* 1830. The whole
street front between the corner blocks on the W side is a
broadly adequate Georgian imitation by the *Covell Matthews
Partnership*, 1975; its ground-floor detail with sparse pilasters
and timid cornice can be compared with the real thing at Nos.
89–90. The balustraded extra storey at Nos. 104–112 is by
Robert Morham, 1880.

HILL STREET *see* THISTLE STREET

HOPE STREET

On the E side, the end garden behind Charlotte Square was
built over with a plain tenement of which half, No. 11, was
extended to the pavement line by *J. R. McKay* in 1938. Enormous building at No. 3, designed for the Royal Bank of
Scotland by *Sydney H. Miller*, 1930, based on a better scheme
of 1922 by *D. W. Crawford*, his colleague in *Dick Peddie &
Walker Todd*. Overbearing Art-Deco Greek, its errors com-
pounded and exceeded by its Princes Street neighbour. The

w side however (like the other views out of Charlotte Square)
is almost intact; good tenements with arched and fanlit main
doors. At its s end Nos. 2-4 still have their double bow with
matching dormers, but have lost their chimneys and are engulfed by a shop. Hope Street had no N section in deference
to the Earl of Moray's right of servitude, but was partly developed as Glenfinlas Street (on the Moray Estate) in the
1820s. This NW corner of the First New Town was never
built up as Craig intended.

THE MOUND

The Mound is a causeway across the valley between the Old
and New Towns, formed from some two million cartloads of
earth and rubbish from the building of the New Town between 1781 and 1830. A road up to the head of the Lawnmarket was proposed in 1824 by *William Burn* and *Thomas
Hamilton* and incorporated into the 1827 Improvement Act.
In 1829 *Alexander Trotter* and *Archibald Elliot II* proposed
a different approach to the Old Town, entering the High
Street at St Giles. Hamilton opposed it, and in 1830 produced
a plan similar to what exists now. *Playfair*'s elaborate scheme
of 1831 was opposed (predictably) by Burn on behalf of the
landowner involved, and in 1834-5 the Town Council carried
out Hamilton's design in its present form. For the townscape,
i.e. the exploitation of the site by means of architecture, the
credit is Playfair's. His galleries on The Mound strike out
from the s side of Princes Street and divide it into two
manageable halves, so that its terminal landmarks are not lost
in the far distance. More positive – indeed breathtaking – is
the s view down Hanover Street over Playfair's R.S.A. portico to the twin Gothic towers of Playfair's New College and
the distant spire of the Tolbooth Church on the Old Town
skyline (for these *see* Old Town, Churches and Public Buildings, above).

RAILWAY TUNNELS lie underneath the National Gallery. The
middle one, on the axis of the E and W porticos, actually
pre-dates the gallery, for it was designed by *Playfair* in 1844-
6, with an entry like Hamilton's King's Bridge (*see* Old
Town, Public Buildings, above). The outer tunnels and the
present rusticated three-arched portal are by *Cunningham,
Blyth & Westland*, 1892.

PRINCES STREET

Craig planned Princes Street, like Queen Street, to be one-sided 6
and outward-looking. Its panoramic s view of the Castle and
Old Town across the valley, which has made it world-famous,
has not been preserved quite intact, or without some trouble.
In 1769-70 a Mr John Hume acquired a 50 m. development site

at the E end of the S side, and began to build. At the same time he and other speculators obtained further feus in the Nor' Loch valley on the condition that no building should rise above street level. But in 1771 the banker Sir William Forbes procured a Bill of Suspension and Interdict, and the case finally went to arbitration. The decision was that the land from the present Waverley Bridge as far as Hanover Street should be laid out as a pleasure garden, but that the completion of the buildings at the E end should be permitted. The North British Hotel, the third development on this site, conceals even more effectively than its predecessors the relationship of North Bridge and the Register House. No feus were ever granted on the S side to the W of Hanover Street, in spite of an intention to do so, and in 1816 an Act of Parliament forbade it.

As in Craig's other main streets, the original houses were of three storeys over basements following the enactment of 1781. Although a good class of residents was attracted, their houses were not comparable with the best in George Street, Queen Street and Castle Street, or the squares: the double-bow front at Nos. 54–59 and the group of three with rather crude Ionic pilasters at Nos. 129–131 were exceptional. Shops and other commercial uses came very soon (especially at the E end), and by the end of the C19 the big hotels and department stores had moved in. A surprising number of the original houses survive, considering the enormous land-values, though some are heavily disguised and overlaid. The worst losses have been of important Victorian buildings replaced according to the formula of the Princes Street Panel.* But picturesque Victorian diversity still prevails, and its value is increasingly acknowledged.

For the North British Hotel and the Register House, *see* Public Buildings, above. Then on the N side WOOLWORTHS,‡ modern classical of 1925 presumably by their own architect *W. Priddle*, extended to the W in 1956. No. 16 with a Tower-of-the-Winds order looks *c.* 1830 but is actually of 1864 by *W. Hamilton Beattie* (of *George Beattie & Son*) in his brief early purity; only the windows give this away. The jolly ROYAL BRITISH HOTEL is by *J. Macintyre Henry*, 1896–8. On the St Andrew Street corner, the former R. W. FORSYTH§ by *John J. Burnet*, begun in 1906, an opulent Edwardian store of six fireproof storeys and the first in Scotland to be fully steel-framed; accordingly there is more expression of the structure than at No. 80 George Street. Ground-floor shop windows and mezzanine framed (as in the earlier building) by a broad architrave. The upright structural members, clad in marble shafts with gilded Ionic capitals, reappear on the third

---

* The Panel was set up in 1954 to regulate the redevelopment of the area of Craig's New Town, and in particular of Princes Street, whose N side was expected to be rebuilt from end to end. The formula included first-floor balconies that would eventually make a continuous walkway, with each individual development cantilevered out overhead. The few isolated examples are of historical rather than architectural interest, and the scheme was abandoned *c.* 1979.

‡ Closed (1984).

§ Now (1984) BURTON.

and fourth floors as attached columns, their cladding banded
into the window frames. Finally an eaves gallery with term
figures by *W. Birnie Rhind* and *W. Reid Dick*, and at the head
of the mullioned corner tower a gilded openwork sphere by
Gilbert Bayes. Much good detail on a small scale, witty and
well made. Plain glazed brick elevation to the back lane. Inside, simple clear floor space and a fine easy-going staircase
of early Renaissance character, the handrails ending Burnet-
style as the heads of beasts. One-way extension to the w along
Princes Street, and a separate building to the N fronting St
Andrew Square (*see* below) connected to the main one by a
service bridge, both by *Burnet*, 1923-5. C & A by *North &
Partners*, 1956, acknowledging the N view with a couple of
recessed balconies,* replaced *David Bryce Jun.*'s Star Hotel
of 1861. Nos. 39-41, by *T. P. Marwick & Son* for Jays the
furnishers, 1938-9, pleasant inter-war modern with vertically
linked windows and sculpture by *Tom Whalen*, was designed
a storey higher, with a roof garden. The OLD WAVERLEY
HOTEL by *J. Armstrong*, 1883, its busy pattern of windows all
Peterhead-granite-shafted, is very high for its time: six
storeys (served by hydraulic lifts) plus two in the mansard
roof.

JENNERS, on the corner of St David Street, by *W. Hamilton* 106
Beattie, 1893-5, is a wondrous Renaissance compilation in
pink stone, just right for what was then one of the biggest
department stores in Britain – impressive by its sheer mass,
interesting and even endearing in its detail, with paired caryatids and lots of strapwork. Splayed corner, borrowed from
the Bodleian Library at Oxford, rising skyward into an octagon with flying buttresses. Inside, a top-lit galleried saloon
and much original detail. As the previous shop (in converted
houses) burned down in 1892, much was made of the fireproof structure, with iron columns and steel beams carrying
Stuart's Granolithic floors only 2-3 in. thick (50-75 mm.) over
areas 14 by 12 ft (4·2 by 3·6 m.) without intermediate joists. N
extension in St David Street by Beattie's partner *A. R. Scott*,
1903. The one in Princes Street is of 1966 by *Tarbolton &
Ochterlony*, who also designed the bay-windowed MOUNT
ROYAL HOTEL next door in 1955. No. 60, a tall narrow
Jacobean frontage by *Hippolyte J. Blanc*, 1903, has two bay-
windows nicely linked by a balcony. Then a happy survival:
Nos. 61-62, an original house with an arcaded dormer and
other gingerbread additions of 1870 by *Robert Raeburn*. The
bottom layer of the cake is a new shopfront. BRITISH HOME
STORES, by *Kenneth Graham* of *Robert Matthew, Johnson-
Marshall & Partners*, 1965, the first and best of the redevelopments that followed the Princes Street Panel guidelines (*see*
above), is fully glazed above the first-floor balcony. Upper
(storage) floors clad in vertical strips of pale granite. The
effect is weakened by the copper-clad parody at No. 63 to the

---

* It is being refronted by *Leach, Rhodes & Walker* (1984).

E. No. 70, built of red sandstone as the Edinburgh Café in 1886, is another of *Hippolyte J. Blanc*'s narrow gabled fronts. After Hanover Street a ragbag of altered houses before two long fronts designed to the Panel formula. The first is by *Newman Levinson & Partners*, its main (W) part built in 1967–9 on the site of David Rhind's Baroque Life Association palazzo of 1855. The second is the NEW CLUB by *Alan Reiach*, 1966. It replaced another valuable building, its sober palace-fronted predecessor by *William Burn*, 1834, extended by *Bryce* in 1859, but is a real attempt to establish a modern equivalent (e.g. in the stepped-out mullions) to the sort of sculptural quality we take for granted in C19 buildings. Inside, *Lorimer*'s dining-room panelling has been re-used from the old club (but without its entablature), and one of Bryce's massive urns from the old skyline has been installed as a decorative feature. The altered house-fronts to the W were successfully unified *c.* 1850 by the simple expedient of a fancy balustrade along the wall-head. At No. 95 an original sculptured doorpiece has somehow survived.

No. 100 beyond the Frederick Street junction, designed as the Windsor Hotel by *Robert Paterson* in 1879 but not as stylish as his Café Royal Hotel (*see* West Register Street, below), still has the iron cresting on its mansard skyline. BOOTS is another dull version of the Panel formula, faced in their old house-material (travertine marble) and designed by their house-architect *C. Sinclair Oakes* in 1966, with a similar extension by *Dick Peddie & McKay*, 1975. Nos. 104–106 began as the Clarendon Hotel, by *W. Hamilton Beattie* (of *George Beattie & Son*), 1875–6, a quiet design under a three-storey mansard. A welcome variation on the Panel formula at No. 107 by *Ian Burke Associates*, 1971, and then another hotel building, the former Palace at Nos. 108–110 by *John Lessels*, 1869, with his favourite barley-sugar shafts framing the centrepiece. The spacious cast-iron galleried saloon in No. 110, originally the showroom of the cabinetmaker John Taylor & Sons, with pretty detail and twisted columns, is the oldest of three surviving examples in Scotland; Jenners in Princes Street and the former Wylie & Lochheads in Glasgow both have frames with fire-resistant cladding.

And now at last some real architectural distinction. The façade of the old CONSERVATIVE CLUB by *R. Rowand Anderson*, 1882–4, is a survival from the second generation of Princes Street buildings. A tall and fastidiously detailed palace-front of calculated asymmetry, it has a canted bay to the l., a bracketed balcony high up to the r., both delicately balustraded. The ground floor with its basement area was mocked by the insertion of a shop *c.* 1960. The far more suitable display window and skilfully adapted entrance date from 1978–81 when *Ketley, Goold & Clark* (with *Simpson & Brown* as consultants for the existing building) designed the new Debenham's store behind the façade, adding a short curtain-wall frontage to the E. At the rear of the new interior (formerly at the club's front door), Anderson's splendid staircase in a two-storey open arcade. Three stained-glass lights in memory of Disraeli (figures of Politics, Imperial Liberty, Literature) by *James Ballantine & Son*, 1884. The PALACE HOTEL at the end of the block, a gigantic makeshift of 1888 by *J. Macintyre Henry* who added bay-windows to the original houses and piled the whole thing up to five storeys with a capacious attic and pyramidal-roofed towers, is weak in terms of architecture, but strong and highly to be prized for its picturesque silhouette.

To the W of Castle Street, three original buildings, including a corner-tenement of 1786, overlaid by Edwardian two-storey shopfronts, No. 118's renewed in simpler form in 1983, Nos. 119–120's still with swirly glazing. No. 125 is a strongly three-dimensional version of the Panel formula by *Ian Burke Associates*, 1970. No. 128, *Peddie & Kinnear*'s former University Club of 1866, is a Graeco-Italian palace, its segmental bow-window divided by superimposed orders which, like all the other details including the deep cavetto cornice, are of precisely the right scale and carved with great delicacy by *John Rhind*. Ground floor built out as shops, with a token show of Doric columns, by *T. W. Marwick*, 1964. Nos. 129–131 have architectural pretensions unusual among the original C18 Princes Street houses, for the outer ones have giant Ionic pilasters, very provincially detailed and now mostly covered up. The gracefully arched timber shopfront at No. 130 is all that remains of *Robert Paterson*'s alterations of 1866.

On the W corner of Charlotte Street, CHARLOTTE HOUSE, built in three instalments for the bakers McVittie Guest. The original L-plan development round the remaining corner house, by *T. Duncan Rhind*, 1903, with narrow fronts of four tightly packed bays on each elevation, powerful neo-Baroque in the manner of J. J. Burnet or Norman Shaw, with niched gables, dizzily tall. Then in 1924 the corner house was bought and replaced by *J. D. Cairns* with a matching (but less confidently detailed) gable on the splay, filling the gaps with glass and bronze-fronted curtain walls. Of the final stage on the corner of the lane, by *Cairns & Ford*, 1935, the good Art Deco stair survives after conversion to office use, but the remarkable decoration of engraved and sandblasted mirror-glass by *Sigmund Pollitzer* was broken up. The front wall of No. 136 was taken down in 1976 and faultlessly replaced, with a big new dormer, by *Morris & Steedman*. No. 139 still has a good early Victorian shopfront. No. 141, the BANK OF SCOTLAND (formerly British Linen Bank), has a hard classical front of 1926, granite with black columns, by *H. O. Tarbolton*. No. 142 is the ROYAL BANK OF SCOTLAND (formerly National Bank), remodelled by *John McLachlan* in 1888 as a prettily detailed miniature palace. Its mere façade survives as a weak collage against the glass curtain wall of the new bank by *Basil Spence, Glover & Ferguson*, 1976. Equally feeble, but more pretentious, the huge, slightly classic store by *J. R. McKay*, 1935, at the end of the street.

PRINCES STREET GARDENS

EAST PRINCES STREET GARDENS were laid out and planted in 1830 under the direction of *Patrick Neill*, rearranged by *David Cousin* in 1849–50 after the construction of the railway (with a stone balustrade along the terrace), and further curtailed in 1892 by the extension of the station beyond Waverley Bridge (*see* Waverley Station, Public Buildings, above). *E. Milner*'s proposal for an earth-covered roof was unfortunately not carried out. – DAVID LIVINGSTONE MONUMENT. Good bronze by *Mrs D. O. Hill* (Amelia Robertson Paton) spoilt by an indifferent base. – ADAM BLACK MONUMENT. By *John Hutchison*, 1876–7. – PROFESSOR JOHN WILSON MONUMENT, at the Royal Scottish Academy corner. By *John Steell*, 1863–5, on a nook-shafted plinth designed by *David Bryce*.

SIR WALTER SCOTT MONUMENT, opposite St David Street. Scott's seated figure, with his deerhound Maida at his side, cut by *John Steell* in 1840–6 from a 30-ton block of Carrara marble, is a fine composition on a plain, low plinth and despite its great size a tellingly modest pose* under the soaring vault. The monument itself, a Gothic steeple of Binny sandstone rising 200 ft (61 m.) from arched diagonal buttresses, is so familiar in the romantic perspective of Princes Street that it would be as hard to imagine Edinburgh without it as Scotland without Scott. Its architect was *George Meikle Kemp*, son of a Border shepherd and a carpenter by trade, who had worked in London and made a study-tour in France. Though reputedly self-taught as an architect, he had also been employed in the office of William Burn. After Scott died in 1832 a committee including Burn and his patron the Duke of Buccleuch had quickly raised £6,000 by subscription, and in 1836 a competition was advertised.‡ Of fifty-five entrants *Thomas Rickman* was placed first, *Charles Fowler* second, and Kemp (under the pseudonym of John Morvo the medieval master mason of Melrose Abbey) third. But the committee continued to argue, further drawings were requested, and Kemp finally got the job. The intended Charlotte Square site (as shown in Kemp's drawing within the monument) was abandoned, and in 1840 work began with the foundation on rock 16 m. below the level of Princes Street. The builder was *David Lind*. In 1844 Kemp was found drowned in the Union Canal. By now the money had run out, but there was no difficulty in raising what was required, and work continued under Kemp's brother-in-law *William Bonnar*. Steell's statue, whose design had been accepted without controversy, was installed in the completed structure in 1846. The total cost was some £15,000.

The great Gothic shrine was not an uncommon theme in

---

* Kemp's own idea had been a standing figure on a Gothic pedestal.
‡ The competition superseded the choice, in 1835, of a design by *David Rhind*.

The Scott Monument
(Grant, *Old and New Edinburgh*)

the early C19 in the minds and the drawings (at least) of
visionary architects such as Schinkel. The Gothic style indeed
was specified in this competition. Kemp's achievement was to
realize this romantic idea in archaeologically correct detail.
For the lowest stage the main source is obviously Melrose;
the diagonal buttresses are related to those in Kemp's own
unexecuted design for the w towers of Glasgow Cathedral,

which in turn were influenced by the w towers at Reims. The complex, rather shaggy spire above, supported by flying buttresses, is a synthesis from other continental sources such as Saint-Maclou at Rouen, with a number of details adapted from the cathedral spire at Antwerp.* Kemp's practical experience and consummate draughtsmanship were the link between his excited experience of the 'gorgeous decorations' of continental Gothic and their execution in the masons' sheds in Princes Street.

Of the STATUES in the niches representing Scott's characters, eight, by *Peter Slater*, *James Ritchie* and *Alexander Handyside Ritchie*, were in place for the inauguration. A further twenty commissioned from *Patric Park* were paid for but never received. Scott's centenary in 1871 revived interest, and twenty-four, by *William Brodie*, *John Hutchison*, *Clark Stanton*, *Mrs D.O. Hill*, *D.W. Stevenson*, *Andrew Currie* and *G.A. Lawson*, were added in 1874, the final thirty-two, by *John Rhind*, *W. Birnie Rhind*, *William Brodie*, *John Hutchison*, *D.W. Stevenson*, *George Webster*, *T.S. Burnett*, *Clark Stanton*, *Fraser Tytler*, *Charles McBride*, *J.S. Gibson*, *W. Sheriffs*, *W. Walker*, *W. Grant Stevenson* and *D. Buchanan*, in 1882. In the chamber at the second stage over the statue (intended by Kemp to be open) is GLASS by *Ballantine* in his usual harsh colours from drawings by *David Roberts* and *James Drummond*, 1855. *Robert Morham* designed the somewhat coarse woodwork, executed by *John Taylor & Son*, in 1871.

WEST PRINCES STREET GARDENS originally extended right round the Castle Rock to the back of the Grassmarket, uninterrupted by the railway or Johnston Terrace, and were laid out by the Princes Street (w section) proprietors who feued the land from the Town under an Act of Parliament of 1816. The works were designed by *James Skene* with *Robert Stevenson* as engineer, and subscription for keys was started in 1821. In 1876, much chopped and changed, the gardens were re-acquired by the Town and re-shaped by *Robert Morham*, who built the pretty red sandstone cottage at the E end ten years later; the nearby greenhouses of 1877 have disappeared. – ALLAN RAMSAY MONUMENT, at the NE corner. Figure of Carrara marble by *John Steell*, 1865. Shafted pedestal on a high Baronial substructure by *David Bryce*. – ROYAL SCOTS GREYS MONUMENT, opposite Frederick Street. A strikingly realistic mounted trooper of bronze on a rocky pedestal, by *Birnie Rhind*, 1906. – DR THOMAS GUTHRIE MONUMENT, opposite Castle Street. Portland stone by *F.W. Pomeroy*, 1910. Bible in hand, the founder of the Ragged Schools takes a boy into his care. – SIR JAMES SIMPSON MONUMENT. Impressive seated bronze figure by *William Brodie*, 1876. – SCOTTISH AMERICAN WAR MEMORIAL, on the terrace below Princes Street. 'The Call', by *R. Tait Mackenzie*, 1924–7; a bronze kilted soldier seated in

56

---

* So Thomas Hamilton pointed out, having cribbed from it himself.

front of a long bas-relief. – ROYAL SCOTS MEMORIAL, down in the garden at the E end. A sort of modern henge by *Frank Mears & Partners*, 1950, the stones carved in very low relief by *C. d'O. Pilkington Jackson*, with bronze medallions of our monarchs between. – The STATUARY GROUP to the W of it, by *William Brodie* for his son-in-law James Gowans and originally sited at the latter's house, Rockville in Napier Road. The Genius of Architecture crowning the Theory and Practice of Art. Unmistakable bits of *Gowans* detail on the polygonal base. – ROSS FOUNTAIN. A colossal Second Empire set piece with voluptuous figures, commissioned (from what sculptor?) and cast in iron by *A. Durenne* of Paris for the International Exhibition of 1862, whence it was purchased by the Edinburgh gunsmith Daniel Ross and bestowed upon a grateful city.*

RUNE STONE. Beside the garden walk just beneath Castle Esplanade, a rune stone of late C11–early C12 date; the stone is from Witting parish, Westmanland, in Central Sweden and was presented to the Princes Street Gardens proprietors by the Society of Antiquaries of Scotland. The inscription, enclosed within the ribbon-like body of a snake, surrounds a splay-armed cross and reads 'Ari put up this stone in memory of his father Hjalm. God help his soul'.

PICTISH SYMBOL STONE. A sandstone slab, decorated with the Pictish symbol known as a crescent and V-rod and part of a circular figure, was found near the Wellhouse Tower below the Castle in use as a footbridge. If originally set up in the neighbourhood, it was outside the main Pictish territory. It is now in the National Museum of Antiquities of Scotland.

QUEEN STREET

Queen Street is by far the longest sequence of C18 architecture in Edinburgh, the design of the four continuous rows of house-fronts pleasantly varied within the discipline of the City's rules. The exact dates (like the names of the individual architects) are mostly hard to find, but one of the earliest is 1769, when Baron Orde took a wide plot near the E end; the house *Robert Adam* designed for him set a standard for the rest. Feuing continued piecemeal towards the W, and was complete by 1792.

Queen Street's outlook is to the N, but thanks to its splendid view over to Fife it not only attracted houses of the best quality but subsequently retained them largely intact, while many of those in the more frequented streets were redeveloped for commercial use. Here the sum of redevelopment consists of a C19 Neo-Classical masterpiece (the College of Physicians), a decent modern office at the W end (at much greater sacrifice of interior than exterior work), and a conscientious replica at the E. The

---

* But Dean Ramsay described it as 'Grossly indecent and disgusting; insulting and offensive to the moral feelings of the community and disgraceful to the City.'

additions to the rear, and the embellishments or even complete
refacings on the front, are of an institutional rather than a commercial kind; their outward effect is to emphasize the quiet
dignity of the originals, which are of three basic types. First is
the street-corner tenement that was standard throughout the
First New Town till Charlotte Square. Second, the main door
and common stair which usually has two main doors serving
individual houses and an intermediate door serving a common
stair (its windows often retain their original six-pane sashes) for
access to the flats overhead. Nos. 18–20, 35–37, 40–42, 45–47
and 55–57 are like this; Nos. 11–12 and 24–25 are two-door
versions on narrower fronts. The third and most important type
is the whole house, between three and five windows in width.
Many are pairs or larger groups of the same design and execution, e.g. the beautiful pair at Nos. 66 and 67. The hand of one
designer is most obvious in the fronts of Nos. 48, 51, 54–58 and
64, all of which have the same big arched doorpiece in contrast
to the usual tripartite design. Many of these houses are now
occupied by professional offices, the principal rooms preserving
their austere domesticity.

We begin with the far E section, which had virtually no Georgian building; the large Venetian Gothic National Portrait
Gallery (*see* Public Buildings, above) is a Victorian bonus.
Facing it is the odd confection of YORK BUILDINGS. The
original E block of *c*. 1801 with giant Tuscan pilasters, set well
back from the street (indeed its address was round the corner
in what is now Dublin Street), was extended in 1878 by *Robert Raeburn* for the upholsterer John Boyd, with an arcade of
shops along Queen Street and offices overhead, crowned with
tall iron-crested roofs. The fussy pedimented porch is by
Herbert Ryle of the *Office of Works*, 1919, who made the
whole thing into a government office, recast as exhibition
space, 1982.

The first section of Queen Street proper, starting from St David
Street, has the largest number of houses claiming public status with added porches and the like. But it begins with the
domestic-seeming replica by *Alan Reiach, Eric Hall & Partners*, in new stone and with an extra storey, of Nos. 2 and 3,
the corner tenement and adjacent house which had become
structurally insecure. The next three house-fronts have a continuous cornice. The first two became part of the Philosophi-
cal Institution, and both had long Jacobethan halls with galleries added at the back (in 1859–60 and 1849–50 respectively)
by *David Bryce*, later altered by *G. Washington Browne*; the
earlier one has survived more complete. No. 5, a long frontage
of five windows, was recast in 1847–8 by *John Dick Peddie*
(his first important commission) as the United Presbyterian
Synod Hall, with a Grecian pedimented porch to the front
and the hall itself to the rear, a noble cube in which the
rounded corners of proscenium, galleries and entablature
form a splendid unity under the coved (and formerly lanterned) ceiling. Nos. 6–7 were built as a pair. On the first

floor of the externally altered No. 7 a good early Adam style
ceiling, geometric at the centre but otherwise still rather Rococo, with a twirling vine.

No. 8 is distinctively the work of *Robert Adam*, 1770–1 for
Baron Orde.* Working within the City's rules, he used the
long frontage for five generously spaced bays and exactly
defined the proportions of the whole with the characteristic
precision of Craigleith stone. Tripartite doorpiece with tiny
guttae under the frieze, its smooth columns set against
square-cut rustication which is separated by a Vitruvian scroll
from the dead-flat upper wall. The mansard, but not the form
of its windows, is original. Adam's interior, reversed from E
to W in execution, has lost some of its detail and (following
incorporation with the Physicians' premises next door in
1957) its internal unity. In the entrance hall the original ceiling (rosette in diamond) and a consoled chimneypiece intended by Adam for the second drawing room. The former
study to the r. still has a chimneypiece with garlands and
paterae (intended for the first drawing room), the apsed dining room to the l. its pilastered sideboard recess, but both
have lost their moulded ceilings. Stair in a square well with
consoled doorheads but otherwise plain; the square-section
balusters may be replacements. In the two first-floor drawing
rooms the woodwork seems original and the ceilings follow
the Adam scheme; the first (possibly a replica) rectangular
with a centre oval and griffons in the end compartments, the
second square and of more delicate execution, with a centre
fan and four painted roundels. In both rooms, plain Grecian
chimneypieces of *c.* 1840. The site of the Adam kitchen at the
bottom of the garden (with access by a passage on basement
level) is now occupied by the Library of the Royal College of
Physicians (*see* Public Buildings, above).

Nos. 11–13 were built as flats, faced with coursed rubble. *W. L.
Moffat* remodelled the ground floor of No. 13 as his own
office in 1860, and in 1874 with his partner *James Aitken* gave
the whole thing an elaborate palace-front with a red granite
columned porch; only the irregularly spaced windows and the
plastered upper walls betray its artisan origin. No. 14 (1787)
started as a fine house with an arcaded ground floor and very
delicate detail. In 1838 as the Caledonian United Club it
acquired an extra bay from No. 13 (refaced to match) and a
coupled Ionic porch; the original showy fanlight seems to
have been resited over the basement door. Nos. 15 and 16
have been coarsely remodelled with large canted bays, the
first in 1897–8 by *Thomas P. Marwick*, the second in 1884
(with a clumsy new doorpiece) by *Robert Paterson & Son*.

After the Hanover Street junction the first altered front, No.
22, got its Jacobethan look from *George Smith* in 1852 and
Kinnear & Peddie in 1892. From here on there is less to say

---

* Boswell wrote 'This respectable English judge will long be remembered in
Scotland where he built an elegant house and lived in it magnificently.'

about Victorian changes and more to admire in the way of
consistent Georgian excellence; individual buildings will only
be remarked upon where there is something to add to the
general description above. No. 27, only three windows wide,
is elegantly finished with square-cut rustication and a triple
doorpiece, emulating Adam's work at No. 8. Upstairs, two
drawing rooms with identical ceilings of the popular late-c18
type, a concave diamond in an oval. Nos. 28 and 29 are a
pair. David Stewart (*see* introduction to the Northern New
Town for his key role in that area) feued the site of No. 29
in 1779. Both houses have suffered from roof alterations, and
No. 28 from the raising of the top windows into the garlanded
frieze. The interiors of Nos. 30 and 31 were removed (and
the doorpiece of No. 31 restored) in 1972–4 by *Ian Burke
Associates*. The masonry of No. 34, an unusually grand house,
has been ruined by brutal 'cleaning' and cement patching.
The ground-floor flats of the otherwise uniform tenements at
Nos. 35–37 are differently designed. Does this suggest that
they were custom-built? Victorian basement shop on the
corner (No. 38), with busts of Burns and Scott among the
jolly collection of sculpture along the top.

After Frederick Street the unexpected Gothic front (like two
bays of Westminster Palace) of St Andrew's and St George's
Church Halls, originally a house (No. 43), made into a sort
of gatehouse by *John Henderson* for his Queen Street Church
to the rear (1851, demolished in 1978). No. 48, the first of a
distinctive Queen Street type with stepped-back cornices in
their arched tripartite doorpieces, was well restored by *Robert
Hurd & Partners* in 1970, though the polychrome scagliola
chimneypieces were replaced with pinewood and composition
ones in the more orthodox taste. Drawing room with a good
ceiling of oval design. The stairwell and cupola are probably
the best in the street.

Beyond Castle Street is the finest of the stepped doorpiece type.
No. 64, four windows wide, built for the Earl of Wemyss in
1790, was one of Edinburgh's grandest houses since those of
Dundas and Crosbie in St Andrew Square and Orde in Queen
Street. The ceilings lack Adam's geometric organization but
are beautifully consistent; in the entrance hall a hexagon in a
circle and six oval reliefs of figures on the walls, in the dining
room an elaborate oval, and in the back room a circle. Square
stairwell with corner landings and a wrought-iron rail. Cupola
on pendentives with more classical reliefs. On the first floor
the front drawing room has a green marble chimneypiece, the
back one an Ionic screen *in antis*. They are connected by
folding doors. Ceilings *en suite*. Nos. 66 and 67,* built in
1791 for General Abercromby of Tullibody and Mr William
Tait, are an elegant pair with exceptional details: columns
and pediments set forward from the triple doorpieces, blind

---

* It is just possible that these are related to the 'house for General Abercromby'
credited to *Thomas Harrison* in the A.P.S.D. Although not in his usual style, they
are of enough sophistication.

balustrades under the first-floor windows and garlands under the top ones, which are framed in very thin pilasters. Good things inside, including front halls like that at No. 64 and corn-sheaves in the cupolas. An outstanding drawing-room ceiling in No. 67.

ERSKINE HOUSE by *Ian Burke & Martin*, 1964, is well considered in detail though it breaks the rhythm of Queen Street's relatively short frontages. It replaces the Mary Erskine School (whose large and much more damaging neo-Palladian front by *Hippolyte Blanc*, 1913, was never more than half built) and, more important, *Thomas Hamilton's* magnificent Hopetoun Rooms of 1827 to the rear. The rest of the street keeps its upper frontages but is chaotic below. No. 74 (first occupied in 1792) has a Greek Ionic porch of *c.* 1830, and at the back the MASONIC HALL by *George Henderson* of *Hay & Henderson*, 1894, with a coarse hammerbeam roof. 'The supreme council do not appear to require anything extra for their lodgement,' says the *Building News*, 'the interior being treated much after the manner of the shopkeeper's saloon.' Nos. 75 and 77 have added porches. The former, very clumsy,* leads to the MASONIC TEMPLE by *Peter L. Henderson*, 1900, one of the most remarkable interiors in Edinburgh until recently, when its elaborate Egyptian decoration was painted out in the usual pastel colours. The lotus-bud and bell-capital columns now seem quite ordinary. The last two buildings, a development by *James Tait* in 1790–2, are on a skew because of Lord Moray's right of servitude (*see* Charlotte Square, above). The nice Georgian shopfront with Soanic detail at No. 78 used to be longer, but is mostly obscured with later fronts. Across the road Queen Street ends, as it began, on a Victorian Gothic note: the CATHERINE SINCLAIR MONUMENT, of Eleanor Cross type, designed by *David Bryce* and carved by *John Rhind*, 1866–8.

ROSE STREET

A narrow street intended for 'the better class of artisans' and well under way by 1781 when the two-storey limit was introduced, so that its three-storey rubble vernacular was allowed to continue all the way to the w end, each row of tenements neatly terminated by the lane entries. Larger-scale later buildings made parts of the street into a canyon. The few surviving Georgian shopfronts date from after 1819, when Kirkwood's elevational map showed none. Many of the more recent shops are overflows from Princes Street in the form of fashionable boutiques or occasionally the backsides of big stores. Pubs are Rose Street's most famous and permanent institution. Against this general background only buildings of special note will be mentioned.

---

* This, together with the Masonic Temple, was demolished, 1984.

Starting from South St David Street, the red sandstone block with a corner turret on the N side was designed by *Peter L. Henderson* as workshops for Charles Jenner, the first part in 1890, the second in 1902 including the ABBOTSFORD BAR with its good Jacobean interior. Large plain Neo-Classical block further on, originally a Burgher Church by *Robert Brown*, 1829, altered and extended as the Eagle Buildings by *G. Washington Browne*, 1905. After Hanover Street two large red sandstone blocks: Nos. 37–45 by *Peter L. Henderson*, 1898, in free style and strongly detailed except at the top; and on the S side MENZIES' HANOVER BUILDINGS, ten bays of impressively plain Art Deco Classical divided by pilasters, by *T. Forbes Maclennan*, 1929, the windows reglazed in 1976 by *Hugh Martin & Partners* who designed the E annexe at the same time.

The section after Frederick Street became a pedestrian precinct in 1968. Nos. 107–109 and 118–136, with cantilevered arcades over shop windows, are by *Ian Burke Associates*, 1972 and 1969. The two lower storeys of Nos. 152–154, basically an original three-storey building, were combined by *T. P. Marwick* in 1893 and 1899 to make the lofty KENILWORTH BAR, with good tiles and Jacobean woodwork (alterations were made 1981). After Castle Street the S side has all its original buildings, though somewhat altered. Facing them the TELEPHONE EXCHANGE, an inexpensive frontage of great elegance by *Leonard Stokes* for the National Telephone Company, 1901–3. Arcaded ground floor (the original entrance canopy removed), harled first and second floors with windows gracefully combined. For the Charlotte Street Baptist Chapel *see* Churches, above. Opposite on the N side the ingenious but regrettable extension of No. 33 Charlotte Square over its own garden, by *Philip Cocker & Partners*, 1976.

ST ANDREW SQUARE

MELVILLE MONUMENT, in the centre of the garden. A fluted Trajan's column, 41 m. high overall, to Lord Melville, Navy Treasurer under Pitt, appropriately designed by the arch-Tory *William Burn*, 1820–3. *Robert Stevenson* was consulted on the foundation. The 4·2 m. statue by *Robert Forrest*, from a model by *Francis Chantrey*, was an afterthought in 1822.

S SIDE (Nos. 1–8). The first side to lose all its original houses. The PRUDENTIAL ASSURANCE office by *Alfred Waterhouse & Son*, 1892–5, is of pink Dumfries-shire stone, the next reddest thing to their customary brick, which had been vetoed by the City. Elaborate early Renaissance detail with a spired corner turret and arcaded ground floor. Fireproof interior with concrete floors on steel beams (but not steel-framed). Public office lined with glazed terracotta in characteristic Waterhouse–Prudential colours. No. 3 next door was designed as an extension of R. W. Forsyth's store by *Burnet*,

Son & Dick, 1923–5, adapting the Princes Street design to a narrow site. Lower part altered. No. 4 is a handsome (but now somewhat eroded) palazzo in the Peddie & Kinnear manner by *John McLachlan*, 1883, with the three central windows grouped together on each floor. Corinthian-columned porches were replaced by consoled ones early in the C20. The narrow frontage of No. 5 is by the school specialist *John A. Carfrae*, 1903, quiet Edwardian Renaissance with a banded first floor and elegant detail at the top. At Nos. 6–7 *John Dick Peddie*'s Reform Club palazzo for the SCOTTISH PROVIDENT INSTITUTION was replaced in 1961 by *Rowand Anderson, Kininmonth & Paul* for the same firm, in glass and marble, with a separately expressed staircase tower, all very wilful and respecting neither the colour nor the building-line of this side of the square. The stone-faced classical block at the corner, No. 8 by *J. R. McKay*, 1954, is wedged between this and the connected Scottish Provident building in St David Street like a diminutive bookend.

w SIDE (Nos. 9–19). At Nos. 9–10 the great palazzo designed by *David Bryce* for the Western Bank in 1846 was later occupied by the SCOTTISH WIDOWS FUND & LIFE ASSURANCE, who in 1962 replaced it with the present building by *Basil Spence, Glover & Ferguson*. A disciplined design, it is of pale Derby marble on a shiny black base, quite flat except for the inset entrance and set-back penthouse, taking its cue constructively from its pre-war neighbour the Guardian Royal Exchange building (for this and the classical Standard Life building opposite, *see* George Street). At Nos. 16–17 the STANDARD LIFE ASSURANCE phase two extension, by *Michael Laird & Partners* in association with *Robert Matthew*, 1968, consists of six stone-faced piers linked by the equally bold horizontal lines of the bright steel window frames. Pitched and slated roof above the crowning steel facia, continuing that of the old building next door. Altogether a masterly updating of the tired theme of the commercial façade. The more conventional SCOTTISH LIFE ASSURANCE SOCIETY building by *Gordon & Dey*, 1960, is enlivened here and there by eccentric details, e.g. the giant pilasters framing the board-room windows and the saw-tooth cornice overhead.

N SIDE (Nos. 21–28). Most of the original houses remain, though much altered and renewed. They will be described in order of building. Control was not yet strict, and the frontages were not of ashlar but of stucco, most of which was later stripped off to reveal the rubble walling. The four central houses, Nos. 23–26, were built in 1770–2 by 'the joint purses of Sir John Whitefoord, Sir Robert Murray and Gilbert Meason'. The architect may be assumed to be *William Chambers*, who designed No. 26 for Meason. All had three-storey, five-bay fronts with architraved windows; the only difference was in the placing of the Roman Doric doorpieces (in the central bay of No. 26, the fourth bay of the others). None now exists in its original form. In 1840 an unknown architect provided

No. 26 with a porch, pediments and balustrade, and in 1878
Peddie & Kinnear extended it to the rear. Some of Chambers's quite simple interior work (including the domed staircase) survives, and in places it has been matched. No. 25 was
remodelled in 1964 with an Ionic porch replacing the long-
lost Chambers doorpiece, and No. 24 in 1970 by *Dick Peddie
& McKay* with an ashlar front, substituting a Roman Doric
porch for the last surviving doorpiece. No. 23, transformed
by *David Bryce* in 1846 for the Exchange Bank of Scotland,
is one of his best Italian Renaissance façades, superbly detailed, with a pedimented Ionic porch and a consoled balcony
under the pedimented first-floor windows. The wall-head balustrade neatly balances that of No. 26. Bryce's interiors and
rear addition are greatly altered. The other original buildings
at Nos. 21 and 22 are by *John Young*, 1775, observing the
height and general arrangement of the four centre houses.
They had main door flats with a second door serving a common stair, and are rubble-built, though the end gable of No.
21 is faced with ashlar. Both have been refaced at the ground
floor, No. 21 in 1845 in ashlar, distinctively detailed with a
Doric porch and entablature, No. 22 in 1848 by *David Bryce*,
Peddie & Kinnear adding the Greek Corinthian porch in
1854. These two houses were extensively restored (without
their stucco facing) and internally adapted for I.B.M. LTD by
Covell Matthews Partnership in 1976–80. The corresponding
houses at the E end, Nos. 27–28, were replaced in 1899 with
the pink sandstone SCOTTISH EQUITABLE LIFE ASSUR-
ANCE building by *J. M. Dick Peddie & George Washington
Browne*, evidently with the recent publications of J. Alfred
Gotch very much in mind. Big gables of shaped Bolsover type
above giant Corinthian pilasters, though of Browne's favourite François I type rather than Robert Smythson's. E end
elevation with superimposed orders, well related to the National Portrait Gallery.

E SIDE (Nos. 29–42). The block at Nos. 29–31 over the bus
station, with a vertical pier treatment derived from Nos. 16–
17 opposite, is by *William Nimmo & Partners*, 1970. The
NORWICH UNION LIFE ASSURANCE building by *R. Seifert
& Partners*, also 1970, is a crisply detailed variant of the
same, with the piers treated as oriels and an awkward mansard
roof overall.

Two similar houses flank the central recession of the
square's E side, i.e. the forecourt of what became the head
office of the Royal Bank. First to be built, and the first architecture on the grand scale to appear in the New Town, was
No. 35 to the N, built in 1769 for Andrew Crosbie of Holm.
On both elevations a giant Ionic order takes in the ground
and first floors: strongly scrolled volutes (diagonally opposed
at the corners), fluted frieze, and a rosette over each pilaster.
Attached columns define the three central bays of the five
facing the square. In 1819 *Archibald Elliot* was engaged by
the Royal Bank to convert the house to their head office; his

are the three E bays, perfectly matched to the original. In 1830 it became the Douglas Hotel, for which in 1865 *Peddie & Kinnear* added the tall bleak bedroom wing to the NE which survives as part of the adjoining office block. The interior is mainly Elliot's. His grand staircase, entered by three-bay columned screens (Corinthian above Ionic), is lit by the oculus of a ribbed dome on wreathed pendentives. Only a few details have the look of Peddie & Kinnear. C18 Doric frieze in the first-floor front room, and a marble Ionic chimneypiece probably by *Elliot*.

The centrepiece of this group, at the E end of the central axis of Craig's New Town, for long the head office of the ROYAL BANK OF SCOTLAND, was designed by *William Chambers* in 1771 as a house for Sir Laurence Dundas. *William Jamieson* was the mason. The large site permitted a free-standing house. Marble Hill was its model (Kew inspiring the back garden, now built over), but this was much grander, ashlar-faced over a rusticated ground floor on all sides, a Corinthian order of pilasters supporting the central pediment in place of Marble Hill's Ionic, and a three-window bow at the back. Inside was the usual tripartite plan, the central stairwell a simpler version of Chambers's contemporary stair at Melbourne House in London (now also replaced). The second floor still has his fret-pattern chimneypieces, but of the C18 first-floor interiors only the NE drawing room (now the board room) remains, the woodwork and tapering pilastered chimneypiece perhaps by *Chambers*, the ceiling by *George Richardson** in the Adam manner, with roundels for paintings in the central oval and the end compartments.

In 1794 the Excise Office acquired the building, adding the gilt Royal Arms (pre-1801 version) to the pediment, and then the two-storey wing (later remodelled, *see* below) at the SE corner. In 1825 the Royal Bank bought it and *Archibald Elliot II* made some internal changes, adding the porch in 1828. In 1836 *William Burn* made a new stair-hall by removing the floor between the vestibule and the room above, with twin stairs ascending to a cantilevered E landing; Chambers's stair was removed.

By 1857 more counter space and probably more grandeur were needed at the bank, and *John Dick Peddie* was brought in. Chambers's exterior was respected but Burn's stair-hall was made into the present vestibule, with a first-floor landing and superimposed Greek Ionic and Corinthian screens of coupled columns. The original stairwell was once again opened up to make a square two-storey hall with a fishscale cove, and the new stair with its Rococo ceiling was built to the N of it. On the E Peddie removed Chambers's bow, rebuilt the NE wing and added the magnificent telling hall on the main axis, 18m. square with a 9m. wide entry to the W and

---

* The design appears in the *Book of Ceilings* as 'executed for Sir Laurence Dundas Bt. at Edinburgh'; the ceiling may have been restored in the C19.

a similar business area to the E. Four wide arches spring from low down in the corners to support a dome pierced by glazed stars which diminish towards the clear central oculus. No columns, no granite, no marble (though the new counters of 1972 have plenty of the last), and very little moulded relief; only anthemion filled pendentives by *James Steele* of Glasgow. The dome is constructed with a large ring and radial ribs of wrought iron.

In front, the dwarf wall separating the forecourt from the square was replaced in 1827 with heavy cast-iron railings and gates made at *Anderson*'s Leith Walk Foundry.* In the following year the lamp-standards cast at Shotts were placed by the porch. In 1834 came the Hopetoun Monument, a dismounted equestrian statue of the fourth Earl (Governor of the Bank 1820-3) in bronze by *Thomas Campbell.*‡ The SE wing seems to have been built by 1804, with a concave quadrant link and three bays which form the W pavilion of an extension built before 1851. The whole row has a distinctive character nearer to the latter date, with the ground-floor window architraves resting on massive panelled sills; an E pavilion was probably intended. The set-back upper storey over the quadrant was added by *Gratton & McLean* in 1958.

Nos. 37-38 on the S side of the forecourt were built by *John Young* in 1781 with instructions to match No. 35 on the N. He did so (with a few mistakes) on the front elevation but omitted the pilasters at the side; *James Craig* seems to have been the architect. The block has been altered internally and to the rear, in 1823 by *William Burn*, in 1851 by *David Bryce*, and again more recently, all for the British Linen Bank.

108   The BANK OF SCOTLAND building next door, like a fragment of Imperial Rome, was commissioned from Burn & Bryce in 1846 by the British Linen Bank to replace their former head office at Nos. 37-38, but Burn was fully occupied in London and the design is by *David Bryce*. The detail is rich and the scale colossal: five identical bays as against the nine bays of the former houses on the site which the bank had acquired in 1825. Over a tall basement six Corinthian columns and their entablatures thrust forward in the Baalbec manner. Statues on the parapet (Navigation, Commerce, Manufacture, Science, Art and Agriculture) by *A. Handyside Ritchie*. The entry is austere: a simple entrance hall leading into a palatial stair-hall with a compartmented ceiling. The stone stair with scrolled and gilded balustrade ascends to the left, its landing supported by consoles, but straight ahead on the entry axis is the telling hall, and a return to the luxuriance of the exterior. It is 22·7m. long, with polished Peterhead granite columns, three bays by five, of which the central three open into side aisles, their mirror-glass arches giving an illu-

---

* Cottingham shows the same design at Cumberland Gate, London.
‡ The statue was made in 1824-9, and in 1834 it was decided to put it here rather than in Charlotte Square.

sion of even greater width than the overall 21·7 m. Above the consoled attic, rich with plaster swags and the busts of eminent Scots, is a flat ceiling with Bryce's favourite Greek-cross coffers and a central dome of engraved glass rising to 15·2 m. Many of the original furnishings survive (but not the counters), and the *Minton* tile floor still exists under the carpet.

The ROYAL BANK OF SCOTLAND at No. 42 was designed as the head office of the National Bank of Scotland in 1936. *Leslie Grahame Thomson* was appointed, but *Arthur Davis* of *Mewès & Davis* was subsequently engaged as consultant; hence the palazzo-front, with giant recessed portico at the entry. But Davis's memories of the Massimi Palace were now growing dim, and clearly too much was asked of the site. Interior by *Thomson* and *F. J. Connell* in an inter-war modern style with much marble, finished in 1942 but now drastically altered.

ST ANDREW STREET

The s section starts from Princes Street. The former Forsyth's on the w side is followed by the ST ANDREW HOTEL, a tall, narrow building with a corner oriel in rich fin-de-siècle gingerbread Renaissance by *H. Ramsay Taylor* of *Cousin, Ormiston & Taylor*, 1900. Then the YMCA by *George Washington Browne*, 1914–15, somewhat in the academic manner of his former partner John M. Dick Peddie, with giant recessed Ionic columns over a channelled base. These and Waterhouse's Prudential Office make a group comparable in scale and character to late Victorian and Edwardian Glasgow. The only building of interest on the other side is Nos. 7–9, by *Knox & Hutton*, 1883, Glaswegian Greek of the non-academic kind with a heavy doorway, the mullions and transoms forming flat crosses, and arched dormers over a chip-carved pilastrade. Nos. 11–17 are by *Ian Burke Associates*, 1978. NORTH ST ANDREW STREET, the other side of St Andrew Square, has only one main frontage, EDINBURGH HOUSE on the e side, a large rectangular frame-up by *F. R. Stovin-Bradford*, 1964.

ST DAVID STREET

The s section again starts from Princes Street and its best thing is the spectacular view past Jenners down to the Scott Monument. Of the two frontages on the e side the upper, faced in pale grey marble, belongs to the Scottish Provident Institution and is by the same architects, *Rowand Anderson, Kininmonth & Paul*, 1961. So is its Portland stone neighbour, IVANHOE HOUSE of 1964. Together they make an acceptable c20 group, without the wilful exhibitionism of the main Scot-

tish Provident frontage round the corner. NORTH ST DAVID
STREET across St Andrew Square is well preserved on its E
side and groups well with Nos. 21-22 in the square. No. 3,
a plain tenement with early Victorian cast-iron doors in its
basement shopfronts, No. 5 with channelled quoins and Nos.
7-9 with a chimney gablet at the wall-head are of the 1770s.
The w side is all by *Alan Reiach, Eric Hall & Partners*, but
not quite all their fault. The old Stock Exchange on the
corner of Thistle Street by *John McLachlan*, 1890, was replaced in 1963 by *Kelly & Surman*. The bald middle block
of 1970 was an attempt to come to terms with the new building, but the latter had to be demolished* before it collapsed;
the relentlessly bay-windowed building now on the site shows
boredom with the whole affair.

ST JAMES CENTRE

Most of the area now occupied by the St James Centre was
known in the C18 as Clelland's Park. The largest owner was
Walter Ferguson W.S., who in 1773 obtained a feuing plan
from James Craig for what became St James's Square, advertising as its main advantage that 'being without the Royalty, it is
free of all the Taxes ... to which the Inhabitants of the City of
Edinburgh are subject'. Only one building from Craig's scheme
still stands (*see* Register House, Public Buildings, above). The
square had a bleak nobility despite its imperfectly levelled site,
and represented, at least on the NE side (1780-6), the City's first
attempt at unified terrace design. Latterly given over to industrial use, including printing, it was demolished for the St James
Centre in 1965. So was the development on Moubray's Feu,
the strip along the w side of Leith Street where *Robert Adam*
produced a magnificent scheme for a three-storey colonnaded
terrace for the Register House Trustees. This found no takers,
and in 1786 he drew up a simpler scheme, still further simplified
(probably by *James Salisbury*) as a terrace which perfectly ra-
tionalized the sudden descent from Waterloo Place into Leith
Walk. It had been drastically altered but it should have stayed.
The only part of Clelland's Park to escape was to the E, where
St Mary's R.C. Chapel had been built on ground belonging to
Mr Ogilvie. Mammon, devoutly wooed by a Town Council
naturally eager for modern development, took the rest.

The ST JAMES CENTRE was designed by *Ian Burke & Martin*
in 1964 and completed, with modifications, by *Hugh Martin
& Partners* in 1970. In its favour is its undoubted efficiency
and the convenience of its covered shopping precinct, handy
to the bus station. The entry from the top of Leith Street is
well contrived, and the precast facing slabs are the result of
careful choice. The spiral CAR PARK to the NE was a happy
addition at a late stage. Against it, there is no need to em-

---

* *Private Eye* undertook a sardonic campaign for its preservation.

phasize its huge intrusive bulk as seen from the Calton Hill and Inverleith, or its callously blank backside to Leith Walk which is partly due to the frustrated plan for an urban motorway on this flank.* The closure of the shops across Leith Street and the building of the FOOTBRIDGE from the Calton (1977) were further conditions attached to the original scheme. Inside the complex, the image of system-built bureaucracy conveyed by NEW ST ANDREW'S HOUSE is suitably frightening. It is the upper part of this building that sticks up at the end of the E vista along George Street, over the roof of the Dundas mansion, and likewise over the dome of Register House in the equally important view down North Bridge.

THISTLE STREET, HILL STREET AND YOUNG STREET

Thistle Street, like its sister Rose Street to the S, was originally intended for occupation by workers and shopkeepers, but a large part of it was built up with modest ashlar-fronted houses for merchants, professional people and even a few landed gentlemen. In 1806 the two W sections were re-named after their builders, Hill and Young. As in Rose Street, some shops were inserted after 1819, but these are concentrated in the Hanover Street–Frederick Street section. Nearly all the C18 buildings have survived in excellent condition.

In THISTLE STREET, starting from St David Street at the E end, THISTLE COURT on the S side is probably the earliest New Town architecture in anything like its original state, reputedly built in 1768; two facing pairs of small but very respectable houses, rubble walled, with freestone dressings including front doors neatly combined under pediments and separated by wrought-iron lamp-brackets. Nos. 1 and 2 to the E have fanlights with arcaded astragals, and a nice set of slate-hung bowed dormers. Nos. 2 and 3 to the W have a blank look; they are an electrical transformer station. Across the street at Nos. 3–9 a very plain block for STANDARD LIFE ASSURANCE by *Michael Laird & Partners*, 1970, strictly continues the scale of W. & R. CHAMBERS's mid-C19 office, an austere frontage of eighteen bays relieved only by a hugely consoled doorpiece. Nos. 17, 21 and 23 are original three-storey houses with Roman Doric doorpieces, not as big as those in George Street but still clearly for better-off people. No. 19 was rebuilt in 1900 to provide halls for St Andrew's Church. The section after Hanover Street, being further from St Andrew Square, is of more workaday character: three-storey tenements like those in Rose Street, faced with rough courses and relieved by the odd arched doorpiece. The late Georgian and early Victorian shops are now mainly devoted

---

* The current proposal by *Basil Spence, Glover & Ferguson* for an extension of John Lewis's store (1984) will be an improvement.

to antiques, but No. 39 has a C19 pub-front with arcaded window and quatrefoil frieze.

HILL STREET, running W from Frederick Street, is named after its builder *James Hill* who was financed by Robert Belsches of Greenyards. The three-storey house elevations, either by Hill himself or by Belsches' architect *Alexander Laing*, were approved by the Town Council and carried out in fine broached ashlar, with unusual doorpieces – two pilasters set in a moulded architrave frame, crowned with a fluted and rosetted entablature. Nos. 2–10 have more conventional doorcases in pairs, and three frontages at the N end are individually designed. Of the end houses, No. 21 on the N side was Belsches' own, with the doorpiece fitted neatly into a recessed bay; it was built in or before 1794, and the Bourbon coat of arms in the middle of the wall records the residence of Louis Philippe's grandsons in 1859–73. No. 24 on the S side is noticeably plainer than the rest of the street. Nos. 17–19, originally of the standard type, remodelled by *George Angus* in 1825–8 as the Subscription Baths and Drawing Academy, are now EDINBURGH LODGE NUMBER ONE, very neat Grecian in smooth ashlar, with an Ionic-columned doorpiece between two other segment-headed entrances.

YOUNG STREET, running W from Castle Street, was named after the builder *John Young*. Feued to him in 1779, it was developed with two-storey houses in droved ashlar, partly by him but one at least by the builder *Peter Marshall*. The doorpieces architraved, those at Nos. 13 and 15 with a cavetto splay, No. 21 of superior quality with an arched doorway. A gap* in the houses on the S side is now filled with a long office block, conforming as nearly to the Georgian pattern as the brief would allow, by *Alan Reiach, Eric Hall & Partners*, 1970. So the only interruption is the SECOND CHURCH OF CHRIST SCIENTIST by *Sir Frank Mears & Partners*, a stone-faced period piece of 1952.

WEST REGISTER STREET

The narrow, zigzag West Register Street, between Princes Street and St Andrew Square, is a foil to the grander spaces and has some good things of its own. The GUILDFORD ARMS is a jolly pub by *R. M. Cameron*, 1896: varnished exterior, lofty interior with ribbed ceiling. On two sides of the block the former CAFÉ ROYAL by *Robert Paterson*, 1861. Planned as a showroom for gas and sanitary fittings, it attracted a neighbouring oyster-restaurant with its swaggering Parisian air and was opened in 1863 as the Café Royal Hotel. Paterson, a pupil of Beattie, was one of the architects who

* Part of this gap was built on by the Unitarians who bought it in 1823; the rest was filled by *William Burn*'s neo-Tudor St Luke's church in 1836. Both buildings were ruinous by 1970.

broke away from Edinburgh's Neo-Classical and Italianate tradition. This building is decidedly wilful, e.g. in the six-window front to Register Place in which the asymmetry of the off-centre door is countered by that of the dormers. The mansard roof, probably the first of its kind in central Edinburgh, is undoubtedly French. It originally had iron cresting at the top. But the three main storeys owe less to the Rue de Rivoli than to contemporary work in England*; basket arches below, a round arcade above, the plate glass on both levels divided by the slimmest of timber mullions. The quadrant corners have many precedents in Edinburgh's Georgian housing, but are an innovation in the architecture of commerce. *A. W. Macnaughtan* altered the building in 1893-5, and it is not clear whether the plasterwork is of this or the earlier date. In 1898 the hotel specialist *J. Macintyre Henry* took over. He inserted the deeply pedimented doorway at the NW corner and in 1900-1 remodelled the interior, designing its sumptuous woodwork. The CIRCLE BAR to the E has lost its central gantry but still has Corinthian lamp-standards of brass on its solid island counter, an aedicular chimneypiece, and six large tile pictures‡ of famous inventors by *Doulton*, designed by *John Eyre* and executed by *K. Sturgeon* and *W. G. W. Nunn*. An arcaded mirror screen divides it from the OYSTER BAR, 105 even more lavish, with small tiled ovals set into the woodwork of the red marble counter. Behind it are eight stained-glass windows (British sportsmen) by *Ballantine & Gardiner*. On the walls three more tile pictures, one by *Nunn* from Eyre's design continuing the Circle Bar series and the others of ships on the Clyde and Mersey by *Esther Lewis*. In contrast the CROWN ROOM upstairs is light and airy, with opulent plasterwork and gilded figurines at the arcade spandrels. Were the big ceiling roundels intended for the hanging of gasoliers in the showroom? They may be Paterson's, but the woodwork is certainly Henry's. He and his partner *T. Forbes Maclennan* added the AMERICAN BAR over the NW corner in 1923, with handsome Wrenaissance woodwork. The large but undistinguished Barbecue Room occupies a Georgian house next door.

The former ROYAL BANK STATIONERY WAREHOUSE, designed by the firm of Paterson's master, *George Beattie & Son*, in 1864 for Cowans the papermakers, is Venetian Gothic in a Ruskinian spirit, and with real feeling for the style. Symmetrical s front, with polychromy still visible through the soot. Large central entry flanked by bronze bas-relief portraits of the Cowans by *William Brodie*. The roof pitch has been changed; originally it was lower, with iron cresting. The N part of this block is plain early C19.

---

* Knowles in London, Picton in Liverpool, Salomons in Manchester and Brodrick in Leeds.

‡ Shown at the Inventions Exhibition in 1885 and perhaps at the Exhibition at the Meadows, Edinburgh, in 1886. The names of the restaurants and bars are those which were used till 1980.

YORK PLACE AND ELDER STREET

These streets are closely connected with the First New Town proper, and half of the s side of York Place appeared in Craig's plan as a continuation of Queen Street. Only in 1793, when the City bought some land from Lord Alva to the NE of St Andrew Square, did feuing begin in York Place and in Clyde Street (parallel on the s side). Part of York Place belonged to the Heriot Trust, who quickly joined in. The street was very soon built, and except for St Paul and St George it seems to have been complete by *c.* 1804.

Nos. 1–73 YORK PLACE (S SIDE). Nos. 1–3 (and Nos. 15–19 North St Andrew Street) are of 1824 by *David Paton*, the son of an Edinburgh builder who later worked for Soane in London and then emigrated to practise in South Carolina. The plans he submitted to the Dean of Guild show the proposed insertion of two pilastered storeys in the existing tenement (probably of the 1770s), but in the end he seems to have rebuilt it completely. Continuous pilastrades (nearly all glazed) are wrapped right round the building, including the round corner tower, and with the fall in the ground there are basement shops in its base and in York Place. Most of the window architraves on the upper levels have been unnecessarily hacked off. Nos. 5–6 were originally *James Adam*'s Episcopal Chapel of St George (*see* Churches, above). No. 7 is again by *James Adam*, a castellated house built in 1793 for the Rev. Alexander Cleeve of St George's but sold by 1795 to the architect Alexander Laing, who owned it till 1818. Three bays with a central over-arch pushing up into the attic like a miniature version of the front of Robert Adam's Dalquharran Castle, Ayrshire (1790), but asymmetrical on the ground floor, which has a clustered-shaft doorpiece to the r. The interior, which may be by *Laing*, has no features of special note.

   After No. 7 the s side consists mainly of three-storey main door and common stair blocks with rusticated ground floors and arched fanlights, stepping down the easy slope. (Nos. 25–27 were shortened in 1969, and the gable made good, for the widening of Elder Street.) The exceptions are the single houses at Nos. 45 and 51 (the former lacking rustication), and the grander front of Nos. 47–49 with a crisp segmental arcade along all five bays of the ground floor. It was built in 1795, and the common stair flat at No. 47 was occupied by the painter-architect *Alexander Nasmyth* who may have had a hand in its design. Nos. 69–73 have a canted bay at the end, facing Broughton Street; the ground floor is built out with a good late C19 pub front.

Nos. 2–40 YORK PLACE (N SIDE). A line of houses of *c.* 1800, of more consistently high quality than any block in Queen Street. All have rusticated ground floors and most have architraved upper windows and a modillion or mutule cornice.

A list of some of their particular features is worthwhile. Nos. 2–4: six bays with overarched ground floor windows, looking from the front like a pair of houses but actually a main door and common stair tenement, with the common stair entered round the corner, where the basement has pilastered shops. No. 6: fluted friezes at the first-floor windows. No. 8 by *Alexander Laing*, 1798. No. 10 has an interesting interior. Built for Lord Craig, it may have been refitted by Admiral Sir David Milne *c*. 1830; front rooms with shallow ribbed vaults and Neo-Perp woodwork, and a back room with more Gothic details. No. 12: a slightly Gothic entrance hall, and a large first-floor back room whose ceiling is a rather heavy version of the fashionable circle-in-diamond type. Rear addition by *J. & F. Johnston*, 1960. No. 18: a tripartite Ionic pilastered doorpiece. No. 20: a fluted Roman Doric doorpiece with a big fanlight. No. 22 (built for Lord Newton): square-sunk rustication like No. 8 Queen Street, and an above-average interior including an entrance hall with an arch resting directly on foliated Roman Doric columns, a graceful curving stair, and an apsed and panelled dining room. No. 32 contained Sir Henry Raeburn's studio and exhibition rooms from 1798 to 1809. Beautifully detailed front with pedimented Roman Doric doorpiece, the centre first-floor window pedimented on consoles; relatively plain interior, the studio having multi-leaved shutters for the control of light. No. 34: an ornamental string course outside, but much alteration inside. No. 36: externally altered with a decently sympathetic doorpiece of Ionic pilasters by *Hippolyte J. Blanc*, 1884; rear extension of 1934 by *Leadbetter, Fairley & Reid*. Nos. 38–40 have a rock-faced basement. No. 44 is a concrete-framed building by *Covell Matthews & Partners*, 1964, pushing irrelevantly between houses and church, and at odds with both. For St Paul and St George, *see* Churches, above.

ELDER STREET. Some feus were bought from the Heriot Trust by the two builders *John Reid* and *John Young* in 1799, but some were still on offer in 1808. Of the excellent row of arcaded shops on the N side all that is left is the gable of the NW corner block plus the symmetrical main door and common stair tenement at Nos. 30–34.

YOUNG STREET *see* THISTLE STREET

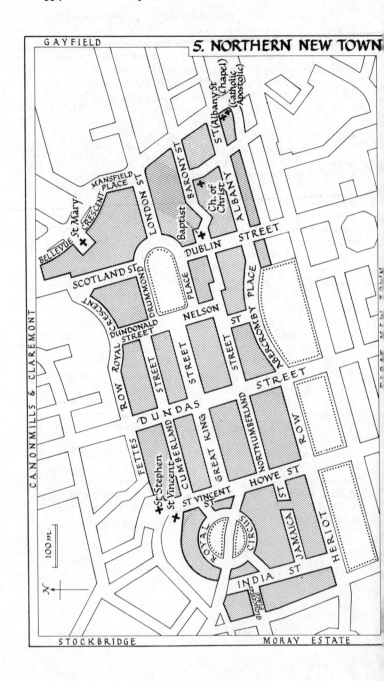

5. NORTHERN NEW TOWN

5. NORTHERN NEW TOWN

Planned by *Robert Reid* and *William Sibbald* in 1801-2, the Northern New Town is by far the largest single scheme in the development of Georgian Edinburgh. Virtually all of it was built, with remarkable unity of design and execution. Only one pair of elevations has been seriously altered (Heriot Row), and only one street lost (the relatively inconspicuous Jamaica Street).

The strong E-W axis, similar to that of the First New Town but running along a hillside instead of a ridge, was a feature of the plan from the start. In 1792 a layout for development to the N of Queen Street Gardens was sent to the Heriot Trust by David Stewart (*see* First New Town, No. 29 Queen Street) who had been Lord Provost in 1780-2. Drawn by Sibbald, the trustees' Surveyor, it covered an area that belonged partly to the Trust and partly to Stewart himself, to the W of the old Gabriel's Road which used to run all the way from the Register House to what later became Saxe-Coburg Place. This plan, on the evidence of a drawing of 1796, had a short central axis joining an E square and a W circus, but as yet no intermediate streets to the N and S.

In 1797 the City acquired the old Customs House (formerly Bellevue House) and its five acres of land to the E of Gabriel's Road, and in 1801 the Heriot Trust asked Sibbald together with Robert Reid to submit a layout for the enlarged site. The following February their new plan for the 'joint ground belonging to the good Town and Mr Stewart* and the Hospital' was received and approved.‡ The earlier plan had been closely contained, with direct entries from Hanover Street and Frederick Street on the S side but only a grudging exit to the N in the direction of Stockbridge. The new one, with its E enlargement, could also join up with St Andrew Street to the S, the Picardy and Gayfield schemes to the E, and (by a later modification) the Moray Estate which was to be developed to the W. There were also two through-routes to the N, the one to Stockbridge greatly improved by *Playfair*'s brilliant management of Royal Circus.

The pattern of architectural responsibility, apart from Playfair's special commission, is complicated. Great King Street, London Street and the intervening Drummond Place (at its E

---

*The reference to Stewart in the Heriot Trust minutes was strictly out of date because he had become bankrupt in 1800 and his land now belonged to two lawyers, James Morison and Maxwell Gordon, and three architect-builders, Thomas Morison, James Nisbet and George Winton.

‡The final scheme seems to have been conflated from four plans of which one was by *Major Stratton*, R.E.

end stood the House of Bellevue on which the axis was fixed)
were designed by *Robert Reid*. So were Heriot Row and Abercromby Place. Reid became increasingly occupied with great
public buildings elsewhere in the City, and after the death of
Sibbald in 1809 the responsibility for architectural control
passed to the next City Superintendent of Works, *Thomas Bonnar*. Bonnar was sacked in 1818 and *Thomas Brown* appointed
in the following year. However by 1821 Bonnar had become
Surveyor to the Heriot Trust, so he designed the important
elevations on the Heriot lands to the w, while Brown undertook
those on the City's lands to the E.

The layout is well served by the elevations, with as much
formality as the site allows. The steep N–S streets, except at
their crossings with the main axis, simply tumble downhill in
a series of massive, flat-fronted tenements. The main E–W
streets, calm and level, are undoubtedly lacking in variety and
bold relief; this was a period of austerity, with Britain at war
and the outcome still in doubt. The unfinished Charlotte Square
was a warning against elaborate elevational designs, but it also
provided the basic palace-front themes for the Northern New
Town. In London Street Reid achieved a Roman solemnity
worthy of Adam himself. It remained for Thomas Brown in
Bellevue Crescent to show what could be done by the addition
of columns to Reid's thrifty vocabulary of pilasters; and for
Playfair in Royal Circus to distil Reid's enforced economy into
the refined spirit of late Georgian Edinburgh, exploiting the
quality of the flat, durable ashlar which is its hallmark. Playfair
also recognized the drama of the steep descent to the N and
made the most of it at St Stephen's Church, whose massive
tower arrests the downward rush of St Vincent Street and rises
four-square against the distant view of the Forth estuary and
the Fife hills beyond.

CHURCHES

ALBANY STREET CHAPEL, 24a Broughton Street. Now an
office. An Independent chapel designed and built in 1816 by
David Skae. The main front is a crowded composition with
an Ionic Venetian window in the middle, flanked by broad
terminal piers with niches; idiosyncratic detail, including
first-floor window aprons with herringbone fluting. The Albany Street front follows the elaborate terrace design probably by *William Sibbald*. The galleried interior, enriched in
1867 and 1891, was lost in 1976–8 when the long-disused
chapel was adapted by *Baron Bercott* as the main Edinburgh
office of the Alliance Building Society; an excusable sacrifice.
CATHOLIC APOSTOLIC CHURCH, 22–24 Broughton Street.
Now a warehouse. A pedimented temple with recessed Ionic
portico, built *c.* 1843–4 for the Rev. Edward Irving. The
name of the young *John Dick Peddie* (b. 1824) has been associated with it; his Trinity Church in Duke Street, Glasgow,

is a richer version of the same theme. In 1876 the Irvingites moved to R. Rowand Anderson's great church down the hill (*see* Gayfield, Churches).

CHURCH OF CHRIST (Glasite or Sandemanian Meeting House), Barony Street. 1835–6. The two-storey street elevation very severe, the interior unchanged, like a faded Victorian photograph. Entrance is by a door in Albany Street Lane, first into a corridor, then into the meeting room with blind-arched walls, BOX PEWS, and a broad PULPIT, curtained under a block-pedimented canopy. Diagonally-beamed ceiling. Low octagonal dome with a central light of gold-tinted glass. Hall on the first floor.

DUBLIN STREET BAPTIST CHURCH, Dublin Street. Middle Pointed, by *Peddie & Kinnear*, 1856–8. The nave lies N–S, fronting the street with an octagonal pinnacle (now truncated) between gables. In the tall N gable a rose window facing the entrance to Broughton Market. Inside, iron columns, elaborate gallery fronts and an open roof on timber arches. – Rich brown PULPIT and ORGAN CASE lightened in 1936. – ORGAN by *Brindley & Foster*, 1898, rebuilt by *F. F. Bell*, 1957. – STAINED GLASS in the rose window by *Ballantine & Gardiner*, 1898.

ST MARY, Bellevue Crescent. The centrepiece of the crescent, 30 grandly Neo-Classical without and notably complete within, designed in 1824 by the City Superintendent of Works *Thomas Brown*, and built for the Town Council. Hexastyle portico, Corinthian instead of the fashionable Doric or Ionic, breaking forward from the three centre bays of the pilastered front; only the central door is therefore aligned with an inter-columniation. Pediment of shallow pitch. The pedimented clock stage of the steeple has Doric columns at the corner, recalling Burn's North Leith Church (*see* Outer Area, Leith), as do the superimposed orders of the upper stages; but their circular tempietto form, crowned by a slim dome and lantern, owes something to Smirke. All this in the finest smooth ashlar, but the body of the church droved in the usual Edinburgh manner. Inside, an arched vestibule and twin stair-halls lead into the rounded E end of the interior, which has a U-plan 31 gallery on fluted Corinthian columns with cantilever consoles. Over the whole ample space a compartmented Neo-Greek ceiling with a large central rose. The layout shows the influence of Elliot's Broughton Place Church (*see* Gayfield). Here only minor alterations have been made – by *John Lessels* in 1874 (platform added, precentor's box removed, pulpit slightly lowered) and *Sydney Mitchell* in 1897 (new seating on the floor of the church, and redecoration which probably included the late Gothic enrichment of the panels round the gallery). Present decoration by *W. G. Dey*, 1974. – PULPIT, on the unobstructed end wall. Drum-shaped. Two free-standing Corinthian columns carry a sounding-board with a reeded dome and cresting of antefixae. Base and double stair altered by *Lessels*. – FONT. A Corinthian column of 1904. –

ORGAN by *Thomas C. Lewis*, 1882. – STAINED GLASS. Two
tall windows flanking the pulpit (St John the Baptist, St Paul
at Athens) by *Francis Barnett* of Leith in the 'Norman-
Mosaic' style, put in 'because of the annoyance of the congregation at having sunlight straight in their faces'. – One to
the far l. of the pulpit (Christ's Entry into Jerusalem) by the
Abbey Studio after 1941. – Bryson memorial windows under
the gallery: to the s Adoration of the Magi, after 1902, to the
N a beautiful Annunciation, after 1880, by *Nathaniel Bryson*.
– Above the gallery to the s the Presentation in the Temple,
good late work by *Robert Burns*, 1924.

ST STEPHEN, St Vincent Street. Built in 1827–8 for £18,975,
a design of vast scale, Baroque power and Grecian severity by
William H. Playfair, dominating the long vista from the lower
end and ingeniously conforming to the oblique line of St
Stephen Street on its W flank. The church was to have been
on the W side of the circus, axial with Great King Street, but
after the change of plan the City bought this new and much
more difficult site in 1822 and commissioned Playfair in the
following year. His plan is basically a square, diagonally sited,
with the N and s corners cut off. Tower to the s, with a
cavernous tunnel entry reached by a stair between giant inverted consoles. The two upper stages are equal in height
with coupled antae at the corners, but otherwise sharply different. One great window with a grille of segmental stone
tracery below, a clock face and a single median anta above.
Corner turrets with crosslets and fretted balustrade, highly
effective from a distance. Oblique flanks with solid end bays
matching the lower part of the tower. The three middle bays,
deeply recessed between antae, have urns above the cornice.
Very plain octagonal interior, the E and W corners cut off by
triangular stairwells. Compartmented ceiling sloping up to
the central lantern. The main entry gives access to the gallery.
The acoustics were bad from the start, and in 1880 *David
Rhind* rearranged the minister's area and installed the broad
Corinthian PULPIT and Ionic-column LECTERN. In 1955–6,
after the church had become too large for its congregation,
Gilbert H. Jenkins of London floored it over with a reinforced
concrete deck at gallery level, keeping the pews but moving
the front panelling to the outer walls. He resited Rhind's
furnishings including the ORGAN which was rebuilt by *Willis*
(the original maker) in its new position. Drastic but successful. In the resulting lower hall the old gallery columns with
Egyptian capitals remain. Below are the five tunnel-vaulted
cellars of the original underbuilding.

ST VINCENT (Episcopal), St Vincent Street. Curvilinear
English Gothic on a small scale by *J., W. H. & J. M. Hay* of
Liverpool, 1857. The N aisle with porch and towerlet faces St
Stephen Street; the chancel gable pokes obliquely into the
grand classical vista down St Vincent Street, just in front of
St Stephen. Inside, a simple arcade with circular piers divides
the nave from the aisle, both with close-packed scissor-braced

roofs. Of the original decorative scheme one frieze survives in the chancel. – ORGAN by *William Townsend*, 1872, rebuilt by *Blackett & Howden*, 1897. – STAINED GLASS. Except for three unattributed late-C19 lights in the five-light E window (Christ preaching), an admirably bright and clear heraldic display by *A. Carrick Whalen* from 1975.

STREETS

ABERCROMBY PLACE

On the s side at the E end a short straight row by the builders *William Cuthbertson* and *James Dobson* without any particular evidence of direction by Reid and Sibbald. No. 1, 1809, is an old-fashioned chimney-gabled tenement built to match its opposite number in Albany Street with excellent effect. The others are a pair of double main door tenements, almost exactly alike, with surprisingly good interiors. No. 7 has a doorcase with birds in relief (cf. No. 32 York Place); the other details, except for the chimneypieces, were altered in 1899 by *Edward Calvert*, who added the oriels on the end gable.

The N side, designed by *Reid* in 1805, approved by the Town Council in 1807 and finished by 1819, is a shallow crescent in two halves embracing the green bulge of Queen Street Gardens, with taller five-bay pavilions all looking straight ahead. Over the rusticated ground floor three of the five windows on each pavilion are discreetly emphasized with blind balustrades and consoled cornices. Smooth ashlar curves between them (slightly marred by a kink at Nos. 24–25), unbroken except for some graceful cast-iron balconies towards the E, the sills lowered to make them usable. Simple but elegant interiors. Nos. 8–13, carried out by *James Gillespie Graham*, have pendentived entrance halls and panelled rooms with doorpieces. No. 13 is particularly good, with an Ionic hall screen and an S-scroll balustered stair lit by a coffered dome on pendentives. Incised panels at each end of the drawing room. Nos. 15 and 16 were entirely rebuilt as offices behind the front wall (and with an incongruous back elevation) by *R. Gerard Walmesley*, 1970. No. 17 was W. H. Playfair's first Edinburgh house.

The houses in the w half of the N side are generally of less interest. No. 30, which belonged to the Riddels of Ardnamurchan and Sunart, has a double columned screen and Parthenon reliefs in the entrance hall. In 1857 *David Bryce* added the massive balustraded porch and recast the interior. In the library a Corinthian overmantel and carrels with Gibbonslike carving; in the drawing room pedimented doorcases, vine-wreathed columns flanking the doorway to the parlour behind.

ALBANY STREET

Feuing from the City Magistrates began in 1801, presumably under *William Sibbald* as Superintendent of Works, but owing to difficulties in clearing the existing feuars the NW quarter was not available till 1815, under *Thomas Bonnar*. In the SW quarter architectural control was at first quite lax. No. 1 is a tenement with an old-style chimney-gable by *George Winton*, 1802. Nos. 3-37, all of two storeys and basement, are nevertheless to different designs, stepped down with the slope of the street. Nos. 11-15 are three of a kind, with rusticated ground floors and pleasant, if rather tentative, internal plasterwork. Nos. 17-23 seem to be the work of one builder but with slightly varied detail; all have the same enriched circles on the entrance-hall ceilings. Nos. 27-37 were all similar, with pretty plasterwork inside, but the last two were drastically altered as a Roman Catholic School, with mansard attic, by *R. T. Currie* in 1907.

To the E of the cross-lane the houses on both sides are presumably to a *Sibbald* design. End pavilions marked by the running together of two recessed doorpieces, as seen at Nos. 39-41 on the S side and Nos. 42-44 on the N. At Nos. 39-41, beautifully carved swags over blind arches with single drops of similar design. The SE pavilion, formed by the flank of the Albany Street Chapel (*see* above), only manages one swag, while the pavilion at the NE corner was supplanted in 1859 by St Mary's Free Church, itself replaced by offices by *David Le Sueur Partnership*, 1983; but the neo-Perp former MANSE at No. 56 survives. The other houses on both sides are regular, without any central accent. In No. 41 a rib-vaulted Gothic entrance hall.

The latest (NW) part, Nos. 2-40, is by *Bonnar*, started in 1815. The corner tenement at Nos. 2-4 is followed by regular house-fronts with rusticated ground floors, stepping downhill in only three stages. Pendentive ceilings in some of the entrance halls. The iron balconies and rock-faced basements vary. In the dining room at No. 34 a neo-Tudor ribbed ceiling and sideboard recess.

BARONY STREET

The name commemorates the old Barony of Broughton, a substantial village whose centre survived till the 1930s. Feus were offered for sale under the direction of *James Milne* for the Heriot Trust in 1821. In 1829 its tolbooth (built in 1582) was demolished and the street begun under *Thomas Bonnar*. It was continued after his death in 1847 by *Alexander Black* with the (unfulfilled) intention of carrying it right through to Dublin Street. Broughton Market was built on the W part of the site and the Dublin Street Baptist Church (*see* Churches, above) closed the intended exit in 1856.

The street could not be built in line with the obliquely sited
Broughton Place to the E, but is neatly centred on its bowed
SW corner and catches a glimpse of the church at the far end.
Plain main door tenements, without basement areas. Nos. 6–
22 on the N side are of the 1830s, under Bonnar, slightly
stepped (with nicely up-swept cornices) to suit the slope.
Plainer mid-C19 S side, under Black. To the NW a rubble-
faced block of council housing, a relic of an attempt by the
City Architect *E. J. MacRae* to finish the street on a new line
in 1933–8.

BELLEVUE CRESCENT AND MANSFIELD PLACE

The crescent, designed by *Bonnar* in 1818 just before his dis-
missal by the City, was taken over in 1819 by *Brown*, who
revised it to incorporate St Mary (*see* Churches, above), built
in 1824. The S part was finished by 1832, but the steep slope
to the N discouraged further building. In 1869 *David Cousin*
modified the design, and in 1882–4 it was finally built under
John Lessels' direction.
The S half is a single unbroken curve. Ionic pilasters on the N
pavilion and beside the church. In the entrance halls at Nos.
3–7 pendentive ceilings, with archways or screens of fluted
Roman Doric columns leading to the stair-hall. Gothic rib-
vault in No. 8. The repeatedly stepped N half consists of main
door tenements looking like houses. Close inspection shows
economies as compared with the other side: simplified Ionic
capitals and no basement rustication. Circular mezzanine
windows in the return elevation to Cornwallis Place. No particular interest inside; when the crescent was finally completed this part of town was no longer fashionable.
MANSFIELD PLACE, though begun in 1820 under *Brown*'s supervision, may, like Bellevue Crescent, have been designed by
Bonnar. End pavilions with a hexastyle anta order, mutual
(though not a very good match) with those of the crescent
and London Street – a fine solid anchor at the NE corner of
the Northern New Town. The main doors have pendentived
entrance halls, but the chief interior interest is at No. 2, where
in 1826 *James West* decorated the walls of a room in his flat.
In 1974 the four large oil-painted landscape panels were restored by *R. L. Snowden*, the other decoration by *James W. T.
Simpson*.

BROUGHTON MARKET

A diagonally sited square formed in the 1840s at the W end of
Barony Street, with an entry from Dublin Street, as a market
for meat, fish and vegetables; much altered and rebuilt for
other purposes. On the NW side a three-storey brick block
with an Artisan Renaissance gable to Dublin Street.

BROUGHTON STREET

W SIDE. Starting at the top, the first houses pre-date Reid and
Sibbald's plan. Nos. 10-12 were built in 1810, with linked
Greek Doric doorpieces and a good flanking elevation to the
S (St Paul came later; *see* First New Town, Churches). Nos.
14-20, plain tenements of similar vintage, are followed by
two pensioned-off churches, the former Catholic Apostolic
Church and Albany Street Chapel (for these *see* Churches,
above). No. 32, built as a George Heriot's District School in
1853, is one of a number designed by *Alexander Black* in the
strapworked Jacobean style of the parent building, and like
the Cowgate one (*see* Old Town, Public Buildings) has a
ground-floor arcade, still to be seen behind the shopfronts
added by *Henry F. Kerr* when it became St Mary's Free
Church Hall in 1889.

Here the grand scheme of the Northern New Town breaks
through, for flanking the entry to Barony Street are two plain
blocks whose circular corner towers, a storey higher, suddenly
bring the whole street to life. Bold cornices encircle them and
then continue along five more blocks (or did, till some of
them were hacked off) to the N, gracefully sweeping downhill
with each step in the building. All this is by *Thomas Bonnar*,
1829-34, following the demolition of the Broughton Tolbooth.

E SIDE. *See* Gayfield: Picardy.

CUMBERLAND STREET

Cumberland Street provided housing of lesser quality than its
S counterpart Northumberland Street, i.e. for the lower-
middle and better-off artisan classes, all in three-storey main
door tenements with basements, and just a few shops. But
even here there is a clear distinction between the grander W
section and the humbler E one. *Thomas Brown* designed the
N side of both, in 1822. In the E section both sides are very
similar, with two plain storeys over a channelled ground floor,
the ends slightly advanced (Nos. 7-15 with their ground-floor
shops were not built till after 1850). To the W the N side adds
some trimmings to this basic formula, e.g. full rustication on
ground-floor level, and architraves and cornices on the windows above; a pity this excellent design was carried out in
poor stone. Nos. 64-70 at the W end are a separate block,
with pilastered shops. On the S side Nos. 59-73, built by
David Paton, look like the work of *Thomas Bonnar* (openings
in sunk borders). The fronts to the E were put up piecemeal
and with slight differences, e.g. the plain shopfronts at Nos.
43-51 which also have a fine set of bow-fronted dormers.

DRUMMOND PLACE

A great U-shaped space, skewered longitudinally by the main 120
London Street–Great King Street axis of the Northern New
Town. These two openings, plus those of the lesser streets to N
and S, posed new and difficult problems in the design of elevations and corner blocks. Three points should be borne in mind
in judging the success of what was done. First, the presence of
Bellevue House by *Robert Adam c.*1775 in the middle of the E
semicircle (undermined by the Scotland Street tunnel and
demolished in the 1840s). Second, the growth of the trees in the
central garden, narrowing the views along the N and S sides and
making it difficult to see the space as a whole. Third, the fact
that when building revived after the Napoleonic wars, something had to be done to give this whole development some fresh
attraction; Drummond Place, which had hardly been started,
offered the best opportunity.

Reid made the designs in 1804. No. 1, the only house to be built
(1806–7) under his and *Sibbald*'s direction, and a perspective
drawing of the entry to Great King Street, give some idea of
Reid's intended elevations, which were revised by *Bonnar* in
1817–18. The superiors were doubtless pleased when most of
the feus were promptly acquired by *Thomas Pringle* and
Thomas Caldwell, largely for resale to other speculative builders. The S side was soon recommenced, followed in 1819 by
the N, partly taken up by the builders *William & Lewis Wal-*
lace, father and son. No. 1 had already fixed the design of the
end pavilions, with Reid's characteristic thermal window in
an upstanding attic, but Bonnar's centrepieces have six
regularly spaced Ionic pilasters. The N side is now more complete than the S, which has lost the cornices over its first-floor
windows. The W side is of 1819, the N section by *Robert*
Watson, the S partly by *William Henry*. Here Reid had intended to flank the Great King Street opening with end pavilions like those of London Street, but Bonnar repeats his
six-pilaster theme on each side – not just once but twice, and
without any particular relation to the N and S roadways of
Drummond Place. The effort to outdo Great King Street is
successful but not very satisfactory in its context.

There is much less doubt about the E end, a semicircle divided
by London Street into two quadrants, of which the N was
built by *Charles Alison* (1818–19), the S by *Charles Black* and
Thomas Ponton. The four end pavilions, slightly broadened
versions of the adjoining ones in London Street, are of polished ashlar with recessed pilasters.

Drummond Place is particularly lucky in having kept (with
Great King Street) its roadway of granite setts, the Georgian
railings, and most of the granite and whin paving round the
central garden. Indoors, the entrance halls are designed as
usual to make an impression. No. 1 is Adamish, and then
they tend to go in pairs, e.g. pendentives at Nos. 17–18 and

22–23, pilasters and coffered ceilings at Nos. 28–29, and a quartet of groin-vaults at Nos. 33–36. No. 23 is probably the finest, with classical figure reliefs and Roman Doric marbled columns. Many varieties of late Georgian chimneypieces. Plasterwork usually of bold design, often with a rose for a pendant lamp in the middle of the ceiling. The interior of No. 4 was recast by *Robert S. Lorimer* for his brother. That of No. 9 was painted in Roman style for Charles Scott, advocate, who owned it from 1868 till the early 1890s. One room survives.

DUBLIN STREET

A steep slope down to Drummond Place, mainly of droved ashlar but varied by the Gothic gables of the Dublin Street Baptist Church (*see* Churches, above) and some pleasant Victorian shops. The s section, formerly Duke Street, was feued from 1799. Building started in 1801 under *Sibbald*'s supervision. On the E side Nos. 11–17, with arched Ionic doorpieces and smooth upper storeys, look like three houses but (like No. 19 with its Roman Doric doorpiece) are actually a variation on the main-door-tenement theme. On the Albany Street corner a pilastered Georgian shop. On the w side the first house, designed to face Queen Street, is now part of York Buildings (*see* First New Town, Queen Street). No. 18 further down is a single house, its superior status emphasized by a rock-faced basement. The N section (i.e. the whole of the original Dublin Street) was added by *Reid & Sibbald* in their plan for the Northern New Town. Building started in 1803.

DUNDAS STREET

Big tenements stepping downhill with minimum architectural ceremony; common droved ashlar over rusticated ground floors. The s section (as far as Great King Street) was started in 1807. The N (originally Pitt Street, begun in 1820) has an exceptional group on the w side, Nos. 78–102, with smooth ashlar and architraved windows above, channelling and set-back window margins below, all in the *Bonnar* manner. It also has fewer interruptions by projecting Victorian shops. Both sections have Georgian shops, mostly pilastered: Nos. 17 (basement), 18–20, 23 (ground floor and basement), 31 (slightly projecting), 35 (ground floor and basement), 38–40, 39–43 (quite plain), 45–49 and 99–103. Much the best of the two-level kind are at No. 23 on the E side. Consoled cornice over the basement shops, the middle one on a small concave curve, reached by its own flight of steps. Immediately to the N Nos. 25–29 by *David Paton*. For the N end of Dundas Street, *see* Canonmills and Claremont, p. 421.

DUNDONALD STREET

Similar in character to Scotland Street. Only the blocks at the top (Drummond Place) end have arched doorways.

FETTES ROW

Like Royal Crescent, offered for feuing by the City Magistrates and thus in the hands of their Surveyor *Thomas Brown*, whose elevations were approved in 1819. Building began in 1821. As first conceived, the W section was to run as far as St Vincent Street, which was to extend to the N and link with it; so the present W pavilion would have been a centrepiece. In the mid 1820s, after the site of St Stephen's church had been decided, a quadrant link was planned. But neither scheme was followed, mainly because of the well-established industries at Silvermills.

The two terraces on each side of Dundas Street, which make such a decisive entry to the New Town from the N, are very similar; plain ashlar ranges of three storeys over a basement. The arched and rusticated ground floors of the taller end pavilions support six giant pilasters – or strictly speaking antae. But the E terrace is superior, with the ground-floor windows architraved and the house doors grouped in pairs. Moreover all the houses (but not the flats in the pavilions) were originally glazed with horizontal panes. The W terrace lacks such refinements, though the spacing of the doorpieces does something to disguise the fact that the main range consists of flats, not houses. Moreover inferior stone was used; but in 1974-6 the whole frontage of the far W pavilion was refaced with Hopeman stone by *Robert Hurd & Partners* under the auspices of the New Town Conservation Committee (the latter's first job on this scale). The E terrace has the better interiors, mostly converted to flats, with refined Grecian cornices, simplified woodwork profiles and monumental chimneypieces.

GLOUCESTER PLACE

Gloucester Place is a late amendment to the Reid & Sibbald scheme which had sited a church (St Stephen's) on the W side of Royal Circus, looking along the Great King Street vista. By early 1822 however the Town Council were negotiating for the St Vincent Street site; presumably there were also consultations with *J. Gillespie Graham* about the link with the Moray Estate (then being designed) which Gloucester Place provides. *Bonnar*, as the Heriot Trust Surveyor, was in charge of it, and 1822 is the date on the surviving drawings. First the entry from India Street, with massive pavilions related to Bonnar's own pair at the entry to Great King Street, but with three bays in the central interval between the pilasters. These pavilions are not even symmetrical, for the s side has some tripartite windows with segmental heads. Is it carelessness, not unknown in Bonnar's work, or is it a deliberate (and for Edinburgh most untypical) wooing of the picturesque, in view of the eccentric lie of the land? Whatever the reason, there are further inconsistencies on the return elevations (of unequal width) round the corner. Then they cease; the houses to N and S have channelled ground floors with Bonnar's distinctive sunk borders, and architraved windows with curving balconies above. At the w end slight advances show where the scheme stops; Gloucester Place hereafter becomes Doune Terrace (*see* Moray Estate). *John Paton* built Nos. 4-14 with his son *David Paton* as architect. The remainder are by *James Ritchie, James Wilkie, James Dobson*, and *William Wallace* and his architect son *Lewis A. Wallace*. Some splendid entrance halls, at No. 4 pilastered with a wreath frieze and compartmented ceiling, at Nos. 6-10 with domes continuous with their arched pendentives.

On the s side Nos. 9 and 11 are arcaded. In No. 13, built by Wallace, a pendentived entrance hall and two drawing rooms *en suite*, the one behind apsed on the mutual wall. The detail, as in the rest of the street, is refined Grecian, of a scale to match the big airy rooms.

GREAT KING STREET

This is the central avenue of the Northern New Town and owes its success to the simplicity of the four identical palace-fronts lining the vista (each some 183 m. long) and the informal prospect of mature trees closing it at each end. Formerly, of course, the trees merely softened it and one could have seen at a glance the longer vista that can now be detected only on the map, or progressively on foot, from London Street to Royal Circus.

Great King Street, designed by Robert Reid in 1804, was not advertised for feuing till 1810. Some feus had been taken by 1812, but it was only in 1817 that building really got under way, supervised by *Bonnar* in accordance with Reid's elevations, which indeed it would have been hard to improve. The similarity between centre and ends (the latter merely omit the flanking pairs of pilasters), the almost complete lack of a central accent, the very shallowness of the projections and the persistence of the main cornice-line from end to end – all these, which might be weaknesses in a single terrace, are perfectly sufficient where terraces succeed and confront each other. Much of the effect comes from the half-rounds of the thermal attic windows in the central and terminal blocks, exactly as in London Street; the only real difference, apart from its added pomp and polish, is that Great King Street has double main door tenements in the centrepiece and pavilions only, with single houses between.

Although he respected Reid's design for the main frontages, *Bonnar* altered the return elevations facing Drummond Place, and probably also those fronting St Vincent Street where he abruptly changed the scale with four colossal Ionic pilasters on each side, making a blatantly grand entry to this big, quiet street.

INTERIORS, E to W. In the entrance hall at No. 22 a rich Grecian centre in an incised Soanic border, and then a columned screen; in the drawing room an Ionic chimneypiece of marble with Flaxman-like figures, and a Tuscan screen on the rear wall. In the drawing room of No. 28 a neo-Rococo painted ceiling of much later date. No. 34 begins like No. 22 and then has a bow-ended dining room decorated all round with paintings in the Watteauesque style popularized by *D.R. Hay*; covered with flat paint as recently as 1956, they were restored in 1981. Pendentived entrance-hall ceilings at Nos. 53, 56 and 58; No. 58 has Roman Doric pilasters too. In the drawing room of No. 53 an enriched ceiling (by this time a rarity) of the oval design familiar in the First New Town. Coffered entrance hall at No. 62. Towards the W the halls become spectacular. At No. 64 a typical screen of two Ionic columns *in antis*, unusual in having a pediment. At No. 68 another repeat of No. 22, but then at No. 72 (the house of the painter Sir William Allan) an exceptional specimen combining a late Adam-type ceiling with a Parthenon frieze. On the stair beyond it roundels with figures and a pendentived cupola. No. 74 has a rib-vault, No. 77 a Tudor fan-vault with a pendant, followed by a tall four-centred archway and graceful curving stair with a statue of Flora in a niche.

HERIOT ROW

With its open S prospect of Queen Street Gardens, Heriot Row 119 enjoys the most privileged site in the Northern New Town. There was keen demand for feus, and both terraces were largely complete by 1808. *Reid* designed the E side with its central pediment in 1802. The centrepiece on the W, designed in 1803, with advanced side bays and central wall-head panel in place of a pediment, was like an astylar version of Adam's design for the E fronts of Charlotte Square. Reid was to use the same theme in Parliament Square (*see* Old Town, Law Courts) and the Inveraray Courthouse, and Robert Brown was to echo it in the Coates development (*see* Western New Town). But Heriot Row's most distinctive feature is its grandly low profile; houses of a mere two storeys, the drawing-room windows all corniced, running between the centrepieces (three-storey houses) and the end pavilions (three-storey main door tenements). Or it would have been; the breaking of the feu-charter began in 1864 when *David Bryce* produced an elevation raising the whole W terrace by one storey between the pavilions. Two of the three houses in the centrepiece were then altered, and some of the linking ones, producing an irretrievably ragged skyline. The short third section to the w of India Street was built under *Bonnar*'s direction by *William & Lewis A. Wallace* in 1817.

INTERIORS, E to W. Best in the E section, particularly in the two-storey houses, of which some are four windows wide. No. 4 was considerably altered by *A. F. Balfour Paul* in 1911. In No. 6 (a wide house), changed and embellished by *Scott Morton & Co.* in 1909 to *Robert S. Lorimer*'s design, a spacious entrance hall opens into a side hall through a Greek Ionic screen; twin ceilings with ovals, and a handsome chimneypiece with overmantel touched up in an early-c18 way. On the first floor an L-plan drawing room with larger and smaller ceiling ovals. Lorimer removed the columned screen between the two parts. No. 7, built for a lawyer, boasts a good Ionic-columned chimneypiece in a drawing room which has the best ceiling of its period in Edinburgh: an elaborate centrepiece flanked by long painted panels of Pompeian scenes, all enclosed within a bow-ended frame with an arabesque border. In the entrance hall at No. 8 the familiar garlanded oval. At No. 10 a pendentived ceiling and Tuscan screen lead to a stairwell with an arcaded first-floor landing; then a plain L-plan drawing room. Nos. 13 and 14 according to tradition were the first houses built in the Northern New Town. Similar interiors, both very showy, but No. 14 slightly grander; a double entrance hall with two screens of columns (the first part groined, the second pendentived), then more columns on the landing of the apsed stairwell, and a cupola on pendentives. On the drawing-room ceiling a large oval pattern of late Adam type, turning Grecian. Finally No. 17, representing the simpler kind of house whose details give grace and ease to the big formal rooms, without architectural drama. The engineer Thomas Stevenson and his son Robert Louis Stevenson lived here from 1857 to 1880, and it has kept its atmosphere (along with its Victorian bathroom) intact. In the w section most of the interiors are likewise simple, No. 32 with its pendentived entrance hall a little more elaborate than the others, even before the installation of earlier chimneypieces in the principal rooms. The one real exception is at No. 26, with a columnar entrance hall like those at Nos. 13 and 14.

HOWE STREET AND ST VINCENT STREET

HOWE STREET, in which some feus had been purchased by 1807, consists almost entirely of main door tenements stepped down the hill. Unlike Dundas Street, there are no main cornices (except opposite the Royal Circus opening) under the top floors. This was the main road to Stockbridge, and most of the pilastered shops survive. On the E side the handsome three-storey tenement at Nos. 9–13 is the most interesting in the street. Recessed bay for the common stair, the blocks on each side differently treated as if they were single houses. Thomas Hamilton lived in the main door flat at No. 9. Nos. 15-19 next to the Northumberland Street junction have pilastered shops. The shops at Nos. 4-10 on the W side begin on the ground floor and continue on basement level, conforming with the fall in the ground. The capacious roof of Nos. 18-22 is part of the reconstruction of 1891 by *John Kinross*. Two-level dormers and bowed doorpiece by *John Jerdan*, 1934. Of the three houses at Nos. 26-30, planned by *Robert Morison* in 1807 as one composition, the middle one has lost its pediment through being raised a storey, and when the flanking houses were built ten years later the one on the r. was given too many architraves on its first-floor windows. At Nos. 32-46 a good row of pilastered shops.

A dilemma follows – whether to sweep informally round to the l. through the trees of Royal Circus to Stockbridge, to accept the very formal invitation of the Great King Street entry to the r., or to go on down St Vincent Street with its two churches; the huge portal of St Stephen straight ahead, the Gothic gables of St Vincent's Episcopal (now the Church of the Knights of St Lazarus) to one side (for these *see* Churches, above). The street was started in 1821, the W side built by *Samuel Pringle & John Edgar*, the E side faced with smooth ashlar for the sake of the Royal Circus *ensemble*. Nos. 4-8 are by *David Paton*, built by his father *John*. Cumberland Street corner blocks of the 1850s, both in inferior stone. Nos. 10-14 are brownish, with most of the mixed Georgian and Victorian detail now missing. Nos. 16-18 on the N corner, partially refaced in 1977-8 by *William A. Cadell*, conform with their Georgian neighbours.

INDIA STREET

Offered for feuing by the Heriot Trust in 1807, India Street was largely built by *William & Lewis A. Wallace* under Bonnar's supervision. More secluded than the other N-S streets of the Northern New Town, it managed to attract houses as well as main door tenements and to achieve some architectural formality on its steep slope. But at the N end the gradient becomes impossible, and the last section is a cul-de-sac ending in mid air, with further surprising effects noted below. The only shop is the discreet basement post office.

Development of the W side began in the spring of 1819 when the *Wallaces* began building Nos. 4-10 at the top, a main door tenement of droved ashlar unusually combined with the status symbol of a rock-faced basement; polished ashlar fronts thereafter become the rule. Single houses at Nos. 12-18 and 32-36. The big intermediate tenements of Nos. 20-30 make an effective centrepiece for this steeply falling group. Cornices over the first-floor windows, the channelled ground floor with Bonnar-type windows in sunk borders. Wallace the builder lived in No. 22. The broad pilastered pavilions are described with Gloucester Place (*see* above). Four-storey tenement to the N at Nos. 48–52, built in 1822 by *Robert Hutchison*, standing six storeys above NW Circus Place, which can be reached on foot down a public stair rebuilt in 1974. From below the view is of Piranesian drama; the towering India Street gable, the deep open gully of its double basement areas bridged by front-door flyovers, and the dog-legged stairway climbing up beneath them.

The E side begins with a Bonnar-type tenement and continues with four more, their ground floors rusticated, not channelled. Nos. 17–21 were built by *Traquair Dobson*, who took a flat for himself at No. 19.

INTERIORS tend to be Grecian, of above-average quality. Prettily decorated groin-vaults in many entrance halls; at No. 34 an oval ceiling on pendentives with a central oval compartment.

JAMAICA STREET

Almost totally demolished in 1960. Built *c.* 1807–19 in the shallow site between Heriot Row and the already projected Royal Circus, it was the only substantial development of workers' housing in the Northern New Town; two long rows of ashlar-fronted tenements, not well built. Compact redevelopment by *Philip Cocker & Partners* for the Link Housing Association, 1979–81. With pitched and slated roofs and conventional window shapes, it is a neat compromise between the C19 and the C20, covering the same area as the old terraces but sealed up at the Howe Street end in an uninteresting way. The reconstituted stone facing with moulded toolmarks looks better than it sounds. To the W a survivor of the old street, KAY'S BAR, formerly an India Street mews building, converted in 1975 from Kay's Wine Shop. A little gable over a simple shopfront.

LONDON STREET

A solemn, symmetrical street built almost exactly as *Reid* designed it in 1806. The N terrace was begun in the following year, the S (slightly revised by *Brown*) in 1819. Charlotte Square provided the basic design of the centrepieces, with the wide middle and narrow ends advanced. The pavilions are a contracted version with pedimented first-floor windows in the end bays. No orders, no central accent, only the semicircular thermal windows in the central and flanking attics to set these grave elevations in motion. Largely main door tenements, with a few single houses in the linking ranges, all showing their secondary status in droved ashlar masonry above the rusticated ground floor. INTERIORS generally plain, with a little more show in the entrance halls and some central rosettes in the main room ceilings.

Nos. 42–54 to the SE, an afterthought designed in 1823 by *Bonnar*, then the Heriot Trust's architect, continue the levels and proportions of Reid's frontage as they sweep round into Broughton Street, but are entirely of polished ashlar with an arcaded ground floor, unfortunately interrupted by a projecting Victorian pub. Some of the curvaceous fanlights survive.

MANSFIELD PLACE *see* BELLEVUE CRESCENT

NELSON STREET

Started in 1812. Main door and common stair tenements of suitably high quality, with some arched and some flat-topped doorways in the rusticated ground floors, running down from Abercromby Place to Drummond Place with a side-step at Northumberland Street.

NORTHUMBERLAND STREET including NORTHUMBERLAND PLACE

Planned as a secondary street, and developed between *c.* 1807 and 1819 with high-class houses, smaller than those of Heriot Row and for the most part less formally composed, but strictly disciplined and not at all inferior in finish: standard types enlivened by small variations. NORTHUMBERLAND PLACE, built to the E in 1804, is near the bottom of the housing scale: two tenements without main door flats, formally designed to fill the view up Nelson Street but lapsing into rubble-faced walls when out of view.

E section all of three storeys plus basement. First-floor windows with architraves and cornices at Nos. 3–5 on the N side (looking up Nelson Street) and Nos. 20–22 in the middle of the S side (Nos. 22 and 36 designed by *Robert Wright* and built by *James McKain*). Other variations include fluted panels or balustrades for the aprons under these windows (or a charming selection of iron balconies, which may have been added a little later),* and a main cornice which makes the second floor into an attic, e.g. at Nos. 19–23 which also surprisingly have some rooms with compartmented ceilings.

In the W section two-storey houses between the lanes, three-storey main door tenements beyond them. On the N side a wide variation of all the options below the wall-head, more

---

*No. 57 had a continuous balcony by 1824 when it was chosen as the model for balconies on the Raeburn Estate (*see* Stockbridge).

or less at random, breaking out at Nos. 63 and 65 into the
maximum show, including Ionic doorpieces. On this side
Adamish entrance halls, apse-ended dining rooms and panelled plaster walls are the fashion. Two-storey terrace between the lanes on the s side planned by the consortium of
George Winton, *Thomas Morison* and *James Nisbet*. Centre
and end pairs of houses advanced and slightly raised; only
these have rusticated ground floors and architraved upper
windows. Between them, arched and pilastered doorpieces
very like those of Forth Street (*see* Gayfield: Picardy), the
middle ones set in pairs. The outbreak of clumsy attics hereabouts could still be corrected. Entrance halls with Adam-
type decoration like those opposite, but a few pendentived.

ROYAL CIRCUS AND NW CIRCUS PLACE

121 *William H. Playfair* was commissioned by the Heriot Trust in
1819 and produced his drawings in 1820. Begun in the following
year and largely complete in 1823. Reid & Sibbald had proposed
a circus traversed by an E-W roadway in line with Great King
Street. Playfair kept the required symmetry, but widened the E
and W openings to accommodate the diagonal line of the road
downhill to Stockbridge. The result is a pair of crescents spaciously disposed on opposite arcs of a great circle – a relationship enhanced by the serpentine road, and by the pronounced
change of level noted by John Britton in *Modern Athens* (1829):
'This, which in other circumstances might have appeared a
blemish, cannot be so considered in the present instance. It
enhances the singular and picturesque grouping of the elegant
streets which lead and look into the circus, and harmonizes so
well with their variety, both in architecture and situation, as to
make the blemish – if it must so be called – essential to the
beauty of the whole.'

The design is very simple: two sweeps of eleven three-bay
houses, the nine middle bays slightly advanced, the central
five bays defined by a giant anta order of shallow projection,
their attic by short antae whose cornice breaks forward over
each one on the skyline. Five similar bays at the main door
tenement pavilions. A calm version of the Drummond Place
–Great King Street theme, it is all dependent on perfect proportion and on the precise execution of flat surfaces and
barely projecting edges which Playfair's supervision achieved.
As to the 'blemish' of differing levels, neither of the crescents,
within itself, is stepped to meet the shape of the ground. The
horizontality is even maintained at the steeply sloping corner
of NW CIRCUS PLACE where Nos. 1–10 (built by *John Hei-
ton*) have a base of pilastered shopfronts, quite unaltered. The
1825 blocks further down are part of James Pedie's development and the other side is on the Raeburn Estate (*see* Stockbridge).

The INTERIORS, none of them necessarily Playfair's concern,

follow the same pattern as those in Great King Street, though
not matching its best examples. Pendentived entrance halls at
Nos. 6-12 on the N side. In No. 14 a compartmented ceiling
with a central rose. No. 28 with its fluted Doric screen also
anticipates the coming Grecian mode. On the S side the best
is at No. 21, with a segmental vault on an anta order. No. 1
is exceptional in its square plan, with a plain groin-vault between segmental arches. Good rooms upstairs too – one with
a painted ceiling, another with a segmentally arched recess
and a big round compartment in the ceiling centre.

ROYAL CRESCENT

The best thing about Royal Crescent is that it was built at all,
and that the outward-looking perimeter of the Northern New
Town was thus adequately, if not triumphantly, completed.
Reid and Sibbald had planned it to have three sections. The
separate building that would have marked the centre had been
dropped by the time *Thomas Brown*, as City Superintendent
of Works, produced elevations for the crescent and Fettes
Row in 1819. Feuing began in 1823, but by 1829 only the E
pavilion with its giant antae plus two pairs of houses with
their massive Greek Doric doorpieces had been built in what
was to have been the middle section (the E one was dropped
after the building of the Scotland Street tunnel in 1847, its
entries still visible). They give an idea of the character of
Brown's scheme. In 1881 *John Lessels*, as architect to the City
Improvement Trust, began to revive interest in the long dor-
mant project. His plans, involving the completion of the crescent with flats throughout, were carried out by his son *James
Lessels* in 1884-8. The pavilions are well enough done but the
rest, although it fulfils Brown's general intentions, is a makeshift, not helped by mistakes in the original setting out of the
plot widths so that some of the windows in the W section are
awkwardly narrow. The stone is different and the curve of
the frontages rather shaky on both sides. Worse still, the
developers of the four-storey W section wanted to give the
upper flats a fair share of the available height, but did not
agree on how to do it; hence the disconcerting changes in the
size of windows and the height of belt-courses. The coffered
ceilings in the entrance halls of the four original houses maintain the neo-Greek theme of the doorpieces.

ST VINCENT STREET *see* HOWE STREET

SCOTLAND STREET

Begun in 1823 as Caledonia Street. Chiefly four-storey tenements, their main cornice at third-floor level. Austere droved

ashlar fronts stepping downhill with a similarly unadorned splay meeting Royal Circus at the NW corner. Five-storey block to the NE, part of the final push to complete the Northern New Town, by *William Hogg*, 1883.

6. MORAY ESTATE

The Earl of Moray's property consisted of a 13 acre (5·3 ha.) estate acquired from the Heriot Trust in 1782 by his father the ninth Earl, who had enlarged the existing house. Despite this, and the natural beauty of the site, he decided early in 1822 that it should be feued for development. *James Gillespie Graham*'s designs were available by July, when the articles of roup were published – the most detailed and stringent ever produced; Lord Moray took every precaution against financial liability even in the laying of roads and pavements. Even so, by 1836 it was almost completely feued; Randolph Cliff, Randolph Place and the N part of the Crescent were the only serious gaps.

This is the most geometrically complicated but also the most unified of all the New Town plans. Three main spaces, crescent, oval and polygon, forming just such a series of 'foliaged compartments' as Lord Cockburn had wished to see in Georgian Edinburgh, are ingeniously linked with the First and the Northern New Towns and as well as possible with that which had been started to the W – all on an awkwardly shaped site and in a suitably noble style. Lord Moray himself considered building a new house in the garden of Randolph Crescent, but settled for No. 28 Moray Place. A good neighbourhood, in short. As to the highly ingenious plan, *William Burn* wrote to the Earl in April 1822 'I have been most anxious to produce something that shall be extremely productive of advantageous speculation and totally different from the monotony of our present streets and squares', enclosing some sketches which were passed on to Gillespie Graham. The result certainly bears the stamp of Graham, though it is clear that he had looked carefully at Playfair's work (especially at the Calton) and intended to rival it. This in commercial terms he certainly did. In its completeness, and in the contrast between its urban enclosures and the open panorama and sylvan walks to the N, the Moray Estate is unequalled. Unfortunately the feudal conditions were later relaxed for a time so that attics were built on many of the linking houses, blurring their relationship with the taller pavilions, and many windows lost their pattern of astragals in favour of plate glass. Balconies and railings however have largely survived, and so have the road setts and a few whinstone pavements.

PERAMBULATION

RANDOLPH CLIFF, although it was built last, is the obvious place to start. It does not seem to be part of Gillespie Gra-

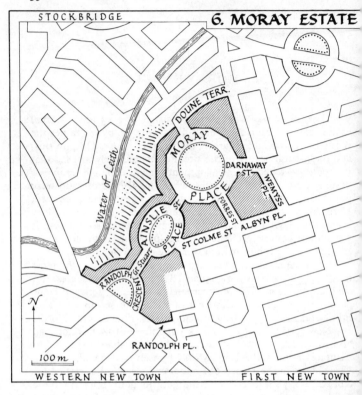

ham's design (it has no orders), but makes an excellent prelude. First the big plain tenement whose massive balconied projection towers over the valley, a masterly design of *c.* 1850 relying on good proportions and on a single point of emphasis in each elevation – a pedimented first-floor window. Ground floor not rusticated but channelled like the rest of Randolph Cliff, which was executed in 1846–9 by *David Rhind* (builder: *James Gowans*) along with the N wing of the crescent, the latter to Gillespie Graham's design. Rhind's hand is seen in the grand stairway and console-supported balcony serving No. 17 Randolph Crescent. To the s of the Crescent, RAN-DOLPH PLACE. Short frontage to QUEENSFERRY STREET (1851), then a cul-de-sac on the axis of St George's church (now West Register House, *see* First New Town, Public Buildings). The N side is by *David Bryce*, 1854, the s side belongs to *Robert Reid*'s modest terrace further along Queensferry Street (*see* Western New Town, Streets). On this sedate grey ensemble *T. Duncan Rhind* intruded characteristically with a half-timbered, red-roofed surprise at the NE end. Tuscan columns on shop level, and a turret of Scots derivation poking up through English-looking gables. Nice iron weath-

ercock. The whole of this little street, and then for a time the
s side only, used to be called Charlotte Place.

In RANDOLPH CRESCENT (s wing built in the 1820s) two curving ranges of three-storey houses between four-storey pavilions repeated at the external angles throughout. Round-
arched openings in the ground floor, then giant Roman Doric
pilasters, and an attic above the main cornice. The only variation is in the number of pilasters: five as a rule, but the
more conventional six flanking the half-circle of the crescent
and, finally, lining the exits from Moray Place. The three
main spaces are linked by GREAT STUART STREET, where
the three houses at Nos. 10-14, slow to feu, were not built
till 1855 – and then of inferior stone. AINSLIE PLACE consists of two facing crescents, the N one with a very restrained
centrepiece – four of the same Roman Doric pilasters slightly
advanced from a similar foursome on each side. No. 23 was
built by *Andrew Wilson*. Finally MORAY PLACE, a prodigious 122
duodecagon (its twelve sides hardly apprehended or related
across 187 m. of sloping ground and mature trees), with three
regularly disposed exits plus an intermediate one, Forres
Street, connecting with North Charlotte Street. Here at last
are columns, first on the six pedimented centrepieces with
their distyle outriggers (a bluff re-statement of Charlotte
Square), then on the hexastyle colonnades between (except at
the Forres Street opening). Of the radiating streets the most
ambitious is DOUNE TERRACE, a detached row of houses
designed as a convex palace-front with pilastered centrepiece.
In the curved DARNAWAY STREET and in FORRES STREET,
continuous houses in the manner of Great Stuart Street.

Two terraces to the s of Moray Place confront the First New
Town. ST COLME STREET, in deference to residents on the
N side of Charlotte Square, was designed to be lower and
plainer than the rest. Channelled ground floor, arched from
end to end, but no orders above (even on the centrepiece)
except for the columned E quadrant. The persistent addition
of attics and other features throughout the Moray Estate has
been particularly damaging to this quiet design. ALBYN
PLACE to the E, relatively intact, is a Roman Doric paraphrase
of the N side of Charlotte Square without Moray Place's
bizarre inward bend of the pavilions and links. The E side of
the same block, the steeply sloping WEMYSS PLACE looking
E along Queen Street Gardens, is a flat version of Ainslie
Place. Middle bay of the centrepiece pierced by an arched
pend to the mews behind. As designed by *George Smith* in
1832 it had a bazaar and gallery. His drawings are consistent
with Gillespie Graham's scheme; the projecting porches,
arched second-floor windows and balustraded parapet may be
due to *J. T. Rochead* who in 1847 reconstructed the building
for the Free St Stephen's congregation.

Private PLEASURE GROUNDS for the use of the Moray Feuars
run down almost to the river, with massive arched retaining
walls and carefully laid paths on the steep slope. Directly

accessible from the back gardens along the N perimeter, they are overlooked by disciplined rear elevations, rubble-built but regular as to string-courses and general fenestration, with touches of personality from later alterations. These cliff-like backs are seen to advantage from the Dean valley and its other side, e.g. from Ann Street.

The INTERIORS are sometimes distinguished (Moray Place and Ainslie Place have the finest) and sometimes quite ordinary. Many houses have suffered by conversion to flats. A Greek Doric theme prevails in the best rooms and the entrance halls, of which MORAY PLACE has a good series at Nos. 2–6 (No. 3 with an unvoluted Corinthianesque order in place of Doric). No. 8 is finished throughout in a post-Adam style of c. 1900, going French in the first-floor drawing room. Notable entrance halls at No. 15 (anthemion frieze) and No. 16 (Ionic order). The Moray house at No. 28 has been drastically subdivided, but its ground-floor rooms are intact and very grand; the stair balustrade is equally grand, apparently genuine late C17, presumably imported c. 1900. No. 41 has a Parthenon frieze (partly removed) in its entrance hall, No. 46, which belonged to Skene of Rubislaw, a groin-vaulted gallery on the second floor. The interior of No. 47, designed for Sir James Wellwood Moncrieff in 1826 by *William H. Playfair*, is conventional in layout except for the lengthening of the stairwell to provide long, easy-going flights. Shallow entrance hall, a coffer-ceiled square. First-floor landing carried through to the front beneath a coffered vault. Arch and consoled doorpiece at the entry to the drawing rooms. The stair, with ladder-like balusters of piled octagons, is lit from a rectangular opening between transverse beams on consoles. In the rooms, ceiling coffers of plain rectangular section, and monumentally simple chimneypieces. The plan is sadly impaired by later partitions. In Nos. 23 and 24 AINSLIE PLACE shallow coffered ceilings of the type favoured by William Burn. The entrance hall at No. 24 (Ionic columns and diagonally coffered ceiling) has an Edwardian chimneypiece and that at No. 23 has been handsomely remodelled, both probably by *Scott Morton*. In GREAT STUART STREET most of the entrance halls are plain, with coffered ceilings. Marbled walls at No. 17. The back ground-floor room, simply treated with ample provision for books, was Playfair's private office, then Lorimer's, then Ian Lindsay's. Fairly standardized entrance halls in RANDOLPH CRESCENT etc., though No. 8 has pilasters and a coffered vault. For the rest, No. 6 in the centre of ALBYN PLACE is a fair example of the good general standard, largely unaltered; entrance hall with plain consoles, coffered dome on pendentives over the stair, and a panelled drawing room with a pendant rosette in the middle of the ceiling. At No. 2 DOUNE TERRACE a Gothic parlour at the back.

7. WESTERN NEW TOWN

For once the site is flat, so the rather complex layout is as clear on the ground as it is on the map. The Western New Town has a memorable entry from the w and a satisfying hierarchy of Georgian streets, their townscape enlivened by St Mary's three spires and the St George's West campanile. These landmarks are Victorian, and so are the streets and crescents to the N and w, though mostly built on a Georgian plan. The mixture of Georgian formality and rich Victorian detail gives a strong impression of the prosperous security of late-c19 Edinburgh. Villas were built at the same time on the sloping ground to the far w, and although this is obviously outside the New Town it is included in this section because it formed part of the Wester Coates estate. The developments are here described in roughly chronological order.

In 1802 the Heriot Trust sold a strip of ground on the s side of the proposed new outlet to Glasgow (now Shandwick Place), and c. 1805 Mrs Jane Cunningham began to develop it as Mait-land Street – a row of plain two-storey houses between three-storey tenement blocks. In 1806 Cockburn Ross of Shandwick, the owner of a similar strip on the N side, advertised house-plots in a crescent to be tangential with the line of Princes Street (i.e. with a convex face to the roadway), with the proviso that 'if it shall appear more eligible to the offerers to build in a straight line, parallel to the road, the plan of the building will be adapted accordingly'. A straight line was preferred, and the original Shandwick Place on the N side was a palace-fronted terrace designed by *James Tait*. Both sides were soon built, but had been largely redeveloped by the end of the C19 when the s side was given the same name as the N.

A large area to the w of what is now Queensferry Street, including the house and grounds of Easter Coates,* had been acquired by William Walker for his son Sir Patrick. In 1808 *Robert Brown* made a plan for developing a large part of it, with Melville Street as its main axis. At its SE corner lay the relatively small Erskine property for which the trustees of James Erskine, Lord Alva, obtained a plan from *James Gillespie Graham* in 1809. It included Stafford Street and William Street (partly on the Walker lands, and jointly developed), and Alva Street whose site was sold in 1825 to James Stuart, a speculating lawyer, and in the following year to a builder who developed it to Graham's design in the 1830s. In 1813 Brown revised the Walker scheme

*Easter Coates was advertised for sale in the *Edinburgh Evening Courant* of 20 May 1786 as 'very commodious for feuing to build on'.

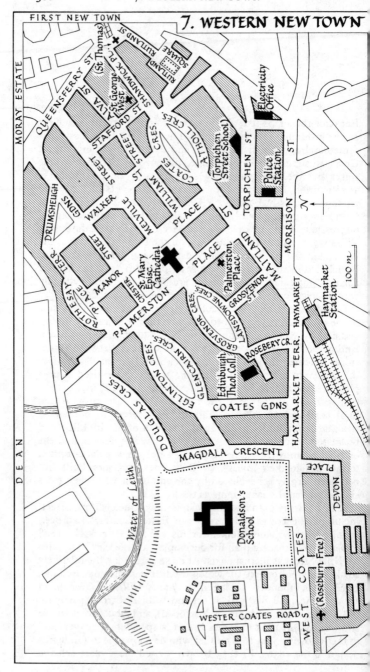

7. WESTERN NEW TOWN

FIRST NEW TOWN

MORAY ESTATE

QUEENSFERRY ST

RUTLAND ST

RUTLAND SQUARE

SHANDWICK PL

+ (St Thomas)

ALVA ST

+ St George's West

STAFFORD ST

ST STREET

COATES CRES

ATHOLL CRES

Electricity Office

(Torpichen Street School)

TORPICHEN ST

Police Station

DRUMSHEUGH GDNS

WALKER STREET

MELVILLE STREET

WILLIAM ST

COATES PLACE

MORRISON ST

ROTHESAY TERR

PLACE

MANOR

CHESTER STREET

St Mary Episc. Cathedral

PALMERSTON PLACE

PLACE

MAITLAND

+ Palmerston Place

GROSVENOR CRES

LANSDOWNE CRES

GROSVENOR ST

HAYMARKET

Haymarket Station

EGLINTON CRES

GLENCAIRN CRES

Edinburgh Theol. Coll.

ROSEBERY CR.

HAYMARKET TERR

100 m

DOUGLAS CRES

COATES GDNS

DEAN

MAGDALA CRESCENT

Water of Leith

Donaldson's School

DEVON PLACE

WEST COATES

(Roseburn Free) +

WESTER COATES ROAD

by adding Coates Crescent, Walker Street and Manor Place. Development started with the crescent, made possible by the purchase of some ground at the w end of Cockburn Ross's property in the same year. From 1820 Major James Weir's trustees developed their small strip of land to the NE with Lynedoch Place, designed by *James Milne*.

The s border was completed in three parts. In 1824 Thomas Morrison's trustees offered feus for the building of *James Haldane*'s bow-cornered block on West Maitland Street; in 1825 came the Heriot Trust's Atholl Crescent, designed by their own architect *Thomas Bonnar*, and finally in 1830 the Learmonth development centred on Rutland Square, where John Learmonth's architect *John Tait* merely revised the scheme prepared by *Archibald Elliot* for James Stuart from whom the site had been purchased in 1825.

Another deal that took place in 1825 was not a pure speculation but an attempt to resolve a conflict of planning interests. The Heriot Trust bought four unfinished houses at the NW end of Lynedoch Place with a view to demolishing them, for they stood in the way of the logical N extension of the Walker scheme and the direct approach to their own unfeued lands of Wester Coates. In the next year *James Gillespie Graham* produced a 'Plan of Sir Patrick Walker's Grounds as laid out in connexion with the Grounds to the West', jointly commissioned by Walker and the Heriot Trust.* He was not the architect usually employed by either, but was well qualified to advise on the relation of the two w developments with his own design for the Moray Estate. Most of his plan (he is not known to have been asked for elevations) was eventually carried out after 1862, with some changes: Chester Street is not aligned with the centre of Randolph Crescent, and the small circus he proposed at its junction with Manor Place was not built, doubtless because Melville Crescent had been so slow in feuing. Rothesay Place went up according to the plan, but since the Lynedoch Place houses had been resold (at a loss) in 1829 its line could not be continued all the way E to Queensferry Street; the result was the rather makeshift triangle of Drumsheugh Gardens, the site of the former Drumsheugh House. Palmerston Place (the boundary between Walker and Heriot lands) was built to the w, but the cathedral site, which seems to have been safeguarded since 1861, prevented the continuation of Melville Street to meet it.

The Heriot Trust's extensive lands to the w of Palmerston Place consisted mainly of the old estate of Wester Coates. The E part, nearest to the city centre, was developed in two stages with continuous terraces. About 1865 *Robert Matheson* produced a plan for a double crescent on the Melville Street axis (Grosvenor and Lansdowne) entered from the s by Grosvenor Street and Rosebery Crescent. The design of the elevations was

---

*The layout virtually as executed is shown in outline on Lothian's map of 1825, the year before Graham's plan. So perhaps Graham was not the inventor of the layout but merely of a desirable deviation that did not come off.

shared between him and the Heriot Trust surveyor *John Chesser*, though the N side of West Maitland Street, on an odd section of Walker property, was by the Walker architect *John Lessels*. By 1872 the Heriot Trust had decided to develop the ground to the N. *Chesser* designed for it another double crescent (Glencairn and Eglinton), deliberately out of line with the Walker layout and thus producing, with its oblique entries, a grandly claustrophobic effect. The outward-facing Douglas and Magdala Crescents, the latter quite modest in scale, provide the N and W boundaries of the whole scheme. The villa development of West Coates began *c.* 1850 in accordance with a layout by the Heriot Trust surveyor *Alexander Black*; a few large houses had been built before the coming of the railway in 1860. The Wester Coates area to the N was supervised by a later surveyor, *Donald A. Gow*, from 1896. The Devon Place working-class development to the S, between West Coates and the main railway line, began in 1864.

CHURCHES

PALMERSTON PLACE CHURCH, 1873–5 by *Peddie & Kinnear* for the United Presbyterian congregation who moved here from the Rose Street Chapel. The street front, with Italianate arcades between almost Georgian stair-towers, tactfully combines the two prevailing styles of the neighbourhood; it may be mere coincidence that the upward continuation of the towers into pedimented tabernacles (with copper domes) makes it look like a domesticated version of the C18 W front of Saint-Sulpice in Paris. Impressive interior, a spacious D-plan continuing the arcaded theme of the porch: seventeen arches on Peterhead granite columns with composite capitals above the gallery. Arcaded clearstorey windows all round. Flat ceiling with delicate Grecian plasterwork; Noah's dove in the central rose. – Elaborate Renaissance PULPIT, and ORGAN CASE in the wide arch at the flat end of the D, both by *J. M. Dick Peddie & G. Washington Browne*, 1901. – ORGAN itself by *Norman & Beard*, rebuilt and enlarged by *Willis*, 1961.

ROSEBURN FREE CHURCH, Hampton Terrace, West Coates. Now the National Bible Society. Small, economical E. E. by *Robert R. Raeburn*, 1867–8. Broad N gable front of three lancets, with a little NE tower and broach-spire, the sculpture left in block. Latterly Wester Coates parish church; converted to its present use by *Dick Peddie & McKay*, 1975.

ST GEORGE'S WEST (originally St George's Free Church), Shandwick Place. 1866–9 by *David Bryce*, expressing the familiar arrangement of the two-storey galleried kirk, entered between stair-halls, in his most wilful Roman Baroque. Gibbsian windows on the W (Stafford Street) front. In the end bays giant Corinthian columns attached to pilasters, the pediments breaking forward on top. The even larger scale of the corner tower is maintained by the whole of the half-symmetrical s front. Divided segmental pediment over the entrance. Over the tower base, which has rusticated quoins instead of a Corinthian order, only the clock stage follows Bryce's design. Structural problems seem to have prevented the building of the rest (two lively Corinthian stages and a scrolled termination of Southern Baroque type), but in 1879–81 *R. Rowand Anderson* supplied the 56-m. Venetian *campanile*, modified from that at S. Giorgio Maggiore. The arches of the octagonal top stage echo those over Bryce's entrance.

Gibbsian interior, translated into cast-iron construction. Spectacular vaulted ceiling, springing from the big consoled entablatures of slim, spirally vaulted Corinthian columns. At the N end an apse, with a more solemn Doric order and a ribbed semi-dome; an open triangular pediment overall. Later organ chambers on each side. – WOODWORK. Excellent, mainly original, with bold curves complementing the brittler richness of the plasterwork. – STAINED GLASS. Only in the wheel window of the apse (Patriarchs, Prophets and Evangelists, a Bible in the centre), after 1878.

ST MARY'S CATHEDRAL (Episcopal), Palmerston Place. 1874– 45 1917. A massive synthesis of early Gothic by *G. Gilbert Scott*, dominating the Georgian vista of Melville Street and, with its three spires, the whole W skyline of the city. The Walker sisters, heirs of Sir Patrick Walker who had developed the lands of Easter Coates, left their whole fortune to the Episcopal Church on condition that a cathedral* should be built for the diocese of Edinburgh on this site. Their trustees invited three architects in Scotland and three in England to design a cathedral seating 1,500 people, with a chapter house holding 150, at a cost of £45,000 (quickly amended to £65,000); the future of the old house (*see* below) was left to their discretion. Drawings were submitted in 1872, and although Alexander Ross's three-spired design was much favoured, the final decision was for one of the three sent in by Scott – variations on the theme of a large central tower and spire.‡ The £89,770 contract was begun in May 1874 by the London builder *G. W. Booth*, with *Edwin Morgan* as clerk of works. Later in the year the trustees, hankering after the cathedral image of Ross's three spires, instructed Scott to add another nave bay, including two W towers with spires to be built only to the height of the nave roof meantime. This raised the contract to £95,016; by 1879 £110,000 had been spent, leaving the chapter house to be executed by *John Oldrid Scott* for £5,000 in 1890–1, and the W spires by *Charles M. Oldrid Scott* for £13,200 in 1913–17, both to their father's designs and with *Edwin Morgan* as contractor.

* St Paul's Church (*see* First New Town) was the pro-Cathedral meantime.
‡ In Scotland the other two competitors were *Lessels* (a crazy late Gothic scheme with a crown spire) and *Peddie & Kinnear* (buttressed spire and crown W spires); in England, *Street* (low central tower and tall W tower) and *Burges* (a reduced version of his Cork Cathedral design, but with no central tower).

A combination of safeness and Scottishness evidently won the day for Scott, who observed in his report that he had been 'most impressed by the earlier phase of the First Pointed period which especially unites the architecture of Scotland with that of Northern England and is one capable, I think, of the greatest possible degree of dignity united with a reasonable amount of simplicity and any amount of beauty'. He went on to specify his sources, and might have listed many more from northern and southern England and northern France, all worked into a cathedral of ample height (roof ridges 26 m., central spire 90 m.) but modest area (80 by 40 m.). Of its ingenuity there is no question. As to dignity, the parts are well related in scale, especially at the transepts and w spires. Since the latter were an afterthought, perhaps it is not Scott's fault that the nave seems a small, prosaic interlude between them. His appreciation of the sculptural and compositional possibilities of his Gothic vocabulary is clear, but the overall effect is firmly earth-bound by the continuity of so many long horizontal lines, and clogged by the hammer-dressed Victorian masonry of the walls. Did this assertion of weight added to already heavy Northern Gothic features, form part of Scott's own idea of dignity?

The w doorway (a variant of that at Holyrood*) is flanked by blind arches (Dunblane) with three gablets above (Elgin). Double opening with panelled jambs and trumeau (Jedburgh). Angels hold drapery on the lintel. Christ in a vesica on the tympanum above. Holyrood is the direct source of the shafts on each side (but here they are alternately of Shap granite), and of the outermost band of formalized leaves in the arch. Whorled wrought-iron door-hinges. w window a rose and four lancets in an arched recess (New Abbey). w towers of three tall stages with intermediate blind arcading, the lower ones double-bayed and rather French, the upper pure E.E. with the angle-buttresses carried up into corbelled turrets and pinnacles at the corners of the octagonal spires (Sutton St Mary, already imitated by Scott at St Matthew in City Road, London, 1847). The central tower, despite its two rivals, is still an effective and original climax. Bold diagonal flying buttresses at the four corners, an intermediate turreted stage, and then a noble octagonal belfry with corner pinnacles, supporting a lucarned and centre-ribbed spire (Chartres) of pronounced entasis. The s transept is the richer. Three tall lancets, their shafts standing out from the wall. Above them a rose window (Lincoln) and gable statuary. In the N transept a wheel window (recalling Chartres) above five lancets, three of them blind. At the E end a crowning vesica (Salisbury's w gable) and five niches with figures over three great lancets, their divisions carried down into the base-course (Whitby).

---

*This and many more allusions are made to Holyrood, e.g. in the bay design from end to end, with especial success in the choir. Scott knew that this site had once belonged to the abbey.

To the N the two-bay passage leading to the square CHAPTER HOUSE, of yellower stone, octagonally roofed with broached corners. The octagonal vault inside, with Shap granite centre column, does not rise into the pointed roof.

If the INTERIOR appears under-lit, that is probably due (1984) to the grime which deadens the upward growth of the nave from its plain round and octagonal piers with stiff-leaf capitals (New Shoreham) into the richer triforium (St Thomas, Canterbury) and the still more intricate clearstorey with its diversely enriched Transitional over-arches. Corbelled shafts sprout eagerly from the wall above the main arcade, but the ribs that spring from them are lost in the gloomy brown of the timber tunnel-roof. Scott's perspective drawing shows no such dead stop, and indeed suggests a painting of Christ in Glory over the crossing arch. On the further (E) side of the crossing the piers are carried down to the floor without corbelled wall-shafts, giving a decisive feeling of entry to the chancel. Rib-vaulted nave and transept aisles, meeting dramatically at the diagonal arches at each corner of the crossing, itself vaulted with a concrete web. The sexpartite concrete chancel vault extends to the triple lancets of the E wall, sweeping it into the semblance of an apse (Tynemouth Priory).

The Victorian furnishings, though lost in the general murk, are of considerable quality and invention. They follow Scott's intentions except that the choir occupies the crossing so as to be near the organ in the N transept. – REREDOS. Alabaster with marble shafts. Beneath a tall gable three superimposed arches; in the middle one (with foliage details from a fragment of Bridlington cloister) a white marble relief of the Crucifixion by *Mary Grant*. – SEPTUM, between nave and crossing. Derbyshire alabaster with diamond inlays between red marble shafts. – PULPIT. Octagonal, with Dumfries-shire stone panels of Christ, St John the Baptist, St Peter and the Evangelists on a shafted cruciform base. – CHOIR STALLS, BISHOP'S THRONE and SEDILIA. Walnut, with ebonized colonnettes; bold and highly original. All by *Farmer & Brindley* to *J. Oldrid Scott*'s designs, 1878–9, based (except for the woodwork) on his father's sketches. So was the alabaster and red marble predecessor (Norman, derived from Winchester and Lincoln) of the present FONT, a tame affair of freestone, with a wrought-iron cover, by *Edith M. B. Hughes*, 1959. – Brass LECTERN. A pious pelican with chicks. – ROOD, above the septum. 1922 by *Robert S. Lorimer*. – CHANCEL FLOOR. Tiled diamonds and whorls (Westminster Abbey) by *William Godwin*, 1878. – SCREENS flanking the altar and chancel. Fanciful wrought-iron by *Skidmore*, 1879. – ORGAN (N transept). By *Henry Willis* to *Herbert Oakeley*'s specification, in a Gothic case presumably by *J. Oldrid Scott*, 1879; rebuilt by *Harrison* in 1929, and again in 1959.

LADY CHAPEL formed in the S chancel aisle by *George Henderson*, 1897–8, with an Italian Romanesque marble

ALTAR and a metal SCREEN by *Singer & Sons* in the diagonal crossing arch. – In the CHAPEL OF THE RESURRECTION (S transept), late Gothic ALTAR and War Memorial REREDOS of oak by *Nathaniel Grieve*, 1922, to *Robert S. Lorimer*'s design. SCREEN to the N. Similar, but made for the chapel of The Hirsel, Berwickshire, in 1928 and moved here in 1959. – SAC-RAMENT HOUSE also by *Lorimer*, the pelican and angels carved by *C. d'O. Pilkington Jackson*. – In the CHAPEL OF ST MARGARET OF SCOTLAND (SW tower) a wrought-iron SCREEN to *Edith M.B. Hughes*' design by *Thomas Bogie*, 1959. – Much contemporary STAINED GLASS by *Clayton & Bell*, *Burlison & Grylls* and *C.E. Kempe* who did the armorial glass in the nave clearstorey. None of note, and much in poor condition (1984). – MONUMENT, chancel N side. Recumbent marble figure of Dean Montgomery †1900 by *Pittendrigh MacGillivray* on a Romanesque base by *Hippolyte J. Blanc*. – BRASSES. A great number, the best on the chancel floor, a figure of Bishop Dowden by *Robert S. Lorimer*, 1911.

ST MARY'S MUSIC SCHOOL occupies the old EASTER COATES to the N of the Cathedral, originally a small two-storey L-plan house built in 1615 for John Byres. Twin turrets on the S gable, tall pedimented dormers, and a corbelled turret in the angle of the NW jamb, all the walling stripped down to rubble. Two-storey mid-C18 N wing, crowstepped to match. The house was repaired in 1813 and altered not long after, acquiring a further N addition with a variety of detail, mainly C17, from Old Town demolitions; the two-light C16 window is said to be from the French Ambassador's chapel in the Cowgate. Reprieved by Scott, it became the Cathedral Choir School in 1887, and in 1903 *George Henderson* recast the N wing around the old details, adding the crowstep gable to the early C19 W porch. Some surprises inside. Mid-C18 staircase in the jamb, with twisted balusters, the ceiling a Tudor rib-vault of *c.* 1830. On the first floor the 'Old Salon' with a coved Jacobethan ceiling of the same Abbotsford vintage, and other rooms with plain panelling and a moulded C17 fireplace.

SONG SCHOOL, further N. A modest hall with crowstep gables and a slated flèche, by *J. Oldrid Scott*, 1885. Tunnel-ceilinged interior, with WALL PAINTINGS by *Phoebe Tra-quair* on the theme of the Benedicite. On the E wall the cath-edral clergy and choir, with panels of Pentecost and Christ's empty tomb. On the S selected verses of the canticle, the second panel with portraits of Mrs Traquair's admired con-temporaries (e.g. Rossetti, Holman Hunt and Watts). On the N birds and choristers singing together, and one panel with a gathering of great men (e.g. Dante, Blake and H.M. Stan-ley). On the W the four beasts, and seraphs singing the Sanc-tus. Happy in expression and frequently in composition, the colours predominantly red and blue as in the Bellevue Baptist Church (*see* Gayfield, Churches, below) but with less gold; altogether more intimate and realistic. ORGAN by *Henry Wil-lis & Sons*, 1887; rebuilt by *Rushworth & Dreaper*.

WALPOLE HALL (Episcopal), still further N. By *Robert S. Lorimer & J. F. Matthew*, completed in 1933 after the former's death. A long buttressed hall with its entrance gable to Chester Street, the gables and dormers colonially shaped over a low wall-head.

ST THOMAS, Rutland Place. Originally Church of England, now (1984) a heritage centre. Neo-Norman by *David Cousin*, 1842-3. Two gables filling a gap in the Georgian development, copiously but knowledgeably enriched (some areas of detail eroded). On the l. gable a bow like a slice off a Templar church, with an elaborate doorway opening into a geometric stair to gallery level. Here a floor was inserted *c.* 1958, but the upper part of the church is intact. Groin-vaulted roof and elaborately arched trusses with pendants where piers would be expected. An even more elaborate arch to the one-bay chancel. The S front originally conformed with the neighbouring houses. After the unity of Rutland Street had been lost to the Caledonian Station (*see* South West, Lothian Road) it was redesigned by *Wardrop & Reid*, 1882, with suitable Norman windows and a porch across the basement area.

PUBLIC BUILDINGS

DONALDSON'S SCHOOL, West Coates. A proudly sited Jacob- 92 ethan palace by *William H. Playfair*, 1841-51. James Donaldson died in 1830, leaving some £210,000 to build and endow an orphan hospital, which subsequently specialized in deaf children. His trustees sought competitive plans from Gillespie Graham and W. H. Playfair and then from David Hamilton, Playfair being finally appointed on a second stage which specified 'Elizabethan' in 1838. Instructed to enlarge his competition design to three storeys, he was in 1839 working on the details of 'a Building, which in the correctness of its parts shall be worthy of comparison with the remains of Old English Architecture. I avoid carefully all mixture of Roman Mouldings with the Gothic.' When the lowest tender of £74,000 was found too high the design was reduced again from three storeys to two as in the 1838 scheme with accommodation for three hundred children. Work began early in 1842, the main contractors being *Young & Trench*, who sorely tried the patience of Playfair and his clerk of works, *Peter Manuel*. The supply of Craigleith stone being too slow, Binny stone was adopted: it is warm in colour, the walling lightly stugged. The building was still not quite complete when the Queen and the Prince Consort visited it in 1850; in that year the balustraded terraces were put in hand, and in February 1851 Playfair's longest job, 'that Eternal Donaldson's Hospital', was finished.

It is a quadrangle 79 by 63 m. overall (54 by 50 m. inside), the central tower on the S front 37 m. high to the finials of its domed octagonal turrets (elaborated from Burghley), the corner towers 30 m. high with square ogee-roofed turrets and bay-windows (developed from Audley End). Buttressed intermediate bays, with the parapet stepped up to the chimney finials – twelve serried buttresses on each of the side elevations, but none on the N, where the basement is exposed and the turreted chapel projects boldly from the centre. Nondescript buildings of the later C20 impair the spectacular views from NW and NE, but thanks to the trees they are easily ignored. Surprisingly friendly COURTYARD. Turreted stairhalls cut in at the corners, tall turreted projections (from Linlithgow Palace or Edinburgh Castle) at the sides. But the big S tower does not loom over it, for it is softened by a canted gatehouse projection at the base, and the whole upper storey is reduced to the cosy proportions of an almshouse by means of a mezzanine arrangement – small staff-rooms off a low corridor for the supervision of the dormitories below. In the middle of the paved square a stone base for a gas light.

Inside, austerity is the predictable rule, e.g. in the minimally Tudor detail of the stair balusters. Late Gothic overmantel in the entrance hall, a memorial to the 1914–18 war by *A.F. Balfour Paul*, made by *Scott Morton & Co*. In the Council room an ogee quatrefoil-ribbed ceiling and a Louis XV chimneypiece. On the W side the seven-bay dining hall with a ribbed ceiling. In the Chapel to the N (now the school hall) the shouldered beam ceiling was no doubt elaborately painted, for in June 1850 Playfair wrote to his friend Rutherfurd 'The ceiling and the stained Glass (by *Ballantine*) superb! Like a Baronial Hall fit to receive Henry VIII, Anna Bullen and Wolsey. Excuse your poor friend's Vanity.' The glass was blown out by a Zeppelin bomb in 1916 and weakly replaced; a fragment is preserved in a sink-room on the first floor of the S range.

EDINBURGH THEOLOGICAL COLLEGE, Rosebery Crescent. Originally COATES HALL, a small Baronial house by *David Bryce* for Sheriff Napier, 1850, of two storeys, with pepperpots on the twin S gables and a round turret in the angle of the NE wing. In 1891 it was bought by the Episcopal Church, and in the next year *Sydney Mitchell* enlarged the wing in a gentler baronial idiom (but the same snecked masonry), crowned the angle-turret with a spired octagon and added a late Gothic chapel lying low to the SE. Bryce's E porch was turned round to become its S entrance. In 1913 *Robert S. Lorimer* added a storey to the main block, much improving the whole group, and bell-roofs to its heightened pepperpots. Harled extensions of *c.* 1970 give the recessed W elevation the look of a back-yard. The CHAPEL is entered through a two-arched aisle with one foliated capital; red sandstone dressings otherwise minimal. *Lorimer* added the panelled E bay (his altar and reredos since removed), its celure an extension of the beamed wagon roof. – STAINED GLASS. At the E end three lights (Crucifixion, with St Mary and St John, St Columba and St Ninian) by *J. Ninian Comper*, beautifully drawn in pale grey-gold with purply blue. – ORGAN by *Rushworth & Dreaper*, 1936. – Pretty LODGE to the E by *Mitchell*.

ELECTRICITY OFFICE, Dewar Place. A flat red sandstone palazzo of sorts, designed in 1894 as the Electric Lighting Central Generating Station by *Robert Morham*, who gave it another storey in 1896. *Alexander Kennedy* of Westminster was the consulting engineer. Arcaded ground floor with alternately projecting voussoirs and centre-columned windows, blocked architraves on the windows above. Long and indeterminate wings, the S one with a domed pepperpot with blocked dwarf columns.

HAYMARKET STATION. 1840. Originally the head office and terminus of the Edinburgh & Glasgow Railway, by the civil engineer *John Miller*, i.e. possibly by *David Bell* who designed station buildings for him in the late 1840s. A rectangular block of five bays, the centre three recessed, domestic in form but heavy in detail except for the tetrastyle Tuscan porch. Upstairs is the old board room with a monumental granite chimneypiece. LODGE in Haymarket Terrace. Low-pitch roof with deep eaves and central chimney, contemporary with the station.

The lines are on a lower level. Original cobbled platforms and iron TRAIN SHED* with tie-rod trusses on fluted columns, their brackets tendrilled Neo-Greek. Trains ran through to Waverley from 1846, but the present arrangement of through platforms is by *James Carswell*, 1894.‡ Redevelopment has been stopped but modernization proceeds (1984).

POLICE STATION, Torphichen Place. An Edwardian Renaissance palazzo designed in the City's office under *Robert Morham*, 1908–9, replacing his own baronial building of 1874. Ground-floor arcade with bands of rock-faced rustication, blocked architraves above. Massive and severe, but nicely linked with a hollow splay to the adjoining terrace.

TORPHICHEN EDUCATION CENTRE (originally the Torphichen Street School). 1886 by *Robert Wilson*. An elaborate classical composition on an obtuse corner. Tall pedimented centrepiece between octagonal turrets with columned cupolas; bulgy Ionic columned doorpieces in the wings. Not elegant, especially after the poor repair of eroded detail, but splendid townscape. The twelve-pane windows show unusual sympathy with the nearby Georgian houses.

STREETS

ALVA STREET

Laid out (and presumably designed) by *James Gillespie Graham* in 1823 and eventually developed by *Robert Hutchison* in the

---

*It is now (1984) at Bo'ness (Lothian).
‡The platform roofs removed, 1982–3.

1830s. Middling in scale, but more substantial and assertive than any of its neighbours. Uniform house-fronts with anthemion balconies bulging from corniced first-floor windows all along (the N side has lost most of its crowning balustrade to top-floor additions). At the E end four-storey tenements with quadrant corners (for the related Queensferry Street elevations *see* below). At the W end only three storeys (with arched doorways for a change), not going right up to Stafford Street, which had already produced its own end pavilions. Simple Neo-Greek interiors, often altered.

ATHOLL CRESCENT AND ATHOLL PLACE

By *Thomas Bonnar*, 1825. ATHOLL CRESCENT, balancing Coates Crescent, shows off its single smooth sweep with ten shallow Ionic pilasters in the middle and five at each end of the arc, and trellis balconies. The centre house and the flat-fronted end ones had Ionic porches, but in 1912 the E end lost a bay (for improved access to Rutland Square) and its porch was moved to No. 5 in the adaptation by *H. Ramsay Taylor* for the College of Domestic Science. The porch was moved again in *Robert Hurd & Partners'* reconstruction of 1982–4. ATHOLL PLACE to the W is a main door and common stair block, with a bow of giant antae curving round the corner to meet a slightly different frontage in Torphichen Street (for the rest of Torphichen Street *see* below, West Maitland Street).

CANNING STREET

Planned as part of the Heriot Trust Atholl development but not built till later, and plain at that. The thirteen-storey CANNING HOUSE by *Gavin Paterson & Son*, 1967, is conspicuous in the Georgian vistas of Rutland Street and Walker Street.

CARBERRY PLACE *see* DEVON PLACE

CHARLOTTE LANE *see* QUEENSFERRY STREET

CHESTER STREET

A highly successful Victorian-Georgian compromise by *John Lessels*, built mainly in 1862–70. Brown-type pavilions, the houses between them with segment-headed first-floor windows (plus consoled cornices on the grander W block facing the cathedral) alternately punctuated with rosettes. Good Victorian versions of the Walker Estate three-bay balcony.

CLIFTON TERRACE *see* HAYMARKET TERRACE

COATES CRESCENT

The building of *Robert Brown*'s Walker scheme began here in
1813. His design owes much to Robert Reid's Northern New
Town; a divided crescent with flat-fronted pavilions (cf.
Abercromby Place), the centrepieces with three out of nine
bays advanced, the pavilions with three out of five recessed
(cf. the centrepieces of E and W Heriot Row respectively). Not
very original but always careful over detail, e.g. in the short
return elevations of the end pavilions. The graceful triple
balconies (here on wrought-iron brackets) frequently reappear in the Walker Estate and further afield. Inside, apse-
ended dining rooms are the general rule, with Corinthian
pilasters at No. 10 and an elaborate frieze at No. 19. Most of
the entrance halls quite simple, but No. 8 has a frieze with
figures and Nos. 9 and 10 have Roman Doric columns *in
antis*. No. 15 similar, with an arch overhead, Nos. 16 and 17
with two-bay groin-vaults.

GLADSTONE MEMORIAL in the gardens. Designed by *J. Pittendrigh MacGillivray* for this site in 1902, but opposed by
the proprietors and relegated to the W side of St Andrew
Square from 1917 to 1955. Gentle, convincing sculpture in
the manner of Alfred Gilbert; W. E. Gladstone in Chancellor's robes and eight other bronze figures representing and
reciting his virtues, on a base of red unpolished granite with
Baroque half-pediments.

COATES GARDENS *see* EGLINTON CRESCENT

COATES PLACE *see* PALMERSTON PLACE

DEVON PLACE DEVELOPMENT

Devon Place leads from West Coates into the workers' settlement developed by the coal merchant James McKelvie from
1864. Unpretentious rows of single-storey cottages in stone
and brick, with cobbled streets and split-whinstone pavements. EGLINTON STREET and SUTHERLAND STREET* to
the E were rather cramped, WEST CATHERINE PLACE, PEM-
BROKE PLACE and CARBERRY PLACE to the W more generously planned with walled backyards, a single cottage closing the view down each cul-de-sac. BALBIRNIE PLACE at the
far W end is more haphazard.

DOUGLAS CRESCENT AND MAGDALA CRESCENT

Both by *John Chesser*, a fancy fringe to the solid fabric of the
Western New Town. DOUGLAS CRESCENT of 1875-9 con-

---

*They were demolished in 1982 and the site redeveloped by the *Scottish Special
Housing Association*.

tinues the sedate design of Palmerston Place at Nos. 23–31, then breaks out with gusto into jolly arched dormers with fish-scale roofs on top of canted bays, only momentarily remembering its dignity at Nos. 11–13. MAGDALA CRESCENT is earlier (1869–76), with the same dormered bays, No. 23 most important because it still has its original cast-iron cresting. *The Builder* in 1876 did not like the 'unvarying recurrence of oriels, identical in form and detail ... an utter negation of art'.

DOUGLAS GARDENS *see* PALMERSTON PLACE

DRUMSHEUGH PLACE AND DRUMSHEUGH GARDENS

DRUMSHEUGH PLACE at the SE angle, a big block with first-floor pediments and a tall Frenchy roof, like Nos. 1–2 Lynedoch Place was built by *Watherston* in 1880–81, possibly to a *Lessels* design. Then MELDRUM HOUSE by *John Drummond*, 1957, equally disastrous from far and near as the replacement for *Campbell Douglas & Sellars'* St Andrew's Free Church of 1884–6. DRUMSHEUGH GARDENS proper consists of tall, grand houses enclosing a triangle of mature trees. The w side, built mainly in 1878, was designed in 1874 by *Peddie & Kinnear*, following Lessels's four-storey scale but translating it into their best Graeco-Italian with a mastery of scale and detail unrivalled in the Western New Town. Channelled ground floor with consoled doorpieces, two-storey rectangular bays with Miletus-type antae and Corinthian-column mullions at the first floor, bracketed Italian cornice and low-pitch roof. Good interior details, starting with columned entrance halls: the external detail has lost some of its quality by overcleaning. The other houses are by *John Lessels*, built by *Watherston*, 1874–82. All have canted bays on the two lower storeys, those on the hypotenuse of the triangle (Nos. 19–37) more successfully handled. Some opulent interiors, e.g. at the broader No. 29, designed and built by *Watherston* for Andrew Wylie, 1887. Entrance hall with brass and polychrome marble fireplace. In the dining room a bold oak sideboard with coupled pilasters, the fireplace red, black and green marble with brass register. Back bedroom with an arched stove. Fantastic Jacobethan stair, the alcove at the half-landing bizarre Second Empire, the conservatory cantilevered from the window as an afterthought.* Domelets in the ceiling. In the pilastered first-floor drawing room two white marble chimneypieces, one with cupids, the other with the earth, the moon and two females. Back bedroom with diapered cove, pink and black columnar chimneypiece and built-in wardrobes. Nos. 34–35 radically altered as the MUIR HALL OF RESIDENCE by *Dunn & Findlay*, 1898.

* Since removed as unsafe.

EGLINTON CRESCENT, GLENCAIRN CRESCENT AND COATES GARDENS

All by *John Chesser*, the two crescents largely built by *Roberts & Son* and by *James Steel* who from 1877 began to challenge the Watherstons in this area. EGLINTON CRESCENT (1875-80) is complex and impressive, with richly consoled tripartite doorpieces and first-floor bay-windows rising from within the balustrades of ground-floor bows. Elaborate interiors, most entrance halls with leaded glass. Towards the E end Corinthian screens and arabesque friezes. At No. 13 a bronze bas-relief with figures. GLENCAIRN CRESCENT (1873-9) merely continues the adjacent Palmerston Place. Mutual corner block designed by *Alexander W. Macnaughtan*, 1879, under Chesser's control but poorly composed. COATES GARDENS (1871-6) links the two crescents with Haymarket Terrace. More modest in scale, with arched doorpieces and alternate broad and narrow dormers behind a crowning balustrade that follows the bay-windows in and out.

EGLINTON STREET *see* DEVON PLACE

GLENCAIRN CRESCENT *see* EGLINTON CRESCENT

GROSVENOR CRESCENT, LANSDOWNE CRESCENT AND GROSVENOR GARDENS

The two facing crescents clinch the huge Gothic vision of St 126 Mary's Cathedral between their E ends. GROSVENOR CRESCENT by *John Chesser*, 1869-71, is much the grander; three-storey houses with two-storey bays and Ionic pilastered doorpieces (columned porches for emphasis in the middle part). The end pavilions are big single houses, each with its porch incorporated in the central bay. This was obviously a sought-after development, for *Peddie & Kinnear* executed Nos. 1-3 (1871) Nos. 5-6 (1869), No. 12 (1869, for Kinnear himself) and Nos. 15-20 (1869-70). *John Watherston & Sons* built Nos. 7-10. Good internal finishings. A few houses embellished later, e.g. No. 10, lavish Edwardian.

LANSDOWNE CRESCENT (1865) is bisected by Grosvenor Street, both designed by *Robert Matheson*. Between the corner pavilions with their Italianate cornices it is virtually late Georgian, with rusticated ground floors and balustraded parapets. GROSVENOR GARDENS, added as an afterthought when Coates Hall had ceased to be a private house, starts with *Sydney Mitchell*'s corner tenement (1891-2) which has some bits of Gibbsian detail. The houses at Nos. 3-6 were added by the civil engineers *Belfrage & Carfrae* at the same time and in the same general style.

GROSVENOR STREET

By *Robert Matheson*, 1865. Lofty corner pavilions at the s (Haymarket) end, with quadrant corners and Matheson's characteristic Italianate cornices, bracketed and consoled. For the rest he proposed two-storey terraces with panelled parapets and pedimented dormers, but the houses as built are tall and severe, of three storeys, with consoled doorpieces.

HAYMARKET TERRACE AND CLIFTON TERRACE

The plainest part of the Heriot Trust development. On the N side of HAYMARKET TERRACE tenements with shops, over which Chesser presumably had general control. ROSEBERY HOUSE, indeterminately sited to the s, by *Michael Laird & Partners*, 1977, is pleated, like a long brown concertina. CLIFTON TERRACE (although the tenement at Nos. 8-15 is probably by *Chesser*) belongs to *Matheson*'s scheme. He was responsible for the row of two-storey bay-windowed houses (Nos. 1-6), for which he originally designed pedimented dormers and iron balustrading at the wall-head. Their modest size contrasts with the large end pavilions of the Grosvenor Street entry and contributes to the small-town scale surrounding the Haymarket junction. The seven-storey HAYMARKET HOUSE by *Covell Matthews & Partners*, 1969, does not.

The pylon with two pedimented clock-faces in the middle of the junction (slightly moved in 1971-2) is the HEART OF MIDLOTHIAN WAR MEMORIAL by *H. S. Gamley*, 1921-2. For Haymarket Station *see* Public Buildings, above.

LANSDOWNE CRESCENT *see* GROSVENOR CRESCENT

LYNEDOCH PLACE

A single-storey terrace development of twenty-one houses in an unbroken curve, designed in 1820 by *James Milne* and largely complete by 1823. Like Ann Street in the Raeburn Estate it has front gardens and a taller centrepiece, every house on each side stepped to suit the slope. No. 23 was reconstructed by *C. S. S. Johnston* with a bay-window in 1893, and the general unity has been upset by many attic additions. On the corner of Drumsheugh Gardens, Nos. 1-2, built by *John Watherston & Sons*, possibly on a *Lessels* design, in 1876-7. LYNEDOCH HOUSE at the NW end (flats for old people) is by *Roland Wedgwood Associates*, 1977, buff brick, with a glass sunroom perched high above Belford Road.

MAGDALA CRESCENT *see* DOUGLAS CRESCENT

MANOR PLACE

Nos. 1–47 on the E side, built from S to N in 1822–67, follow *Robert Brown*'s design, a slightly different version of his Walker Street houses. Tenements at the entry to William Street bluntly indicate their lower status with rubble gables. When the W side was undertaken in 1864 *John Lessels* was in charge. Victorian splay to the Coates Place corner at the S end, quite unrelated to Brown's pavilion opposite. At Nos. 4–24 Lessels follows Brown's design but introduces round-headed doorways and (for the first time) a regular procession of dormers along the skyline.

The N part, mainly 1870–74 but not finished till 1892, is again by *Lessels*. Slightly elaborated Brown-type pavilions at Chester Street, then houses with arched doorpieces and triple first-floor windows, centrally pedimented – pleasant enough details, but the change in rhythm from floor to floor makes nonsense of the attempted overall symmetry. The N pavilions an equally messy compromise.

MELVILLE PLACE *see* QUEENSFERRY STREET

MELVILLE STREET AND MELVILLE CRESCENT

Designed by *Robert Brown* in 1814, MELVILLE STREET is the main vista of the Walker development, 366 m. long and 33 m. wide between the house-fronts which repeat the Coates Crescent design with one extra storey. The first incident is the three-house centrepiece on the N side, opposite the entry of Stafford Street. The middle house has a central front door, giant Ionic columns and a swagged parapet panel. Complete original glazing, including the graceful mouchette fanlight. Then MELVILLE CRESCENT, not a crescent at all but a diagonal square (cf. Laura Place on the vista of Great Pulteney Street in Bath), on each of whose splayed frontages Brown intended a still grander display, with pedimented columns and outlying pilasters. As executed it is an inadequate focus for the layout, upstaged by the ever-surprising E gable and spired silhouette of Gilbert Scott's cathedral (*see* Churches, above).

The houses in Melville Street were quickly feued, and by 1825 only the far SW terrace was unbuilt (finished by 1833). The end pavilions were less popular: only those to the E are Georgian, with one-bay quadrant corners to Queensferry Street (Stafford Street corners 1856 and 1859; Manor Place corners 1860–61). Of the houses in the crescent only No. 1 is to Brown's design, *c.* 1843, complete with rock-faced basement. In 1855 the Walkers' new architect *John Lessels* simplified the details in order to get the scheme finished, reducing the columns to pilasters and omitting the pediments and basement rustication. Plate-glass, by then the norm, has also replaced many of the original six-pane sashes in the street itself. Attic additions and ill-judged stone-cleaning have spoiled the unity of the street but not its spatial quality. Well preserved iron-work, e.g. the arched lamp-holders over front steps.

The Melville Street INTERIORS are modest. At No. 25 coffered ceilings in the main rooms. The best entrance halls on the N side at Nos. 35 and 57 (arched and coffered) and No. 49 (Greek Doric columns and triglyph frieze), on the S side at No. 32 (arcaded walls and ornate ceiling), Nos. 42 and 46 (pendentive corners) and No. 44 (pilasters and wreaths). No. 54 was altered by *Robert S. Lorimer* for his own occupation in 1903, with small-paned glazing and a shaped stone balcony. Rear ground-floor dining room Neo-Tudor with a stone fire-place, a ribbed and bossed ceiling and a latticed bay-window.

The crescent interiors are much grander. At No. 1 (*c.* 1843) a tunnel-vaulted entrance hall leading to an oval-domed stair. Nos. 2 and 3 are by *Peddie & Kinnear*, 1862, No. 2 for the railway engineer John Miller of Leithen. Ionic entrance hall, consoled stair, Corinthian-screened drawing room. At No. 3 an entrance hall with double-coved ceiling. Classical reliefs in the stair-hall and drawing room. Nos. 4–6 were built in 1856 by *John Watherston & Sons* with simpler detail. Nos. 7–9 by *J. Dick Peddie* have rich palmette friezes in their drawing rooms. Nos. 10–12 by *Lessels* himself, with coffer-vaulted entrance halls. The novel arrangement in No. 12 of an L-plan service stair to the drawing room reappears in houses of the 1870s and 1880s, e.g. in Drumsheugh Gardens.

STATUE of the first Viscount Melville on a tall stone plinth at the centre of Melville Crescent by *John Steell*, 1857.

MORRISON STREET *see* WEST MAITLAND STREET

OSBORNE TERRACE *see* WEST COATES

PALMERSTON PLACE, COATES PLACE AND DOUGLAS GARDENS

PALMERSTON PLACE is an eventful street with two important churches, St Mary's Episcopal Cathedral and the twin-domed Palmerston Place Church (*see* above). A funny start at the SE corner, where *Lessels* has come along COATES PLACE (1864) with a four-storey block of flats and rounded the bend with two pairs of incredibly meagre pilasters. The bold Ionic porch of the ROYAL BANK OF SCOTLAND by *T. P. Marwick*, 1894, happily diverts attention. At the SW corner in 1880 *Thornton Shiells & Thomson* used the same pilaster theme, but the ground floor has been less lucky; the granite Art Deco BANK OF SCOTLAND with pseudo-Miletus capitals is by *Reid & Forbes*, 1932.

On the E side Nos. 3–21, with advanced centre but not quite symmetrical, show *Lessels* at his best. Doorpieces standing proud of the horizontal channelling, segment-headed first-floor windows with cornices, the middle one on each house having a little flourish. Beyond the Cathedral No. 25, a single large mansion of 1881 (architect unknown). Curved bay integrated with a Roman Doric porch, tall French roof added in 1886. Outstanding interior with Baroque doorcases, half filled by a massive stair-hall with an engraved glass dome on pendentives. Nos. 27–37, with canted bays, boldly projecting doorpieces clasped by Roman Doric half-pilasters, and a modillioned cornice overall, and No. 39 at the Rothesay Place corner were built in 1881–4 by *Alexander White*, evidently helped by the *Watherston* drawing office. Finally DOUGLAS GARDENS by *John Watherston & Sons*, 1890, a terrace of bay-windowed, steeply-gabled frontages stepping effectively downhill towards the Water of Leith.

John Chesser's performance on the W side of Palmerston Place (for the Heriot Trust) is relatively dull. Nos. 4–10 and 16–26 are mainly of 1872–8, with two-storey bays, iron-balustraded like the porches. Several were executed by *Peddie & Kinnear*, who also designed the Palmerston Place Church (*see* above). Then PALMERSTON COURT, a spectacular block of Glaswegian character (architect unknown), built as a pair of houses in 1880–81. Rectangular bays integrated with the porches as a base for canted bays above, iron balconies of intersecting hoops, and a steep roof with the only formally designed dormers in the street. Finally back to *Chesser* with Nos. 36–48 and 54–62, designed in 1872 and built mainly in 1877–80. Full-height bays and depressed arch doorpieces.

PEMBROKE PLACE *see* DEVON PLACE

QUEENSFERRY STREET AND MELVILLE PLACE

After the corner of Shandwick Place the notable mid Victorian shopfront of YOUNG & SAUNDERS, Italian Warehousemen (now ODDBINS), at No. 5. The houses behind presumably by *James Tait* for Cockburn Ross of Shandwick, after 1809. The fronts on each side of Alva Street belong to *J. Gillespie Graham*'s Erskine development of the 1830s, the S one elaborately refaced c. 1860. Then the pavilions of Melville Street, with recessed quadrant corners ingeniously built up to the required four storeys by wall-head panels. A Greek Doric doorpiece survives on the S side. The rusticated arches of the CLYDESDALE BANK at No. 21 are an anachronistic pastiche by the *Rowand Anderson Partnership*, 1977, replacing an original shop. The N corner continues as MELVILLE PLACE with original shopfronts at Nos. 12 and 13, all part of *Robert Brown*'s Walker development.

The long two-storey frontage on the E side of Queensferry Street, with characteristic lunettes in two wall-head chimney-gables, is by *Robert Reid*, from 1807. The Randolph

Place section (originally Charlotte Place) has been raised to three storeys and almost all the ground-floor shopfronts are later. Over the s quadrant a nice attic studio with Art Nouveau copper roof and finial, by *William H. Ross*, 1909. Small glass-bayed office building in CHARLOTTE LANE by *Alan Reiach, Eric Hall & Partners*, 1967.

ROSEBERY CRESCENT

The E side was the W boundary of *Matheson*'s Heriot Trust scheme, plain bay-windowed houses with half-pilaster door-pieces, of two and three storeys. The w side a more consistent job by the civil engineer *A. W. Belfrage*, 1890. For the Edinburgh Theological College *see* Public Buildings, above.

ROTHESAY PLACE AND ROTHESAY TERRACE

This part of the Walker development was entrusted in 1872 to *Peddie & Kinnear*, who designed the three terraces of ROTHESAY PLACE where each trio of drawing-room windows is linked together as a Corinthian arcade, and actually executed Nos. 1, 4-9 and 14. Nos. 17 and 18 (1888) do not follow their scheme and have been maimed by decay and over-cleaning. ROTHESAY TERRACE begins at the E end with Nos. 1 and 2, again by *Peddie & Kinnear*, with smug bow-windows echoing their University Club (*see* First New Town, Princes Street). The wider and slightly taller No. 3 is by *Sydney Mitchell*, 1883,* for John R. Findlay of the Scotsman newspaper. He continues the neighbouring wall-plane and even some of the moulded courses, but brings the whole frontage to life with purposefully distorted symmetry, e.g. with balanced but dissimilar bay-windows. No orders; all the detail rather blunt and smooth except where there is a special point to be made, e.g. with the flared iron balconies, the tightly patterned glazing and the central timber porch with intricate early Renaissance carving. The interior continues this theme in Franco-Italian vein. Walnut-panelled entrance hall, with a scroll-pedimented chimneypiece of red and white marble. In the dining room at the back an oak dado with round brass display frames, a two-stage chimneypiece and a bay-window with stained glass. Beamed ceiling, with a plaster frieze of putti. Square staircase, entered through an arcade, the steps marble, the balusters wrought brass and the newels walnut, carved as shield-bearing griffons. Upstairs, the drawing room with a bay-window is again at the back, the ceiling painted with astrological symbols and rural scenes. Two chimney-pieces, one Italian Renaissance in alabaster and coloured stones by *Farmer & Brindley*, the other less formal, of ma-

125

---

* Mitchell had just left Anderson & Browne to set up on his own.

hogany in an arched recess. In the morning room more mahogany, in the library (at the front) cedar. The rear rooms survey the Dean valley, with Findlay's personal townscape of Well Court (also by Mitchell, *see* Dean: Dean Village) nestling at the bottom.

The rest of Rothesay Terrace is by *John Watherston & Sons*. Nos. 4–6 keep up something of the style of No. 3, and Nos. 7–8 (after an awkward gap) at least maintain the scale. By now the terrace has become a shallow crescent and the other houses, started in 1898, show many lapses in discipline. At No. 13 some interior work by *Lorimer*, executed by *Scott Morton & Co.* Nos. 19–24 are a six-storey block of flats, 1906–7, designed from the start with a lift.

RUTLAND PLACE, RUTLAND STREET AND RUTLAND SQUARE

A secluded square with a monumental entry from the busy West End. *Archibald Elliot* made the plan for James Stuart in 1819, drawing palace-fronted elevations for Rutland Street. John Learmonth bought the ground in 1825 and developed it from 1830. His architect *John Tait* adopted Elliot's giant pilaster motif (Corinthian for a change) at the entry; it looks old-fashioned despite its crisp detail. RUTLAND PLACE begins with the former St Thomas's Church (*see* Churches, above). Then a four-bay pilastrade with an attic, joined by a plain bow (the original plain shops underneath) to the pilastered end-pavilion of RUTLAND STREET. This N side of the street is still fairly complete despite some Neo-Norman remodelling for the back of the church. Five-bay pavilion fronts with the same unfluted pilasters, the centre three bays breaking forward under a single-windowed attic; the houses between them bold and astylar (Elliot's centrepiece omitted) with big consoles at the doors, continuous trellis balconies and balustraded parapet. More than half the S side was replaced by the Caledonian Hotel and Station (*see* South West, Lothian Road), but at the entrance to RUTLAND SQUARE the original pavilions are returned with a five-bay pilastrade and a three-bay attic, the flanking houses quite plain except for the wide architraves characteristic of Tait. On the N and S sides three-storey houses with Ionic porches, the end ones slightly advanced. On the W the pavilions are tenements. Advanced five-bay centrepiece; no giant order, but an Ionic ground-floor colonnade linked to the flanking porches and standing forward from them. More emphasis is given by balustrades, and more still (unhappily) by an extra storey added to the middle house by *F. W. Deas*, 1907. Most of the interiors are above-average neo-Greek with plenty of coffered ceilings; Nos. 14 and 15 in the square by *Tait* himself, No. 16 by *William Burn*.

SHANDWICK PLACE

Very little is left of the original Georgian terraces, and this is now the most Victorian of Edinburgh's commercial streets, with as much variety as any in central Glasgow. If both Edinburgh scholarship and Glasgow inventiveness are lacking, it is because this slightly off-centre street did not demand first-rate architecture. But of commercial show there is plenty.

N SIDE. On the Queensferry Street corner the former Commercial Bank* (with the Caledonian United Services Club above) by *Sydney Mitchell & Wilson*, 1901. Serried Gibbsian windows, big shaped gables and a pimple of a dome at the angle, the ground floor redesigned in red granite by *Tarbolton & Ochterlony*, 1938-40. At Nos. 6-8 a narrow bay-windowed front by *Robert Paterson*, 1880, solidly classical in a Glasgow 1840s manner and quite unsuited by *John McLaren*'s top-floor arcade of 1896. The curious frontage of No. 18, with a wide-arched first-floor window and huge blind balustrade at the top, is by *George Fortune*, 1894. ALBERT BUILDINGS at Nos. 22-30, built as the Albert Gallery in 1876-7 for selling the works of contemporary artists, are by *Hamilton Beattie* (by this time no longer an artist himself), with a swagged entablature and a Frenchy roof. In the conversion soon after, by *Frank Simon* for the Army & Navy Stores, the three-domed saloon was lost but the entrance kept. Bas-relief of Prince Albert in the pediment, a thistly shield on top, and life-size figures of Painting and Poetry by *Mrs D. O. Hill* sitting on the ends. No. 32 with its broad front and two shallow bays is by *MacGibbon & Ross*, 1887. Painted compo, slightly Jacobean with a broken pedimented gable, but the slender construction and generous glazing suggest some knowledge of contemporary American fashion. Then some remnants of *James Tait*'s original Shandwick Place; Nos. 34-36 formed part of the centrepiece, and Nos. 38-50 were given an extra storey, with a fancy iron parapet and mansard roof, by *W. Hamilton Beattie* in 1873. Finally at Nos. 52-56 a well detailed Victorian Renaissance block with pedimented stone dormers over bay-windows, by the minor master *John McLachlan*, 1878 - a good neighbour to St George's West Church (*see* above).

S SIDE (formerly Maitland Street). First an original house-block, somewhat altered and conspicuously lacking the chimneystack from its E gable. Nos. 13-23 are also basically original, reconstructed in 1880 by *Robert Morham* with window trimmings and segmental pediments. The former Wylie & Lochhead building at Nos. 25-27 is by the Edinburgh building firm of *William Turner & Sons*, 1905, lean classical, with two storeys of display windows. Much more entertaining the

---

*The telling room of 1940 with a painted ceiling by *Henry Lintott* (Scottish industry, a cherub scattering the bank's customers with gold coin) was altered in 1981.

MAITLAND HOTEL by *MacGibbon & Ross* in painted compo, 1876, its florid centre combining Romanesque and Renaissance motifs and rising between bay-windows to a pilastered attic and a still higher gablet. At No. 45 the upper storeys of an original house. WILKIES (Nos. 53–61) has an Art Deco front by *Reid & Forbes*, 1937, beautifully executed in ashlar, with a recessed centre bay and fanciful metalwork. In 1979 the canopy underneath it was removed and the overall symmetry lost by moving the entrance to one side. Another original house at Nos. 63–65, almost lost behind a glazed outshot of 1913. Top floor still later. Nos. 67–81 are united by *J. R. McKay*'s long shopfront of 1924 extended by *Cowie & Hardie* in 1937 (both for Frosts). Of the upper parts the first is by *William Bell*, 1879, with chip-carved bay-windows, the second by *P. R. McLaren*, plain Scots Classical of 1901 which could quite well be of the mid C19 except for the red sandstone balustrade on top. Nos. 85–87 are also of red stone, a debased version of Washington Browne's François I manner by *R. Thornton Shiells & Thomson*, 1889. The symmetrical Renaissance block at Nos. 89–93 by *W. F. Rollo-Wilkie*, 1896, closes the s end of Stafford Street well enough but the detail is thin. At the far w end the original block, its ground floor built out as shops, terminates the street at the entry to Atholl Crescent.

STAFFORD STREET

A street of middling status and much charm leading up to the grand frontage of No. 25 Melville Street. Built mainly in 1819–24, but begun a decade earlier when Cockburn Ross developed the SE corner (now the site of St George's West, *see* above) as part of his Shandwick Place scheme. Neat two-storey terraces, the rusticated ground floors obscured here and there by shops built out over the areas. The junction half-way along has four corner pavilions rising higher, with cheerful pediments, and the slightly crooked entry from Alva Street gives the whole thing an informal nudge.

Stafford Street was developed jointly by Sir Patrick Walker and the Erskine Trustees. Which of their architects designed it? Probably *Robert Brown*, for Gillespie Graham's Alva Street (designed in 1823) is pompous and stand-offish.

SUTHERLAND STREET *see* DEVON PLACE

TORPHICHEN STREET *see* WEST MAITLAND STREET

WALKER STREET

The central cross-axis of Robert Brown's scheme, the part s of Melville Street built in 1822–7, the shorter N part in 1827–

45. Two-storey houses, the crowning balustrades often replaced by attics. At William Street the corners are marked
with three-storey houses, slightly advanced, but the main
junctions have full-dress corner pavilions. *John Lessels*'s two
pavilions at the far N end are curiously inconsistent, the W
one (1862) simplified, the E one (1874) taller, to match
Drumsheugh Gardens.

WEST CATHERINE PLACE *see* DEVON PLACE

WEST COATES AND WESTER COATES

The ground to the W and immediately to the S of Donaldson's
Hospital (*see* Public Buildings, above) was developed with
large suburban villas from *c.* 1850 under the general control
of successive Heriot Trust surveyors, who may sometimes
have influenced their design. In WEST COATES itself Nos. 1–
6 on the N side (mainly Jacobethan and baronial) were built
under *Alexander Black*, who died in 1858. No. 7, large and
plain, shows the influence of his successor *John Chesser*. The
three 'terraces' on the S side were similarly developed in the
1860s. In OSBORNE TERRACE Nos. 14–17 have been recast
as a symmetrical composition by *A. E. Horsfield*, 1923, and
the GENERAL ACCIDENT building is by *Morris & Steedman*,
1961, precast concrete with tall, frequent mullions. For the
former Roseburn Free Church in Hampton Terrace *see*
Churches, above. For the working-class housing by the railway to the S, *see* Devon Place.

Villa development to the N of West Coates, inhibited for a time
by the building of the railway along its outer edge in 1860,
revived in 1896 under another Heriot Trust Surveyor, *Donald
A. Gow.* In WESTER COATES ROAD No. 6 (REDMOUNT) is
by *Henry F. Kerr*, 1896, red sandstone baronial with an octagonal entrance turret in the angle, round ones on the S
gable. In WESTER COATES AVENUE No. 2, Scottish Renaissance with a Gibbsian doorpiece, again by *Kerr*, 1899. No. 6,
a broad house with bits of half-timbering, by *Marshall &
Dick*, 1897. No. 14, L-plan, with piend roofs and shaped
dormers, by *Thomas T. Paterson*, 1899. No. 27 by *McArthy
& Watson*, 1905, with a nice pedimented doorpiece. WESTER
COATES GARDENS starts with No. 1 by *T. Duncan Rhind*,
1907, harled Arts-and-Crafts with a red-tiled roof. Nos. 7–9
ambitious Neo-Jacobean by *John Watherston & Sons*, 1906.
In the crescent on the N side they also designed (and meticulously built) No. 8 with rubble masonry and leaded lights.
More half-timbering at No. 6, by *Archibald Macpherson*,
1906.

WEST MAITLAND STREET, MORRISON STREET AND TORPHICHEN STREET

James Haldane's Morrison development (1825) is elegant but unlucky, its severe Neo-Greek palace-fronts unbalanced or incomplete, and many of the rusticated ground floors obscured by later shops. On the S side of WEST MAITLAND STREET (mainly of 1828-9) a six-bay anta centrepiece and well composed pavilions with paired antae. The intermediate houses on the E side, built earlier, are not a good match. To the W the same double antae are used to flank the semicircular bow facing Haymarket, but this splendid marker of the entry to the town centre is spoiled by ground-floor projections. Round the corner in MORRISON STREET, large astylar blocks merge into a palace-front with a particularly blank and blatant pub-front under the pedimented centrepiece. The design goes no further. To the E, an awkward change of scale at the entry to TORPHICHEN STREET. Two pavilions here (one upset by an irrelevant Victorian porch at No. 12), and then the pavilion and centrepiece of another frustrated palace-front, all four with regularly placed antae but each, as it happens, with a different number of them. Two office blocks of impoverished design do not help, the one at the E end by the *Covell Matthews Partnership*, 1964. For the turreted Torphichen Education Centre on the N side *see* Public Buildings, above.

WILLIAM STREET

1824-5, presumably by *Robert Brown*. A street of shops and artisan flats (equivalent to Rose Street in the First New Town) between Coates Crescent and Melville Street, its E half at an odd angle in order to meet the awkwardly aligned Alva Street. Nothing elaborate; four rectangular three-storey terraces of droved ashlar with open ends for access to the lanes behind, though the E terraces are joined to the corner pavilions of Stafford Street. In this half the N side (Nos. 5-31) is very like Brown's exactly contemporary design in St Stephen Street (*see* Stockbridge), with basement areas, small iron balconies for window-shoppers and a fascia and cornice over the shops. The S side (Nos. 6-26) has no basement, and the shops have no cornice. In the W half the shops on the N side (Nos. 33-51) have not only a fascia and cornice but a proper pilastrade; those on the S (Nos. 28-36) have basement areas but only a plain fascia. The shopfronts, with few exceptions, are remarkably well preserved.

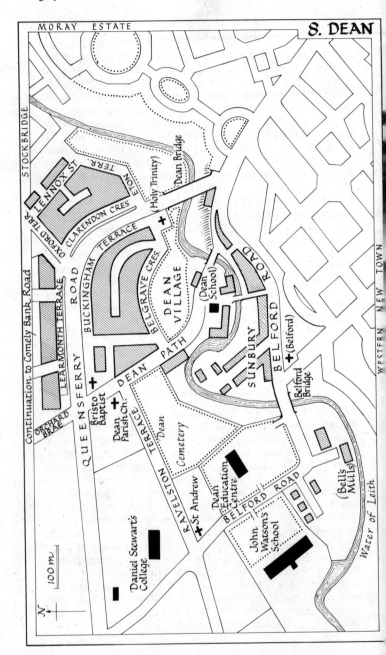

8. DEAN

MORAY ESTATE

STOCKBRIDGE

OXFORD TERR

LENNOX ST

ESTON TERR

CLARENDON CRES

(Holy Trinity)

Dean Bridge

Continuation to Comely Bank Road

ORCHARD BRAE

LEARMONTH TERRACE

QUEENSFERRY ROAD

BUCKINGHAM TERRACE

BELGRAVE CRES

DEAN VILLAGE

DEAN PATH

Bristo Baptist

Dean Parish Ch.

TERRACE

Dean

RAVELSTON

Cemetery

St Andrew

Dean Education Centre

BELFORD ROAD

John Watson's School

Daniel Stewart's College

100 m

N

(Dean School)

SUNBURY

BELFORD ROAD

(Belford)

Belford Bridge

(Bell's Mills)

Water of Leith

WESTERN NEW TOWN

1. *South Side and Old Town*
from Holyrood Park: on the
skyline the McEwan Hall, Castle,
Tolbooth Church, University
Old Quad dome, St Giles' crown,
Tron Church

2. *Old Town*: Bakehouse Close, Canongate, 1648, restored 1927–32

4. *Old Town*: High Street, St G
and late Georgian teneme

3. *Old Town*: the Royal Mile running down from the Castle to the
Palace of Holyroodhouse

5. *Old Town*: West Bow,
seventeenth-century tenements
early eighteenth-century houses at
entry from Grassma

6. *Old Town and New Town*: Lawnmarket, the Mound and Princes Street (1959, before the loss of the nineteenth-century New Club and Life Association buildings in Princes Street)

7. *First New Town*:
George Street from St Andrew Square

8. *Leith*: Bernard Street,
Burns statue and north side

9. *Calton*: Waterloo Place
by Archibald Elliot, 1815

10. *Dean*: Well Court
by Sydney Mitchell & Wilson, 1883–6

11. *Duddingston*: the loch and
seventeenth-century Parish Church tower

12. St Margaret's Chapel at the Castle, early twelfth century

13. Holyrood Abbey from the south-east (photo *c.* 1900)

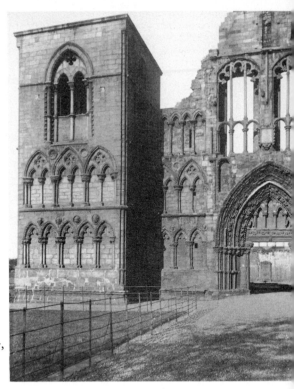

15. Holyrood Abbey, the nave, thirteenth century, terminated by east window of 1633 (photo *c*. 1900)

. Holyrood Abbey, the west front, early thirteenth
ntury with seventeenth-century embellishments
hoto *c.* 1900)

16. St Giles, High Street, from the north-east,
the crown spire late fifteenth century,
the remainder re-cased 1829

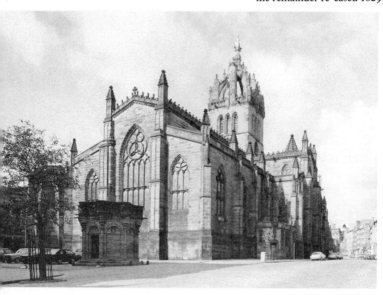

17. St Giles,
the Albany Aisle,
early fifteenth century

18. Trinity College Church, Chalmers Close, late fifteenth to early sixteenth century (engraving showing original location from R. W. Billings, *Baronial and Ecclesiastical Antiquities*, 1847)

19. Trinity College Church, capital of fifteenth-century fireplace from demolished house

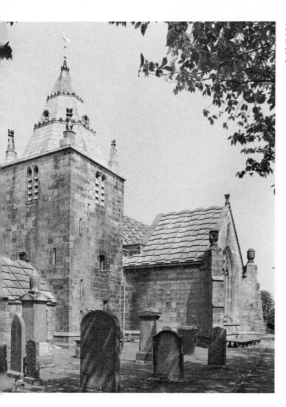

20. Corstorphine Parish Church, fifteenth century with later additions

21. St Triduana's Chapel, Restalrig Parish Church, c. 1477–87, undercroft

22. St Ninian's Manse, Leith,
the belfry of 1675

24. Greyfriars Church,
Candlemaker Row,
west gable, 1718-21

25. Magdalen Chapel, Cowgate, interior

3. Tron Church, High Street,
John Mylne, 1636-46,
duced 1785

26. Canongate Church, Canongate, by James Smith, 1688-91

27. Canongate Church, Canongate

28. St Andrew and St George's Church, George Street, by Major Andrew Frazer, 1782-7

29. West Register House (former St George's Church), Charlotte Square, by Robert Reid, 1811

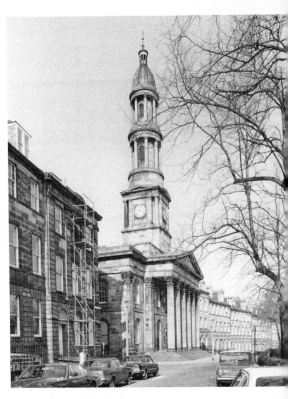

30. St Mary,
Bellevue Crescent,
by Thomas Brown,
1824

31. St Mary, Bellevue Crescent, by Thomas Brown, 1824

32. St John's Episcopal Church, Princes Street, by William Burn, 1815

33. St Paul's and St George's Episcopal Church, York Place, by Archibald Elliot, 1816

34. Newhaven
Parish Church,
Craighall Road, by
John Henderson,
1836

35. Liberton Parish Church, Kirkgate,
by James Gillespie Graham, 1815

36. Tolbooth Church, Castlehill, by James Gillespie Graham and A. W. N. Pugin, 1839

37. St Mark's Unitarian Church, Castle Terrace, by David Bryce, 1834

38. Mayfield Church,
Mayfield Road,
by Hippolyte J. Blanc,
1876

39. St Michael's Parish Church,
Slateford Road, by John Honeyman, 1881

40. Barclay-Bruntsfield Church,
Barclay Place, by F. T. Pilkington, 1862

41. Bellevue Reformed Baptist (former Catholic Apostolic) Church, Mansfield Place, by R. Rowand Anderson, 1872

42. St Michael and All Saints' Episcopal Church, Brougham Street, by R. Rowand Anderson, 1866

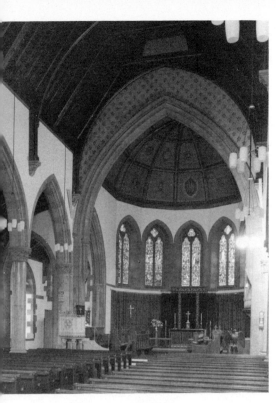

43. St Peter's Episcopal Church, Lutton Place, by William Slater, 1857

44. St Giles, High Street, Thistle Chapel, stall canopies, by Robert Lorimer, 1909

45. St Mary's Episcopal Cathedral, Palmerston Place,
by George Gilbert Scott, 1874

46. St Anne, St John's Road, Corstorphine,
by Peter MacGregor Chalmers, 1912

47. Craigsbank Church, Craigs Bank,
by Rowand Anderson, Kininmonth & Paul, 1964

48. Greyfriars
Churchyard (right to left):
Alexander Miller 1616,
Alexander Beatton by
Robert Mylne, 1674 (half
hidden), John Nasmyth
1614, Richard Doby 1613,
James Struthers *c.* 1807
(by the path), John and
Isaac Morrison 1615,
'Ray's tomb' 1610, George
Heriot by Richard Doby,
1610

49. Greyfriars
Churchyard, early
seventeenth-century
monuments of Byres of
Coates, Henryson, and
Foulis of Ravelston

50. Greyfriars Churchyard,
Mackenzie Mausoleum, 1691

51. Greyfriars Churchya
Bayne of Pitcarley enclosure, 1

53. Old Calton Burying Ground,
David Hume Monument
by Robert Adam, 1777

52. Calton Hill,
Playfair Monument
by W. H. Playfair,
1825, National
Monument by
W. H. Playfair and
C. R. Cockerell,
1824, Nelson
Monument by
Robert Burn, 1807

54. Calton Hill, Dugald
Stewart's Monument
by W. H. Playfair, 1831

Register House,
llington Monument
John Steell, 1848

West Princes Street Gardens, Royal Scots
Greys Monument by Birnie Rhind

57. Edinburgh Castle from the north-east
   a. Gatehouse
   b. Portcullis Gate
   c. St Margaret's Chapel
   d. Half Moon Battery
   e. Palace
   f. Great Hall
   g. Scottish United Service
      Museum
   h. Scottish National War
      Memorial
   j. Cisterns
   k. Military Prison
   l. New Barracks
   m. Governor's House
   n. Hospital
   o. Tearoom

58. Edinburgh Castle,
Portcullis Gate,
c. 1577

59. Edinburgh Castle, Great Hall roof,
early sixteenth century

60. Craigmillar Castle,
fifteenth to seventeenth century

61. Castle Gogar, 1625

62. Palace of Holyroodhouse from the north-west,
the north-west tower 1528,
the remainder with the south-west tower
by Sir William Bruce, 1671

63. Palace of Holyroodhouse,
ceiling of West Drawing Room, 1674

64. Caroline Park House,
West Granton Road,
south front, c. 1693

65. Prestonfield House, Priestfield Road, c. 1685

66. The Drum, Gilmerton, by William Adam, 1726

67. The Drum, Gilmerton, plasterwork by Samuel Calderwood in the hall

68. Gayfield House, East London Street, built by
Charles and William Butter, wrights, 1765

69. Duddingston House, Milton Road West,
by William Chambers, 1763

70. Muirhouse, Marine Drive,
by R. & R. Dickson, 1830

71. Lauriston Castle, Cramond Road South,
late sixteenth century,
extended by William Burn, 1827

72. Southfield (Hospital), Lasswade Road,
by John Chesser, 1875

73. Kingston Clinic,
Kingston Avenue,
by Frederick T. Pilkington,
1867

74. Canongate Tolbooth, Canongate, 1591

75. Parliament House, Parliament Square, roof by John Scott, 1637

76. George Heriot's School, Lauriston Place,
begun by William Wallace, 1628

77. George Heriot's School,
Lauriston Place,
the main (north) entrance

79. Register House, Waterloo Place,
by Robert Adam, 1774

80. University of Edinburgh
Old Quad, South Bridge,
by Robert Adam, 1789

81. Assembly Rooms, George Street,
by John Henderson, 1782,
the portico added by William Burn, 1817

82. University of
Edinburgh upper
library, Old Quad,
South Bridge, by
W. H. Playfair, 1819

83. Customs House, Commercial
Street, Leith, by Robert Reid, 1810

84. Law Courts,
Parliament Square,
upper vestibule of
the Signet Library

85. Parliament Square, by Robert Reid, 1803–38

86. John Watson's School, Belford Road, by William Burn, 1825

87. Royal High School, Regent Road, by Thomas Hamilton, 1825

88. Royal Scottish Academy, by W.H. Playfair, 1822 and 1831

89. Royal College of Physicians, Queen Street, by Thomas Hamilton, 1844

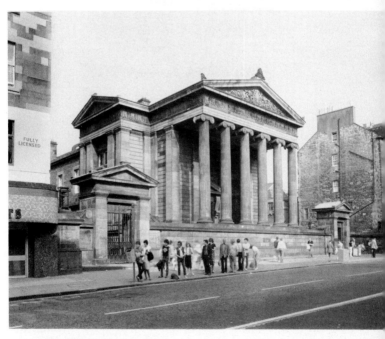

90. Surgeons' Hall, Nicolson Street, by W. H. Playfair, 1829

93. Fettes College, East Fettes Aven by David Bryce, 1

91. Dean Education Centre, Belford Road, by Thomas Hamilton, 1831

92. Donaldson's School, West Coates, by W. H. Playfair, 1841

94. Dr Bell's
School, Great
Junction Street,
Leith, by R. & R.
Dickson, 1839

95. Boroughmuir School, Viewforth,
by J. A. Carfrae, 1911

96. Royal Scottish Museum, Chambers Street, by Francis Fowke, 1861

97. Royal Scottish Museum, Chambers Street, by Francis Fowke, 1861

98. McEwan Hall, Teviot Place,
by R. Rowand Anderson, 1888

99. Edinburgh,
Central Public
Library, George IV
Bridge, by George
Washington
Browne, 1887

101. University of
Edinburgh Library,
George Square, by
Basil Spence,
Glover & Ferguson,
1965

102. Royal
Commonwealth
Pool, Dalkeith
Road, by Robert
Matthew, Johnson-
Marshall &
Partners, 1967

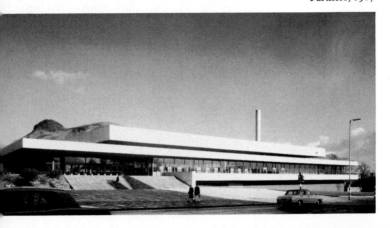

103. No. 45 George Street (formerly Blackwood's office) by Thomas Hamilton, 1829

104. St Stephen Street, two-level shopfronts, 1824

105. Café Royal, West Register Street, Oyster Bar, by J. Macintyre Henry, 1900

106. Jenners, Princes Street, by W. Hamilton Beattie, 1893

107. Royal (former Commercial) Bank of Scotland,
George Street, by David Rhind, 1843

108. Bank of
Scotland (former
British Linen
Bank), St Andrew
Square, by David
Bryce, 1846

109. Bank of Scotland, George Street, by J. M. Dick Peddie, 1883

110. Standard Life Assurance Co. extension, phase one, George Street, by Michael Laird, 1964

111. Gladstone's Land, Lawnmarket, stone frontage of c. 1621

112. Lamb's House, Water's Close, Leith, early seventeenth century

113. John Knox House, High Street, sixteenth century

114. Moray House, Canongate, *c.* 1625

115. George Square, laid out by
James Brown, 1766, the west side

116. Dundas House (now Royal Bank of Scotland),
St Andrew Square, by William Chambers, 1771

117. Charlotte Square, by Robert Adam, 1791, centrepiece on the north side

118. Castle Street, bow windows on the east side, late eighteenth century

119. Heriot Row, by Robert Reid, 1802 (second floor added between centrepiece and east pavilion)

120. Drummond Place by Robert Reid, 1804

121. Royal Circus
by W. H. Playfair, 1820

122. Moray Place
by James Gillespie
Graham, 1822

123. St Bernard's Crescent by James Milne, 1824

124. Royal Terrace by W. H. Playfair, 1821

125. No. 3 Rothesay Terrace
by Sydney Mitchell,
1883

126. Grosvenor Crescent by John Chesser, 1869

127. Blacket Place, *c.* 1830

128. Lammerburn,
Napier Road,
by James Gowans,
1860

129. Rustic Cottages, Colinton Road, by Robert Lorimer, 1900

130. No. 53
Pentland Terrace
by John Gordon &
Bennet Dobson,
1904

131. Moncreiff
Terrace, housing by
Nicholas Groves-
Raines, 1979

132. Nos. 65-67 Ravelston Dykes Road by Morris & Steedman, 1960

8. DEAN

The Dean estate was bought for development by John Learmonth from the Nisbets of Dean in 1825. As Lord Provost he
had in the previous year proposed a high-level bridge for improved access to this ground and to Queensferry. He obtained
plans from *James Jardine* in 1825 and *Gillespie Graham* in 1828,
but when the Cramond Road Trustees agreed to help with the
cost it was on condition that the bridge should be designed by
Telford, and free of tolls. It was built in 1831-2, largely paid
for by Learmonth. The Orphan Hospital Trustees immediately
took ground for their new building close by John Watson's
School, the Western Cemetery Company bought Dean House
and its neighbouring park in 1845, and Daniel Stewart's Trust
purchased their site in 1847. So the w half of the Dean estate
became a territory of 'pauper palaces' and woodland, an entirely
happy outcome. In the E half Learmonth had hoped for a quick
return on the capital spent on the bridge from a housing development like Lord Moray's. In this he was disappointed and
most of the ground was sold to the Heriot Trust who eventually
developed it. The only Learmonth scheme was that which bears
the family name to the N of Queensferry Road. Even Learmonth
Terrace was not finished, and no elevational designs were enforced to the N of it. In 1894 the 33 ha. running downhill to
Comely Bank were sold to the builder James Steel. Despite
some recent intrusions along Queensferry Road, the Dean estate
still provides a green, uncluttered prelude to the dramatic
high-level entry over the Dean Bridge; it contributes to the
city's fantastic skyline as seen from the w and N; and its houses
show the beginning and the best maturity of Victorian terrace
design in Edinburgh, unembarrassed by a formal Georgian layout.

CHURCHES

BRISTO BAPTIST CHURCH, Queensferry Road, Buckingham
Terrace and Dean Path. Large and bold in a thrifty
Scandinavian-cum-Dutch-Colonial style (harled walls enriched with stone-carving) by *William Paterson* of *Oldrieve,
Bell & Paterson*, 1932-5. In plan it is an obtuse L to fit the
road pattern, the tall shaped gable of the church looking
downhill, with an arcaded and Corinthian-columned porch
and a lofty High Renaissance window, the hall standing back
in line with Buckingham Terrace. Gabled porch in the angle.
The Dean Path entrance is in a shaped gable, effectively or-

namented with a stone cartouche from the previous church of
1836. Simple interior with a coombed ceiling and marble bap-
tismal tank. Flat-shouldered arch splayed into the Art Deco
organ-screen. – ORGAN by *D. & T. Hamilton*, 1888, for the
St James Place Church (*see* First New Town, St Mary's R. C.
Cathedral), rebuilt by *J. J. Binns* in 1907, and rebuilt here by
C. P. Scovell, 1935.

DEAN FREE CHURCH, Belford Road and Douglas Gardens.
Now in secular use. Free Gothic in red sandstone by *Sydney
Mitchell & Wilson*, 1888, skilfully fitted into a steeply falling
corner site and an important element in the townscape from
near and far, e.g. in the view from Bell's Mills. The basement
area is bridged (the halls are underneath) to reach a handsome
double portal with a burning-bush tympanum. Unbuttressed
tower above, terminated by two intricate octagonal stages, the
lower with flying buttresses, the upper with a red-tiled conical
roof. Five-bay nave with continuous clearstorey windows between the buttresses. S aisle of only three bays, for the E end
of the church comes up against the neighbouring houses.
Three-sided apse to the E. Excellently proportioned and detailed interior. Nave arcade with alternate round and octagonal piers and moulded capitals. Clustered and corbelled
wall-shafts support the hammerbeams of the timber-lined
roof. – MEMORIAL in the porch, moved from St Cuthbert's
Free Church in Spittal Street in 1911. Marble Gothic tablet
with a relief portrait of Sir Henry Wellwood Moncrieff †
1883, by *Hippolyte J. Blanc*. – STAINED GLASS. In the apse,
two lights to the S (War Memorial, with Madonna and soldiers) and two to the N (Magdalen anointing Christ's feet), in
the N transept two more (the Good Shepherd and the Sower),
all by the *Bromsgrove Guild* in the early 1920s; stippled
colours and beautiful drawing.

DEAN PARISH CHURCH, Dean Path and Ravelston Terrace.
1902–3 by *Dunn & Findlay* to replace an established church
of 1835–6. Quite ambitious, in rough-faced yellow-grey stone
with the red stone dressings predominating, the detail from
Scottish rather than English sources. Cruciform, with a shallow chancel and piend-roofed halls at the W end. E front
of Dunblane type, its ample width cleverly narrowed with
gabled buttresses (repeated at the SE porch). On the NE tower
(with another doorway) single lancets at the belfry stage and
then a pinnacled stone spire, rather bald and hesitant.
   Interior handsome in proportion if sparse in detail. Wide
nave with timber wagon-vault and plastered clearstorey over
four-bay arcades. The mouldings die into octagonal piers.
Moulded capitals at the chancel arch and twin arches of the
galleried transepts. In the big chancel window Y-tracery of
Aberdeen Greyfriars type over a blind arcade. – ORGAN by
Charles & Frederick Hamilton, 1903. – STAINED GLASS. In
the chancel window, providing just the required focus of
colour and interest, three lights (Christ appearing to the Magdalen) of *Morris & Co.* type, but not known to be theirs, after

1908. – Four lancets in the N transept (SS. Mark, Luke, Peter and Paul), 1962, and two in the S (SS. John and Mungo), 1949, by *William Wilson*. – In the S aisle a lancet (the Good Shepherd) and two further lights as a War Memorial (Abraham and David), all of 1947–8, by *R. Douglas McLundie* of the *Abbey Studio*. – WAR MEMORIAL TABLET in the S aisle by *Reginald Fairlie*, 1922.

HOLY TRINITY (Episcopal), Dean Bridge, Queensferry Road. Preserved as an electricity transformer station without drastic change, so its original designation is justified. Neo-Perp by *John Henderson*, 1837–8, an important landmark with a good but not very original pinnacled profile, raised to the level of the bridge by a cloistral arcade like that of St John, Princes Street. The rest derived from Barry's early churches (e.g. All Saints at Stand, Lancashire, 1822). Five-bay rectangle with a twin-lanceted tower flanked by high staircase projections. The main differences are that the tall archway at the bottom of the tower is not recessed in Barry fashion but filled in with a door and window, and that the tracery is of wood. In 1900 *John Robertson* extended the very shallow chancel, giving it quite unsuitably three thickly moulded lancets and a vesica in a depressed arch. In 1909 *Dunn & Findlay* proposed to correct the orientation of the church and insert stone arcades, but neither was done. In 1957 the South of Scotland Electricity Board removed the galleries and cast-iron arcades. – STAINED GLASS. Three superb lights (the Ascension) by *Henry Holiday*, 1899–1900. The rest by *Ballantine*, 1860s. Holiday's enamel-work altarpiece is now in St David, Boswall Parkway (*see* Outer Area, Granton, Churches).

PUBLIC BUILDINGS

BELFORD BRIDGE AND DEAN BRIDGE. Low- and high-level bridges over the Water of Leith. Belford Bridge is by the engineers *Blyth & Cunningham*, 1885–7. One large semicircular arch between pilaster buttresses with panels of the city arms. Red granite crenellations and other mildly castellated details. The Dean Bridge (for its planning *see* above) is by *Thomas Telford*, 1829–31, and one of his boldest masonry designs, with a total length of 136 m. made up of four segmental arches of 29 m. span carrying the road 32 m. above the river bed. Footpaths borne on very flat segmental arches springing from slim panelled piers attached to the main ones, the same elegant formula that Telford had used for the smaller road-bridge at Pathhead, Midlothian (1827). Castellated approaches and decorative spandrel panels were planned but not executed. Parapets made higher in 1912, hiding the view but making it more difficult to jump off.

DANIEL STEWART'S AND MELVILLE COLLEGE (originally Daniel Stewart's College), Queensferry Road. Abundantly towered and turreted Jacobethan by *David Rhind*, 1848, set grandly back from its axially sited lodge and double gateway. Stewart died in 1814, and on the death of his niece in 1845 the Trustees had accumulated £80,000 for the building of the school. Rhind, chosen on the strength of his Commercial Bank in George Street (*see* First New Town), produced three schemes on the same basic plan* but in different styles: Italian, Westminster Palace Gothic (for which the drawings still exist) and the one that was chosen.

Basically it is of two storeys on a U-plan, the forecourt cut off by an arcaded screen. In the middle twin lodges with octagonal pinnacles and canted bay-windows; the doorway between them is the focus of the whole thing, in which the (English) Elizabethan predominates over the (Scottish) Jacobean. Twin staircase towers rise from the internal angles of the court, the top stage set back between corner bartizans, all with ogee lead roofs. Copious detail, with canted bays, hood-moulds, and mullions and transoms diverting the attention from shortcomings in compositon. The silhouette is magnificent, greatly enhanced by its elevated setting on a terrace above the road, where a central lodge stands between two gates on the entry axis. WAR MEMORIAL on the same axis, an obelisk with bronze panels by *William C. Laidlaw*, 1921.

In 1972 *Rowand Anderson, Kininmonth & Paul* made a good job of remodelling the HALL which *MacGibbon & Ross* had formed by roofing the forecourt in 1894; it is now quite an effective foil to Rhind's work. Former entrance hall and stair-halls quite simple, with coffered ceilings. At the centre of the upper corridor the WAR MEMORIAL (formerly ante-chapel) of 1934, lined with Lorimerian Gothic panelling designed by *C. E. Tweedie & Sons* and executed by *Nathaniel Grieve & Co*. Stained glass of saints by *Margaret Chilton & Marjorie Kemp*. The LIBRARY projecting from the rear of the building was originally the chapel. Seven-bay roof of angel hammerbeams effectively coloured in black, red and gold by *Basil Spence*. Many furnishings are still *in situ*: *Rhind*'s gallery front with painted shields, and *Tweedie*'s panelling, stall-work and pulpit canopy of 1932. Armorial stained glass, again by *Chilton & Kemp*. Gothic tablets flanking the s window, including one to Longmore † 1849. The other first-floor rooms were originally dormitories.

ART HALL to the W of the main building, 1908–9 by *George Washington Browne* in a slightly updated version of Rhind's Jacobethan, a turreted three-bay, one-storey rectangle with canted bays flanking the E entrance. Later C20 buildings, of varying style and quality, encroach undesirably at the SE on the original layout.

DANIEL STEWART'S BOARDING HOUSE, Queensferry Road, to the W of the College. Formerly Dean Park House by *Frederick T. Pilkington* in his later (Second Empire) style, 1874,

---

*A smaller version of Playfair's 1835 scheme for Donaldson's School (*see* Western New Town, Public Buildings).

for the geologist, S. L. Jolly. Jolly had feued the ground from
the College, who in 1962–3 bought it back and converted the
house to its present use. It is Pilkington's best work in this
manner, ably worked up from good pattern-books, set in a
smallish garden but swaggeringly large in scale, dwarfing its
immediate neighbour (the quite substantial villa built for the
headmaster in 1865, now a hotel). On the N front a big central
bow with a slated dome, arcaded on both levels. Upper arches
with *trompe l'œil* splays and coupled Corinthianesque columns. Very elaborate end bays, and a parapet of bold curvaceous profile overall, with ball finials and dormers.

The interior has been modified but there is still plenty to
see. Pilastered porte-cochère with massive doors, now used as
a room with lowered ceiling and raised floor. Recessed front
door flanked by huge urns. T-plan HALL, intact. A wide corridor, with more Corinthianesque pilasters and richly consoled cornice, opens under an arch into a colossal imperial
staircase with carved scrollwork balustrades ending in winged
dragons, a coved ceiling with consoles (their swags detachable
for cleaning), and a huge Venetian window elaborately
painted with black linear patterns.

The principal rooms have all been changed and their coves
ceiled in. In the DINING ROOM to the W a wide sideboard
recess framed in pearwood, but no longer any chimneypiece.
DRAWING ROOM to the N, its L-plan extending into the bow,
subdivided, but the Louis XV panelling and white marble
chimneypiece with a relief panel of the trial of Charles I,
conventionally late Victorian and perhaps not by Pilkington.
The doorcases throughout, double-leaved for the main rooms,
sustain the larger-than-life quality.

Outside again, the cobbled driveway sweeps through the
porte-cochère and turns a quarter-circle to the former STABLE
BLOCK at No. 3 Queensferry Terrace, large and plain, with
banded masonry faintly reminiscent of Gowans. Bold mullions give some hint of Pilkington's own powers of invention.

DEAN BRIDGE. *See* Belford Bridge.

DEAN CEMETERY. Laid out by *David Cousin* in 1845 on the
policies of Dean House, with much of the sculptured detail
of that notable early C17 mansion built into the S retaining
wall. The S of the twin bowed entrances on Dean Path by
Cousin: good decorative cast-ironwork between piers capped
by pyramids on ball feet. Inside, a neat LODGE, single storey
and attic, with fretted bargeboards and some Tudorish detail.
The cemetery was extended N to Ravelston Terrace in 1871,
and identical gates to Dean Path were built on the axis of the
new N avenue.

This is Edinburgh's nearest approach to Glasgow's Firpark
Necropolis. Although neither so large nor so well endowed
with monuments of an architectural nature, it is richer in
sculpture, particularly bronze portrait reliefs, with *Brodie* and
Hutchison well represented. The only memorial on the full
Glasgow Necropolis scale is that of the Glasgow magnate

James Buchanan, a very fine version of Playfair's choragic monument to Dugald Stewart on Calton Hill, designed and sculptured by *William Brodie* (builder *T. McEwen*), 1860. In it a bust on a channelled base, with a marble bas-relief of a mourning woman and a surrounding balustrade of scrolled foliage.

On the w wall a group of monuments of more than ordinary interest. – William Henry Playfair † 1857 is commemorated in the midst of monuments to his legal friends and employers by an arched recess with a pedestal. – Lord Cockburn † 1854. Three cusped arches with bronze relief portraits (the former clearly not by Playfair). – Lord Rutherfurd † 1852. Peterhead granite pyramid by *Playfair* with a double medallion portrait by *Sir John Steell*. – Lord Jeffrey † 1850. Sarcophagus by *Playfair* with bas-relief portrait. – On the same wall two monuments by *Peddie & Kinnear*, Findlay Anderson's Gothic with three pointed arches in a segmental arch, Auldjo's Jamieson's *Rundbogen* with a good bas-relief of angels. – Also on this wall, an elaborate monument by *John Rhind*, 1872, to John Buchanan, three cusped arches with red Inverness granite shafts and panels.

Impressive monuments in the N extension of 1871, on the axis of the N gate. To the E of the avenue a huge Runic cross to the Nasmyth family, 6·8 m. high, designed and executed by *John Rhind*, 1880. – To the w a colossal plain obelisk to Alexander Russell † 1876, the editor of The Scotsman. – In the same area *J. S. Rhind*'s fussy obelisk of 1906 to Sir James Steel, the house-building tycoon, with a portrait bust flanked by lions. – Practitioners of the arts are well represented and their monuments are generally the most interesting. Robert Reid † 1856. Large slab with a bronze medallion in an arched recess. – Near by Alexander Black † 1858, a massive Classic sarcophagus. – David Scott. Bronze high-relief portrait on a suitably intense Celtic cross design by his brother *William Bell Scott*, 1860. – Thomas Bonnar † 1873. Bronze relief by *W. G. Stevenson*. – Sam Bough, by *William Brodie*, 1879. – James Cassie. A West Highland cross by *Sir George Reid*, 1880. – George Paul Chalmers. Quarter-length marble by *John Hutchison*, 1880. – John Lessels † 1883. Small and weird, with a domical top. – D. O. Hill. Bronze bust by his wife *Amelia Paton*, 1886. – T. S. Burnett † 1888 by *John Rhind*.

Others are worth searching out, for example *William Brodie*'s Gothic monument with a huge marble bas-relief on the back for the historian John Hill Burton † 1881, who had commissioned it during his life-time. – Frances Barry † 1850. Depressed Gothic arch with a beautiful marble relief of the girl lying dead, by *Sir John Steell*. – Lord Fraser † 1889. Red stone; very fine early Renaissance of the Kinross–Washington Browne school. – Lord Belhaven and Stenton. A Corinthian-pilastered design by *W. Birnie Rhind*, 1896, with bas-relief angels flanking a roundel (replaced in bronze by

C. d'O. Pilkington Jackson, 1924). – Sir William Fraser, by *A. F. Balfour Paul*, 1900, a small elevated sarcophagus of sandstone based on English Renaissance examples. – Sir Hector Mac-Donald. Red stone Renaissance obelisk with a bronze bust by *W. Birnie Rhind*, 1904. – Captain James Marshall McLaren. Granite, with a fine bronze figure holding a wreath, by *Sir George Frampton*, 1910. – For oddity the honour must go to the monument of John Leishman † 1861 (?), with a tripod of winged lions supporting a pedestal with rams' heads which in turn supports a garlanded column surrounded by pelicans.

In the N part of the cemetery across Ravelston Terrace, added in 1877 but not developed until 1909, fewer monuments of interest. Handsome Renaissance walls and gates and neat single-storey lodge with bow-windows and central chimney by *James Jerdan & Son*, 1910.

DEAN EDUCATION CENTRE (originally the Dean Orphanage), 91 Belford Road. In wooded grounds on the rise to the N of Belford Bridge. Characteristically original work of *Thomas Hamilton*, 1831-3, English Baroque in concept but Neo-Classical in detail, carried out with the utmost precision in Craigleith stone. A single long block of two storeys on a terrace with plain walls and urns. Central steps between scrolls (like inverted consoles) lead up to the tetrastyle Tuscan portico, the wide intercolumniation emphasized by a massive attic in two stages, bearing a clock-face (the clock salvaged from the demolition of the Netherbow Port) on scrolls. At the ends tall pavilions with paired arches confined between the plain corner pilasters. To the rear two strange openwork towers; glimpsed previously over the trees, they may already have mystified the visitor. They mark the twin staircases, for which their lowest stages provide clearstorey light by arched windows. Scrolls and urns initiate the upper stages; four tall octagonal chimney-shafts united by arches. The idea must have come from Vanbrugh, but the late Classical detail is closer to George Dance at Cole Orton and Ashburnham. Other details typify Hamilton and his age, e.g. the proportions of the windows and their glazing, with narrow panes bordering the large ones, accentuating the sharpness of the whole building.

Inside there is predictably less to wonder at, but the monumental theme continues in the entrance hall with its depressed arches and niches on massive ram's-headed and swagged podia. A shallow inner hall, its ceiling filled with a single line of coffers, leads to the corridors (for boys and girls respectively) and the square stair-halls, their great height exaggerated by inward inclination at the clearstorey stage. In Victorian times the W corridor became part of a large hall.

DEAN SCHOOL (now Telford College of Further Education Annexe), Dean Village. Gothic, by *Robert Wilson*, 1874-5, extended by him in 1892. Symmetrical front; a high two-storey block with a central gable and belfry flanked by gablets, and short lower wings, all with piended roofs. A small

triangular-plan janitor's house adjoins Well Court. Apart
from the usual board-school roundel with its sculptured relief
of Education, the detail is all of Wilson's simple chamfer
variety.

FLORA STEVENSON PRIMARY SCHOOL, Comely Bank. Spirited Renaissance in snecked rubble with ashlar dressings, by
John A. Carfrae (nominally by his chief *Robert Wilson*), 1899–
1900. Tall centre block with alternate oval and pedimented
top-floor windows, Venetian-windowed pavilions and a Doric
cupola. Boys' and girls' entrances in the wings, with carved
roundels of Education in deep semicircular pediments.

86 JOHN WATSON'S SCHOOL,* Belford Road. Greek Doric, long
and grey in a half-rural setting, by *William Burn*, 1825. When
Watson died in 1762 he left £5,000 to the Writers to the
Signet for charitable purposes. In 1822, with £110,000 at
their disposal, they obtained an Act of Parliament for a
school, with boarding accommodation, for the fatherless
children of the professional classes. Burn's first design was
for a very plain E-plan building. As carried out, it is a lengthened and refined version of his unexecuted project of 1820
for the remodelling of George Watson's Hospital off Lauriston Place. Two storeys on a basement with square windows
(not the arched ones of the 1820 design). Hexastyle portico
with middle bays recessed into the building. Then five-bay
links and three-bay pavilions, the whole united by a triglyph
entablature. Conventional Smirke classicism in fact, but very
exactly proportioned and executed. In the screen-bay end
elevations of the pavilions the outside bays repeat the pilastered treatment of the front. Astylar centre with two tripartite
windows on ground-floor level. Severe rear elevation in rough
coursed stonework, the hall in the raised centre section.

Absolutely plain inside, but there is much dignity in Burn's
logical and well proportioned plan which follows that of his
Merchant Maiden Hospital (1816, demolished 1935, *see*
South West, Public Buildings, Royal Infirmary). The entrance hall occupies the three centre bays behind the portico.
Niche on each side, flanked by doors in arched recesses, the
inner ones entering the long central corridors. To the rear the
main hall, with a compartmented ceiling and an anta chimneypiece at each end. Twin stair-halls behind the unrecessed
bays of the portico. The first-floor rooms were originally dormitories. Bronze tablet to George Rowe † 1909 with a good
bas-relief head, by *Percy Portsmouth*, 1911.

The building in its park looks like a long country house;
indeed Burn's first scheme for Garscube in 1826 was an Ionic
variant of it. On the road a neat LODGE with a Doric porch
between pedimented gables. Simple gatepiers with original
ironwork. The WINDMILL behind the school to the w was
described as 'old' in 1759 but is probably not earlier than

---

*Converted as the National Gallery of Modern Art, 1981–4. Burn's stairs have
been removed.

1700. About 4 m. in diameter, 7 m. remains of its probable 9 m. height.

PERAMBULATIONS

1. Dean Village

What is now called the Dean Village* was originally the Water of Leith Village, the largest of Edinburgh's milling settlements. Deep in the valley, it developed round the mills that had existed in some form at the time of the foundation of Holyrood Abbey in the reign of David I, and in course of time straggled up Bell's Brae (the approach from the town on the SE) and Dean Path (towards Dean House on the NW), both routes shelved into the steep banks. The old Queensferry Road (now Belford Road) ran along the S bank at a higher level and crossed the river at Bell's Mills. In 1830 the new Dean Bridge carried the flow of traffic (and residential development) across the valley high overhead, but the village continued to flourish until the rise of the giant flourmills of Leith in the late C19. It was kept alive by the tannery which closed in *c.* 1970 and by repeated injections of picturesque architecture, but this also began to decay, and the lead taken by the painter Alexander Zyw in restoring Bell's Brae House in 1946 was only very slowly followed until the 1980s. The character of the village depends less on architectural consistency than on purposeful siting and on countless details from the skyline down to the iron railings and granite setts. Its uniqueness lies in its quiet seclusion in the valley – so remote from the city but so near to its centre.

In the middle of the village a single-arch C18 stone BRIDGE. To the E the large early C19 WEST MILL, the only one still standing and roofed, completely remodelled internally by *Philip Cocker & Partners* for the Link Housing Association in 1972–3. There was a mill here by 1573. In 1734–5 the City sold the Dean mills to the Baxter (Baker) Incorporation, who rebuilt this one from 1805. The names of their Deacon and other officers are recorded on a finely carved wheatsheaf roundel in the SW gable. Externally the best of the surviving Scots burgh grain-mills. Two broad contiguous ranges, four storeys high to the road and five over the twin sluice arches to the Water of Leith, of rust-tinted rubble with droved freestone dressings, the pattern of small squarish openings relieved by round ones. Inside were wooden floors on cast-iron columns and two breastshot wheels, 18 ft in diameter and 12 ft wide (4·3 by 3·6 m.), dismantled in 1937 by the City, who had bought the mill and closed it in 1891 as part of an attempt to reduce pollution in the river. For the former school *see* Public Buildings, above.

---

*The original Dean Village was on the Dean House estate, where Belgrave Mews are now.

10 DAMSIDE leads to the site of the tannery,* a large late-C18 pantiled group cleared in 1976, and to WELL COURT of 1883-6, a picturesque fantasy designed by *Sydney Mitchell* for John R. Findlay to be viewed from the back windows of his house at No. 3 Rothesay Terrace (*see* Western New Town) but also as a benefaction to the Village, then losing its trade to the big new mills elsewhere. The cost was some £14,000. It is a quadrangle of two- and three-roomed flats with a detached community hall (for reading and recreation) and a resident factor's house at the SE corner. Hailes stone with red Corsehill dressings in a small-windowed C17 Scots style, with deep-eaved, romantically profiled roofs of red Broseley tiles. On the N front to Damside a tall shaped gable and a five-storey tower over the pend entry, with a semi-octagonal stair-turret just inside. Most of the flats are in the symmetrical W side, where stair-towers with iron-grilled arches flank the piend-roofed centrepiece. The rest of the court is a picturesque, beautifully composed jumble of crowstepped gables and turrets. Outside, the S range, with a big chimney flanked by tall dormers, is set back from the river on a narrow terrace garden with a miniature bastion wall and a seat under a sloping pentice. Mullioned oriels (inspired by the Earl's Palace at Kirkwall, Orkney) in the hall to the E, at present an architect's office, the inside unaltered except for the slight deepening of the minstrels' gallery at the N end. Within the court the clock-tower, with a timber and lead belfry rather like that of St Ninian's (*see* Leith, Perambulations, North Leith), commands the whole group.

Immediately to the N DEAN PATH BUILDINGS of 1885, also for Findlay, by his son *James L. Findlay* (a former pupil of Mitchell), in the same general style as Well Court but with slated roofs. Stair-turrets on the S (towards Rothesay Terrace), basement areas to the N. The E end is unfinished. At the bottom of DEAN PATH a mixture of new and old by *Ian G. Lindsay & Partners*, 1960–3; No. 4 a smooth rendered block of flats with cantilevered balconies over an (artificial) stone base, No. 6 a later C18 tenement with a stair-tower, No. 8 another replacement with a large stone commemorating its predecessor of 1883, and No. 10 a regular rubble front of the late C18 – all very sensible rather than what is called sensitive. The restorer of the Dean Tannery shop, further up on the S side, carried this principle to excess by lopping off the big chimneys, and with them most of its character. No. 39 was much better restored in 1970, but the gable still shows the scar of the removal of its E extension.

Now for the S bank. Across the iron footbridge (1877) HAWTHORN BUILDINGS by *Dunn & Findlay*, 1895, a harled row built along the slope with a half-timbered top floor and tall red-brick chimneys. Good Scots C17 moulded doorpieces on

---

*This large area is now (1984) being redeveloped with housing by *Smart*, paying lip-service to its location with much repetition of 'vernacular' features.

the N, with shouldered fanlights. Restoration by *Philip Cocker & Partners*, 1978–80, along with an early-C19 block of the same address.* Further along HAWTHORNBANK LANE No. 12, a simple early-C19 cottage to the front but with two more storeys below, showing quite a notable elevation to the river at the back. No. 3, HAWTHORNBANK HOUSE, is by *H. Anthony Wheeler* for himself, 1974, a straightforward harled block with a low-pitch roof and some reasonable admissions of modernity (e.g. the window carried round the corner for the view). At the junction with Bell's Brae, BELL'S BRAE HOUSE, L-plan early-C18, restored by *Basil Spence* for Alexander Zyw in 1946–8, incorporating the adjacent house and altering its elevation with balconies and French windows (with small-pane glazing), again for the sake of the view.

MILLER ROW along the s side of the river was lined with mills. Marr's Mill disappeared in the late C19 and other buildings (including Lindsay's Mill and a number of cottages) in the 1930s and 50s, and the gaunt, close-built character of this bank was lost. Some of it will be regained with a stone-walled office by *Robert Matthew, Johnson-Marshall & Partners*, 1984. At the E end, close under the Dean Bridge, the former squash court (now a factory), by *Cousin, Ormiston & Taylor*, 1913, with a crenellated top, strapwork window-heads and a corbelled pepperpot.

BELL'S BRAE starts near the centre with the splendid four-storey range of Nos. 11–13, built in 1675 as a granary for the Baxters' Incorporation. Two rectangular stair-turrets with notable doorways, to the E heavily moulded with the date on the keyblock, to the W also moulded, the overdoor panel with a wheatsheaf, cherubs' heads, two crossed peels with a pie and three cakes, and a pair of scales. The larger inscription reads:

> GOD BLESS THE BAXTERS OF EDIN
> BRUGH UHO BULT THIS HOUS 1675

Arched wall-head belfry added by *Robert S. Lorimer* c. 1900 for the Cathedral Mission, for whom he adapted a large room as a chapel. Its fittings were moved elsewhere in 1976 when *Frederick R. Stevenson* made it into flats (the floors etc. had already been renewed) and re-harled the exterior, carefully restoring the crowsteps to the stair-turrets and fitting half-shutters in the windows. No. 6, bent to the curve of a very narrow site, was designed by *Thomas Moncur* as stables in 1881. Dormered on the gambrel roof to the N, mildly baronial towards the river and crowstepped Gothick at the W end, it was skilfully converted by *Robert Matthew, Johnson-Marshall & Partners* for their own use in 1972–3. At the very top KIRKBRAE HOUSE (No. 10 Randolph Cliff), originally a C17 or C18 tavern for the village baxters, now incorporating two

---

* The High Green site to the E is to be developed (1984) with an ingeniously picturesque housing scheme by *T. M. Gray Associates*.

earlier stones; to the s a sculptured early c17 dormer-head portraying a judge (from the demolished Dean House), and to the n a cartouche dated 1619 from one of the baxters' buildings in the village. In 1892 *J. Graham Fairley* included this modest structure in a much larger Scottish baronial house of L-plan. Two storeys show above bridge level, nicely detailed, with a broken pedimented doorpiece and a circular nw turret, but from Miller Row it is seen as a fantastic composition towering five storeys up the precipice at the sw abutment of the bridge, with the turret boldly corbelled out on the salient angle.

BELFORD ROAD starts from here, with the brown-brick Lynedoch House (*see* Western New Town, Lynedoch Place) peering over the long retaining wall on the up-hill side. First on the n is DRUMSHEUGH TOLL by *George Washington Browne*, 1891, in a free Tudor style as a studio house for Martin Hardie; stables and another house planned to the e were not built. The steep site is brilliantly exploited. It is stolid and cosy towards Belford Road, with broad eaves, a squat crenellated tower, a four-light half-timbered bay-window to the w, and a canopy over the door in the angle; highly picturesque towards Bell's Brae, with more half-timbering, a big studio-windowed gable, a red sandstone octagonal turret and a dizzily elevated balcony (the terrace was partly reconstructed and extended in 1975). The detail has much charm, e.g. the cement base-course stamped diaper-fashion with a Gothic capital H, the beautifully leaded glass and a modicum of ironwork. The 'Dean Studio' gatepiers next door are a relic of the neo-Norman Free Church by *David Cousin*, 1844 (converted to a studio in 1890 and demolished in the 1950s). Its tower and that of Drumsheugh Toll were related.

Next appears the Moorish façade, deeply shadowed under a low-pitch stone-bracketed roof, of the DRUMSHEUGH BATHS by *John J. Burnet*, 1882 and (after a fire) 1892–3. An early sketch shows the Belford Road section with two storeys. There is now one, formerly of rubble (now harled) over an ashlar base, with four grilled windows in red-brick horseshoe arches and a fifth as the doorway, red stone shafts and beautifully carved capitals. Inside, a janitor's box with a stained-glass window; then the arched vestibule leading to the stair that descends on four sides of a hollow, arcaded newel; the baths themselves are on a much lower level, and externally rubble and pantile 'vernacular', being hardly visible from the road. Main bath with open timber roof. Seven Moorish arches on cast-iron columns to the w; three to the e, with a mezzanine gallery for access to the diving niche (now closed), and then the three vaulted bays of the hot and cold baths (now the children's training pool). Mezzanine Turkish bath (now a lounge) through a timber screen to the s. After the Baths, just red sandstone tenements by *Edward Calvert*, 1890, and *William MacLeod*, 1893.

At this point is the entry to SUNBURY, a small neighbourhood of mews buildings and granite cobbles taking its name from Sunbury House of which the last remnants (and those of the associated distillery) disappeared soon after the Second World War. Sunbury Mews starts with the round-turreted building at the head of the brae by *John C. Hay*, 1886, and leads down past Sunbury Place, a row of artisan housing of *c.* 1865, to *Whytock & Reid's* SUNBURY WORKS, a three-storey cabinet-factory built in brick for Robert and Hugh Reid in 1886. Towards the river their contemporary wood storage shed, openwork timber with a pantiled roof; to the s the firm's office and showroom by *Henry Wylie & Partners*, 1973. The stone urn in front is one of those that adorned the skyline of Burn's New Club in Princes Street (*see* First New Town). Belford Mews are red sandstone neo-Jacobean with mansard roofs, shaped gables and pedimented dormers. Two-storey harled warehouse to the E, with a machicolated centre, by *George Fortune*, 1893. Belford Road continues with the buff brick flats and houses of SUNBURY PLACE by *Ian H. Rolland Associates*, 1981. All are carefully connected in neighbourly fashion but come to grief in a series of awkward roofs.

Of BELL'S MILLS to the s of Belford Bridge, wrecked by an explosion in 1975, only the two-storey rubble-walled GRAN-ARY survives, with its central pediment dated 1807, now part of the DRAGONARA HOTEL by *Crerar & Partners*, 1978. To the W BELL'S MILLS HOUSE, a villa built *c.* 1780 of large cleft stones with exactly finished dressings. Moulded architraves round the front openings and a cornice over the front door.

After the bridge (*see* Public Buildings, above) a small development of 1877; connected houses in Belford Terrace (built by a Mr *Forbes*) and some large but not specially distinguished villas in Belford Place. No. 1 and No. 4 (called Belford House and enlarged by *James McLachlan* in 1922) are more elaborate than the others.

2. The Heriot Trust and Steel Development SW of Queensferry Road

BUCKINGHAM TERRACE was begun in 1860 and feued very quickly. The first in the West End to offer bay-windows, it was also the first and perhaps the best of *Chesser's* terraces, benefiting from Tait's example across the road but introducing a system of symmetrically paired houses, the doors grouped together in the advanced and balustraded pavilions, the bays together in the links. The detail is equally well considered: consoled balconies over the front doors, and two-storey canted bays providing balustraded balconies for alternate second-floor windows. The main frontage of thirty-four houses has a convex curve at Nos. 11–20, corresponding with the line of Queensferry Road, with sloping gardens between. Two houses are of special interest. No. 8, recast by *Robert S. Lorimer* in 1893 and easily recognized by the nicely detailed front door, wrought-iron balcony and small-paned windows, is simple and elegant inside. No. 34 by *Peddie & Kinnear*, 1865, has a special doorpiece and more elaborate interiors than the general run. Nos. 18–20 also by *Peddie & Kinnear*. The site of Nos. 35–40 to the w of Belgrave Place, originally designed by *Chesser* for Colonel Learmonth in 1876, was taken by the builder *James Steel* whose architect *Alexander W. Macnaughtan* departed from the agreed scheme. Steel was threatened with proceedings through the Lord Advocate, and Nos. 41–44 were never built; their place was taken by the Bristo Baptist Church (*see* Churches, above). The executed houses are of greyer stone than the rest, without Chesser's trick of balancing the elevations. Full-height bays, and pedimented dormers exploiting the attic space.

BELGRAVE PLACE, begun in 1880, was also designed by *Macnaughtan* for Steel (presumably with Chesser's approval): an insensitive arrangement of full-height bays with cornices on every level. BELGRAVE CRESCENT is of 1874 by *Chesser*, using the successful Eglinton Crescent formula of 'telescopic' two-storey bays, balustraded parapet and pedimented dormers but the lower part of each bay is rectangular instead of bowed. Whichever is preferred, Belgrave Crescent has a splendidly spacious outlook. The gardens in front were laid out by *James Jeffrey* in 1876. Plainer interiors than at Eglinton Crescent, many of the entrance halls and staircases subdivided. But *Robert S. Lorimer* did some work at No. 8 (small-pane glazing again), *Scott Morton & Co.* at Nos. 17, 22 and 24. In No. 13 a neo-Adam ceiling. Beyond Belgrave Place Nos. 22–25, a more elaborate design by *Chesser* for *James Steel*, very muddled, with clumsy porches on the end houses. No. 22 is advanced to make a corner pavilion, its canted bay pushed up to the full height of the wall.

3. The Heriot Trust Development NE of Queensferry Road

A small area bought by the Heriot Trust from Learmonth whose architect, *John Tait*, remained in charge. His carefully detailed elevations form an outward-facing polygon, all the houses looking on to gardens except in Lennox Street, which is two-sided and rather different in character.

The three main terraces have many features in common. All are of three storeys, with flat-faced architraves at the front doors, stone-consoled balconies of single-house (mostly three-bay) width and elegant classical ironwork. Pavilions and centre-pieces, crowned with balustrades (some missing, or replaced with dormers), project boldly so that the bracketed main cornice butts neatly into them at any necessary change in level; Tait had studied Playfair's Regent Terrace. The windows show a transition between crown and plate glass. On the second floor the conventional six panes to each sash; the lower ones have four, with thick uprights and thin cross-bars.

What gives each terrace its distinctive character is the pattern of the first-floor window-heads. CLARENDON CRESCENT (1850–53) has segmental pediments, except in the outer bays of each of the houses flanking the centrepiece. OXFORD TERRACE (mainly 1858–9, shorter and a little steeper) has no centrepiece, but each house in the central link and its two pavilions has a segmental pediment between triangular ones. ETON TERRACE (1855), with triangular pediments on the centrepiece and pavilions and a channelled ground floor, is cranked in plan. Overlooking the private DEAN GARDENS which run down to the Water of Leith, it is connected to the crescent by a monumental screen wall of three blind arches. All three terraces have well proportioned but not elaborate interiors, with many good chimneypieces. Nos. 8 and 12 Oxford Terrace and No. 5 Eton Terrace are by *Peddie & Kinnear*. LENNOX STREET was carried out in 1868–9 to a revision of Tait's design by *John Chesser*. It shows in the relatively coarser detail of the two-bay houses with canted bay-windows and crowning balustrades. Two storeys, rising to three at the S end where Nos. 9–11, 14–20 and 24–26 were again executed by *Peddie & Kinnear*.

4. *The Learmonth Development N of Queensferry Road*

LEARMONTH TERRACE on the N side of Queensferry Road, designed by *John Chesser* for Colonel Learmonth in 1873, is another variation on the exactly contemporary Eglinton Crescent theme (cf. Belgrave Crescent, above), with canted bays on top of ground-floor bows. Nos. 4–8 and 9–24 follow it closely, the former varied by an extra storey at the centre. To the E Nos. 1–3, which have no private driveway or screening plantation, form a plainer endpiece (again cf. Eglinton Crescent, Western New Town). The break in the terrace at Learmonth View is better than Chesser usually managed in his later years. Beyond it in the much altered second section a narrow W pavilion. The interiors of Nos. 5–7 look like *Steel*: compartmented ceilings, coarse Corinthianesque columns in the entrance halls (where not divided), and oval windows in the back walls of the rear dining rooms. Nos. 9–24 by *MacGibbon & Ross** from 1877, first for the Leith Heritages Company and then for the builder *George Gilroy*. Most have plain entrance halls leading straight to the stair, the ceilings compartmented or with elaborate cornices to the E, ribbed Jacobean to the W. At No. 9 a gilded cornice and grisaille ceiling painting; No. 24 arched, with Corinthian pilasters in inner and outer halls.

The final W section did not get beyond No. 25, a house so grandiose that no-one could hope to follow it. By *James Simpson* of Leith, 1891–3, for Arthur Sanderson the wine-mer-

---

* David MacGibbon was a tenant in No. 17 after his financial *débâcle* of 1878–81, moving to No. 23 in the mid 1880s.

chant, it is an elaborate version of Chesser's basic theme: four
bays with two bow-windows, anthemion friezes and a columned doorpiece, all in the Greek Corinthian Peddie & Kinnear manner. The sharp carving has survived on the asymmetrical Learmonth Avenue frontage. The interior, the most
sumptuous in the city, less subtle than No. 3 Rothesay Place
(*see* Western New Town) but much more expensive, was decorated by *W. Scott Morton* in 1893. Front door with stained
glass designed by *Hart* (the Panathenaic festival) and made
by *Cottier*. In the ENTRANCE HALL mahogany panelling, an
Ionic-columned chimneypiece and a compartmented ceiling
brilliant with mosaic and gold. A screen of square Doric columns, with bronze reliefs of figures on the entablature blocks,
opens into the main STAIR, the handrail supported by winged
horses and scrolls, the landing by Corinthian columns continuing upwards as caryatid figures of Athena and Hera. Attic
overall, with a gilded Parthenon frieze and quotations from
Homer and Plato. Back on the ground floor, the DINING
ROOM at the front was described at the time as Renaissance,
though of what type it would be hard to say. Ribbed Jacobean
ceiling, plenty of oak and rosewood, and a large ingle-neuk
with superimposed orders and an arched tympanum. In the
lower windows more glass (the Seasons) by *Cottier*. The LIB-
RARY, called Italian, is square and aisled, with slim Doric
columns of American walnut. One bay is an ingle with complex Jacobean woodwork. The walls were originally covered
in leather. In the relatively plain BREAKFAST ROOM at the NE
corner a bronze pilastered chimneypiece with Adamish capitals and boldly carved putti in the frieze; Dutch tiles round
the grate. Upstairs the L-shaped 'Adam–style' DRAWING
ROOM indeed has richly carved pilasters of Adam–Pergolesi
type, and a ceiling of two ovals, a circle worked into the bow.
The arched alabaster chimneypiece with caryatids unhappily
cuts off the lower parts of the pilaster and overmantel. Enclosed iron grate with brass sphinxes. Elm woodwork with
inset ceramic ovals. Two BEDROOMS to the rear, the main
one ('French, Louis XIII') Corinthian-columned and pilastered (a small area of the original tapestry survives by the
door), with embossed Tynecastle canvas on the close-beamed
ceiling. In the guest bedroom, an arcaded octagon with landscapes painted in alternate tympana, an Adamish chimneypiece and a ceiling filled with arabesques. A smaller stair
(replaced in the 1950s after a fire) leads to the neo-Eliza-
bethan BILLIARD ROOM, lined and ceiled in oak, with more
embossed canvas between. Three-arched screen at the dais.
Chimneypiece at each end, as richly detailed as the rest. At
attic level the long NURSERY or Young Ladies' Room is
'Early English', i.e. relatively plain Jacobean, with a coomb
ceiling, a baluster screen at the entrance end and a canopied
chimneypiece with fireside seats at the other.

LEARMONTH COURT at Nos. 26–27, a block of inter-war modern flats by *T. Bowhill Gibson*, 1935, is a good enough com-

position, with recessed bay-windows over the two canopied entries and a recessed bow turning the corner into Orchard Brae. Granite-like blockwork walls relieved by areas of harling, the roof pitched and slated.

The area N of Learmonth Terrace as far as Comely Bank Road was bought for development by Sir James Steel, the last 32 ha. in 1894. DEAN PARK CRESCENT to the E (1879–90) is presumably by *A. W. Macnaughtan*, the rest by Steel's next architect *Alexander Allan*. Mostly superior bay-windowed tenements of fine smooth ashlar but standardized detail, e.g. in the long switchback vista of COMELY BANK AVENUE (1893), but in the middle a strip of garden overlooked by houses that may reflect *MacGibbon & Ross*'s unexecuted scheme of 1877: SOUTH LEARMONTH GARDENS (1901) like a plain version of Buckingham Terrace, and down the hill the mansarded LEARMONTH GARDENS (1899), Nos. 1–9 almost early Victorian with their steep gablets, Nos. 10–19 with pedimented dormers and no basements (the servants lived in the small back wings). Steel's development (all for rented occupation) was completed by the Dean Property Investment Co. with *Stewart Kaye* as architect in 1938 and (with synthetic stone facing) 1946: stiff survivals of the old bay-windowed tenement type, but with tall, narrow windows to light the stairs. Much more interesting is *Kaye*'s earlier LEARMONTH COURT for the builder *James Miller*, 1937, long red-brick flats with steel windows and stone trim, really enjoying the site. In ORCHARD BRAE a big intrusive office with black fins over the entrance, FINANCE HOUSE by *J. & F. Johnston*, 1968, enlarged to the rear in 1978.

9. STOCKBRIDGE

Although it continues the Georgian development of the Northern New Town without a break (or did so until the destruction of Kerr Street and some adjacent terraces), Stockbridge is a distinctive place with more of the character of a small town than a suburb, albeit quite transformed from the pre-1813 village of riverside cottages, mills and villas. Today its landmark from a distance is the big Victorian church tower; most of the other buildings are on an intimate Georgian scale, reflecting social status by their charming variations on a few architectural themes (e.g. the plain anta, the Ionic pilaster and the fluted Doric column) and by their different house-types, spaces and prospects. The focal point is the Stock Bridge itself, spanning the Water of Leith. The savings bank at one corner is like a miniature town hall, and the main road on both sides of the river is a busy shopping centre, Georgian in its beginnings but extended later at the expense of the double villas in Raeburn Place. Looking w from the bridge, the view softens into the densely wooded slopes below the Moray Estate, a semi-rural boundary which helps to distinguish Stockbridge as a separate place.

The three Perambulations correspond with the main Georgian schemes; the Raeburn Estate (which originally included some streets on the w side of the Water of Leith), plus the modest development of the grounds of Malta House; the Saxe-Coburg precinct to the N of Hamilton Place; and to the s of it the St Stephen Street–Clarence Street area which includes the Victorian Co-operative Society buildings of Patriothall.

CHURCHES

St Bernard's Parish Church, Saxe-Coburg Street. Originally St Cuthbert's Chapel of Ease. 1823 by *James Milne* in his earlier, flatter style, as in Ann Street and Saxe-Coburg Place itself. Pedimented façade with pairs of giant Ionic pilasters looking rather small between the three-storey tenements. The two stages of the steeple have the same sort of flatness, emphasized by the concave corner treatment but nicely tied together at the top by a stone crown like an openwork dome. A domed vestibule with Greek Doric columns on all four sides leads into a very simple interior with a U-plan gallery on slim iron columns. In 1888 *Hardy & Wight* decorated the plain ceiling with geometric ribs and added the broad, shallow apse with blind arcading and a correctly cof-

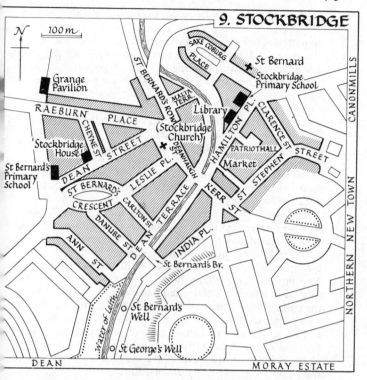

9. STOCKBRIDGE

fered vault. Their elaborate Renaissance set-piece of varnished wood was split up in 1961-2 by *James Beveridge*, who pushed the communion table back into the apse, re-sited the pulpit to one side, and banished the organ to a no-nonsense case in the gallery and most of the elders' seats to oblivion. – ORGAN by *D. & T. Hamilton*, 1881; rebuilt by *W. Gledhill* in 1907, and by *Rushworth & Dreaper* in 1961.

STOCKBRIDGE FREE CHURCH, Deanhaugh Street. Demolished 1980 except for the tower. This was basically St George's Free Church by *David Cousin*, 1844-5, displaced by the railway from Lothian Road and partially re-erected in 1867-8 by *Peddie & Kinnear*, who used the left-over stone for the large, well-proportioned tower, capped with a slated pyramid spire. The gable front was completely masked by the tower and its flanking stair-towers. – Brick faced HOUSING by *Matthew, Hamilton & Maclean*, 1980, incorporating the tower.

PUBLIC BUILDINGS

GRANGE CRICKET CLUB PAVILION, off Raeburn Place and Portgower Place. 1892 by the civil engineers *Cunningham,*

Blyth & Westland, a jolly half-timbered affair with a veranda on turned columns of art-furniture type. Tiers of seats in front of the clock-tower on the lopsided, red-tiled roof.

ST BERNARD'S BRIDGE. 1824, presumably by *James Milne*. A segmental arch with alternately raised voussoirs, plus a smaller land-arch. Iron railings instead of a solid parapet. A flight of steps in Jacobean style, 1887, leads down to the riverside walk.

ST BERNARD'S PRIMARY SCHOOL, Dean Street. A George Heriot's Trust school designed by *John Chesser*, 1874–7. Gabled blocks in the style of the parent institution, but with square pepperpots. Ground-floor windows with nicely varied pediments, some with the initials GH, but many of these good details sadly eroded and in places chopped off. E extension by *Robert Wilson*, 1887.

ST BERNARD'S WELL, on the S bank of the Water of Leith. A circular Roman temple among the trees, commissioned from *Alexander Nasmyth* in 1788 by Lord Gardenstone (a wealthy Law Lord who thought he had benefited from the mineral spring) as a replacement for the small well-house of 1760. The builder *John Wilson* began work in 1789. The pump room is in a base of boldly cleft rustication below the level of the path. Above it ten tall Doric columns, unfluted, support a meticulously detailed entablature with paterae between triglyphs. Under the lead dome a STATUE of Hygeia, the original figure of *Coade* stone, 1791, replaced with another carved by *D. W. Stevenson* in 1888, when the building was restored and the pump-room refitted by *Thomas Bonnar*.

ST GEORGE'S WELL, to the S of it. Dated 1810, and named in allusion to the jubilee of George III. A small gable to the front and a windowless bow on a high rustic base to the rear, towards the water.

STOCKBRIDGE HOUSE DAY CENTRE, Cheyne Street. An old people's club by *Robert Hurd & Partners*, 1974–5. Semi-traditional, mainly harled, with an octagonal hall. Nicely complementary to its old and new surroundings.

STOCKBRIDGE LIBRARY, Hamilton Place. One of Thomas Nelson's recreation and library buildings. Early Renaissance by *H. Ramsay Taylor* of *Lessels & Taylor*, 1898–1900. Single storey of red sandstone, with a good pilastered doorpiece, a perfunctory row of three stepped gables to the E and a two-storey crenellated octagon at the W corner. Inside, open timber roofs over arcades on spindly coupled columns.

STOCKBRIDGE MARKET, Hamilton Place and St Stephen's Place. The Greek Doric entrances are all that survives of the building of 1824–5 designed by *Archibald Scott* for Captain David Carnegie on the model of the Liverpool market. The Hamilton Place entry is domestic in scale – indeed the centre bay gives access to the common stair of the four-storey tenement at Nos. 18–26, part of the same development. The outer bays are pends leading to the market and converging behind the bowed rear wall of the stair-well. S entry grander, an arched gateway with a short symmetrical approach along St Stephen's Place. The plan was for fish stalls behind the Hamilton Place tenement, the s part to have a central block of stalls divided in four by a cruciform walk, and more around the perimeter; this was for flesh, poultry, fruit and vegetables. The Ordnance map of 1852 shows only the e half of this layout, and before the market finally closed in 1906 it had already been encroached upon by the building of No. 13 St Stephen's Place in 1846 and Nos. 16–22 in the 1850s.

STOCKBRIDGE PRIMARY SCHOOL, Hamilton Place. Gothic, by *R. Rowand Anderson*, 1874–7. Designed for 600 pupils, it is the best of all the first generation of Board Schools; snecked masonry with refined early Dec dressings, each of the giant arches (with Anderson's characteristic rectangular top-lights) encompassing a pair below. The gabled profile builds up to the slated flèche of the central ventilator, but the symmetry of the front is decisively broken by an extra gable bearing a double-cylinder chimney-stalk (typical early Anderson) with the usual high relief roundel of Education with her pupils set below it. JANITOR'S HOUSE to the e. A neat matching design.

PERAMBULATIONS

1. The Raeburn Estate

Henry Raeburn was born of an artisan family in Stockbridge. His marriage in 1780 to Ann Edgar, widow of Count James Leslie, brought him the house and grounds of Deanhaugh, to which he added the neighbouring estate of St Bernard's.* He began to feu his property for building *c*. 1813, but continued to live in St Bernard's House till his death in 1823. The layout was then revised and the house demolished in 1826 to make way for the e side of Carlton Street. It is only in this last phase, on the evidence so far discovered, that the design of any part of the Raeburn Estate can be attributed with absolute certainty to *James Milne*. The case for his authorship of at least some of the original scheme rests on its similarity to his known work elsewhere, e.g. that of Ann Street to Lynedoch Place. Slightly less convincing is the tradition that Raeburn himself had some responsibility for this varied and interesting layout. The following description deals first with the high-class terraces to the s of Dean Street and then with the mixed development from Dean Street to the n.

ANN STREET is presumably by *James Milne*. By 1817 only the w half had been built. As originally planned *c*. 1814 it was to be the westernmost of three parallel streets between Dean Street and the Water of Leith, all of similar layout: symmetrical terraces, their stepped-in ends giving an air of seclusion,

---

* Walter Ross died at St Bernard's in 1789. The record of Raeburn's acquisition of some land from his trustees in 1798 mentions a previous purchase.

facing each other across the front gardens which were then a
novelty in Edinburgh. But Ann Street would always have
been the best, thanks to its elevated site. The tall pedimented
centrepieces, rather thinly monumental with seven giant Ionic
pilasters, are raised on the brow of the hill from which there
is a constricted but nonetheless dramatic view across the valley to the s. Each is a pair of three-storey houses, with small
porches of coupled Greek Doric columns, flanked by two-
storey houses with architraved upper windows, and then by
rows of five houses of smaller scale but distinctively detailed;
fluted aprons under the first-floor windows and paired doorpieces with consoles ending in square blocks and guttae. End
houses stepped forward on both sides, adding to the intimacy
of the street and incidentally making more room for back
gardens at the corners, the N end sweeping round into Dean
Park Crescent, the s end making a very formal approach to
the brink of the valley. The SE corner block of 1869-70 leads
into UPPER DEAN TERRACE, three pairs of simple houses
with steeply banked front gardens, built in 1816-17. All the
INTERIORS are quite modest, but it is noticeable that the twin
houses of Ann Street's E centrepiece (Nos. 28 and 30) are
deeper than their opposite numbers and have apsed back
rooms on ground and first floors.

123 ST BERNARD'S CRESCENT and its associated terraces follow
James Milne's revised scheme of 1824, by which time the
enthusiasm for New Town house-building had reached its
height. Grant's *Old and New Edinburgh* refers to 'the double
crescent called St Bernard's, suggested by Sir David Wilkie
... and adorned with the grandest Grecian Doric pillars that
are to be found in any edifice not a public one'. The three-
storey centrepiece is indeed of astounding grandeur, with
giant Doric columns rising from pavement level, arranged in
2-4-2 sequence between four single bays of giant antae. The
supporting houses, of two storeys, share the same cornice-
line, but with balustrades instead of an attic. Except for their
continuous ground-floor colonnade they resemble the rest of
the scheme in their flat surfaces and bold detail, and the
strong horizontal emphasis of both; the horizontal window-
panes (where they have not been replaced) contribute to this
effect. The s side of the crescent was designed to match the
N, with four giant anta pavilions, but the E segment lacks its
proper pavilion at the corner of Danube Street. Its twin on
the other side was built, but nothing more till the gap was
filled in 1879-82 by *John Webster*, who also completed the
Danube Street corner in 1883-4 to a design by *MacGibbon
& Ross* which is decidedly less well managed. The N side was
not quite finished either. The final termination of the W tenement of 1879 is an economical but just adequate design by
Philip Cocker Associates, 1970, for the Link Benevolent Housing Association. At the Leslie Place end, where the Leslies
had been in much less of a hurry to vacate their lands (Count
Leslie living in Deanhaugh well into the second half of the

century), No. 1 was built as a decent late classical tenement
in 1880. Another four-storey tenement at the corresponding
s corner by *Robert Paterson & Son*, 1881, with the grace to
continue the rusticated ground floor of Carlton Street; the
tops of the windows are higher than the ceilings within, and
the difference is made up with inset courses of masonry. LES-
LIE PLACE itself is of the early 1880s, a tenemented canyon
with bay-windows. Only the Deanhaugh Street corner was
built to Milne's design.

DANUBE STREET starts parallel with Ann Street, but its head
is curved round to meet the crescent's grand centrepiece.
Channelling in place of a colonnade on the ground floor, but
the same continuous balcony* above, broken only by the two
slightly advanced houses in the middle of each side. With its
two contrasting vistas, rural and monumental, this is the most
attractive of Edinburgh's neo-Greek streets. CARLTON
STREET is straight, leading the E end of the crescent down to
the river, and short, so the ground floor is appropriately rusticated. DEAN TERRACE (originally Mineral Street, with reference to the well) follows the same model with interesting
variations, e.g. continuous balconies to the W, individual ones
on the gently curved E section. Both have channelled ground
floors, the openings in square-headed recesses (cf. Bonnar's
later work in the Northern New Town). The side elevations
of the three-storey corner tenements are modified to conform
with their respective streets. On the W side of DEANHAUGH
STREET Nos. 14–26 are a continuous unaltered row of pilastered shopfronts, with basement shops below them and two
storeys of flats above.

The INTERIORS of Milne's second phase, like the first, are
fairly simple but with more neo-Greek detail. Predictably
those of the N side of the crescent are exceptional, with monumental Grecian entrance halls: Doric columns in No. 13.
The houses towards the W are of shallow plan allowing tall
staircase windows at the back. Danube Street has some of the
finest stairwells; at Nos. 3–9 the cupolas are enriched with
luxuriant Grecian plasterwork. Few of the corner tenements
have anything of special note, but the flats at No. 1 Carlton
Street have circular entrance halls.

Now to the main road, which begins as DEANHAUGH STREET,
very much the centre of Stockbridge. After the bridge itself
(*see* Public Buildings, above), Milne's row of pilastered shops
and the tower of the former Stockbridge Free Church (for
both *see* above). The E side starts with the EDINBURGH SAV-
INGS BANK, a plain block of *c.* 1840 transformed by *Mac-
Gibbon & Ross* in 1900 with balustrades and a corbelled-out
clock tower. Interior later remodelled by *William Paterson*,
with woodwork by *Scott Morton & Co*. At the other end Nos.
39–51, a large hammer-dressed tenement by *Frederick T.*

---

* The balconies in Danube Street and Carlton Street were copied, not very
faithfully, from one at 57 Northumberland Street (*see* Northern New Town).

Pilkington, 1880–1, an economical version of his original design for a fantastic hotel with elongated domes and elaborate dormers, and well related to the junction, with a giant bowed chimney-gable looking down Raeburn Place.

Here a digression from the Raeburn Estate into ST BERNARD'S ROW. No. 1 is a three-storey rubble house with a late-C18 look. Then a small tenement by *Kantel Design*, 1982; the V-shaped balconies on its pedimented front make it Edinburgh's best post-modern joke. The former grounds of Malta House were developed piecemeal from the early C19. MALTA GREEN COTTAGE, *c.* 1830, its first-floor centre bay corbelled and battlemented, was extricated from use as a garage in 1981 and is to be restored as the centrepiece of some new houses by *Robert Hurd & Partners*. MALTA HOUSE itself is set back by the river, late Georgian with a mid-Victorian mansard and red stone dressings. N wing with a Venetian window and crenellated parapet. To the N the one-sided MALTA TERRACE, a short cul-de-sac with a corner tenement of *c.* 1869 and then a standard row of *c.* 1822 with rusticated ground floors and individual balconies. On the W side of St Bernard's Row, after the gusset end-block, a two-storey front-gardened row of houses in which Nos. 8 and 10 have elegantly panelled doorpieces (diamond and oval) and Nos. 12–16 are progressively plainer; all *c.* 1820. Nos. 18 and 20, Roseburn Cottage and St Bernard's Cottage standing back in their gardens, are rubble-built with piend roofs and tripartite ground-floor windows. One of them was first advertised for sale with a 'flower plot in front, small garden at the rear' in 1807, having been built by *Mr Johnston*, wright.

RAEBURN PLACE was built in 1814–25 as a mixed development of tenements and villas. First the tenements at the E end. Nos. 2–26 of *c.* 1820 have a bow at the corner of St Bernard's Row and a very odd skew-line between Nos. 14 and 16, presumably following the boundary between the Raeburn and Malta House properties. For Nos. 1–7 on the S side *see* Dean Street etc. below. Then, further out of town, the street was lined with elegant double villas and their front gardens. Those on the S side, built by 1817, now poke over the top of a continuous row of single-storey shops. The N side, built a little later (except for Nos. 28–30, *c.* 1850), has been swamped in more piecemeal fashion. Nos. 40–42 survive with some alterations and Nos. 44–46 still have most of their ground floors lurking behind the shops, but Nos. 36–38 were demolished for Woolworths in 1962. Finally on what was the very edge of the town there were three single villas of which two were demolished for Victorian tenements. The survivor is the RAEBURN HOUSE HOTEL, formerly Somerset Cottage, *c.* 1832, very pretty with its arched doorpiece and rock-faced links to the single-storey pavilions. MARY'S PLACE on the S side, a small development feued not by Raeburn but by John Learmonth (*see* Dean), is a rather haphazard terrace of houses of 1821–2. At Nos. 3–6 a ground floor with droved rustication (for another example *see* Gayfield: Gayfield Place). Thanks to the elevated site, the shops built over the front gardens of Nos. 7–12 only hide the basements.

Next a charming small-scale development of modest but quite showy houses beginning with Nos. 1–7 Raeburn Place, an acute-angled tenement of 1813 with twin bow-windows at the corner. Fluted surrounds to surviving doorpieces, with domino blocks at the corners, set in over-arches. RAEBURN STREET (built in 1816–19 as Hermitage Place) has gatepiers at each end and was presumably locked up at night. As it is so close behind Cheyne Street it has only one side; two-storey, front-gardened houses with fluted aprons under the upper windows and Greek Doric doorpieces in pairs with mutual cornices. A continuous rank of the same half-columns frames all the ground-floor openings of the pedimented centre house (No. 6).

At the corner of DEAN STREET another tenement with domino-blocked doorpieces. Here the houses on the N side (1813) continue the Raeburn Street pattern with a small difference; not only the cornice but also the fluted frieze is continuous over each doorpiece. One such doorpiece still exists within the shop extension of Nos. 11–19. Many interiors in both streets have been subdivided, but No. 25 Dean Street still has a double-arched entrance hall with a central column. Who designed these little houses? They have a family relationship with Ann Street, so perhaps *James Milne* was the architect, but *William Bryce* is known to have had something to do with Dean Street. The influence of Raeburn himself must not be forgotten, for this is neither professional academic architecture nor mere builder's work.

On the other (s) side of Dean Street, the former SECESSION CHURCH of 1828–9, large and plain, with two storeys of arched windows, the middle bay slightly advanced. To the E ST BERNARD'S CHURCH SCHOOL by *Robert Wright*, 1826, with pendant-bracketed cornices over the doors on each side of a tall double window. At its W end this side of Dean Street is bounded by the backs of St Bernard's Crescent; some of the basements contain little shops.

CHEYNE STREET of 1827, now a single terrace of tenements backing on to Raeburn Street, is long and dour, with a four-storey centrepiece and s pavilion, the former shaggy from the flaking of its poor-quality stone. Main door flats distinguished by pilastered doorcases. No front gardens and no basement areas; decidedly for the lower middle class. The w side of the street, started at the s end, has been demolished. So has Bedford Court, cottagey terraces of 1900, now replaced by *Michael Laird & Partners'* decent housing, cement-rendered with coloured margins, and by the old people's centre at Stockbridge House (*see* Public Buildings, above).

Virtually the whole of the Raeburn development to the s of the Water of Leith was demolished in 1966–7. Not much was said about its loss at the time; it would not be so meekly

accepted now. India Place and MacKenzie Place were less
ambitious than any of the Raeburn terraces to the N except
for Cheyne Street, but they had considerable charm thanks
to their serpentine line along the natural contours of the river
bank. INDIA PLACE (1823-5) consisted of long ashlar fronts
with simple architrave-and-cornice doorpieces and an almost
unbroken cornice-line, but no front gardens or basement
areas. A curved front with pilastered endpieces joined it to
MACKENZIE PLACE, a plain terrace with basement areas to
the W of St Bernard's Bridge; a villa of *c.* 1800 still stands,
with a C20 sun-porch, at the far W end. The E part of SAUN-
DERS STREET (1825-30) was similar; it ran along the river
front. Much of this was in poor condition, but there was no
such reason for the clearance of the W side of KERR STREET,
a main-road terrace of five storeys stepped downhill with
tower-like canted bays at the ends, joining Stockbridge to the
Northern New Town. The parallel five-storey housing blocks
built across the contours made the best of what could only be
(within local authority cost limits) an indifferent job. Their
walls are ingeniously relieved by shallow splays, but their
grey concrete blocks provoke unfavourable comparison (especially after rain) with the stone buildings all around. The
architects were *Michael Laird & Partners*, 1974-5. Their
monopitch STOCKBRIDGE CLINIC in India Street is part of
the same scheme.

The W side of NW CIRCUS PLACE, at the SE corner of this
section, was formerly called Spring Gardens. At the S end
(Nos. 30-31) it is a homely two-storey block with a shop built
out at the corner, but it continues (Nos. 25-29) as a smooth
ashlar curve, concave to the main street and then convex
round the corner into Gloucester Street, with nice shops on
the way. Built *c.* 1850 on the site of earlier houses, it gracefully terminates the Georgian sequence before the C20 housing begins. In GLOUCESTER STREET itself (formerly Church
Street, i.e. the road to St Cuthbert's) the painter David Roberts was born in DUNCAN'S LAND in 1796, when it was
quite new. Two storeys and a mansard attic with a bowed
staircase at the back, built with rubble and dressed stone from
demolitions in Bank Street (the carved lintel inscribed FEAR
GOD ONLY 1605 comes from there), and restored by *Robert
Hurd & Partners* in 1973-4.

2. *St Stephen Street and Clarence Street, Hamilton Place and Patriothall*

This area comprises one main development and several small
ones. In 1817 the NE bank of the river below the Stock Bridge
was occupied by the Stockbridge Mills and farm steading. E of
it was Mr Kedslie's house, which became the site of Stockbridge
Market. The rest was garden ground and open field with a
scattering of rural houses. The mill lade ran through the property, dividing it into roughly equal areas. The N half was

Patriothall, a small property with a mansion house belonging to a Mr Muir; on the s were fields belonging to a Mr Bell.

Patriothall was staked out for building by *William Burn* c. 1818 and proposals were made for developing the property of Mr Kedslie, but he became insolvent. Nothing more was done until in the early 1820s James Pedie, W.S., assembled an L-plan development site from Mr Bell's property and the E section of Mr Muir's, and laid out St Stephen Street (then Brunswick Street) and Clarence Street (briefly Silvermills Street) with *Robert Brown* as his architect. Under agreements of 1824–5 Captain David Carnegie bought the Kedslie property and an entry to St Stephen Street from Pedie and constructed the Stockbridge Market. Meantime to the E *Thomas Brown*, the City Superintendent of Works (perhaps in consultation with Playfair), had designed a quadrant (originally called St Stephen Street) linking the scheme to St Vincent Street and thus integrating it into the Northern New Town. On the w the perimeter of the Stockbridge Mills site was developed as Glanville Place and Bakers' Place. The Patriothall area was not built up till Victorian and Edwardian times.

ST STEPHEN STREET, largely by *Robert Brown* for James Pedie, begins with two plain four-storey blocks of 1825 in NW Circus Place. The ground floors of Nos. 11–15 have been built out as two banks (the Bank of Scotland Art Deco Classical by *Reid & Forbes*, 1933), but Nos. 17–22 still have their pilastraded shopfronts. Gracefully bowed block of 1824 on the corner for the carver and gilder David Hatton who had his shop there. The other corner block was built by *John Paton* and probably designed by his son *David Paton*; the lack of a second-floor sill-course and references to consultation with him suggest that it is not Brown's. Next the opening into St Stephen's Place (1825–6, formerly Market Place), with twin quadrant corners and pilastraded shopfronts flanking the grand entry to the former Stockbridge Market (*see* Public Buildings, above); one side formed part of Captain Carnegie's market development. Then Nos. 41–61, built to Brown's design by *John Cunningham* in 1824–9 and very like Brown's William Street (*see* Western New Town), with two storeys above the pilastered shop windows which have little bracketed iron walkways over the basement areas. Further on, the unity breaks down. Nos. 79–87 at the E end are plainer, of the 1850s, Nos. 75–77 (c. 1860) depart further from Brown's design and even have a wall-head chimney, and Nos. 63–73 (c. 1870) cram in an extra storey under the cornice with two chimneys above.

The s side is much more complete. Nos. 22–102 with their pilastered shops are similar to Nos. 41–61 across the road, but on higher ground, so that Brown was able to contrive shops on two levels, ground floor and basement, with steps up to one and down to the other – the most extensive example of what was once a common Edinburgh arrangement. This

long block was the work of two builders, *Andrew Wilson* up
to No. 58 and *Robert Gilkison* beyond. Wilson used inferior
stone above the shopfronts, and Nos. 22–58 were refaced by
John C. Hope in 1976–80. All these blocks consist of flats,
some small, many further subdivided. The shops came to new
life during the 1970s, but the smart ones have not yet ousted
the brightly eccentric or the conscientiously shabby. At the
E end of St Stephen Street the oddities are architectural, all
on the S side. First the former ST STEPHEN'S SCHOOL by
George Smith, 1835–6, big and plain with an open book on
top, bold Playfair-inspired consoles enclosing the middle windows. Then the red-and-yellow-brick Episcopal Hall with a
pediment, built for St Vincent's Church in the early 1860s,
and finally *Sydney Mitchell*'s ST STEPHEN'S CHURCH
HALLS, 1883, incongruously Gothic in the Rowand Anderson
manner. The stationery factory of *c.* 1875 which closes the
Clarence Street vista is prosaic but decently proportioned.

The E end of St Stephen Street is really part of the Northern
New Town, included here because of its name and history
(*see* above). On the corner of Clarence Street a big block by
Thomas Brown, 1829–30. Beset by structural troubles from
the start, it is a *locus classicus* in Edinburgh conservation, its
basic soundness vindicated by *Robert Hurd & Partners*' re-
medial work in 1975–6. Next to it the curved red sandstone
frontage of the large and unsuccessful skating rink designed
in 1895 by *Peter L. Henderson* and converted to a theatre in
1899–1901 by *T. P. Marwick*, who heightened the elevation.
It is now a ballroom. Across the road are Victorian tenements
bent to fit the curve, with long-and-short dressings of red
stone.

CLARENCE STREET is nicely aligned with the tower of St Bernard's church, drawing the rather isolated Saxe-Coburg
scheme into the larger plan. By September 1825 *Robert Brown*
had designed it all, with the exception of Thomas Brown's SE
corner noted above, as main door and common stair tenements. Unfortunately the quality of the stone is among the
worst in the New Town. Nos. 22–26 have had their rusticated
and polished surfaces rendered right over. Nos. 21–25 were
not built at all, and remain an unsightly gap. Both sites strad-
dle the line of the old Stockbridge mill lade. The pavilion on
the corner of St Stephen Street was built by *William Cullen*
in 1829–30. Those to the N have bowed corners, pilastered
ground floors, and basement shops, but differ in detail. The
NE one was built by *Alexander Smith* in 1825–6; the NW one
(1830–1) states the theme for Nos. 70–88 Hamilton Place,
where the ground floor is rusticated.

In the middle of HAMILTON PLACE crushingly large and plain
tenements by *T. P. Marwick* for the St Cuthbert's Co-operative Society, 1901–9; a disappointing work. Brick-built bakery and warehouses behind. The pend at No. 54 leads into
PATRIOTHALL, a symmetrical U-plan block of brick industrial housing, *c.* 1860. Like other model schemes of its date it

has been well thought out as institutional architecture, with three round-arched stair-towers, the middle one with a pyramid roof. In the main range, cantilevered galleries for access. Further along Hamilton Place Nos. 28-34 of the 1820s, with a rusticated ground floor. Next comes *Archibald Scott*'s tenement over the entrance to the former Stockbridge Market (*see* Public Buildings, above), and then Nos. 12-16 with pedimented first-floor windows.

Now the site of the old Stockbridge Mills. Nos. 6-10, with GLANVILLE PLACE, were built in 1823-4 in place of the old steading, quite plain except for some cast-iron balconies. BAKER'S PLACE round the corner on the main road, a small two-storey block, abutted the W gables of the mill buildings, which worked till 1901 when they were largely wrecked by an explosion; a fragment can still be seen (1984), but most of the site was covered with housing by *Christopher Dinnis Associates*, 1983-4.

3. Saxe-Coburg and Deanbank

DEANBANK HOUSE, concealed from Saxe-Coburg Street by a stone wall, is a late-C18 villa of two bays and three storeys, with piend roof, rustication and urns at the corners, and a large cavetto round the front door. The single-storey wings project at the back, and their ball-finialled gables are joined by a wall over which appears the Gothick-glazed staircase window; a pleasing, nearly symmetrical composition. In DEANBANK LANE two other villas of the same period, less interesting and somewhat altered: DEANBANK COTTAGE and the former DEANBANK LODGE.

In 1802 a site of four acres (1·6 ha.) at Deanbank was advertised for feuing to a plan by *Robert Burn*, but nothing seems to have been built. The present scheme was laid out in 1821 for the Trustees of James Rose. SAXE-COBURG STREET (originally East Claremont Street), developed on the NE side by the architect-builder *Adam O. Turnbull*, starts with a four-storey block of 1826 on the corner of Henderson Row, to which it presents pilastered shopfronts. Nos. 3-7 (1825) and 8-12 (1831-2, with unevenly spaced windows) are of only three storeys, but nonetheless higher than St Bernard's in between (*see* Churches, above). At the end Nos. 13-15, plain post-Georgian of *c.*1867; DEANBANK TERRACE on the SW side, turning the corner into Hamilton Place, is a similar development of 1870-6. If the terrace planned by Turnbull on this side (corresponding with Nos. 1-12 over the way) had been built, it would have involved the demolition of Deanbank House.

SAXE-COBURG PLACE is charming but sadly unfinished. *James Milne*'s scheme of 1821 was for a long rectangular layout of two-storey houses with basements, the centre and end houses on each long side slightly higher, with four giant, but friendly, Ionic pilasters. The short NW side was to have just the end houses advanced and presumably pilastered. Building started at once, and of the nine houses planned on the SW side Nos. 1–8 were completed, but not the pilastered No. 9. In 1828 its site, and that of its opposite number on the NE side, was taken over by *Turnbull* along with the whole NW end, which he replanned as a three-storey semicircular crescent with double-house pavilions. Milne's design (minus the end house) was carried out on the NE side, though Nos. 25–27 were not built till after 1852. But only half Turnbull's crescent was up when he was bankrupted in 1834, and in 1897 the N part was clumsily filled with the red sandstone Glenogle Baths whose front is to Glenogle Road (*see* Canonmills, Public Buildings). Nos. 7 and 8 were unhappily remodelled by *John Ingram*, 1919, as a single building with an extra storey. Otherwise there has been little change except for some altered glazing and a few attic additions.

10. CANONMILLS AND CLAREMONT

A series of modest-sized Georgian developments, none of them completed, on the N fringe of the New Town. Maps of the 1820s show that a formal layout was intended between Fettes Row and Henderson Row, with St Vincent Street continuing downhill to finish opposite the portico of Edinburgh Academy. A good start was made in Henderson Row itself, but then the scheme stagnated. In 1822 *Robert Brown* designed a scheme for the estate of James Eyre near Canonmills on the Water of Leith (the old milling settlement of the Abbey of Holyroodhouse). It did better, but the high-density Victorian completion of Eyre Crescent is particularly unhappy. The Heriot Trust's Bellevue and East Claremont scheme was attractively sited to the E, with a view over the wooded grounds of Broughton Hall and Broughton Park (since built over). But it was remote and overambitious. The long vistas from St Mary's church (Northern New Town) brings expectations of further Georgian achievements but does not fulfil them. The most complete development in this area is in fact Victorian – the pioneer artisan housing-scheme known as the Colonies on the S bank of the Water of Leith.

CHURCHES

BELLEVUE CHAPEL, Rodney Street. By *James B. Wemyss* of Leith. A little Gothic church with a spire, 1878–81, originally for Herr Blumenreich's German congregation. 'Bare and uninteresting', said *The Builder*.

DAVIDSON CHURCH, Eyre Place and Eyre Crescent. Now a warehouse. Middle-Pointed Gothic by *John Starforth*, 1879–81, the halls at the back added on the lines he intended, but by *G. Washington Browne* ten years later. Starforth was a pupil of Bryce but his Edinburgh churches are not among his best.* This one is of six bays N to S, broad and bulky in relation to the crescent in which it stands, its SW tower meant to have a steeple but given a pyramidal roof instead. However it has many interesting details; the 2–4–2 arrangement of the S gable windows, the SE porch-stair with its wheel window and L-plan roof, the trefoil-headed main windows and the dormers in the main roof.

ST BERNARD'S FREE CHURCH, Henderson Row. Disused. Gothic, by *John Milne* of St Andrews‡ (a pupil of David

---

* Cf. his churches at Dumfries, Moffat, Kelso and Greenock.

‡ It is a replica of the Martyrs' Free Church in St Andrews (since rebuilt) also by Milne.

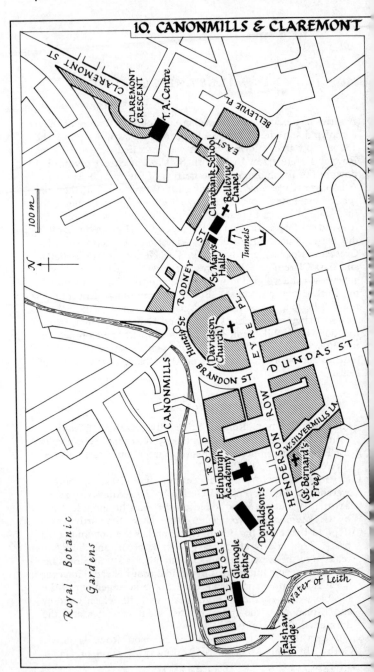

10. CANONMILLS & CLAREMONT

Bryce), 1854–6, incorporating the s gable of the previous brick church of 1844. Milne's N front is a very respectable piece of early Dec: ashlar, buttressed and pinnacled, the central doorway with three orders of shafts, blind flanking arches, and a three-light window above. Spired belfry corbelled from the apex of the gable. Five aisled bays, the clearstorey framed up in timber. Galleried interior with cast-iron columns supporting shouldered beam 'arcades' and a good plaster ribvault. – Between the wars Milne's octagonal PULPIT was moved forward in front of a large organ case. – STAINED GLASS above it: a war memorial in a vesica (the Risen Christ with a pelican and a phoenix) by *Douglas Hamilton*, 1949. – HALLS to the w. A small edition of the old church, of brick with low-pitch roofs, built as a school in 1845–6, possibly by *Robert Wright*, who was an office-bearer in the congregation.

ST MARY'S CHURCH HALLS, Rodney Street. By *Sydney Mitchell*, 1885, reconstructed from *George Smith*'s old Canonmills Parish School of 1827–30. A decent two-storey late Gothic gable front with high Flemish crowsteps and a square NW projection, broached to octagonal, containing the staircase. For St Mary's Church *see* Northern New Town.

PUBLIC BUILDINGS

CLAREBANK SCHOOL, Rodney Street. By *Robert Wilson*, 1880. Minimal Gothic. Gablets flank a big centre gable with the Edinburgh board-school roundel of a figure of Education. The bellcote at the top has been removed.

EDINBURGH ACADEMY, Henderson Row. Basic Greek by *William Burn*, 1823–4, for the committee of subscribers set up by Henry Cockburn and Leonard Horner in 1822. The first design for a two-storey school, probably related to Burn's Merchant Maiden School of 1816, was found too expensive even when reduced to a single storey. The City offered to build it, but finally decided on a different site (*see* Calton, Public Buildings, Royal High School), so the committee went on with their own project on the Henderson Row site which was acquired from the Heriot Trust. Burn again revised his plans in June 1823 and the building was substantially complete by October 1824, at the modest cost of £13,000.

The enforced economy makes the Academy, with its low profile and primitive Greek Doric order, the most interesting of Burn's classical public buildings, though the plan has been obscured by the subdivision and knocking together of rooms. It is an inverted T, the stem formed by the hall, the cross-bar by a double-pile arrangement of classrooms, with a suite of two small rooms at each end, entered from outside; at the far end of the hall a single pile consisting of the Rector's classroom, large waiting-room, and two more small classrooms. The large W room on the main front remains intact. Portico and pediment of deep projection with four unfluted columns, the 'temple' axis maintained by the long oval of the hall's clearstorey lantern popping up behind. The contrary emphasis of the long frontage is acknowledged, however, by a single-column porch attached to each side. End pavilions, after three regular bays, defined by antae at the corners.

Inside, the long oval HALL was originally quite plain, relieved only by the niches and cantilevered balcony, and the shallow coffered dome with central oculus. The floor was tiered down to the central well in which sat the Rector and his staff. In 1911–12 *A. F. Balfour Paul* added columns at each end below the balcony, rosettes in the coffers, and at the N end a mahogany case for the organ by *Lewis & Co.*, 1913, rebuilt by *Compton* in 1962. Stained glass (the Signs of the Zodiac) by *Ballantine* in the lantern above. On the portico are bold inscriptions in Latin and Greek, an allusion to the committee's insistence on classical education; the first announces that the Edinburgh Academy was dedicated to the studies of youth in 1824, the second that Education is the Mother of Wisdom and Virtue. Alabaster tablet in the vestibule to James Carmichael † 1895, by *Robert S. Lorimer*.

Burn's original arrangement included covered ways with slim cast-iron columns leading from the end doors and returning along the sides of the forecourt to the lodges on Henderson Row. Only two bays survive, to the E of the building; also the JANITOR'S LODGE, a two-storey cottage with low-pitch roofs and jerkin-headed gables. MASTER'S LODGE rebuilt by *R. S. Reid* of *Leadbetter, Fairley & Reid* in 1924 after a fire; two storeys with a balconied porch, perfunctorily classical. At the far NW corner of the site the L-plan OLD MATHEMATICAL (from 1888 OLD PREP), single-storey ashlar with a piend roof, joined on by *Alan Reiach*'s low slate-hung link to the long single-storey block on the W side of the forecourt, an easy-going design by *MacGibbon & Ross*, 1892–3, with a pedimented frontispiece and pretty diagonal-boarded porches to the classrooms. Across the court the LIBRARY. Severely Neo-Classical centre block by *Leadbetter & Fairley*, 1898–1900 (the clock later); lower symmetrical wings with key-blocked tripartite windows by *R. S. Reid*, 1930. To the N the plain LABORATORIES, 1890 by *MacGibbon & Ross*, who also designed the Venetian-windowed LECTURE THEATRE in 1908.

The other buildings line the N side of the site, facing the two courts formed by Burn's hall range. To the W *A. F. Balfour Paul*'s dormered DINING HALL BLOCK, 1911, with a deep bracketed balcony, symmetrical except for the off-centre sculptured doorpiece; interior modified by *Stanley P. Ross-Smith*, 1973. To the E the WAR MEMORIAL BUILDING by *R. S. Reid*, 1922, a monumental single-storey frontage over a channelled basement. Inside, the gymnasium, with an arched steel truss roof and some Doric details. None of these buildings has anything like the merit of the original, but at least they do not embarrass it; the best is the library.

DONALDSON BUILDING (former Deaf and Dumb Institution), to the W, set well back from Henderson Row where only the lodge and gates are visible. Original building of 1823 by *J. Gillespie Graham*, quite severe; three storeys with advanced and pedimented centre and fanlit doorpiece of coupled Roman Doric pilasters. In 1893 *Charles S. S. Johnston* added two-storey wings with attics, neo-Jacobean with ogee-roofed angle towers; a curious choice both of style and material (red sandstone).

FALSHAW BRIDGE (across the Water of Leith), W end of Glenogle Road. 1877 by *David C. Proudfoot*, engineer, with iron handrails, the thistle-topped posts reinstated in 1956 when the structure was renewed by the *City Engineer* with prestressed concrete beams.

GLENOGLE BATHS, Glenogle Road. A castellated composition (adapted from his Dalry baths design) by *Robert Morham*, 1897–1900, towering above the road. Buttressed towers on three of the corners but not on the one nearest to Saxe-Coburg Place, where the curved classical frontage is in yellow ashlar instead of the rock-faced red sandstone of the rest; this does not camouflage the huge roof looming up irrelevantly behind.

TERRITORIAL ARMY CENTRE, East Claremont Street. Free, indeed wilful, Renaissance by *T. Duncan Rhind*, 1912. Pedimented centrepiece with chunky squared-off details; the upper-floor semi-dormers look as if they are still waiting for the wall to be built up between and over them. Predictably, no thought for the surroundings.

PERAMBULATION

On the W side of BRANDON STREET the former PRINTING WORKS of R. & R. Clark, symmetrical Jacobean by *John Chesser*, 1883, with shaped gables, bays and bows, became in 1976 the dignified frontage of a very large Fyfestone-clad office block by *Covell Matthews Partnership*. In HENDERSON ROW Nos. 2–28 and 32–42 on the N side are by *William Burn*, all 1825–6 except the corner block at No. 28 of 1887 by *MacGibbon & Ross* (its front conforming to Burn's design, its Perth Street flank bay-windowed). Plain, impressive tenements of main door and common stair type, with channelled ground floor and Ionic porches at the main doors, the crowning balustrade formerly continuous except at the end pavilions, which have a fourth storey. In the entrance hall of the main door flat at No. 6 two pendentived bays with wreaths. On the S side a motley collection, with a couple of minor public buildings. POLICE GARAGE designed by *W. Hamilton Beattie* in 1886 as a depot for the Northern Cable Tramway Company, with a broad vehicle entrance supported by cast-iron pilasters, some fussy architecture on top; adjoining public WASH HOUSE, with chimney, of 1904. After St Ber-

nard's Free Church (*see* above), West Silvermills Lane leads
past the carcase of SILVERMILLS HOUSE of *c.* 1760, three
rubble storeys with narrow dressed margins and an architraved doorpiece of bold profile. Parts of the mills themselves
still stand on both sides of the lane to the S of the house, with
some remnants of the tannery which did much to inhibit the
progress of New Town development.

Saxe-Coburg Street (*see* Stockbridge) and Gabriel's Road lead
to GLENOGLE ROAD. On the S side the Glenogle Baths
(*see* Public Buildings, above), on the N the COLONIES,
eleven parallel terraces laid out in 1861 by the Edinburgh
Co-operative Building Association, promoted by the Rev.
James Begg* and managed by James Colville. At the E end
the converted C18 GLENOGLE HOUSE. REID TERRACE
(named after Sir Hugh Gelzean Reid of the *Evening News*,
who gave much encouragement to the scheme) was begun on
23 October 1861: two-storey terrace of 'flatted cottages', the
ground floor entered from one side, the first floor from the
other by means of outside stairs. Front gardens on both sides,
with the original iron clothes-poles. The scheme proved a
success, and the similar HUGH MILLER PLACE was put in
hand in 1863, RINTOUL PLACE and COLVILLE PLACE in
the next two years. The later terraces have bay-windows. All
are of stugged and snecked masonry with rock-faced gables
to Glenogle Road, the keystones of the ground-floor windows
carved with the tools of various trades. Obelisk piers flank the
entries to the intermediate streets, all blind alleys except the
easternmost, which has a footbridge with rustic parapet crossing the Water of Leith to Rocheid Path. At its W end the road
crosses the river by Falshaw Bridge (*see* Public Buildings,
above); at its E end it returns, past some high-density *Barratt*
housing of 1978–81, to Brandon Street.

Now a circuit of a very mixed block. The E side of BRANDON
STREET (1822) was the main part of *Robert Brown*'s Eyre
Estate development to be executed. The three-storey corner
pavilion follows the example of his earlier work in Melville
Street (*see* Western New Town), with over-arched ground-
floor windows in the advanced end bays. First a two-storey
row, with a rib-vaulted entrance hall at No. 7. Then Nos. 10–
16, a four-storey tenement on a convex curve and a gentle
slope, in gently advanced and recessed planes with a panelled
parapet over the five central bays (cf. the similar but concave
treatment at Brown's Coates Crescent). Brandon Terrace is
late Victorian, with canted bays over shops. *Brown* then reappears at the tenement of HUNTLY STREET, 1825, another
generously curved frontage with a centre panel on the parapet
and a plain arcaded ground floor; graceful fanlights. It turns
a flat front to the foot of CANON STREET, where Nos. 1–7
are again by *Brown*, internally reconstructed by *Philip Cocker
Associates* for the Link Housing Association in 1974. The

---

* Begg describes the enterprise in *Happy Homes for Working Men.*

heavily altered four-storey mill buildings of Canonmills on the E side lost their original function in 1865. In the adjoining filling-station a lintel from one of the two buildings formerly on the site, cursively inscribed 'the Baxters land 1686'.

Round the corner EYRE CRESCENT, a deep and oppressive U of four-storey tenements mainly by *George A. Lyle*,* 1891–4, awkwardly filled with the former Davidson Church (*see* above). To the S a strange hinterland with three items of interest. At Nos. 3–5 EYRE TERRACE an improbable tenement of 1904, four rendered storeys, the surrounds stuck with bits of road-metal, a centre panel of a lion rampant between diamond panels with a thistle and a rose, all picked out with little coloured rocks.‡ In DUNDAS STREET, on the corner of Eyre Place, the TRUSTEE SAVINGS BANK, which consists of a warehouse designed by *Covell Matthews & Partners*, 1966, wrapped up in brown anodized facing panels by *Alan Reiach, Eric Hall & Partners* in 1982. A smart, rather crinkly parcel with pink string on top. The former Alexander's Garage, cement-faced Wembley Art Deco of 1931 by *Reid & Forbes*. Uphill on the E side, the ROYAL BANK OF SCOTLAND COMPUTER CENTRE by *Michael Laird & Partners*, 1978, a three-decker sandwich rising from well below street level, both the long sides canted inwards at a continuous angle in deference to Fettes Row as the monumental entry to the Northern New Town. Its success is parodied by the slightly later buildings (by other architects) across the street. For the main (S) part of Dundas Street, *see* Northern New Town, p. 344.

At the Canonmills junction a four-faced CLOCK on an Art Deco dolmen by *L. Grahame Thomson*, 1947. The street bearing the name of CANONMILLS starts with a hammer-dressed baronial tenement of 1863 on the corner of Warriston Road (bakery on the ground floor). Further uphill the former Youth Centre of the Dublin Street Baptist Church (*see* Northern New Town), a nice remodelling of the school attended by Robert Louis Stevenson, as recorded on a plaque designed by *Tom Curr*. The architect was *David McArthy*, the date 1906. A long retaining wall leads up to HERIOT HILL HOUSE, secluded behind a gateway on the corner of Broughton Road. Very plain, built by 1788 but soon afterwards given a new front range with tripartite windows and single-storey wings.

Rodney Street leads to what exists of the Heriot Trust's Bellevue and East Claremont development, begun at the N end in 1823 with CLAREMONT CRESCENT by *William Burn*. Segmental plan, with short parallel wings making it into a shallow U, open to East Claremont Street; plain but distinctively proportioned, with square-sunk rustication on the ground floor. By 1852 only half the houses in the segment were finished,

---

* Lyle was assistant and successor to *Robert Raeburn*, who designed the Canon Street corner and possibly also the crescent.

‡ *Lorimer* supported the Dean of Guild petition, but can hardly have been the architect.

but eventually all were built except one; the later date is revealed indoors, and at the tall backs where bay-windows appear.

In EAST CLAREMONT STREET a N wing with a surprisingly plain elevation. The S wing was not built; the Territorial Army Centre took its site (*see* Public Buildings, above). On the E side No. 118 (originally the Civil Service Supply Association warehouse), a well proportioned front by *John Lumsdaine*, 1886, and CLAREMONT COURT, a civilized block of council flats by *Basil Spence, Glover & Ferguson*, 1960. The rest of the W side by *Thomas Bonnar*, from 1824, Nos. 1–41 (1824–30) a splendid range of four-storey tenements, more like Glasgow than Edinburgh in the overall rhythm of ground-floor arches without rustication, and the pedimenting of every third window at first-floor level. Nos. 43–85 are slightly later (1825–7) and more orthodox except for the abrupt change in scale; two-storey houses with a channelled and recessed ground floor and emphasized pavilions.

BELLEVUE TERRACE, designed by *Bonnar* just before he died, was built mainly under the control of *Alexander Black* in 1834–56. Nos. 1–3, a large tenement rounding the corner, echo the arched ground floor of East Claremont Street but add giant Roman Doric pilasters to the plain first and second floors; again an above-average performance by Bonnar. Nos. 4–11, a mixture of houses and flats with identical square-headed doors, form a straight range grandly raised on a terraced site, with crowning balustrades. The gable at No. 11 shows that further building was intended (it would have turned NE into a large crescent facing NW), but at least enough was finished to appear complete from Bellevue Crescent. After Black's death, Bonnar's ambitious scheme was given up. Their successor *John Chesser* designed the simple two-storey U-plan terrace of houses on the SE side of East Claremont Street (Nos. 2–24) and in BELLEVUE PLACE. Most of the latter was not built till the 1890s. The rest of the area was partly developed with four-storey tenements from the 1870s and then filled up with a motley sprinkling of two-storey suburban houses.

11. GAYFIELD, HOPE AND PICARDY

A large range of time and character, from the stolid late C18 to
the showiest late Georgian; and of type, from the single tenement to the palace-fronted terrace, the urban frontage complete
with shops, and even some surprisingly early suburban villas.
All have had their troubles, both in their building and their
subsequent history. As a bonus, the section includes a great
Victorian church whose future, in 1984, is regrettably uncertain.

CHURCHES

BELLEVUE REFORMED BAPTIST CHURCH (formerly Catholic 41
Apostolic), East London Street, facing Mansfield Place. Norman, as required in the competition* which was won by *R.
Rowand Anderson*, 1872. The lawyer W.F. Pitcairn was chief
promoter. Big, simple roofs and grey, hammer-dressed walls,
composed and detailed with authority. The church is built up
to street level on a base consisting of a hall, library and
offices, to make the most of a very conspicuous site. Work
began in 1873 and stopped three years later, after £17,000
had been spent, with a temporary wall in the middle of the w
gable where a square tower had been proposed. In 1884 Anderson revised this end, substituting a large narthex and circular sw baptistery; a round s tower was proposed but again
not built. The structure was finished by 1885, and in 1893
work started on the paintings which had been intended from
the start. The choir capitals, left in block, were carved in the
following year.

The exterior is dominated by the nave, five tall aisleless
bays with paired clearstorey windows, and square corner-
turrets which have blind arcaded tops and stone pyramid
spires. In the w gable a giant wheel window with scalloped
edge and colonnette spokes. Large gabled narthex beneath it,
the windows flanked by narrower blind ones as in the
conical-roofed baptistery. The three-bay chancel meets the E
end of the nave Gerona-style, its last bay aisleless and running
into the semicircular E apse whose clearstorey windows are
incorporated in a blind arcade. At London Street level an
iron gallery runs round the apse to the two-storeyed neo-
Norman house adjoining the NE nave bay. A very spacious
interior of simple geometry with well-judged decoration.

---

* For the earlier Catholic Apostolic Church in Broughton Street *see* Northern
New Town.

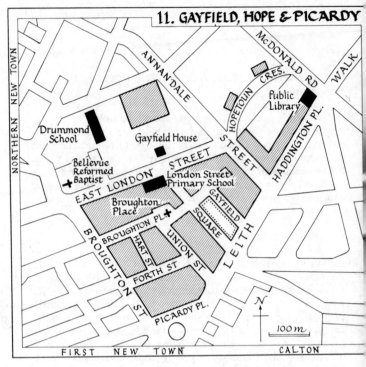

Rib-vaulted narthex leading through a large doorway to the
nave, a double cube with a tunnel roof. Plain walls, interrupted only by single wall-shafts supporting the arch-braces.
Clearstorey windows high up in deep splays, linked by a
wall-passage which is reached by spiral stairs in the turrets.
Tall chancel arch of four orders flanked by much smaller aisle
arches; aisle arcades with stiff-leaf capitals. In chancel and
apse the clearstorey forms part of an arcade with clustered
and ringed shafts, and once again a wall-passage behind.
Ribbed tunnel roof painted with formalized trees by *Andrew
Hutton*.

The MURAL DECORATION is by *Phoebe Traquair* (a
Dublin-born artist married to a Scots scientist), who began
over the chancel arch (1893–4) with the Worship of Heaven
from the Book of Revelation; at the top, a multitude of saints
over the sea of glass mingled with fire, then the four-and-
twenty elders beneath canopies, and finally choirs of singing
and trumpeting angels. Haloes, crowns and trumpets
moulded in relief and gilded. s chapel with tunnel ceiling and
N aisle with close-beamed lean-to roof painted with the Wise
and Foolish Virgins in 1895–7, when work also began on the
continuous narrative of the origins and life of Christ in the
triforium zone of the nave. w wall with Christ in Glory sur-

rounded by hosts of trumpeting angels, like the E wall bright with gold. Phoebe Traquair painted in oils with a water-colour technique, and at the time her style was described as early Florentine; it certainly has freshness and impact, with reminiscences of Puvis de Chavannes and of the Edinburgh artist William Hole. She was not so good a draughtsman as Hole but, as Sir James Caw* remarked, she has much greater charm of colour and a Blake-like command in representing the supernatural. Her paintings are essential to the great plain surfaces of Anderson's church.

STAINED GLASS. An elaborate scheme, the W wheel window with decorative glass by *Ballantine*, 1885, the authorship of the remainder (New Testament scenes) unknown. Three lights in the E window of the S chapel (the Transfiguration) successful, rich in colour though somewhat blunt in drawing. – Anderson's BALDACCHINO of 1893–4 is arched and vaulted with gabled angle-turrets and a spired octagonal superstructure; carved angels, apostles and prophets by *W. Birnie Rhind*. Of the ORGAN only the fanciful Romanesque case survives, cantilevered from the S nave wall. The relatively modest PULPIT is of oak, linenfold panelled. The other furnishings including the stalls, all of much significance in Catholic Apostolic ritual, have been dispersed and the church is now (1984) used as a store, only the narthex for worship.

BROUGHTON PLACE CHURCH, at the E end of Broughton Place. Greek Doric, built in 1820–1 as the Rev. James Hall's United Associate Synod Chapel (an offshoot from the Burgher Congregation in Rose Street), but best known as Dr John Brown's Chapel, after its second minister. *Archibald Elliot's* design is unusually pretentious for a Secession Church: square in plan, with two storeys of arched openings and a tetrastyle Greek Doric portico, the columns two-thirds fluted with the lower third of polygonal section down to the two-step stylobate. Plain rubble flanks, and at the E end a semi-lozenge organ bay, cantilevered over the lane, by *G. Washington Browne*, 1890. Simple platform roof. Tower and spire planned but not built.

Inside, square vestibule and twin stair-halls with simple round arches and reeded doorcases. Auditorium recast by *John Paterson* in his characteristic Romanesque manner, 1870, giving segmental heads and colonnettes to Elliot's windows, rich arcading to the fronts of the U-plan gallery and elaborate foliated capitals to its cast-iron columns. Elliot's flush-panelled pews were remodelled. – PULPIT of very generous proportions (as usual in United Presbyterian churches), with elaborate Paterson detailing. – Plain Renaissance case above it by *Browne* containing the ORGAN by *Henry Willis & Sons*, 1890, rebuilt in 1901 by *Norman & Beard*. The central area was rearranged and the whole interior lightened by the removal of varnish in 1952. – MEMORIALS. Tudor double

* *Scottish Painting*, 1908.

tablet to the Rev. James Hall † 1826 and Dr John Brown
†1858. – Good marble roundel of Dr John Smith by *W.
Grant Stevenson,* 1906.

CHURCH HALL AND OFFICES of 1878 at the nearby corner
of Union and Gayfield Streets by *Archibald Macpherson,*
usually a Roman Catholic architect. Renaissance, with a distinctive two-storey symmetrical front; consoled doorpiece,
arched first-floor windows and pedimented dormers. The hall
behind is single-storeyed with an elaborate Venetian window
to Gayfield Street. Interior with Roman Doric colonnades
and cupola lights.

PUBLIC BUILDINGS

DRUMMOND SECONDARY SCHOOL (formerly Bellevue),
Cochran Terrace. Economical Palladian by *John A. Carfrae,*
1911, in harl and red brick, with a central cupola.

LONDON STREET PRIMARY SCHOOL, East London Street.
Debased late classical by *Robert Wilson,* 1887, enlarged to the
rear by *John A. Carfrae,* 1910.

POLICE STATION, Gayfield Square. 1961 by *Michael Laird.*
Forecourt between rubbly gables. Externally framed sports
hall at the back.

PUBLIC LIBRARY, Leith Walk and McDonald Road. Baronial
Renaissance, designed as the Nelson Hall and East Branch
Library by *H. Ramsay Taylor,* 1902. Mullioned windows and
a big corner turret with candle-snuffer roof.

TELEPHONE EXCHANGE, East London Street. 1962 by the
Ministry of Works, a big simple block with an officious vertically emphasized frontage.

MANSION

68 GAYFIELD HOUSE was built shortly before 1765 by *Charles
& William Butter,* wrights. The first occupant was the Earl
of Leven. Now unhappily isolated beyond East London
Street, it has two storeys over a full basement – hence its
upstanding look. Rubble built, originally harled, the centre
three of its five bays set forward under a bullseyed pediment
topped with urns. Chimney gables of curly profile on the
flanks, their small windows lighting the attics whose roofs run
into the piends of the main one. Lugged architraves on the
windows above the basement, and a Roman Ionic doorpiece
reached by a flight of steps. Inside there is good but not
elaborate woodwork, and modest Rococo plasterwork, in the
entrance hall and the upper-floor drawing room to the NE.
Geometrical staircase with turned balusters.

PERAMBULATIONS

1. Gayfield

The solicitor James Jollie began feuing the grounds of Gayfield
House (*see* above) in 1785. Development began (on the NE side
of its front drive) with Gayfield Place, some of which was later
re-named Gayfield Square. By 1807, if not before, *Hugh Cairncross* (an ex-assistant of Robert Adam) was being employed; he
was later joined by his son *George*. The Gayfield Estate is an
engaging mixture of formal and informal, elegant and austere,
and not only retains the mid-Georgian villa from which it took
its name (*see* above) but includes some of the earliest of the
villas (in the lesser sense) which were to become so popular
elsewhere in the 1820s.

The large and magnificent tenement of GAYFIELD PLACE was
begun in 1790 by the obscure architect *James Begg*; no design
by Cairncross is known. The massive five-bay centrepiece has
four storeys like the rest, but then continues with a fifth
shallow one at the attic, in which the advanced end bays have
semicircular lunettes crowned with pediments. Then four-bay
flanking ranges, and finally another projection with a bow like
a corner-tower at each end; in each bow a tall over-arch taking
in three storeys of windows – tripartite on the ground floor,
Venetian on the first and second. Still unfinished in 1804, the
building has certain inconsistencies – e.g. the turning of the
SW end and its bow to line up with the square, and the narrowing of the adjacent windows which are mere slits – but is
executed with obsessive attention to detail. The ground-floor
rustication and the Venetian window shafts are not polished
but droved, and stranger still, their arches are made of only
three stones; unfortunately the keystones have tended to slip.
Garlanded ceilings and a Venetian hall-screen in the main
door flat at No. 4.

GAYFIELD SQUARE began on the SW side. No. 1, and the little
row of houses that formerly adjoined the square, were replaced in 1961–5 by the Police Station (*see* Public Buildings,
above). The remaining houses were built from *c.* 1790–1800,
at least one by *Alexander Laing*. Nos. 3–5 are two-storey villas
four windows wide with front gardens, each slightly different
in detail; No. 3 of plain droved ashlar with a Roman Doric
pilastered doorpiece whose shafts and frieze are fluted; No. 4
of polished ashlar with rusticated ground floor and detached
Roman Doric column doorpiece; No. 5 with only an architraved doorpiece, but notable for an elaborate wrought-iron
lamp-holder bridging the gatepiers. The other houses on the
NW side run out of the square towards Gayfield House, with
basements and areas but no front gardens. No. 6 detached,
No. 7 with a cavetto-framed and Corinthian pilastered doorpiece, Nos. 8 and 9 a double houseblock (since divided, with
a peculiar alteration to the door of No. 8), and No. 10 only
two windows wide.

The NW SIDE is by *Hugh Cairncross*. Nos. 12–17, designed in 1807 and built by *John Fraser*, are a virtually symmetrical main door and common stair block of three storeys and basement with a rusticated ground floor, the ends and pedimented centre slightly advanced; quite plain, and now even more so with the cornices cut back from the pediment and l. side. Nos. 18–20 and 21–23 (1808) run out of the square to the NE, their design more basic as they get further away. Both blocks are of the two main door and central common stair type, the latter without string-courses. No. 24, built on the falling ground with five absolutely plain storeys, became derelict and was demolished in 1976. On the NE SIDE Nos. 24–26, 27–29 and 30–32 are again by *Cairncross*, 1807, an austere but effective group of tenements of the same type but with four storeys. The arched doorpieces of the main door flats are variously treated (No. 32 quite special with filigree jambs), and the ground floor rustication stops at the recessed common-stair bays, into which the cornice is neatly returned at the top. Some unexpectedly elaborate interiors, e.g. with apse-ended rooms and Corinthian pilasters. *David Skae* and *John & Alexander Drysdale* were the builders.

ANTIGUA STREET, in progress in 1800, lies on Leith Walk. Starting with a blank gable to the square, it consists of four plain tenements with an extra storey above the cornice at Nos. 1–5. The canted bay at No. 1 turns the corner into UNION STREET, whose development was shared by the Gayfield and Picardy estates. The Gayfield (NE) side was built in 1804–6 by *John Williamson*, *John Inglis* and *John Aitchison*, probably to *Cairncross*'s design, as they are the three-storey equivalent of the NE side of Gayfield Square. They also have similar interiors, of which Nos. 17–21 are most interesting: concave diamond motifs on the entrance hall ceilings, and twin-arched screens (with slim shafts and long-leafed Adamesque capitals) at the basement stairs. In the main door flat at No. 5 an unusually designed recess in its principal room; clustered Gothic shafts and a frieze with an urn and griffons. Further downhill the street becomes BROUGHTON PLACE EAST, where No. 2 was built in 1808 and Nos. 3–5 in 1819–20. Ahead is the oblique view of the Doric portico of the Broughton Place Church (*see* Churches, above) seen past its Victorian Renaissance Halls.

BROUGHTON PLACE was offered for feuing in 1807 to *Cairncross*'s design. The N SIDE is a long palace-front of two-storey houses, with three-storey main door and common stair blocks forming the ends and pedimented centrepiece. Rusticated ground floor, with over-arches in the flatted blocks only, and rock-faced basement. A distinguished terrace indeed, obviously influenced by the E section of Heriot Row (*see* Northern New Town) but slightly smaller in scale. E pavilion memorable for the bow on its E gable with balustered Venetian windows on ground and first floors. In the main door flat (No. 30) a pendentived entrance hall with busts in the lunettes. The W pavilion, built in 1819 as the St James' Episcopal Chapel and School, was converted to shops and houses some time after 1888. The S SIDE is less unified and of smaller scale, with plain basements but rock-faced ground floors, all with main doors and common stairs. Two shallow bows face each other at the entry into HART STREET, built in 1808, the E side by *Robert & Henry Paterson*, the W by *Walter Paterson*; they signed the plans and the architect did not, but he was probably *Cairncross* again. Two-storey houses of various widths (from four to seven windows) stepped uphill to Forth Street. EAST LONDON STREET marks the N edge of the estate. On the S side the London Street Primary School spoils the view towards Gayfield House. To the W the fascist-looking Telephone Exchange, and the large tenement block at Nos. 2-10, late Georgian in its intention but 1872 in its turgid execution. Finally R. Rowand Anderson's Romanesque Catholic Apostolic (now Reformed Baptist) Church. For these churches and public buildings, *see* above.

2. *The Hope Estate*

In 1824-5, encouraged no doubt by the early success of the Calton scheme, Major John Hope offered this land for feuing to a scheme by *Robert Brown*, whom he had already employed at Clerk Street and Rankeillor Street (*see* South Side) and who here produced some of the most highly finished terraces in the New Town. Unfortunately the demand quickly slackened, and the result is a number of graceful fragments. The projected square to the N of Hope (now Hopetoun) Crescent was not started or even named.

HADDINGTON PLACE is part of the NW side of Leith Walk. Begun in 1825, only its first section was completed (Nos. 1-8); four storeys over the basement, the ground-floor shops defined by coupled antae and the common stair doors by Ionic columns *in antis*. First-floor windows with a continuous trellis balcony, their cornices modulated to pediments at the centre of each pavilion. Main cornice at second-floor level; the attic storey has a solid parapet with St Andrew's crosses over the pavilions (cf. Western New Town, Melville Crescent) and balustrades between. At the corner a majestic three-window bow with coupled Ionic columns at the ground floor and a scrolled panel at the wall-head. Of the similar corner on the other side of Annandale Street nothing was built, and of the longer, downhill section only enough (Nos. 17-32) to reveal the intended design of the centrepiece, whose three middle bays would have had coupled Ionic columns on shop level; only two bays exist, and a later tenement extends to the r. as far as the baronial Public Library on the corner of McDonald Road (*see* Public Buildings, above). To the l. the bland stone-faced office block with modified classical cornices and a rounded corner to Annandale Street is APEX

HOUSE by *Philip Cocker & Partners* (the interiors by the *Comprehensive Design Group*), 1976–8.

ANNANDALE STREET was planned with four-storey tenements. Two exist on the SW side, continuing from the bowed corner, with fanlit doors to the main door flats, Ionic columned doorpieces to the common stairs. On the NE side two similar but disconnected blocks with an Ionic columned doorpiece at Nos. 6–10 and a Greek Doric one at Nos. 18–22. For the rest, *Michael Laird & Partners* designed the STANDARD LIFE office to the SW in 1976, and to the NE its elegant covered car park with a deep corrugated facia in 1978. At the far SW end is the Lothian Region Transport CENTRAL GARAGE. With a symmetrical red brick façade and red stone dressings, Neo-Classical of sorts, surmounted by a huge glass dome, it is the shell of the extraordinary folly designed for the Edinburgh Exhibition Association by *G. M. Holmes Douglas* in 1922 when the Waverley Market (*see* First New Town, Public Buildings) was considered no longer suitable for large industrial shows. Converted to its present use and extended by the City Architect *E. J. MacRae* in 1934.

HOPETOUN CRESCENT is a tragedy. An Ionic paraphrase of Playfair's Hillside Crescent (*see* Calton, Perambulation), it was designed by *Brown* in 1825 and begun as a speculation by the architect *Patrick Wilson*, but of its two-storey houses only Nos. 7 and 8, 17 and 18 were built. So the full sweep of paired Ionic columns and first-floor balcony, cornice and crowning balustrade was never realized; these fragments stand forlorn in a mixed area of industrial development.

3. Picardy

This was a 5 acre (2 ha.) feu acquired by the City from the Heriot Trust in 1730 for a colony of silk-weavers who had fled from France after the Edict of Nantes. Their efforts to grow mulberry trees on the slopes E of the present St Andrew Square were not successful, and the village passed into the hands of the Commissioners for the Improvement of Manufactures in Scotland. In 1800 they made arrangements for its feuing with *Robert Burn*, and building went on to his designs from *c.* 1803–9. The triangle to the S of Picardy Place was demolished in 1969 in preparation for a huge traffic-interchange on the projected inner ring road. All that actually happened was a very large roundabout.

PICARDY PLACE (named after the old Weavers' Village) continues the line of York Place. The three-storey tenements of the S side, with taller blocks at the ends, have been demolished. The surviving N side, thus thrown into prominence, was designed as a long palace-front with a five-bay Ionic pilastered centrepiece, the middle bays set forward beneath a pediment. Pavilions with pedimented windows in the middle of the first floor, nicely connected to the adjacent streets with a splay to Union Place and a bow window to Broughton Street; this is where Robert Burn conducted a drawing academy. In 1973-5 Nos. 16-26 (E of the centre-piece) were gutted and reconstructed as an office-block with large rear additions. The fronts were stripped of later accre-tions but the restored ground floor has fewer doors, careless detail, and obvious c20 glazing. No party walls, no skews or chimneys. The centrepiece at No. 12 remains intact, and No. 14 to the E is only impaired by the projecting late Gothic shopfront by *Dunn & Findlay*, 1895. W part (despite shop-fronts) in better shape. The houses were built for well-to-do people, and some rather standardized plasterwork of late Adam type can still be seen in the main rooms. UNION PLACE, facing Leith Walk, consists of plain ashlar tenements. UNION STREET is similar.

Burn designed FORTH STREET symmetrically, but the detail is much less academic than in Picardy Place and the general height is two storeys. On the palace-fronted S side a centre-piece and pavilions of three storeys with rusticated ground floors. In the nine-bay centrepiece four giant panelled pilas-ters with pretty rosetted tops and a pediment, the end bays advanced without pilasters, all recalling the centrepiece on the N side of Charlotte Square on a much more intimate scale. Doorpieces in the intermediate bays, i.e. the third and seventh, replaced by windows in 1974-5 when *William Holford & Associates* remodelled the whole interior of the centrepiece, previously gutted for use as a warehouse. The two-storey houses on each side have doorpieces with rosetted pilasters against their plain ground floors. Interiors radically altered but with some fragments of Adamish plasterwork. At the W end the symmetry has been upset by the addition of an extra storey to one house and (less harmfully) by the insertion of a pilastered shop in the ground floor of the pavilion.

The N side of Forth Street is more fragmentary. E end block (1804) and Nos. 4-10 (1820) corresponding to the S side but much altered. Nos. 12-30, beyond Hart Street, were among the first to be built and are better preserved despite some mansard attics. Nos. 20 and 22 match the S side but the others do not. No. 24 similar, but altered with a continuous Victo-rian balcony and pilastered entrance hall. No. 26, of polished ashlar, is the most handsome house in the street, with the grandest of all the doorpieces, Ionic columned with the en-tablature fluted between rosettes. The fanlight arch, and those of the two windows to the side, spring from an ornamented string-course. Balustraded first-floor windows and rock-faced basement; good Adamish plasterwork inside. No. 28 at the E end, an equally well detailed house with a bow to Union Street, was built by *James Spadin*, architect, and finished in 1803.

The E side of this part of BROUGHTON STREET, *Burn*'s work as far as No. 41, was built in 1808-9. Later shops obliterate all the main door flats but Nos. 35-37 and the earlier block at Nos. 55-63 still have their arched ground floors. The coarse rubble late C18 blocks at Nos. 65-71 and 73-79 were on part of the Gayfield Estate.

12. CALTON

James Stuart in the preface to the *Antiquities of Athens* (1762)
compared the two cities in respect of their setting of hills by the
sea. But even in the early C19, after the building of two New
Towns and the starting of a third, there was no civic architecture to match the nickname Athens of the North, which Lord
Cockburn described as 'a sarcasm, or piece of affected flattery'.
The expansive years after the end of the Napoleonic wars in
1815 saw a dramatic change. By 1829, when Thomas Shepherd
published his *Modern Athens! Displayed in a Series of Views*
(the equivalent of the London views in *Metropolitan Improvements*), the number and combination of Greek Revival buildings
in the city fully justified the title. Although the temptation to
liken the Calton Hill to the Acropolis should be resisted (it
usurps the status of the Castle), the greatest concentration of
such buildings is here. The architecture on the hill itself is a
mixture of greatness and idiosyncrasy – a sort of windy outdoor
Valhalla, where most of the decisions about style and siting
were made piecemeal, with an eye more to picturesque relation-
ships than to formal ones (e.g. when *Thomas Hamilton* gave his
great school the aspect of a propylaeon, and related the telescopic profile of his Burns monument to that of the peculiar
Nelson monument). The absence of a master plan means that
the hill, as a natural feature, still dominates. Likewise *Playfair*'s
Calton Scheme defers to the landscape, though much more deliberately. The very formal prelude to all this, entirely urban in
its monumental combination of public and commercial buildings, is *Elliot*'s Waterloo Place.

CHURCHES

GREENSIDE CHURCH, Royal Terrace. Stiff Gothic by *James
Gillespie Graham*, 1830–9, the tower completed in 1851–2.
Rather the poor relation of Playfair's great terraces, and interesting mainly for its adoption of the T-plan and the lancet
style; earlier Gillespie Graham churches are almost invariably
neo-Perp rectangles. The tower with its depressed three-light
belfry windows and battlemented parapet with pinnacles is a
stock pattern of his, familiar from the 1820s onwards. The
gallery stair-halls flanking it are of 1885 by *David Robertson*,
who at the same time removed the transeptal galleries, recast
the furnishings and reglazed the church with cathedral glass.
– LECTERN. Bronze eagle by *Charles Henshaw*, 1939. –
ORGAN by *Harrison & Harrison* of Durham, 1885, rebuilt by

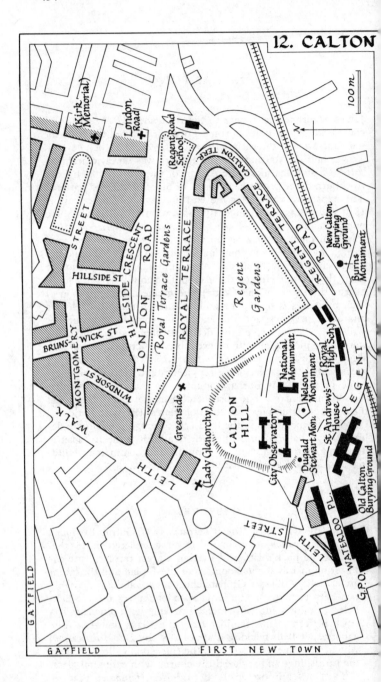

12. CALTON

100 m

N

(Kirk Memorial)
London Road
Street
Hillside St
Hillside Crescent
London Road
Montgomery
Wick St
Bruns
Windsor St
Walk
Leith
Gayfield
Gayfield
(Regent Road School)
Royal Terrace Gardens
Royal Terrace
Carlton Terr.
Regent Terrace
Regent Gardens
Road
New Calton Burying Ground
Burns Monument
(Royal High Sch.)
National Monument
Nelson Monument
St Andrews House
Regent
Greenside
(Lady Glenorchy)
Calton Hill
City Observatory
Dugald Stewart Mon.
Waterloo Pl.
Old Calton Burying Ground
G.P.O.
Leith Street
First New Town

Ingram, 1933. – MONUMENT. Wall-tablet to Dr William
Glover, with a high-relief portrait in white on a grey ground
by *John Hutchison,* 1871.

KIRK MEMORIAL EVANGELICAL UNION CHURCH, Montgomery Street and Elgin Terrace. Now in secular use. Crisply
detailed Perp, by *Hippolyte J. Blanc,* 1895.

LADY GLENORCHY'S LOW CALTON CHURCH, Greenside
Place. Secularized. Tudor collegiate front by *John Henderson,*
1846. Broad crenellated tower with a canted bay rising from
the shallow porch. Shops in the wings. The church itself is
earlier, built in 1844 to replace one which was to be demolished for the railway in 1846. Simple and spacious classical
interior with cast-iron arcades, galleries, and an arched ceiling
renovated in 1893 by *G. Washington Browne.* Extensive basements underneath, making the sides five storeys in height.

LONDON ROAD CHURCH (formerly United Presbyterian),
London Road and Easter Road. Gothic, by *John Starforth,*
1874. Plate tracery, lancets and SE spire, all rather French.
The wide interior, with iron bracketed galleries, became unsafe and was consolidated and modernized by *Norman Reid,*
1965.

PUBLIC BUILDINGS AND MONUMENTS

BURNS MONUMENT, s side of Regent Road. An amplified version of the Choragic Monument of Lysicrates by *Thomas
Hamilton,* 1830, differing most obviously from the Athenian
original and from his earlier version at Alloway (1820) in that
its columns surround (in temple style) a cylindrical cella, ornamented with lyres and carried upwards to form an attic,
with wreaths. The finial also follows its model, but three
supporting griffons are introduced to suit the increased girth
below. In the base, with its three angle-pedestals, a chamber
which formerly enshrined Flaxman's statue* and various relics of the poet; it used to be lit by windows at the bottom of
the cella.

CALTON GAOL GOVERNOR'S HOUSE, *see* St Andrew's House.

CITY OBSERVATORY, on the w summit of the Calton Hill. A
domed Greek cross by *William H. Playfair,* 1818, for the
Astronomical Institution founded in 1812 with Professor
John Playfair as president. One of the main objects was to
give accurate time. The engineer *James Jardine* produced a
design in 1816 but Playfair, the president's nephew and the
university's architect, got the job.‡ Each arm of the cross has
two pilastered bays and a hexastyle Roman Doric portico
facing one of the points of the compass, with a central observatory dome. Within this, the telescope is mounted on a con-

---

*The statue is now in the National Portrait Gallery, the relics in Lady Stair's
House.

‡Michael Langdon says that his scheme is based on an earlier one by *William
Stark.*

ical masonry pillar unconnected with the upper floor through which it rises. The E and W arms, cleft from the rest, housed on the E the transit instrument and astronomical clock, on the W the mural circle and clock. Interior 'overhauled' by *Robert*
52　　*Morham* in 1895–8. In 1825–6 *Playfair* designed the MONU-MENT in his uncle's memory to the SE, a tetrastyle Greek Doric mass on a high podium, square and solid, somewhat after the Lion Tomb at Cnidos but with fluted columns and no lion, and in 1827 the channelled boundary wall taking in the monument at its SE corner and slightly bowed on the S side. Pedimented entries to the S and E and a small transit house to the W. In 1895, after railway smoke had forced the Astronomer Royal to depart to Blackford Hill (*see* Outer Area: Blackford, Public Buildings, Royal Observatory), the City acquired the buildings and *Robert Morham* designed the octagonal CITY DOME at the NE corner, built by *Howard Grubb* of Dublin, rather fussy late classical, larger in scale than the rest but thinner in modelling.

The Gothic-towered OBSERVATORY HOUSE, at the SW corner of the boundary wall, was started in 1776 by Thomas Short (an optician-astronomer) with help from the City and University, but money ran out, and in 1788 the City took over, finishing the building in 1792 in a style 'far inferior' to what had been intended. Short's architect was *James Craig*, with the benefit of advice (and possibly a sketch) from *Robert Adam*, who suggested it should look like a fortification. To a three-storey round tower is attached a short wing, coarsely built of rubble with buttresses, Gothick windows, and wall-head corbels perhaps intended to support battlements. Addition at the NE of 1893, partly battlemented and partly crow-stepped, with pointed windows to match Craig's.

54　DUGALD STEWART'S MONUMENT, on the Calton Hill, SW of the Observatory. By *William H. Playfair*, 1831. A more literal version than Hamilton's (*see* the Burns Monument above) of the Athenian original. Circular base. The colonnade is relatively taller, enclosing an urn.

GENERAL POST OFFICE. High Renaissance Italian by the government architect *Robert Matheson*, 1861–6, much enlarged later. In spite of its address the G.P.O. really belongs to the First New Town, for it occupies the site of Shakespeare Square and the old Theatre Royal.* Matheson's building, with its hint of the garden front of Vulliamy's Dorchester House in London, was originally of two storeys with three-storey corner pavilions, the SW one prolonged to form a taller S frontage. To him therefore belong the rusticated ground floor (interrupted by the entrance loggia facing Waterloo Place) and the Corinthian order and alternating pediments of the first floor. Prince Albert, at the laying of the foundation stone, prescribed the urns on the crowning balustrade. By

---

*The Theatre Royal was built in 1768, refronted by *Burn* in 1830, and closed in 1859.

1890 the space was inadequate and *W. W. Robertson* doubled
the s front, setting the new work slightly back. In 1908-9
W. T. Oldrieve extended it still further, on a different line to
avoid the railway, and in different stone (pink Duddingston
Hill instead of the original yellow Binny). His building rises
seven storeys, the bottom two completely underground, the
top two picking up the rhythm of Matheson's design in a
simplified way. He also heightened the original building with
a columnar second floor, but preserved its outline by adding
a plain pilastered storey to the pavilions. The public office
was remodelled first by him, and again by *Eric Hall & Partners* in 1965.

LEITH WALK PRIMARY SCHOOL, Brunswick Road. Gothic,
by *W. L. Moffat & Aitken*, 1875. A large-scale symmetrical
board-school in what *The Builder* calls the 'decorated collegiate style', enlarged by *Robert Wilson* in 1894 and *John A.
Carfrae* in 1903.

MORAY HOUSE SCHOOL OF COMMUNITY STUDIES, *see* Regent Road School.

NATIONAL MONUMENT, on the summit of the Calton Hill. 52
An unfinished Parthenon for which *C. R. Cockerell* and
William H. Playfair were responsible. The project for a monument to those who had fallen in the Napoleonic Wars had
been in the air since 1815 when *Archibald Elliot* proposed a
triumphal arch at the E end of Waterloo Place. His later design for a Pantheon did not find favour, and in 1822 the
promoters (including Scott, Cockburn and Lord Elgin) ap-
pealed for £42,000 'to erect a facsimile of the Parthenon'; less
than half was ever subscribed. Cockerell was appointed in
1823 to ensure the accuracy of the reproduction, Playfair as
resident architect in the following year. They intended to set
the building on the spacious platform of a massive pilastraded
substructure containing catacombs, with square pylons at the
E corners, the hill being made up to the stylobate at the W
end. The temple would have been a church. Work began in
1826 and came to a halt in 1829, with only part of the stylobate, twelve columns at the w end and their architrave faultlessly completed in Craigleith stone.*

NELSON MONUMENT, on the Calton Hill, SE of the Observa- 52
tory. One of Edinburgh's odder things, designed in 1807 by
Robert Burn, over 30 m. high, of five stages, with a hatched
frieze and a corbelled and battlemented parapet. Within this
a sixth stage, similarly detailed, supports cross-trees and a
time ball (giving a visual signal at noon to ships in the Forth).
Base enclosed in a five-sided structure added in 1814-16 by
Thomas Bonnar to Burn's design, castellated in the Adam
style, with a boldly carved relief of the *San Josef* over the
entrance. 'Originally intended to give accommodation to a

*Proposals in 1907 to complete the monument as a National Gallery (with
funicular railway from Waterloo Place) or to mark the bicentenary of the Act of
Union, and in 1908 to make it part of the buildings for a proposed Scottish
Parliament came to nothing.

few disabled seamen', the rooms were subsequently 'leased to a vendor of soups and sweetmeats ... and the visitors to the monument have the opportunity of eating in them ... and drinking, under certain restrictions, to the memory of the great hero they commemorate.' The tower is still accessible, but the rooms are now a private house.

NEW CALTON BURYING GROUND, S side of Regent Road. Instituted for the purpose of re-interring the remains disturbed by the cutting of Waterloo Place through the Calton Burying Ground (*see* below) and opened to visitors in 1820. Well laid out, presumably by the City Superintendent of Works *Thomas Brown*, with terraces to the SW and a crenellated circular WATCH TOWER of coursed rubble with a cantilevered external stair, effective both pictorially and functionally. – MONUMENTS. Andrew Milne †1835. Relief of Wisdom consoling Misfortune by *Patric Park*. – *David Bryce* †1876. Roman Doric, probably by himself. – Call enclosure (1833) and Ranken enclosure, Greek Doric and Egyptian respectively. – Some good early C18 monuments brought from the Old Burying Ground.

OBSERVATORY HOUSE, *see* City Observatory.

OLD CALTON BURYING GROUND. Bisected by the road between Elliot's screen walls. The best things are in the larger S part, given here in order of date, with an indication of their relation to the central path. First a wall-tabernacle with Ionic columns to John Morton, heelmaker, †1728 (E). – Some very primitive headstones also commemorate shoemakers and their families and bear their badge, e.g. one with a naive cursive inscription to Mary Thomson, spouse to James Forsyth, †
1762 (E). – The finest work is the DAVID HUME MONUMENT by *Robert Adam*, 1777 (E), a grandly Roman cylinder of rough ashlar with a fluted frieze on the lower stage, a bold Doric entablature on the upper. Big urn in a niche above the doorpiece. Adam's preliminary sketches show that the tomb of Theodoric at Ravenna was the starting point for his design. – The shared enclosure of Charles and Isaac Salters, brewers, and John Wilkie, mason, 1786 (E), combines modern swags and paterae with an old-fashioned rendering of skull and bones. – The Spottiswood enclosure, *c.*1800 (E), has a *Batty Langley* Gothic front, the neighbouring tabernacle to Francis Allan, upholsterer, †1815, a flaming urn. – Not far away the elegant enclosure of William Raeburn, perfumer, †1812, with a fluted and domed sarcophagus like a bottle (erected 1817). – ROBERT BURN MAUSOLEUM, 1816 (W) presumably by his son *William Burn*, in the Gothic style of St John, Princes Street. – Tall obelisk on the central eminence by *Thomas Hamilton*, 1844, commemorating the Political Martyrs of 1793. – Near it, the bronze relief portrait of the painter David Allan by *John Hutchison*, 1874. – The EMANCIPATION MONUMENT (E) commemorates Scottish-American soldiers who took part in the Civil War. Red granite pedestal with a standing figure of Abraham Lincoln, a freed slave looking up

to him, in bronze by *George E. Bissell* of New York, unveiled in August 1893.

PLAYHOUSE THEATRE, Leith Walk. A large dual purpose cinema-theatre by *John Fairweather* of Glasgow, 1927–9. The modest classical façade of two storeys, including shops, gives little idea of the size of the auditorium built out over the falling ground to the rear. The stalls are entered via the basement, the circle from the ground floor, the balcony and restaurant from the first floor and the ballroom from the second. The first of the two foyers is Ionic-pilastered. The auditorium was designed to hold 3,048, following a study tour in the U.S.A. with a view to planning the Playhouses in Edinburgh, Glasgow and Dundee. Circle and balcony both cantilevered. The proscenium arch has a cavetto frame with scrolled decoration and boxes at circle level in the splay; above, Corinthian aedicule features with organ screenwork of somewhat Adamesque detail. Double-coved ceiling, with more scrollwork. Decoratively uninspired, and offering nothing to the devotees of the intimate theatre, it is nonetheless admirably spacious. Rehabilitation of 1978–80 by the *Lothian Region Architects' Department*.

POST OFFICE LETTER SORTING DEPOT, Brunswick Road. 1980 by *Basil Spence, Glover & Ferguson*. White-clad, elegant and anonymous, the roof sweeping down with the slope. Group of three chimneys like red pencils.

REGENT ROAD SCHOOL (originally a Heriot Trust School, now MORAY HOUSE SCHOOL OF COMMUNITY STUDIES), London Road and Montrose Terrace. Mixed Jacobethan by *John Chesser*, 1874, extended by *Robert Wilson*, 1894. Two storeys, with near-symmetrical frontages, the main one of ashlar with an elaborate armorial tympanum in the centre gable.

ROYAL HIGH SCHOOL, N side of Regent Road. Greek Doric 87 by *Thomas Hamilton*, 1825–9, and a monument of high importance in the history of the Greek Revival. Its genesis is complex but instructive. In 1822 a committee of subscribers, including Scott and Cockburn, proposed a new and independent school at Canonmills, but were persuaded that it should actually be built by the City and associated with the existing Royal High School in Infirmary Street. The committee's site was accepted, and later in the year *William Burn* was engaged to make a design. When the tenders came in they were well over the expected £12,000. A loan of a further £9,000 was arranged and *Thomas Hamilton* was asked for an alternative plan, but it was then suggested that the arrangement of two schools would be educationally and socially divisive, and in 1823 the City decided on a single school on a central site. At this the original subscribers went their own way with Burn's Edinburgh Academy scheme (*see* Canonmills, Public Buildings). The City, no doubt with the idea of eclipsing the rival institution, gave Hamilton a new cost-limit of £20,000. He designed a massive square building with a dome for the grounds of the Excise Office (the former Dundas mansion in St Andrew Square), but while it was being considered the Royal Bank put in an offer of £33,000 for the site. In 1825 the s slope of the Calton Hill, a difficult site because of the amount of underbuilding required, was accepted as the only possibility. The final cost was £24,000.

The site has a curved frontage to Regent Road, and falls from w to e as well as from n to s. Hamilton used it to exploit the picturesque capabilities of a monumental composition, taking as his main elements the temple, the lesser temple (e.g. that of Unwinged Victory in its relation to the Propylaeon at the Acropolis), and the *stoa* or market colonnade; all Greek Doric. To begin on the smallest scale, two small temples at the ends, with unfluted prostyle porticos, do not quite face each other but look slightly outwards, being aligned with the bend in the road. Their base is a long, channelled retaining wall interrupted at the centre by pedimented gateways of massive projection. Two more gateways, without pediments, set back on top of them. The wall on this level does not sweep right across the site but is carried back as a plain basement for the central temple; a temple indeed, not a mere portico, for it rises clear of the rest, with an entablature all round. Wings with stoa colonnades, tetrastyle anta-fronted pavilions with an arched window in the basement underneath – an un-Grecian touch of movement in what is decidedly (despite the thrilling deployment of its composition before the moving spectator) a static ensemble. Hamilton's watercolours show that he had thought of a row of circular windows under the main portico. He also tried a sculptural frieze, but in the end left this wall blank, veiled by a line of railings between the two upper gateways. Round-headed windows again on the e and w elevations. n side of one large storey only, since the ground has risen to the main floor level. Pedimented n end of the central temple fronted with six antae, the pavilions with four, the links punctuated by the octagonal clearstories of the writing classroom and library. The detailing is simpler than on the s side but of the same exactitude, e.g. in the careful pattern of windows and glazing. – SCULPTURE. At the NW door into the central hall a carved stone from the original High School with the City's heraldic castle and the inscription IR6. MUSIS RES PUBLICA FLOREAT 1578. – Also a bronze plaque with a relief portrait bust of Hamilton by *D. A. Francis*, 1929.

The hall within the central temple is lit by five windows above the galleries each side, with antae between them. On the end walls the intervals between antae are decisively wider towards the middle. Over the dentilled entablature a plaster vault with a very low curve, rosettes in the square coffers. Galleries on iron columns with branched capitals, the seats tiered down to the central apsidal-ended *orchestra* with its gilded anthemion railing. In 1977–80 the *Property Services Agency* (project manager *W. Pritchard*) adapted the school for use by the Scottish Assembly, whose establishment failed to be confirmed in the referendum of 1978. In the hall, which would have been the debating chamber, a concave gallery was added at the s end and modern seating substituted for the original benches. Much woodwork was renewed (including all the windows with Hamilton's ingenious 'disappearing' sashes) and left unpainted, the grain of the pitch-pine exposed.

OTHER BUILDINGS. To the w the tapering, panelled gate-piers are by *Hamilton*, the lodge a good imitation of 1885 by *Robert Wilson*, cross-planned, with a temple roof and antae at the corners. – SCULPTURE in the courtyard. Good female bronze by *J.-A.-J. Falguière*. – To the E *Wilson*'s symmetrical classroom block of 1894 incorporating his gymnasium of 1885, quietly following the style of the main building.

ST ANDREW'S HOUSE, s of Regent Road. International modern, and by far the most impressive work of architecture in Scotland between the wars, built in 1936–9 to designs by *Thomas S. Tait* of *John Burnet, Tait & Lorne* to accommodate the principal departments of the Scottish Office. Its stylistic origins are diverse, but as a whole it is closest to Nénot's League of Nations building at Geneva; strictly symmetrical in the Beaux-Arts tradition, but much less classical and, in its exploitation of the dramatic view from the s, much more rhetorical; also, vast as it is, by no means so large. 100

Entrance (N) front to Regent Road unashamedly authoritarian, the scale of the central block displaying to the full Tait's love of the colossal. Massive lower projection, bastion-like features with thistle decoration flanking the bronze relief doors ('And I will make you Fishers of Men') by *Walter Gilbert*. Royal arms on top by *Alexander Carrick*, the lion and unicorn reliefs by *Phyllis Bone*. From here rise seven vertically emphasized bays, their soaring mullions ending in half-length figures (Architecture, Statecraft, Health, Agriculture, Fisheries and Education) by *W. Reid Dick*. Staircase bays on each side, their windows split by tall granite mullions, and beyond them long wings of twelve bays, with broad piers stopping short of the wall-head. Set-back top floors with chamfered piers and cantilevered roofs whose long shadows contrast with the unemphasized wall-head at the centre. At the ends cantilevered canopies, and metal and glass staircase bays sheltered by projecting roofs on stone spheres. Whatever is thought about the politics of this architecture, or of a style that was at least ten years behind the mainstream of the modern movement,* its abstract qualities and consummate handling of detail cannot be denied.

About the s front there need be no qualifications. Seven-storey central block flanked by lower staircase bays and then by long four-storey wings, their top floors set back. Two

---

*Indeed there is little advance on Burnet's Wallace Scott Institute (1913) at Cathcart, Glasgow.

more wings project to the S from the ends, and the resulting courtyard is closed by a long bow-fronted range on the cliff-edge. This is a calm composition, tellingly detailed (e.g. in the chimney pylons which are echoed in the bold mullions of the advanced wings) and well related to the site with the help of the wall and Governor's House (*see* below) of the old Calton Gaol. Tait's S front is a work of real imagination and grandeur, meriting comparison with the old Royal High School to the E. The inside, however, is disappointing: dry and colourless Art Deco with a decent entrance hall and twin staircases of moderate interest, with little of the adroit and economical detailing which sharpens the proportions and accentuates the light and shade of the exterior.

GAOL GOVERNOR'S HOUSE, to the w. Battlemented, towered and turreted, this and the great wall below, by *Archibald Elliot*, 1815–17, are all that remains of what was in its time Scotland's largest prison. First came the D-plan Bridewell by *Robert Adam*, 1791, using his castle style to relate to the rocky site and Craig's castellated Observatory. Then Elliot's gaol (replacing the old Tolbooth in the High Street), a long crenellated block with upstanding centre and pavilions, of no special interest; but the towered curtain wall he wrapped round both buildings, rising sheer from the rocky slope, stepping up to the Governor's House and linking with the retaining wall of the Old Calton Burying Ground, is still one of the most successful castellated compositions of late Georgian times. *Tait* demolished the Adam and Elliot gaols and later buildings, and truncated the towers with good reason, but his plan to remove the Governor's House was not implemented. At the time of writing it has long been an empty shell.

WATERLOO PLACE. The idea of extending Princes Street to the E, with a viaduct over the Low Calton ravine (like the new South Bridge) and a cutting through the Old Calton Burying Ground, seems to have originated with *John Paterson* in 1790. For reasons of cost nothing was done at the time, but in 1813–14 the necessary Acts were passed and commissioners appointed with *Robert Stevenson* as their engineer. Late in 1815 *Archibald Elliot*'s design was preferred to those of *Gillespie Graham* and *Crichton*. Stevenson was in favour of a fully open bridge 'for the sake of the views it would command', but in the end only one arch was left without flanking buildings. The success of Elliot's ensemble is partly due to its faultless execution by *Peter Lorimer*, who took all the building lots in 1817. Although he disposed of three of them in 1818 (the SW block to the Stamp Office, the SE block to the Post Office and part of the NE block to the Waterloo Hotel Company), he retained all the contracts until completion in 1822. Pale close-grained stone from the Hailes quarry was used throughout. There has been virtually no external alteration; indeed the setting of the twin w porticos was enhanced when Matheson drew back the building line of Shakespeare Square for his new Post Office.

This triumphal E exit from Princes Street shares its name 9
with Waterloo Place in London, also begun in 1815; clearly
Elliot had Nash's design in mind. Twin porticos at the w
end, fluted Ionic on plain basements, are a frame for the view
of the Calton Hill. Along the street two pairs of palace-fronts
with the Ionic order continued as antae of Miletus form. Both
frontages on the s side have recessed columnar porticos; tetrastyle over the grand entry of the Stamp Office, distyle at the
old Post Office to the E, in which their London surveyor
Joseph Kay had a hand. Ground floors arched throughout,
with no rustication. Nos. 23–25 in the NE block are dignified
with informally placed doorpieces of fluted Doric columns –
a theme picked up again in primitive, unfluted form in the
niched screen and retaining walls of the burying ground, and
in the former CALTON CONVENING ROOMS (now Clarinda's
Bar, a gracefully top-lit haven for midday bureaucrats), built
in 1818–19 with a half-round colonnade at the sharp angle
with High Calton.

Elliot's REGENT BRIDGE of 1816–19 crosses Calton Road
with a lofty semicircular arch and connects the palace-fronts
with triumphal screens commemorating the battle of Waterloo: Ionic colonnades with taller Corinthian columns in the
central arch, rather like a late-C18 country-house gateway
(e.g. Adam's at Syon).

INTERIORS, where they survive, fairly plain. Nos. 1–21 on the
N side severely altered in commercial use, Nos. 16–20 entirely
replaced in the reconstruction and extension as Inland Re-
venue offices by *W. W. Robertson* of *H.M. Office of Works* in
1898–1902. The most complete are at the former Stamp
Office on the s side, the most interesting were at No. 23, now
the City Housing Department, built as the Waterloo Hotel
and the first large purpose-made hotel in the city, its pros-
pectus stating that Edinburgh had never had 'an establishment like the Tontine at Glasgow where Strangers could see
the manners of the People and mix with the Society of the
place'. The entrance hall and spacious front rooms on Waterloo Place remain, but the tall rear wing was rebuilt with dry
concrete units to suit the new floor levels when *Williamson
& Hubbard* recast the interior in 1971–3. In the wing was the
long Ionic-columned dining room, later adapted as an oper-
etta house and then again for dining, and finally partitioned
off as the North British Railway office in 1894. No. 25, altered
by *Peter L. Henderson* in 1889 as Gas Offices, was recast by
Williamson & Hubbard in 1974. A large attic room with dome
and top-lighting was unfortunately subdivided.

WILSON, TEMPLETON AND KENNEDY MONUMENT, Regent
Road, at the entry to the footpath up to the Calton Hill. A
modest freestone wall-slab by *Thomas Bonnar*, 1894. Three
portrait medallions by *W. Grant Stevenson*.

PERAMBULATIONS

1. The Calton Scheme

Playfair's great scheme occupies the E spur of Calton Hill and
part of its long N slope towards Leith. Had the latter section
been completed, the whole development would have been by
far the most magnificent in the New Town. The City had owned
the Calton itself since 1723. In 1811 they persuaded the three
other landowners (Heriot's and Trinity Hospitals and Mr Allan
of Hillside) to join in a single scheme, and a competition was
advertised in the following year. Reports on the entries were
invited from the foremost architects resident in Edinburgh, including *William Stark* who wrote a cogent report condemning
the imposition of formal plans on uneven ground, stressing the
beauty of the site and the importance of following natural contours, and of combining architecture with trees. He maintained
that amenities of this kind would prove a 'vendable commodity',
and gave some clear hints as to what he would have done with
the site.

Stark died in 1813 but the Commissioners were persuaded by
his arguments, despite the £900 they had spent on plans that
did not respect them. In February 1818, encouraged by the fact
that Waterloo Place would soon provide a splendid new access,
they commissioned his former pupil *W. H. Playfair* to produce
a plan for the 'Proposed New Town between Edinburgh and
Leith' in accordance with his ideas. Presented just over a year
later, in December 1819 it was accepted. To the S it provided
for two long, convergent terraces (Royal and Regent) and a
third as their hinge (Carlton) enjoying the slope of the hill at
the rear as well as the open views from their fronts; to the N a
public garden; and finally, on the gentle incline across London
Road, a vast radial layout centred on the segmental garden of
Hillside Crescent. It was intended to include a square, and
houses for all classes except the poorest, with markets enclosed
by the fronts of fourth-rate houses. The terraces to the S were
feued quite briskly, though the enormous houses in Royal Terrace were only completed by 1860. Elm Row, looking on to the
long-vanished elms of Leith Walk, was also successful. So were
Leopold Place and Hillside Crescent with their garden prospects, but the latter was checked by geological problems, and
confidence in the lower area began to falter. In 1838 development was virtually stopped for more than thirty years by a
decision that feuars in Hillside had to pay poor-rates to both
Edinburgh and Leith. When it was resumed there seems to have
been no attempt to enforce the Playfair design except in the case
of blocks already begun. But little building was done till 1883,
when the Heriot Trust architect *John Chesser*, the prime expo-
nent of terrace design at the time, produced modified designs
for the rest of the crescent and the neighbouring streets, with
flats instead of houses. To the N of Montgomery Street a goods
yard invaded the site, and the radial street-plan was abandoned.

In the Calton scheme Playfair rejected the tyranny of the palace-front. Royal Terrace does have a centrepiece but it is hardly different from the outer pavilions – an impressive architectural episode to be glimpsed through the trees without the symmetrical implications of a pediment. Elsewhere he preferred a simple duality of pavilions or even, as in Regent Terrace, a pair of dualities. The important thing is the progress from end to end, often quickened by the repetition of Neo-Classical porches and never embarrassed by makeshift changes of level; these changes are dealt with in the proper place, where the lowered cornice can butt into a projecting pavilion. Playfair also had a distinctive way with chimneys, but very few of the original ranks of octagonal flues can now be seen. He attracted with grand, uphill houses the landscape-loving 'Circle of fashionable and wealthy people' to whom he referred in his report. But without the lesser members of the architectural hierarchy – the dramatic perspective of streets from Hillside Crescent – the vision is sadly incomplete.

REGENT TERRACE is approached by an inconspicuous branch 124 off Regent Road. Designed in 1825 and begun in the following year, with its fine s view it was not long in building. The symmetry of each of the two pavilioned terraces is not obvious, and the main impression is of a well ordered build-up along the gentle slope, emphasized by continuous trellis balconies and punctuated by Greek Doric porches. Its perfect clarity has been marred by a number of second-floor additions to the two-storey houses. CARLTON TERRACE curves round the hairpin at its E end, designed in 1821 on the same system but with different details, complementing the smooth curve of the wall: consoled porches and single-window balconies, heavy panelled parapets on the pavilions and crowning balustrades between them. Nos. 5–13 on the curve are four-bay houses, their irregular pattern of doors and windows reversed between Nos. 9 and 10. Consistently good neo-Greek interiors, many (especially in their entrance halls and staircases) spoiled by subdivision.

The climax is ROYAL TERRACE, facing N over Leith to the sea. It was begun in 1821, but Playfair seems to have recast his design in 1824, as the surviving elevational drawing bears that date. Forty houses and 360 m. long, its ground floor arched and rusticated from end to end, it consists of three main units. The middle is of three very lofty storeys, the fifty-seven bays interrupted by three giant Corinthian colonnades supporting attics, with balustrades between; seven attached columns on each side, ten in the centre which do not form a distinct centrepiece but sufficiently acknowledge the grand axis of the whole layout. Outer units similar but lower, each with four groups of six giant Ionic columns. Curiously the W unit has two more bays than the E, but this is not noticeable; nor is the fact that their end houses are part two-storey and part four-storey. Unfortunately most of the

windows are plate-glass (some re-glazed, some original), but
the balconies survive and not a single house has been heightened. The coursed rubble rear elevations, neatly ordered but
not quite symmetrical, with cornices at the wall-head, are
seen from REGENT GARDENS, laid out for the proprietors
by Professor *Robert Graham* and Dr *Patrick Neill*, 1830, their
w boundary separated by a ha-ha from the public ground on
Calton Hill. Behind Carlton Terrace an irregular pentagon of
lanes and mews buildings.

The scale of the Royal Terrace interiors is enormous. The
degree of enrichment varies greatly, as does the style (Nos.
15–22 and 31–34 are of 1852–60). In one, the extra large No.
35, the Adam style lingers on with a Roman Ionic screen in
the first-floor drawing room, but the majority have neo-Greek
detail of very high quality, the grandest with elaborately compartmented ceilings and Grecian columns in the drawing
rooms. Entrance halls are of particular interest, notably at
No. 4 with Greek Doric columns; Nos. 21–22 with three-bay
groin-vaults; No. 27 with an equestrian relief; Nos. 29 and
38 with pendentives; Nos. 30–31 with tunnel-vaults; No. 34
circular; No. 37 groin-vaulted; and Nos. 39–40 where the
groin-vaults are fluted.

Then an interval of grass and trees in which Greenside Church
(*see* Churches, above), having provided an eye-catcher from
the far end of Royal Terrace, pretends to be a country kirk.
BLENHEIM PLACE, designed in 1821, is so curious and extravagant that the wonder is that it was built at all. Nos. 6–
10, in deference to the view of Calton Hill, have only one
storey with coupled antae above pavement level plus three
basement storeys below, the lower flats entered from the rear;
hence the surprising number of chimneys. Built in 1824 for
John Dickson, they act as a base for the solemn Ionic portico
on the gable of the corner block. More giant Ionic columns
turn the corner into Leith Walk; the readiness of the feuars
to build such a monument of civic design is proof of the early
popularity of Playfair's scheme. Most of the ground-floor
arcades of this section survive, pretentiously refaced on the
curve but quite plain and with graceful fanlights at No. 5.
ELM ROW across the road, also designed in 1821, has a
similar corner quadrant except that it is Roman Doric. The
relation between the two is progressive in an uphill direction,
but the Ionic pedimented cornerpiece at the lower end never
got a Doric partner on the other side of Montgomery Street.
For the rest, Elm Row follows the plain pavilioned terrace
theme, formerly enlivened (but now only at the top quadrant)
by a regular ground-floor arcade for shops. A notable survivor, even without its arches, is the chemist's shop at No. 11,
with two Ionic columns in a symmetrical but somewhat altered interior.

ROYAL TERRACE GARDENS slope down to London Road. The
grandly named ROYAL TERRACE GARDENS HOUSE of 1836
is actually a cottage designed by *Playfair* with a boldly pedi-

mented central bay and blocky, primitivist window architraves. To the N of the road LEOPOLD PLACE, designed in
1820, with conventional houses in the middle, flats at the
ends. Once again symmetry is rejected, for the Doric quadrant at the Elm Row end has an Ionic counterpart at the
Windsor Street end. HILLSIDE CRESCENT, designed in 1823
with very grand houses linked by a Greek Doric ground-floor
colonnade, was begun in 1825. The W part (Nos. 1–7) was
completed to Playfair's design. In the next part Nos. 8–11
were executed by *W. Hamilton Beattie* in 1880–3 but suffered
badly from subsidence, and in 1967 the first three were replaced with the cynical irrelevance of ELLIOT HOUSE by
Leslie D. Morrison & Partners. The rest of this part, and of
the whole crescent to the E, is a clumsy four-storey improv-
isation on Playfair's theme by *John Chesser*, 1884.

Three of the N–S streets are more or less by Playfair. The first
from the W, WINDSOR STREET, designed in 1822 and begun
in the following year, is the prototype of Regent Terrace (*see
above*), with Doric doorpieces but a less bold cornice and
rather a sudden jump from two to four storeys at the ends.
It is all complete, but unfortunately inferior stone was used,
most of it now painted in assorted colours. Greek Doric columns in most of the entrance halls. BRUNSWICK STREET,
designed *c.* 1824, is one of those radiating from the crescent.
Two-storey houses of highly unusual design, balustraded
along the top, with Ionic porches projecting far out from a
continuous cantilever balcony, also balustraded. On the W
side BRUNSWICK HOUSE, a bland stone-faced office by
Cairns Munro, 1977, on a previously vacant site. At the
Montgomery Street crossing four corner-blocks by *John
Chesser*, of the mid 1880s, with Doric doorpieces to Brunswick Street. In HILLSIDE STREET and WELLINGTON
STREET, the other radials, no such attempt was made to imitate Playfair; they have four-storey tenements with bay-windows, dated 1878–92. To the E BRUNTON PLACE, designed
in 1823 to balance Leopold Place. Nos. 4–9, by the Leith
architect-builder *Thomas Beattie*, are tenements, with main
doors and common stair doors neatly grouped in compound
doorpieces of antae and columns. Pavilions reduced both in
scale and elegance, following the Chesser scheme. Nos. 13–
24 also by *Chesser*, with a quadrant corner into Brunton Terrace. For John Starforth's London Road Church at the
corner of Easter Road *see above*.

To the N in BRUNSWICK ROAD, four-storey plum brick terraces by the *City Architect's Department*, 1979, with ner-
vously jumping sills. For Leith Walk Primary School *see*
Public Buildings, above. Beyond the disused railway yard of
1881, the former Cochrane's golfball factory in MURANO
PLACE, red and yellow brick by *P. & J. Henderson*, 1910–
12.

2. Calton Hill and Leith Street

CALTON HILL (formerly High Calton) winds steeply down to Leith Street. Nos. 20-26 on the N side are the oldest houses surviving in the area, built in the 1760s on an irregular line with a picturesque conglomeration of paved ramp, steps and gatepiers penetrating high rubble retaining walls. ROCK HOUSE, notable in photographic history as the home of D. O. Hill, Archibald Burns and F. C. Inglis, is the best, with a stuccoed front and stone margins. On the S side, much more urban, an obliquely sited offcut of *Elliot*'s Waterloo Place and the concrete slab replacement of the N wing of the old Waterloo Hotel (*see* above). Most of the W half of Calton Hill, long ruinous, was bulldozed in 1974, but in 1979-81 this rough amputation was made good by *Robert Hurd & Partners* who restored Nos. 16-18 for the Cockburn Conservation Trust and designed the new end house for the Viewpoint Housing Association, in a semi-vernacular manner, with a salvaged doorpiece from George Square (*see* South Side).

On the E side of LEITH STREET, the top section of the main road, all that remains of the piecemeal development of the City's ground after *c.* 1790 is a valuable group of tenements descending in a serpentine line from Waterloo Place (masking its workaday rear elevations) and picturesquely negotiating the awkward junction with Calton Road by means of a bow-ended gusset. One block with shops to Calton Road (probably the next one up) was started in 1803. Plain ashlar fronts with occasional tripartite windows. Some interiors much altered as shops and even factories in the later C19-20. The shops were put out of business by agreement by the St James Centre developers (*see* First New Town), but the whole group was repaired for the City by *Bamber, Gray & Partners* in 1979-80. Further downhill the tenements on this side, including a handsome pedimented block by *Robert Burn*, 1800-3 (sometime the Imperial Hotel), fell into poor condition and were demolished in 1973 under the threat of a huge traffic interchange required for an inner ring road.

The main road now becomes LEITH WALK, and the present long gap comes to an end with the Tudor frontage of Lady Glenorchy's Church (*see* Churches, above). Next to it the unremarkable Classical front of the Playhouse Theatre (*see* Public Buildings, above).

The only survivors of GREENSIDE PLACE are Nos. 23-27, a double tenement once with urns above the eaves, spoiled by shops below. It is by *John Baxter*, *c.* 1798, and so is BAXTER'S PLACE, a not quite symmetrical block of three pairs of houses, the outer pairs Doric-pilastered with triglyph blocks instead of a continuous frieze, the ground floor rusticated. The composition was splendidly reunited by piend roofs and the S section freed of shops and restored by *Robert Hurd & Partners* in 1976-8. Playfair's Blenheim Place with its corner quadrant is neatly joined to this.

LEITH

INTRODUCTION

The natural harbour formed by the mouth of the Water of Leith
became the port of the burgh of Edinburgh in 1329, though the
land on the E of the river belonged to the Logans of Restalrig
and on the W to the Abbey of Holyrood. Houses on the E bank
were sufficiently numerous by 1413 for Edinburgh to feel it
necessary to get a charter from Sir Robert Logan restraining
the inhabitants from trading on their own account. But the
settlement seems to have grown through the C15 and a chapel
was built here *c.* 1490. Development of the W bank began in
1493 when Abbot Robert Bellenden bridged the river and
founded St Ninian's Chapel.

In 1548 Mary of Guise moved the seat of government to
Leith and built fortifications enclosing most of the area now
bounded by Bernard Street, Constitution Street and Great
Junction Street and a small stretch of the W bank around Sandport Place. Eight years later the parish church of Restalrig was
abandoned in favour of St Mary's Chapel, which became the
church of a new parish of South Leith. The virtual independence of Leith did not survive the Protestant siege of 1560 and
the subsequent demolition of its walls. But although Edinburgh
re-established its superiority, Leith developed as a merchant
port with its own craftsmen, their houses covering the land
within the line of the 1548 walls.

Development outside the walls began in the later C17. In
1656–7 a large Cromwellian fort, Leith Citadel, was built W of
the river. After the Restoration it was converted into housing
and its parade ground 'as large as Trinity Great Court' subsequently largely built over. On the E bank *Robert Mylne*, Master Mason to the Crown, built a windmill and a row of tenements S of the old walls in 1686.

In the second half of the C18 regular streets (Bernard Street
and Constitution Street) were formed on the edges of the town,
and Queen Charlotte Street (then Quality Street) pushed into
the old layout. At the same time villas were built nearby and
Leith became a fashionable seaside resort which, as early as
1767, was able to boast a golf clubhouse built by the Honourable
Company of Edinburgh Golfers at the W end of the Links.

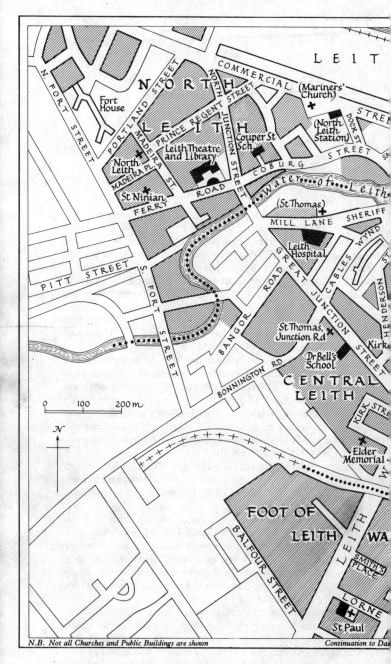

N.B. *Not all Churches and Public Buildings are shown*

Continuation to Da

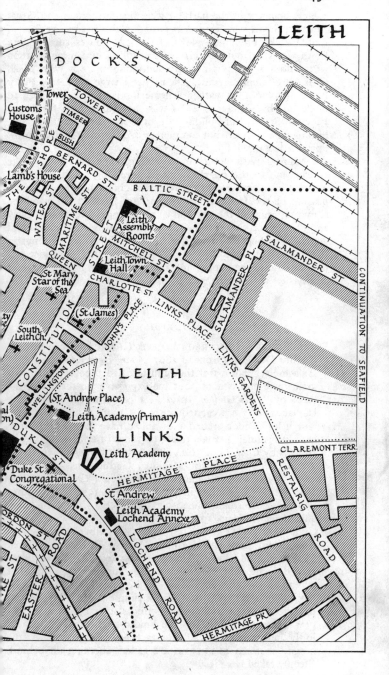

LEITH

DOCKS

Tower
Customs
House
TOWER ST.
TIMBER
BUSH
BERNARD ST.
Lamb's House
THE SHORE
WATER ST.
MARITIME ST.
STREET
BALTIC STREET
SALAMANDER ST.
Leith
Assembly
Rooms
MITCHELL ST.
QUEEN
St Mary
Star of the
Sea
Leith Town
Hall
CHARLOTTE ST.
SALAMANDER PL.
CONTINUATION TO SEAFIELD

ty
South
Leith Ch.
(St James)
JOHN'S PLACE
LINKS PLACE
LINKS GARDENS

CONSTITUTION
WELLINGTON PL.
(St Andrew Place)
LEITH
Leith Academy (Primary)
LINKS
CLAREMONT TERR.

on)
DUKE ST.
Leith Academy
HERMITAGE PLACE
RESTALRIG ROAD

Duke St
Congregational
St Andrew
Leith Academy
Lochend Annexe

GORDON ST.
EASTER ST.
ROAD
LOCHEND ROAD
HERMITAGE PK.

New docks w of the harbour were begun in 1800 and Great
Junction Street was formed as a road to them from the foot of
Leith Walk. The small parks of the C18 houses surrounding
Leith were laid out for terraces and villas, beginning in 1800
with land s of Leith Links and continuing in 1807 with *James
Gillespie Graham*'s feuing scheme for a large area N of Ferry
Road, then in 1808 with a scheme for land s of Ferry Road
made out by *Robert Burn*, as was the feuing plan for Great
Junction Street. But building was only sporadic, and these am-
bitious schemes were not completed (in drastically revised form)
until the late C19.

Piecemeal redevelopment, including some grand buildings
appropriate to the burgh status acquired by Leith in 1833,*
went on in the centre of the town throughout the C19. After the
passing of the Leith Improvement Act in 1880 many of the
slums and most of the C16 and C17 buildings were cleared away
and Henderson Street forced through the pattern of closes and
wynds. The belief in the virtue of demolishing old buildings in
the interest of slum clearance or sometimes just clearance has
continued into the C20, giving Leith more than its fair share of
empty sites and massive new blocks of flats.

CHURCHES

DUKE STREET CONGREGATIONAL CHURCH, Duke Street.
Thrifty Dec gable front of 1867. *Adam Herbertson & Son* of
Galashiels, relations of the minister, had prepared 'plans of
great taste and beauty', but too expensive, so they were altered by *James Goalen*. Inside, the cast-iron columns of the
U-plan gallery are carried up to the roof to suggest a nave
and aisles. Tudor-arched and vaulted nave roof. Furnishings
mostly original. – Elaborately carved PULPIT. – Behind it,
ORGAN by *Conacher & Co.*, 1867 (rebuilt by *Ingram* in 1930–
2 and *Willis* in 1960), in a spindly Gothic case. – STAINED
GLASS. N window (Evangelists) by *Barnett & Son*, 1902. –
War Memorial window in the vestibule, *c.* 1920. – The other
windows have small stained-glass panels by *Margaret Chilton*
and *Marjorie Kemp*, 1933.

ELDER MEMORIAL FREE CHURCH, Casselbank Street. Accomplished Scots late Gothic by *Sydney Mitchell & Wilson*,
1901. Long and low, the roof-line broken only by an ogee-
roofed flèche. The buttressed and parapeted N aisle does not
extend to the end bays. Full-height gabled porch in the w
bay. Tall E bellcote. Beautifully simple interior. Nave and
passage-aisles, the tall arcades with octagonal piers, their depressed arches echoed by the braced timber nave roof. An
individual transverse vault for each bay of the aisles. At the
E end, platform PULPIT with a gallery shooting off behind.
Steeply raked w gallery.

*Leith was reincorporated in Edinburgh in 1920.

ELIM PENTECOSTAL CHURCH, Casselbank Street. *See* Perambulation 1.

LEITH BAPTIST CHURCH, Madeira Street. Plainest lancet style by *Robert Wilson*, 1884-5. – In the galleried interior two STAINED GLASS windows by *Alexander Kerr*, 1945.

LEITH METHODIST CHURCH, Great Junction Street. *See* Perambulation 1.

LEITH-ST ANDREW (originally Free Church), Easter Road. By *Hardy & Wight*, 1880-1. A rubble-built lanceted box with shallow s transepts, passage-aisles and a tall NE tower partly balanced by a transeptal stair-projection. The small octagonal spire, intended from the start, was built in 1902 when the hall was added at the s. Inside are pointed arcades with squat piers; a scissor-roof over the nave. – FURNISHINGS mostly of 1902, but plain pews of 1880. – STAINED GLASS at the w end and in transepts, by *James Ballantine & Son*, 1881.

MARINERS' CHURCH OF SCOTLAND, Dock Street. Secularized. A Gothic chapel-of-ease by *John Henderson*, built in 1839 with a school behind. Tudor arched door and tall Perp window contained in an extravagantly crocketed ogee arch and flanked by twin octagonal towers of three diminishing stages, with tall lancets at the lowest stage and smaller ones at the belfry. The towers have lost their spires and the interior has not survived conversion to offices.

NORTH LEITH (ST NINIAN'S) CHURCH, Quayside Street. *See* Perambulation 4.

NORTH LEITH FREE CHURCH (now NORTH LEITH PARISH CHURCH HALLS), Ferry Road. Germanic Gothic by *Campbell Douglas*, 1858-9, the broad gable masked by the (truncated) broach steeple on the r. and a gable on the l.

NORTH LEITH PARISH CHURCH, Madeira Street. Assured neo-classical by *William Burn*, 1813-16. Two-storey country-house front with a full-height Ionic portico in the middle and pilasters at the corners. It is based on Wilkins' hall block at Downing College, Cambridge, but with over-arched segment-headed windows and niches flanking the door. A more conspicuous departure from its prototype is the addition of a tall steeple to proclaim that it is a parish church. Three-stage tower with superimposed orders in the cut-out corners. Pedimented first stage, ox-skulls on the clock-stage, octagonal belfry and spire. David Hamilton's Falkirk Town Steeple, begun in the same year, is very similar. In the flanks, segment-headed windows below, round-arched above. w end a canted bay, its (blocked) Venetian window old-fashioned in this context.

The interior is reached conventionally enough through a vestibule flanked by stair-halls to the galleries. Less conventional is the placing of the pulpit against the E (entrance) wall, and the vestry above the vestibule. From the vestry the minister stepped directly into his pulpit, skied at gallery level with stairs down to the ground on each side. Round the other three sides a gallery on Ionic columns. In 1880-1 the original pulpit was replaced by an organ with a lower pulpit in front. Burn's arrangement was restored by *Ian G. Lindsay & Partners* in 1948–50 when the organ was moved to the w gallery. The present PULPIT is by *Scott Morton & Co.*, 1950, a parody of the original with only one flight of steps; its height a compromise between common sense and architectural sense. – STAINED GLASS. On the s side the end windows (Gloria in Excelsis and the Transfiguration) by *James Ballantine*, 1909–10 and 1912–13. The windows between them by *A. Ballantine & Gardiner* (Suffer Little Children) after 1892, and, much more vigorous, by *Douglas Strachan* (Christ preaching from a boat), 1907. w window (The Last Supper) by *James Ballantine & Son*, 1884. On the n side re-set glass of 1883 by *Barnett & Son* and one light (St Hilda) of 1939. – ORGAN by *Ernest Wadsworth*, 1880; rebuilt by *A. E. Ingram*, 1920, and in 1950 by *Rushworth & Dreaper*. – Classical ORGAN CASE by *Alexander Kent*, 1950.

Along the s wall of the small GRAVEYARD, pedimented enclosures; very Greek, with garlanded friezes.

NORTH LEITH PARISH CHURCH HALLS. *See* NORTH LEITH FREE CHURCH.

ST ANDREW, Easter Road. *See* LEITH-ST ANDREW.

ST ANDREW PLACE CHURCH (originally Secession Church; now disused), St Andrew Place. The builders were *John & James Rutherford*,* 1826–7. A full-height pedimented portico with giant Ionic columns at the centre of the five-bay front, angle-pilasters at the ends. Lugged doorpiece between niches behind the portico, lugged blind windows in the outer bays; the upper storey panelled. (Galleried interior.)

ST JAMES (Episcopal), Constitution Street. Disused. By *G. Gilbert Scott*, 1862–5; *R. Rowand Anderson* was the executant architect. Built of snecked Bishopbriggs rubble, it is cruciform with a pinnacle-buttressed tower of four stages in the angle of the s transept and choir. A stair-turret climbs within the protection of the SE angle buttress, and an octagonal spire with lucarnes rises above it (the top of the spire was lopped off in 1977). Dunblane Cathedral was specified as the model for the design, and the three tall lancets beneath a vesica at the w front are a faithful enough adaptation of the w front of Dunblane; the lean-to narthex beneath is not.

The interior is spacious. Aisleless three-bay nave spanned by a wagon roof braced with lattice-trusses ('more like the work of an engineer than that of an architect', complained *The Builder*) supported by wall-shafts. Attenuated engaged columns with foliage caps support the chancel arch. Round the barrel-vaulted chancel is blind arcading stopped rather awkwardly at the arch into the organ chamber under the tower. In the panels of the arcade figures (SS. Columba, Didimus, Mark, Peter, Andrew, James, Paul, Luke and Mar-

---

*Four architects, James or John Tait, William Bell, Archibald Scott and James Anderson, submitted designs for the church in 1826. It is not known whose design was used.

garet of Scotland) painted by *E. F. C. Clarke*, 1893 (replacing paintings of 1869 designed by Clarke but executed by Ballantine & Son).

REREDOS of 1873 also designed by *Clarke* and executed by *Thomas Earp*; alabaster, statuary marble and mosaic with at the centre a carved scene of the Ascension. – Octagonal PULPIT given in 1907; white marble with grey-veined columns at the corners, the faces carved with panels (the Good Shepherd, the Transfiguration and the Good Samaritan) and Christian symbols. – STAINED GLASS.* In the chancel three lights (the Passion, Crucifixion and Entombment) probably by *Clayton & Bell* after 1865. – Nave w window (scenes from the life of St Peter) by *Clayton & Bell*, 1865. – N transept E windows (scenes from the life of Christ) and w window (the Ascension) again probably *Clayton & Bell*, *c.* 1870. – On the N side of the nave Abraham and Isaac, St John the Baptist and the Resurrection by *Francis Barnett*, 1868.

VESTRY added to the E of the N transept in 1881. The inoffensive HALL extending E from it is by *D. J. Chisholm* of *Dick Peddie, Todd & Jamieson*, 1936–7; built into its porch a stone taken from a house in which Episcopalians worshipped in the last years of the C17 and inscribed:

TF·THAY·AR·WELCUM·HEIR·THAT·
AM GOD·DOIS·LOVE·AND·FEIR·1590

ST JOHN'S CHURCH OF SCOTLAND, Constitution Street. Secularized. A Tudor front was added in 1843 by *David Rhind* to the plain preaching-box built in 1773. At the centre of the front a tower of two stages, the lower square with pinnacled buttresses, the upper octagonal with a pierced parapet and truncated pinnacles; a spire was planned but not built. Hoodmoulded door set beneath a band of blind quatrefoils. The centre was flanked by boldly advancing one-storey schoolroom pavilions with pinnacles and canted-bay centres; the s one has gone. Inside is a broad single-span roof, the trusses springing from corbels carved with heads. – At the E end a STAINED GLASS roundel (Angels) by *Dickson & Walker*, 1897.

ST MARY STAR OF THE SEA (R.C.), Constitution Street. A large upturned snecked-rubble ship of a church. Aisled and clearstoried nave with an apsidal chancel at the E, transepts at the w and small stone boxes (housing confessionals) protruding from the s flank. It looks convincingly of a piece but is not. *E. W. Pugin* and *Joseph A. Hansom*'s church, built in 1852–4, had no chancel, no N aisle and was orientated to the w. The N aisle was added in 1900 and the chancel in 1910–12 when the church was turned round and the present w entrance made.

Inside, it is a splendidly high barn with simple pointed arcades and a braced collar roof. Chancel arch flanked by two

*Now (1984) mostly broken or removed.

tiers of STATUES of saints; chancel ceiling decorated with faded paintings; low SEPTUM of alabaster with green marble columns. The REREDOS behind the high altar has blind arcading and statues of saints at the angles. In the Lady Chapel to the S alabaster REREDOS with canopied niches containing statues of Our Lady and saints. On the front of the ALTAR a high-relief carving of the Annunciation. At the Chapel of the Sacred Heart, the representation of the Sacred Heart stands in front of a REREDOS whose canopied niches contain kneeling angels. All these furnishings look early C20.

STAINED GLASS. E window of three lights (the Crucifixion) by *The Cloky Stained Glass Studios*, 1955, flanked by two-light windows, their glass resited here in 1912; on the N SS. Francis Xavier, Anne, Francis and Edmund, 1881, on the S SS. Abundi, Joanna, Charles Borromeo and Mary Magdalen, 1882. The other windows (mainly saints) are of the late C19 with a set of *c.* 1920 in the N aisle, complete but not of specially good quality. – MONUMENT. The Very Rev. John Noble †1867; effigy on a tomb-chest.

ST PAUL, Lorne Street. Early Dec by *J. Graham Fairley*, 1884-5. Gabled front with angle buttresses rising into octagonal pinnacles. Stair-halls each side, the larger r. one intended as the base of a tower. Transepts at the flanks. S halls. Inside, a U-plan gallery. Hammerbeam roof strengthened with tie-beams and kingposts. Pine-panelled sanctuary deepened by *Fairley* in 1903. – Octagonal wooden PULPIT. – COMMUNION TABLE of red English alabaster with relief of the Last Supper by *W. Birnie Rhind*. – Angel LECTERN. – ORGAN by *Brindley & Foster*, 1903.

ST THOMAS' CHURCH, MANSE, SCHOOLS AND ASYLUM, Sheriff Brae. By *John Henderson*, 1840-3. Founded by Sir John Gladstone of Fasque, a native of Leith, as a memorial to his family; now GURU NANAK GURDAWARA SINGH SABHA SIKH TEMPLE. At the head of Sheriff Brae, a droved ashlar Georgian box with a steeple against the gable. The thinly Romanesque windows and doors go happily enough with the tower's pinnacles and octagonal spire. It would not look very different had it all been Perp. The back forms one side of a U-plan courtyard. On its N side the manse and schools, on its W the asylum for ten women incurables. Jacobean, with string-courses forming hoodmoulds over the windows. Parapet jumping up into shaped gables and pedimented dormer-heads.

ST THOMAS JUNCTION ROAD (originally Secession Church), Great Junction Street. Classical by *William Bell*, 1824-5. Front with coupled giant Roman Doric pilasters at the angles and the pedimented centre; windows segment-headed at the ground floor and round-arched above. Inside, a groin-vaulted VESTIBULE opens into the D-plan auditorium; the gallery with slender cast-iron Corinthian columns follows the shape of the building. – Of the refurnishing of *c.* 1930 the Wrenaissance PULPIT with an ORGAN by *Rushworth & Dreaper*

behind. - Mural MONUMENT to the Rev. Francis Muir
†1871 in the vestibule; marble carved in high relief with an
open book and shepherd's staff in front of a tomb. - Brick
HALLS at the rear by *Peter L. Henderson*, 1894.

SCANDINAVIAN LUTHERAN CHURCH, North Junction Street.
Small and Gothic, by *James Simpson*, adapting a design by
Johan Schröder of Copenhagen, 1868-9. Spiky Scandinavian
steeple on the r. of the gable. Inside, a scissor-roofed nave
and semicircular chancel. - ORGAN in the W gallery probably
by *Hamilton & Müller*, rebuilt here* by *D. & T. Hamilton*,
1868.

SOUTH LEITH BAPTIST CHURCH, Casselbank Street. 1893-4.
Two storeys in the height of the adjoining three-storey
houses. At the tall ground floor an extravagantly console-
pedimented door between meanly pilastered and corniced
windows. Round-arched windows light the upper floor (intended as the manse).

SOUTH LEITH PARISH CHURCH, Kirkgate. Stodgy Gothic by
Thomas Hamilton, 1847-8. It was not an entirely new church.
A chapel dedicated to Our Lady built here *c.* 1483 consisted
of an aisled nave, a crossing and a chancel. The chancel and
crossing were destroyed during the bombardment of Leith in
1560, the same year in which the chapel took over the functions of a parish church, which it formally became in 1609.
Galleries were erected on all four sides, the aisle roofs being
raised to accommodate them to N and S. The steeple built
above the W gable in 1615 and rebuilt in 1674 was demolished
as unsafe in 1836, and in 1838 the Presbytery ordered repairs
estimated at £3,000. An Act of Parliament providing for restoration was passed in 1846. The present church is the result.

Except for removing the N and S galleries Hamilton respected the existing arrangement of the church, with the pulpit in front of the W gallery, and made no attempt to rebuild
the chancel. Of the original fabric he kept only the heavily
stuccoed nave arcades and the lower walls of the aisles. The
outside was cased in ashlar and the aisle roofs were lowered.
In place of the original square-headed clearstorey openings
Hamilton provided traceried Gothic windows. Flamboyant
tracery replaced the Y-tracery of the aisle windows and the E
window. The fine loop tracery of the W window was removed
and a replica installed.‡ The gables were rebuilt, the E gable
slightly further out so as to include the W piers of the crossing, and crocketed pinnacles replaced the obelisks on the buttresses at both ends. A square tower, buttressed at the lower
stages and with a pierced parapet, was built at the NW. SW
vestry of 1902.

Inside there is the same mixture of restoration, reconstruction and new work. Despite the stucco the minimally pointed
nave arcades are substantially original. Panelled aisle roofs

---

*Originally built for Old St Paul's (*see* Old Town, Churches).
‡The original was re-erected at St Conan, Loch Awe.

braced with trusses springing from corbels carved with
human heads similar to those supporting the heavy hammerbeams adorned with pendant bosses and angels of the nave
roof, derived from St Isaac's Leningrad. Movement is para-
lysed by the end galleries.

The FURNISHINGS are later. Octagonal PULPIT of marble,
with alabaster statues in niches, COMMUNION TABLE, a
marble slab on clustered columns, and PEWS, all by *Sydney
Mitchell & Wilson*, 1893-4. – Brass eagle LECTERN, Tudor
gallery fronts and W SCREEN, 1909. – ORGAN in the W gallery
by *Brindley & Foster*, 1887, rebuilt by *Peter Conacher* in 1964
and by *Rushworth & Dreaper* in 1972. – STAINED GLASS. An
extensive scheme was intended from the start; *Ballantine &
Allan* are recorded as working on it in 1848. The present
windows, none of much quality, are of 1889-93 by *Ballantine
& Son* and *Ballantine & Gardiner*.

MONUMENTS. A large number, only some worth mention.
N aisle: at the ends Alexander Henderson †1819 and James
Miller †1855 and his family; Commissioners' Gothic tablets
– the Very Rev. John White †1951, a bronze relief portrait
by *J. Mortimer*, 1952. – Lieutenant John Spence †1845; relief
of a tomb with crossed swords and a scabbard. – S aisle: at
the W end James Reoch †1845, designed by *Thomas Hamilton*
and executed by *A. Handyside Ritchie*, 1848; cusped niches
containing figures of Charity and Justice each side of a
crocketed-pinnacled arch containing a roundel carved with a
portrait of Reoch. – At the E end, the Very Rev. James Mitchell †1911, with a bronze relief portrait and surmounted by a
figure of Charity in an aedicule. – SE vestibule: James Jameson †1760 by *George Jameson*, an inscription tablet placed in
an elaborate picture frame with a ship and coat of arms, all of
stone. – In the oak PANELLING (1967) of the NW vestibule
two stone PANELS: one, dated 1560, bearing the arms of Mary
of Guise, is said to have been originally built into her house
in Water Lane; the other, dated 1565, with the royal arms of
Mary Queen of Scots, was originally at the Leith Tolbooth.
– In the floors of the NE and SE porches worn GRAVE SLABS
of the C16, C17 and C18.

CHURCHYARD. E wall 1792-5. W wall largely built by *John
Russell*, 1825, with crosslets and blind Perp windows. In it,
a stone inscribed 'IR6' (for James VI). In both walls tall
octagonal Perp panelled gatepiers presumably by *Thomas
Hamilton*, *c.* 1848. Against the W wall, S of the gates, a pedimented stone of 1802 from the Convening House of the Incorporation of Carters. In the tympanum a carved horse and
cart. Inscription:

> Great God, whose potent Arm drives the sun,
> The Carters bless while wheels of Time shall run,
> of old they Drove thy Sacred Ark O God,
> Guide thou their hands and Steps in every road,
> protect this house we Dedicate to thee.
> Increase and sanctify our Charity,

Thy blessing Lord be its foundation stone,
And we'll ascribe the praise to thee alone.

In front, the headstone of Alexander Abercromby, dated 1656
and adorned with emblems of mortality. – To the s, a pair of
heraldic stones, one from the Coopers' almshouse, dated
1723. – Beyond, a stone with skull, crossbones and hourglass
impaling workmen's tools. – Near by, a group of four headstones, all with scrolly broken pediments, skull and crossbones. The monument to John Pew †1750 and Beatrix
Thomson †1729 was put up in 1731. – On the s wall Anthony
Henry Geutzener †1832, an obelisk with a high relief bust by
Thomas Goodwillie, 1841. – Sticking out from the wall, clum-
pish Gothick enclosures of *c.* 1830. On its E side John Patison
†1808, round-arched, the tympanum carved with a headless
figure among classical ruins. – Near the s flank of the church,
a couple of urns on tall pedestals: Anthony Dickson's (†1814)
is swagged, Hannah King's (†1798) fluted, with the inscription:

Affliction sore
Long time she bore,
Physicians art
prov'd vain.
At length it pleas'd
her Saviour God
kindly to move
the smarting rod,
And ease her
dust from pain.

Immediately E, Euphemia Grant †1720. Headstone with foliage, putti and skulls. – On the N, Andrew Vauch †1759, an
aedicule, the scrolly pediment formed by a cherub's wings;
on its ends an angel head and a skull. – At the E end of the
church, large obelisk to Richard Scougall † 1800. – On the E
boundary wall three large tripartite monuments, Gothick for
Adam White †1843 on a site bought in 1805, Egyptian for
William Dudgeon †1857 and sober classical of 1860 for John
Watson. – Against the N wall, a row of Tudor-arched enclosures of *c.* 1825. – Tapering gatepiers with elongated vases,
all very Greek, at the entrance to an extension of 1839 – Early
C19 battlemented enclosures continue to the NW corner. –
Near by, Andrew Park †1814, a swagged urn on a pedestal of
the same type as Anthony Dickson's (*see* above).

UKRAINIAN CATHOLIC CHURCH OF ST ANDREW, Dalmeny
Street. An angular church built for the United Presbyterians
in 1882 to a design supplied by the American architects *Sloan
& Balderston* and adapted by *Archibald Thomson* of Leith.
Nearly identical fronts to Dalmeny Street and Buchanan
Street, each with a large gable and a tiny spire. Slate and
timber belfry above the third gable on the splayed corner.
Plate-traceried windows. Horseshoe gallery inside.

HARBOUR AND DOCKS

The original HARBOUR of Leith was merely the sheltered an-
chorage of the mouth of the Water of Leith. Here during the
Earl of Hertford's invasion of 1544 a wooden pier was made
for the unloading of stores. A wharf was built on the E in the
early C17 and extended 300 ft (91 m.) seaward c. 1720-30. At
the same time a small dock was built on the W. Dry docks on
the W followed in 1772 and 1787. A small part of *Robert
Whitworth*'s scheme of 1786* for a 7 acre (2·8 hectares) wet
dock upstream was carried out in 1788-9 when the old bridge
at Sandport Place was replaced by a DRAWBRIDGE with
chunky cutwaters. A QUAY along Coalhill s of the bridge was
built to *William Sibbald*'s specification in 1791.

Whitworth's scheme was dropped in 1799 when *John Rennie* was asked for fresh proposals. He saw that the major
obstacle to Leith's development as a harbour was its lack of
deep water, made worse by the encroachment of a sand bar
E of the river mouth. Rennie proposed blocking the progress
of the bar by a long E pier and gaining a deep-water approach
through three connected wet docks stretching from the mouth
of the Water of Leith to the deep water at Newhaven with an
entrance at each end. A second drawbridge at the foot of
Bernard Street was built in 1800. In the same year was begun
the OLD EAST DOCK, opened in 1806. Now filled in, its
LOCK GATES survive, replacements by *James Leslie*, 1842-4,
of those of 1800-6. The WEST DOCK (also infilled), for which
John Paterson was resident engineer, followed in 1811-17.
The third and much larger dock reaching to Newhaven was
not built (for the warehouses associated with Rennie's
scheme, *see* Perambulations 4, North Leith).

In 1824 *William Chapman* designed further extensions.
The East Pier was lengthened by about 1,500 ft (457 m.) in
1826-30 and a West Pier and Breakwater built out from the
W end of the West Dock to form an outer harbour in 1829.

Chapman's scheme led to the bankruptcy of the City of
Edinburgh in 1833; even so, schemes for further works
poured out, five of them in 1834-5, all concerned with taking
the harbour into deep water. William Cubitt and James Anderson proposed extensions W to Newhaven; James Walker
the least ambitious, a T-shaped pier at Newhaven; R. & R.
Dickson and John Milne an extension of the East Pier by
about 2,000 ft (610 m.) and a new dock at its seaward end.
Further schemes followed, among them one by *John Milne*
for a new harbour to the E. In 1838 Leith Docks and Harbour
were vested in a Commission, five of its eleven members
appointed by the Treasury, and in 1839 *James Walker* and
William Cubitt reported to the Treasury on how the harbour
might be enlarged. Cubitt stuck to his 1834 proposal for a W

---

*This was one of two alternative schemes put forward by Whitworth. The other
was for a dock covering roughly the area of the Old East Dock.

extension to Newhaven. Walker proposed a large extension of the outer harbour to the NW served by a new quay N of the existing West Docks. Walker's scheme was adopted by the Treasury but not executed.

Pressure for enlargement of the docks and harbour continued, and in 1847 *James M. Rendel* produced a new scheme for development to the N. Its main features were to be a new wet dock N of the Old East Dock; a new pier running from the W side of the new dock and past the W breakwater for 1,750 ft (534 m.), with a low-water pier at its end carrying a railway line; and the extension of the East Pier by a further 1,000 ft (305 m.). Work began in 1847 and in 1851 the VICTORIA DOCK was opened. The SHEDS along its N and E sides are of 1899, brick and timber with ashlar dressings, punctuated on the N front of the N range by timber canopies. Higher shed of 1900 of brick and corrugated iron behind to the N. The Rendel scheme was completed in 1855 with the opening of the low water pier. The large PRINCE OF WALES GRAVING DOCK (*Alexander M. Rendel* and *George Robertson*, engineers) was built at the E side of the harbour in 1858–63. Immediately to its N a brick-built HYDRAULIC PUMPING STATION of the same date, Italianate, its central tower with bracketed eaves and blind arcading.

The Harbour and Docks Act of 1860 cancelled the City of Edinburgh's debt to the Treasury in return for an immediate payment of £50,000, and in 1862 an ambitious scheme for the expansion of the docks was prepared by *Alexander M. Rendel* and *George Robertson*. They proposed a 3,480 ft (1060 m.) EMBANKMENT along the East Sands, allowing the reclamation of 84 acres on which to build docks. Work began in 1863; the contractor was *William Scott*. In 1869 the ALBERT DOCK was opened, a wet dock with a water-area of 4.4 ha.; at its E end survives a HYDRAULIC CRANE (the first in Scotland) with a timber sentry-box beside it. Brick SHED of 1900 at the NE. The hydraulically-operated VICTORIA SWING BRIDGE across the Inner Harbour, linking the Albert Dock to the Victoria Dock, also by *Rendel* and *Robertson*, 1871–4, was replaced later with a bowstring swing bridge.

E of the Albert Dock the EDINBURGH DOCK, once more by *Rendel* and *Robertson*, 1873–81, with a water-area of 6.8 ha. On the jetty divided by a dry dock at the E end the ENGINE HOUSE of 1891, Renaissance, with a pedimented W gable and windows in over-arches. To the N of the dock the SAI FACTORY, by *Basil Spence & Partners* in consultation with *Kinnear & Gordon*, 1955–7, dominated by the 900-ft length of the raw materials store, an unbroken stretch of corrugated asbestos-cement sheeting curving towards the pitched-roofed elevator running along the top.

Expansion began again in 1891 when plans by *Peter Whyte*, superintendent of Leith Harbour and Docks, were approved. Whyte's scheme, in which *Rendel* had played a part, was to build an embankment in order to reclaim 54 acres N of the

Albert Dock. Here Whyte proposed a wet dock entered from
Leith Harbour and connected to the Albert Dock, and a dry
dock at the NW corner. The embankment was begun in 1893
and completed by 1896; *Rendel* was officially the engineer,
Whyte the superintending engineer. Meanwhile another dry
dock, the ALEXANDRA GRAVING DOCK by *Peter Whyte*
with *Rendel* as consultant engineer, had been built beside the
Prince of Wales Graving Dock in 1894-6. Wrought-iron
GATES by *W. G. Armstrong & Co.* The new wet dock proposed by Whyte in 1891 was built in 1896-1904 at a cost of
c. £750,000, its steel and iron GATES again by *W. G. Armstrong & Co.*, its walls of masonry with a granite coping. The
East Pier was breached to provide an opening from the harbour to the new dock, and the dry dock at its NW was built
in 1909-12, *Whyte* still the engineer and *Brand & Sons* the
contractors. At the E end of the Imperial Dock the massive
grey concrete lump of a GRAIN WAREHOUSE by *Alfred H.
Roberts*, Superintendent and Engineer to Leith Dock Commission, 1933-4, extended N in the same style in 1957-8 by
Kinnear & Gordon and *M. C. White*, Chief Engineer to Leith
Docks Commission.

The deep-water harbour at Newhaven, first projected by
Rennie in 1799, was finally incorporated into Leith Harbour
in 1936-43. *J. Dalgleish Easton*, Superintendent and Engineer
to Leith Dock Commission, produced the scheme, a massive
WEST BREAKWATER running NE from Newhaven Harbour,
plus a further extension of the EAST PIER to the NW (impri-
soning the Martello Tower). The entrance to the greatly expanded Leith Harbour was by a LOCK between the ends of
the new breakwater and pier extension. LIGHTHOUSES of
1950 at the entrance. The HARBOUR MASTER'S OFFICE at
the E of the lock is of 1969, brick, with boldly swept-up eaves.
DEEP WATER QUAYS at the S of the new WESTERN HAR-
BOUR of 1947-50, joint engineers *M. C. White*, Chief Engineer
to Leith Dock Commission, and *L. G. Mouchel & Partners*.
On the quays the huge bulk of the CHANCELOT MILLS,
1953-4.

At the main entrance to the Docks in Tower Place the
PORTS OFFICE of 1892, free Renaissance, with a pedimented
centre and a porch with coupled Roman Doric piers.

For the MARTELLO TOWER, *see* Public Buildings, below.

PUBLIC BUILDINGS

COUPER STREET SCHOOL, Admiralty Street. By *George Craig*,
1889-90. Horribly plain except for iron cresting round the
flat glass roof.

83 CUSTOMS HOUSE, Commercial Street. Brutalist neo-classical
by *Robert Reid*, 1810-12. The Customs House is of two tall
storeys above a windowless base, the advanced ends raised
higher with a panelled attic storey. Balustraded links join

them to the massive temple centrepiece, its pediment, containing the royal arms of George III, supported at the ends by masonry slabs whose niches and panels serve only to emphasize their solidity. Between them are two Greek Doric columns; no antae to soften the severity. The dumbbell-balustered perron in front of the centre was added by *William Burn* in 1824; so were the single-storey pavilions which break forward from the ends and are tied to the centre by tall spearhead railings. At the gables recessed balustraded centres imprisoned between masonry. Burn again weakened the starkness by adding one-storey links to the simply detailed stable range at the rear.

Inside, the oblong central STAIR-HALL with a balcony at the upper level is by *Burn*. Imperial stair with acanthus balusters embossed with lions rampant; above, an oval dome on pendentives. Elliptical arches, their soffits coffered, open to the rooms each side. Here *Reid*'s work survives. To the w the LONG ROOM, again with an oval dome on pendentives, opens through a triple arcade of round arches into a room to the s; the two arches to the N are later slappings. At the E of the stair-hall the oval BOARD ROOM with another pendentived dome. A segmental-arched recess in the E wall is its focus.

DR BELL'S SCHOOL, Great Junction Street. A long Tudor 94 front by *R. & R. Dickson*, 1839. At the ends, crowstepped screen walls with octagonal piers and hoodmoulded entries. In the middle, battlemented angle-buttressed towers clasping the tall stepped gable of the schoolroom. Here, over hoodmoulded windows, an ornately canopied niche containing a statue of Dr Andrew Bell who endowed the school in 1831. It was taken over by the Leith School Board in 1891 (becoming the Great Junction Street School), and the three-storey rear wing by *George Craig* was opened in 1892. At the r. of the original building and attempting to copy its style is a SWIMMING BATH dated 1896.

DRILL HALL, Dalmeny Street. Free Wrenaissance, by *Anderson, Simon & Crawford*, 1900–1. Long and symmetrical, with corniced doors flanking a rusticated segmental pend arch topped by obelisks. At the top a bracketed cornice with a segmental pediment at the centre.

EASTERN CEMETERY, Easter Road. Laid out in 1883. Pilastered gatepiers with ball finials. Cottagey lodge.

EASTERN GENERAL HOSPITAL, Seafield Street. By *J. M. Johnston*, 1903–7, as the Leith Poorhouse. A large group of tall buildings, white-harled with red dressings. Mild Art Nouveau detail. Post-war alterations and discreet new buildings by *Alison & Hutchison & Partners*.

FORT PRIMARY SCHOOL, North Fort Street. By the *City Architect's Department*, 1967–8. Friendly but undistinguished in brick and harl. Across the street the original building (now ANNEXE) by *James Simpson*, 1875. Two tall storeys, with crowstepped centre and ends.

LEITH ACADEMY PRIMARY SCHOOL, St Andrew Place.

Large-scale Free Renaissance by *George Craig*, 1895-8. Three storeys and basement, the pedimented ends pilastered at each floor, the pilastered centrepiece taller, with a bracketed semi-circular balcony above the door and a truncated pyramid roof surmounted by a cupola. The GYMNASIUM of 1920 behind is also by *Craig*, harled, with brick dressings.

LEITH ACADEMY SECONDARY SCHOOL, Duke Street. By *Reid & Forbes*, 1931. The plan, a hollow pentagon with a central hall cutting across the courtyard, is slightly more interesting than the brick-faced elevations with their stone dressings, timid modernistic detail, and cupola.

LEITH ACADEMY SECONDARY SCHOOL LOCHEND ANNEXE, Lochend Road. Built as Lochend Road School in 1885-7; the architect was *George Craig*. Large and Gothic, with octagonal pinnacled buttresses at the gabled centre and steep gabled dormers.

LEITH ASSEMBLY ROOMS AND EXCHANGE, Nos. 37-43 Constitution Street. By *Thomas Brown*, 1809-10, and now (1984) in commercial use. A long three-storey front with a rusticated ground floor. At the centre and ends doors with Doric columns *in antis* under segmental fanlights flanked by round-headed windows set in over-arches. Pedimented centre with giant Ionic columns and first-floor tripartite window under a blind segmental fanlight. The coursed rubble rear wing to Assembly Street is the old Assembly Rooms of 1783-5 with a tall one-storey centre and narrow two-storey ends; here the Adamesque ceiling is now hidden by a suspended one. In Brown's Assembly Rooms, the Ball Room on the first floor is impressive, rising through two full storeys with the openings set in over-arches. Tripartite window at the centre of the long s wall with Corinthianesque columns *in antis* – an arrangement originally repeated at the door opposite, which is flanked by consoled and corniced doors and was once surmounted by an opening to the Orchestra above.

LEITH CENTRAL STATION, Leith Walk. 1898-1903, the bulk of the huge train-shed with its steel-framed roof disguised from the street by weak Renaissance frontages. Small tower at the bowed NW corner. Interior of the Central Bar by *Peter L. Henderson*, 1899, with tiled murals (sporting activities) by *Minton, Hollins & Co*.

LEITH HOSPITAL, Taylor Gardens. The earliest part is in Mill Lane, a plain block by *Peter Hamilton*, 1850, with Roman Doric pedimented portico; originally two storeys, raised to three in 1894. To its NE an extension of 1873-5 by *James Simpson*, raised in 1888-9 with a French mansard. To its s a large Renaissance block by *W. N. Thomson*, 1898-1903, built to commemorate the Diamond Jubilee. Facing it across King Street is a harled Nurses' Home of the same date and also by *Thomson*, weak early C17 Scottish style with some crowsteps. The front building to Taylor Gardens is by *George Simpson*, 1923-7; stripped Tudor.

LEITH THEATRE AND PUBLIC LIBRARY, Ferry Road. By

Bradshaw, Gass & Hope, 1929–32.* Driest Classical survival on a wedge-shaped site. The straight front of the D-plan Library is to Ferry Road, balustraded with a pair of columns at the entrance. Inside, a shallow dome with glazed coffers over the lending library. Behind but off-axis is the taller theatre (originally town hall). Curved loggia projecting from between pedimented ends. The same uninspired detail inside.

LEITH TOWN HALL AND POLICE STATION, Nos. 75–81 Constitution Street and 29–41 Queen Charlotte Street. The Neo-Classical main block, built as the Leith Sheriff Court in 1827–8, was designed by *R. & R. Dickson*, whose name is prominently displayed on the Queen Charlotte Street front. To Constitution Street the ground floor is rusticated with segmentally arched openings. Above, giant pilasters frame the end bays; the centre is set back behind Ionic columns with on their entablature a shallow block pediment with scrolled sides. The centre of the narrower front to Queen Charlotte Street is rusticated from top to bottom. It has an unfluted Greek Doric porch, a round-arched first-floor window with heavy brackets in a similar over-arch, and then again a shallow block pediment buttressed by scrolls.

After Leith became a parliamentary burgh in 1833 the pressure on the limited space of the Sheriff Court building increased. In 1868 the adjoining house at No. 31 Queen Charlotte Street (*c.* 1820) was reconstructed as an annexe (with a Corinthian doorpiece) to designs by *James Simpson*. A few years later a small addition was built to the N, very classical, with unfluted Greek Doric columns *in antis* at ground floor, Ionic columns *in antis* above, and urns on top.

Inside, the old SHERIFF COURT ROOM survives with shallow-relief panelled plasterwork on the ceiling, a deep anthemion and palmette frieze and plain classical doorpieces. Behind it is the CELL BLOCK of *c.* 1870; two tiers of cells round a central well, a balcony at the upper tier with tall and thick railings, their spiked ends curved alternately inwards and outwards. The old COUNCIL CHAMBER is reached by a ceremonial stair from the Queen Charlotte Street entrance with armorial stained glass at the half-landing. The chamber in its present form was designed by *James Simpson* and sumptuously decorated by *Thomas Bonnar Jun.* in 1891–2. Plaster ceiling panelled in deep relief, a bay-leaf roundel at the centre and ovals at the ends from which drop large foliaged pendants with light fittings. Painted shields everywhere, with the arms of the famous connected with Leith.

LEITH VICTORIA PUBLIC BATHS, Junction Place. By *George Simpson*, 1896–9. Red sandstone Free Renaissance with a tall pediment at the centre of the two-storey main block. Broken segmental pediment over the entrance in the one-storey wing to the r.

---

*Restored to the original design after war-time bomb damage and reopened in 1961.

LORNE PRIMARY SCHOOL, Lorne Street. 1875–6 and presumably by *James Simpson*. Raised to three storeys in the starkest
possible style in 1898 (by *A. & R. McCulloch*). Crowstepped
lodge at the W gate.

MARTELLO TOWER, Leith Docks. Built in 1809 to defend the
entrance to Leith Harbour, now half-buried in the E breakwater, it rises as a circular ashlar tower from a battered base
to a cordon and parapet. Segment-headed windows, door protected by gunloops. The trefoil gun-emplacement at the platform was added by *Lieutenant-Colonel Yule* in 1850 when the
accommodation inside was reorganized. Inside, a segmental
tunnel-vault ringing a central pillar.

NORTH LEITH STATION, Commercial Street. *See* Perambulation 4.

ST MARY'S (R.C.) PRIMARY SCHOOL, Links Gardens. By
J. M. Johnston, 1926. Stripped neo-Georgian in brick.

SEAFIELD CEMETERY, Seafield Road. *See* Perambulation 3.

SEAFIELD SEWAGE TREATMENT WORKS, Seafield Road. A
discreet complex, its buildings by *Lothian Region Department
of Architectural Services*, 1973–8. Administration block with
an oversailing first floor of pre-cast concrete units.

TRINITY ACADEMY ANNEXE, North Junction Street. Built as
the David Kilpatrick School in 1913–15, a red sandstone
monster by *George Craig* with a less than acceptable minimum
of classical and sub-baronial detail.

TRINITY HOUSE, Kirkgate. Expensive classicism of 1816–18,
with single-storey pavilions flanking the main block. *Thomas
Brown* was the architect, *Thomas Beattie* the builder. Rusticated ground floor, and a balustraded portico with coupled
Greek Doric columns. The upper order is Ionic, with coupled
pilasters at the ends and coupled columns supporting the
central pediment carved with the arms of Trinity House; the
central window tripartite, with Ionic columns *in antis* and a
round-arched fanlight, the outer windows pedimented. Inside, a Roman-Doric-columned screen opens from the square
Vestibule into the oval Stair-hall, where a geometric Imperial
stair rises to the first floor; STAINED GLASS War Memorial
window by *J. R. Cook*, 1933.

The whole of the first floor is occupied by the CONVENING
ROOM. Its centre window is framed in Ionic pilasters, its
doorpiece corniced, the chimneypieces at each end (supplied
by *Dewar & Pitcaithly*) of black marble; all these fairly plain,
but not the ceiling, which is Adamesque. Brown's original
design was rejected on the ground that 'the principal ornaments would have no prominence or relieve'. As executed,
the modelling is unusually deep for Edinburgh work; three
compartments, a central octagon enclosing a foliaged pendant,
rectangular end-panels with figures of a sailor, an admiral,
Neptune, dolphins, ships and nautical emblems, and a frieze
with figures of Neptune, ships and flying fish.

In the Master's Room on the ground floor a plain black
marble chimneypiece containing a superb cast-iron surround

of portraits, tridents, fouled anchors and cannon. Fragments still exist of the hospital built by the Fraternity of Masters and Mariners of Leith in 1555; its vaulted cellars can be reached from the courtyard at the rear. Above the gate to the courtyard is a stone with a steep pediment carved with a fouled anchor and the date 1570. Its inscription was recut in 1883:

> They that goe down to the sea in shippes
> That doe business in the great Waters
> These see the works of the Lord
> And his wonders in the deep
> (Psalm 107 Verses 23 and 24)

Built into the s wall is another stone, inscribed

> IN · THE · NAME · OF · THE
> LORD · VE · MASTERIS ·
> AND · MARENERS · BYLIS
> THIS · HOUS · TO · YE · POUR
> ANNO · DOMINI · 1555 ·

YARDHEADS SCHOOL, Giles Street. Originally by *James Simpson*, 1875–6, massively reconstructed in 1888 by *George Craig*, who raised it to three storeys with sparing French detail.

PERAMBULATIONS

1. Central Leith

The obvious starting-point is the bronze QUEEN VICTORIA STATUE at the foot of Leith Walk, by *John S. Rhind*, 1907. His panels on the plinth (the entry of the Queen and Prince Consort to Leith in 1842, and the departure of volunteers for the South African War) were added in 1913. The Queen looks across to Leith Central Station (*see* Public Buildings). Behind her a low tenement (Nos. 1–5 DUKE STREET) of *c.* 1810 with a bow projecting at one end, bullied by a later C19 block beside it; both bullied by Kirkgate House (*see* below).

KIRKGATE begins with the NEWKIRKGATE SHOPPING CENTRE by *Ian Burke, Martin & Partners*, 1965. Beyond, a vestige of the old street with two piously preserved sacred cows, Trinity House and South Leith Parish Church (*see* Public Buildings and Churches, above). Kirkgate now becomes a courtyard of housing by *Alison & Hutchison & Partners*, 1962–75. Low rise with zigzag rendered fronts in GILES STREET and COLTFIELD LANE; LINKSVIEW HOUSE is a slab varied by the pattern of its balconies.

At the top of CONSTITUTION STREET a brick cinema of 1912. Architecture starts with No. 161, a superior villa of 1802 with a pebble-rusticated basement and Roman Doric doorpiece. Built over vaulted cellarage and with a warehouse wing behind, it is a combined house and commercial premises. The rubble-built No. 159 bows its corner on the acute angle of Laurie Street. Austere tenements of *c.* 1805 at Nos. 141–149

followed by a warehouse at Nos. 137–139, 1864 with minimal
Renaissance detail. Then a gap site.

On the w side of Constitution Street a full frontal view of
KIRKGATE HOUSE, eighteen storeys of brick by *Ian Burke,
Martin & Partners*, 1965–8, before the South Leith churchyard. Its wall forms one side of the forecourt of No. 138, a
classy villa of *c.* 1790. Corinthian-columned doorpiece with
griffons on the frieze. The N side of the forecourt is occupied by the early C19 one-storey Nos. 134–136; corniced windows in over-arches. Narrow swept dormers on the mid-C18
No. 132.

On the E side, buildings resume with Nos. 121–125, bulbous
Renaissance of *c.* 1890, probably by *James Simpson*. Then St
James (*see* Churches, above), its forecourt with stumpily
spired gatepiers and a crowstepped church officer's house.
Beyond, an early C19 tenement, a later C19 Renaissance
counting house and a narrow balustraded block of *c.* 1890
with a recessed oriel at its centre. A solidly Georgian gable
announces Queen Charlotte Street.

Opposite, after St Mary Star of the Sea (*see* Churches, above)
and a late C19 row of shops under a scrolly cast-iron balustrade (Nos. 96–102), the bookend of No. 94 appears to be the
chimney-gableted front of a tenement. But it is only the gable
of a sixteen-bay block fronting QUEEN CHARLOTTE
STREET, built *c.* 1800–5, in general conception very like Baxter's Place (*see* Calton, Calton Hill and Leith Street) but the
detail more delicate. Giant Corinthianesque pilasters, each
with its own frieze, at the end pavilions. Fluted second-floor
band-course studded with rosettes. Rusticated ground floor
overlaid with Victorian shopfronts, the corner one quite exuberant. Further w a large tenement of 1878, Second Empire
in inspiration, Third Republic in execution. In MARITIME
STREET C19 warehouses. On the w Nos. 3–6, 1899; shallow
canted oriels, shell tympanum in the pedimented doorpiece.
Nos. 7–8 plain Renaissance by *James Simpson*, 1893–5. The
front of Nos. 11–14 (by *James Simpson*, 1898) breaks into
oriels, the corner one resting on a corbel carved with a Bacchus head and rising to an octagonal turret, its oculi draped
with bunches of grapes.

No. 92 CONSTITUTION STREET, at the NW corner with Queen
Charlotte Street, the grandest late C18 house in Leith, was
built in 1793 for the merchant Thomas Williamson, 'under
the immediate inspection of an eminent architect'.* Above
the rusticated ground floor, giant Corinthianesque pilasters
topped with urns at the corners. Pediment across the full
width of the five-bay front. Frieze with rosettes; at the second
floor band-course, portraits in roundels. The architraves of
the first-floor windows break through pilastered and corniced
surrounds. In the stair-hall an enriched ceiling and on the
walls roundels with low-relief classical figures.

* So said a sale advertisement in the *Edinburgh Evening Courant.*

Across Constitution Street is Leith Town Hall (*see* Public Buildings, above). To its E in QUEEN CHARLOTTE STREET, late C18 houses (Nos. 45-49) with consoled doorpieces. No. 51 of *c.* 1790 is grander; giant Roman Doric pilasters, each with an individual frieze, and a Leith-Corinthian pilastered doorpiece. Opposite, the tall harled MASONIC LODGE, its present post-Wrenaissance appearance dating from *T. Aikman Swan's* 1922 reconstruction.

The W side of CONSTITUTION STREET continues with late Georgian houses, plain except for a columned doorpiece at No. 84, before the scale drops with a late Victorian block (Nos. 74-80). Then a towering early C19 slab. In its centrepiece, very broad pilastered and segmental-arched doorpieces flank a pend arch under a blind-fanlit tripartite window. Even with a mansard roof (by *James Simpson*, 1878) it is wonderfully stark. Next door, the genteel early C19 ROYAL BANK, Italianate, with scrolled foliage on the band-course below the first-floor windows, their friezes carved with honeysuckle. Rather pompous Roman Doric porch.

Across the street St John (*see* Churches, above) is followed by the plain front of Nos. 59-61 which became the Gas Company offices *c.* 1860. Behind, a courtyard of industrial buildings. Then a dumpy Renaissance POST OFFICE by *Robert Matheson*, 1875-6. Among the warehouses of MITCHELL STREET a late C19 one-storey counting-house at Nos. 36-39; arcaded windows and pedimented door. A central hoist on the early C19 Nos. 32-35. Opposite, an early C19 house with a pilastered doorpiece.

On the W side of CONSTITUTION STREET after Maritime Lane, a touch of late Victorian exuberance. The red sandstone balustered shopfront of No. 46 has a Corinthianesque arcade. Pub-front (by *W. N. Thomson*, 1897-8) at No. 44, the parapet carved with swags, the round arch of the centre window flanked by doors with pedimented transoms. Inside, a pub-Jacobean bar-counter, thinly ribbed ceiling and frieze with sailing ships. The C18 block next door was dressed up with scrolled broken pediments in 1886. Then, the tall end of Waterloo Buildings (*see* below).

On the Mitchell Street corner, No. 55 Constitution Street was built by a merchant, William Ainslie, in 1799. Typical Leith-Corinthian columns at the doorpiece, balustered aprons to the first-floor windows. Originally of four bays, it has been extended to six. The old Post Office (Nos. 49-53), built *c.* 1805, is long and low with Greek-key friezes at the pilastered doorpieces. Tripartite windows (the l. one destroyed by a crude slapping) at the ends. The Leith Exchange Buildings (*see* Public Buildings, above) lead to Baltic Street. On the N corner is the Italianate former CORN EXCHANGE by *Peddie & Kinnear*, 1860-3. Office block with stilted segmental arches below, round-headed above, and an octagonal domed tower. Hall along Constitution Street pierced with tall round-arched openings under a strip-cartoon carved by *John*

Rhind of *putti* bringing grain to Leith for sale. Inside, a massive single-span roof braced by pierced trusses. To the E in BALTIC STREET, remains of the old GASWORKS begun in 1835.

8 BERNARD STREET is Leith's most formal space, a broad triangle with the combined atmosphere of a street and a square, narrowing at its w end where it jinks to the l. for its exit to the Shore. At the base of the triangle the bronze BURNS STATUE by *D. W. Stevenson*, 1898. At the s corner with Constitution Street WATERLOO BUILDINGS by the architect-contractor *William Lamb*, c. 1820. A massive five storeys and nine bays to Bernard Street and three to Constitution Street, with a set-back bowed corner, it is the largest of Leith's Georgian tenements, and the grandest, with a pilastrade of shopfronts breaking into Ionic columns at the corner, first-floor window architraves set between half-pilasters, and a distinctive saw-tooth cornice crowning the second and fourth floors.

The centrepiece of Bernard Street is the former LEITH BANK, probably by *John Paterson*, 1804–6.* In appearance a very smart villa, it is only two storeys high. Ionic-columned bow with a shallow dome (its rolled lead unhappily replaced with copper), flanked by a single pilastered bay each side. Pale stone for the details to contrast with the droved ashlar walling. At the flanks the full entablature of the front is reduced to a cornice but with a pediment at the E. Stable building behind, its w gable pedimented. Inside, the circular vestibule opens through a groin-vaulted square passage into the oval banking hall. Here the frieze is decorated with Adam motifs – affronted griffons, winged ladies and scrolls. Above the stiff-leaf acanthus cornice a Vitruvian scroll border. The saucer dome, originally 'ornamented with various figures and devices, painted in a very tasteful manner', has a top-lit cupola; round it, another Vitruvian scroll border. Behind the elegant (but later) mahogany counter the central doorcase is crowned by a gilded clock on the backs of griffons, with cornucopias down its sides. In the room to the r., the original built-in cupboards. On the upper floor, two rooms of domestic scale but exceptional quality, one bow-ended, with a husk-garlanded and thistled chimneypiece, the other (above the vestibule) circular, its wooden chimneypiece enriched with a figure of Hope (?) who leans on an anchor and looks mournfully at a pile of shells. The ceiling decoration has been painted over. The flanking three-storey tenements were designed (presumably by Paterson) to show off the bank towards which their roofs are deferentially piended (cf. the tenements flanking the Assembly Rooms in George Street). At the first floor the windows of the recessed three-bay centres are set in pilastered over-arches; the central windows of the flanking

*The façade is almost identical with Paterson's (demolished) Montgomerie House, Ayrshire.

three bays have consoled pediments of the same type as the bank's.

Nos. 27–29 Bernard Street were built for James Alison in 1807 (the drawings signed 'J. R. J. Leith', probably the builder *John Russell Jun.*); Nos. 11–23 by *Thomas Beattie* in 1815. In MARITIME STREET, running between the E block and the bank, Nos. 27–29, the birthplace of John Home (†1808) the author of *Douglas*, was reconstructed with a segmental pend arch in the early C19. At the narrowing of Bernard Street the early C19 No. 33 is followed by No. 37 built in 1873 as the Leith Merchants' Club, the label-stops of its doorpiece carved with heads of Bacchus and Neptune.

The N side of BERNARD STREET is more varied, with no shortage of banks. At the E end, the Italianate ROYAL BANK OF SCOTLAND by *Peddie & Kinnear*, 1871–2, with a heavy bracketed pediment over the door (originally in the middle but soon moved to one end) and broad eaves. Next to it, the CLYDESDALE BANK, modernistic neo-Georgian by *J. M. Johnston*, 1923. Then the early C19 Nos. 8–14 with a segmental pend arch, and next door a mid-Victorian palazzo. The twin bows of Nos. 22–24 show what Nos. 1–5 Duke Street (*see* above) could have looked like. The canted bay-window and polished granite doorpiece of the BANK OF SCOTLAND (by *James Simpson*, 1871) do their best to give presence to a narrow frontage.

Round the corner of the old Leith Merchants' Club, CARPET LANE sneaks off to the S. On the l. an early C19 pilastered gateway. On the r. a huge flour mill of 1828: Z-plan main block of six storeys and attic, with an arcaded ground floor to Carpet Lane and five-storey brick-filled arcades to Broad Wynd. Back in BERNARD STREET, a ground-floor pilastrade at the early C19 Nos. 41–45, stilted arches at the Italianate Nos. 49–55 (by *John Paterson*, 1868). The harled wing of the King's Wark (*see* below) leads to the Shore.

The N side of the final section of Bernard Street is lined with late Georgian buildings. Consoled pediment over the central first-floor window of No. 44, whose pilastered doorpiece is outdone by the later addition of a broken pediment and Ionic pilasters to the door of Nos. 46–48. Georgian reticence is broken by undisciplined baronial at Nos. 50–58 by *J. Anderson Hamilton*, 1864; restless string-courses, chimneys corbelled out from far down the wall-face. On the bowed corner a two-storey cap-house with a truncated octagonal spire, the angle-turrets bristling with cannon-spouts. As townscape it works well.

Not much townscape at the SHORE – a few buildings among gap sites. N of the Bernard Street junction the multi-gableted mid-C19 front of the OLD SHIP INN followed by the arched pend to TIMBER BUSH. Here a collection of warehouses, among them an early C19 pair (Nos. 50–53), each with a central hoist. Of the tenement at Nos. 18–22 Shore built by

Robert Mylne in 1678, only the ground floor survives, its moulded doorpiece inscribed

Christus R[ex] Regum, qui non dormita[t] in aevum
Protega [h]anc aedem, necnon sine crimine plebem

MARITIME HOUSE beyond is by *J. & F. Johnston*, 1957, respectable and inappropriate. A tenement built by *John Russell Jun.* in 1802 abuts the circular SIGNAL TOWER, originally a windmill for making rape-seed oil, built by *Robert Mylne* in 1686. Five receding stages, the domed roof replaced *c.* 1805 with a battlemented parapet and blind quatrefoils. Its cheerfully martial aspect does something to relieve the ponderous Baronial of the ANGEL HOTEL (formerly Sailors' Home) by *C. S. S. Johnston*, 1883–5. More enjoyable the EAGLE BUILDINGS in TOWER STREET, *c.* 1900, with a sculptured eagle between two gables.

s of Bernard Street the SHORE begins with the early C18 KING'S WARK, restored by *Robert Hurd & Partners*, 1972–8. Central gablet and scrolled skewputts. Only the ground floor of its very similar neighbour survives; lugged and architraved door, its scrolled pediment broken by a cartouche dated 1711. Then a tall crowstepped warehouse of 1912 (No. 41) and a bleak baronial lodging-house of 1898 by *J. W. Maclean* (Nos. 52–55). The late C18 front of No. 56 is only two bays; depressed arches at the ground floor, tripartite windows above. The later wing to BURGESS STREET was raised with a slated hat in the reconstruction of 1979–80. The view up Burgess Street is closed by a late C19 bonded warehouse, two of its seven bays with giant aedicules.

112 In WATER'S CLOSE off Burgess Street is LAMB'S HOUSE, built in the first years of the C17 and the best large merchant's house of its date in Edinburgh. The scale is impressive: four storeys and attic with a seven-bay front. The symmetrical 2:3:2 grouping of the windows is wilfully disturbed by the corbels of the flattened stair-tower climbing up the middle to end in a chimney-gabled cap-house. Asymmetrical gablets, the l. one halted against a chimney. Gables all crowstepped, walls (almost as inevitably) harled. The pantiled roof was restored by *Neil & Hurd* in 1937–9. In a further restoration by *Robert Hurd & Partners*, 1959–61, the windows were put back to their original size with fixed leaded upper lights and shutters below. More conjectural was the provision of a hoist over the door in the high l. gablet. The 1959 work, converting the house into an old people's day centre, provided also the discreet lift-tower at the back and the low hall slightly overlapping the front. Inside, a few original features (some much restored). On the stair, two ogee-headed slop-recesses. On the upper floors, large stone fireplaces in the s wall and small simply-moulded early C18 chimneypieces in the E gable. The w part of the third floor has loft-doors to front and back, so presumably it was a store.

Back at the SHORE the comfortable baronial No. 65, *c.* 1900,

looks quite at home: not so the desperately polite UN-
EMPLOYMENT BENEFIT OFFICE by *H.M. Office of Works*,
1929, embarrassed at having to slum it in Leith. Up TOL-
BOOTH WYND, after a plain late Georgian tenement (No. 77
Shore), boxy low-rise housing by *Alison & Hutchison &
Partners*, 1974, as an approach to their Linksview House (*see*
above). Late Victorian model housing in HENDERSON
STREET. Nos. 59-61 (by *James Simpson*, 1890-1) acknow-
ledges the importance of its position at the Shore corner with
a wealth of Scots Renaissance detail.

COALHILL begins with the bowed corner of a late Georgian
block. Then a small C18 warehouse, rubble-built and pantiled. Two first-floor windows still of their original tiny dimensions. To the l. the view along Parliament Street is closed
by THE VAULTS (No. 87 Giles Street), a rubble warehouse
of 1682, given a fourth storey and central gablet in 1785. The
lift-tower against the front is C20. Inside, the undercroft may
be C16; a vaulted passage flanked by vaulted cellars.

Opposite The Vaults is the splay-ended and aggregate-panelled
CABLES WYND HOUSE by *Alison & Hutchison & Partners*,
1963-6, its ten storeys insignificant compared with its length.
Behind, CABLES WYND and SHERIFF BRAE lead through
drab inter-war housing to St Thomas (*see* Churches, above).
MILL LANE squeezes between St Thomas and Leith Hospital (*see* above). On the r. a low mid-C19 range ending with
a birdcage bellcote.

On GREAT JUNCTION STREET, the former STATE CINEMA is
by *James Miller & Partners*, 1938, jazz-modern with a
Spanish-inspired tower; the interior more than fulfils expec-
tation. After the open space of Taylor Gardens a large block
of 1911 (Nos. 170-174), squared-up Art Nouveau with an
octagonal corner-tower. More tentative Art Nouveau detail of
1905 at the angle oriel of Nos. 160-168. TELECTRA HOUSE,
a rectangular frame filled with glass, is by *J. & F. Johnston*,
1963. On the opposite side of Great Junction Street, housing
by the *Scottish Special Housing Association*, 1980. After BAN-
GOR ROAD with its red sandstone SALVATION ARMY HALL
of 1910, a long procession of late C19 tenements with sparse
classical detail before St Thomas Junction Road Church and
the former Dr Bell's School (qq.v.).

On the NE side of Great Junction Street, after Cables Wynd, a
couple of bonded warehouses: No. 124 later C19, five storeys;
Nos. 108-118 rather earlier, three storeys, with centre bays
recessed and first-floor windows in over-arches. Then, late
C19 tenements, their monotony relieved by the slightly cottagey look of the two gablets and steep dormer of Nos. 66-70
of 1879. In Henderson Street, Yardheads School (*see* Public
Buildings, above) and in ST ANTHONY PLACE the LODGE
TRAFALGAR, stodgy Gothic of 1888 by *George Craig*.

In Great Junction Street the tenement on the Henderson Street
corner (Nos. 48-52) is of 1885, the first building put up under
the Leith Improvement Scheme and designed presumably by

James Simpson. A Butterfieldian chimney and Gothic colonnettes at the windows of the late C19 Nos. 18–46. Nos. 2–16
are deadly plain.

Across the street, Nos. 81–87, incorporating the LEITH METH-
ODIST CHURCH by *Maclennan & Cunningham*, 1931–3,
artificial stone and harl with a few ill-judged modernistic
touches. Late C19 Georgian survival tenements at Nos.
47–67, a two-storey late Georgian house overpowered by its
shopfront at Nos. 35–39. The austere block of Nos. 1–17 is
deceptively of a piece. Nos. 1–5 are early C19; the rest came
in 1863.

Round the corner in Leith Walk, KIRK STREET runs off to the
w. Georgian survival terraces of 1863–4 but with Nos. 22–24
of 1866 built in brick, and Nos. 44–46 early C19 with pilastered doorpieces. In CASSELBANK STREET more Georgian
survival, but with columned and pilastered doorpieces. Beside
the Elder Memorial Free Church (*see* Churches, above), the
ELIM PENTECOSTAL CHURCH, built in 1886 as Turkish
baths; pediment between lead-covered ogee domes.

Nos. 12–62 LEITH WALK were built *c.* 1800. The short two-
storey terrace at Nos. 52–62 is distinctly smart, with columned doorpieces, Leith-Corinthian at No. 52, Ionic at Nos.
60 and 62. Nos. 12–42 are of three storeys but simpler. Pilastered doorpieces, the best at No. 12, with stiff acanthus-leaf
capitals and an ornamented frieze. *George Anderson* was the
builder of at least one of these houses.

2. *Foot of Leith Walk*

A late C19 tenement area with a few Georgian currants and one
plum. It was still almost entirely rural in 1785 when *John
Baxter* prepared a scheme for development E of Leith Walk.
Scattered development (not to Baxter's plan) followed in the
late C18 and the first years of the C19 on both sides of LEITH
WALK. On the w side No. 212 of *c.* 1800, a plain cottage with
a front garden. Of the same date a couple of tenements at
Nos. 236–264 and a three-storey terrace, Nos. 294–308, its
ground floor hidden by shops but with a bracketed doorpiece
at No. 306. Tripartite windows at No. 308, given thin columns and a pediment at the second floor. The mansard-
roofed No. 324 is late C18, with architraved and corniced
windows. Early C19 Roman Doric pilastered and block-
pedimented doorpiece. Another terrace of *c.* 1800, Nos. 326–
346, has been quite classy; two storeys above an unsunk basement with a segmental pend arch and quoins. Protruding
shops lower the tone.

James Smith, a merchant, bought the site of SMITH'S PLACE
in 1800. By 1814 he had laid out a *cul-de-sac* and the next
year built a house for himself at its end. Smith's villa is
memorable. Two storeys above a pebble-rusticated basement.
Only three bays, Venetian windows in over-arches flanking
the slightly advanced centre. Thermal window in the pedi-

ment, swagged urns above. Inside, fluted anta pilasters in the vestibule. Oval stair-hall, the cantilevered geometric stair rising from the basement to the top floor. In the front ground-floor rooms, Corinthianesque pilasters at the windows. Pilastered doorcases in the r. room. In both, elaborate friezes.

The N side of Smith's Place is a palace-fronted block begun in 1814. Pedimented ends and a taller centre. Nos. 3–5 at the w end look altered: they are in fact by E. J. MacRae, 1936, built as part of the Tramway Depot Offices, a belated completion of Smith's Place. Less welcome the 'Fyfestone' third floor of No. 11 and the gaudy paint of No. 1. The s side of the street is of c. 1825. Intended from the start, its layout was changed after 1822, perhaps to bring it into line with W. H. Playfair's 1819 feuing scheme for the Heriot Trust and Trinity Hospital lands stretching s to Calton Hill. Plain tenements with one house squeezed in at No. 4. Broad pedimented gable at No. 2.

BALFOUR STREET on the w of Leith Walk was begun by R. Rowand Anderson in 1868. Rubble tenements with rogue Gothic detail at Nos. 36–38 and 46, their chimneys extravagantly corbelled out from the wall. Eventually the Heriot Trust and Trinity Hospital lands from Leith Walk to Easter Road were developed from the 1870s with utilitarian tenements. No reminder of Playfair except in the Georgian survival blocks on the E side of LEITH WALK between Smith's Place and Albert Street, by John Chesser, 1873–96. Of the sporadic Victorian industrial development a curiosity survives, Nos. 380–382 EASTER ROAD (N end), built as a wool store in 1876; would-be Beaux-Arts classical with keyblocked ground-floor openings, the doors tall carriage arches. Blind first floor under a bracketed cornice, the frieze decorated with metopes. The Italianate counting-house at the s end is contemporary.

The C20 contribution has been small. In LEITH WALK, Nos. 106–154 by H. Gildard White, 1933, two storeys of red sandstone with pilasters stuck on the front. Hardly architecture. Boxy housing development in CROWN STREET, GORDON STREET and MANDERSTON STREET, 1973 by the City Architect's Department.

3. Leith Links

ACADEMY STREET begins with a red sandstone tenement (1898) at the Duke Street corner. Then Nos. 5–13, early C19, with a projecting bow at one end. No. 15, its front garden all but filled with the harled box of the LEITH DOCKERS SOCIAL CLUB, is the classy villa built by a Leith merchant, James Scott, in 1801. Corinthianesque columns at the door and balustered aprons under the ground-floor windows. ST ANDREW PLACE is shared by the St Andrew Place Church and Leith Academy Primary School (qq.v.). N of Laurie Street, WELLINGTON PLACE begins with a tall tenement (Nos. 1–3) of c. 1820, its starkness relieved by the channelled ground floor and the placing of the cornice below the third floor. The height drops at No. 4, a house of c. 1815 brutally reconstructed c. 1900 as a small warehouse. Also of c. 1815 is the low tenement of Nos. 5–7, its ground-floor windows set in over-arches and its centre bay slightly recessed with a wall-head chimney. Quite stylish except for the broader spacing of the windows r. of the centre. The asymmetry suggests miscalculation of the width of the plot rather than a deliberate quirk of design. Then, higher blocks of c. 1815–20 at Nos. 8–11. The crowstepped gablet of Nos. 12–13 of c. 1870 is not enough to make it architecture. A large gap site follows.

JOHN'S PLACE begins with a muscular bonded warehouse (No. 13) by *J. Anderson Hamilton*, 1862. Outsize rope-mouldings over the doors, their ends most professionally knotted. The splay-fronted bonded warehouse of 1898 next door is a weakling by comparison. Gentility resumes with St James's churchyard (*see* Churches, above). Its former parsonage (No. 11) is by *G. Gilbert Scott*, 1862–3, prosperously clerical, with a comfortable bay-window and a touch of polychrome. Beyond is a terrace (Nos. 3–10) of unified design built in 1825. Paired Roman Doric and Ionic doorpieces, No. 4 with columns rather than mere pilasters. At the end of the terrace the pedimented No. 2 is the surviving pavilion of an 1825 villa replaced by a 'Fyfestone' and pebbledash nonentity. The view is closed by the three E houses of Queen Charlotte Street, c. 1775, No. 65 with Venetian windows to the attic and a front door to both N and S, No. 61 with a flashy bow-ended drawing room added c. 1820.

At Nos. 1–4 LINKS PLACE a large tenement of 1900. Then a couple of late C18 villas flanking the simple classic entrance to the old LINKS PLACE SCHOOL (by *James Simpson*, 1875). Across Poplar Lane, the vast free Renaissance warehouse of the SCOTTISH CO-OPERATIVE WELFARE SOCIETY. Its l. half, by *James Simpson*, came in 1878–9; pilastered centre with an oriel and French pavilion roof, channel-pilastered ends with pedimented gablets. The r. gablet was moved E when the block was almost doubled in length with a second pavilion roof, c. 1920. Unexciting classic additions of 1885 to the N.

The two matching terraces of Nos. 1–4 and 6–10 LINKS GARDENS were built c. 1805 flanking the front garden of an earlier mansion. Enjoyable outsize balconies at No. 7. Fan-vaulted entrance halls at Nos. 6–7 and Adamesque plasterwork in the first-floor drawing room of No. 9. The ground between the terraces was filled with a tall tenement in 1898. Similar tenements (Nos. 11–27, 1893) march away from the Links. Beyond the Links Primary School (*see* Public Buildings, above) and the brick backdrop of a rope walk (1937), the former SEAFIELD BATHS* stand at the corner of Seafield Place and SEAFIELD ROAD. Designed by *John Paterson* and built in

---

*The baths were built by shareholders who had each subscribed £50 towards the £8,000 cost, gaining the right to use the baths in perpetuity. Seventeen baths of varying temperature and a swimming pool were provided.

1810-13, the baths have all the suavity and many of the
elements of the Leith Bank of ten years before. The two main
fronts are identical, each with a Greek Doric portico projecting from a slightly recessed centre. Rusticated ground floor
with overarched end windows. Alternate cornices and consoled pediments at the first-floor windows. Plain frieze-band
with guttae beneath the cornice at the end bays. The two
fronts are joined by a rounded corner with a ribbed lead
dome. The domed room inside survived a rough conversion
to housing c. 1914. A lower section curves back to join Nos.
6-8 Seafield Road, a pair of semi-detached houses built in
1830. Pedimented centre and gablets at the ends. Block-con-
soled doorpieces with pendants at the links. On the N side of
Seafield Road and SALAMANDER STREET a large bonded
warehouse, 1885, and a maltings with two pagoda-roofed
kilns, 1900.

SEAFIELD CEMETERY at the E end of Leith Links was laid out
in 1889. The approach shows a late C19 attempt to revive
Scottish Renaissance architecture but uncertainty as to the
date of that renaissance. From the N, first a store dressed up
as a late C17 garden pavilion from Kinross House. Then rusticated gatepiers with obelisk finials of the early C17 Pinkie
House type. Bargeboarded LODGE with an ogee-roofed
stair-tower. The reconstituted granite CREMATORIUM at the
E end of the cemetery is by *W. N. Thomson*, 1938-9, decorous
jazz-modern inside and out.

At the SE corner of the Links, BOOTHACRE COTTAGES, 1864
Georgian survival, are followed by PIRNIEFIELD PLACE.
Here is a tenement of c. 1804 (Nos. 11-13) with round-arched
fanlights to the main doors. Off SEAFIELD AVENUE is SEA-
COTE HOUSE, a villa of c. 1800. The centre bay, which has
lost its portico, is flanked by over-arched windows with
dumbbell balusters. W of Pirniefield Place, inter-war and
post-war housing illustrates changing fashions among speculative builders. In this mixture No. 16 PROSPECT BANK
ROAD is a late C18 survivor.

Back at Leith Links the E end of CLAREMONT PARK is unpromising. Dull houses of c. 1890, red sandstone predominating. But there follows a line of villas whose concentrated
architectural quality makes it among the best such group in
Edinburgh. They are built on land offered to feuars from
1827, the feu-plan and elevations of the individual houses
being provided by *Thomas Hamilton*. Designs vary but unity
is given by gatepiers with shallow pyramidal tops and linking
screen walls separating the back and front gardens. At No. 12
a balustraded porch with pilastered piers. Panelled aprons
under the windows. The double house of Nos. 10-11 has a
single curved and balustraded Roman Doric portico, its projection echoed vertically by the pediment above. Only pilastered doorpieces at Nos. 8-9, not built until c. 1850. At No.
7 a Tuscan-columned porch and corniced windows with
panelled aprons.

Across CLAREMONT ROAD (in which the one-storey No. 45 is early C19 with a Roman Doric porch), Nos. 5 and 6 Claremont Park were originally identical (No. 5 has acquired a canted bay-window) with Ionic columns *in antis* at the doors and panelled aprons under the windows. But different screen walls. Plain builders' designs of *c.* 1830 conclude the row.

W of Summerfield Gardens, the massive development of GLADSTONE PLACE by *James Simpson*, 1880, austere Italianate much in the style of David Rhind. Canted bay-windows at the ends of each tenement, the junctions marked at the eaves by urns on heavy consoles. The W end breaks slightly into a monumental composition and turns the corner with a generous curve. In RESTALRIG ROAD early C20 tenements lead to a villa of *c.* 1820 (No. 67) with pilasters. Nos. 69–77 of *c.* 1810 form a short terrace, Nos. 69–71 with corniced ground-floor openings, Nos. 73–77 with a rusticated ground floor, its masonry droved. After Prospect Bank School (*see* Public Buildings, above), the Georgian-survival Nos. 87–89 are of *c.* 1863, No. 87 with a faintly Italianate tower. Opposite, No. 92, the former VICTORIA INDUSTRIAL SCHOOL, 1885. Italian Romanesque detail. No. 90, set back behind a long front garden, is early C19, built of rendered brickwork. Off-centre Roman Doric columned doorpiece and a segmental pend-arch.

The S side of Leith Links continues with EAST HERMITAGE PLACE, two-storey and attic terraces begun by the Industrial Co-operative Building Society in 1868, continued after 1875 by the builders *W. & A. Fingzies*, and completed in 1883. The corniced doorpieces are still Georgian, the canted bay-windows are not. Behind, the terraces off INDUSTRIAL ROAD are part of the same development. The view up Somerset Place is closed by the butterfly-roofed harled boxes of BURNS STREET and PRIMROSE STREET, by the *City Architect's Department*, 1972.

Building plots in WEST HERMITAGE PLACE were put up for sale in 1800. The plan (but not necessarily the elevations) was by *Robert Burn*. In 1825 *Thomas Bonnar* prepared elevations for the unfeued plots. First, a terrace of *c.* 1805. No. 1 has a columned doorpiece flanked by a tripartite window and a late bay-window. Nos. 2–3 are a grander double house with fluted aprons under the first-floor windows, the centre window originally tripartite under a segmental blind fanlight. After the simple Nos. 4–5, No. 6 appears to be a forerunner of the Bonnar scheme with its rusticated ground floor and pebble-faced basement. Nos. 7–13 are undoubtedly by *Bonnar*, like a chunk of Melville Street (*see* Western New Town, Streets). Fan-vaulted entrance hall at No. 13. No. 14, *c.* 1805, is a typical Leith villa of the better class with an Ionic-columned doorpiece. VANBURGH PLACE was designed and built by *William Lamb* from 1825. Unusually for Leith it is a unified terrace all of which was built. Paired doors set in screens of Ionic columns *in antis*. At the bottom of LOCHEND ROAD, the Leith Academy Secondary School Lochend Annexe and St Andrew's Church (qq.v.). To the w, Leith Academy (*see* Public Buildings, above) begins DUKE STREET. The rogue baronial tenement (1861) with extravagant crosslets and arrowslits must be by *J. Anderson Hamilton*. By contrast, the early C19 Nos. 79–83 form a droved ashlar slab above a rusticated ground floor. Next to this, SOUTH LEITH PARISH CHURCH HALLS, blocky Art Nouveau by *J. M. Johnston*, 1906–7.

4. North Leith

Starting at SANDPORT PLACE the view across a vast gap site focusses on the Mariners' Church (q.v.). The entrance to QUAYSIDE STREET is framed by late C19 tenements, No. 17 with outsize scrolled skewputts and carved plaques. QUAYSIDE MILLS incorporate parts of the old St Ninian's or North Leith Church and Manse. The chantry chapel founded by Robert Bellenden *c.* 1493, virtually rebuilt in 1595 and 'in a great measure rebuilt'* in 1736, in 1825 became a granary. The four-storey block at the E end of the complex is the heavily reconstructed church. At its N flank a moulded elliptical arch, probably late C16, rising from below street level. w of the church is the manse, early C17 with moulded window margins and crowstepped gables. The stair-tower was given a pilastered wooden belfry with a lead-covered ogee spire in 1675. S of the manse an early C18 tenement. Rusticated pend arch, its scrolled keystone carved with a grotesque head. Above a first-floor window a lintel, perhaps removed from the entrance to the church, inscribed

BLESSED AR THEY YAT HEIR YE VORD OF GOD AND KEIP IT
LUK XI 1600

At Nos. 3–5 Quayside Street the mills' Renaissance counting-house, 1863.

In SANDPORT STREET, Nos. 28–44 form part of a massive Italianate tenement development built by *George Roberts & Son*, 1870–5. Generously bowed corner to COMMERCIAL STREET, where it becomes very grand with shopfronts forming a podium between the advanced ends. In COMMERCIAL WHARF an early C19 warehouse with a central hoist. The Customs House (*see* Public Buildings, above) begins the N side of Commercial Street. In DOCK PLACE Nos. 1–11 are by *John Paterson*, the resident engineer for Leith Docks, *c.* 1810. Housing at the ends, a warehouse in the centre. The Tudor gatepiers of the old East Dock (*see* Harbour and Docks, above) stand between it and the blandly pompous gable front added (by *Archibald Thomson*, 1882) to the first of two warehouses running along Commercial Street. They are of thirty-five and thirty bays, both by *Paterson*, *c.* 1810.

* *Statistical Account of Scotland*, vi (1793), 574.

In DOCK STREET, immediately s of the Mariners' Church, a wire fence defends the surviving E gate of LEITH CITADEL of 1656–7. Vaulted segment-arched pend with hoodmoulds at the outer faces. The parapet is a conjectural restoration by the *City Architect's Department*, 1964. At the corner of Commercial Street and CITADEL STREET the chunky NORTH LEITH STATION, 1846 by *Grainger & Miller*, very Greek with a Corinthianesque order. Entrance screen with columns *in antis* and angular vases on the parapet. At the W end a piered portico. Across Commercial Street, the English Baroque former LEITH NAUTICAL COLLEGE (by *William C. Laidlaw*, 1901–3) precedes a row of late C19 bonded warehouses.

North Leith's post-war housing begins at CITADEL PLACE, by *T. Harley Haddow & Partners*, 1978–9, low-rise with brick garden walls and timber fences along the winding lanes. Less twee is the straight terrace at WEST CROMWELL STREET by the same architects, 1980. Behind is the COUPER STREET development by *Alison & Hutchison & Partners*, 1961–5, a pair of grid-fronted twenty-storey towers (THOMAS FRASER COURT and JOHN RUSSELL COURT). Quartz-aggregate cladding above a brick base. At their feet, a splay-fronted brick and glass block. No. 199 Commercial Street, an office block in glazed red brick, is by *Covell Matthews & Partners*, 1978. Shallow projecting top floor and a suggestion of towers. The low-rise HAMBURGH PLACE (by *T. Harley Haddow & Partners*, 1979) contrasts with the brave new world of the LEITH FORT scheme, 1957–63 by *Shaw-Stewart, Baikie & Perry*. At the N of the site, two twenty-storey point-blocks (CAIRNGORM HOUSE and GRAMPIAN HOUSE). Pre-cast concrete cladding pierced by a few small metal windows. Behind, in HAMILTON WYND and CANNON WYND, low courtyard houses almost hidden by high walls panelled with enthusiastically pointed boulder rubble. The s defence is provided by the seven-storey FORT HOUSE, brown brick with cream-coloured painted bands and balconies, and a hint of battlements at the top. In NORTH FORT STREET the rubble wall behind Fort House is broken by corniced gatepiers and round-arched foot-gates, the entrance to Leith Fort by *James Craig*, 1780. Inside, a pair of guardhouses with open-pedimented gables. Along their fronts, Roman Doric verandas with pedimented centres.

The new housing schemes embrace C19 terraces. PRINCE REGENT STREET, focused on North Leith Parish Church (*see* Churches, above), is a disappointing procession of block-pedimented doorpieces, 1868–73. But Nos. 36–40 are of *c.* 1825 with a delicate fanlight. More late Georgian at Nos. 76–78 NORTH JUNCTION STREET with projecting bowed ends. Opposite is the PORTLAND development of *c.* 1820, tall tenements set above a podium of shopfronts, all rather spoiled by the Georgian-survival Nos. 9–20 PORTLAND PLACE which elbowed its way into the block, *c.* 1870. Sporadic Georgian

development in PORTLAND STREET. The grandest house
was at Nos. 1–3 but the perron to its pilastered front door
(now a window) has gone, and the door in the unsunk rusticated basement has been given a concrete portico. A humbler
version, but intact with a Roman-Doric-columned doorpiece,
appears at Nos. 35–37 of *c.* 1855. Much more consciously
urban than the rest is No. 45 of *c.* 1830. Segmental fanlight
over the door and fluted aprons at the first-floor windows.
After Georgian pilastered doorpieces (Nos. 49–53), Nos. 55–
57 (1891) at the Madeira Street corner seem horribly crude.
Across Madeira Street, No. 87 is a red-brick cottage in the
style of *T. Duncan Rhind*, *c.* 1890. Pedimented timber porch
and large segmental-pedimented dormers. Georgian respectability resumes with Nos. 99–101 of 1815, a terrace scheme
continuing round the corner with Nos. 20–30 NORTH FORT
STREET and completed in much modified form with Nos. 2–
18 in 1860–6.

MADEIRA PLACE, a terrace of *c.* 1825 on its N side, box-dorm-
ers on the S, leads to MADEIRA STREET. North Leith Parish
Church (*see* Churches, above) is its centrepiece. The *c.* 1830
block of Nos. 33–47 tries to live up to the church, the three
bays of No. 45 slightly advanced as a pavilion. Rusticated
ground floor and aprons to the first-floor windows of No. 68
(*c.* 1820). The rest was built between 1859 and 1876, enlivened only by No. 20's anxiety to fit a bay-window into its
narrow plot. (For the Leith Baptist Church, *see* Churches.)
In FERRY ROAD, Georgian-survival terraces flank the old
North Leith Free Church (*see* Churches) on the N side. Late
Georgian terraces at Nos. 57–61 and 89–93 on the S. SOUTH
FORT STREET begins with fragments of an 1815 scheme
(Nos. 1–7 and 8–10). Rusticated ground floor and fluted
aprons at the first floor. Shallow-relief Adamesque plasterwork at the entrance hall of No. 10. But at the W corner a
massive 1889 block with a two-storey rectangular oriel.
No. 23, originally DR BELL'S SCHOOL by *James Simpson*,
1869, was refronted as an Italianate villa *c.* 1890. In FERRY
ROAD E of Madeira Street, the Leith Theatre and Public
Baths (*see* Public Buildings, above). In COBURG STREET a
free Renaissance warehouse (No. 50) dated 1900. Beyond, on
the S side, the old NORTH LEITH CHURCHYARD.

OUTER AREA

BLACKFORD AND LIBERTON

Standing at the Royal Observatory on Blackford Hill one sees to the N perhaps the finest of all panoramas of the city, to the S unspoiled countryside in which Liberton is still a solitary landmark. In the E part of the area the A701 (Nether Liberton and Liberton Brae) climbs out of Edinburgh through pleasant suburbia and then descends for Peebles, with a sight of the monumental lime kilns near Burdiehouse Farm. Kirkbrae is the best approach to the village of Liberton with its spiky Gothick church tower, and then goes on to Lasswade. Both roads have attracted housing developments, and the municipal scheme at Gracemount, including high-rise blocks, is one of the more successful of its kind.

CHURCHES

BURDIEHOUSE CHURCH, Gracemount Drive. By *Harry Taylor*, 1960. A harled box, the E window looking at an outdoor cross against a rubble wall. STAINED GLASS by *Mary Wood*.

CONVENT OF THE POOR CLARES COLETTINES (R.C.), Lasswade Road. By *A. E. Purdie* of London, 1896. Gothic, of snecked Craigmillar stone with grey Dunfermline dressings. Slated roofs, red ridge-tiles and flowery iron finials. Lanceted CHAPEL with bellcote at S (liturgical E) end. Quadripartite rib-vault. Spiky Gothic REREDOS with statues of St Anthony and St Francis, an alabaster Madonna to the l. The main convent building adjoins the chapel at right angles, gabled and dormered and symmetrical except for the priest's house at the W end.

35 LIBERTON PARISH CHURCH, Kirkgate. A rectangular semi-Gothic* box by *J. Gillespie Graham*, 1815, after the old church was burned and then demolished. The three-stage W tower with corbelled parapet and thin pinnacles is a landmark. Except for this, every elevation is symmetrical. Two steep gables on the S (pulpit) side, one on the N, all crossy and crenellated and diagonally buttressed. Shallow crowsteps at the E and W ends. The windows and tracery are more plausible. Galleried interior, reduced to a T by stair-halls at the N corners. Re-cast in 1882, it received its plain compartmented ceiling and bland oak furnishings *c*. 1930. – MONUMENT on the W wall to William Purdie †1834, signed by *A. Ritchie*. Urn with marble portrait head in low relief, over a tablet flanked by two boys. – STAINED GLASS. On the S side, E end, two lights (Cornelius) by *Ballantine*, 1905. – MONUMENTS in the old churchyard (newer ones are in a W extension). – To the W the elegant Peacock family monument, a pedestal dated 1738. – Also the table-tomb first occupied by the wife (†1753) of William Straiton of Tower Farm; on the W endpiece a relief of ploughing with oxen and harrowing with horses, on the E a swanky monogram. At the sides two fat balusters with swirling flutes, and between them the damaged recumbent figure of a man holding a skull, his head on a corn-sheaf. – To the SW a pedestal to James Baxter, 'Taylor in Gilmertoun', †1737. On the faces, crude Corinthian pilasters and pediments with strange masks; on the ends, very thin caryatids. – To the E a nice group of headstones with inscriptions on carved drapery, e.g. to Mark Haliburton, farmer, †1708. Gates and small SESSION HOUSE (here called an offertory house) contemporary with the church.

REID MEMORIAL CHURCH, West Savile Terrace and Blackford Avenue. Lorimerian Gothic, by *L. Grahame Thomson*, 1929–33. Church, hall and church officer's cottage form an architectural oasis at an otherwise nondescript junction, all of Craigmillar rubble with slightly warmer-coloured Dodding-

---

*The apt description in Groome's *Ordnance Gazetteer*, *c*. 1890.

ton dressings and copious ironwork by *Thomas Hadden*. 'The principal aim', said *The Architect and Building News*, 'was to secure, without unnecessary ornament, a dignity in the cathedral tradition by that feeling of height and aspiration which indicates the theme ... of the Ascension'. It is a lofty, cruciform church with stiff neo-Perp detail, meticulous but affectionate. w window deeply recessed, segmental-headed windows over low aisles, and very tall pointed windows at the shallow transepts and semi-octagonal E apse. Blunt gables of shallow pitch, plain buttresses slightly battered. At the apse the buttresses are crowned with angels below the wall-head. The main roof behind the parapet was covered with Caithness slates (now replaced with concrete tiles). Battlemented NE tower built in a single stage with angle-buttresses. Octagonal SE belltower with a pretty ogee dome of copper. The interior is of rough plaster, relieved by Doddington stone and pale oak. Big clearstorey over a segmental arcade, with a compartmented wagon ceiling of pointed section; it is suspended from a steel roof structure whose design justifies the buttresses. To the E an effective change of mood, building up to the elevated chancel which has a rib-vault of oak with carved and coloured bosses. – Plain PULPIT, LECTERN and COMMUNION TABLE, all of stone. Painted REREDOS (the Last Supper) by *William R. Lawson*. – ELDERS' STALLS and other carved oak fittings by *Scott Morton & Tynecastle Company*. – ORGAN in the tower (the pipes concealed behind grilles) by *Rushworth & Dreaper*. – STAINED GLASS. Three tall windows in the apse (Nativity, Crucifixion and Ascension) by *James Ballantine II*. The colours are symbolic of their subjects, culminating in rose-coloured angels at the centre, and appear more diffused at a distance. To the E the subsidiary buildings, including a turreted two-storey cottage in the Lorimer manner, form a courtyard with a fountain, dominated by the apse. In the base of the apse a carved PANEL in low relief (Christ and the Woman of Samaria) by *Alexander Carrick*.

PUBLIC BUILDINGS

ALNWICKHILL HOUSE, Alnwickhill. By *Robert Wilson* as the Industrial Home for Fallen Women, 1890, but now used as local-authority housing. Mild Queen Anne in yellow sandstone.

CRAIGMILLAR PARK GOLF CLUB, Observatory Road. By *Edward Birrell*, 1980, after a fire. A simple and sensible design, retaining the old street frontage of 1906.

DR GUTHRIE'S BOYS' SCHOOL, Lasswade Road. By *Sydney Mitchell* as the Edinburgh Industrial Ragged School, 1885. Plain Gothic in pink and red sandstone, the N part slightly later. Gymnasium by *Esmé Gordon*, 1965.

FIRE STATION, Kirkbrae. By *Bamber, Gray & Partners*, 1974–6. Smart plastic top, multi-balconied concrete tower.

KAIMES SCHOOL, Lasswade Road. By *E. Alexander*, 1973. A school for the partially sighted. Small-scale, with tile-hung walls.

LIBERTON HOSPITAL, Lasswade Road. Lodge and former Cottage Hospital by *Dick Peddie & Washington Browne*, 1906, with warm masonry and red-tiled roof. Two-storey administrative block, single-storey wings with six oblong bay-windows apiece. This is now an annexe to the Geriatric Hospital by *John Holt*, 1963. Four storeys, with grey vertical fins, suspended by an external frame over a single-storey service block.

MORTONHALL CREMATORIUM, Howdenhall Road. By *Basil Spence, Glover & Ferguson*, 1964. The main chapel is a calmly expressionist cluster of quartz-faced pylons, unevenly coursed, the intermediate slits providing light for the funnel-shaped auditorium, and a crowning tetrahedron transmitting it downwards into the 'sanctuary'; an impressive interior, entered by a timber porte cochère. The smaller Pentland Chapel is relatively fussy and pokey. Only the woodland setting and stony pathway recall Asplund's Forest Crematorium, but these buildings and their dependencies achieve their effect in a much smaller context.

MOUNT VERNON R.C. CEMETERY, Mount Vernon Road. A granite Calvary Cross by *Whitehead & Sons* of Aberdeen, 1913, with a life-size figure.

POLICE STATION, Mayfield Road. By *Morris & Steedman*, 1963. Brick, with a deep copper facia, well related to the slope.

ROYAL OBSERVATORY, Observatory Road, Blackford Hill. By *W. W. Robertson* of H.M. Office of Works, 1892, opulent Graeco-Italian in aubergine-coloured stone. Panels with the signs of the Zodiac along the N range between the larger and smaller telescope towers, which are crowned with green copper cylinders. Library wing and Astronomer's house to S. W additions of singular incongruity by *J. Malcolm Mackintosh*, 1967. ARCHWAY at the foot of Observatory Road. By *Sydney Mitchell*, 1887, in memory of Lord Provost Harrison †1885. Red sandstone, with attached Ionic columns.

ST CRISPIN'S R.C. SCHOOL, Watertoun Road. By *Law & Dunbar-Nasmith*, 1963. Brick, with a timber clearstorey.

72 SOUTHFIELD HOSPITAL, Lasswade Road. A showy baronial country house by *John Chesser*, 1875. S (entrance) front with bows and fancy crowsteps, W front with a tall lucarned turret and John o'Groats-style dormered and finialled bay. WALLED GARDEN to S.

UNIVERSITY OF EDINBURGH: KING'S BUILDINGS, West Mains Road and Mayfield Road. A 35 ha. site; the N side is level, the S rises into the open hills. Plenty of trees (perhaps not big enough) and interesting ground-cover make peace between the buildings without much favour to their individual qualities. The pre-1939 buildings are lined up along the two roads, with monumental frontages advertising the dignity of science. The earliest is CHEMISTRY in West Mains Road by *Rowand Anderson & Balfour Paul*, 1920-4, red stock brick with red sandstone dressings and yawning Wrenaissance centrepiece (the rear part vapidly heightened by *Rowand Anderson, Kininmonth & Paul*, 1949). Then *John F. Matthew* of *Lorimer & Matthew* took over, with *Alexander Carrick* supplying appropriate sculptural motifs, e.g. on the horizontal bands between two-storey giant orders. On the corner of the two roads ZOOLOGY, 1927-8, with a high arched entrance in the splayed centrepiece (three-storey extension of H-shaped concrete units, 1969, and single-storey GENOME UNIT, 1975, both by *Robert Matthew, Johnson-Marshall & Partners*). Within the site, the less formal ANIMAL GENETICS building, 1929-30, harl-fronted with a colonial gable and Lorimerish balcony over the entrance. Back in West Mains Road, GEOLOGY, 1930-1, conscientiously stone-faced all round, with a severely simplified giant order and another colonial centrepiece (w extension for EXPERIMENTAL PETROLOGY by *Alan Reiach & Partners*, 1965). In Mayfield Road, ENGINEERING, 1929-32, with a massive central pylon (brick extension, and a lecture theatre free-standing like a timber-clad mushroom, by *Robert Gardner-Medwin* and *Kingham, Knight*, 1961). Inside the site, the KING'S BUILDINGS UNION, 1938-9, thinly formal with the same coved cornice as the adjacent Geology building.

The post-war era began feebly with the (former) POULTRY RESEARCH building by *A. G. Ingham* of the Department of Agriculture; more bravely with AGRICULTURE itself, designed by *Alan Reiach* and *Ralph Cowan* in 1948, executed in 1955-60 with a concrete frame under its plum-coloured brick skin. Main block with three storeys above an open cloister, subsequently glazed in because of the wind. Through this, but without any explicit symmetry, the only formal vista on the whole site (planned by *William H. Kininmonth* and now oddly blocked by a clump of shrubs) flows out to the open fields and Liberton Tower. At the SE corner off Mayfield Road, two buildings by *Robert Gardner-Medwin* with *Kingham, Knight*. In the two-storey BOTANY building, 1965, the concrete frame is infilled with concrete panels or large windows. At the DARWIN building (Molecular Biology, Forestry and Natural Resources), 1968, concrete stanchions rise the whole height of an eight-storey tower with a varied pattern of glazed panels between. At ANIMAL BREEDING RESEARCH on a hump in the middle of the site, by *Basil Spence & Partners*, 1962, the frame comes right outside; black steel uprights carrying panelled walls, all elegantly related and detailed. The s boundary is completed by the JAMES CLERK MAXWELL BUILDING (Physics, Maths, Computer Science) by *Hardie Glover* of *Basil Spence, Glover & Ferguson*, 1966. Much less preoccupation with the supporting structure; here the main theme is the artfully punctuated brickwork of the tall slab, the two-storey Computer Centre, and the lecture-theatre wing curving round from the main (W) entrance. Planting, for once, in complete harmony. Meticulous interior of white painted brick, but spartan except for the laminated timber stair-rails. Near the NW corner the four-storey EPI-GENETICS by *Robert Matthew, Johnson-Marshall & Partners*, 1966, four storeys of big slabs faced with graph-paper mosaic. To the W the INSTITUTE OF GEOLOGICAL SCIENCE by *M. J. Mannings, Department of the Environment*, 1971, a strong composition of ochre brickwork with much use of stair-towers, chamfered corners and bellying glass. In the centre of the site *Michael Laird* designed the REFECTORY in 1971, using the same bowed concrete units as at his reconstruction of the BOILER HOUSE just before; the bright convergent tubes of the new chimney (built round the old one) make a fine landmarking signature for the whole heterogeneous assembly of buildings.

MANSIONS

GRACEMOUNT HOUSE, Lasswade Road. Now a youth centre. Mostly *c*. 1800. E entrance front of one storey and basement, smooth ashlar with two deep bows connected by a broad open pediment in which an elegant tripartite doorpiece is set in a shallow over-arch. The clumsy mansard and treatment of the front steps are later. Gothick N front (formerly symmetrical) *c*. 1790 with moustachioed terms of impressively archaic aspect, and a female bust and an angel on top. Additions and alterations *c*. 1890 (by *G. S. Aitken*) and 1932 have removed most of the Georgian interior. GATEWAY in Howdenhall Road with geometric cast-iron piers and wrought-iron gates, *c*. 1800.

LIBERTON HOUSE, Liberton Drive. A harled L-plan house built *c*. 1600 for the Littles of Liberton, who bought the estate in 1587. Original window margins with rounded arrises, and a sundial inscribed W.L. 1683 at the SE corner. In the reentrant (NW) angle a round stair-turret corbelled out to the square at the second floor, its crowstepped gable restored *c*. 1890. The crowsteps of the main gables are of 1936, when *Rowand Anderson, Paul & Partners* removed a Georgian top floor and restored the wall-head with dormers of late C17 type, but left the plain porch at the base of the turret and the E bay-window, both of *c*. 1840. Against the N gable a crowstepped and pedimented lean-to, probably *c*. 1890. Two-storey extension of the W jamb probably late C17; the dormer-head dated 1675 was moved here *c*. 1890 from the W range, which has swept dormers of 1936 and over the door a resited lintel (from where?) inscribed WILLIAM. 1570. LITIL in lacy characters.

Inside the porch the original moulded entrance doorway of *c*. 1600, with an empty panel overhead. Unusually for a country house it opens not into the stair-turret but into the hall (cf. Tweeddale House; *see* Old Town, Royal Mile: High Street), but is well guarded by gun loops. The planning is again that of a town house. Unvaulted ground floor hall and chamber in the main block, their height curtailing that of the bedrooms above. In the hall three tall windows to the E, two high ones to the S flanking a stone chimneypiece with sparsely fluted attached columns, very deep frieze and squidgy cornice – the intention perhaps classical, the result still Gothic. In the W and N walls segmentally arched buffet recesses. Similar recesses in the S wall of the adjoining chamber and right along its E and W walls, that on the E extended by the bay-window of *c*. 1840. Original kitchen in the W jamb; segmental-arched fireplace and a recess in the N wall with a gun loop covering the approach. Beamed ceiling with heraldic decoration by *Thomas Bonnar, Jun.*, 1892. Upstairs, chimneypieces of the later C17 and massive Arts and Crafts timberwork of 1936 in the first-floor NE room.

Beside the avenue leading to the house, a tall lectern DOO-COT, probably of the late C17, harled with moulded string and eaves courses. A large circular opening over the door.

LIBERTON TOWER, Liberton Drive. Perched on a ridge running W from Liberton, with a splendid S panorama of Edinburgh. Suburbia barely keeps its distance. Despite being left to fend for itself in the corner of a farmyard, this is an exceptionally complete late medieval tower house. Rectangular plan, four storeys, carefully coursed rubble with dressings reserved for openings and corners. The windows are still mostly the original chamfered loops, a worn carved panel high up on the S wall the sole decorative concession. The basement door has been enlarged and is not similar to the main second-floor entrance in the E wall. Below the latter, a corbel for a wooden stair. Some ancient harling still clings to the E side. The wall-head is plain apart from spouts draining the parapet walk (cf. Craigmillar). The slab roof rests on a pointed tunnel-vault below which were the residential storeys. Under these a lower barrel-vaulted basement for storage. The wooden floors that made two storeys within each space have gone.[*] The raising of the basement door has interrupted the corbels for the joists. The hatch in the vault was presumably made when the tower was put to agricultural uses.

From the entresol a stair in the NW corner leads to the hall on the second, main floor. Plain fireplace in the long S wall, largish windows, an aumbry and a garderobe in the NE corner (with thoughtful provision for a close-fitting door). The aumbry is an original feature, and its depressed ogee head (damaged when a door was fitted later) suggests a date for the tower of *c*. 1500. A blocked original opening is beside the aumbry. It was anticipated that any intruders would come up from the basement rather than through the E door, whose

---

[*] MacGibbon & Ross show the joists of the upper floor in place.

outside stair could be removed. To continue upwards they would have to come into the hall and cross to the SW, in full view of an efficient spyhole in the E wall. Access to this is from the straight stair in the thickness of the E wall, the alternative approach to the next floor and the more direct way to the roof. The top floor has a small and a large fireplace, suggesting subdivision into two private rooms. Adjoining the tower are two farmhouses, one with a lintel dated 1701 in its older r. part.

MORTONHALL HOUSE, Frogston Road East. Designed and built for the Trotters of Mortonhall, probably by *John Baxter Jun.*, 1769. Grey and austere with five broad bays, quite plain at the basement and ground floor but with rusticated quoins at the two upper floors. Advanced and pedimented centre, in which the *piano nobile* windows have alternate triangular and segmental pediments; on the S side the pediments go right across. In the main N pediment a bullseye window in uncarved blocks, in the S pediment a whole uncarved tympanum. Five narrower bays at each end. Later additions are inconspicuous (a low service wing to the E, a light iron staircase to the S), except for the Greek Doric porch built *c.* 1835 at the front door; the original consoled doorway survives.

Original interior of outstanding quality, the two main rooms re-cast at the end of the C18. In the square entrance hall a curiously bracketed cornice and a rococo centrepiece of quasi-Gothic line. In the middle of the house two cantilevered stone staircases side by side, the main one in a square well with the landings at the corners and S side. The outer end of each step is shaped (over a flat soffit), the inner end has a returned nosing; another old-fashioned feature is the spindly design of the turned wooden balusters, alternately straight and serpentine. Coved ceiling with scrolled foliage in the corners, and a central lantern. Service stair to the W, with plain straight balusters. Dining room in the middle three bays of the S front, the black marble chimneypiece *c.* 1820. First drawing room above, with original white marble chimneypiece; lugged frame with boy-headed flanking consoles, a garlanded female mask above. Delicate ceiling of 1795–1800 with corn-ears in a long oval.* Oval miniature pastoral scenes in gilt arabesques, by *Thomas Bonnar* of *D.R. Hay & Co.*, *c.* 1840, on door and shutter panels. Second drawing room at the SE, the chimneypiece Louis XV type of 1843, the ceiling with star pattern and twelve low-relief roundels of classical figures in the centre square, double diamonds in the ends. Gilt coat of arms painted over the door and a gilt stencilled wreath pattern apparently *c.* 1840, beneath the blue damask Victorian wallpaper. At the W side a two-window bedroom with a Louis XV chimneypiece of liver-coloured marble, perhaps C18. On the second floor (over the first drawing room)

*cf. the corn-ears in a long oval at No. 6 Charlotte Square and at No. 1, which also has a star ceiling with roundels (*see* Central Area, First New Town: Streets).

the library. Original coved ceiling with two-headed eagles in leafy sprays at the corners, more foliage and fruit-filled horns halfway along, all immaculately wood-grained in the C19 and matching the bookcases, which leave ample wall-height for the display of busts etc. on top. An extraordinary chimney-piece of fine-grain stone and uncertain C18 date. Male and female caryatid terms, their features regular but not idealized, their pedestals very tenuously curved. On their heads leafy concave capitals with diagonally projecting abaci, joined by a concave fluted cornice.

STABLES in view of the house to the N with a tall Doric archway and pyramid-roofed pavilions. Paved quadrangle, sloped down to a central circle. WALLED GARDEN with corner pavilion nearby, and outbuildings including a hay-loft with lobed ventilator slits.

ST CATHERINE'S, Howdenhall Road. Now a boys' home. A triple-pile Georgian house whose development is hard to work out. The castellated N front with tripartite main-storey windows probably belongs to the house designed by *John Simpson* for himself and built by *David Bell* in 1806. The third (s) range of rooms must have been added soon after. It includes a new entrance hall in the middle, leading to the staircase, which had to be turned back-to-front. The plain new façade was given a fancy porch and two bay-windows *c.* 1835; *c.* 1880 the entrance was moved to its final position at the W end, with a large single-storey classical extension by *George S. Aitken.* The E extension was put on in 1914.

BALM WELL to the W. Early C19 gable incorporating a convex lintel from a moulded doorway inscribed AP 1563. Inside, the opening is flanked by stones with attached shafts, possibly related to the original well built by order of James V in 1517.

FARMS

BROOMHILLS, Frogston Road East. A picturesque group, built *c.* 1830 of squared rubble with swept and roughly corbelled corners along the road which runs down to the Burdiehouse Burn.

BURDIEHOUSE MAINS, Burdiehouse Road. Built *c.* 1830, a three-bay farmhouse with advanced and block-topped centre-piece. Behind it (to the E) a farm courtyard of elaborate symmetry, the rear part traditionally a lace-factory. LIME KILNS to the S. Three connected kilns, polygonal, segmental and rectangular in plan, built on to the side of the hill. Stone-faced, brick-lined.

LIBERTON TOWER MAINS, Liberton Brae. Built *c.* 1830, a three-bay farmhouse as at Burdiehouse (*see* above) but the symmetrical courtyard to the rear is more compact and highly finished.

MEADOWHEAD, Liberton Drive. By *David Bryce Jun.* A large

group, complete except for the engine-house chimney (whose base remains), all built in 1854-5, when the nearby C18 cottages were up-graded as a farmhouse.

PERAMBULATIONS

NETHER LIBERTON is a little settlement entered not from the street of that name but from the N end of Gilmerton Road. OLD MILL LANE begins with NETHER LIBERTON HOUSE, originally C18 but enlarged c. 1840 into a double pile with Tudor trimmings. Then INCH COTTAGE, c. 1880 with a pretty white-painted porch. Two architects' houses to the rear: *Stuart Renton*'s CLAPPERFIELD in white-painted brick, 1971, and *Fraser Bowman*'s ingeniously simple YARD HOUSE, 1975. OLD MILL COTTAGE above the Braid Burn was refronted c. 1880 but still has its mill-wheel. WHITE HOUSE is a row of pantiled cottages converted for himself by *R. Scott Morton* in 1957. To the W LIBERTON BANK HOUSE, single-storey C18 with big attic windows in the gables, and down in the valley LIBERTON GREEN HOUSE, C18 but much altered. To the W of the main road (Craigmillar Park) the big rubble and pantile DOOCOT of Inch House (*see* Gilmerton: Mansions, below), of early C17 double-lectern type, and the C18 DOVECOT COTTAGE.

KIRKBRAE starts with the Fire Station (*see* Public Buildings, above). The long climb becomes interesting with a group of four villas on the E side; No. 75, dated 1868, with fat barge-boards and ornamental beam-ends of cast metal, No. 77 Tudor, both with pretty conservatories retaining some coloured glass. ST HILDA'S is mostly mid-C19 with a mad mansard, spindly slated candle-snuffers coming straight down on chunky corner corbels. On the W side AUCHINDOUNE (No. 64) in red-tiled estate-agent style by *J. R. McKay*, 1925. On the hilltop, the real feeling of a village. To the E a couple of single-storey cottages, to the W the mid-C19 LIBERTON INN turning the corner into KIRKGATE, where its harled C18 annexe is named after Reuben Butler, the schoolmaster in Scott's *Heart of Midlothian*. Behind the wall lurks the Parish Church (*see* above). HALL on the opposite side with wheel-windowed N gable, 1882, and little spiky villas of the same period.

The main street goes on as LASSWADE ROAD, its village scale maintained by the whitewashed single-storey cottage (formerly double) at No. 4, the view narrowed by a projecting outhouse of the former KIRK FARM; C18 farmhouse with gable to road, overlooking a single-storey courtyard, all now in commercial use. Finally a petrol station, and across the road a pair of decent harled tenements c. 1925, with corner turrets. Altogether a good group, thanks to plenty of old walls and slate roofs and a bit of luck. For Dr Guthrie's Boys' School and other public buildings in Lasswade Road, *see*

above. On the E side two pleasant groups of houses. LOCK-
ERBY COTTAGES by *McWhannel & Rogerson*, 1892–4, all
semi-detached and built of cream stone, but varied as to
dormer pediments and other red sandstone dressings. In
LOCKERBY CRESCENT, villas of uniform design in plum-
coloured brick by *Miller*, 1977. Off GRACEMOUNT DRIVE to
the W, multi-storey blocks (GARVALD COURT, FALA
COURT, SOUTRA COURT) by *Crudens Ltd* in association with
the *City Architect's Department*, 1962.

BRUNTSFIELD AND MERCHISTON

Late Georgian and early Victorian maps show villas creeping
along Bruntsfield Place and spreading out E into Greenhill (*see*
Morningside) and W into Leamington Terrace and Viewforth.
From the 1850s the favoured area for villa building became
Merchiston, where the Merchant Company sold feus on the
lands of Merchiston Castle, *David Rhind* supervising the de-
velopment until *c.* 1864, when he was replaced by *David Mac-
Gibbon*.

In the late 1850s the Warrender family's estate of Bruntsfield
was laid out for good-class tenements. Building here continued
into the C20, when the original name had been superseded by
that of Marchmont after the main N–S road. Before then almost
all the Georgian villas of Bruntsfield Place had fallen victim to
tenement expansion.

CHURCHES

BRUNTSFIELD EVANGELICAL (originally United Presbyterian), Westhall Gardens and Leamington Terrace. Tough
early French Gothic by *J. Russell Walker*, 1882–3. Main gable
to Leamington Terrace, with a round mincer-plate window.
Tower at the corner, an octagonal belfry with octagonal turrets at the angles and capped with 'a dumpy extinguisher in
a manner which is neither quaint nor beautiful' (*The Builder*,
unfairly). Complicated side elevation with a vestigial transept.
Big-scale interior, with timber tunnel roof on iron-shafted
arcades, the side galleries carried by timber trusses. – PULPIT
in a big semicircular arcade, French Gothic in the Burges
manner. – ORGAN overhead by *Norman & Beard*.
CANDLISH CHURCH (originally Free Church), Polwarth Terrace and Harrison Road. By *Sydney Mitchell & Wilson*, 1900.
Late Dec in deep red sandstone with smooth dressings and
nicely varied detail, the chancel added by the same architects
in 1902, the square SW tower by *James Jerdan & Son* in 1913;
a less confident design with a top-stage belfry, pinnacles and
gargoyles. A finely proportioned interior with red stone dressings; chamfered nave arcade below the clearstorey, taller
arches opening into the transepts. Timber tunnel roof, W

gallery reached by a staircase in the tower. – PULPIT. Octagonal, of variegated stone; statuettes of Dr Candlish and John Knox in a blind arcade, bright red colonnettes below, a timber sounding-board above. – FONT. Red stone with white marble bowl and cherubs' heads, 1887. – ORGAN by *Forster & Andrews*, 1903. – STAINED GLASS. In the E window five lights (scenes following the Resurrection, the Transfiguration as the main subject), 1903. – HALL to the N by *Jerdan*, 1913.

GERMAN LUTHERAN CHURCH, Chalmers Crescent. By *Alfred Schildt* of Frankfurt, with *Reiach & Hall* as executant architects, 1967. Stone-faced, with the minister's house cantilevered out from the adjoining wing. – STAINED GLASS by *George Garson*.

GILMORE PLACE FREE PRESBYTERIAN (originally United Presbyterian), Gilmore Place. A compact Gothic church by *Thornton Shiells & Thomson*, 1880. Rose-windowed gable to the front, gables suggestive of transepts to the side. Galleried interior with clear-span open roof.

JESUS CHRIST OF THE LATTER-DAY SAINTS CHURCH, Colinton Road. The expressionist production of their own architects, 1963.

ST JOSEPH'S CONVENT OF THE LITTLE SISTERS OF THE POOR (R.C.), Gilmore Place. By *J. M. Monro* of Glasgow, 1889. A symmetrical crowstepped front incorporating a Georgian house and using its central Venetian windows. CHAPEL to the rear; Romanesque, added by Monro in 1897.

ST KENTIGERN (Episcopal, in secular use in 1984), St Peter's Place (entered by a pend from Viewforth). A tiny roundarched church by *John M. Dick Peddie*, 1897; nave, one aisle and narthex.

ST OSWALD (originally St Mark, now Boroughmuir School Annexe), Montpelier and Montpelier Park. Original church of 1894, a modest gable and doorway with red dressings. New church of brown stone, 1899, adjacent to it but much more sophisticated. E.E. lancets in aisles and clearstorey but round windows with geometric tracery in the (liturgical) NE chapel. Against the W gable a wide two-storey narthex, pinnacled and buttressed, ceremoniously entered from N or S. Impressive interior with plain clearstorey windows over a slightly richer arcade, the three tall arches of the W gallery looking up to the crossing and half-round chancel arch. Gerona-style chancel, its aisles within the width of the nave. Gothic reredos of red sandstone. Under the tunnel roof, kingpost trusses crossbraced to form big Iona crosses. – STAINED GLASS. In the chancel two lancets and a vesica (Christ's Crucifixion, Resurrection and Ascension) by *C. E. Kempe*, *c.* 1899. One rose window in the NE chapel (the Trinity) in the same manner. In the N aisle one light (St Ninian) by *William Wilson*, 1950. Some other glass (unattributed) of moderate quality.

VIEWFORTH ST DAVID AND ST OSWALD (originally Free Church), Gilmore Place and Viewforth. Gothic, by *Frederick T. Pilkington*, 1871. Unexpectedly orthodox four-square plan and restrained detail as compared with what *The Builder* called 'the restless efforts at originality which characterized his former works'. Effective nonetheless in its massive upward growth (a battered base and then a further constriction at the steep sill-course) and in the contrasting fragility of the shafted geometric window in the big central gable. To the W a rose-windowed stair-hall and quirky dormered HALL. To the E the tower; over its colonnetted doorway thin vertical strips forming three blind arches of prodigious height before breaking into six smaller arches. An octagonal belfry, in a pure C13 French manner with tall shafts and gablets, complemented this rude pedestal but was taken down in 1976. Interior still largely by Pilkington, a powerful variation of a basically Georgian form. Very thin iron columns with burgeoning capitals and big four-way consoles; they support not a nave arcade but huge transverse beams over the side galleries. Simple plaster groin-vault above. Gallery front with blind balustrade divisions, richly carved. – PULPIT and large traceried organ case by *T.P. Marwick*, 1899, following a serious fire. – ORGAN by *Blackett & Howden*.

PUBLIC BUILDINGS

BOROUGHMUIR SCHOOL, Viewforth. Largest and cleverest of *John A. Carfrae*'s board schools, 1911. Simple rectangular plan with two light-wells, each containing a gymnasium at basement level. A stone base stepping downhill, then a giant Roman Ionic order taking in the first and thermal windowed second floors and topped by Palladian vases sprouting gilded flames. Central tower with Doric porch and a high arcade, and very tall flanking towers with an arched entry, the arches with intricate Byzantinesque carving by *Joseph Hayes*.

BOROUGHMUIR SCHOOL ANNEXE, Warrender Park Crescent. A large board school by *John A. Carfrae*, 1902, the cross-bar of the T plan presenting a lofty and complex Renaissance elevation of pale orange sandstone (obscured by later planting) to Bruntsfield Links; the rest picturesquely composed with orange dressings on deep pink rock-faced masonry.

BRUNTSFIELD PRIMARY SCHOOL, Montpelier. By *Robert Wilson* (but effectively by his successor as School Board architect, *John A. Carfrae*), 1893. Rubble with red sandstone dressings, the symmetrical S front with the windows of two superimposed halls, central lantern and gabled pavilions, looking down Bruntsfield Avenue.

GEORGE WATSON'S COLLEGE, Colinton Road. By *James B. Dunn*, 1930. Two-storey H plan with linking hall, the pilastered N (entrance) front efficiently detailed in hard purple stone, with a galleon wind-vane* (for the Merchant Company) over the central pediment.‡ S front vestigially classical

---

*From the hall block of the old school.

‡Burn's portico at the old school was meant to be re-erected here, but this was not done.

and very dull, inward-facing elevations harled with cheerful red brick arches. To the E the WAR MEMORIAL, by *J. A. Carfrae*, 1920, a severe pedimented portal with an open Greek Doric apse behind. Nearby, a bronze figure of a sleeping boy ('Summer') by *G. A. Lawson*. MUSIC SCHOOL to the SE by *Michael Laird*, 1962, single-storey practice rooms and square, stone-based hall with hyperbolic paraboloid roof. SPORTS PAVILION, Myreside Road, by *Walker Todd*, 1932.

JAMES GILLESPIE'S HIGH SCHOOL, Warrender Park Road and Lauderdale Street. A sympathetic mixture of old and new. *William H. Kininmonth*'s school buildings, 1962–4, are of domestic scale with regular patterns of large windows, and composed as three informal quadrangles with a plain brick clock-tower where they meet. The last quadrangle is entered obliquely. On the E side is the school hall. On the N, with a discreet bridge link, BRUNTSFIELD HOUSE, built in the late

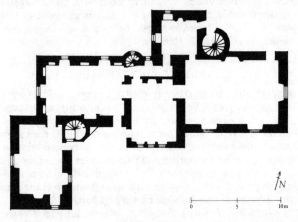

Bruntsfield House,
plan of first floor

C16 by the Lauder family and acquired in 1695 by the Warrenders of Lochend. Plain three-storey Z plan, i.e. with a long main block running E to W and jambs at the NE and SW corners. Crowsteps, pedimented dormers and finials. Stair-turrets in the internal angles on corbels enriched with rope and billet moulding, but the NE turret is a little distance away from the jamb and finishes with a shallow projecting cap-house, presumably once providing a passage past the main block into the top floor of the jamb. In the C17 the SE internal angle was filled with a slightly projecting block. C20 pediments over the big C18 windows. Inside, a vaulted basement, but only a few moulded second-floor fireplaces and the internal corbel of the NE stair-turret survive from the earlier work. On the first floor, two grand rooms *en suite*, of *c.* 1700. The Headmistress's Room in the body of the house is completely panelled. In the C17 addition, the Music Room with big diagonally voluted pilasters at the fireplace, and lugged doors. Richly coffered ceiling of *c.* 1830 with oddly skinny ribs. In both rooms, late C18 chimneypieces of exceptional quality, with yellow marble-shafted Ionic columns, *putti* in the centre panels.

JAMES GILLESPIE'S SCHOOL ANNEXE, Upper Gilmore Place. Probably by *Carfrae*, *c.* 1895. Red sandstone Renaissance, the symmetrical Gillespie Street frontage with twin gables whose top floors have attached columns and obelisk finials.

MARCHMONT ROAD SCHOOL, Marchmont Road and Marchmont Crescent. Plain School Board Gothic by *Robert Wilson*, 1882, with a bellcote on the S gable. Very effective on its corner site.

NAPIER COLLEGE, Colinton Road. Designed round Merchiston Castle by *Alison & Hutchison & Partners*, 1961. Brick-faced E block of seven storeys, the S gable brick-faced with high triangular oriels, the rest built of quartz-faced slabs in horizontal bands. Otherwise a workaday S elevation, but with an open entry to the upper courtyard, which is separated from the lower one by the tower and an elevated link.

Exhibited like a trophy in the middle of the college is MERCHISTON CASTLE, the late medieval L-plan tower house of the Napiers, almost certainly the tower mentioned in a sasine of 1495. As if to dispel undue awe in the face of antiquity, a concrete dog-leg stair leaps up to the second-floor S entrance and an elevated corridor slices through the projecting N jamb. Rubble walls, with dressings reserved for corners and openings; the original windows simply chamfered. Corbelled parapet with bartizans on the main block and rounded corners on the jamb. A single machicolation on the N side. Crow-stepped cap-houses with some later dormers, and a conical roof indicating the stair within the SW angle. The recessed entrance is mostly from 1961, when *Alison & Hutchison & Partners* restored the tower. Entirely of that date are the incised Napier arms and bogus drawbridge slots. In the re-entrant angle a rounded projection for garderobes, the position of its outlet marked by new corbels inside the elevated corridor. Real rock on the N side, supplemented by rockery. An external cellar below ground belonged no doubt to an addition shown in C18 views as filling the re-entrant angle.

Within the tower there have been five unvaulted storeys, all linked by the newel stair in the SW corner. The two lower levels would doubtless be used for storage. On the second floor the external entrance reaches a lobby which may perpetuate a screens passage. Fielded panelling and painted wood heraldic ceiling of 1963. The hall (now Principal's Room) has a plaster ceiling with the monogram of Charles II; four rectangular compartments cut into by a central circle and arcs of others, and in each division a smaller circle and a moulded motif, e.g. busts labelled 'Alexander' and 'King David'. Big central pendant. The wide fireplace in the S wall is mostly of

c. 1962 but incorporates parts of the original C15 work. In the
NE corner, near where the high table would have stood, a
newel stair leads to the private rooms above. The kitchen in
the wing has the usual big fireplace, lockers and serving hatch,
but also a shot-hole in a corner of the fireplace. From the
lobby a straight service stair in the thickness of the W wall
descends towards the lower rooms in the wing. The first exit
from the SW turnpike leads into a cramped space over the
lobby where probably there was a minstrels' gallery. The
third-floor room now takes in the former fourth floor, the
corbels for which run inconsequentially across the long walls.
The eccentric placing of the bolection-moulded fireplace is
evidence of a subdivision now suppressed. The painted
beamed CEILING was brought here in 1964 from Prestongrange near Tranent (Lothian). It has been shortened by five
panels. Date 1581 on a tablet near the W end. In design and
execution it is so much more accomplished than any other
Scottish ceiling paintings of the late C16 or early C17 that
attribution to a French or Flemish artist seems unavoidable.
The use of grisaille on a red lead ground has no parallel in
Scotland. The arabesques on the ceiling boards are extraordinarily inventive. At the W end, where the gallery between
turnpike and wing casts a shadow, four nightmarish 'drolli-
ties' sport outsize penises. The identification of their source
in designs by *François Rabelais* published in 1565 disposes of
an earlier theory that they reflect a period of witchcraft and
necromancy at Prestongrange. The repetitive strapwork on
the soffits of the beams is evidently later. A little to the W, on
Colinton Road, a late C17 GATEWAY. Recumbent lions flanking a narrow arch, the effect of the chunky rustication spoiled
by re-setting in new 'rustic' masonry.

WARRENDER BATHS, Thirlestane Road. By *R. Paterson &
Son*, 1886-7. Single-storey rogue Jacobean with spoke-
tracery in the tall round-arched windows.

BRUNTSFIELD

BRUNTSFIELD PLACE. The main route begins with the tall
Gothic landmark of the Barclay Church (*see* Central Area,
South West) and the adjoining BARCLAY PLACE. Two
daring tenement schemes by *Thomas P. Marwick*, each with
four storeys and mansard attic. Nos. 1-19, 1885, with a fancy
Corinthian order framing the first and second floors, long
fluted chimneys shooting up between bullseyed gables. The
other, 1890, with a symmetrical front to BARCLAY TER-
RACE; corner oriels shafted and domed, full-height chimneys
and boldly stepped gables, all lightened at the head with panels of swirling fronds. Round the corner the GOLF TAVERN
overlooking the Links, early C19 given a mullioned red sandstone ground floor (and contemporary interior) by *R. M.
Cameron* in 1899. To the W GILLESPIE CRESCENT with hori-

zontally emphasized tenements by *David MacGibbon*, 1870; Gillespie's Hospital for the Blind by *Robert Burn*, 1801, was replaced with sheltered housing by *Ian H. Rolland Associates* in 1976. Back in Bruntsfield Place, the w side has a row of grand villas with a clear view over the park. Nos. 46–55 an identical trio with recessed doorpieces. No. 65 pedimented; all built for John Walker, 1826–7, and followed by three double villas (the N pair by *David MacGibbon*, c. 1861–3) now joined as the Bruntsfield Hotel. Then tenements on both sides. On the w Nos. 118–130 by *A. W. Macnaughtan*, 1889, with a lanterned corner, and Nos. 158–174 by *Edward Calvert*, 1887, adding incised patterns to his usual rollicking vocabulary. Finally Nos. 198–206 by *Dunn & Findlay*, 1902, a light-hearted view-stopper with an oriel gable between two ogee-topped turrets. To the E BRUNTSFIELD CRESCENT overlooking the park, a bold baronial terrace by *MacGibbon & Ross* for the builders *W. & D. McGregor*, 1870–3. Pink rubble quarried on the site, with battlemented bays and crowstep gables, arched iron railings and deeply recessed front doors (the Lorimer family lived at No. 1 from 1873). BRUNTSFIELD TERRACE alongside with stolid villas c. 1855, No. 8 Italian. On the E side of Bruntsfield Place the tenements resume with Nos. 131–151, relaxed but artful Queen Anne by *G. Washington Browne*, 1887, and Nos. 155–195 by *Hippolyte J. Blanc* for *Beattie* the builder, 1882, with a nice rhythm of baywindows, pediments and gables round the convex curve of the street.

MARCHMONT

A square site, 0·5 km. each way, sloping down to Bruntsfield Links and filled with long blocks of four-storey baronial tenements. All but the narrowest streets are lined with tall baywindows which are Scoticized either with candle-snuffer roofs or with crowstepped gables, frequently supported by corbels that project both outwards and sideways, colliding at the corners. Turrets (especially at street corners), pediments, string courses and wall-head chimneys are all used to produce the maximum diversity between the numerous schemes and also – with one striking exception in Warrender Park Road – within them, as if to assure the prospective buyer that his tenement flat can have as much individuality as a villa. Many schemes are quite small, e.g. of only two adjacent numbers in a street, so the builders and their architects cannot all be mentioned – only those who within the prescribed formula managed to be more different than others. The winner, with his fondness for quirky detail, asymmetrical chimney stalks and tablets carved with his initials, is Edward Calvert.

An erratic but alphabetically ordered tour can begin with MEADOW PLACE, a terrace of c. 1805 facing the Links, the front gardens partly built as shops.

ARGYLE PARK TERRACE. No. 10 (on the site of *Hardy & Wight*'s West St Giles' Church of 1881) consists of four-storey flats by *Michael Calthrop & Campbell Mars*, 1979, the eccentric windows quite at home in this company. Nos. 1–5 by *W. Hamilton Beattie*, 1873, with crowstepped bays and timber dormers, turn the corner into the w side of ARGYLE PLACE by *John C. Hay*, 1876, all for the builder *John Pyper*. Flats in this block were intended to sell at £700, 'half flats' (three or four rooms plus kitchen) at £350–500. Continuous ground-floor shops with leaf-capitalled colonnettes. On the E side Nos. 2–9 are severely detailed semi-detached villas of c. 1860, later made continuous and then cheated of their view. One block to the w is MARCHMONT CRESCENT, climbing steadily from N to S. In the N half are cheaper tenements (five storeys, without bay-windows) of 1877–81 by *A. W. Macnaughtan* and *David McArthy*, forming a continuous baronial curve with big chimney stalks over corbelled arches. The grander s half is by nine different architects. The cool grey stone of Nos. 25–29 by *Hay*, 1880, stands out from the rest, but the most inventive are No. 41 by *Peter L. Henderson*, 1883 (crowstepped gables oddly superimposed on piends), Nos. 56–66 with the initials of *Edward Calvert* and the date 1881 (massive L-plan chimney-stalks at the wall-head), and Nos. 32–42 by *Thornton Shiells & Thomson*, 1880, their pointed roofs and fancy pediments commanding the street. MARCHMONT ROAD climbs out of town with a long straight vista focused on the Castle. On the E side Nos. 21–23 by *Hippolyte J. Blanc*, 1880, with a variety of pediments. The same with ogee-topped turrets at Nos. 11–19, 1879. Nos. 43–59 with the bays grouped in pairs, one crowstepped and one snuffered, are by *William Hogg*, 1887. *R. Roberts* had already done the same trick at Nos. 83–99, 1883, probably as a deliberate variation on the two-gable theme at Nos. 105–121 by *Hay*, 1880. For the Marchmont Road School, *see* Public Buildings, above. On the w side Nos. 2–16 by *Calvert*, 1890–1, a frenzied pink and cream block with a big corner turret and some of the bay-windows perversely triangular in plan. Nos. 18–20 by *Macnaughtan*, 1880, with Jacobean overdoors. Nos. 30–38 pink and white by *T. P. Marwick*, 1888, Nos. 102–122 pink by *Hogg*, 1886.

In WARRENDER PARK ROAD (from the E end) Nos. 45–49 are by *Marwick*, 1881–2, a long hypnotic curve of gabled bays. Nos. 85–95 by *George Wilson*, 1886, with an ogee-roofed octagon corner. Nos. 113–151 in grey and cream stone by *Thomas Gibson*, 1878, turning the corner with a lucarned conical roof into the w side of MARCHMONT STREET; on its E side more high jinks at No. 9 by *Macnaughtan*, 1892 (vesica in gable), and Nos. 10–13 by *Calvert*, 1883 (scrolled skewputts on top of colliding corbels). Back in Warrender Park Road, a weird pink block at the far w end by *Gibson*, 1878, the conical corner roof lopsided and its pyramidal companion now unhappily truncated. On the s side Nos. 2–24, 1878, and

Nos. 36–46, 1879, are big near-symmetrical compositions with boldly recessed centres. In the five-storey WARRENDER PARK TERRACE, facing the Links, Nos. 2–4 are of 1878, Nos. 17–19 of 1880 and Nos. 20–22 of 1881, all by *Calvert*. Nos. 36–41 by *Marwick*, 1880, with knotted ropes over arched front doors. In ALVANLEY TERRACE the two-storey Nos. 2 and 3 are by *David Bryce*, 1870, severely bayed and pedimented. Nos. 5–11, four storeys with a good row of shops, are by *Gibson* for the builders *W. & D. McGregor*, 1877. So is WARRENDER PARK CRESCENT with four storeys plus basement, 1877–81; Nos. 1–8 in grey stone from Blair quarry, Culross (Fife), with red colonnettes at the arched doorways, Nos. 9–20 with conical roofed bays and some Jacobean detail.

MERCHISTON

A quick look at MERCHISTON PLACE (No. 12 by *Rhind*), MERCHISTON PARK (mostly late classical) and MERCHISTON AVENUE (No. 20 1874, Gothic with grotesque heads in relief). Then COLINTON ROAD. On the N side Napier House, flats by *John Jerdan* in horizontal bands of harl and red brick, 1934. After Napier College and Merchiston Tower (*see* above) No. 16 is MERCHISTON COTTAGE, *c.* 1840, No. 18 the quirky lodge of a villa replaced in 1966 with a block of *Mowlem* flats. Next a succession of important villas. No. 20, REDHOLME, 1888, the most elaborate of those designed by *Edward Calvert* for *Renton* the builder (for the first, *see* No. 3 Ettrick Road, below). All are predominantly French (e.g. the superimposed corner pilasters crowned by inverted consoles) but with incised classical ornament for extra definition; here a scroll frieze at the ground floor and Greek key at the wallhead. Median window shafts of red granite, and likewise the Corinthian columns of the porch, which has opulent swags overhead. Entrance hall with caryatid corbels and anthemion frieze, stair with mezzanine gallery and four-light stained-glass window (the Seasons). Other *Calvert* villas of the same date at Nos. 22, 38 and 40. No. 28 spired Jacobean, No. 32 (BOROUGHFIELD, Sir James Steel's house) austere, with an arcaded parapet. No. 34 (HOLLYWOOD) apparently a Bruntsfield Place villa of the late 1820s transplanted here in the 1870s and enhanced by a central chimney stack. No. 36 a simple harled house by *Begg & Lorne Campbell*, 1924. No. 42 (CRANLEY) with stained glass of 1902 by *Henry Holiday* at the front door (Oberon and Titania) and the stair (Science, Art and Charity).

On the S side of Colinton Road the mansarded Nos. 9–19 (part of the Morningside Road corner block), 1868, and the bargeboarded baronial Nos. 21–33, all by *David MacGibbon*. After George Watson's College (*see* above) the houses go red. No. 73 (DUART LODGE) by *George Henderson*, *c.* 1902, with red tiles and half timbering, and two houses (Nos. 1 and 2

South Gillsland Road), neo-Jacobean by *Frank Simon*, 1897.
Nos. 75-77 by *MacGibbon & Ross*, 1897, and three double
villas with Jacobean gables at Nos. 79-89 by *Calvert*. No. 95
by *Simon* again, COLDSTREAM LODGE by *G. Mackie Watson*, 1900, and No. 99 by *J. Macintyre Henry*, 1903. Side-
roads on the S side. In ABBOTSFORD PARK No. 12 by *D.
Richardson*, 1858 (his unsuccessful entry for the Dean Cemetery lodge competition), and Nos. 14-16 with pilaster
mullions, Glasgow fashion. Classicism in ABBOTSFORD
CRESCENT and at the start of TIPPERLIN ROAD, where No. 5
is symmetrical Graeco-Italian by *Robert Wilson* in the Peddie
& Kinnear style, 1881. No. 11 quite different by *John
McLachlan*, 1888, with bold rubbly gables and a timber porch
(plus a luggage porch round the side). Nos. 4-8 by the builder
David Adamson, 1894. No. 12 (VIEWFIELD) with classical
iron gates is indigenous Georgian *c.* 1830, but Victorianized.
In ALBERT TERRACE Nos. 1-9, 1863, are perfectly Georgian
in detail except for the pottery balustrade with a heron stand-
ing on each end. MERCHISTON GARDENS by *MacGibbon
& Ross*, 1898-1903, and finally MYRESIDE ROAD, where
No. 84 is a small block of flats by *Alan Reiach*, 1956.

SPYLAW ROAD long and straight, the villas mostly late classical
and barricaded by trees and hedges. No. 8 apparently by
Frederick T. Pilkington in the mid 1870s; recessed corner
porch (glazed in 1981) with square piers and huge florid heads
without any abacus (cf. Pilkington's Eastern Club in Dundee,
now demolished). No. 16 (REDWOOD) very like No. 34 Colinton Road and likewise transplanted; *MacGibbon & Ross*
designed the stables in 1878 and made further additions, perhaps including the Italian tower, in 1883. Good things in the
three intersecting roads. At the GILLSLAND ROAD corner,
TORNAVEEN by *Robert Raeburn*, *c.* 1875, with scrolly window
heads and a thin tower with a tapering hat. No. 11 ETTRICK
ROAD very similar but of more sustained fantasy. No. 3 by
Edward Calvert, *c.* 1885, with corner pilasters (cf. No. 20 Colinton Road) but recessed in the middle and not quite symmetrical. As St Denis School it has been enlarged with classrooms in 1932 and 1959. On the other side No. 8 by
Sutherland & Walker, 1876, and No. 14 by *J. R. & E. E.
Pearson*, 1892, red marble shafts at its triple-arched doorpiece. At the NAPIER ROAD intersection, LAMMERBURN by
James Gowans, 1860 (later enlarged in the same style); a happy
composition in his peculiar formula* with steep gables, bracketed eaves and banded chimneys. No. 5, diagonally opposite,
is by *James C. Walker*, 1863, also of banded rubble but cosier,
of one storey plus an attic in the bargeboarded roof (cf. his

128

*Sir James Gowans, Lord Dean of Guild from 1885, was obsessed by stone and
by the elaboration of construction, especially at corners; this formula was based
on a stone grid, usually of 2 ft (0·6 m.) squares of Cyclopean rubble, with angles
based on the diagonal or bisected diagonal of the square. His own house, Rockville
(1858), on the other side of Napier Road, had a five-stage tower with his initials
in the wrought-iron railings, plus a lodge and stables. All except the boundary
wall was demolished in 1965.

Kirtle Lodge, Trinity; *see* Granton, Newhaven and Trinity: Perambulations).

GILMORE PLACE has a mixed bag of houses made friendly by front gardens, a feature of the original development. The s side begins handsomely with Nos. 1–21, a bowed corner block and three-storey terrace of 1823; the N side with Lochrin Buildings (*see* p. 266) from round the corner, followed by a heavy early Victorian terrace. Then on both sides two-storey artisan Georgian, Nos. 31–35 brutally reconstructed, No. 43 incorporated in St Joseph's Convent (*see* above); the rest with pleasantly varied detail, e.g. the old-style restricted door-pieces at Nos. 71–73. To the s HAILES STREET, a single terrace of 1821 with a veritable catalogue of different door-pieces, and GILLESPIE STREET, plainer but with a terminal pediment (both Gillespie Trust developments). UPPER GIL-MORE PLACE is partly of 1810 (a rubbly pedimented row at Nos. 7–13) and partly infill by *David MacGibbon*, who also designed Nos. 106–136 on the N side of Gilmore Place, both in 1877. On both sides some modest villas including a craggy Gothic pair at Nos. 201–203. For the Gilmore Place Free Presbyterian and St Oswald's Churches, *see* above.

Then a territory of big board schools (*see* above) and still bigger tenements. In LEAMINGTON TERRACE a pair of powerful baronial blocks at Nos. 1–21, by *James Bell*, 1880. In VIEW-FORTH a solitary late Georgian bungalow at No. 104, round which *Edward Calvert* designed VIEWFORTH SQUARE in 1891, five storeys high with corbel-topped bays and ladder-like chimneys. At Nos. 2–24 between Westhall Gardens and Bruntsfield Place a much tamer tenement by *R. M. Cameron*, 1885. In BRUNTSFIELD AVENUE another giant block by *Calvert*, 1887, its far-fetched classical detail more elaborate on the Bruntsfield Place frontage. In MONTPELIER PARK Nos. 6–28 with spired bays are by *Dunn & Findlay*, 1893.

POLWARTH GARDENS. Mostly four-storey tenements of the 1880s, with some good townscape incidents. A bluff corner block at the junction with POLWARTH CRESCENT, whose next crossing has two baronial corners with red sandstone dressings, by *James M. Thomson*, 1897, crowned with a spire and a compound ogee; the same scheme goes on into Temple Park Crescent.

POLWARTH TERRACE (W of Napier Road). For the Candlish Church *see* above. No. 24 (QUINTON) on the N side has bargeboards and Bryce-like bay-windows. Nos. 26–28, 1896, are by *McArthy & Watson*, as are Nos. 1–10 Polwarth Grove, 1891. No. 30 by *Calvert*, 1892, with a gable of salvaged bits and pieces. Nos. 32–34 and 54–56 (1897) by *J. B. Bennett*; Nos. 42 and 50–52 (1893) by *MacGibbon & Ross*. No. 44 a transplanted Georgian villa. Nos. 58–60 by *J. D. Cairns*, 1894. No. 66 by *James Jerdan*, 1897, with an asymmetrical gable and Renaissance detail. Nos. 72–74 by *John A. Liddle*, 1900. Nos. 76–78 by *James Jerdan*, 1896, composed like a single villa and much the best of this semi-detached bunch. Nos. 80–

110 and 120–122 by *Calvert* in the 1890s, Nos. 116–118 by *J. Walker Todd* and *W. N. Thomson*, 1923. On the s side No. 27 by *R. Thornton Shiells*, 1858, formerly at No. 2 Bruntsfield Terrace and transplanted here in 1899; Gothic, with a vegetable porch and bulbous columns. No. 41 by the R. C. church architect *Archibald Macpherson*, *c.* 1910, with rubble walls, a bold doorpiece and curved pediment; many alterations.

CALDER AND LANARK ROADS

Victorian working-class housing, crossed by railway lines and the Union Canal, spreads along the Dalry, Gorgie and Slateford Roads. Then, inter-war housing followed by post-war estates. At the beginning of Lanark Road, a fragment of old Slateford survives. At its exit from Edinburgh into the Pentland foothills, prosperous villas make a tail to the village of Juniper Green, carefully kept apart from the high-rise blocks of Wester Hailes.

CHURCHES

CONGREGATIONAL CHURCH (now disused), Caledonian Road. Gawky French Gothic by *Alexander Heron*, 1872, with polychrome arches and a smallish spire. His 'first effort', says *The Builder*.

DALRY CHURCH (now St Bride's Community Centre), Orwell Terrace. By *Sydney Mitchell & Wilson*, 1908. Rock-faced neo-Perp, with a flèche on the canted s apse. – STAINED GLASS. Two lights (War Memorial) by *John Blyth*, 1949.

HOLY TRINITY, Hailesland Road. By *Cairns & Ford*, 1972. A sturdy brick cube on a hillock by the roundabout. Deep roof-beams project at the bevelled corners, one of them carrying the bell. – STAINED GLASS, in the vestibule. Three lights (the message of the Gospel) by *William Wilson*, 1939, from Lady Glenorchy's Church in Roxburgh Place (*see* Central Area, South Side, Churches).

JUNIPER GREEN (originally Free Church), Lanark Road. Lumpy transitional by *James Fairley*, 1879, with a bellcote on the s gable. Very wide-span roof with arched principals.

LONGSTONE PARISH CHURCH, Kingsknowe Road North. By *Leslie Grahame MacDougall*, 1954. Mildly Italian, the circular e tower seen as a light-flooded chancel from the portal-arched nave. At the other end a stage, for this was originally a dual-purpose hall-church.

NORTH MERCHISTON (former Free Church), Slateford Road and Shandon Crescent. Competent Dec by *McArthy & Watson*, 1895. Pink and white, with hall sited at an oblique angle.

ST AIDAN, Stenhouse Grove. By *J. Inch Morrison*, 1933. Church and hall in variegated, English-looking red brick, with Art Deco window shapes.

ST COLM, Dalry Road. Mongrel Gothic by *Robert Raeburn*,

1881. Geometric tracery, clock-faces corbelled out at the base of a lucarned broach spire. Triple-arched roof trusses carried by iron shafts rising through the gallery.

ST CUTHBERT (R.C.), Slateford Road and Hutchison Crossway. Clumsy geometric, lacking the intended SE spire, by *J.B. Bennett*, 1894. HALL to the NW by the same architect, enlarged later.

ST DAVID, Broomhouse Crescent. A harled octagon with pointed central lantern, by *Gordon & Dey*, 1960. – ORGAN by *Rushworth & Dreaper*, 1963.

ST MARTIN OF TOURS (Episcopal), Dalry Road and Murieston Crescent. Originally Evangelical Union. Simplified Dec by *Simon & Tweedie*, finished in 1894, its rough and smooth polychrome obscured by soot. Verticality is emphasized by long triangular fillets, and by the tall diagonal buttresses of the SE tower and spire. – ORGAN by *W.G. Vowles*, 1870, rebuilt by *Ronald L. Smith*, 1971, and brought here in 1982.

ST MARTIN OF TOURS (Episcopal; disused), Gorgie Road and Murieston Road. An ambitious but unfinished composition by *John Robertson* of Inverness, 1898. Red and white with geometric tracery, the S (liturgical W) end elaborated with a SW baptistery and only two walls of the intended SE tower. The chancel later, externally a makeshift. Rubble-lined interior, with quatrefoil iron piers sending out timber arches in all directions, the aisle arches colliding with plaster half-vaults. – STAINED GLASS. At the W end three lights (St Martin) by *Heaton, Butler & Bayne*, c. 1900. At the E end three lights (Christ transfigured, SS. Martin and Adrian) by *R. S. Forrester*, c. 1935. To the N the temporary IRON CHURCH of 1883. Both buildings are now threatened (1984).

ST MICHAEL'S PARISH CHURCH, E end of Slateford Road. 39 Large and very perfect E.E. by *John Honeyman* of Glasgow, 1881–3, replacing the Iron Church of North Merchiston.* Aisles and clearstoried nave, N transept and 41 m. NW tower. This has angle-buttresses modified to clasping buttresses at the tall belfry stage (one lancet on the E face, two on each of the others), and was to have carried a broach spire. Stugged masonry with smooth dressings, stiff-leaf capitals and dog-tooth carving at the E gable and tower doorway. Inside, a C13 arcade on round piers right up to the E end, with one taller and richer arch into the transept (organ chamber). Timber roof with purlin trusses over clearstorey wall-shafts. The furnishings original, and likewise dark-stained. – COMMUNION TABLE with Lord's Prayer and Creed on reredos, PULPIT and LECTERN painted with fruits of the Bible by *Gertrude Hope*. – ORGAN by *Brindley & Foster*, 1895. – STAINED GLASS. In the three E lancets (Deposition etc., in memory of Mrs Hope), by *A. Ballantine & Gardiner*, 1895. In the S aisle, at the E end one light (Christ and children), at the W end

---

*This was built in 1876 at the junction of Ardmillan and Angle Park Terraces, and sold in 1884 (*see* Morningside: Royal Edinburgh Hospital, below).

three lights (Jairus's daughter) by *James Ballantine & Son*, 1886, and on the s side a lancet (Nunc Dimittis) by *Douglas Strachan*, 1925. HALL and beadle's house to the w.

ST NICHOLAS, Calder Road and Wester Hailes Road. By *Archibald M. Doak & Alexander R. Whitelaw*, 1955. – ORGAN of 1929 by *Andrew Watt*, who rebuilt it here in 1963.

ST SALVADOR (Episcopal), Saughton Mains Street. Plain but impressive, by *Tarbolton & Ochterlony*, 1939-42. Only the battered E tower (with slated spire), chancel and porch were built, with a hall to the N. All harled and minimally Gothic, with the carvings left in block.

SLATEFORD SECESSION CHURCH, Lanark Road (to the rear of Slateford House). Now a factory. 1785, re-cast in 1826. A plain box with arched windows and a bellcote.

STENHOUSE SAUGHTON CHURCH, Gorgie Road and Chesser Avenue. By *T. Aikman Swan*, 1935. Neat rubble, with tweaky N gable and copper-topped tower. – ORGAN by *H. S. Vincent*, 1897; rebuilt here by *Ingram*, 1935.

TYNECASTLE CHURCH (former, now disused), Gorgie Road. By *Hardy & Wight*, 1900. An orange and white stone front with blind arcade under the gable window. Assorted buttresses, one of which was a belfry.

PUBLIC BUILDINGS

BABERTON GOLF CLUB, Baberton Avenue. By *J. N. Scott & A. Lorne Campbell*, 1902. Variegated red sandstone, engulfed in thoughtless extensions.

BROOMHOUSE PRIMARY SCHOOL, Broomhouse Crescent. By the *City Architect's Department*, 1955.

CHESSER HOUSE, Gorgie Road. Huge Government office block, by *Michael Laird*, 1967.

CLOVENSTONE PRIMARY SCHOOL, Clovenstone Park. By the *City Architect's Department*, 1974. Brick, with clearstorey lighting.

CRAIGLOCKHART PRIMARY SCHOOL, Ashley Terrace. By *Robert Wilson* and *John A. Carfrae*, 1901. Big raised hall with jolly cupola between gables. The usual imaginative Renaissance detail towards the top.

DALRY BATHS, Caledonian Crescent. By *Robert Morham*, 1893-5. Like a Georgian survival villa with Italianate detail.

DALRY CEMETERY, Dalry Road. Now a waste land. Laid out, with an elaborate lodge and central catacombs, by *David Cousin*, 1846.

DALRY GIRLS' REFORMATORY, Ardmillan Terrace and Gorgie Road. 1861, severe and domestic-looking, like a farmhouse of twenty years earlier.

DALRY PRIMARY SCHOOL, Dalry Road. By *George Beattie & Son*, 1876-7. Upper floor added by *Robert Wilson*, 1890.

FOUNTAINBRIDGE PUBLIC LIBRARY, Dundee Street and Murdoch Terrace. By *John A. W. Grant*, 1938. Smooth Art

Deco classical, with a giant pilaster order to the sides, stair-tower and entrance on the corner.

GORGIE WAR MEMORIAL HALL, Gorgie Road. Originally Gorgie Free Church. By *David Robertson*, 1887. Gothic, with a flèche. Harled E extension.

HAILESLAND PRIMARY SCHOOL, Hailesland Place. Minimal in brick, by the *City Architect's Department*, 1972.

JUNIPER GREEN PRIMARY SCHOOL, Baberton Avenue. By *John A. Carfrae*, 1910.

KINGSKNOWE GOLF CLUB, Lanark Road. By *J. N. Scott & A. Lorne Campbell*, 1909. White-harled and red-tiled, a verandah between twin bays.

LONGSTONE PRIMARY SCHOOL, Redhall Grove. By the *City Architect's Department*, 1954-7.

MAGDALENE ASYLUM, Gorgie Road. Now a social work office. By *Leadbetter & Smith*, 1861. Symmetrical baronial with a central crowstep gable. No turrets, but a big handsome one on the lodge.

MARKETS AND SLAUGHTERHOUSES, New Market Road, off Slateford Road. A parade of buildings of 1909 (except where stated) behind a long strip of fenced grass. First on the l. the modest gates and lodges leading to the old CORPORATION SLAUGHTERHOUSE, by the City Superintendent of Works *James A. Williamson*, and to its smart red-brick successor by the City Architect *Brian Annable*, 1977. Next, the grand quadrilateral of ST CUTHBERT'S ASSOCIATION SLAUGH-TERHOUSES, by *T. P. Marwick*, modern and yet monumental with arched and saucer-domed corner pavilions, exploiting the contrast of smooth yellow and rough purple stone. *Williamson*'s MARKET RESTAURANT (now a bar) is rubble-faced but tame. To the rear, his five-aisled, steel-framed SHELTER for store cattle, 1912. Finally, his CORN EX-CHANGE, rubbly again but with a Roman Doric loggia, the spacious hall glass-roofed and aisled.

MURRAYBURN PRIMARY SCHOOL, Sighthill Loan. Stripped neo-Georgian by *E. J. MacRae*, 1938-9.

NAPIER COLLEGE (formerly College of Commerce), Sighthill Court. A vari-coloured slab by *J. & F. Johnston*, 1965-8, the saucer-dome gymnasium to the N modelled on the Dome of Discovery at the 1951 Festival of Britain.

NORTH MERCHISTON CEMETERY, Ardmillan Terrace and Slateford Road. Laid out *c.* 1875.

NORTH MERCHISTON SCHOOL, Bryson Road. Now in other use. By *Robert Wilson*, 1882; enlarged 1897. Very simple Gothic.

ROXY CINEMA (former), Gorgie Road. Red brick, the bowed endpiece rendered and painted, by *Chadwick, Watson & Co.* of Leeds, 1937.

ST CUTHBERT'S (R.C.) HIGH SCHOOL, Hutchison Cross-way. By the *City Architect's Department*, 1956-7.

ST GILES' SCHOOL, Broomhouse Crescent. Harled boxes with some brick panels, by *Stanley Poole, Brand Associates*, 1973-8.

St Nicholas School, Gorgie Road. *c.* 1920. Single-storey, with verandahs and red-tiled roofs.

Saughton Park, Gorgie Road. Laid out 1905–14. BRIDGE over the Water of Leith by *Robert Morham*, 1908. Among the parterres, miscellaneous salvaged STATUARY. Further on, an elaborate C17 baluster SUNDIAL, all restored except the four-dialled finial. To the w the iron BANDSTAND by *James A. Williamson*, 1909, made by the *Lion Foundry*.

Saughton Prison, off Gorgie Road. By *H.M. Office of Works*, 1925. Harled with red sandstone dressings. Shaped gables and crenellations give a false jollity.

Sighthill Health Centre, Calder Road. By *R. Gardner-Medwin* of the Department of Health for Scotland, 1951. Picturesque and cheerful, with big windows and shallow-pitch copper roofs.

Sighthill Primary School, Calder Park. By the *City Architect's Department*, 1968.

Slateford Station. *See* Perambulations, below.

Stenhouse Primary School, Stevenson Drive. By *John A. Carfrae*, 1929.

Stevenson College, Sighthill Court. A grey slab by *J. & F. Johnston*, 1966–70.

Stevenson College Annexe, Stenhouse Street West. Originally Whinhill School, by *Alexander A. Foote*, 1954.

Telephone House, 357 Gorgie Road. Two brick blocks by *Covell Matthews & Partners*, 1973, the rear one with an exposed concrete frame.

Tivoli Cinema (former), Gorgie Road. Red sandstone, including the flashy Art Deco entrance, by *John McKissack & Sons* of Glasgow, 1933.

Tynecastle High School, McLeod Street. Uninspired harled Wrenaissance by *John A. Carfrae*, 1910–11.

Tynecastle Secondary School Pentland Annexe, Gorgie Road. Built as Gorgie School, 1876. *Robert Wilson* added the upper floor in 1890–1.

Westburn Primary School, Sighthill Road. Low, with aggregate cladding, by the *City Architect's Department*, 1974–7.

Wester Hailes Centre. *See* Perambulations, below.

Wester Hailes Education Centre, Murrayburn Drive. Large and stylish, by *Robert Matthew, Johnson-Marshall & Partners*, 1975–8.

MANSIONS

Dalry House, Orwell Place. A classy villa institutionalized in a back street. It began as an early C17 Z-plan block with a short se jamb and an octagonal stair-tower jutting out from the nw corner. Three storeys, with chamfered window margins. In the early C18 two bays were added to the n and an ogee-roofed tower built at the sw corner. The ogee roof of the original tower is presumably of the same date. S extension of *c.* 1800, two storeys in the height of the original three. Bullseye window in the S front's centre pediment. Crude school addition to the E of this added in 1877 by *John Wath-erston & Sons*, who also replaced the S part's roof with a huge slated box retained in *Robert Hurd & Partners'* alterations of 1965. E wing behind the N part also of 1965, replacing a 1900 wing.

Inside, the line of the early C17 kitchen fireplace is exposed but a door has been slapped through it. In the door jamb is the original oven. The C17 first-floor hall has a compart-mented ceiling dated 1661; its emblems, including the Hon-ours of Scotland, a crowned saltire and Charles II's initials, are from the same moulds as were used at Stenhouse (*see* below), Merchiston Castle (*see* Napier College under Brunts-field and Merchiston: Public Buildings) and Gorgie House (demolished).

EASTER DALRY HOUSE, Distillery Lane. A small early-mid-C18 mansion stuck in a car-park. Two-storey and attic main block; single-storey wings. The entrance front faces S, with a Venetian-windowed gablet. The N (garden) front is grander, with a flat corniced porch topped by balls. Are the bracketed cornices over the windows original? Stair with twisted ma-hogany balusters and panelled rooms inside.

HAILES HOUSE, Hailes Avenue. Plain three-bay mansion by *Sir James Clerk* of Penicuik, *c.* 1765. Two storeys above an unsunk basement. Large scrolled end chimneys. The red-tiled roof is an unfortunate alteration. Also altered is the twisty balustered staircase inside. Low stable court to the SE, with new roof-tiles and windows.

MILLBANK, Redhall Bank Road. Mid-C18. Modest, of rough masonry with a centre pediment and single-storey wings.

STENHOUSE, Stenhouse Mill Crescent. A rubbly F-plan laird's house saved from dereliction by the National Trust for Scot-land, who were given it by the Greyhound Racing Association in 1937. Restored by *Ian G. Lindsay* in 1937–9 and 1962–5, it is now used as a Conservation Centre.*

The name comes from the Stanhope family, who were granted a tack of the adjacent Saughton Mills by Holyrood Abbey in 1511. The part N of the central stair-tower was probably built soon after. On the ground floor, two tunnel-vaulted rooms, each with an outside door to the E (both now blocked). The N room was a hen-house with a couple of holes for the birds in the gable and sixteen rectangular roosting boxes in the inside wall. The room on the floor above, with a small aumbry in the E wall, a garderobe in the W, and a

---

* The Stenhouse Conservation Centre was opened in 1966 under the joint aegis of the National Trust for Scotland and the Ministry of Public Building and Works. In 1969 the Ministry of Public Building and Works assumed full re-sponsibility for the centre, which is now (1984) part of the Ancient Monuments Division of the Scottish Development Department.

fireplace at each end, was probably originally two (hall and chamber).

In 1623 an Edinburgh merchant, Patrick Ellis, extended the house to a T plan, doubling the main block's length to the S, adding a W stair-tower to the middle of the W side, and reconstructing the old top floor. From the stair-tower a range of offices (their line marked by a dwarf wall) ran N to form a narrow entrance court. In the jamb, corniced doors to the stair and a store beside it. Their lintel is inscribed BLISIT. BE.GOD.FOR.AL.HIS.GIFTIS. Above the main door, the arms and initials of Ellis and the date 1623. Pedimented dormer-heads reconstructed in the 1960s from the evidence of fragments. A second jamb to the S with a huge chimney was added c. 1700.

Ellis's S extension provided a kitchen with a large E fireplace and oven. Smaller C17 fireplace in the S gable. Above was a new hall. Two aumbries, rectangular in the S wall but the S one still Gothic with an ogee arch. The barley-sugar columns (removed) of the fireplace struck a would-be classical note but they narrowed to the bottom rather than the top.*

Tight stair, minimally projecting in the internal angle of the jamb and main block, to the second floor. In the two N rooms, late C17 moulded plaster ceilings restored by *Albert Cramb* in the 1960s. N one very simple. The S one, much grander, with a small pendant, royal emblems and female figures and angels in the compartments, is made from the same moulds as were used at Dalry House in 1661 (*see* above), Merchiston Castle and Gorgie House. On the wall, plaster panel with Charles II's monogram, and the royal crest flanked by the Honours of Scotland and a crowned saltire. The fireplace lintel's l. end is supported by a heavy double corbel, presumably early C16 rather than C17.

PERAMBULATIONS

DALRY ROAD runs SW from Haymarket. On the S side nine terraces of flatted cottages called after great reformers (COB-DEN, BRIGHT etc.) and parts of Scotland (DOUGLAS, AR-GYLL etc.), built for the Edinburgh Co-operative Building Company in 1870. Then glum four-storey tenements of the same date. For the churches buried among them, and for the numerous others hereabouts, *see* above. For the Public Baths in Caledonian Crescent and for Dalry Cemetery *see* Public Buildings, and for Dalry House in Orwell Place *see* Mansions. On the N side a narrow lane to Easter Dalry House (again *see* Mansions, above), and the CALEDONIAN DISTILLERY, an important group comprising (E to W) a baronial whisky bond of c. 1870, a tall brick chimney exactly on the axis of Shand-

---

* Information from Mr R. L. Snowden. Fragments of the columns are at Sten-house.

wick Place, the huge hump-topped still building of 1855 and its associated and older maltings, all of stone. In WEST PARK PLACE the former LETTER SORTING OFFICE of 1915 by *Oldrieve*, official classical in red brick and yellow trim. No. 94 Dalry Road was Dalry Station, 1900.

DUNDEE STREET is the W continuation of Fountainbridge, mostly tenements of the 1870s plus one very dry public building, the C20 Fountainbridge Public Library (*see* above). Then a tenemented triangle in which ANGLE PARK TERRACE contains SLATEFORD STATION (Caledonian Railway, now disused), 1882, quite countrified with its rough red sandstone and deep gables. In BRYSON ROAD to the S the former EDINBURGH & DUMFRIES-SHIRE DAIRY (now Kennarty), all bright red brick trimmed with yellow. Georgian revival head office of 1920, taken over from another firm in 1924 when the pantiled cooler-house was built to the rear. To the W a late C19 cabinet works also taken over, and to the NE their own 'hygienic bakery' (1937, now disused) with three storeys and a vertically expressed stair-tower. For the former North Merchiston School, *see* Public Buildings. The other two sides of the Angle Park triangle are ARDMILLAN TERRACE with a Jubilee corner tenement by *J. C. Hay*, 1887 ('Let the earth rejoice'), and the earlier HENDERSON TERRACE, a picturesque uphill composition of turreted tenements and semi-dormered houses in the Pilkington manner.

SLATEFORD ROAD starts with St Michael's Church (*see* above), by far the best in the area and, of its kind, in Edinburgh. On the N side the CALEDONIAN BREWERY of Lorimer and Clark, founded and built (of red stock brick) in 1868. Original office like a plain stone cottage to the l., and a new bright red-brick show-front to the r. (*c*. 1910) masking the end of the four-storey maltings, which have two kilns at the back. Next to them the brick-chimneyed brewhouse (still using coal to fire the copper pots). The site made use of the railway and a specially sunk well. On the S side another Edinburgh Co-operative Building Company scheme (PRIMROSE, MYRTLE and BAY TERRACES), 1877. Then, just off the main road, SHANDON CRESCENT, part of an unusual scheme of *c*. 1880, two-storey terraces nicely combining Georgian discipline and Victorian entertainment. Shandon Road becomes ASHLEY TERRACE, the name commemorating the great housing reformer. So does SHAFTESBURY PARK, yet another of the Co-operative Building Company's projects, 1884–5. The usual serried gables and parallel terraces (Hazelbank, Hollybank etc.), but here the plan is different, with the front doors all on one side and one level, producing a repetition of four doors (two for upstairs), two bay-windows, four doors again, and so on. For Craiglockhart Primary School, *see* Public Buildings. Back in Slateford Road the politely eclectic No. 97 was designed for Henderson's biscuit factory by *R. R. Hagg* in 1910. On the N side the former BERNARD'S BREWERY, mixed Renaissance but with a round corner tower, by *Blanc*

& Gordon, 1887. Then MOAT PLACE and HUTCHISON PLACE, excellent City housing of 1927. On the s side two spectacular blocks of MCEWAN'S MALTINGS, *c.* 1900. Six storeys with tall blind arcades and mutuled cornices. For the Markets and Slaughterhouses at the end of Slateford Road, *see* Public Buildings.

LANARK ROAD begins with the UNION CANAL AQUEDUCTS. The first (a concrete arch) crosses it. The second, of eight arches with battered piers (by *Hugh Baird,* 1818) runs alongside it, with the fourteen-arched RAILWAY VIADUCT (1847) just beyond. On the s side a neat Tudor LODGE (formerly of Craiglockhart House; *see* Craiglockhart: Mansions), and then at Nos. 43–53 the C18 CROSS KEYS and SLATEFORD HOUSE with symmetrical architraved windows, *c.* 1770. They are linked into a continuous group with a hall-over-shop and battlemented gateway (both 1899), the gateway leading to the former Seccssion Church (*see* above). Pockets of inter-war bungalows for 2 km., and in the midst of them REDHALL BANK ROAD, with quarrymen's* cottages of the 1850s by *James Gowans.* INGLIS BANK with piend roofs, Nos. 8–10 a terrace with swept dormers and hooded chimneys. Back in Lanark Road, and nearly opposite the Kingsknowe Golf Club (*see* Public Buildings), No. 327 is TROQUEER by *James Morris* of Ayr, *c.* 1914, with random block window-surrounds. For Hailes House in Hailes Avenue, *see* Mansions. No. 434 on the corner of Wester Hailes Road (formerly FAWSIDE) is by *Edward C. H. Maidman,* 1902. Square tower of red Lancashire bricks, the remainder half-timbered and tile-hung, with a lead-domed porch. No such roguery at No. 442, THE GAIR, stolid red sandstone by *Maidman* again, 1904. No. 491 is TORDUFF by *Robert S. Lorimer,* 1905, a compact arrangement of all manner of red-tiled gables over white harl. This is the edge of Colinton and the beginning of JUNIPER GREEN, with little Georgian villas on the N side (No. 500, CASTLEBANK, a castellated Gothic box) and Victorian on the s. Also on the s, an outstandingly coarse block of flats for the elderly by *Johnson Turnbull,* 1979. They replace St Margaret's Church, red sandstone Gothic by *R. M. Cameron,* 1895, and adjoin its surviving hall. The village straggles on regardless (the bay-windowed shop at No. 538 still unspoiled) till it reaches Currie at the old city boundary.

INGLIS GREEN ROAD takes its name from the bleachfield started by Mr Inglis in 1649. The present LAUNDRY includes an C18 house with elaborate scrolled skewputts. Victorian Longstone is a bedraggled workers' village. Most of the C20 council housing is by *Miller,* 1962, but a group of houses in LONGSTONE ROAD is by *Eric Hall & Partners,* of the same date. The round tower of Longstone Church (*see* above) is a welcome landmark.

---

* Gowans's father had a lease of the quarry, which earlier supplied the warm yellow sandstone for St John's, Princes Street, and St Paul's, York Place.

At the E end of GORGIE ROAD the former Magdalene Asylum; for this and all public buildings and churches, *see* above. Unexpected festivity at Gorgie railway bridge (*c.* 1860), with iron garlands hung on the span between swanky piers. On the N side at WESTFIELD ROAD a long and dignified pink sandstone palace block – not Georgian but of 1925 by *Alex. A. Foote*, with a continuous canopy over the ground-floor shops. Opposite Saughton Park, good housing of 1922 with random rubble gables at Chesser Gardens etc. Then to the N of CALDER ROAD great oblong swatches of housing – STENHOUSE of 1928-9, SAUGHTON of 1949 (N part 1963), BROOMHOUSE of 1946 along with *Stewart Sim*'s low-rise offices of 1951 for the Ministry of Works; SIGHTHILL of the mid 1960s (mixed high- and low-rise) providing some patients for the hitherto isolated Health Centre, whose architect, *Robert Gardner-Medwin*, also designed the red-roughcast housing in WESTER HAILES ROAD to the S, 1951. The backlands of Sighthill are a dump for various public buildings (*see* above), and the final swatch is an industrial estate where the best thing is *Michael Laird*'s ETHICON FACTORY of 1968. WESTER HAILES, to the S of Calder Road, a great horseshoe of council housing by *Frank Mears & Partners* in collaboration with the *City Architect*, mostly of 1966-7, with Kingsknowe Golf Course jutting into the middle. Holy Trinity Church (*see* above) is a vantagepoint from which the sameness of some high-rise slabs and the cranky diversity of others can be surveyed. Nearby, the HAILESLAND COMMUNITY CAMPUS includes brightly painted wooden fun-buildings for children, 1979. The WESTER HAILES CENTRE, by *Marshall Morrison & Associates*, 1972-4, has an impregnable ribbed concrete exterior, an impeccable interior with moving walkways between the shops on two levels.

COLINTON

Old Colinton lay in the valley of the Water of Leith, surrounded by large estates. Its late C18 parish church still flourishes (transformed), its own 'big house' of Spylaw still exists, and the buildings of Spylaw Farm are still used. But its paper and grain mills have virtually disappeared (or been badly modernized). Redhall Mill, adapted for wood-flour, blew up in 1976. But the C19-20 industrial decline coincided with the picturesque exploitation of the heights above the Dell. Georgian villas were followed after the coming of the railway by Victorian and Edwardian, at first quite ordinary and then very distinguished. *Rowand Anderson* came to live here, and designed some of the finest. In 1893 *Robert Lorimer* built a cottage for Miss Guthrie Wright (Colinton Cottage in Pentland Avenue), and started a fashion. Other architects worked in styles more mannered but less sophisticated. As Groome says (*Ordnance Gazetteer*, 1895), 'The village has changed a little ... but always for the better, a good many comfortable, old-English looking houses having arisen upon its upper outskirts ...'. It is not without its later C20 bungalow fringe, but still has the feeling of being next to the country. In short, the perfect suburb – or nearly so. The by-pass that will relieve the traffic problems of Bridge Road will also cut it off from the Pentland Hills which rise to the s, within the parish.

CHURCHES

St Cuthbert's Church (Episcopal), Westgarth Avenue. A simple church by *R. Rowand Anderson*, 1888–9, of variegated Hailes rubble with late Gothic detail worked in slightly redder Dumfriesshire sandstone, the roof red-tiled. In 1893, instead of the intended spire, Anderson completed the attached NE tower with a lead-covered belfry which has a concave roof and lantern in the C17 Scots manner of St Ninian's Manse (*see* Leith, Perambulations: North Leith) rising behind a gargoyled parapet and carefully detailed to suit the Gothic church. A stone porch was built instead of the original timber one in what was then the end bay of the nave. It was lengthened in 1934, but the later stonework is exactly matched with the old, and what was added can best be explained from inside.

A joyous interior, much extended from the original four-bay aisle-less nave and small chancel. In 1894 Anderson added the s transept (already provided for), installing the tracery of the original E window in its s wall. This is the Lady Chapel, and the organ chamber formed at the same time has become its sanctuary. Benefactions came quickly and when the church was re-opened in 1898 it had been decorated to Anderson's design by *Powell* of Lincoln. In 1939 the walls were covered with a dense coating of cream paint, but their colour-scheme is known; in the nave a green diaper pattern with scriptural frieze over a deep chocolate dado, in the chancel a red and yellow diaper on grey-green with superimposed angels on the side walls and the Annunciation on the E wall, all the figures done by *Phoebe Traquair*. The roof decoration, however, is intact. In the nave, where the basic kingpost structure was supplemented in 1894 by two tiers of arch braces, it is extremely lively; drab green complementing Chinese red, with sacred monograms in black letter, all stencilled. In the wagon roof of the chancel it is more solemn; foliage and heraldry with angel supporters, vigorously drawn. All the furnishings, except those otherwise dated, belong to this scheme. In 1934 *Matthew M. Ochterlony*, a member of the vestry, added three bays to the nave; the first bay extends s into the new baptistery, N into the porch, both being lined with rubble. He united the interior by repeating the roof structure (but not its decoration) and by the dark green floor of Ailsa Craig granite throughout. The choir vestry was built

to his design in 1940. – STAINED GLASS. Good, but mostly
unattributed. In the E window three lights (the Resurrection),
1897, and on the N side of the chancel one light (St Cuthbert),
competently drawn. In the Lady Chapel three lights (Our
Lady, SS. Cuthbert and George) by *Margaret Chilton*, 1935.
In the NE nave window two lights (Hope and Love) in the
manner of *Nathaniel Bryson*, after 1895. At the W end four
lights (King David I and other church builders), 1923.

ST CUTHBERT'S PARISH CHURCH, Dell Road. In its present
form largely by *Sydney Mitchell*, 1907–8. The church of 1650
was replaced in 1771 by *Robert Weir*, mason, and *William
Watters*, wright, to their own design. In 1837 *David Bryce*
broadened the stem of the T-plan and made new external
stair-towers; the simple campanile is probably his too. Mitchell's reconstruction (presumably assisted by *E. Auldjo Jamieson*) ingeniously diversified the exterior (e.g. with a livelier
arrangement of gables), reusing Bryce's tower over a new
porch. The interior was transformed to neo-Byzantine. Pink
sandstone columns with angel capitals carry the nave
tunnel-vault and the transverse aisle vaults over the galleries.
Dark woodwork is confidently combined with pale plaster
(low-relief angels in the spandrels of the nave roof), large scale
with small. The E apse is framed with dove-grey marble and
boldly screened with an inscribed oak cross-beam; its panelling is of 1929. – PULPIT, oak COMMUNION TABLE and marble FONT all 1908. – ORGAN by *Norman & Beard*, 1908,
rebuilt in a new case in the W gallery by *Rushworth &
Dreaper*, 1928. – STAINED GLASS. In the apse nine small
niched lights (the Christian virtues) to a scheme begun in
1925. At the W end (Suffer the little children) of *Ballantine*
character, before 1907. Under the W gallery three windows
(King David and two pairs of angels) by *William Wilson*,
1960. – MONUMENTS in the churchyard. Notable C18 stones
including scrolly table-tops and later Rococo headstones. C19
monuments austere except for a well-placed Gothic pinnacle
to George Porteous, builder, 1876, by his son *George M.
Porteous*. To the N the rusticated and pedimented mausoleum
of James Gillespie of Spylaw †1797; permission to build it
was given in 1794.

OFFERTORY HOUSE at the churchyard entry. Probably
mid-C18 and repaired (with the wall) in 1807; the Session
House (it may then have been such) was re-roofed and enlarged in 1852. Former PARISH SCHOOLHOUSE to the S, built
by *John Fraser* of Colinton in 1811–13 from a sketch by
Alexander Trotter of Dreghorn. MANSE to the SE, built in
1783 by *Robert Weir*, mason, and *Thomas Jack*, wright; additions in 1823 from drawings by *Trotter* again (but executed
by *Archibald Elliot II*) and in 1861 by *John Chesser*.

PUBLIC BUILDINGS

BONALY PRIMARY SCHOOL ANNEXE, Thorburn Road. L-plan with low eaves and big gables, by *Robert Wilson*, 1891. Quite the village school, with a hint of churchiness in the hall windows.

BRIDGES over the Water of Leith. COLINTON BRIDGE, Dell Road. One stone arch, probably c18. VIADUCT, Bridge Road. Built *c.* 1874 but later widened with a projecting footpath and nasty concrete parapet.

COVENANTERS' MONUMENT, Redford Road, s side. Four engaged Ionic columns from *William Adam*'s Royal Infirmary (1738, demolished 1884) effectively assembled into a cluster beneath a deep entablature with pulvinated frieze, pyramid cap and weathercock. The work was done *c.* 1884 for R. A. Macfie of Dreghorn. *See also* the Drummond Scrolls, Redford House (Mansions, below).

MERCHISTON CASTLE SCHOOL, Colinton Road. A monumental group, not quite at ease in the noble parkland of Colinton House, having moved here in 1929-31 after the Dean of Guild Court's refusal to allow the building of the WAR MEMORIAL HALL in the grounds of Merchiston Castle (*see* Napier College, under Bruntsfield and Merchiston: Public Buildings). This hall, by the Old Merchistonian *Norman A. Dick*, was built as the centrepiece of the new school. Grandiose Corinthian order, pediment and tall central lantern, the Baroque Lutyens-type dressings and roughcast walls crying rich and poor at the same time. The interior, successfully doubling as a chapel, is a long space with side galleries, lit by dormers between massive arched principals on beast-headed hammerbeams. Showy woodwork relieved by touches of ironwork, e.g. the original hanging lights. Splayed back from the hall are the much plainer, dormered wings by *W. J. Walker Todd*.

Immediately to the w, the former COLINTON HOUSE, the distinguished Edinburgh villa of the banker Sir William Forbes of Pitsligo built in 1801-6. Five-bay polished Craigleith ashlar, with a front of broad, relaxed proportions. Large central porch with coupled Ionic columns, the wide segmental fanlight repeated in each wing beneath a plain attic panel with guttae. Forbes bought the estate from the Foulises in 1800 and first consulted the mason-architect John Fraser of Colinton, who suggested the repair and extension of the existing castle. Plans in the Adam castellated manner were accordingly produced (architect unknown), but at the same time Thomas Harrison, Richard Crichton, Robert Burn, John Paterson and others produced plans for a new house. On 21 April 1801 Forbes wrote to his eldest son 'Tomorrow I go out to lay the foundation-stone of our new house. We have got now, I think, an excellent plan, chiefly Mr Harrison's only somewhat more expensive than I had reckoned on!' So the exterior at least is by *Harrison*,[*] the bowed rear elevation resembling that of Kennet (Central Region, 1793, demolished 1967) with the addition of a continuous balcony suggested by one of Forbes's many advisers, for Forbes himself managed everything and everybody. For the house *John Fraser* was the mason, *John Young* the carpenter, *William Scott* the plumber, *Charles Stewart* the slater, *John Baxter* the glazier and *James Bryce* the painter, the work being measured by *Hugh Cairncross*. The house was adapted by *Todd* as the science laboratory, with a Venetian-windowed addition to the w (the disastrous extra storey on the w wing is later) and careful changes to the rear, e.g. tripartite windows each side of the bow. The interior has fared worse. The entrance hall and Ionic pilastered corridor survive, both groin-vaulted. The staircase a simple dog-leg, its network balustrade damaged.

STABLE COURT, near the Colinton Road entry, with arched blocks at the corners and central gateway, built and possibly designed by *John Fraser c.* 1802-4.

COLINTON CASTLE. Buried in ivy. A house here was mentioned in 1545 and the L plan with stair in the angle could be of that date, with the second (s) stair-tower added in the early c17. The castle was repaired after the fire of 1650, but unroofed in 1801 and partly demolished at *Alexander Nasmyth*'s instructions of 15 December 1804 to make a picturesque ruin. WALLED GARDEN, the walls with red-brick lining built by *John Fraser*, 1801-2, with the advice of the London nurseryman *William Forsyth*, who also supervised the layout and designed hot-houses, the vinery built by *Samuel Butler* of London, the rest by *John Young*. Nothing left of these, but within the garden the school SANATORIUM and outside it PRINGLE HOUSE, good harled buildings of minimum cost and formality by *Todd*. SWIMMING POOL by *David Carr*, 1960.

The PARK, like the house, seems to come from decisions by Forbes, who in 1801 obtained a plan from *Matthew Stobie* and recommendations from *William Alexander* but attributed the result to his own gardener at Colinton, *James Rintoul*.

REDFORD BARRACKS, between Colinton Road and Colinton Mains Drive. The largest display of military architecture in Scotland since the c18 Fort George, but here it is Imperial free-style Renaissance by the Director of Barrack Construction *Harry B. Measures*, 1909-15, making up in monumental confidence whatever it lacks in refinement of composition. CAVALRY BARRACKS, facing Colinton Road between colonnetted gate-piers, a very tall domed clock-tower in the middle of a 91 m. frontage with recessed balconies overlooking the parade-ground. CAVALRY OFFICERS' MESS to the NE, with ogee-roofed towers in the angles of the canted wings. To the SW the much humbler INFANTRY OFFICERS' MESS, and the

---

[*] But the front elevation as executed was drawn by *Richard Crichton*, probably from sketches by Harrison.

INFANTRY BARRACKS with verandahs between towers. Guard-houses, senior officers' houses and stabling complete the group.

MANSIONS

BONALY TOWER, Bonaly Road. A tower house by *William H. Playfair*, 1836, for Lord Cockburn, who had bought the property in 1811 and had first considered a neo-Tudor design by William Burn. Playfair's tower (adjoining the original farmhouse) is effectively simple, tall and square with crenellated parapet and rounded corners, the staircase jamb bulging out into a five-storey circular turret with a dormered conical roof. It is built of large rubble to a pleasantly irregular face and with minimal enrichment, e.g. at the architraved doorway. Cockburn died in 1854. In 1866 *David Bryce* baronialized the old farmhouse with the usual pair of pepperpots to the w, and in 1888 *Sydney Mitchell* extended it to the s with a library wing and two more pepperpots whose regular snecked masonry and refined detail make Playfair's work look still more genuine by contrast. Playfair's interiors are modest. Mitchell's first-floor library has a large Gothic ingle on the long side, and a corner wash-room lined with Dutch tiles. LODGE to the N. 1836, enlarged in 1975. GATE-PIERS. Octagonal, neo-Gothic with iron tops.

COLINTON CASTLE and COLINTON HOUSE. See Public Buildings, above.

FERNIELAW HOUSE, Fernielaw Avenue. A modest house of the later C18 with a Venetian window on the N front, and mid-C19 attachments including a crowstepped NE wing, all harled and ochre-washed to distinguish it from the white-harled early C20 extension.

LAVEROCKDALE HOUSE, Dreghorn Loan. By *Robert S. Lorimer*, 1912–14, in C17 Scots style, rubble-walled and stone-slated. The N front tall and rather aloof with very irregular windows, the entrance lurking at the side of the central stair-tower. Apple-house and generating-house to E and W. To the N a garage and store (not by Lorimer), weatherboarded and pantiled, quite extensive on a smaller scale. Two-storey STABLES with arched entry and adjoining house.

REDFORD HOUSE, Redford Road. Originally the late C17 house of James, Lord Redford, but now a strung-out building of many periods with a roughly symmetrical NW front in a shallow forecourt, all smartly whitewashed, with an upstanding canted centre. This contains the stair, with detail c. 1820.

DRUMMOND SCROLLS. This is the name of the stable block built c. 1884 by the then owner of Redford House, R. A. Macfie of Dreghorn, with parts of the frontispiece of *William Adam*'s Royal Infirmary (1738, demolished 1884). At the W end the top halves of Ionic pilasters and a niche with the inscription GEORGIUS II REX (for the statue it contained, *see*

p. 260). On the s side the attic section, three bays divided by piers and flanked by huge leafy scrolls, one with thistles and the other with roses. It was repaired and internally modernized in 1966, a new garden fence concealing it from the road. More Royal Infirmary architraves on the LODGE (FORDEL), whose gable has a tablet commemorating General Gordon at great length. For another building from the same source, *see* the Covenanters' Monument (Public Buildings, above).

SPYLAW HOUSE, Spylaw Park, off Spylaw Street. Built in 1773 for the snuff-maker James Gillespie, replacing an earlier house of *c.* 1650 but apparently retaining its oblique rear wing. Two storeys over a basement and perron stair, in rubble with freestone dressings, the front unusual because the quoined centrepiece takes up nearly the whole width, with no outer bay. A gracefully arched window in the pediment.

WOODHALL HOUSE, w end of Woodhall Road. Built *c.* 1630 for Adam Cunningham, Lord Woodhall, and castellated *c.* 1820 with hoodmoulds over the windows and a buttressed central tower containing a rib-vaulted porch. In the l. room of the main storey an early C17 moulded plaster CEILING with roundels of David and Alexander and the inscription NOBIS HAEC INVICTA MISERUNT 108 PROAVI. On the rear (N) side, a late Georgian wing with horizontal glazing. To the E a huge stone-fronted wing including a centrally planned chapel built in 1960–6 for the Society of Jesus, who have now departed.

PERAMBULATION

COLINTON ROAD. On the w side the perimeter wall of Colinton House (now Merchiston Castle School; *see* Public Buildings, above), almost concealing a decent TELEPHONE EXCHANGE of 1960, and ending with HEATHER COTTAGE, a pedimented lodge of *c.* 1810. On the E side, after the imperial grandeur of the Barracks (*see* Public Buildings), INCHDREWER is a big villa with tapering 'rectory' chimneys by *David Robertson*, 1876, but much altered by *Robert S. Lorimer*, who added the elaborate billiard room in 1901. Then OLD FARM COURT by *H. Anthony Wheeler* for the Viewpoint Housing Association, 1976; 'Fyfestone' fronts and lead-clad bay-windows. *Lorimer's* white-harled RUSTIC 129 COTTAGES with boat-shaped dormers, 1900–2, make a pretty group with St Cuthbert's Episcopal Church (*see* Churches, above). REDFORD ROAD begins with a group of deep-eaved COLINTON COTTAGE HOMES by *R. Wilson*, 1891. Leafy wrought-iron gate-posts. Then No. 26, *c.* 1900, forms the centrepiece of a group of flats by *Wheeler & Sproson* for the Viewpoint Housing Association, 1978, well composed in brick. No. 28, SHERWOOD, is probably by *James B. Dunn*, 1892 and 1910, a mixture of half-timber and varicoloured

stone. In THORBURN ROAD No. 1 is the LADY ROWANI
ANDERSON MEMORIAL COTTAGE, polite baronial by *Anderson & Paul*, 1922. Then two cottage groups for the Aged
Christian Friend Society, the first in a lightweight Renaissance style with playful carved door-heads, by *John A. Carfrae*, 1907, the second with outside stairs and a central brick
arch, 1928. For the Bonaly Primary School Annexe, *see*
Public Buildings, above.

WOODHALL ROAD begins with fancy late Georgian. On the
side No. 1, with Ionic porch and twin bays, looks N over the
Dell. Then in the thickening trees a notable series of large
Victorian villas by *Anderson*. Nos. 11 and 13, 1877, are a
single block with two half-timbered brick gables, deep-eaved
and originally with wooden balconies. THIRLESTANE
(originally Torduff, on the corner of Barnshot Road) is austerely Gothic, with a gazebo turret to the S. It was built for
Anderson himself in 1879, but his wife did not like it and the
result was No. 15, ALLERMUIR, more orthodox baronial with
crowsteps, 1880-2. In BARNSHOT ROAD Nos. 4 and 6, 1895-
6, are also by him, their stone and timber detail very crisp
against roughcast walls.

Further along Woodhall Road and outside this perambulation, Nos. 47-53 are another group of white-harled cottages
designed by *Lorimer* in 1907, executed by *R. R. Grieve* in
1910. Various gable forms, including the inverted w. Opposite, WEST COLINTON COTTAGE, late Georgian remodelled
c. 1935, with a jerkin head roof, by *John J. Burnet* and *Edith
Hughes*. On the N side of WOODHALL ROAD No. 2 is a
castellated Gothic miniature (once a library), No. 4 a bungalow of false-rusticated ashlar, with a little forecourt. Both are
late Georgian. No. 12 is early Victorian picturesque, with
Gothic porch, and after the next house a path descends
through woods to BRIDGE ROAD. Notable wrought-iron railings on the ramp up to No. 25. Here we have Colinton's
shopping centre, a cheerful shanty-village clinging preca-
riously to the edge of the Dell, the N side slightly dignified
by the more permanent-looking COLINTON ARMS of *c.* 1880
a pair of pedimented Tudor lodges *c.* 1810 in the middle, and
at the w end the ROYAL BANK OF SCOTLAND, single-storey
c. 1920, with pairs of miniature columns.

The bank building marks the sharp corner of SPYLAW
STREET, No. 23 (bright red brick) providing a much less decorous entry on the other side. Nos. 5-16 are a row of harled
cottages stepping down the steep slope, No. 17 at the head
slightly more elaborate. They are by *MacGibbon & Ross*
1900, with deep pantiled roofs and some fancy porches spanning the pavement.* On the N side the entry to Spylaw House
(*see* Mansions, above). The late C19 LAUREL BANK is a nice
termination, just where the road turns to cross the single-arch
(C18?) bridge. For St Cuthbert's Parish Church *see* Churches

---

* Nos. 5-14 are remodelled earlier cottages.

[Digression up the Water of Leith WALKWAY to Craiglockhart Dell and Lanark Road.]
A sharp climb to SPYLAW BANK ROAD, with No. 1 a solid C18
house at the corner, then early C19 cottages at Nos. 2 and 3.
Much charm, some oddity, with mad half-timbered end
gables at Nos. 44–46, c. 1920. At No. 52 the SIR WILLIAM
FRASER HOMES by *A.F. Balfour Paul*, 1898–9, C17 Scots
with open ogee-roofed pavilions flanking the court, harled
with red sandstone dressings. No. 47 is GLENLYON by *Lorimer*, 1906, Anglo-Scots traditional with a corbelled bow. No.
49, ALMORA, by *Lorimer*, 1899, more manorial, with a red-
tiled cat-slide roof. STONEHOUSE (originally Dunnottar, No.
1 Pentland Road) is substantial and nearly symmetrical, with
rubble walls and stone slates, again by *Lorimer*, 1914–15.
GLENLINDEN (No. 1 Spylaw Avenue) is brash red-and-
white, 1910. Square tower with triangular oriels. SPYLAW
BANK HOUSE is stolid, ashlar-trimmed Georgian, c. 1810
with later extensions. Finally No. 65, BALMADIES by *Matthew M. Ochterlony*, 1915. A sensitive mixture of harl and
stone, with green slate roofs and a dormered turret.
In SPYLAW AVENUE (for No. 1, *see* above), No. 3 is ACHARRA
by *Lorimer*, 1897. Corbelled first floor and snug piend roofs.
No. 4 is by *Dunn & Findlay*, 1902. HARTFELL (No. 10 Spylaw Park) is by *Lorimer*, 1899 and 1905–9, with gables to the
N and balconied turrets to the s. GILLESPIE ROAD is a country lane heavily used (1980) as a by-pass. [Digression to the
w for the large MUIREND by *Hippolyte J. Blanc*, 1897, with
additions by *John Butters* of Ludlow, 1908. Also No. 39 by
Barbour & Bowie of Dumfries, 1905.] To the E, more cottage
houses by *Lorimer*: No. 21 (PENTLAND COTTAGE, 1895),
No. 32 (HUNTLY, 1899), No. 26 (HERMITAGE, 1898), No.
14 (ROXOBEL, 1895). And so back to Bridge Road.

OTHER VILLAS

BONALY ROAD. No. 2 is by *Lorimer*, 1907, part of the Woodhall Road group, *see* Perambulation, above. No. 6 is FUL-
LARTON by *Ochterlony*, 1927, with red tiles and white harl.
At the far s end DRUIM by *Norman McGlashan*, 1906. Red-
and-white, witty Art Nouveau with rough red sandstone at
the corner turrets and droopy-buttressed front door. A timber
verandah faces the garden.
CASTLELAW ROAD. No. 6 was originally GORTONLEE by *Kininmonth & Spence*, 1933. Smart but comfy colonial.
GRANT AVENUE. No. 1 by *Alexander A. Foote*, 1922–3. A
rubbly M gable amid red roofs and tile-hung walls.
PENTLAND AVENUE. Nos. 4–6, a red sandstone double villa by
James Jerdan & Son, 1914. No. 8 by *James M. Thomson*,
1904, symmetrical red-and-cream with three glazed bays.
Then three cottages by *Lorimer*, each harled and red-tiled,
with a round turret: No. 21 (ROWANS, 1901), No. 23 (COL-

INTON COTTAGE, 1893) and No. 40 (WESTFIELD, 1901). No. 42 is also by *Lorimer*, 1897 and 1910, with a verandah between gabled bays on the garden front.

WEST CARNETHY AVENUE. Two houses by *Ochterlony*. No. 3 (HAREFIELD, dated 1928), and No. 7 (formerly FALINGE, dated 1931), both with brick-trimmed entrance gables.

CORSTORPHINE

A large area stretching from the main railway line on the S, over Corstorphine Hill (its upper slopes still well wooded) to Clermiston, it is now the epitome of suburban sprawl, cut off by golf courses from direct contact with its parent town.

The medieval settlement around the church and castle (long gone) became an C18 watering-place with its own mineral well. By 1800 there were several villas, each in its own park, on both sides of Corstorphine Hill, those on the S with views to the Pentlands, those on the N to the Firth of Forth. A few more came in the C19 but it was only after the arrival of the railway in 1901 that commuting became easy. Since 1920 Corstorphine has been the speculative builder's demesne. Perhaps as a symbol of suzerainty the Edinburgh District Council has designated a Conservation Area around Kirk Loan.

CHURCHES

20 OLD PARISH CHURCH, Kirk Loan. Late medieval, brooding in its village churchyard just behind the main road. The manor of Corstorphine was acquired in 1376 by Sir Adam Forrester, several times Lord Provost of Edinburgh. Some time before his death in 1405 he built a chapel dedicated to St John the Baptist beside the parish church. In 1426 three chaplaincies were founded there; in 1429 the chapel became collegiate with two more chaplains and two clerks; and in 1444 it acquired a further four chaplains. It is this private foundation whose church has survived; the parish church adjoining on the N side was pulled down in 1646 to make way for a new N aisle, itself replaced by a larger extension in 1828. Sir Adam's building must be the existing nave including the chapel projecting S from the W end. The chancel and W tower came later, probably after 1444. Their greater height relative to the nave gives the church its distinctively broken-backed appearance.

The chancel has a slabbed roof and excessively deep buttresses at the angles. A bizarre touch is the C18 replacement of their pinnacles with cubic sundials, some of them dummies. E window with three lights, rather perfunctory Perp tracery (two lozenges) and triple chamfered reveals. In the gable an image niche. The S windows are paired lights set flush with the wall. On the N side a contemporary sacristy with rectangular windows and inserted mullions. The slabbed roof of the nave, together with the tunnel-vault that carries it, is by *George Henderson*, 1903–5. On the s side of the nave *William Burn* repeated the design of the chancel windows in 1828. The s chapel projects from the w end of the nave rather than from the e end as was normal (e.g. Borthwick, Lothian). The explanation must be that the e part of what one now reads as the nave was built as the chancel of Sir Adam Forrester's chapel. Presumably it was thrown into the nave only when the existing chancel was added to house the enlarged college. The three-light window of the s chapel is carefully detailed and in this respect resembles the early Perp work in the presbytery at Melrose Abbey (from 1385) and St John's Chapel at St Giles (*c.* 1395; *see* Old Town); the basic pattern is common in late c14 and early c15 English work, but the elongated diamond shape over the outer lights is a specifically Lincolnshire and Fenland motif. Beside the window small shields, and above it another under a helm and a fancy ogee head. The slabbed roof does not join on to the roof of the nave (cf. the similar arrangement at St Michael's, Linlithgow, Lothian). The tower is detached from the w gable of the nave, and carries a dumpy octagonal stone spire enlivened by three crenellated bands, lucarnes in the main faces and meagre crocketed pinnacles at the corners. The bell-stage has paired lights like those in the chancel s wall. On the w side a plain porch, probably mid-c17, with one round-headed window, reused medieval shields and an illegible fragment of a Gothic inscription. The arch into the tower is that of the former w window. The n side of the church is Burn's 1828 rationalization of the n aisle built in 1646 on the site of the parochial part of the medieval building.

The interior of the nave and n aisle is virtually all by *Henderson*, who made a radical restoration in 1903–5, removing Burn's n and e galleries and replacing his plaster vault with twin tunnel-vaults of granolithic slabs (the exterior slabs are of the same material) on chamfered stone ribs. Six of the nave corbels are carved by *Birnie Rhind* with heads derived from Leonardo's Last Supper. n nave arcade on square piers with chamfered corners, and chancel arch to match. The chancel has a plain, steeply pointed tunnel-vault. On the w wall, above Henderson's chancel arch, the line of the medieval arch is visible. On the e wall a foliage-topped inscription commemorating Provost Nicholas Bannatyne †after 1470 (the last figure not filled in) and mentioning the founding of the college in 1429. Fine SEDILIA with basket arches and oddly stretched cusping under crocketed ogee gables alternating with shields. Miniature rib-vaults inside. The sacristy to the n has a rough tunnel-vault and corbels for two floors. Most of the MENSA of the medieval altar survives within the reveals of the e window. The s chapel has a tunnel-vault from which surface ribs in a diamond pattern have been removed; the area of the diamond projects slightly in relation to the rest of the vault surface.

MONUMENTS. In the S chapel Sir Adam Forrester †1405. A plain depressed pointed arch over a tomb-chest of Perp type with shields in cusped panels. Male effigy only, the feet on a grimacing dog. – On the W wall the tomb-slab of James Watson of Saughton †1620, with a long Roman-lettered inscription from Ezekiel chapter 37. – In the chancel, W end of N wall, Sir John Forrester I †1440, James I's Master of the Household. Continuously moulded basket arch with bases, the tomb-chest like Sir Adam's only bigger. Male and female effigies, the latter holding a book. – To the E Sir John Forrester II †c. 1454. The architecture is particularly good, a broad moulded arch of almost triangular profile, and hood-mould with shield-carrying angels as terminations and vigorously carved small and large crockets. Male and female effigies wearing cloaks and a few traces of original black and red paint. – Also in the chancel, S wall, the grave slabs of Alexander Tod †1499 and Robert Heriot, rector of Gogar, †1444, the latter with a chalice and wafer in shallow relief. – WAR MEMORIAL in the W arch leading into the tower, by *William Davidson*, 1919–23, including figures in the spandrels by *Alexander Carrick*, all in Ravelston stone.

FURNISHINGS. In the S chapel a circular stone late medieval FONT of bulging profile brought from Gogar in 1955, and on the E wall a small TAPESTRY by *Sax Shaw* of *Dovecote Studios*, also 1955. – Stone pillar LECTERN by *Henderson*, and likewise the timber furnishings, including the case for the ORGAN by *Ingram*, all in his blunt Scots Gothic style except for the stumpy Romanesque COMMUNION TABLE. – STAINED GLASS. A large set by *Ballantine*, variously signed and dated 1904–5. – In the SE chancel window two lights (the Lamb of God), after 1876, and in the SE nave window two lights (Consider the Lilies), 1904, by *Nathaniel Bryson*. – In the S chapel three lights (Christ in Majesty) by *Gordon Webster*, 1970. – In the first-floor tower window one light (St John's cross) to the architect George Henderson †1905.

MONUMENTS in the churchyard. – To the NW Jane Muirhead †1751, with a primitive finial of angel and trumpet. To the SW Francis Glog †1732, with spirited rococo carving and figures of a sower and reaper and Father Time, and a handsome pedestal to Thomas Louriston †1751, missing its vase finial. – On the S wall of the chancel a pedimented monument to Walker †1751 on which the name *Wm. Don* may be that of the sculptor.

ST ANDREW, Clermiston View. A simple harled church by *Basil Spence & Partners*, 1957–9, making the most of the site. Its low-pitch gable stands back on a terrace. Hall projecting forward to the l., its gable rising from the rubble retaining wall, its roof made interesting by a simple trick; the ridge is not quite parallel to the wall, so the eaves have a slight slope. Bell-tower to the r., a concrete tripod with golden ball and cross. A plain, elegant interior; timber-lined roof, rubble end-wall with climbing plants.

St Anne, St John's Road and Kaimes Road. By *P. MacGregor* 46
Chalmers, 1912. This is a brilliant presbyterian essay in the
Early Christian manner, built of rough-faced Hailes stone in
regular courses, with corbelled eaves and narrow, round-
arched windows. A tall main body 100ft (30m.) long, plain
and uniform from end to end. Aisles running into parallel
side-chapels, and a five-sided E apse with blind arcades at the
head. The SW campanile (with the two top stages arcaded)
would have completed the composition, but only the bottom
stage was built, a porch with portal elaborately carved by
James C. Young; Christ in Glory in the tympanum. It is
groined inside, the lintel at the wing carved with Christ's
entry into Jerusalem by *Tom Whalen*, 1953. A notable interior, continuously arcaded, with a pair of clearstorey windows
over each arch. Monolith columns of Cullaloe stone with basket capitals, but square piers are used at the ends, and at the
point where the aisles open through arches into the broader
chapels. The pews and the flat board-and-beam ceiling are of
oak, perfectly plain. A big round arch into the apse, which is
arcaded over the seats of the minister and twelve elders; floor
of Iona marble. The principal furnishings were designed by
Chalmers. – Oak COMMUNION TABLE, with a carved sycamore roundel of Christ at Emmaus. – Oak LECTERN STALL,
and PULPIT on four columns. – Stone FONT. – Furnishings
in N chapel designed by *William G. Dey*, 1953. – ORGAN by
Ingram (specification by *Whalley* of St George's, Charlotte
Square), 1922. – STAINED GLASS. A united but far from
monotonous collection which brightens the sobriety of the
church and effectively lights it. – In the apse the three centre
lights (Christ's Baptism, Crucifixion and Resurrection) by
Alfred A. Webster of the *Stephen Adam Studio*, Glasgow,
1917. The other two (Christ's infancy and Ascension) by *Gordon Webster*, 1953, adopting his father's basic composition
but with a broader and less realistic technique. Gordon
Webster did all the others in the church, 1932–63. – In the
porch two lights (Jacob and David) by *William Wilson* in his
sharpest and most vivid manner, 1947. The HALL to the N is
by *T. Bowhill Gibson*, 1928, in complete harmony with Chalmers' work.

St John the Baptist (R.C.), St Ninian's Road. By *Charles
W. Gray*, 1926. Rubbly but tame, especially when its NE
tower is seen beside St Ninian's. Spacious interior with aisles
alongside portal arches, a baldacchino in the apse. ORGAN by
Walker, 1964.

St Kentigern (R.C.), Parkgrove Avenue. By *T. Harley Haddow*, 1966. An elegant square with clearstorey glazing, each
quarter of the roof falling to its corner in a zinc-covered
catenary curve. Harled outbuildings to match, and a brick
and timber interior, full of light.

St Ninian (former Free Church), St John's Road and St
Ninian's Road. A plain box of 1844–5, dressed up in 1869.
The new front is mixed Gothic tending to French. Stumpy

SE spire with heavy pinnacles on the broaches. T-plan interior with queenpost arch-braced roof. The N apse for the organ and pulpit was built in 1888-9; in 1911-14 *J. Macintyre Henry* added the transepts. – FURNISHINGS by *William G. Dey*, 1953. – ORGAN by *E. F. Walcker*, 1902, rebuilt in the E wing by *Ingram*, 1957.

PUBLIC BUILDINGS

CLERMISTON ADULT TRAINING CENTRE, Parkgrove Terrace. By *A. C. M. Forward*, 1963. An industrial box with octagonal pavilions on the E.

CORSTORPHINE HOSPITAL (formerly Royal Infirmary Convalescent Home), Corstorphine Road. A long Italian spread on the sunny hillside, built in two stages. The first by *Peddie & Kinnear*, 1866, 'for an anonymous gentleman* who is to present it to the managers', two-storey and attic centrepiece with arcaded wings obscured, 1960-2, by glass curtain walling. The second by *Kinnear & Peddie*, 1891, providing the end pavilions and bullseyed towers, plus a new porch in the middle, all much richer.

CORSTORPHINE PUBLIC HALL, Kirk Loan. By *J. Robart Pearson*. Dated 1903 but the foundation stone was laid in 1891. Cheap Scots style with red sandstone dressings. Salamanders climbing the door pediments give a jolly touch.

PUBLIC LIBRARY, Kirk Loan. Squared up vernacular with a cupola, by *E. J. MacRae*, 1927.

QUEEN MARGARET COLLEGE, Clerwood Terrace. By *Andrew Renton*, 1973. Slate and glass horizontals sitting well on the site of the demolished Clermiston House. Fully-glazed lecture halls on the W. At the NW corner, LIBRARY by *Stewart Brown* of Andrew Renton's Edinburgh office, 1977, the slate dominant. – TEACHING BUILDING AND STUDENTS' UNION in the style of the original, by *Simpson & Brown*, 1979-82.

SCHOOLS. As indicative of changing educational ideas as of architectural fashions. The barrack-like CORSTORPHINE PRIMARY SCHOOL, Corstorphine High Street, with thinnest Scots Renaissance detail, is by *James A. Williamson*, 1893-4. Festival of Britain priggishness appears at CARRICK KNOWE, Lampacre Road, by *Walls & Duncan*, 1952-4, DRUMBRAE, Drumbrae Avenue, 1957, and CLERMISTON PRIMARY, Parkgrove Place, 1954-8, both by the *City Architect's Department*. Friendly boxes with not much style for FOX COVERT (R.C.) PRIMARY, Rannoch Road, by the *City Architect's Department*, 1964.

SCOTTISH NATIONAL ZOOLOGICAL PARK, Corstorphine Road. The Zoological Society of Scotland acquired the Corstorphine Hill House estate in 1913 and immediately laid out

---

* Later identified as Mr William Seton Brown.

the s part to a plan by *Patrick Geddes* and *F. C. Mears*. In 1927 Mears laid out the N part. The main inspiration was Carl Hagenbeck's Stellingen Zoo near Hamburg, where animals were seen in something approaching their natural surroundings. At Corstorphine, quarries opened for bottoming for the zoo roads were converted into pools or animal pits with rocky ledges. The POOLS near the entrance, the LION ROCK, and the BROWN BEAR ENCLOSURE, made in 1913-15, were followed by the ROCK DENS (1928), BABOON ROCK (1929), PENGUIN POOL (1930), TIGER ENCLOSURES (1936-7), and PRAIRIE DOG ROCK (1958).

In the middle of the complex is CORSTORPHINE HILL HOUSE (MEMBERS' HOUSE), begun in 1793 as a whinstone villa with a central bow on the s front. On the N, a classy tripartite window with Adamesque pilasters. In 1891 *A. W. Macnaughtan* baronialized the house, heightening the bow to a heavily castellated tower and adding a large but uninspired E block. Inside, his octagonal Entrance Hall (leafy enriched ceiling) opens into an opulent Stair-hall with stained-glass figures of Art, Commerce and Literature on the half-landing. First-floor Drawing Room with *pâtisserie* decoration. The tight oval stair in the middle of the original house survives with a Roman Doric screen on the landing. Public Restaurant on the w added by *Mears*, 1936-7. – STABLES (MAINTENANCE SECTION) by *Macnaughtan* to the NW. – To the SE, WALLED GARDEN (PARROT GARDEN) with AVIARIES against the N and E walls and the TROPICAL BIRD AND REPTILE HOUSE (by *Mears*, 1925) on the s.

LODGE on Corstorphine Road by *Alexander N. Paterson*, 1923-6, Beaux-Arts classical. On each end, an early C19 stone falcon originally at Falcon Hall (Morningside). – Also from Falcon Hall the rusticated GATE-PIERS and heavy cast-iron gates, widened in 1974-5. – Piend-roofed CARNEGIE AQUARIUM beside the Lodge, by *Paterson*, 1924-7,* dressed up with a round-arched blind arcade and coloured cement roundels. – N of the Walled Garden, brick CHIMPANZEE HOUSE (1981). – CHILDREN'S FARM, diminutive Cape Dutch ranges by *J. Wilson Paterson*, 1956-8. – Broad-eaved COTTAGE behind. – LION HOUSE, a tactful adjunct to the Lion Rock by *Thain Contracts Ltd*, 1976. – On the w side of the park, Spanish Colonial BOOK SHOP, by *Mears*, 1913, built as a restaurant. – ORANG UTAN HOUSE, 1980. – MONKEY HOUSE, 1970-1, Fyfestone and drydash with conservatory-like cages at the ends.

DESCRIPTION

The entry from CORSTORPHINE ROAD is guarded by two sentinels, the POST HOUSE HOTEL by *Nelson Foley*, 1971-3, on

---

*Paterson was appointed after a competition in 1919 but later modified the design.

the N and the FORESTRY COMMISSION by *Hugh Martin & Partners*, 1972, on the S, the one boxy in concrete aggregate, the other a brown glass semicircle. More brown glass by *Hugh Martin & Partners*, 1975, on CIVIL AVIATION HOUSE in TRAQUAIR PARK EAST. For the Scottish National Zoological Park and Corstorphine Hospital, *see* Public Buildings, above. A second line of defence is provided by No. 235, an Arts and Crafts children's home by *James Jerdan*, 1891, in brick and harl, facing St Anne's Church (*see* above). After St Anne's, more harl and half-timbering at Nos. 18-20 ST JOHN'S ROAD. In CORSTORPHINE HOUSE AVENUE to the S, CORSTORPHINE HOUSE of 1832, still Georgian but with bay-windows. St John's Road now becomes meanest commercial. For St Ninian's Church, *see* above. Opposite, THE CEDARS, large with bargeboards, retreats behind a wall, but the ROYAL BANK OF SCOTLAND by *Waters Jamieson Partnership*, 1978, flaunts its wealth in tiles and brown glass. Brown glass again but in a neo-vernacular concrete frame on the BANK OF SCOTLAND by *James Gray & Associates*, 1974, at the corner of Drum Brae North.

Near the top of Meadowplace Road, MURRAY COTTAGES, a picturesque group round a green, by *Henry F. Kerr*, 1910. The buff brick LADYWELL HOUSE on the N side of LADYWELL ROAD, by *J. Gray*, 1968, tries hard to keep a domestic scale. For Corstorphine Primary School in CORSTORPHINE HIGH STREET, *see* Public Buildings (Schools). ST MARGARET'S PARK opposite was laid out by *E. J. MacRae*, 1927. In its NE corner, the white-harled DOWER HOUSE of *c.* 1660. Originally L-shaped, it was extended to a T plan in the early C18 and raised to three storeys. In the N jamb, corniced door with a moulded panel-frame above. Crowsteps on the main block, scrolled skewputts on the jamb.

Nos. 5-7 Corstorphine High Street are a harled pair of early C19 piend-roofed houses facing away from the street. Outsize Ionic porches. The stone over the central pend, carved with a cusped ogee arch and coats of arms, looks early C16. Corstorphine Public Hall and Public Library mark out KIRK LOAN as a centre for the area. The parish churchyard and a cottage in HALL TERRACE do their best to give it a village atmosphere.

At the E end of DOVECOT ROAD, a C16 flat-topped beehive DOOCOT. Behind, the DOVECOTE STUDIO, picturesque of 1910. In TRAQUAIR PARK WEST, a detached house dated 1903 on the Station Road corner followed by two red sandstone terraces of 1903-7, all with Arts and Crafts detail.

CLERMISTON ROAD leads to grand villas on Corstorphine Hill. On the corner of Gordon Road, No. 26, beautifully composed Art Nouveau of *c.* 1910 with broad eaves and battered chimneys. Set back in their own grounds, two large villas, HILLWOOD, aggressive and unscholarly baronial by *MacGibbon & Ross*, *c.* 1873, with strongly corbelled oriels and a huge circular entrance tower, and CLERWOOD by *Thomas McGuf-*

fie, c. 1860, with two large gables and Gothic detail. Between and behind, CORSTORPHINE HILL TOWER, with diagonally set buttresses and a cap-house, was built by William Macfie of Dreghorn in 1871 to commemorate the centenary of the birth of Sir Walter Scott. On the W side of the road, Nos. 177–81 were the lodges of Clermiston Mains. Mono-pitch rear extensions of 1963 successfully keep the symmetry. CLERMISTON MAINS itself in OAK LANE has a comfortable ogee-roofed stair-tower, *c.* 1900. On the approach, No. 1 with a low domestic block set back from a studio and garage is by *H. H. Haswell-Smith, c.* 1960. At the top of Clermiston Road the lumpy FOX COVERT HOTEL's rear surprisingly incorporates a tower of the Victorian CLERMOUNT which stood on the site.

CLERMISTON CRESCENT gives the entry to the CLERMISTON HOUSING SCHEME by *John A. W. Grant,* 1952–61, its generous layout and unpretentious humanity putting Corstorphine's private housing to shame. In PARKGROVE LOAN, CLERMISTON HOUSE by *Scott & McIntosh,* 1966–9, with huge copper-roofed stone stair-towers.

CRAIGLEITH AND RAVELSTON

Until the late C19 this was farmland disturbed only by the huge Craigleith Quarry, the largest in Scotland, from which most of the stone for the New Town was taken. Then development spread from Dean into the E edge of Ravelston, and W from Craigleith Railway Station (opened for passenger traffic in 1879) to form the detached suburb of Blackhall. Since the 1920s there has been an invasion of speculative house-builders, halted by the green crescent under the slopes of Corstorphine Hill.

CHURCH

ST COLUMBA, Queensferry Road. By *P. MacGregor Chalmers,* 1903. Built of snecked masonry with some Norman detail, but elaborately composed with the N aisle running into a NE chapel which has an apsidal E end alongside that of the chancel. The NW tower contains the porch and was meant to have an octagonal stone spirelet. A chaste but highly original interior. The nave, with steep arch-braced roof, has a low arcade and clearstorey on the N side, but on the S a tall galleried arcade through which is glimpsed a single-bay SW tribune. High chancel arch, the dome of the apse lacking its intended mosaic decoration. – FONT in the apse of the NE chapel. A carved stone cylinder. – WOODWORK by *Scott Morton & Co.,* designed by *Jeffrey Waddell.* – STAINED GLASS. In the chancel two lights (bread and wine), over the arch three lights (Crucifixion) and in the NE chapel one light (Emmanuel), all by *Heaton, Butler & Bayne,* small in size but richly coloured and realistic.

PUBLIC BUILDINGS

BLACKHALL LIBRARY, Hillhouse Road. By *Bradshaw, Gass & Hope*, 1966. Low, with fully glazed walls on to an internal courtyard.

BLACKHALL PRIMARY SCHOOL, Maidencraig Crescent. 1907, by *John Watson*, whose design surprisingly won a competition.

MARY ERSKINE SCHOOL, Ravelston Dykes Road. By *William H. Kininmonth*, 1964–7. Strong composition of straightforward harled blocks in a parkland setting.

The new buildings are joined to RAVELSTON HOUSE, a swish villa in the late Adam manner, built by Alexander Keith, c. 1790. Standard Palladian composition of a main block with blind-arcaded links to low Venetian-windowed pavilions. But the main block's centrepieces are a semi-octagon on the N and a bow on the S, both carried up as towers above the eaves. On the N (entrance) tower, a blind balustrade below the first-floor windows; perron with elaborate S-scrolled ironwork. The same S-scrolls on the drawing-room balcony and garden stair on the garden front. Behind the N wall of the roofless E garden pavilion, Kininmonth's canopy link makes a brutal horizontal. The W pavilion's link was raised to three floors and deepened towards the garden, c. 1875, in a would-be tactful style.

The interior was gone over in expensive Adam-revival taste in 1915–16, the new work not always easy to distinguish from the old. Octagonal entrance hall with classical plaster roundels of c. 1790. The white marble chimneypiece with a ram led to sacrifice on the central panel is the first of many – far too many for all to have been originally in the house. Straight ahead, the double bow-ended morning room (? originally drawing room). On the E, and running the full depth of the house, the drawing room, presumably formed from two rooms with pilasters supporting a beam to mark the original division. Prettily plaster-panelled walls and a sunburst on the ceiling. On the W side, stair-hall of 1915–16 with Doric friezes on the walls. Skimpy twisted stair-balusters. Behind, the dining room pushed through a columned screen into the Victorian extension. In a small top-floor bedroom, a smart pine and gesso chimneypiece of c. 1810 decorated with reliefs of the Nelson Monument and St Cuthbert's steeple.

To the NW, picturesque stable and coach-house buildings of c. 1875. Among them, reminders of the earlier Ravelston House. Early C18 ball-finialled lectern DOOCOT (now part of a house). – Entrance arch in the BARMKIN WALL flanked by gun loops, one a quatrefoil. – Crowstep-gabled STAIR-TOWER of the house itself. Sub-classical door dated 1626 with large floral decoration on the jambs. In a niche in the W wall, fountain made up of a legless lady (perhaps late C17) squeezing one breast to fill the basin below. – Door surround in the WALLED GARDEN with scrolls, a dormer pediment and a finial of the sun in glory, all presumably from the old house. Against the N wall, GARDEN HOUSE, its entrance made from a C17 fireplace, with a Greek key border surrounding small-scale decoration, topped by parts of three dormer-heads.

ROYAL VICTORIA HOSPITAL, Craigleith Road. The little pedimented WEST LODGE belonged to the late Georgian villa of Craigleith House, converted in 1894 by *S. Henbest Capper* into a hospital for consumptives. A pleasant arrangement of buff brick single-storey wards by *Alan Reiach & Partners,* 1966, now occupies its site. Other buildings by the same firm, and more now in progress to the E (1981) by *Alan Reiach, Eric Hall & Partners.* The intermediate phase by *Sydney Mitchell & Wilson* starts with the Arts and Crafts EAST LODGE of 1906. Rubble ground floor beside a Tudor arched pend; to the rear a half-sunk stair-tower up to a slate-hung top hamper of nice asymmetry. Up the drive one survivor of a group of small Y-plan red-brick pavilions – three of 1903, two more of 1906, which is also the date of the central service building. ADMINISTRATION BLOCK in C17 Scots style with a huge, swanky bas-relief of the Royal Arms covering the whole of the entrance gable. Former DINING HALL to the rear, its entrance front like a dry but whimsical Georgian orangery. Between them an Italianate campanile, completing a mixture that foreshadows Clough Williams-Ellis's adventures at Portmeirion.

ST GEORGE'S SCHOOL, Upper Coltbridge Terrace. Colonial neo-Georgian by *A. F. Balfour Paul,* 1911–14. Sensible PRIMARY DEPARTMENT in pale brick by *Eric Hall & Partners,* 1964.

WESTERN GENERAL HOSPITAL, Crewe Road. Conscientious architecture, but mostly at cross purposes, adding up to a tangled makeshift. The combined Poor House of St Cuthbert's and Canongate (*see* Paediatric Department, below) was turned into a hospital in 1927 and grew in the 1950s and 60s under the control of John Holt, architect to the South Eastern Regional Hospital Board. This clockwise tour begins at the S entry from Crewe Road. On the S side the single-storey SCOTTISH HEALTH SERVICE CENTRE by the *SERHB Architect's Department,* 1969, with a lodge-like E extension of concrete blockwork, 1974. The NUFFIELD TRANSPLANT UNIT by *Peter Womersley* expresses the isolated mystique of kidney surgery in 1955; a fastidious assembly of smooth (but patchy yellow-coloured) concrete units with a tall ventilation stack and a long access bridge over the roadway. On the N side the modular concrete CYCLOTRON UNIT, 1975. The adjoining RADIOTHERAPY UNIT and related wards are by the *SERHB Architect's Department,* 1952–6; conventional brown brick walls alternating with white framed curtain walls of glass and green slate. Temporary laboratories of *c.* 1969 and the two-storey steel faced LIBRARY by the *Common Services Agency Building Division,* 1979, obstruct the three-storey frontage of the PAEDIATRIC DEPARTMENT (the original

Poor House) by *Peddie & Kinnear*, 1867, enlarged with a Frenchy forecourt by *D. & J. Bryce*, 1880. Its otherwise bold detail pales beside *Peddie & Kinnear*'s detached w wing (now the SURGICAL WARDS), with a big corbelled arch in the centre block. On the front a giddy spiral stair of cast iron, to the rear the GASTRO-INTESTINAL UNIT by *Scott & McIntosh*, 1966, and to the N the MAIN OPERATING THEATRES (originally built on legs over the old theatres) by *Basil Spence & Partners*, 1956. Further w the five-storey SURGICAL NEUROLOGY block by the *SERHB Architect's Department*, 1952, with stone gable and green slate panelled flanks; timber-clad drum over the operating theatre. To the N the copper-roofed TEACHING AND RESEARCH CENTRE by *Alison & Hutchison & Partners*, 1953.

At the NW corner of the site the CENTRAL MICROBIOLOGY LABORATORY by the *SERHB Architect's Department*, 1959 (their mixture much as before), and in front of it the ANIMAL HOUSE, one smartly detailed brick storey by *Scott & McIntosh*, 1977. BOILER HOUSE AND LAUNDRY by *Basil Spence, Glover & Ferguson*, 1966, with white steel-clad walls and concrete chimney; OLD BOILER HOUSE (superseded) by *Basil Spence & Partners*, 1956, brick with shell concrete roofs. Along the N side the four-storey brick NURSES' HOME by the *City Architect's Department*, 1935; COLLEGE OF NURSING added to the N by the *SERHB Architect's Department*, 1958. Then the RECREATION HALL, like a brick chapel, *c.* 1920. Facing it, the OUTPATIENT CASUALTY AND DIAGNOSTIC block by the *SERHB Architect's Department*, 1966–8, the PATHOLOGY block by the *City Architect's Department*, 1939, and the four-storey HUMAN GENETICS block by *Alan Reiach, Eric Hall & Partners*, 1970. Finally the OLD OUTPATIENT building designed as a children's home by *R. M. Cameron*, 1912, a harled single-storey pavilion block with jolly red tile roofs and stone dressings; house to the E facing Crewe Road (now the MIDWIFERY CENTRE) to match.

MANSION

CRAIGCROOK CASTLE, off Craigcrook Road. A C16 tower house with large C19 additions. William Adamson, an Edinburgh merchant, bought the estate in 1542, and the earliest part of the house was probably built by him or his son in the next few years. This was Z-plan, with the four-storey main block lying E-W, a round tower at the SW corner and a square stair-tower at the NE. Tight stair-turrets corbelled out at the SE corner and above a large gun loop in the N corner of the round tower. A bristle of cannon-spouts below the round tower's corbelled parapet, their martial effect belied by the main block's pedimented dormer-heads. Inside, tunnel-vaulted ground-floor rooms in the main block and the round tower. Above were a first-floor hall with a chamber in the round tower, each with a private stair to the floors above.

Full-height E extension, again with dormer-heads, probably of 1626. This had tall conical-roofed turrets flanking the crowstepped gable.

Under his will of 1712, John Strachan (†1719) left the estate to endow the charitable Craigcrook Mortification which in 1736 gave the Constable family a ninety-nine-year lease of the house. The *Scots Magazine* reported in April 1810 that Archibald Constable, the then tenant, had, 'Without injuring the appearance of antiquity ... rendered it completely commodious and agreeable as a modern residence.'

Five years later the lease was taken over by the judge Lord Jeffrey, who immediately added the awkwardly castellated drawing-room wing N of the C16 main block. In 1835 Jeffrey employed *William H. Playfair* to carry out a major reconstruction of the C17 E extension. Its S wall was partly rebuilt, its N wall completely so, on a new line further N. At the same time, the two top floors of the C16 main block were thrown into one, the wall-head raised and new pedimented dormer-heads provided. The N stair-turret was heightened with a tall conical cap. All this is quite relaxed, but Playfair's new stair-tower NE of the original is stark baronial, an octagon ruthlessly corbelled out to the square.

In 1891 *Thomas Leadbetter* added a listless billiard-room extension to the E, joined to Playfair's stair-tower by a corridor link across the N front.

Inside the front door a comfortable clockwise turnpike of 1835 leads to the first-floor circular lobby formed by removal of the C16 turnpike. Drawing room of 1815, plain classical with a late C19 Holyrood revival chimneypiece. Morning room (the C16 hall) with console-corniced doorcases, perhaps of 1815 but probably *c.* 1800. Watteauesque decoration on the E wall, presumably of 1835, when an oriel window was formed opposite. Shallow-relief late C17-style ceiling enrichment, probably of 1891, contrasting with the swagged frieze. The study in the tower was gothicized in 1817. Plaster ribs across the flat ceiling, blind arcading on the walls and blind traceried window embrasures; heraldic stained glass. The oak graining of the walls executed by *David Roberts* and *John Jackson* as a background for the C16 Stirling Heads (now back at Stirling) is no more. Jacobean ceiling in the 1835 dining room. Stained-glass window with two female figures in the NE corner.

Remains of the BARMKIN WALL on the E approach. Round-arched gateway, dated 1626, with a semicircular strapworked pediment and obelisks. In the large WALLED GARDEN on the S, low OFFICE BLOCK by *Alison & Hutchison & Partners*, 1969.

DESCRIPTION

In RAVELSTON PARK plump villas. No. 1 on the S corner, with a canted bay and bargeboards, of 1865. No. 2 opposite is

Gothic. The rest are of the 1880s. No. 6 is by *Kinnear & Peddie*, 1885; No. 23 by *George Henderson*, 1884. Barge-boarded No. 18 dated 1881.

RAVELSTON DYKES is broad and arboreal, the trees too often a substitute for architecture. The tiled roof of No. 72, by *John Dall*, 1924, is flanked by large brick chimneys at right angles to each other. Nos. 78–84, again by *Dall*, 1924, two double houses with half-timbering in the gabled ends and a curly pedimented dormer-head in the centre. Voyseyish touches but with tall ground-floor windows at Nos. 104–106 of 1927. For the Mary Erskine School, *see* Public Buildings, above. At its entrance, a pair of strong but very simple houses
132   (Nos. 65–67 RAVELSTON DYKES ROAD) by *Morris & Steedman*, 1960. Beside them, a stepped terrace (Nos. 69–85) by *Roland Wedgwood Associates*, 1969. On the bend of the road, RAVELRIG MANOR by *Hart Bros.*, 1966, with a timber-clad clearstoried pavilion. For the stables of Ravelston House, *see* under the Mary Erskine School, above.

N of Ravelston Dykes, RAVELSTON RISE by *James Miller & Partners*, 1974, straightforward in buff brick. RAVELSTON GARDEN, three flat-roofed white-harled blocks of four-storey flats by *Neil & Hurd*, 1936, with horizontal windows and heavy balconies. RAVELSTON HOUSE PARK leads to RAVELSTON HEIGHTS, nine storeys with a fussy grid front, by *T. Boland & Co. Ltd*, 1965.

QUEENSFERRY ROAD divides Ravelston from Craigleith. At the E, ORCHARD BRAE HOUSE, by *Reiach & Hall*, 1974, heavy with purplish brick and brown glass. Below it in ORCHARD BRAE AVENUE, flats by *Miller*, 1965, still Festival of Britain but without the butterfly roofs. On the corner of CRAIGLEITH CRESCENT, the CREST HOTEL by *Morris & Steedman*, 1968, enjoys the view but spoils it for others. On the N side of Queensferry Road, MAIDENCRAIG COURT, gutless by *Leslie Grahame MacDougall*, 1954–5.

CRAIGLOCKHART

Rurally sited institutions to the E of Colinton Road, suburbia to the W, and to the far W the arcadia of Glenlockhart Dell.

FORT, Wester Craiglockhart Hill. The rocky summit is occupied by the remains of a small prehistoric D-plan fort, *c.* 27 m. by 18 m. Drystone wall at least 2·5 m. thick, severely wasted. Additional protection by a broad rock-cut ditch *c.* 20 m. to the SW. The interior of the fort was mutilated by the building of gun emplacements during the First World War, but trial excavation in 1970–1 revealed that there had been at least two periods of occupation, the latter during the Roman Iron Age, when the wall appears to have been deliberately cast down.

CHURCH

CRAIGLOCKHART PARISH CHURCH, Craiglockhart Avenue. Late Scots Gothic by *George Henderson*, 1889, when this was still a rural site. Aisleless, of rock-faced white stone, the dressings and Dec tracery red. The upper part of the steeple all red, built to a revised design in 1899. It has reticulated windows and battlemented parapet, corbelled angle-buttresses and crowstepped flyers supporting a belted and lucarned spire. Copious sculpture, with gargoyles and sejant beasts, making a distinctive prickly silhouette. Square turret between tower and porch, containing a nicely detailed stair. The interior plain except for the variety of tracery and carved corbels under the simplest kind of timber ceiling. – STAINED GLASS. In E window three lights (Supper at Emmaus), 1904.

PUBLIC BUILDINGS

CITY HOSPITAL, Greenbank Drive. By the City Architect *Robert Morham*, 1896–1903. Deep red sandstone, two symmetrical and parallel ranges of pavilions projecting to the S. Except for the central administrative block and some ancillary buildings (e.g. the mortuary and octagonal Gothic chapel to the NE) the effect is industrial, a Japanese distillery to judge by the big pagoda ventilators. Japan is also evoked by the covered walkways with prettily fretted wooden canopies. Many of the paired S turrets were brutally built-across in 1935, and the later C20 has contributed more brash infill, e.g. the glazed screen of the Ear, Nose and Throat Department by *Alison & Hutchison & Partners*, 1963. To the SW, a broad-eaved timber building for consumptives, by *J.A. Williamson*, 1913 (now disused, 1984). To the W of the entrance, flats for resident staff by *Alan Reiach, Eric Hall & Partners*, 1963. Buff brick, with slate-hung aprons under the windows. To the E, a more informal brick range for non-resident staff by *M. Shaw-Stewart*, 1966.

CRAIGHOUSE (Thomas Clouston Clinic, Royal Edinburgh Hospital), Craighouse Road. This huge château by *Sydney Mitchell*, dominating the N slope of Easter Craiglockhart Hill, was built in 1889–94 for the Royal Edinburgh Asylum. Dr *Clouston**★* made the preliminary sketch-plans. The builder was *John Lownie*, the materials rough-faced orange sandstone with warm yellow dressings, and soft-green N of England slates. Externally, Craighouse exploits the picturesque qualities of the François I style without becoming diffuse or unscholarly. It is basically of E plan, the middle stroke projecting to the N, where the composition builds up from the

★ 'It is one of Dr Clouston's leading principles that in the treatment of the insane, their surroundings should be made as bright and as pleasant as possible' (*Journal of Decorative Art*, December 1894).

workshop to the kitchen block to the clearstoried hall and attendant tower (30 m. high, 10 m. square) which is the climax of the bell-roofed and dormered skyline. Internally there is no decline of quality. Rooms and corridors neatly domestic, communal rooms palatial. From porch to main storey, a white marble STAIR, one straight flight. HALL, 19 m. by 10 m. by 14 m. high, pilastered above a deep oak dado, semicircular clearstorey windows breaking into the vault, a balustered gallery to the S. The colours are original above frieze level. DRAWING ROOM, adjoining. Lighter and more leisurely, with a corner turret annexe. Separate pavilions and a picturesque LODGE are designed *en suite*.

OLD CRAIG HOUSE, to the E. Built by the Symsounes of Craighouse. White-harled and crowstepped, originally one range with a N stair-tower, 1565, the N jamb added in 1746. It was altered in 1878 for the Royal Edinburgh Asylum (date on the ingle of the former dining room) and subsequently by *Sydney Mitchell*. Vaulted ground-floor rooms. In the first-floor end room a grey and white marble chimneypiece with gadrooned top, presumably 1746.

CRAIGLOCKHART COLLEGE OF EDUCATION, Colinton Road. Originally the Craiglockhart Hydropathic Institution, by *Peddie & Kinnear*, 1877-80. A giant Italian villa. Central tower with high loggia and lantern, pavilions and links with solemn Neo-Classical antae under the deep eaves. CHAPEL to the S by *Reginald Fairlie & J. Chisholm Cameron*, 1933. Rough, snecked walls. Over the entry on the canted porch, a SCULPTURE of the baptized Christ by *Michael Snowden*, 1968. Plain interior, with arches rising from wall-shafts. Square, saucer-domed chancel with SCULPTURES of SS. Michael and Raphael by *Alexander Carrick*. Apsidal sanctuary with grey marble reredos. The modish TEACHING BLOCK, farther to the S, is by *Cameron*, 1965.

GREENLEA OLD PEOPLE'S HOME, Craighouse Road. Originally the City Poor House, by *George Beattie & Son*, 1867-9, a competent baronial exercise in which the central block with John o' Groats tower was to house the merely poor, the E of the long crowstepped wings the sick, and the W the lunatic. Other classifications were later adopted and amenities added, with the City Parks Department making a good contribution from the first.

MANSIONS

CRAIGLOCKHART HOUSE, Craiglockhart Dell Road. Bald Tudor Gothic of *c.* 1830 and later, now stranded among the bungalows in much reduced grounds adjoining the Dell.

REDHALL HOUSE, Craiglockhart Drive South. By *James Robertson*, 1758, for George Inglis of Auchendinny, who had bought the property in 1755. Five bays, advanced and pedimented centre with urns. The porch and canted W wing *c.* 1900, when most of the interior was renewed. The heavy cantilever stair with turned wood balusters is original. Also a chimneypiece on the upper floor, E end, of timber with enriched pulvinated frieze. STABLES to the SW. Simple V plan, *c.* 1758, with a later ashlar wing, a panel carved with a horse at the pilastered end. DOOCOT. Hexagonal, 1756. A C16 panel with the Otterburn arms. SPECIAL SCHOOLS. Both of yellow brick with dark timber trim, too near the house but not rivalling it in bulk or formality. GRAYSMILL by *Lothian Region Architectural Services Department (A. S. D. Swanson),* 1978, and CAIRNPARK, designed for the Region by *Baxter, Clark & Paul,* 1978. WALLED GARDEN. Red-brick lined, with a pedimented brick summerhouse, *c.* 1756, by *Robert Bowie,* who also designed the rustic grottoes in the adjoining CRAIGLOCKHART DELL (accessible from Lanark Road).

DESCRIPTION

In COLINTON ROAD the major events, apart from Craiglockhart College (*see* Public Buildings, above), are provided by *James Gowans.* On the w side WAVERLEY at No. 82, designed in 1884 for the pen-maker Duncan Cameron. Symmetrical front, with massive central pediment and set-back dormers, subdivided and extended *c.* 1970. To the N, with an obvious family resemblance, the heavily pedimented terrace of Nos. 68–78, of which Nos. 68 and 70 are dated 1886 on the rear bargeboards. The smaller and plainer pair at Nos. 64–66 are probably the model dwellings for four workmen's families built at the 1886 Edinburgh Exhibition and re-erected as a double house in 1887. On the E side, two semi-detached blocks at the entry of LOCKHARTON GARDENS. Nos. 1 and 2 ponderous, with massive dormers over plain, smooth bows. Nos. 3 and 4 dated 1884, in a polite version of Gowans's stick-style, with linked porches. Nos. 157–159 Colinton Road are still less aggressive in the same manner.

CRAIGMILLAR

All this was gently rolling countryside, with a couple of small industrial pockets, till 1930, when the N part (the Niddrie estate) became a receptacle for families cleared from the slums of St Leonards.

CHURCHES

BRISTO MEMORIAL CHURCH, Peffermill Road. By *J. Inch Morrison,* 1904. A rubbly gable facing the street, with simplified Gothic windows.

NEWCRAIGHALL CHURCH, Newcraighall Road. Gothic, by

Henry Hardy, 1876. Stark yellow brick with red stripes, lanceted and gableted.

RICHMOND CRAIGMILLAR CHURCH, Niddrie Mains Road and Wauchope Road. Mixed Italian and Romanesque in pale rubble, by *Reid & Forbes*, 1934. Cruciform, with a canted chancel and sticking up w gable.

ROBIN CHAPEL (Interdenominational) at the Thistle Foundation in Niddrie Mains Road (*see* Public Buildings, below). By *John F. Matthew*, 1950–3, in snecked Doddington stone and Ballachulish slates, as a memorial to Robin Tudsbery, killed in the war in 1945. A broad w front with three entrance arches. Over them in the gable a cross-shaped window formed of thin radiating stones. Oblong N tower, rounded to the N and crowstepped to the S, with a high door and balcony overlooking the court. The interior ingeniously collegiate in plan; three-bayed aisles at the W end only, the capitals carved by *Maxwell Allan*. Plaster tunnel-vault with painted bosses, an inscription ('So long Thy power hath blest me ...') below the cornice. The FURNISHINGS were commissioned with considerable taste. – ALTAR of creamy Italian marble, matching the squared floor. – Sheffield plate CANDLESTICKS, pottery VASES by *Lydia Barge* of the Glasgow School of Art. – CANDELABRA and eagle LECTERN of wrought iron by *James Finnegan*. – FONT in N aisle, a replica of the font at the Old Church, Chelsea. – Oak CHOIR STALLS with animal ends by *Thomas Good*, Edinburgh. – STAINED GLASS. At the E end (the young soldier borne up to God) and nine other windows (the Pilgrim's Progress), all by *Sadie McLennan*.

ST ANDREW (formerly Episcopal, now in secular use), Newcraighall Road. Lanceted Gothic, by *John Robertson* of Inverness, 1900. Economical in construction (brick covered with fake cement masonry) but not in its eccentric plan. Baptistery adjoining w end, NE chapel and NW porch with tall candle-snuffered turret – all circular, to liven it up.

ST ANDREW AND ST AIDAN (Episcopal), Hay Drive. By *Dick Peddie & Walker Todd*, 1935. Harl and salmon-pink sandstone, Gothic in form but not in detail. A pair of gables make a sort of transept on each flank, each divided by a mullion and transom forming a cross. HALL to the E with tall dormered windows, beautifully simple like a harled Highland kirk.

ST TERESA (R.C.), Niddrie Mains Road. A pebbledashed, expressionist octagon by *Charles W. Gray*, 1963. Shallow-pitch gables, green copper roof and central flèche bearing a cross. Priest's house adjoining.

CRAIGMILLAR CASTLE

60 Like all the most enjoyable ruins, Craigmillar is instructively complete and picturesquely placed. The setting, still tenuously rural despite encirclement by council housing, is excellent militarily as well as scenically. To the N is a clear view

of gradually shelving ground, and below the s walls protrudes the rock face that gives the castle part of its name. All but the latest work is due to the Preston family, who acquired the barony in 1374 and who later presented St Giles's armbone to Edinburgh's parish church. In 1544 Craigmillar was looted and burned after its surrender to the English invasion force. From the late C15 to the early C17 there are references to the use of the castle by the Crown. The property was bought in 1660 by Sir John Gilmour, later President of the Court of Session, and the Gilmours lived here until the late C18, when they moved to the Inch (*see* Gilmerton: Mansions, below).

The core of the castle visually and historically is the late C15 L-plan TOWER HOUSE, with its ground-floor entrance in the small s jamb, covered by a single gun loop. Access from the s was hindered by a steep drop of 11 m. and by a wide cleft cut into the rock; the N approach involved passing close to at least two sides of the tower. Both plan and siting owe an obvious debt to the great tower (David's Tower) added to Edinburgh Castle from 1362, which for two centuries was the most conspicuous landmark in the view from Craigmillar. The severe general impression is due largely to the plainness of the wall-head. Parapets flush with the wall below, simple embrasures and water spouts. Original openings rectangular and chamfered. Over the round entrance arch a panel carved with the Preston arms. The tunnel-vaulted lobby within has had, at mid-height, a floor that would have made a good vantagepoint for dropping missiles on to intruders. On the l. a door into a barrel-vaulted basement also formerly subdivided by a wooden floor. Partition walls were inserted later, possibly when the windows in the end walls became doors connecting with the adjoining wings. The upper basement room was entered originally from the space over the entrance lobby.

Straight ahead in the lobby is the door to the turnpike, its arch low enough to force any sizeable assailant to stoop. The first exit from the stair is an inconvenient one to the room over the lobby. A few steps on, the stair suddenly changes direction, a device to surprise intruders, no doubt, though the stonework looks too chaotic to be homogeneous. Emerging into another lobby made shapeless by the intrusion of a stair to the C16 E extensions, one has the choice of going on upwards (with another change of direction in the spiral) or into the HALL. Lacking its beamed ceiling, this room is open to the barrel-vault covering the third floor and carrying the roof. The corbels for the ceiling joists have been painted with a pattern of diamonds. A splendidly ample fireplace takes up most of the w wall. The sloping hood and coupled jamb shafts recall the fireplaces at Borthwick Castle, Lothian (*c.* 1430), though the coarse mouldings here suggest a greater distance from French prototypes. In fact, the detailing is sufficiently diagnostic of mid- to late-C15 date to dispose of the usual dating of the tower to *c.* 1374. To the r. a door contemporary

with the fireplace opens into the C17 W range but must originally have led to a privy. L. of the fireplace a plain shield, re-
set in the N wall part of another, with fleur-de-lys and English
leopards, found in the SE curtain tower. Wide segment-
headed embrasures with seats whose outer limits mark the
position of the original window walls. Openings enlarged in
the C16 for fixed glazing above folding shutters. Off the S
window a small mural chamber – a C15 snug? The now demolished C15 tower house of Elphinstone, Lothian, whose walls
were honeycombed to an exceptional degree, had three such
rooms. A larger space hollowed out of the NE corner may
have been for secure storage of tableware. The original
kitchen is in the jamb, its wide fireplace contracted after ampler kitchens were added in the E wing. Queen Mary is supposed to have recuperated in this room after Rizzio's murder.
Two round-headed wall cupboards with provision for
shelves. The poorly-lit space over the hall was probably the
main bedroom. The room in the jamb at this level has S-
facing windows and a fireplace, and could have been the
Great Chamber where the laird and his family dined. At the
head of the turnpike a lobby gives on to the low-pitched slab
roof, now partly replaced in concrete. The other door in the
lobby leads to a cap-house of a type added to other C15 towers
in the early C16 (e.g. Newark near Selkirk). Crowstepped
gables, the E one with two windows flanking the kitchen chimney stack. The larger opening commands the main entrance.
Fireplace in the S wall.

Craigmillar's most memorable feature is its rectangular
CURTAIN. Relatively low, it surrounds the tower house on
three sides and joins on to its S angles. Unlike simple
barmkins, it is backed by more or less continuous ranges of
building. The deceptively powerful impression it gives externally is due to the survival of all four towers and most of the
machicolations. The early C15 dating usually given is based
on an early C19 record* that the date 1427 was inscribed on
the panel with the Preston arms over the main N entrance. If
this ever existed, it is not visible now. On the top of the
frame, however, the date 1508 in arabic numerals appears
between a coronet and a now featureless disc. If 1508 is the
date of building, it robs the curtain of its status as a pioneer-
ing work of artillery fortification in Scotland, putting it about
fifty years behind James II's Ravenscraig Castle in Fife. On
the bottom of the frame the somewhat otiose legend CRAG-
MYLLOR. Royal arms on the merlon above. The wide round
entrance arch looks vulnerable but there may originally have
been guardrooms, portcullis etc. behind. The small blocked
windows lit a range of building extending the full length of
the N curtain. Near the NE tower a water trough rather high
up connects with the kitchens in the E range. Here and on the
E curtain the machicolations project far enough to leave room

---

* A. Nisbet, *A System of Heraldry* (Edinburgh, 1816).

for a broad wall-walk. Some of the merlons have fancy gun loops such as one usually associates with the late C16 (three holes, a trefoil, holes framed by letters). The NE tower faced directly the main approach and is well equipped with ground-floor gunports of the inverted keyhole type used in SE English town defences from c. 1380 and at Ravenscraig c. 1460. The round openings higher up in this and two other towers would be for handguns. In the E curtain a plain door leads out to the chapel. Over it a panel with the Preston arms and the initials SP (for Simon Preston). These and the letter S inlaid in a stone to the r. confirm the 1508 date for the curtain. In the SE tower three more inverted keyhole loops. Its W face is flattened to accommodate the postern. Within the parapet, stairs lead to an upper battlement such as existed on the other curtain towers. A wall-walk much lower than the machicolations of the SE tower ends at a much corbelled oriel-cum-bretasche. W of the tower house is a blocked arch that must have given access to the tower entrance via a dis-mountable wooden stair set in the man-made cleft in the rock face. The blocking is probably later C17 and was carried, according to MacGibbon and Ross, on timber beams before the present arch was built. W of the cleft a projecting privy. The main defence of the S approach was a projecting timber gallery or hoarding whose joist and roof corbels and access doors remain. The curtain here is well in advance of the S side of the tower house and has had a S extension of some kind. The SW tower has simpler machicolations than the others, but their modest projection echoes the SE tower. The machicolations of the W curtain were replaced by dormers and chimneys in 1661. Large windows, heavily barred, look out on to a walled garden. From here a stair (formerly with a late C17 balustrade) descended S to a pleasance incorporat-ing a pond in the shape of the letter P. Some of the S curtain has as yet escaped the deadening recessed pointing and pebbly mortar universally prescribed for Ancient Monuments in state care.

A door by the NW tower leads to the irregular OUTER COURT. Over the outer face a re-set panel of the Preston arms between a rebus (a press and a tun) and the date 1510 or 1570 (the third digit has been tampered with). The walls of the outer court are usually dated after the sack of 1544. The N wall is broken by an E-facing entrance arch. The barn-like building filling the W side of the court housed a Presbyterian congregation in 1687. At the NE corner of the court is a round tower with unobtrusively placed wide-mouthed gunloops. The upper floor was a doocot. A conical roof is shown in an engraving of 1788. From here the wall runs S to enclose a second garden and the small early C16 CHAPEL. Crowstepped gables, no buttresses and no N windows. The chancel has one straight-headed two-lighter, the nave one rectangular window and a plain door under an image niche. Oculus high up in the N wall. Inside, traces of a screen and holes for fixing the retable to the E wall. There is a straight joint between the NW corner and the wall of the outer court that continues almost to the NE tower. Behind this wall has been a well and an upper floor. The purpose of the round window is unexplained.

The COURTYARD BUILDINGS within the curtain represent a vast improvement on the services and private rooms available in the tower house. It is perhaps not going too far to see the curtain itself as a by-product of this typically late medieval quest for comfort. Most of the ranges added E and W of the tower are later than the curtain, but it seems likely that the existing arrangement of kitchen quarters off the 'low' end of the hall and private rooms off the high-table end was intended from the start. Probably contemporary with the curtain are the tunnel-vaulted cellars extending from the tower house to the middle of the E range. The room nearest the tower has a ceiling hatch and a later bread oven contrived under the turnpike. The window seats in the ground-floor rooms behind the S curtain must indicate a domestic function before their inclusion in the kitchen area. The rest of the SE and E ranges was rebuilt at one go – in the late C16, to judge from the door next to the tower. Straight head, bold mouldings stopped high up on the jambs. The only other ornament is the Preston achievement between first and second floors. The pediment with the initials of Dame Margaret Cockburn, wife of Sir John Gilmour, does not belong here, and late C19 photographs show it above one of the 1661 windows at the N end of the W range. A plain door on the l. leads to the cellarage. Immediately inside the main door, on the l., a straight stair mounts to the kitchens. The broad easy turnpike farther in connects the storage floors in the tower basement and the ground floor of the SE range, and the passage-like servery linked to the kitchen by a door and two hatches. The kitchen, like all the rooms in the E range, is barrel-vaulted. The second floor has a spacious room with a fireplace and an oriel next to the tower house. Earlier buildings against the curtain have left a single roof-line on the tower. This room and those in the attic of the E range may have been bedrooms.

Beside the blocked S entrance to the curtain is a small lean-to entered directly from the court and provided with a privy commanding views of the S approach as well as a proper window with seats. It may have been a porter's lodge. Next to the door a stray bit of a rectangular multi-light Late Gothic window. The W range was remodelled in 1661 by Sir John Gilmour, leaving an earlier cellar at the S end, a Late Gothic fireplace in the room above (which could have been the 1508 Great Chamber) and most of a late C16 or early C17 mullion-and-transom window in the E wall. The passage to the tower house seems to be Gilmour's, doubtless succeeding an earlier link. His certainly is the adjoining stair, which allowed one to by-pass the tower. Canted entrance with rather thin pediment and modern date stone. The N ground-floor room was Gilmour's kitchen: see the big fireplace with rather gross roll mouldings. The dining room (?) to the s has been the best-appointed room in the w range. Two big windows with segment-headed rear arches flank a wide fireplace with simple panels and a shield on the lintel. The N range has left many traces on the N curtain but none on the E and w ranges, so it must have been pulled down by the later C16. If it was timber it may not have been rebuilt after the 1544 sack. There seem to be two periods of openings, the later going with a low rectangular door built into the N entrance arch and removed fairly recently. Two spectacularly contorted pines provide a welcome foil to the manicured rubble of the court.

PUBLIC BUILDINGS

JACK KANE COMMUNITY AND SPORTS CENTRE in the public park of the Niddrie Policies, Niddrie Mains Road. By the City Architect *Brian Annable*, 1973–5. A near-abstract group of halls, windowless in most views, elegantly composed on the rising grassland and built of pale grey blockwork with projecting triangular eaves. These are related to the triangular steel grid of the roof construction, which is most notably visible in the huge main hall.

SCHOOLS. A large number, best listed together. The earliest is NIDDRIE MAINS PRIMARY at the E end of Niddrie Mains Road. Symmetrical red-brick Renaissance with a lantern, by *Robert Wilson*, 1894. In front, a Celtic cross MEMORIAL to General Wauchope of Niddrie, designed by *T. T. Paterson* and carved in pink Corrennie granite by *William Beveridge*, 1900. Then NEWCRAIGHALL PRIMARY to the E of the village. Two elegantly linked red sandstone gables by *A. Murray Hardie*, 1905. A series of schools by the City Architect *E. J. MacRae* begins with what is now the COMMUNITY CENTRE in Niddrie Mains Terrace, mildly Classical with red brick and tiles, 1932. ADVENTURE PLAYGROUND nearby, incorporating a disused post-war church, appropriately fortress-like. For the new mass settlements MacRae used the common formula of a long symmetrical two-storey range, economical but decently varied. CRAIGMILLAR PRIMARY in Harewood Road, 1936, and ST FRANCIS R.C. PRIMARY in Niddrie Mains Road, 1937, have wings slightly canted forward. PEFFERMILL in Craigmillar Castle Avenue, 1938, is straight-fronted with an old-fashioned central lantern. The surprise is CASTLEBRAE HIGH (JUNIOR) in Harewood Road, by *Reid & Forbes*, 1937. Large and very flashy International Modern, well built in harl and concrete with horizontally emphasized windows and a central tower of Art Deco profile and ornament. The best post-war school is the GREENDYKES CHILDREN'S CENTRE, Craigmillar Castle Avenue, civilized buff brick by *Alan Reiach & Partners*, 1967. GREENDYKES PRIMARY in Greendykes Road by the *City Architect's Department*, 1969, is admirably simple, with piend roofs over big windows, but spoiled by extension. CASTLEBRAE HIGH on the other side is of bigger scale in grey blockwork by *Glen Gibb*, 1972. The PEFFERBANK ADVANCED TRAINING CENTRE, Duddingston Road West, is by *John D. Robertson*, 1980. Well detailed red brick, not at all institutional.

THISTLE FOUNDATION, Craigmillar Castle Avenue. For the Robin Chapel, whose crowstepped tower is a minor landmark, *see* Churches, above. It is the centrepiece of the community village by *Stuart R. Matthew*, 1947, for disabled people and their families. Terraced cottages with tiled roofs and shaped dormers lining a long grassy court. To the s a fan-shaped layout of similar cottages, all linked together by covered ways with ramps at the gradients. Self-opening doors at the entry to the central clinic and other communal buildings. Hostel for single people, with a common room lit from the clearstorey of an eccentric laminated timber roof, by *Robert Rogerson*, 1969.

MANSIONS

NIDDRIE MARISCHAL HOUSE. A small fragment among the new flats of Niddrie Mains Drive. The house (demolished) lay immediately to the E. This is on the site of a chapel built to the Virgin Mary in 1502. (The vaulted interior incorporates some fragments of it, according to RCAHMS.) The front has a rusticated and pedimented central arch between keystoned niches. Set in the pavement, a tablet inscribed 'This Pavilion is Found[ed] by Andrew Waucho[pe] of Niddrie Esqr the 8th day of October 1735 years'.

PEFFERMILL HOUSE, Peffermill Road. L-plan, built for Edward Edgar and dated 1636 on the long NW side. Semi-dormered second floor above a string course, with elaborate pediments. The three wall sundials supported on cherubs' heads are very similar to those of George Heriot's School (*see* Old Town: Public Buildings). In the angle a circular string-coursed stair-turret with moulded and heraldically pedimented doorway to the wide turnpike stair. Next to it, the corbelled chimney of the first-floor HALL. This has been repeatedly altered, but the fireplace lintel and some stone corbels and wall-plates on this level were revealed in the restoration by *Nicholas Groves-Raines*, which started in 1980. Beyond the hall, a fragment of C17 decorative WALL PAINTING of big red flowers over a trompe-l'œil masonry dado. The room in the jamb has two stone-framed cupboards.

DESCRIPTION

In the s part of Craigmillar a green wedge of farmland provides a setting for Craigmillar Castle (*see* above). Its s boundary is OLD DALKEITH ROAD (A68), which has a messy start and then becomes passably rural. The long row of single-storey BRIDGEND COTTAGES at the Braid Burn leads up to the picturesque rubble walls and red pantile roofs of the late C18 BRIDGEND FARM. Then a continuous estate wall (but with some unfortunate breaches, 1984) to the grey early C19 farm buildings at Little France, and on to the late C18 quadrant gateway of Edmonstone House (the house itself demolished). For the S side of the road, *see* Gilmerton. The wall then turns N along The Wisp, which marks the city boundary, to the pink brick mid-C19 CLOVERFOOT COTTAGES.

In the N part an equally long grey wedge of local-authority housing was pushed out to the E on the axis of an unremarkable main road which starts at the C17 Peffermill House (*see* above). This part of PEFFERMILL ROAD has little else except the HEALTHY LIFE BISCUIT FACTORY to the S by *Alan L. Goodwin*, 1935, and to the N a panorama of DRYBROUGH'S BREWERY, incorporating a mid-C19 warehouse and the former Blyth & Cameron Brewery with red sandstone trimmings fronting Duddingston Road West, by *Peter L. Henderson*, 1897. The route continues as NIDDRIE MAINS ROAD, whose W part makes a brave attempt to be a street. Its little shops are helped by the WHITE HOUSE, a cockeyed Art Deco roadhouse in white plaster by *Patterson & Broom*, 1936–8, in hopes of a cocktail clientele. Wauchope Avenue to the N has a kindred building, the former REGAL CINEMA by *T. Bowhill Gibson*, 1934 (now the County, but disused), with a square, slit-windowed frontage above the entrance canopy. On a hummock to the S, along Craigmillar Castle Avenue, the oasis of the THISTLE FOUNDATION (*see* Public Buildings, above).

For the scattering of churches and public buildings, *see* above. The main thing is HOUSING and it happened as follows, taking most of its street-names from the demolished C17–19 mansion of Niddrie Marischal and its owners the Wauchopes. All is by the *City Architect's Department*, all perfectly acceptable by the standards of its time, but hopelessly deprived of urban amenities (save churches and schools) from the start. The substantial three-storey blocks to the N of Niddrie Mains Road, either harled with classical trimmings or smooth-rendered minimal Art Deco, were built in 1930–4 and completed with the basically similar Niddrie Mill development at the E end in 1957. To the S the Craigmillar Castle houses were built in 1937–8 and those with Niddrie Marischal addresses (to a smaller scale) from 1950. The Greendykes flats, with their stark horizontal bands, followed in 1964 and those of Niddrie Marischal with their bleakly picturesque mono-pitch roofs in 1968. The two tower-blocks here and two more at Craigmillar Castle Gardens (intrusive in the view from Duddingston) are of the same generation.

The last part of the axis is NEWCRAIGHALL ROAD which begins with the East Duddingston *Miller* development to the N, the Castle Park *Barratt* scheme to the S. Both were built in 1981. QUARRY COTTAGES and NIDDRY COTTAGES are nice rows of *c.* 1880, built with pink bricks from the still flourishing NIDDRIE BRICKWORKS further on to the s. The former St Andrew's Church (*see* above) is also brick-built under fake masonry. The colliery of NEWCRAIGHALL is now defunct, leaving a huge black waste-bing and to the s (just before the railway) the PITHEAD BATHS of simple geometric design in brick by *James Benzies*, 1936 (derelict 1984). Of the formally planned colliers' village only the N edge survives (1984), a good row of rubble and rendered cottages. To the s of the road the *Scottish Special Housing Association* redevelopment of neat two-storey houses is nearly complete; for the Victorian church and Edwardian school, *see* above. The NEWCRAIGHALL MINERS WELFARE SOCIETY to the s is polite but very old-fashioned with red stone trimmings, by *Alexander Allan*, 1925.

CRAMOND AND DAVIDSON'S MAINS

Two villages tenuously linked by villas. Cramond, a mill and harbour settlement, has the authentic Colour Supplement village appearance; Davidson's Mains, despite an 1827 attempt to make the old hamlet of Muttonholes into a miniature 'New Town', only a hangdog core. The railway's arrival in 1894 brought villadom and villa-dwellers, the plushest grouped round the golf courses laid out on the Barnton estate. Silverknowes Farm, cut off from the best golf by Lauriston Castle estate, was divided into two parcels in the 1920s, one sold to the City, the other to the builders *Mactaggart & Mickel*. Tightknit development followed, the City's layout more spacious, the private housing more varied. The large villas and gardens on the w are now giving way to flats and small houses.

CRAMOND ROMAN FORT. Excavation in 1954–66 revealed parts of the *principia* (on which the church stands), workshops and *horrea* (granaries) and showed the outline of the fort; part of the interior is landscaped to show the surviving remains of the rampart and the layout of the buildings. The finds are in the National Museum of Antiquities of Scotland and Huntly House Museum, Edinburgh. *See* Introduction, pp. 30–1.

CHURCHES

CRAMOND PARISH CHURCH, Cramond Glebe Road. A rubbly, cruciform kirk with early C19 flat Gothic windows. Basically 1656, on the site of the medieval church, which had become ruinous. The C15 tower of two plain stages still stands at the w end, and likewise the Cramond vault at the E, with stone-slabbed roof and smooth ashlar walls on a chamfered base-course. The new church had aisles, sited like transepts, but the N aisle was widened to the w in 1701 and then lengthened in 1911 by *James Mather* so as to form a nave. The S aisle was lengthened to form the Barnton vault in 1701, then widened and given a tiny castellated porch by *Robert Burn* in 1811; a century later it was heightened and became the chancel. Further C19 alterations by *William Burn* in 1828, *Robert Bell* in 1843, *David Bryce* in 1851 and 1868. The inside is virtually all of 1911, the four limbs of the cross uniformly galleried and roofed with pitchpine hammerbeams. Bland oak furnishings, except for the FONT, *c.* 1900, a white marble pedestal with cherubs' heads. – MONUMENT on the E wall. A marble portrait bust, in a cartouche, of Lord James Hope †1670, chief benefactor of the new church. – ORGAN by *Norman & Beard*, 1911. – STAINED GLASS. Mercifully unattributed except for two lights under the W gallery, one (Peace) by *Alexander Strachan*, 1939, and one (Christ and children) by the *Abbey Studio* after 1928. – MONUMENTS in the churchyard. A nice intermingling of type and date, many of the earlier headstones set firmly in moulded bases. – On the S wall a large slab to George Sheiell † 1687. – Nearby, an indecipherable early C18 headstone with mermaid-like caryatids. – To the S a massive pedestal with pretty drapery and a swagged vase, 1762, and an iron obelisk to Andrew Reoch †1854, engineer in Demerara. – To the S an unnamed early C18 headstone with cumbrous draperies, two weepers and a tree, 'repaired by *Robert Haig & Sons*, Upper Cramond, 1827'. – To the E a sluggish rococo headstone to George Wright, dated 1742. – On the E wall a pedimented marble monument to William Davidson of Muirhouse †1794 in a Batty Langley Gothic enclosure; and a mural slab inscribed to one side

> HEIR·LYIS·IOHN·STAL
> KER·OF·EASTER·DRY-
> LAW·AN·TRUE·AND
> LIVELY·PATERNE·OF
> PIETY·AND·PROBITY
> WHA·DIED·6·FEBR
> AET·60·AN·DO·1608·

Above it a starkly simplified pediment inscribed with the attributes of death and some remarkably good Trajanic lettering. Of three crowning obelisks the middle one has a grinning skull.

DAVIDSON'S MAINS PARISH CHURCH, Quality Street. Originally Cramond Free Church. A small T-plan kirk with flat Gothic windows, by *David Cousin*, 1843. The timber bellcote with a prickly slated hat that was added to the centre (s) gable in 1866. Featureless interior enlarged to the N in 1970. To the E, the little school and house by *Robert R. Raeburn*, 1845-6, were extended with a HALL by *Auldjo Jamieson & Arnott*, 1933, maintaining the domestic scale by means of a dormered roof.

HOLY CROSS (Episcopal), Quality Street. Simple Romanesque

by *J. M. Dick Peddie*, 1912. Cruciform, of natural-faced stone with large brown slates, the chancel eaves slightly lower than the rest. Inside, four chamfered arches at the crossing, all with scissor-braced roofs, the E roof of the S transept (next to the vestry) resting on heavy corbels. – STAINED GLASS. In the E chancel wall three lights with delicate old-fashioned drawing on a clear ground (the Nativity) by *Christopher Webb*, 1930.

ST MARGARET (R.C.), Main Street, Davidson's Mains. By *Peter Whiston*, 1950. A tall triangular prism, excellently detailed, lit from the S gable, which faces the street.

PUBLIC BUILDINGS

BRUNTSFIELD GOLF CLUB, Garden Terrace. Dated 1898. Subdued cottage style.

CARGILFIELD SCHOOL, Gamekeeper's Road. Large and stylish English picturesque by *Peddie & Washington Browne*, 1899. Asymmetrical tile-hung U-plan front with half-timbering and big Venetian windows. – LIBRARY-CHAPEL behind, a pallid version of the original style by *E. A. O. Auldjo Jamieson*, 1923.

CRAMOND INFANT SCHOOL, Whitehouse Road. By *E. E. Pearson*, 1913–14.

CRAMOND OLD BRIDGE, Brae Park Road. *c.* 1500, heavily repaired in 1617–19, and again by *Robert Mylne*, 1687–91. Further repairs 1761, 1776 and 1854. Three obtusely pointed arches with a string course jumping over them. Heavy triangular cutwaters.

CRAMOND PRIMARY SCHOOL, Cramond Crescent. By *David Carr*, 1967–71; extended, 1974. Self-effacing, with a prominent boiler chimney.

DAVIDSON'S MAINS PRIMARY SCHOOL, Corbiehill Road. By the *City Architect's Department*, 1965–6.

DUNFERMLINE COLLEGE OF PHYSICAL EDUCATION, Cramond Road North. By *Robert Matthew, Johnson-Marshall & Partners* (partner-in-charge: *T. R. Spaven*), 1964–6; extended, 1972. Sensible but unexciting, with harled and slate-hung walls.

ROYAL BURGESS GOLF CLUB, Whitehouse Road. By *R. M. Cameron*, 1896–7. Best Jacobean in harl and half-timber.

ROYAL HIGH SCHOOL, East Barnton Avenue. By *Reid & Forbes*, 1964–8. Four-storey brick main building, just like a decent office block. Additions by *J. D. Cairns & Ford*, 1973.

SILVERKNOWES GOLF CLUB, Silverknowes Parkway. By *Alan Reiach & Partners*, 1962. Low and rambling, with large windows taking in the view over the course.

SILVERKNOWES PRIMARY SCHOOL, Silverknowes Eastway. By the *City Architect's Department*, 1957–9, in the Festival of Britain style.

MANSIONS

CRAMOND HOUSE, Cramond Glebe Road. Built for the family of Inglis of Cramond. The original house, a harled double pile of *c.*1680 with crowstep gables and moulded eaves course, was probably entered at the E end. Here, a symmetrical nine-bay range was added *c.*1760 to form a T plan. One grand storey over a basement, the centre advanced and pedimented, all in polished ashlar with tall arched and keyblocked windows. The square balusters of the spreading stair to the centre door were added *c.*1850 along with the Jacobean screen wall and belfry, these at least by *William Burn*. The T became an H in 1818, when *Charles Black* added the W range with a central bow.

The principal rooms are all of *c.*1760. Square entrance hall with a coved ceiling. On the S, drawing room with a modillion cornice and shell and foliage frieze; on the N, dining room with a mutule cornice, but the chimneypieces *c.*1850. Vaulted basement.

Large WALLED GARDEN to the S with much brick-facing.

CRAMOND TOWER, off Cramond Glebe Road. A small late medieval tower house, part of a residence of the Bishops of Dunkeld. Repairs are recorded in 1507, though not specifically to the tower. Four storeys, the wall-head rawly curtailed. At the SE corner is a rounded stair projection with two loops, one covering the ground-floor entrance. This is round-arched with two chamfered orders, the outer one partly cut away to take a rectangular flush door. Later additions to the other sides have long since disappeared, leaving tuskings of a wall extending S in a line with the E side. Parts of the foundations of an E extension were exposed at the time of writing (1981). On the N side two long openings, now blocked. The ground floor is lit by a small window over the door. The larger windows on the next two levels acquired square-paned sashes on the conversion to domestic use by *Robert Hurd & Partners*, 1979. The inner arch of the entrance lobby is a depressed pointed arch. The ground floor is down five steps. Pointed tunnel-vault. On the first floor the S wall has a wide recess whose purpose may have been to give extra floor-space. The wall above is carried on timber lintels. The fireplace with a lintelled hood on corbels has been built into a larger one flush with the wall. The second floor has a fireplace with a segmental arched hood (cf. Dundas Old Castle, Lothian). Window seats in the S wall, a garderobe within the E wall. As so often, the uppermost floor is ill-lit and barrel-vaulted. Unusually, the axis of the vault is at right angles to the basement. (The National Monuments Record for Scotland has photographs of late medieval wall painting found in 1979.)

LAURISTON CASTLE, Cramond Road South. A late C16 tower [71] with large early C19 additions and a mostly Edwardian interior. The house and contents were left to the nation in 1926 and are now looked after by Edinburgh District Council.

The castle of the Lauristons of that Ilk was burned by the Earl of Hertford in 1544. *c.* 1590 the lands were bought by Sir Archibald Napier of Edenbellie and Merchiston, apparently as an estate for the eldest son of his second marriage, and soon afterwards a new tower house was built w of the derelict tower. Napier's T-plan house is the w accent of the present mansion. Four-storey main block with a stair-tower at the back. s front with two-storey corner turrets decorated with gun loops. Their curvaceous tall roofs are by *William Burn*, 1827. Window in the w turret with a boldly projecting sill, perhaps for a lantern. Huge wall-head chimney flanked by pedimented dormer-heads, one with the initials D.E.M. for Dame Elizabeth Mowbray, Napier's wife, the other an 1856 replacement of a stone with Napier's initials. Off-centre door, very old-fashioned if it was made *c.* 1650 by Robert Dalgleish (the Napiers' successor at Lauriston), who erected a tablet above it to record how he owed his wealth to God, not the stars. To its l. a tablet (*c.* 1610) inscribed with Sir Alexander Napier's horoscope, found in the grounds and put up here *c.* 1905. Between the tablets, a space for a third. More dormer-heads flanking the stair-tower. One has a segmental pediment with Dalgleish's arms.

In 1827 *William Burn* designed suave Jacobean extensions for Thomas Allan. Extending E of the tower's s front are a gabled entrance hall and a three-bay dining room whose dormer pediments are large editions of Napier's. Then, a low coach-house and stable court. Burn's N range extends across that face of the tower. Broad two-storey bay-windows linked by a balcony. Screen wall hiding the stable court; broad-eaved octagonal tower as an E stop. Later owners have tampered with Burn's elevations but not improved them. Gabled porches on the s and w, by *W. H. Playfair*, 1845. Library built above the N screen wall, 1872, when the panel carved with the Crawfurd arms was inserted.* In 1927 an over-emphatic CURATOR'S HOUSE was added by *E. J. MacRae* to the E end of the stable court.

The interior is a mixture of Burn and *William R. Reid*, who bought the house in 1903. Entrance hall by *Burn* with a straight flight of stone stairs to the *piano nobile*. Armorial stained glass in the doors at the top, *c.* 1872. Top-lit inner hall with a small Frenchy chimneypiece, also by Burn. On the r., dining room by *Reid*. Oak-grained plaster panelling, Wrenaissance but with swagged urns over the doors. Inset C17 Brussels tapestries, the largest signed by *H. Reydams*. Grisaille painting of putti by *Jacob van Strij* in the overmantel. Arts and Crafts chimneypiece with a Spanish embroidery frieze. Corridor with C16–17 painted glass leading to the wooden-ceiled library, again altered by Reid with a Holyrood-style chimneypiece.

Burn's sitting room and drawing room are *en suite*. Heavy

---

* Brought from Cartsburn, Greenock.

compartmented drawing-room ceiling with a shallow dome. The Adam-revival chimneypieces are by Reid, who also added Ionic pilasters on the walls and carved panels over the doors. Another Adam-revival chimneypiece in the adjoining bedroom. Off it, a magnificent bathroom, c. 1905; the plumbers were *William Barton & Sons*. S of the inner hall, the Oak Room, the C16 hall. Reid gave it a thin Jacobean ceiling and wooden chimneypiece incorporating a carved panel dated 1616. Behind a shutter of the W window, tiny stair to a room above which had a 'laird's lug' into the hall. Narrow service room on the W with a stair to the ground floor. The tower's upper rooms all done by Reid with Holyrood-type chimneypieces. Under Burn's sitting room, a ground-floor room (perhaps the boudoir) with Watteauesque paintings of c. 1840 on the window ingoes, perhaps by *D. R. Hay* (cf. Mortonhall House, Blackford and Liberton).

Broad-eaved LODGE, by *Playfair*, 1846, on the approach. – Beside it, a pair of SPHINXES flanking the drive. – Overlooking the pond, bronze STATUE ('Diane') by *J.-A.-J. Falguière*. – On the S lawn, multi-faceted SUNDIAL dated 1684, on a late C19 pillar. – To the W, two Doric COLUMNS. – NE of the house, late C19 GREENHOUSE with thistle cresting. – Nearby, bargeboarded DAIRY (now lavatories), c. 1860. – On its SE, GARDEN STORES, c. 1845, in a small courtyard whose GATE-PIERS are topped by heraldic lions. – In woodland to the S, WELL, rebuilt c. 1930, with two dormer-heads from Cartsburn, one inscribed 'TC.IS' (for Thomas Crawfurd and his wife Jean Semple), the other '1672', the strapwork decoration surprising for that date.

PERAMBULATIONS

1. Barnton

The BARNTON HOTEL on the corner of QUEENSFERRY ROAD and Whitehouse Road is by *George A. Lyle*, 1895, almost fun with a pagoda tower. *See* above for the Royal Burgess Golf Club in WHITEHOUSE ROAD, from whose S end BRAEHEAD ROAD leads to ALMOND COURT, red-brick flats decorated with concrete, by *T. Boland & Co.*, 1956. The crowstepped BRAEHEAD HOUSE, c. 1700, at the end of BRAEHEAD DRIVE, has sad baronial additions of c. 1890 at one end and GATE-PIERS topped by obelisks of heaped-up stones. On the W side of Whitehouse Road, THE WHITEHOUSE, perhaps begun c. 1615 (the date on a stone, not *in situ*) as a plain L-plan laird's house with a stair-tower in the re-entrant and a second stair at the SW corner. It was extended N and S in the C18; in 1895–1901 *MacGibbon & Ross* filled in the corner between the jamb and N extension and added bay-windows on the W. – In the garden, a baluster SUNDIAL dated 1732. – Stone PILLAR with JOUGS, and an ARCHWAY rebuilt here, *c.* 1900. In ESSEX ROAD, No. 4 (ALMONDALE), *c.* 1935, carefully composed neo-Georgian with ogee-roofed towers in the corners of the U-plan entrance front.

On the corner of BARNTON AVENUE WEST, Tudor GATE-PIERS to Barnton House (demolished) by *David Hamilton, c.* 1810; curved screen wall on N with round-arched arrow-slits. On the S side of the street, houses in variegated brick by *W. & J. R. Watson,* 1982. Then No. 10 (THE SHAWS), Arts and Crafts in flush-pointed rubble, *c.* 1914. No. 4 (ALMOND LODGE) by *James Miller* of Glasgow, 1939, heavy-handed asymmetrical neo-Georgian in brick.

BARNTON AVENUE across the golf courses is dry martini country. No. 53 (HARMONY) by *Dick Peddie & Walker Todd, c.* 1930, asymmetrical U-plan with tall dormer-heads and a diagonally set centre chimney. No. 46 (COTSWOLD), plump with pink harl and red-tiled roofs, dated 1903. Shaped dormer-heads and a cartouche over the door of No. 39 (WOODCROFT), dated 1909. No. 42 (WHITE LODGE), large, with half-timbering, is by *Hamilton-Paterson & Rhind,* 1900. The white-harled gables of No. 37 are no competition for those on No. 31, by *J. B. Dunn, c.* 1906, stopped against chimneys or curvaceously swept. In EASTER PARK DRIVE to the N, a barracks for senior executives by *Norman Collison Construction Group Ltd,* 1971, surrounding EASTER PARK, a beautifully detailed neo-Georgian villa by *William R. Reid,* 1905-6. Adamesque pilasters and rosettes on the frieze; a huge rosette instead of a centre window on the garden front. The main rooms, with Louis XV chimneypieces stirred into the neo-Adam mixture, survived the conversion into flats. On the approach, corniced GATE-PIERS with eagles. For Bruntsfield Golf Club, *see* above. No. 35 EAST BARNTON AVENUE, by *George Henderson,* 1901, was built as the Holy Cross parsonage; large quirky Tudor with a wavy-topped SE tower and a rustic balcony. Barnton Avenue's opulence ends with the large but plain No. 16 (BRACKENRIG). The red-tiled tall mansards of No. 6 (REDRIG) squeak a protest at the *petit bourgeois* sobriety of the road's late Victorian E end.

2. Cramond

In CRAMOND ROAD NORTH the GATES of Cramond House (*see* above), *c.* 1790, with a pedimented arch and outsize rosettes. On top of the pediment, a chimney for the LODGE's two rooms, one each side of the carriageway. Hiding in its garden, No. 12 (AVISFIELD) by *Morris & Steedman,* 1955, and extended by the same firm in 1964, its heavy stone chimney just the right contrast to its white-walled simplicity. For Dunfermline College of Physical Education, *see* above. On the bend of the road to the S, CRAMOND GREEN, pale brick terraced housing by *Philip Cocker Associates, c.* 1965. Opposite in THE GLEBE, two pairs of broad-eaved cottages. CRAMOND GLEBE ROAD goes down the hill to the N. On the r.

the drydashed CRAMOND GLEBE GARDENS by *Albert Thain Ltd*, 1972, followed by the large garden of CRAMOND MANSE, whose piend-roofed core of 1745 is swallowed up in cottagey additions by *David Bryce*, 1857, and a plain back wing of *c.* 1770. Then the Parish Church and Cramond House and Tower (*see* above). CRAMOND INN's pantiled N block was built in 1670, but its black-painted crowsteps were probably added in 1887, when it was given a jolly Queen Anne addition, dressed up with Rosemary tiles and crowsteps to show that it is Scottish. Crowstepped and pantiled E extension of 1977.

Across the street, the OLD SCHOOLHOUSE, designed and built by *James Robb*, mason, 1778, with its gable butting into the road, and No. 51 (BALNAGARROW), boxy Modern Movement by *James Miller*, 1936, announce CRAMOND VILLAGE. Parallel rows of late C18 housing along the steeply sloping brae to the Almond, their crisp white harl and black margins part of *Ian G. Lindsay & Partners'* facelift and evisceration of 1959–61. The tidy promenade which they overlook was provided in 1935. At its N end, a very discreet SEWAGE PUMPING STATION of 1951, with a flagpole on top. Upstream, an early C19 stone QUAY. Then the remains of the mills along the Almond. All were originally grain mills, converted to iron mills *c.* 1750–82. COCKLE MILL has an early C19 office range (now a house) with its own little harbour and millworkers' cottages (CADELL'S ROW). Roofless W forge and dramatic WEIR of *c.* 1800 at FAIR-A-FAR MILL. Only a bow-ended early C19 cottage at PEGGY'S MILL. A pair of pantiled cottages at DOWIE'S MILL.

3. Davidson's Mains and Silverknowes

QUALITY STREET begins with a couple of piend-roofed houses, outliers of *James Gillespie Graham's* scheme of 1827. The basic unit is a three-bay single-storey and basement flatted block with ground-floor tripartite windows. Semi-detached blocks at Nos. 11–27. Detail varies – mutuled cornice on Nos. 29–31; timber mullions at Nos. 7–9 and 29–31; stone mullions for the rest. The chamfered margins of Nos. 21–27 reveal that they were not built until *c.* 1855. Then plain terraces of *c.* 1890. For Holy Cross Episcopal Church opposite, *see* above. Beside it, a round WELL with a crenellated parapet, dated 1832. Its little dome is repeated on the GATE-PIERS to the demolished Barnton House. In CRAMOND ROAD SOUTH, the angular ROYAL BANK by *J. D. Cairns & Ford*, 1976, fails to hold the corner. After the shed of SAFEWAYS, Nos. 12–22, an orange-tiled Tudor terrace, *c.* 1914.

The S side of MAIN STREET begins promisingly with an early C19 house, mucked up by a protruding café extension but saved by its pilastered doorpiece. Then plain cottages. Opposite, an Artisan Art Nouveau pub (YE OLDE INN) and the CLYDESDALE BANK, by the *Waters Jamieson Partnership*,

1982, neo-vernacular to fit in but set back in case it does not. Another C19 cottage (No. 55), and the attempt to be a village is given up.

In CORBIEHILL PARK to the s, MARCHFIELD HOUSE, 1810–13 but looking fifty years earlier. Statue in a niche above the porch; round-arched attic windows in the large end chimneys. Mid-C19 crowstepped coach-house (MARCHFIELD LODGE) on the N.

SILVERKNOWES ROAD bisects the Silverknowes developments, council housing on the w, private on the E. Both sides are laid out in crescents but they avoid meeting to form circuses. No. 29 (SILVERKNOWES), c. 1840, with horizontal panes. At the N end, Silverknowes Golf Club (see above); in the middle of the course, dumpy baronial offices of SILVERKNOWE (demolished). In LAURISTON FARM ROAD, LAURISTON FARM, Tudor of c. 1840, with an octagonal horsemill in the steading.

DUDDINGSTON AND WILLOWBRAE

The A1 leads out of town, starting with the close-packed factories and tenements of London Road but soon emerging into multicoloured suburbia. Some of the best and worst of Edinburgh's local-authority housing lies back from the road. To the s is the almost unspoiled feudal ensemble of Duddingston – the village and kirk by the loch, the house in its park, all seen against the wilder terrain of Arthur's Seat and Whinny Hill.

CHURCHES

DUDDINGSTON PARISH CHURCH, Old Church Lane. The initial picture is of a spiky pinnacled C17 kirk with C18 Gothick windows, and it needs a second look to see the basic structure of a C12 two-cell church. Short chancel with clasping buttresses and original corbel tables on the side walls. The E gable has C17 crowsteps and pinnacles. Of the higher and wider nave, the s wall is the best preserved part. Norman buttresses overlaid by C17 ones define four bays. In the E bay a blocked lancet, in the w bay a richly decorated but much weathered Norman door. Chevron on the voussoirs, herringbone and lozenge patterns on the jamb shafts. On the l. shaft, tiny figure groups in relief. At the top are Christ Crucified in a long robe, a cockerel and another robed figure looking towards the cross and raising one arm (Peter's denial of Christ?). Lower down are a soldier holding an axe and sword with a monster at his feet, and another figure in a tunic and overmantle. The capitals have been quite ambitious but the designs are now impossible to make out properly. The stocky C17 w tower is plain apart from its lively cresting with obelisks and concave-sided pyramids. The N (Prestonfield) aisle has a blocked E doorway dated 1631 (the access stair now missing), and two N windows with crude loop tracery. Inside, the chancel arch has chevron on the outer order and billet on the hood-mould. The jambs have three half-shafts with scallop capitals. The chancel, with the galleried aisle and tower-space, are the limbs of the little T-plan kirk interior as formed by *R. Rowand Anderson* in 1889 and chastened in 1968, with furnishings by *Whytock & Reid*. The chancel was stripped of its plaster. – STAINED GLASS. On the S side one light to the l. of the pulpit (the Good Shepherd) and another to the r. (St Luke, in memory of the painter-minister John Thomson of Duddingston), both 1903 with the look of *Ballantine*. In the Prestonfield loft the two central lights (Christ and children) and a pair on each side (the works of Mercy) all by *Douglas Strachan, c.* 1935. – MONUMENTS in the churchyard. A good collection with some early C18 headstones and table-tops, but mostly later. On the S wall a strapworked and pedimented Ionic tabernacle to David Scott and his wife Margaret Gourley †1693. To the NW a Gothic tomb-chest to Isabella Ramsay, the first wife of John Thomson of Duddingston, †1809 and to Thomson himself †1840. It is signed by *David Ness*, but hard to date. Also an early C19 pyramid on a pedestal, its marble facing detached (1981) but elegantly carved with an urn, a low relief of a shipwreck and the signature of *A. Gowan*. It is dedicated to Patrick Haldane of Gleneagles by his grandson, who left £200 for the purpose.

To the E, adjoining the pyramid-topped gate-piers, an octagonal SESSION HOUSE cum watch-tower by *Robert Brown*, 1824. Round-arched windows, corbelled and battlemented parapet. Just outside, a stepped C17 LOUPIN-ON-STANE (platform for mounting a horse).

GUTHRIE MEMORIAL CHURCH, Easter Road. In secular use. By *Charles S. S. Johnston*, 1881. A big brother to its neighbour St Margaret's (*see* below). Gable with geometric tracery in triple lancets, the steeple to the l. and pinnacle to the r. both truncated. To the rear, fancy dormers over the aisles and ventilator over the nave. A distinctive interior, with iron piers and traceried arcades beneath a timber clearstorey.

HOLYROOD ABBEY CHURCH (formerly United Presbyterian), London Road and Marionville Road. Late Gothic in red sandstone by *R. M. Cameron*, 1899, with W entrance gable between two low towers, N and S transepts. A jolly interior, arcaded and galleried, with the later C19 arrangement of pulpit beneath a spiky ORGAN by *E. F. Walcker* of Ludwigsburg, 1901. – STAINED GLASS. On the S side two lights as a war memorial (SS. Michael and Andrew) by *John Blyth*, 1949.

LOCKHART MEMORIAL CHURCH, Albion Road. Gothic revival-survival by *Jeffrey Waddell & Young*, 1927, the congregation having previously worshipped in the hall to the E, 1900. An aisled church with N transept, NE porch and canted chapel, all rock-faced with smoother edges, but the specifically Gothic detail is restricted to the W and transept windows; the rest concedes to some sort of modernity. Interior all stone and oak, lit by plain glass quarries. Rubble walls and chamfered arcades, the piers awkwardly rounded towards the half-arched aisles. Round-arched clearstorey, the windows continuous on the S side. Massive pews, dark stained. – COM-MUNION TABLE from the Guthrie Memorial Church (*see* above) and SCREEN at the W end from the Kirk Memorial Church (*see* p. 435), both Gothic. – ORGAN in the arched NE chamber, adjoining the chancel, by *Evans & Barr* of Belfast.

NEW RESTALRIG PARISH CHURCH (formerly Parson's Green Free Church), Willowbrae Road and Portobello Road. Dec Gothic in red Corncockle stone by *Sydney Mitchell & Wilson*, 1890. Low aisles swept round to form a porch at the W gable, on the acute-angled road junction. NE tower with corbelled parapet and red tiled spire. Galleried interior, the nave arcade jumping up into two big arches at each transept. – ORGAN by *J. W. Walker*, removed from the former Catholic Apostolic Church (*see* Central Area, Northern New Town) in 1884 and rebuilt here, its fourth location, by *Ronald L. Smith* in 1974. HALL with much glazing added to the S side in 1977.

ST MARGARET (Episcopal), Easter Road. A village-scale church by *Hippolyte J. Blanc*, 1879. Aisleless, with a flèche over the crossing, the W (liturgical S) transept built slightly later and meeting the street-line. A broad but cosy interior with a braced wagon-roof. – PULPIT. Elaborately pinnacled Gothic, *c*. 1818, from St Paul's in York Place, of which this was originally a mission church. – ORGAN by *Eustace Ingram*, 1893, rebuilt by the same firm in 1945. – STAINED GLASS. In the nave the first pair of lancets (SS. Andrew and Margaret) by *William Wilson*, 1947. The second pair (SS. Margaret and Michael, as a 1914–18 war memorial) by *G. Brodrick* of Twickenham.

WILSON MEMORIAL CHURCH (PORTOBELLO UNITED FREE CHURCH), Portobello Road. By *James Johnstone*, 1933. Smart and symmetrical in red brick and white render, the slim tower vertically striped.

PUBLIC BUILDINGS

ELSIE INGLIS MEMORIAL HOSPITAL, Spring Gardens. Begun in 1923 with the irregularly composed HOSPICE or ward block by *H. O. Tarbolton*, who designed the other 1920s buildings. Brick NURSES' HOME (1927), symmetrical with jerkin-headed end-gables and a copper roofed porch. Dutch-gabled OUT PATIENTS' block (1924; extended, 1933). ISO-LATION UNIT and STAFF QUARTERS by *Alison & Hutchison & Partners*, 1963.

LEITH NAUTICAL COLLEGE, Milton Road East. By *J. & F. Johnston & Partners*, 1974–7.

MEADOWBANK SPORTS CENTRE, London Road. A large complex by *Stuart Harris*, *Thomas R. Hughes* and *Brian T.*

Armitstead of the *City Architect's Department*, 1968, for the
1970 Commonwealth Games.

PORTOBELLO GOLF CLUB, Park Avenue. By *J. A. Williamson*,
1910.

SCHOOLS are numerous. The finest is LEITH ACADEMY
ANNEXE on a hemmed-in site in Albion Road, by *John
A. Carfrae*, 1903. Four-storey baroque in red and yellow
stone, picturesquely composed. In Duddingston Road,
DUDDINGSTON PRIMARY by *Carr & Matthew*, 1955-8,
PORTOBELLO HIGH by *Fairbrother, Hall & Hedges*, 1959-
64, concrete and curtain wall with a nine-storey slab, and ST
JOHN'S R.C., by *Reid & Forbes*, 1924, two-storey economi-
cal classic. In Duddingston Park, PORTOBELLO ANNEXE of
1875-6, extensive and accomplished Gothic like a Victorian
monastery. In Duddingston Road West, HOLY ROOD R.C.
SCHOOL by *Bamber & Hall*, 1967-71. In Meadowfield
Drive, PARSON'S GREEN PRIMARY by the *City Architect's
Department*, 1959-61, with rendered walls, big windows and
copper roof. In the desert of Bingham Avenue, LISMORE
PRIMARY by *Alison & Hutchison*, 1958-9. In Northfield
Broadway, ROYAL HIGH PRIMARY by *Reid & Forbes*, 1931,
as refined in its way as the parent building (*see* Central Area,
Calton: Public Buildings), but genteel Roman instead of
Greek. Single-storey to the N with a columned segmental
portico, two-storey to the S.

WATER DEPOT, Drumpark Yard, off Albion Road. Picturesque
polychrome sheds and associated housing by *James Jerdan*,
1893-5.

MANSIONS

BRUNSTANE HOUSE, Brunstane Road South. A rather ordinary
C16 and C17 house transformed into an exceptional villa in
the C18. Demolition of the tower built here by the Crichtons
of Brunstane was ordered in 1547, but a new L-plan house
was probably built *c.* 1565.* In 1632 this passed to John,
Lord Maitland, later second Earl and first Duke of Lauderdale. By 1639 he had remodelled the house, probably extending the N jamb (really NE, but N for clarity) to the W and
adding a tower at the NE corner. In 1672 Lauderdale consulted *Sir William Bruce* about a major extension. 'I do not
intend', Lauderdale stated, 'a house of much receite' (i.e.
there was to be no State Apartment) but 'will only patch what
is already built, and make myself a very convenient lodge'.
Lauderdale's 'lodge' was at first intended to be twice the size
of the existing, with the principal apartment‡ filling the first
floor of the N and E ranges and a second apartment above the

---

* John Crichton was given a new charter in that year.
‡ Consisting of great stair, vestibule, great chamber, Countess of Lauderdale's
closet, drawing room, Countess's bedchamber, Earl's bedchamber, drawing room,
dressing room and Earl's closet.

kitchen in a new s range. Extensive building work was carried out in 1672–4 with *James Stark* as overseer, *Patrick Wotherspoon* as mason and *John Young* as wright, but the E range was shorter than first envisaged and the new s range may have been no more than an office-wing. In 1733 Brunstane was bought by Lord Milton, who employed *William Adam* to rebuild the s range and make a new office court in 1735–44.

The approach is from the w over the MAITLAND BRIDGE built by *Patrick Wotherspoon* in 1672, the parapets nipped in over the broad abutments over the single arch. The first impression is of symmetry: projecting wings with octagonal stair-towers in the corners. But the N tower has an octagonal roof, the s a flattened ogee; the purplish rubble of the noticeably broader and longer s wing and its short N jamb contrasts with the yellower stone of the C16 and C17 N and E ranges. William Adam's single-storey corridor across the E range bisects the Artisan Mannerist NE stair-tower door of 1639, corniced with a segmental pediment enclosing the arms of Maitland and Home and the IMAH* monogram. On the E front to the garden, full-height corner towers; the N one has a bell-cast pyramid roof, the s a flat ogee. In the middle a round-arched door, probably of 1672–4. At the NE corner, C16 corbelling above the ground floor. The N flank was altered in 1672–4 with a long stair up to the first-floor dining room. Over the door an open pediment enclosing a carved head.

The interior is best understood if the C19 division into two dwellings is ignored. The mid-C18 entrance was by a central door (now blocked) into the passage across the E range. At each end a turnpike stair, the C16 one leading to the principal rooms, the larger s one with moulded risers (probably of 1735–44 rather than 1672–4) to the family wing. In the NW corner is the 1639 kitchen, with a huge segmental-arched fireplace. The ceiling with shallow vaults springing from diagonal beams is by *Adam*. At the SE corner of the ground floor is Adam's panelled octagonal parlour. Landscapes by *James Norie* over the lugged-architrave doors. Round-arched cupboards with fluted pilasters and heavy keyblocks. Chimneypiece with a pulvinated frieze and vast trophied overmantel richly stuccoed by *Thomas Clayton*‡ with a massive urn in the middle and the arms of Lord Milton on one of the banners. The pair of intersecting beams across the ceiling are presumably structural, although dressed up with leafy decoration.

On the first floor, the N stair opens into the dining room (now subdivided).§ Mid-C18 marble chimneypiece with lugged architrave. Its flanking wooden consoles carved with

* For John Maitland and Anne Home, his first wife.

‡ Probably. The only payments for stucco work are to Clayton, but other plasterers (*Samuel Calderwood, Joseph Enzer* and *Alexander Morison*) were also employed at Brunstane.

§ Originally the hall. The C18 room-names are used in this description.

leaves look like an afterthought but are shown in a sketch design by *Robert Adam*. Drawing room to the w with a typically William Adam basket-arched chimneypiece. In the NE tower a closet. Fragment of a frieze with stiff roses, apparently of 1639. s of the dining room is the bedchamber (subdivided), again by Adam. Basket-arched chimneypiece and stucco overmantel with urns and baskets of fruits. On the r. a stuccoed harp and trumpets; over the door on the l. a trophy. Then Lady Milton's dressing room, partly plaster-panelled, the rest of the walls being meant for tapestries. Stucco drapery over the fireplace, its incised wooden frieze probably the base of an overmantel.* The stucco work is probably by *Clayton*. So too is the overmantel of shells and flowers framing the scene of a naval battle in Lord Milton's dressing-room beyond. In the closet of the SE tower the in-goes of the mid-C18 fireplace are carved with hands ready to grasp the tongs and poker.

On the second floor the square SE room has just such a coomb ceiling as William Adam had proposed for this end of a two-storey gallery (abandoned in favour of bedrooms) occupying the whole of the s range. Another coomb ceiling in the next-door closet. In the middle room of the E range a frieze with fleur-de-lys, thistles and roses, of the same type as in the NE closet below and again probably of 1639. The three-panelled door to the NE closet on this floor is distinctively late C17. So probably is the pulvinated frieze incongruously poised on an C18 chimneypiece in the NW room.

In the single-storey s range of OFFICES added by *Adam* the coved ceiling of the dairy is enriched with stuccoed garlands by *Clayton*, 1742. – To the S, simple U-plan STEADING by *Robert Brown*, 1824, with a vast octagonal horsemill projecting from the piend-roofed centre block. Dreary Victorian block of FARMWORKERS' HOUSING to the w.

DUDDINGSTON HOUSE,‡ Milton Road West. The superb 69 Edinburgh villa by *William Chambers*, 1763, of the eighth Earl of Abercorn, who had bought the barony of Duddingston from the Duke of Argyll in 1745. Two storeys, basically a plain block in polished grey ashlar,§ but with all the Classical elements and enrichments precisely carved in pale creamy stone. Pedimented E-facing Corinthian portico of four fluted and filleted Corinthian columns of the same height and with the same entablature as the block, which has a pedestal string course (no basement) and crowning balustrade. Architraved windows, tall and corniced on the ground (principal)

---

* Perhaps the picture frame carved by *William Strachan* in 1737–8.

‡ Now the Mansion House Hotel (1984). David Walker in *Country Life* (24 September 1959) records its neglected state after wartime use. Rescued by the hotel owner, it has suffered only minor permanent damage in its conversion and new use.

§ The use of wrought-iron cramps between the facing stones led to spalling at the corners, which were then patched with cement and the whole surface painted (1963).

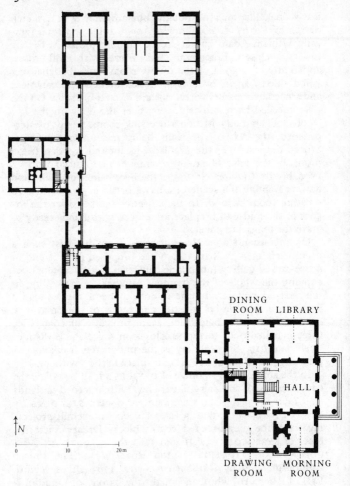

Duddingston House,
plan of ground floor

floor, and further emphasized by consoles and balustered
aprons in the single broad bays each side of the portico. To
the N the office courtyard, open to the E and complementing
the main block with its hollow space and smaller scale. Pedimented N range (stables) and S range (kitchen, connected to
the house by a covered passage) facing each other across a
piazza which is bounded on the W side by a Roman Doric
colonnade with pedimented centre block and cupola belfry.

Three shallow steps into the portico, whose end columns
are answered by pilasters against the wall. Richly coffered
ceiling. Inside, a two-storey hall of the same height and
width, but without orders. Axial stair, the kinked handrail
supported by alternately straight and serpentine balusters.

The first flight leads up to a long mirror in which the reflected columns of the portico are glimpsed, as if they formed the other end of the temple. Here the stair divides, leading to small cantilevered landings on the N and S sides, not integrated with the overall design; awkward in themselves, but not necessarily an oversight. Swagged frieze, hexagonal coffered ceiling (cf. the Adam brothers' Dumfries House, Strathclyde, 1755) interrupted by a big centre oval. Chimneypiece against the S wall with Ionic term-pilasters and swagged, boxy overmantel. In the SE morning room crossed palm-leaf overdoors. In the SW drawing room reeded and wreathed wall panels and a white marble chimneypiece with egg-and-dart frame, swagged frieze and antelope-headed terms. The lobby between them, its dome prettily lined with corn stalks and ears, has been lost. NW dining room (enlarged and then much altered) and NE library with centre panel ceiling in diagonal compartments, the shelves long ago removed and the chimneypiece modified. A variety of interesting chimneypieces in the first-floor bedrooms.

Most of the park laid out by *James Robertson, c.* 1768, survives as a golf course, but Holy Rood R.C. School (*see* Public Buildings (Schools), above) intrudes on the site of the walled garden to the W. Domed TEMPLE to the E, with coupled Roman Doric columns at the splayed corners. ENTRANCE at the corner of Willowbrae Road and Duddingston Road. Concave screen wall, the two crowning antelopes vandalized.

DUDDINGSTON VILLAGE

A beautiful approach from Holyrood Park. Below the road on the r. lies Duddingston Loch. Beyond it, a deep belt of scrub and then (except for two tower-blocks, *see* p. 545) a clear horizon from Craigmillar Castle to Blackford Hill and the Pentlands. Straight ahead, the village; not architecturally distinguished but at least small and compact, with a dominating kirk (*see* above), some decent Georgian villas, plenty of trees and excellent rubble WALLS. The first of these is the boundary between park and village, starting in the loch, picking its way up to the road and then resuming, with a pantiled C18 out-house and a mysterious narrow entry (a short cut to the pub), for the long climb to the N up Dunsapie Hill. Only the Tudor-gabled LODGE of the park, *c.* 1840, stands outside it. Inside, two early C20 houses, GATESIDE with picturesque gables and CRAIGNEUK getting in the way of the church with no excuse at all. After the church gateway OLD CHURCH LANE has a high wall on the S side, broken only by the swept-in gateway of the manse garden. The MANSE itself was built in 1805 of rubble with neat dressings; three bays, plus an extra E bay built on by *Allan Livingston* in 1821 with delicate ironwork of anthemion and rosette pattern. It faces the loch-side, where the octagonal studio and curling house is by *W. H. Playfair*, 1823, built for the Rev. John Thomson, who called it EDINBURGH so that the servants could truthfully say he was not at home. The N side of the lane has lower walls (some with railings of the same design as the manse balcony) revealing front gardens and small villas. DUNERNE (with an added bay-window) and LOCHSIDE HOUSE are a pair, *c*. 1815, with consoled doorpieces. The others are contemporary but more sophisticated: DUDDINGSTON LODGE very flat-faced, with polished ashlar and pilaster doorpiece; CHALFONT ST ARTHUR single-storey with architraved openings and shallow piend roof; GLENARTHUR, picturesquely enhanced *c*. 1840 with an octagonal end tower (plus a square one at the back) and solid gate-piers, ball-finialled; and HOME HOUSE, which has been expanded to five bays, harled and colour-washed.

The short stretch along DUDDINGSTON ROAD WEST passes the 1914–18 WAR MEMORIAL, a Celtic cross by *G. Washington Browne*, 1921, and the Holy Rood R.C. School dumped in 1967 on the tattered fringe of the policies of Duddingston House (*see* above). Corner-shop at the entry to THE CAUSEWAY, where the zealous restoration of No. 8 does not add to its credibility as PRINCE CHARLIE'S HOUSE (his lodging before Prestonpans in 1745), though the restored houses along the close to the l. are still effective. A little precinct of unpretentious semis, and at the corner a steep lane up to SYCAMORE BANK, rubble with slim Classical dressings by *Robert Kay*, *c*. 1810. No. 42, back in the Causeway, is similar but badly eroded. No. 46 is HAWTHORN BRAE, a standard villa of *c*. 1820 whose raised site has been exploited by fruity Victorian additions and pompous gate-piers. Nos. 58–60 are POPLAR BANK and the adjoining DAIRY, early C19 with a pilastered doorpiece in the rubble street-front, the most village-like building in this tiny suburb. On the S side the early C18 IAN HILL'S HOUSE is aloof from the street. At the W end a strangely brash block of flats proudly dated 1929 and finally the SHEEP HEID, still basically an C18 inn but with a nice Edwardian ground floor and a skittle-alley to the rear. Round the corner LOCHSIDE COTTAGE, *c*. 1815, is best seen from the park entry, to which it shows a bow window. Another landmark is BELLA VISTA uphill to the N, built in 1801 but showily enlarged in 1875 with an ogee slated dome. On its E side a stone-built billiards-house lined with elided pairs of bellied pilasters, the finials apparently missing. To its W an octagonal battlemented pavilion with the doorway formed in a shell-headed niche.

STREETS AND NEIGHBOURHOODS

EASTER ROAD

EASTER ROAD is the further E of the two roads from Edinburgh to Leith. The S part is a steep canyon of tenements built *c.* 1900 with uniform bay-windows projecting above the shops and framing, to the s, the rocky profile of Salisbury Crags. For St Margaret's and the former Guthrie Memorial Church, *see* above. To the e in Edina Place the former EDINA WORKS of the printers W. & A. K. Johnston, 1878, a large two-storey pilastered block of red brick with yellow terracotta brackets under the cornice; EDINA HOUSE at the end of the street is of red brick with suburban gables. BOTHWELL STREET begins with Andrew Whyte & Son's BOTHWELL WORKS. A plain block of 1893 like a tenement on the corner, then a palatial façade by *J. P. Goodsir*, 1912; the rusticated ground floor quite conventional, the three upper floors united by subtly combined pilasters, the cornice relieved by two small segmental pediments. It was built in reinforced concrete by *Robert Bruce* and somewhat spoiled by the addition of a fourth floor in 1920. Close-packed tenements, those at the end (Nos. 26–34 next to the railway) of bizarre design in red sandstone *c.* 1900, with deep overhanging mansards and tall-hatted corner oriels. Over a footbridge to ALBION ROAD. To the n a tenement with the inscription HERI SOLITUDO. HODIE VICUS. CRAS CIVITAS. [yesterday solitude, today a village, tomorrow a city] 1902. H.M. For the Lockhart Memorial Church, Leith Academy Annexe and the Water Depot, *see* above.

LONDON ROAD AND WILLOWBRAE ROAD

LONDON ROAD enters this section at the Easter Road junction, and the n side begins with the fruity corner block at Nos. 1–12, 1893; ground-floor shops with delicate cast-iron arcading. Then the variously ornamented gable-ends of seven parallel terraces built by the Edinburgh Co-Operative Building Company. That of REGENT PLACE is dated 1871, and its ground floor contains the excellent late Victorian ARTISAN BAR. Only that of LADY MENZIES PLACE has been spoiled – with a crass bank frontage by *Oldrieve, Bell & Paterson*, 1934. The terraces themselves are two-storey flatted cottages stepping downhill to the n, but the e terrace is continued along the street as a tenement at Nos. 1–11 EARLSTON PLACE. Nos. 12–17 by *Peter L. Henderson*, 1882, a massive tenement with ponderous dormers and fantastic end-turrets, containing the pilastered ground-floor frontage of MILLER'S FOUNDRY: this continues as the arcaded wall of the rolling-mill by *John McLachlan*, 1890. At the e end an impressively simple stone addition by *W. Beattie-Brown*, 1914. Holyrood Abbey Church marks the junction of Marionville Road, and the Meadowbank Sports Centre soon follows; for both *see* above. The monster MEADOWBANK HOUSE is by the *Property Services Agency*, 1974.

The s side of LONDON ROAD (starting again at the Easter Road junction) begins with the four-storey Georgian tenements of

EAST NORTON PLACE, 1819–20, of which Nos. 2–6 were
built by *John Nicholson*, wright; No. 2 is crowned with a
vestigial open pediment. The bowed end belongs to MONT-
ROSE TERRACE on the other side of the gusset block; three-
storey tenements of the same date whose pilastered doorpieces
have recessed Gothic panels at Nos. 33 and 37. At the W end
SINCLAIR'S BAR, *c.* 1880, with a jolly Scotch turret and
fancy dormers (one inspired by Maybole Castle, Strathclyde).
The next part of London Road is less interesting than
what happens behind. First a forbidding hinterland with
T. B. McFadzen's brick Episcopal Chapel (1885, now
disused) in SUNNYBANK PLACE, and two good terraces of
1829 in COMELY GREEN PLACE, chopped off and blighted
by the railway. Then into the open at SPRING GARDENS,
where No. 17, ST ANN'S BANK, overlooks Holyrood Park
with an upright chimney-gabled frontage and Roman Doric
doorpiece; No. 19 is hood-moulded Tudor, *c.* 1850; and No.
39 is a very late Georgian villa with little wings. A terrace of
the same vintage to the r. Nos. 2–4 and 41–43 are cottagey,
dormered terraces of *c.* 1840. For the Elsie Inglis Memorial
Hospital, *see* above. ROYAL PARK TERRACE, 1877, with its
long repetition of crowstepped chimney-gables, leads back
into London Road. The last part of the S side, PARSON'S
GREEN TERRACE, consists of fussy baronial tenements by
Edward Calvert, 1878. The area on the hill behind is tight-
packed suburbia. Some vigour, e.g. at Nos. 8–10 WOLSELEY
CRESCENT, which are deep-eaved Gothic in two shades of
red stone, *c.* 1880; and some liveliness, e.g. at the cottage-style
Manse (of New Restalrig Parish Church) in LILYHILL
TERRACE by *Sydney Mitchell & Wilson*, 1894. But a lot of
Victorian styles and types came here to die, e.g. the bay-
windowed terrace at Nos. 3–21 KENMURE AVENUE by *J. R.
McKay*, 1933.

WILLOWBRAE ROAD in itself has little of note till the far E end,
just before Duddingston Cross Roads. On the N side the early
C19 DUDDINGSTON MILLS COTTAGES lead down to the
remains of the C18 mill on the Figgate Burn. Then the early
C20 SMITHY, picturesquely symmetrical, and at the corner
the former MAYFIELD by *R. S. Reid*, *c.* 1912, a pretty little
L-plan house of rubble with a turret in the angle. At the S
corner the former LOUISFIELD, built as a house by Louis
Cauvin, *c.* 1810 (for his monument, *see* Restalrig Parish
Church, below), and enlarged as a school by his trustees in
1833, now half-way between a villa and an institution; projecting ends, advanced and pedimented centre with Greek
Doric porch. Elbowing into its garden some sheltered housing
by the *City Architect's Department*, 1980. Its neighbour is the
former NAIRNE LODGE, built of rubble *c.* 1805, with two
gentle bows but now submerged (as a hotel) in thoughtless
extensions. The former BELFIELD nearby is a slightly later
and more orthodox villa with a pilastered doorpiece between
over-arched windows.

To the N of Willowbrae Road two large areas of housing. First NORTHFIELD, mainly three-storey blocks designed and laid out for the City by *Fairlie, Reid & Forbes* after a competition held in 1919. The neutral colour of harled walls is relieved with red brick and red tiles. Rubble walls here and there, e.g. at Northfield Gardens and Nos. 53–57 Northfield Broadway, where both design and composition are outstanding. For Reid & Forbes's equally distinguished Royal High Primary School, *see* above. The second area is MOUNTCASTLE, mainly private housing of the 1930s by *James Miller*. The houses to the S of Willowbrae Road are also by Miller; private (1930s) from Abercorn Crescent to Paisley Drive, then public (1958) as far as Duddingston Road.

MILTON ROAD

The next stage of the A1, and a similar story. For the gateway of Duddingston House, *see* above. Otherwise nothing notable before the E end. On the N side QUEENS BAY LODGE, a happy semi-baronial jumble of 1890. A rosetted iron fence to the road, inscribed 'The Scaliger Railing, Verona. This exact copy was made at Portobello Midlothian 1890 by James Ross Blacksmith ...'. The house is a Church of Scotland Eventide Home. To the rear, in QUEEN'S BAY CRESCENT, a pleasant terrace for the Kirk Care Housing Association by *Matthew, Hamilton & Maclean*, 1978. On the S side the KING'S MANOR HOTEL (originally Milton House and subsequently a convent), whose main aspect is *c.* 1840. At its W end the former chapel, C20 Romanesque, the interior adapted as a bar. At No. 44 the vaguely grandiose former office of Dobbies the nurserymen by *Robert F. Sherar*, 1909, a baronial turret with triglyphs at its E end. Set back from the road the flashy Leith Nautical College (*see* above).

Milton Road is skirted with a variety of housing. To the S an arid two-storey local-authority housing scheme of concrete block work, *c.* 1950, centred on BINGHAM BROADWAY, the depression raised to nightmare by *William Kininmonth*'s apparently windowless geometric church, 1965, now abandoned. Little of interest to the N, but a good clutch of four schools in Duddingston Road and Duddingston Park (*see* above). Duddingston Road ends at SOUTHFIELD PLACE, with tenements in a rubbly version of Greek Thomson's Glasgow idiom, *c.* 1880, and the solid Italianate station (disused) of 1867, before squeezing under the railway to Portobello. At the N end of DUDDINGSTON PARK, some big semi-detached villas of typically strong Abercorn Estate style, *c.* 1880. Nos. 1–6 have giant timber bay-windows with attic verandahs; Nos. 15–30 stone bays with flowery iron verandahs (cf. Morton Street; *see* Portobello and Joppa: Perambulation).

PORTOBELLO ROAD

After New Restalrig Church at the V-junction (*see* above), the
s side has a good plain Co-op shop by *Thomas P. Marwick
& Son*, 1938, and the long frontage of the PIERSHILL TAV-
ERN, *c.*1890, inserted in a vernacular two-storey row. On
the N side the rubble-and-harl tenements of PIERSHILL
SQUARES by the *City Architect's Department*, 1937–8, open to
the street. Further out, the Wilson Memorial Church (*see*
above) and finally on the s side a big red-brick block designed
as a chocolate factory in 1906.

WILLOWBRAE ROAD *see* LONDON ROAD

FAIRMILEHEAD

Here Edinburgh spills out toward the Pentland Hills. Until the
1950s it was farmland with a sprinkling of mansions and rural
settlements. Now, the land as far south as the Green Belt has
been almost covered with housing, private on the east, local-
authority on the west. Perhaps the new (1984) Outer By-Pass
will act as a Berlin Wall to prevent the city's inhabitants escap-
ing to new homes in the lusher pastures beyond.

CAIYSTANE,* in Caiystane View, off N side of Oxgangs Road.
An impressive, well-proportioned standing stone 3·1 m. in
height. The E face is decorated with a small linear group of
cup-marks 0·5 m. from the ground; other depressions are
natural.

CHURCHES

COLINTON MAINS PARISH CHURCH, Oxgangs Road North
and Oxgangs Drive. A white-harled kirk by *Ian G. Lindsay
& Partners*, 1954. Square, lanterned tower adjoining the
w gable, the windows round-headed and bullseye. Simple
interior, the galleried N jamb facing the painted PULPIT
with hexagonal sounding-board. Hall and session room also to
the N.

FAIRMILEHEAD CHURCH, Frogston Road and Comiston
Road. Rubbly Scots colonial by *L. Grahame Thomson*, 1937.
Aisleless and cruciform. Dumpy SW tower with gently
rounded corners, the corbelled upper stage crowned with an
ogee slated roof and shaped semi-dormers. Simple interior of
plain elliptical section throughout, the pulpit and lectern in-

---

* Property of the National Trust for Scotland.

tegrated into the textured plaster walls. – WOODWORK by *Scott Morton & Co.* – STAINED GLASS, all single lights. On the s side of the nave, two by *William Wilson* (Charity, 1957; 'Thou madest Him to have dominion', 1959), and two (The Pure in Heart, 1952; Light of the World, 1964) by *Abbey Studio*, who also did the w window over the gallery (David and Jonathan, 1952).

ST HILDA (Episcopal), Oxgangs Road North and Oxgangs Avenue. By *Frederick R. Stevenson*, 1965. Economical and geometrical, the church adjoining the rectory. Both roofs are eccentrically pitched, but in opposite directions, the church identifiable by its buttresses and token lancets.

ST JOHN'S PARISH CHURCH, Oxgangs Road North and Oxgangs Path. By *Alan Reiach*, 1956. A brave group near the top of the hill, the long, clearstoried church and its hall on two sides of a paved court, the saddleback belltower between them. Elegant interior marred by altered lighting.

ST MARK (R.C.), Oxgangs Avenue and Oxgangs Crescent. A distinguished church by *Peter Whiston*, 1959. Aisle wall of whin setts (reused from roadways) forming a base for the plain slated roof. Inside, channelled stanchions form the nave colonnades, and beams of the same section divide the timber-lined roof. Big triangular w window. – STATIONS OF THE CROSS in the shallow nave walls over the aisles. High-relief bronzes on flat panels, by *Vincent Butler*. – STAINED GLASS. Equally impressive, five closely-set lights in each aisle (scenes from St Mark's Gospel).

PUBLIC BUILDINGS

BUCKSTONE PRIMARY SCHOOL, Buckstone Loan East. By the *City Architect's Department*, 1975–7. Drydash and black plastic panels.

COMISTON SPRINGS WATERWORKS, Buckstone Terrace. Originally Fairmilehead Waterworks. FILTER HOUSE by *J. & A. Leslie & Reid*, 1910, with a bullseye window in the pedimented gable. – Two pairs of rubbly COTTAGES of the same date. – LOTHIAN REGIONAL COUNCIL WATER DEPARTMENT by *Bamber & Hall*, 1971–2, smart in dark brick and aggregate.

FAIRMILE NURSING HOME, Frogston Road West. By *Stanley Peach, Brown & Partners*, 1963.

FIRRHILL HIGH SCHOOL, Colinton Mains Drive. By *Robert Matthew, Johnson-Marshall & Partners*, 1957–9, and extended by the same architects, 1968–70. Five-storey main block with bands of harl and glass. Timber cladding and glass for the minor blocks.

HUNTER'S TRYST PRIMARY SCHOOL, Oxgangs Green. By the *City Architect's Department*, 1957–9. Three storeys of concrete panels with huge windows. In the playground, a late C17 gadroon-topped WELL.

LOTHIANBURN GOLF CLUB, Biggar Road. By *J. Inch Morrison*, 1909. Relaxed in white harl and red-tiled roofs. Small spire over the entrance.

MORTONHALL GOLF CLUB, Braid Road. Picturesque cottage style by *Sydney Mitchell*, 1892, who doubled its size and added another floor in 1903–4.

OXGANGS COMMUNITY CENTRE, Oxgangs Path. By *B.L. Matthew & Haswell-Smith*, 1965. Harl and timber, with bold beam ends carrying the roofs.

OXGANGS PRIMARY SCHOOL, Colinton Mains Drive. By *Gordon & Dey*, 1953–4. Temporary looking but colourfully rendered.

PRINCESS MARGARET ROSE HOSPITAL, Frogston Road West. Founded as a children's orthopaedic hospital in 1929 and now for adults too. The first buildings (1929–38) are by *Reginald Fairlie*, polite but cheap neo-Georgian. The WARD BLOCK in the middle of the site must have looked better before glazed outshots were added to the front.* – Cheerless NURSES' HOME. – Tightly composed double LODGE with a large expanse of roof and strong centre chimney. – The Ward Block was extended E in timber and glass in 1952. – Additions since 1960 all by *Morris & Steedman*. – CLINICAL UNIT (1960–5), a harled platform carrying elegant black glass stepping up the hill. – Behind the wards, the almost invisible THEATRE BLOCK (1967) and black-glass PLANT ROOM. – On the W, NURSES' RECREATION HALL (1968) with a clear-storey. On the E, BOILER HOUSE (1966), with a tall chimney.

ST MARK'S R.C. PRIMARY SCHOOL, Firrhill Crescent. By the *City Architect's Department*, 1972–4. Quite tightly composed in pale brick.

MANSIONS

COMISTON HOUSE, Camus Avenue. Built for Lord Provost James Forrest in 1815; now a hotel. Giant corner pilasters, couple-columned doorpiece in the pedimented centre, all unfluted Greek Ionic with angled volutes. Consoled ground-floor windows in the two outer bays. Double groin-vaulted entrance hall, dining room to E with original black marble chimneypiece, central bow-windowed room to the rear (N) and narrow stairwell to the W. Contemporary STABLES to the SW, U-plan with central archway. At the SE corner a circular angle-turret with gun loops and corbelled upper stage, a C16 or C17 survival from the old house.

MORTON HOUSE, Winton Loan. Early C18, becoming the dower house of Mortonhall House (*see* Blackford and Liberton) and fashionably enlarged in the early C19. Original two-storey range dated 1702 (or 1707?), its E front having a

---

* Originally the wards, with one exception, were open to the S to admit healthy breezes from the hills.

central chimney-gable with two windows and scrolled skew-putts, an old-fashioned semi-dormer on each side. Its prospect of the East Lothian coast is flanked by obelisks. Office wing to the N, joined to it at right angles, with the date 1713 on a sundial; at the E end a large fireplace and oven, at the W a wooden stair with cut-out balusters up to the first floor (now only a gallery). A new two-storey range and entrance front were added to the E side of the original one in (traditionally) 1806. Rubble walls (formerly harled), Roman Doric doorpiece in the pedimented centre, and unusually wide segmental-headed windows on each side of it. Central rectangular stairwell with corner landings, cornice of miniature fan-vault pendants, and a round cupola. In the ground-floor dining room to the S a pine chimneypiece with intricate shell and seaweed decoration, the tiny initials R and T alternating in the frieze. Similar chimneypiece with rural subjects in the small room to the N, brought from the first-floor S drawing room. On the W axis of the house, twin early C18 PAVILIONS with ogee roofs, and later rusticated GATE-PIERS with urns. Early C18 whitewashed COTTAGES in a semi-formal group nearby. BELVEDERE on the hilltop to the SE, of rubble with a bullseyed and spike-ended gable rising from two blunt-topped turrets; probably early C18, formerly with painted panelling. For Morton Mains, *see* the Description below.

DESCRIPTION

The OXGANGS DEVELOPMENT was laid out for housing by the *City Architect* in 1954. To its N, off COLINTON MAINS DRIVE, FIRRHILL, a large Edwardian villa with a pedimented Venetian window in the middle of the S front. A village centre is given by Colinton Mains Parish Church (*see* above), looking across Colinton Mains Park to the grid-fronted blocks of CAPELAW COURT, ALLERMUIR COURT and CAERKETTON COURT, all by the *City Architect*, 1961. In OXGANGS DRIVE, OXGANGS PLACE and OXGANGS AVENUE, a wall of housing with huge stair windows, by *Wheeler & Sproson*, 1964. Low-rise flats and terraced houses, the asbestos tile-hanging an unnecessary touch, in DREGHORN DRIVE and DREGHORN PLACE. In OXGANGS ROAD NORTH, the Georgian gate-piers of the demolished Dreghorn House and its broad-eaved EAST LODGE of *c.* 1860. THE HUNTER'S TRYST of *c.* 1800 puts a vernacular stop to the local-authority development.

The access lane from Oxgangs Road to SWANSTON VILLAGE was replaced by broad tarmac in 1979. SWANSTON COTTAGE, where R. L. Stevenson lived from 1867 to 1880, was built by the Town Council in 1761 in connexion with the city waterworks (square WATER HOUSE of that date to the E). It was given a first floor in 1820 and bow windows in 1867, and altered by *Lorimer* for Lord Guthrie in 1908. Mid-C19 FARM

STEADING with steep gables and arched entry. FARMHOUSE uphill to the S, early C18, L-plan, with crowstep gables. Nearby, a half-square of mid-C19 farmworkers' housing, and the eight single-storey THATCHED COTTAGES of old Swanston Village in five whitewashed blocks. Their Tay-reed thatch and concrete ridges belong to *J. Wilson's Paterson*'s restoration of 1964. Adjoining, the two-storey C18 WHITE HOUSE (former schoolhouse). All inward-facing in a little dip, a picturesque entry to the bare Pentland Hills.

OXGANGS ROAD divides two private developments, CAIY-STANE by *Mactaggart & Mickel*, *c.* 1960, and SWANSTON AVENUE etc. by *Wimpey*, *c.* 1955. *Miller* homes from *c.* 1960 on both sides of COMISTON ROAD to the S. In PENTLAND DRIVE, COMISTON, a plain farmhouse of *c.* 1840. For Comiston House, *see* above. No. 53 PENTLAND TERRACE stands high up to get the view over the city. Art Nouveau by *John Gordon & Bennet Dobson* of Glasgow, 1904, with a pagoda-roofed tower at one corner and strong battered chimneys.

More *Miller* housing N of FROGSTON ROAD WEST. In WIN-TON LOAN on the S, Nos. 1 and 3 are by *Alan Reiach*, 1962–3, No. 3 for himself, self-effacing in grey brick. For Morton House, *see* above. Lumpy farmhouse of *c.* 1840 at MORTON MAINS. HORSEMILL on the S of the steading.

Cottagey ROYAL BANK at the top of BIGGAR ROAD. Then the modernistic FAIRMILE INN by *T. Bowhill Gibson*, 1938, with big bows and green tiles. Lothianburn Golf Club (*see* above) marks the city boundary.

FETTES, INVERLEITH AND WARRISTON

A wide plain, chequered with parks and playing-fields, only 1 km. downhill from the George Street ridge. A big gridiron of roads, with here and there a string of terraced houses or villas, Georgian and Victorian; all very quiet and leisurely, except Inverleith Row, which carries northbound traffic from the city centre to the busy artery of Ferry Road. There has been a mild invasion of C20 public buildings and offices, but nothing to rival the huge baronial presence of Fettes College, either in size or in architectural distinction.

CHURCHES

FIRST CHURCH OF CHRIST SCIENTIST, Inverleith Terrace. Scots Romanesque by *Ramsay R. Traquair* (son of the painter Phoebe Traquair and a pupil of Lorimer), 1910–11. Based on old St Giles at Elgin, tall and compact, the N end formed as a transverse saddleback tower with apsidal stair-turrets at the gables. HALLS below, where the ground falls towards the Water of Leith, and to the SE a picturesquely composed service wing with a 'pencil' chimney. The sides of the church

are weakened by the transparency of the large windows, but
the N front is strongly composed and detailed. Parapet with
crowned Celtic cross, cornice terminated by St Mark's lion
and St John's eagle, and three splayed windows over the
porch which has a bas-relief of a galleon in its gable.
Wrought-ironwork in coiled patterns by *Thomas Hadden*.
The interior tunnel-vaulted and very simple, flooded with
light. Twin lecterns flank the segmental S arch in which the
screenwork is by *Frank C. Mears* and the ORGAN by *William
Hill & Son & Norman & Beard*, 1925.

INVERLEITH PARISH CHURCH (originally Granton and Wardie Free Church), Ferry Road. Perfunctory rock-faced Gothic
by *Hardy & Wight*, 1881. Pinnacled NE tower adjoining the
centrally buttressed N gable, a poor termination to Granton
Road. Interior with plain arcades, plainer clearstorey, and
depressed arches opening into transepts. Panelled wagon roof,
pulpit, organ case in S apse, all by *J. R. McKay*, 1937, following a fire. ORGAN by *Henry Willis & Sons*, 1931, rebuilt by
J. W. Walker, 1969. These and the earlier war memorial
COMMUNION TABLE are all of oak, carved by *Scott Morton*.
Large MANSE to the W, also by *Hardy & Wight*, 1881. Minimal Gothic, much more confident but needlessly quirky.

ST JAMES (Episcopal), Inverleith Row. C14 Gothic (cf. Bodley's late churches) in red Corsehill stone by *R. Rowand Anderson*, who won the competition in 1885, the congregation
having moved in 1883 from Broughton Place into the hall at
the W end of the site. *John Beattie & Son* were the builders.
E gable with Curvilinear traceried window to the street,
flanked by a SE tower (the 37 m. spire unexecuted). Only three
of the five nave bays were built, with an open kingpost roof,
but the interior is wonderfully spacious. An arcade with filleted quatrefoil piers and naturalistic leafy capitals divides the
S aisle from the nave, and the chancel arch is of similar late
Dec character. – PAINTED DECORATION. In the nave a stencilled turquoise dado, the upper walls stone-coloured, with
stencilled monograms and fleurs-de-lys. A lettered frieze of
the *Te Deum* unites the nave and the chancel, which is painted
in spirit fresco by *William Hole*, c. 1892–1902. Vines and pea-
cocks below, apostles, prophets and martyrs above. The
whole scheme consolidated (in the nave renewed) by *Ian Hod-
kinson* and *Colin McWilliam*, 1963. The late C19 hanging
lights were designed for electricity and painted to match. –
FURNISHINGS. The PULPIT by *Anderson*, c. 1893, was
followed in general style by *John J. Burnet*'s paving and fur-
nishing of the chancel in 1902. His are the ALTAR and its
RAIL, the CHOIR STALLS and the organ case (the organ by
Brindley & Foster, 1896) in the arched chamber to the S, a
splendid *ensemble*. – ALTARPIECE. A pedimented triptych
(Christ with SS. George and Stephen) by *William Hole*. In
1921–3 *Burnet* added the simple ROOD BEAM with figures by
Gilbert Bayes, and the BAPTISTERY with its traceried screen
through which the church is entered. White marble FONT

and deep dado by *C. d'O. Pilkington Jackson*. – STAINED
GLASS. Not in every window (the nave is well lit) but very
colourful, mostly by *Ballantine & Gardiner*, including the
five lights of the E window (life of Christ). In the NE chancel
window, two lights with intricate, graceful drawing (the Good
Samaritan) by *Henry Payne* of Amberley, *c.* 1910. In the baptistery two single lights (Christ and little children) by *Douglas
Strachan*, simple and direct.

ST LUKE, East Fettes Avenue. Romanesque, by *P. MacGregor
Chalmers*, 1907–8, for the former Young Street congregation.
Strongly composed, with careful use of masonry texture, the
archaeologically-minded detail concentrated on the SE porch
and the square-turreted E gable facing the road. The single-
storey HALL to the S was not built till *c.* 1920. Inside, giant
arcades encompass the clearstorey (cf. Romsey or Jedburgh,
but without triforium), with aisle arcades corbelled from the
round piers. Timber-lined tunnel roof with transverse ribs.
SW baptistery chapel and N transept. W chancel and apse with
blind arcade (the capitals carved with scenes from the life of
Christ) and concrete rib-vault intended for mosaics. Walls
and piers have incised texts and consecration-crosses. – Furnishings in oak, by *Chalmers*. – ORGAN in the transept, by
Ingram, 1912. – STAINED GLASS. In the apse three lights
(Christ the healer), 1958, and at the W end of the N transept
five lights (St Luke), all by *William Wilson*. – In the baptistery chapel one light (the Madonna) by *Margaret Chilton* and
Marjorie Kemp, 1937.

ST NINIAN (Episcopal), Comely Bank. The original church,
harled with minimum slate dressings, is by *Dick Peddie &
Walker Todd*, 1921. It is now the hall, having been supplanted in 1952 by *R. H. Taylor*'s featureless but correctly
orientated church.

ST STEPHEN, Comely Bank. Obliquely sited at the corner of
East Fettes Avenue. Red sandstone with neo-Perp detail by
J. N. Scott & A. Lorne Campbell, 1901, for the former Wemyss Place U.F. congregation, following a competition. The
porch between the wide nave and W transept was intended as
the base of a tower. Inside, a hammerbeamed and compartmented roof. – ORGAN by *J. J. Binns* of Leeds, 1902. –
STAINED GLASS. In the W transept three lights (St Michael,
Moses, David) by *R. Douglas McLundie* of *Abbey Studio*. In
the E transept three lights (St Stephen) by *George Garson*,
1968.

PUBLIC BUILDINGS

BROUGHTON HIGH SCHOOL, East Fettes Avenue. Brick and
harl, by *George L. Walls*, 1972. Four-storey extension by
Sandy Brown Associates, 1979.

EDINBURGH ACADEMY PREPARATORY DEPARTMENT. By
Morton J. Cowie, 1958. Serried windows, brick spine walls

and a brick-faced clocktower, all in the lightweight style of its time but with a touch of formality. Dining-room wing by *Stanley P. Ross-Smith*, 1971.

FETTES COLLEGE, East Fettes Avenue. The Scottish baronial-French Gothic masterpiece of *David Bryce*, 1864–70, built of hard grey Cullalo stone by *Alexander Morrison*, with sculpture by *John Rhind*. The merchant and underwriter Sir William Fettes (†1836) had left £166,000 for the establishment of a school. The main building (at a total cost of £150,000, including accommodation for fifty foundationers) is superbly confident in organization, lively and scholarly in detail. Its distant skyline is encountered at its most picturesque from the E side, along Inverleith Place, and at its most powerful from the S, head-on down the tenemented vista of Learmonth Avenue to the Carrington Road gateway. From here a stairway ascends the terrace to the monumental show-front. The central tower* has a high arch over the entry (cf. Fyvie Castle and Bryce's Craigends, Strathclyde) and is carried up through five storeys (the belfry at Douai) to a two-tier lucarned roof and spired Gothic clock-stage, flanked by massive chimneys. More chimneys march along the ridge (the E section unhappily stripped of its iron cresting), over the wings whose inner bays push forward to reinforce the projection of the tower. In their ground floors, arcaded loggias (Blois), resourcefully detailed. At the wall-head Gothic dormers (the Hôtel de Cluny). Crowstepped and orielled pavilions advance boldly from the ends, but are dominated by large towers on their E and W flanks (Blois again).

This S range forms one of the stalks of the H plan which Bryce said he adopted for good ventilation. Seen from the NW the composition is wholly picturesque, its silhouette descending from the big W tower to the Gothic intricacy of the chapel (part of the cross-bar of the H) with its flying buttresses and tall, traceried gablets; the base of the chapel is the former dining hall. In the angle an octagonal turret (after Victor Petit's drawing of La Verdière?) builds up towards the giant central tower of the S range; it is repeated on the E side of the cross-bar. The N range has the crowstepped headmaster's house at its W end (relatively modest but with an octagonal Gothic turret) and the laundry at its E end, with bedrooms overhead.

The inside is sparer in detail (fern and other leafy cornices in the main rooms) but no less impressive in scale. In the entrance or CALL-OVER HALL a marble bust of Bryce by *George McCallum*. Imperial STAIR with Gothic ironwork leading to a spacious first-floor landing. LIBRARY in the central tower, with barley-sugar-columned bookcases, acorn frieze and Gothic marble chimneypiece, the Fettes arms on the overmantel. Wide corridors leading to CLASSROOMS, those in the end pavilions very large, undulating into their

* The tower contains a gigantic iron cistern.

bay-windows and corner turrets. In the middle range the
former dining hall (now a library) with traceried windows,
linenfold dado and beamed ceiling on carved angel brackets.
Gothic-cum-Renaissance white marble mantel with the Fettes
arms again. The former servery (now opened into the library)
leads to the semi-octagonal former kitchen, with arched fireplace bay. CHAPEL on the first floor. S gallery, three-sided N
apse, the roof a steeper version of that of Parliament House
(see Old Town: Law Courts). In 1948–50 the walls were
stripped down to a fussy pattern of rubble, the sills lowered,
the N rose window knocked out and replaced with a pokey
sort of chancel reached by a lot of steps. – STAINED GLASS.
Mixed in quality, the best being three lights (Theology) by
Henry Holiday, 1893. Two more triplets (Resurrection, 1881;
David, 1887) by Ballantine, who may have done the rest. To
the E of the main building, the WAR MEMORIAL by W.
Birnie Rhind, 1919. Large bronze figure of a fallen officer who
cries 'Carry on' to his men.

Ancillary buildings to the E. CONCERT HALL (former
gymnasium) by John Bryce, 1878, with a muscular open roof
of pitch pine,* between two rubbly ranges by William H.
Kininmonth, 1950. Further away, the plain brick SWIMMING
BATHS by John Bryce, 1878, rebuilt after a fire in 1890.
Henceforth the trustees employed R. Rowand Anderson and
his successors, William H. Kininmonth supplying the DIN-
ING HALL, 1967, an elegant foil to the main building with
its simple glazing, deep lead fascia and battered slate base.
The exception is the CRICKET PAVILION to the N by the old
Fettesian W. L. Carruthers, 1906, with red roof and Roman
Doric verandah.

The grounds were laid out by Archibald Campbell-Swinton
of Kimmerghame (a trustee) and enclosed with iron fences by
David Bryce in 1874; his are the main S gate, the terraces and
the E and W LODGES. His too are the three first boarding
houses, MOREDUN (1869–70) to the E of the main gate, CAR-
RINGTON (1871–2) balancing it to the W, and GLENCORSE
(1873) further to the E. All anglicized baronial with canted
bays and bargeboarded gables; Carrington the most altered
(1883, 1892 and more drastically after a fire in 1963). In 1880
R. Rowand Anderson designed the red-roofed Gothic N
LODGE and MALCOLM HOUSE (Junior School, former Sanatorium), whose W part remained unfinished. KIMMER-
GHAME to the SW was designed by A. F. Balfour Paul in
1928. Neo-Jacobean Arts and Crafts, the last attempt to build
in character with the original buildings; a new chapel was
designed by Reginald Fairlie in 1932 but not carried out.

GEORGE HERIOT'S SCHOOL SPORTS GROUND, Inverleith
Row. GRANDSTAND with its back to the street, cardboard
early Georgian by John Anderson, 1925.

* Inside, ORGAN by D. and T. Hamilton, 1873, rebuilt by H. S. Vincent, 1900,
and Rushworth & Dreaper, 1928. Moved here from the Chapel in 1953.

INVERLEITH PARK. Laid out by the City in 1890. N GATE (dated 1891) arched and pedimented, E GATE with rusticated piers and sejant lions; both by *Sydney Mitchell*. The park is quartered by two paths. At their intersection the memorial FOUNTAIN to Bailie J. C. Dunlop, a rough Peterhead granite obelisk by *William Hole*, 1900, with portrait medallion by *George Webster*. To the S a serpentine path with a pond and small formal garden. At its E end the old farmhouse of Inverleith, C18 but brought up to date *c.* 1900 with red roof and chimneys.

POLICE HEADQUARTERS, Fettes Avenue. By *Alan Reiach, Eric Hall & Partners*, 1971. The timid and economical pink-brick ghost of a good building.

ROYAL BOTANIC GARDEN, Inverleith Row and Arboretum Road. An outstanding gardenesque layout on a modest (25 ha.) site, including a surprising quantity of architecture. The move from Leith Walk in 1822–4 was carried out by *William McNab*, supervised by the Professor of Botany *Robert Graham*, and involved the transplanting of some large specimen trees. Also of the LINNAEUS MONUMENT designed by *Robert Adam* in 1778 and now (after many subsequent moves at Inverleith) in a formal setting to the N of the new glass-houses; a pretty oval urn on a square pedestal, with a portrait head in low relief over John Hope's Latin dedication.

INVERLEITH HOUSE stands on a gentle hillock in the W part of the garden, an austere mansion of three storeys and basement by *David Henderson* for James Rocheid, 1774. On the N side a forecourt formed by diagonal screen walls and pyramid-roofed pavilions. Bluntly bowed stair-tower with windows on each side; the porch at its base an addition, but the mutuled main cornice shows that this was always the entrance front. S front five windows wide (grouped 2:1:2), enjoying a matchless panorama of the city. Lugged central doorpiece whose entablature (inspired by Henderson's son John, then in Rome?) has curious fluted triglyphs. The interior was partly re-finished in 1877 (after a fire) by *W. W. Robertson*, and further modified in 1960 during conversion to its use (until 1984) as the National Gallery of Modern Art.* D-plan geometrical stair, imported late C18 pine chimneypieces with composition ornament in some of the rooms. GATE-PIERS to the SW, at the entry to Arboretum Avenue. Broken pediment type with grotesque lions, early C18.

The OLD PALM STOVE, 1834, is an octagon 18 m. across. In 1859–60 *Robert Matheson* substituted iron shafts for the intermediate stone mullions (the recessed glazing is still more recent) and a glass dome for the original conical roof; this was to suit his adjoining NEW PALM HOUSE of 1856–8, a Roman

---

* Ian Gow points out that the first-floor library in the middle of the N front had an apse at the S end, as noted in Robert Mylne's sketchbook (Scottish Record Office). It was noted by RCAHMS (1951) but destroyed in 1960.

Doric pilastered rectangle 30 m. by 17 m. by 11 m. high. Inside, slim iron arcades support the two superimposed convex roofs. NEW GLASS HOUSES by *George A. H. Pearce* and *John Johnson* of the *Department of the Environment*, 1965–7. Mansard profile on a concrete base, braced by an external frame leaning outwards and connected to the glazed frame with tensional cables. The result is a wide unimpeded space, the specimens in the w part explored by an irregular elevated walkway.

LABORATORIES to the E by *W. T. Oldrieve* of the *Office of Works*, 1909, with a complex but impoverished Free Renaissance frontage to Inverleith Row. On the garden side is *Matheson*'s octagonal classroom and museum building of 1848–51, late Classical with pedimented faces. Further to the w, the new HERBARIUM and LIBRARY by *R. Saddler* of the *D.O.E.*, 1960–4, a big but lightweight box made almost graceful by superimposed arcades.

At the SE by the Rock Garden, the former ROYAL CALE-DONIAN HORTICULTURAL SOCIETY HALL (then for a time the Herbarium) by *David Cousin*, 1842–3; cottage-style on a big scale, with Jacobean brackets under the deep, low-pitch eaves.

ST COLM'S COLLEGE. *See* Streets and Neighbourhoods (Inverleith), below.

TELFORD COLLEGE. Crewe Road South. By *Alison & Hutchison & Partners*, 1966–8. Large and disciplined but very boring; the band of green slate does not enliven the plum brickwork.

WARRISTON CEMETERY, Warriston Road. Laid out in 1842 by *David Cousin*, who designed the neo-Tudor CATACOMBS in the N section, their long buttressed front concealing a vaulted corridor for mural monuments, top-lit by gratings in the terrace above. *J. Dick Peddie* doubled their length in 1862. Also by *Peddie* the neo-Tudor TUNNEL with handsome Gothic archways, 1845, connecting the N and S sections under the former Edinburgh and North Leith Railway embankment. The N extension of the cemetery, 1905, is approached from Warriston Gardens under a railway bridge by *Grainger & Miller*, *c.* 1845. LODGE with Roman Doric verandah by *J. R. McKay*, 1931.

MONUMENTS. Beautifully sited by serpentine walks through overgrown trees and shrubs, but now sadly vandalized (1984). Much good portrait sculpture. Most curious is the Robertson mortuary chapel by *Henry S. Liefchild* of London, *c.* 1865, an arcaded Gothic shrine of white marble with incised foliage in the spandrels. Tall hipped roof of ruby glass lighting a female figure recumbent on her tomb-chest. The other sizeable building is the arched pedestal (its urn overthrown) to the Revd James Peddie †1845, by *John Dick Peddie*, who also designed the monument to Thomas Scott on the w wall. – Doric column to Alexander Wilson, contractor, †1866. – The painter Scott Lauder †1869. Sicilian marble

slab by *John Hutchison*. – The painter Horatio McCulloch
†1872, by *James Drummond*. – Alexander Smith. Large Iona
cross designed by Drummond and executed by *John Rhind*
with a *Brodie* medallion, 1868. – The sculptor John Rhind
†1892 and his wife and family. Double portrait in low relief
by *John M. Rhind*. – Robert Bryson. Neo-Greek by *Stuart
Burnett*, 1887. – Robert MacLean †1871. 8 m. West Highland
cross by *McGlashan*.

WARRISTON CREMATORIUM, Warriston Road. Square plan,
two storeys, built *c*.1818 as East Warriston House for the
banker Andrew Bonar and converted by *Lorimer & Matthew*,
1928–9. N side original (except for the chimney), with an
arched tripartite window, S side completely remodelled with
Lorimer & Matthew's tall arched windows. The same firm
designed the round-arched SE cloister in 1946 but it remained
unfinished. The NW cloister is part of *Esmé Gordon*'s modern-
ish extensions, 1967.

STREETS AND NEIGHBOURHOODS

FETTES

Sir William Fettes's estate was Comely Bank, an area slightly
larger than that which is now bounded by East Fettes Avenue
and Crewe Road South. The name of COMELY BANK now
applies to the street along its S boundary, where *Thomas
Brown* provided Sir William with the plan and elevation for
a terrace along the N side in 1817. Two-storey houses with
front gardens, the ground floor rusticated, with a three-storey
centrepiece of flats at Nos. 15–17; the three-storey E pavilion
at Nos. 1–3 was built in 1888 to Brown's design but with an
added bay-window. No W pavilion, but two red sandstone
terraces; a similar one round the corner at Nos. 1–8 EAST
FETTES AVENUE was designed by *McArthy & Watson*, 1889,
for the Fettes Building Association. Further to the N the
CHRISTIAN SALVESEN office by *Morris & Steedman*, 1969,
its two-storey blocks defined by buff brick walls and elegantly
subdivided by concrete fins and panels. Similar residential
blocks in FETTES PLACE, part of the same development.

All the late C19 feuing on the Fettes Estate was supervised by
R. Rowand Anderson, beginning in 1883 with Moredun Crescent on the W side of Crewe Road (demolished for the Western General Hospital; *see* Craigleith and Ravelston, Public
Buildings). Most adventurous is NORTH PARK TERRACE to
the SE. Nos. 14–15 semi-detached baronial on a mighty scale
(1893–4), Nos. 16–19 a single block with the middle gables
curvilinear, the outer ones half-timbered (1897); all by *John
C. Hay*. For Fettes College itself, *see* Public Buildings, above.

INVERLEITH

The Inverleith estate was acquired by the Rocheid family in
1665. In 1822–4 the Botanic Garden was moved from the
Hope estate in Leith Walk to a new site on the E side of
Inverleith House. In 1877 the government and the City
bought the house and its policies from the Fettes Trust and
added them to the Botanic Garden; the extension was opened
in 1881, with the house occupied by the Regius Keeper. Inverleith Park to the W was bought by the City from Carl
Rocheid in 1889 and laid out as tree-lined public playing-
fields with a little garden and pond on the S (Stockbridge)
side. Finally, house-sites to the N of Inverleith Place were
feued under the supervision of *R. Rowand Anderson*. Between
them are the playing-fields of more or less distant schools.

The road from Canonmills Bridge to Trinity (W side) starts
with some smaller-scale developments. HOWARD STREET
consists of one long bay-windowed tenement by *George Beattie & Sons*, 1895. Then the cul-de-sac of TANFIELD LANE,
with the much altered buildings of two rival gas companies
established in the 1820s. On the S side the Oil Gas Co., of
which Sir Walter Scott was the chairman, *William Burn* the
architect. It failed in 1839 and became the Tanfield Hall,
scene of the first Free Church assembly in 1843. One of the
four bowed arms of the cruciform plan survives. On the N the
Portable Gas Works, the remaining part now a bonded warehouse; the building now fronting TANFIELD (on the main
road) is Morrison & Gibb's printing works by *Robert Wilson*,
1896, a single-storey free-Renaissance range in red sandstone
with a factory of earlier date behind. At SUMMER PLACE the
plain three-storey block by *John Tait* at Nos. 1–5 was built
c. 1830 and soon acquired projecting shops. At Nos. 6–8 a big
gawky tenement with shops, *c.* 1870 in the style of *Beattie*,
dressed up with pediments and busts and a corner oriel to cut
a respectable figure with its neighbours.

INVERLEITH ROW was laid out with sites for a row of villas
(minimum cost £500) along the edge of the gardens (*see* Royal
Botanic Garden, Public Buildings, above). Building began in
1823, but seems to have been inhibited at the S end by the
nearby industries of Tanfield. Quadrant-bayed house at
No. 1a and terrace at Nos. 1–4, both by *David MacGibbon*,
1862, in the dry Italianate style of William Burn, from whose
London office he had lately come. The ensuing Georgian
villas are an outstanding series, all built in the 1820s with
front gardens and nearly all of two storeys. Three main types:
Nos. 5–6 a double villa unified by a tetrastyle Greek Doric
porch; Nos. 9–10 similar but Ionic; Nos. 11–12 and 13–14
(cf. Nos. 21–25 Inverleith Place) pilastered from end to end
but with separate Doric porches. No. 8 a single villa by
William H. Playfair for his kinsman Daniel Ellis the military
surgeon, 1824–5; continuous pilasters and a central Doric
porch between tripartite windows, the crowning balustrade

restored in 1975. Other single villas with ground-floor orders at Nos. 15-16 and 18-20. The third type (single villa with giant anta order) spoiled by a clumsy mansard at No. 7 but intact at Nos. 17 and 19. After the Royal Botanic Garden Laboratories (*see* above), Nos. 21-22 are exceptional in having three storeys and basement and only four bays, tall and cubical with Tower-of-the-Winds porches. Nos. 23-24 also neo-Greek but more severe, with anta porches to the sides of the main block. The remainder, except for some Victorian villas, repeat and vary these themes. For St James's Church, *see* above. The W side of Inverleith Row ends with a later C19 tenement; for the E side, *see* the description of Warriston, below.

INVERLEITH TERRACE is built up only on the S side, the houses overlooking the Royal Botanic Garden in front, the Water of Leith at the back. Bay-windowed terrace at Nos. 3-8 by *R. Rowand Anderson*, *c.* 1869, then a short terrace of Georgian type at Nos. 9-11 by *John Tait*, 1834, continued *c.* 1860 with broader details, all climbing the slope. No. 16 by *F. W. Deas*, 1912, very pretty and precise with curved symmetrical gables to the front and harled bays to the side, well related to the First Church of Christ Scientist (*see* above). At No. 23 ST COLM'S COLLEGE, designed as the United Free Church Training Institute for Lady Missionaries by *Gordon L. Wright*, 1908. Dormered boarding-school style with some red sandstone enrichment, e.g. the oriel above the chapel, which has one stained-glass window by *William Hole* (Christ the Light of the World, with eastern buildings across the water). Further W No. 34 (EDZELL LODGE) by *S. Henbest Capper*, 1895, refined baronial with a turret in the angle, delicate upright cusping over the door. No. 35 by *Thomas T. Paterson*, 1897, very free Renaissance in red sandstone behind the shrubs, with a symmetrical front to Arboretum Avenue; discreet orange brick extension by *Stanley P. Ross-Smith*, 1980.

INVERLEITH PLACE begins two-sided. To the S Nos. 1-11 (not houses but wide-plan maisonettes) commissioned from *Wardrop & Anderson* in 1887 by the builders *Sutherland & Sons*; Queen Anne style in an austerer Edinburgh version, with an irregular arrangement of tall gables and bay-windows. Then a short sequence built *c.* 1825 (stipulated minimum cost £1,000 each), all with Doric porches. At least one house is by *John Tait*. Nos. 21-25 a pair with pilastered ground floor but much altered, as is No. 37. No. 39 by *Thomas Brown*, unspoiled, with pedimented centre and panelled giant pilasters at the ends. Nothing more on the S side except Nos. 59-61 on the corner of Arboretum Road by *Dunn & Findlay*, 1894; red sandstone, François I doorpiece, two dissimilar gables linked by a balustrade.

On the N side of Inverleith Place the much longer stretch of villas includes few of much size or interest despite their good position. Nos. 12-14 an old-fashioned pair by *J. R. & E. E.*

Pearson, 1897. Nos. 18–20 by *John A. Carfrae*, 1897, and single villas at Nos. 22–26 and 30 by *Dunn & Findlay* from 1899, all commissioned by *Sutherland* the builders. No. 28 more exciting, by *C. S. S. Johnston* for the shipowner Duncan McIntyre, 1898; big gable to the r., bay-window roofs linked as a porch, steel-framed internal structure. No. 32 by *Anderson, Simon & Crawford* (Rowand Anderson's brief partnership with Frank Simon & A. Hunter Crawford), 1900; suave English Jacobean, complete with leaded windows and obelisk finials. Nos. 36–46 all to a basic design by *John McLaren* with finicking variations by *G. D. Forsyth* and built by *Robert Forbes*. No. 48 half-timbered by *S. Henbest Capper*, No. 50 plain red sandstone by *T. T. Paterson*, both 1895. Of the same year No. 58 on the corner of Arboretum Road, by *R. M. Cameron* for the Town Clerk Thomas Hunter, but it looks earlier: opulent Victorian Renaissance with Peterhead granite columns at the porch and iron cresting on the platform roof. In the last section Nos. 74–76, semi-detached but asymmetrical by *William N. Thomson*, 1895 (No. 74 for himself), with mullion windows and scallop-topped bays.

To the N of Inverleith Place, a few good things. In INVERLEITH AVENUE SOUTH, No. 5 by *J. Inch Morrison*, 1924 (since altered), and No. 7 by *Henry & Maclennan*, 1915. Smaller but more interesting No. 18, by *A. E. Horsfield*, 1909; neat English Arts and Crafts with Roman tiles and leaded glass. In the N part of Arboretum Road FAIRFIELD by *John Kinross* and *Harold O. Tarbolton*, 1901; plain Scots, beautifully proportioned and detailed with cornucopias over the moulded doorpiece. Round the corner in KINNEAR ROAD the three Edinburgh Academy boarding-houses. JEFFREY HOUSE and SCOTT HOUSE by *Alexander N. Paterson*, 1899, the plans reversed to achieve overall symmetry. Pink Corncockle and red Locharbriggs dressings, with bay-windowed gables and truncated corner towers; portrait medallions over the staircase in between. MACKENZIE HOUSE by *Ramsay Traquair*, 1910, rubbly Lorimerian Scots with bits of classical detail. To the W big bungalows: No. 22 by *A. F. Balfour Paul*, 1926; No. 26 by *Oldrieve, Bell & Paterson* with a mansard and ogee dormer, 1932. In INVERLEITH GROVE only WESTERING by *Matthew M. Ochterlony*, 1939, harled and pantiled.

In INVERLEITH GARDENS (S side of Ferry Road) the twin late-Georgian villa at Nos. 22–23 set a pattern for its neighbours. Nos. 9–21 probably by *Anderson & Browne*, *c.* 1883, with plenty of arty detail (cf. their Nile Grove, Morningside). For Inverleith Parish Church and Manse, *see* above. To the W, ROSETTA, a tall and crisp freestyle villa by *Robert R. Raeburn*, 1880.

WARRISTON (AND GOLDENACRE)

The estate of Warriston (formerly West Warriston) lay on the E side of the road from Canonmills to Trinity. It was laid out for building by *James Gillespie Graham* in 1807. Starting from Canonmills Bridge, the Georgian development begins with the plain three-storey tenement of WARRISTON PLACE, *c.* 1818. WARRISTON CRESCENT provides its slightly monumental elevation round the corner (Nos. 1–4), and continues with a long shallow curve of two-storey broached ashlar (Nos. 5–33), nearly all built by 1830. A nice variety of entrance halls, including Gothic vaults and domes on pendentives. No building on the N side, except at the entry where Nos. 51–53* are part of the tenement designed by *J. Gillespie Graham, c.* 1809. On the quadrant corner an Ionic pilastered pub by *R. M. Cameron*, 1903, and more commercial extensions on the ground floor at Nos. 1–4 HOWARD PLACE (back on the main road), where Graham's design continues with two-storey houses at Nos. 5–32. Front gardens (the first for an Edinburgh terrace?) and rusticated ground floors. EILDON STREET on Heriot Trust land to the E (facing Warriston Crescent over the playground) is another single terrace with tenemented entry, but with bay-windows and heavy attics; Nos. 1–18 by *A. Bennet*, 1879, the rest by *George Grant*, 1906, with pilastered doorways and Edwardian glazing. Then in the main road, opposite Inverleith Row, a single gate-pier from Warriston House, built in 1784 and demolished in 1966. On its site *Miller* villas of 1970, and to the N (Warriston Gardens) inter-war houses by *A. E. Horsfield*.

The name GOLDENACRE is now applied to the whole neighbourhood at the N end of the main road, but strictly belongs only to the land on the E side, owned by the Duke of Buccleuch, extending as far S as Goldenacre Terrace and developed in the late C19 with street-names taken from Buccleuch titles and properties. Those at the N end form a compact group of four-storey tenements by *George Beattie & Son*, 1879, except for the S corner of Royston Terrace, which is by *Thomas T. Paterson*, 1898.

GILMERTON

The village of Gilmerton was a coal-mining settlement in the C17, a centre of lime working by the C19. On the SE is open country, on the NW broad bands of C20 housing separated by parkland.

RAVENSWOOD AVENUE. Standing stone in small enclosure at E end of Ravenswood Avenue, 1·95 m. in height.

CHURCHES

GILMERTON PARISH CHURCH, Ravenscroft Street. Innocent Romanesque, built in 1837 as a chapel of ease from Liberton.

* The gap in the numbers allowed for still more houses in the crescent, but the railway came instead. Nos. 52–53 were built in 1860.

Shallow-pitch gable with buttresses, triple window and conical-topped bellcote. Porch added in 1882 by *John G. Adams*, along with the lean-to transepts which enhance the interior; also the oak Gothic pulpit. – STAINED GLASS. Five bible-storey windows and a central rose window, *c.* 1883, perfectly suited to the church.

LIBERTON NORTHFIELD PARISH CHURCH (originally Free Church), Gilmerton Road and Mount Vernon Road. Robust Gothic, by *J. W. Smith*, 1869. E gable to road with plate-tracery in red-striped lancets, NE tower with a much politer broach spire added by *Peddie & Kinnear* in 1873. Interior with raked floor, the arch-braced roof with radial bosses springing from stumpy colonnettes which have a variety of leafy capitals. Low N and S transepts entered by triple arches and expressed on the outside by triple gables. Tiny clear-storey lights, and more small windows enlivening the W wall around the chancel arch, which is now filled by the organ.

ST JOHN VIANNEY (R.C.), Fernieside Gardens. Red brick, by *Reginald Fairlie*, 1952. Porch with big round arch projecting from a segmental gable. The acoustic ceiling and adjacent presbytery later.

TRON MOREDUN, Craigour Gardens. By *Cairns & Ford*, 1951. Roughcast with stone and concrete dressings, a cross in the gable over the round-arched porch.

PUBLIC BUILDINGS

DR GUTHRIE'S GIRLS' SCHOOL, Gilmerton Road. By *McArthy & Watson*, 1903. Picturesque Renaissance, harled with red sandstone dressings, the advanced ends clasping a single-storey entrance hall with steeply pedimented door-piece. Additions by *Esmé Gordon*, 1962.

GEORGE AND AGNES MURRAY HOME, Gilmerton Road. By *Thomas W. Turnbull*, 1929. Harl and artificial stone. Single-storey Y-plan wings on each end of a two-storey main block, with a nice build-up of slated piend roofs. Incorporated in the S front two small Ionic columns from Moredun House, whose garden walls and mid-C19 office courtyard are still *in situ*. Baluster SUNDIAL on the lawn to the S, early C18.

GILMERTON BOARD SCHOOL (disused), Gilmerton Road and Newtoft Street. By *J. Inch Morrison*, 1912. Discreet Renaissance in pale sandstone, a lantern on the red tile roof.

KINGSINCH SCHOOL, Inch Park, Gilmerton Road. By *Law & Dunbar-Nasmith*, 1968–9. CLASP-system* panels effectively placed on a hillock. *See also* p. 27.

MOREDUN RESEARCH INSTITUTE, Gilmerton Road. By *A. K. Robertson*, 1924–7; wings added 1938–9. Major expansion since 1960, the new buildings (Microbiology Institute, 1961;

---

* System of prefabricated unit construction developed for the Consortium of Local Authorities Special Programme, started in 1957.

Radio Isotope and Metabolism, 1963; Farm Animals Isolation Unit, 1966; Pathology, 1972; Biochemistry, 1976) all by *Moira & Moira & Wann*.

NATIONAL COAL BOARD SCOTTISH AREA H.Q., Gilmerton Road. The core is Green Park, early Victorian, mixing Jacobean detail with a Doric porch. Large, plain extensions, rendered by *Egon Riss*, 1947, concrete-panelled by *Sydney Greenwood*, 1968.

MANSIONS

THE DRUM (formerly Somerville House*), between Gilmerton 66
Road and Old Dalkeith Road. By *William Adam*, still inexperienced as a designer, for Lord Somerville, 1726-34. The arrangement is Palladian, with the three-storey w pavilion incorporating part of the house built by *John Mylne* in 1584-5; an E pavilion was intended but not built. Straight links, monumentally composed with shell-headed niches, make a fine spread from side to side but detract from the corps-de-logis, which consequently has to be made interesting and important by every conceivable means, including a few that can only have been conceived in ignorance. The basement is channelled, the ground floor rusticated, with Gibbs-surround windows superimposed on the rustication. The taller first floor, on an awkwardly shallow plinth, is treated in the same way but with pediments over the windows and blocked Ionic pilasters at the edges, teasing up the rusticated wall to yet another sculptural effect. Finally a deep entablature, a widely spaced balustrade, and over the projecting centrepiece a steep pediment in which Somerville's arms are quartered with those of his first wife, Ann Baynton. The real surprise, in the midst of all this business, is a large and bland Venetian window whose cornices project further than the main cornice above; its calm geometry is echoed by the arch of the perron stair, a late C18 modification. A pity that this ambitious ashlar front makes such efforts to be different from the five-bayed ends. On these and on the rear elevation, with its canted bay for the main entrance, Gibbsian windows are deployed to much greater effect against plain harling. The big chimney-stalks, carved with fireplace-like basket arches, are impressive from all directions.

Everything inside works better if not exactly more smoothly, the plan neatly divided in three with clear views through the middle of the house,‡ the plaster decoration rumbustious but admirably relevant to the architecture. On the ground floor it is by *Samuel Calderwood*. HALL with a big trophy of arms over the chimneypiece, luxuriant twirls over 67

---

* 'Somerville House' in *Vitruvius Scoticus*.
‡ Ian Gow points out its similarity to that of Roger Morris's Marble Hill, Twickenham, 1724.

the doors, but all in the disciplined framework of an Ionic
order beneath a coved ceiling. In the DINING ROOM to the
l. the same order is used with basket arches as a screen for
the alcove, and to frame the fireplace and pedimented overmantel, which are carved with much refinement in grey marble. White marble architraves to the doors each side. On the
opposite wall a trophy of mason's instruments; the rest panelled in plaster with jolly enrichments, including Europa and
the bull, the bull metamorphosed by stages into the Som-
ervilles' heraldic dragon. Here the cove is diapered, the ceiling lined with foliage and rosettes. To the r. of the hall the
PANELLED ROOM, its ceiling of similar character but probably of 1860, followed in the E link by the BOOK ROOM with
cupboard doors cusp-panelled and keyblocked. In the corner
an overmantel painting of a grotto. To the NE of the main
block is the LIBRARY, with a fireplace architrave of curious
pale brown marble, full of fossils. But the main sequence is
N from the hall through a deep basket archway (realistic
overdoor trophies of music and naval warfare crammed into
little groin vaults on each side) to the circular STAIRWELL;
the service stair is fitted into its SE corner. Rustication on the
lower stage, through which the timber cantilever stair climbs
in a single sweep, starting at an inviting angle and turning
through 180° in plan. Elegance and fretwork in the upper
stage, which has a swirled ceiling rosette and is lit by a huge
Venetian window. The plaster from here on is by *Thomas
Clayton*. Along the whole E side is the DRAWING ROOM. The
ceiling is coved again, but within the cove, along with routine
patterning quoted from downstairs, are scrolls and foliage of
a more delicate rococo sweep, nicely related to the windows.
The soffit is even more modern, divided structurally into
three parts, with an octagonal relief of Jupiter and Juno in
the middle one. Lugged chimneypiece, and in the lugged
frame of the overmantel a relief of Neptune drawn out of the
waves by sea-horses. Facing it, a Venetian window of the now
familiar Ionic order. The SMALL DRAWING ROOM (adjoining) is in fact a lofty room lit by the big Venetian window of
the S centrepiece; this was grandly Corinthianized in the late
C18 and the matching chimneypiece installed along with the
other finishings, quite plain except for a patera frieze and a
plain oval in the ceiling. On the E side the principal BED-
CHAMBER and its dressing room, both with original coves
and cornices.

The upper floors of the W pavilion are likewise early C18,
the ground floor presumably before 1698; this date and the
initials J S (for James Somerville) appear on the pierced iron
latch of the N door into the old rooms. Vaulted chambers on
each side of a thick chimney-wall, the shallow groin vaults
springing from square piers on the E side, from stone columns
elsewhere. The W side of the pavilion received its purely
ornamental doorpiece in the late C18, its bay-windows in
1860.

SUNDIAL to the W of the house, a C20 replica of a large
diapered baluster of c. 1730. – GARDEN WALL further W. In
the remaining part a stone heraldic tablet inscribed 'Arms of
Hugh 6th Lord Somerville, 1524, brought from Cowthally
Castle to Drum in 1694'. – STABLES to the S, 1806. A cupola
over the rusticated arch door, bullseye windows on each side
to light the passage past the stalls. Between them the original
cast-iron screens, decorative arcades of flat section. – Nearby,
a shaft and CROSS of 1892 with the inscription 'In memory
of the Old Mercat Cross of Edinburgh which stood at the
Drum from 1756–1866'. – EAST LODGE, Old Dalkeith Road.
Late C18. A pair of square lodges with Venetian windows and
pyramidal roofs. Concave screen wall and rusticated gateway.

DRUMBANK HOUSE, Old Dalkeith Road. Built c. 1845 on the
edge of the Drum estate, a solemn little villa with eccentric
Georgian survival details. Window margins rusticated on the
ground floor, Egyptian on the first floor, where the middle
bay has pilasters and the bevelled corners have columned
aedicules – all oafish Ionic with block pediments. Interior
slightly less odd. Walled garden adjoining to the N, stables to
the S.

INCH HOUSE (in use as a community centre, 1984), Glenallan
Drive, between Old Dalkeith Road and Gilmerton Road. The
original house is of L-plan with three storeys and attic, a
square five-storey stair-turret in the angle, with the date 1617
in the pediment over the door. It was built for James Winram,
Keeper of the Great Seal of Scotland, who added a two-storey
N extension to the NE jamb in 1634 (the date on one of the
carved dormers). In 1660 Inch was acquired by the Gilmours,
who added a W wing to the main S range, probably in the late
C18. In 1891 (exhorted by the Society of Antiquaries of Scotland) they employed *MacGibbon & Ross* to restore the house
and extend its character to the wing, which they did in no
uncertain way. Most of the frontage remained distinctively
Georgian, but the bay next to the old work was transformed
with a pilastered porch, its pediment breaking up into an
oriel, and a heavy baronial top-hamper was loaded on to the
harled wall-head. More excitement to the rear, where the
wing was thickened and given a diagonally projecting NW
turret. Also a new N range with ogee-roofed tower. Inside,
the new front door leads into the hall where one of the re-
sited stone TABLETS is carved with a castle and the initials
GH 1612, and then to MacGibbon & Ross's main stair (the
colonnette balusters not restored after the fire of 1979). The
room treatment is theirs too, but without consistency or outstanding quality. Some Georgian chimneypieces reused, including one in the NW turret, pine and composition, c. 1800,
with thin Gothick shafts and a relief of a fox and hounds.
The old building has vaulted cellars and a doorway with
lugged architrave, probably re-sited. On the turnpike stair
the doorways are framed with early C17 oak tabernacles whose
pilasters are thin, fluted and crudely voluted. SUNDIAL to the

NE of the house; 1660, on a square pier, brought from Craig-millar and restored in 1894. WALLED GARDEN to the NE. Stone wall with carved skewputts and rope-moulded piers and archway re-sited at the N entry.

KINGSTON CLINIC, Kingston Avenue. Designed by *Pilkington & Bell* for the tailor William Christie (as Craigend Park), 1867–9. Powerful but nonetheless charming Ruskinian Gothic, of rockfaced pink sandstone with yellow incised bands and florid dressings, on a terraced eminence enjoying a panorama of the city to the N and W. At the SW corner a swept-round porch with pairs of leaf-capitalled shafts, as a base for the round tower, whose Gothic windows are crowned by a vine in high relief, spilling upwards over the cranked string course. Flanking bow windows, and an attached stair-turret with concave candle-snuffer roof. At the NW, canted bay-windows springing from bell-topped bows. N front quasi-symmetrical, with a smaller-scale E extension. Entrance hall with a round arch on Peterhead granite shafts. NW draw-ing room with deep trellised cove flowing into the two bows. Huge imperial staircase, deeply carved in dark timber but far from heavy withal, top-lit by a dome with yellow etched grif-fons. The landing leads into a top-lit billiard room. STABLES to the SE. L-plan, of the same stone but plainer, with stepped and arched gateway into the yard. LODGE at the Gilmerton Road entry. Low-pitched roofs with elaborate bargeboards.

KINGSTON GRANGE, Kingston Avenue. Originally Sunnyside, by *Robert Adam*, 1785–8. S (entrance) front transformed in a plain Jacobean manner *c.* 1840, so that a chimneyed gable sticks up oddly over the Roman Doric porch. The harled S front survives, with its original cornice and centre bow; like-wise the cornice of the dining room inside it, but no other C18 finishings on the ground floor. LODGES. In Kingston Avenue late C18, harled, with a dome at each end and tall picturesque roof. In Gilmerton Road *c.* 1840 and stone-faced, Tudor-Gothic with central pediment.

DESCRIPTION

Gilmerton has retained many of the buildings and some of the cohesion of its old hilltop village, though strung out along the busy A7, which approaches from the N along Gilmerton Road.* On the W side Dr Guthrie's Girls' School and the former Gilmerton Board School (*see* Public Buildings, above). Round the corner in NEWTOFT STREET a Tudor cottage, *c.* 1840 (probably related to the Anderson Female School which used to stand on the Board School site). Further on, the former Gilmerton Convalescent Home, plain Gothic by

---

* To the S of Lady Road the SHOPPING CENTRE by *Michael Laird & Partners* is now under construction (1984). This is Edinburgh's first U.S.-type shopping mall, united and abstracted into a huge polygonal mushroom whose glass head is sometimes nipped into a yellow brick stalk, sometimes swept downwards.

Campbell Douglas & Sellars, 1886. Back to the main road,
which here becomes DRUM STREET. Nos. 8-14 are two-
storey with shops, *c.* 1960, a townscape disaster. Nos. 16-18,
pantiled single-storey cottages, restore both street-line and
character. To the r. the entry to THE COVE, an underground
network of passages and rooms excavated in the pinkish rock
by the plumber *George Paterson*, 1719-24. Steep serpentine
stair down to a central passage *c.* 15 m. long. Numerous
rooms, three with long tables and side-benches formed in the
stone, the largest with a pillar joining the roof to the table,
which has a hollowed-out bowl and seating for a party of
twenty. No. 22 after the lane a single-storey cottage with horizontal panes, *c.* 1840, and then the MECHANIC ARMS, two-
storey, *c.* 1800.

On the E side of Drum Street the Gothic hall of the Junior
Friendly Society, 1888, and after the garage a good row of
pantiled, street-hugging cottages converted to shops. The
ROYAL BANK a model of stone-fronted gentility, *c.* 1935,
with a curly gable and Quality-Street bow windows. RAV-
ENSCROFT STREET branches to the W, starting with Nos. 1-
3, *c.* 1840, obliquely sited and rather grand, with an advanced
centrepiece. On the N side the Parish Church (*see* above) and
a row of cottages at Nos. 12-26, *c.* 1840, with gabled twin
porches. Across the street the bargeboarded MANSE, *c.* 1890.
Uphill, the ghosts of Georgian prosperity. On the S side the
five-bay WESTLAND HOUSE and then JOFFVILLE, with its
gable to the street; behind them the steading of SOUTH
FARM. Fronting the N side the gable of No. 32. All these late
C18 and harled; so is the piend-roofed RAVENSCROFT
HOUSE to the rear, one wall now masked with Fyfestone.
No. 96 (ANNVILLE) is early C19 with a Roman Doric door-
piece. A forlorn collection (1984) cheered up by DEAN COT-
TAGE at No. 92, 1867. To the S of Newtoft Street some relics
of Gilmerton House (demolished *c.* 1950), including an early
C18 gazebo platform on an arched shelter. The last part of
Drum Street has a good long tenement range on the W side,
curving downhill to the GARDENER'S ARMS, all built *c.* 1880.
Across the road, the entry to East Farm.

GILMERTON ROAD then resumes. After Inch Park and House
(*see* above) the road is straddled by the large INCH HOUSING
SCHEME by *Stratton Davis & Yates*, from 1951. Street-
names from Sir Walter Scott, but more of an English feeling
about these rendered terraces with slight variations in their
graceful, lightweight detail. The NW corner (names from
Robert Burns) was added in the 1970s. A golf course interlude (*see* Kingston Grange, above) and then the MOREDUN
SCHEME of one- and two-storey prefabricated houses, 1948-
50 (still in good shape), supplemented by the conventional
red-roofed houses of Fernieside. The tall flats were added
later. The housing at the Ferniehill and Drum addresses to
the S was built in 1965 by *James Miller*. The FERNIEHILL
INN, Ferniehill Road, is a neat early C19 villa with a mad

castellated extension and a beleaguered look. Gilmerton Road then enters the village (*see* above).

GLASGOW ROAD

Edinburgh's w fringe. A sprawl of housing, with factories on the s, halted for the time being by the river Almond and the Green Belt.

CATSTANE, 600 m. NE of Boathouse Bridge on the right bank of the river Almond, a standing stone with an early Christian inscription. A C17 account described the stone as the only upright of the contiguous kerb of a low mound about 6·4 m. in diameter, and excavation in 1861 showed that it had been set over a short cist, both presumably of Bronze Age date. The standing stone and cairn may be compared to the kerb-cairn at Cairnpapple (West Lothian). Further excavation in 1864 discovered that the stone had formed the focus of a cemetery of fifty early Christian burials in long cists, found in nine parallel rows; one short cist was also found. The inscription, which dates to late C5 or early C6:

> IN OC T/(V)MVLO IAC(E)T/ VETTA F/ VICTR
> In this tomb lies Vetta daughter of Victricius.

CHURCHES

47 CRAIGSBANK, Craigs Bank. By *Rowand Anderson, Kininmonth & Paul*, 1964–7. Abstract in white drydash with a curved belfry at the NW. Square interior with raised seating round three sides, lit from concealed windows near the roof. At the back, rubbly HALL of 1937.

GOGAR PARISH CHURCH, off Glasgow Road. Disused and boarded up. By *J. A. Williamson*, 1890–1. Small and sturdy in crazy-paved whinstone. Buttressed three-bay 'nave' with a broad-eaved roof; squat NW tower. The crowstepped 'transept' across the s end is the C16 chancel of the old church, which fell out of use in 1602. The line of the E window can be traced. Williamson re-roofed it, and added the W porch and s gablet.

MONUMENTS in the churchyard. On the w, headstone of Alexander Ferguson †1761, cartouche in the segmental pediment, flanked by hourglasses. – On the s, John Bell (?) and Isabel Begg, both †1724, round-headed with his face on one side, hers on the other, both set in lots of leaves. – Frieda MacGillivray †1910 and her family on the E. Tall granite pier with a bronze relief portrait by *J. Pittendrigh MacGillivray*.

ST THOMAS (Episcopal), Glasgow Road. By the Rev. *D. E. Hart-Davies*, 1937–8. – STAINED GLASS. E window by *Heaton, Butler & Bayne*.

PUBLIC BUILDINGS

CRAIGMOUNT HIGH SCHOOL, Craigs Road. By *Alison & Hutchison & Partners*, 1968–70. Segment-shaped main building enclosing a round block.

CRAMOND BRIG GOLF CLUB, Cammo Road. Now a farmhouse. Picturesque, by *Bailey S. Murphy* and *D. M. Kinross*, c. 1910.

EAST CRAIGS AGRICULTURAL STATION, Craigs Road. Neo-Georgian main block of 1925. Behind, EAST CRAIGS HOUSE of 1768, with a semi-octagonal stair-tower added to the middle of the s front c. 1800.

EAST CRAIGS PRIMARY SCHOOL, Craigmount Brae. By *Lothian Region Department of Architectural Services*, 1978.

EDINBURGH AIRPORT, off Glasgow Road. By *Robert Matthew, Johnson-Marshall & Partners* (partner-in-charge: *John Richards*), 1975, the central block and one wing of the planned U-shaped Terminal Building. Sensible with a touch of elegance, the brown vitreous-enamelled panels smart from close to but fading into the fields in the view from the main road. – The old TERMINAL (now Project Terminal), 1954, by the same firm, the steel frame clad in vertical mahogany boarding, was one of Edinburgh's first modern buildings of distinction without pomposity.

FORRESTER HIGH SCHOOL, Broomhouse Road. By the *City Architect's Department*, 1959.

GOGARBURN HOSPITAL, Glasgow Road. Rambling collection of cheap neo-Georgian buildings begun by *Stewart Kaye* with the Administration Block in 1929, and continued after 1933 by *E. J. MacRae*. – CHILDREN'S UNIT on the s by *John Holt*, 1970. – GOGARBURN HOUSE on the w, stolid Scots Renaissance, by *James Jerdan*, 1893.

GYLEMUIR PRIMARY SCHOOL, Wester Broom Place. By the *City Architect's Department*, 1967–8.

MAYBURY ROADHOUSE, Maybury Road. Jazz-modern with a vengeance by *Patterson & Broom*, 1935. Outside now a bit tatty, but the interior a ghastly memorial to inter-war taste.

ROYAL SCOT HOTEL, Glasgow Road. By *Building Design Associates*, 1971–3; extended 1976. A large but sorry introduction to the city.

ST AUGUSTINE'S (R.C.) HIGH SCHOOL, Broomhouse Road. Abstract in white render, by the *City Architect's Department*, 1968–9.

SECUREX FACTORY (GYLEMUIR WORKS), Glasgow Road. By *J. B. Dunn & Martin*, 1935, with an Art Deco clocktower.

MANSIONS

CAMMO, Cammo Walk. A collection of fragments. The house was built by John Menzies in 1693, the park laid out by *Sir John Clerk*, 1710–26. The estate passed in 1741 to the Watsons of Saughton, in 1980 to the National Trust for Scotland. It is managed in association with the City of Edinburgh.

Approach from the N across a single-span BRIDGE dated 1762, with stepped finials on the piers. Ruin of an earlier bridge beside it. – GATE-PIERS with fluted friezes, and a roofless LODGE, dated 1789, with rosettes on the doorpiece. – Only the lower part of the HOUSE walls survive. Artisan Mannerist doorpiece, the pediment broken by a coat of arms, very much in the manner of *Robert Mylne*. – CANAL on the S. – U-plan STABLES, dated 1811; semi-elliptical blind fanlights over the doors and an octagonal centre tower. – Outside the park, round early C19 WATERTOWER with a battlemented parapet.

61 CASTLE GOGAR, off Glasgow Road. Built in 1625 by John Cowper, whose father had bought the estate in 1601. Its towers, turrets and crowsteps make this the most baronial of Edinburgh's late C16–early C17 mansions.

The plan is an L but with the jamb joined to the main block only by its SE corner. In the inner angle a large octagonal stair-tower corbelled out to the square at eaves level and balustraded (cf. Winton House (Lothian) and Innes House (Grampian), the similarity suggesting *William Ayton* as the designer). On the NE corner of the main block a fat round tower with splayed gun loops. Pair of unequal candle-snuffer-roofed turrets on the S gable; another on the jamb's NW corner, all with gunholes. Monograms of Cowper and his

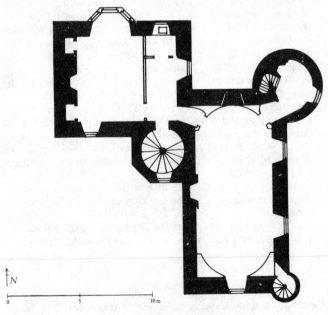

Castle Gogar,
plan of first floor

wife on the pedimented dormer-heads. A rough entrance court open to the S is formed by a W extension of *c.* 1700 and a near-contemporary cottage. They may be on the line of the original barmkin. Early C19 Jacobean porch; late Victorian N bay-window.

The interior has semicircular tunnel-vaulted ground-floor rooms in the main block. In the jamb the elliptically arched kitchen fireplace has been dressed up in the early C18 and the vault replaced by a coved ceiling. Generous turnpike stair supplemented by an awkward service stair to the first floor mostly in the wall-thickness of the NE tower. In the SE turret, stair from the first floor to the bedrooms above. The first-floor hall was made into a bow-ended drawing room, *c.* 1790. The jamb's chamber had been altered about sixty years earlier, its E part becoming a pine-panelled parlour with paintings of landscapes and ruins in the overmantel and overdoors. The thin rococo plasterwork in the corners looks early C19 rather than C18. Adam revival surround to the basket-arched marble chimneypiece of typically William Adam type.

Cushion-rusticated GATEPIERS of *c.* 1730 with rather small urn finials. The exuberant late C17 wrought-iron GATES are said to have come from Caroline Park (*see* Granton, Newhaven and Trinity: Mansions).

CRAIGIEHALL, off Queensferry Road. A villa of *c.* 1695–9 sitting among the offices and houses of H.Q. Scottish Command. This is Edinburgh's only example of the comfortable Dutch-classical country house popularized in England by Hugh May and Sir Roger Pratt. The client was the third Earl (later first Marquess) of Annandale; the architect *Sir William Bruce.* Six-bay two-storey and basement fronts to E and W, both with two-bay pedimented centrepieces. Swanky coats of arms in the tympana. Front door squeezed between two windows; above it, an urn set in a swagged bullseye. The original roof was bell-cast, with a cupola. The N pavilion, now minus its chimneys, may have been balanced by one on the S. The quadrant link was demolished in 1828 to make way for a dining-room extension by *William Burn.* Bow at the back; the projecting front lost its pediment in 1953. N offices by *David Bryce,* 1852. *Robert S. Lorimer* added a bay-window on the S in 1926. The top-heavy roof over the main block came in 1953.

Bruce's interior was planned with two ground-floor apartments, a state apartment (dining room, drawing room, bedchamber and dressing room) on the N and W, and a second apartment (ante-room, bedchamber and closet) on the S. Panelled entrance vestibule with an angular arch into the central stair-hall. The stair has an elaborate wrought-iron balustrade, very like that at Caroline Park (*see* Granton, Newhaven and Trinity), with thistles, roses, tulips and oakleaves. On the S, full-depth drawing room made by Burn from the second apartment. The sandstone chimneypiece carved with monkeys is by Lorimer. In the W recess, the panelled N wall of

Bruce's dressing room survives. Foliaged door architrave and chimney frieze. Skimpily draped cherub set on the swagged overmantel. N of the vestibule, a small front room with reused 1690s panelling; three of the doorcases match, one does not. Landscapes set in the panels above the doors, probably mid-C18. In the Blue Room behind, C17 fluted pilasters flanking the fireplace. White marble chimneypiece, its frieze carved with a floral swag suspended from clenched teeth lions' masks. Huge brackets under the small shelf. Overmantel with superb woodwork; high-relief dead ducks and fruit at the sides, deeply undercut stiff foliage on top. These frame a C17 view of Edinburgh, probably an insert.

On the front lawn, tall early C17 pillar SUNDIAL with a multi-faceted head and obelisk finial. The stepped base and globe on which it stands are of c. 1760. On the back lawn, baluster sundial of c. 1710, the iron dial made by *England* of London. – To the NW, roofless DOOCOT, dated 1672. – In the WALLED GARDEN on the NE, OFFICE BLOCK by *Bowhill Gibson & Laing*, 1966. – Mid-C19 STABLES; at their entrance, GATES placed here by Charles Hope-Weir in 1749.

After his return from accompanying Robert Adam to Italy in 1754–5, Hope-Weir replanned and extended the park, abolishing an early C18 forecourt in front of the house. To reach his new deer park S of the Almond he built an extravagantly rock-faced BRIDGE in 1757. Beside it, a barrel-vaulted Roman GROTTO and BATH-HOUSE under a round GARDEN ROOM. The thatched roof is no more. In the middle of the deer park on the top of Leny Hill, the circular CRAIGIEHALL TEMPLE, dated 1759. Its top floor, thought a hazard to aircraft, was removed in 1975. Stair-tower at the back. At the front, Doric portico with a massive segmental pediment carved with the arms and monograms of the third Earl of Annandale and his wife Sophia Fairholm, so it presumably pre-dates Sophia's death in 1716. Was this one of the forecourt gates designed by the *Earl of Mar* and made by *Alexander McGill* in 1708? Octagonal interior, stripped of panelling but still with plain classical chimneypieces and a tiled floor inlaid with marble.

GOGAR PARK, off Glasgow Road. Early Victorian overgrown cottage, probably incorporating a late Georgian villa.

GOGARMOUNT, Glasgow Road. Smart villa, dated 1817. Single-storey with bows flanking the paired columns of the Doric porch. Italianate tower behind. (Inside, round hall under the tower, its walls painted with rural scenes. The Corinthian columns must be late Victorian.)

DESCRIPTION

The churches, public buildings and mansions are snug in the Green Belt or buried in housing, both speculative and for associations. The best of the post-war development is tucked in behind Queensferry Road, e.g. the mono-pitched blocks by *Roland Wedgwood Associates* for the Southfield Housing Association, 1968, in CRAIGMOUNT AVENUE NORTH. In QUEENSFERRY ROAD, No. 565, opposite the Barnton Hotel, English Arts and Crafts with a gambrel roof, is by *Hedley*, *c.* 1905. In CAMMO CRESCENT, Edwardian red-tiled villas, their bay-windows pretending to be towers. In the plain steading (now offices) of BRAEHEAD MAINS a large sculptured group by *Robert Forrest, c.* 1836, of James V at Cramond Bridge, formerly at Clermiston House. Across Cramond Bridge (*see* Cramond and Davidson's Mains), CRAMOND BRIG COTTAGES, a neat three-sided courtyard by *Law & Dunbar-Nasmith*, 1963, hidden below the dual-carriageway. Among trees beyond Craigiehall (*see* above), the Scots Renaissance LOWOOD by *R. Weir Schultz*, 1910–12, with a round entrance tower on the hinge of the L plan.

GRANGE

Predominantly a Victorian area built over several small estates. The N part near the Meadows was laid out for development in 1825. Grange Road itself was made in 1845, and the area to the S was laid out in streets to plans made successively by *David Cousin* in 1851, and *Robert R. Raeburn* in 1858 and 1864. On this S part where the ground slopes down to the Pow Burn valley giving views of Blackford Hill and the Pentlands, the plots are larger and the houses grander. Throughout, the garden walls and trees play as big a part as the architecture.

CHURCHES

MARCHMONT ST GILES (originally Robertson Memorial), Kilgraston Road. Economical Gothic by *Robert Morham*, 1869, on an open site. Spindly W steeple, gabled and pinnacled, with clock faces over wide belfry arches; porch in its base, with touches of pink stone and flanking stair-halls. Broad wagon-roofed interior on iron-framed timber arches; arched transepts and splayed apse. – FONT. Art Nouveau Gothic. – ORGAN by *Brindley & Foster*, rebuilt by *N.P. Mander*, 1963. – STAINED GLASS. Sentimental, e.g. on the S side one light at the W end (Christ and little children, 1902), two in the nave (Supper at Emmaus, *c.* 1889), and two in the transept (Martha and Mary, 1902) by *A. Ballantine & Gardiner*. – Gothic MANSE to N, contemporary with the church.
ST CATHERINE ARGYLE (originally Chalmers Memorial Free Church), Beaufort Road. Fussy Dec by *Patrick Wilson*, 1865. T plan, with an octagonal belfry in one of the angles distracting attention from the incomplete stump of a steeple in the other. Two-colour masonry and an abundance of pink granite shafts, effective only in the elaborate entry at the base of the

T. Interior modernized as a hall in 1972 (after the fire at the
Argyle Place Church in Sciennes Road, since demolished) but
reinstated after the demolition of West St Giles; only a few
Ruskinian corbels still show beneath the ceiling.

St Margaret's Convent of the Ursulines of Jesus,
Whitehouse Loan. The first religious house in Scotland since
the Reformation, founded by the Canadian born Fr James
Gillis after he had raised the money in France. The architect
was *J. Gillespie Graham*, 1835, and he incorporated in the
new buildings the three-storey mansion of Whitehouse,
c. 1670, adding to its N end the tall square gatehouse; ogee
roof with deep eaves and lacy Jacobean flashings, and a
rope-moulded archway entered from Whitehouse Loan. At
the S end a block of mild Tudor character with twin gables
also adjacent to the road (subsequently altered). Single-storey
office wing with belfry (still *in situ*) connected to the Chapel
in the Saxon style, i.e. a very innocent version of Norman;
this description gives its liturgical orientation, but the W front
actually faces S. Stiff and pretty like a German toy, with
pinnacled and nook-shafted buttresses, triple nave window
and octagonal belicote; pious heads as label-stops, and plenty
more at the other round-arched windows along the sides.
Gothic E end, tall and complicated with snecked masonry and
Dec tracery, by *Archibald Macpherson*, 1893-5. Graham's
neo-Norman is more consistent inside. Four bays with round
stone piers, scalloped and rope-moulded capitals, nave and
aisles rib-vaulted in plaster. Through the tall E arch, Macpherson's chancel is of two bays with a three-sided apse,
rib-vaulted in stone with bosses at the diagonal intersections
but a more central European confluence of the transverse and
ridge-ribs. In the lower part of the apse a quicker rhythm of
blind arcades alternating with statues by *William Vickers* of
Glasgow. Below it, the crypt where Gillis is buried; moulded
ribs dying into three plain cylindrical piers. Lady Chapel to
the S of the chancel, organ gallery to the N. – Altar. Traceried, with panels of green Genoa marble, and now moved
away from its setting before the gold and jewelled sacrament
house and elaborate alabaster reredos of angels between flying
buttresses. – Lady Chapel reredos. By *George Goldie*,
executed by *Earp*, 1877. Our Lady in a marble-shafted tabernacle with a jolly turreted castle overhead, flanked by interlaced Norman arcades. – Rood screen, formerly right across
the W bay of the nave and aisles but now removed to the W
end. Neo-Norman in stained timber, but was it part of Graham's design? The three crowning figures and the florid carving between them must be of later period, but perhaps they
were added. The stalls that filled the nave were likewise extravagant in style, but have been moved to St Mary's R.C.
Cathedral (*see* Central Area, First New Town: Churches). –
Stained glass. Eight clearstorey lights in bright colours
(figures of saints), 1862.

School to the S. By *E. W. Pugin*, 1861, a long Gothic

range whose austerity is barely relieved by cusped hood-moulds at the main storey; long corridor on the ground floor, forming an indoor cloister. N extension of the old house and a separate house known as the HERMITAGE, both baronial, c. 1856. – SUNDIAL in the garden overlooked by school and chapel. Early C18 baluster type, with cut-out hemispheres. – GROTTO to the S. A replica of the grotto at Lourdes, 1880.

SALISBURY CHURCH (originally United Presbyterian), Cause-wayside and Grange Road. By *Robert Paterson*, 1862. It is a snecked stone box of two storeys with Frenchified detail, partly Gothic. Windows with alternate smooth and knobbly voussoirs, colonnettes and plate-tracery. Steep wheel-win-dowed gable between stair-halls, the hall at the SE corner forming a tower with angle-shafts, short belfry and lucarned pavilion roof (minus its original iron cresting and finial). A jolly interior, like a permanent harvest-festival. Aisles from end to end, formed by iron pillars with diversely foliaged capitals of *carton-pierre* under the thin, ball-flowered arcade. Gothic roof-trusses on leafy corbels, and a deep cornice of serpentine vine. The steep rake of the gallery to the E and the pierced ventilators in the roof (the sixty-three-jet sun-burners underneath them, by *Robertson & Cairns*, are missing) add a theatrical feeling. Of the original furnishings, only the bul-bous Gothic pulpit remains amid genteel screen-work of 1958. – Original CLOCK in the gallery opposite. – ORGAN by *Wadsworth*, much altered. – STAINED GLASS. The original glazing is clear (with coloured borders) to N and S, abstract in jewel colours to E and W. On the S side two lights (the Raising of the Young Man; the Baptism of Christ) by *Douglas Stra-chan*, after 1928.

PUBLIC BUILDINGS

ASTLEY AINSLIE HOSPITAL, Grange Loan. Founded as a convalescent and recreational institution under the will of John Ainslie †1900. The site acquired in 1921 consisted of a nine-hole golf course and four substantial villas. The charac-ter of an exclusive villa development has been kept, as have most of the garden walls. LODGES in Grange Loan: at the E, ST ROQUE LODGE of c. 1870 with broad eaves: then the hos-pital lodges by *Auldjo Jamieson & Arnott*, 1932, square pav-ilions with bullseye windows and wrought-iron gates of late C17 type. The main entrance is from Canaan Lane, the lodge pavilions again by *Jamieson & Arnott*, 1932, cribbing from Reginald Fairlie's Floors Castle lodges (Borders).

Of the original villas, CANAAN HOUSE (ADMINISTRA-TION DEPARTMENT), c. 1805, with a giant over-arch in its parapeted centre, was almost doubled in size in 1877. Addi-tions by *John Jerdan*, 1922, swamp the Italianate CANAAN PARK of c. 1845. Also Italianate of the same date but classier is ST ROQUE. The new buildings provided by *Auldjo Jamie-*

son & Arnott between 1925 and 1939 are in a cheap stock-
brokers' cottage style with harled walls and tiled roofs. Only
the NURSES' HOME of 1925 rises above one storey. A
squidgy Doric order along the front of the SCIENTIFIC DE-
PARTMENT (1929) and an eccentrically placed scrolled chimney on the RESIDENCY attempt a touch of swagger.

Minimal cottage style again for the SCHOOL by *Stuart
Matthew*, 1957. Much tougher with strong horizontals and
vertical fins is *Michael Laird & Partners'* CHILDREN'S
UNIT, 1963-5. The BALFOUR PAVILION by the *Scottish
Health Service Common Services Agency: Building Division*,
1980, returns to the cottage theme but on a large scale, with
mono-pitch roofs and a busy mixture of materials.

In the grounds are several medieval ARCHITECTURAL
FRAGMENTS of fine quality. Eight vaulting bosses with Late
Gothic foliage (both swirling and crinkly), the Crown of
Thorns, the Arma Christi and the arms of the Royal Burgh.
St Giles and Trinity College Church are likely sources. Reset
in the walls of an arbour are three large slabs with cusped
loop tracery under crocketed ogee heads. On the richest panel
two shields have been given the date 1728. The ogee points
of the shields and the loop tracery suggest the early C16.
Wilson's *Memorials of Edinburgh in the Olden Time* records
several very similar panels decorating the heads of niches in
the wall beside chimneypieces. Simpler niches in this position
survive at the Earl of Morton's House in Blackfriars Street
(Old Town) and in numerous tower houses, e.g. Liberton,
Borthwick (Lothian).

GRANGE CEMETERY, Beaufort Road. Layout, lodge, and
vaulted catacombs sombrely bisecting the ground from E to
W, all by *David Bryce*, 1846. Rigidly planned and well-tended
MONUMENTS. Against the N wall an austere block pediment
to Dr Thomas Chalmers †1847; an Egyptian portal with a
date-palm by *Robert Thomson* to the wife of William Stewart
†1868; a characteristic monument to Sir James Gowans
†1890, in his own style with an equilateral triangular monolith under bracketed eaves. At the centre of the S wall, seen
through the round arch of the catacombs, a large Grecian
memorial in bright red Corrennie granite to Dr Thomas
Guthrie, by *Pittendrigh MacGillivray*, 1908, with a bronze
medallion portrait.

POLICE STATION, Causewayside. By *Robert Morham*, 1885.
Baronial with a corner turret.

ROYAL HOSPITAL FOR SICK CHILDREN, Sciennes Road. By
G. *Washington Browne*, 1892, on the site of the Trades Maidens' Hospital (the old premises at Meadowside House were
redeveloped as an extension of the Royal Infirmary). 'English
Renaissance', said *The Builder*, i.e. mostly Jacobean, in red
Corsehill sandstone. Central administrative block with a rich
armorial doorway between very tall mullioned bays with
shaped tabernacle gables. A front courtyard is formed by
gabled wings with octagonal corner towers, the first-floor log-

gias between the towers unhappily filled in *c.* 1960. MORTU-
ARY to the NE, a small room lined with paintings by *Phoebe
Traquair*, 1885, originally at Meadowside and reinstated here
by her in 1895. Above the dado life-size angels singing the
Sanctus on a background of horizontal bands representing the
six orders (or days) of creation. At the N end a panel of
'Maternity', at the S end 'The Cup of Life' and 'The Bridge
of Life'. Diaper ceiling painted down into the cove. All very
colourful and charming, with lots of appealing detail. OUT-
PATIENTS department in Sylvan Place, Edwardian Renaissance by *Browne*, 1903, this time in grey stone. Additions to
the N of the main building (and with no attempt to suit it) by
Cullen, Lochhead & Brown of Glasgow, 1960.

SCIENNES PRIMARY SCHOOL, Sciennes Road. By *Robert Wilson*, 1889. Large and symmetrical Jacobean Renaissance with
a central cupola.

PERAMBULATION

FINGAL PLACE overlooking the Meadows is a terrace of *c.* 1825
with channelled ground floors. Running back, two more terraces, the broad-eaved Nos. 2–9 ARGYLE PLACE (*c.* 1860)
and the Georgian SYLVAN PLACE (*c.* 1835). Imprisoned behind, SYLVAN HOUSE (No. 13 Sylvan Place), *c.* 1760, with
a grand doorpiece. Bay-windowed terraces built from *c.* 1860
in RILLBANK CRESCENT, RILLBANK TERRACE and MILL-
ERFIELD PLACE give way to plain mid-Victorian tenements.

Still further E in MONCREIFF TERRACE is a big tenement by 131
Groves-Raines & Spens, 1979. Five concrete block storeys
with brown stained wooden windows and set-back attic. The
fun is in the bright blue painted steel balconies which make
a right angle at each of the splayed corners, and the scarlet
frameworks that hem them in from first floor up (the use of
single vertical timbers from top to bottom is remarkable) and
continue right along the attic. The method, which is to make
a pattern over the larger windows and define their private
outdoor space, is equally enjoyable.

CAUSEWAYSIDE is entered past LORD RUSSELL PLACE, a
large Georgian tenement with a bowed centre to its narrow
N front. Then some *Barratt* flats of 1981, lamb dressed as
mutton. In SCIENNES the front of SCIENNES HILL HOUSE
is visible, elaborated with mid-C19 architraves and absorbed
into working-class housing, *c.* 1880. Back in Causewayside,
after the Police Station on the corner of Sciennes House Place
(*see* above), No. 120, *c.* 1800, pilastered shopfronts now with
Quality Street glazing. Through the pend, GRANGE COURT,
its late C18 N range improved as artisan housing in the late
C19 with bowed towers for stairs and sanitation. In 1969
Cameron & Gibb modernized the interiors, demolished a central block and built new houses on the S and W sides.

GRANGE ROAD begins at the E end with Salisbury Church (*see* above), facing a row of old-fashioned shop-fronted tenements by *Robert R. Raeburn*, 1877. Nos. 30-32, 34, 40 and 46 were built by 1852, all solid villas in the old Georgian tradition. Then a diversion into the s part of MANSIONHOUSE ROAD (referring to the old house of Grange, formerly at its s end), where Nos. 28, 30-32 and 43 were being built in 1845; also No. 31, whose single raised storey and central pediment were imitated at No. 29 in 1848. *See* above for Grange Cemetery and St Catherine Argyle Church in Beaufort Road, and for Marchmont St Giles Church in KILGRASTON ROAD, where No. 11 (ESDAILE) is large and plain baronial, *c.* 1860; as the College for Ministers' Daughters it was given stained glass on the stair (St Joan and Florence Nightingale, 1925) and in the hall (St Columba, 1930) by *Marjorie Kemp*. In BLACK-FORD ROAD, No. 35, austerely pebbledashed with red dress-ings, is by *G. Washington Browne* for himself, 1899; on the N front a tall gable with the initials GWB. JBB at the apex, on the other fronts red sandstone bay-windows.

DICK PLACE was mostly built up with polite villas by 1852, then acquired some picturesque fancies like the bargeboarded No. 57, and finally some Gothic seasoning - mild at No. 55 by *R. Thornton Shiells* in 1862, wild at Nos. 48-50 by *Frederick T. Pilkington*, 1864, a symmetrical pair in which totter-ing crowstepped porches and skeleton chimneys contrast with massive bald outshots. Set back in the trees is *Pilkington*'s own house at No. 38 (EGREMONT, originally Park House), 1864, with masonry patterns more elaborate and modelling more perverse than ever; on the E side a round-arched and crested canopy at the porch (cf. his Lloyd's Bank in Victoria Street, London, now demolished), on the s a dizzy build-up of stilted arches and encrusting foliage. Ingeniously planned interior with Louis XVI detail. Equally hidden (in the garden of the old house of Grange), No. 46a by *Kininmonth & Spence* for William Kininmonth, 1933, a small abstract composition, now white-harled, originally whitewashed brick with horizon-tally emphasized joints; open-plan interior, the living room enjoying the s view with a continuously glazed semicircular bow. Near the E end of Dick Place, No. 25 FINDHORN PLACE (RATHAN) is by *Charles Leadbetter* for Robert Mid-dlemass the biscuit-maker, 1876.*

In LAUDER ROAD, No. 15 (ST ANDREW'S COTTAGE) is dated 1852; Nos. 27-29 are an Italianate pair, one with a balcony on its bay-window, the other with a tower. No. 18 is opulent classical on a corner site; in its garden, an over-large brick block by *Roland Wedgwood Associates*, 1981. No. 2 (DOUG-LAS HOUSE) weighty Italian. On the opposite corner of Grange Loan, No. 2 SOUTH LAUDER ROAD (MASSON HALL OF RESIDENCE) by *Sydney Mitchell & Wilson*, 1892,

---

*Dull classical outside, but *The Journal of Decorative Art* in April 1877 de-scribed the luxurious decorative scheme by *Joseph Shaw & Co*. Middlemass in-vented the digestive biscuit.

well composed in harl and red trimmings with big curvaceous gables and a mansard roof; additions at rear by *Frank Perry*, 1966. In ST ALBAN'S ROAD, No. 61 on the S side is by *Roland Wedgwood Associates* for Viewpoint Housing Association, 1975, much the best of the C20 redevelopments in Grange; variegated red brick with upright stretcher courses from end to end over the windows. In ST THOMAS ROAD, No. 10 by *Morris & Steedman*, 1961, a single-storey patio house almost invisible in the trees. The E section of GRANGE LOAN is fragmentary. On the N side, Nos. 108–122 by *Lyle & Constable*, 1933, but still clinging to stone fronts and crowsteps. To their E a fluted and rusticated Ionic gate-pier from the house of Grange, with a coronet and griffon as finial; another further W. On the S side a would-be classical water-tower on harled pilaster legs, a clumsy oddity of *c.* 1900, and WEST GRANGE GARDENS, buff brick flats with blunt copper roofs, by *J. & J. A. Carrick*, 1971. GRANGE TERRACE to the S is composed as a Victorian palace front with bay-windows and an iron crested centrepiece, probably by *Robert R. Raeburn*, *c.* 1865.

In BLACKFORD AVENUE, ST RAPHAEL'S (formerly Kilravock Lodge) by *MacGibbon & Ross*, *c.* 1874, a landmark with its tall baronial turret, enlarged as a hospital with an Art Deco W wing by *J. Douglas Miller*, 1934; adjoining chapel converted from a laundry by *A. Murray Hardie*, 1919, and enlarged by *W. J. Devlin*, 1928. Also by *MacGibbon & Ross* No. 1 OSWALD ROAD (formerly ST OSWALD'S), its entrance front cleverly composed with an octagonal turret over the porch and picturesque dormers on each side. No. 5 round the corner is prosperous Classical with a weighty balcony over the door and a lead-roofed bay-window to one side, probably by *John Chesser*, *c.* 1860. No. 24 is by *John M. Kinross*, *c.* 1888, as are its three close neighbours at Nos. 31–35 MORTONHALL ROAD (No. 33 for himself), in a rubbly Scots style striking just the right balance between grandeur and domesticity. On the N side of Mortonhall Road, No. 4 (CARDON) by *T. T. Paterson*, 1902, aggressively red all over, and No. 8 (formerly OUTWOOD) by *Frank W. Simon* for his father Professor Simon, 1889, beautifully detailed in pale orange sandstone with spreading piend roofs. To the S, GLENISLA GARDENS, a cosy terrace with twin porches and piended dormers in the *Sydney Mitchell* style, *c.* 1890, curving down into the valley.

Back at the N end of Blackford Avenue, the W and more interesting part of GRANGE LOAN. On the S side, No. 123 (formerly DUNARD) by *Robert R. Raeburn*, *c.* 1865, a large lump of a house with an Ionic porch between dissimilar bays, and Nos. 129 and 131, surprisingly restrained designs by *Frederick T. Pilkington* for Alexander Monteith, 1872. For the rest, *see* Astley Ainslie Hospital above. The N side is here called WHITEHOUSE TERRACE and numbered W to E. No. 8 with a lodge is boldly composed with a tall candle-snuffer turret beside a crested French roof; the others likewise secluded and confident in their several styles but less showy – all *c.* 1870. In the s part of WHITEHOUSE LOAN, No. 21 (SYDNEY LODGE), crisply harled with piended wings, and No. 17 (THE WHITEHOUSE) with a pedimented front, both apparently *c.* 1840. Opposite, THE ELMS by *William Notman*, 1858, with a baronial s front, the double bartizan entrance less convincing, and the big CLINTON HOUSE, *c.* 1870, dramatically gabled and bargeboarded with a two-storey conservatory. A pretty Tudor double house (Nos. 1–3) on the corner of BLACKFORD ROAD. Quadrant-cornered lodge on the corner of HOPE TERRACE, where Nos. 9–11 are a long plain pair built of whinstone, *c.* 1840, and the WHITEHOUSE AND GRANGE BOWLING CLUB, *c.* 1912, enjoys half-timbering and red tiles. In STRATHEARN ROAD, No. 88 is baronial of 1856 and Nos. 12–19 are a fragment of a hugely mansarded and dormered terrace, *c.* 1880; but tenements prevail. The Greek Doric embellishment of No. 20 for the ROYAL BANK is by *Dick Peddie & Walker Todd*, 1934. Petit bureaucrat POST OFFICE by *H.M. Office of Works*, 1919, and so back to Grange Road.

In CHALMERS CRESCENT, No. 5 of *c.* 1866 with a square steeple. Opposite, two houses have round corner towers, No. 8 (dated 1877) with a conical spire, No. 10 (*c.* 1868) with battlements. Nos. 2 and 9 PALMERSTON ROAD (both dated 1868) are fiercely baronial, No. 2 even boasting a gun loop.

GRANTON, NEWHAVEN AND TRINITY

Two harbour villages, one C16, the other C19. The Georgian and Victorian villas which enjoy the view from the high ground behind have been joined by a large inter-war housing scheme on the w.

CHURCHES

CHRIST CHURCH (Episcopal), Trinity Road. Now a house. A little Dec village church by *Hay* of Liverpool, 1854, of squared Fife rubble with Craigleith dressings. s porch and transept, sw steeple continuous with the w gable, in which the r. label-stop is traditionally a portrait of the mason (an incised mark underneath). N aisle by *Thomas Leadbetter* 1889. Conversion in a modern idiom by *Gordon & Dey*, 1980, retaining some decent stained glass and allowing the full internal height to be seen at the two staircases.

GRANTON CONGREGATIONAL CHURCH, Boswall Parkway. Built in 1936 by the *Coltmuir Stone Company* of Glasgow. Economical but ambitious Gothic with aisles, clearstorey and apse, the interior a little more convincing.

GRANTON METHODIST CHURCH, Boswall Parkway. Designed

as a hall (but the church was never built) by *A. H. Mottram*, 1937. Harled and slated, a red-brick porch on the gambrel-roofed front.

GRANTON PARISH CHURCH, Boswall Parkway. By *John F. Matthew*, 1934. A round-arched cruciform church of pink Craigmillar rubble with rustic dressings of dark brown Doddington stone; NE tower and E hall. Very plain interior, the wagon roof cedar-framed and panelled with oak, pulpit and stalls also of oak.

NEWHAVEN PARISH CHURCH, Craighall Road. A Gothic box 34 by *John Henderson*, opened in 1836. Standard firescreen-gabled W front of chunky polished ashlar with crowning bellcote, ideally sited at the head of a sloping garden. The interior a plain four-bay prism of flat-topped aisles and arched nave, no side galleries. In 1899 *William H. McLachlan* added the chancel, reusing the old E window. – Pitch-pine PULPIT by *William Watson & Sons*, 1890. – Oak COMMUNION TABLE, 1900. – ORGAN by *Conacher & Co.*, 1883, rebuilt in the W gallery by *Gray & Davison*, 1936. – STAINED GLASS by *Ballantine & Son*, the figures naive in one N aisle window of 1858 ('I was sick and ye visited Me ...'), colourful but vapid in two S aisle windows of *c.* 1899 (the Good Samaritan, Christ and the little children). The purely decorative windows are mainly of the 1870s, the colours jewelled in the chancel, more subdued in the aisles. – WAR MEMORIAL in the porch by *Hamilton* of Glasgow, 1919; unusually happy, a bronze plaque framed in green mosaic and flanked by oak Gothic tabernacles with small figures of a soldier and sailor.

OLD GRANTON PARISH CHURCH, Granton Road. Now disused. Simple E.E. in rockfaced masonry, 1877.

OLD NEWHAVEN FREE CHURCH, Pier Place, Newhaven. Now in secular use. By *J. Anderson Hamilton*, 1852, re-cast and enlarged by *Wallace & Flockhart* of London, 1883, with halls and a 37 m. steeple whose gablets rise higher than the corner pinnacles. Plenty of architectural features, but all the detail simple and geometric.

ST DAVID OF SCOTLAND (Episcopal), Boswall Parkway. By *Harold O. Tarbolton*, 1939. Church and hall in two white-harled sheds, very simple but nicely composed, and a modern-looking rectory facing the main road. – Inside the church, on the (liturgical) W wall, three panels (the Passion and Crucifixion) of the enamel-tiled ALTARPIECE from Holy Trinity, Dean Bridge (*see* Central Area, Dean, Churches). It is by *Henry Holiday*, *c.* 1910, strongly composed with lovely deep colours but insipid detail.

ST MARGARET MARY (R.C.), Boswall Parkway. By *Reginald Fairlie*, 1939. A shaped gable rising from single-storey porch and aisles, and a single-storey presbytery to the W, all white-harled with orange brick.

ST MARY AND ST JAMES'S CHAPEL, Westmost Close, Newhaven. Built in 1506–8 on a roughly rectangular plan 7 m. long, a ruin by 1611 and now reduced to fragmentary walls, of which the w gable is the most complete. It contains a rectangular C17 window with chamfered edge and glass check and holes for vertical bars.

ST SERF, Ferry Road, on the corner of Clark Road. Gentle Dec by *G. Mackie Watson*, 1901 after a competition, the chancel completed *c.* 1925, the hall to the N in blocky style, 1959, the N transept and (copper-covered) spire not at all. White masonry, pink dressings, green North of England slates. Wide nave with tall arcades, passage aisles and a tunnel roof. – Gothic PULPIT of oak by *Watson*, stiffly imitated in the chancel CHOIR SCREEN by *C. d'O. Pilkington Jackson*, 1926. – STAINED GLASS. In the chancel three windows of two lights each (the Te Deum) by *Gordon Webster*, 1970.

WARDIE PARISH CHURCH (originally United Presbyterian), Primrose Bank Road and Netherby Road. A jolly Gothic church with Francophile detail, by *John McLachlan*, 1892. Distinctive silhouette, with central lantern and conical pinnacles. Inside, a clear-span tunnel roof over the galleries, without any illusion of aisles. – A complete and perfect set of Gothic oak FURNISHINGS by *Scott Morton & Co.*, 1935, including the ORGAN CASE in the S gable arch (the organ reconstructed by *Rushworth & Dreaper*). – STAINED GLASS over the arch. A roundel (Christ in Glory).

PUBLIC BUILDINGS

AINSLIE PARK SCHOOL ANNEXE, Ferry Road and Craighall Road. By *E. J. MacRae* at his most economical, 1939.

GRANTON HARBOUR. The Duke of Buccleuch consulted *Robert Stevenson* in 1834, and the Middle Pier was started to his design in 1836 but was taken over by *Burgess & Walker* of London in 1837. Finished in 1844, it served the ferry (and for some time the train-ferry) to Burntisland in Fife. A reinforced concrete coaling-jetty was added to the end by *J. H. Hannay-Thompson* and the *Yorkshire Hennebique Co.* in 1937. The harbour is formed by two breakwaters which enclose the water on each side, that to the w begun immediately after the Granton Harbour Act of 1842 (timber coal-wharves of *c.* 1860 survive at the far end), and the interlocked rubble E breakwater in 1852–63.

NEWHAVEN HARBOUR. A much longer history than Granton Harbour (the *Great Michael* was built here in 1511), but what now exists is partly of the same date (sea wall by *Grainger & Miller*, 1837) and partly of 1864, when *Stevenson* built the breakwater. It was enlarged in 1876, with a lighthouse on the extended E wall, which was widened in 1893–6 with an arcaded timber fish-house.

NORTHERN GENERAL HOSPITAL, Ferry Road. Designed in 1893 as the Leith Public Health Hospital by the Burgh Architect *James Simpson*, and finished by his son *George Simpson*. All of brick, the lodge and economically manorial reception block fronting the road, the four original single-storey wards, with square corner pavilions, behind.

SCOTTISH GAS BOARD. Head office in Marine Drive by *Thomas Hughes*, 1965, with long white horizontals beautifully composed to present the ideal image of a public corporation. Huge open office surrounded by smaller ones. Training centre extension by *James Parr*, 1968. To the E, GRANTON GAS-WORKS, West Granton Road. A large site on which today's prosaic installations have little connexion with the bizarre and stately architecture designed for the Edinburgh and Leith Corporation Gas Commissioners by *W. R. Herring* in 1898, all red brick with yellow trim. Main gate, originally arched, then four rows of buildings. Coal-stores with French hats on top, retort houses behind (No. 2 only survives). Purifying houses (all gone). Laboratory, meter house and pumping station, three big identical rectangles with bulging pavilion roofs (carried on delicate space-frame). Finally, tall gas-holders; one of a projected row of eight was built to Herring's design, with a steel frame of the same extraordinary delicacy, then the fixed and louvred one to the W in 1933 and another to the E in 1966. Along the E side of the site the gasworks' own passenger station and seventeen-bay, two-aisle work-shops.

STARBANK PARK, Starbank Road and Laverockbank Road. Laid out, *c.* 1890, on the shoreward slope of the garden of Starbank House (*see* Perambulations, below), with a memorial fountain by *George Simpson*, 1910.

TRINITY ACADEMY, Craighall Avenue and Newhaven Road. Ambitious Renaissance by the Leith School Board architect *George Craig*, 1891, in brown stone with red dressings. Giant pilastered ends and a figure of Youth with the torch of learn-ing high above the arcaded central porch. Extensions to the E by *Stanley P. Ross-Smith*, 1957 and 1962.

VICTORIA PARK, Newhaven Road. Bronze statue of Edward VII in Thistle robes by *John S. Rhind*, 1913. VICTORIA PARK HOUSE (formerly Bonnington Park House, now a children's centre), 1789. Many additions, starting with later Georgian pedimented wings. Original lodge.

VICTORIA PRIMARY SCHOOL, Newhaven Main Street. Gothic, by *George Craig*, 1896, on the basis of the school by *John Lessels*, 1861, which had already been enlarged in 1875 and 1884. A much lower E extension by *Reid & Forbes*, 1930, is stiff classical.

MANSIONS

CAROLINE PARK HOUSE, off West Granton Road. A late C17 house of major importance and surprising complexity, set in industrial wasteland. In 1683 Sir George Mackenzie of Tar-bat bought the estate of Royston, on which stood a substantial mansion built by Andrew Logan *c.* 1585. By 1685, when

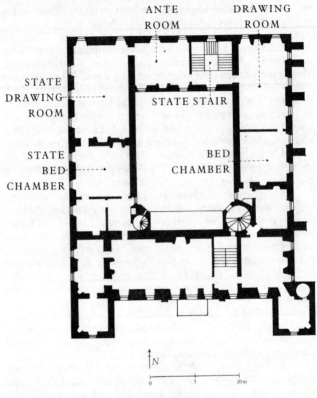

Caroline Park House,
plan of first floor

Mackenzie was made Viscount Tarbat, he had converted the
C16 house (apparently L-plan) into a quadrangle by extending
the E jamb and adding N and W ranges. In 1693 the main
approach to the house was moved from the N to the S, and
about the same time the old S front was refaced and remodelled, work being finished in 1696. The building accounts*
are maddeningly silent as to the architect or masons involved
in the work,‡ although *Alexander Eizat* seems to have been
the principal wright involved in the 1680s.

What was Tarbat's purpose in rebuilding Royston? An inscription (now removed) on the N front recorded that since
wealth is of no use unless it is spent, George and Anne,

* I am very grateful to Mrs Monica Clough for discussing the house with me
and generously giving me copies of her notes from the Cromartie muniments at
Castle Leod; and to the Earl of Cromartie for allowing this material to be made
available. J.G.

‡ The Robert Mylne who held a registered bond dated 23 June 1694, requiring
Viscount Tarbat to pay him £2,800 Scots, may have been the mason and architect
of that name, but the bond is not necessarily for payment for building work.

Viscount and Viscountess Tarbat, built this cottage (*tuguriolum*) for their own enjoyment and that of their friends. But a house containing a state apartment is no conventional country cottage, and Royston was a villa of the grandest sort, designed to display the owners' importance to those with business in Edinburgh (Tarbat's main estates were in Ross-shire) whilst affording the necessary privacy for political intrigue. Certainly, Tarbat saw it as a show house in 1705, when he tried unsuccessfully to get the government to buy it as an official residence for the Lord Chancellor. In 1739 the estate was sold by Tarbat's younger son, Sir James Mackenzie, Lord Royston, to the second Duke of Argyll, who renamed it Caroline Park in honour of his daughter, the Countess of Dalkeith. Argyll employed *William Adam* in 1740–1 to alter the house and add a range of offices. After the Duke's death Caroline Park was let to a succession of tenants, among them Lord Cockburn's father and Lady John Scott, who produced the standard version of 'Annie Laurie'.

The house is best understood by beginning at the harled N front of 1683–5. A pair of angular shaped gables with scrolled skewputts clasp the broad three-bay centre, an arrangement used at quite a number of late C17 houses (e.g. Prestonfield; *see* Newington: Mansions), but here the balustraded parapet is very awkwardly related to the gables and the W gable is broader than the E one. In the middle of the balustrade an inscription panel,* its frame carved with scrolls of typical late C17 type (cf. Greyfriars Churchyard; *see* Old Town: Churches). The only ground-floor opening is the basket-arched door, the top of whose lintel rises to a small point, a Gothic touch belied by the cornice above. The flanks are utilitarian, but the E range has been given sturdy buttresses, probably part of the repairs by *Alexander Laing* in 1790. The top of the E gable of the S range has been cut about as if the E range had been lowered. High up in the gable, a C16 cannon spout.

The S front is without parallel in Scotland. The general 64 outline is French, the detail Edinburgh. Seven-bay main block, its three-bay centrepiece marked off by giant pilasters, rusticated with pulvinated bands. Above the centre, a fat ogee roof enlivened by a stone dormer, its jambs corbelled out above the main cornice. Semicircular pediment, its finial a flaming mountain (part of Tarbat's coat of arms). Frieze carved with the date 1696. Boldly advanced end pavilions, their ogee roofs‡ topped with small square cupolas (cf. Mansart's Château de Berny). On the frieze of the l. pavilion, the inscription ANNE VICOUNTES TARBAT, on the r. GEORGE VICOUNT TARBAT. All this is ashlar-fronted, and the rusticated quoins seem an unnecessary embellishment. Much more peculiar is the heavy base-course, carved with very

---

* The inscription (no longer visible) is given in full by the RCAHMS.
‡ These have been remodelled. Originally they were steeper at the bottom.

old-fashioned floral and abstract designs but including rock-faced blocks. Is this an attempt to suggest a rusticated basement, and have stones from the C16 house been incorporated? Low basket-arched doors in the inward-facing pavilion walls, with small pendants in the middle of their lintels. Curious detail at the front door too. Bracketed lintel with a keystone dropping through it as a pendant. Set behind this is a door of the same design as the one in the N front, but without the cornice, the only part of the old walls to show through the new facings. Roman Doric porch, its wrought-iron balustrade decorated with a coroneted GT MW monogram (for George, Viscount Tarbat, and his second wife, Margaret, Countess of Wemyss), the thistle and rose, and the Wemyss swan and Mackenzie stag's head. This must be of 1700–5,* but the design is not symmetrical, so was it meant to go somewhere else? And is the porch what it seems? On to its flat roof opens a pedimented door with a pulvinated frieze and finial carved with Tarbat's crest of the sun in glory. This is much grander than the ground-floor door and suggests that it was intended to be the principal entrance approached by a double stair, the arrangement provided by James Smith at Newhailes‡ in 1686. But this would have meant a complete replanning of the house, a likely enough reason for dropping the idea.

From 1696 the main entrance was through the s door. The formal route then lay across the paved courtyard to the N range (cf. Drumlanrig, Dumfries and Galloway). On the s side of the courtyard clear evidence of the C16 house. Massive off-centre chimney. Octagonal SE stair-tower, its upper stage corbelled out to the square and its top lopped off.§ The lean-to corridor (probably early C18) linking it to the smaller late C17 SW stair cannot hide the irregularity of this side. Cornice on the other three sides, the regular three bays of the N range a not very compelling focus.

The N door opens on to the state stair. Wrought-iron balustrade with circles of roses between the plain uprights, perhaps by *Alexander Gairdner*, who was paid for smith work here in 1685. On the landing chunky foliaged wooden balusters. The state apartment opens to the r. First the ante-room or dining room, now quite plain.‖ Then, in the w range, the drawing room. Heavily moulded ceiling. Cornice of downward-pointing soggy leaves. In the corners of the cove, huge upward-pointing leaves; in the middle of each side, foliaged scrolls flanking a circle of bayleaves in which is the coroneted monogram of Lord Tarbat and his first wife. On the flat, a compartmented scheme including roses of the same design as had appeared in wrought-iron on the stair. In the middle, set in an oakleaf border, a gaily painted Aurora by *Nicolas Heude*. This is a puzzle. It can only be seen properly

---

* They married in 1700, and she died in 1705.
‡ *See The Buildings of Scotland: Lothian.*
§ The stair inside seems to have originally gone up one floor higher.
‖ The RCAHMS reported pine panelling in 1921.

from the middle of the w wall; on the approach from the NE it is upside-down, but even turned through 180° it would not make its full impact on someone entering or passing through the room. Was it painted as part of another (abandoned) scheme? The plasterwork must have been done before Anne, Viscountess Tarbat's death in 1699. Although George Dunsterfield entered into an agreement to do plasterwork at Tarbat House, this does not look like his work. It may well be by *William Baine*, who was paid for plasterwork done at Royston before November 1690. Wooden chimneypiece with panelled pilasters and a corniced lintel by *William Adam*, 1740–1. Dado and doorcases of the same date. The panelling above is C19.* Over the fireplace and the s doors, early C18 landscapes with classical ruins. In the square bedchamber beyond, another coved ceiling modelled with the same motifs. In the round centre a painting by *Heude*, this time of Diana and Endymion and correctly positioned to be seen on the approach. Doorcases, dado and fireplace surround of 1740–1; C19 panelling on the upper part of the walls. More landscapes over the doors and fireplace. The three-panel door to the closet is distinctively late C17. So too is the other door in the closet, but its wall panelling looks mid-C18. Immediately E of the closet, a tight service stair. Beside it the RCAHMS reported a lift (now plastered over).

The E range contained Lord Tarbat's apartment. L. of the state stair is the drawing room. The pulvinated frieze over the stone fireplace looks late C17, but the dado is of 1740–1. So too are the doorcases, deprived of their cornices when the crude panelling of the upper walls was put in. Two more C18 landscapes above doors. In the bedchamber the C18 doorcases are intact, with another C18 chimneypiece and yet more landscapes.

The principal access to the first floor of the s range is by a stair of *c.* 1700 immediately beside the entrance hall. Wrought-iron balustrade with roses and thistles of the same sort as on the balustrade of the porch. Near the bottom of this stair a stone fireplace in the E wall, probably C16. This range was damaged by fire in 1934, and most of its first floor is now one large room, featureless except for a huge C16 stone fireplace. The two w rooms have been thrown into one. Late C17 corner fireplace with a stepped overmantel. Of the same date the lugged architraved doorcases, but they have lost their cornices. C18 landscapes inserted in the 1930s panelling. The late C16 beams painted with designs of fruit were uncovered after the fire and inserted here. On the walls of the room in the SW pavilion more landscapes, of *c.* 1740 and apparently by a different artist. These are painted on the plaster; so too are their frames, decorated with trophies, foliage, lions, doves, and the Argyll monogram and coronet.

On the ground floor none of the panelling reported by the

‡ The room was originally tapestry-hung.

RCAHMS survives. Semi-elliptical tunnel-vault in the NW kitchen.

Simple piend-roofed NW range of OFFICES by *William Adam*, 1740–1, now rather altered. WALLED GARDEN to the N. Against its W wall a lectern DOOCOT with crowstepped gables, probably early C18.

Tall GATE-PIERS to the NE, with the same pulvinated bands of rustication as the pilasters of the S front, and presumably built in the 1690s. They used to have finials of scrolls forming crown spires. Mid-C18 foot-gates inserted between them.

CRAIGROYSTON HOUSE, West Shore Road. A flat, castellated joke of *c*. 1800. Two storeys and five bays, of which the second and fourth have tall parapets to look like towers. Gothic porch and centrepiece, spindly square turrets at the corners, battlements overall. Whatever fun the inside may have possessed was replaced by *Lorimer*'s compartmented plasterwork in 1907. The E extension is probably his.

GRANTON

Granton itself is the creation of the Dukes of Buccleuch, based on the Victorian harbour, whose main function was the export of their coal. The ducal grandeur of its buildings (always isolated, and now invaded by industrial sprawl) is due to its other job as a ferry terminal connecting Edinburgh to Fife and the north of Scotland. The flat land to the S is a huge rectangle of local-authority housing.

GRANTON SQUARE, its N side open to the harbour and its S side to a skyline of public housing, is flanked by two similar buildings of pale grey Granton stone by *William Burn*, 1838, in the dignified Georgian survival manner that was never to lose its popularity in Victorian Scotland. To the W a big tenement of three storeys and eleven bays, the ends advanced with rusticated quoins, with the entry to the harbour office on the N elevation. Further to the W along the shore is a bonded warehouse with hoists, *c*. 1860, and a brick warehouse of *c*. 1880 whose corner (possibly older) is broached in to form a lighthouse. To the E the former GRANTON INN (now H.M.S. Claverhouse), of the same bulk but more ample scale, with only seven bays and a central porch of coupled Roman Doric columns. On the N elevation a long consoled balcony viewing the sea, and immediately to the E the stables and coachyard. LOWER GRANTON ROAD continues with an incomplete terrace (Nos. 153–155) whose heavy cornice and ground-floor bay-windows suggest *William Burn* again. Ferranti's BELLESK HOUSE, by *Bamber, Gray & Partners*, 1978, dispels the feudal image, but it returns with the long, gently serpentine line of EAST COTTAGES, plain and well proportioned, of red Granton brick, *c*. 1840. Uphill from the Square are the former Board School by *Robert Wilson*, 1885, and to the E the former parish church and a pair of whin and red sandstone houses of 1891, one of which was originally the police station.

EAST PILTON, to the S of Granton proper, was laid out by the City Architect *E. J. MacRae* in 1930, on the E-W axis of Boswall Parkway. With its mixture of two- and three-storey houses and flats, it owes its present stability (compared with West Pilton) to a good provision of churches and shops as well as the extremely boring schools of which MacRae was the master. Traditional methods of house design and construction have helped too.

GRANTON ROAD, laid out in 1836 for access to the harbour, divides East Pilton from Trinity. No. 2, *c.* 1835, has two blockish pediments to the front, and one over the bay-window to Ferry Road. No. 174 (GRANTONS, 1855) has many of the tricks and all the vigour of *David Bryce*. On the E side the former Granton Road Station (now a workshop) of *c.* 1844. Just before the drop to Granton, BOSWALL ROAD turns sharply off to the r., along the brink of the high ground above the Forth. First the single-storey but very grand CHALLENGER LODGE, *c.* 1830, with unfluted Greek Doric portico. SW wing (for St Columba's Hospice) by *Alan Reiach, Eric Hall & Partners*, 1978. Then three symmetrically composed villas, also of *c.* 1830 but more adventurous: BOSWALL HOUSE in the middle, with a three-storey pedimented centrepiece set back behind a semicircular Doric porch, MANOR HOUSE (somewhat remodelled) and FORTHVIEW to W and E. Monumental front garden walls with extraordinary ironwork. To the rear, each house has a canted bay with delicate iron balcony, and the two outer ones are picturesquely composed with a suggestion of towers. Further E in PRIMROSE BANK ROAD, an odd mixture: Nos. 16–18 highly skilful Queen Anne, by *A. Hunter Crawford*, *c.* 1895–6, of purpose-made red Midland brick with stone dressings; CRAIGFORTH very dry and stylish, *c.* 1890, with a skinny porch uniting canted bays; No. 34 (CRAIGALLAN) respectable-rustic early Georgian revival, by *Crawford*, 1905; and Nos. 36–42 red brick and half timber, 1920. TRINITY LODGE, a little late Georgian villa on the corner of Stirling Road, has pebbledashed itself in despair.

LOWER GRANTON ROAD (E section) can be reached from Granton Road by Wardie Steps. The elaborately Jacobean WARDIE HOTEL, 1881, has a nicely detailed baronial extension by *Reid & Forbes*, 1935. WARDIE SQUARE, *c.* 1840, with cottagey semi-dormers, lies behind East Cottages (for which *see* above).

NEWHAVEN AND TRINITY

Newhaven had a prosperous shipyard in the early C16, and there is evidence of at least one important building to suggest that it was still a substantial place under James VI. But its feudal superiority had already been purchased from James V by the City of Edinburgh, and from the C17 to the C19 it was little more than a fishing village. There are now more pleasure boats than fishing boats in the harbour, but the village itself has been successfully – if drastically – preserved by the City. Trinity, on the plateau above the shore, is a large, placid suburb developed with modest villas from the late C18 to late C19. In 1785 *David Henderson* advertised building plots on a large site to the N of Ferry Road, to a plan 'constructed in a new and beautiful manner, as an assemblage of Gentlemen's Villas, bounded upon the outer line by a plantation of forest trees, and the internal boundaries of each lot by a continuation of flowering shrubs; and each Villa situated in such a manner as not to overlook another' (*Edinburgh Evening Courant*). This scheme did not get very far, but it gives a fair description of most of Trinity today, though the large gardens of the first generation of villas have all been subdivided to provide more villa sites. Trinity Chain Pier, to the W of Newhaven, was built to Captain *Samuel Brown*'s design in 1820 and became the terminus of the Edinburgh and Trinity Railway, with a later branch to Granton; its site is now marked only by a pub of some character but nondescript design.

PERAMBULATIONS

FERRY ROAD (E of Crewe Toll) is not a recommended walk but has some decent buildings and some curiosities, e.g. near the E end in PITT STREET, two early C20 folk-art warehouses, one with a pair of carved demons sticking out their tongues, another with a low-relief sculpture of soldiers slaughtering women and children, entitled 'The Valour of German Culture 1914'. Near-vernacular of 1859 at Nos. 88–96, block-pedimented doors at Nos. 46–76. Then late Victorian tenements till TRAFALGAR LANE, whose vista is closed by the C19 corniced doorpiece of No. 90. On each side of the lane entry, tenement blocks of a plain Georgian scheme, Nos. 1–13 *c.* 1825, Nos. 23–29 of 1859 a careful repeat. In FERRY ROAD itself, another Georgian fragment at Nos. 140–148, with tripartite windows in the bowed corner to Summerside Place. Then a stretch of placid villas, of which the oldest is BONNINGTON PARK HOUSE, twin-pedimented Georgian luxuriantly modernized in 1883. No. 219 is TAAP HALL, a seven-bay tenement of 1790 with consoled doorpiece in the recessed centre, Nos. 200–202 a tall semi-detached pair built *c.* 1830 with segment-headed ground-floor windows. On the s side the Tudor VICTORIA PARK HOTEL and Italian ACRA LODGE (No. 223), both *c.* 1860, with towers. Opposite, the Ainslie Park School Annexe (*see* Public Buildings, above). Nos. 218–240 and 241–243 are flats of 1920, ambitiously pedimented, by the City Architect *E. J. MacRae*. On the N side BANGHOLM VILLAS by *George Simpson*, 1925, white-harled

and red-tiled rows. Then at the Goldenacre junction the
grand lava-topped walls and gates and rustic lodge of TRIN-
ITY COTTAGE *c*. 1830. Behind them, TRINITY PARK
HOUSE by *Morris & Steedman*, 1971, a large three-storey
office block whose serpentine plan, reeded concrete horizontals and recessed ground floor make it a far from unpleasant
surprise in the trees. For Inverleith Gardens on the S, *see*
Fettes, Inverleith and Warriston: Streets and Neighbourhoods (Inverleith). On the N side CASTLEHAVEN, cloddish
baronial of 1888 with solid pepperpots, and ASHBROOK (now
a Church of Scotland Eventide Home), clumping Italian with
the required tower and arcaded windows, by *Robert R. Raeburn*, 1869. Finally the Northern General Hospital (*see* Public
Buildings, above) and the FERRANTI factory and offices at
Crewe Toll by *Douglas H. Bamber* from 1955.

NEWHAVEN ROAD (N part, starting from Ferry Road) is lined
with good Georgian villas at the N end, all on the E side; No.
176 a piended cottage at an oblique angle, Nos. 184 and 186
very grand with pedimented windows over Ionic porches.
Then Nos. 190-192 with roughly coursed masonry, Nos.
202-204 with Roman Doric columned doorpieces, and Nos.
212 (covered by shops) to 216 set back to make a front-gardened enclave, all with cherry-cocked pointing and rosetted
doorpieces. Their ground-floor tripartite windows have blank
outer lights but those at Nos. 232-236 are fully glazed; No.
232 (JESSFIELD) was begun *c*. 1817 as an office for the naval
commander in chief. On the W side Victoria Park and its
House (*see* Public Buildings, above), and before the plunge
down to Newhaven, a curiosity in the wall of the builder's
yard at Nos. 217-219; a stone rose finial from a dormer-head,
the small triangle underneath inscribed I BEL 1593.* Under
the window a stone thistle finial, apparently from the same
building.

To the E, the DUDLEY AVENUE development, *c*. 1892, flat-
roofed terraces with fancy iron crests and urn or ball finials
weaving in and out over the bay-windows. In SUMMERSIDE
STREET twenty-five villas by *Robert Meldrum*, 1874, with
showy doorpieces on the W side; eagle and snake consoles at
Nos. 11-13, florid vegetation at Nos. 17-19. *James Goodwillie*
was the builder. The U.P. Church by *Starforth* (1878,
demolished in 1977) stood at the NE. In SUMMERSIDE
PLACE (originally Great Wellington Street) the red sandstone
Gothic hall of North Leith Parish Church by *Hippolyte J.
Blanc*, 1885. Also the bowed end of a Georgian terrace in
FERRY ROAD; Nos. 142-144 three-storey, *c*. 1820, Nos. 146-
148 with droved ground-floor rustication, and No. 150 very
smooth, *c*. 1835.

To the W, PARK ROAD with No. 46 (DUNFORTH) in its own

---

*The name of I. (*sc*. John) Bel is carved under the heraldic frontispiece at
Castle Fraser, Grampian; the mason George Bell (†1575), buried in Midmar
churchyard, is assumed to be his father. The Newhaven stone was dug up on the
site *c*. 1970 and the date slightly emphasized by recutting.

grounds at the w end, baronial, *c.* 1860, with an octagonal NW turret. To the s, BELVEDERE PARK, well-detailed three-storey flats in buff brick by *Johnston & Groves-Raines*, 1978.

NEWHAVEN is in planning terms a Comprehensive Development Area, for which *Ian G. Lindsay & Partners* were appointed as architects by the City of Edinburgh in 1960. Their conservation policy was of a no-nonsense kind, with much sacrifice of individual character and much redevelopment, yet the result is intelligible and even subtle. The village starts at the e end with ANNFIELD, a long three-storey artisan terrace begun *c.* 1806 but not complete until *c.* 1850 and then with a hiccup at No. 14, two-storey with a pedimented chimney-gable. New three-storey flats to the w (and in Great Michael Rise) by *Basil Spence*, 1957; walls of granite setts (salvaged from the roads) alternating with coloured harl. More setts as a base for a huge iron anchor outside the AN-CHOR BAR. Then MAIN STREET, granite-paved and blocked to vehicles at the w end, starting on the N side with the vital townscape focus of the Victoria Primary School (*see* above), and a chunky stone-fronted house with a general store underneath. On the s side, harled three-storey flats by *Ian G. Lindsay & Partners*, who are in command from here on. More flats uphill to the s, and on the blank gable of No. 6 (AUCHINLECK COURT) a large overdoor stone (re-sited here for the second time) inscribed IN THE NEAM OF GOD 1588 and carved with a big ship, two globes and navigational instruments. On the N side a long fish-shaped island of buildings, the older inhabitants including the pantiled AULD HAVEN bar at No. 14, the slate-roofed No. 22, and No. 40 with a rear stair-turret. The fish is transfixed by GREAT MICHAEL CLOSE, FISHMARKET SQUARE, WESTER CLOSE, LAMB'S COURT (for the walls of St Mary and St James's Chapel, *see* above) and WESTMOST CLOSE. The new housing is virtually uniform, with timber-railed forestairs; most of the old houses conform to its brown-painted margins and woodwork. At the w end the bluff, chimney-headed end of the former Marine Hotel, which also forms the w end of PIER PLACE, the fish's N side. No. 10 is severely sandblasted Gothic, converted to a house from the hall of the Old Newhaven Free Church (*see* above), the town's chief landmark. Then the STONE PIER INN, with C19 crowsteps, and No. 4, a three-storey stone-fronted tenement built for the Society of the Free Fishermen, 1868; a clock in the pediment for ships entering harbour, and to the l. a stone barometer case, 1900, incorporating a panel of a ship carved in 1775. No. 3 is a late C18 two-storey tenement with rendered walls and tripartite windows. The PEACOCK INN has fancily restored itself with the same new red pantiles as the rest. To the rear in PEACOCK COURT an C18 house whose bare N gable reveals its red-brick construction. For Newhaven Harbour, *see* Public Buildings, above.

Main Street has a short continuation along the sea front with Nos. 39–47, *c.* 1840. Across the foot of Craighall Road these

are balanced by a slightly later tenement and terrace at Nos.
1–3 STARBANK ROAD. For Starbank Park, *see* Public Buildings, above. Not much joy in the rest, but TRINITY CRES-
CENT by *Thomas Brown* made a brave start in 1824 and strug-
gled on into the mid-C19; on the W side (Nos. 6–16) complete
pavilion tenements and only one gap in the houses; on the E
side only one house.

EAST TRINITY ROAD runs E to W with four-storey tenements,
1897–1902, along much of the S side; iron balconies give Nos.
17–37 quite a seaside look, but the effect is of a high barrier
at the frontier of the choice villadom to the N. Trinity House
has been redeveloped but has left a very grand gateway. On
the N side delightful villas with erratic garden walls; No. 68
(LANGDALE) combines a bay-window with a ground-floor
pilastrade, No. 66 (ST MARIE'S) has an Ionic doorpiece and
an espaliered pear-tree, No. 64 (ROSE COTTAGE, 1826) owls
on the gate-piers, No. 62 (CORBIESTEPS, *c.* 1840) not only
crowsteps but some Tudor detail. Of three Georgian bungalows, No. 56 (HEATHERLIE) acquired its cheerful red mansard *c.* 1920 and the bow-fronted No. 50 an extra floor *c.* 1890,
but No. 40 (LAVEROCKBANK COTTAGE) is intact, with a
Gothick doorway. To the W, EARL HAIG GARDENS, Scottish Veterans' Garden City housing by *Henry & Maclennan*,
1925. A pretty quadrangle of harled two-storey cottages, the
N and S sides with bullseyed open pediments, the E and W in
C17 West of England style.

In CRAIGHALL ROAD are the former Newhaven Station at No.
33 and Newhaven Parish Church (*see* above). Two other
roads are comfortably lined with villas. In LAVEROCKBANK
TERRACE, No. 4, by *Kinnear & Peddie*, 1883, has pedimented stone dormers over dissimilar bay-windows; Nos. 6–
7 have the *Peddie & Kinnear* monogram and the date 1857 in
one of their copious gables. Round the corner at No. 11 the
former Free Church Manse, *c.* 1870. On the E corner of LAV-
EROCKBANK AVENUE a group of shops by *Matthew Steele* of
Bo'ness, 1933. On the E side of LAVEROCKBANK ROAD a
pretty group, *c.* 1810: Nos. 1–2 with unusual ground-floor
rustication on the face only, Nos. 3–4 with ground-floor windows segmentally over-arched, Nos. 5, 6 and 7 with corner-
blocked architraves, and a graceful fanlight at No. 9. No. 12
(BANKHEAD, originally Mayville) was given a big blockish
extension with a belvedere on the roof by *Peddie & Kinnear*
c. 1860. Next to it MAYVILLE GARDENS by *Hippolyte J.
Blanc*, 1881, a cul-de-sac of two cottagey terraces with larger,
deep-eaved houses at the entry. Finally No. 17 (STARBANK),
a deep-eaved Regency villa with a Gothic doorway; its garden
is Starbank Park, with rose-beds to the S (for the N part, *see*
Public Buildings, above). On the W side five Georgian villas
in their own grounds; No. 46 (STRATHAVON LODGE, originally Viewfield) was built at the beginning of the C19 and
much extended later. No. 52 is a simple brick and concrete
house designed for himself by the engineer *Jerrold Slade*. At

the bottom the STARBANK ARMS at No. 64, with a quatrefoil carved in the N gable.

Next YORK ROAD. On the W side No. 3 with horizontal window panes and No. 5 with a delicate bowed porch of cast iron, both *c.* 1820. Then oafish recent houses. On the E side Nos. 12 (ST ANDREW'S LODGE) and 14 (YORK LODGE) both Tudor, *c.* 1850, and differing only in their first-floor conservatories. No. 16 (HOLLY LODGE) smart and plain, but spoilt by a cement bay, No. 22 (GRANGE HOUSE) very grand, with a Doric porch and balcony between pedimented bays, and No. 24 (GOTHIC HOUSE) with big pinnacles and castellated porch; all *c.* 1820. The tall CAIRNEY HOUSE (No. 26) by *J. Dick Peddie*, 1854, has fretwork quoins. To the N two towered villas of *c.* 1870, sharing a twin-arched gateway; FORTHLAND HOUSE baronial, LOMOND HOUSE with scoop-corbelled bay-windows viewing the firth down below. To the NW the former TRINITY STATION of 1843 (well preserved as a house), with a massive retaining wall on the approach.

RUSSELL PLACE begins on the W side with a red-brick garden wall, divided but still effective. On the E, No. 10 (ST HELEN'S), *c.* 1860, has a half-circular bow window with curved glass and cast-iron lotus balcony and cresting. No. 12 (CLAIRINCH) is one of a number of bargeboarded villas. To the N of Lennox Row a notable group of GOTHIC COTTAGES of *c.* 1820, deep in the trees: No. 22 with a mullioned bay, No. 24 with a smart cast-iron verandah, and No. 23, altered to form part of the stables of North Trinity House (*see* below). In LENNOX ROW itself No. 6 (GRECIAN COTTAGE, of similar date) has a Doric porch. *Grainger & Miller*'s monumental bridge (1843) carries the street over the railway.

In TRINITY ROAD, No. 70 (TRINITY GROVE) was a first-generation Trinity villa, built with harled walls and stone margins for David Hunter of Blackness in 1789. C19 additions, including a square tower. To the N the villas have grass verges in front of their garden walls; No. 76 (BIRNAM LODGE), with polychrome relieving arches over arcaded windows, and No. 90 (SILVERTON), neo-Jacobean with an ogee-topped gazebo tower surveying the neighbourhood, both *c.* 1860. Then No. 102 (KIRTLE LODGE) at the Lennox Row corner, by *James C. Walker*, 1862; deep eaves and long-and-short rustic quoins. At the N end, No. 110 of Peddie & Kinnear type, with a Tudor Gothic porch added later, and Nos. 114–116 (NORTH TRINITY HOUSE) *Peddie*'s own house of 1858, bearing their PK monogram. For the former Christ Church Episcopal Church, *see* above.

MORNINGSIDE

After the disputing churches of Holy Corner, a steady downward slope of 1 km. to the S and the Braid Hills. The scene is nicely varied between the anonymity of tenements and the fun of local shops, and a little group of mid-C19 buildings on the main road still provides a recognizable centre. Villa development came rather late, and the character of Church Hill (just N of the Parish Church) and Greenhill, which belonged to Sir William Forbes of Pitsligo, is on the threshold between Georgian and Victorian. Heavyweight Victorian villas filled up the gaps, and the later tidal wave of tenements hardly penetrated these cosy neighbourhoods. To the S, *R. Rowand Anderson* supervised the feuing of the salubrious Braid estate, the property of another Aberdeenshire family; their house, the Hermitage, still stands in its riverside park. Morningside is a byword for Edinburgh gentility.

CHURCHES

ARCHIEPISCOPAL CHAPEL (R.C.), Greenhill Gardens. By *R. Weir Schultz*, 1904–7, built under the will of the third Marquess of Bute as a shell for an interior originally designed by *William Frame* in 1889 for the chapel at House of Falkland (Fife). Outside, it is a tiny Greek-looking church in snecked rubble, cruciform with green copper roofs and clearstoried dome. Arcaded narthex with Celtic-Byzantine carving. Intricate classical interior with four composite pilaster orders under the dome, four diapered arches, very small extra bays with matching columns to E and W. Walls arcaded in plaster, pedestals and dado of polished wood, and a plain semi-domed E apse. – Wooden CHAIR and PRIE-DIEU, both by *Schultz*. – STAINED GLASS. In the apse, three small lights (the Crucifixion, SS. Andrew and Margaret) and to the S three more (St Clare) by *Gabriel Loire* of Chartres, 1970; thick, rough glass without surface drawing, the colour and portrayal perfectly judged. The house to which the chapel is attached is by *John Henderson*, c. 1859. Between them a new porch by *Reginald Fairlie*, 1934, blocking the chapel's N windows.

BAPTIST CHURCH (originally Free Church), Morningside Road. Economical Gothic by *MacGibbon & Ross* following a competition in 1872. Pinnacled SE steeple, plate-traceried W window over the porch. Burnt out in 1973, the interior was re-cast by *David Carr* as a simple, steeply raked auditorium.

BRAID CHURCH (formerly United Presbyterian), Nile Grove and Hermitage Terrace. A two-storey Classical octagon like a baptistery,* by *G. Washington Browne*, 1886. Entrance front diagonal to the street corner, with a bowed portico and steep crowning pediment between little towers which have pyram-

---

* In 1893 the church was decorated with marbling which explicitly continued the Italian baptistery theme, with *Robert Gibb* as adviser; the lower walls marbled red-brown, the upper parts buff, cream and blue-grey. None of this remains, and of the sage-green vestibule only the 'pavonazzo' marbling of the attached columns on the twin staircases.

idal stone roofs. Simple detail, but careful gradations of
colour from creamy Hailes to red Prudham sandstone. The
interior has a shallow dome, clearstorey windows, and a
curved gallery looking across to the pulpit, organ and communion table; a very neat plan. ORGAN by *Brindley & Foster*,
1898, rebuilt by *John Compton*, 1951.

CHRIST CHURCH (Episcopal), Bruntsfield Place. Ambitious
French Gothic by *Hippolyte J. Blanc* (a member of the congregation), 1875–8. Cruciform plan, without aisles or clearstorey except at the busy E end, which has a five-sided chevet
towards the road; gablets and flying buttresses above, ambulatory with small cinquefoil windows below. More cinquefoils
over the numerous double lancets, and larger ones as rose
windows at the nave and transept gables. Tower in the angle
of the N transept, containing the main door and organ chamber. Tall belfry and 43 m. spire with lucarnes and two-stage
pinnacles (their finials removed as dangerous in 1933, followed
by those of the chevet gablets *c.* 1960). A more confident
interior. Plain nave (plainer since 1949, when the pictorial
panels were painted over) with a clear-span roof (still decorated), whose hammerbeam principals spring from corbelled
red stone wall-shafts and are ingeniously splayed at the transepts. Rich and intricate chancel in a personal early-French
manner, the lower arcade of the chevet with big leafy capitals
and diapered spandrels, the clearstorey windows soaring up
into the timber vault; their form is repeated on the side walls
(with figures of saints) as part of the original decorative
scheme. – PULPIT and FONT. Both original, with angels at
the corners. – CHANCEL SCREEN. Modest E.E., designed by
Blanc and carved in oak on a marble base, both by *Beveridge*.
– MEMORIAL TABLET on N side of chancel arch. To Mr Al-
cock the organist, designed by *Blanc* and carved in alabaster
by *Beveridge*. – ORGAN by *Peter Conacher*, 1875; rebuilt by *C.
& F. Hamilton* in 1902 and again by *Ronald L. Smith* in 1971.
– STAINED GLASS. An extensive scheme installed and later
supplemented by *Ballantine*, beginning in the chancel (Nativity, Crucifixion and Resurrection), 1877. W rose window
(Christ as teacher) by *A. E. Borthwick*, 1926.

CLUNY CHURCH CENTRE (originally South Morningside Free
Church), Cluny Drive and Braid Road. Confident mixed
Gothic by *R. Rowand Anderson*, 1890, in red sandstone.
Square NW tower becoming more elaborate in successive
stages, the top windows and solid parapet having Perp tracery. Corner stair-turret and slim lead spire. In 1976–7 *R. D.
Cameron & Gibb* divided the interior, forming small rooms
and offices on the ground floor and aisles. The nave piers
were already articulated at gallery level and the arcades are
still seen in the HALL above. Timber-lined tunnel-roof concealing a steel structure. – STAINED GLASS. In the surviving
E window seven lights ('Come unto Me . . .').

CLUNY PARISH CHURCH (formerly St Matthew's), Braid
Road and Cluny Gardens. A red sandstone church on the

grassy terraced corner, by *Hippolyte J. Blanc*, 1889–90.* Cruciform, with nave aisles and a central Gothic flèche, the E.E. detail concentrated on the w and transept gables. A NW tower was projected but not built. Inside, a w gallery over the vestibule, nave arcades with spandrels diapered in relief, and tall twin arches opening into each transept. Boarded wagon roof over clearstorey wall-shafts. Blanc added the arcaded chancel some years later, with a variegated marble floor, oak dado and furnishings *en suite*, all made by *Scott Morton & Co*. – Stone FONT carved by *W. H. Kerr*. – Wrought-iron hanging gasoliers in the nave, designed by *Blanc*. – ORGAN by *Henry Willis & Sons*, 1901, rebuilt by *Rushworth & Dreaper*, 1929. – STAINED GLASS. In the E window four lights (the Evangelists; scenes from the life of Christ) by *E. Burne-Jones* and made by *Morris & Co*., 1901. In the w window four lights whose colours blend less well with the bluish pink stonework (Christ as friend, preacher, philanthropist and missionary) by *Percy Bacon & Co*., 1905. In the s aisle two lights (SS. Columba and Ninian) by *William Wilson*, 1961.

GREENBANK CHURCH (originally Greenbank United Free Church), Braidburn Terrace and Comiston Road. Bland but substantial Gothic by *A. Lorne Campbell* (finished in 1927), with red sandstone edges. A gentle arcaded interior, flattened by a plain wagon roof. – FURNISHINGS to *Campbell*'s design by *Scott Morton & Co*. – FONT. Gothic, of stone, 1927. – ORGAN by *A. E. Ingram*., 1927, rebuilt by *R. L. Smith*, 1972. – STAINED GLASS. In the E window and carefully related to its broad mullions, five lights (Revelation), 1928; in the s transept four lights (Pilgrim's Progress), 1934, all by *Alexander Strachan*. In the N transept four lights (parables) with the inscribed names of *W. Wilson, W. Blair, D. Saunders, C. Whalen*, 1954. In the N aisle three lights (Nativity, Kings and Shepherds) by *William Wilson*, 1957. In the s aisle three lights (St Cecilia) by *Ballantine*, after 1915. – HALL to the E with Perp doorway, built in 1900 and used as a temporary church.

MORNINGSIDE PARISH CHURCH, Morningside Road. By *John Henderson*, opened in 1838, with a toy Romanesque gable facing the street. In the middle an engaged tower, tall and slim, surmounted by a simple spirelet and four plain pinnacles. In 1868 *Peddie & Kinnear* added the transepts and E apse, and theirs presumably is the ingenious roof of wide, wall-braced trusses uniting the nave and transepts, with diagonal trusses and central kingpost at the crossing. In 1888 *Hardy & Wight* replaced the apse with a chancel. – COMMUNION TABLE, 1877, altered 1897. – Brass LECTERN and octagonal Caen stone FONT by *Cox & Sons, Buckley & Co*., 1888. – Other furnishings of oak by *L. Grahame Thomson*, 1931–3. – ORGAN on s side of chancel by *Henry Willis &*

---

* The congregation had previously used an iron church in Cluny Avenue, built by *Isaac Dixon* of Liverpool and subsequently demolished.

Sons, 1921, replacing that of 1875. - STAINED GLASS. A complete set of 1868–74 telling Bible stories in vivid magic-lantern panels, e.g. in the N transept three lights (parables), 1872. Three lights on the N side of the nave (King David with his harp) by *A. Ballantine & Gardiner*, 1902, and the next three (David and Jonathan) by *James Ballantine & Son*, in the same spirit. The HALL with elaborate classical frontage in Newbattle Terrace was built in 1899.

MORNINGSIDE UNITED* (originally Congregational), Bruntsfield Place and Chamberlain Road. Pinkish, rock-faced Early Christian revival by *James McLachlan*, 1927–9, elaborately composed with arcades and a campanile, but small in scale. A bland, light interior with plaster vaults on stone piers. - ORGAN by *Cousans & Sons*, 1904, rebuilt by *Rushworth & Dreaper*, 1955. - STAINED GLASS. In the S aisle two lights (Nativity etc. as a 1914–18 war memorial) by *Ballantine*. Also two lights (scenes from the life of Christ as a 1939–45 war memorial) by *William Wilson*.

NORTH MORNINGSIDE (United Presbyterian, now disused), Morningside Road and Chamberlain Road. Ponderous neo-Norman by *David Robertson*, 1879–81. Stair-halls flank the N (Chamberlain Road) end, the one to the W carried up into a pyramid-roofed tower. The interior unexpectedly impressive. Minimal aisles and low nave arcades, but a lofty clearstorey whose shafted triple windows enliven the glass. Very wide timber-lined tunnel-roof, made even wider by hammerbeams concealed in groins along the edges. At the N end a gallery with porch beneath, at the S a huge arched recess for the ORGAN by *Bryceson Brothers & Ellis*, 1881. Beneath it, a massive build-up of PULPIT and choir gallery, all in simplified Norman woodwork. - STAINED GLASS. A remarkable but mixed collection. In the clearstorey, three lights each. W side, at the N end (St Paul at Athens) still Art Nouveau, 1925; at the S end (the Acts of Mercy) neo-primitive, 1930; both by *Margaret Chilton* and *Marjorie Kemp*. E side, at the S end (Christ with animal creation), 1930, unattributed. The others (Sacrifice, Peace and Victory as a 1914–18 war memorial) by *Clayton & Bell*. In the E aisle some unsigned lights of the 1960s in the style of *William Wilson*, that of Dorcas especially colourful. In the N aisle two sombre and impressive lights (the Resurrection) by *John Duncan*, 1935. In the W gable three very tall lights (Psalm 23 and other texts), in memory of the architect John Paterson, by *William Wilson*, 1957.

ST PETER (R.C.), Falcon Avenue. An austere church by *Robert S. Lorimer*, 1906 (the nave completed in 1928–9), with tall arched windows and shallow buttresses, the roof originally

---

* This was the first case in Edinburgh (1979) of a Congregational church uniting with the Church of Scotland. A Union in the more frequent sense (i.e. into one building) has since taken place between the congregations of North Morningside and Morningside United, and the latter building was the one to be chosen. It occupies the site of a French Gothic United Presbyterian church by *Robert Paterson*, 1863, demolished in 1927.

slated (now copper-covered). The Presbytery and former
School make an arcaded forecourt; they are built of the same
variegated masonry with warmer-coloured Prudham dressings, but their roofs are red-pantiled, their detail cosily
Gothic. In the NE angle of the court, i.e. of the nave and S
transept, a tall and thin campanile ending with a stripy bell-
stage and Chinese-looking roof. Touches of SCULPTURE, e.g.
an angel cherishing a model of the Presbytery in a panel on
the Presbytery wall, an Annunciation on the nave wall, and
rainwater heads carved as grotesque beasts clinging preca-
riously to the tops of two buttresses, but only the Crucifixion
on the canted apse is definitely the work of *Joseph Hayes*.
Inside, lofty nave arcades of whitewashed brick, with
wrought-iron monograms as anchors for tie-rods across the
narrow aisles. Bigger arches at the crossing, that of the N
transept cut across by the organ gallery. Massive cross-beams
above, with a wagon roof in the middle and flat panels along
the edge, all of Oregon pine. The furnishings much disturbed
by Vatican II.* – ROOD of painted wood on the E wall of the
sanctuary (formerly in the arch) in the medieval German
manner, by *Joseph Hayes*. – FONT in the baptistery to the SW.
An enriched lead cistern by *G. P. Bankart*. – PAINTINGS. In
the former St Andrew's Chapel to the NW, a mural (the Feed-
ing of the Five Thousand, with red-headed angels) by *Morris
Meredith Williams*. (The green marble altar now in the S transept.) On the W wall a huge canvas (the Progression of St
Peter) by *Frank Brangwyn*; this and its princely gilt frame
were formerly the climax of the church on the E wall of the
sanctuary. – STAINED GLASS. In the sanctuary two lights
(Christ's Ministry) and in the N transept two lights (Our
Lady) by *Morris and Gertrude A. Meredith Williams*. Lovely
colour and very small-scale drawing. In the S transept one
light (the Life of St Giles) by *Nina M. Davidson*, executed
by *Guthrie & Wells*, by comparison flashy and mannered. In
the NE chapel three large lights set in concrete (memorial to
Canon John Gray) by *Pierre Fourmaintraux* of the Whitefriars
Studios, 1963.

PUBLIC BUILDINGS

CHURCH HILL THEATRE (originally Morningside Free
Church), Morningside Road. By *Hippolyte J. Blanc*, 1892.
Bold Renaissance (as requested by the congregation), in pink
Corsehill sandstone. Pedimented two-storey centrepiece with
Venetian window over the entrance, flanked by pavilions, of
which the S one was intended as the base of a 55 m. campanile.
Conversion to theatre use (1965) retained the W part of the
interior, with a curved plaster vault.

* Lorimer's altar, iron altar-rail and timber pulpit have disappeared, along with
eleven Stations of the Cross by *John Duncan*.

DOMINION CINEMA, Newbattle Terrace. Marble-fronted *moderne* by *T. Bowhill Gibson*, 1937–8. Horizontal canopy and vertical fin. Interior divided into two cinemas, 1972, and into three, 1979.

PUBLIC LIBRARY, Morningside Road. By *James A. Williamson*, 1917. A hard, officious frontage of Blackpastures (Northumberland) stone with pedimented ends, the carving by *Joseph Hayes*. Domed reading room with plasterwork by *Mackenzie* of Glasgow.

ROYAL EDINBURGH HOSPITAL, Tipperlin Road. Known also as West House and designed by *William Burn* in 1839 to supplement the old East House asylum (1809 by Robert Reid, demolished 1896) and to accommodate the pauper lunatics of Edinburgh and Leith. Three-storey H plan, open to the S as a grassy court with tripartite windows which go Venetian in the three-bay centrepiece. Small-pane sashes, often with an iron grille of the same pattern behind. On the E side of the H a canted centrepiece, large and dour, between quasi-octagonal towers, outer canted bays between depressed over-arch links; the arches seem originally to have been open. On the W side a similar centrepiece, but the SW range was carried out by *David Bryce* from 1852, the NW range by *Robert Paterson* in 1867 with a tall iron-crested hat on its central canted bay. To the N the former entrance courtyard with a head of Philippe Pinel on the inner keystone of the pend arch; also a two-storey wing by *W. L. Moffat*, 1874. To the W the laundry and former house for refractory patients, both by *Bryce* before 1861. Further W the CHURCH CENTRE, a cruciform Gothic chapel of corrugated iron bought from St Michael's Slateford (*see* Calder and Lanark Roads, above), in 1884. The quadrangular pavilion behind it is by *Henry & Maclennan*, 1912.

The main C20 contribution is to the E, starting with the JORDANBURN LECTURE HALL, wan Art Deco by *Auldjo Jamieson & Arnott*, 1934. The big square of the ANDREW DUNCAN CLINIC and the nine-storey UNIVERSITY OF EDINBURGH DEPARTMENT OF PSYCHIATRY are by *John Holt*, 1966, all horizontally emphasized sandwiches of glass and concrete and all linked by a covered way to the already spoiled E face of the old building. It is further confused by the PINEL MEMORIAL of 1930, with a bronze bust of Pinel († 1826) and bronze reliefs of famous doctors and nurses.

SOUTH MORNINGSIDE PRIMARY SCHOOL, Comiston Road. By *Robert Wilson*, 1891. Rock-faced Hailes stonework with red dressings; a big central gable and lantern.

MANSION

HERMITAGE OF BRAID, off Braid Road. Now a countryside information centre. Stolid but romantic in the trees by the Braid Burn, the Edinburgh villa of Charles Gordon of Cluny, perhaps by *Robert Burn*, 1785. A three-bay ashlar front with machicolated centrepiece, battlements and pointed dummy bartizans. Prettily arched and fanlit front door between Venetian windows, the arched rhythm continuing along the four bays of the rubble s flank, over a deep basement. The plan is three rooms thick, with a central passage to the dog-leg stair at the back. Fancy plaster friezes, and in the first room to the r. an enriched pine chimneypiece with marble slip and original tiles. DOOCOT to the w, of lectern type, perhaps C18 with a pediment added to the rear wall.

PERAMBULATION

MORNINGSIDE ROAD begins with 'Holy Corner', actually a crossroads with four corners and four oddly assorted churches (for these, see above). On the E side the puny Early Christian Morningside United and the big neo-Norman North Morningside Church. On the W, two spired Gothic churches, Christ Church complicated French and the Baptist Church much simpler; between them (representing Mammon) the classical banking-house of the BANK OF SCOTLAND (formerly Commercial Bank) by *Peddie & Kinnear*, 1873, and the grand French-roofed sweep of No. 12 MORNINGSIDE ROAD (on the corner of Colinton Road) by *David MacGibbon*, 1868 (but based on Rhind's giant scheme of 1862). Ordinary tenements till No. 104; a valuable shopfront at No. 66, arcaded and pedimented. On the E side a row of plain villas and then the red sandstone Church Hill Theatre (see above).

Side roads to the E. In CHAMBERLAIN ROAD assorted villas of the 1860s; in the front garden of No. 1 the Burial Enclosure, 1645, of John Livingstone, who bought the lands of Greenhill in 1631. In FORBES ROAD, *J. Maitland Wardrop*'s own bayed and bargeboarded house, c. 1865. Then the Arcadian formality of GREENHILL GARDENS. On the W side, No. 7 by *David Cousin* (for himself), 1849. On the E, No. 2 (LINK-FIELD HOUSE) with scooped bays in the Bryce style, c. 1860. Nos. 8 and 10 with incised ornament and low-pitched, deep-eaved roofs, c. 1850, No. 14 solid but refined Georgian survival, its twin at No. 12 much altered, No. 16 prettiest Jacobean, with strapwork and all, and No. 18 in bargeboard cottage style; all under construction in 1849. Nos. 32–34 very refined and swanky classic, with mutuled cornice and generous tripartite windows, more glass than wall. No. 42 (ST BENNET'S), the largest of the later houses, crowstepped baronial by *John Henderson*, c. 1859 (for the domed Archiepiscopal Chapel later attached to it, see above). On the other side, No. 29, c. 1855, with an Italian tower on a battered base. GREENHILL PARK was laid out by *John Henderson*. By him No. 5, bay-windowed classic of 1859, and the more old-fashioned Nos. 2–4 and 7–9, both with over-arched pediments, 1853. No. 6 Italian, c. 1861. No. 10a a plain harled box in a secluded corner by *Esmé Gordon* (for himself), 1968.

To the E a scheme by *Robert Raeburn*, 1877, with villas surrounded on three sides by terraces: GREENHILL TERRACE, GREENHILL PLACE with a mansard-hatted centrepiece, and STRATHEARN PLACE.

CHURCH HILL is another layout by *John Henderson*, 1842, and his are the fancy-classical No. 1, with a central pediment, the undecided Nos. 3–5, whose pediment crowns a Tudor bay-window, and No. 7, with a bayed central tower (spoiled by a C20 top storey), all 1843; the even numbers (s side) are a little later. In PITSLIGO ROAD a plain block of flats by *Esmé Gordon*, 1969, with heraldic trimmings at the door. In CLINTON ROAD, EAST MORNINGSIDE HOUSE, with its original C18 gate-piers but otherwise much altered, and No. 2 (AVALLON), big-scale baronial in red sandstone rubble with yellow dressings, c. 1862.

MORNINGSIDE ROAD goes noisily on, but the buildings on both sides now have a village look. On the W, No. 65, barge-boarded Gothic, and Nos. 67–69, playful classic, before Morningside Parish Church (*see* above); all toylike, with front gardens. On the E of Morningside Road, Nos. 108–112, a picturesque ramble of rubbly houses with mid-C19 crowsteps, plus iron railings mounted on a high stone wall that becomes steeper with the slope. At Nos. 122–130 a pretty row of single-storey shops with arches on leaf-capital shafts. Rubble garden walls, and then the OLD SCHOOLHOUSE of 1823, with a large clock over the middle of three small ashlar bays.

Side roads. To the W, MORNINGSIDE PLACE, laid out by *Robert Wright* for William Deuchar of Morningside in 1823. No. 2 at the corner, piend-roofed. Nos. 1, 3 and 11 all 1824. Nos. 13–15 with striped masonry and 17–19 rustic, in the style of Gowans but quieter, by *J. T. Rochead*, c. 1870. No. 5 (STROWAN LODGE), standing back from the road, c. 1830, with coursed rubble walls and Roman Doric porch. No. 5a by *Robert W. Naismith* (for himself), 1976; buff Leicester brick and glass, the front kept carefully down to one storey. MORNINGSIDE PARK turns back to the main road with a little gingerbread terrace (by *Pilkington & Bell*, c. 1870) on the way, No. 10 important because still iron-crested. For the Royal Edinburgh Hospital, *see* Public Buildings, above. To the E, NEWBATTLE TERRACE breaks the village scale of the main road pleasantly enough with a big turreted tenement on the corner. Then the Church Hall and the Dominion Cinema (*see* above). On the N side Nos. 5 and 7, 1848. In FALCON AVENUE four-storey concrete flats with long balconies, by *J. R. McKay*, 1938; for St Peter's Church, *see* above. CANAAN LANE a narrow slit, the string of cottages at Nos. 8–22 rudely confronted by the C20 block of Falcon Court opposite. MILLBURN HOUSE, c. 1820, with two gabled garden-houses. DEAN BANK HOUSE (Girls' Institution), skinny classic by *David McArthy*, 1912. In JORDAN LANE a small group of houses, c. 1800, trying to ignore a large garage. Further to the

E a sudden change of scale with the four-storey chip-carved tenements of WOODBURN TERRACE.

In the last stretch of Morningside Road the E side is disturbed by the *Waters Jamieson Partnership*'s SAFEWAY SUPERMARKET, 1978, an asbestos-tiled mansard on legs. On the W a two-storey stretch, *c.* 1850, before the pompous Public Library (*see* above). Nos. 200–210 go up to five storeys in honour of Queen Victoria's jubilee, 1877, and the final tenement block is of red sandstone by *George Wilson*, 1887. Nos. 422–424 are the old Morningside Station, now shops. The smart, blank front of the BANK OF SCOTLAND by *Hugh Martin & Partners*, 1977, turns the corner into Balcarres Street. Finally, behind the trees on the E side, a picturesque Queen Anne development by *Anderson & Browne* (*G. Washington Browne* probably in charge) for the builder *James Slater*, from *c.* 1880. In NILE GROVE, Nos. 4–6 dated 1881, and a single big villa at No. 8; on the N side, Nos. 5–7 with piend roof, Nos. 25–27 gabled, the rest in three symmetrical but charmingly varied terraces up to No. 53. Likewise HERMITAGE TERRACE, 1884–7, with prettily assorted bays and dormers between two-storey end gables. For Braid Church, also by Browne, *see* above.

COMISTON ROAD climbs S into the Braid Hills without much architecture on the way (for Greenbank Church, *see* above; and for the S part of the road, *see* Fairmilehead, above). But it starts with a bang – a giant red sandstone Renaissance block of 1889 (including the richly sculptured HERMITAGE BAR) at the join with BRAID ROAD, which climbs alongside it to Cluny Parish Church and the Cluny Church Centre (*see* above). Between the two roads, Nos. 3–7, 9–11 and 13 (BRAIDFOOT) discreet rubbly Renaissance by *R. Rowand Anderson*, 1889–90. BRAID CRESCENT, *c.* 1887, deep red sandstone with the grandest two-storey bay-windows in Edinburgh, each crowned with an octagonal lead dome. To the E the long, airy roads of the BRAID ESTATE, where *R. Rowand Anderson* was 'feuing architect', with control over design, and his firm seems to have been directly responsible for the general run of the houses. No. 1 CLUNY GARDENS (formerly RED HOUSE) with very polite Renaissance detail is by *John Kinross*, 1886. But No. 33 and presumably its neighbours are by *G. Washington Browne*, 1886, and the quite ordinary double villas of BRAID AVENUE are by *Wardrop & Anderson*, 1888, all for the builder *James Slater*. The finest and latest are towards the N and the valley of the Braid Burn, e.g. in CORRENNIE GARDENS No. 18 by *Sydney Mitchell*, 1897, remarkably plain and horizontal with a red roof and deep eaves, and No. 23 (BRAIDWOOD) by *James Jerdan*, much more conservative Queen Anne. In HERMITAGE DRIVE two informal classical houses; No. 16 (DRUMEARN) by *Sydney Mitchell & Wilson*, 1902, with giant pilasters at the angles, and No. 24 (SHEILDAIG) by *Robert S. Lorimer*, 1905, with a big curly gable and piended wing. S of the Braid Burn a patchy area dominated by the BRAID HILLS HOTEL, spiky red-dressed baronial by *W. Hamilton Beattie*, 1886, with modern additions by *Richardson & McKay*, 1937.

To the W of Comiston Road, MORNINGSIDE DRIVE. Nos. 11–23 a hall with shops underneath, fruity red sandstone by *W. Hamilton Beattie*, 1888. On the N side Morningside Cemetery (1876) masked by new houses, and at No. 204 a neat block of flats in buff brick by *Kingham, Knight* for the Viewpoint Housing Association, 1978. A cottagey row in CRAIGHOUSE TERRACE by *Dunn & Findlay*, 1899, followed in 1925 by *Dunn*'s plain terrace in PLEWLANDS GARDENS and his commonplace semis in PLEWLANDS AVENUE. In COMISTON DRIVE a long three-storey block with horizontally integrated windows by *James A. Gray* for the Spur Comiston Housing Society, 1969. And to the S in GREENBANK a maze of stone-fronted and Welsh-slated bungalows; GREENBANK LOAN by *G. M. Campbell* of Portobello, 1933, is typical. BRAIDBURN VALLEY PARK, with its terraced open-air theatre, was laid out in 1934–7.

MUIRHOUSE AND DRYLAW

The names belong to the estates of two existing mansions: Drylaw to the S hemmed in by post-war housing, Muirhouse to the NW standing aloof from it in a green strip by the shore. The notoriety belongs to the contemporary development of a third area, West Pilton, a graveyard of good intentions in local-authority housing, with indifferent planning as its congenital disease, poor design and management as undertakers. Crewe Road North divides it from the pre-war suburb of East Pilton.

CHURCHES

DRYLAW PARISH CHURCH, Groathill Road North. By *William Kininmonth*, 1956. White-harled and slated, with a stone cross on the W gable facing the gates of Drylaw House – a nostalgically feudal arrangement. W saddleback tower and octagonal S meeting-room.

MUIRHOUSE PARISH CHURCH, Pennywell Gardens. By the Church of Scotland's own architect *Harry Taylor*, 1963. Harled as usual, an expressionist composition with the S end canted up to a sharp point over the entry.

OLD KIRK, Pennywell Road. By *Stanley Ross-Smith* of *Gordon & Dey*, 1952, determined to be new and ingenious. White rendered walls and deep eaves, the porch splayed invitingly out from the N aisle, its centre mullion forming a cross with its transom.

ST PAUL (R.C.), Pennywell Road and Muirhouse Avenue. By *Peter Whiston*, 1968. Harled and slated, with parallel mono-pitch roofs. A splendid interior, the timber-lined roof like a tent running across the liturgical axis, the floor raked down to the altar with views beyond it into a lower-level chapel. Over the chapel altar a cross formed of relief panels (scenes of the Passion) by *Vincent Butler*. On the E end wall of the church a painted panel of St Paul by *Steven Foster*, 1975.

PUBLIC BUILDINGS

CRAIGROYSTON HIGH SCHOOL, Pennywell Road. One to three storeys, red brick and glass panels, by *Mottram, Patrick & Dalgleish*, 1960 and 1972.

FIRE STATION, Crewe Toll. Engineering brick, white hose-tower, by *Bamber & Hall*, 1966–9.

INCHVIEW PRIMARY SCHOOL, West Pilton Avenue. Modest white harl, low-pitch roofs, by *J. & F. Johnston*, 1948.

PIRNIEHALL PRIMARY SCHOOL, West Pilton Crescent. Low-rise, with long black facias over big windows, by the *City Architect's Department*, 1966.

ST DAVID'S PRIMARY SCHOOL, West Pilton Place. Prefabricated timber classrooms from Finland, conventional hall, by the *City Architect's Department*, 1950.

SILVERLEA OLD PEOPLE'S HOME, Muirhouse Parkway. By the City Architect *Alexander Steele*, 1961. Traditional-modern compromise with picture-frame windows, butterfly roofs, odd panels of rubble.

MANSIONS

DRYLAW HOUSE, off Groathill Road North. This is the modest-sized mansion of George Loch of Drylaw, who was a Commissioner of Supply for Midlothian and began building it, according to the armorial brass plate over the front door, on 10 April 1718. It was originally a simple oblong in plan, but a projecting centrepiece was added to the entrance (E) front soon after 1786, when William Ramsay of Barnton bought the estate, including the quarry at Craigleith. The addition has harled walls and plain stone dressings to match the rest, but its pediment and Roman Doric doorpiece, with graceful fanlight, give Drylaw a decidedly late C18 look. The W front, however, is almost untouched; two floors, each with six windows placed for internal convenience rather than outside effect, over a half-sunk basement that still has some of its eight-pane (as opposed to six-pane) sashes. A central door on the ground floor has a spreading flight of steps to the garden, with the remains of a twisty wrought-iron balustrade. The dominating feature is the moulded cornice; the deep piend roof above it has two big chimneystacks indicating the position of the internal cross-walls. At the N end a little office court was added *c.*1744 on the sunk level adjoining the kitchen, which has a wide keyblocked arch over the fireplace.

Also in the basement are a bolection-moulded door and a segmental stone arch beautifully chamfered at its junction with a rounded wall at the foot of the stair.

Within the later E extension is an entrance hall leading straight to the original staircase, its main flights ascending N to S with three moulded windows at the bottom to light the basement one. It is a splendid affair, with stone steps to the first floor and leafy wrought-iron balusters – little heads spewing out different sprays of foliage – in provincial William and Mary style. The top flight (to the attic) is of oak, with Dutch-looking turned balusters, and it is all lit from a cupola, the new extension having blocked the windows. The panelled rooms on the main floors are mostly original, complete with their timber cornices, but there were minor changes *c.* 1744-5, when *William Coleburn* made and fitted some marble chimneypieces which are recognizable from the description in his bill. On the ground floor the NW room still has the basic moulded fireplace, but the dining room (NE) has a keystoned basket arch. Less orthodox for their time are those with paterae in the corner panels, a detail usually associated with 1810-20; but the grandest is in the best current style with black and yellow marble frame and a 'frieze with Eagles heads and Raffle leaves', i.e. a rinceau with beaked ends. This is in the first-floor (W) drawing room, which was fitted up with a modillioned cornice at the same time. Architectural adornments were also added to the other important rooms, the most ambitious being in the ground-floor (W) parlour. Here the lugged doors are original, but the cornice is full-dress Roman Doric and the pilasters flanking Coleburn's chimneypiece support a triglyph frieze; between them is a panel with an imaginary landscape in the manner of the Norie family but attributed to *William Delacour*. There are painted embellishments on the woodwork here, and two more overmantel landscapes in the dining room and (S) drawing room.

A building to the N, with what seems to be a skewputt crudely carved as a large head, is a fragment of an earlier house containing a C17 classical chimneypiece of stone, with garlanded frieze. Fluted GATE-PIERS to the N and E, the former with alternate rock-faced blocks. To the S the WALLED GARDEN, whose trees and bushes were inventoried in 1760.

70 MUIRHOUSE, Marine Drive. By *R. & R. Dickson*, 1830-2. Asymmetrical Tudor Gothic, with a tower over the entrance and elaborately decorated chimneys. Inside, entrance hall with a hammerbeam roof and N gallery. The fiercely detailed chimneypiece looks late Victorian. Heraldic ceiling and large Frenchy chimneypiece in the dining room. Only one of the front drawing room's trompe-l'œil ceiling roundels, painted by *J. Zephaniah Bell* in 1833, survives. Thin Jacobean ceiling in the back drawing room.

DESCRIPTION

WEST PILTON consists mainly of two- and three-storey blocks of City housing. It was started in the area N of Ferry Road by *Stewart Kaye* and the *City Architect*, 1936-7. Traditional roofs, rubbly trim on the more conspicuous blocks. Elsewhere economical modernism – rendered horizontal strips linking the windows. CREWE ROAD WEST by *T. Bowhill Gibson*, 1937, is surprisingly traditional. Contracts were stopped by the war, and when development restarted West Pilton became an area of experiment in timber-free construction, all on a grand layout like a parody of the New Town; the wooden Swedish houses in WEST PILTON PLACE look odd in this company. Floors and flat roofs of concrete (water tanks in boxes on top), steel window frames, visually effective emphasis here and there on the concrete walls, especially at the corners. The *City Architect's Department* was responsible, but designs may have come from outside. Two large flat greens. WEST PILTON PARK has two landmarks on its E side, ten-storey blocks of 1955. To the N, WEST PILTON CIRCUS (originally the site of a reservoir serving Granton) has three-storey maisonette blocks all round, started in 1951 and now (1984) in process of conversion by *The Todd Jamieson Partnership* for *Barratt*, with improved insulation, wood-framed windows and grey-tile pitched roofs. More *Barratt* housing on a random lay-out is to fill the huge circle in the middle. To the N, fronting West Granton Road, two fashionably brutalist 'precinct' schemes of 1971.

MUIRHOUSE lies to the W, and its W part is quite traditional, started in 1953 by *John A.W. Grant*. Its E part (Pennywell Place, Gardens etc.) began in 1963; simple blocks of varied heights with low-pitch roofs, smartened with white horizontal strips and coloured panels. Also of the early 60s are the multi-storey blocks to the N, and the slabs on the S side of Muirhouse Parkway, overlooking the Forth. On the N side, Silverlea Old People's Home (*see* Public Buildings, above), the late C18 MUIRHOUSE MAINS, and two welfare housing schemes, SALVESEN CRESCENT for retired lighthouse keepers, white-harled with elaborate traditional detail, by the *Scottish Special Housing Association*, 1954, and SALVESEN GARDENS for disabled ex-servicemen, harled and red-tiled, by *John A.W. Grant*, 1948. Muirhouse did not get its modest 'shopping centre' (in Pennywell Road) till 1970-1.

DRYLAW began with private housing by *Miller*, and was completed by the City from 1951. Private and public have some interesting encounters, e.g. in Easter Drylaw Gardens. THE DOOCOT on the corner of Ferry Road and Groathill Road North is a pebbledashed pub with a coolie-hatted corner quadrant, by *W.N. Thomson*, 1953.

MURRAYFIELD

On a s slope. The land N of Corstorphine Road was laid out for
villa and terrace development from the 1860s; industry and
working-class tenements followed on the s, squeezed against the
railway.

CHURCHES

GOOD SHEPHERD (Episcopal), Murrayfield Avenue. By *Robert
S. Lorimer*, 1897. A little church on a suburban hillock, built
of rough Hailes stone with red dressings; late Gothic with a
distinct Scots accent, e.g. in the central buttress interrupting
the W window facing the road, the loop tracery and pendant
mullions of the E window and the little windows of the SW
porch. A squat SE tower and N aisle were intended but not
built. The interior has a plain tunnel-roof of timber, with a
cross-ribbed celure at the E end. Chancel arch corbelled from
chamfered piers which are carved with angels before they die
into the roof. More stone-carving over the robust and charming SEDILIA. – Stone FONT at the W end, a drum with incised
reliefs on a fluted Gothic pedestal. – SCREEN and ORGAN
CASE of loving Perp detail, simpler PULPIT, all of oak. –
ORGAN by *Brindley & Foster*, 1884, moved here from a private house, 1905; rebuilt by *Henry Willis & Sons*, 1966. –
STAINED GLASS. In the E window three lights in archaic
style (Crucifixion) by *Oscar Paterson*, who also did the porch
windows. On the s side two lights (Christ's Nativity and Baptism), 1935, and two more (Christ healing the sick and washing His disciples' feet), 1943, by *Margaret Chilton*. On the N
side (Lansdowne School window, on the theme of a fish-
pond) by *Douglas Hogg*, 1977.

MURRAYFIELD PARISH CHURCH, Abinger Gardens and Or-
midale Terrace. By *A. Hunter Crawford*, 1905. Cruciform
and Dec, with delicate Prudham stone tracery in plain walls
of biscuit-coloured Hailes rubble, the tall aisles giving it the
simplicity of a hall-church. The angle-buttressed SW tower
containing a wide-arched porch is still abruptly incomplete,
but in 1929–31 *A. Balfour Paul* finished the N transept and
chancel and added an intrusive SE organ chamber. The hall
was designed in 1956 by *J. Wilson Paterson*, an aggressively
horizontal rubbly box which did not improve the already un-
comfortably wide W front with stumpy stair-tower to the W
gallery. The width is more effective inside, with high chamfered arcades opening into the aisles and transepts. High-
pitched oak roof with arched hammerbeam trusses, and a
wagon roof over the chancel. – Perp COMMUNION TABLE. –
Light oak CHOIR STALLS with inset low-relief carving by *J.
Murray Reid*, 1930. – ORGAN by *Brooke* of Glasgow, 1870,
rebuilt by *A. E. Ingram*, 1925; moved here from the Holy
Rude, Stirling, in 1936; rebuilt by *Rushworth & Dreaper*,

1962. – STAINED GLASS. In the Y-traceried E window five lights (Last Supper and Crucifixion) by *Douglas Strachan*, 1934. In the N chancel wall two lights (Fortitude, Courage, Faith and Hope), 1930, and in the S wall two more (Christ calling His disciples), 1936, all by *Herbert Hendrie*. In the S transept four lights with figures (SS. Columba, Ninian, Cuthbert and Margaret) on pale backgrounds, by *James Ballantine*, completed in 1933. – In the N transept four lights (Nativity) by *William Wilson*, 1964. – In the vestibule four pairs of lights (Old Testament figures), also by *William Wilson*, 1961. – WAR MEMORIAL (1914–18) to S of chancel arch by *Robert S. Lorimer*, 1921, of carved oak with a canopy. Beside it, the equivalent memorial from West Coates Parish Church, and in the vestibule the memorial from Roseburn Free Church (*see* Western New Town).

PUBLIC BUILDINGS

BRIDGES, Roseburn Terrace. The broad segment-arched New Bridge carrying the A8 was built in 1841 and widened in 1930, when its ashlar parapets were given rubbly extensions. – The much smaller C18 Old Bridge leaves its E end at an acute angle.

ROSEBURN PRIMARY SCHOOL, Roseburn Street. By *Robert Wilson*, 1893. Plain mullioned Jacobean with a tempietto lantern, of white Hailes stone with pink Corsehill dressings and green Tilberthwaite slates.

MANSIONS

BEECHMOUNT, Corstorphine Road. By *John Watson*, 1900. Flabby classical, the NW turret colonnetted and domed as a gazebo. Impressive but coarse corridors and a huge stair with colourless Art Nouveau glass.

BEECHWOOD, Corstorphine Road. Built in 1780 for Francis Scott, second son of the laird of Harden. Five-bay main block of smooth ashlar on a basement, a divided stair leading up to the tripartite doorpiece. Three-bay wings of one main storey, by *William Sibbald*, c. 1799, with continuous blind balustrade and bowed ends; their wide chimney-stalks join those of the main house at right angles. (Double-pile plan with centre stair, drawing room in W wing, dining room in E wing, white marble chimneypieces, described in RCAHMS Edinburgh.) WALLED GARDEN to the NW, with a garden-house at the SE corner. The house is now being adapted (1984) as part of the MURRAYFIELD INDEPENDENT HOSPITAL by *Gordon & Latimer*.

BELMONT, Belmont Avenue. A villa on a noble scale by *William H. Playfair* for the judge Lord Mackenzie, 1828, commanding the S view over the suburban plain to the Pentland Hills. The composition is Italian, the masonry of great

precision with the simplest possible detail. A two-storey range
with massive paired consoles under the continuous balcony of
the *piano nobile*; large balustrades along the balcony and
wall-head (pent-house behind added in 1964). Taller end
blocks which appear from the s as balconied towers with
single first-floor windows and tripartite attics, mutuled eaves
and shallow piend roofs. Large semicircular-arched porte
cochère, linked to the E end by a plain hall. Corridor from end
to end (some 40m., now unfortunately divided), with stone
pavement and segmental coffered vault; square stairwell at
the centre of the N side. On the s side first the library (the
shelves removed 1964), with full-width s bay framed by
pilasters. White marble Neo-Classic chimneypiece brought
from Fordell House, Fife, in 1955; foliage frieze and male
and female figures, inscribed '*Ettore Albercini* fecit Roma
1854'. Dining room of four bays now divided, but the cornice
reproduced and a late C18 enriched pine chimneypiece installed in the first half; in the second the original one still *in
situ*, black marble, yellow-figured, with anta order between
pedestals. Last the drawing room, a square with three bays
framed in lotus-headed pilasters, forming a blunt T. Compartmented ceiling, pedestal chimneypiece of white marble.
STABLES to the E, altered *c.* 1964.

MURRAYFIELD HOUSE, at the head of Murrayfield Avenue.
Built *c.* 1735 by Archibald Murray, second son of Alexander
Murray of Cringletie, near Peebles (Borders). Five bays and
three storeys, harled with crisp stone dressings. Lugged door
with segmental pediment, a central Venetian window under
a small open pediment crowned with urns, and scrolled skewputts. To the E a two-storey ashlar wing, *c.* 1780. Dining room
to the E of the entry, formed from two rooms *c.* 1780, with
the typical bowed end of that period but retaining and extending the original detail. Arched china-cupboard on the E
wall. To the rear the original dog-leg stair with turned
wooden balusters. On the first floor an ante-room with lugged
panelling and the basket-arched fireplace which is repeated
elsewhere. In the wing the drawing room, with late C18 timber and composition chimneypiece and a plain oval in the
coved ceiling.

ROSEBURN HOUSE, Roseburn Street. An unpretentious harled
mansion in the shadow of Murrayfield Stadium. Mungo Russell, merchant burgess, bought land here in 1576, and in 1582
(the date over the entrance door) built a small three-storey
house with a round stair-tower at its SE corner. Soon after,
the house was extended s with a two-storey range, the lower
part of whose W wall survives. In the mid C17 the rectangle
became a U by the addition of an L-plan E wing, extended s
in the C18. At the foot of the large stair-tower (now with a
late Georgian roof) protruding from its E flank, a skinny
lugged-architraved doorpiece. Built into the courtyard's N
wall, a fireplace lintel dated 1562, inscribed with pious texts
and a shield containing the Royal Arms.

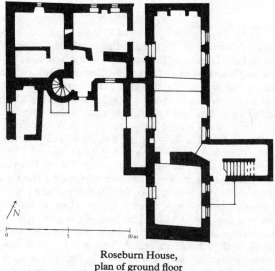

Roseburn House,
plan of ground floor

Vaulted ground floor inside. The end of the C17 stair's spinewall has vestigial capitals and bases. First-floor SE room with mid-C18 panelling.

STREETS AND NEIGHBOURHOODS

COLTBRIDGE

For the old and new bridges, *see* Public Buildings, above. The red-tiled PAPE'S COTTAGES to the N, 1895, were endowed by the owner of old Coltbridge House. At Nos. 1–7 ROSE-BURN CLIFF a terrace by *McArthy & Watson* for Patrick Geddes, 1911, in similar style; harl and red dressings, jettied upper storey with half-timber gables. COLTBRIDGE AVENUE begins with a tall baronial tenement on the W side, 1881, and a two-storey dormered terrace with shops on the E, 1869. Then single-storey workers' houses of the later C19. In COLTBRIDGE TERRACE, Nos. 1–7 by *Frederick T. Pilking-ton*, 1869; a rubbly dormered row with colonnetted bays, naturalistic carving fanned out over the windows. At the corner of Henderland Road a fussy, square-towered house (later Lansdowne House School, now part of St George's School, for which *see* Craigleith and Ravelston) by *T. B. McFadzen*, 1875; bargeboarded lodge. For the former Coltbridge School, *see* below.

CORSTORPHINE ROAD

A wide and noisy speedway (A8) to Corstorphine en route for Glasgow. Starting at the E end, the S side has a few stolid villas and the Italianate (former) Coltbridge School at No. 17, all early Victorian, as is Greenside Lodge at No. 55. Much more on the N side. At the E end the terrace of ABINGER GARDENS, by *Dunn & Findlay*, 1898, set back from the main road behind trees; snecked rubble contrasting with smooth stone bays on to whose tops one can walk out from the French-windowed attic to enjoy the view. For Murrayfield Parish Church, *see* above. Next a prosaic line of Victorian villas, followed by the long wall (originally of Murrayfield House) concealing earlier villas and pierced by their showy gateways. No. 18, *c.* 1820; No. 20 (ORMELIE) of similar date but unbalanced by a Victorian bay-window and then extended by *Lorimer* in 1895. The best of the others is No. 30 (THE TOR, a Baptist Eventide Home, 1984), gabled Jacobean of 1866 with a lodge to match, the porch added and the interior re-cast in 1896. Two-storey galleried entrance hall with carved Renaissance woodwork, a stained-glass window with a figure of Health on the stair landing; all very cosy in scale, excellent in quality.

Within the angle of Corstorphine Road and Ellersly Road, the offices of the DISTILLERS' COMPANY by *Robert Matthew, Johnson-Marshall & Partners*, 1981. A large, aggressive building, with stone walls refusing to be pierced by windows but at the same time denying any structural role. The stone surfaces interlock with lead cladding, in roughly equal proportion. For the spaciously sited mansions of Beechwood and Beechmount, *see* above.

EASTER BELMONT ROAD

Very select inter-war villas climbing the hill; mown verges instead of pavements. On the S side a series by *Orphoot, Whiting & Bryce*, including No. 3 (WELL HOUSE) with big plastered gables and some classical detail, 1931, and No. 5 (BRUCE-HILL) with harled gables, 1932. Two adventurous houses by *Kininmonth & Spence*, No. 11 (LISMHOR) very horizontal early modern, No. 4 very vertical with odd Georgian quotations, both 1935. No. 8 Monte Carlo vernacular of the same period. No. 6 (ARDNASAID) of more civilized Mediterranean inspiration by *L. Grahame Thomson*, 1932; central loggia and canted wings, beautifully detailed.

ELLERSLY ROAD AND KINELLAN ROAD

On the N side, ELLERSLY HOUSE by *R. H. Watherston* (for himself), 1910, placid early-Georgian revival but swamped by extension as a hotel. On the S, WESTERLEA by *Campbell Douglas* and *J. J. Stevenson*, 1860-9, a big Jacobean composition remodelled internally by *Lorimer*, 1913, and later extended as a children's home. On the N side of KINELLAN ROAD are RESTALRIG, a cottagey villa of *c.* 1840, and ST LEONARDS, altered by *Lorimer* in 1912. Round the corner on the W side, McNEIL HOUSE by *Rowand Anderson & Paul*, 1913; rubble from the Rattlebags quarry, leaded windows.

MURRAYFIELD DRIVE AND MURRAYFIELD ROAD

In MURRAYFIELD DRIVE, BALNAGOWAN by *Parker & Unwin* (of garden city fame) for W. A. Smith, 1906-7. White-harled walls with groups of small windows delicately placed, a strong composition of hipped grey roofs, white chimney-stalks with corner lugs under thin moulded copes. The two-storey hall survived the later subdivision into flats by *A. H. Mottram* (a former assistant in the Parker & Unwin office). In MURRAYFIELD ROAD, No. 23 (REDCROFT), *c.* 1910: snecked masonry, moulded dressings, red-tiled roofs with Lorimer-style dormers on the wings. No. 33 (KINELLAN) by *R. & R. Dickson*, 1846, enlarged in 1913 by *Lorimer*, who artfully repeated the giant pilaster order and gave the front door a big Dutch rococo fanlight. In the garden a life-size lead statuary group of a lion protecting a lamb and a young girl. No. 42 (GLION, originally the Ravelston Dykes Golf Club) by *Cooper & Taylor*, 1897, looking much newer except for its heavy red-brick chimneys. Plinth of the same pressed brick, a lead-roofed porch between two bay-windows, half-timbered gables; conversion by *Basil Spence*, *c.* 1935, retaining the main club-room. At the N end, the MURRAYFIELD GOLF CLUB by *Rowand Anderson & Balfour Paul*, 1934; smart white harl and grey slates, with plinth and tapering chimney-stalks of blue engineering brick.

ROSEBURN AND SAUGHTONHALL

Except for Roseburn House (*see* above) this area to the S of Corstorphine Road has little to notice. Roseburn is industrial (a good pair of red-brick Post Office buildings in Russell Road, *c.* 1910) and recreational (Murrayfield Rugby Stadium, 1924-5). Saughtonhall to the W is all housing; three hundred semi-detached houses for the City (pebbledashed with pink stone bays), 1925, by *C. E. Tweedie*, who also designed twenty private semis off GLENDEVON PLACE with imitation stonework, 1934. The monotony is relieved by a cottagey terrace of real stone and fake half-timber at Nos. 30-42 BALGREEN ROAD, *c.* 1895, and a group of buff brick mono-pitch houses in SAUGHTON CRESCENT by *Kingham, Knight* for the Crescent Housing Society, 1971.

NEWINGTON

Three roads out of Edinburgh to the s, attracting villas and terraces and then subjecting them to the pressures of commerce and traffic. But between the roads quiet Georgian cross-streets (Duncan and Middleby) and just enough room for a series of self-contained developments, beginning in 1825 with George Bell's Blacket Place, named after his family seat and laid out (and to some extent designed) by *James Gillespie Graham*. Further s is Mayfield, the property of Duncan McLaren (Lord Provost 1851–4). *David Cousin*'s 1862 scheme for the E (Waverley Park) section was an old-fashioned grid, but his final one perfected the Blacket idea of the private arcadia; the w section is a more conventional gridiron and crescent. Both were drawn in 1870 and showed single villas only; many double ones were eventually allowed. The Craigmillar Park area was laid out by *Cousin* in 1877. To the E, despite a big incursion of C20 public and private housing into the Prestonfield estate, the golf course survives as an important link in the city's inner Green Belt and a setting for Prestonfield House.

CHURCHES

CRAIGMILLAR PARK CHURCH (originally Mayfield Church), Craigmillar Park. Blunt, knobbly Gothic by *Hardy & Wight*, 1878. Twin doorways in the E gable facing the street, a steeple intended but not built. Inside, E.E. nave arcades, spacious transepts and a braced open roof. At the E end a gallery, at the w the chancel, quietly transformed by *Ian G. Lindsay*, 1956. He left on the N side the ORGAN, 1892, by *Brindley & Foster*, in its spiky Gothic case, but redesigned the PULPIT with a pretty strapworked sounding-board, and installed a large draped COMMUNION TABLE with a rose-coloured velvet reredos. This simplicity accords with the STAINED GLASS. In the s transept three lights (St Michael, Christ with children and healing the sick) after 1933, and two lights below (John the Baptist and Zacchaeus), 1938, by *Margaret Chilton* and *Marjorie Kemp*. In the aisles eight pairs of lancet lights (a mixture of large figures and miniature subjects) by the same artists, 1927–45. In the chancel w wall three tall lights (Christ's life and ministry), too small in scale but effective in their soft colours, respectively blue, pink and green. They could also be by *Chilton and Kemp*.

CRAIGMILLAR PARK FREE CHURCH, closing the vista of East Suffolk Road. Now in secular use. Imaginative Perp by *Sydney Mitchell & Wilson*, 1898. Cruciform, with NW tower containing the porch and intended to have a turreted belfry and octagonal spire. Red sandstone crockets and blind tracery partly left in block, but nonetheless making a graceful pattern against the paler masonry. In 1976 *R. D. Cameron* divided the interior into a school hall above (the timber-lined roof still

exposed) and offices below, and converted the octagonal
HALL into the art department. *See also* St Margaret's School,
below.

DUNCAN STREET BAPTIST CHURCH, Duncan Street. *c.* 1843.
Heavy two-storey classical villa front. Giant anta pilasters and
a centre pediment. (Interior recast, 1888.)

MAYFIELD CHURCH (originally Free Church), Mayfield Road 38
and West Mayfield. Stylish Gothic by *Hippolyte J. Blanc*,
1876–9, after a competition. It is his best church in Edinburgh. The style is French, the 48 m. spire of Normandy type
with tall, shafted pinnacles at the angles being a South Edinburgh landmark; it was added in 1894 to the plain tower,
which is a good foil to the arcaded W gable alongside (the
main doorway was enlarged by the removal of the trumeau in
1970). Low aisles, double-gabled transepts and a long nave
roof which was punctuated, till 1969, by a flèche at the crossing. Inside, a stumpy French arcade and wall-shafted clearstorey. At the transepts, taller piers with free-standing
corner-shafts, and big leafy corbels at the peaks of the arches.
Five-sided apse with timber rib-vault, enlarged in 1894. The
main roof was unusual, with a high round-arched vault rising
from a hammerbeamed soffit on each side. It was destroyed
by fire in 1969 and replaced with a reticulated vault in white
plaster by *David Carr* and *Stewart Tod*, successful in itself
but unrelated to the walls except by means of some awkward
plaster groins. – Gothic timber PULPIT by *A. F. Balfour
Paul*, 1932; the rest of the furnishings plain but effective
replacements. – ORGAN by *H. S. Vincent* of Sunderland,
1895, moved out of the apse in 1932 and completely rebuilt
in the W gallery in 1970. – STAINED GLASS. An outstanding
collection, undamaged by the fire. In the apse four lancet
lights (the Evangelists) by *William Meikle*, 1900. In the S
transept two triple lights (the Ascension, 1899, Christ in
glory, 1902) by *Ballantine & Gardiner*. – In the N transept a
similar trio (Transfiguration) by *Ballantine*, 1904, and another (Nativity) by *Oscar Paterson*, 1912. In the S clearstorey
two pairs of lights (Hope and Faith, Liberality and Praise),
1901, and another pair (David), 1903, all by *Ballantine &
Gardiner*. The series is completed (Humility and Joy, Gentle-
ness and Fortitude) by *Guthrie & Wells*, 1922. In the S aisle
four pairs of two lights (the Beatitudes) by *Guthrie & Wells*,
one signed by *Charles L. Davidson*, 1927(?). In the N aisle
three pairs (praise of creation, from the Psalms) and a single
light (Gloria), also by *Guthrie & Wells*, about the same date.
– HALL to the SE by *Blanc*, 1875–6, extended in 1894 and
again by *David Carr* in 1968. The original manse, built with
the church, is now incorporated in the halls.

PRIESTFIELD CHURCH (originally Rosehall United Presbyterian), Dalkeith Road and Marchhall Place. Formidably Lombardic, by *Sutherland & Walker*, 1877, after a competition.
Pedimented W front with flanking porches leading into stair-
towers of five arcaded storeys, pedimented transept and hall

on the rival N front, all enlivened by arches and plate-tracer-ied rose windows. A simpler interior with a low-pitch beamed ceiling and giant arches over the N and S transept galleries, which have arcaded timber fronts like the W gallery. Radial seating below. – Gothic COMMUNION TABLE, of oak (as a First World War memorial), moved from Prestonfield Church* in 1975. – PULPIT, arcaded, moved from its central position in 1975. – FONT. A kneeling angel with a clam-shell, by *John Rhind*, 1881, in Caen stone after Thorwaldsen. – ORGAN in the E arch by *Binns* of Sheffield, *c.* 1900. – STAINED GLASS, all given in 1921. Over the W gallery three lights as a First World War memorial (Christ and the leper, 'These are they that came ...', and Christ bearing His Cross) by *Alexander Strachan*. Under the gallery and elsewhere a series of biblical trees by *Mary Wood* and *Douglas Hamilton*, with rich colours and sturdy drawing on pale grounds.

ST COLUMBA'S R.C. CHURCH, Upper Gray Street. By *R. M. Cameron*, 1888. A small-scale pedimented front with François I trimmings. The rubbly Presbytery and the Hall further down the street are by *Reginald Fairlie*, 1927.

SYNAGOGUE, Salisbury Road. Post-Georgian in variegated red brick by *James Miller* of Glasgow, 1929–32. *Dick Peddie & McKay* divided the interior at gallery level in 1979. Very simple T-plan with raked seating, a separate central bema (platform) under a top-lit dome. – STAINED GLASS. In the vestibule four lights by *William Wilson*, 1957.

PUBLIC BUILDINGS

LONGMORE HOSPITAL, Salisbury Place. By *J. M. Dick Peddie*, 1879, the rear extension 1891. Solemnly classical, with broad pilasters between the windows, the upper floor relieved by paired Roman Doric columns. Three-storey pedimented centrepiece.

MARCHHALL NURSING HOME, Marchhall Place. 1854. Tall gables and scrolly bargeboards.

NEWINGTON CEMETERY, Dalkeith Road. Laid out semi-for-mally in 1848 by *David Cousin*, who designed the Gothic lodge and neo-Norman CATACOMBS beneath the W-facing terrace.

ROYAL BLIND ASYLUM, NW end of Craigmillar Park. By *Charles Leadbetter*, 1874. A startling S front with three rubbly sash-windowed storeys and a mansard, the style described by *The Building News* as 'light French'. *The Builder* said that 'an ornamental effect is to be aimed at without incurring much expense', but the central round turret with a clock in the parapet is not particularly subtle.

---

*This Gothic church by *Thomas Ross* was built in 1900 at the junction of Dalkeith Road and Lady Road, and demolished in 1975 when the congregations united.

ROYAL COMMONWEALTH POOL, Dalkeith Road and Holy- 102
rood Park Road. By *John Richards* of *Robert Matthew,
Johnson-Marshall & Partners,* 1967, for the 1970 Commonwealth Games. Olympic-length pool and diving and learning
pools, beautifully combined with a large vestibule and viewing spaces. External glazing in three diminishing tiers recessed beneath long facias. Bright steel chimney to the S,
entrance by a wide-stepped platform from the W and N.

ST MARGARET'S SCHOOL, East Suffolk Road. A stolid Victorian villa, *c.* 1880, with a two-storey extension to the S by
Law & Dunbar-Nasmith, 1971; slate roof and slate-hung
walls, the windows vertically linked and finished at the top
(except over the staircase) with shallow gablets. The school
hall is the former Craigmillar Park Free Church (*see* above).

UNIVERSITY OF EDINBURGH, POLLOCK HALLS OF RESID-
ENCE, Dalkeith Road and Holyrood Park Road. Named after
Sir Donald Pollock, and built in the wooded grounds of three
large suburban mansions which he gave to the University.
Excellent small-scale planting between the buildings on the
close-packed site, and dramatic E views of Salisbury Crags.

Of the three mansions, ABDEN HOUSE is spiritless Jaco-
bean by *Thomas Davies,* 1855, the others bold baronial by
John Lessels for the sons of the printer and publisher Thomas
Nelson. (Nelson's Parkside Works, also by Lessels, stood on
the site of the Scottish Widows Fund building adjoining
Dalkeith Road; *see* Perambulations, below.) SALISBURY
GREEN (1860–7, for William Nelson) was based on a small
mansion of *c.* 1780. This was refronted, with an oriel over a
Roman Doric porch, and extended to the NW with a cap-
housed tower, new wing and service wing. Vigorous dormers
and turrets overall, but plenty of more civilized detail, e.g.
pious texts and cherub corbels, beautifully carved. To the S,
a single-storey wing of *c.* 1820, and a careful extension by
Gordon, Duncan, Somerville, 1979, on the site of Lessels's
conservatory. Top-lit inner hall with scholarly Jacobean
doorcases, and a small dog-leg stair in the original position,
wrought brasswork supporting the handrail. In the bowed
drawing room a rich ceiling on segmental arches, the main
oval painted with clouds and cherubs, the semi-dome with a
classical plaque in grisaille. The earliest date on the painting
is 1861, and it is attributed to *Charles Fréchou,* who worked at
Carbet Castle, Broughty Ferry, Tayside. Two impressive
rooms of 1882, the top-lit oak billiard room, and in the SE
part of the old house an ebonized room by *Alexander Dingwall* and *John Haddon* of *Bonnar & Carfrae,* black and gold
with red velvet panels. French rococo enrichments in the
corners of the ceiling, black marble chimneypiece and ingeniously folding shutters. ST LEONARD'S to the N (1869–70,
for Thomas Nelson, Jun.) is Lessels from the start, fiercest
hammer-dressed baronial on a more compact plan, with basement offices. Lion-bracketed oriel over the entrance, and an
awesome four-storey tower. The interior rather heavy-handed

Art Movement. Colossal stair-hall, birds and beasts lurking in the carved scrolls of the stair, for which that at Kinross House was the starting point. Neo-Jacobean ceilings, the compartments painted presumably by *Thomas Bonnar*, more striking in quantity than quality; olive green the prevailing colour.

The new halls are by *Rowand Anderson, Kininmonth & Paul*. First the Scandinavian-looking HOLLAND and FRASER, 1959, each of U plan and linked on the S side by the (former) refectory which has a lofty shell-concrete arcade; formal N entry between towers with concrete finials like some sort of lifting apparatus. Then a large group of five-storey towers, 1967, faced with vertical reddish slabs, all the horizontal elements suppressed – perhaps to avoid any challenge to the solid permanence of the crags; the view from Queen's Park is less successful.

UNIVERSITY OF EDINBURGH, SUFFOLK ROAD HALLS OF RESIDENCE, East Suffolk Road. By *A. K. Robertson*, begun in 1914, for women students. Five two-storey blocks of Georgian domestic character (symmetrical with bowed ends) but with rubble walls, mansard roofs and ornamental dormers. Formal composition round four sides of a green, with NW entrance lodge.

MANSIONS

CAMERON HOUSE, Cameron House Avenue. Built for the Dicks of Prestonfield in 1770. Three-storey main block with two-storey wings. Projecting single-storey pavilions with Venetian windows in their gables. Divided into flats in 1973 by the *City Architect's Department*, who linked the house to a new block on the E.

65 PRESTONFIELD HOUSE, Priestfield Road. Now a hotel. A compact but classy mansion built for Sir James Dick, Lord Provost of Edinburgh, to replace a house burnt down by a student demonstration in 1681. The house was occupied in 1689, although two years later Charles Brand was commissioned to buy Flemish or Dutch pictures 'in bright colours' for the stair-hall.

Prestonfield is the last of a group of houses, beginning with Methven Castle (Tayside) in 1664, characterized by a U plan wrapped round a flat-roofed block. Main front to the W, its balustraded two-storey centre gripped between three-storey curvilinear gables. The stone detail contrasting with the harled walls is still Artisan: elaborate strapwork buckle quoins (cf. George Heriot's School, Old Town: Public Buildings) and lugged architraves. Some of the vertical emphasis has been lost by the early C19 banking of ground to hide the basement and the addition of a beautifully detailed Roman Doric porte cochère. Three-bay S flank with the eaves entablature forming pulvinated friezes for broken pediments over the second-floor windows. Triple-gabled E front, the outer gables curvilinear, the centre concave. Simply chamfered margins. Across this front a large single-storey and basement extension with bowed N and S ends was built c. 1830. More chamfered margins on the N elevation, which was originally a repeat of the S. In c. 1890 *MacGibbon & Ross* added a full-height bathroom extension to the middle, placing the central pediment on top of their curvilinear gable.

From the front door (an early C19 segmental arched replacement) the original processional route led across a vestibule to a grand stair up to the main apartment. C17 black and white marble floors survive. The segmental arch from the vestibule into the stair-hall was made in the early C19 when the stair was removed, the top of the stair-hall floored over and a Roman Doric screen inserted on the E as an entry to the new drawing room and dining room beyond. At the same time the W stair landing was made a balcony, reusing the original balusters over a semi-elliptical arch springing from paired consoles. The first floor is now reached by the secondary N stair. Three doors on the old stair-hall balcony. The middle one, richly consoled and pedimented, opens into the Tapestry Room (original drawing room) running across the S three-fifths of the W front. Its Artisan Mannerist exuberance is slightly bizarre. Lugged marble chimneypiece set in an extravagant wooden surround. On the jambs, consoles carrying realistic male heads with pots of lilies above. Foliaged frieze with putti supporting Dick's coat of arms. In the overmantel a landscape framed by swags and putti. The W wall and most of the N and S walls are panelled. On the E and returning to the W, Mortlake tapestries, apparently here from the start. Extraordinary doorcases with pulvinated friezes stepped up over the lugs of the architraves. Lugged panelled doors. The low but deeply modelled ceiling gives the knockout. Around the foliaged centrepiece, circles with animals and a pot of lilies in a grotesque cartouche. Another cartouche with vines in one of the oblong end panels; in the other, merpeople.

To the N, the Leather Room (original bedchamber). In the panelling, red leather embossed in high relief with flowers, shells, insects, snakes and putti, made in 1676 at Cordova for Dick's Lawnmarket house and moved when Prestonfield was rebuilt. Fireplace with squares of roses in the consoled lugs. Above it the main cornice breaks forward as if a pilastered overmantel had been intended. In the second-floor Cupid Room, the C17 stair-hall ceiling with a dangling cupid in the middle. The two front rooms on this floor have paintings in the overmantels, one showing a storm at sea.

The ground floor must originally have contained family apartments. In the Italian Room a C17 fireplace in a stepped architrave: Ionic pilastered overmantel with boldly screwed-out volutes. Classical landscapes attributed to the *Nories* in the panelling. Doorcases with pulvinated friezes. In the Old

Bar a late C18 bookcase adapted as a gantry. C17 chimney-piece in the New Bar. The S extension of *c.*1830 added a drawing room and dining room, one on each side of an oval-domed vestibule, both with dished ceilings and bowed ends. Curved mahogany doors. Anta doorpieces with palmette entablature. Plaster-panelled walls, the fields outlined with bound reeding. The pine and gesso dining-room chimney-piece of *c.*1800 with Corinthian pilasters and a marine frieze is presumably an import. Drawing-room chimneypiece of white marble.

Roofless two-storey round STABLES N of the house, by *James Gillespie Graham*, 1816. Externally the circle is squared off at the NW, NE, SW and SE. Pend arch in the pedimented SE projection. Inside, the court is a perfect circle. Pedimented loft doocot facing the entrance.

PERAMBULATIONS

CAUSEWAYSIDE is narrow and bitty. On the E side two wall-head chimney gables at Nos. 21–23, late C18. Moderne GARAGE by *Basil Spence*, 1937. Nos. 45–79 four-storey late Georgian. After the Salisbury Place corner the four-storey WIGHT'S PLACE at Nos. 169–179, *c.*1835, titled in capital letters over the pend. At Nos. 227–231 a little C17 or C18 house with pantiled roof and shops below. For the W side as far as Grange Road, *see* Grange: Perambulation. Then perfunctory concrete grids of the later C20 at Nos. 140 and 160. On the E side of RATCLIFFE TERRACE a small-scale C18 composition of rubble and pantiles; Nos. 33–37 with a wide gable and C19 pedimented shopfronts, No. 39 set back, No. 43 with a hipped roof. A solitary villa at No. 59, nudged by a tall warehouse and half swamped by a shanty shop. The street ends with the respectable suburbia of MAYFIELD ROAD. *Menzies & Cockburn* designed the terraces at Nos. 1–18 and 28–32, 1910–11. For Mayfield Church, *see* above.

DALKEITH ROAD is a fragmentary 1·5 km. long, pleasantly close to Queen's Park. At the N end (on the site of Nelson's printing works) the SCOTTISH WIDOWS FUND & LIFE ASSURANCE head office by *Basil Spence, Glover & Ferguson*, 1972, an elegant polygonal composition mounting up from one to four storeys, though the storeys are defined only by thin bronze lines on the brown glass curtain wall. Colourless glass at the entry, reached by a bridge over a pebble-bottomed sheet of water. York stone boundary wall and basement carpark; *Sylvia Crowe* was landscape consultant. At the E end of HOLYROOD PARK ROAD the massive gable of J. & G. STEWART'S WHISKY BOND, which also has a regally pedimented centrepiece inscribed AU (for Andrew Usher), 1902. LODGE to Holyrood inscribed VR 1863. Back to Dalkeith Road for the Royal Commonwealth Pool and then the University's Pollock Halls, standing in trees behind a long wall with the respective lodges of St Leonard's, Salisbury Green (*c.* 1830, with pediment) and Abden House; for all these, *see* above. On the W side No. 58, a grand villa of *c.* 1820 indecently exposed and enlarged as a pub. Then the three lodges of the Blacket development, and a side view of Arthur Lodge (*see* Blacket Place, below); also three outward-looking villas, No. 66 on the very edge of Victorian and predictably dated 1837. Two more lodges, to the Waverley Park development and then to Newington Cemetery (*see* above). The E side finishes with a downhill rush of four-storey tenements heralded by Priestfield Church (*see* above). PRESTONFIELD AVENUE to the E, and the big triangle to the S of it, were built up with harled three-storey flats by the *City Architect's Department*, 1928–9; very plain but with arched canopies, the more conspicuous gable ends also arched. Much of the private housing to the N is by *Miller*. For Cameron House and Prestonfield House, *see* above.

At the S end of Dalkeith Road is CAMERON CRESCENT with ingenious polychrome flats by *Nicholas Groves-Raines*, 1981. Four storeys of red brick with yellow brick stripes along lintels and cornice, long-and-short yellow quoins at the windows and obtuse angles. The emphasis is horizontal in the window glazing, vertical in the framework that shoots up the front of each bay to make a triangular balcony on top.

NEWINGTON ROAD (main route) has a double personality – late Georgian grace overlaid by Victorian and C20 commerce, but with less damage than at first appears. No. 10 on the W side is the former West Newington House, *c.* 1805; Roman Doric doorpiece in the recessed centre bay, the outer windows tripartite between rosetted giant pilasters, now incorporated in a fruity bay-windowed terrace of *c.* 1867. At No. 28 a good chemist's shopfront projecting from the Victorian corner tenement. After West Newington Place, Nos. 56–68 by *Thomas Bonnar*, *c.* 1825, three-storey with outshot shops whose centrepiece is a pedimented entry to No. 62. On the E side Nos. 1–37, *c.* 1825, two-storey with higher pavilions. After East Newington Place, Nos. 39–71, also *c.* 1825, a three-storey terrace with architraved windows; finally Nos. 81–109, *c.* 1811, with two storeys, the centre prettily marked by tripartite windows and a swagged wall-head panel, the ends by plain panels. All these are built on high basements, so their ground floors are not quite hidden by the chaotic shops built (except at Nos. 53–57) over the old front gardens. At No. 33 the stiff classical ROYAL BANK by *W. J. Walker Todd*, 1932. In EAST NEWINGTON PLACE, an incomplete terrace at Nos. 1–3, *c.* 1835, and at the end a sawmill with sheds and yellow brick chimney, *c.* 1893. In WEST NEWINGTON PLACE, Nos. 3–6 by *Thomas Brown*, *c.* 1825, and a handsome mid-C19 tenement closing the W vista.

MINTO STREET (main route again) is a sedate procession of front-gardened villas, 1808–30. On the E side Nos. 7–8, 10 and 13 have been updated with Victorian bays, and nearly all have lost some dignity as hotels, e.g. with shoddy links between Nos. 17–18 and Nos. 21–22, the latter called the Doric Hotel despite an Ionic porch. For Blacket Avenue, *see* below. At the s end a terrace of 1827, its terminal houses marked by urns on a balustrade (No. 24) and an extra storey (No. 30). On the w side the same general pattern, with a terrace at Nos. 40–43, but the villas more sporadic, e.g. No. 39 with its Ionic doorpiece on a Duncan Street gable-end, No. 44 completely Victorianized *c.* 1880 with arches and leafy capitals.

To the e of Minto Street, SALISBURY ROAD. On its n side Nos. 17 and 21, *c.* 1825, with recessed Ionic doorpieces and a Victorian garden fence of tapering stone pylons. No. 2, *c.* 1815, with over-arched ground floor. Then, standing back, the five-storey Longmore Hospital Nurses' Home by *J. Douglas Miller*, 1935. Nos. 35–37 and 41–45, both *c.* 1825, with Ionic and Greek Doric doorpieces. On the s side No. 2 (William Blackwood's house), 1815 but altered. No. 6, 1817, rubble-fronted, altered as St David's R.C. Convent with a new hall and chapel by *Frank Mears & Partners*, 1967. After the Synagogue (*see* above), No. 8, a long villa with Roman Doric doorpiece *in antis*, No. 10 with pilastered doorpiece, both *c.* 1815.

To the w of Minto Street, SALISBURY PLACE. On the n side the Longmore Hospital (*see* Public Buildings, above), on the s a jumble at whose w end has been begun (1984) the NATIONAL LIBRARY FOR SCOTLAND EXTENSION by *Basil Spence, Glover & Ferguson*. Two Georgian villas, *c.* 1810, informally sited; No. 7 swamped by shops, No. 21 turning the corner into UPPER GRAY STREET, a pretty little arcadia with industrial intrusions. On the e side single-storey cottages at Nos. 3 and 5, *c.* 1810, their scale respected by St Columba's Church (*see* above) but not by its Presbytery. At Nos. 31–39 a modest terrace, *c.* 1810, prolonged to No. 23, *c.* 1850. On the w side stolid villas and a big tenement at Nos. 32–34 (now a builder's store), Frenchy in front, red-and-yellow brick behind.

DUNCAN STREET. On the n side Nos. 1–9, *c.* 1825, with arched ground-floor windows in the centrepiece. Then a pompous classical TELEPHONE BUILDING by *J. Wilson Paterson*, 1923, and the Duncan Street Baptist Church (*see* above). On the s the office of JOHN BARTHOLOMEW designed as the Edinburgh Geographical Institute by *H. Ramsay Taylor*, 1909. Worthy Palladian in plum-coloured sandstone, not very suitable for the elegant portico of 1815 with coupled columns (Corinthian above, Tower-of-the-Winds below) brought here from Falconhall, Dr Bartholomew's house in Morningside. To the w the School Dental Centre, formerly the Duncan Street School, improvised from two Georgian villas by *John A. Carfrae*, 1910.

SOUTH GRAY STREET. A nice parade of villas, *c.* 1815, mostly on the w side.

MIDDLEBY STREET. On the N side two-storey villas, c. 1817. On the S Nos. 2–12 c. 1827. Paired single-storey houses with Greek Doric doorpieces, joined into a continuous row by balustrade-topped links: an unusual idea, but quite practicable because sunk basements give another storey on the back-garden side.

BLACKET AVENUE enters *Gillespie Graham*'s intimate layout through his Tudor Gothic gate-piers on the E side of Minto Street, and runs between the trees to Dalkeith Road. Its main function was access to Newington House (demolished 1966), whose modest gateway is on the S side; on the N, only No. 15, c. 1825, with an Ionic doorpiece approached through a monumental gate in the high garden wall, and the austere BELLEVILLE LODGE, c. 1840, with twin bay-windowed gables. BLACKET PLACE with similar gate-piers and a 127 picturesque LODGE in Dalkeith Road. On the N side massive gate-piers (now blocked) formerly serving ARTHUR LODGE, 1827–30, for the jeweller William Cunningham, probably by *Thomas Hamilton*; uncommonly elegant, with a tall pedimented centrepiece between block-pedimented wings, their single windows in tapered architraves between perfectly smooth panels incised with an anthemion motif. Covered atrium plan. Later colonnettes at the stair. No. 1 Blacket Place (S side), Jacobean, c. 1840, No. 7 with Greek Doric porch. After the plain cottage at No. 2, Greek Doric is also the rule on the N side (the double villas having either separate or combined porches) till the Ionic double villa at Nos. 26–28 which turns the corner. Doric resumes on what is now the W side, with a triple villa at Nos. 38–42; most of these 1825 or soon after, but a final kick from Nos. 60–62, c. 1870, gabled and bayed in the Bryce manner. On the E side Nos. 9–11, c. 1850, gravely classical; across Blacket Avenue Nos. 15 and 17, single-storey with deep eaves and Tuscan porches. More bland Roman Doric, then a bold shock from *James Gowans*, the double villa at Nos. 23–25 (1859–60), whose ashlar is framed with his usual polychrome crazy-work; round-arched windows on the ground floor and again as dormers on the picturesque skyline. The vista of Blacket Place is closed by the Jacobean villa, c. 1845, at No. 10 MAYFIELD TERRACE. This street forms another entry from Dalkeith Road (lodge and gate-piers matching those of Blacket Place and Blacket Avenue) and one first-generation villa, the Greek Doric bungalow at No. 28, 1828. Nos. 12–14 Graeco-Italian, Nos. 1, 3 and 16 in the Bryce manner; the other villas stodgy, becoming respectably uniform in ALFRED PLACE, where the Thomas Burns Home for Blind Women was built with smug red brick and roughcast in 1928.

MAYFIELD GARDENS is the next name for the main route. On the E side Nos. 1–19 are a grand classical terrace by *David Cousin*, 1862, with consoled front doors and a long rank of pedimented dormers between the pavilions. This and the still more massive terrace at Nos. 31–39 are all that was built of

Cousin's 1862 plan. The w side has nothing to rival it, but ends with the former Newington Station (1884), now used as shops.

To the E of Mayfield Gardens, the WAVERLEY PARK development: Waverley Lodge (1871) and the blank garden walls further down Dalkeith Road recall the exclusiveness of Blacket Place, but the internal layout is more picturesque – based on a loop of villas with their backs to a small public garden. Most are semi-detached (not single houses, as Cousin intended), but with just enough variety – and trees – to sweeten the substantial Victorian pudding; e.g. in QUEEN'S CRESCENT, No. 2 with an arcaded bow, Nos. 3 and 16 with Italian towers, No. 31 (1876) with curly bargeboards, and Nos. 32-33 with a pair of highly original bay-windows; No. 18a is an artfully simple insertion in Fyfestone by *Morris & Steedman*, 1970. In VENTNOR TERRACE, Nos. 8-11 by *John McLachlan*, 1883, have a big quartet of steep, timber-filled gables. Nos. 4-5 by *William Potts*, 1900, are the (red sandstone) cherry in an otherwise grey mixture. For NEWINGTON CEMETERY (to the SE), *see* above.

To the w of Mayfield Gardens, WEST MAYFIELD. The street of that name has a Georgian N side, all *c.* 1830. Nos. 1-4 have a bow at the corner of Minto Street, originally with a balustrade on top, now with a good Victorian shop below. Unusual w section with a full-height basement, the outside stairs to the 'ground floor' (actually the first) divided by the original railings and curly lamp-holder; No. 4 has a pretty iron balcony. Nos. 5-10 a single-storey terrace. No. 11 (in its own garden) was symmetrically enlarged in the mid C19. On the S side Mayfield Church and its Gothic gabled manse (*see* above). The glum Renaissance villa at No. 21, with its iron-crested roof, dominates the solid but unremarkable West Mayfield development, most of which was designed in the 1870s by *W. Hamilton Beattie* and *J. C. Hay*. On the w side of MOSTON TERRACE a long bay-windowed tenement with crested dormers.

CRAIGMILLAR PARK continues the main route. The builder *D. M. Dunlop* developed the E side from 1877, and No. 19 (ANNESLEY) is one of the more interesting villas in a dull lot. Another tower opposite (No. 12), but the best villa on the w side is No. 8 (BELMONT) by *Archibald Macpherson* in a bold and well-detailed François I style, the porch framed by pink sandstone antae with arabesque panels. Stained glass with the signs of the Zodiac at the side entry. The streets to the w were mostly built in the late 1880s, though some are earlier, e.g. WEST SAVILE ROAD by *David Cousin* for the builder *D. M. Dunlop*, 1877. For the Royal Blind Asylum and the University's Suffolk Road Halls of Residence on the E side of Craigmillar Park, *see* above.

PILRIG

A small area straddling the old boundary between the burghs of Edinburgh and Leith. The ruined Pilrig House fails to give focus to this mixture of classy Georgian terraces, Victorian and later working-class housing, and factories.

CHURCHES

PILRIG AND DALMENY STREET (former Free Church), Leith Walk and Pilrig Street. Splendidly bold French Gothic by *Peddie & Kinnear*, 1861–3. *George Lorimer* was the builder. Rock-faced rubble with plate tracery and heavy ornament, compactly planned with a lucarned steeple filling the corner between the double s transept and wheel-windowed E gable. A spectacular interior. E gallery, transeptal galleries with iron columns and leafy stone capitals carrying a diagonal arch-braced roof of laminated timber. A fire in 1892 destroyed the original decorative scheme. The chancel FURNISHINGS were reorganized in 1963 but still make an impressive pitchpine Gothic display incorporating communion table and pulpit beneath the ORGAN by *Forster & Andrews*, 1903. – STAINED GLASS. The original non-figurative scheme is complete. Rose window in chancel by *Ballantine & Son*, the rest by *Field & Allan* of Leith. Adjoining HALL in Pilrig Street, turreted Gothic by *Sydney Mitchell & Wilson*, 1892.

ST JAMES (now disused), McDonald Road. E.E. by *Hardy & Wight*, 1894. Rockfaced Hailes stone with red dressings. An elaborate gabled front with a tower over the l. stair-hall, the weak but interesting spire not built till 1906.

ST PHILIP (Episcopal), Logie Green Road. By *John J. Burnet*, 1908. Red brick, except for the harled and cottage-windowed nave, which is built on top of the arched and massively buttressed hall. Porch and vestry added 1922. Brick inside, with the narrow raftered nave leading through a round arch into the broad, calm chancel. – SCULPTURE (the Tree of Life) as a reredos in the Children's Chapel, carved in wood by *A. Carrick Whalen*, 1950.

PUBLIC BUILDINGS

BONNINGTON PRIMARY SCHOOL, Bonnington Road. By *James Simpson*, 1875. Large plain Gothic, with a prickly skyline of ventilators.

BROUGHTON PRIMARY SCHOOL, Broughton Road and McDonald Road. Monumental Queen Anne by *Robert Wilson*, 1897, with red sandstone dressings. A masterly skyline. McDonald Road extension by *John A. Carfrae*, 1902.

McDONALD ROAD FIRE STATION, McDonald Road. By *Bamber & Hall*, 1964–6. Buff brick in a concrete frame. Behind, a 'ship' for practice.

POWDERHALL REFUSE DEPOT, Broughton Road. Scots baronial by the City Engineer *John Cooper*, 1893. Symmetrical, with red sandstone dressings, central tower and lots of pepperpots.

RAILWAY BRIDGE (disused) over Warriston Road and the Water of Leith. By *Grainger & Miller* for the Edinburgh, Leith & Newhaven Railway, 1841–3. Three segmental arches on high cutwaters, with plain pilasters at the spandrels.

TERRITORIAL ARMY HALL, 124 McDonald Road. Unorthodox Renaissance by *T. Duncan Rhind* for the Royal Artillery Regiment, 1912.

MANSION

PILRIG HOUSE, Pilrig Street. A roofless L-plan house built by Gilbert Kirkwood, 1638. In the re-entrant, round stair-tower corbelled out to the square at the top. Moulded doorpiece missing its pediment. Early C19 doorpiece on the s front, which used to have a curly gable of *c.* 1700. Set into the wall, armorial stone with angel supporters, the base for a sundial.

STREETS

BONNINGTON ROAD

Opposite Bonnington Primary School (*see* above), a large mid-C19 stone warehouse.

LEITH WALK

After the late C19 SHRUB PLACE, with an iron-crested corner to McDonald Road, this stretch has some good Georgian fragments but is otherwise chaotic. The Lothian Region Transport Depot (including the TRANSPORT MUSEUM) is a haphazard collection of grey brick boxes, 1974, quite unrelated to the street. SHRUBHILL HOUSE by *Marshall, Morrison & Associates*, 1970, is a decent office block with long horizontals of vertically textured concrete, its set-back building line excused by a garage forecourt. Then MIDDLEFIELD, a three-storey house of 1793 combining old and new fashions in sharply carved masonry; a pedimented first-floor window between Gothic-glazed Venetians, and a pedimented chimney-gable over a blank panel with large guttae. Unfortunately a later block stands in front. Nos. 372–376 (formerly George Place, *c.* 1810) are a long tenement with rusticated ground floor and recessed centre. For Pilrig Place, with its rounded corner, *see* Pilrig Street below.

McDONALD ROAD

A mixed bag. For the Public Library on the S corner, *see* Gay-field, Hope and Picardy: Public Buildings, and for St James's Church and the Fire Station on the N side, *see* Churches and Public Buildings, above. Next to the Fire Station a huge shed with a showy classical gable designed as an electricity gener-ating station by the City Engineer *John Cooper*, 1899, with adjacent offices. Red-brick boiler-house chimney to rear. The BRIDGESIDE WORKS, quietly dignified red sandstone with Renaissance details, by *Cooper & Taylor* for Brown the prin-ter, 1898. For the Territorial Army Hall on the S side, *see* above.

NEWHAVEN ROAD

Mostly faceless C20 industry and warehousing, but Nos. 48–58 are a modest row of houses, *c.* 1850, and the C20 warehouse to the N retains the façade of the former tannery. Immediately after the bridge over the Water of Leith, BONNINGTON MILLS HOUSE, late C18 with open-pedimented gable. BON-NYHAUGH HOUSE, built in 1621 by the Town Council for a Dutch dyer and much altered, with a brick stair-turret and a pantiled wing. In BONNINGTON AVENUE two harled blocks of updated Georgian character by *A. H. Mottram*, 1937. At the N end of Newhaven Road, BONNINGTON TERRACE with strapped window surrounds and regular dormers, *c.* 1866, faces a two-storey late Georgian row. For the N part of Newhaven Road, *see* Granton, Newhaven and Trinity: Perambulations.

PILRIG STREET

A showy start with the round tower of PILRIG PLACE, *c.* 1810, on the corner of Leith Walk. Rock-faced basement, rusticated ground floor and a slated circular dormer. Nos. 2–6 Pilrig Street follow suit. All were built by *David Sutherland*. Then Nos. 1–27 on the S side (*c.* 1821), stepping down the gradual slope and ringing the changes between doorpieces and lower-storey rustication. Nos. 46–48, with Ionic pilastered doorpieces, *c.* 1823, are stranded among the later work over-looking Pilrig Park; for what is left of Pilrig House, *see* above. To the S two very individual precincts, the first by *Patrick Wilson* for the Pilrig Model Dwellings Company, 1849, in four two-storey terraces of flatted cottages, of which SHAW'S PLACE and SHAW'S TERRACE have nicked and pedimented ends and cornised door-heads. Between them, two parallel terraces forming the cross-bar of the H layout, the front one with pedimented pavilions. It faces the three-storey tene-ments of SPEY TERRACE, still with minimal Classical detail and bearing the monogram of the Edinburgh Artisan Building Company, 1867. In SPEY STREET a polychrome high-rise block by the *City Architect's Department*, 1960. DRYDEN STREET has an excellent red-brick warehouse with giant arches, *c.* 1900. At its w end, the grandiose former TRANSPORT DEPOT in red brick with stone dressings, *c.* 1910. The second precinct is ROSSLYN CRESCENT, 1888, a bottle-shaped development of middle-class houses opening direct from Pilrig Street. At the entry, four semi-detached houses with rustic dormers; then two serpentine two-storey terraces with bay-windows, enclosing trees and leading to a three-storey block with copious bays and a couple of slated hats, startlingly upright. To the N of Pilrig Street, ARTHUR STREET has a row of houses and flats by *Leslie D. Morrison & Partners* for the Port of Leith Housing Association, 1980, and behind it the single-storey early C19 row of PILRIG COTTAGES.

WARRISTON ROAD

Starting at the Canonmills end, a row of cottages (probably late C18) once the CANONMILLS POTTERY. Under the railway bridge (*see* Public Buildings, above) to LADY HAIG'S POPPY FACTORY by *A. Hunter Crawford*, 1912, and the original part of Waterston's LOGIE GREEN works by *John Breingan*, 1901, a mixture of straightforward modern design for use, stodgy Renaissance for show; both buildings are of red sandstone. Industry finally gives way to Corporation housing of 1937. For Warriston Crematorium on the other side of the Water of Leith, *see* Fettes, Inverleith and Warriston: Public Buildings.

PORTOBELLO AND JOPPA

Portobello was the name of a thatched cottage built *c.* 1742 by a veteran of Admiral Vernon's victory against the Spanish at Puerto Bello (1739). It stood by the Musselburgh road in the village of Figgate, then part of the Brunstane Estate, and was replaced in 1862 by the Town Hall (now the Baptist Church). In 1763 the Edinburgh builder William Jamieson bought forty acres (7·3 ha.) of the estate, started a brickworks to the E of the Figgate Burn, and built seven villas in large gardens, including Rosefield for himself; only the oddest, The Tower, survives. About 1786 he also founded two potteries at the mouth of the burn. In the *Statistical Account* (1796) the village is called 'Portobello and Brickfield'.

Bathing machines were to be seen on the beach by 1795, and by 1804 (Groome's *Ordnance Gazetteer*) 'The beauty of the beach, the fineness of its sands, and its general eligibility as a bathing-place, began to draw the attention of the City of Edin-

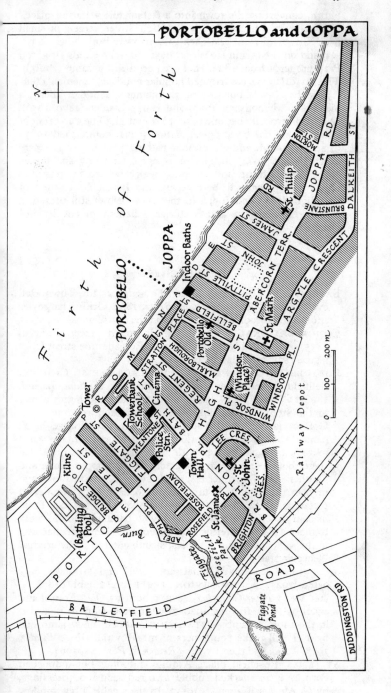

PORTOBELLO and JOPPA

burgh, converting the town into a fashionable watering place.'
The main road became a regular High Street, streets of small
neat villas with front and back gardens were built down to the
sea, and on the inland side John Baxter developed his Brighton
Park property from 1823. In 1832 Portobello became a burgh.
The Victorian age contributed popular holidays, tenements (enjoying the seaside but jostling the demure Georgian villas), a
pier (1870, demolished 1917) and Harry Lauder (1870–1950).
In 1896 Portobello became part of Edinburgh. The c20 brought
a formidable red-brick power station (1934, demolished 1977–
9) at the w end, and an outdoor bathing pool to use its spare
heat (disused 1984); little else except catchpenny shabbiness
along the sea-front, and creeping neglect whose progress has
only recently begun to be reversed. But Portobello to the s of
the High Street and Joppa to the E (see below) still present a
picture of Georgian and Victorian villadom practically unchanged.

CHURCHES

BAPTIST CHURCH, High Street. Designed as the Town Hall
over a row of shops, by *David Bryce*, 1862. Griffon gargoyles
and lucarned roof, a Gothic clock in the centre gable.

CONGREGATIONAL CHURCH, Marlborough Street. Built in
1835, remodelled with an ambitious Romanesque street frontage *c.* 1870 and enlarged *c.* 1885.

PORTOBELLO OLD AND WINDSOR PLACE PARISH CHURCH,
Bellfield Street. The original building by *William Sibbald*,
1808–10 (dated 1809), has an E frontage of smooth grey ashlar
to the street. In the upper storeys of the two outer bays
Gothic glazing. In the advanced centre bay a large blank
panel as if for an inscription; over it a pediment crowned
in 1839 by a clock-stage with antae and a further octagonal
stage, both perfectly in character, with a copper dome and
weathercock. The other elevations are of coursed rubble, and
in plan the original church seems to have been a galleried
rectangle. w jamb of 1839. N jamb of 1878 in rock-faced
masonry by *J. Macintyre Henry*, who trimmed the old work
to make a T-plan interior with galleries of Georgian character
in the N, E, and s jambs, the last s jamb entered by its original
Georgian stair.

PULPIT in a tame Renaissance style and FONT *en suite*
dated 1925. – COMMUNION TABLE presumably 1878. –
ORGAN by *Peter Conacher*, 1872; rebuilt by *C. P. Scovell* and
again by *A. E. Ingram*, 1920–2, when *J. A. Carfrae* placed it
in the short w jamb. – STAINED GLASS. In the w jamb one
light (I will make you fishers of men) by the *Abbey Studio*,
1948. – HALL to the s by *Alan Reiach & Partners*, 1964.

ST JAMES, Rosefield Place. A quite ambitious but unfinished
Perp essay in snecked rubble with red sandstone dressings,
by *G. Mackie Watson*, 1910–12. In the s gable a big window

whose blind lower half conceals the gallery. The sw tower with copper spire was not built; nor was the w of the two transepts. Interesting interior, with tall arcades (alternate red and cream stones) embracing the clearstorey and the flatter arches of the aisles. The capitals remain uncarved. Plain tunnel-roof. In 1934 the semi-octagonal chancel was added to *F. E. B. Blanc*'s design to house the new ORGAN by *Rushworth & Draper*. – FONT of Caen stone on a pedestal, the bowl carved with cherubic heads; formerly in St Cuthbert, Princes Street. – STAINED GLASS. In the chancel two lights (Suffer the little children) by *John Blyth*, 1949.

ST JOHN THE EVANGELIST (R.C.), Brighton Place and Sandford Gardens. An idiosyncratic work of C20 Gothic, jolting the calm of Brighton Place and an enigmatic landmark on the entry by rail from London. The architect was *J. T. Walford*, 1903–6; masons *J. Smith & Sons*. Steeple with four blunt-headed octagonal turrets, a fifth rising still taller in the middle. Mass (Winchburgh rubble) and precision (smooth Auchenheath dressings) contribute to the upward endeavour of the whole composition; likewise the concave gablets and huge louvres of the tower, the emphasized mullions of the w window and the tall attic of the attendant baptistery to the N. Tracery on the N and S sides distinctively Scottish, with loops and central mullions.

The inside is less brilliant but nonetheless distinctive. Angels lean out above the octagonal piers, and there are more at the spring of the chancel arch, all of Grange stone from Burntisland, which also lines the semi-octagonal chancel but comes to a sudden stop above the arcade; the clearstorey windows are groined into pitchpine vaults with pendants at the apex of each. – Furnishings of mixed quality, with PEWS in sympathy but oak PULPIT conventionally Germanic. – ORGAN rebuilt by *Rushworth & Draper* when moved here from Hawick in 1961. – STAINED GLASS in the chancel of good colour but trite drawing. – Other windows of clear glass in ruby borders.

ST MARK (Episcopal), at the E end of the High Street. A villa-like Neo-Classical church, 1824, standing small and stolid in a well planted churchyard discreetly lined with monuments, including many military ones. Grand entry on the axis with serpentine walls and miniature porticos which would be more impressive if it did not face N. Semicircular bowed centrepiece with engaged Roman Doric columns, a flat-topped dome, and a circular porch with geometric stair (formerly to the galleries) top-lit from the ribbed dome; crisp Grecian detail.

In 1892 *Hay & Henderson* altered the church; to them is due the Venetian glazing pattern in the two side windows of the N front. Inside, they removed the galleries (but left the circular windows that lit them along each side) and reinforced the ceiling with beams that cut into the Grecian cornice. To the S they added a chancel with a beamed roof of shallow pitch sloping further down on the W side to form an organ chamber. During the work that followed a fire in 1967 a vestry and a tiny stone-lined chapel were formed underneath. – Oak ALTAR and brown marble REREDOS of 1892. – ORGAN by *D. & T. Hamilton*, 1872; rebuilt by *Ingram*, 1899, and again by *Ronald L. Smith*, 1972. – STAINED GLASS. Two windows on the lower level (the Good Samaritan to the W, David and Jonathan to the E) by *Ballantine & Son*, 1881, have their characteristic Renaissance borders.

ST PHILIP (former Free Church), Abercorn Gardens and Brunstane Road North. A very competent E.E. church of Binny stone by *John Honeyman*, 1875–7, strongly composed on the grassy platform of its corner site. Aisled nave with a well-detailed entry in the S gable. In place of the SE aisle bay a massively buttressed tower (containing the stair to the gallery) with a lucarned broach-spire over a lofty traceried belfry of later Gothic type (like the larger windows). The interior is equally good. Clustered piers with assorted leafy capitals support the nave arcade; clearstorey wall-shafts on deep foliated corbels run into the wood-lined tunnel-roof. No chancel, but a splendid window in the N (liturgical E) gable and another in the S over the gallery. – PULPIT. Octagonal, of Caen stone with figures, by *Honeyman*, 1885. – STAINED GLASS. Remarkably complete; almost entirely decorated texts, with no figures. – The small frontage of the HALL to the N by *James W. Maclean*, 1888, is remarkably modern for its date.

WILSON MEMORIAL (Portobello United Free Church). *See* Duddingston and Willowbrae.

WINDSOR PLACE CHURCH (originally United Presbyterian), High Street and Windsor Place. Now disused and under sentence of demolition (1984). A confused Gothic church with a very effective spire, by *Stewart & Menzies*, 1878.

PUBLIC BUILDINGS

COUNTY CINEMA (former), Bath Street. 1938 by *T. Bowhill Gibson*, originally with a pale blue slab frontage outlined in neon, the 10m. tower window illuminated from inside by changing lights; now roughcast all over. Slightly better preserved interior.

POLICE STATION, High Street. Designed as the Town Council Office by *Robert Paterson*, 1877. Franco-baronial with a mansarded tower and iron crown. 'The composition is stilted, the detail heavy, and every angle possesses its own little pepperbox turret – a useless appendage' (*The Builder*); but very nice townscape.

PORTOBELLO CEMETERY, Milton Road East. Layout and buildings by *Robert Paterson & Sons*, 1876. – MEMORIAL to Dr Balfour by *John S. Rhind*, 1907; granite obelisk and bronze relief portrait.

PORTOBELLO GOLF CLUB. *See* Duddingston and Willowbrae, Public Buildings.

POST OFFICE, Windsor Place. Pretty neo-Jacobean by *W. W. Robertson*, 1904.

PUBLIC BATHS (indoor), Promenade, at the foot of Marlborough Street. By *Robert Morham*, 1898. Queen Anne, in red Dumfriesshire sandstone; a long front with two curving gables. Balconies with excellent ironwork.

SCHOOLS. For Portobello Secondary and St John's R.C. Schools *see* Duddingston and Willowbrae, Public Buildings. TOWERBANK SCHOOL, Beach Lane. Very plain, by *J. Macintyre Henry*, 1885, extended by *J. A. Carfrae*, 1906.

TOWN HALL, High Street. A public hall, well turned out by the City Architect *James A. Williamson*, 1909-12. Giant Roman Ionic columns at the entrance. Stage with proscenium arch.

PORTOBELLO: STREETS

ADELPHI PLACE

Formerly Adelaide Place. The quadrant on the E High Street corner is followed by a simple terrace with a bullseyed pediment (but lacking a wing), both of *c.* 1830. The rest is informal, narrowing at the HOME MISSION HALL of 1863 (economical brick Gothic) and going on as a winding lane between continuous cottage fronts, some brick and some stone, of about the same date. At the bridge over the Figgate Burn a good view of brick garden walls jostling for the maximum ground, and a square brick cottage with rounded corners, *c.* 1840.

BATH STREET AND BATH PLACE

Graceful Georgian, embarrassed by hearty Victorian and degraded by ramshackle C20. BATH STREET, the first to be laid out N of the High Street (1801), became the most important, running from the Royal Hotel (*see* High Street, below) to the Hot and Cold Sea Water Baths on the Promenade (opened in 1805, replaced in the mid C19 by the Marine Bar). Feus of 45 ft (13.7 m) width were still being advertised in 1805-6. Well finished two-storey houses of *c.* 1820 at Nos. 5-11 on the E side, Nos. 22-24 and 42-44 on the W, but Nos. 18-20 are outstanding – a double villa whose twin bows have a patera string-course and railed tops. On the E side most of the single-storey villas are swamped by shops, but there are notable Victorian tenements: the bay-windowed ST JAMES'S TERRACE in the style of *J. C. Walker*, *c.* 1870, with blocked mullions and multiple jerkin-head dormers, and the red sandstone BRIGHTON and WINDSOR MANSIONS, lavish neo-

Jacobean by *Edward Calvert*, 1899. At the NW corner a
tenement of 1877, with festive corner domes fronting the Promenade. For the former County (subsequently George)
Cinema *see* Public Buildings, above.

BATH PLACE to the NW is a single-storey terrace built before
1824, with Greek Doric doorpieces and motley alterations, its
sea view blocked in the mid C19.

BELLFIELD TERRACE

Opening off Bellfield Lane to the w of Bellfield Street, for which
see Joppa, below. The terrace seems to have started with the
two-storey villa in the middle. Pediment and suavely recessed
doorpiece. Brick-walled wings added before 1824 made it into
an E, whose l. half was then filled in with an ashlar front. A
N extension to the back of the E forms Nos. 20–26 Straiton
Place (*see* below).

BRIDGE STREET, PIPE STREET AND FIGGATE STREET

To the w of BRIDGE STREET the Figgate Burn, emerging from
under the High Street, flows down to the Forth between high
rubble walls. A cottage has been preserved because Harry
Lauder was born there in 1870. PIPE STREET leads to the
two bottle-shaped brick kilns (the red one dated 1906, the
yellow one 1909) which are all that remain of Jamieson's
brickworks and their successor, Buchan's Thistle Pottery.
New two-storey housing by the *City Architects' Department*,
1976, decent but quite unrelated to the Portobello tradition
in its layout. A further scheme of 1980 obliterated FIGGATE
STREET, laid out in 1802 and gradually developed with elegant classical villas, mainly of brick. Not one survives.

BRIGHTON PLACE AND ROSEFIELD

A choice neighbourhood till 1846, when the railway came so
close to the s, but still a very pretty one, with varied late
Georgian development and two green spaces. Of Rosefield
House, built by William Jamieson for himself in 1769, nothing is left except some garden walls at ROSEFIELD PARK,
one of them red brick with a pointed archway. This whole
area to the E of the Figgate Burn was acquired by the architect
John Baxter, who laid it out and designed the elevations.
Sixteen houses were built in 1820–3.

Of the E side of BRIGHTON PLACE only the N half is built up.
After the High Street corner block, a monumental bay-windowed tenement by *William Hay*, 1869, still Georgian in its
masonry finishes. Then the tall pinnacles of St John's (*see*
Churches, above). Nearly all the rest is Baxter's design. On

the w side, a long procession of semi-detached villas. Those to the s enjoy an open view across BRIGHTON PARK, whose other sides are lined with the similar villas of EAST BRIGHTON CRESCENT and the continuous terrace of SANDFORD GARDENS with Greek-key iron balcony. All are of two storeys, with rusticated ground floors and linking screen walls. In the park a massive C18 stone SUNDIAL with thistle finial, and from it a distant view of Arthur's Seat.

Similar houses in WEST BRIGHTON CRESCENT, and two rows of linked single-storey villas, cleverly detailed, with the walls treated like broad antae supporting segmental arches over the openings. In ROSEFIELD PLACE six more of a slightly different variety, with architraved windows, are confronted by St James's (see Churches, above). At the end is the much altered BURNSIDE HOUSE, plain classical with a bow, mostly c. 1840. ROSEFIELD AVENUE has five villas of the arched kind. At its N end a startling head-on view of the baronial Police Station (see Public Buildings, above) across the High Street.

FIGGATE STREET see BRIDGE STREET

HIGH STREET

Portobello High Street is a 1 km. section of the road from Leith to Musselburgh; a slight bend in the middle makes it more interesting. The buildings are a mixture of small-scale late Georgian and bigger, often fruity Victorian. The main C20 contribution (demolished in 1977–9) was the vast red-brick Power Station at the w end, so monumentally dressed up by the City Architect *E. J. MacRae*, 1934, that it made the High Street look like a string of ragged camp-followers. After this and more vacancy, the High Street proper begins as soon as it has crossed the Figgate Burn. Even numbers are on the N side. The CO-OPERATIVE SOCIETY at No. 46, with flats above the shopfronts and a fishscale-slated corner tower, is by *James Simpson* of Leith, 1882. Then at No. 62 (Pipe Street junction) the first of the recessed quadrant corners of the late Georgian High Street; a mere two storeys with flats again over shops. Others survive at No. 79 (Adelphi Place, with blind attic), Nos. 140–152 (intermediate frontages without the corners) and Nos. 164–208 (continuous from Bath Street to Regent Street, with some breaks where older buildings were left). No. 186 still has its pair of Ionic pilasters, and Nos. 190 and 194 have their plainer pilastered shopfronts. No. 208 was built c. 1820. E of Regent Street Nos. 210–240 (1822) also remain, including the excellent butcher's shop of W. J. HUNTER at No. 228 with its small Roman Doric order inside. After Bellfield Lane Nos. 288–304, a symmetrical composition with canted corners instead of quadrants. This is, or was, the Georgian norm; now back to the w end for the variations.

No. 74 is the front of a hall, red sandstone, *c.* 1900, with a
Perp window. Nos. 100–102 are of a still earlier generation,
with a pantiled roof. Then the astonishing baronial Police
Station (*see* Public Buildings, above).

Meanwhile on the S side an unsuitably varied composition of
rubbly council housing of *c.* 1960 before the street's wide
central section, which is politely dominated by the Edwardian
Town Hall (*see* Public Buildings, above). It narrows again,
and three frontages are shown off by the gentle curve: the
Georgian-survival ROYAL BANK with Renaissance trimmings (formerly National Bank) by *T.P. Marwick*, *c.* 1900;
the Franco-Flemish Baptist Church (formerly the Town Hall;
see Churches, above); and the CLYDESDALE BANK, part of
the same Gothic design except for the incongruous Baroque
ground floor. Then a former Royal Bank with the Italianate
confidence of *Peddie & Kinnear*, 1864. Heavy cornice, triple
arcade on the first floor, the ground floor with later mourning
bands of black marble. The Windsor Place Church with its
important spire (*see* Churches, above) may have disappeared
by the time this is read. The massive BLUEBELL INN of 1883
is more likely to survive. St Mark (*see* Churches) is set back
in a well planted churchyard.

On the N side at the corner of Bath Street the ROYAL HOTEL
of *c.* 1825, now including the former Assembly Rooms with
a clumsy mansard and shaped gable of *c.* 1910 over their pilastered Bath Street frontage. At Nos. 328–332 at the corner
of Pittville Street a mid-Victorian block with one of its iron-
columned shopfronts intact. The street continues as Abercorn
Terrace (*see* Joppa, below).

MARLBOROUGH STREET *see* REGENT STREET

MENTONE AVENUE

A strange backwater to the W of Bath Street, shared by two nice
terraces of gabled cottages of *c.* 1890, and two formidably tall
tenements with ashlar fronts, flat roofs and galleried brick
backs, *c.* 1860 but with much Georgian detail. One horizontally channelled throughout, the other crowned with iron
Georgian urns. At the end, new housing of 1980. To the N
Towerbank School (*see* Public Buildings, above).

PIPE STREET *see* BRIDGE STREET

PROMENADE

The N exposure is redeemed by a tremendous view across the
Forth estuary, the sad buildings by some late Georgian survivors and a few bits of real fun. Gone is the 381 m. pier at
the end of Bath Street by *John Stewart & Son* of Irvine,
1870, where the excursion steamers called. Probably going

(1981) is the 100 by 45 m. outdoor BATHING POOL of cream-and-green-painted concrete by the City Engineer *W. A. Macartney*, 1934-7, with its canopied stands and wave-machinery. To the rescue, though impeded by a shabby amusement hall, comes PORTOBELLO TOWER, a highly irregular castellated Gothic octagon of rubble with playfully laid red-brick dressings. Built in 1785 for the lawyer John Cunningham (perhaps by *William Jamieson*, from whom he feued the site), it incorporates all manner of architectural scraps from late medieval to late C17. On the angles at the top (second-floor) level, Late Gothic triple shafts with elided bases and capitals, apparently jambs of chimneypieces. On the S side of the stair turret a rich pot-pourri including Late Gothic foliage capitals, spiralling nook shafts, and a lintel with the motto LETARE [rejoice] and a shield supported by putti. On the N side, low down, an aedicule concocted from a Romanesque voussoir with chevron, a shield with a merchant's mark, medieval fireplace jambs with fleuron between the shafts, and an early C17 pediment of fanciful profile on which stand two more putti with a shield.* The adjoining house is relatively dull Tudor-Gothic of 1863. On the W corner of Bath Street, a festive tenement by *Robert Paterson & Son*, 1877, each turret with a cluster of humped dormers, fishscale roof and weathervane. The MARINE BAR is mid C19 but still in the Georgian tradition. At the end of Marlborough Street the PRINCE OF WALES FOUNTAIN, 1860, a swagged stone drum on a base that once had water-jets. To the E of Nos. 51-56, a severe mid-C19 Jacobean terrace, the Public Baths (q.v.), red sandstone with verandahs.

The E part of the Promenade belongs to Joppa, but is included here for convenience. After a spectacular but hardly light-hearted baronial tenement, four large seaside villas at the foot of Brunstane Road. HAMILTON LODGE is Italian on a grand scale with an arcaded tower, c. 1840, distinguished in composition and detail. Who was the architect? Then three baronial oddities by *J. C. Walker*, 1865-8, RABBIT HALL somewhat Frenchified (spoiled by *William Hay*'s weak NW addition), the other two very much so, with tall mansards coming to a frilly iron termination over the porch. The one to the E has a graceful cast-iron fence. ESPLANADE TERRACE at the far E end, c. 1890, has serried dormers suggesting seaside lodgings.

REGENT STREET, MARLBOROUGH STREET AND STRAITON PLACE

Laid out by the architect-builder *Lewis A. Wallace*, starting in 1815. Some feus were bought by the builder *George Birnie*.

---

* According to *William Baird* (*Annals of Duddingston and Portobello*, 1898) this includes fragments of the Old College (*see* p. 188 and n.) and Mercat Cross of Edinburgh (*see* Old Town: Public Buildings), and of the cathedral of St Andrews.

REGENT STREET is the most complete. On the W side a mixture of small villas, some two-storey and all with door-pieces (diagonally voluted pilasters at No. 36) except for WAVERLEY COTTAGE, which has traceried and hood-moulded windows in an attached Ionic colonnade of minia-ture scale. No. 36 on the E side has crinkly rustication. MARLBOROUGH (originally Wellington) STREET has been invaded by tenements and a jolly neo-Norman Congrega-tional Church (q.v.), but the W side still has a trim pair of cottages at Nos. 43–45 (formerly RAEFIELD). On the E side No. 24 (WELLINGTON COTTAGE) with a fanlit tripartite door. No. 28 was built by *Roderick Morrison*, 1823. In the dining room extensive remains of stencilled decoration, prob-ably original. Then Nos. 34–36 (WELLINGTON LODGE), built in 1816 for the City Chamberlain Thomas Henderson, of one storey with bowed wings and horizontal glazing.

No. 38 (LEVEN LODGE) on the corner of STRAITON PLACE is single-sided, but its clear view of the sea is now blocked, e.g. by the red sandstone Brighton and Windsor Mansions (*see* Bath Street, above). At the W end one of the original cottages grotesquely refronted with Fyfestone; at the E a good row with Greek Doric doorpieces *in antis* at Nos. 14–16, No. 18 slightly different with crinkly rusticated quoins instead of col-umns. Nos. 20–26, tacked on to the back of Bellfield Terrace (*see* above), have a modest flat frontage with skinny door-pieces.

ROSEFIELD *see* BRIGHTON PLACE

WINDSOR PLACE

Formerly Jamieson Street, laid out on land belonging to William Jamieson's trustees. On the E side the Windsor Place Church and the Post Office (*see* Churches and Public Build-ings, above). Then WINDSOR PLACE LODGE, built before 1824, the grandest single house in Portobello. Two storeys and basement, with Ionic porch between arched tripartite windows; single-storey wings. On the W side No. 7 two-storey, No. 9 single-storey with piend roof and architraved windows. Nos. 15–17 are a two-storey Gothick villa with val-anced bay-windows and delicate ornamental glazing (some tinted). Crinkly rustication extends to the gatepiers. At the far end a nine-bay fragment of a sophisticated classical terrace of *c*. 1840.

JOPPA: PERAMBULATION

Joppa was built on the Marquess of Abercorn's land imme-diately to the E of Portobello, starting about the same time but growing more slowly. In 1801 building lots were advertised in the formal street-plan by *Robert Brown* to the N of the main road (Abercorn Terrace). The S side, to which the railway had come in 1846, was hardly developed till *c.* 1860. Its villas have a hard Victorian consistency which suggests that the estate provided designs.

On the w side of BELLFIELD STREET (formerly Melville Street) Portobello Old Church (*see* Churches, above) flanked by two-storey houses of *c.* 1815 at Nos. 8–16 and 18–26, continuous but slightly varied (No. 24 with gateposts). On the E side a similar row at Nos. 31–37 but with rubble walls and pretty detail (scalloped fanlight at No. 33). At No. 37 Scott visited his son-in-law Lockhart in 1827. Then VERNON VILLAS at Nos. 39–47, of *c.* 1880 with quirky roofs over canted bays.

The green square of ABERCORN PARK is bounded on the w by PITTVILLE STREET, in which the grandest house (now Nos. 13–17) was not built till *c.* 1835, with a portico of coupled Greek Doric columns; on the E by JOHN STREET, mainly of 1820–30, but No. 5 *c.* 1840 with distinguished proportions and a Roman Doric porch. To the N ELCHO TERRACE of *c.* 1860, and on the open s side the pyramidal DEWAR MEMORIAL of 1914. JAMES STREET, further to the E, continues the friendly mixture of Georgian and Victorian. To the s of the main road, here called ABERCORN TERRACE, a series of villas linking behind stone walls and illustrating the change from Georgian parade to Victorian privacy, No. 1 built as the MANSE *c.* 1850, the rest of *c.* 1860 with variations on the theme of the canted bay beneath a steep gable. Nos. 25–25a semi-detached, with paired doorpieces but dissimilar bays. For St Philip's on the N side *see* Churches, above.

In ST MARK'S PLACE three villas of 1881, bargeboarded baronial of grim precision. In ARGYLE CRESCENT pretentious late C19 semi-detached houses on the s side enjoying the view down to the sea, their opposite numbers much humbler. Up Brunstane Road and JOPPA TERRACE (a bay-windowed artisan tenement of *c.* 1850) to the former STATION of *c.* 1846, snecked rubble with low-pitch roofs. In DALKEITH STREET more grand semis on the s side, the N houses (including a bungalow row *c.* 1850) retreating downhill behind long front gardens. On the E side of MORTON STREET a powerful tenement on the Joppa Road corner and then Nos. 35–57, gaily bargeboarded semis with cast-iron balconies of potted sunflower design spanning the gap between their bay-windows. In COILLESDENE AVENUE (and running s to Milton Road) a big private housing scheme by *Alan Reiach*, 1955, buff brick, Derby spar lintels and tile roofs, the houses linked by slatted stairwells.

RESTALRIG

Until 1925 this was farmland with one small village. Now it is an untidy museum showing the different varieties of medium-density low-rise housing.

CHURCHES

LOCHEND PARISH CHURCH, Restalrig Road South and Sleigh Drive. By *A. Lorne Campbell*, 1929, in hard red brick with mixed Gothic windows of stone tracery. A gentler interior of buff brick, with segmental arcades and a wagon roof on transverse arches. ORGAN by *E. H. Lawton* of Aberdeen. The harled HALL to the NW has boat-shaped dormers in the Lorimer manner.

PARISH CHURCH, Restalrig Road South and Restalrig Avenue. Rectangular and plain, with a minimum of C15 details, including flowing tracery, correctly renewed by *William Burn* in 1836. The w wall, restored by Burn, stands on the old foundations. w porch, 1884, and a vestry on the N side occupying the site of the medieval sacristy. Inside, a w gallery and thinly ribbed timber vault. Woodwork at the E end as a war memorial designed by *P. R. McLaren*, 1922. – STAINED GLASS. In the w window three lights (SS. Triduana and Margaret; Dorcas) by *William Wilson*, 1966. – On S side two lights (heavenly and earthly choirs) by *Sax Shaw*, 1979.

Attached to the SW corner by the C18 Grant burial enclosure is a low hexagonal structure which formed the lower storey of a two-tier chapel built for James III. Work was probably in progress by 1477, when a chaplaincy was endowed for an altar in the upper chapel. Payments for the stone roofing slabs were entered in the Exchequer Rolls for 1486–7, and in 1487 the parish church was made collegiate. Nothing is known of James's particular interest in Restalrig, nor does there seem to be any obvious explanation or parallel for the two-tier arrangement. The hexagonal plan recurs in the well-house from Restalrig now in Holyrood Park (*see* p. 147), and it is often said that the lower chapel also functioned as a well. The difficulty with this theory is that the building makes no provision for a well or spring. The water which floods the interior unless it is pumped out has to be explained by a rise in the water-table, since an altar is known to have stood here in 1515. The dedication of this altar was to the obscure St Triduana, who by the late Middle Ages had acquired a reputation for curing eye complaints. Her cult at Restalrig is supposed to have involved healing waters, and it is possible that they flowed from the well now in Holyrood Park. Externally the only medieval features are the three-light windows under four-centred arches. The steeply pitched roof was added by *Thomas Ross* in 1906, and his are the buttresses replacing original ones removed much earlier. The interior is reached down a flight of steps and through a door in the NW face. As in a chapter house, the vault springs from a central pier. Its ribs make a six-point star enclosing twelve equilateral triangles, so that in the centre of each side the apex of the vault is much further from the pier than from the window. The pier has six shafts with fillet, four slimmer shafts in each angle. Elided bell-bases and capitals with nicely carved

crinkly foliage. Foliage on all bosses and shields on two. On
the floor lie bosses from the upper chapel, with tracery fragments from there and the church. From the position of ribs
on the bosses it has been deduced that the upper vault was in
one span with no central column. The base of a respond
similar to the base of the centre pier was found in 1962 at the
E end of the N wall of the church. This and another base cut
into the NE side of the hexagon must have belonged to the
arcades of a projected choir with aisles. Work cannot have
progressed far, as the E wall of the church is still medieval.
Only 50 cm. remain of the walls of the upper chapel, enough
to show that there was an aumbry in the NE side.

MONUMENTS in the churchyard. To the S, Charles Hunter,
'Brewer in the Abbeyhill', †1769 (erected 1791), with broom
and shovels. To the SW, James Arbuthnot, cordiner, †1670,
with his knife, and William Waters, 'Smith in Abbeyhill',
†1734, with a crowned hammer. Masons are also represented.
On the side of the Grant enclosure an inscription to Louis
Cauvin †1778 and his namesake †1825, both teachers of
French. A stone cabin for the sexton, and rusticated GATE-
PIERS at the entry. Across the road, a section of wall and two
massive projecting piers belonging to the C16 DEANERY.

ST CHRISTOPHER, Craigentinny Road and Craigentinny Avenue. By *James McLachlan*, 1934–8. Variegated red brick,
with round-arched windows and red-tiled roof. A thin square
tower with a copper hat adjoins the double gable of the S
transept. Calm interior of darker, plum-coloured brick, with
a low wagon roof and segmental arcades running continuously
past the narrow aisles and spacious transepts. ORGAN from St
Catherine's, Grange, rebuilt here with artfully placed pipes
(all speaking) by *Ronald L. Smith*, 1975. The HALL to the S
was built before the church.

ST NINIAN (R.C.), Marionville Road. A highly original but
unfinished church by *Giles Gilbert Scott*, 1929, of snecked
Craigmillar rubble with Darney and Blaxter dressings. Blind
clearstorey, blind aisles returned as porches on to the
crowstepped W gable, whose large window has a heavy centre
mullion. Transeptal chapels to the W of what would have
been the square tower, with tall N and S windows. Temporary
E end. Inside, the nave has plain plastered arcades corbelled
from smooth ashlar piers of lozenge plan, oak roof-trusses
and oak lintelled aisles. The E arch of the tower is barely
started. Unfortunately the church is used in reverse, with the
entry at the E end and the people facing W, so the effect of
the dramatic lighting is lost. MARIONVILLE HOUSE to the E
is used as a church house; mid-C18, a single massive block of
three storeys with an architraved doorpiece.

PUBLIC BUILDINGS

CHRISTIE MILLER MAUSOLEUM, Craigentinny Crescent. By
David Rhind, 1848–56. A huge segmental pedimented Roman

mausoleum shocking the prim houses surrounding it. In his will William Henry Miller of Craigentinny directed that he was to be buried in a 20-foot-deep pit above which, *The Scotsman* reported, was to be raised a monument 'in commemoration of the private virtues of the deceased, for, as a public character, he was unknown.' On the sides, marble panels carved in low relief by *Alfred Gatley* with 'The Overthrow of Pharaoh in the Red Sea' and 'The Song of Moses and Miriam'.

CRAIGENTINNY PRIMARY SCHOOL, Loaning Road. By *E. J. MacRae*, 1935. Its S front with flabby wings is the death-rattle of inter-war classicism.

FIRE STATION, Restalrig Drive. By *Bamber & Hall*, 1964.

MANSIONS

CRAIGENTINNY HOUSE, Loaning Road. The large C16-17 baronial mansion of the Nisbets of Craigentinny, bought *c.* 1760 by William Miller, seedsman, and modernized for Christie Miller by *David Rhind*, 1849-50. Rubble, the freestone dressings largely restored. Pepperpots at the W gable, a fussy square bartizan at the SE corner. On the S side the hall chimney is corbelled out at the first floor. The stair-tower to the W of it has an entrance in its base and formerly had a small room at its head; in place of this, Rhind continued the scale-and-platt stair to the third floor, so the corbelled stairturret in the angle is no longer functional. On the N side a pilastered late C18 entrance. Inside, a strapworked stone chimneypiece by Rhind in the position of the old hall fireplace. On the second floor a suite of late C18 rooms in one of which the plaster has been cut away to show two pious metrical inscriptions, presumably C17 but carelessly restored. A wing by Rhind was demolished after bomb damage; the present unsuitable E extension was carried out by Lothian Regional Council for social work offices in 1978. The house stands towards the front of a high walled enclosure, with rusticated gate-piers of *c.* 1700 to the road. At the SE corner the stump of a small pavilion. For the Christie Miller Mausoleum, *see* above.

LOCHEND HOUSE, Lochend Park. The tower house of the Logans of Restalrig was largely destroyed at the end of the C16. Whatever its subsequent history, only a picturesque fragment with a huge stepped-off ingle still stands at the W end of the present five-bay house, *c.* 1820, with pilaster doorpiece. DOOCOT on the other side of the loch. C16 beehive type, the large doorway and cylindrical top both later.

DESCRIPTION

At first sight Restalrig and its neighbour Craigentinny are simply a left-over territory to the N of the railway between

Leith and Portobello, and thus a natural dumping-ground for inter-war housing designed by the *City Architect's Department*; three-storey flatted blocks of generous scale but less generous style (mildly Scots Renaissance or jazz-modern) on the tree-lined main roads, smaller two-storey blocks on the network between. It began to the w of the dreary RESTALRIG ROAD in 1925-6 and continued to the E in 1926-7, including some two-storey steel blocks (harled, with tile or slate roofs) in Restalrig Crescent and Findlay Gardens. Around CRAIG-ENTINNY AVENUE and further to the E the scale is reduced to genteel single-storey; pebbledashed bungalows built by *James Miller*, starting in 1932 with CRAIGENTINNY CRES-CENT, where they are bizarrely dominated by the Christie Miller Mausoleum. More bungalows and bungaloid corner-shops in Britwell Crescent and Vandeleur Avenue were designed by *Peter R. MacLaren* in 1933. Industry provides a few landmarks, notably the corbelled red-brick tower of the former MUNRO factory at the w end of Restalrig Drive by *J.R. & E.E. Pearson*, 1910. The office extension of WALKER'S SAWMILL at No. 122 Restalrig Road is by *J.E. Arnott*, 1970; nicely composed in rustic brick, but lost in unfriendly surroundings. The presiding feature of the area is the low, distant profile of Arthur's Seat, across the railway and uphill to the sw.

But an older structure still exists. The C17 Craigentinny House adjoins the stranded village of RESTALRIG, whose medieval church is too closely nudged by the showy modern Fire Station (for all these, *see* above). To the E of the churchyard an odd little street which is the bottom end of RESTALRIG ROAD SOUTH. Built into the stone-and-brick wall, a country-looking harled house with semi-dormers. Opposite, a row of cottages remodelled as a church hall with cement crowsteps, *c.* 1900. More crowsteps over a row of shops, ending with a C17 stair-tower at No. 62; moulded doorway to the N. The old Deanery wall (*see* Churches, above) now screens a workshop. No. 66 (St Triduana's) and No. 78 (St Margaret's) are in the harled and half-timbered cottage-style of *c.* 1900. On the w side some flashy semi-detached houses, then No. 75, originally plain early C19 but much enlarged in 1879 as BROOKLYN HOUSE. Strapworked and crowstepped porch projecting from the front, bay-windowed extension and formidable stair-tower at the back, all done in stone except where it doesn't show. No. 77 is unembellished late Georgian, its rural character contradicted by the big red-brick warehouse on the corner of Loaning Road; this is the way to Craigentinny House (*see* above).

GLOSSARY

Particular types of an architectural element are often defined under the name of the element itself, e.g. for 'dog-leg stair' see STAIR. Literal meanings, where specially relevant, are indicated by the abbreviation *lit*.

ABACUS (*lit*. tablet): flat slab forming the top of a capital, *see* Orders (fig. 16).

ABUTMENT: the meeting of an arch or vault with its solid lateral support, or the support itself.

ACANTHUS: formalized leaf ornament with thick veins and frilled edge, e.g. on a Corinthian capital.

ACHIEVEMENT OF ARMS: in heraldry, a complete display of armorial bearings.

ACROTERION (*lit*. peak): pointed ornament projecting above the apex or ends of a pediment.

ADDORSED: description of two figures placed symmetrically back to back.

AEDICULE (*lit*. little building): term used in classical architecture to describe the unit formed by a pair of orders, an entablature, and usually a pediment, placed against a wall to frame an opening.

AFFRONTED: description of two figures placed symmetrically face to face.

AGGER (*lit*. rampart): Latin term for the built-up foundations of Roman roads.

AGGREGATE: small stones added to a binding material, e.g. in harling or concrete.

AISLE (*lit*. wing): (1) passage alongside the nave, choir or transept of a church, or the main body of some other building, separated from it by col-

umns or piers; (2) (Scots) projecting wing of a church for special use, e.g. by a guild or by a landed family whose burial place it may contain.

AMBULATORY (*lit*. walkway): aisle at the E end of a chancel, usually surrounding an apse and therefore semicircular or polygonal in plan.

ANNULET (*lit*. ring): shaft-ring (q.v.).

ANSE DE PANIER (*lit*. basket handle): basket arch (*see* Arch).

ANTA: classical order of oblong section employed at the ends of a colonnade which is then called *In Antis*. See Orders (fig. 16).

ANTEFIXAE: ornaments projecting at regular intervals above a classical cornice. See Orders (fig. 16).

ANTHEMION (*lit*. honeysuckle): classical ornament like a honeysuckle flower (*see* fig. 1).

A   P   A   P   A

Fig. 1. Anthemion and
Palmette Frieze

APSE: semicircular (i.e. apsidal) extension of an apartment. A term first used of the magistrate's end of a Roman basilica, and thence especially of the vaulted semicircular or polygonal end of a chancel or a chapel.

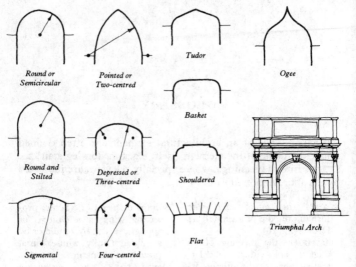

Round or Semicircular

Pointed or Two-centred

Tudor

Ogee

Round and Stilted

Depressed or Three-centred

Basket

Shouldered

Triumphal Arch

Segmental

Four-centred

Flat

Fig. 2.   Arch

ARABESQUE: light and fanciful surface decoration. *See* Grotesque.

ARCADE: series of arches supported by piers or columns. *Blind Arcade:* the same applied to the surface of a wall. *Wall Arcade:* in medieval churches, a blind arcade forming a dado below windows.

ARCH: for the various forms *see* fig. 2. The term *Basket Arch* refers to a basket handle and is sometimes applied to a three-centred or depressed arch as well as the type with a flat middle. *Transverse Arch:* across the main axis of an interior space. A term used especially for the arches between the compartments of tunnel- or groin-vaulting. *Diaphragm Arch:* transverse arch with solid spandrels spanning an otherwise wooden-roofed interior. *Chancel Arch:* across the w end of a chancel. *Relieving Arch:* incorporated in a wall, to carry some of its weight, some way above an opening. *Strainer Arch:* inserted across an opening to resist any inward pressure of the side members. *Triumphal Arch:* Imperial Roman monument whose elevation supplied a motif for many later classical compositions. *Blind Arch:* framing a wall which has no opening. *Over-arch:* framing a wall which has an opening, e.g. a window or door.

ARCHITRAVE: (1) formalized lintel, the lowest member of the classical entablature (*see* Orders, fig. 16); (2) moulded frame of a door or window. Also *Lugged* or *Shouldered Architrave*, whose top is prolonged into lugs (*lit.* ears).

ARCHIVOLT: continuous mouldings of an arch.

ARRIS (*lit.* stop): sharp edge at the meeting of two surfaces.

ASHLAR: masonry of large blocks wrought to even faces and square edges. *Droved Ashlar* (Scots) is finished with sharp horizontal tool-marks.

ASTRAGAL (*lit.* knuckle): moulding of round section, and hence (Scots) wooden glazing-bar between window-panes.

ASTYLAR: term used to describe an elevation that has no columns or similar vertical features.

ATLANTES: male counterparts of caryatids, often in a more demonstrative attitude of support. In sculpture, a single figure of the god Atlas may be seen supporting a globe.

ATTACHED: description of a shaft or column that is partly merged into a wall or pier.

ATTIC: (1) small top storey, especially behind a sloping roof; (2) in classical architecture, a storey above the main cornice, as in a triumphal arch.

AUMBRY: recess or cupboard to hold sacred vessels for Mass.

BAILEY: open space or court of a stone-built castle; *see also* Motte-and-Bailey.

BALDACCHINO: tent-like roof supported by columns, e.g. over some monuments of the C17–18.

BALLFLOWER: globular flower of three petals enclosing a small ball. A decoration used in the first quarter of the C14.

BALUSTER (*lit.* pomegranate): hence a pillar or pedestal of bellied form. *Balusters:* vertical supports of this or any other form, for a handrail or coping, the whole being called a *Balustrade*. *Blind Balustrade:* the same with a wall behind.

BARBICAN: outwork defending the entrance to a castle.

BARGEBOARDS: boards, often carved or fretted, hanging clear of the wall under sloping eaves.

BARMKIN (Scots): enclosing wall.

BARONY: *see* Burgh.

BARROW: burial mound.

BARTIZAN (*lit.* battlement): corbelled turret, square or round, at the top angle of a building.

BASE: moulded foot of a column or other order. For its use in classical architecture *see* Orders (fig. 16). *Elided Bases:* bases of a compound pier whose lower parts are run together, ignoring the arrangement of the shafts above. Capitals may be treated in the same way.

BASEMENT: lowest, subordinate storey of a building, and hence the lowest part of an elevation, below the piano nobile.

BASILICA (*lit.* royal building): a Roman public hall; hence an aisled church with a clearstorey.

BASTION: projection at the angle of a fortification.

BATTER: inward inclination of a wall.

BATTLEMENT: fortified parapet with upstanding pieces called merlons along the top. Also called Crenellation.

BAYS: divisions of an elevation or interior space as defined by any regular vertical features.

BAY-WINDOW: window in a recess, with a consequent projection on the outside, named according to the form of the latter. A *Canted Bay-window* has a straight front and bevelled sides. A *Bow Window* is curved. An *Oriel Window* does not start from the ground.

BEAKER: type of pottery vessel used in the late third and early second millennia B.C.

BEAKHEAD: Norman ornamental motif consisting of a row of bird or beast heads with beaks biting usually into a roll moulding.

BELFRY (*lit.* tower): (1) bell-turret set on a roof or gable (*see also* Bellcote); (2) room or stage in a tower where bells are hung; (3) bell-tower in a general sense.

BELL-CAST: *see* Roof.

BELLCOTE: belfry as (1) above, with the character of a small house for the bell(s), e.g. *Birdcage Bellcote:* framed structure, usually of stone.

BERM: level area separating ditch from bank on a hill fort or barrow.

BILLET (*lit.* log or block) FRIEZE: Norman ornament consisting of small blocks placed at regular intervals (*see* fig. 3).

Fig. 3. Billet Frieze

English

Flemish

Fig. 4. Bond

BIVALLATE: of a hill fort: defended by two concentric banks and ditches.

BLIND: *see* Arcade, Arch Balustrade, Portico.

BLOCKED: term applied to columns etc. that are interrupted by regular projecting blocks, e.g. to the sides of a Gibbs surround (*see* fig. 10).

BLOCKING COURSE: plain course of stones, or equivalent, on top of a cornice and crowning the wall.

BOLECTION MOULDING: moulding covering the joint between two different planes and overlapping the higher as well as the lower one, especially on panelling and fireplace surrounds of the late C17 and early C18.

BOND: in brickwork, the pattern of long sides (stretchers) and short ends (headers) produced on the face of a wall by laying bricks in a particular way (*see* fig. 4).

BOSS: knob or projection usually placed to cover the intersection of ribs in a vault.

BOW WINDOW: *see* Bay-window.

BOX PEW: pew enclosed by a high wooden back and ends, the latter having doors.

BRACE: *see* Roof (fig. 22).

BRACKET: small supporting piece of stone, etc., to carry a projecting horizontal member.

BRESSUMER: (*lit.* breast-beam): big horizontal beam, usually set forward from the lower part of a building, supporting the timber superstructure.

BRETASCHE (*lit.* battlement): defensive wooden gallery on a wall.

BROCH (Scots): circular tower-like structure, open in the middle, the double wall of dry-stone masonry linked by slabs forming internal galleries at varying levels; found in W and N Scotland and probably dating from the earliest centuries of the Christian era.

BRONZE AGE: in Britain, the period from *c.* 2000 to 600 B.C.

BUCRANIUM: ox skull.

BULLSEYE WINDOW: small circular window, e.g. in the tympanum of a pediment.

BURGH: formally constituted town with trading privileges. *Royal Burghs*, which still hold this courtesy title, monopolized imports and exports till the C17 and paid duty to the Crown. *Burghs of Barony* were founded by secular or ecclesiastical barons to whom they paid duty on their local trade.

BUT-AND-BEN (Scots, *lit.* outer and inner rooms): two-room cottage.

BUTTRESS: vertical member projecting from a wall to stabilize it or to resist the lateral thrust of an arch, roof or vault. For different types used at the corners of a building, especially a tower, *see* fig. 5. A *Flying Buttress* transmits the thrust to a heavy abutment by means of an arch or half-arch.

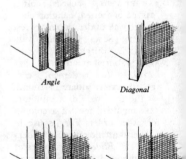

Angle

Diagonal

Set-back

Clasping

Fig. 5. Buttresses at a corner

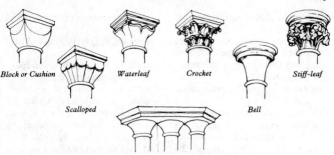

Block or Cushion *Waterleaf* *Crocket* *Stiff-leaf*

Scalloped *Bell*

Fig. 6. Capitals *Elided*

CABLE MOULDING or ROPE MOULDING: originally a Norman moulding, imitating the twisted strands of a rope.

CALEFACTORY: room in a monastery where a fire burned for the comfort of the monks.

CAMBER: slight rise or upward curve in place of a horizontal line or plane.

CAMES: *see* Quarries.

CAMPANILE: free-standing bell-tower.

CANDLE-SNUFFER ROOF: conical roof of a turret.

CANOPY: projection or hood over an altar, pulpit, niche, statue, etc.

CANTED: tilted, generally on a vertical axis to produce an obtuse angle on plan, e.g. of a canted bay-window.

CAP-HOUSE (Scots): (1) small chamber at the head of a turnpike stair, opening onto the parapet walk; (2) chamber rising from within the parapet walk.

CAPITAL: head or top part of a column or other order; for classical types *see* Orders (fig. 16); for medieval types *see* fig. 6. *Elided Capitals:* capitals of a compound pier whose upper parts are run together, ignoring the arrangement of the shafts below.

CARTOUCHE: tablet with ornate frame, usually of elliptical shape and bearing a coat of arms or inscription.

CARYATIDS (*lit.* daughters of the village of Caryae): female figures supporting an entablature, counterparts of Atlantes.

CASEMENT: (1) window hinged at the side; (2) in Gothic architecture, a concave moulding framing a window.

CASTELLATED: battlemented.

CAVETTO: concave moulding of quarter-round section.

CELURE or CEILURE: panelled and adorned part of a wagon roof above the rood or the altar.

CENOTAPH (*lit.* empty tomb): funerary monument which is not a burying place.

CENSER: vessel for the burning of incense, frequently of architectural form.

CENTERING: wooden support for the building of an arch or vault, removed after completion.

CHAMBERED TOMB: burial mound of the Neolithic Age having a stone-built chamber and entrance passage covered by an earthen barrow or stone cairn.

CHAMFER (*lit.* corner-break): surface formed by cutting off a square edge, usually at an angle of forty-five degrees.

CHANCEL (*lit.* enclosure): that part of the E end of a church in which the altar is placed, usually applied to the whole continuation of the nave E of the crossing.

CHANTRY CHAPEL: chapel attached to, or inside, a church, endowed for the celebration of masses for the soul of the founder or some other individual.

CHECK (Scots): rebate.

CHERRY-CAULKING or CHERRY-COCKING (Scots): masonry techniques using a line of pinstones in the vertical joints between blocks.

CHEVET (*lit.* head): French term for the E end of a church (chancel and ambulatory with radiating chapels).

CHEVRON: zigzag Norman ornament.

CHOIR: (1) the part of a church where services are sung; in monastic churches this can occupy the crossing and/or the easternmost bays of the nave, but in cathedral churches it is usually in the E arm: (2) the E arm of a cruciform church (a usage of long standing though liturgically anomalous).

CIBORIUM: canopied shrine for the reserved sacrament.

CINQUEFOIL: *see* Foil.

CIST: stone-lined or slab-built grave. First appears in Late Neolithic times. It continued to be used in the Early Christian period.

CLAPPER BRIDGE: bridge made of large slabs of stone, some built up to make rough piers and other longer ones laid on top to make the roadway.

CLASSIC: term for the moment of highest achievement of a style.

CLASSICAL: term for Greek and Roman architecture and any subsequent styles inspired by it.

CLEARSTOREY: upper storey of the walls of a church, pierced by windows.

CLOSE (Scots): courtyard or passage giving access to a number of buildings.

COADE STONE: artificial (cast) stone made in the late C18 and the early C19 by Coade and Sealy in London.

COB: walling material made of mixed clay and straw.

COFFERING: sunken panels, square or polygonal, decorating a ceiling, vault or arch.

COLLAR: *see* Roof (fig. 22).

COLLEGIATE CHURCH: a church endowed for the support of a college of priests, especially for the singing of masses for the soul of the founder. Some collegiate churches were founded in connection with universities, e.g. three at St Andrews and one at King's College, Aberdeen.

COLONNADE: range of columns.

COLONNETTE: small column.

COLUMN: in classical architecture, an upright structural member of round section with a shaft, a capital and usually a base. *See* Orders (fig. 16).

COLUMNA ROSTRATA: column decorated with carved prows of ships to celebrate a naval victory.

COMMENDATOR: one who holds the revenues of an abbey *in commendam* (medieval Latin for 'in trust' or 'in custody') for a period in which no regular abbot is appointed. During the Middle Ages most Commendators were bishops, but in Scotland during and after the Reformation they were laymen who performed no religious duties.

COMPOSITE: *see* Orders.

CONDUCTOR (Scots): down-pipe for rainwater; *see also* Rhone.

CONSERVATION: a modern term employed in two, sometimes conflicting, senses: (1) work to prolong the life of the historic fabric of a building or other work of art, without alteration; (2) work to make a building or a place more viable. Good conservation is a combination of the two.

CONSOLE: ornamental bracket of compound curved outline (*see* fig. 7). Its height is usually greater than its projection, as in (*a*).

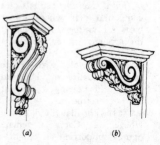

(*a*)   (*b*)

Fig. 7. Console

COOMB CEILING or COMB CEIL-
ING (Scots): ceiling whose slope
corresponds to that of the roof.
COPING (*lit.* capping): course of
stones, or equivalent, on top of
a wall.
CORBEL: block of stone projecting
from a wall, supporting some
feature on its horizontal top
surface. *Corbel Course:* continuous projecting course of stones
fulfilling the same function.
Corbel Table: series of corbels
to carry a parapet or a wall-
plate; for the latter *see* Roof (fig.
22).
CORBIE-STEPS (Scots, *lit.* crowsteps): *see* Gable (fig. 9).
CORINTHIAN: *see* Orders (fig.
16).
CORNICE: (1) moulded ledge, decorative and/or practical, projecting along the top of a building or feature, especially as the
highest member of the classical
entablature (*see* Orders, fig. 16);
(2) decorative moulding in the
angle between wall and ceiling.
CORPS-DE-LOGIS: French term
for the main building(s) as distinct from the wings or pavilions.
COUNTERSCARP BANK: small
bank on the down-hill or outer
side of a hill-fort ditch.
COURSE: continuous layer of
stones etc. in a wall.
COVE: concave soffit like a hollow
moulding but on a larger scale.
A *Cove Ceiling* has a pronounced curve joining the walls
to a flat surface in the middle.
CREDENCE: in a church or chapel,
a side table, often a niche, for
the sacramental elements before
consecration.
CRENELLATION: *see* Battlement.
CREST, CRESTING: ornamental
finish along the top of a screen,
etc.
CROCKETS (*lit.* hooks), CROCK-
ETING: in Gothic architecture,
leafy knobs on the edges of any
sloping feature. *Crocket Capital: see* Capital (fig. 6).
CROSSING: in a church, central
space opening into the nave,
chancel and transepts. *Crossing*

Tower: central tower supported
by the piers at its corners.
CROWSTEPS (Scots): squared
stones set like steps to form a
skew, *see* Gable (fig. 9).
CRUCK (*lit.* crooked): piece of
naturally curved timber combining the structural roles of an
upright post and a sloping rafter, e.g. in the building of a cottage, where each pair of crucks
is joined at the ridge.
CRYPT: underground room
usually below the E end of a
church.
CUPOLA (*lit.* dome): (1) small
polygonal or circular domed
turret crowning a roof; (2)
(Scots) small dome or skylight
as an internal feature, especially
over a stairwell.
CURTAIN WALL: (1) connecting
wall between the towers of a
castle; (2) in modern building,
thin wall attached to the main
structure, usually outside it.
CURVILINEAR: *see* Tracery.
CUSP: projecting point formed by
the foils within the divisions of
Gothic tracery, also used to
decorate the soffits of the
Gothic arches of tomb recesses,
sedilias, etc.
CYCLOPEAN MASONRY: built
with large irregular polygonal
stones, but smooth and finely
jointed.

DADO: lower part of a wall or its
decorative treatment; *see also*
Pedestal (fig. 17).
DAGGER: *see* Tracery.
DAIS, or DEIS (Scots): raised platform at one end of a room.
DEC (DECORATED): historical
division of English Gothic architecture covering the period
from *c.* 1290 to *c.* 1350.
DEMI-COLUMNS: engaged columns, only half of whose cir-
cumference projects from the
wall.
DIAPER (*lit.* figured cloth): repetitive surface decoration.
DISTYLE: having two columns; cf.
Portico.

DOGTOOTH: typical E.E. decoration applied to a moulding. It consists of a series of squares, their centres raised like pyramids and their edges indented (*see* fig. 8).

Fig. 8.   Dogtooth

DONJON: *see* Keep.

DOOCOT (Scots): dovecot. Freestanding doocots are usually of *Lectern* type, rectangular in plan with single-pitch roof, or *Beehive* type, circular in plan and growing small towards the top.

DORIC: *see* Orders (fig. 16).

DORMER WINDOW: window standing up vertically from the slope of a roof and lighting a room within it. *Dormer Head:* gable above this window, often formed as a pediment.

DORTER: dormitory, sleeping quarters of a monastery.

DOUBLE PILE: *see* Pile.

DRESSINGS: features made of smoothly worked stones, e.g. quoins or string courses, projecting from the wall which may be of different material, colour or texture.

DRIPSTONE: moulded stone projecting from a wall to protect the lower parts from water; *see also* Hoodmould.

DROVED ASHLAR: *see* Ashlar.

DRUM: (1) circular or polygonal vertical wall of a dome or cupola; (2) one of the stones forming the shaft of a column.

DRYSTONE: stone construction without mortar.

DUN (Scots): a small stone-walled fort.

E. E. (EARLY ENGLISH): historical division of English Gothic architecture covering the period 1200–1250.

EASTER SEPULCHRE: recess with tomb-chest, usually in the wall

of a chancel, the tomb-chest to receive the Sacrament after the Mass of Maundy Thursday.

EAVES: overhanging edge of a roof; hence *Eaves Cornice* in this position.

ECHINUS (*lit.* sea-urchin): lower part of a Greek Doric capital; *see* Orders (fig. 16).

EDGE-ROLL: moulding of semicircular or more than semicircular section at the edge of an opening.

ELEVATION: (1) any side of a building; (2) in a drawing, the same or any part of it, accurately represented in two dimensions.

ELIDED: term used to describe (1) a compound architectural feature, e.g. an entablature, in which some parts have been omitted; (2) a number of similar parts which have been combined to form a single larger one (*see* Capital, fig. 6).

EMBATTLED: furnished with battlements.

EMBRASURE (*lit.* splay): small splayed opening in the wall or battlement of a fortified building.

ENCAUSTIC TILES: glazed and decorated earthenware tiles used for paving.

EN DÉLIT: term used in Gothic architecture to describe attached stone shafts whose grain runs vertically instead of horizontally, against normal building practice.

ENGAGED: description of a column that is partly merged into a wall or pier.

ENTABLATURE: in classical architecture, collective name for the three horizontal members (architrave, frieze and cornice) above a column; *see* Orders (fig. 16).

ENTASIS: very slight convex deviation from a straight line; used on classical columns and sometimes on spires to prevent an optical illusion of concavity.

ENTRESOL: mezzanine storey within or above the ground storey.

EPITAPH (*lit.* on a tomb): inscription in that position.

ESCUTCHEON: shield for armorial bearings.

EXEDRA: apsidal end of an apartment; *see* Apse.

FERETORY: (1) place behind the high altar where the chief shrine of a church is kept; (2) wooden or metal container for relics.

FESTOON: ornament, usually in high or low relief, in the form of a garland of flowers and/or fruit, hung up at both ends; *see also* Swag.

FEU (Scots): land granted, e.g. by sale, by the *Feudal Superior* to the *Vassal* or *Feuar*, on conditions that include the annual payment of a fixed sum of *Feu-duty*. The paramount superior of all land is the Crown. Any subsequent proprietor of the land becomes the feuar and is subject to the same obligations. Although many superiors have disposed of their feudal rights, others, both private and corporate, still make good use of the power of feudal control which has produced many well-disciplined developments in Scotland.

FIBREGLASS (cf. glass-reinforced plastic): synthetic resin reinforced with glass fibre, formed in moulds, often simulating the outward appearance of traditional materials.

FILLET: narrow flat band running down a shaft or along a roll moulding.

FINIAL: topmost feature, e.g. above a gable, spire or cupola.

FLAMBOYANT: properly the latest phase of French Gothic architecture, where the window tracery takes on undulating lines, based on the use of flowing curves.

FLATTED: divided into apartments. But flat (Scots) is also used with a special colloquial meaning. 'He stays on the first flat' means that he lives on the first floor.

FLÈCHE (*lit.* arrow): slender spire on the centre of a roof.

FLEUR-DE-LYS: in heraldry, a formalized lily as in the royal arms of France.

FLEURON: decorative carved flower or leaf.

FLOWING: *see* Tracery (Curvilinear).

FLUTING: series of concave grooves, their common edges sharp (arris) or blunt (fillet).

FOIL (*lit.* leaf): lobe formed by the cusping of a circular or other shape in tracery. *Trefoil* (three), *Quatrefoil* (four), *Cinquefoil* (five) and *Multifoil* express the number of lobes in a shape; *see* Tracery (fig. 25).

FOLIATED: decorated, especially carved, with leaves.

FORE- (*lit.* in front): *Fore-building:* structure protecting an entrance. *Forestair:* external stair, usually unenclosed.

FOSSE: ditch.

FRATER: refectory or dining hall of a monastery.

FREESTONE: stone that is cut, or can be cut, in all directions, usually fine-grained sandstone or limestone.

FRESCO: painting executed on wet plaster.

FRIEZE: horizontal band of ornament, especially the middle member of the classical entablature; *see* Orders (fig. 16). *Pulvinated Frieze* (*lit.* cushioned): frieze of bold double convex profile.

FRONTAL: covering for the front of an altar.

GABLE: (1) peaked wall or other vertical surface, often triangular, at the end of a double-pitch roof; (2) (Scots) the same, very often with a chimney at the apex, but also in a wider sense: end wall, of whatever shape. *See* fig. 9. *Gablet:* small gable. *See also* Roof, Skew.

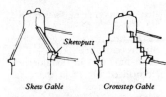

Skewputt

Skew Gable   Crowstep Gable

Dutch Gable

Curvilinear or Shaped
Gable at wall-head

Fig. 9.   Gables

GADROONING: ribbed ornament, e.g. on the lid or base of an urn, flowing into a lobed edge.

GAIT (Scots) or GATE: street, usually with a prefix indicating its use, direction or destination.

GALILEE: chapel or vestibule usually at the W end of a church enclosing the porch; *see also* Narthex.

GALLERY: balcony or passage, but with certain special meanings, e.g. (1) upper storey above the aisle of a church, looking through arches to the nave; also called tribune and often erroneously triforium. (2) balcony or mezzanine, often with seats, overlooking the main interior space of a building. (3) external walkway projecting from a wall.

GARDEROBE (*lit.* wardrobe): medieval privy.

GARGOYLE: water spout projecting from the parapet of a wall or tower, often carved into human or animal shape.

GAZEBO (jocular Latin, 'I shall gaze'): lookout tower or raised summer house overlooking a garden.

GEOMETRIC: historical division of English Gothic architecture covering the period *c.* 1250–90.

See also Tracery. For another meaning, *see* Staircase.

GIBBS SURROUND: C18 treatment of door or window surround, seen particularly in the work of James Gibbs (1682–1754) (*see* fig. 10).

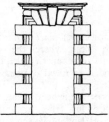

Fig. 10.   Gibbs Surround

GNOMON: vane or indicator casting a shadow on to a sundial.

GROIN: sharp edge at the meeting of two cells of a cross-vault; *see* Vault (fig. 26a).

GROTESQUE (*lit.* grotto-esque): classical wall decoration of spindly, whimsical character adopted from Roman examples, particularly by Raphael, and further developed in the C18.

GUILLOCHE: running classical ornament formed by a series of circles with linked and interlaced borders (see fig. 11).

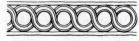

Fig. 11.   Guilloche

GUN LOOP: opening for a firearm.
GUTTAE: *see* Orders (fig. 16).

HAGIOSCOPE: *see* Squint.
HALF-TIMBERING: timber framing with the spaces filled in by plaster, stones or brickwork.
HALL CHURCH: (1) church whose nave and aisles are of equal height or approximately so. (2) (Scots C20): church convertible into a hall.
HAMMERBEAM: *see* Roof.
HARLING (Scots, *lit.* hurling): wet dash, i.e. a form of roughcasting

in which the mixture of aggregate and binding material (e.g. lime) is dashed onto a rubble wall as protection against weather.

HEADER: *see* Bond.

HENGE: ritual earthwork with a surrounding bank and ditch, the bank being on the outer side.

HERITORS (Scots): proprietors of a heritable subject, especially church heritors who till 1925 were responsible for each parish church and its manse.

HERM (*lit*. the god Hermes): male head or bust on a pedestal.

HERRINGBONE WORK: masonry or brickwork in zigzag courses.

HEXASTYLE: term used to describe a portico with six columns.

HILL FORT: Iron Age earthwork enclosed by a ditch and bank system; in the later part of the period the defences multiplied in size and complexity. They vary in area and are usually built with careful regard to natural elevations or promontories.

HOODMOULD or label: projecting moulding above an arch or lintel to throw off water.

HORSE-MILL: circular or polygonal farm building in which a central shaft is turned by a horse to drive agricultural machinery.

HUNGRY JOINTS: *see* Pointing.

HUSK GARLAND: festoon of nutshells diminishing towards the ends (*see* fig. 12).

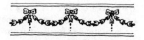

Fig. 12.   Husk Garland

HYPOCAUST (*lit*. under-burning): Roman underfloor heating system. The floor is supported on pillars and the space thus formed is connected to a flue.

ICONOGRAPHY: description of the subject matter of works of the visual arts.

IMPOST (*lit*. imposition): horizontal moulding at the spring of an arch.

IN ANTIS: *see* Anta.

INDENT: (1) shape chiselled out of a stone to match and receive a brass; (2) in restoration, a secretion of new stone inserted as a patch into older work.

INGLENOOK (*lit*. fire-corner): recess for a hearth with provision for seating.

INTERCOLUMNIATION: interval between columns.

IONIC: *see* Orders (fig. 16).

JAMB (*lit*. leg): (1) one of the straight sides of an opening; (2) (Scots) wing or extension adjoining one side of a rectangular plan, making it into an L or T plan.

KEEL MOULDING: *see* fig. 13.

Fig. 13.   Keel Moulding

KEEP: principal tower of a castle. Also called Donjon.

KEY PATTERN: *see* fig. 14.

Fig. 14.   Key Pattern

KEYSTONE: middle and topmost stone in an arch or vault.

KINGPOST: *see* Roof (fig. 22).

LABEL: *see* Hoodmould. *Label Stop:* ornamental boss at the end of a hoodmould.

LADY CHAPEL: chapel dedicated to the Virgin Mary (Our Lady).

LAIGH, or LAICH (Scots): low.

LAIRD (Scots): landowner.

LANCET WINDOW: slender pointed-arched window.

LANTERN: a small circular or polygonal turret with windows all round crowning a roof (*see* Cupola) or a dome.

LAVATORIUM: in a monastery, a washing place adjacent to the refectory.

LEAN-TO: term commonly applied not only to a single-pitch roof but to the building it covers.

LESENE (*lit.* a mean thing): pilaster without base or capital. Also called pilaster strip.

LIERNE: *see* Vault (fig. 26b).

LIGHT: compartment of a window.

LINENFOLD: Tudor panelling ornamented with a conventional representation of a piece of linen laid in vertical folds. The piece is repeated in each panel.

LINTEL: horizontal beam or stone bridging an opening.

LOFT: three special senses: (1) *Organ Loft* in which the organ, or sometimes only the console (keyboard), is placed; (2) *Rood Loft:* narrow gallery over rood screen, q.v.; (3) (Scots) reserved gallery in a church, e.g. a *Laird's Loft,* or a *Trades Loft* for members of one of the incorporated trades of a burgh.

LOGGIA: sheltered space behind a colonnade.

LONG-AND-SHORT WORK: quoins consisting of stones placed with the long sides alternately upright and horizontal, especially in Saxon building.

LOUIS: convenient term used in the antique trade to describe a curvaceous chimneypiece of Louis XV character.

LOUVRE: (1) opening, often with lantern over, in the roof of a room to let the smoke from a central hearth escape; (2) one of a series of overlapping boards to allow ventilation but keep the rain out.

LOZENGE: diamond shape.

LUCARNE (*lit.* dormer): small window in a roof or spire.

LUCKENBOOTH (Scots): lock-up booth or shop.

LUGGED: *see* Architrave.

LUNETTE (*lit.* half or crescent moon): (1) semicircular window; (2) semicircular or crescent-shaped surface.

LYCHGATE (*lit.* corpse-gate): wooden gate structure with a roof and open sides placed at the entrance to a churchyard to provide space for the reception of a coffin.

LYNCHET: long terraced strip of soil accumulating on the downward side of prehistoric and medieval fields due to soil creep from continuous ploughing along the contours.

MACHICOLATIONS (*lit.* mashing devices): on a castle, downward openings through which missiles can be dropped, under a parapet or battlement supported by deep corbels.

MAINS (Scots): home farm on an estate.

MAJOLICA: ornamented glazed earthenware.

MANSARD: *see* Roof (fig. 21).

MANSE: house of a minister of religion, especially in Scotland.

MARGINS (Scots): dressed stones at the edges of an opening. 'Back-set margins' (RCAHMS) is a misleading term because they are actually set forward from a rubble-built wall to act as a stop for the harling. Also called Rybats.

MARRIAGE LINTEL (Scots): on a house, a door or window lintel carved with the initials of the owner and his wife and the date of the work – only coincidentally of their marriage.

MAUSOLEUM: monumental tomb, so named after that of Mauso-

lus, king of Caria, at Halicar-
nassus.

MEGALITHIC (*lit.* of large stones):
archaeological term referring to
the use of such stones, singly or
together.

MERCAT (Scots): market. The
Mercat Cross was erected in a
Scottish burgh, generally in
a wide street, as the focus of
market activity and local ceremonial. Most examples are of
post-Reformation date and have
heraldic or other finials (not
crosses), but the name per-
sisted.

MERLON: *see* Battlement.

MESOLITHIC: term applied to the
Middle Stone Age, dating in
Britain from *c.* 5000 to *c.* 3500
B.C., and to the hunting and
gathering activities of the
earliest communities. *See also*
Neolithic.

METOPES: spaces between the triglyphs in a Doric frieze; *see*
Orders (fig. 16).

MEZZANINE: (1) low storey between two higher ones; (2) low
upper storey within the height
of a high one, not extending
over its whole area.

MISERERE: *see* Misericord.

MISERICORD (*lit.* mercy): ledge
placed on the underside of a
hinged choir stall seat which,
when turned up, provided the
occupant with support during
long periods of standing. Also
called Miserere.

MODILLIONS: small consoles at
regular intervals along the
underside of some types of
classical cornice.

MORT-SAFE (Scots): device to assure the security of a corpse or
corpses: (1) iron frame over a
grave; (2) building or room
where bodies were kept during
decomposition.

MOTTE: steep mound forming the
main feature of C11 and C12
castles.

MOTTE-AND-BAILEY: post-
Roman and Norman defence
system consisting of an earthen
mound (motte) topped with a
wooden tower within a bailey,
with enclosure ditch and palisade, and with the rare addition
of an internal bank.

MOUCHETTE: motif in curvilinear
tracery, a curved version of the
dagger form, specially popular
in the early C14 in England but
in the early C15 in Scotland; *see*
Tracery (fig. 25).

MOULDING: ornament of continuous section; *see* the various
types.

MULLION: vertical member between the lights in a window
opening.

MULTI-STOREY: modern term
denoting five or more storeys.

MULTIVALLATE: of a hill fort:
defended by three or more concentric banks and ditches.

MUNTIN: post forming part of a
screen.

NAILHEAD MOULDING: E.E. ornamental motif, consisting of
small pyramids regularly repeated (*see* fig. 15).

Fig. 15. Nailhead Moulding

NARTHEX: enclosed vestibule or
covered porch at the main
entrance to a church; *see also*
Galilee.

NECESSARIUM: medieval euphemism for latrines in a monastery.

NEOLITHIC: term applied to the
New Stone Age, dating in Britain from the appearance of the
first settled farming communities from the continent *c.* 3500
B.C. until the beginning of the
Bronze Age. *See also* Mesolithic.

NEWEL: central post in a circular
or winding staircase, also the
principal post when a flight of
stairs meets a landing.

NICHE (*lit.* shell): vertical recess
in a wall, sometimes for a statue.

NIGHT STAIR: stair by which

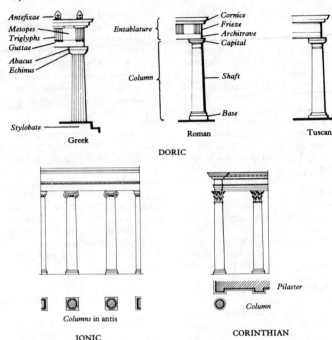

Fig. 16.   Orders

monks entered the transepts of
their church from their dormitory to celebrate night services.
NOOK-SHAFT: shaft set in an
angle formed by other members.
NORMAN: *see* Romanesque.
NOSING: projection of the tread
of a step. A *Bottle Nosing* is half
round in section.

OBELISK: lofty pillar of square
section tapering at the top and
ending pyramidally.
OGEE: double curve, bending first
one way and then the other.
Ogee or *Ogival Arch: see* Arch.
ORATORY: small private chapel in
a house.
ORDER: (1) upright structural
member formally related to
others, e.g. in classical architecture a column, pilaster, or anta;
(2) one of a series of recessed
arches and jambs forming a
splayed opening. *Giant* or

Colossal Order: classical order
whose height is that of two or
more storeys of a building.
ORDERS: in classical architecture,
the differently formalized versions of the basic post-and-
lintel structure, each having its
own rules of design and proportion. For examples of the main
types *see* fig. 16. Others include
the primitive Tuscan, which
has a plain frieze and simple
torus-moulded base, and the
Composite, whose capital combines Ionic volutes with Corinthian foliage. *Superimposed
Orders:* term for the use of
Orders on successive levels,
usually in the upward sequence
of Doric, Ionic, Corinthian.
ORIEL: *see* Bay-window.
OVER-ARCH: *see* Arch.
OVERHANG: projection of the
upper storey(s) of a building.
OVERSAILING COURSES: series of
stone or brick courses, each one
projecting beyond the one
below it; *see also* Corbel course.

PALIMPSEST (*lit.* erased work): re-use of a surface, e.g. a wall for another painting; also used to describe a brass plate which has been re-used by engraving on the back.

PALLADIAN: architecture following the ideas and principles of Andrea Palladio, 1508–80.

PALMETTE: classical ornament like a symmetrical palm shoot; for illustration *see* Anthemion, fig. 1.

PANTILE: roof tile of curved S-shaped section.

PARAPET: wall for protection at any sudden drop, e.g. on a bridge or at the wall-head of a castle; in the latter case it protects the *Parapet Walk* or wall walk.

PARCLOSE: *see* Screen.

PARGETING (*lit.* plastering): usually of moulded plaster panels in half-timbering.

PATERA (*lit.* plate): round or oval ornament in shallow relief, especially in classical architecture.

PEDESTAL: in classical architecture, a stand sometimes used to support the base of an order (*see* fig. 17).

Fig. 17. Pedestal

PEDIMENT: in classical architecture, a formalized gable derived from that of a temple, also used over doors, windows, etc. For the generally accepted meanings of *Broken Pediment* and *Open Pediment see* fig. 18.

PEEL (*lit.* palisade): stone tower, e.g. near the Scottish–English border.

PEND (Scots): open-ended passage through a building on ground level.

PENDANT: hanging-down feature of a vault or ceiling, usually ending in a boss.

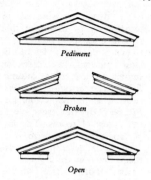

Pediment

Broken

Open

Fig. 18. Pediments

PENDENTIVE: spandrel between adjacent arches supporting a drum or dome, formed as part of a hemisphere (*see* fig. 19).

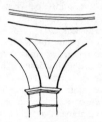

Fig. 19. Pendentive

PEPPERPOT TURRET: bartizan with conical or pyramidal roof.

PERISTYLE: in classical architecture, a range of columns all round a building, e.g. a temple, or an interior space, e.g. a courtyard.

PERP (PERPENDICULAR): historical division of English Gothic architecture covering the period from *c.* 1335–50 to *c.* 1530.

PERRON: *see* Stair.

PIANO NOBILE: principal floor, usually with a ground floor or basement underneath and a lesser storey overhead.

PIAZZA: open space surrounded by buildings; in the C17 and C18 sometimes employed to mean a long colonnade or loggia.

PIEND: *see* Roof.

PIER: strong, solid support, frequently square in section. *Compound Pier:* of composite section, e.g. formed of a bundle of shafts.

PIETRA DURA: ornamental or scenic inlay by means of thin slabs of stone.

PILASTER: classical order of oblong section, its elevation similar to that of a column. *Pilastrade:* series of pilasters, equivalent to a colonnade. *Pilaster Strip: see* Lesene.

PILE: a row of rooms. The important use of the term is in *Double Pile*, describing a house that is two rows thick.

PILLAR PISCINA: free-standing piscina on a pillar.

PINNACLE: tapering finial, e.g. on a buttress or the corner of a tower, sometimes decorated with crockets.

PINS (Scots): small stones pushed into the joints between large ones, a technique called cherry-caulking.

PISCINA: basin for washing the communion or mass vessels, provided with a drain; generally set in or against the wall to the s of an altar.

PIT PRISON: sunk chamber with access above through a hatch.

PLAISANCE: summer house, pleasure house near a mansion.

PLATT (Scots): platform, doorstep or landing. *Scale-and-Platt Stair: see* Stair.

PLEASANCE (Scots): close or walled garden.

PLINTH: projecting base beneath a wall or column, generally chamfered or moulded at the top.

POINTING: exposed mortar joints of masonry or brickwork. The finished form is of various types, e.g. *Flush Pointing*, *Recessed Pointing*. *Bag-rubbed Pointing* is flush at the edges and gently recessed in the middle of the joint. *Hungry Joints* are either without any pointing at all, or deeply recessed to show the outline of each stone. *Ribbon Pointing* is a nasty practice in the modern vernacular, the joints being formed with a trowel so that they stand out.

POPPYHEAD: carved ornament of leaves and flowers as a finial for the end of a bench or stall.

PORCH: covered projecting entrance to a building.

PORTCULLIS: gate constructed to rise and fall in vertical grooves at the entry to a castle.

PORTE COCHÈRE: porch large enough to admit wheeled vehicles.

PORTICO: in classical architecture, a porch with detached columns or other orders. *Blind Portico:* the front features of a portico attached to a wall so that it is no longer a proper porch.

POSTERN: small gateway at the back of a building.

POTENCE (Scots): rotating ladder for access to the nesting boxes of a round doocot.

PREDELLA: in an altarpiece the horizontal strip below the main representation, often used for a number of subsidiary representations in a row.

PRESBYTERY: the part of the church lying E of the choir stalls.

PRESS (Scots): cupboard.

PRINCIPAL: *see* Roof (fig. 22).

PRIORY: monastic house whose head is a prior or prioress, not an abbot or abbess.

PROSTYLE: with a row of columns in front.

PULPITUM: stone screen in a major church provided to shut off the choir from the nave and also as a backing for the return choir stalls.

PULVINATED: *see* Frieze.

PURLIN: *see* Roof (fig. 22).

PUTHOLE or PUTLOCK HOLE: putlocks are the short horizontal timbers on which during construction the boards of scaffolding rest. Putholes or putlock holes are the holes in the wall for putlocks, and often are not filled in after construction is complete.

PUTTO: small naked boy (plural: putti).

QUADRANGLE: inner courtyard in a large building.

QUARRIES (*lit.* squares): (1) square (or sometimes diamond-shaped) panes of glass supported by lead strips which are called *Cames*; (2) square floor-slabs or tiles.

QUATREFOIL: *see* Foil.

QUEENPOSTS: *see* Roof (fig. 22).

QUIRK: sharp groove to one side of a convex moulding, e.g. beside a roll moulding, which is then said to be quirked.

QUOINS: dressed stones at the angles of a building. When rusticated they may be alternately long and short.

RADIATING CHAPELS: chapels projecting radially from an ambulatory or an apse; *see* Chevet.

RAFTER: *see* Roof (fig. 22).

RAGGLE: groove cut in masonry, especially to receive the edge of glass or roof-covering.

RAKE: slope or pitch.

RAMPART: stone wall or wall of earth surrounding a castle, fortress, or fortified city. *Rampart Walk:* path along the inner face of a rampart.

RANDOM: *see* Rubble.

REBATE: rectangular section cut out of a masonry edge.

REBUS: a heraldic pun, e.g. a fiery cock as a badge for Cockburn.

REEDING: series of convex mouldings; the reverse of fluting.

REFECTORY: dining hall (or frater) of a monastery or similar establishment.

REREDORTER (*lit.* behind the dormitory): medieval euphemism for latrines in a monastery.

REREDOS: painted and/or sculptured screen behind and above an altar.

RESPOND: half-pier bonded into a wall and carrying one end of an arch.

RETABLE: altarpiece; a picture or piece of carving standing behind and attached to an altar.

RETROCHOIR: in a major church, an aisle between the high altar and an E chapel, like a square ambulatory.

REVEAL: the inward plane of a jamb, between the edge of an external wall and the frame of a door or window that is set in it.

RHONE (Scots): gutter along the eaves for rainwater; *see also* Conductor.

RIB-VAULT: *see* Vault.

RINCEAU (*lit.* little branch) or antique foliage: classical ornament, usually on a frieze, of leafy scrolls branching alternately to left and right (*see* fig. 20).

Fig. 20.   Rinceau

RISER: vertical face of a step.

ROCK-FACED: term used to describe masonry which is cleft to produce a natural, rugged appearance.

ROCOCO (*lit.* rocky): latest phase of the Baroque style, current in most Continental countries between *c.* 1720 and *c.* 1760, and showing itself in Britain mainly in playful, scrolled decoration, especially plasterwork.

ROLL MOULDING: moulding of semicircular or more than semicircular section.

ROMANESQUE: style in architecture current in the C11 and C12 and preceded the Gothic style (in England often called Norman). (Some scholars extend the use of the term Romanesque back to the C10 or C9.)

ROOD: cross or crucifix, usually over the entry into the chancel. The *Rood Screen* beneath it may have a *Rood Loft* along the top, reached by a *Rood Stair*.

ROOF: for external forms *see* fig. 21; for construction and components *see* fig. 22. *Wagon Roof:* lined with timber on the inside, giving the appearance of a curved or polygonal vault.

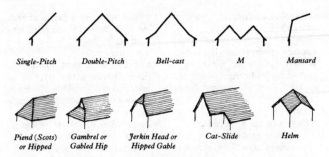

Single-Pitch   Double-Pitch   Bell-cast   M   Mansard

Piend (Scots)   Gambrel or   Jerkin Head or   Cat-Slide   Helm
or Hipped   Gabled Hip   Hipped Gable

Fig. 21.   Roof Forms

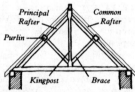

Ridge Piece
Rafter   Rafter
Collar
Tie-beam
Wall-plates

Common Roof Components

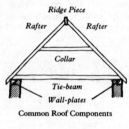

Principal   Common
Rafter   Rafter
Purlin
Kingpost   Brace

Roof with Kingpost Truss

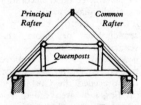

Principal   Common
Rafter   Rafter
Queenposts

Roof with Queenpost Truss

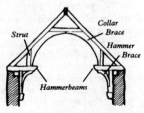

Collar
Brace
Strut   Hammer
Brace
Hammerbeams

Hammerbeam Roof

Fig. 22.   Roof Construction

ROPE MOULDING: *see* Cable Moulding.

ROSE WINDOW: circular window with patterned tracery about the centre.

ROTUNDA: building circular in plan.

ROUND (Scots): useful term employed by the RCAHMS for a bartizan, usually roofless.

RUBBLE: masonry whose stones are wholly or partly in a rough state. *Coursed Rubble:* of coursed stones with rough faces. *Random Rubble:* of uncoursed stones in a random pattern. *Snecked Rubble* has courses frequently broken by smaller stones (snecks).

RUSTICATION: treatment of joints and/or faces of masonry to give an effect of strength. In the most usual kind the joints are recessed by V-section chamfering or square-section channelling. *Banded Rustication* has only the horizontal joints emphasized in this way. The faces may be flat but there are many other forms, e.g. *Diamond-faced*, like a shallow pyramid, *Vermiculated*, with a stylized texture like worms or worm-holes, or *Glacial*, like icicles or stalactites. *Rusticated Columns* may have their joints and drums treated in any of these ways.

RYBATS (Scots): *see* Margins.

SACRAMENT HOUSE: safe cupboard for the reserved sacrament.

SACRISTY: room in a church for sacred vessels and vestments.

SALTIRE or ST ANDREW'S CROSS: with diagonal limbs. As the flag of Scotland it is coloured white on a blue ground.

SANCTUARY: (1) area around the main altar of a church (*see* Presbytery); (2) sacred site consisting of wood or stone uprights enclosed by a circular bank and ditch. Beginning in the Neolithic, they were elaborated in the succeeding Bronze Age. The best known examples are Stonehenge and Avebury.

SARCOPHAGUS (*lit.* flesh-consuming): coffin of stone or other durable material.

SARKING (Scots): boards laid on the rafters (*see* Roof, fig. 22) to support the covering, e.g. metal or slates.

SCAGLIOLA: composition imitating marble.

SCALE-AND-PLATT (*lit.* stair and landing): *see* Stair (fig. 24).

SCARCEMENT: extra thickness of the lower part of a wall, e.g. to carry a floor.

SCARP: artificial cutting away of the ground to form a steep slope.

SCREEN: in a church, usually at the entry to the chancel; *see* Rood Screen and Pulpitum. *Parclose Screen:* separating a chapel from the rest of the church.

SCREENS or SCREENS PASSAGE: screened-off entrance passage between the hall and the kitchen in a medieval house, adjoining the kitchen, buttery, etc.; *see also* Transe.

SCUNTION (Scots): equivalent of a reveal on the indoor side of a door or window opening.

SECTION: view of a building, moulding, etc. revealed by cutting across it.

SEDILIA: seats for the priests (usually three) on the s side of the chancel of a church; a plural

word that has become a singular, collective one.

SESSION HOUSE (Scots): (1) room or separate building for meetings of the elders who form a kirk session; (2) shelter by entrance to church or churchyard for an elder receiving the collection for relief of the poor, built at expense of kirk session.

SET-OFF: *see* Weathering.

SGRAFFITO: scratched pattern, often in plaster.

SHAFT: upright member of round section, especially the main part of a classical column. *Shaftring:* motif of the C12 and C13 consisting of a ring like a belt round a circular pier or a circular shaft attached to a pier.

SHEILA-NA-GIG: female fertility figure, usually with legs wide open.

SHOULDERED: *see* Arch (fig. 2), Architrave.

SILL: horizontal projection at the bottom of a window.

SKEW (Scots): sloping or shaped stones finishing a gable which is upstanding above the roof. *Skewputt:* bracket at the bottom end of a skew.

SLATE-HANGING: covering of overlapping slates on a wall, which is then said to be *slate-hung*.

SNECKED: *see* Rubble.

SOFFIT (*lit.* ceiling): underside of an arch, lintel, etc.

SOLAR (*lit.* sun-room): upper living room or withdrawing room of a medieval house, accessible from the high table end of the hall.

SOUNDING-BOARD: horizontal board or canopy over a pulpit; also called Tester.

SOUTERRAIN: underground stone-lined passage and chamber.

SPANDRELS: surfaces left over between an arch and its containing rectangle, or between adjacent arches.

SPIRE: tall pyramidal or conical feature built on a tower or turret. *Broach Spire:* starting from a square base, then carried into an octagonal section by means of triangular faces. *Needle Spire:* thin spire rising from the centre of a tower roof, well inside the parapet. *Helm Spire:* see Roof (fig. 21).

SPIRELET: *see* Flèche.

SPLAY: chamfer, usually of a reveal or scuntion.

SPRING: level at which an arch or vault rises from its supports. *Springers:* the first stones of an arch or vaulting-rib above the spring.

SQUINCH: arch thrown across an angle between two walls to support a superstructure, e.g. a dome (*see* fig. 23).

Fig. 23. Squinch

SQUINT: hole cut in a wall or through a pier to allow a view of the main altar of a church from places whence it could not otherwise be seen. Also called Hagioscope.

STAIR: *see* fig. 24. The term *Perron* (*lit.* of stone) applies to the external stair leading to a doorway, usually of double-curved plan as shown. *Spiral*, *Turnpike* (Scots) or *Newel Stair:* ascending round a central supporting newel, usually in a circular shaft. *Flying Stair:* cantilevered from the wall of a stairwell, without newels. *Geometric Stair:* flying stair whose inner edge describes a curve. *Well*

Stair: term applied to any stair contained in an open well, but generally to one that climbs up three sides of a well, with corner landings.

STALL: seat for clergy, choir, etc., distinctively treated in its own right or as one of a row.

STANCHION: upright structural member, of iron or steel or reinforced concrete.

STEADING (Scots): farm building or buildings. A term most often used to describe the principal group of agricultural buildings on a farm.

STEEPLE: a tower together with a spire or other tall feature on top of it.

STOUP: vessel for the reception of holy water, usually placed near a door.

STRAINER: *see* Arch.

STRAPWORK: C16 and C17 decoration used also in the C19 Jacobean revival, resembling interlaced bands of cut leather.

STRING COURSE: intermediate stone course or moulding projecting from the surface of a wall.

STUCCO (*lit.* plaster): (1) smooth external rendering of a wall etc.; (2) decorative plaster-work.

STUDS: intermediate vertical members of a timber-framed wall or partition.

STUGGED (Scots): of masonry that is hacked or picked as a key for rendering; used as a type of surface finish in the C19.

STYLOBATE: solid structure on which a colonnade stands.

SWAG (*lit.* bundle): like a festoon, but also a cloth bundle in relief, hung up at both ends.

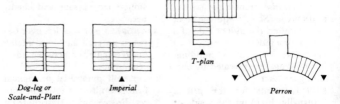

Dog-leg or Scale-and-Platt   Imperial   T-plan   Perron

Fig. 24. Stair

TABERNACLE (*lit.* tent): (1) canopied structure, especially on a small scale, to contain the reserved sacrament or a relic; (2) architectural frame, e.g. of a monument on a wall or free-standing, with flanking orders. Also called an Aedicule.

TAS-DE-CHARGE: coursed stone(s) forming the springers of more than one vaulting-rib.

TERMINAL FIGURE or TERM: upper part of a human figure growing out of a pier, pilaster, etc. which tapers towards the bottom.

TERRACOTTA: moulded and fired clay ornament or cladding, usually unglazed.

TESSELLATED PAVEMENT: mosaic flooring, particularly Roman, consisting of small *Tesserae* or cubes of glass, stone, or brick.

TESTER (*lit.* head): bracketed canopy, especially over a pulpit, where it is also called a sounding-board.

TETRASTYLE: term used to describe a portico with four columns.

THERMAL WINDOW (*lit.* of a Roman bath): semicircular, with two mullions.

THREE-DECKER PULPIT: pulpit with clerk's stall below and reading desk below the clerk's stall.

TIE-BEAM: *see* Roof (fig. 22).

TIERCERON: *see* Vault (fig. 26b).

TILE-HANGING: *see* Slate-hanging.

TIMBER FRAMING: method of construction where walls are built of timber framework with the spaces filled in by plaster or brickwork. Sometimes the timber is covered over with plaster or boarding laid horizontally.

TOLBOOTH (Scots): tax office containing a burgh council chamber and a prison.

TOMB-CHEST: chest-shaped stone coffin, the most usual medieval form of funerary monument.

TOUCH: soft black marble quarried near Tournai.

TOURELLE: turret corbelled out from the wall.

TOWER HOUSE (Scots): compact fortified house with the main hall raised above the ground and at least one more storey above it. A medieval Scots type continuing well into the C17 in its modified forms, the L plan and so-called Z plan, the former having a jamb at one corner, the latter at each diagonally opposite corner.

TRACERY: pattern of arches and geometrical figures supporting the glass in the upper part of a window, or applied decoratively to wall surfaces or vaults. *Plate Tracery* is the most primitive form of tracery, being formed of openings cut through stone slabs or plates. In *Bar Tracery* the openings are separated not by flat areas of stonework but by relatively slender divisions or bars which are constructed of voussoirs like arches. Later developments of bar tracery are classified according to the character of the decorative pattern used. For generalized illustrations of the main types *see* fig. 25.

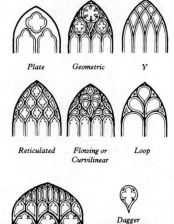

Plate	*Geometric*	*Y*
Reticulated	*Flowing or Curvilinear*	*Loop*
Perpendicular		*Dagger*
	Quatrefoil	*Mouchette*

Fig. 25. Tracery

TRANSE (Scots): passage, especially screens passage.

TRANSEPTS (*lit.* cross-enclosures): transverse portions of a cross-shaped church.

TRANSOM: horizontal member between the lights in a window opening.

TREFOIL: *see* Foil.

TRIBUNE: *see* Gallery (1).

TRICIPUT, SIGNUM TRICIPUT: sign of the Trinity expressed by three faces belonging to one head.

TRIFORIUM: middle storey of a church treated as an arcaded wall passage or blind arcade, its height corresponding to that of the aisle roof.

TRIGLYPHS (*lit.* three-grooved tablets): stylized beam-ends in the Doric frieze, with metopes between; *see* Orders (fig. 16).

TRIUMPHAL ARCH: *see* Arch.

TROPHY: sculptured group of arms or armour as a memorial of victory.

TRUMEAU: stone pillar supporting the tympanum of a wide doorway.

TUMULUS (*lit.* mound): barrow.

TURNPIKE: *see* Stair.

TURRET: small tower, often attached to a building.

TUSCAN: *see* Orders (fig. 16).

TYMPANUM (*lit.* drum): as of a drum-skin, the surface framed by an arch or pediment.

UNDERCROFT: vaulted room, sometimes underground, below the main upper room.

UNIVALLATE: of a hill fort: defended by a single bank and ditch.

VASSAL: *see* Feu.

VAULT: ceiling of stone formed like arches (sometimes imitated in timber or plaster); *see* fig. 26. *Tunnel-* or *Barrel-Vault:* the simplest kind of vault, in effect

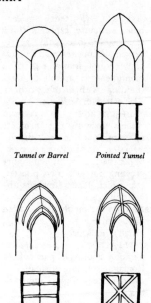

Tunnel or Barrel   *Pointed Tunnel*

Pointed Tunnels with Surface Ribs

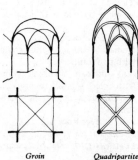

Groin   *Quadripartite*

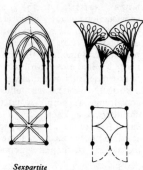

Sexpartite   *Fan*

Fig. 26. (a) Vaults

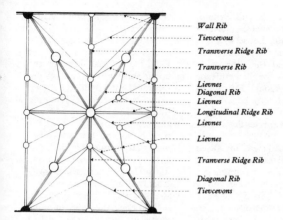

Wall Rib
Tievcevous
Transverse Ridge Rib
Transverse Rib
Lievnes
Diagonal Rib
Lievnes
Longitudinal Ridge Rib
Lievnes
Lievnes
Tranverse Ridge Rib
Diagonal Rib
Tievcevons

Fig. 26. (b) Ribs of a Late Gothic Vault

a continuous semicircular arch. *Pointed Tunnel-Vaults* are frequent in Scottish late medieval architecture but otherwise rare. A Scottish peculiarity is the *Pointed Tunnel-Vault with Surface Ribs* which are purely decorative in intention. *Groin-Vaults* (usually called *Cross-Vaults* in classical architecture) have four curving triangular surfaces produced by the intersection of two tunnel-vaults at right angles. The curved lines at the intersections are called groins. In *Quadripartite Rib-Vaults* the four sections are divided by their arches or ribs springing from the corners of the bay. *Sexpartite Rib-Vaults* are most often used over paired bays. The main types of rib are shown in fig. 26b; *transverse ribs, wall ribs, diagonal ribs,* and *ridge ribs. Tiercerons* are extra, decorative ribs springing from the corners of a bay. *Liernes* are decorative ribs in the crown of a vault which are not linked to any of the springing points. In a *stellar vault* the liernes are arranged in a star formation as in fig. 26b. *Fan-vaults* are peculiar to English Perpendicular architecture and differ from rib-vaults in consisting not of ribs and infilling but of halved concave cones with decorative

blind tracery carved on their surfaces.

VAULTING-SHAFT: shaft leading up to the springer of a vault.

VENETIAN WINDOW: *see* fig. 27.

Fig. 27.   Venetian Window

VERANDA(H): shelter or gallery against a building, its roof supported by thin vertical members.

VERMICULATION: *see* Rustication.

VESICA (*lit.* bladder): usually of a window, with curved sides and pointed at top and bottom like a rugger-ball.

VESTIBULE: anteroom or entrance hall.

VILLA: originally (1) Roman country-house-cum-farmhouse, developed into (2) the similar C16 Venetian type with office wings, made grander by Palladio's varied application of a central portico. This became an important type in C18 Britain, often with the special meaning of (3) a country house which is not a principal residence. Gwilt (1842) defined the villa as 'a country house for the residence of opulent persons'. But devaluation had already begun, and the term implied, as now, (4) a more or less pretentious suburban house.

VITRIFIED: hardened or fused into a glass-like state.

VITRUVIAN SCROLL: running ornament of curly waves on a classical frieze. (*See* fig. 28.)

VOLUTES: spiral scrolls on the front and back of a Greek Ionic capital, also on the sides of a Roman one. *Angle Volute:* pair of volutes turned outwards to meet at the corner of a capital.

VOUSSOIRS: wedge-shaped stones forming an arch.

WAINSCOT: timber lining on an internal wall.

WALLED GARDEN: C17 type whose formal layout is still seen in the combined vegetable and flower gardens of C18 and C19 Scotland. They are usually sited at a considerable distance from a house.

WALL-PLATE: *see* Roof (fig. 22).

WATERHOLDING BASE: type of Early Gothic base in which the upper and lower mouldings are separated by a hollow so deep as to be capable of retaining water.

WEATHERBOARDING: overlapping horizontal boards, covering a timber-framed wall.

WEATHERING: inclined, projecting surface to keep water away from wall and joints below.

WEEPERS: small figures placed in niches along the sides of some medieval tombs; also called mourners.

WHEEL WINDOW: circular window with tracery of radiating shafts like the spokes of a wheel; *see also* Rose Window.

WYND (Scots): subsidiary street or lane, often running into a main street or gait.

YETT (Scots, *lit.* gate): hinged openwork gate at a main doorway, made of wrought-iron bars alternately penetrating and penetrated.

Fig. 28. Vitruvian Scroll

INDEX OF ARTISTS

INDEX OF STREETS AND BUILDINGS

This index includes streets and major buildings. Principal references are in **bold** type; demolished buildings are shown in *italic*.

Monuments and statues are listed by surname (e.g. 'Pitt (William) Statue'), institutions by full name (e.g. 'George Heriot's School').

ADDENDA

p. 225 [OLD TOWN: OTHER STREETS]

FORREST HILL

An unpromising cul-de-sac, but the plain harled tenements on
the r. are the altered N wing of the former CHARITY
WORKHOUSE built in 1739–43 by *Samuel Neilson,* mason,
and *William McVey* and *James Heriot,* wrights.* At the end
of the street the old DRILL HALL, bare Scots Renaissance by
Cooper & Taylor, 1902–4. In front of the entrances a wide
semi-elliptical arch with rope hoodmould and an aedicule on
the parapet. To the l. the original Hall by *Duncan Menzies* of
Stewart & Menzies, 1872, a single-span girder roof across its
29m. width. Cast-iron balcony at the N end.

FORREST ROAD

Nos. 1–61, S SIDE. A plain late Georgian three-storey front with
a bow on the corner of Greyfriars Place. Then Baronial sets
in, with four-storey and attic tenements of varied design by
R. Thornton Shiells, 1870. Comfortably large angle-turret at
Nos. 7–9. Balanced asymmetry at Nos. 11–17, with a heavily
corbelled central chimney and a corbelled and crowstepped
gablet on the canted S corner. Full-height canted bay-windows at Nos. 19–25, the r. one corbelled out with a crowstepped gablet, the l. one with a spire. After Forrest Hill the
style is plainer though still Baronial, Nos. 51–61 making a
bleak corner to Lauriston Place.

Nos. 2–34, N SIDE. All Baronial, 1872. Only the
ODDFELLOWS HALL by *J.C. Hay* (Nos. 12–16) is enjoyable.
Three bays, nearly symmetrical. Pilastered shopfront with
foliaged capitals and elaborately carved shields over its centre.
Stilted round arches at the double first-floor windows, and at
the second floor a high relief of Faith, Hope and Charity.
Trefoil-pierced parapet with tall square turrets, the l. one
with a spire (now truncated). In the centre a statue of Charity
on a crowstepped gablet. Inside, the hall has been floored
over at gallery level but still has its cast-iron columns.

---

* It was a large U-plan building with a pedimented centrepiece.

The National Trust for Scotland is proud to be associated with Penguin Books Limited in the preparation of *The Buildings of Scotland*.

The Trust exists to care for fine buildings and beautiful scenery. It was brought into being in 1931 by a few prominent Scots concerned at the destruction of much of the country's heritage of landscape and architecture.

In its care are some 97 properties covering 36,500 hectares. These include castles and great houses, gardens, mountains, islands, historic sites and a wide variety of small properties.

The Trust has won widespread recognition for its pioneer work in the restoration of the 'little houses' of towns and villages. The 'buy, restore, sell' cycle, using a special fund, which it initiated, has been widely imitated.

Like the National Trust, it is incorporated by Act of Parliament and is dependent for finance on legacies, donations and the subscriptions of its members.

The Trust's offices, from which fuller details may be obtained, are at 5 Charlotte Square, Edinburgh.